EUROPEAN UNION LAW

ERRATUM

The publishers would like to correct the following errors in chapter 17 of
the Third Edition of *European Union Law*:

p.698
The second sentence on p.698 (eighth sentence of paragraph 17–012)
should read:
It set out the different procedures between which the Council and the
European Parliament could choose when conferring implementing powers
on the Commission.

p.704
The final two sentences of paragraph 17–016 should read:
In case of a negative opinion, the Commission is not allowed to adopt the
draft implementing act. Where no opinion is delivered, the Commission
may adopt the draft implementing act, unless the act concerns the adoption
of definitive multilateral safeguard measures (Comitology Regulation, Art.
6(3)). In that case, the Commission always needs a positive opinion before
it can adopt the draft implementing act (Comitology Regulation, Art. 6(4)).
The third sentence in paragraph 17–017 should read:
The same goes for all measures on which the regulatory procedure with
scrutiny was applicable.
The sixth and seventh sentences of paragraph 17–017 should read:
Where the Union legislator had set up a regulatory committee with
scrutiny, the implementing measures which the Commission proposed to
the committee were scrutinised by both the Council and the European
Parliament. If the Committee voted by a qualified majority (determined in
the same way as in the case of a management committee) in favour of the
measures envisaged, they had to be submitted for scrutiny to the European
Parliament and the Council (Second Comitology Decision, Arts 5a(2) and
(3)a)).

EUROPEAN UNION LAW

Third edition

By

KOEN LENAERTS
Judge of the Court of Justice of the European Union
Professor of European Law at Leuven University

PIET VAN NUFFEL
Member of the Legal Service of the European Commission
Professor of European Law at Leuven University and Visiting
Professor at the College of Europe (Natolin)

Editors

ROBERT BRAY
Principal Administrator in the Secretariat of the Committee on Legal
Affairs of the European Parliament

NATHAN CAMBIEN
Research Fellow at the Institute for European Law, Leuven University

SWEET & MAXWELL

 THOMSON REUTERS

First edition   (1999) by K Lenaerts & P Van Nuffel
Second edition   (2005) by K Lenaerts & P Van Nuffel
Third edition   (2011) by K Lenaerts & P Van Nuffel

Published in 2011 by
Sweet & Maxwell, 100 Avenue Road, London NW3 3PF
Part of Thomson Reuters (Professional) UK Limited
(Registered in England & Wales, Company No. 1679046. Registered Office and address
for service: Aldgate House, 33 Aldgate High Street, London EC3N 1DL)

For further information on our products and services, visit
www.sweetandmaxwell.co.uk

Typeset by LBJ Typesetting Ltd of Kingsclere
Printed and bound in Great Britain by
CPI William Clowes Ltd, Beccles, NR34 7TL

No natural forests were destroyed to make this product;
only farmed timber was used and re-planted.

A CIP catalogue record for this book
is available from the British Library

ISBN 978 0 414 04816 4 (Hardback)
ISBN 978 1 847 03743 5 (Paperback)

PREFACE

Since December 1, 2009—the date when the Lisbon Treaty entered into force—
the European Union has been operating on the basis of new constitutional foundations. Those foundations are the Treaty on European Union, as modified by the
Lisbon Treaty, the Treaty on the Functioning of the European Union and the
Charter of Fundamental Rights of the European Union. These are the texts that
now determine the competences and govern the functioning of the Union and that
define the fundamental rights enjoyed by the Union's citizens and other subjects
of Union law.

We have sought to provide readers with a comprehensive and systematic
analysis of the Union's constitutional law, in the broadest sense of that expression. We deal not only with the Union's competences, institutional structure, procedures and legal instruments, but also with the main substantive provisions of
Union law. In considering each aspect of that law, we have endeavoured to concentrate on those issues which lawyers are likely to encounter in practice, and
have included numerous references to documents available on the Internet, realising that this new medium is invaluable as a freely-available source of materials
for practitioners, academics and students world-wide.

Our work opens with an historical survey covering the converging paths taken
towards integration in the European Union and culminating in its current structure, the procedure for amending the Treaties and the conditions for accession
to the Union (Part I). This is followed by an outline of the Union's jurisdiction
(Part II). The starting point is a discussion of the objectives of the Union, followed by an examination of the general principles of Union law encompassing
conferral of competences, subsidiarity, proportionality, sincere cooperation and
equal treatment, which together constitute the overarching legal framework
within which the Union exercises its competences in order to achieve those objectives. Part II goes on to provide an extensive overview of substantive Union law,
which follows the order of the Treaties themselves and places particular emphasis on citizenship of the Union, the free movement of goods, persons, services and
capital and the area of freedom, security and justice. Owing to space constraints,
certain discrete fields of Union law that are worthy of study in their own right
(such as competition law) are dealt with only in outline, but those sections are
accompanied by numerous references to learned articles and textbooks, should
readers wish to learn more.

Part III identifies the actors that shape the European Union and its activities,
that is, the institutions, bodies, offices and agencies of the Union (with detailed
overviews of its political and other institutions and of its administrative organisation) and the Member States (with particular reference to the increasingly important role played by national parliaments in monitoring the Union's activities). Part
IV sets out the decision-making process in the European Union, which

includes—but is not limited to—the adoption of legislative acts and the implementation of legislation.

In our survey of the sources of Union law (Part V), efforts have been made not only to explain the principles of primacy and direct effect of that law, but to provide clear, practical guidance concerning their application, with particular attention being paid to the way in which each of the twenty-seven Member States ensures the implementation of Union law at national level.

Regarding European Union action in the international arena, Part VI comprehensively explores the Union's external competences and its external representation—an area where significant changes have been introduced by the Lisbon Treaty. In that context, we discuss the Union's only remaining "intergovernmental" area of activity—the common foreign and security policy.

The question of judicial protection within the European Union continues to be dealt with in a companion volume: Koen Lenaerts, Dirk Arts and Ignace Maselis (Robert Bray and Kathleen Gutman, eds), *Procedural Law of the European Union*.

For this third edition, the authors are very grateful for the contribution of a special editor, Nathan Cambien, research fellow at the Institute for European Law of Leuven University, who provided invaluable assistance with the meticulous adaptation of the text to reflect the changes introduced by the Lisbon Treaty and other recent legal developments. Furthermore, we would like to express our gratitude to Robert Bray, principal administrator at the European Parliament, whose English translation of our Dutch-language handbook formed at the time the basis of the first edition of this work and who so kindly volunteered to be associated with its second and third editions as general editor.

This book reflects the state of the law on November 1, 2010.

All views expressed are our own and should not be ascribed to the institutions to which we belong.

Koen Lenaerts
Piet Van Nuffel

Luxembourg and Brussels
November 30, 2010

TABLE OF CONTENTS

PART I

THE EUROPEAN UNION: DIFFERENT PATHS
TOWARDS INTEGRATION

CHAPTER 1. THE ESTABLISHMENT OF THE EUROPEAN
COMMUNITIES

PART II

JURISDICTION OF THE EUROPEAN UNION

CHAPTER 7.   PRINCIPLES GOVERNING THE COMPETENCES OF
THE EUROPEAN UNION

CHAPTER 10. AREA OF FREEDOM, SECURITY AND JUSTICE

CHAPTER 11.   OTHER AREAS OF UNION POLICY

CHAPTER 12.   LIMITS AND EXCEPTIONS TO THE APPLICATION
OF THE TREATIES

CHAPTER 14.   THE MEMBER STATES OF THE UNION

PART IV

THE DECISION-MAKING PROCESS WITHIN THE EUROPEAN UNION

CHAPTER 16. LEGISLATION

PART V

SOURCES OF LAW OF THE EUROPEAN UNION

INTRODUCTION TO THE SOURCE MATERIAL

A. OFFICIAL PUBLICATIONS

http://europa.eu
The Internet is the easiest way to find information about the European Union. The "europa" website is a source of news and information about the history and activities of the Union and leads visitors to the websites of the various institutions and to several databases containing official information, including "Eur-Lex":

http://eur-lex.europa.eu
The "Eur-Lex" site is the starting point for any enquiry for legal information about the European Union. This site provides access in all official languages to the Treaties on which the Union is based and to legislation and to the case law of the Union Courts. It is also a conduit to a number of other official documents, including the *Official Journal of the European Union*.

1. Treaties

Under the heading "Treaties" of the "Eur-Lex" site, can be found the text of the Treaty on European Union (TEU, as amended by the Treaty of Lisbon) and the Treaty on the Functioning of the European Union (TFEU, the new name of the EC Treaty since the Treaty of Lisbon), the Charter of Fundamental Rights of the European Union, as well as the original EC Treaty, EU Treaty and the amending treaties, including the Treaty of Lisbon.

In the United Kingdom, the legislation necessary to implement EU Treaties and acts can be found on the site of Her Majesty's Stationery Office: *http://www.hmso.gov.uk/*

2. Legislation

The "Eur-Lex" provides access to the *Official Journal of the European Union*, which is the official source for acts of the European Union (before February 1, 2003, its official name was *Official Journal of the European Communities*).

The *Official Journal* is published in all of the official languages (before May 1, 2004, the English version could be recognised by its mauve-coloured spine). As from the 1998 issues, it is available free of charge from "Eur-Lex". It is also available monthly or annually on CD ROM. The paper version is still available.

Before 1968, the *Official Journal* appeared in one part, whose page numbers initially ran on from one issue to the next ([1962] O.J. 1). Since July 1, 1967, the pagination of each volume starts from page 1 (e.g. [1967] O.J. 100/1). Since January 1, 1968, the *Official Journal* has been published in two parts and a supplement.

The *English Special Editions of the Official Journal* cover the period before the United Kingdom and Ireland joined the Community (until the end of 1972), but not all acts adopted were published therein.[1] Furthermore, there is no official list of *English Special Editions* and they have never been codified.[2]

---

[1] If an English version of a measure exists, the *English Special Edition* is cited in the European Court Reports. Otherwise the practice is to cite the French *Journal Officiel* reference.

[2] However, the list below (drawn up by the English Translation Division of the ECJ over the years) is believed to be complete.

First series
1952–1958
1959–1962
1963–1964
1965–1966
1965–1972 (omissions)
1966–1972
1967
1968 (I)
1968 (II)
1969 (I)
1969 (II)
1970 (I)
1970 (II)
1970 (III)
1971 (I)
1971 (II)
1971 (III)
1972 (I)
1972 (II)
1972 (III)
1972 (March 27) = J.O. L. 73 (documents concerning accession)
1972 (October 10–31)
1972 (November)
1972 (December 1–8)
1972 (December 9–28)
1972 (December 28–30)
1972 (December 30–31) = J.O. L. 297–299
1972 (December 31) = J.O. L. 296
1972 (December 31) = J.O. L. 300
1972 (December 31) = J.O. L. 301
1972 (December 31) = J.O. L. 302
1972 (December 31) = J.O. L. 303 & 306
1972 (December 31) = J.O. L. 307 (Budget 1973)

The *Official Journals* whose numbers are preceded by the letter L (*législation*, Legislation, cited as [2008] O.J. L14/1) contain decisions of the institutions and bodies, divided into "legislative acts" (inter alia, regulations, directives and decisions addressed to all Member States) and "non-legislative acts" (international agreements, other regulations, directives and decisions, recommendations, guidelines, rules of procedure and acts adopted by bodies created by international agreements).

The *Official Journals* whose numbers are preceded by the letter C (*communications*, Information and Notices, cited as [2008] O.J. C12/1) publish resolutions, recommendations and opinions; information (section with inter alia interinstitutional agreements); preparatory acts (initiatives or proposals of the Member States or the Institutions); notices from the institutions, bodies, offices and agencies and announcements (such as summaries of judgments of the Union Courts and notices of cases brought before the Union Courts). C-series issues indicated with a terminal "A" or "E" (e.g. [2002] O.J. C 228 E/1) exist only in electronic form and contain inter alia administrative notices (such as competitions organised for recruitment of staff) and minutes of the sittings of the European Parliament, preparatory acts (such as positions adopted by the Council in the course of the legislative procedure) and written questions put by MEPs and their answers.

The Supplement to the *Official Journal* (numbers preceded by the letter S) publishes public procurement contracts exceeding specified limits. Since July 1998 the supplement may be consulted only electronically either through the "Eur-Lex" site (TED database) or on CD ROM.

On the "Eur-Lex" site, the heading "Legislation in force" leads to the *Directory of European Union legislation in force*, a list of all legislation in force including

---

Supplement to the first series of Special Editions (1952–72) Consolidated edition of corrigenda

Second series
I   External Relations (1)
        External Relations (2)
II   Agriculture and Food Aid
III   European Agricultural Guidance and Guarantee Fund
IV   Transport
V   Euratom
VI   Competition (a) and (b)
VII   Institutional Questions
VIII   European Coal and Steel Community
IX   Resolutions of the Council and of the Representatives of the Member States
X   Miscellaneous

Supplement
1959–1962 (Court of Justice)
(1959 J.O. 18 Rules of Procedure
1962 J.O. 34 Supplementary Rules
1960 J.O. 72 Instructions to the Registrar)

consolidated legislation, which is available in full. The *Directory* is also published in paper form half-yearly with a chronological index and an index of key words.

The link on "Eur-Lex" to "Preparatory acts" leads to proposals for legislation of the Commission and to opinions provided by other institutions and bodies in the legislative process. Documents originating with the Commission are classified as "COM-documents" or "SEC-documents". In order to find out where matters stand with a given proposal for legislation, it is possible to consult the "PreLex" database ("Monitoring the decision-making process between institutions") in any official language or "OEIL", the "legislative observatory" of the European Parliament (in English or French only).

3. Case law

Since June 1997 the most important decisions of the Court of Justice, the General Court (previously the Court of First Instance) and (since 2006) the Civil Service Tribunal are available on the day of pronouncement from the "curia" website: *http://curia.europa.eu/*. A search form allows users to search for cases by case number, date or name of the parties, fields and words in the text. All decisions (including those from before June 17, 1997) can be found on the "Eur-Lex" website under the heading "Case law" (search for case number, date or the names of parties).

A paper version of the case law of the Court of Justice and the General Court is published in all the official languages in the *Reports of Cases before the Court of Justice of the European Union (European Court Reports* or *E.C.R.*—the English version is mauve).

Since 1990 the reports have been in two, separately paginated parts—Part I containing reports of cases of the Court of Justice, Part II those of the General Court (previously Court of First Instance). The case number is preceded by the letter C (*Cour*) where the proceedings were brought before the Court of Justice, by the letter T (*Tribunal*) where they were brought before the General Court and by the letter F (*Fonction publique*) where they were brought before the Civil Service Tribunal. Where the case number is followed by "- P" (*pourvoi*), the case is an appeal against a decision of the General Court, where it is followed by "- R" (*référé*), the decision relates to an application for interim measures.

Since January 1, 1994 staff cases (proceedings brought by officials before the Civil Service Tribunal or before the General Court under European Union civil-service law) are no longer reported in the *European Court Reports* (except where they are of general interest or important in principle), but separately in the language of the case, with an abstract in the other languages, in the *European Court Reports—Reports of European Staff Cases (ECR-SC)*.

The "curia" website is also a source of other useful information. Under the heading "case law" links are provided to the Digest of case law (systematic summaries of judgments and orders) an alphabetical index of subject-matter and a useful survey of annotations of judgments.

4. Other documents

The "europa.eu" portal guides the site visitor to a number of official documents which have been available for some years in both paper and electronic form.

Each month the Commission publishes the *Bulletin of the European Union* (EU Bull., prior to 1994: *Bulletin of the European Communities*, EC Bull.). That publication provides an overview of major events at Union level, describes the activities of the institutions and embodies a "documentation" section, including a list of infringement proceedings brought by the Commission against Member States alleged to be in breach of their obligations. Additionally, there are regular supplements to the *Bulletin* dealing with specific subjects. Issues of the *Bulletin* since 1996 are available in electronic form.

Each year the Commission issues a *General Report on the Activities of the European Union* (available in electronic form since 1997), together with other reports, including the *Report on Competition Policy*, which is available from the website of the Commission's Competition Directorate General: *http://ec.europa.eu/ competition/*.

An interesting feature is the catalogue of the Commission's library, which contains references to more than 200,000 publications and gives access to a search engine: *http://ec.europa.eu/eclas/*.

The historical archives may be consulted (partially also via the internet) at the European University Institute in Florence: *http://www.iue.it/ECArchives/*. Interesting historic documents are also to be found at the websites of the European Navigator (*http://ena.lu*) and the Archive of European Integration (*http://aei.pitt.edu*).

B. FURTHER INFORMATION

In most of the Member States there are a number of learned journals specialising in European law. Those published in English include principally *Common Market Law Review* (C.M.L.Rev.), *European Law Review* (E.L.Rev.), *Columbia Journal of European Law* (Col.J.E.L.) and *Legal Issues of European Integration* (L.I.E.I.). Among other journals, there are *Cahiers de droit européen* (C.D.E.), *Europarecht* (EuR.), *Journal de droit européen* (J.Dr.Eur.), *Revue du Marché Commun et de l'Union européenne* (R.M.C.U.E.), *Revue trimestrielle de droit européen* (R.T.D.E.) and *Sociaal-Economische Wetgeving* (S.E.W.). Major European Union and national judicial decisions are reported in many of those journals and especially in *Common Market Law Reports* (C.M.L.R.). General and specialist law journals increasingly contain articles on European law. A number of daily newspapers, including *The Times* and the *Financial Times* regularly report cases of the Court of Justice.

Up-to-date information on the activities of the European Union can be found in *Europe*, a daily publication in several languages (including English) of the press agency *Agence Europe*. The weekly publication *European Voice* gives an excellent insight into current events on the European scene. The very latest news can be found on the web page *EU news*, which publishes press releases from the institutions as they are issued. This web page also provides links to the press services of the institutions and bodies: *http://europa.eu/press_room/index_en.htm.*

C. SOURCES CITED IN ABBREVIATED FORM

Lenaerts, Arts and Maselis (Bray and Gutman eds), *Procedural Law of the European Union* (3rd edn, London, Sweet and Maxwell, 2012): Lenaerts, Arts and Maselis, *Procedural Law of the European Union.*

Accession Treaty 1972	Treaty of January 22, 1972 between the Member States of the European Communities, the Kingdom of Denmark, Ireland, the Kingdom of Norway and the United Kingdom of Great Britain and Northern Ireland concerning the accession of the Kingdom of Denmark, Ireland, the Kingdom of Norway and the United Kingdom of Great Britain and Northern Ireland to the European Economic Community and to the European Atomic Energy Community (see para. 6–002)
Accession Treaty 1979	Treaty of May 28, 1979 between the Member States of the European Communities and the Hellenic Republic concerning the accession of the Hellenic Republic to the European Economic Community and to the European Atomic Energy Community (see para. 6–003)
Accession Treaty 1985	Treaty of June 12, 1985 between the Member States of the European Communities and the Kingdom of Spain and the Portuguese Republic concerning the accession of the Kingdom of Spain and the Portuguese Republic to the European Economic Community and to the European Atomic Energy Community (see para. 6–004)
Accession Treaty 1994	Treaty of June 24, 1994 between the Member States of the European Union and the Kingdom of Norway, the Republic of Austria, the Republic of Finland and the Kingdom of Sweden concerning the accession of the Kingdom of Norway, the Republic of Austria, the Republic of Finland and the Kingdom of Sweden to the European Union (see para. 6–005)
Accession Treaty 2003	Treaty of April 16, 2003 between the Member States of the European Union and the Czech

Republic, the Republic of Estonia, the Republic of Cyprus, the Republic of Latvia, the Republic of Lithuania, the Republic of Hungary, the Republic of Malta, the Republic of Poland, the Republic of Slovenia, the Slovak Republic, concerning the accession of the Czech Republic, the Republic of Estonia, the Republic of Cyprus, the Republic of Latvia, the Republic of Lithuania, the Republic of Hungary, the Republic of Malta, the Republic of Poland, the Republic of Slovenia and the Slovak Republic to the European Union (see para. 6–006)

Accession Treaty 2005   Treaty of April 25, 2005 between the Kingdom of Belgium, the Czech Republic, the Kingdom of Denmark, the Federal Republic of Germany, the Republic of Estonia, the Hellenic Republic, the Kingdom of Spain, the French Republic, Ireland, the Italian Republic, the Republic of Cyprus, the Republic of Latvia, the Republic of Lithuania, the Grand Duchy of Luxembourg, the Republic of Hungary, the Republic of Malta, the Kingdom of the Netherlands, the Republic of Austria, the Republic of Poland, the Portuguese Republic, the Republic of Slovenia, the Slovak Republic, the Republic of Finland, the Kingdom of Sweden, the United Kingdom of Great Britain and Northern Ireland (Member States of the European Union) and the Republic of Bulgaria and Romania, concerning the accession of the Republic of Bulgaria and Romania to the European Union, [2005] O.J. L157/11 (see para. 6–007)

Act of Accession 1972   Act appended to the 1972 Accession Treaty (see para. 6–002)

Act of Accession 1979   Act appended to the 1979 Accession Treaty (see para. 6–003)

Act of Accession 1985   Act appended to the 1985 Accession Treaty (see para. 6–004)

Act of Accession 1994   Act concerning the conditions of accession of the Republic of Austria, the Republic of Finland and the Kingdom of Sweden and the adjustments to the Treaties on which the Union is founded (see para. 6–005)

Act of Accession 2003   Act concerning the conditions of accession of the Czech Republic, the Republic of Estonia, the Republic of Cyprus, the Republic of Latvia, the Republic of Lithuania, the Republic of Hungary,

	the Republic of Malta, the Republic of Poland, the Republic of Slovenia and the Slovak Republic and the adjustments to the Treaties on which the European Union is founded (see para. 6–006)
Act of Accession 2005	Act concerning the conditions of accession of the Republic of Bulgaria and Romania and the adjustments to the Treaties on which the European Union is founded (see para. 6–006)
Act on the Direct Election of the European Parliament	Act concerning the election of the European Parliament by direct universal suffrage (see para. 13–017)
Amsterdam Treaty	Treaty of Amsterdam of October 2, 1997 amending the Treaty on European Union, the Treaties establishing the European Communities and certain related acts (see para. 3–020)
Brussels Convention	Convention of September 27, 1968 on jurisdiction and the enforcement of judgments in civil and commercial matters (see para. 10–017)
Charter of Fundamental Rights	Charter of Fundamental Rights of the European Union of December 7, 2000 (see para. 22–021)
CFI Decision	Council Decision 88/591/ECSC, EEC, Euratom of October 24, 1988 establishing a Court of First Instance of the European Communities (see para. 13–077)
Comitology Decision	Council Decision 1999/468/EC of June 28, 1999 laying down the procedures for the implementing powers conferred on the Commission (see para. 17–012)
Comitology Regulation	Regulation (EU) No. 182/2011 of the European Parliament and of the Council of February 16, 2011 laying down the rules and general principles concerning mechanisms for control by Member States of the Commission's exercise of implementing powers (see para. 17–012)
Commission Rules of Procedure	Rules of Procedure of the Commission (see para. 13–074)
Conditions of Employment	Conditions of employment of other servants of the European Union (see para. 13–158)
Council Rules of Procedure	Rules of Procedure of the Council (see para. 13–033)
Decision on Provisional Location	Decision of the Representatives of the Governments of the Member States on the provisional location of certain institutions and departments of the Communities (see para. 13–152)
EAEC Treaty	Treaty establishing the European Atomic Energy Community (see para. 1–014)

EC Treaty	Treaty establishing the European Community (see para. 1–013)
ECHR	European Convention for the Protection of Human Rights and Fundamental Freedoms (see para. 1–006)
ECJ Rules of Procedure	Rules of Procedure of the Court of Justice (see para. 13–094)
ECJ Statute	Protocol on the Statute of the Court of Justice of the European Union (see para. 13–077)
ECSC Treaty	Treaty establishing the European Coal and Steel Community (see para. 1–008)
EEA Agreement	Agreement on the European Economic Area (see para. 25–029)
EEC Treaty	Treaty establishing the European Economic Community (see para. 1–013)
EIB Statute	Protocol on the Statute of the European Investment Bank (see para. 13–116)
EMI Statute	Protocol on the Statute of the European Monetary Institute (see para. 13–096)
EP Rules of Procedure	Rules of Procedure of the European Parliament (see para. 13–020)
ESC Rules of Procedure	Rules of Procedure of the European Economic and Social Committee (see para. 13–109)
ESCB Statute	Protocol on the Statute of the European System of Central Banks and of the European Central Bank (see para. 13–001)
EU Constitution	Treaty establishing a Constitution for Europe (see para. 4–003)
EU Treaty	Treaty on European Union, as applicable until the entry into force of the Lisbon Treaty (see para. 13–010; "TEU" is used for references to the Treaty on European Union as amended by the Lisbon Treaty)
European Council Rules of Procedure	Rules of Procedure of the European Council (see para. 13–032)
Financial Regulation	Financial Regulation applicable to the general budget of the European Communities (see para. 13–129)
First Decision on Own Resources	Council Decision 70/243 of April 21, 1970 on the replacement of financial contributions from Member States by the Communities' own resources (see para. 13–134)
First Decision on the Seats of the Institutions	Decision of December 12, 1992 taken by common agreement between the Representatives of the Governments of the Member States on the location of the seats of the institutions and of certain bodies

and departments of the European Communities (see para. 13–153)

First Treaty on
Budgetary Provisions
: Treaty of April 22, 1970 amending certain Budgetary Provisions of the Treaties establishing the European Communities and of the Treaty establishing a Single Council and a Single Commission of the European Communities (see para. 13–141)

Fourth Decision on
Own Resources
: Council Decision 94/728 of October 31, 1994 on the system of the Communities' own resources (see para. 13–134)

Fifth Decision on
Own Resources
: Council Decision 2000/597 of September 29, 2000 on the system of the Communities' own resources (see para. 13–134)

General Court Rules
of Procedure
: Rules of Procedure of the General Court (see para. 13–094)

Lisbon Treaty
: Treaty of December 13, 2007 amending the Treaty on European Union and the Treaty establishing the European Community (see para. 4–008)

Merger Treaty
: Treaty establishing a Single Council and a Single Commission of the European Communities (see para. 1–016)

Nice Treaty
: Treaty of Nice of February 26, 2001 amending the Treaty on European Union, the Treaties establishing the European Communities and certain related acts (see para. 3–024)

Ombudsman Regulations
: Decision of the European Parliament of March 9, 1994 on the regulations and general conditions governing the performance of the Ombudsman's duties (see para. 13–118)

Protocol on Privileges
and Immunities
: Protocol on the Privileges and Immunities of the European Union (see para. 13–128)

Protocol on Seats
: Protocol on the location of the seats of the institutions and of certain bodies, offices, agencies and departments of the European Union (see para. 13–153)

Rome Convention
: Convention of June 19, 1980 on the law applicable to contractual obligations (see para. 10–018)

Rules of Procedure—
Court of Auditors
: Rules of Procedure of the Court of Auditors (see para. 13–105)

Schengen Protocol
: Protocol integrating the Schengen acquis into the framework of the European Union (see para. 10–011)

Second Decision on
Own Resources
: Council Decision 85/257 of May 7, 1985 on the system of the Communities' own resources (see para. 13–134)

Second Decision on the
Seats of the Institutions
: Decision of October 29, 1993 taken by common agreement between the Representatives of the

	Governments of the Member States, meeting at Head of State and Government level, on the location of the seats of certain bodies and departments of the European Communities and of Europol (see para. 13–153)
Second Treaty on Budgetary Provisions	Treaty of July 22, 1975 amending Certain Budgetary Provisions of the Treaties establishing the European Communities and of the Treaty establishing a Single Council and a Single Commission of the European Communities (see para. 13–141)
Single European Act	Single European act (para. 3–006)
Sixth Decision on Own Resources	Council Decision 2007/436/EC, Euratom of June 7, 2007 on the system of the European Communities' own resources, [2007] O.J. L163/17 (see para. 13–134)
Social Agreement	Agreement on social policy concluded between the Member States of the European Community with the exception of the United Kingdom of Great Britain and Northern Ireland (see para. 11–043)
Social Protocol	Protocol on social policy (see para. 11–043)
Staff Regulations	Staff Regulations of Officials of the European Union (see para. 13–158)
TEU	Treaty on European Union as amended by the Lisbon Treaty (see para. 4–009)
TFEU	Treaty on the Functioning of the European Union (see para. 4–009)
Third Decision on Own Resources	Council Decision 88/376 of June 24, 1988 on the system of the Communities' own resources (see para. 13–134)
Third Decision on the Seats of the Institutions	Decision taken by common agreement between the Representatives of the Member States, meeting at Head of State or Government level, of December 13, 2003 on the location of the seats of certain offices and agencies of the European Union (see para. 13–154)

LIST OF ABBREVIATIONS

A.A.	Judgments of the Belgian *Arbitragehof/Cour d'arbitrage*
A.Ae.	*Ars Aequi*
ACP	African, Caribbean, Pacific
A.D.	*Actualités du droit*
A.J.C.L.	*American Journal of Comparative Law*
A.J.D.A.	*L'actualité juridique—droit administratif*
A.J.I.L.	*American Journal of International Law*
A.J.T.	*Algemeen Juridisch Tijdschrift*
Ann.Dr.Louv.	*Annales de droit de Louvain*
Ann.Dr.Lux.	*Annales du droit luxembourgeois*
Ann.Fac.Dr.Liège	*Annales de la Faculté de droit, d'économie et de sciences sociales de Liège*
A.ö.R.	*Archiv des öffentlichen Rechts*
Arr.Cass.	Judgments of the Belgian *Hof van Cassatie/Cour de Cassation*
A.Völkerr.	*Archiv des Völkerrechts*
B.S.	*Belgisch Staatsblad/Moniteur belge*
B.T.I.R.	*Belgisch Tijdschrift voor internationaal recht*
BVerfGE	Decisions of the *Bundesverfassungsgericht*
B.Y.I.L.	*British Yearbook of International Law*
Cambridge L.J.	*Cambridge Law Journal*
C.D.E.	*Cahiers de droit européen*
CFI	Court of First Instance of the European Communities
CFSP	Common foreign and security policy
C.M.L.Rep.	*Common Market Law Reports*
C.M.L.Rev.	*Common Market Law Review*
Cm	Command paper
Col.J.E.L.	*Columbia Journal of European Law*
Col.L.Rev.	*Columbia Law Review*
Coreper	Committee of Permanent Representatives
Cornell I.L.J.	*Cornell International Law Journal*
CSCE	Conference for Security and Cooperation in Europe
C.Y.E.L.P.	*Croatian Yearbook of European Law & Policy*
D.ö.V.	*Die öffentliche Verwaltung*
D.R.	Decisions and Reports of the European Commission on Human Rights
D.Vbl.	*Deutsches Verwaltungsblatt*

EAEC	European Atomic Energy Community
EBRD	European Bank for Reconstruction and Development
E.Bus.L.Rev.	*European Business Law Review*
E.Bus.Org.L.R.	*European Business Organisation Law Review*
EC	European Community
ECB	European Central Bank
EC Bull.	*Bulletin of the European Communities*
ECHR	European Convention for the Protection of Human Rights and Fundamental Freedoms
ECSC	European Coal and Steel Community
ECJ	Court of Justice of the European Communities
E.Comp.L.Rev.	*European Competition Law Review*
E.Const.L.Rev.	*European Constitutional Law Review*
E.C.R.	*European Court Reports*
EDC	European Defence Community
EEA	European Economic Area
EEC	European Economic Community
E.En.Env.L.Rev.	*European Energy and Environmental Law Review*
E.Env.L.Rev.	*European Environmental Law Review*
EFTA	European Free Trade Association
E.For.Aff.Rev.	*European Foreign Affairs Review*
E.H.R.L.R.	*European Human Rights Law Review*
EIB	European Investment Bank
E.J.C.C.L. & C.J.	*European Journal of Crime, Criminal Law and Criminal Justice*
E.J.I.L.	*European Journal of International Law*
E.J.L.Ref.	*European Journal of Law Reform*
E.J.M.L.	*European Journal on Migration and Law*
E.J.Soc.Sec.	*European Journal of Social Security*
E.L.J.	*European Law Journal*
E.L.Rev.	*European Law Review*
EMI	European Monetary Institute
EMS	European Monetary System
EMU	economic and monetary union
Env.L.Rev.	*Environmental Law Review*
EPC	European Political Co-operation
EPC Bulletin	*European Political Co-operation Documentation Bulletin*
EPSO	European Personel Selection Office
E.Pub.L.	*European Public Law*
E.R.C.L.	*European Review of Contract Law*
E.Rev.Priv.L.	*European Review of Private Law*
ERPL/REDP	*European Review of Private Law / Revue européenne de droit privé*
ESCB	European System of Central Banks

ESDP	European Security and Defence Policy
E.St.A.L.Q.	*European State Aid Law Quarterly*
E.T.S.	*European Treaty Series*
EU	European Union
EU Bull.	*Bulletin of the European Union*
Eu.GR.Z.	*Europäische Grundrechte Zeitschrift*
EUMC	Military Committee of the European Union
EUMS	Military Staff of the European Union
EuR.	*Europarecht*
Euredia	*Revue Européenne de Droit Bancaire et Financier/ European Banking and Financial Law Journal*
Eur. L. F.	*European Legal Forum*
Europe	*Europe. Daily news bulletin*
Eu.Z.W.	*Europäische Zeitschrift für Wirtschaftsrecht*
E.W.S.	*Europäisches Wirtschafts- und Steuerrecht*
FAO	Food and Agricultural Organisation
Fordham I.L.J.	*Fordham International Law Journal*
GATT	General Agreement on Tariffs and Trade
GDP	gross domestic product
G.L.J.	*German Law Journal*
GNP	gross national product
G.J.	*Gaceta Jurídica*
G.Y.I.L.	*German Yearbook of International Law*
Harv.I.L.J.	*Harvard International Law Journal*
Human Rights L.J.	*Human Rights Law Journal*
I.C.L.Q.	*International and Comparative Law Quarterly*
IGC	Intergovernemental Conference
I.J.C.L.	*International Journal of Constitutional Law*
I.J.N.L.	*International Journal of Nuclear Law*
I.L.M.	*International Legal Materials*
ILO	International Labour Organisation
Intertax	*Intertax: international tax review*
Int'l J.Comp.Lab.L.	*International Journal of Comparative Labour Law and Industrial Relations*
Ind.Rel.	
IMF	International Monetary Fund
I.O.L.R.	*International Organizations Law Review*
IPRax.	*Praxis des Internationalen Privat- und Verfahrensrechts*
I.P.S.	*Irish Political Studies*
Ir.J.E.L.	*Irish Journal of European Law*
J.C.E.R.	*Journal of Contemporary European Research*

J.C.M.S.	*Journal of Common Market Studies*
J.C.P.	*Jurisclasseur périodique—La semaine juridique*
J.E.I.	*Journal of European Integration*
J.Env.L.	*Journal of Environmental Law*
JHA	justice and home affairs
J.I.E.L	*Journal of International Economic Law*
J. Legis. Stud.	*The Journal of Legislative Studies*
JRC	Joint Research Centre
J.T.	*Journal des tribunaux*
J.T.D.E.	*Journal des tribunaux—Droit européen*
J.T.T.	*Journal des tribunaux de travail*
Jura Falc.	*Jura Falconis*
J.W.T.	*Journal of World Trade*
J.Z.	*Juristen-Zeitung*
Kst.	*Kamerstukken* (Netherlands Parliament)
L.I.E.I.	*Legal Issues of European Integration* (since 2000: *Legal Issues of Economic Integration*)
Leiden J.I.L.	*Leiden Journal of International Law*
L.Q.R.	*Law Quarterly Review*
MEP	Member of the European Parliament
M.J.E.C.L.	*Maastricht Journal of European and Comparative Law*
Mich.L.Rev.	*Michigan Law Review*
Mod.L.Rev.	*Modern Law Review*
NATO	North Atlantic Treaty Organisation
N.I.L.R.	*Netherlands International Law Review*
N.J./A.B.	*Nederlandse Jurisprudentie. Administratiefrechtelijke beslissingen*
N.J.B.	*Nederlands Juristenblad*
N.J.W.	*Neue Juristische Wochenschrift*
N.J.Wb.	*Nieuw Juridisch Weekblad*
Nordic J.I.L.	*Nordic Journal of International Law*
Not.U.Eur.	*Noticias de la Unión Europea*
N.T.B.	*Nederlands Tijdschrift voor bestuursrecht*
N.T.E.R.	*Nederlands Tijdschrift voor Europees Recht*
N.T.I.R.	*Nederlands Tijdschrift voor internationaal recht*
OECD	Organisation for Economic Cooperation and Development
OJ	*Official Journal of the European Union*
O.J.L.S.	*Oxford Journal of Legal Studies*
OLAF	European Anti-Fraud Office

OSCE	Organisation for Security and Co-operation in Europe
Pas.lux.	*Pasicrisie luxembourgeoise*
Pet.Aff.	*Les petites affiches*
PJCC	Police and judicial co-operation in criminal matters
Publ. ECHR	Publications of the European Court of Human Rights
Pub.L.	*Public Law*
PSC	Political and Security Committee
RabelsZ	*Rabels Zeitschrift für ausländisches und internationales Privatrecht*
R.A.E.	*Revue des affaires européennes*
R.B.D.C.	*Revue belge de droit constitutionnel*
R.C.C.	*Revue de la concurrence et de la consommation*
R.C.D.I.P.	*Revue critique de droit international privé*
R.D.Etr.	*Revue de droit des étrangers*
R.D.I.D.C.	*Revue de droit international et de droit comparé*
Rec.C.E.	*Recueil des décisions du Conseil d'Etat statuant au contentieux, du Tribunal des conflits et des jugements des Tribunaux administratifs*
Rec.Con.const.	*Conseil constitutionnel—Recueil des décisions*
Rec. Dalloz	*Recueil Dalloz-Sirey*
R.E.C.I.E.L.	*Review of European Community and International Environmental law*
R.D.U.E.	*Revue du droit de l'Union européenne*
R.D.ULB	*Revue du droit de l'Université Libre de Bruxelles*
R.D.Unif.	*Revue de droit uniforme/Uniform Law Review*
R.E.D.P.	*Revue européenne de droit public*
Rev.E.D.E.	*Revista española de Derecho Europeo*
Rev.I.S.	*Review of International Studies*
R.F.D.A.	*Revue française de droit administratif*
R.F.D.C.	*Revue française de droit constitutionnel*
R.G.D.I.P.	*Revue générale de droit international public*
R.I.D.C.	*Revue internationale de droit comparé*
R.I.E.J.	*Revue interdisciplinaire d'études juridiques*
Riv.D.E.	*Rivista di diritto europeo*
R.I.W.	*Recht der internationalen Wirtschaft*
R.M.C.	*Revue du Marché Commun*
R.M.C.U.E.	*Revue du Marché Commun et de l'Union européenne*
R.M.U.E.	*Revue du Marché Unique européen*
R.T.D.E.	*Revue trimestrielle de droit européen*
R.T.D.H.	*Revue trimestrielle des droits de l'homme*
R.U.D.H.	*Revue universelle des droits de l'homme*
R.W.	*Rechtskundig Weekblad*

S.E.W.	*Sociaal-economische wetgeving. Tijdschrift voor Europees en economisch recht*
Stat.L.Rev.	*Statute Law Review*
Stb.	*Netherlands official gazette*
Stud. Dipl.	*Studia Diplomatica*
Swiss Rev.I.Comp.L.	*Swiss Review of International Competition Law*
T.Agr.R.	*Tijdschrift voor Agrarisch Recht*
T.B.H.	*Tijdschrift voor Belgisch handelsrecht*
T.B.P.	*Tijdschrift voor bestuurswetenschappen en publiekrecht*
Tex. Int'l L.J.	*Texas International Law Journal*
Themis	*Rechtsgeleerd Magazijn Themis*
Tilburg For.L.Rev.	*Tilburg Foreign Law Review*
T.O.R.B.	*Tijdschrift voor onderwijsrecht en onderwijsbeleid*
T.P.R.	*Tijdschrift voor privaatrecht*
Trb.	*Tractatenblad van het Koninkrijk der Nederlanden*
T.R.V.	*Tijdschrift voor rechtspersonen en vennootschappen*
Tulane E. & Civ. L. F.	*Tulane European and Civil Law Forum*
T.V.V.S.	*TVVS. Maandblad voor ondernemingsrecht en rechtspersonen*
UN	United Nations
U.N.T.S.	*United Nations—Treaty Series*
VAT	value added tax
V.U.W.L.R.	*Victoria University of Wellington Law Review*
WEAG	Western European Armaments Group
WEU	Western European Union
World Comp.	*World Competition*
WTO	World Trade Organisation
W.u.W.	*Wirtschaft und Wettbewerb*
Y.ECHR	*Yearbook of the European Convention on Human Rights*
Y.E.L.	*Yearbook of European Law*
Z.a.ö.R.V.	*Zeitschrift für ausländisches öffentliches Recht und Völkerrecht*
Z.Eu.P.	*Zeitschrift für Europäisches Privatrecht*
Z.Eu.S.	*Zeitschrift für Europarechtliche Studien*
Z.f.RV.	*Zeitschrift für Rechtsvergleichung, internationales Privatrecht und Europarecht*
Z.H.W.	*Zeitschrift für das gesamte Handelsrecht und Wirtschaftsrecht*
Z.ö.R.	*Zeitschrift für öffentliches Recht*
Z.Vgl.RW.	*Zeitschrift für vergleichende Rechtswissenschaft*

xl

NUMERICAL TABLE OF EUROPEAN CASES

GENERAL COURT

ALPHABETICAL TABLE OF
EUROPEAN CASES

TABLE OF NATIONAL CASES

TABLE OF TREATIES, PROTOCOLS AND DECLARATIONS

Declarations annexed to the EU Treaty

TABLE OF EUROPEAN UNION AND COMMUNITY ACTS

DIRECTIVES

DECISIONS

RULES OF PROCEDURE

INTERINSTITUTIONAL AGREEMENTS

TABLE OF CONVENTIONS AND AGREEMENTS CONCLUDED BY THE EU OR THE FORMER EC

CONVENTIONS AND AGREEMENTS CONCLUDED AMONG EU MEMBER STATES

OTHER INTERNATIONAL TREATIES AND CONVENTIONS

TABLE OF UK LEGISLATION

TABLE OF NON-UK LEGISLATION

Part I

THE EUROPEAN UNION: DIFFERENT PATHS TOWARDS INTEGRATION

CHAPTER 1

THE ESTABLISHMENT OF THE EUROPEAN COMMUNITIES

European Communities and European Union. The origin of the European 1–001
Union goes back to the three European Communities, which were established
by treaty: the European Coal and Steel Community (ECSC), the European
Community (EC) and the European Atomic Energy Community (Euratom or
EAEC). The EC (until 1992, the European Economic Community, or EEC) was
the most prominent of these international legal persons owing to its general
sphere of operation. Prior to this "Community" integration process and in
parallel thereto, European States had engaged in other forms of cooperation.
Indeed, the Member States of the European Communities had concluded agreements amongst themselves concerning cooperation in areas falling outside the
Communities' sphere of operation with which they did not associate the same
legal consequences as they attached to Community action. In 1992 the link which
existed in practice between the two integration paths was institutionalised by
packaging them into the European Union, yet without altering the specific legal
character of either path. As a result, the distinction remained between Community
and non-Community action, whereby only acts of the institutions based on one of
the Community Treaties constituted a source of "Community law". This distinction largely disappeared with the entry into force on December 1, 2009 of the
Lisbon Treaty, which merged both Community and non-Community provisions
into one European Union with legal personality. As a result, the EC was replaced
by the European Union. Since the ECSC Treaty ceased to exist in 2002, the
EAEC is the only one of the three Communities which continues in being.[1]

The first part of this book describes the parallel emergence of the Communities
(Ch. 1) and the non-Community integration process (Ch. 2), and explains how the
European Union has combined the two paths towards integration (Ch. 3). The
succeeding chapters provide an overview of recent Treaty amendments (Ch. 4)
and of the procedures for amending the Treaties (Ch. 5) and for the accession of
Member States to the European Union (Ch. 6).

---

[1] See Protocol (No. 2) annexed to the Treaty of Lisbon amending the Treaty establishing the
European Atomic Energy Community, [2007] O.J. C306/199.

I. Post-war Initiatives for European Integration

1–002 **European integration.** Europe's history is punctuated by attempts to bring peoples and States together in larger entities. At various times, powerful leaders have tried to establish a pan-European State by conquering and annexing neighbouring territories. The common factor in all these attempts was that they tried to unify peoples or States by force. Gradually, however, the idea emerged that European States could benefit from a process of peaceful cooperation. In the first half of the twentieth century, prominent politicians and intellectuals developed concrete proposals to achieve "European integration" by step-by-step voluntary cooperation. The chaos of Europe in the aftermath of the Second World War turned out to be the ideal setting to turn this political idea into reality.

1–003 **Economic and military cooperation.** The idea of "European integration" was brought back to the attention of the public on September 19, 1946 by a speech made by Winston Churchill at the University of Zürich in which he called for the establishment of "a kind of United States of Europe" on the continent.[2] This call was in line with the desire on the part of the United States and the United Kingdom to establish cooperation between western European States as a counterweight to the Soviet Union's increasing power.

On a more limited scale, the Benelux countries (Belgium, Luxembourg and the Netherlands) had already set an example by founding a customs union in 1948, which was later converted into an economic union in which their economic, financial and social policies were coordinated.[3] The Committee of Ministers of the Benelux Union is assisted by a general secretariat and advisory bodies, including the Advisory Benelux Interparliamentary Council. A Benelux Court of Justice is responsible for ensuring the uniform interpretation of agreements concluded between the Benelux countries.[4] A first step towards economic cooperation

---

[2] For the text of the speech, see *http://www.ena.lu* [Accessed November 11, 2010].

[3] Treaty of The Hague of February 3, 1958 establishing a Benelux Economic Union (*UNTS* No. 5471,) which succeeded the Customs Convention between Belgium, Luxembourg and the Netherlands signed in London on September 5, 1944. The Treaty of 1958 was replaced in 2010 by a renewed Benelux Treaty signed at The Hague on June 17, 2008, which changed the official name from Benelux Economic Union to Benelux Union. The leading role played by Benelux (recognised in Art. 350 TFEU [*ex Art. 306 EC*], para. 22–050, *infra*), has now been largely assumed by the EU. For an analysis, see Rood, "Een nieuw Benelux-verdrag: een nieuw élan voor de samenwerking? (2010) S.E.W.186–191; Wouters, Van Langenhove, Vidal, De Lombaerde and De Vriendt, *De Benelux: tijd voor een wedergeboorte?* (Antwerp, Intersentia, 2007), 279 pp.; Wouters and Vidal, "Towards a rebirth of Benelux?" (2007) B.T.I.R. 533–568; Leclerq, "Le droit Benelux sous un jour nouveau, droit inconnu?" (2006) J.T. 613–624; Oosterkamp, "Is er naast de Europese Unie nog toekomst voor de Benelux?" (2002) S.E.W. 237–240; Mortelmans, "Benelux 50 jaar: voorlopen, gelijklopen of doodlopen?" (1995) S.E.W. 399–403.

[4] Treaty on the establishment and statute of the Benelux Court of Justice, signed at Brussels on March 31, 1965, as supplemented by the Protocol of April 29, 1969. It has been in force since January 1, 1974. The Benelux Court of Justice—composed of Judges of the highest courts of each

was taken on April 16, 1948, when the Organisation for European Economic Cooperation (OEEC) was set up to coordinate economic recovery in Europe and in particular to distribute aid granted under the Marshall Plan.[5] Military cooperation was also initiated when France, the United Kingdom and the Benelux countries signed the Brussels Treaty of March 17, 1948.[6] This was followed by the establishment of the North Atlantic Treaty Organisation (NATO), set up by the North Atlantic Treaty of April 4, 1949.[7]

Congress of Europe. In May 1948 prominent persons from different social, cultural and political circles meeting at the "Congress of Europe" held in The Hague passed a number of resolutions working out the idea of European integration in two ways. First, they called for a European organisation to be set up to safeguard the democratic systems of the European countries through multilateral supervision of compliance with human rights. Secondly, they called for a pooling of the crucial components of economic, industrial and—hence also to some extent—political life with a view to forestalling the threat of war in Western Europe.

1–004

The Council of Europe. With the signature of the Statute of the Council of Europe on May 5, 1949, the ideas formulated at the Congress of Europe gave rise to an international organisation.[8] The Council of Europe, which is based in Strasbourg, has at present 47 member countries.[9] It may concern itself with all

1–005

---

of the three countries—is itself a court against whose decisions there is no remedy under national law and hence is required by the third para. of Art. 267 TFEU [*ex Art. 234 EC*] to make a reference for a preliminary ruling to the Court of Justice of the EU whenever a question of Union law is raised before it: ECJ, Case C-337/95 *Parfums Christian Dior* [1997] E.C.R. I-6013, paras 15–31.

[5] Convention on European Economic Cooperation, signed at Paris on April 16, 1948, UNTS (1949) 59, Cmnd. 7796. The OEEC was replaced on September 30, 1961 by the Organisation for Economic Cooperation and Development (OECD), which seeks to promote, alongside economic growth, employment and rising living standards in member countries, also the well-being of developing countries and other States. The Convention on the Organisation for Economic Cooperation and Development was signed at Paris on December 14, 1960, (1961) UNTS 21, Cmnd. 1646. Its website is at *http://www.oecd.org* [Accessed November 11, 2010]. Art. 220(1) TFEU [*ex Art. 304 EC*] makes provision for cooperation between the European Union and the OECD. See also Art. 202 EAEC.

[6] Treaty between Belgium, France, Luxembourg, the Netherlands and the United Kingdom, (1949) UNTS 1, Cmnd. 7599.

[7] North Atlantic Treaty, (1949) UNTS 56, Cmnd. 7789. NATO's website is to be found at *http://www.nato.int* [Accessed November 11, 2010].

[8] (1949) UNTS 61, Cmnd. 7778. The Council of Europe's website is at *http://www.coe.int* [Accessed November 11, 2010].

[9] The founder members were Belgium, Denmark, France, Greece (which withdrew from the Council of Europe in 1970 to be readmitted in 1974), Ireland, Italy, Luxembourg, the Netherlands, Norway, Sweden and the United Kingdom. The Federal Republic of Germany, Iceland and Turkey joined in 1950, Austria in 1956, Cyprus in 1961, Switzerland in 1963, Malta in 1965, Portugal in 1976, Spain in 1977, Liechtenstein in 1978, San Marino in 1988, Finland in 1989, Hungary in 1990, Poland in 1991, Bulgaria in 1992, the Czech Republic, Estonia, Lithuania, Romania, Slovakia and Slovenia in 1993 (Czechoslovakia had already joined as a unitary State in 1991), Andorra in 1994, Albania, Latvia, Macedonia, Moldova, the Ukraine and the Former Yugoslav Republic of Macedonia in

political, economic and social matters of European interest and hence has a more extensive field of activity than the European Union.[10] The organisation has a Committee of Ministers, which is advised by the Parliamentary Assembly (formerly the Consultative Assembly). Although the Assembly has been made up of delegates from the national parliaments since 1951, the Council of Europe is still organised on an intergovernmental model. It does not have any actual power to make laws. The two instruments employed in the context of the Council of Europe are non-binding resolutions and draft conventions, which take effect only between States which have ratified them. As a result, it has not evolved any further than a forum for discussion, providing interesting ideas for European cooperation, but not affording any genuine prospects of realising them.

1–006 **European Convention on Human Rights.** The most important convention which has come into being under the auspices of the Council of Europe is the European Convention for the Protection of Human Rights and Fundamental Freedoms (ECHR) of November 4, 1950.[11] The distinct place occupied by the ECHR within the Council of Europe is clear from two special characteristics.

First and foremost, the Council of Europe is identified with the ECHR. No State can join the Council of Europe unless it agrees to accede to the ECHR. At the same time, States may accede to the ECHR only if they are members of the Council of Europe (ECHR, Art. 59(1)). The preamble to the ECHR states that the central aim of the Council of Europe is "the collective enforcement of certain of the rights stated in the Universal Declaration" of Human Rights proclaimed by the General Assembly of the United Nations on December 10, 1948. Accordingly, every person within the jurisdiction of the Contracting States is ipso facto protected by the ECHR, irrespective of his or her nationality or place of residence.

The ECHR constitutes a first expression of supranationalism in the European integration process. With the creation of the European Court of Human Rights, the

---

1995, Croatia and Russia in 1996, Georgia in 1999, Armenia and Azerbaijan in 2001, Bosnia and Herzegovina in 2002, Serbia in 2003 (originally joined as Serbia and Montenegro), Monaco in 2004 and Montenegro in 2007.

[10] Article 220(1) TFEU [*ex Art. 303 EC*] makes provision for cooperation between the European Union and the Council of Europe. See also Art. 200 EAEC. See already Ouchterlony, "The European Communities and the Council of Europe" (1984) 1 L.I.E.I. 59–74.

[11] Cmnd. 8969. The ECHR and Protocols Nos 1 and 6 thereto are set out in Schedule to the Human Rights Act 1998. For an exhaustive discussion of the rights set out in the ECHR, see Ovey and White, *Jacobs, White & Ovey: The European Convention on Human Rights* (Oxford, Oxford University Press, 2010), 720 pp.; Harris, O'Boyle, Bates and Buckley, *Harris, O'Boyle & Warbrick: Law of the European Convention on Human Rights* (Oxford, Oxford University Press, 2009), 914 pp.; Reid, *A practitioner's guide to the European Convention on Human Rights* (London, Sweet & Maxwell, 2008), 709 pp.; Grabenwarter, *Europäische Menschenrechtskonvention: ein Studienbuch* (Munich, Beck, 2008), 451 pp.; Mowbray, *Cases and materials on the European Convention on Human Rights* (Oxford, Oxford University Press, 2007), 1058 pp.; van Dijk, Van Hoof, van Rijn and Zwaak, *Theory and practice of the European Convention on Human Rights* (Antwerp, Intersentia, 2006), 1190 pp.; Vande Lanotte and Haeck, *Handboek EVRM* (Antwerp, Intersentia, 2005), 949 pp.

ECHR provides an enforcement structure which subjects the States to "European" supervision of their compliance with the provisions of the Convention. Ratification of the ECHR has the result that any Contracting Party may refer to the European Court of Human Rights any alleged breach of the provisions of the ECHR and the protocols thereto (ECHR, Art. 33). More importantly, any person, non-governmental organisation or group of individuals claiming to be the victim of a violation by one of the Contracting Parties of the rights set forth in the ECHR may submit an application to the European Court of Human Rights (ECHR, Art. 34). The procedure for dealing with individual applications has been radically altered by Protocol No. 11 to the ECHR, which has been in force since November 1, 1998.[12] If an individual application is not declared inadmissible by a committee of the Court consisting of three Judges, it will be referred to a Chamber of seven Judges which decides on its admissibility and merits (ECHR, Arts 28 and 29).[13] After the Chamber has given judgment, any party may request that the case be referred to the Grand Chamber of seventeen Judges (ECHR, Art. 43(1)). The Grand Chamber will accept such a request only if a panel of five Judges determines that the case raises a serious question affecting the interpretation or application of the Convention or the Protocols thereto, or a serious issue of general importance (ECHR, Art. 43(2)). Judgments of the Grand Chamber and—in so far as no request is made to refer the case to the Grand Chamber or such a request is refused—of the Chambers are final and the Contracting Parties have to abide by them (ECHR, Arts 44 and 46).

As a result of Protocol No. 11, the Strasbourg procedure has come a long way from the original enforcement procedure, which severely limited direct access to the European Court of Human Rights by individual victims of violations. Originally, persons or groups of individuals lodged a complaint with the European Commission of Human Rights, which had to decide whether to consider the petition admissible and whether to remit the case to the Court of Human Rights. It could only do so if the Contracting State against which the petition was lodged had made a separate declaration that it recognised the competence of the Commission to receive such complaints and accepted the Court's jurisdiction. Under the present system, the individual right to submit applications and the jurisdiction of the Strasbourg Court is accepted by all the Contracting States.

---

[12] Protocol No. 11 to the European Convention for the Protection of Human Rights and Fundamental Freedoms restructuring the control machinery established thereby, signed on May 11, 1994. For the position of the United Kingdom, see the Human Rights Act 1998. The Protocol is discussed in Wachsmann, Eissen and Flauss (eds), *Le Protocole No 11 à la Convention européenne des droits de l'homme* (Brussels, Bruylant, 1995), 194 pp; Verrijdt, "De gevolgen van het Elfde Protocol bij het E.V.R.M. Dilemma tussen de kwaliteit en de kwantiteit van de (grond)rechtsbedeling" (2002–2003) Jura Falc. 571–651; Drzemczewski, "The European Human Rights Convention: Protocol No. 11—Entry into force and first year of application" (2000) Human Rights L.J. 1–17; De Schutter, "La nouvelle Cour européenne des droits de l'homme" (1998) C.D.E. 319–352; Schermers, "The Eleventh Protocol to the European Convention on Human Rights" (1994) E.L.Rev. 367–384.

[13] In certain cases, the Chamber may, before it has rendered its judgment, relinquish jurisdiction in favour of the Grand Chamber of seventeen Judges, see ECHR, Art. 30.

II. THE ECSC TREATY

1–007 **Schuman plan.** The most successful initiative for European integration, which would lead to the establishment of the European Communities and, eventually, the European Union, was tabled on May 9, 1950, when the French Foreign Minister Robert Schuman launched a proposal to bring the coal and steel sectors of European States under one common policy. This proposal, which had earlier been conceived by Jean Monnet, a senior French civil servant, satisfied the French Government's concern to avoid a third resurgence of the German war machine and, at the same time, sought to reinforce the political clout of the western European States in the face of Soviet expansionism in central and eastern Europe. The solemn declaration by Schuman on May 9, 1950 made clear that this initiative was considered to be a first step in a process of integration which would develop further and was open to other States. Schuman deliberately opted to start that process of integration by concrete cooperation in a defined field. He famously stated that:

> "Europe will not be made all at once, or according to a single plan. It will be built upon concrete achievements which first create a de facto solidarity".[14]

The aim was to transfer the administration of two basic industries to an independent supranational institution, the High Authority, which would be empowered to take decisions binding on both the Member States and coal and steel undertakings. Accordingly, the Schuman plan was based on a functional approach to the process of European integration which set specific aims and conferred genuine decision-making power on common institutions in designated fields in order to achieve them.

1–008 **European Coal and Steel Community.** Only five States responded to the French invitation to participate in the Schuman plan by attending the preparatory conference which opened in Paris on June 20, 1950. On April 18, 1951 Belgium, France, Germany, Italy, Luxembourg and the Netherlands signed in Paris the Treaty establishing the European Coal and Steel Community (ECSC Treaty) for a period of fifty years (the ECSC entered into force on July 23, 1952 and came to an end on July 23, 2002).[15] Since the tasks of the ECSC could be taken over by the

---

[14] The text of the declaration is available at *http://www.ena.lu* [Accessed November 11, 2010]. This declaration was echoed in the preamble to the ECSC Treaty: "recognising that Europe can be built only through practical achievements which will first of all create real solidarity, and through the establishment of common bases for economic development".

[15] See Art. 97 ECSC. Upon the expiry of the Treaty, the net assets of the ECSC were earmarked for research in sectors related to the coal and steel industry; see the Protocol annexed to the EC Treaty by the Treaty of Nice ([2001] O.J. C80/67) and Decision 2002/234/ECSC of the Representatives of the Governments of the Member States, meeting within the Council, of February 27, 2002 on the financial consequences of the expiry of the ECSC Treaty and on the research fund for coal and steel ([2002] O.J. L79/42). See Obwexer, "Das Ende der Europäischen Gemeinschaft für Kohle und Stahl" (2002) Eu.Z.W. 517–524.

European Community, the ECSC Treaty was not extended.[16] The ECSC Treaty established a common market in coal and steel by abolishing and prohibiting within the Community all import and export duties and charges having equivalent effect and, likewise, all quantitative restrictions on the movement of products, together with all measures discriminating between producers, purchasers or consumers or interfering with the purchaser's free choice of supplier. Under the provisions of the Treaty, state aid and restrictive practices were prohibited. The ECSC institutions were given the task of ensuring an orderly supply to the market, equal access to sources of production, the lowest possible prices, the encouragement of more efficient and modernised production and resource utilisation, improved working conditions and the growth of international trade.[17]

By accepting joint administration of sectors of their national economies, the founding States went further than the international consultation which had previously taken place within the Council of Europe (see para. 1–005). This new form of cooperation was referred to from the outset as "supranational" (see para. 1–020 *et seq.*).

ECSC Institutions. The ECSC Treaty was a textbook example of a *traité-loi*. **1–009** It contained virtually all the rules which the Member States deemed necessary for the smooth operation of a common market in the coal and steel sector. Since the Member States considered that their respective interests were sufficiently protected by the detailed Treaty provisions, they were prepared to place their confidence in an expert authority responsible for ensuring that those provisions were implemented. The Treaty therefore empowered a High Authority, composed of experts required to be independent *vis-à-vis* both the Member States and industry, to take binding decisions and make recommendations.[18]

The Treaty further set up a Special Council of Ministers, composed of representatives of the Member States, which was responsible for harmonising the action of the High Authority with the general economic policies of the Member States. The Contracting Parties limited the High Authority's autonomous power to take decisions to matters already extensively regulated by the Treaty and created a regulatory interaction between the High Authority and the Council where more fundamental political and economic options—often in specified circumstances—were to be decided upon.[19]

---

[16] See the Resolution of the Council of the European Union and the representatives of the governments of the Member States, meeting within the Council of July 20, 1998 concerning the expiry of the Treaty establishing the European Coal and Steel Community, [1998] O.J. C247/5. For the continuity of the Community legal order and the succession of the ECSC, see CFI, Case T-24/07 *ThyssenKrupp Stainless v Commission* [2009] E.C.R. II-2309, paras 75–80 and 83.

[17] For an evaluation of the extent to which these objectives were achieved, see Hosman, "Bij het afscheid van het EGKS-Verdrag: Droom en werkelijkheid" (2002) S.E.W. 134–144.

[18] Articles 8 and 14 ECSC.

[19] See, on the one hand, Art. 26 and, on the other, Arts 85 and 95, first para., ECSC. For a retrospective look at the application of those provisions, see Meunier, "La Communauté européenne du charbon et de l'acier est morte, vive la fédération européenne!" (2001) R.M.C.U.E. 509–515.

The ECSC Treaty also set up two supervisory institutions, a Common Assembly, composed of representatives from the national parliaments, and a Court of Justice which was given the task of ensuring that,

> "in the interpretation and application of this Treaty, and of the rules laid down for the implementation thereof, the law is observed".[20]

III. PROPOSALS FOR POLITICAL COOPERATION

1–010 **European Defence Community.** The success of the ECSC initially led to plans to bring political matters, such as defence and foreign policy, also under the umbrella of a supranational organisation. On May 27, 1952 the ECSC Member States signed the Treaty establishing the European Defence Community (EDC).[21] The Member States of the EDC were to make army divisions available to the European Defence Forces under a Commissariat. The EDC was also to have a Council, a Parliamentary Assembly (the ECSC Common Assembly plus nine delegates) and to use the Court of Justice of the ECSC. The EDC was based on a plan put forward by the French Minister of Defence René Pleven which offered a solution enabling a military security structure to be put in place in continental Europe as a counterweight to the expansion of communism—a present threat in view of the Korean War—yet without ignoring French resistance to German rearmament.

Prior to the entry into force of the EDC Treaty, the Ministers of Foreign Affairs of the ECSC decided to implement Art. 38 of the EDC Treaty, which charged the Common Assembly with considering any changes eventually to be made to the Treaty, having regard to the principle that,

> "the final organisation which will replace the present provisional organisa- tion should be so conceived as to be able to constitute one of the elements in a federal or confederal structure".

The aim of the changes was to coordinate the agencies for European cooperation, already existing or which might be established, within the framework of a federal or confederal structure (EDC Treaty, Art. 38(1)). The Common Assembly of the ECSC—meeting as the "*Ad Hoc* Assembly"—proposed that a European Political Community should be set up to coordinate Member States' foreign policy and establish a common market. The institutional structure of the ECSC was to be taken over and more extensive powers were to be given to the "supranational" institutions, namely the independent policy institution and the Parliamentary Assembly.[22] Both the EDC Treaty and the draft Statute of the European Political

---

[20] See Arts 24 and 31 ECSC.

[21] See Fursdon, *The European Defence Community: A History* (London, Macmillan, 1980), 360 pp.

[22] For the draft text, see *http://www.ena.lu* [Accessed November 11, 2010].

Community expressly set out to establish a Community of a "supranational character".[23]

The whole plan fell through when, on August 29, 1954, the French National Assembly voted to postpone ratification of the EDC Treaty sine die. The Gaullists and Communists had opposed the EDC, the former fearful of surrendering French sovereignty, the latter shrinking from German rearmament.

Defence cooperation. In October 1954, a solution was found to the problem of growing German strength. The North Atlantic Treaty Organisation (NATO) accepted the Federal Republic of Germany as a member. In addition, the Paris Protocol of October 23, 1954 amended the Brussels Treaty (see para. 1–003) and set up the Western European Union (WEU),[24] which was joined by Germany, together with Italy. That organisation continued in being until it was decided on March 31, 2010 to have it dismantled.[25] A subsequent development was the participation of all Member States of the European Communities in the Conference for Security and Cooperation in Europe (CSCE), which met for the first time in 1973, resulting in the signing of the Helsinki Final Act.[26] The CSCE was institutionalised by the 1990 Charter of Paris[27] and has been renamed since January 1, 1995 the Organisation for Security and Cooperation in Europe (OSCE).[28]

1–011

---

[23] Article 1 of the EDC Treaty; Art. 1 of the Draft Statute. See Von Lindeiner-Wildau, *La supranationalité en tant que principe de droit* (Leiden, Sijthoff, 1970), at 9.

[24] The Treaty establishing the Western European Union and Protocols thereto, signed in Paris on October 23, 1954 (1955) UNTS 39, Cmnd. 9498. See Dumoulin and Remacle, *L'Union de l'Europe occidentale. Phénix de la défense européenne* (Brussels, Bruylant, 1998) 604 pp. The WEU website was at *http://www.weu.int/* [Accessed November 11, 2010].

[25] See the Statement of March 13, 2010 of the Presidency of the Permanent Council of the WEU on behalf of the High Contracting Parties to the modified Brussels Treaty (Belgium, France, Germany, Greece, Italy, Luxembourg, The Netherlands, Portugal, Spain and the United Kingdom), according to which the WEU Permanent Council is charged with organising the cessation of WEU activities preferably by June 2011. The Statement recalls that, since the entry into force of the Lisbon Treaty, Art. 42(7) of the TEU commits the Member States to mutual aid and assistance in case of armed aggression.

[26] Final Act of Helsinki of August 1, 1975, for the English text see *From Helsinki to Vienna. Basic documents of the Helsinki Process*, 1990, IEE/39 (the text was not subject to ratification). The Final Act consists of the conclusions of the Conference on Security and Cooperation in Europe, which opened in Helsinki on July 3, 1973. It embodies a political declaration setting out principles for the conduct of relations between the States party to it (including respect for human rights), a document on "confidence-building measures and certain aspects of security and disarmament", together with provisions on cooperation in the fields of economics, science and technology and of the environment.

[27] Charter of Paris of November 19–21, 1990 for a New Europe (1990) 11 EC. Bull point 2.2.1.

[28] See the final declaration of the meeting of Heads of State or Government held on December 6, 1994 in Budapest, *Europe*, doc. No. 1917, December 28, 1994. OSCE's website is at *http://www.osce.org/* [Accessed November 11, 2010].

IV. The EEC Treaty and The EAEC Treaty

1–012 **Spaak Report.** Following the failure of the European Defence Community, the advocates of European integration switched to a more realistic economic and social approach. Encouraged by the Benelux countries and the influential Action Committee for the United States of Europe, the way was open to a *relance européenne*. Starting from a plan which had been put forward by the Dutch Foreign Minister Johan Willem Beyen, the Benelux countries proposed establishing a common market and coordinating policy decisions relating to market support. By the Resolution of Messina of June 2, 1955, the Member States subscribed to these proposals and charged an intergovernmental committee, chaired by the Belgian Foreign Minister Paul-Henri Spaak, with working out the still embryonic ideas. The Spaak Report amounted to an all-embracing programme for the establishment of a common market, which was too detailed to be enshrined in a treaty. The resultant broad substantive approach made it necessary to rethink the regulatory process capable of reacting to economic and social developments.

1–013 **European Economic Community.** The Treaty establishing the European Economic Community (EEC Treaty, commonly referred to as the Treaty of Rome), which was signed in Rome on March 25, 1957 and entered into force on January 1, 1958,[29] took over the substantive aims and institutional structure proposed in the Spaak Report. The preamble and Arts 2 and 3 EEC set forth the objectives contemplated by the Contracting Parties. Article 2 EEC announced ambitious aims to be achieved through the establishment of a common market and the progressive approximation of the Member States' economic policies.[30] Article 3 EEC specified those objectives by listing the tasks of the Community. First, Art. 3 EEC looked forward to the achievement of four economic freedoms. Free movement of goods, persons, services, and capital (including payments) formed the pillars on which the common market was based.[31] The "activities of the Community" also included "the approximation of the laws of Member States to the extent required for the proper functioning of the common market"[32] and "the establishment of a common customs

---

[29] Article 8 of the Treaty on European Union of February 7, 1992 amended the Treaty establishing the European Economic Community so as to establish a European Community (EC). The abbreviation "EEC" is therefore used in this work only where express reference is made to the original EEC Treaty.

[30] Four of the dynamically formulated aims were of an economic and social nature—(1) harmonious development of economic activities throughout the Community, (2) continuous and balanced expansion, (3) an increase in stability and (4) an accelerated raising of the standard of living—, whilst the fifth was simply a policy of seeking "closer relations between the States belonging to [the Community]".

[31] Free movement of goods (Arts 9 to 37 EEC) formed, together with free movement of persons, services and capital (Arts 48 to 73 EEC), the common agricultural policy (Arts 38 to 47 EEC) and the common transport policy (Arts 74 to 84 EEC), the "foundations of the Community" (Part Two of the EEC Treaty).

[32] See Arts 99 to 102 EEC.

tariff and of a common commercial policy towards third countries".[33] In order to prevent undertakings and Member States from frustrating the common market, free competition was to be secured.[34] Article 3 further provided for the adoption of common policies in the spheres of agriculture and transport. Lastly, Art. 3 made provision for the coordination of the Member States' economic policies.[35]

European Atomic Energy Community. At the same time as the EEC Treaty, the Treaty establishing a European Atomic Energy Community (EAEC also known as Euratom) was signed. It also entered into force on January 1, 1958. Its aim was to create the conditions necessary for the speedy establishment and growth of nuclear industries. To this end, Art. 2 EAEC provided for common policies on research, safety standards, investment and installations, supplies of ores and fuels, application of the nuclear industry, right of ownership in fissile materials and international relations in the field of nuclear energy, and introduced a common market.[36]   1–014

Traité-cadre. Since in principle the EEC Treaty covered all sectors of the economy and sought to attain the chosen policy objectives progressively, it was impossible to lay down the requisite rules of law exhaustively in the Treaty itself. Accordingly, it was not a *traité-loi* but a *traité-cadre* containing provisions relating to the functioning of the institutions and decision-making, alongside basic substantive rules which had to be complied with by the Community and the Member States. Within the framework of the EEC Treaty—and pursuant thereto—a substantial corpus of rules had been formulated, with the result that it could be said to be a *traité-fondation*[37] or a *traité-constitution* (see para. 1–027).   1–015

---

[33] See the section "Setting up of the common customs tariff" (Arts 18 to 29 EEC) in the title on the free movement of goods and the chapter entitled "Commercial policy" (Arts 110 to 116 EEC) in the title on the economic policy of the Community.

[34] See Arts 85 to 98 EEC.

[35] This related to conjunctural policy (Art. 103 EEC) and balance of payments (Arts 104 to 109 EEC). "Social policy" (Arts 117 to 122 EEC) was not mentioned as such in Art. 3, although it did refer to the "creation of a European Social Fund" (Arts 123 to 128 EEC) and to the "establishment of a European Investment Bank" (Arts 129 and 130 EEC). The last "activity of the Community" set out in Art. 3 is "association of the overseas countries and territories" (Arts 131 to 136 EEC).

[36] For a good description of the EAEC Treaty, see Cusak, "A Tale of Two Treaties: An Assessment of the Euratom Treaty in Relation to the EC Treaty" (2003) C.M.L.Rev. 117–142; True, "Legislative competences of Euratom and the European Community in the energy sector: the "Nuclear Package" of the Commission" (2003) E.L.Rev. 664–685. See also, *http://books.google.com/books?id= AFQvAAAAYAAJ&cd=1&source=gbs_ViewAPI* [Accessed November 11, 2010] *Euratom: 50 years of nuclear energy serving Europe* (Luxembourg, Office for Official Publications of the European Communities, 2007), 63 pp. For a call for the integration of Euratom into a comprehensive European Union, see Trüe, "The Euratom Community Treaty's prospects at the start of the new millennium" (2006) I.J.N.L. 247–260.

[37] Lesguillons, *L'application d'un traité-fondation: le traité instituant la C.E.E.* (Paris, Librairie Générale de Droit et de Jurisprudence, 1968), 320 pp.

The EAEC Treaty does not embody the detailed market rules of the ECSC Treaty, but does share that Treaty's sectoral approach.

1–016 **Institutions.** The EEC Treaty and EAEC Treaty built on the institutional structure of the ECSC Treaty. The institutional set up of the EEC and the EAEC also consisted of a Commission (the equivalent of the ECSC High Authority), a Council, an Assembly and a Court of Justice. The parallel with the ECSC Treaty, however, did not extend any further than the organisational level, since the extensive programme to be achieved by the establishment of the EEC and the EAEC necessitated other roles for the institutions with decision-making powers.

The hub of the decision-making process was located in the Council. The Member States did not wish to vest any legislative powers in the Commission, because substantive policy choices had often been deliberately left open in the EEC Treaty. The ultimate policy choices were therefore to be determined by the Member States, within the Council. For those reasons, too, the role of the Assembly (which later became the European Parliament) was not extended either. The Commission's task, in principle at least, was confined to making proposals, implementing legislation and supervising compliance with Community law.

The three Treaties (ECSC, EEC and EAEC) provided for different powers for the institutions, although this was not reflected at the organisational level, since the institutions which each Treaty brought into being in parallel were merged. As long ago as when the EEC Treaty and the EAEC Treaty came into being, the Member States concluded the Convention on certain institutions common to the European Communities.[38] That convention provided that there should be one Parliament and one Court of Justice serving the three Communities in accordance with the powers conferred on those institutions by the different Treaties (Convention, Arts 1–2 and 3–4). At the same time it was provided that one Economic and Social Committee was to perform such tasks as the EEC Treaty and the EAEC Treaty conferred on it (Convention, Art. 5). The Treaty establishing a Single Council and a Single Commission of the European Communities, known as the Merger Treaty, which was concluded on April 8, 1965 and entered into effect on July 1, 1967, was a further step in that direction.[39] It provided that one Council and one Commission would play the roles specifically ascribed to them by the various treaties. In addition, the Merger Treaty unified the Staff Regulations (Art. 24) and laid down the principle that there should be a single budget of the European Communities (Art. 20).

---

[38] See [1967] O.J. 152/5. Not printed in the English Special Edition of the O.J.; for the English text, see *http://www.ena.lu* [Accessed November 11, 2010].

[39] See [1967] O.J. 152/2. Not printed in the English Special Edition of the O.J.; for the English text, see *http://www.ena.lu* [Accessed November 11, 2010]. See further Linthorst Homan, "The Merger of the European Communities" (1965–66) C.M.L.Rev. 397–419; Bleckmann, "Die Einheit der Europäischen Gemeinschaftsrechtsordnung. Einheit oder Mehrheit der Europäischen Gemeinschaften" (1978) EuR. 95–104. As regards the merger idea, see also: Van Stempel, "Die Fusion der Organe der Europäischen Gemeinschaften", in Hallstein and Schlochauer (eds), *Zur Integration Europas. Festschrift für C.F. Ophüls* (Karlsruhe, Müller, 1965), 229–241.

The Convention and the Merger Treaty were repealed by Art. 9 of the Treaty of Amsterdam, which, however, confirmed the rule that the same institutions would act under each of the Treaties on the basis of the specific powers that such Treaty conferred to them.[40]

Subsequent changes. The Community's objectives and competences laid down in the EEC Treaty were supplemented by the Single European Act (SEA), the EU Treaty, the Treaty of Amsterdam and the Treaty of Nice (see paras 3–006 *et seq.*). In contrast, the objectives and competences of the ECSC and the EAEC remained unchanged. At the institutional level, the initial Treaty structure was largely preserved, although significant changes have been made to the respective roles of the institutions by subsequent amending Treaties.   1–017

Reaction. Shortly after the EEC Treaty was signed, seven other western European countries (Austria, Denmark, Norway, Portugal, the United Kingdom, Sweden and Switzerland) decided to cooperate economically. They were unwilling to go as far as the cooperation established by the EEC Treaty, which set up a customs union. Instead, they preferred to set up a free-trade area, without common external tariffs or supplementary harmonisation of economic and social legislation.[41] On January 4, 1960, those seven States concluded the Convention establishing the European Free Trade Association (EFTA).[42] Later, Finland, Iceland and Liechtenstein joined,[43] but first Denmark and the United Kingdom, then Portugal, and finally Austria, Finland and Sweden left the organisation to accede to the Communities and the Union (see para. 6–005.). EFTA's Council of Ministers and Committee of Parliamentarians have been supplemented—as far as the EFTA States belonging to the European Economic Area (Iceland, Liechtenstein and Norway) are concerned—by a Standing Committee, a Joint Parliamentary Committee, a Surveillance Authority and a Court of Justice (see para. 25–031).   1–018

---

[40] Amsterdam Treaty, Art. 9(1), (2) and (3).

[41] According to Art. XXIV(8) of the General Agreement on Tariffs and Trade (GATT, para. 25–011, *infra*), a free-trade area is a group of two or more customs territories in which the duties and other restrictive regulations of trade are eliminated on substantially all the trade between the constituent territories in products originating in such territories. A free-trade area differs from a customs union, in which the reciprocal abolition of restrictions on trade is coupled with a common external tariff; see the discussion in para. 9–016, *infra*.

[42] *Convention establishing the European Free Trade Association*, signed at Stockholm on January 4, 1960, (1960) UNTS 30, Cmnd. 1026. EFTA's website is at *http://www.efta.int/* [Accessed November 11, 2010]. The EFTA States did not only aim at removing barriers to trade between themselves, but also referred expressly to the EEC Member States as potential members of a future multilateral economic cooperation association: see Jacot-Guillarmod, "Expressions juridiques, au sein du système européen de libre-échange, du rapprochement de l'AELE et de la Communauté", in Capotorti, Ehlermann, Frowein, Jacobs, Joliet, Koopmans and Kovar (eds), *Du droit international au droit de l'intégration. Liber Amicorum P. Pescatore* (Baden-Baden, Nomos, 1987), 317–318.

[43] Iceland became a member of EFTA on March 1, 1970, Finland (having been an associate member since 1961) on January 1, 1986 and Liechtenstein on September 1, 1991.

V. THE SUPRANATIONAL CHARACTER OF COMMUNITY LAW

1–019 **Community law.** The EC Treaty and the EAEC Treaty constituted the foundation of "Community law", which additionally consisted of the legislative and implementing measures adopted on the basis of the Treaties and the judicial interpretation of those provisions, supplemented by the unwritten general principles of superior law. Since the entry into force of the Lisbon Treaty on December 1, 2009, the EC has been replaced by the European Union and Community law—with its specific characteristics—has become Union law (see para. 4–009). Community/Union law has its origin in international law, since the European Communities/Union constitutes an "international" organisation based on treaties concluded between sovereign States. As a subject of law, the Community/Union acts vis-à-vis third countries in accordance with the rules of international law (see para. 24–002). In contrast, relations between Member States (within the field of application of Community/Union law) and between Member States and the Communities/Union are no longer governed by international law. Those relations are governed by Community/Union law. This is illustrated by the fact that the Court of Justice has given a different interpretation to provisions of the EC Treaty, on the one hand, and to corresponding provisions of international agreements concluded by the Community on the basis of the EC Treaty, on the other. The Court bases itself in this connection on the more extensive objectives of the EC Treaty, the specific characteristics of decision-making within the Community and the possibilities of enforcing Community law.[44] The same reasoning holds good with regard to Union law since the entry into force of the Lisbon Treaty.

1–020 **Supranational.** With a view to distinguishing the Communities/Union and the Community/Union legal order more clearly from other forms of international organisations and from general international law, they are commonly referred to as a "supranational" organisation and as "supranational" law. It is generally accepted that the term "supranational"[45] refers to the particular set of relationships between Member States, Community/Union institutions and individuals, of which the principal characteristics are as follows:

    (a) the Community/Union has institutions which act independently of the Member States in terms of their composition and manner of operation;

---

[44] See ECJ, Case 270/80 *Polydor* [1982] E.C.R. 329, paras 14–20; Opinion 1/91 *Draft agreement between the Community, on the one hand, and the countries of the European Free Trade Association, on the other, relating to the creation of the European Economic Area* [1991] E.C.R. I-6079, paras 13–21. See para. 22–048, *infra*.

[45] The origin, meaning and application of the term "supranationality" are discussed extensively in von Lindeiner-Wildau, *La supranationalité en tant que principe de droit* (Leiden, Sijthoff, 1970), 178 pp.

   (b) the Community/Union may take decisions by a majority, yet they will bind all the Member States;

   (c) the institutions of the Community/Union implement those decisions or are responsible for supervising that they are properly implemented by the Member States;

   (d) the founding Treaties and decisions of the Community/Union may give rise to rights and obligations on the part of individuals which are directly enforceable by courts in the Member States, even in the presence of conflicting provisions of national law.[46]

Consequently, the term "supranationalism" fits the *sui generis* nature of the European Communities/Union perfectly. In addition, those factors express the dynamic nature of the integration process which has been taking place within the Communities/Union.[47]

(a) Independent institutions. The authentic French version of the ECSC Treaty   **1–021** used the term *"supranational"* in referring to the independent status of the High Authority (the Commission).[48] Indeed, the Commission is not made up of representatives of the governments of the Member States in the traditional manner of international institutions, as is still the case with the Council and the European Council. Members of the European Parliament, the Court of Justice and the Court of Auditors are also independent of the governments of the Member States. In addition, the European Parliament is the only institution whose Members are not appointed by the national governments (or the Council/European Council) but directly elected.[49]

(b) Autonomous decision-making. In international law, there is a principle of   **1–022** decision-making that States cannot be bound against their will. Although that

---

[46] *Cf., ibid.*, at 45–61; Schermers and Blokker, *International Institutional Law* (The Hague, Martinus Nijhoff, 1995), para. 61, (who mention, as additional requirements for supranational organisations, that the organisation should be financially independent and that participating States must have the approval of all the States and the supranational institutions in order to leave the organisation, wind it up or change its powers); Hay, *Federalism and Supranational Organisations, Patterns for New Legal Structures* (Urbana/London, University of Illinois Press, 1966), at 30–34 (who sets out additional political qualifications, such as the compass of the organisation's powers).

[47] Weiler, "The Community System: the Dual Character of Supranationalism" (1981) Y.E.L. 267–306.

[48] See the original fifth and sixth paras of Art. 9 ECSC (removed by Art. 19 of the Merger Treaty and replaced by Art. 10 of that Treaty, the wording of which was introduced as the new Art. 9 ECSC by Art. 9(2) of the EU Treaty). For an earlier use of the term and for its intentional omission from the EEC and EAEC Treaties, see Hay (n.46, *supra*), at 29–30; Jaenicke, "Die Supranationalität der Europäischen Gemeinschaften", *Zur Integration Europas. Festschrift für C.F. Ophüls* (n.39, *supra*), 85, at 88.

[49] See para. 13–015, *infra*.

principle is reflected in the contractual nature of the Treaties underlying the Communities/Union and in the requirement that certain votes in the Council have to be unanimous, in many respects it does not apply in the Community/Union legal order. In numerous cases a majority decision of the Council binds all Member States. In addition, the Court rejects the technique of international law whereby a State may enter a "reservation" when a decision is taken and so avoid being bound by a provision of a treaty or a decision. The Court stresses that measures of the Communities/Union cannot be regarded as international agreements because of the independent institutional framework within which they are drawn up.[50] It further emphasises that the rules laid down by the common institutions must be interpreted in a uniform manner. That requirement would be detracted from if Community/Union law were to take account of reservations or objections entered by Member States at the preparatory stage.[51]

1–023　(c) Implementation of decisions. Member States of the Communities/Union must take all necessary measures to ensure fulfilment of the obligations arising for them under Community/Union law (see para. 7–042). They are generally charged with implementing Community/Union law, unless implementation is specifically entrusted to an institution of the Communities/Union (see para. 17–001). Under Community/Union law, Member States are subject to more far-reaching supervision than is generally the case under international law. Thus, the *exceptio non adimpleti contractus* (the defence of a material breach of a treaty)[52] used in international law is not employed as a mechanism for enforcing reciprocal obligations; Community/Union law has procedures of its own for determining infringements and imposing sanctions therefor.[53] Under Art. 344 TFEU [*ex Art. 292 EC*], Member States must submit any dispute concerning the interpretation or application of the Treaty to the methods of resolution provided for therein. The jurisdiction of the Court of Justice is compulsory and its judgments are binding throughout the Community/Union. In contrast, within the international legal order, the International Court of Justice adjudicates only if there is voluntary—general or specific—acceptance of the court's jurisdiction on the part of the parties.

1–024　(d) Separate legal order. The Communities/Union constitute a legal order in their own right, which is different from the legal orders commonly created by international treaties. The essential characteristics of the Community/Union legal

---

[50] ECJ, Case 38/69 *Commission v Italy* [1970] E.C.R. 47, paras 10–11.
[51] ECJ, Case 143/83 *Commission v Denmark* [1985] E.C.R. 427, paras 12–13 (para. 22–105, *infra*).
[52] See Art. 60 of the Vienna Convention of May 23, 1969 on the Law of Treaties (for that Convention, see para. 22–055, *infra*).
[53] ECJ, Joined Cases 90/63 and 91/63 *Commission v Luxembourg and Belgium* [1964] E.C.R. 625, at 631–632; ECJ, Case C-5/94 *Hedley Lomas* [1996] E.C.R. I-2553, para. 20; ECJ, Case C-11/95 *Commission v Belgium* [1996] E.C.R. I-4115, paras 37–39; ECJ, Case C-14/96 *Denuit* [1997] E.C.R. I-2785, paras 34–35; ECJ, Case C-45/07 *Commission v Greece* [2009] E.C.R. I-701, para. 26; ECJ, Case C-118/07 *Commission v Finland* [2009] E.C.R. I-10889, para. 48.

order include the fact that individuals can rely in legal proceedings on a series of provisions of Community/Union law and the primacy of Community/Union law over the law of the Member States.[54] The Court of Justice established those basic principles in 1963 and 1964 in two ground-breaking judgments: *Van Gend & Loos* and *Costa v ENEL*.[55] In the latter judgment, the Court observed that,

> "the EEC Treaty has created its own legal system which, on the entry into force of the treaty, became an integral part of the legal systems of the Member States and which their courts are bound to apply".

The Court considered that the Member States brought that legal order into being and at the same time limited their sovereignty, albeit within limited fields,

> "[b]y creating a Community of unlimited duration, having its own institutions, its own personality, its own legal capacity and capacity of representation on the international plane and, more particularly, real powers [as a result of the Member States' having limited their own powers or transferred them to the Communities]."[56]

Whereas that judgment and the judgment in *Van Gend & Loos* (para. 1–018, *infra*) refer to a limitation of sovereignty "within limited fields", more recent judgments speak of a limitation of sovereign rights "in ever wider fields".[57]

Rights for individuals. In *Van Gend & Loos*, the Court held for the first time that Community law not only imposes obligations on individuals but is also intended to confer upon them "rights which become part of their legal heritage".[58] In so doing, it referred to "the spirit, the general scheme and the wording" of the EEC Treaty. The Court first considered that,   1–025

> "[t]he objective of the EEC Treaty, which is to establish a Common Market, the functioning of which is of direct concern to interested parties in the Community, implies that this Treaty is more than an agreement which merely creates mutual obligations between the contracting States".

---

[54] ECJ, Opinion 1/91 *Draft agreement between the Community, on the one hand, and the countries of the European Free Trade Association, on the other, relating to the creation of the European Economic Area* [1991] E.C.R. I-6079, para. 21.

[55] ECJ, Case 26/62 *Van Gend & Loos* [1963] E.C.R. 1; ECJ, Case 6/64 *Costa v ENEL* [1964] E.C.R. 585. See, among others, Lecourt, "Quel eût été le droit des Communautés sans les arrêts de 1963 et 1964?", in *L'Europe et le Droit, Mélanges en hommage à J. Boulouis* (Paris, Dalloz, 1991), 349–361.

[56] ECJ, Case 6/64 *Costa* [1964] E.C.R. 585, at 593.

[57] ECJ, Opinion 1/91 *Draft agreement between the Community, on the one hand, and the countries of the European Free Trade Association, on the other, relating to the creation of the European Economic Area* [1991] E.C.R. I-6079, para. 21.

[58] ECJ, Case 26/62 *Van Gend & Loos* [1963] E.C.R. 1, at 12–13.

The Court averred that this "view" was "confirmed" by "the preamble to the Treaty which refers not only to governments but to peoples" and,

> "more specifically by the establishment of institutions endowed with sovereign rights, the exercise of which affects Member States and also their citizens".

Two further indicia led the Court to conclude that,

> "the Community constitutes a new legal order of international law for the benefit of which the States have limited their sovereign rights, albeit within limited fields, and the subjects of which comprise not only Member States but also their nationals".

The first was the fact that,

> "the nationals of the States brought together in the Community are called upon to cooperate in the functioning of this Community through the intermediary of the European Parliament and the Economic and Social Committee".

The second was that

> "the task assigned to the Court of Justice under Article 177 [*now Art. 267 TFEU*], the object of which is to secure uniform interpretation of the Treaty by national courts and tribunals, confirms that the States have acknowledged that Community law has an authority which can be invoked by their nationals before those courts and tribunals".

Van Gend & Loos had to come to terms with the view then held by the Member States that Community law constituted a form of international law and, accordingly, that only subjects of that law could take the initiative of seeking a declaration that the agreed rules had been breached. *Van Gend & Loos*, a Dutch company, had brought an action in the competent national court in which it sought to recover an import duty which it considered that the Netherlands tax authorities had charged contrary to (the former) Art. 12 EEC. The national court made a reference for a preliminary ruling on the interpretation of Art. 12, pursuant to what is now Art. 267 TFEU. The Belgian, Netherlands and German Governments argued before the Court that the reference was not concerned with the interpretation of the Treaty but with a Member State's compliance therewith. They contended that the Court could declare that national legislation was contrary to the Treaty only through the proper procedures provided for in Arts 169 and 170 EEC [*now Arts 258 and 259 TFEU*]. The Court's response was to hold that the fact that Arts 169 and 170 EEC enabled the Commission and the Member States to bring an action did not mean that individuals could not plead a Member State's infringement of Community law before a national court, which might result in a question being referred for an interpretation of Community law. The Court held that,

> "[t]he vigilance of individuals concerned to protect their rights amounts to an effective supervision in addition to the supervision entrusted by Articles 169 and 170 [*now Arts 258 and 259 TFEU*] to the diligence of the Commission and the Member States".

Consequently, the individual legal subject enforces the rights that he or she draws from Union law through the national courts which, in accordance with Art. 267 TFEU, "cooperate" with the Court of Justice with the aim of ensuring that Union law is applied in a uniform manner in all the Member States.[59] In this way, the Treaties establish a complete system of legal remedies in order to secure compliance with Union law by Union institutions, Member States and individuals.[60]

Primacy of Community/Union law. Among the various legal orders which have   1–026
been established by treaty, the Community/Union legal order is special inasmuch
as it takes away from Member States the freedom to determine the position
of Community/Union law vis-à-vis domestic law. National courts and tribunals
are automatically required to apply Community/Union law in the context of the
national legal system. In the leading case of *Costa v ENEL* the Court inferred from,

> "the integration into the laws of each Member State of provisions which derive from the Community, and more generally the terms and the spirit of the Treaty"

that it is

> "impossible for the States, as a corollary, to accord precedence to a unilateral and subsequent measure over a legal system accepted by them on a basis of reciprocity."[61]

The Court was answering a preliminary question from an Italian court concerning the compatibility with the EEC Treaty of an Italian law of December 6, 1962

---

[59] ECJ, Case 16/65 *Schwarze* [1965] E.C.R. 877, at 886; ECJ, Case C-221/88 *Busseni* [1990] E.C.R. I-495, para. 13. See, in addition, Lenaerts, "Form and Substance of the Preliminary Rulings Procedure", in Curtin and Heukels (eds), *Institutional Dynamics of European Integration. Essays in Honour of Henry G. Schermers*, Vol. II (Dordrecht, Martinus Nijhoff, 1994), 355–380.

[60] ECJ, Case 294/83 *Les Verts* v *European Parliament* [1986] E.C.R. 1339, para. 23. See Lenaerts, "Case 294/83 *Parti écologiste 'Les Verts' v European Parliament* [1986] ECR 1339. The Basic Constitutional Charter of a Community Based on the Rule of Law", in Poiares Maudoro and Azoulai (eds), *The Past and Future of EU Law. The classics of EU Law Revisited on the 50th Anniversary of the Rome Treaty* (Oxford, Hart Publishing, 2009) 295–342.

[61] ECJ, Case 6/64 *Costa v ENEL* [1964] E.C.R. 585, at 593–594.

nationalising the electricity industry. The Italian Government submitted written observations to the Court in which it argued that the national court had no jurisdiction to make a reference under Art. 177 EEC [*now Art. 267 TFEU*], because it was obliged to apply the national law. The Court rejected that argument on the ground that to take such a view would deprive the law stemming from the Treaty of its character as Community law and call in question the legal basis of the Community itself.

> "The executive force of Community law cannot vary from one State to another in deference to subsequent domestic laws, without jeopardising the attainment of the objectives of the Treaty set out in Article 5(2) [*of the EEC Treaty, now Art. 3(3) TEU*] and giving rise to the discrimination prohibited by Article 7 [*now Art. 18 TFEU*]".

The Court concluded from this that, if Member States were entitled to renounce their obligations unilaterally, those obligations would be merely contingent and the authorisation provisions which enable a Member State to derogate from the Treaty in particular cases would lose their purpose. Lastly, the Court expressed the view that,

> "the precedence of Community law is confirmed by Article 189 [*now Art. 288 TFEU*], whereby a regulation 'shall be binding' and 'directly applicable in the Member States' ".

1–027   **Constitutional basis.** As a result of its complete system of legal remedies, the Community has been called a community based on the rule of law, whose foundation is the "constitutional charter" constituted by the Treaties.[62] For this reason, the texts of the Treaties have been described as the constitution of the Communities[63] and the Court of Justice as a constitutional court.[64] Even before the entry into force of the Lisbon Treaty, this work and other commentators referred to the

---

[62] ECJ, Case 294/83 *Les Verts v European Parliament* [1986] E.C.R. 1339, para. 23; ECJ, Opinion 1/91 *Draft agreement between the Community, on the one hand, and the countries of the European Free Trade Association, on the other, relating to the creation of the European Economic Area* [1991] E.C.R. I-6079, para. 21 ("the EEC Treaty, albeit concluded in the form of an international agreement, none the less constitutes the constitutional charter of a Community based on the rule of law").

[63] Gerkrath, *L'émergence d'un droit constitutionnel pour l'Europe*, (Brussels, Editions de l'Université de Bruxelles, 1997), 425 pp; Lenaerts, "Constitutionalism and the Many Faces of Federalism" (1990) A.J.C.L. 205–263; Mancini, "The Making of a Constitution for Europe" (1989) C.M.L.Rev. 595; Ipsen, "Europäische Verfassung—Nationale Verfassung" (1987) EuR. 195–213; Lenaerts, *Le juge et la constitution aux Etats-Unis d'Amérique et dans l'ordre juridique européen* (Brussels, Bruylant, 1988), paras 243–245, at 257–263; Hartley, "Federalism, Courts and Legal Systems: The Emerging Constitution of the European Community" (1986) A.J.C.L. 229–247; Stein, "Lawyers, Judges, and the Making of a Transnational Constitution" (1981) A.J.I.L. 1–27.

[64] See Lenaerts, Arts and Maselis, *Procedural Law of the European Union* (3rd edn, London, Sweet & Maxwell, 2012) Ch. 1.

constitutional law *of the European Union*, extending thereby the analysis to cover the areas in which the Union does not act as the Community.[65] The "constitutional law" of the European Union consists of all the rules of Union law relating to the general objectives, the allocation of competences and the way in which the legislative, executive and judicial functions are performed within the Union. In view of the supranational character of the Union, Union law employs concepts taken from international law[66] and national constitutional law,[67] in particular the constitutional law of federal States.[68]

A number of initiatives have been undertaken to provide the European Union with a true constitution in its own right in order to clarify the constitutional elements of the supranational legal order and confer greater democratic legitimacy on them. The European Parliament prepared on its own motion a formal Constitution of the European Union (see para. 3–020). Constitutional questions were also raised in the Declaration adopted by the European Council of December 14 and 15, 2001 at Laeken. That declaration led to the convening of a "Convention", which ultimately produced a Draft Treaty establishing a Constitution for Europe, which was later approved in the Intergovernmental Conference (see para. 4–003, *infra*). However, it proved not possible for this "Constitution" to be ratified by all the

---

[65] See, for example, Weiler, *The Constitution of Europe* (Cambridge, Cambridge University Press, 1999), 364 pp.; Rossi, "'Constitutionalisation' de l'Union européenne et des droits fondamentaux" (2002) R.T.D.E. 27–52; Arnold, "European Constitutional Law: Some Reflections on a Concept that Emerged in the Second Half of the Twentieth Century" (1999) Tulane E. & Civ. L.F. 49–64; Piris, "Does the European Union have a Constitution? Does it need one?" (1999) E.L.Rev. 557–585; Snyder, "General Course on Constitutional Law of the European Union", in European University Institute, *Collected Courses of the Academy of European Law (1995—Volume VI-1)* (Dordrecht, Nijhoff, 1998), 41–155; Favret, "Le traité d'Amsterdam: une révision *a minima* de la 'charte constitutionnelle' de l'Union européenne" (1997) C.D.E. 555–605; Curtin, "The Constitutional Structure of the Union: A Europe of Bits and Pieces" (1993) C.M.L.Rev. 17–69; Pliakos, "La nature juridique de l'Union européenne" (1993) R.T.D.E. 187–224; VerLoren van Themaat, "De constitutionele problematiek van een Europese politieke Unie" (1991) S.E.W. 436–454.

[66] See the privileges and immunities of the Union in the national systems (para. 13–128); the legal concept of the direct effect of Treaty provisions (para. 21–055); the status of international law in the Union legal order (paras 22–043—22–058); the position in international law of the Union (paras 24–002—24–011).

[67] See, for instance, the allocation of the three classic functions of a State (paras 15–011—15–013); the distinction between legislation and the implementation of legislation (paras 17–006—17–007); democratic legitimacy (paras 20–004—20–008) and the role of the Parliament (paras 20–010—20–016); citizenship (paras 8–001—8–014); the principle of equal treatment (paras 7–050—7–060) and other general principles of law (paras 22–036—22–038) and fundamental rights (paras 22–017—22–019); the rules on public funding (paras 13–130—13–133); the procedure for concluding international agreements (paras 26–003—26–018).

[68] See the discussion of exclusive and non-exclusive competence (paras 7–020—7–025); the principles of subsidiarity (paras 7–026—7–027) and proportionality (paras 7–033—7–034); the duty of sincere cooperation (para. 7–042 *et seq.*); the allocation of powers of implementation (para. 17–001 *et seq.*); the primacy of Union law (para. 21–004 *et seq.*); the relationship between the external powers of the Union and those of the Member States (paras 25–058—25–059 and paras 26–014—26–016).

Member States. Hence, the 2007 IGC chose to abandon the Constitutional Treaty and to incorporate many of the changes it would have introduced in a new treaty, the Treaty of Lisbon, which modified the existing treaties on which the European Union was based, while leaving out any references to the constitutional character of the Treaties (see para. 4–007 *et seq.*).

CHAPTER 2

INTERGOVERNMENTAL COOPERATION BETWEEN EC MEMBER STATES

Intergovernmental cooperation. From the outset, the momentum of supra-national integration led the Member States to become involved in cooperation in areas which did not (as yet) fall within the competence of the Communities. The adjective "intergovernmental" appropriately describes those forms of international cooperation: the international agreements involved were generally made between representatives of the executives or of the "governments" (hence "governmental") of the States party to them. By having recourse to such "intergovernmental" cooperation, the EC Member States succeeded in cooperating amongst all or some of them in fields where they were not (yet) willing to act under the "supranational" decision-making procedures provided for in the Community Treaties. In contradis-tinction to decisions taken within supranational organisations, intergovernmental decisions do not in principle have the force of law within national legal systems unless they are specifically adopted therein, and generally do not confer any rights on individuals.[1]

2–001

I. EUROPEAN POLITICAL COOPERATION

Fouchet Plan. After the first years of operation of the EEC and the EAEC, plans began to emerge anew to extend integration to less socio-economically oriented areas.[2] The French President de Gaulle presented plans for forming a Political Union, which were discussed in 1961 and 1962, first at summit conferences and subsequently in the Fouchet Committee.[3] Under the structure proposed by de Gaulle, the Heads of State or Government meeting within the Council of the Union would conduct common foreign and defence policy by unanimous vote and

2–002

---

[1] Schermers and Blokker, *International Institutional Law* (The Hague, Martinus Nijhoff, 1995), paras 58–59, at 39–40, and paras 1330–1331, at 819–820.

[2] Lang, "Die Bemühungen um die politische Einigung Europas seit dem Scheitern der Europäischen Verteidigungsgemeinschaft", in Hallstein and Schlochauer (eds), *Zur Integration Europas. Festschrift für C.F. Ophüls* (Karlsruhe, Müller, 1965), 125–141.

[3] These plans are annexed to Bloes, *Le "Plan Fouchet" et le problème de l'Europe politique* (Bruges, College of Europe, 1970), at 487–510; see also *http://www.ena.lu* [Accessed November 10, 2010].

cooperate on culture, science and safeguarding human rights, fundamental freedoms and democracy. The Union was also to have a Political Commission and a Parliamentary Assembly, but no Court of Justice. Made up of national civil servants, the Political Commission was to confine itself to preparing and, where necessary, carrying out the decisions of the Council. The Parliamentary Assembly was to play an advisory role. Under the first proposal of November 1961, this *Union d'Etats* was to operate alongside the existing Communities. Under a subsequent proposal, this organisation was also to have powers in the economic field and foresaw the institutions of the Communities being bound by decisions of the Heads of State or Government. The "Fouchet Plan" ultimately came to grief because of the fears of the smaller Member States that this would erode the powers and supranational character which the Communities had acquired. A further decisive factor was de Gaulle's refusal to have the United Kingdom (which applied in 1961 for membership of the Communities) involved in the negotiations.

2–003   **European Political Cooperation.** The field in which Member States agreed to coordinate their policies outside the sphere of competence of the Communities was foreign policy, resulting in the emergence of European Political Cooperation (EPC).[4] At a meeting of the Council held in Luxembourg on October 27, 1970, the Foreign Ministers gave their approval to the Davignon Report, which proposed that there should be half-yearly meetings of the Foreign Ministers, to which a member of the Commission could also be invited.[5] It was in this way that European Political Cooperation (EPC) came about. It was further developed on the basis of reports of the Foreign Ministers[6] and of the Heads of State or Government.[7]

Initially, the Foreign Ministers deliberately kept their EPC meetings separate from meetings of the Council of the European Communities.[8] But gradually a link grew up between them.[9] Because having a special body for EPC was still reminiscent of the Political Committee proposed in the Fouchet Plan, the EPC secretariat was given purely administrative functions under the authority of the Presidency.

---

[4] De Schoutheete, *La coopération politique européenne* (Paris/Brussels, Nathan/Labor, 1986), 334 pp.; Ifestos, *European Political Cooperation—Towards a Framework of Supranational Diplomacy?* (Aldershot, Avebury, 1987), 635 pp.

[5] Report of the Ministers of Foreign Affairs of the Member States on the question of political integration (1970) 11 EC Bull. 9–14.

[6] Copenhagen, 1973, (1973) 9 EC Bull. 13 and 20–23; London, 1981, (1981) EC Bull., Suppl. 3, 14–18 (see also (1981) 10 EC Bull. point 2.2.59).

[7] Solemn Declaration of Stuttgart on European Union of June 19, 1983, (1983) 6 EC Bull. Point 1.6.1.

[8] The most striking example is one day in 1973 when the Foreign Ministers met in the morning in Copenhagen under EPC auspices and in the afternoon in Brussels as the Council of the European Communities.

[9] See Nuttall, "Interaction between European Political Co-operation and the European Community" (1987) Y.E.L. 211–249.

Legal status. All EPC decisions were taken by consensus and the Court of Justice   **2–004**
had no jurisdiction to supervise the fulfilment by Member States of the obligations which they assumed in the context of EPC. Accordingly, the rules of conduct governing EPC constituted a species of soft law influencing the international
action of the Member States. It was not until 1986 that the Member States gave
EPC practice a legal basis under a treaty by means of the Single European Act
(Art.1; Art.3(2); Art.30 or Title III of the Single European Act). In 1992, the EU
Treaty converted EPC into the non-Community "second pillar" of the Union, the
common foreign and security policy based on Title V of the EU Treaty (CFSP;
see paras 25–039—25–048).[10] In December 2009, the Lisbon Treaty abolished
the pillar-structure in which the Union had been organised, although special provisions remain in place as regards the former "second pillar".

European Council. From 1961 onwards, the Heads of State or Government of   **2–005**
the Member States held regular meetings in order to discuss political sticking
points in Community policy.[11] At the Paris summit conference on December 9
and 10, 1974, they decided to hold such meetings from then on at least three times
a year, accompanied by the Foreign Ministers.[12] The institution created thereby,
the European Council, was intended not only to give impetus to European
Political Cooperation, but also to take political decisions regarding matters coming within the sphere of competence of the Communities.[13] Although the
European Council also made pronouncements about matters for which the
Communities were competent, it did not play a formal role in Community decision-making and did not constitute an institution hierarchically superior to the
Community institutions. The Single European Act caused the European Council
to be acknowledged for the first time in the Treaties. The EU Treaty conferred a
number of tasks on the European Council in the context of the Community decision-making process and the CFSP. Consequently, since the EU Treaty and the
Treaty of Amsterdam the European Council acted as a specific organ of the Union
alongside the Community institutions (see para. 13–025). The Treaty of Lisbon
included the European Council among the institutions of the Union (see
Art.13(1), second subpara., TEU).

---

[10] Title V of the EU Treaty. Article 50(2) EU repealed Arts 2, 3(2) and 30 (Title III) of the Single
European Act.
[11] Such summit conferences took place twice in 1961 (Paris and Bonn) and thereafter in 1967 (Rome),
1969 (The Hague), 1972 (Paris) and 1973 (Copenhagen), each time at the prompting of the French
President.
[12] Communiqué of the Heads of State or Government meeting in Paris on December 9 and 10, 1974,
(1974) 12 EC Bull. point 1104(3).
[13] See Tindemans, "Le Conseil européen: un premier bilan, quelques réflexions", Mélanges Fernand
Dehousse; Vol. II. *La construction européenne* (Paris/Brussels, Nathan/Labor, 1979), 167–173;
Wessels, *Der Europäische Rat* (Bonn, Europa Union, 1980), 472 pp.

II. EUROPEAN MONETARY COOPERATION

2–006 **Initial steps.** The initial successes of the Communities prompted the Heads of State or Government in December 1969 to investigate transforming the customs union, which had only just been introduced, into an economic and monetary union (EMU).[14] The Council set up the Werner Committee, which put forward proposals in October 1970 for achieving EMU in stages.[15] With a view to achieving the first stage, a resolution of March 22, 1971 of the Council and the representatives of the Governments of the Member States looked forward to increased coordination of economic and monetary policies and limitation of the fluctuation margins between the Member States' currencies.[16] Since not all the measures seemed feasible—the economic climate became more unfavourable after the oil crisis—EMU remained at the starting blocks. In the monetary sphere, the Council nevertheless set up the European Monetary Cooperation Fund as planned.[17] Following the collapse of the international system of fixed exchange rates (the Bretton Woods system), the Member States endeavoured, with varying degrees of success, to coordinate their intervention on the currency markets (the "Snake").

2–007 **European Monetary System.** Monetary cooperation as between the Member States came into being on the basis of the resolution of the European Council of December 5, 1978 on the establishment of the European Monetary System (EMS).[18] Within the EMS, bilateral exchange rates were set as between the various currencies. Initially, the EMS operated on the basis of the intergovernmental agreements contained in the resolution of the European Council and in agreements between the central banks. For the coordination of their general monetary policy, representatives of the central banks also met in institutions of the Communities, such as the Monetary Committee and the Committee of Governors of the central banks.[19] By a regulation, the Council subsequently entrusted the

---

[14] Final communiqué of the Conference (December 2, 1969), EC Bull., 1-1970, 16, point 8.

[15] The final report of the Werner Committee of October 8, 1970 was published in (1970) EC Bull. Suppl. 11, and in [1970] O.J. C136.

[16] Resolution of the Council and of the Representatives of the Governments of the Member States of March 22, 1971 on the attainment by stages of economic and monetary union in the Community, [1974] O.J., English Spec. Edn, Second Series, IX. Resolutions of the Council and of the Representatives of the Member States, p. 40.

[17] Regulation (EEC) No. 907/73 of the Council of April 3, 1973 establishing a European Monetary Cooperation Fund, [1973] O.J. L 89/2.

[18] Resolution of the European Council of December 5, 1978 on the establishment of the European Monetary System (EMS) and related matters (1978) 12 EC Bull. point 1.1.11.

[19] For these bodies, see the Rules governing the Monetary Committee, [1952–1958] O.J., English Spec. Edn, p. 60; Council Decision 64/300/EEC of May 8, 1964 on cooperation between the Central Banks of the Member States of the European Economic Community, [1963–1964] O.J., English Spec. Edn, p. 141.

management of the EMS to the Monetary Cooperation Fund.[20] In 1978 the Council had adopted, in connection with monetary cooperation, a regulation introducing the ECU (European Currency Unit) as a unit of account for the exchange rate mechanism and a means of settling transactions between national authorities and the Fund.[21] The ECU was a basket of currencies whose value was determined by the value of the national currencies, weighted according to their share of the basket. That share was fixed commensurately with each Member State's share of the Union's Gross National Product and of internal Community trade. By means of a regulation, the Council introduced the ECU as the means of account for the Communities' budget.[22]

Economic and Monetary Union. The EU Treaty laid the foundations for the introduction of economic and monetary Union, thereby bringing monetary cooperation within the ambit of "supranational" Community decision-making. On December 31, 1998 the conversion rates between the common currency—now named the euro—and the currencies of the Member States taking part in EMU were irrevocably fixed.[23] Since January 1, 1999 the euro has been the currency of the Member States participating in EMU (see paras 11–031 *et seq.*).

2–008

III. POLICE AND JUDICIAL COOPERATION

First cooperation and agreements. Equally outside the ambit of the Communities, forms of cooperation grew up between ministerial departments of the Member States with regard to trans-frontier aspects of justice and home affairs. In December 1975, the European Council meeting in Rome approved the initiative of ministers from the Member States meeting twice a year in order to discuss questions of law and order, such as terrorism and other forms of international lawlessness.[24] Various other intergovernmental bodies coordinated and

2–009

---

[20] Council Regulation (EEC) No. 3181/78 of December 18, 1978 relating to the European Monetary System, [1978] O.J. L379/2 (repealed by Council Regulation (EC) No. 640/2006 of April 10, 2006, [2006] O.J. L115/1).

[21] Council Regulation (EEC) No. 3180/78 of December 18, 1978 changing the value of the unit of account used by the European Monetary Cooperation Fund, [1978] O.J. L 379/1).

[22] Council Regulation (EEC, Euratom) No. 3308/80 of December 16, 1980 on the replacement of the European unit of account by the ECU in Community legal instruments, [1980] O.J. L345/1.

[23] Council Regulation (EC) No. 2866/98 of December 31, 1998 on the conversion rates between the euro and the currencies of the Member States adopting the euro, [1998] O.J. L 359/1.

[24] See (1975) 11 EC. Bull. point 1104. These meetings were known as the Trevi Group. "Trevi" refers to the Roman fountain and has been turned into an acronym for *Terrorisme, Radicalisme, Extrémisme et Violence Internationale*. For the structure and operation of Trevi, see Le Jeune, *La coopération policière européenne contre le terrorisme* (Brussels, Bruylant, 1992), 105–148.

studied national police policy.[25] Agreements were also concluded between the Member States on police and judicial cooperation in criminal matters and on judicial cooperation in civil matters, including the Brussels Convention.[26] Similar conventions are also concluded under the auspices of the Council of Europe.[27]

2–010 **Cooperation extended to migration issues.** The internal-market programme (see para. 9–009) looked forward to the abolition of checks on persons at the internal frontiers of the Community by the end of 1992. Cooperation between the Member States in the sphere of customs controls and combating criminality therefore became essential. Free movement of persons meant that non-EC nationals could move freely within the Community once they had crossed the external frontiers. The Member States accordingly sought to arrive at forms of cooperation enabling a common control policy at the external frontiers and a uniform policy with regard to the access, movement and residence of nationals of third countries in the Community. The European Council meeting at Rhodes on December 2 and 3, 1988 set up a Coordinators Group to coordinate the various activities in the sphere of the free movement of persons.[28] The activities of an ad hoc working group on immigration[29] resulted in agreements which were

---

[25] For example, Celad (*Comité européen pour la lutte anti-drogue*), which was set up on the initiative of the French to coordinate national anti-drugs policies (1989) 12 EC Bull. point 1.1.9., and Interpol, an intergovernmental cooperative association which has been operating since 1923 not on the basis of a treaty. See Fijnaut, "The 'Communitisation' of Police Cooperation in Western Europe", in Schermers, Flinterman, Kellermann, Van Haersolte and Van de Meent (eds), *Free Movement of Persons in Europe. Legal Problems and Experiences*, (Dordrecht, Martinus Nijhoff, 1993), at 75–92.

[26] Brussels Convention of September 27, 1968 on jurisdiction and the enforcement of judgments in civil and commercial matters (Accession Convention for Denmark, Ireland and the United Kingdom: [1978] O.J. L304/77; a codified text of the Convention can be found in [1998] O.J. C17/1), implemented in the United Kingdom by the Civil Jurisdiction and Judgments Act 1982. The Brussels Convention has since been replaced, except as far as Denmark is concerned, by Council Regulation (EC) No. 44/2001 of December 22, 2000 on jurisdiction and the recognition and enforcement of judgments in civil and commercial matters ([2001] O.J. L12/1; implemented in the United Kingdom by the Civil Jurisdiction and Judgments Order 2001 (SI 2001/3929)); see para. 10–017, *infra*, and for the interpretation of the Brussels Convention by the Court of Justice, para. 22–049, *infra*. See also the Brussels Convention of May 25, 1987 abolishing the Legalisation of Documents in the Member States of the European Communities, (1987) 5 EC Bull. 3.4.3, and the Rome Convention of November 6, 1990 between the Member States of the European Communities on the Simplification of Procedures for the Enforcement of Maintenance Payments (1990) Trb. 54.

[27] For an overview of those conventions, see Oschinsky and Jenard, *L'espace juridique et judiciaire européen*, (Brussels, Bruylant, 1993), 860 pp..

[28] See (1988) 12 EC Bull. point 1.1.3. The Coordinators Group drew a distinction as regards the various areas of cooperation between priority and ancillary measures. This resulted in the Palma document of June 1989, which was approved by the European Council held in Madrid in June 1989, (1989) 6 EC Bull. point 1.1.7.

[29] The ad hoc group consisted of national officials meeting in various working parties: policy on asylum, external frontiers, admission/deportation, visa policy and forged papers. See (1986) 10 EC Bull. point 2.4.7.

submitted to the Member States for ratification. The Dublin Convention of June 15, 1990, which determines which Member State should examine applications for asylum, entered into force on September 1, 1997 (see para. 10–013). A draft Convention on the crossing of external borders of the Member States failed to be signed on account of differences between Spain and the United Kingdom relating to the application of the Convention to Gibraltar.[30]

After the EU Treaty entered into force, on November 1, 1993, intergovernmental cooperation between the Member States in the fields of the police and justice was conducted on the basis of the non-Community third pillar of the Union, namely Title VI of the EU Treaty. In this way, a convention was drawn up pursuant to the EU Treaty to supplement the Brussels Convention as regards jurisdiction and the recognition and enforcement of judgments in matrimonial matters.[31] In 1999, the Treaty of Amsterdam brought judicial cooperation in civil matters and immigration and asylum policy within the sphere of the EC Treaty, while retaining police and judicial cooperation in criminal matters in Title VI of the EU Treaty (see para. 10–016 *et seq.*). In December 2009, the Lisbon Treaty brought the provisions of Title VI of the EU Treaty and the Community competence on "visa, asylum, immigration and other policies related to the free movement of persons" (Part Three, Title IV of the EC Treaty) together in a single title (Part Three, Title V of the TFEU) on the "area of freedom, security and justice" (see para. 10–008).

Schengen Agreements. Some Member States had already taken the decision to replace frontier controls amongst themselves by a common policy at their external frontiers. The Benelux Treaty of April 11, 1960 obtained that outcome with effect from July 1, 1960.[32] National courts in the Benelux countries may refer questions on the interpretation of that treaty to the Benelux Court of Justice (see para. 1–018).   **2–011**

On June 19, 1990, France, Germany and the Benelux countries concluded the Convention on the application of the Schengen Agreement of June 14, 1985 on the gradual abolition of checks at the common borders.[33] The Schengen

---

[30] See the discussion in para. 10–003, *infra*.

[31] Convention of May 28, 1998, drawn up on the basis of the former Article K.3 of the EU Treaty, on Jurisdiction and the Recognition and Enforcement of Judgments in Matrimonial Matters ([1998] O.J. C221/2; the "Brussels II Convention", see para. 10–017, *infra*).

[32] Agreement between the Kingdom of Belgium, the Grand Duchy of Luxembourg and the Kingdom of the Netherlands on the displacement of checks on persons to the external frontiers of the Benelux area, signed at Brussels on April 11, 1960 (B.S., July 1, 1960, Trb., 1960, 40).

[33] Schengen Convention of June 19, 1990 implementing the Schengen Agreement of June 14, 1985 between the Governments of the States of the Benelux Economic Union, the Federal Republic of Germany and the French Republic on the gradual abolition of checks at their common borders ([2000] O.J. L239/19; for the Schengen Agreement of June 14, 1985: *ibid.*, p. 13). See the discussion in Fijnaut, Stuyck and Wytinck (eds), *Schengen: Proeftuin voor de Europese Gemeenschap?* (Antwerp/Arnhem, Kluwer/Gouda Quint, 1992), 212 pp.; Schutte, "Schengen: Its Meaning for the Free Movement of Persons in Europe" (1991) C.M.L.Rev. 549–570.

Convention established free movement of persons without checks at internal borders and stepped up checks at the external borders of the Schengen countries. It introduced common rules on the grant of visas and a uniform visa for nationals of third States (i.e. non-EC nationals) intending to stay in the Schengen area for less than three months. In order to offset the disappearance of internal borders, the Convention introduced a system for the exchange of information and cooperation between police forces and the judicial authorities, together with the Schengen Information System (SIS), which enables authorities to consult personal data held by authorities in other States via a central computer in Strasbourg. Upon the entry into effect of the Amsterdam Treaty, in May 1999, all EU Member States, with the exception of Ireland and the United Kingdom, were parties to the Schengen Convention and the agreements concluded pursuant to it.[34] The "Schengen *acquis*" did not enter into effect in all the States at the same time.[35] Since Denmark, Finland and Sweden, together with Iceland and Norway, had already abolished checks on persons moving between them under the auspices of the Nordic Council, the Schengen *acquis* could not be applied until Iceland and Norway had been enabled to take part in the Schengen cooperation by means of an agreement concluded with the Community.[36] The Treaty of Amsterdam incorporated the Schengen *acquis* into the European Union (see para. 10–010). The Schengen agreement applies to most of the Member States that acceded in 2004 and 2007, but not as yet to Bulgaria, Cyprus and Romania (see para. 10–011). Since December 2008 it also applies to Switzerland (see para. 10–011).

---

[34] Italy signed the convention on November 27, 1990, Portugal and Spain on June 25, 1991, Greece on November 6, 1992, Austria on April 28, 1995 and Denmark, Finland and Sweden on December 19, 1996.

[35] For the last States, see Council Decision 1999/848/EC of December 13, 1999 on the full application of the Schengen *acquis* in Greece, [1999] O.J. L327/58 (entry into force on January 1, 2000), and Council Decision 2000/777/EC of December 1, 2000 on the application of the Schengen *acquis* in Denmark, Finland and Sweden, and in Iceland and Norway, [2000] O.J. L309/24 (entry into force on March 25, 2001).

[36] See para. 10–011, *infra*.

CHAPTER 3

BRINGING TOGETHER THE PATHS OF INTEGRATION INTO ONE EUROPEAN UNION

I. First Proposals for a European Union

Towards European Union. Ten years after the Fouchet Plan, there was a resurgence of the idea of expanding the area of activity of the Communities and, at the same time, of unifying the existing Community and non-Community integration paths. At the Paris summit conference held in October 1972, the Heads of State or Government set themselves the major objective of

> "transforming, before the end of the present decade and with the fullest respect for the Treaties already signed, the whole complex of the relations of the Member States into a *European Union*."[1]

From that point on, the framework to be established was referred to as the "European Union", regardless of its legal nature.

Tindemans Report. At the Paris summit conference held in December 1974, the Heads of State or Government of the Member States invited the then Prime Minister of Belgium, Leo Tindemans, to draw up a report on European Union on the basis of reports to be prepared by the European Parliament, the Commission and the Court of Justice and after consulting "with the governments and a wide range of public opinion in the Community".[2] The Tindemans Report on European Union of December 1975 listed policy priorities for the Communities, but did not propose any real institutional reforms. It did make the case for meetings dealing with European Political Cooperation (EPC) to coincide as far as possible with Council meetings and for conferring formal legal force on the procedures relating to EPC.[3] The only achievement of the report was that the European Council instructed the Commission and the Foreign Ministers to report once a year on progress made

3–001

3–002

---

[1] (1972) 10 EC Bull. 25, point 16 (italics supplied).
[2] (1974) 12 EC Bull. point 1104, No. 13.
[3] Tindemans Report (1976) EC Bull. Suppl. 1, 14–15.

towards achieving European Union.[4] No more did the European Council follow up the "Report of the Three Wise Men" drawn up at its request in 1979.[5]

3–003 Stuttgart Declaration. In 1981 the German and Italian Foreign Ministers, Hans-Dietrich Genscher and Emilio Colombo, came up with a Draft European Act.[6] The draft proposed unifying all decision-making procedures of the Communities and EPC by conferring competence for all matters on the European Council and various subdivisions of the Council, which would be answerable to the European Council. It was also proposed to give more powers to the European Parliament, including the right to be consulted on the appointment of the President of the Commission and on the conclusion of international agreements. In the end, the European Council held in Stuttgart on June 19, 1983 merely adopted a Solemn Declaration on European Union, which, on the institutional level, contained little that was of any substance or novelty.[7] The Declaration confirmed that the European Council acted within the ambit of the Communities and EPC and likewise in other spheres (culture, law and order and lawlessness were mentioned), but that in so doing Community matters and matters coming under the heading of EPC were to continue to be governed by their respective procedures.

3–004 Draft Treaty on European Union. The proposal which attracted the most interest was the Draft Treaty establishing the European Union which was approved by the European Parliament on February 14, 1984.[8] The Draft Treaty proposed to eliminate the distinction between the Communities and EPC. The European Communities were to be converted into a European Union which was to have general competence in respect of external relations, yet retain the intergovernmental method of decision-making alongside the supranational one. It was proposed that the European Union would conduct its policy through common action in some fields and through cooperation between the Member States in the European Council in others.

The Draft Treaty proposed that the European Council should be recognised as an institution of the Union alongside the four existing institutions (European Parliament, Council, Commission, Court of Justice). Common action of the Union would invariably have to be based on a law. In principle, legislative power

---

[4] (1976) 11 EC Bull. 109, point 2501.

[5] For a summary of that report, see (1979) 11 EC Bull. point 1.5.2. The "Wise Men" were Barend Biesheuvel, Edmund Dell and Robert Marjolin. For the Council's comments, see (1980) 12 EC Bull. point 1.1.11. See VerLoren van Themaat, "Enkele kanttekeningen bij de rapporten van drie Wijzen en van de Commissie Spierenburg" (1980) S.E.W. 144–153.

[6] Neville-Jones, "The Genscher-Colombo Proposals on European Union" (1983) C.M.L.Rev. 658–699.

[7] Solemn Declaration of Stuttgart on European Union of June 19, 1983, (1983) 6 EC Bull. Point 1.6.1.

[8] [1984] O.J. C77/33, and (1984) 2 EC Bull. point 1.1.2. For commentaries on the Draft Treaty, see Bieber, Jacqué and Weiler, *An ever closer Union—A critical analysis of the Draft Treaty establishing the European Union* (Brussels, Commission of the EC, 1985), 345 pp.; Capotorti, Hilf, Jacobs and Jacqué, *Le Traité d'Union européenne—Commentaire du project adopté par le Parlement européen*, (Brussels, Editions de l'Université de Bruxelles, 1985), 307 pp. See also Nickel, "Le projet de traité instituant l'Union européenne élaboré par le Parlement européen" (1984) C.D.E. 511–542.

would be exercised jointly by the Council and the European Parliament. The Union would obtain extensive powers in relation to economic policy (including conjunctural and credit policy) and to "societal policies" (consumer, environmental, education and research, cultural, and information policies). As far as external relations policy was concerned, it was proposed that the Union would undertake common actions in respect of aspects already falling within the competence of the Communities, but cooperation between the Member States would continue to apply to the remaining aspects. Obligations entered into by the Member States under mutual cooperation would not form part of the law of the Union, but would be governed by international law.

Adonnino and Dooge Committees. Although the Draft Treaty was not approved, it did set in motion a political debate on amending the existing Treaties. The European Council held in Fontainebleau in June 1984 set up two ad hoc committees, one to prepare and coordinate measures "to strengthen and promote [the Community's] identity and its image for its citizens and for the rest of the world" (the Adonnino Committee) and the second on institutional affairs (the Dooge Committee).[9] The Dooge Committee concluded that negotiations should be held on a treaty to establish a European Union.[10] In June 1985, the Milan European Council decided to convene a conference of representatives of the governments of the Member States within the meaning of Art. 236 EEC to discuss amendments to the Treaties.[11] In September 1985 the proceedings of the Intergovernmental Conference began. Portugal and Spain, as candidates for accession, were involved from the outset. The result was the Single European Act.

3–005

II. THE SINGLE EUROPEAN ACT

Single European Act. On February 17, 1986, nine Member States signed the Single European Act (SEA).[12] The Danish Government wished first to hold a

3–006

---

[9] (1984) 6 EC Bull. point 1.1.9. For the Adonnino Committee's report, see the discussion of citizenship, para. 8–003, *infra*.

[10] (1985) 3 EC Bull. point 3.5.1. See Lauwaars, "De Europese Unie: Het Ontwerp-Verdrag van het Europese Parlement en het rapport van het Comité-Dooge" (1985) S.E.W. 398–409.

[11] (1985) 6 EC Bull. point I.2.2.

[12] For a general discussion, see De Ruyt, *L'Acte unique européen*, (Brussels, Editions de l'Université de Bruxelles, 1987), 355 pp.; Bosco, "Commentaire de l'Acte unique européen des 17–28 février 1986" (1987) C.D.E. 355–382; VerLoren van Themaat, "De Europese Akte" (1986) S.E.W. 464–483; Krenzler, "Die Einheitliche Europäische Akte als Schritt auf dem Wege zu einer Gemeinsamen Europäischen Außenpolitik" (1986) EuR. 384–391; Jacqué, "L'Acte unique européen" (1986) R.T.D.E. 575–612; Pescatore, "Some Critical Remarks on the Single European Act" (1986) C.M.L.Rev. 9–18; Edward, "The Impact of the Single European Act on the Institutions" (1986) C.M.L.Rev. 19–30; De Zwaan, "The Single European Act: Conclusion of a Unique Document" (1986) C.M.L.Rev. 747–765; Glaesner, "L'Acte unique européen" (1986) R.M.C. 307–321; Nuttall, "European Political Cooperation and the Single European Act" (1985) Y.E.L. 203–232.

referendum and both Greece and Italy decided to await the outcome of that referendum before signing. Although the Danish Parliament voted to reject the Single European Act on January 21, 1986, the Danish people voted in a referendum on February 27, 1986 by 56.2 per cent to accept the results of the negotiations. On the following day, Denmark, Greece and Italy signed the SEA. Although in Ireland the Parliament (the Dail) had voted in favour of the Single European Act, the Government could not deposit the instrument of ratification because an action was brought challenging the constitutionality of the new treaty. Because the Supreme Court ruled that the SEA necessitated a change in the Constitution, the latter was amended after a referendum held on May 26, 1987.[13] As a result, the Single European Act did not enter into force until July 1, 1987.[14] The SEA for the first time brought the Community and non-Community paths together into one text, although it kept the two integration paths separate in Title II (Arts 4 to 29) and Title III (Art. 30 only), respectively, supplemented by common provisions (Title I: Arts 1, 2 and 3) and general and final provisions (Title IV: Arts 31 to 34).[15]

3–007 **Amendments to Community Treaties.** The Single European Act was a heterogeneous text. First, it made major changes to the ECSC, EEC and EAEC Treaties. It conferred new competences on the Community,[16] but did not alter the general objectives of the Community (Art. 2 EEC) or the list of the Community's tasks (Art. 3 EEC). In addition, the SEA looked forward to the completion of the common market by adding an Art. 8a, which heralded the achievement by December 31, 1992 of an "internal market", defined as,

> "an area without internal frontiers in which the free movement of goods, persons, services and capital is ensured in accordance with the provisions of this Treaty" (see now Art. 26 TFEU [*ex Art. 14 EC*]).

At the institutional level, the SEA made decision-taking more flexible by introducing qualified majority voting in the Council. The introduction of the cooperation procedure (Art. 149, second para., EEC; now repealed) made for increased involvement of the Assembly, henceforward referred to in the Treaty as the European Parliament.

---

[13] Murphy and Cras, "L'affaire Crotty: la Cour Suprême d'Irlande rejette l'Acte Unique Européen" (1988) C.D.E. 276–305; McCutcheon, "The Irish Supreme Court, European Political Co-operation and the Single European Act" (1988) L.I.E.I. 93–100; Temple Lang, "The Irish Court Case Which Delayed the Single European Act: *Crotty v An Taoiseach and others*" (1987) C.M.L.Rev. 709–718.

[14] Implemented in the United Kingdom by the European Communities (Amendment) Act 1986.

[15] Hence its title "Single European Act" (*Acte unique européen, Einheitliche Europäische Akte*).

[16] The most important areas entrusted to the Community by the SEA were: (1) increased Community competence with regard to social policy (Arts 118a and 118b EEC); (2) economic and social cohesion (Arts 130a to 130e EEC); (3) research and technological development (Arts 130f to 130q EEC) and (4) the environment (Arts 130r to 130t EEC).

Codification of EPC. Secondly, the SEA codified for the first time existing prac- **3–008** tice in the matter of European Political Cooperation (see para. 2–003). EPC became thus enshrined in a treaty which was the outcome of a procedure initiated in the context of the Communities. At the same time, the Intergovernmental Conference made sure that EPC would not interfere with Community action. The SEA emphasised the differing legal bases of the European Communities and EPC (SEA, second and third paras of Art. 1) and the various conditions and purposes which the Community institutions and the EPC institutions and bodies had to take into account when taking action (SEA, Art. 3(1) and (2)). In order to give Member States the last word on any further integration in the context of EPC, Art. 31 of the SEA denied any jurisdiction to the Court of Justice to rule on acts taken by EPC institutions or bodies or by Member States within the framework of EPC.[17] Nevertheless, the Single European Act established for the first time a number of institutional links between the two integration paths. The European Council was empowered to act in both spheres under Art. 2 of the SEA. The SEA made it also easier for decision-making of the Communities and EPC to be concentrated within the Council on the initiative of the Member State holding the Presidency, with the permanent involvement of the Commission and the European Parliament. Above all, the establishment of the EPC secretariat in Brussels was of practical signifi-cance in this regard. The SEA shared responsibility for attaining consistency between the external policies of the Communities and of EPC by providing that both the Presidency and the Commission should have special responsibility in that regard "each within its own sphere of competence".

III. THE ESTABLISHMENT OF THE EUROPEAN UNION

A. THE TREATY ON EUROPEAN UNION

Intergovernmental conference. In December 1989 the European Council held **3–009** in Strasbourg decided to convene "a conference of representatives of the govern-ments of the Member States" within the meaning of Art. 236 EEC.[18] This

---

[17] Article 31 provided that the provisions of the ECSC Treaty, the EEC Treaty and the EAEC Treaty concerning the powers of the Court of Justice and the exercise of those powers applied only to the provisions of Title II and to Art. 32. Consequently, that article ruled out the common provisions (Title I), the provisions on European cooperation in the sphere of foreign policy (Title III) and the general and final provisions (Title IV), with the exception of Art. 32, which provided that, apart from Art. 31 and the provisions of the Community Treaties, nothing in the Single European Act was to affect the Community Treaties. For the lack of jurisdiction of the ECJ to rule on an act of the European Council, see CFI (order of July 14, 1994), Case T-584/93 *Roujansky v Council* [1994] E.C.R. II-585, paras 12–14, confirmed by ECJ (order of January 13, 1995), Case C-253/94 P *Roujansky* [1995] E.C.R. I-7.
[18] (1989) 12 EC Bull. point I.1.11.

intergovernmental conference was to determine the changes which needed to be made to the EEC Treaty in order to achieve economic and monetary union. The unification of Germany and political developments in central and eastern Europe, however, triggered debate about the further development of the Community's political dimension, both internally and externally. Following the collapse of the communist state machinery of the eastern bloc, the question arose as to whether the Member States could allow the new democracies to join the Community or whether it was necessary first to improve the Community's institutional structure.[19] Subjects were put forward from various quarters for an additional intergovernmental conference. Following a memorandum from the Belgian Government and a joint letter from the French President François Mitterand and the German Chancellor Helmut Kohl, addressed to the Irish Presidency, the Commission and the European Parliament also lodged proposals.[20] In June 1990 the European Council decided to hold both a Conference on Economic and Monetary Union and a Conference on Political Union.[21] These Intergovernmental Conferences were opened at the meeting of the European Council held in Rome on December 14–15, 1990.

The proceedings were rounded off at the European Council held in Maastricht on December 9–10, 1991.[22] The two texts on which the European Council had reached agreement, namely provisions on Economic and Monetary Union and provisions on Political Union, were fused into one Treaty on European Union, which was signed on February 7, 1992 by all the Member States. Particular heed was paid during the conferences to the form in which the different texts were to be amalgamated. In April 1991, the Luxembourg Presidency compiled the views of the Member States in a non-paper, which traced out a structure in which the Union was based on three pillars, namely provisions on the Communities, provisions on a common foreign and security policy, and provisions on cooperation in the fields of justice and home affairs.[23] In September 1991, the Netherlands

---

[19] See the preamble to the EU Treaty, where the High Contracting Parties refer to "the historic importance of ending the division of the European continent and the need to create firm bases for the construction of the future Europe".

[20] All these texts are reproduced as annexes to Laursen and Vanhoonacker (eds), *The Intergovernmental Conference on Political Union* (Maastricht, European Institute of Public Administration/Martinus Nijhoff, 1992), 505 pp., and in Corbett, *The Treaty of Maastricht. From Conception to Ratification: A Comprehensive Reference Guide* (Harlow (Essex), Longman, 1993), 512 pp.

[21] (1990) 6 EC Bull. point I.1., No I.11.

[22] For commentaries on the negotiations, see Corbett, "The Intergovernmental Conference on Political Union" (1992) J.C.M.S. 271–298; VerLoren van Themaat, "De constitutionele problematiek van een Europese politieke Unie" (1991) S.E.W. 436–454; VerLoren van Themaat, "Some Preliminary Observations on the Intergovernmental Conferences: The Relations between the Concepts of a Common Market, a Monetary Union, an Economic Union, a Political Union and Sovereignty" (1991) C.M.L.Rev. 291–318; Vignes, "Le project de la Présidence luxembourgeoise d'un Traité sur l'Union" (1991) R.M.C. 504–517; Reich, "Le développement de l'Union européenne dans le cadre des conférences intergouvernementales" (1991) R.M.C. 704–709.

[23] For the text of the non-paper, see *Europe*, No. 1709/1710, May 3, 1991.

Presidency unexpectedly proposed that discussion should proceed on the basis of a non-paper which assumed as its destination, not the "European Union", but the "European Community".[24] Under this proposal, both the common foreign and security policy and cooperation in the fields of justice and home affairs were to be brought within the sphere of competence of the European Community. This approach was supported by the European Parliament and the Commission. In the conference room, the Presidency was backed only by Belgium, with the result that preference was given to pursuing the negotiations on the basis of the Luxembourg proposal of a European Union founded on three pillars.

Treaty of Maastricht. The Treaty on European Union (EU Treaty, sometimes referred to as the Maastricht Treaty) was signed at Maastricht on February 7, 1992.[25] Just as in the case of the Single European Act, the entry into force of the EU Treaty was delayed by complications in the national ratification procedures.[26] In Denmark, 50.7 per cent of the votes cast in the referendum held on June 2, 1992 were against the Treaty, although the Danish Parliament had voted in favour on May 12, 1992.[27] The Treaty was approved, however, by referendum on June 18, 1992 in Ireland (69.05 per cent voted yes) and on September 20, 1992 in France, albeit narrowly (51.05 per cent). In order to enable the Treaty to be ratified in Denmark, the European Council held in Edinburgh on December 11–12, 1992 laid down a number of special rules which would apply only to Denmark and enter into force at the same time as the Treaty itself.[28] Those rules are embodied partly in a

3–010

---

[24] For the text of the Netherlands Draft Treaty, see *Europe*, No. 1734/1734, October 3, 1991.

[25] [1992] O.J. C191; implemented in the United Kingdom by the European Communities (Amendment) Act 1993. The Treaty was republished, together with a complete, revised text of the EC Treaty in [1992] O.J. C224. For general commentaries on the EU Treaty, see Cloos, Reinesch, Vignes and Weyland, *Le traité de Maastricht. Genèse, analyse, commentaires* (2nd edn, Brussels, Bruylant, 1994), 814 pp.; Constantinesco, "La structure du Traité instituant l'Union européenne— Les dispositions communes et finales. Les nouvelles compétences" (1993) C.D.E. 251–294; Curtin, "The Constitutional Structure of the Union: A Europe of Bits and Pieces" (1993) C.M.L.Rev. 17–69; Hartley, "Constitutional and Institutional Aspects of the Maastricht Agreement" (1993) I.C.L.Q. 213–237; Everling, "Reflections on the Structure of the European Union" (1992) C.M.L.Rev. 1053–1077; Melchior, "Le Traité de Maastricht sur l'Union européenne (essai de présentation synthétique)" (1992) A.D. 1207–1255.

[26] For a survey of the national ratification procedures, see (1993) 10 EC Bull. point 2.3.1. See the discussion in Rideau, "Les procédures de ratification du traité sur l'Union Européenne" (1992) R.F.D.C. 611–624; Arts *et al.*, "Ratification Process of the Treaty on European Union" (1993) E.L.Rev. 228–253, 356–360, 448–451 and 541–544.

[27] For the situation after the referendum, see Kapteyn, "Denemarken en het Verdrag van Maastricht" (1992) N.J.B. 781–783. Without Danish ratification, the EU Treaty could not enter into force (see Art. 52 EU). *Cf.* Rideau, "La ratification et l'entrée en vigueur du Traité de Maastricht. Aspects internationaux" (1992) R.F.D.C. 479–491.

[28] (1992) 12 EC Bull. points I.33–I.44.

decision of the Heads of State or Government meeting within the European Council,[29] and partly in unilateral "declarations" of the European Council and Denmark itself.[30] The provisions helped to ease Denmark's obligations, yet without encroaching upon the EU Treaty. In a second referendum held on May 18, 1993, 56.8 per cent of Danes voted in favour of ratifying the EU Treaty.[31]

The Constitutions of Germany,[32] France,[33] Ireland,[34] Spain,[35] Luxembourg[36] and Portugal[37] were amended, principally to enable those countries to participate in economic and monetary union and to give the vote to nationals of other

---

[29] Decision of the Heads of State or Government, meeting within the European Council, concerning certain problems raised by Denmark on the Treaty on European Union, [1992] O.J. C348/2.

[30] Declarations of the European Council, [1992] O.J. C348/3; Unilateral Declarations of Denmark, to be associated to the Danish instrument of ratification of the Treaty on European Union and of which the 11 other Member States will take cognisance, [1992] O.J. C348/4.

[31] Glistrup, "Le traité sur l'Union européenne: la ratification du Danemark" (1994) R.M.C.U.E. 9–16; Howarth, "The Compromise on Denmark and the Treaty on European Union: A Legal and Political Analysis" (1994) C.M.L.Rev. 765–805. Gjørtler, "Ratifying the Treaty on European Union: An Interim Report" (1993) E.L.Rev. 356–360. For this and other Danish referendums concerning European integration, see Simoulin, "L'Europe au miroir danois" (2002) R.M.C.U.E. 83–88.

[32] For the amendment of the *Grundgesetz* (Basic Law), see Autexier, "Le traité de Maastricht et l'ordre constitutionnel allemand" (1992) R.F.D.C. 625–641; Hahn, *Der Vertrag von Maastricht als völkerrechtliche Übereinkunft und Verfassung* (Nomos, Baden-Baden, 1992), 141 pp.; Arnold, "La loi fondamentale de la RFA et l'Union européenne: le nouvel article 23 de la loi fondamentale" (1993) R.I.D.C. 673–678; Scholz, "Europäische Union und Verfassungsreform" (1993) N.J.W. 1690–1692; Scholz, "Grundgesetz und europäische Einigung" (1992) N.J.W. 2593–2601.

[33] For the judgment of the *Conseil constitutionnel* of April 9, 1992 which prompted the amendment of the Constitution, see (1993) C.M.L.R 345–358, the commentaries of Jacqué (1992) R.T.D.E. 251–264 and Genevois (1992) R.F.D.A. 373, and, in addition, Favoreu and Gaïa, "Les décisions du Conseil constitutionnel relatives au traité sur l'Union européenne" (1992) R.F.D.C. 389–412; Grewe, "La révision constitutionnelle en vue de la ratification du traité de Maastricht" (1992) R.F.D.C. 413–438; for the second judgment of the *Conseil constitutionnel* of September 2, 1992, see Genevois, "Le Traité sur l'Union européenne et la Constitution révisée" (1992) R.F.D.A. 937; for a discussion of those judgments and the third judgment of September 23, 1992, see L. Favoreu, "Le contrôle de constitutionnalité du traité de Maastricht et le développement du 'droit constitutionnel international' " (1993) R.G.D.I.P. 39–66; Blumann, "La ratification par la France du traité de Maastricht" (1994) R.M.C.U.E. 393–406; Oliver, "The French Constitution and the Treaty of Maastricht" (1994) I.C.L.Q. 1–25.

[34] Murphy, "Maastricht: Implementation in Ireland" (1994) E.L.Rev. 94, at 100.

[35] For the judgment of the *Tribunal constitucional* and the amendment of the Spanish Constitution, see Rubio Llorente, "La constitution espagnole et le traité de Maastricht" (1992) R.F.D.C. 651–662; Lopez Castillo and Polakiewicz, "Verfassung und Gemeinschaftsrecht in Spanien—Zur Maastricht-Erklärung des Spanischen Verfassungsgerichts" (1993) Eu.GR.Z. 277–285.

[36] Delpérée, "La Constitution belge, la Constitution luxembourgeoise et le Traité sur l'Union européenne" (1993) Ann.Dr.Lux. 15–33; Arendt, "Le traité sur l'Union européenne et la Constitution du Grand-Duché de Luxembourg" (1993) Ann.Dr.Lux. 35–52; Frieden, "L'Union européenne et la Constitution luxembourgeoise: une cohabitation nécessaire" (1993) Ann.Dr.Lux. 53–63; Thewes, "La Constitution luxembourgeoise et l'Europe" (1993) Ann.Dr.Lux. 65–78.

[37] Miranda, "La constitution portugaise et le traité de Maastricht" (1992) R.F.D.C. 679–688; Alves Vieira, "Ratifying the Treaty on European Union" (1993) E.L.Rev. 448–451.

Member States. In Belgium and Italy the necessary constitutional changes were to be made after the event.[38] In the Netherlands the government considered that the EU Treaty was not incompatible with the Constitution.[39] In the United Kingdom[40] and Germany[41] ratification hinged on a judicial pronouncement on the constitutional implications of the EU Treaty.

Eventually, the Treaty on European Union entered into force on November 1, 1993.

B. EUROPEAN UNION

European Union. By the EU Treaty, the Contracting Parties established a European Union, founded on the European Communities and supplemented by the policies and forms of cooperation established by the new Treaty (Art. 1, first and third paras, EU). The EU Treaty left the European Communities in place, but supplemented them with a new, overarching structure, the European Union.

3–011

---

[38] Van Ginderachter, "De goedkeuring van het Verdrag van Maastricht" (1992–93) R.W. 670–673; Gaudissart, "La ratification du traité sur l'Union européenne: l'exemple de la Belgique" (1994) R.M.C.U.E. 86–93. See the opinion of the *Raad van State/Conseil d'Etat* (1991–1992) Gedr.St., Kamer, B.Z, No. 482/1, 69–89. The *Arbitragehof/Cour d'Arbitrage* (the Belgian constitutional court, as it was then named) declared an application for annulment of the law approving the EU Treaty inadmissible on the ground that persons claiming that the introduction of voting rights for the non-Belgians would diminish the weight of their own votes had no specific interest: *Arbitragehof/Cour d'Arbitrage*, October 18, 1994, No. 76/94, (1994) A.A. 901–910. For the situation in Italy, see Luciani, "La Constitution italienne et les obstacles à l'intégration européenne" (1992) R.F.D.C. 663–676.

[39] Ter Kuile, "Tussen Brussel en Maastricht" (1992) N.J.B. 1040–1044; Brouwer, "Wijkt het Unie-Verdrag van Maastricht af van de Grondwet of van het Statuut?" (1992) N.J.B. 1045–1049; Besselink, "De constitutie van Europa: de verenigbaarheid van het Verdrag betreffende de Europese Unie met de Nederlandse Constitutie" (1993) T.B.P. 370–376. But see Heringa, "De verdragen van Maastricht in strijd met de Grondwet" (1992) N.J.B. 749–752. For the advice of the *Raad van State* to the Queen of May 27, 1992, see *Kst.*, Tweede Kamer, 1991–92, 22 647 (R1437), A.

[40] On July 30, 1993 the Divisional Court dismissed an action brought against the intended ratification of the EU Treaty: Denza, "La ratification du traité de Maastricht par le Royaume-Uni" (1994) R.M.C.U.E. 172–180; Marshall, "The Maastricht Proceedings" (1993) P.L. 402–407; Szyszczak, "Ratifying the Treaty on European Union: a final report" (1993) E.L.Rev. 541–544.

[41] The *Bundesverfassungsgericht* held on October 12, 1993 that the ratification of the EU Treaty did not raise any constitutional objections. For the relevant judgment, see para. 21–028, *infra*. On the following day, the Federal Republic of Germany deposited the instrument of ratification, it being the last Member State to do so, after which the EU Treaty entered into force on November 1, 1993 pursuant to Art. 52(2) EU. See the notice concerning the date of entry into force, [1993] O.J. L293/61. In a judgment of March 31, 1998, the *Bundesverfassungsgericht* further held that participation in Economic and Monetary Union was compatible with the German Basic Law; see (1998) EuR. 324–339 and Mengelkoch, "Bundesverfassungsgericht lässt Euro rollen" (1998) EuR. 563–570; see also Kempen, "Die Europäische Währungsunion und der Streit um die Geltung des Gemeinschaftsrechts" (1997) A.Völkerr. 273, at 290–292.

It was initially suggested that the whole entity should be called a "Union with a federal mission", but some Member States were strongly opposed to this.[42] In the end, the Intergovernmental Conference characterised the Treaty as

"a new stage in the process of creating an ever closer union among the peoples of Europe, in which decisions are taken as closely as possible to the citizen."[43]

Accordingly, the Contracting Parties did not regard the European Union as completing the integration process, but as a new step towards "union among the peoples of Europe", as mentioned already in the preamble to the EEC Treaty. The EU Treaty established a legal link between the Communities and the supplementary policies and forms of cooperation: henceforward, there was to be one procedure for acceding to the Union, supplanting the various accession procedures provided for in the ECSC, EEC and EAEC Treaties (Art. 49 EU) and one procedure for amending the various Treaties on which the Union was founded (Art. 48 EU). Yet the EU Treaty did not confer legal personality on the Union as a whole.

3–012 **Treaty structure.** The Communities and the supplementary policies and forms of cooperation subsisted within the European Union as different integration paths. The type of integration was not immediately apparent from the structure of the EU Treaty, which contained, preceded by common provisions (Title I: Arts 1 to 7) and followed by final provisions (Title VIII: Arts 46 to 53):

— provisions amending the Treaty establishing the European Economic Community with a view to establishing the European Community (Title II: Art. 8);

— provisions amending the Treaty establishing the European Coal and Steel Community (Title III: Art. 9);

— provisions amending the Treaty establishing the European Economic Energy Community (Title IV: Art. 10);

— provisions on a common foreign and security policy (Title V: Arts 11 to 28);

— provisions on police and judicial cooperation in criminal matters (Title VI: Arts 29 to 42).

— provisions on closer cooperation (Title VII: Arts 43 to 45).

---

[42] Principally, the United Kingdom, Denmark and Portugal strongly objected to the term "federal", often wrongly interpreting it as a synonym for centralism. See Lenaerts, "Federalism: Essential Concepts in Evolution—The Case of the European Union" (1998) Fordham I.L.J. 746–798.

[43] In 1997 the Treaty of Amsterdam added that "decisions are [to be] taken as openly as possible and as closely as possible to the citizen": Art. 1, second para., EU.

The common provisions covered the establishment, definition, foundation and task of the Union (Art. 1), its objectives (Art. 2, first para.) and the manner of achieving them (Art. 2, second para.), the institutional framework and its tasks (Arts 3 and 4), the manner in which the Community institutions exercise their powers (Art. 5), the principles respected by the Union (Art. 6(1), (2) and (3)), providing the Union with the necessary means (Art. 6(4)) and the possibility of imposing sanctions for a serious and persistent breach by a Member State of the principles of liberty, democracy, respect for human rights and fundamental freedoms, and the rule of law (Art. 7).

The final provisions consisted inter alia of rules on the powers of the Court of Justice (Art. 46), the relationship between the EU Treaty and the Community Treaties (Art. 47), the amendment of the Treaties on which the Union is founded (Art. 48) and the admission of States to the Union (Art. 49).

Three pillars. The legal structure of the European Union was best understood as an **3–013** entity supported by three pillars. The first pillar of the Union consisted of the Community Treaties, as significantly modified by Titles II, III and IV of the EU Treaty. Community action under the first pillar was subject to the provisions of these Treaties and to the common provisions and the final provisions of the EU Treaty. The second pillar of the Union consisted of the provisions on a common foreign and security policy laid down in Title V of the EU Treaty. The third pillar of the Union (Title VI of the EU Treaty) consisted initially of the provisions on "cooperation in the fields of justice and home affairs" (JHA cooperation). The Treaty of Amsterdam conferred on the Community competence to adopt measures in various fields falling under JHA cooperation, thereby reducing the scope of application of Title VI of the EU Treaty to police and judicial cooperation in criminal matters (PJCC). For both the CFSP and PJCC—the second and third pillars of the Union— the legal bases were laid down exhaustively in the EU Treaty, namely in Titles V and VI, respectively, and in the common provisions and the final provisions.

A key indication as to the relationship between the different pillars was afforded by Art. 2, fifth indent, EU, which set out the objective of the Union to maintain in full the *acquis communautaire* and build on it. The EU Treaty was the first of the Treaties to use the expression *acquis communautaire*. Whereas, generally speaking, that expression referred to existing Community law as interpreted and applied by the Court of Justice, here it denoted the specific institutional and substantive bases of the Community legal order, on which the Union could not go back.[44] Accordingly, it clearly followed from Art. 2 EU that neither the CFSP nor PJCC could go back on the integration achieved under the Community Treaties.[45]

---

[44] In the context of the accession of new Member States to the Union, *acquis communautaire* (now referred to as "Union *acquis*") is used to describe the whole corpus of Community law which new Member States have to take over; para. 6–010, *infra*. For a critical view of the different meanings ascribed to this expression, see Delcourt, "The *acquis communautaire*: has the concept had its day?" (2001) C.M.L.Rev. 829–870.

[45] For PJCC, see para. 10–022, *infra*; for the CFSP, see para. 27–005, *infra*.

3–014 **Amendments to Community Treaties.** As regards the first pillar, the EU Treaty extended the sphere of action of the Community to such an extent that the title "European Economic Community" was replaced by "European Community". The competences of the Community were considerably enlarged, also outside the economic sphere.[46] In addition, the EU Treaty clarified and extended the scope of existing Community powers under the original EEC Treaty and as added by the Single European Act.[47] What attracted the most attention was the decision to introduce, starting in 1997 and by no later than January 1, 1999, an economic and monetary union between Member States fulfilling the necessary conditions for the adoption of a single currency.[48] At the same time, the actual objectives of the Community were extended for the first time by expanding Arts 2 and 3 EC and introducing an Art. 3a (see paras 7–003—7–004). At the institutional level, the EU Treaty advanced further into the territory opened up by the Single European Act. On the one hand, the EU Treaty further extended the scope of qualified majority voting in the Council.[49] On the other, further steps were taken to give the European Parliament a greater say in the legislative process, in particular through the introduction of a co-decision procedure (Art. 189b EC, now replaced by the ordinary legislative procedure (see Art. 294 TFEU)) and more extensive application of the cooperation procedure and procedures requiring the Parliament to give its assent or to deliver advisory opinions.[50]

3–015 **CFSP.** Title V of the EU Treaty constituted the legal basis for the Union's common foreign and security policy (CFSP), the Union's "second pillar". That policy replaced European Political Cooperation between the Member States (EPC; see

---

[46] The EU Treaty conferred competence on the European Community with regard to (1) citizenship of the Union (Arts 8 to 8e EC, later—with the Treaty of Amsterdam—renumbered as Arts 17 to 22); (2) the common policy on visas (Art. 100c EC, later repealed); (3) economic and monetary policy (Arts 102a to 109m, later Arts 98 to 124 EC); (4) education (Art. 126, later Art. 149 EC); (5) culture (Art. 128, later Art. 151 EC); (6) public health (Art. 129, later Art. 152 EC); (7) consumer protection (Art. 129a, later Art. 153 EC); (8) trans-European networks (Arts 129b to 129d, later Arts 154 to 156 EC); (9) industry (Art. 130, later Art. 157 EC); (10) development cooperation (Arts 130u to 130y, later Arts 177 to 181 EC) and (11) extended powers in the social policy sphere as a result of the "Protocol on social policy", with the same status as the EC Treaty, and the "Agreement on social policy concluded between the Member States of the European Community with the exception of the United Kingdom of Great Britain and Northern Ireland" to which the Social Protocol refers. See Lane, "New Community Competences under the Maastricht Treaty" (1993) C.M.L.Rev. 939–979.

[47] See Art. 127 (vocational training, later Art. 150), Arts 130a to 130e (economic and social cohesion, later Arts 158 to 162), Arts 130f to 130p (research and technological development, later Arts 163 to 173) and Arts 130r to 130t (environment, later Arts 174 to 176) EC.

[48] Art. 109j [later *Art. 121*](3) and (4) EC.

[49] See para. 16–009, *infra*.

[50] See Art. 192, first para., EC for this enumeration (para. 14–012 *et seq., infra*). It is also noteworthy that the practice by which the nominated President and other Members of the Commission collectively are to be subject to a vote of approval by the European Parliament was enshrined in the Treaty (Art. 214(2) EC).

para. 2–003)[51] and was based both on action by the institutions of the Union and on cooperation between the Member States. Article 11(1) of the EU Treaty set out objectives supplementing the general objectives of Art. 2 EU (see para. 25–039). Title V of the EU Treaty did not determine in greater detail how the CFSP was to take substantive shape, but elaborated the procedures and instruments pursuant to which the institutions and the Member States were to conduct a foreign and security policy (Arts 12 to 15). Pursuant to general guidelines and common strategies determined by the European Council, the Council was to adopt joint actions, common positions or other decisions and conclude agreements with third countries and international organisations (for a survey of the CFSP, see paras 5–039—25–048). The Member States were to consult one another on any matter of foreign and security policy of general interest (Art. 16 EU). The CFSP covered all matters bearing on the security of the Union and could lead to a "common defence", should the European Council so decide (Art. 17(1) EU; see para. 25–043).

PJCC. Title VI of the EU Treaty provided the framework for police and judicial cooperation in criminal matters between Member States (PJCC), the third "pillar".[52] The area originally covered by Title VI, "cooperation in the fields of justice and home affairs" ("JHA cooperation")[53] contemplated primarily such police and judicial cooperation as was necessary to accompany the liberalisation of the movement of persons in the internal market.[54] Since the Treaty of   **3–016**

---

[51] Article 50(2) EU repealed Arts 2 and 3(2) and Title III of the Single European Act.

[52] In decisions adopted pursuant to Title VI of the EU Treaty, the—less precise—abbreviation "JHA" was used even after the Treaty of Amsterdam. For a discussion of the PJCC provisions, see the relevant sections in Peers, *EU justice and home affairs law* (Oxford, Oxford University Press, 2006), 588 pp; Anderson and Apap, *Police and Justice Co-operation and the New European Borders* (The Hague, Kluwer Law International, 2002), 303 pp.; Monar, "Justice and Home Affairs in the Treaty of Amsterdam: Reform at the Price of Fragmentation" (1998) E.L.Rev. 320–335; Margue, "La coopération européenne en matière de lutte contre la criminalité organisée dans le contexte du traité d'Amsterdam" (1997) 3 R.M.U.E. 91–117. For the implementation of these provisions in the various legal orders of the Member States, see Moore and Chiavario (eds), *Police and judicial co-operation in the European Union* (Cambridge, Cambridge University Press, 2004), 397 pp.

[53] Ever since the Treaty of Amsterdam, cooperation in the fields of justice and home affairs under Title VI of the EU Treaty has been confined to police and judicial cooperation in criminal matters. Since the expression "justice and home affairs" (JHA) bears on both the "communitarised" competences (EC Treaty, Title IV) and on non-Community cooperation in criminal matters (EU Treaty, Title VI), the authors have elected in this work to refer to cooperation pursuant to Title VI of the EU Treaty as police and judicial cooperation in criminal matters (PJCC) in line with the wording of the Treaty.

[54] See Müller-Graff, "The Legal Base of the Third Pillar and its Position in the Framework of the Union Treaty" (1994) C.M.L.Rev. 493–503. For the first results and the need to reform the third pillar, see Labayle, "La coopération européenne en matière de justice et d'affaires intérieures et la Conférence intergouvernementale" (1997) R.T.D.E. 1–35; Den Boer, "Police Cooperation in the TEU: Tiger in a Trojan Horse?" (1995) C.M.L.Rev. 555–578; Lepoivre, "Le domaine de la justice et des affaires intérieures dans la perspective de la Conférence intergouvernementale" (1995) C.D.E. 323–349; O'Keeffe, "Recasting the Third Pillar" (1995) C.M.L.Rev. 893–920. Compare Vignes, "Plaidoyer pour le IIIème pilier" (1996) R.M.C.U.E. 273–281, with Dehousse and Van den Hende, "Plaidoyer pour la réforme du troisième pilier" (1996) R.M.C.U.E. 714–718.

Amsterdam, cooperation under Title VI of the EU Treaty was aimed at preventing and combating crime, organised or otherwise. Pursuant to Art. 29 EU, the Council could act in various ways in order to prevent and combat crime, organised or otherwise, in particular terrorism, trafficking in persons and offences against children, illicit drug trafficking and illicit arms trafficking, corruption and fraud (see Art. 29, second para., EU).[55] As a result, the European Union became the pre-eminent forum for bringing Member States' criminal law policy closer together and to make a start with European criminal law.[56] Title VI of the EU Treaty constituted part of the legal basis for integrating the Schengen *acquis* into the European Union and its further development (see para. 10–010). Article 29, first para., EU further mentioned preventing and combating racism and xenophobia as a means—without prejudice to the powers of the Community—of achieving the Union's objective of "providing citizens with a high level of safety within an area of freedom, security and justice". Article 42 EU provided that action in areas referred to in Art. 29 EU could be brought within the scope of Title IV of the EC Treaty. In the event that this was done, the Council was to determine the relevant voting conditions.

3–017 **Single institutional framework.** Institutional links between the Communities and the second and third "pillars" of the Union made it possible to achieve the common objectives of the Union using a heterogeneous structure. Under the first para. of Art. 3 EU, the Union had an

> "institutional framework which shall ensure the consistency and the continuity of the activities carried out in order to attain its objectives while respecting and building upon the *acquis communautaire*."

By that institutional framework was meant the European Council and the institutions of the Communities (the European Parliament, the Council, the Commission, the Court of Justice and the Court of Auditors; see Art. 5). Article 4 EU gave the European Council the task of providing the Union with the necessary impetus for its development and of defining the general political guidelines. The EU Treaty assigned the European Council with a few specific tasks in Title II (provisions amending the EC Treaty) and Title V (CFSP), which were later supplemented by

---

[55] Mitsilegas, "Defining organised crime in the European Union: the limits of European criminal law in an area of 'freedom, security and justice' " (2001) E.L.Rev. 565–581 ; Margue, "La coopération en matière de prévention et de lutte contre le crime dans le cadre du nouveau troisième pilier" (2000) R.D.U.E. 729–747;.

[56] See also Mitsilegas, *EU Criminal Law* (Oxford, Hart Publishing, 2009), 352pp.; Barents, "De denationalisering van het strafrecht" (2006) S.E.W. 358–374; Guild, "Crime and the EU's Constitutional Future in an Area of Freedom, Security and Justice" (2004) E.L.J. 218–234; von Bubnoff, "Institutionelle Kriminalitätsbekämpfung in der EU—Schritte auf dem Weg zu einem europäischen Ermittlungs—und Strafverfolgungsraum" (2002) Z.Eu.S. 185–237; Harding, "Exploring the intersection of European law and national criminal law" (2000) E.L.Rev. 374–390.

the Treaty of Amsterdam (see para. 13–026). Henceforth, the Community institutions had not only the powers which they had under the Community Treaties, but also the task of determining and implementing the CFSP of the Union and the Member States and of organising PJCC among the Member States. As far as the CFSP and PJCC were concerned, it was the Council, the most "intergovernmental" institution of the Communities, which was to organise consultations among the Member States, adopt common positions and joint actions (in the context of the CFSP) and adopt common positions, framework decisions and decisions, and establish conventions (in the context of PJCC).[57]

Under Article 28(1), Art. 41(1) and Art. 44, respectively, of the EU Treaty, the composition and manner of operation of the European Parliament, the Council and the Commission as laid down in the EC Treaty were to apply when these institutions acted under Titles V or Title VI of the EU Treaty, with the exception of the rules on voting in the Council. In addition, the Community budgetary procedure was to apply to all administrative and operational expenditure occasioned by actions taken under Title V or Title VI, unless the Council decided otherwise by a unanimous vote in the case of operational expenditure.[58] In this way, the European Parliament, which had a power of decision relating to non-compulsory expenditure (see para. 13–141), exercised supervision over non-Community action on the part of the Union.

No uniform decision-making. The fact that there was a "single" institutional framework did not signify, however, that the institutions performed the same functions within each of the two integration paths.[59] Article 5 EU stated that the Community institutions were to exercise their powers under the conditions provided for and in order to achieve the objectives laid down, on the one hand, in the Community Treaties and, on the other, in the other provisions of the EU Treaty. Consequently, in the context of Title V, Title VI and Title VII the institutions were to operate in accordance with the procedural rules laid down therein. As a result,   **3–018**

---

[57] Articles 14 to 16 EU (CFSP) and Art.34 EU (PJCC).

[58] Article 268, second para., EC; Art.28(2) to (4) EU and Art. 41(2) to (4) EU. Art. 248 EC conferred powers on the Court of Auditors for the purposes of verifying the Communities' accounts; that institution also exercised powers in connection with Title V, Title VI and Title VII of the EU Treaty. For an application of the original version of Art. 41 (the former Art. K.8(1)) of the EU Treaty, see CFI, Case T-174/95 *Svenska Journalistförbundet v Council* [1998] E.C.R. II-2289, para. 82.

[59] *Cf.* Curtin (n. 25, *supra*), at 27–30, who referred to the single institutional framework as a "fiction" and as "being given the lie". As regards the logistical support provided by the Community for the non-Community forms of cooperation, see Isaac, "Le 'pilier' communautaire de l'Union européenne, un 'pilier' pas comme les autres" (2001) C.D.E. 45, at 49–63. With regard to the heterogeneous structure perpetuated by the Treaty of Amsterdam, see the commentaries in (1998) EuR. Beiheft 2: Zuleeg, "Die Organisationsstruktur der Europäischen Union—Eine Analyse der Klammerbestimmungen des Vertrags von Amsterdam", 151–163; von Bogdandy, "Die Europäische Union als einheitlicher Verband", 165–183. See also von Bogandy, "The Legal Case for Unity: The European Union as a Single Organisation with a Single Legal System"*(1999) C.M.L.Rev. 887–910.

for CFSP and PJCC matters, in principle the requirement that the Council must take decisions by a unanimous vote applied (Art. 23 and Art. 34 EU). Under the second and third pillars, the Commission did not have an exclusive right of initiative and exercised no supervision as to the Member States' compliance with the obligations which they entered into. The European Parliament, for its part, was entitled only to be consulted and kept informed.[60]

3–019 **Community and non-Community provisions.** The different decision-making procedures clearly demonstrate that the second and third pillars did not satisfy the criteria of the definition of supranational cooperation set out above. They exhibited the characteristics of an intergovernmental form of cooperation, with decision-making in the hands of the Council, and hence of the national governments collectively, although the European Parliament had the right to be consulted on PJCC measures adopted by the Council. In view of the task conferred on the Court of Justice with regard to police and judicial cooperation in criminal matters (PJCC or JHA), this was less true of that form of cooperation, which was introduced by the Treaty of Amsterdam in place of the characteristically intergovernmental cooperation in the fields of justice and home affairs.

As far as Union action under the CFSP was concerned, any supervision by the Court of Justice was ruled out. In accordance with Art. 46 EU the Court exercised no supervision over the fulfilment by Member States of obligations laid down in the common provisions and in the provisions concerning the CFSP (Title V) of the EU Treaty.[61] The Court also had no jurisdiction to rule whether an act of the Union was lawfully based on the common provisions or on the provisions of Title V of the EU Treaty.[62] Furthermore, it could not give a preliminary ruling on the validity of such an act in the light of those provisions, on its interpretation or on the interpretation of the relevant Treaty provisions.[63] This also took acts of the European Council, which as such did not adopt acts of Community law (see para. 13–028), outside the scope of judicial review.[64] As far as PJCC (Title VI) was concerned, although the Court of Justice was not empowered to review whether Member States fulfilled their Treaty obligations, Art. 35 EU conferred jurisdiction on it to review, under certain conditions, acts adopted by the Union

---

[60] Article 18(4), Art. 21, Art. 22 and Art. 27 (CFSP) and Art. 34(2), Art. 36(2) and Art. 39 (PJCC) EU.

[61] Para. 23–006, *infra*; compare the powers of the Court of Justice under Arts 226 to 228 EC.

[62] Subject, however, to the enforcement by the Court of Art. 47 EU (see n. 45, *infra*, and the associated text). Compare the powers of the Court under Arts 230 to 233 EC.

[63] *Cf.* the preliminary ruling procedure under Art. 234 EC. See ECJ (order of April 7, 1995), Case C-167/94 *Grau Gomis and Others* [1995] E.C.R. I-1023, para. 6, where the Court held that it had no jurisdiction to interpret Art. 2 EU.

[64] See CFI (order of July 14, 1994), Case T-584/93 *Roujansky v Council* [1994] E.C.R. II-585, paras 12–14 (and the parallel order given on the same day in Case T-179/94 *Bonnamy v Council*, paras 10–12, not reported), upheld by ECJ (order of January 13, 1995), Case C-235/94 P *Roujansky* [1995] E.C.R. I-7.

under Title VI (see para. 13–085).[65] Closer cooperation between Member States could also be the subject of judicial review on the conditions laid down in Art. 35 EU as far as police and judicial cooperation was concerned; where such closer cooperation related to matters coming under the EC Treaty, the provisions of that Treaty applied (Art. 40(4) EU and Art. 11(4) EC; see para. 19–011).

Since the non-Community provisions of the EU Treaty were not to affect the Community Treaties or the Treaties and acts modifying or supplementing them (Art. 47 EU), the Union had always to respect the *acquis communautaire*. The Court of Justice could enforce compliance with that obligation using the proper procedures against institutions of the Communities acting for the Union and against Member States (Art. 47 was among the final provisions of the EU Treaty which were enforceable by the Court).[66]

IV. SUBSEQUENT AMENDMENTS

A. THE TREATY OF AMSTERDAM

Treaty of Amsterdam. The EU Treaty of February 7, 1992 stated that a confer-   **3–020**
ence of representatives of the governments of the Member States was to meet in 1996 to examine the provisions of the Treaty for which revision was provided.[67] Members of the European Parliament produced a proposal for consolidating the texts of the Treaties into a formal Constitution of the European Union, although

---

[65] See ECJ, Case C-354/04 P *Gestoras Pro Amnistía and Others v Council* [2007] E.C.R. I-1579, paras 44–57; ECJ, Case C-355/04 P *Segi and Others v Council* [2007] E.C.R. I-1657, paras 44–57.

[66] See, to that effect, ECJ, Case C-170/96 *Commission v Council* [1998] E.C.R. I-2763, paras 12–18; ECJ, Case C-176/03 *Commission v Council* [2005] E.C.R. I-7879, paras 37–38; ECJ, Case C-91/05 *Commission v Council* [2008] E.C.R. I-3651, paras 32–34. See Isaac, "Le 'pilier' communautaire de l'Union européenne, un 'pilier' pas comme les autres" (2001) C.D.E. 45–89.

[67] Article N(2) of the original EU Treaty. The articles concerned were the original Article B, last indent (policies and forms of cooperation introduced by the EU Treaty), Art. J.4(6) and Art. J.10 (CFSP, particularly security policy) of the EU Treaty and the former Art.189b(8) EC (scope of the co-decision procedure). See also the declarations annexed to the EU Treaty relating to the commitment to examining the incorporation into the EC Treaty of specific titles on energy, civil protection and tourism (Declaration No. 1) and the establishment of a hierarchy between the different categories of Community acts (Declaration No. 16). Reference was also made to the 1996 Intergovernmental Conference in a statement annexed to the Interinstitutional Agreement of October 29, 1993 on budgetary discipline and improvement of the budgetary procedure to the effect that the budgetary procedure should be reviewed at the Conference in order to achieve interinstitutional cooperation on a partnership basis ([1993] O.J. C331/10) and in the *modus vivendi* between the European Parliament, the Council and the Commission of December 20, 1994 concerning the implementing measures for acts adopted in accordance with the procedure laid down in Art. 189b EC [*now Art. 291 TFEU*] ([1995] O.J. C43/40), where the three institutions referred to the review of the comitology question.

it failed to trigger a political debate.[68] When the accession negotiations were being rounded off in 1994, the Member State governments committed themselves to discussing at the intergovernmental conference (IGC) scheduled for 1996 how the institutions should be adapted in order to operate effectively after the forthcoming and subsequent enlargements of the Union.[69] In order to prepare for the IGC, the European Council, meeting at Corfu on June 24 and 25, 1994, established a Reflection Group, consisting of representatives of the Ministers for Foreign Affairs, a representative of the President of the Commission and two representatives of the European Parliament.[70] On the basis of reports which the institutions had been asked to draw up on the functioning of the Union[71] and of the priorities sketched out by the European Council held in Cannes on June 26 and 27, 1995 with a view to responding to citizens' expectations,[72] the Reflection Group submitted its final report on December 5, 1995.[73] On March 29, 1996 the IGC opened, resulting in the Treaty on which the Heads of State or Government reached agreement on June 16 and 17, 1997 at Amsterdam.[74]

---

[68] Draft Constitution of the European Union, not approved by the European Parliament, but published as an annex to a resolution of February 10, 1994, [1994] O.J. C61/155. See Petersmann, "Proposals for a New Constitution for the European Union: Building-Blocks for a Constitutional Theory and Constitutional Law of the EU" (1995) C.M.L.Rev. 1123–1175; Gouad, "Le projet de Constitution européenne" (1995) R.F.D.C. 287–318.

[69] (1993) 12 EU Bull. point I.18 and (1994) 3 EU Bull. point I.3.28. For the challenges facing the IGC, see Dashwood, *Reviewing Maastricht issues for the 1996 IGC: Seminar series organised by the Centre for European Legal Studies Cambridge* (London, Sweet & Maxwell, 1996), 341 pp.; Louis, "La réforme des institutions" (1995) 3 R.M.U.E. 233–242; Justus Lipsius, "The 1996 Intergovernmental Conference" (1995) E.L.Rev. 235–242; Chaltiel, "Enjeux et perspectives de la conférence intergouvernementale de 1996" (1995) R.M.C.U.E. 625–636;.

[70] (1994) 6 EU Bull. point I.25. The Reflection Group was chaired by a Spanish State Secretary, Carlos Westendorp.

[71] See the reports of the Council of April 10, 1995 ((1995) 4 EU Bull. point 1.9.1) and of the Commission of May 10, 1995 ((1995) 5 EU Bull. point 1.9.1), the resolution of the European Parliament of May 17, 1995 ([1995] O.J. C151/55; (1995) 5 EU Bull. point 1.9.2), the report of the Court of Justice of May 17, 1995 ((1995) EU Bull. point 1.9.3), the contribution of the Court of First Instance of May 17, 1995 ((1995) 5 EU Bull. point 1.9.4) and the report of the Court of Auditors ((1995) 6 EU Bull. point 1.9.4). See also the Opinions of the Economic and Social Committee of November 23, 1995 ([1995] O.J. C39/85) and of the Committee of the Regions of April 21, 1995 ([1996] O.J. C100/1). For commentaries on the contributions of the Court of Justice and the Court of First Instance, see Arnull (1995) E.L.Rev. 599–611, and Craig (1996) Pub.L. 13–17.

[72] (1995) 6 EU Bull. point I.28 (strengthening the CFSP and JHA cooperation, making the institutions more efficient, democratic and open; meeting the needs of citizens, who are concerned about employment and environment questions; putting the principle of subsidiarity into practice more effectively).

[73] (1995) 12 EU Bull. point 1.9.2 (for the text of the first part, "A Strategy for Europe", see point I.97 *et seq.*).

[74] (1997) 6 EU Bull. points I.3 and II.4. For further discussion of the IGC, see Lenaerts and De Smijter, "La conférence intergouvernementale de 1996" (1996) J.T.D.E. 217–229; Dehousse, "Evolution ou révolution des institutions européennes: le débat fondamental de la Conférence intergouvernementale de 1996" (1996) J.T. 593–596; Kortenberg, "Le Traité d'Amsterdam. La négotiation du Traité. Une vue cavalière" (1997) R.T.D.E. 709–719.

On October 2, 1997 the Treaty of Amsterdam amending the Treaty on European Union, the Treaties establishing the European Communities and certain related acts was signed.[75] The Treaty of Amsterdam was the subject of a referendum in Ireland on May 22, 1998 (61.7 per cent in favour) and in Denmark on May 28, 1998 (55.1 per cent in favour) and prompted an amendment of the Constitution in Austria, France and Ireland.[76] The Treaty entered into force on May 1, 1999.[77]

Amendments to the Treaties. The Treaty of Amsterdam did not interfere with the structure of the European Union as described above. It amended the common and final provisions of the EU Treaty and each of the three Community Treaties, restructured the CFSP (EU Treaty, Title V) and radically reformed Title VI of the EU Treaty (covering police and judicial cooperation in criminal matters).[78]

3–021

---

[75] [1997] O.J. C 340/1. The Treaty of Amsterdam was enacted into United Kingdom law by the European Communities (Amendment) Act 1998. For commentaries, see Barents, *Het Verdrag van Amsterdam in werking* (Deventer, Kluwer, 1999), 452 pp.; Hummer, Obwexer and Schweitzer, "Die Europäische Union nach dem Vertrag von Amsterdam. Gegenwärtige Stand and künftige Entwicklung" (1999) Z.f.R.V. 132–146; De Zwaan, "Het Verdrag van Amsterdam. Etappe in het proces van Europese integratie" (1999) N.J.B. 492–500; Hilf and Pache, "Der Vertrag von Amsterdam" (1998) N.J.W. 705–713; Lenaerts and De Smijter, "Le traité d'Amsterdam" (1998) J.T.D.E. 25–36; Manin, "The Treaty of Amsterdam" (1998) Col.J.E.L. 1–26; Sauron, "Le traité d'Amsterdam: une réforme inachevée?" (1998) Rec. Dalloz 69–78; Timmermans, "Het Verdrag van Amsterdam. Enkele inleidende kanttekeningen" (1997) S.E.W. 344–351; Blumann, "Le traité d'Amsterdam. Aspects institutionnels" (1997) R.T.D.E. 721–749; Petite, "Le traité d'Amsterdam: ambition et réalisme" (1997) 3 R.M.U.E. 17–52; Favret, "Le traité d'Amsterdam: une révision *a minima* de la 'charte constitutionnelle' de l'Union européenne" (1997) C.D.E. 555–605.

[76] See the survey in Lepka and Terrebus, "Les ratifications nationales, manifestations d'un projet politique européen—la face cachée du Traité d'Amsterdam" (2003) R.T.D.E. 365–388; Hoffmeister, "Europäisches Verfassungsrecht nach Amsterdam" (1999) EuR. 280–288. In France the *Conseil constitutionnel* held on December 31, 1997 that some provisions of Title IV of the EU Treaty introduced by the Amsterdam Treaty conflicted with the Constitution: see Chaltiel, "Commentaire de la décision du Conseil constitutionnel relative au traité d'Amsterdam" (1998) R.M.C.U.E. 73–84. For the French law ratifying the Amsterdam Treaty, see Karagiannis, "Observations sur la loi française n° 99–229 du 23 mars 1999 autorisant la ratification du traité d'Amsterdam" (2001) R.T.D.E. 19–47. For the constitutional situation in Germany, see Bothe and Lohmann, "Verfahrensfragen der deutschen Zustimmung zum Vertrag von Amsterdam" (1998) Z.a.ö.R.V. 1–44.

[77] Under Art. 14 of the Amsterdam Treaty, it entered into force on the first day of the second month following that in which the instrument of ratification was deposited by the last signatory State to fulfil that formality. See information about the date of entry into force of the Treaty of Amsterdam, [1999] O.J. L114/56.

[78] Bardenhewer, "Die Einheitlichkeit der Organisationsstruktur der Europäischen Union" (1998) EuR. Beiheft 2, 125–138. See also Vedder, "Die Unterscheidung von Unionsrecht und Gemeinschaftsrecht nach dem Vertrag von Amsterdam" (1999) EuR. Beiheft 1, 7–44; Isaac, "Le 'pilier' communautaire de l'Union européenne, un 'pilier' pas comme les autres" (2001) C.D.E. 45–89. For the first time, a Treaty also amended the preamble to the EU Treaty (references to fundamental social rights, sustainable development and the establishment of an area of freedom, security and justice; see Art. 1(1) to (3) of the Treaty of Amsterdam) and the preamble to the EC Treaty (reference to access to education; see Art. 2(1) of the Treaty of Amsterdam).

As far as the common and final provisions of the EU Treaty are concerned, States wishing to accede to the Union were henceforth expressly required to respect the principles of liberty, democracy, respect for human rights and fundamental freedoms, and the rule of law (Art. 6(1) and Art. 49 EU). In order to secure compliance therewith, the Treaty of Amsterdam made it possible, in the event of a Member State's committing a serious and persistent breach of those principles, to suspend certain of the rights deriving from the application of the EU Treaty and the EC Treaty to the Member State in question (Art. 7 EU; see also Art. 309 EC).

The Treaty of Amsterdam of October 2, 1997 further supplemented the objectives of the Community (see paras 7–003—7–004) and conferred some new areas of competence on it.[79] The most important change made by the Amsterdam Treaty with regard to the Community Treaties was the introduction in the EC Treaty of powers relating to visas, asylum, immigration and other policies related to free movement of persons, to employment and to customs cooperation.[80] On the institutional level, the Amsterdam Treaty refined the co-decision procedure (Art. 251 EC), but deferred the promised review of the composition and functioning of the institutions to a subsequent intergovernmental conference.[81]

The provisions on the CFSP (EU Treaty, Title V) were completely redrafted. Primarily, the procedure and instruments for determining and implementing the CFSP were clarified. As a result of the incorporation in the EC Treaty of a number of fields relating to justice and home affairs which have to do with free movement of persons and customs, only police and judicial cooperation in criminal matters fell within the field of application of Title VI of the EU Treaty (PJCC). However, the Amsterdam Treaty did not confine such cooperation to that which was necessary in connection with the abolition of frontier checks, but placed it in the broader context of the Union's objective of providing "citizens with a high level of safety within an area of freedom, security and justice".[82] At the same time,

---

[79] The areas of competence taken up in the EC Treaty are visas, asylum, immigration and other policies related to free movement of persons (Arts 61 to 69), employment (Arts 125 to 130) and customs cooperation (Art. 135). At the same time, the powers conferred by the Social Protocol and the Social Agreement (n. 48, *supra*) were incorporated into the EC Treaty (Arts 136 to 143) in place of the former Treaty provisions on social policy. See Golsalbo Bono, "Le Traité d'Amsterdam. Les politiques et actions communautaires" (1997) R.T.D.E. 769–800. Remarkably enough, the Amsterdam Treaty even made a minor amendment to the preamble of the EC Treaty (introduction of a recital concerning education, see para. 11–048, *infra*).

[80] EC Treaty, Title IV (Arts 61 to 69, Title VIII (Arts 125 to 130) and Title X (Art. 135), respectively.

[81] Article 2 of the Protocol, annexed to the EU Treaty and the Community Treaties, on the institutions with the prospect of enlargement of the European Union, [1997] O.J. C340/111. In addition, the promised review (see n. 67, *supra*) of the incorporation into the EC Treaty of specific titles on energy, civil protection and tourism, the determination of a hierarchy between the different categories of Community acts and the question of comitology were also postponed. However, a declaration was annexed to the Amsterdam Treaty, calling on the Commission to submit a proposal for the revision of the existing Comitology Decision by no later than the end of 1998 ([1998] O.J. C340/137; on the basis of the proposal submitted by the Commission on July 16, 1998, the Council approved a new Comitology Decision on June 28, 1999, see para. 17–012 *et seq., infra*).

[82] See Art. 29, first para., EU.

maintaining and developing the Union as an area of freedom, security and justice continued to be an objective of the Union itself (Art. 2, fourth indent, EU), which was to be pursued both by Community policy and by action in the context of PJCC.[83] The Treaty of Amsterdam cautiously subjected action on the part of the Union to achieve this objective to review by the Court of Justice. On the one hand, Art. 35 EU conferred jurisdiction on the Court, subject to certain conditions, to give preliminary rulings on the validity and interpretation of acts of the institutions in connection with PJCC (see para. 13–085). On the other, review by the Court of the exercise of Community powers conferred in pursuance of this objective (EC Treaty, Title IV) was limited, since the Court's jurisdiction to give preliminary rulings in this connection under Art. 234 EC was confined to requests from national courts and tribunals against whose decisions there is no judicial remedy.[84] In view of the fact that most of the provisions of Title IV of the EC Treaty required the Council to act, in a transitional period, by a unanimous vote and provided for only limited powers on the part of the Commission and the European Parliament in the decision-making process,[85] the Amsterdam Treaty accentuated the intergovernmental features of these Community provisions.

Closer cooperation. In addition, the Treaty of Amsterdam provided for general mechanisms for Member States wishing to cooperate more closely with each other in Community matters or in matters covered by Title VI of the EU Treaty (PJCC), where not all the Member States show the same readiness to cooperate (EU Treaty, Title VII). These mechanisms enabled Member States to cooperate more closely, under certain conditions, while using the institutions, procedures and mechanisms laid down by the EU Treaty and the EC Treaty (see para. 10–004).   **3–022**

Forms of cooperation in which not all the Member States take part had already materialised before (see para. 12–013) both outside the context of the EU Treaty (e.g. Schengen) and within it, particularly pursuant to the EC Treaty (EMU) or a protocol to that Treaty authorising Member States to engage in cooperation while using the Community institutions (Social Protocol). The Amsterdam Treaty reordered some of these forms of cooperation. It incorporated Schengen cooperation into the European Union by introducing Community powers in this sphere, enlarging the scope of Title VI of the EU Treaty and adopting the Schengen *acquis*, partly as Community law, partly as Union law (with Denmark being given a special status and with exceptions being provided for Ireland and the United Kingdom; see para. 10–010, *et seq.*). Furthermore, the Treaty repealed the Social Protocol and transformed the corresponding cooperation entirely into Community competence (see para. 11–043).

---

[83] See Art. 61 EC, para. 10–004, *infra*.
[84] Art. 68(1) EC.
[85] See Art. 67(1) EC (the Commission did not have the sole right of initiative; requirement to "consult" the European Parliament).

3–023 **Renumbering.** The most conspicuous change introduced by the Amsterdam Treaty for practitioners and students was the renumbering of the articles, titles and sections of the EU Treaty and the EC Treaty in order to reduce their complexity and make them more accessible.[86] In the course of this exercise, lapsed provisions of the EU Treaty and of the then three Community Treaties were deleted.[87]

B. THE TREATY OF NICE

3–024 **Treaty of Nice.** The Protocol on the institutions with the prospect of enlargement of the European Union annexed to the Treaty of Amsterdam already signalled that it was necessary to reform the institutions with a view to the further enlargement of the Union.[88] The European Council held at Cologne on June 3 and 4, 1999 announced that a new Intergovernmental Conference (IGC) would be convened in early 2000 "[i]n order to ensure that the European Union's institutions can continue to work efficiently after enlargement". The President of the Commission convened a group of experts under the chairmanship of the former Belgian Prime Minister Jean-Luc Dehaene to report on the "institutional implications of enlargement". On February 14, 2000 the Portuguese Presidency of the Council convened the Intergovernmental Conference,[89] after the Council had obtained the opinion

---

[86] Article 12 of the Amsterdam Treaty, which refers to the tables of equivalences set out in the Annex thereto. A consolidated version of the EU Treaty and the EC Treaty was published together with the Treaty of Amsterdam, [1997] O.J. C340/145 (EU Treaty) and p.173 (EC Treaty).

[87] See Art. 6 (for the EC Treaty), Art. 7 (ECSC Treaty) and Art. 8 (EAEC Treaty) of the Amsterdam Treaty. Article 9 repealed the Convention of March 25, 1957 on certain institutions common to the European Communities and the Merger Treaty of April 8, 1965 (see para. 1–016, *supra*). In order to ensure that the repeal or deletion of such provisions did not bring about any change in existing Community law, Art. 10 provided that there was to be no change in the legal effects of the provisions of the Treaties and acts adopted pursuant thereto. See the Explanatory Report from the General Secretariat of the Council on the simplification of the Community Treaties, [1997] O.J. C353/1, and Jacqué, "Le Traité d'Amsterdam. La simplification et la consolidation des traités" (1997) R.T.D.E. 903–913; for earlier proposals for the consolidation of the Treaties, see Schmid, "Konsolidierung und Vereinfachung des europäischen Primärrechts—wissenschaftliche Modelle, aktueller Stand und Perspektiven" (1998) EuR. Beiheft 2, 17–38; von Bogdandy and Ehlermann, "Consolidation of the European Treaties: feasibility, costs and benefits" (1996) C.M.L.Rev. 1107–1116.

[88] For that protocol, see n. 81, *supra*. See also the Declaration by Belgium, France and Italy on the Protocol annexed to the EU Treaty and the Community Treaties on the institutions with the prospect of enlargement of the European Union, [1997] O.J. C340/144, in which those Member States stated that the Treaty of Amsterdam did not meet the need for substantial progress towards reinforcing the institutions, this being an indispensable condition for the conclusion of the first accession negotiations.

[89] (2000) 1/2 EU Bull. point 1.1.5.

of the Commission and the European Parliament.[90] The IGC concluded on December 10, 2000 at Nice when the Heads of State or Government reached agreement on a new treaty.[91]

On February 26, 2001 the Treaty of Nice amending the Treaty on European Union, the Treaties establishing the European Communities and certain related acts was signed.[92] The Treaty was put to a first referendum in Ireland on June 7, 2001 and rejected by 53.87 per cent of the votes. Following this, the Irish Government launched a national debate, which culminated in a second referendum on October 19, 2002, in which 62.89 per cent voted in favour.[93] The Treaty entered into effect on February 1, 2003.

Amendments to the Treaties. For its part too, the Treaty of Nice did not change the structure of the European Union as it was laid down in the EU Treaty. The Treaty did not result in the comprehensive reform sought in some quarters, but was limited primarily to adjustments in the composition and operation of the European Parliament, the Council and the Commission following the accession of new Member States and to a reform of the Community judicature.[94]

First, the Treaty provided that the Council was to nominate the President of the Commission by a qualified majority vote.[95] The powers of the President of the

3–025

---

[90] See the resolution of the European Parliament on the convening of the Intergovernmental Conference, [2000] O.J. C309/85 and the Commission's opinion of January 26, 2000, "Adapting the institutions to make a success of enlargement" ((2000) EU Bull., Suppl. 2/2000), which was obtained by the Council under Art. 48 EU.

[91] (2000) 12 EU Bull. point 1.1.3. As to how the Treaty came about, see Wiedmann, "Der Vertrag von Nizza—Genesis einer Reform" (2001) EuR. 185–215.

[92] [2001] O.J. C80/1. The Treaty of Nice was ratified in the United Kingdom by the European Communities (Amendment) Act 2002. For general commentaries, see Lenaerts and Desomer, "Het Verdrag van Nice en het 'post-Nice'-debat over de toekomst van de Europese Unie" (2001–2002) R.W. 73–90; Bradley, "Institutional design in the Treaty of Nice" (2001) C.M.L.Rev. 1095–1124; Favret, "Le traité de Nice du 26 février 2001: vers un affaiblissement irréversible de la capacité d'action de l'Union européenne?" (2001) R.T.D.E. 271–304; Pieter Van Nuffel, "Le Traité de Nice. Un commentaire" (2001) R.D.U.E. 329–387; Louis, "Le Traité de Nice" (2001) J.T.D.E. 25–34; Hatje, "Die institutionelle Reform der Europäischen Union—der Vertrag von Nizza auf dem Prüfstand" (2001) EuR. 143–184; Shaw, "The Treaty of Nice: Legal and Constitutional Implications" (2001) E.Pub.L. 195–215. For critical commentaries, see Pescatore, "Nice—Aftermath" (2001) C.M.L.Rev. 265–271; De Zwaan, "Het Verdrag van Nice" (2001) S.E.W. 42–52.

[93] For these referendums, see Gilland, "Ireland's (First) Referendum on the Treaty of Nice" (2002) J.C.M.S. 527–535; Kämmerer, "Das Déjà-vu von Dublin—Gedanken zum Ausgang des zweiten irischen Referendums über den Vertrag von Nizza" (2002) N.J.W. 3596–3598. For ratification in France, see Chaltiel, "La ratification du Traité de Nice par la France" (2001) R.M.C.U.E. 442–446; for ratification in Germany, see Streinz, "(EG)-Verfassungsrechtliche Aspekte des Vertrags von Nizza" (2003) Z.ö.R. 137–161.

[94] Furthermore, the Treaty of Nice modified the provisions of the EC Treaty on the common commercial policy (Art. 133 EC) and introduced provisions on economic, financial and technical cooperation with third countries (Art. 181a EC).

[95] Article 214(2) EC.

Commission were also strengthened. In addition, the Treaty provided that from 2005 the number of Members of the Commission would be limited to one per Member State. Once the twenty-seventh Member State acceded, the number of Members of the Commission would be further limited insofar as the Member States having a national as a Member would be chosen by rotation.[96] By way of compensation for losing their right to have a second national as Member of the Commission, the large Member States demanded that the weighting of votes in the Council be adjusted. The upshot was a compromise whereby the weighted percentage of votes necessary to attain a qualified majority would be gradually increased.[97] At the same time, half of the Member States had to vote in favour of any decision and any Member State could request verification that the Member States constituting the qualified majority represented at least 62 per cent of the total population of the Union.[98] The number of Members of the European Parliament would be gradually increased to 732, against the wishes of Parliament itself.[99]

The Court of Justice and the Court of First Instance were radically reformed. Since the entry into force of the Treaty of Nice, both courts were in principle to sit as chambers. Institutions and Member States were still entitled to bring a case before the "Grand Chamber" of the Court of Justice. The Court of Justice would sit as a full Court only in very exceptional circumstances.[100] The number of advocates-general was still limited to eight, but they were to be involved only in cases where required by the Statute of the Court of Justice.[101] The possibility was created to set up specialised chambers ("judicial panels") for specific matters. An appeal would lie from those "judicial panels" to the Court of First Instance.[102] The Court of First Instance could see its range of tasks expanded, since the Treaties allowed all direct actions to be concentrated in that court and enabled requests for preliminary rulings to be referred to it in respect of certain matters to be indicated in the Statute.[103]

Lastly, the Treaty of Nice increased the possibilities for enhanced cooperation, whilst laying down more flexible conditions.[104] For instance, the minimum number of Member States required for enhanced cooperation was reduced to eight.

---

[96] Article 4 of the Protocol, annexed to the EU Treaty and the Community Treaties by the Treaty of Nice, on the enlargement of the European Union.

[97] Article 3 of the Protocol on the enlargement of the European Union. See also Declaration (No. 20) on the enlargement of the European Union and Declaration (No. 21) on the qualified majority threshold and the number of votes for a blocking majority in an enlarged Union.

[98] Protocol on the enlargement of the European Union, Art. 3(a)(ii).

[99] Article 189, second para., EC.

[100] Article 221 EC, and Art. 16 of the Protocol, annexed to the EU Treaty, EC Treaty and EAEC Treaty by the Treaty of Nice, on the Statute of the Court of Justice.

[101] Article 222 EC.

[102] Article 225a EC.

[103] Article 225 EC.

[104] Articles 43–45 EU.

Enhanced cooperation also became possible in the field of the common foreign and security policy, albeit on stricter conditions (see para. 19–006 *et seq.*).

Charter of Fundamental Rights. In the margins of the Nice European Council, **3–026** a Charter of Fundamental Rights[105] was adopted. That list of fundamental rights was not incorporated in the Treaty itself, but jointly proclaimed by the European Parliament, the Council and the Commission. Nevertheless, the Charter gained immediate acceptance as an authoritative description of the fundamental rights to which everyone in the European Union is entitled (see para. 22–021).

---

[105] EU Bull. (2000) 12 point 1.2.2; for the text of the Charter, see *ibid.*, point 2.2.1 and [2000] O.J. C364/1.

CHAPTER 4

FROM THE CONSTITUTION FOR EUROPE TO THE TREATY OF LISBON

I. THE CONVENTION ON THE FUTURE OF EUROPE

Laeken Declaration. When the Treaty of Nice was signed, it was clear that this **4–001** text would be just another step in the ongoing process of reforming the European Union.[1] In a declaration annexed to the Nice Treaty, the 2000 Intergovernmental Conference proposed that further discussion on the future of the Union should cover four areas: a more precise delimitation of competences between Member States and the Union, the status of the Charter of Fundamental Rights, simplification of the Treaties and the role of national parliaments.

As announced at the Nice European Council, the European Council held in Laeken (Brussels) on December 14 and 15, 2001 adopted a Declaration on the future of the European Union.[2] The "Laeken Declaration" convened a "Convention" composed of representatives of the Heads of State or Government and the parliaments of the Member States and the candidate Member States, the European Parliament and the Commission, together with observers from the European Economic and Social Committee, the Committee of the Regions, the European Ombudsman and the European social partners.[3] The composition of the Convention, which was largely inspired by the group which had drawn up the Charter of Fundamental Rights (see para. 22–020), made it clear that there was a genuine willingness to see the future of the Union debated in a broader and more transparent way, rather than behind the closed doors of an intergovernmental

---

[1] Brand, "Quo vadis Europa? Thoughts on the Future of the Union" (2002) Tilburg For.L.Rev. 106–143; Prechal, "Een constitutionele 'post-Nice' agenda?" (2001) N.J.B. 384–389; Touscoz, "Un large débat. L'avenir de l'Europe après la conférence intergouvernementale de Nice (CIG-2000)" (2001) R.M.C.U.E. 225–236.

[2] For the text of this Declaration, see (2001) 12 EU Bull. point I.27. See also Lenaerts, "La déclaration de Laeken: premier jalon d'une Constitution européenne?" (2002) J.T.D.E. 29–43.

[3] (2001) 12 EU Bull. point I.1. See also the resolution of the European Parliament of November 29, 2001 on the constitutional process and the future of the Union, ([2002] O.J. C153E/310) and Grawert, "Wie soll Europa organisiert werden?—Zur konstitutionellen 'Zukunft Europas' nach dem Vertrag von Nizza" (2003) EuR. 971–991; Hobe, "Bedingungen, Verfahren, und Chancen europäischer Verfassunggebung: Zur Arbeit des Brüsseler Verfassungskonvents" (2003) EuR. 1–16; Rieder, "Der Konvent zur Zukunft Europas" (2002) Zeitschrift für Rechtspolitik 241–280.

conference.[4] According to the Laeken Declaration, the Convention's discussions and all official documents were to be in the public domain. Moreover, the Convention was to work in all the Union's working languages. The terms of reference given to the Convention by the Laeken Declaration expanded upon the four issues mentioned above, whilst adding the question whether the simplification and reorganisation of the Treaties might not lead in the long run to the adoption of a constitutional text for the Union.[5]

4–002   **Convention.** On February 28, 2002, the Convention on the future of Europe started its work, with Valéry Giscard d'Estaing acting as Chair and Giuliano Amato and Jean-Luc Dehaene as Vice-Chairs. The Praesidium of the Convention[6] steered the discussions, which were conducted in a number of working groups and discussion circles.[7] At the same time, the Convention gave rise to a broader debate in the Member States.[8] In order to give impetus to the discussion, a "Contribution to a Preliminary Draft Constitution of the European Union" was prepared in December 2000 at the request of the President of the Commission and the Commissioners participating in the Convention.[9] On the basis of the conclusions and suggestions of the working groups, the Praesidium of the Convention ultimately formulated a Draft Treaty establishing a Constitution for Europe, which obtained a broad consensus at the plenary session of the Convention held on June 13, 2003.[10] On June 20, 2003

---

[4] See Lenaerts and Desomer, "New Models of Constitution-Making in Europe: The Quest for Legitimacy" (2002) C.M.L.Rev. 1217, at 1234–1243; Walker, "Europe's constitutional passion play" (2003) E.L.Rev. 905–908.

[5] See De Witte, "Simplification and Reorganisation of the European Treaties" (2002) C.M.L.Rev. 1255–1287; Pache, "Eine Verfassung für Europa—Krönung oder Kollaps der europäischen Integration?" (2002) EuR. 767–784.

[6] Pursuant to the Laeken Declaration, the Praesidium was composed of the Convention Chair and Vice-Chairs, the representatives of the Spanish, Danish and Greek governments occupying the Presidency of the Council during the Convention, two representatives of national parliaments, two European Parliament representatives and two Commission representatives.

[7] Within the framework of the Convention, working groups were set up on "subsidiarity", the "Charter of Fundamental Rights of the European Union", "legal personality" of the Union, "national parliaments", "complementary competences", "economic governance", "external action", "defence", "simplification" of legislative procedures and instruments, the area of "freedom, security and justice", and "social Europe". In addition, discussion circles addressed the role of the Court of Justice, the budgetary procedure and the own resources of the Union. See Barents, "Naar een Europese constitutie?" (2002) N.T.E.R. 305–311 and (2003) N.T.E.R. 39–47. All Convention documents can be consulted on the Convention's website: *http://european-convention.eu.int/bienvenue.asp?lang=EN&Content=* [Accessed November 17, 2010].

[8] In accordance with the Laeken Declaration, a forum was created in order to enable organisations representing civil society (e.g. the social partners, the business world, non-governmental organisations and academia) to be involved in the debate.

[9] This document, known as "Penelope", can be consulted on *http://www.ena.lu* [Accessed November 17, 2010] alongside the contributions from the Commission. For a commentary by the chair of the working group that prepared the document, see Lamoureux, "La Constitution 'Penelope': une refondation pour en finir avec les replâtrages" (2003) R.D.U.E. 13–37.

[10] A draft of the 16 opening articles was presented in February 2003, see (2003) C.M.L.Rev. 267–277.

the first two parts of the Draft Treaty establishing a Constitution for Europe were submitted to the European Council meeting in Thessaloniki[11]; the third and fourth parts of the Draft Constitution were adopted by the Convention on July 10, 2003. Given the fact that the Treaty establishing a Constitution for Europe was intended to amend the existing Treaties, it had to be adopted in accordance with the procedure for the amendment of the Treaties laid down in Art. 48 of the EU Treaty. As a result, the changes needed to be approved by the representatives of the national governments meeting in an Intergovernmental Conference (IGC) and the new text was to be ratified by all Member States in accordance with their respective constitutional requirements (see para. 5–002).

II. THE CONSTITUTION FOR EUROPE AND ITS FAILED RATIFICATION

IGC. On July 18, 2003 the Draft Constitution was submitted to the Italian Presidency of the Council in Rome. The Draft Constitution was further published in the *Official Journal*[12] and was widely debated by academics.[13] On October 4, 2003, the Italian Presidency of the Council convened an IGC.[14] Under the Irish Presidency, the IGC reached agreement on the Treaty establishing a Constitution

4–003

---

[11] According to the European Council held in Thessaloniki on June 19 and 20, 2003, this marked "a historic step in the direction of furthering the objectives of European integration". Nevertheless, the European Council considered the text of the draft constitutional treaty to be no more than "a good basis" for starting the intergovernmental conference: (2003) 6 EU Bull. points I.3.2–I.3.5.

[12] [2003] O.J. C169.

[13] For general comments, see Lenaerts and Gerard, "The structure of the Union according to the Constitution for Europe: the emperor is getting dressed" (2004) E.L.Rev. 289–322; Arnull, "The Member States of the European Union and Giscard's Blueprint for its Future" (2004) Fordham I.L.J. 503–543; Temple Lang; "The Main Issues After the Convention on the Constitutional Treaty for Europe" (2004) Fordham I.L.J. 544–589; Ruffert, "Schlüsselfragen der Europäischen Verfassung der Zukunft: Grundrechte—Institutionen—Kompetenz—Ratifizierung" (2004) EuR. 165–201; Kokott and Rüth, "The European Convention and its Draft Treaty establishing a Constitution for Europe: Appropriate Answers to the Laeken Questions?" (2003) C.M.L.Rev. 1315–1343; Dougan, "The Convention's Draft Constitutional Treaty: bringing Europe closer to its lawyers?" (2003) E.L.Rev. 763–793; Schwarze, "Ein pragmatischer Verfassungsentwurf—Analyse und Bewertung des vom Europäischen Verfassungskonvent vorgelegten Entwurfs eines Vertrags über eine Verfassung für Europa" (2003) EuR. 535–573; Epping, "Die Verfassung Europas?" (2003) J.Z. 821–831; Geelhoed, "Een Europawijde Europese Unie: een grondwet zonder staat?" (2003) S.E.W. 284–310; Eijsbouts, "Presidenten, parlementen, fundamenten—Europa's komende constitutie en het Hollands ongemak" (2003) N.J.B. 662–673; Lenaerts, Binon and Van Nuffel, "L'Union européenne en quête d'une Constitution: bilan des travaux de la Convention sur l'avenir de l'Europe" (2003) J.T.D.E. 289–299.

[14] Pursuant to Art. 48 EU, the IGC was convened following consultation of the European Parliament (Resolution of September 24, 2003 on the draft Treaty establishing a Constitution for Europe and on the convening of the Intergovernmental Conference), the Commission (Opinion of September 17, 2003 "A Constitution for the Union", COM (2003) 548 final) and the European Central Bank (Opinion of September 19, 2003, [2003] O.J. C229/7), the Council having delivered an opinion in favour on September 29, 2003.

for Europe (the "EU Constitution") within the framework of the European Council held in Brussels on June 18, 2004. After signature by the representatives of the Member States on October 29, 2004, the Treaty establishing a Constitution for Europe was published in the *Official Journal*[15] and submitted for ratification to the Member States.[16]

4–004 **Constitution for the EU.** The Treaty establishing a Constitution for Europe sought to replace the EC Treaty and the EU Treaty by a new Treaty.[17] It was proposed that the new Treaty would be the "Constitution" of the new European Union, with legal personality, which would take the place of the European Community and the European Union. The EU Constitution was designed to simplify the legal structure of the Union by abolishing the pillar structure and by merging the Union's intergovernmental field of action with the field covered by the Community. Only the European Atomic Energy Community would continue to exist as a separate legal entity.

As mentioned before, the EU Constitution consisted of four parts. Part I set out the objectives of the Union, referred to fundamental rights and citizenship of the Union, catalogued the Union's competences, described its institutions and the way how the Union's competences were to be exercised (institutionally and financially) and set forth the conditions for membership of the Union. Part II of the EU Constitution incorporated the Charter of Fundamental Rights of the Union, virtually unmodified. Part III of the EU Constitution entered at length into the policies and functioning of the Union. It took over the various legal bases from the EC Treaty and the EU Treaty—with or without amendments and additions—and contained detailed provisions on the operation and internal organisation of the institutions and bodies of the Union. The general and final provisions of Part IV determined the territorial scope of the Constitution, the procedure for amending it and the conditions under which the Constitution would enter into force. Initially, the idea had been to give a different status to the various parts of the Constitution with the principal aim of enabling Part III to be more easily amended than Part I. Ultimately, however, the EU Constitution did not introduce any hierarchy as between the various parts.

---

[15] [2004] O.J. C310.

[16] For a discussion, see Closa, "Constitution and Democracy in the Treaty Establishing a Constitution for Europe", (2005) 11 E.Pub.L. 145–164; Lenaerts, "The Constitution for Europe: fiction or reality?" (2005) Col.J.E.L. 465–479; Lenaerts and Gerard, "The structure of the Union according to the Constitution for Europe: the emperor is getting dressed", in Van Thiel, De Gucht & Lewis (eds), *Understanding the new European Constitutional Treaty* (Brussels, VUB Press, 2005) 43–92; Lenaerts and Van Nuffel, "La constitution pour l'Europe et l'Union comme entité politique et ordre juridique" (2005) C.D.E. 13–125; Lever, "The Treaty establishing a Constitution for Europe" (2005) 28 Fordham I.L.J 1091–1108; Toulemon, "La Constitution européenne. Son origine, ses vertus, ses faiblesses", (2005) R.M.C.U.E. 213–219; Ziller, "National Constitutional Concepts in the New Constitution for Europe" (2005) E.Const.L.Rev. 247–271.

[17] See the repeal of earlier Treaties envisaged by Art. IV-437 of the EU Constitution.

Constitutional innovations. The EU Constitution contained some remarkable   **4–005** innovations, such as the incorporation of the Charter of Fundamental Rights of the Union,[18] the fact that Member States would have the right to withdraw from the Union,[19] a clearer allocation of competences as between the Union and the Member States,[20] the explicit statement of the principle of primacy of Union law over the law of the Member States, the fact that the co-decision procedure was to become the "ordinary legislative procedure" and the introduction of new legislative instruments for the Union, such as "European laws" and "European framework laws", corresponding to the present regulations and directives, respectively.[21] Moreover, the EU Constitution proposed to reinforce the arrangements on the basis of which the Union is to pursue its external policies,[22] inter alia by providing for the appointment of a Union Minister for Foreign Affairs who would conduct the CFSP and be responsible, at the same time, as Vice-President of the Commission, for handling external relations and coordinating other aspects of the Union's external action. On the institutional level, the EU Constitution proposed changes to the voting requirements in the Council and the composition of the Commission and formally recognised the European Council as an institution of the Union in its own right.[23] In order to strengthen the Union's identity, the EU Constitution expressly referred to the existing symbols of the Union, namely its flag, anthem, motto, the euro as its currency and May 9, as Europe Day (see para. 8–003).[24]

---

[18] See Arnull, "Protecting fundamental rights in Europe's new constitutional order", in Tridimas and Nebbia (eds), *EU Law for the Twenty-First Century: Re-Thinking the New Legal Order*, (Oxford, Hart, 2004) 95–112; Young, "The Charter, Constitution and Human Rights: is this the Beginning or the End for Human Rights Protection by Community Law?", (2005) 11 E.Pub.L. 219–239; Kapteyn, "De reikwijdte van het Handvest van de grondrechten van de Europese Unie als onderdeel van een Grondwet voor Europa" (2004) Themis 111–19.

[19] See De Witte, "The European Constitutional Treaty: Towards an Exit Strategy for Recalcitrant Member States?" (2003) M.J.E.C.L 3–8.

[20] See Goucha Soares, "The division of competences in the European Constitution" (2005) 11 E.Pub.L. 603–621; Craig, "Competence: clarity, conferral, containment and consideration" (2004) E.L.Rev 323–344.

[21] See Lenaerts and Desomer, "Towards a hierarchy of legal acts in the European Union? Simplification of legal instruments and procedures" (2005) 11 E.L.J. 744–765; Blanchet, "Les instruments juridiques de l'Union et la rédaction des bases juridiques: situation actuelle et rationalisation dans la Constitution" (2005) R.T.D.E. 319–343.

[22] See Bulterman, "De externe betrekkingen van de Europese Unie in de Europese Grondwet" (2005) A.Ae. 121–128; Cremona, "The Draft Constitutional Treaty: External relations and external action" (2003) C.M.L.Rev. 1347–1366; Thym, "Reforming Europe's Common Foreign and Security Policy" (2004) E.L.J. 5–22; Pernice and Thym, "A New Institutional Balance for European Foreign Policy?" (2002) E.For.Aff.Rev. 369–400.

[23] See Blumann, "Les institutions de l'Union dans le cadre du Traité établissant une Constitution pour l'Europe" (2005) R.T.D.E. 345–374; Dashwood and Johnston, "The institutions of the enlarged EU under the regime of the Constitutional treaty" (2004) C.M.L.Rev. 1481–1518.

[24] For the EU Constitution as a step towards the building of a "European" identity, see von Bogdandy, "Europäische Verfassung und europäische Identität" (2004) J.Z. 53–104; for the link between the EU Constitution and the citizens of Europe, see Schmitz, "Das europäische Volk und seine Rolle bei einer Verfassunggebung in der Europäischen Union" (2003) EuR. 217–243.

4–006   **No ratification by all Member States.** As already mentioned, the EU Constitution was to replace the existing Treaties only if it was ratified by all the Member States in accordance with their respective constitutional requirements. In several Member States ratification of the EU Constitution was made dependent on the positive outcome of a referendum. After the negative referendums in France (May 29, 2005; 55 per cent against)[25] and the Netherlands (June 1, 2005; 61.6 per cent against),[26] the fate of the EU Constitution became unclear.[27] The European Council of June 16 and 17, 2005 announced a period of reflection, during which several of the Member States suspended the ratification process. In other Member States, the ratification process was continued, with the result that the EU Constitution was eventually ratified by a majority of the Member States.[28] On the political level, however, it became clear that the EU Constitution would never be ratified by all Member States.[29] At the same time, most leaders agreed that there was a need to reform the existing institutional structure of the Union, especially because of the accession in 2004 of ten new Member States, followed by two more on January 1, 2007.

III. THE TREATY OF LISBON

A. NEGOTIATION AND RATIFICATION OF THE TREATY OF LISBON

4–007   **New negotiations on a Reform Treaty.** In early 2007, the German Chancellor Angela Merkel initiated a new round of discussions on the reform of the Treaties. The German Presidency of the Council aimed at finding a consensus on the necessary amendments to the existing Treaties that would sufficiently accommodate the political objections in certain Member States which had prevented the EU

---

[25] See Ziller, "The end of Europe? A flavour of déjà-vu. Reflections on the French Referendum and Its Aftermath" in Wouters, Verhey and Kiiver (eds), *European Constitutionalism beyond Lisbon* (Antwerp-Oxford-Portland, Intersentia, 2009) 17–31.

[26] Bursens and Meijer, "Beyond first order versus second order explanations of European referendum outcomes. Understanding the Dutch 'Neen' and the Luxembourg 'Jo' ", in Wouters, Verhey and Kiiver (eds), *European Constitutionalism beyond Lisbon* (Antwerp-Oxford-Portland, Intersentia, 2009) 33–57; Besselink, "Double Dutch: the referendum on the European Constitution" (2006) E.Pub.L. 345–351.

[27] By contrast, the consultative referendums in Spain on February 20, 2005 and in Luxembourg on July 10, 2005 had a positive outcome (76.7 per cent and 56.5 per cent in favour, respectively).

[28] The Constitution was ratified by 15 of the (then) 25 Member States: Austria, Belgium, Cyprus, Estonia, Germany, Greece, Hungary, Italy, Latvia, Lithuania, Luxembourg, Malta, Slovakia, Slovenia and Spain. After the negative referendums in France and the Netherlands, the ratification process was suspended and eventually cancelled in the Czech Republic, Denmark, Ireland, Finland, Poland, Portugal, Sweden and the United Kingdom.

[29] See Hurrelmann, "European democracy, the permissive consensus and the collapse of the EU Constitution" (2007) 13 E.L.J. 343–359.

Constitution from entering into force. Eventually, the Brussels European Council of July 21 and 22, 2007 agreed to convene an IGC, which was to draft a Reform Treaty amending the EU and EC Treaties and merging the Community and the EU into one European Union with legal personality, but without conferring on the Treaties a constitutional nature. The European Council adopted a precise and detailed mandate on the basis of which the IGC had to draft the amendments to the existing Treaties. The IGC started on July 23, 2007 and reached an agreement on October 18, 2007 on a number of important modifications to the EU Treaty and the EC Treaty, most of which were drawn from the text of the EU Constitution. This agreement could be reached only after certain derogations had been granted to Poland and the United Kingdom with respect to the application of the Charter of Fundamental Rights of the European Union and, again, to the United Kingdom on the judicial enforcement of measures in the field of police and judicial cooperation in criminal matters (see paras 4–009—4–010).

Treaty of Lisbon. On December 13, 2007, the Heads of State or Government of the Member States signed in Lisbon the Treaty amending the Treaty on European Union and the Treaty establishing the European Community (hereinafter, the Treaty of Lisbon or Lisbon Treaty).[30] The Treaty was set to enter into force on January 1, 2009, after ratification by all the Member States in accordance with their constitutional requirements, or—failing ratification by all Member States by that date—on the first day of the month following the deposit of the instrument of ratification by the last signatory State to take this step (Art. 6(2) of the Treaty of Lisbon). After the negative referendum in Ireland on June 12, 2008 (53.4 per cent against), it became clear that the Treaty would not enter into force on January 1, 2009. Cases brought before the constitutional courts of the Czech Republic[31]

4–008

---

[30] [2007] O.J. C306. For general discussions, see the contributions in Wouters, Verhey and Kiiver (eds), *European constitutionalism beyond Lisbon* (Antwerp, Intersentia, 2009), 306 pp.; the contributions in Griller and Ziller (eds), *The Lisbon Treaty: EU constitutionalism without a Constitutional Treaty?* (Vienna, Springer Verlag, 2008), 383 pp.; Cambien and Roes, "Het Verdrag van Lissabon: *anywhere as long as it's forward?* Een overzicht voor de rechtspraktijk" (2010) T.B.P. 195–206; Reh, "The Lisbon Treaty: De-Constitutionalizing the European Union?" (2009) J.C.M.S. 625–650; Dougan, "The Treaty of Lisbon 2007: winning minds, not hearts" (2008) C.M.L.Rev. 617–703; Craig, "The Treaty of Lisbon: Process, architecture and substance" (2008) E.L.Rev. 137–166; Rood, "De EU na het Verdrag van Lissabon: naar een nieuw politiek en institutioneel evenwicht?" (2008) S.E.W. 132–135; Eijsbouts, "Fundering en geleiding. Opmerkingen over Lissabon en de institutionele evolutie van de Unie" (2008) S.E.W. 82–88.

[31] In a first judgment of November 26, 2008 (PL ÚS 19/08, available at *http://www.usoud.cz* [Accessed November 17, 2010]), the Czech Constitutional Court ruled on the constitutionality of a number of specific articles of the Treaty of Lisbon and of the Charter of Fundamental Rights and found that these were compatible with the Czech constitutional order. In a second judgment of November 3, 2009 (Pl. ÚS 29/09, available at *http://www.usoud.cz* [Accessed November 17, 2010]), the Czech Constitutional Court ruled on a challenge to the Treaty of Lisbon as a whole, and found that it was consistent with the Czech constitutional order. See further para. 21–047, *infra*.

and Germany[32] also delayed ratification by those Member States. A new referendum in Ireland was organised on October 2, 2009, with a positive outcome this time (67.1 per cent in favour), which allowed Ireland to proceed with ratification.[33] The second referendum was only held after Ireland received guarantees on a number of specific Irish concerns.[34] To that end, the European Council agreed that, after the entry into force of the Lisbon Treaty, the Commission would continue to include one national of each Member State.[35] Furthermore, agreement was reached on a Decision of the Heads of State or Government of the Member States on the concerns of the Irish people on the Treaty of Lisbon and on a Solemn Declaration on Workers' Rights, Social Policy and other issues.[36] It was agreed that this Decision would take effect on the date of entry into force of the Lisbon Treaty and that its provisions would be set out in a protocol to the TEU and the TFEU, to be adopted at the time of conclusion of the next accession treaty.[37] Poland, on October 12, 2009, and the Czech Republic, on November 13, 2009, were the last Member States to deposit their instruments of ratification. The Czech Republic did so only after receiving an assurance from the European Council that it would get the same exceptional treatment as Poland and the United Kingdom with respect to the application of the Charter of Fundamental Rights of

---

[32] Judgment of June 30, 2009, (2009) BVerfGE, 2 BvE 2/08, 2 BvE 5/08, 2 BvR 1010/08, 2 BvR 1022/08, 2 BvR 1259/08 and 2 BvR 182/09, available at *http://www.bundesverfassungsgericht.de/entscheidungen.html* [Accessed November 17, 2010]. See Doukas, "The verdict of the German Federal Constitutional Court on the Lisbon Treaty: Not guilty, but don't do it again!" (2009) 34 E.L.Rev. 866–888; Schorkopf, "The European Union as an Association of Sovereign States: Karlsruhe's Ruling on the Treaty of Lisbon" (2009) G.L.J. 1219–1240; Niedobitek, "The Lisbon Case of 30 June 2009—A Comment from the European Law Perspective" (2009) G.L.J. 1267–1275. See further para. 21–030, *infra*.

[33] See Carbone, "From Paris to Dublin: Domestic Politics and the Treaty of Lisbon" (2009) J.C.E.R. 43–60; Quinlan, "The Lisbon Treaty Referendum 2008" (2009) I.P.S. 107–121; Kingston, "Ireland's options after the Lisbon referendum: strategies, implications and competing visions of Europe" (2009) 34 E.L.Rev. 455–475; Cahill, "Ireland's Constitutional Amendability and Europe's Constitutional Ambition: the Lisbon Referendum in Context" (2008) G.L.J. 1191–1218. See further para. 21–034, *infra*.

[34] See the Statement of the Concerns of the Irish People on the Treaty of Lisbon as set out by the Taoiseach in Annex 1 to the European Council Presidency Conclusions of December 11 and 12, 2008 (17271/108 REV 1).

[35] See the European Council Presidency Conclusions of December 11 and 12, 2008 (17271/108 REV 1) and of June 18 and 19, 2009 (11225/2/09 REV 2). See also para. 13–068, *infra*.

[36] See the Decision of the Heads of State or Government of the 27 Member States of the EU, meeting within the European Council on the concerns of the Irish people on the Treaty of Lisbon set out in Annex 1 and the Solemn Declaration on Workers' Rights, Social Policy and other issues set out in Annex 2 to the European Council Presidency Conclusions of June 18 and 19, 2009 (11225/2/09 REV 2).

[37] Point 5 of the European Council Presidency Conclusions of June 18 and 19, 2009 (11225/2/09 REV 2).

the Union.[38] In accordance with Art. 6(2), the Treaty of Lisbon entered into force on December 1, 2009.

B. NEW STRUCTURE OF THE BASIC TREATIES

New structure of the Treaties. As the EU Constitution had proposed, the Treaty of Lisbon abolished the pillar structure on which the European Union was based, and replaced the European Community and the European Union by a new European Union, with legal personality, which exercises both the former Community and non-Community competences. Unlike the EU Constitution set out to do, the Treaty of Lisbon did not replace the existing Treaties by one single Treaty. Union action continues to be based on the amended Treaty on European Union (TEU), on the one hand, and the amended Treaty establishing the European Community—renamed the Treaty on the Functioning of the European Union (TFEU)—on the other hand. Both Treaties were published in consolidated versions in the *Official Journal*.[39] The two Treaties have the same legal value.[40] The new European Union replaces and succeeds to, the European Community (Art. 1, third para., TEU). Only the European Atomic Energy Community continues to exist as a separate legal entity, based on the (amended) EAEC Treaty.[41]

4–009

Most of the amendments proposed by the EU Constitution were taken over by the Treaty of Lisbon.[42] Some of them were introduced in the new Treaty on European Union, while others appear in the Treaty on the Functioning of the European Union.

As the EU Constitution had proposed, the Treaty of Lisbon merged the Union's intergovernmental field of action with the field previously covered by the Community. The Union's competence in the field of police and judicial cooperation in criminal matters (PJCC), previously based on Title VI of the EU Treaty, was incorporated into the Treaty on the Functioning of the European Union, together with the existing Community competence for "visa, asylum, immigration and other

---

[38] See the Protocol on the Application of the Charter of Fundamental Rights of the European Union to the Czech Republic set out in Annex I to the European Council Presidency Conclusions of October 29 and 30, 2009 (15265/1/09 REV 1). The Protocol will be annexed to the TEU and the TFEU at the time of the conclusion of the next accession treaty (Point 2 of the Presidency Conclusions).

[39] See [2010] O.J. C83 (following a first publication in [2008] O.J. C115).

[40] Article 1, third para., TEU and Art. 1(2) TFEU.

[41] For a consolidated version, see [2010] O.J. C84 (erratum: [2010] O.J. C 181/1).

[42] Jacobs, "Het Verdrag van Lissabon en de Europese Grondwet. Is er een overtuigend onderscheid?" (2008) N.J.B. 320–329; Lenaerts, "De Rome à Lisbonne, la constitution européenne en marche?" (2008) C.D.E. 229–253. See also Barents, "De Europese Grondwet is dood—leve de Europese Grondwet" (2007) N.T.E.R. 174–184; Corthaut, "Plus ça change, plus c'est la même chose? A Comparison with the Constitutional Treaty" (2008) M.J.E.C.L. 21–34.

policies related to the free movement of persons" (Part Three, Title IV of the EC Treaty), resulting in a single Title of the TFEU (Part Three, Title V) on the "area of freedom, security and justice" (see para. 10–001). PJCC thus becomes fully subject to the Community method—namely legislation is to be adopted by the European Parliament and the Council under the co-decision procedure, whilst there is the possibility of judicial review by the Court of Justice, even though PJCC decision-making retains some specific characteristics of its own (see paras 16–015 and 16–034). However, account must be taken of the transitional arrangements in place with regard to the former third pillar (see the discussion in paras 4–014—4–015). Moreover, the United Kingdom negotiated a special status for itself as regards the judicial enforcement of PJCC measures.[43] The provisions on the common foreign and security policy (CFSP) remain to be found in Title V of the Treaty on European Union, but the Treaty of Lisbon added a number of general provisions, applicable to the whole of the Union's external action.[44] In the field of the CFSP, decision-making continues to exhibit significant features of intergovernmentalism (see para. 18–001 *et seq.*). In this field, Union action is subject to judicial review by the Court of Justice solely as regards restrictive measures against natural or legal persons (see para. 13–086).

C. CONSTITUTIONAL INNOVATIONS

4–010   **Constitutional innovations.** The Treaty of Lisbon took up most of the innovations proposed by the EU Constitution, with the exception of the term "Constitution" and a number of other elements considered by the IGC to be of a constitutional nature.[45]

In the first place, the Treaty of Lisbon updated the values and objectives of the Union (Arts 2 and 3 TEU; see para. 7–007). A major difference as compared with the EU Constitution is that the Lisbon Treaty did not incorporate the Charter of Fundamental Rights of the Union into the Treaties, although an explicit statement was introduced to confirm that the Union recognises the rights, freedoms and principles set out in the Charter, which have the same legal value as the Treaties (see Art. 6(1) TEU). Here too, the United Kingdom, together with Poland, has obtained exceptional arrangements (see para. 22–022). The Treaty of Lisbon took over from the EU Constitution the democratic principles on which the functioning of the Union is based (see para. 20–004 *et seq.*). A notable novelty, which also appeared in the EU Constitution, lies in the fact that any Member State that no longer subscribes to the objectives and/or policies of the Union now has the right

---

[43] See para. 10–029, *infra*.

[44] Articles 21–22.

[45] See the IGC mandate in Annex I to the Presidency Conclusions of the European Council of June 21 and 22, 2007 (11177/1/07 REV 1), at 3.

to withdraw from the Union (see para. 6–015). This right of withdrawal has a clear symbolic value. Even if, on the face of it, the right of withdrawal may seem to endanger the internal cohesion of the Union, it also underscores the deliberate choice made by each Member State belonging to the Union. The Treaty of Lisbon did not take over the express reference in the EU Constitution to the existing symbols of the Union, namely its flag, anthem, motto, the euro as its currency and May 9, as Europe Day (see para. 8–003).[46]

Secondly, the Treaty of Lisbon clarified the allocation of competences as between the Union and the Member States, as well as the extent to which the institutions of the Union can make use of the Union's competences. To this end, the Treaty of Lisbon classified the Union's competences, largely on the basis of principles elaborated in the case law of the Court of Justice (see paras 7–020 *et seq.*). In contrast to the EU Constitution, the Treaty of Lisbon did not explicitly enshrine the principle of primacy of Union law over the law of the Member States (see para. 21–002). As to the legal instruments of the Union, the Treaty of Lisbon made a clear distinction between legislative acts and other acts. All legislative acts are now adopted, in principle, by the European Parliament and the Council under the co-decision procedure—now called the "ordinary legislative procedure" (see para. 16–022).[47] The Treaty of Lisbon also extended the substantive scope of application of this procedure. However, it did not take up the new terminology proposed by the EU Constitution, which provided that legislative acts would take the form of a "European law" or a "European framework law", corresponding to the existing regulation and directive, respectively (see para. 22–063). As regards other acts to be adopted by the Union for the implementation of the Treaties or for the implementation of legislative acts or other implementing acts, the Treaty of Lisbon reorganised the division of powers between the institutions (see para. 16–006 *et seq.*).

Thirdly, the Treaty of Lisbon reinforced the arrangements on the basis of which the Union is to pursue its external policies—in like manner to the EU Constitution.[48] As already mentioned, the Treaty of Lisbon brought together all external policies in one title on the Union's external action, for which specific objectives are formulated. In order to ensure consistency between the various external policies, the Treaty of Lisbon provided for the appointment of a High Representative of the Union for Foreign Affairs and Security Policy, who is to conduct the CFSP and will be responsible, at the same time, as Vice-President of the Commission, for handling external relations and coordinating other aspects of

---

[46] See, however, Declaration (No. 52), annexed to the Treaty of Lisbon ([2010] O.J. C83/355), in which 16 of the Member States declare that these symbols will for them continue as symbols to express the sense of community of the people in the European Union and their allegiance to it.

[47] Best, "Legislative procedures after Lisbon: fewer, simpler, clearer" (2008) 15 M.J.E.C.L. 85–96.

[48] See Thym, "Reforming Europe's Common Foreign and Security Policy" (2004) E.L.J. 5–22; Pernice and Thym, "A New Institutional Balance for European Foreign Policy?" (2002) E.For.Aff.Rev. 369–400.

the Union's external action (see para. 13–070). This means that the Lisbon Treaty takes over the functions of "Union Minister of Foreign Affairs", as proposed in the EU Constitution, but with a title that no longer refers to a state-like entity. The High Representative is to chair the meetings of the Foreign Affairs Council. In addition, the Treaty of Lisbon created a single procedure for the negotiation and conclusion of international agreements which applies in the field of CFSP as well as in all other fields of external action (see para. 26–003). Moreover, the Treaty of Lisbon took a number of significant steps towards a European security and defence policy. The Treaty of Lisbon extended the list of tasks that can be accomplished by the Union in this respect and consolidated the Member States' commitment to make civilian and military capabilities available to the Union. Furthermore, it provided for a species of "structured cooperation" among those Member States which are capable of contributing thereto (see para. 25–045).

Fourthly, with respect to the procedure for future amendments of the Treaties, the Treaty of Lisbon determined that the intergovernmental stage of the amendment procedure is to be preceded by a Convention composed of representatives of the national governments, the national parliaments, the European Parliament and the Commission (see para. 5–003).

D. AMENDING THE INSTITUTIONAL FRAMEWORK

4–011 **Institutional changes.** The Treaty of Lisbon introduced a great number of amendments to the institutional framework of the Union, most of which were already set forth in the EU Constitution.[49] First of all, the Treaty of Lisbon stepped up the role played by the European Parliament in the legislative and budgetary process (see paras 13–006 and 13–138). It is also important that for the first time the European Council was formally recognised as an institution of the Union in its own right, even though its function continues to be confined to issuing general policy guidelines without any participation in the legislative process (see para. 13–025). A further novelty is that the European Council elects a permanent president (see para. 13–031). The most controversial changes introduced by the Treaty of Lisbon were those directly affecting the balance of power between the Member States, in particular the number of seats allocated to each of

---

[49] For an overview, see Bribosia, The Main Institutional Innovations in the Lisbon Treaty, in Griller and Ziller (eds), *The Lisbon Treaty: EU constitutionalism without a Constitutional Treaty?* (Vienna, Springer Verlag, 2008) 57–78. For the amendments to the institutional framework proposed by the EU Constitution, see Chaltiel, "Une Constitution pour l'Europe, an I de la République européenne", (2003) R.M.C.U.E. 493–501; Huber, "Das institutionnelle Gleichgewicht zwischen Rat und Europäischem Parlament in der künftigen Verfassung für Europa" (2003) EuR. 574–599; Moussis, "For a drastic reform of European institutions" (2003) E.L.Rev. 250–258; Smulders, "Kritische kanttekeningen bij de gevolgen van het 'ontwerp-Verdrag tot vaststelling van een grondwet voor Europa' voor het institutionele evenwicht" (2003) N.T.E.R. 246–252.

the Member States in the European Parliament (see para. 13–016), the arrangements relating to the presidency of the Council formations, the number of votes required for the Council to take decisions by a qualified majority (see para. 13–052 *et seq.*) and the question whether or not the college of Commissioners should comprise at least one national of every Member State (see para. 13–090). On October 18, 2007, the IGC managed to achieve a compromise on each of these items, although not without a number of last-minute concessions, such as the enlargement of the European Parliament by one seat and the special arrangements, set out in a Declaration annexed to the Treaties, under which a minority of the Member States in the Council is empowered to suspend the adoption of an act by a qualified majority (see paras 13–016 and 13–054, respectively).

E. Union law and its relationship to previous Community and non-Community law

New Union law. With the entry into force of the Treaty of Lisbon, the European   **4–012**
Union no longer acts through either measures of Community law or non-Community measures. The Union's action in each of its fields of competence now gives rise to measures of "Union law". Consequently, the expression "Union law" has taken on a new and unequivocal meaning. Before the entry into force of the Lisbon Treaty, the expression was used ambiguously, either to refer to the whole body of law governing the European Union (Community and non-Community law) or to refer solely to those provisions that did not constitute Community law, that is to say the largely "intergovernmental" provisions of the EU Treaty that did not modify the EC Treaty or the EAEC Treaty (in particular, Titles V and VI on the common foreign and security policy and on police and judicial cooperation in criminal matters, respectively) and the measures adopted pursuant to those provisions. Since December 1, 2009, Union law refers unambiguously to the Union's new legal order, that is to say, to all provisions of the TEU and the TFEU, all measures adopted pursuant to those provisions and to all other legal rules and principles that are applicable to the Member States and the Union institutions whenever they apply those provisions and measures.

Even where the Union institutions act within the framework of the EAEC—the only remaining "Community"—one could say that their action also gives rise to acts of "Union law" as the legal status of measures adopted pursuant to the EAEC Treaty is not any different from the status of previous Community law, which has now become Union law.

Continuity of previous Community law. Although the Treaty of Lisbon has   **4–013**
brought under the common denominator of "Union law" both previous Community law and non-Community law, it does not change the characteristics and legal effects that the Union Courts have attributed to previous Community law. Indeed, the reordering and renumbering of the provisions of the previous EC Treaty—now the TFEU—does not affect their legal status at all. Moreover, given the unity of the new Union legal order, the characteristics and legal effects of previous Community law

71

now apply to all provisions of Union law. As a general rule, that goes for any provision of the Treaties and the measures adopted pursuant to them, irrespective of whether they are based upon the TEU or the TFEU, since both Treaties have the same legal value.[50] Hence, the general principles that the Union Courts have derived from the EC Treaty as principles of Community law (e.g. primacy of Community law) become principles of Union law (primacy of Union law).[51] The Union's current legal order thus replaces the pre-existing Community legal order while carrying over all its "supranational" and "constitutional" characteristics (see paras 1–024—1–027). Likewise, the considerations on the basis of which the European Community could be called a "supranational" organisation continue to apply to the new European Union (see paras 1–020—1–023).

4–014   **Status of previous non-Community law.** With respect to those fields that, before December 1, 2009, did not form part of Community law, the Lisbon Treaty provides for some transitional arrangements laid down in Protocol (No. 36) on transitional provisions attached to the TEU, TFEU and EAEC Treaty.[52] They concern acts adopted pursuant to the EU Treaty before December 1, 2009 (in practice, the pre-existing CFSP and PJCC measures).

According to Art. 9 of that Protocol, the legal effects of the acts adopted by the institutions, bodies, offices and agencies of the Union on the basis of the EU Treaty prior to the entry into force of the Lisbon Treaty, are preserved until those acts are repealed, annulled or amended in implementation of the current Treaties. The same applies to agreements concluded by the Member States on the basis of the former Arts 24 and 38 EU.[53] Consequently, when applying and interpreting measures adopted on the basis of Title V and Title VI of the EU Treaty before December 1, 2009, account has to be taken of the specific legal status of these CFSP and PJCC instruments (see paras 23–001 *et seq.*).

Moreover, with regard to non-Community acts adopted in the field of PJCC prior to the entry into force of the Lisbon Treaty, Art. 10(1) of the Protocol provides for reduced powers for the Commission and the Court of Justice for a transitional period of five years. On the one hand, the Commission cannot enforce the application of such acts by bringing infringement proceedings under Art. 258 TFEU [*ex Art. 226 EC*]. On the other hand, with respect to those acts, the Court of Justice has only the powers that were attributed to it by Title VI of the EU Treaty before December 1, 2009, that is to say the powers attributed to the Court under Art. 35 EU (see para. 13–085).

---

[50] However, the Court of Justice continues not to have jurisdiction in respect of most measures adopted within the framework of the CFSP (para. 13–086, *infra*). See also the transitional regime that applies to PJCC measures adopted prior to December 1, 2009 (see para. 4–015, *infra*).

[51] E.g. ECJ (judgment of January 19, 2010), Case C-555/07, *Kücükdeveci* [2010] 2 C.L.M.R. 33, paras 21 and 27 (principle of non-discrimination on grounds of age as a general principle of European Union law), 48 (duty to interpret national law in conformity with European Union law) and 54 (principle of primacy of European Union law). See the case note by Roes, (2010) Col.J.E.L. 497–519.

[52] Protocol (No. 36) on Transitional Provisions, [2010] O.J. C83/349.

[53] *Ibid.*, Art. 9.

However, where such PJCC acts are amended, the reduction in the powers of both the Commission and the Court no longer applies with respect to the amended act and for those Member States to which that amended act is to apply.[54] Accordingly, with regard to the provisions of the amended act, the Commission and the Court enjoy the full scope of powers they have under the Treaties with regard to acts adopted in the field of PJCC (Art. 10(2) of Protocol (No.36)). In any event, the reduced powers will cease to apply on December 1, 2014 (Art. 10(3) of the Protocol).

The same protocol lays down specific transitional provisions with regard to the United Kingdom, in view of the special position it has obtained in relation to PJCC acts (see para. 10–029).

In contrast, the Lisbon Treaty does not provide for any different legal regime with respect to the current provisions of the Treaties on the CFSP (Arts 23 to 46 TEU), judicial cooperation in criminal matters (Arts 82 to 86 and 89 TFEU) and police cooperation (Arts 87 to 89 TFEU) and measures adopted by the Union institutions and bodies pursuant to those provisions. Consequently, Union law in those fields has the same legal effects as Union law in fields that, before the entry into force of the Lisbon Treaty, formed part of Community law. With respect to the CFSP, however, the Treaties still do not confer any general jurisdiction on the Court of Justice to rule on the interpretation and application of the relevant Treaty provisions and Union measures (see para 13–086).

Transitional provisions. Protocol (No. 36) on transitional provisions contains   **4–015** some further institutional arrangements aimed at ensuring a smooth transition from the arrangements in place before the entry into force of the Lisbon Treaty to the ones contained in that Treaty. These apply in particular to the qualified majority voting requirement in the Council, the configurations of the Council (para. 13–044) and the composition of the European Parliament (para. 13–016) and various advisory bodies (paras 13–108 and 13–112). In the absence of transitional provisions, the application of provisions of the TEU and TFEU or the protocols attached, introduced or amended by the Treaty of Lisbon in a field which was originally governed by the EC Treaty must take effect in conformity with the principles governing the temporal application of the law. Accordingly, the substantive rules will apply to the future effects of situations which arose under previous Treaty provisions (see para. 12–003). In contrast, procedural rules are generally held to apply to all disputes pending at the time when they enter into force.[55]

---

[54] With respect to such an "amended act", the Protocol does not distinguish between the parts amended and other, unamended, parts, with the result that any amendment to pre-existing PJCC acts may result in the Commission and Court no longer having reduced powers.

[55] See ECJ, Joined Cases 212/80 to 217/80 *Meridionale Industria Salumi and Others* [1981] E.C.R. 2735, para. 9; ECJ, Case 21/81 *Bout* [1982] E.C.R. 381, para. 13; CFI, Case T-334/07 *Denka International v Commission* [2009] E.C.R. II-4205, para. 45.

CHAPTER 5

AMENDMENT OF THE TREATIES

Amendment. An amendment to the Treaties enables amending or supplementing   5–001
provisions to be adopted that have the same legal force as the original Treaty provisions.[1] In this way, the original Community Treaties were amended and supplemented by the Single European Act and the EU Treaty. Both the EC Treaty as so
amended and the provisions which the EU Treaty added to it were subsequently
amended by the Treaty of Amsterdam, the Treaty of Nice and, most recently,
the Treaty of Lisbon. Alongside the ordinary revision procedure, the Treaties
make provision for amending specific provisions by means of simplified procedures. After a discussion of these procedures, it will be considered whether the
Treaties subject their amendment not only to procedural, but also to substantive
constraints.

I. PROCEDURE FOR AMENDING THE TREATIES

Ordinary and simplified procedures. Article 48 TEU defines the procedures for   5–002
amending the TEU and TFEU. It sets out both the "ordinary revision procedure"
and "simplified revision procedures". The former procedure constitutes the general amendment procedure, which was introduced by the EU Treaty (Art. 48 EU)
to replace the different manners of amendment originally contained in the ECSC
Treaty (Art. 96), the EEC Treaty (Art. 236) and the EAEC Treaty (Art. 204). The
Treaty of Amsterdam and the Treaty of Nice were concluded under the procedure
laid down by *ex* Art. 48 EU. The same procedure applied to the amendments proposed by the EU Constitution Treaty and to the amendments introduced by the
Treaty of Lisbon. The simplified revision procedures allow certain Treaty provisions to be amended without having to follow all the requirements of the ordinary
revision procedure, such as convening an intergovernmental conference or having
the amendments ratified by all the Member States.

---

[1] Para. 22–008, *infra*.

A. ORDINARY REVISION PROCEDURE

5–003 **From two to three stages.** Initially, the ordinary revision procedure consisted of two stages. Amendments under Art. 48 EU first required the Council to consult the European Parliament and, where proposals for amendment did not emanate from the Commission, the latter, and to deliver an opinion in favour of calling a conference of representatives of the Member State governments (the Community/Union stage). Second, the amendments were determined by the conference of representatives of the Member State governments, the intergovernmental conference or "IGC" (the intergovernmental stage). In December 2001, the European Council meeting in Laeken (Brussels) decided that the intergovernmental conference to be set up for the next amendment of the Treaties would be prepared by a "Convention" consisting of representatives of the national governments, the national parliaments, the European Parliament and the Commission. The discussions in the Convention resulted in the draft EU Constitution, which was submitted to the Intergovernmental Conference and approved by it on June 18, 2004 (see para. 4–003). Since the participants felt that the Convention constituted an improvement over the traditional procedure for amending the Treaties, an obligatory "convention stage" was enshrined in the EU Constitution for every future amendment of the Constitution. This procedure was taken over in the Treaty of Lisbon in the provisions on the "ordinary revision procedure" in respect of future changes to the Treaties. This means that amendments are negotiated not only in the intergovernmental conference, but also in a broader political forum. The Lisbon Treaty also gave a central role to the European Council in the revision procedure.

5–004 **Proposals for amendment.** Since the Lisbon Treaty, not only any Member State government and the European Commission, but also the European Parliament may submit proposals for amendment. These proposals may, inter alia, serve either to increase or to reduce the competences conferred on the Union in the Treaties. They are submitted to the European Council by the Council, which is also to notify the national parliaments (Art. 48(2) TEU). The European Council has to consult the European Parliament[2] and the Commission. In the event that institutional changes in the monetary area are proposed, the European Central Bank must also be consulted by the Council.[3]

5–005 **Negotiations.** Proposals for amendment will be the subject of negotiations only if the European Council, by a simple majority, adopts a decision in favour of

---

[2] Only Art. 96 ECSC did not contain this requirement.

[3] The EU Treaty introduced that requirement into the revision procedure. Article 102a(2) EEC, however, already required the Monetary Committee and the Committee of Central Bank Governors to be consulted on such amendments.

examining the proposed amendments (Art. 48(3) TEU). In that event, the President of the European Council convenes a Convention composed of representatives of the national Parliaments, of the Heads of State or Government of the Member States, of the European Parliament and of the Commission. The Convention is to adopt by consensus a recommendation to the intergovernmental conference. Indeed, the ultimate decision on Treaty amendments is still left to the "conference of representatives of the governments of the Member States", which is convened by the President of the Council for the purpose of determining by common accord the amendments to be made to the Treaties (Art. 48(2), (3), first subpara., and (4), first subpara., TEU). The European Council may decide, however, after obtaining the consent of the European Parliament, that the extent of the proposed amendments does not justify convening a Convention. If so, the European Council refers the proposed amendments directly to the conference of representatives of the governments of the Member States (Art. 48(3), second subpara., TEU). That was the case with the first amendment proposed after the Lisbon Treaty, which would allow the number of Members of the European Parliament to be increased for a transitional period.[4]

Entry into force. The amendments do not enter into force until they have been ratified by all the Member States in accordance with their respective constitutional requirements (Art. 48(4), second subpara., TEU). The consent of the European Parliament is therefore not required.[5] National constitutions will normally require the national parliament to give its approval. Furthermore, in some Member States amendments must also be approved by parliaments of federated entities or in a referendum. In any event, Member States only have a right to approve or reject the amendments, without any possibility of making changes to the amendments proposed.

5–006

---

[4] See European Council Decision 2010/350/EU of June 17, 2010 on the examination by a conference of representatives of the governments of the Member States of the amendments to the Treaties proposed by the Spanish Government concerning the composition of the European Parliament and not to convene a Convention, [2010] O.J. L160/5 (see para. 13–016).

[5] Article 84 of the European Parliament's Draft Treaty establishing the European Union provided for a revision procedure whereby the "two arms of the legislative authority" (European Parliament and Council) had to approve any "draft law amending one or more provisions of this Treaty". Such amendments could be submitted by a representation in the Council or one-third of MEPs or the Commission. The draft law was to come into force when all the Member States had ratified it ([1984] O.J. C77/52). The 1994 Draft Constitution of the European Union would also have involved the European Parliament and the Council in making the amendment. Such an amendment would have to be made by a "constitutional law" on the initiative of the European Parliament, the Commission, the Council or a Member State. See Art. 32 of the Draft Constitution; para. 3–020, *supra*.

Unless all the Member States ratify the amending Treaty, it cannot enter into force.[6] Consequently, the rejection of the EU Treaty by a referendum held in Denmark held up its entry into force until that country proceeded to ratify it after a positive vote in a new referendum.[7] The problem recurred with the Treaty of Nice, which Ireland could not ratify until after the positive outcome of a second referendum.[8] Similarly, the EU Constitution never entered into force given the negative outcome of the referendums in France and the Netherlands.[9] By the same token, the entry into force of the Treaty of Lisbon had to be delayed in view of the negative outcome of the referendum in Ireland in June 2008, which made it impossible for Ireland to proceed with its ratification until after the positive outcome of the second referendum held in October 2009.[10]

The Treaty of Lisbon introduced a clause that seeks to avoid future amendments to the Treaties coming up against such impasse. Article 48(5) provides that if, two years after the signature of a treaty amending the Treaties, four-fifths of the Member States have ratified it and one or more Member States have encountered difficulties in proceeding with ratification, the matter "shall be referred to the European Council". In that event, consultations in the European Council may perhaps create the appropriate political climate for the Member States to proceed with ratification. However, it does not alter the fact that an amendment to the Treaties cannot enter into force unless it is ratified by all the Member States.

All the same, in order to increase the likelihood of ratification by each Member State, an amending Treaty will often contain opt-out provisions for particular Member States (see para. 12–013).

---

[6] Nevertheless, in theory, a treaty may enter into force between some of the parties if it allows for this possibility (Art. 24(2) of the Vienna Convention on the Law of Treaties of May 23, 1969, para. 22–055, *infra*). The second para. of Art. 82 of the Draft Treaty establishing the European Union (para. 3–004, *supra*) would have allowed the Treaty to enter into force as soon as it had been ratified by a majority of the Member States of the Communities whose population represented two-thirds of the total population of the Communities. In that case, the governments of the Member States which had ratified the Treaty were to meet in order to decide by common accord on the procedures by and the date on which the Treaty should enter into force and to decide on their relations with the other Member States ([1984] O.J. C77/52). Article 47 of the 1994 Draft Constitution of the European Union was similar, although it provided for a majority of four-fifths of the total population of the Union; para. 3–020, *supra*.

[7] Para. 3–010, *supra*. The procedure for Treaty amendment laid down in Art. 236 EEC did not allow the EU Treaty to enter into force as between the other Member States: Rideau, "La ratification et l'entrée en vigueur du traité de Maastricht" (1992) R.F.D.C. 479–491.

[8] Para. 3–024, *supra*.

[9] Para. 4–006, *supra*.

[10] Para. 4–008, *supra*.

B. Simplified procedures for specific Treaty amendments

Simplified revision procedures. The Treaty of Lisbon introduced a simplified   **5–007**
revision procedure for amendments to the provisions of Part Three of the TFEU,
relating to the internal policies and action of the Union, provided that they do
not increase the competences of the Union. Under this procedure, the European
Council is competent to take a decision to amend these provisions without
having to convene an IGC. A proposal thereto is to emanate from a national
government, the European Parliament or the Commission. The European Council
is to act by unanimity after consulting the European Parliament and the
Commission, and the European Central Bank in the case of institutional changes
in the monetary area.[11] However, such a European Council decision will not come
into force until it has been approved by the Member States in accordance with
their respective constitutional requirements (Art. 48(6) TEU).

Another simplified revision procedure introduced by the Treaty of Lisbon
enables the European Council to adopt a decision authorising the Council to act by
a qualified majority in an area or case where the TFEU or Title V of the TEU provides for the Council to act unanimously (Art. 48(7), first subpara.).[12] Likewise, the
European Council may adopt a decision allowing for the adoption of legislative acts
according to the ordinary legislative procedure where the TFEU provides for such
acts to be adopted by the Council according to a special legislative procedure
(Art. 48(7) second subpara.) These amendments can therefore be undertaken without having to convene an IGC or having the amendments ratified in each of the
Member States. However, the possibility to use Art. 48(7) is explicitly excluded for
a number of Treaty provisions (see Art. 353 TFEU).[13] Moreover, any initiative
taken by the European Council in this connection must be notified to the national
parliaments. The European Council decision cannot be adopted if a national parliament makes known its opposition within six months of the date of notification of
the initiative. This gives every national parliament de facto the same right to veto
the adoption of decisions under Art. 48(7) TEU as it would have where the constitutional system of the Member State concerned requires Treaty amendments to
be approved by the national parliaments.[14] In the absence of opposition, the

---

[11] For the legal force of a decision of the European Council under Art. 48 TEU, see para. 22–015, *infra*.

[12] This possibility does not apply to decisions with military implications or those in the area of
defence: Art. 48(7), first subpara., TEU.

[13] According to Art. 353 TFEU, the possibilities afforded by Art. 48(7) TEU cannot be used with regard
to Art. 311, third and fourth paras, TFEU (decisions on "own resources"); Art. 312(2), first subpara.,
TFEU (regulations laying down a multiannual framework), Art. 352 TFEU (the "flexibility clause"),
and Art. 354 TFEU (on the suspension of Treaty rights). However, Art. 312(2), second subpara., TFEU
does enable the European Council, acting unanimously, to authorise the Council to adopt
regulations laying down a multiannual financial framework by a qualified majority.

[14] See also Art. 6 of Protocol (No. 1) on the role of National Parliaments in the European Union
([2010] O.J. C83/203), which provides that national parliaments must be informed of an initiative
of the European Council at least six months before any decision is adopted.

European Council may adopt its decision, acting unanimously after obtaining the consent of the European Parliament, which is to be given by a majority of its component members (Art. 48(7) third and fourth subparas).

5–008 **Other amendments without an intergovernmental conference.** Alongside the procedures laid down in Art. 48 TEU, some other Treaty articles may be amended without convening an intergovernmental conference. In such a case, it is not the European Council, but the Council which determines the amendment by a unanimous vote pursuant to an ad hoc decision-making procedure. Nevertheless, under the Treaty, the entry into force of the amendment in question is dependent upon its "approval by the Member States in accordance with their constitutional requirements".[15] There are five cases in which this may be done. First, the Council may, on a proposal from the Commission and after obtaining the consent of the European Parliament, strengthen or add to the rights attaching to citizenship of the Union listed in Art. 20(2) TFEU (Art. 25, second para., TFEU [*ex Art. 22, second para., EC*]). Second, the Council, after obtaining the consent of the European Parliament, is to adopt a decision on the accession of the Union to the European Convention for the Protection of Human Rights and Fundamental Freedoms (Art. 218(8), second subpara., TFEU).[16] Third, the Council, after obtaining the consent of the European Parliament, which is to act by a majority of its component members, lays down the provisions for the election of the European Parliament by direct universal suffrage in accordance with a uniform procedure or with principles common to all Member States (Art. 223(1), second subpara., TFEU [*ex Art. 190(4), second subpara., EC*]).[17] Fourth, the Council, acting on a proposal from the Commission and after consulting the European Parliament, may adopt provisions to confer jurisdiction on the Court of Justice in disputes relating to European intellectual property rights (Art. 262 TFEU [*ex Art. 229a EC*]). Fifth, the Council, acting on a proposal from the Commission and

---

[15] For the legal force of such a Council decision, see para. 22–015, *infra*. Denmark has notified the constitutional procedure which has to be followed in the case of decisions taken under Art. 22 EC [*now Art. 25 TFEU*]. These decisions are seen as a "case of a transfer of sovereignty, as defined in the Danish Constitution, [which requires] . . . either a majority of 5/6 of Members of the Folketing or both a majority of Members of the Folketing and a majority of voters in a referendum". See the Unilateral Declarations to be annexed to the Danish act of ratification of the EU Treaty of which the other Member States will take cognisance ([1992] O.J. C 348/4),

[16] This provision was added by the Lisbon Treaty.

[17] On the basis of Art. 108 EAEC and Art. 190 EC, the Council adopted Decision 76/787/ECSC, EEC, Euratom of September 20, 1976 and the Act annexed to it concerning the election of the representatives of the Assembly by direct universal suffrage ([1976] O.J. L278/1 and 278/5, respectively). This decision was approved in all the Member States (for the United Kingdom, see the 1978 European Parliamentary Elections Act). In accordance with the procedure laid down in the Treaty, the Act was amended by Council Decision of February 1, 1993 ([1993] O.J. L33/15), which adjusted the number of seats of each Member State in the European Parliament (para. 13–016, *infra*) and by Council Decision of June 25, 2002 and September 23, 2002 laying down common principles for the election procedure in the Member States ([2002] O.J. L283/1) (para. 13–018, *infra*).

after consulting the European Parliament, lays down provisions relating to the system of own resources of the Union (Art. 311, third para., TFEU [*ex Art. 269, second para., EC*]).[18]

The EU Treaty provides for a similar procedure for the decision taken by the European Council for the realisation of a common defence, whereby the European Council recommends to the Member States the adoption of a such decision in accordance with their respective constitutional requirements (Art. 42(2), first subpara., TEU [*ex Art. 17(1), first subpara., EC*]).

Other amendments without national ratification. The Treaties also allow   **5–009**
amendments to be fully implemented at Union level without ratification by the Member States. Mention has already been made of the general possibility for the European Council to extend qualified majority voting or the field of application of the ordinary legislative procedure (see para. 5–007). Besides, the European Council has the power, acting unanimously, to extend the application of qualified majority voting in the field of the CFSP.[19] Furthermore, the Treaties permit the Council to extend the field of application of the ordinary legislative procedure by a unanimous vote and after consulting the European Parliament[20] or to extend qualified majority voting by a unanimous vote.[21] However, insofar as the extension of the ordinary legislative procedure to aspects of family law is concerned, the decision of the Council cannot be adopted if a national parliament makes known its opposition, just as the decision of the European Council to extend the scope of application of the ordinary legislative procedure and qualified majority voting can be blocked if it is opposed by a national parliament.[22] In addition, the Treaties enable the Council, acting unanimously after obtaining the consent of the European Parliament to enlarge the scope of action of the Union in the field of judicial

---

[18] See the "own-resources" decisions; para. 13–134, *infra*. Before the Lisbon Treaty, a Treaty amendment without an IGC was also possible if the Council, acting on the initiative of the Commission or a Member State, decided that action in areas of police and judicial cooperation in criminal matters was to fall under Title IV of the EC Treaty, rather than be the subject of non-Community cooperation (see *ex Art. 42 EU*). See also the Declaration by Denmark on Art. K.14 of the Treaty on European Union, annexed to the Treaty of Amsterdam ([1997] O.J. C340/143).

[19] Article 31(3) TEU. This possibility does not exist for decisions having military or defence implications (Art. 31(4) TEU).

[20] Article 81(3), second subpara., TFEU (judicial cooperation in civil matters—aspects of family law with cross-border implications, see para. 10–016, *infra*); Art. 153(2), fourth subpara., TFEU [*ex Art. 137(2), second subpara., EC*) (social policy, see para. 11–044, *infra*); Art. 192(2), second subpara., TFEU (environment, see para. 11–060, *infra*); Art. 333(2) TFEU (enhanced cooperation, see para. 19–009, *infra*). Unanimity under Art. 333(2) refers to the votes of the participating Member States (see Art. 330 TFEU). The article cannot be applied to decisions having military or defence implications (Art. 333(3) TFEU).

[21] Article 333(1) TFEU (enhanced cooperation; see para. 19–009, *infra*). Unanimity is again calculated in accordance with Art. 330 TFEU. Article 333(1) cannot be applied to decisions having military or defence implications (Art. 333(3) TFEU).

[22] Article 81(3), third subpara., TFEU. See also para. 5–005, *supra*.

cooperation in criminal matters.[23] The Council[24] or the Council and the European Parliament[25] may also amend provisions of a number of the Protocols annexed to the Treaty, acting in accordance with specific procedures, and confer new powers on the European Central Bank.[26] The Council, acting unanimously, may increase the number of Advocates General of the Court of Justice (Art. 252, first para., TFEU [*ex Art. 222, first para., EC*]) and, acting together with the European Parliament under the ordinary legislative procedure, create judicial panels with particular jurisdiction (Art. 257, first para., TFEU [*ex Art. 225a, first para., EC*]).[27]

Under the "minor amendments procedure" laid down in Art. 76, 85 and 90 of the EAEC Treaty, the Council may amend the chapters "Special provisions", "Safeguards" and "Property ownership", respectively, in exceptional circumstances on the initiative of a Member State or the Commission. Such an amendment has to be adopted unanimously by the Council on a proposal from the Commission and after consulting the European Parliament.[28]

II. LIMITS TO THE POSSIBILITY TO AMEND THE TREATIES

5–010   **Procedural constraints.** Under international law, a treaty may be amended at any time by agreement between the parties.[29] Some commentators have taken the view

---

[23] Article 82(2)(d) TFEU (which allows the Council to add aspects of criminal procedure for which the European Parliament and the Council may establish minimum rules); Art. 83(1), third subpara., TFEU (which allows the Council to add further areas of crime in respect of which the European Parliament and the Council may establish minimum rules concerning the definition of offences and sanctions). See also Art. 86(4) TFEU (which enables the European Council, acting unanimously after obtaining the consent of the European Parliament and consulting the Commission, to extend the powers of the European Public Prosecutor's Office).

[24] See the second subpara. of Art. 126(14) TFEU (Protocol (No. 12), annexed to the TEU, TFEU and EAEC Treaty, on the excessive deficit procedure, [2010] O.J. C83/279); Art. 308, third para., TFEU (Protocol (No. 5), annexed to the TEU and TFEU, on the statute of the European Investment Bank, [2010] O.J. C83/251).

[25] See Art. 129(3) TFEU (Protocol (No. 4), annexed to the TEU and TFEU, on the statute of the European System of Central Banks and of the European Central Bank, [2010] O.J. C83/230; para. 13–097, *infra*); Art. 281 TFEU (Protocol (No. 3), annexed to the TEU, TFEU and EAC Treaty, on the statute of Court of Justice of the European Union, [2010] O.J. C83/210; para. 13–077, *infra*).

[26] Article 127(6) TFEU [*ex Art. 105(6) EC*] (the Council is to adopt regulations, acting unanimously and after consulting the European Parliament and the European Central Bank; para. 11–040, *infra*).

[27] For the Council decisions altering the number of Members of the Court of Justice, see the discussion of the composition of those institutions (paras 13–068 and 13–090, *infra*); see also Council Decision 74/584/EEC, Euratom, ECSC of November 26, 1974 on the adjustment of Art. 32 of the ECSC Treaty, Art. 165 of the EEC Treaty and Art. 137 of the Euratom Treaty, [1974] O.J. L318/22.

[28] The second para. of Art. 76 EAEC further requires the Council to apply the provisions of Chapter VI in accordance with the same procedure in the event that it fails to confirm them within seven years of their entry into force. The fact that the Council did not proceed to confirm or amend the provisions in question does not mean that they must have lapsed: ECJ, Case 7/71 *Commission v France* [1971] E.C.R. 1003, paras 18–29.

[29] See Art. 39 of the 1969 Vienna Convention (para. 22–055, *infra*).

that it is implicit in the rules embodied in the Union legal order that the Member States as "masters of the Treaties" may amend the Treaties without having to comply with the procedure set out in Art. 48 TEU.[30] It is a fact that the ECSC Treaty has been amended on two occasions outwith Art. 96 ECSC.[31] The amendments were made during the transitional period in which it was not possible to amend the Treaty pursuant to Art. 96.[32] Nevertheless, the Court of Justice has held that the Member States cannot amend provisions of primary Union law by means of Art. 308 EC [*now Art. 352 TFEU*],[33] a joint resolution[34] or an agreement jointly concluded with third countries[35] and that the Treaty rules regarding the manner in which the Union institutions arrive at their decisions are not at the disposal of the Member States.[36] The fact that the Member States are subject in their "constituent" function to the rules governing the amendment of the Treaties ensues from the specific character of the Union legal order. The Court of Justice has ruled that,

> "apart from any specific provisions, the Treaty can only be modified by means of the amendment procedure carried out in accordance with the Treaty."[37]

---

[30] E.g. Everling, "Sind die Mitgliedstaaten der Europäischen Gemeinschaften noch Herren der Verträge?", *Völkerrecht als Rechtsordnung. Internationale Gerichtsbarkeit. Menschenrechte. Festschrift H. Mosler* (Berlin, Springer, 1983), 173, at 186–190; Zuleeg, "Der Bestand der Europäischen Gemeinschaft", in Bieber, Bleckmann, Capotori *et al.* (eds), *Das Europa der zweiten Generation. Gedächtnisschrift für C. Sasse* (Baden-Baden, Nomos, 1981), Vol. 2, at 58–59, and see the commentary by Louis (1980) C.D.E. 553–558; König and Pechstein, "Die EU-Vertragsänderung" (1998) EuR. 130–150 (who argue that the resultant treaty would be valid only under international law); Deliège-Sequaris, "Révision des traités européens en dehors des procédures prévues" (1980) C.D.E. 539–552;

[31] Treaty of October 27, 1956 amending the ECSC Treaty (change in the distribution of votes in Art. 28 following the cession of the Saar to the Federal Republic of Germany) and the Convention of March 25, 1957 on certain institutions common to the European Communities (para. 1–009, *supra*).

[32] In the debate held in the Dutch Second Chamber prior to the Law approving the Treaty of October 27, 1956, the Second Chamber passed a motion deploring the fact that it was possible for the Community Treaties to be amended otherwise than by recourse to the procedures provided for in the Treaties themselves to that end (*Handelingen*, Tweede Kamer, 1957–58, Annex I, 1957–58, 4763 No. 9) and the government stated that it would in practice comply with the motion (*Handelingen*, Tweede Kamer, 1957–58, 1092). See Van der Goes van Naters, "La révision des traités supranationaux" in *N.T.I.R.* (*Varia Ius Gentium. Liber Amicorum J.P.A. François*) (Leyden, Sijthoff, 1959), at 120–131.

[33] ECJ, Opinion 2/94 *Accession by the Communities to the Convention for the Protection of Human Rights and Fundamental Freedoms* [1996] E.C.R. I-1759, para. 30.

[34] ECJ, Case 59/75 *Manghera* [1976] E.C.R. 91, paras 19–21; ECJ, Case 43/75 *Defrenne* [1976] E.C.R. 455, paras 57–58.

[35] ECJ, Case 22/70 *Commission v Council* [1971] E.C.R. 263, paras 17 and 22.

[36] ECJ, Case 68/86 *United Kingdom v Council* [1988] E.C.R. 855, para. 38.

[37] ECJ, Case 43/75 *Defrenne* [1976] E.C.R. 455, para. 58. In Opinion 1/92, the Court of Justice observed that "[t]he powers conferred on the Court by the Treaty may be modified pursuant only to the procedure provided for by Article 236 of the Treaty [*now Article 48 TEU*]", ECJ, Opinion 1/92 *Draft Agreement between the Community, on the one hand, and the countries of the European Free Trade Association, on the other, relating to the creation of the European Economic Area* [1992] E.C.R. I-2821, para. 32.

5–011 **Substantive constraints.** A further question is whether there are also substantive, in addition to procedural, limits imposed by Union law on amendments to the Treaties. Where a Treaty article provides for a specific amendment procedure, the amendment remains confined to the content of that article. In addition, it appears from the Treaty articles which refer to the "irrevocable" fixing of exchange rates and of the value of the euro for the third stage of EMU[38] that any later revision of the Treaty reversing that situation is precluded.

Under the EC Treaty, some commentators have taken the view that Community law debarred the Member States from introducing amendments detracting from the fundamental values of respect for human rights, democracy and the rule of law or amendments affecting the identity and the very existence of the Community.[39] Although the Court of Justice has not ruled on any principles or specific Treaty articles which are purportedly not open to amendment, it nevertheless stressed the importance of the Court's function under Art. 220 EC [*see now Art. 19 TFEU*] of guaranteeing the autonomy of the Community legal order, alongside other "foundations of the Community".[40] There is no reason why this would not also apply to the Union legal order after the entry into force of the Lisbon Treaty.

5–012 **Judicial review.** Since an amending Treaty concluded between the Member States is not an act of the institutions and has the same legal force as the Treaty sought to be amended, the Court of the Justice is not entitled to review the legality or validity of an amending Treaty.[41] However, the Commission is entitled to bring a Member State which has failed to fulfil its obligations under the Treaties before the Court of Justice. That Court also reviews the conduct of all the governments of the Member States for compliance with their Treaty obligations.[42] The commentators

---

[38] See Art. 140(3) TFEU (see also *ex Art. 4(2), Art. 118, second para.*, and *Art. 123(4) EC*) and Art. 49 of Protocol (No. 4), annexed to the TEU and TFEU, on the statute of the European System of Central Banks and of the European Central Bank, [2010] O.J. C83/230.

[39] Curti Gialdino, "Some Reflections on the *Acquis Communautaire*" (1995) C.M.L.Rev. 1089, at 1109–1114. See also Heintzen, "Hierarchisierungsprozesse innerhalb des Primärrechts der Europäischen Gemeinschaft" (1994) EuR. 35–49 (who regards only the principles of democracy and the rule of law at Union level as inviolable on the ground that the Member States themselves are constituted on the basis thereof). See also Bieber, "Les limites matérielles et formelles à la révision des traités établissant la Communauté européenne" (1993) R.M.C.U.E. 343–350; Da Cruz Vilaça and Piçarra, "Y a-t-il des limites matérielles à la révision des traités instituant les Communautés européennes?" (1993) C.D.E. 3–37.

[40] ECJ, Opinion 1/91 *Draft Agreement between the Community, on the one hand, and the countries of the European Free Trade Association, on the other, relating to the creation of the European Economic Area* [1991] E.C.R. I-6079, paras 35 and 69–72; see also ECJ, Opinion 1/00 *Proposed agreement between the European Community and non-Member States on the establishment of a European Common Aviation Area* [2002] E.C.R. I-3493, para. 5.

[41] See CFI (order of July 14, 1994), Case T-584/93 *Roujansky v Council* [1994] E.C.R. II-585, para. 15 (para. 22–009, *infra*).

[42] See ECJ, Case 230/81 *Luxembourg v European Parliament* [1983] E.C.R. 255, paras 36–37.

in question infer from this that the Court of Justice is entitled to act against the Member States as a whole in the event that they should disregard the procedural or substantive limits set with regard to the revision of the Treaties. They also argue that the Court would construe an amending Treaty which transgresses the substantive limits in such a way as to keep that Treaty within the bounds of Union law.[43]

---

[43] Bieber (n. 39, *supra*), at 348–349; see also Da Cruz Vilaça and Piçarra (n. 39, *supra*), at 17–18. See further König and Pechstein, "Die EU-Vertragsänderung" (1998) EuR. 130, at 138–142 (who argue that such an amendment of the Treaties would be inapplicable).

CHAPTER 6

ACCESSION TO THE EUROPEAN UNION

I. MEMBER STATES OF THE EUROPEAN UNION

Member States. Six waves of accession have enlarged the number of Member **6–001**
States from six to 27. Since January 1, 2007, the European Union has consisted
of 27 Member States: Austria, Belgium, Bulgaria, Cyprus, the Czech Republic,
Denmark, Estonia, Finland, France, Germany, Greece, Hungary, Ireland, Italy,
Latvia, Lithuania, Luxembourg, Malta, the Netherlands, Poland, Portugal,
Romania, Slovakia, Slovenia, Spain, Sweden and the United Kingdom.

January 1, 1973. In 1961 Denmark, Ireland, Norway and the United Kingdom **6–002**
applied for accession to the European Communities. After the UK accession
negotiations foundered in January 1963 on the veto of the French President,
General de Gaulle, it was not until June 1970 that accession negotiations started
up again with Denmark, Ireland, Norway and the United Kingdom. On January
22, 1972 the six Member States concluded with those four States an Accession
Treaty and signed related documents setting out the conditions of accession.[1]
France made ratification of the treaty conditional upon the result of a referendum,
which was held on April 23, 1972. Accession was also approved by referendum
in Ireland (May 10, 1972) and Denmark (October 2, 1972). Following the adverse
outcome of a national referendum held on May 24–25, 1972 in Norway (53.6 per
cent against accession), on January 1, 1973 only Denmark, Ireland and the United
Kingdom acceded to the three Communities.[2] EC membership was the subject of

---

[1] Treaty of January 22, 1972 between the Member States of the European Communities, the
Kingdom of Denmark, Ireland, the Kingdom of Norway and the United Kingdom of Great Britain
and Northern Ireland concerning the accession of the Kingdom of Denmark, Ireland, the Kingdom
of Norway and the United Kingdom of Great Britain and Northern Ireland to the European
Economic Community and to the European Atomic Energy Community, [1972] O.J. English Spec.
Edn, 5, and the appended Acts, Protocols, Exchanges of letters, Final Acts and Declarations. For
the accession to the ECSC, see the Decision of the Council of the European Communities of
January 22, 1972 concerning the accession of the Kingdom of Denmark, Ireland, the Kingdom of
Norway and the United Kingdom of Great Britain and Northern Ireland to the European Coal and
Steel Community, [1972] O.J. English Spec. Edn, 12. The Treaty obligations were incorporated
into domestic law in the United Kingdom by the European Communities Act 1972.
[2] See the Decision of the Council of the European Communities of January 1, 1973 adjusting the
documents concerning the accession of the new Member States to the European Communities,
[1973] O.J. L2/1.

a referendum in the United Kingdom on June 5, 1975, where the result was in favour of that country's remaining in the European Community. In a referendum held on February 23, 1982 the population of Greenland expressed the wish to leave the European Communities. This wish was subsequently carried out by an amendment to the Treaties (see para. 12–007).

6–003 **January 1, 1981.** Greece was the first country to conclude an Association Agreement with the Communities, on July 9, 1961. The Agreement was considered as a precursor to accession of Greece to the Communities. However, the military coup of 1967 rendered accession impossible. In 1975, after democracy was reinstated, Greece renewed its bid for accession. On May 28, 1979 the nine Member States concluded an Accession Treaty with Greece,[3] resulting in the Hellenic Republic becoming a member of the Communities on January 1, 1981.

6–004 **January 1, 1986.** Spain and Portugal applied for accession to the Communities after democracy was restored in these countries. In Spain the death of Franco (1975) gave the impetus for democratic reforms resulting in the 1978 Constitution. In Portugal, the Carnation Revolution in 1974 opened the way to restoration of democracy. Portugal and Spain joined the Communities on January 1, 1986 following signature of the Accession Treaty on June 12, 1985.[4]

6–005 **January 1, 1995.** Following the entry into force of the EU Treaty, States have become members of the Communities by acceding to the European Union (see para. 6–008). Following the signature of the EU Treaty in 1991, it was agreed to deal with the applications to accede made by the States which, as members of the European Free Trade Area (EFTA), had signed the Agreement on the European

---

[3] Treaty of May 28, 1979 between the Member States of the European Communities and the Hellenic Republic concerning the accession of the Hellenic Republic to the European Economic Community and the European Atomic Energy Community, [1979] O.J. L291/9, and the appended Acts, Protocols, Final Acts and Declarations; Decision of the Council of the European Communities of May 24, 1979 on the accession of the Hellenic Republic to the European Coal and Steel Community, [1979] O.J. L291/5; this was incorporated into domestic law in the United Kingdom by the European Communities (Greek Accession) Act 1979.

[4] Treaty of June 12, 1985 between the Member States of the European Communities and the Kingdom of Spain and the Portuguese Republic concerning the accession of the Kingdom of Spain and the Portuguese Republic to the European Economic Community and the European Atomic Energy Community, [1985] O.J. L302/9, and the appended Acts, Protocols, Final Acts and Declarations; Decision of the Council of the European Communities of June 11, 1985 on the accession of the Kingdom of Spain and the Portuguese Republic to the European Coal and Steel Community, [1985] O.J. L302/5; this was incorporated into domestic law in the United Kingdom by the European Communities (Spanish and Portuguese Accession) Act 1985.

Economic Area (EEA) (see para. 25–029). The negotiations which started in February 1993 with Austria, Finland and Sweden and in April 1993 with Norway resulted in the Accession Treaty signed in Corfu on June 24, 1994.[5] The accession was approved by referendum in Austria on June 12, 1994 (66.36 per cent in favour), in Finland on October 16, 1994 (56.9 per cent in favour) and in Sweden on November 13, 1994 (52.2 per cent in favour). Following another adverse referendum in Norway on November 27 and 28, 1994 (52.5 per cent against), on January 1, 1995, only Austria, Finland and Sweden acceded to the European Union (EU).[6]

May 1, 2004. The European Council considered that negotiations on additional accessions to the Union could not commence until after the conclusion of the Intergovernmental Conference scheduled to open in 1996.[7] In accordance with the decision taken by the European Council in Luxembourg on December 12 and 13, 1997, the enlargement process was started on March 30, 1998 with ten central and eastern European States and Cyprus.[8] On March 31, 1998 accession negotiations were commenced with Cyprus, the Czech Republic, Estonia, Hungary, Poland and Slovenia and on February 15, 2000 also with Bulgaria, Latvia, Lithuania, Malta, Romania, and Slovakia.[9] The negotiations resulted in the Accession Treaty signed in Athens on April 16, 2003 by the Member States

6–006

---

[5] Treaty of June 24, 1994 between the Member States of the European Union and the Kingdom of Norway, the Republic of Austria, the Republic of Finland and the Kingdom of Sweden concerning the accession of the Kingdom of Norway, the Republic of Austria, the Republic of Finland and the Kingdom of Sweden to the European Union, [1994] O.J. C241/9, and the Act concerning the conditions of accession of the Republic of Austria, the Republic of Finland and the Kingdom of Sweden and the adjustments to the Treaties on which the European Union is founded, *ibid.*, p. 9, and the Final Act, [1994] C241/371 (title amended by Decision 95/1 (see following n.), ratified in the United Kingdom by the European Union (Accessions) Act 1994.

[6] Decision 95/1/EC, Euratom, ECSC of the Council of the European Communities of January 1, 1995 adjusting the instruments concerning the accession of new Member States to the European Union, [1995] O.J. L1/1. Further particulars may be found in Goebel, "The European Union Grows: The Constitutional Impact of the Accession of Austria, Finland and Sweden" (1995) Fordham I.L.J. 1092–1190; Jorna, "The Accession Negotiations with Austria, Sweden, Finland and Norway: A Guided Tour" (1995) E.L.Rev. 131–158.

[7] See the European Council held in Corfu on June 24–25, 1994 ((1994) 6 EU Bull. point I.13), the European Council held in Essen on December 9–10, 1994 ((1994) 12 EU Bull. point I.13) and the European Council held in Cannes on June 26–27, 1995 ((1995) 6 EU Bull. point I.12).

[8] See (1997) 12 EU Bull. point I.2–6 (European Council) and (1998) 3 EU Bull. point 1.3.49. In Malta the government formed after the elections on October 26, 1996 "froze" the Maltese application to accede (*Europe*, No. 6860, November 25/26, 1996, 2); at the end of 1998 the application was "reactivated".

[9] For the negotiations, see Ott and Inglis (eds), *Handbook on European Enlargement—A Commentary on the Enlargement process* (The Hague, T.M.C. Asser Press, 2002), 1150 pp.

and ten candidate Member States (Cyprus, the Czech Republic, Estonia, Hungary, Latvia, Lithuania, Malta, Poland, Slovenia and the Slovak Republic).[10] Referendums were held on accession in nine of the candidate Member States. Each of them was in favour of joining the European Union: Malta on March 8, 2003 (53.6 per cent in favour), Slovenia on March 23, 2003 (89.6 per cent in favour), Hungary on April 12, 2003 (83.8 per cent in favour), Lithuania on May 10 and 11, 2003 (91.1 per cent in favour), the Slovak Republic on May 16 and 17, 2003 (92.5 per cent in favour), Poland on June 7 and 8, 2003 (77.4 per cent in favour), the Czech Republic on June 13 and 14, 2003 (77.3 per cent in favour), Estonia on September 14, 2003 (66.9 per cent in favour) and Latvia on September 20, 2003 (67 per cent in favour). On May 1, 2004 these States acceded to the European Union.

6–007 **January 1, 2007.** As explained above, negotiations for the accession of Bulgaria and Romania were initiated in 2000, together with other candidate Member States. However, unlike the other candidate Member States, Bulgaria and Romania had not made sufficient progress in relation to the accession criteria in order to be able to accede to the EU in 2004. The European Council noted this backlog and proposed January 2007 as the date for their accession.[11] On April 25, 2005 an Accession Treaty was signed, in which it was agreed that Bulgaria and Romania would become parties to the EU Constitution, unless it was not in force at the time of their accession, in which case they would become party to the

---

[10] Treaty of April 16, 2003 between the Member States of the European Union and the Czech Republic, the Republic of Estonia, the Republic of Cyprus, the Republic of Latvia, the Republic of Lithuania, the Republic of Hungary, the Republic of Malta, the Republic of Poland, the Republic of Slovenia, the Slovak Republic, concerning the accession of the Czech Republic, the Republic of Estonia, the Republic of Cyprus, the Republic of Latvia, the Republic of Lithuania, the Republic of Hungary, the Republic of Malta, the Republic of Poland, the Republic of Slovenia and the Slovak Republic to the European Union, [2003] O.J. L236/17, together with the Act concerning the conditions of accession of the Czech Republic, the Republic of Estonia, the Republic of Cyprus, the Republic of Latvia, the Republic of Lithuania, the Republic of Hungary, the Republic of Malta, the Republic of Poland, the Republic of Slovenia and the Slovak Republic and the adjustments to the Treaties on which the European Union is founded, [2003] O.J. L236/33, and the Final Act, [2003] O.J. L236/959. For some rectifications to the Treaty, see [2004] O.J. L126. The Treaty was ratified in the United Kingdom by the European Union (Accessions) Act 2003 (c.35). For an appraisal, see the articles in Cremona (ed.), *The enlargement of the European Union (Collected Courses of the Academy of European Law)* (Oxford, Oxford University Press, 2003), 260 pp.

[11] See the conclusions of the European Council held in Brussels on June 17 and 18, 2004, point 20–24.

existing Treaties.[12] Since that was the case, the two countries acceded to the European Union on January 1, 2007 by becoming party to the existing Treaties. Since their accession, the EU consists of 27 Member States.[13]

II. ACCESSION OF MEMBER STATES

Accession. Article 49 TEU [*ex Art. 49 EU*] governs the accession of States to the   6–008
European Union. That provision was introduced by the EU Treaty in 1992 and repealed the respective provisions of Art. 98 ECSC, Art. 237 EEC and Art. 205 EAEC.[14] As a result, the accessions to the Communities in 1973 (Denmark, Ireland and the United Kingdom), 1981 (Greece) and 1985 (Portugal and Spain) were based on the specific rules contained in each of the Community Treaties, whereas the accessions to the European Union in 1995, 2004 and 2007 were based on *ex Art. 49 EU*. By becoming a member of the Union, a State accedes to all the Treaties on which the Union is based.[15]

A. CONDITIONS FOR ACCESSION TO THE EUROPEAN UNION

Essential conditions. Article 49 TEU provides that "[a]ny European State which   6–009
respects the values referred to in Article 2 and is committed to promoting them" may apply to become a member of the Union.

---

[12] Treaty of April 25, 2005 between the Kingdom of Belgium, the Czech Republic, the Kingdom of Denmark, the Federal Republic of Germany, the Republic of Estonia, the Hellenic Republic, the Kingdom of Spain, the French Republic, Ireland, the Italian Republic, the Republic of Cyprus, the Republic of Latvia, the Republic of Lithuania, the Grand Duchy of Luxembourg, the Republic of Hungary, the Republic of Malta, the Kingdom of the Netherlands, the Republic of Austria, the Republic of Poland, the Portuguese Republic, the Republic of Slovenia, the Slovak Republic, the Republic of Finland, the Kingdom of Sweden, the United Kingdom of Great Britain and Northern Ireland (Member States of the European Union) and the Republic of Bulgaria and Romania, concerning the accession of the Republic of Bulgaria and Romania to the European Union, [2005] O.J. L157/11; together with the Act concerning the conditions of accession of the Republic of Bulgaria and Romania and the adjustments to the Treaties on which the European Union is founded, [2005] O.J. L157/203 and the Final Act, [2005] O.J. L157/377. The Treaty was ratified in the United Kingdom by the European Union (Accessions) Act 2006 (c.2). For an appraisal, see Lazowski, "And then they were twenty-seven . . . a legal appraisal of the sixth accession treaty", (2007) 44 C.M.L.Rev. 401–430; van den Oosterkamp and Galama, "De toetreding tot de Europese Unie van Bulgarije en Roemenië" (2007) S.E.W. 8–22.

[13] For a general comment on the enlargement, see Falkner and Treib, "Three Worlds of Compliance or Four? The EU-15 compared to New Member States" (2008) 46 J.C.M.S. 293–313; Petit, "Quelques réflexions sur la capacité d'intégration de l'Union européenne" (2007) R.M.C.U.E. 153–162; Rasmussen, "Present and future European judicial problems after enlargement and the post-2005 ideological revolt" (2007) C.M.L.Rev. 1661–1687.

[14] Repealed by EU Treaty, Arts 9(21), 8(83) and 10(28), respectively.

[15] Likewise, before the EU Treaty, a would-be Member State always had to accede to all three Communities because of their institutional and political unity.

As far as what is meant by "European" is concerned, it should be mentioned that in 1987 the Council did not accede to Morocco's request to join the Communities in all probability because Morocco was not regarded as a European State.[16] The Commission takes the view that not only geographical, but also historical factors contribute to the "European identity" and that the essence of that notion is likely to be regarded differently by each succeeding generation.[17]

The requirement that a candidate State should respect "the values referred to in Article 2" was introduced by the Treaty of Lisbon and refers to the values of respect for human dignity, freedom, democracy, equality, the rule of law and respect for human rights, including the rights of persons belonging to minorities.[18] Even before such an explicit provision was added to the Treaties, respect for these values was deemed to be a fundamental requirement for accession to the Union.[19] In a Joint Declaration of April 5, 1977, the European Parliament, the Council and the Commission stressed,

> "the prime importance they attach to the protection of fundamental rights, as derived in particular from the constitutions of the Member States and the European Convention for the Protection of Human Rights and Fundamental Freedoms".[20]

The European Council, meeting in Copenhagen on April 7 and 8, 1978, associated itself with that declaration and affirmed that,

> "respect for and maintenance of representative democracy and human rights in each Member State are essential elements of membership of the European Communities".[21]

---

[16] See the wording of the application (1987) 7/8 EC Bull. point 2.2.35, and the Council's veiled answer (1987) 9 EC Bull. point 2.2.19. See also Dorau, "Die Öffnung der Europäischen Union für europäische Staaten. 'Europäisch' als Bedingung für einen EU-Beitritt nach Art. 49 EUV" (1999) EuR. 736–753.

[17] Commission of the European Communities, *Europe and the challenge of enlargement* (1992) EC Bull., Suppl. 3, 11.

[18] This requirement replaces the requirement introduced by the Treaty of Amsterdam for respect for "the principles set out in Article 6(1)", which already referred to the principles of liberty, democracy, respect for human rights and fundamental freedoms, and the rule of law (see Art. 49 EU).

[19] In the preamble to the EEC Treaty, the Contracting Parties called upon "the other peoples of Europe who share their ideal" to join in their efforts towards integration. Admittedly, the Court of Justice held in 1978 that it had no jurisdiction to answer questions referred for a preliminary ruling on the form and content of the conditions for accession to the Community on the ground that "the legal conditions for such accession remain to be defined in the context of [the procedure laid down by Art. 237 EEC] without its being possible to determine the content judicially in advance" (ECJ, Case 93/78 *Mattheus* [1978] E.C.R. 2203, para. 8).

[20] Joint Declaration by the European Parliament, the Council and the Commission, [1977] O.J. C103/1 (para. 22–018, *infra*).

[21] (1978) 3 EC Bull. 5–6.

The European Council took over that requirement at Copenhagen on June 21 and 22, 1993 and coupled it with other criteria which candidate countries had to fulfil (the so-called "Copenhagen criteria"). First, membership of the Union requires the candidate country to have achieved stability of institutions guaranteeing democracy, the rule of law, human rights, and respect for and protection of minorities. Secondly, there must be the existence of a functioning market economy together with the capacity to cope with competitive pressures and market forces within the Union. Thirdly, the candidate country must have the ability to take on the obligations of membership, including adherence to the aims of political, economic and monetary union.[22]

Since the Treaty of Lisbon, Art. 49 TEU states that "the conditions of eligibility for accession agreed upon by the European Council shall be taken into account", which is a clear reference to the Copenhagen criteria.

Other requirements. Traditionally, membership of the European Union has   6–010
always implied acceptance of the so-called *acquis communautaire*, which the Commission has defined as "the rights and obligations, actual and potential, of the Community system and its institutional framework".[23] Since the replacement of the Community by the Union, reference should be made in this connection to the "Union *acquis*".

The would-be Member State has to accept the provisions of the Treaties, the decisions taken by the institutions pursuant to the Treaties (including agreements concluded by the Communities or the Union) and the case law of the Court of Justice. It has to accede to the declarations, resolutions, decisions and agreements made by the Member States, meeting within the Council, in the European

---

[22] European Council meeting at Copenhagen on June 21 and 22, 1993 ((1993) 6 EC Bull. point I.13); *Europe and the challenge of enlargement*, (n. 17, *supra*), 12; Katz, "Les critères de Copenhague" (2000) R.M.C.U.E. 483–486. See also Tatham, *Enlargement of the European Union* (The Hague, Kluwer Law International, 2009), at ch. 8; Kochenov, *EU enlargement and the failure of conditionality: pre-accession conditionality in the fields of democracy and the rule of law* (The Hague, Kluwer Law International, 2008), 358 pp.; Ingis, EU enlargement: Membership Conditions applied to future and potential Member States", in Blockmans and Łazowski, *The European Union and its neighbours: a legal appraisal of the EU's policies of stabilisation, partnership and integration* (Cambridge, Cambridge University Press, 2006), 61–93; Hoffmeister, "Changing requirements for membership" in Ott and Inglis (eds), *Handbook on European Enlargement—A Commentary on the Enlargement Process* (The Hague, T.M.C. Asser Press, 2002), at 90–102; Cremona, "EU Enlargement: Solidarity and Conditionality" (2005) E.L.Rev. 3–22; Nettesheim, "EU-Beitritt und Unrechtsaufarbeitung" (2003) EuR. 36–64; Šarčević, "EU-Erweiterung nach Art. 49 EUV: Ermessensentscheidungen und Beitrittsrecht" (2002) EuR. 461–482; Williams, "Enlargement of the Union and human rights conditionality: a policy of distinction?" (2000) E.L.Rev. 601–617.

[23] *Europe and the challenge of enlargement*, (n. 17, *supra*), 12. For the origin and meaning of the term *acquis communautaire* in this context, see Goebel, "The European Union Grows: The Constitutional Impact of the Accession of Austria, Finland and Sweden" (1995) Fordham I.L.J. 1092, at 1140–1157.

Council, in the Council or elsewhere which relate to the Communities or the Union. At the same time, it must undertake to accede to agreements concluded by the Member States which affect the functioning of the Union or are closely connected with action by the Union, international agreements concluded by the Member States jointly with the Union and agreements concluded between the Member States relating to such agreements or implementing them.[24] Candidate Member States also accede to the provisions of the Schengen *acquis* as integrated into Union law and the acts building upon it or otherwise related to it.[25] Difficulties of adjustment are resolved by temporary derogations and transitional measures; only those derogations that have been expressly laid down can be validly invoked before the Court of Justice.[26]

The establishment of the internal market means that transitional measures which might have the effect of maintaining the frontiers between established and new Member States must be kept to the strict minimum. Countries applying to accede to the Union are to take the necessary measures to satisfy the conditions of accession in good time. After the Act of Accession has been signed, they must refrain from adopting measures interfering with the functioning of the Union.[27]

B. Procedure for Acceding to the European Union

6–011 **Application and negotiations.** The accession procedure begins with an application to become a member of the Union. The request is to be addressed to the Council. At the same time, the European Parliament and national parliaments have to be notified of this application. Under the first paragraph of Art. 49 TEU, the Council is to take its decision by a unanimous vote after consulting the Commission and receiving the consent of the European Parliament acting by a majority of its component members.[28] The Member States and the candidate

---

[24] See Arts 2 to 4 of the 1972, 1979 and 1985 Acts of Accession, Arts 2 to 5 of the 1994 Act of Accession, Arts 2 to 6 of the 2003 Act of Accession and Arts 2 to 6 of the 2005 Act of Accession. For further discussion of the legal force of the various instruments which new Member States have to accept, see paras 22–103 and 23–004 *et seq., infra*.

[25] 2003 Act of Accession, Art. 3(1) and 2005 Act of Accession, Art. 4(1) (see para. 10–010).

[26] See ECJ, Case C-420/07 *Apostolides* [2009] E.C.R. I-3571, para. 33; ECJ (judgment of October 28, 2010), Case C-350/08 *Commission v Lithuania*, not yet reported, paras 54–79.

[27] See ECJ, Case C-27/96 *Danisco Sugar* [1997] E.C.R. I-6653, paras 24–31 (see also para. 22–055, *infra*).

[28] The Single European Act introduced the requirement for the assent of the European Parliament in Art. 237 EEC. The accession procedures laid down in Art. 98 ECSC and Art. 205 EAEC required the Council only to seek the opinion of the Commission. During the procedure for the accession of Portugal and Spain, the Economic and Social Committee delivered an own-initiative Opinion ([1984] O.J. C23/51). Since the Council had consulted the European Parliament in accordance with point 2.3.7. of the Solemn Declaration of Stuttgart, the Parliament gave its views on the conclusion of the negotiations with Portugal and Spain in a resolution, [1985] O.J. C141/130.

Member State agree intergovernmentally on the terms of accession and the resulting application of the Treaties (Art. 49, second para., TEU).[29]

In practice the Commission delivers an initial opinion and the Council takes an initial decision to open the procedure. The actual opinion of the Commission and the decisions of the European Parliament and the Council are not given until after the negotiations with the candidate Member State have been concluded. In accordance with the working procedure adopted by the Council on June 8 and 9, 1970, the candidate Member State negotiates in fact with the Union institutions (and therefore not with the Member States as such): the Council negotiates on the basis of common positions which it determines beforehand and, as far as some matters are concerned, it requires the Commission to negotiate with the candidate Member State.[30] The final agreement is concluded between the Member States and all the candidate Member States, and enters into force after ratification by all the States in accordance with their respective constitutional requirements (Art. 49, second para., TEU).[31]

Accession Treaty. The conditions for accession and the resulting adjustments to the Treaties are laid down in an Act annexed to the Accession Treaty ("the Act of Accession"), as supplemented by Protocols, Declarations and a Final Act.[32] Since at the moment of signature of the 2005 Accession Treaty it was not clear whether the Treaty establishing a Constitution for Europe would enter into force, that Accession Treaty laid down in a "Protocol" the conditions for accession in the event that it would enter into force before the moment of accession and specified   **6–012**

---

[29] Under the procedure laid down by Art. 98 ECSC, the Council was to determine the terms of accession by a unanimous vote. As a result, the three rounds of accession negotiations prior to the entry into force of EU Treaty resulted in a Council decision on accession to the ECSC alongside a Treaty between the Member States and the applicant Member State with regard to accession to the EC and the EAEC.

[30] For the procedure, see Puissochet, *L'élargissement des Communautés européennes: présentation et commentaire du Traité et des Actes relatifs à l'adhésion du Royaume-Uni, du Danemark et de l'Irlande* (Paris, Editions techniques et économiques, 1974), at 21–22; for the application of the procedure during the more recent accession negotiations, see Tatham, *Enlargement of the European Union* (The Hague, Kluwer Law International, 2009), at ch. 9; Maurer, "Negotiations in progress" and "Progress of the negotiations" in Ott and Inglis (eds), *Handbook on European Enlargement— A Commentary on the Enlargement Process* (The Hague, T.M.C. Asser Press, 2002) at 113–129; Joly, "Le processus de l'élargissement de l'Union européenne" (2002) R.M.C.U.E. 239–246; Landaburu, "The Fifth Enlargement of the European Union: The Power of Example" (2002) Fordham I.L.J. 1–11.

[31] For where all the applicant States do not ratify the Treaty, see para. 5–006, *supra*. The European Parliament's draft Treaty (Art. 2) and its 1994 Draft Constitution (Art. 45) would have made accession to the Union dependent on the conclusion of a treaty by the applicant State directly with the Union.

[32] For full references to the documents relating to preceding accessions, see para. 6–001 *et seq.*, *supra*.

in an "Act" the conditions for accession in the case where that would not be the case, which was the situation that ultimately materialised.[33]

In 1978, the Commission argued that the adjustments could encompass amendments of the Treaties going further than mere technical adjustments.[34] Nevertheless, the 1972, 1979, 1985, 1994, 2003 and 2005 Accession Treaties confined the institutional amendments to an appropriate representation of the new Member States in the institutions and bodies of the Communities. The Court of Justice takes the view that the conditions of admission and the adjustments to the Treaties entailed thereby include adjustments to Union secondary legislation agreed by the Member States upon accession.[35] For every enlargement by which several countries accede, a single Accession Treaty has been drawn up which stipulates that the new Member States are to become members of the European Union subject to the conditions set out in an Act of Accession annexed to the Treaty.[36] In the course of ratification by each of the Member States, the national parliaments (and, in the event of a referendum, the people) cannot therefore confine their approval to only some of the new Member States mentioned in the Accession Treaty. Since, however, it is impossible to tell beforehand whether an Accession Treaty will be approved in all the would-be Member States, such a Treaty will generally contain a provision empowering the Council to make the necessary adjustments in the event that a smaller number of States actually join.[37]

---

[33] See Art. 2(1)–(2) of the 2005 Accession Treaty, the annexed Protocol concerning the conditions and arrangements for admission of the Republic of Bulgaria and Romania to the European Union and the annexed Act concerning the conditions of accession of the Republic of Bulgaria and Romania and the adjustments to the Treaties on which the European Union is founded.

[34] See the Communication of the Commission to the Council (supplementing its Communication of April 20, 1978) (1978) EC Bull., Suppl. 1), *Enlargement of the Community—Transitional period and institutional implications* (1978) EC Bull. Suppl. 2, points 30–53.

[35] ECJ, Joined Cases 31–35/86 *LAISA and Others v Council* [1988] E.C.R. 2285, paras 9–12, with a critical note by Vandersanden (1989) C.M.L.Rev. 551–561. The Court has specified that the adaptation measures provided for by acts of accession, as a general rule, authorise only adaptations intended to render earlier Union measures applicable in the new Member States, to the exclusion of all other amendments (ECJ, Case C-413/04 *European Parliament v Council* [2006] E.C.R. I-11221, paras 31 to 38, and ECJ, Case C-414/04 *European Parliament v Council* [2006] E.C.R. I-11279, paras 29 to 36; ECJ, Case C-273/04 *Poland v Council* [2007] E.C.R. I-8925, paras 45–51).

[36] See the Council's answer of December 19, 2002 and the Commission's answer of August 20, 2002 to questions E-2069/02 and E-2070/02, respectively (Van den Bos and Van der Laan), [2003] O.J. C92 E/131 and C192 E/47, respectively.

[37] Pursuant to the third para. of Art. 2 of the 1972 Accession Treaty and the second subpara. of Art. 2(2) of the 1994 Accession Treaty, the Council adopted a decision each time Norway found it impossible to ratify the Accession Treaty (on January 1, 1973 and January 1, 1995, respectively), adjusting the instruments concerning the accession of new Member States to the European Communities/European Union ([1973] O.J. L2/1, and [1995] O.J. L1/1). See also the second subpara. of Art. 2(2) of the 1985 Accession Treaty, the second subpara. of Art. 2(2) of the 2003 Accession Treaty and the second subpara. of Art. 4(2) of the 2005 Accession Treaty.

C. PENDING APPLICATIONS

Pending applications. Various countries have applied for membership. **6–013**
Following the recent accession of new Member States in 2004 and 2007, the
following countries' applications remain outstanding: Turkey (April 14, 1987),
Switzerland (May 26, 1992), Croatia (February 21, 2003), the Former Yugoslav
Republic of Macedonia (March 22, 2004), Montenegro (December 15, 2008),
Albania (April 28, 2009), Iceland (July 16, 2009) and Serbia (December 22,
2009). An application from Norway led to negotiations which culminated in the
1972 Accession Treaty, which, however, was rejected by a majority of voters in a
referendum (see para. 6–002). The same thing happened with the negotiations on
Norway's second application, which resulted in the 1994 Accession Treaty.[38] As
long as there is no majority in Switzerland for joining the EEA, it is difficult to
see it acceding to the Union (see para. 25–029).

Currently, Croatia, Turkey and the Former Yugoslav Republic of Macedonia
have the status of "candidate Member State". The European Council held in
Luxembourg on December 12 and 13, 1997 confirmed Turkey's eligibility for
accession to the European Union and that it would be judged on the basis of the
same criteria as the other applicant States.[39] In June 2004, the European Council
declared that Croatia met the requisite conditions to start accession negotiations
in 2005.[40] On October 3, 2005 accession negotiations were started with Turkey
and Croatia. The Former Yugoslav Republic of Macedonia was recognised as a
candidate Member State by the European Council of December 15 and 16,
2005.[41] To date, accession negotiations have not yet started.

The other countries of the Western Balkans (Albania, Bosnia and Herzegovina,
Montenegro, Serbia and Kosovo) are recognised as being potential candidates for
membership of the Union.[42] Whether they accede or not will depend upon
whether they comply with the general accession criteria and upon the progress
they make in the stabilisation and association process (see para. 25–022).

---

[38] Para. 6–005, *supra*. Norway had applied to join on November 25, 1992.

[39] (1997) 12 EU Bull. point I.6.31. See also the position expressed by the President of the Council at
the meeting of the EC-Turkey Association Council of April 29, 1997 ((1997) 4 EU Bull. point
1.4.74).

[40] Conclusions of the European Council held in Brussels on June 17 and 18, 2004, points 31–36. See
Yakemtchouk, "La Croatie: deviendra-t-elle membre de l'Union européenne?" (2005) R.M.C.U.E.
317–324.

[41] Conclusions of the European Council held in Brussels on December 15 and 16, 2005, points 23–25.

[42] See the Presidency conclusions following the European Councils held at Santa Maria da Feira on
June 19–20, 2000 ((2000) 6 EU Bull. point I.49.67) and at Nice on December 7–9, 2000 ((2000)
12 EU Bull. point I.36.60), where express reference is made to "potential candidates for EU membership" and "a clear prospect of accession"; see (with respect to Kosovo) the Presidency conclusions following the European Council held on June 19–20, 2008 (2008 EU Bull., Annex to the
Presidency conclusions, point 1/1).

Through an instrument for Pre-Accession Assistance, the Union provides specific assistance to candidate countries as well as potential candidate countries.[43]

III. MEMBER STATES LEAVING THE UNION

6–014   **Traditional situation.** The traditional view was that Member States could not voluntarily leave the Union. Since the Treaties (with the exception of the ECSC Treaty) were concluded for an unlimited time, Member States were not entitled unqualifiedly to revoke their membership in the absence of an explicit Treaty provision allowing this. Moreover, within the European Union—which confers enforceable rights directly on Member States and individuals, possesses institutions entitled to deal with economic, social and political issues and has a compulsory system for the judicial resolution of disputes—revocation of membership is not possible for one of the specific reasons accepted by international law as justifying the unilateral termination of a relationship established by treaty, namely breach of the Treaty by other Member States, supervening impossibility of performance on the part of the Member State seeking to withdraw, or fundamental change of circumstances with respect to those existing at the time when the Treaty was concluded.[44] A Member State could leave the Union only following "amendment" of the Treaty (procedure set out in Art. 48 TEU).

6–015   **Possibility to withdraw.** This situation has changed completely with the entry into force of the Treaty of Lisbon. The Treaties now provide for an express possibility for any Member State to withdraw voluntarily from the European Union (Art. 50 TEU).[45] This right of withdrawal has a clear symbolic value. Even if, on the face of it, the right of withdrawal may seem to endanger the internal cohesion of the Union, it also underscores the deliberate choice made by each Member State belonging to the Union.

The following rules apply in this connection. If a Member State has taken the decision to withdraw, in accordance with its own constitutional requirements, it has to notify the European Council of its intention and negotiate and conclude

---

[43] Council Regulation (EC) No. 1085/2006 of July 17, 2006 establishing an Instrument for Pre-Accession Assistance (IPA), [2006] O.J. L210/82.

[44] See Arts 60, 61 and 62 of the 1969 Vienna Convention on the Law of Treaties (para. 22–055, *infra*). However, for agreements concluded by the Union with third countries, see para. 22–055, *infra*. Moreover, a Member State cannot unilaterally change the delimitation of powers between the Union and its Member States: see the Commission's answer of September 7, 2001 to question E-2399/01 (Huhne), [2001] O.J. C364E/252.

[45] The Treaty of Lisbon takes over the rules proposed by the Constitution in this regard: see Art. I-60. See Malathouni, "Should I stay or should I go: the sunset clause as self-confidence or suicide?" (2008) 15 M.J.E.C.L. 115–124; Bruha and Nowak, "Recht auf Austritt aus der Europäischen Union?" (2004) A. Völkerr. 1–25; Friel, "Secession from the European Union: Checking out of the Proverbal 'Cockroach Motel'" (2004) Fordham I.L.J. 590–641.

an agreement with the Union setting out the arrangements for its withdrawal and taking account of the framework for its future relationship with the Union. That agreement is to be concluded on behalf of the Union by the Council, acting by a qualified majority after obtaining the consent of the European Parliament (Art. 50(1) and (2) TEU).[46] In this connection, it will have to be determined to what extent rights and obligations stemming from Union law may continue to apply to citizens of the withdrawing Member State. However, a Member State cannot be forced to await the outcome of the negotiations on the conditions accompanying its withdrawal. In the absence of any agreement, the Treaties will cease to apply to the Member State in question two years after the notification of the intention to withdraw, unless the European Council, in agreement with the Member State concerned, unanimously decides to extend this period (Art. 50(3) TEU).

In the event that a State which has withdrawn from the Union should apply to rejoin, the procedure laid down in Art. 49 TEU would apply (Art. 50(5) TEU).

IV. SUSPENSION OF TREATY RIGHTS AND OBLIGATIONS

No unilateral suspension. Member States may not suspend their own Treaty obligations vis-à-vis a Member State which is in persistent breach. No more do the Treaties permit a Member State to be excluded or compelled to leave the Union.[47] A Member State which fails to fulfil its obligations may be brought before the Court of Justice by the Commission or another Member State, and possibly fined (Arts 258 to 260 TFEU).[48] Commentators have been divided as to whether a unilateral suspension of Treaty obligations may be justified under international law where no solution can be found using the dispute-settlement procedures or the safeguard clauses of Arts 346 to 348 TFEU.[49]

6–016

---

[46] The Council has to take into account the guidelines provided by the European Council (Art. 50(2) TEU). The member of the European Council or of the Council representing the withdrawing Member State does not participate in the discussions of the European Council or Council or in decisions concerning it (Art. 50(4) TEU).

[47] Likewise, when Denmark was unable to ratify the EU Treaty after a negative vote in a first referendum, the other Member States could not exclude it from the Community or replace the Community by some other organisation: Kapteyn, "Denemarken en het Verdrag van Maastricht" (1992) N.J.B. 781–783; see to the same effect, Rideau, "La ratification et l'entrée en vigueur du traité de Maastricht" (1992) R.F.D.C. 479, at 490–491.

[48] For further details, see Lenaerts, Arts and Maselis, *Procedural Law of the European Union*, (London, Sweet & Maxwell, 2012) Ch. 5. In the event of an excessive deficit, the Council, excluding the representative of the Member State concerned, may impose sanctions (Art. 126(11) TFEU [*ex Art. 104(11) EC*]; para. 11–038, *supra*).

[49] The view that such measures would run counter to the Union legal order is discussed in Everling, "Sind die Mitgliedstaaten der Europäischen Gemeinschaften noch Herren der Verträge?", in *Völkerrecht als Rechtsordnung. Internationale Gerichtsbarkeit. Menschenrechte. Festschrift H. Mosler* (Berlin, Springer, 1983), 173–191.

For further literature and a number of scenarios for exceptional measures, see Ehlermann, "Mitgliedschaft in der Europäischen Gemeinschaft—Rechtsproblem der Erweiterung, der Mitgliedschaft und der Verkleinerung" (1984) EuR. 113, at 120–121.

6–017 **Suspension of Treaty rights.** If a Member State commits a "serious and persistent breach" of the values referred to in Art. 2 TEU,[50] the Council may decide to suspend certain of its rights deriving from the application of the Treaties (Art. 7 TEU). The values concerned are respect for human dignity, freedom, democracy, equality, the rule of law and respect for human rights, including the rights of persons belonging to minorities.[51] The European Council determines such a breach after inviting the Member State in question to submit its observations. It makes that determination unanimously at the proposal of one-third of the Member States or the Commission, after obtaining the consent of the European Parliament (Art. 7(2) TEU).[52]

The Treaty of Nice supplemented this procedure by a warning procedure under which the Council may determine that there is a "clear risk" of a serious breach by a Member State of the said values. This requires a reasoned proposal by one-third of the Member States, by the European Parliament or by the Commission which the Council must adopt by a majority of four-fifths of its members after obtaining the consent of the European Parliament. The Council must hear the Member State concerned and may address recommendations to it. It must regularly verify that the grounds on which such a determination was made continue to apply (Art. 7(1) TEU). This procedure affords a legal basis for Member States to act where the political situation in a Member State is at risk of no longer affording all the guarantees for the protection of fundamental rights.[53] The

---

[50] Before the Treaty of Lisbon, Art. 7 EU referred to breach of the principles mentioned in Art. 6(1) EU, namely the principles of liberty, democracy, respect for human rights and fundamental freedoms, and the rule of law.

[51] For the violation of fundamental rights, see De Witte and Toggenburg, "Human Rights and Membership of the European Union", in Peers and Ward (eds), *The EU Charter of Fundamental Rights* (Oxford, Hart, 2004) 59–82; Wachsmann, "Le traité d'Amsterdam. Les droits de l'homme" (1997) R.T.D.E. 883, at 895–897; for breaches of the principle of democracy, see Verhoeven, "How Democratic Need European Union Members Be? Some Thoughts After Amsterdam" (1998) E.L.Rev. 217–234.

[52] For a detailed study of the possibility of suspending Member States, see Schmitt von Sydow, "Liberté, démocratie, droits fondamentaux et Etat de droit: analyses de l'article 7 du traité EU" (2001) R.D.U.E. 285–328. The Commission is convinced that this possibility should not have to be applied; see the Commission's communication to the Council and the European Parliament of October 15, 2003 on Art. 7 of the EU Treaty: "Respect for and promotion of the values on which the Union is based" (COM (2003) 606 fin.).

[53] A rather extreme example is afforded by the reaction of 14 Member States on January 31, 2000 following the formation of a government including an extreme right-wing party in Austria where bilateral contacts with members of the Austrian Government were broken off. See Gilliaux, "L'Union européenne à l'épreuve de gouvernements liberticides?" (2000) J.T. 449-454; Leidenmühler, "Zur Legalität der Massnahmen gegen die österreichische Bundesregierung" (2000) Zeitschrift für öffentliches Recht 299–322; Regan, "Are EU Sanctions Against Austria Legal?" (2000) Zeitschrift für öffentliches Recht 323–336; Schmahl, "Die Reaktionen auf den Einzug der Freiheitlichen Partei Österreichs in das österreichische Regierungskabinett" (2000) EuR. 819–835. Following a situation report drawn up by a number of "wise men", these "sanctions" were lifted. See Adamovich, "Juristische Aspekte der 'Sanktionen' der EU-14 und des 'Weisenberichtes'" (2001) Eu.GR.Z.

Treaties do not specify that there must have been a determination of a clear risk of a serious breach of the values referred to in Art. 2 TEU before the European Council can determine that a serious and persistent breach exists.

When the European Council has determined that there is a serious and persistent breach, the Council may decide by a qualified majority to suspend certain of the rights deriving from the application of the Treaties, including the voting rights of the representative of the government in question in the Council. The Council has to take into account the possible consequences of such a suspension on the rights and obligations of natural and legal persons. The obligations of the Member State in question under the Treaties[54] continue in any case to be binding on that State (Art. 7(3) TEU). Subsequently, the Council may decide by a qualified majority to vary or revoke the suspension of rights in response to changes in the situation which led to its being imposed (Art. 7(4) TEU).

Throughout the procedure referred to in Art. 7 TEU, decisions of the European Council or the Council are taken without taking into account the vote of the representative of the Member State concerned. By the same token, that Member State is not counted in the calculation of the one-third or four-fifths of Member States referred to in Art. 7(1) and (2) TEU (see Art. 7(5) TEU and Art. 354, first para., TFEU).[55] The European Parliament is to act by a two-thirds majority of the votes cast, representing the majority of its component Members (Art. 7(5) TEU and Art. 354, fourth para., TFEU).

Within one month from the date of the determination that there is a "serious and persistent breach" or a "clear risk" of a serious breach, the Court of Justice may, at the request of the Member State concerned, rule on whether the purely procedural stipulations of Art. 7 have been complied with. The Court is to decide within one month from the date of the request (Art. 269 TFEU).

89–92; Burchill, "The Promotion and Protection of Democracy by Regional Organisations in Europe: The Case of Austria" (2001) E.Pub.L. 79–102; Hummer, "The End of EU Sanctions Against Austria—A Precedent for New Sanctions Procedures?" (2000/01) European Legal Forum 77–83.

[54] The English version of the TEU seems to contain a mistake: it refers to "this Treaty" instead of "the Treaties".

[55] Abstentions by members present in person or represented do not prevent the adoption of decisions referred to in Art. 7(2) TEU (Art. 354, first para., TFEU).

Part II

JURISDICTION OF THE
EUROPEAN UNION

CHAPTER 7

PRINCIPLES GOVERNING THE COMPETENCES OF THE EUROPEAN UNION

Jurisdiction. The jurisdiction of the Union is laid down in the Treaty on European   **7–001**
Union (TEU), as amended by the Lisbon Treaty, and in the Treaty on the Functioning
of the European Union (TFEU), which is the new title of the EC Treaty as amended
by the Lisbon Treaty. The fundamental principles governing the Union competences
are set out in Title I of the TEU ("Common Provisions") and in Title I of the TFEU
("Categories and Areas of Union Competence"). Further details about these competences are to be found in the provisions of the TFEU relating to each area, which take
over the provisions relating to the relevant areas that were set out in the EC Treaty,
as amended by the Lisbon Treaty and supplemented by the provisions on police and
judicial cooperation in criminal matters that were previously contained in
Title VI of the EU Treaty. The common foreign and security policy (CFSP) is the
only area set out in the TEU (Title V TEU, building upon Title V of the original EU
Treaty). The EAEC Treaty remains relevant for the competences of the European
Atomic Energy Community. After explaining the fundamental principles governing
the Union competences (Ch. 7), this Part sets out the Union's competence and
substantive rules relating to the citizenship of the Union (Ch. 8), the internal market
(Ch. 9), the area of freedom, security and justice (Ch. 10), other internal policies
(Ch. 11) and the limits and exceptions to the application of the Treaties (Ch. 12).
Whereas the fundamental principles set out in this Part also apply to the CFSP
and other external competences of the Union, the detailed scope of those external
competences are dealt with in Part VI.

Functional approach. The Community Treaties set the Communities "tasks" with   **7–002**
a view to attaining clearly circumscribed objectives.[1] The Lisbon Treaty replaced

---

[1] Accordingly, the task of the ECSC was to "contribute . . . through the establishment of a common
market . . . to economic expansion, growth of employment and a rising standard of living in the
Member States" (Art. 2, first para., ECSC). Article 3 ECSC briefly indicated what this entailed.
Art. 2 EC likewise prescribed objectives and tasks, which were enlarged upon in Arts 3 and 4 of
that Treaty. Article 1 EAEC provides that the EAEC is to "contribute to the raising of the standard
of living in the Member States and to the development of relations with other countries by creating
the conditions necessary for the speedy establishment and growth of nuclear industries", this
objective being enlarged upon in Art. 2 EAEC.

these objectives and tasks with a whole range of objectives for the European Union that apply both to the former Community competences and to the former non-Community fields of action (see para. 7–007). Following this description of objectives, the TEU and the TFEU set out the legal rules pursuant to which the tasks indicated are to be carried out (the "legal basis" for Union action). These rules are to be followed both in the TEU and the TFEU, which have the same legal value (Art.1, second subpara., TEU). In addition, the Treaties contain a supplementary legal basis for Union action for which specific provision is not made therein but which is necessary to attain one of the objectives set out in the Treaties (Art. 352 TFEU [*ex Art. 308 EC*]; Art. 203 EAEC). Consequently, Union competence is not divided up according to subject-matter, but "functionally" limited to what is required by the objectives set out in the Treaties (see Art. 1, first subpara., TEU).[2] This "functional" approach also underpins the EAEC Treaty, which contains the legal basis for action of the (only remaining) Community on Atomic Energy.[3] The Union's competence is further subject to compliance with the principles of subsidiarity (where the competence in question is non-exclusive) and proportionality. Other important principles with which Union action has to comply are the principles of sincere cooperation and equal treatment.

I. VALUES AND OBJECTIVES OF THE EUROPEAN UNION

7–003   **Evolution.** Before the Treaty of Lisbon entered into force, the objectives of the Community were listed in Art. 2 EC,[4] which afforded the Community three instruments for achieving these objectives: the establishment of a common market, the establishment of an economic and monetary union and the implementation of "flanking" common policies and activities. Those instruments were enlarged upon in Art. 3(1) EC,[5] which provided an overview in its twenty-one paragraphs of the

---

[2] See Reimer, "Ziele und Zuständigkeiten—Die Funktionen der Unionszielbestimmungen" (2003) EuR. 992–1012.

[3] See para. 1–014, *supra*.

[4] Although Art. 2 referred to the "task" of the Community, Art. 3(1) EC used the expression "the purposes set out in Article 2". However, the terminology used in the various languages differed.

[5] According to Art. 3(1) EC, the activities of the Community were to include: (a) the prohibition, as between Member States, of customs duties and quantitative restrictions on the import and export of goods, and of all other measures having equivalent effect; (b) a common commercial policy; (c) an internal market; (d) measures concerning the entry and movement of persons; (e) a common policy in the sphere of agriculture and fisheries; (f) a common policy in the sphere of transport; (g) a system ensuring that competition in the internal market is not distorted; (h) the approximation of the laws of Member States to the extent required for the functioning of the common market; (i) the promotion of coordination between employment policies of the Member States; (j) a social policy; (k) the strengthening of economic and social cohesion; (l) an environment policy; (m) the strengthening of the competitiveness of Community industry; (n) the promotion of research and technological development; (o) encouragement for the establishment and development of trans-European networks; (p) a contribution to the attainment of a high level of health protection; (q) a contribution to education and training

Community's activities, and in Art. 4 EC, which outlined the economic, monetary and exchange rate policies which the Member States and the Community were to conduct. The EC Treaty expanded on all these tasks in the twenty-one titles of Part Three, "Community Policies". The EU Treaty for its part listed the objectives of the Union in Art. 2 EU.

The Treaty of Lisbon replaced the list of Union and Community objectives, instruments and tasks by an introductory title of the TEU (Title I "Common Provisions") that sets out the values of the Union (Art. 2 TEU) and provides the Union with a list of objectives (Art. 3 TEU). This list focuses on non-economic goals to a far greater extent than the EC Treaty. The Union is to pursue its objectives by appropriate means commensurate with the competences which are conferred upon it in the Treaties (Art. 3(6) TEU).

Values. Article 2 TEU proclaims that the Union is founded on the values of respect   **7–004** for human dignity, freedom, democracy, equality, the rule of law and respect for human rights, including the rights of persons belonging to minorities. It further adds that these values are common to the Member States "in a society in which pluralism, non-discrimination, tolerance, justice, solidarity and equality between women and men prevail". The value of equality finds its most important expressions in the equality of the Member States before the Treaties, which the Union has to respect, and the equality of its citizens, who shall receive equal attention from its institutions, bodies, offices and agencies (Arts 4(2) and 9 TEU; see paras 7–050 *et seq.*). As regards respect for fundamental rights, Title I of the TEU expressly provides that the Union recognises the rights, freedoms and principles set out in the Charter of Fundamental Rights of the European Union (Art. 6(1) TEU), that the Union must accede to the European Convention for the Protection of Human Rights and Fundamental Freedoms (Art. 6(2) TEU) and that fundamental rights, as guaranteed by the European Convention for the Protection of Human Rights and Fundamental Freedoms and as they result from the constitutional traditions common to the Member States, shall constitute general principles of the Union's law (Art. 6(3) TEU).[6]

A request made in some quarters to emphasise the Christian roots of European civilisation in the Treaties, or at least in the preamble to the Treaties, was a much debated issue in civil society.[7] Ultimately, a compromise solution was reached, and the preamble to the TEU refers to the Contracting Parties "drawing inspiration from the cultural, religious and humanist inheritance of Europe".

---

of quality and to the flowering of the cultures of the Member States; (r) a development cooperation policy; (s) the association of the overseas countries and territories; (t) a contribution to the strengthening of consumer protection; (u) measures in the spheres of energy, civil protection and tourism.

[6] See the discussion in paras 22–016 *et seq., infra.*

[7] See, for example, Weiler, "A Christian Europe? Europe and Christianity: rules of commitment" (2007) 6 European View 143–150; Menendez, "A pious Europe? Why Europe should not define itself as Christian" (2005) 30 E.L.Rev. 133–148; Mattera, "L'européanité est-elle chrétienne?" (2003) R.M.C.U.E. 325–342.

7–005 **Main objectives.** The Union's first aim is to promote peace, the Union's values and the well-being of its peoples (Art. 3(1) TEU). Next, the Treaty refers to

"an area of freedom, security and justice without internal frontiers, in which the free movement of persons is ensured in conjunction with appropriate measures with respect to external border controls, asylum, immigration and the prevention and combating of crime." (Art. 3(2) TEU).

Thirdly, reference is made to the establishment of an internal market,[8] to

"the sustainable development of Europe based on balanced economic growth and price stability, a highly competitive social market economy, aiming at full employment and social progress, and a high level of protection and improvement of the quality of the environment."

To the promotion of scientific and technological advance, to combating social exclusion and discrimination, to the promotion of social justice and protection, equality between women and men, solidarity between generations and protection of the rights of the child, to the promotion of economic, social and territorial cohesion, and solidarity among Member States, to respect for the Union's rich cultural and linguistic diversity and to the safeguarding and enhancement of Europe's cultural heritage (Art. 3(3) TEU). Lastly, Art. 3(4) TEU refers to the establishment of an economic and monetary union whose currency is the euro.[9]

Unlike the EC Treaty,[10] the TEU as amended by the Treaty of Lisbon also provides the Union with specific objectives as to its external action. In its relations with the wider world, the Union is to uphold and promote its values and interests and contribute to the protection of its citizens. It must contribute to peace, security, the sustainable development of the Earth, solidarity and mutual respect among peoples, free and fair trade, eradication of poverty and the protection of human rights, in particular the rights of the child, as well as to the strict observance and the development of international law, including respect for the principles of the United Nations Charter (Art. 3(5) TEU). Union action on the international scene must be guided by the principles which have inspired its own creation, development and

---

[8] At the instigation of the newly elected French President Nicolas Sarkozy, reference to "free and undistorted competition" was removed from the final text of the Treaty. However, Protocol (No. 27), annexed to the TEU and TFEU, on the internal market and competition ([2010] O.J. C83/309), annexed to the Treaties explicitly states that "the internal market as set out in Article 3 TEU includes a system ensuring that competition is not distorted".

[9] See also Art. 119 TFEU [*ex Art. 4 EC*].

[10] Article 2, second indent, EU referred to the objective of the Union's asserting its identity on the international scene, but that objective was only enlarged upon in specific provisions of the EC Treaty (see, e.g., Art. 131, first para., Art. 177 and Arts 300 and 301 EC) and in the provisions relating to the common foreign and security policy (see Art. 11(1) EU).

enlargement[11] and the Union must seek to develop relations and build partnerships with third countries, and international, regional or global organisations which share these principles (Art. 21(1) TEU). Article 21(2) TEU provides a list of nine objectives which the Union is to pursue in its external action. These objectives and the principles referred to in Art. 21(1) TEU must be taken into account not only in the development and implementation of the different areas of Union external action, but also in the external aspects of its other policies (Art. 21(3) TEU).

Before the Lisbon Treaty, the list of objectives laid down in the Treaties was largely concerned with economic goals, although this economic focus had become less predominant even before the Lisbon Treaty. The initial, mainly economic objectives of the Community[12] were amended for the first time only by the EU Treaty. The EU Treaty introduced objectives such as economic and social cohesion and environmental protection, which the Member States already regarded as important for Community policy before and for which Community action already had an express legal basis in the Treaty as a result of the Single European Act.[13] By adopting the objectives of non-inflationary growth and a high level of employment and social protection, the Community followed in the direction already taken by cooperation between the Member States and Community social policy.[14] Convergence of economic performance and improvement of the "quality of life" constituted completely new objectives. The Treaty of Amsterdam made promoting equality between men and women—a general principle of Community law—a Community task,[15] added a high degree of competitiveness to the task of promoting economic convergence, and enlarged upon the existing principles of sustainable growth and protection of the environment.[16]

---

[11] Article 21(1) TEU refers in this regard to democracy, the rule of law, the universality and indivisibility of human rights and fundamental freedoms, respect for human dignity, the principles of equality and solidarity, and respect for the principles of the United Nations Charter and international law.

[12] According to Art. 2 EEC, the Community's objectives were "to promote throughout the Community a harmonious development of economic activities, a continuous and balanced expansion, an increase in stability, an accelerated raising of the standard of living and closer relations between the States belonging to it".

[13] As far as economic and social cohesion is concerned, see the reference to "reducing the differences existing between the various regions and the backwardness of the less-favoured regions" in the preamble to the EEC Treaty and Arts 130a to 130e of that treaty. As for environment protection, see the declaration of the Paris Summit Conference held in October 1972, which launched an environmental policy (1972) 10 EC Bull. 21 point 8; the recognition of environmental protection as "one of the Community's essential objectives" in ECJ, Case 240/83 *Procureur de la République v ADBHU* [1995] E.C.R. 531, para. 13, and Arts 130r to 130t EEC.

[14] See Art. 104 EEC, which required the Member States "to ensure a high level of employment and a stable level of prices" in their economic policies, the first para of Art. 117 and Art. 118a(1) EEC (social policy).

[15] For that principle of law, see para. 7–050, *infra*.

[16] In its latest version, Art. 2 EC set out accordingly the following objectives for the Community: to promote throughout the Community (1) a harmonious, balanced and sustainable development of economic activities, (2) a high level of employment and of social protection, (3) equality between men and women, (4) sustainable and non-inflationary growth, (5) a high degree of competitiveness

7–006 **Horizontal objectives.** The objectives set out in Art. 3 TEU have to be complemented by further objectives, laid down in the "provisions of general application" of Title II of the TFEU, which the Union must take into account in the implementation of its policies. First of all, it must aim, in all its activities, to eliminate inequalities and to promote equality between men and women (Art. 8 TFEU). Furthermore, the Union must respect requirements relating to the promotion of a high level of employment, adequate social protection, the fight against social exclusion, and a high level of education, training and protection of human health (Art. 9 TFEU) and aim to combat all forms of discrimination referred to in Art. 19 TFEU (Art. 10 TFEU). It must also take into account environmental protection, in particular with a view to promoting sustainable development (Art. 11 TFEU)[17] and consumer protection (Art. 12 TFEU). In formulating and implementing the Union's agriculture, fisheries, transport, internal market, research and technological development and space policies, the Union and the Member States must pay full regard to the welfare requirements of animals (as "sentient beings"), while respecting the legislative or administrative provisions and customs of the Member States relating in particular to religious rites, cultural traditions and regional heritage (Art. 13 TFEU).[18] Other horizontal objectives are ensuring the provision and good functioning of services of general economic interest (Art. 14 TFEU; see para. 11–017) the promotion of good governance and ensuring the participation of civil society (Art. 15 TFEU) and the protection of personal data (Art. 16 TFEU). Finally, Art. 17 TFEU states that the Union is to respect the status of churches and religious associations or communities and of philosophical and non-confessional organisations in the Member States.[19]

---

and convergence of economic performance, (6) a high level of protection and improvement of the quality of the environment, (7) the raising of the standard of living and quality of life and (8) economic and social cohesion and solidarity among Member States.

[17] Scott, *Environmental protection: European law and governance* (Oxford, Oxford University Press, 2009), 225 pp.; Holder and Lee, *Environmental protection, law and policy: text and materials* (Cambridge, Cambridge University Press, 2007), Ch. 4; Schumacher, "The environmental integration clause in Article 6 of the EU Treaty: prioritising environmental protection" (2001) Env.L.Rev. 29–43; Wasmeier, "The integration of environmental protection as a general rule for interpreting Community law" (2001) C.M.L.Rev. 159–177.

[18] This objective was inserted in the Treaties by the Treaty of Lisbon. See, however, already Protocol (No. 33), annexed to the EC Treaty by the Treaty of Amsterdam, on protection and welfare of animals, ([1997] O.J. C340/110). Ensuring the welfare of animals did not for all that constitute a general principle of Union law: ECJ, Case C-189/01 *Jippes and Others* [2001] E.C.R. I-5689, paras 71–79. For the objectives of environmental and animal protection, see Camm and Bowles, "Animal Welfare and the Treaty of Rome—A Legal Analysis of the Protocol on Animal Welfare and Welfare Standards in the European Union" (2000) J.Env.L. 197–205; Van Calster and Deketelaere, "Amsterdam, the Intergovernmental Conference and Greening the EU Treaty" (1998) 12 E.Env.L.Rev. 17–19.

[19] See Art. 17(1) and (2) TFEU. Article 17(3) adds: "Recognising their identity and their specific contribution, the Union shall maintain an open, transparent and regular dialogue with these churches and organisations".

Other provisions of the Treaty mention further objectives which the Union must invariably take into account in its activities, such as cultural aspects (Art. 167(4) TFEU) and development cooperation objectives (Art. 208(1) TFEU).

All these objectives are to be treated on an equal footing with the objectives set for the Union in other specific provisions of the Treaties. Indeed, in accordance with Art. 7 TFEU, the Union has to ensure consistency between its different policies and activities "taking all of its objectives into account".

Legal status of objectives. According to the Court of Justice, the aims on which the establishment of the Union is based cannot have the effect of "imposing legal obligations on the Member States or of conferring rights on individuals".[20] They depend for their implementation on the policies pursued by the Union and the Member States, with the result that their legal impact is limited to guiding the interpretation of Union law.[21] Thus, Union competence is often inferred from specific Treaty provisions read together with the "objectives of the Union" or, before the Treaty of Lisbon entered into force, the "requirements of the common market" enshrined in Art. 3 EC.[22] The Court interprets the Treaty provisions in the light of the Union's objectives.[23] Accordingly, the Court has inferred from the objective of ensuring undistorted competition in the internal market (listed in Art. 3(g) EC), read in conjunction with Arts 10, 81 and 82 EC [*now Art. 4(3) TEU and Arts 101 and 102 TFEU*] an obligation for Member States not to adopt any measures which may render ineffective the competition rules for undertakings set out in Arts 81 and 82 EC [*now Arts 101 and 102 TFEU*].[24] Conversely, an objective such as an "open market economy with free competition" (Art. 119 TFEU [*ex Art. 4 EC*]) must be read in conjunction with the provisions of the Treaty designed to implement it.[25]

7–007

---

[20] ECJ, Case C-339/89 *Alsthom Atlantique* [1991] E.C.R. I-107, para. 9; ECJ, Case C-9/99 *Echirolles Distribution* [2000] E.C.R. I-8207, para. 25; ECJ (judgment of June 3, 2010), Case C-484/08 *Caja de Ahorros y Monte de Piedad de Madrid*, not yet reported, paras 46–47. For their legal force, see Reimer (n. 2, supra); Durand, "Les principes", in de Cockborne, Defalque, Durand, Prahl and Vandersanden, *Commentaire Mégret—Le droit de la CEE. 1. Préambule. Principes. Libre circulation des marchandises* (Brussels, Editions de l'Université de Bruxelles, 1992), Nos 12–18, at 13–19; Pescatore, "Les objectifs de la Communauté européenne comme principes d'interprétation dans la jurisprudence de la Cour de Justice" in *Miscellanea W.J. Ganshof van der Meersch* Tome 2 (Brussels, Bruylant, 1972), Part II, at 325–369.

[21] ECJ, Case C-149/96 *Portugal v Council* [1999] E.C.R. I-8395, paras 86–87 (objective of economic and social cohesion).

[22] For the common transport policy, see ECJ, Case 22/70 *Commission v Council* [1971] E.C.R. 263, para. 20; for compliance with the conditions of competition, see ECJ, Case 97/78 *Schumalla* [1978] E.C.R. 2311, para. 6.

[23] ECJ, Case 270/80 *Polydor* [1982] E.C.R. 329, para. 16.

[24] ECJ, Case 311/85 *VVR v Sociale Dienst van de Plaatselijke en Gewestelijke Overheidsdiensten* [1987] E.C.R. 3801, para. 24; ECJ, Case 267/86 *Van Eycke* [1988] E.C.R. 4769, para. 20 (see para. 11–010, *infra*).

[25] ECJ, Case C-9/99 *Echirolles Distribution* [2000] E.C.R. I-8207, para. 24.

II. THE PRINCIPLE OF CONFERRAL OF COMPETENCES

7–008   **Fundamental principles.** The Union may act only within the limits of the competences conferred upon it by the Treaties (the principle of conferral). Furthermore, the exercise by the Union of its competences is governed by the principles of subsidiarity and proportionality. These fundamental principles governing the division of competence between the Union and the Member States are set out in Title I ("Common provisions") of the Treaty on European Union (See Arts 4 and 5 TEU). Competences not conferred upon the Union by the Treaties remain with the Member States (Arts 4(1) and 5(2) TEU).

  The Treaty on the Functioning of the European Union determines the areas of, delimitation of, and arrangements for exercising Union competences (Art. 1(1) TFEU). In Title I, the TFEU sets out the categories and areas of competences (Arts 2 to 6 TFEU). Further details about the scope of these competences and the procedural arrangements for exercising them are to be found in the subsequent provisions of the TFEU relating to each area (Art. 2(6) TFEU).[26] However, the scope of and the procedural arrangements relating to the common foreign and security policy continue to be set out in Title V TEU.

A. NEED FOR A LEGAL BASIS

7–009   **Principle of conferral.** Article 5(1) TEU states that the limits of Union competences are governed by the principle of conferral (which is also known as the principle of "attribution of competence"). Pursuant to that principle,

> "the Union shall act only within the limits of the competences conferred upon it by the Member States in the Treaties to attain the objectives set out therein"

(Art. 5(2) TEU [*ex Art. 5, first para., EC*]). This principle must be respected in both the internal action and the international action of the Union.[27] All Union

---

[26] See Part Two ("Non-discrimination and citizenship of the Union"), Part Three ("Union policies and internal actions"), Part Four ("Association of the overseas countries and territories") and Part Five ("External action by the Union") of the TFEU. For the discussion of the scope of the various Union competences, see Chs 10 and 11, *infra*, and, for external action, Ch. 25, *infra*.

[27] ECJ, Opinion 2/94, *Accession by the Communities to the Convention for the Protection of Human Rights and Fundamental Freedoms* [1996] E.C.R. I-1759, para. 24; ECJ, Opinion 2/00, *Cartagena Protocol* [2001] E.C.R. I-9713, para. 5; ECJ, Case C-370/07 *Commission v Council* [2009] E.C.R. I-8917, para. 46. For legal basis as the precondition for legislative and executive action on the part of the Union, see Van Ooik, *De keuze van rechtsgrondslag voor besluiten van de Europese Unie* (Deventer, Kluwer, 1999), 483 pp.; Triantafyllou, *Des compétences d'attribution au domaine de la loi. Etude sur les fondements juridiques de l'activité administrative Communautaire* (Brussels,

action must be founded upon a legal basis laid down in the Treaties. Naturally, the legal basis for Union acts may also be found in another Union act which they are designed to implement. In those circumstances, too, an institution or a body cannot act unless its action is based on a basic act having a legal basis in the Treaties which (1) defines the Union's competence *ratione materiae* and (2) specifies the means of exercise of that competence, that is to say, the legislative instruments and the decision-making procedure.

(1) Competence *ratione materiae*. In the first place, the legal basis determines   **7–010** the extent of the competence conferred on the Union in a certain field or for the realisation of certain objectives. Most Treaty articles conferring a certain competence on the Union, at the same time specify the objectives to be pursued by the Union in that field.

The legal basis thus determines the "vertical" division of competence between the Union and the Member States.[28] Certain competences conferred on the Union are "exclusive" (see Art. 2(1) TFEU), which means that the Union alone has jurisdiction. However, in most fields both the Union and the Member States are competent to act (see paras 7–020—7–025). Where the Union is not empowered to act, such action comes within the residuary competence of the Member States.[29] However, the principle of conferral has in practice placed few limits on the action of the Union, inter alia because of the existence of the "supplementary" legal basis of Art. 352 TEU [*ex Art. 308 EC*] and the teleological interpretation which the Court of Justice has given to various legal bases.[30]

The attribution of ever more competences to the Union has given rise to a continual debate about the most appropriate distribution of competence as between the Union and the Member States, which has found expression in particular in the introduction of principle of subsidiarity (see para. 7–026 *et seq.*) and in the call

---

Bruylant, 1997), 432 pp. See also Lenaerts, *Le juge et la constitution aux Etats-Unis d'Amérique et dans l'ordre juridique européen* (Brussels, Bruylant, 1988), No. 300, at 346–349, and Nos 309–311, at 357–362; Emiliou, "Opening Pandora's Box: The Legal Basis of Community Measures Before the Court of Justice" (1994) E.L.Rev. 488–507; Lenaerts and van Ypersele, "Le principe de subsidiarité et son contexte: étude de l'article 3 B du traité CE" (1994) C.D.E. 13–30 and 35–44; Peter, "La base juridique des actes en droit communautaire" (1994) R.M.C.U.E. 324–333; Craig, "Competence: clarity, conferral, containment and consideration" (2004) E.L.Rev. 323–344; Barents, "The Internal Market Unlimited: Some Observations on the Legal Basis of Community Legislation" (1993) C.M.L.Rev. 85–109; Bradley, "The European Court and the Legal Basis of Community Legislation" (1988) E.L.Rev. 379–402.

[28] ECJ, Case C-370/07 *Commission v Council* (n. 27, *supra*), para. 49. See von Bogdandy and Bast, "Die vertikale Kompetenzordnung der Europäischen Union—Rechtsdogmatischer Bestand und verfassungsrechtliche Reformperspektiven" (2001) Eu.GR.Z. 441–458.

[29] This corollary of the principle of conferral is expressly mentioned in Art. 4(1) and 5(2) TEU ("Competences not conferred upon the Union in the Treaties remain with the Member States").

[30] See Van Nuffel, *De rechtsbescherming van nationale overheden in het Europees recht* (Deventer, Kluwer, 2000), 84–102 pp. Nevertheless, the Council can use the "supplementary" legal basis of Art. 352 TFEU only if it remains within the limits traced by the Treaties; see para. 5–018.

for a more precise delimitation of competences.[31] The Treaty of Lisbon has partially responded to this call in so far as it codifies some of the principles that were to be found only in the case law of the Court of Justice and sets out a limitative list of exclusive competences (see para. 7–020 *et seq.*).

7–011   **(2) Exercise of competence.** In addition, the legal basis determines the way in which the Union exercises its competence *ratione materiae* (together with the principle of subsidiarity, para. 5–028, and the principle of proportionality, para. 5–036).[32] As far as the appropriate legislative instrument is concerned, some Treaty articles restrict action on the part of the Union to "directives", "directives or regulations", "recommendations" or "incentive measures", whilst others authorise any "measures" to be taken.[33] As far as the decision-making procedure is concerned, the Treaty articles determine what institutions are to be involved in the adoption of an act and how this is to take place.[34] A dispute as to the correct legal basis for an act is not a purely formal one inasmuch as a different decision-making procedure may affect the determination of the content of the act adopted.[35] This will be the case, for example, where a Treaty article requiring the Council to decide by unanimity rather than by qualified majority is wrongly used.[36] However, an argument contesting the legal basis of an act may indeed have only formal significance where the legal basis argued for does not entail any stricter procedural requirements than the one on which the act is actually founded.[37]

The decision-making procedure and any limitation as to the legislative instruments which may be used determine the horizontal allocation of powers among the Union institutions according to which

---

[31] See the call for a wide debate in Declaration (No. 23), annexed to the Treaty of Nice, on the future of the Union, ([2001] O.J. C80/85) and the "Declaration of Laeken" of the European Council of December 14 and 15, 2001. For the question of lack of transparency in the delimitation of powers, see para. 20–009. For further discussion of the delimitation of powers as between the Union and the Member States, see von Bogdandy and Bast, "The European Union's Vertical Order of Competences: The Current Law and Proposals for its Reform" (2002) C.M.L.Rev. 227–268.

[32] See Art. 2(6) TFEU, which provides that "The scope of and arrangements for exercising the Union's competences shall be determined by the provisions of the Treaties relating to each area".

[33] See the lists of instruments in Arts 218 and 288 TFEU and the discussion of acts of the institutions and bodies, para. 22–059 *et seq.*

[34] ECJ, Case C-370/07 *Commission v Council* (n. 27, *supra*), para. 48. See the discussion of decision-making, para. 16–004 *et seq.*

[35] See, for example, ECJ, Case 45/86 *Commission v Council* [1987] E.C.R. 1493, para. 12; ECJ, Case 68/86 *United Kingdom v Council* [1988] E.C.R. 855, para. 6; ECJ, Case 131/86 *United Kingdom v Council* [1988] E.C.R. 905, para. 11.

[36] E.g. ECJ, Case C-211/01 *Commission v Council* [2003] E.C.R. I-8913, para. 52.

[37] ECJ, Case 165/87 *Commission v Council* [1988] E.C.R. 5545, para. 19; ECJ, Case C-268/94 *Portugal v Council* [1996] E.C.R. I-6177, para. 79; ECJ, Case C-491/01 *British American Tobacco (Investments) and Imperial Tobacco* [2002] E.C.R. I-11453, paras 97–98.

"each institution shall act within the limits of the powers conferred on it in the Treaties, and in conformity with the procedures, conditions and objectives set out in them" (Art. 13(2) TEU).

At the same time, this allocation of powers influences the vertical relationship between the Union and the Member States. Where the decision-making procedure requires there to be a unanimous vote in the Council, each Member State has a right of veto. Where an institution is entitled to adopt a regulation, it may restrict the power of the Member States to a greater degree than where it is empowered only to adopt directives, since, in principle, a directive leaves the Member States with more latitude than a regulation.

Choice of legal basis. It is an essential procedural requirement of any Union act   7–012
that it should state its legal basis.[38] The duty to indicate the legal basis does not only follow from the duty to state reasons, but also from the requirement of legal certainty and the principle of conferral.[39] The absence of such an indication is tolerated only if the legal basis of the act may be determined unambiguously from other factors.[40] Given the consequences of the legal basis in terms of substantive competence and the procedure, the choice of the correct legal basis is of constitutional importance.[41] The choice of the legal basis for an act does not turn on the relevant institution's conviction as to the objective pursued but must be "based on objective factors which are amenable to judicial review",[42] such as the aim and content of the measure.[43] It follows that the Union must make the aim of the act completely clear.[44]

Institutions, Member States and, to a lesser extent, individuals have often challenged the legal basis of Union acts, with the parties adopting a stance reflecting their differing (political) interests. In such cases, the Court of Justice acts

---

[38] ECJ, Case C-325/91 *France v Commission* [1993] E.C.R. I-3283, para. 26.

[39] ECJ, Case C-370/07 *Commission v Council* (n. 27, *supra*), paras 37–55.

[40] ECJ, Case 45/86 *Commission v Council* [1987] E.C.R. 1493, para. 9; CFI, Case T-70/99 *Alpharma v Council* [2002] E.C.R. II-3495, paras 110–121.

[41] ECJ, Opinion 2/00 *Cartagena Protocol* [2001] E.C.R. I-9713, para. 5; ECJ, Case C-370/07 *Commission v Council* (n. 27, *supra*), paras 46–49; ECJ, Opinion 1/08, *General Agreement on Trade in Services* [2009] E.C.R. I-11129, para. 110.

[42] ECJ, Case 45/86 *Commission v Council* [1987] E.C.R. 1493, para. 11.

[43] ECJ, Case C-300/89 *Commission v Council* [1991] E.C.R. I-2867, para. 10. For the practical interpretation of the "objective factors", see Van Nuffel (n. 30, *supra*), 180–211.

[44] The choice of aim is reviewed only marginally by the Court. The Union is free to determine whether the measure is suitable for the purpose of achieving the intended aim and the Court will consider only whether the Union was guilty of an error, manifestly exceeded its powers or misused its powers: ECJ, Case C-331/88 *Fedesa and Others* [1990] E.C.R. I-4023, para. 8; see also para. 5–039. Where the act affects the residuary powers of the Member States, the principles of subsidiarity and proportionality require the aim and content of the act and likewise the choice of legislative instrument to be specifically reasoned, paras 5–033 and 5–044.

as a constitutional court, reviewing the horizontal and vertical division of powers within the Union.[45] In this way, the Court of Justice annulled a directive of the European Parliament and the Council on tobacco advertising on the ground that those institutions had adopted a piece of legislation—at the Commission's proposal—which exceeded the bounds set by the Treaties for harmonisation.[46] However, the question whether an act should have been adopted on a different legal basis will not need to be answered by the Court where this has no effect on the procedure followed for its adoption.[47] Moreover, an error as to the legal basis will not affect the validity of the act in question where the persons affected enjoyed all of the procedural guarantees which may have been applicable and the error did not have any adverse effect on their legal position.[48]

B. COMPETENCES DISTINGUISHED ACCORDING TO THE LEGAL BASIS

7–013 **Distinction depending on legal basis.** In accordance with Art. 5(2) TEU, the Union acts only within the limits of the competences conferred upon it by the Member States in the Treaties to attain the objectives set out therein. The Union exercises the competences conferred upon it, first and foremost, when its action falls, expressly or impliedly, within the scope of one or more specific Treaty provisions. In addition, the Union may act outside the scope of specific Treaty provisions where such action is necessary to attain the "objectives set out [in the Treaties]". This refers to the "flexibility clause" laid down in Art. 352 TFEU [*ex Art. 308 EC*].

1. Competences conferred expressly or impliedly by the Treaties

7–014 **Legal basis.** Action by the Union is founded in principle on a "specific" provision of the Treaties which confers the competence to act. The latter is defined by

---

[45] Lenaerts (n. 27, *supra*), Nos 309–311, at 357–362.

[46] ECJ, Case C-376/98 *Germany v European Parliament and Council* [2000] E.C.R. I-8419; see commentaries by Cornides, "Eine Richtlinie löst sich in Rauch auf" (2001) Z.f.RV. 130–135; Hervey, "Up in Smoke? Community (anti-)tobacco law and policy" (2001) E.L.Rev. 101–125; Gosalbo Bono, "L'arrêt 'tabac' ou l'apport de la Cour de justice au débat sur la délimitation de compétences" (2001) R.T.D.E. 790–808; Mortelmans and van Ooik, "Het Europese verbod op tabaksreclame: verbetering van de interne markt of verbetering van de volksgezondheid?" (2001) A.A. 114–130; Usher (2001) C.M.L.Rev. 1519–1543; Amtenbrink and Appeldoorn, "Is er leven na het Tabaksreclamearrest?" (2000) S.E.W. 413–420; Barents, "De tabaksrichtlijn in rook opgegaan" (2000) N.T.E.R. 327–331.

[47] E.g. ECJ, Joined Cases C-184/02 and C-223/02 *Spain and Finland v European Parliament and Council* [2004] E.C.R. I-7789.

[48] CFI, Case T-213/00 *CMA CGM and Others v Commission* [2003] E.C.R. II-913, paras 65–103. For the possibility that a dispute concerning the legal basis has merely formal significance, see also para. 5–011.

the list of its aims and the means which may be employed in order to attain them.[49] The aims and means mentioned act as the demarcation of competence as it ensues from the Treaty provision in question. Some Treaty articles allow the Union to act in so far as certain policy areas of the Member States are respected[50] or there is no harmonisation of national laws and regulations.[51]

The Treaties also contain "general" provisions empowering the Union to adopt the "measures for the approximation of the provisions laid down by law, regulation or administrative action in Member States which have as their object the establishment and functioning of the internal market" (Art. 114(1) TFEU [*ex Art. 95(1) EC*] or to issue, in any field,

> "directives for the approximation of such laws, regulations or administrative provisions of the Member States as directly affect the establishment or functioning of the internal market" (Art. 115 TFEU [*ex Art. 94 EC*]).

Such provisions may not, however, be used as a legal basis in order to circumvent an express exclusion of harmonisation laid down in specific articles of the Treaties.[52]

Applicable legal basis. In many instances, a measure is intended to attain objectives set out in a specific Treaty article, whilst at the same time influencing the functioning of the internal market (e.g. an environment protection measure harmonising product or production standards and thereby promoting the free movement of goods and/or free competition). If the measure has a twofold purpose or if it has a twofold component and if one of those is identifiable as the main or predominant purpose or component, the legal basis must be determined on the basis of the Treaty article corresponding to the main purpose or the main component of the act. Where, for example, harmonisation of national legislation is only an incidental effect of a measure which primarily pursues another objective, the measure must be adopted only

7–015

---

[49] *Cf.* ECJ, Case 242/87 *Commission v Council* [1989] E.C.R. 1425, paras 6–37.

[50] See, for example, the areas reserved to the Member States in Art. 165(1) (content of teaching and organisation of education systems) and Art. 166(1) (content and organisation of vocational training) TFEU. See in this regard Van Nuffel (n. 30, *supra*), at 102–121. See also the areas in which the application of certain legal bases is precluded, particularly Art. 153(4) (fundamental principles of national social security systems) and (5) (pay, the right of association, the right to strike and the right to impose lock-outs) and Art. 173(3), second subpara. (tax provisions and provisions relating to the rights and interests of employed persons) TFEU.

[51] See Art. 19(2) (action to combat discrimination); Art. 149 (employment); Art. 153(2), first subpara., indent (a) (social policy); Art. 165(4) (education), Art. 166(3) (vocational training), Art. 167(5) (culture) Art. 168(5) (public health) Art. 173(3) (industry); Art. 195(2) (tourism); Art. 196(2) (civil protection) and Art. 197(2) (administrative cooperation) TFEU; Van Nuffel (n. 30, *supra*), at 267–268. As far as the external powers of the Union are concerned, this is confirmed in Art. 207(6) (common commercial policy) TFEU.

[52] ECJ, Case C-376/98 *Germany v European Parliament and Council* [2000] E.C.R. I-8419, para. 79 (for commentaries, see n. 46).

on the basis of the specific Treaty article which corresponds to its main or predominant purpose or component.[53] This criterion is often referred to as the "centre of gravity" test.

Conversely, a general Treaty article, such as Art. 114 TFEU, constitutes a sufficient legal basis where a measure aims to harmonise national measures, even if that measure also seeks, in a subordinate manner, to attain an aim sought by specific Treaty articles.[54] The same is true of the Union's external powers where agreements coming under the common commercial policy, development cooperation or environment protection are based on Treaty provisions relating to the chief subject-matter of the agreement.[55]

Before the entry into force of the Lisbon Treaty, the "centre of gravity" criterion also applied to determine whether a measure had to be adopted on the basis of the EC Treaty rather than within the framework of Title V (common foreign and security policy) or Title VI (police and judicial cooperation in criminal matters) of the EU Treaty.[56] Under the current Treaties, the same criterion would appear to apply so as to determine, in order to respect the delimitation between the common foreign and security policy and the other Union policies laid down in Art. 40 TEU, whether a measure has as its main aim or contents the implementation of the common foreign and security policy or the implementation of other Union policies.

7–016 **Multiple legal bases.** Where a measure has several contemporaneous objectives or components which are indissolubly linked with each other without one being

---

[53] ECJ, Case 68/86 *United Kingdom v Council* [1988] E.C.R. 855, paras 14–16; ECJ, Case C-70/88 *European Parliament v Council* [1991] E.C.R. I-4529, paras 16–18; ECJ, Case C-155/91 *Commission v Council* [1993] E.C.R. I-939, paras 18–20; ECJ, Case C-187/93 *European Parliament v Council* [1994] E.C.R. I-2857, paras 23–26; ECJ, Case C-426/93 *Germany v Council* [1995] E.C.R. I-3723, para. 33; ECJ, Case C-271/94 *European Parliament v Council* [1996] E.C.R. I-1689, paras 28–32; ECJ, Case C-84/94 *United Kingdom v Council* [1996] E.C.R. I-5755, paras 11–12 and 22; ECJ, Joined Cases C-164–165/97 *European Parliament v Council* [1999] E.C.R. I-1339, para. 16; ECJ, Case C-36/98 *Spain v Council* [2001] E.C.R. I-779, para. 59; ECJ, Case C-281/01 *Commission v Council* [2002] E.C.R. I-12649, paras 33–49; ECJ, Case C-338/01 *Commission v Council* [2004] E.C.R. I-4829, para. 55. See Lenaerts, "The Principle of Subsidiarity and the Environment in the European Union: Keeping the Balance of Federalism" (1994) Fordham I.L.J. 846, at 871–873.

[54] ECJ, Case C-377/98 *Netherlands v European Parliament and Council* [2001] E.C.R. I-7079, paras 27–28; ECJ, Case C-491/01 *British American Tobacco (Investments) and Imperial Tobacco* [2002] E.C.R. I-11453, paras 93–94.

[55] ECJ, Opinion 2/00 *Cartagena Protocol* [2001] E.C.R. I-9713, paras 22–44; ECJ, Case C-411/06 *Commission v European Parliament and Council* [2009] E.C.R. I-7585 (environment protection). See also paras 20–002 (common commercial policy) and 20–027 (development cooperation).

[56] With respect to the delimitation between Community powers and the Union's competence in the field of police and judicial cooperation in criminal matters, see ECJ, Case C-176/03 *Commission v Council* [2005] E.C.R. I-7879, paras 51–53; ECJ, Case C-440/05 *Commission v Council* [2007] E.C.R. I-9097, paras 71–73; with respect to the delimitation between Community powers and the Union's competence with respect to the common foreign and security policy, see ECJ, Case C-91/05 *Commission v Council* [2008] E.C.R. I-3651, paras 73–74 (see para. 27–005, *infra*).

secondary and indirect in respect of the others, the measure must be based on the various relevant Treaty provisions.[57] However, recourse to a dual legal basis is not possible where the procedures laid down for each legal basis are incompatible with each other or where the use of two legal bases is liable to undermine the rights of the Parliament.[58] In that event, it must be determined in the light of the general scope of the Treaties which Treaty provision affords the appropriate legal basis by itself. If there is no provision that provides a legal basis supporting the whole of the intended measure, the measure will have to be split into parts, each based on the appropriate legal basis for that particular part.[59]

In the *titanium dioxide* case,[60] the Court of Justice held that the directive which the Council had adopted on the basis of Art. 130s EEC [*now Art. 192 TFEU*] on procedures for harmonising the programmes for the reduction and eventual elimination of waste from the titanium dioxide industry displayed,

> "in view of its aim and content, . . . the features both of action relating to the environment with which Article 130s of the Treaty is concerned and of a harmonising measure which has as its object the establishment and functioning of the internal market, within the meaning of Article 100a of the Treaty [*now Art. 114 TFEU*]".

It was impossible to have such a dual legal basis, however, because then the cooperation procedure with the European Parliament required by Art. 100a would have been jeopardised (see the discussion of the cooperation procedure in para. 16–012). The Court went on to hold that Art. 100a was the proper legal basis, thereby giving preference to the provision which afforded the European Parliament the greater say in the legislative process. By contrast, the use of a dual legal basis was held to be valid where it did not lead to an encroachment upon the European Parliament's rights, in particular because the combination of the relevant procedural requirements assured the European Parliament the highest degree of involvement provided by the relevant Treaty articles.[61]

Similarly, the Court has considered that the fact that the ordinary legislative procedure laid down by Art. 114 TFEU was combined with the qualified majority vote prescribed by Art. 207 TFEU [*ex Art. 133 EC*] did not prejudice the substance

---

[57] ECJ, Case 165/87 *Commission v Council* [1988] E.C.R. 5545, para. 11; ECJ, Case C-178/03 *Commission v European Parliament and Council* [2006] E.C.R. I-107, paras 43–56.

[58] ECJ, Case C-178/03 *Commission v European Parliament and Council* [2006] E.C.R. I-107, para. 57.

[59] This may be the case where one of the relevant Treaty provisions concerns a field in which certain Member States do not participate in the Union's action, and therefore do not participate in the decision-making.

[60] ECJ, Case C-300/89 *Commission v Council* [1991] E.C.R. I-2867, paras 17–25.

[61] E.g. ECJ, Case C-178/03 *Commission v European Parliament and Council* [2006] E.C.R. I-107, para. 59; ECJ, Case C-155/07 *European Parliament v Council* [2008] E.C.R. I-8103, paras 75–79 (co-decision procedure rendered applicable).

of the legislative procedure.[62] However, the Court has held that Art. 114 TFEU cannot be applied in conjunction with Arts 113 and 115 TFEU since unanimity is required for the adoption of a measure on the basis of Arts 113 and 115 TFEU whereas a qualified majority is sufficient for a measure to be adopted on the basis of Art. 114 TFEU.[63]

7–017 **Implied competence.** Where the Union acts on the basis of a specific or a general Treaty provision, it exercises its powers using the means and by the procedure laid down in the relevant provision. Some Treaty provisions do not expressly provide for all necessary means in order to attain the objectives of the relevant competence *ratione materiae*. In such cases, the Court of Justice has recognised that it is implicit in the Union competence that additional means may be used in order to achieve the objectives.

In this way, it fell to the Court to determine whether the Community had the power to negotiate and conclude the European Agreement concerning the work of crews of vehicles engaged in international road transport (AETR).[64] By judgment of March 31, 1971, it held that although the Treaty provisions empowering the Community to take measures within the framework of the common transport policy,

> "do not expressly confer on the Community authority to enter into international agreements, nevertheless the bringing into force . . . of Regulation No 543/69 of the Council on the harmonisation of certain social legislation relating to road transport . . . necessarily vested in the Community power to enter into any agreements with third countries relating to the subject-matter governed by that regulation."[65]

Whenever Union law has conferred on the institutions competences within the internal system of the Union for the purpose of attaining a specific objective, the Union has authority to enter into the international commitments necessary for the attainment of that object even in the absence of an express provision concerning the matter.[66]

The existence of an implied competence derogates from the principle of conferral. Therefore, it must be appraised strictly. The Union is entitled to rely on an

---

[62] ECJ, Case C-491/01 *British American Tobacco (Investments) and Imperial Tobacco* [2002] E.C.R. I-11453, paras 103–111 (on the combination of the co-decision procedure of *ex Art. 251 EC* with qualified majority voting).

[63] ECJ, Case C-338/01 *Commission v Council* [2004] E.C.R. I-4829, para. 58.

[64] ECJ, Case 22/70 *Commission v Council* [1971] E.C.R. 263. The acronym "AETR" stands for "Accord européen sur les transport routiers" (European Agreement on Road Transport).

[65] *Ibid.*, para. 28.

[66] ECJ, Opinion 1/76 *Draft Agreement establishing a European laying-up fund for inland waterway vessels* [1977] E.C.R. 741, para. 3. See also the discussion of the external powers of the Union: para. 25–055.

implied competence only where it is necessary to ensure the practical effect of the provisions of the Treaty or the Union act at issue.[67] The close relationship between the implied competence and the express competence which it supplements must be shown by objective evidence which the Court of Justice can review. Thus, the Court held that the professional and social integration of workers from third countries was directly linked with the social questions for which the former Art. 118 EEC provided for cooperation between the Member States.[68] More recently, the Court considered that the Union's competence to issue legislation in fields such as environmental protection or maritime safety entails the competence to require the Member States to introduce criminal sanctions in order to ensure that the rules which it lays down in that field are fully effective, i.e. when the application of effective, proportionate and dissuasive criminal penalties by the competent national authorities is an "essential measure" for combating serious offences.[69]

The Treaty provision providing for the express competence with which the implied competence is associated determines the decision-making procedure which the Union has to follow in exercising that competence. Accordingly, whenever the Union legislates on the right of residence of students and dependants pursuant to an implied competence contained in Art. 18 TFEU [*ex Art. 12 EC*], which empowers the Union to adopt rules designed to prohibit any discrimination on grounds of nationality, it has to do so in accordance with the procedure prescribed by the second para. of Art. 18 TFEU.[70]

---

[67] ECJ, Case C-295/90 *European Parliament v Council* [1992] E.C.R. I-4193, paras 18–20; CFI, Case T-240/04 *France v Commission* [2007] E.C.R. II-4035, para. 37; CFI, Case T-143/06 *MTZ Polyfilms v Council* [2009] E.C.R. II-4133, para 47. See also ECJ, Case 9/74 *Casagrande* [1974] E.C.R. 773, paras 4–6.

[68] ECJ, Joined Cases 281/85, 283–285/85 and 287/85 *Germany, France, Netherlands, Denmark and United Kingdom v Commission* [1987] E.C.R. 3203. However, the Court found no legal basis for the cultural integration of such workers in that former Community power on the ground that the link was "extremely tenuous", *ibid.*, para. 22.

[69] ECJ, Case C-176/03 *Commission v Council* [2005] E.C.R. I-7879, paras 48–51, with case notes by Tobler (2006) C.M.L.Rev. 835–854; van Ooik, (2006) S.E.W. 78–85 and Apps (2006) Col.J.E.L. 625–637. See further White, "Harmonisation of criminal law under the first pillar" (2006) E.L.Rev. 81–92. By contrast, the Court held that the (then) Community was not competent to determine the type and level of the criminal penalties to be applied: ECJ, Case C-440/05 *Commission v Council* [2007] E.C.R. I-9097, paras 66–70. For an example, see Directive 2008/99/EC of the European Parliament and of the Council of November 19, 2008 on the protection of the environment through criminal law, [2008] O.J. L328/28. The Lisbon Treaty has provided for explicit powers to establish minimum rules with regard to the definition of criminal offences and sanctions to ensure the effective implementation of Union harmonisation measures (see Art. 83(2) TFEU). Nevertheless, outside the ambit of Art. 83(2) TFEU a Union competence may still entail the implied power to require the Member States to introduce criminal sanctions in order to ensure the effective implementation of Union rules.

[70] *Cf.* ECJ, Case C-295/90 *European Parliament v Council* [1992] E.C.R. I-4193, paras 18–20.

2. Supplementary competence to achieve Union objectives (Art. 352 TFEU)

7–018   **Supplementary competence.** Article 352 TFEU [*ex Art. 308 EC*] gives the Union an ancillary legal basis in order to take the appropriate measures,

> "if action by the Union should prove necessary, within the framework of the policies defined in the Treaties, to attain one of the objectives set out in the Treaties, and the Treaties have not provided the necessary powers."[71]

Consequently, action pursuant to Art. 352 is justified only where no other Treaty provision gives the Union the necessary express or implied competence.[72] The Union may refer to the supplementary legal basis in combination with other, specific Treaty provisions where these provisions do not confer on the Union the necessary powers to attain the objectives pursued.[73] However, Art. 352 may not be used to supplement a specific Treaty provision which limits Union competence by excluding coverage of certain policy areas or the use of certain instruments.[74] Accordingly, measures based on Art. 352 may not entail harmonisation of Member States' laws or regulations in cases where the Treaties exclude such harmonisation (see Art. 352(3)).

In addition, the action must be necessary to attain one of the objectives set out in the Treaties. For a long time, it was assumed that it fell to the Council to determine

---

[71] Article 308 EC provided for a legal basis where action should prove necessary "to attain, in the course of the operation of the common market, one of the objectives of the Community and this Treaty has not provided the necessary powers".

[72] ECJ, Case 45/86 *Commission v Council* [1987] E.C.R. 1493, para. 13; ECJ, Case C-436/03 *European Parliament v Council* [2006] E.C.R. I-3733, paras 36–46; ECJ, Case C-166/07 *European Parliament v Council* [2009] E.C.R. I-7135, paras 40–41. See also Case 242/87 *Commission v Council* [1989] E.C.R. 1425, in which the Court of Justice dismissed an application for annulment of the decision by which the Council had adopted the European Community action scheme for the mobility of university students (Erasmus) on the basis of Arts 128 and 235 EEC (Art. 235 EEC being the predecessor of Art. 308 EC, which has itself now been renumbered as Art. 352 TFEU). The Court held that the dual legal basis of Arts 128 and 235 was lawful inasmuch as the decision also concerned scientific research. This fell outside the scope of Art. 128, which—as it was worded in the EEC Treaty—authorised the Council to adopt "a common vocational training policy". The Council adopted a second Erasmus decision solely on the basis of Art. 128 EEC following the omission of the research aspect from the Commission proposal. *Cf.* Joined Cases C-51/89, C-90/89 and C-94/89 *United Kingdom, France and Germany v Council* [1991] E.C.R. I-2757. For the extension of Community competence made possible by Art. 308 EC, see Bungenberg, "Dynamische Integration, Art. 308 und die Forderung nach dem Kompetenzkatalog" (2000) EuR. 819–900.

[73] ECJ, Joined Cases C-402/05 P and C-415/05 P *Kadi and Al Barakaat International Foundation* [2008] E.C.R. I-6351, paras 211–214; ECJ, Case C-166/07 *European Parliament v Council* (n. 72, *supra*), para. 69.

[74] See Van Nuffel (n. 30, *supra*), 90, No 117.

(by unanimous vote) that action was necessary and that its decision to this effect was in principle not justiciable.[75] But in a 1996 opinion the Court of Justice unambiguously held that Art. 308 EC [*now Art. 352 TFEU*],

> "cannot serve as a basis for widening the scope of Community powers beyond the general framework created by the provisions of the Treaty as a whole and, in particular, by those that define the tasks and the activities of the Community."[76]

Since the institutional system of the Union is based on the principle of conferral, Art. 352 cannot be used as the legal basis for the adoption of provisions whose effect would, in substance, be to amend the Treaties without following the procedure which it provides for that purpose.[77]

Moreover, as it expressly states, Art. 352 may not be used for the purpose of attaining objectives pertaining to the CFSP and that action based on Art. 352 must respect the limits on the Union's competence set out in the second paragraph of Art. 40 TEU, that is to say, it must not affect the procedures and powers provided for in the TEU with respect to the CFSP (see Art. 352(4)).[78] Before the entry into force of the Lisbon Treaty, the Court of Justice ruled that whereas Art. 308 EC [*now Art. 352 TFEU*] could not be used to attain CFSP objectives,[79] it could be used to adopt Community measures necessary for the implementation of actions decided under the CFSP where these measures were linked to the operation of the common market.[80] Accordingly, the Court found that a regulation freezing the financial assets of persons or entities suspected of contributing to the funding of terrorism was validly based on Arts 60, 301 and 308 EC [*now Arts 75, 215 and 352 TFEU*].[81] Likewise, it would appear that Art. 352 TFEU can be used to adopt

---

[75] For the latitude which the Court allows the Council in assessing "necessity", see ECJ, Case 8/73 *Massey-Ferguson* [1973] E.C.R. 897, para. 3.

[76] ECJ, Opinion 2/94, *Accession by the Communities to the Convention for the Protection of Human Rights and Fundamental Freedoms* [1996] E.C.R. I-1759, para. 30.

[77] *Ibid.* (Opinion holding that the accession of the Community to the ECHR would exceed the limits of Art. 308 EC [*now Art. 352 TFEU*] of para. 22–031, *infra*). See also Declaration (No. 42), annexed to the Lisbon Treaty, on Art. 352 of the Treaty on the Functioning of the European Union ([2010] O.J. C83/351).

[78] See also Declaration (No. 41), annexed to the Lisbon Treaty, on Art. 352 of the Treaty on the Functioning of the European Union ([2010] O.J. C83/350), according to which an action based on Art. 352 TFEU can relate to the Union's objectives set out in Art. 3(2), 3(3) and—within the framework of non-CFSP external competences—Art. 3(5), but cannot only pursue the objectives set out in Art. 3(1) TEU ("to promote peace, [the Union's] values and the well-being of its peoples"). In the same Declaration, the Intergovernmental Conference recalls that in accordance with Art. 31(1) TEU, no legislative acts may be adopted in the area of CFSP.

[79] ECJ, Joined Cases C-402/05 P and C-415/05 P *Kadi and Al Barakaat International Foundation* [2008] E.C.R. I-6351, paras 194–204.

[80] *Ibid.*, paras 218–231.

[81] *Ibid.*, para. 235.

Union measures necessary for the implementation of actions decided under the CFSP where those measures have as their main aim or contents the attainment of Union objectives other than those related to the CFSP.

Article 352 TFEU creates a supplementary competence and does not contain any obligation for the Union to use it.[82]

7–019 **Procedure.** Article 352 TFEU lays down the precise decision-making procedure which the Union must follow whenever it exercises this supplementary competence. The Council must act unanimously on a proposal from the Commission and after obtaining the consent of the European Parliament (Art. 352(1)). Before the entry into force of the Lisbon Treaty, the European Parliament was only consulted in this connection.[83] Where recourse is made to Art. 352 TFEU in combination with other Treaty provisions, the relevant procedural requirements are to be combined. However, since recourse to Art. 352 TFEU necessarily implies that no other legal basis is available which would be appropriate and sufficient by itself, the issue of the compatibility of the procedural requirements does not arise. Contrary to its case law relating to the use of a dual legal basis, the Court thus allows for the unanimity requirement of Art. 352 TFEU to be combined with other procedures—such as the ordinary legislative procedure—that would otherwise provide for qualified majority voting.[84]

In the same way as *ex Art. 308 EC*, Art. 352 TFEU does not specify any particular types of legislative measure ("the appropriate measures"), as a result of which all means are possible and recourse will never have to be made to implicit powers. However, the Lisbon Treaty introduced the obligation for the Commission to draw national parliaments' attention to proposals based on Art. 352 (Art. 352(2)).

C. EXCLUSIVE AND NON-EXCLUSIVE COMPETENCE

7–020 **Classification.** Depending on their relationship to the competences of the Member States, the Union's competences are subdivided into exclusive and non-exclusive competences. In areas of exclusive competence, only the Union may legislate and adopt legally binding acts. Member States may act only if so

---

[82] ECJ, Case 22/70 *Commission v Council* [1971] E.C.R. 263, para. 95 ("Although Article 235 [*now Art. 352 TFEU*] empowers the Council to take any 'appropriate measures' . . ., it does not create an obligation, but confers on the Council an option, failure to exercise which cannot affect the validity" of a decision).

[83] See Art. 308 EC.

[84] ECJ, Case C-166/07 *European Parliament v Council* (n. 72, *supra*), para. 69 (combination of unanimity voting with the co-decision procedure required by Art. 159 EC [*now Art. 175 TFEU*]). See, e.g., Regulation (EU) No. 1232/2010 of the European Parliament and the Council of 15 December 2010 concerning European Union financial contributions to the International Fund for Ireland (2007–2010), [2010] O.J. L346/1.

empowered by the Union or for the implementation of Union acts (Art. 2(1) TFEU). In areas where the Union is not exclusively competent, both the Union and the Member States may act with a view to attaining the objectives of the Treaties. The Treaties distinguish between two types of non-exclusive competence. On the one hand, there are areas in which the Union "shares" competence with the Member States (Arts 2(2) and 4 TFEU). In areas of "shared competence" Member States may act to the extent that the Union has not exercised its competence. They lose this power to the extent that the Union actually exercises its own competence (the pre-emption principle; see para. 7–024). On the other hand, there are areas in which the Union has competence to carry out actions to support, coordinate or supplement the actions of the Member States (Arts 2(5) and 6 TFEU). These actions may not supersede the competences of the Member States in these areas.

In this way, the Treaty of Lisbon introduced for the first time a clear definition of the different categories of competence in the Treaties (see Art. 2 TFEU). Moreover, it added lists of the most important areas of competence by category of competence (Arts 3 to 6 TFEU). Areas not so listed fall under the general category of "shared competence" (Art. 4(1) TFEU).

7–021

Exclusive competences. Exclusive competences are those which have been definitively and irreversibly forfeited by the Member States by reason of their straightforward transfer to the Union. In that event, Member States may act only if so empowered by the Union or to implement measures adopted by the Union. Article 3 TFEU sums up the areas in which the Union has exclusive competence. These are:

(1) the customs union;

(2) the establishing of the competition rules necessary for the functioning of the internal market;

(3) monetary policy for the Member States whose currency is the euro;

(4) the conservation of marine biological resources under the common fisheries policy; and

(5) common commercial policy (see Art. 3(1) TFEU).

In addition, the Union has exclusive competence for the conclusion of an international agreement when its conclusion is provided for in a legislative act of the Union or is necessary to enable the Union to exercise its internal competence or in so far as its conclusion may affect common rules or alter their scope (see Art. 3(2) TFEU).

Before the Treaty of Lisbon introduced this explicit list of exclusive Union competences, the Court of Justice had already established the exclusive nature of the Union's competence under Art. 133 EC [*now Art. 207 TFEU*] to conduct a common commercial policy vis-à-vis third countries with regard to trade in goods[85] and of the Union's competence conferred by Art. 102 of the 1972 Act of Accession to determine conditions for fishing with a view to ensuring protection of fishing grounds and the conservation of the biological resources of the sea.[86] For the Court, it appeared from the wording and the context of the Treaty provisions in question that any parallel action of the Member States would conflict therewith. In addition, two other areas were generally accepted to be exclusive Union competences, namely the Union's competence for the customs union[87] and the Union's monetary policy as regards the Member States participating in the third stage of Economic and Monetary Union (see para. 11–027 *et seq.*). Accordingly, Art. 3(1) TFEU largely confirms the existing position with regard to exclusive Union competences while including for the first time the exclusive competence to establish the competition rules necessary for the functioning of the internal market (Art. 3(1)(b) TFEU).[88] Moreover, as far as the common commercial policy is concerned, Art. 3(1)(e) makes no distinction between goods and services, which means that both are covered by the exclusive competence, in contrast to the Court's pre-Lisbon case law. For its part, Art. 3(2) confirms the case law of the Court of Justice by establishing an "exclusive competence" for the Union to conclude an international agreement where its conclusion is provided for in a legislative act of the Union or is necessary to enable the Union to exercise its internal competence, or in so far as its conclusion may affect common rules or alter their scope (see para. 25–055).

The Treaties preclude Member States from establishing enhanced cooperation between themselves in areas which fall within the exclusive competence of the Union (see Art. 329(1) TFEU). Furthermore, the Union cannot transfer a field in which it has exclusive competence back to the Member States because the text of the Treaties itself definitively rules out competence on the part of the Member States.

7–022   Authorisation. Where the Union has exclusive competence, this means that any action by a Member State in the same field is a priori in conflict with the Treaties.

---

[85] ECJ, Opinion 1/75 *Draft OECD Understanding on a Local Cost Standard* [1975] E.C.R. 1355, at 1363–1365 (para. 7–021, *supra*); ECJ, Case 41/76 *Donckerwolcke* [1976] E.C.R. 1921, para. 32; ECJ, Opinion 1/78 *International Agreement on Natural Rubber* [1979] E.C.R. 2871, paras 52–60; ECJ, Opinion 2/91 *Convention No. 170 of the International Labour Organisation concerning safety in the use of chemicals at work* [1993] E.C.R. I-1061, para. 8; ECJ, Case C-347/03 *Regione autonoma Friuli-Venezia Giulia* [2005] E.C.R. I-3785, paras 71–83.

[86] ECJ, Joined Cases 3–4/76 and 6/76 *Kramer* [1976] E.C.R. 1279, paras 39–41; ECJ, Case 804/79 *Commission v United Kingdom* [1981] E.C.R. 1045, paras 17–18; ECJ, Opinion 2/91 (n. 85, *supra*), para. 8.

[87] It was generally accepted that, as a result of the introduction of the common customs tariff, Art. 26 EC on the customs union precluded any parallel competence on the part of the Member States.

[88] ECJ (judgment of September 14, 2010), Case C-550/07 P *AkzoNobel Chemicals and Akcros Chemicals v Commission*, not yet reported, para. 116. The exclusive character of the Union's competence to legislate in this matter does not affect the Member States' competence to implement the Union's rules on competition (see paras 11–012—11–013, *infra*) or to take legislative action themselves with respect to situations that fall outside the "competition rules necessary for the functioning of the internal market" (thus, Arts 101 and 102 TFEU apply only if trade between Member States is affected: paras 5–112 and 5–115, *infra*).

This is liable to raise problems. If the Union omits to act, a measure deemed to be necessary may remain untaken in the absence of any other competent authority. Furthermore, changed political and economic circumstances may make action on the part of the Member States desirable. Accordingly, the exclusive character of a Union competence should remain limited to what is essential in order to attain the objectives of the Union.

The fact that a particular competence is exclusive does not preclude the Union from delegating certain means of exercising that competence to the Member States (see Art. 2(1) TFEU). In so doing, the Member States may act as agents of the Union pursuant to a "specific authorisation".[89] In such a case, the Union specifies in what way and according to what procedure the Member States are to act.[90] Accordingly, the Court of Justice was prepared in principle to accept Member States taking measures to preserve fish stocks "as trustees of the common interest" since the Council had not yet formulated any policy following the entry into effect of Art. 102 of the 1972 Act of Accession. They had to do so,

> "as part of a process of collaboration with the Commission and with due regard to the general task of supervision which Article 155 EEC [now Art. 17(1) TEU] . . . gives to the Commission."[91]

In 1986 the Court went very far in this direction when it decided that the United Kingdom had a "specific authorisation" to prohibit oil exports to Israel by derogation from the exclusive competence with regard to the common commercial policy. It inferred that authorisation from the fact that there was no express prohibition of export restrictions in the EEC-Israel Agreement and that oil was excluded from the Council regulation establishing common rules for exports.[92] However, where a specific authorisation can exist without the Union's having genuinely endorsed the national measures taken, the very exclusivity of the relevant competence is called in question.[93]

Shared competences. By means of a non-exhaustive list,[94] Art. 4(2) TFEU enumerates the most important competences that the Union shares with the Member States: **7–023**

---

[89] ECJ, Case 41/76 *Donckerwolcke* [1976] E.C.R. 1921, para. 32.

[90] Lenaerts, "Regulating the Regulatory Process: 'Delegation of Powers' in the European Community" (1993) E.L.Rev. 23–49, in particular at 27–32.

[91] ECJ, Case 804/79 *Commission v United Kingdom* [1981] E.C.R. 1045, para. 30.

[92] ECJ, Case 174/84 *Bulk Oil* [1986] E.C.R. 559, paras 15–19 and 33.

[93] See Lenaerts, "Les répercussions des compétences de la Communauté européenne sur les compétences externes des Etats membres et la question de la 'preemption' ", in Demaret, *Relations extérieures de la Communauté européenne et marché intérieur: aspects juridiques et fonctionnels* (Bruges, College of Europe/Story, 1988) 39, at 47–54. For the "specific authorisation" by which Union export rules permit Member States to subject dual-use goods to export controls, see paras 25–006—25–007, *infra*. Another example is Council Decision 1999/405/EC of June 10, 1999 authorising the Kingdom of Spain to accede to the Convention establishing the Inter-American Tropical Tuna Commission on a temporary basis (IATTC), [1999] O.J. L155/37.

[94] Article 4(2) TFEU refers in this respect to "the following principal areas".

(1) internal market;

(2) social policy, for the aspects defined in that Treaty[95];

(3) economic, social and territorial cohesion;

(4) agriculture and fisheries, excluding the conservation of marine biological resources;

(5) environment;

(6) consumer protection;

(7) transport;

(8) trans-European networks;

(9) energy;

(10) area of freedom, security and justice; and

(11) common safety concerns in public health matters, for the aspects defined in the Treaty on the Functioning of the European Union.

Articles 4(3) and 4(4) TFEU mention other competences falling within the category of "shared competences" with respect to which the Treaty expressly provides that the exercise of these competences by the Union "shall not result in Member States being prevented from exercising theirs". This applies to the areas of research, technological development and space (Art. 4(3) TFEU) and development cooperation and humanitarian aid (Art. 4(4) TFEU).

Moreover, the Treaty mentions two other policy areas, for which no further classification is given. These are the coordination of the economic and employment policies of the Member States (Art. 2(3) and 5(1) and (2) TFEU) and the definition and implementation of a common foreign and security policy, including the progressive framing of a common defence policy (Art. 2(4) TFEU). Since all competences outside the areas referred to in Arts 3 and 6 are shared by the Union with the Member States (see Art. 4(1) TFEU), these two policy areas can only be classified as falling within the general category of shared competences.

In an area of shared competence, the Union may in principle repeal the Union measure, leaving the Member States in a position to exercise their powers in full again. The repeal must accord, however, with the objectives of the Treaty provision forming the legal basis of the measure and with the principle of subsidiarity (see para. 7–029).

7–024   **Pre-emption.** In areas of shared competence the Member States may only exercise their competence to the extent that the Union has not exercised its

---

[95] See also Art. 5(3) TFEU, which provides that the Union may take initiatives to ensure coordination of Member States' social policies.

competence. The Member States may again exercise their competence to the extent that the Union has decided to cease exercising its competence (Art. 2(2) TFEU). With this provision, the Lisbon Treaty codified the doctrine of pre-emption, according to which Member States lose their power to enact rules in an area of shared competence to the extent that the Union has exercised its competence.[96]

Once the Union has exercised its competence, national rules must give way to the Union's provision in so far as there is a conflict between them (primacy of Union law, see para. 7–048). In accordance with the pre-emption doctrine, the Union's exercise of its competence in a given field will limit the Member State's competence to act to matters that have not yet been regulated by the Union. In any given case, it is to be determined to what extent Union action still leaves room for the Member States to legislate. Accordingly, the Court of Justice held in the *AETR* case that the Union's exercise of its powers in regard to the common transport policy,

> "excludes the possibility of concurrent powers on the part of the Member States, since any steps taken outside the framework of the [Union] institutions would be incompatible with the unity of the common market and the uniform application of [Union] law."[97]

Depending upon the extent to which the Union exercises its competence to regulate a given matter, that exercise may confer upon it an "exclusive nature",[98] even though there is no question of an "exclusive competence" being transferred to the Union within the meaning of Art. 2(1) TFEU.[99]

So as to limit the instances where the Union's action in a given area would have the effect of excluding the Member States' power still to enact rules in that

---

[96] Schütze, "Supremacy without pre-emption? The very slowly emergent doctrine of Community pre-emption" (2006) C.M.L.Rev. 1023–1048; Cross, "Pre-emption of Member State Law in the European Economic Community: A Framework for Analysis" (1992) C.M.L.Rev. 447–472. For comparisons with the pre-emption principle in the constitutional law of the United States, see Lenaerts (n. 27, *supra*), Nos 436–468, at 525–566 (for the doctrine of pre-emption, see Nos 167–174, at 176–185).

[97] ECJ, Case 22/70 *Commission v Council* [1971] E.C.R. 263, para. 31. See also ECJ, Opinion 1/03 *New Lugano Convention on jurisdiction and the recognition and enforcement of judgments in civil and commercial matters* [2006] E.C.R. I-1145, paras 115–132 and the "open skies" judgments discussed in para. 25–058, *infra*.

[98] ECJ, Opinion 2/91 *Convention No. 170 of the International Labour Organisation concerning safety in the use of chemicals at work* [1993] E.C.R. I-1061, para. 9; see also ECJ, Opinion 1/94 *Agreement establishing the World Trade Organisation* [1994] E.C.R. I-5267, paras 72–105; ECJ, Opinion 2/92 *Third Revised Decision of the OECD on national treatment* [1995] E.C.R. I-521, paras 31–36 (para. 25–058, *infra*).

[99] See ECJ, Case C-491/01 *British American Tobacco (Investments) and Imperial Tobacco* [2002] E.C.R. I-11453, para. 179 (competence to harmonise under Art. 95 EC [*now Art. 114 TFEU*] is not exclusive). For these so-called *compétences exclusives par exercice*, see also Lenaerts and van Ypersele (n. 27, *supra*), at 20–28.

area, the Lisbon Treaty has specified in a Protocol on the exercise of shared competence that "when the Union has taken action in a certain area, the scope of this exercise of competence only covers those elements governed by the Union act in question and therefore does not cover the whole area".[100] Likewise, with respect to the areas of shared competence mentioned in Arts 4(3) and 4(4) TFEU (research, technological development, space, development cooperation and humanitarian aid), the TFEU provides that "the exercise of that competence shall not result in Member States being prevented from exercising theirs".

7–025 **Supporting competences.** Finally, the Treaties mention areas where the Union is competent to "support, coordinate or complement the actions of the Member States, without thereby superseding their competence in these areas" (Art. 2(5) TFEU). The areas in question are:

(1) protection and improvement of human health;

(2) industry;

(3) culture;

(4) tourism;

(5) education, vocational training, youth and sport;

(6) civil protection; and

(7) administrative cooperation (Art. 6 TFEU).

It follows from Art. 4(1) TFEU, that these areas are not regarded as "shared competences" in the sense of Art. 2(2) TFEU. Within this distinct category of "supporting" competences, the Union may take action but its legally binding acts may not entail harmonisation of Member States' laws or regulations (Art. 2(5) TFEU). The provision according to which the Union's action in these areas shall not supersede Member States' competence indicates that, even if Member States do not adopt rules that conflict with provisions of Union law (principle of primacy), the Union's action is not to restrict the Member States' regulating power in the areas concerned (i.e. the doctrine of pre-emption does not apply). Nevertheless, in accordance with the principles of primacy of Union law and of sincere cooperation, Member States are not to adopt measures which would put at risk the uniform application of the acts adopted by the Union in the areas concerned.

---

[100] Protocol (No. 25), annexed to the TEU and TFEU, on the exercise of shared competence, [2010] O.J. C83/307.

III. THE PRINCIPLE OF SUBSIDIARITY

A. ROLE PLAYED BY THE PRINCIPLE

Limit to the exercise of power. The principle of subsidiarity signifies that, in areas which do not fall within its exclusive competence, the Union

7–026

> "shall act only if and in so far as the objectives of the proposed action cannot be sufficiently achieved by the Member States, either at central level or at regional and local level, but can rather, by reason of the scale or effects of the proposed action, be better achieved at Union level."[101]

In this way the principle of subsidiarity constitutes a filter between Union competence and the possibility of exercising that competence. When the Union has competence, it can nonetheless only use that competence if the principle of subsidiarity so allows. The EU Treaty introduced the principle into the EC Treaty as a reaction to a degree of dissatisfaction in some Member States about the way in which the Community was exercising its powers. Above all, following the extension of majority voting in the Council, there was a growing feeling that the Member States might be caught unaware by Community action markedly restricting their freedom to frame their own policies, even in areas not directly targeted by that action. In federal Member States, moreover, the constituent entities felt the loss of "national" sovereignty rather as an encroachment of the Community on their powers, whilst they themselves had no say in the matter.

When the Single European Act conferred competence on the Community with regard to the environment, Art. 130r(4) EEC at the same time laid down the principle that the Community was to take action relating to the environment,

> "to the extent to which the objectives . . . can be attained better at Community level than at the level of the individual Member States."[102]

---

[101] For general discussions, see Tridimas, *The General Principles of EU Law* (Oxford, Oxford University Press, 2007), Ch. 4; Davies, "Subsidiarity: the wrong idea, in the wrong place, at the wrong time" (2006) C.M.L.Rev. 63–84; Syrpis, "In Defence of Subsidiarity" (2004) O.J.L.S. 323–334; Bermann, "Proportionality and Subsidiarity", in Barnard and Scott (eds), *The Law of the Single European Market* (Oxford/Portland, Hart, 2002), 75–100; de Búrca, "Proportionality and Subsidiarity as General Principles of Law", in Bernitz and Nergelius (eds), *General Principles of European Community Law* (The Hague-London-Boston, Kluwer Law International, 2000), 93–112; Barber, "The Limited Modesty of Subsidiarity" (2005) E.L.J. 308–325; Bermann, "Taking Subsidiarity Seriously: Federalism in the European Community and the United States" (1994) Col.L.Rev. 331–456; von Börries, "Das Subsidiaritätsprinzip im Recht der Europäischen Union" (1994) EuR. 263–300; Toth, "The Principle of Subsidiarity in the Maastricht Treaty" (1992) C.M.L.Rev. 1079–1105.

[102] See also Art. 12(2) of the Draft Treaty establishing the European Union (para. 3–004, *supra*), [1984] O.J. C77/33. As to the success of this principle, see Cass, "The Word that Saves Maastricht? The Principle of Subsidiarity and the Division of Powers Within the European

The EU Treaty deleted this specific mention of the principle of subsidiarity when the principle set out in general terms in Art. 5 EC [*now Art. 5 TEU*] was introduced for all Community competences. With only minor changes, the Treaty of Lisbon retained the definition of the subsidiarity principle in Art. 5(3) TEU.

The principle of subsidiarity formulated in Art. 5(3) TEU constitutes a guide as to how powers at Union level have to be exercised, as was already emphasised in the criteria for applying the principle set forth by the European Council held at Edinburgh on December 11 and 12, 1992[103] and subsequently incorporated in a protocol annexed to the EC Treaty by the Treaty of Amsterdam.[104] The Treaty of Lisbon retained this approach, although the concrete guidelines for applying the subsidiarity test were not taken over in the new protocol annexed to the Treaties (see para. 7–031).[105]

7–027   **Limit to conferral of power.** At the same time, subsidiarity implicitly underpins the Treaties as a political principle which does not govern the exercise of powers which have been conferred but oversees the actual conferral of powers.[106] The principle arose in a socio-economic context as limiting intervention by the authorities to such matters as the persons or groups concerned could not deal with themselves. Later, it acquired the additional meaning of an obligation for the authorities whenever taking action to weigh up the different levels of authority at

---

Community" (1992) C.M.L.Rev. 1107–1136; Emiliou (n. 144, *supra*), at 384–399; Hummer, "Subsidiarität und Föderalismus als Strukturprinzipien der Europäischen Gemeinschaften?" (1992) Z.f.R.V. 81–91.

[103] Overall approach to the application by the Council of the subsidiarity principle and Art. 3b [*now Art. 5(3) TEU*] (1992) 12 EC Bull. points I.15–I.22, which was adopted by the European Council held in Edinburgh on December 11 and 12, 1992 even before that Treaty provision entered into force (*ibid.*, point I.4). The European Council had been provided with the Commission's communication to the Council and the European Parliament of October 27, 1992 on the principle of subsidiarity (1992) 10 EC Bull. point 2.2.1; for a commentary, see Ehlermann, "Quelques réflexions sur la communication de la Commission relative au principe de subsidiarité" (1992) 4 R.M.U.E. 215–220.

[104] Protocol (No. 30), annexed to the EC Treaty, on the application of the principles of subsidiarity and proportionality, [1997] O.J. C340/105. See Feral, "Le principe de subsidiarité: progrès ou statu quo après le traité d'Amsterdam?" (1998) 1 R.M.U.E. 95–117; Constantinesco, "Le traité d'Amsterdam. Les clauses de 'coopération renforcée'. Le protocole sur l'application des principes de subsidiarité et de proportionalité" (1997) R.T.D.E. 751–767.

[105] Protocol (No. 2), annexed to the TEU and TFEU, on the application of the principles of subsidiarity and proportionality ([2010] O.J. C83/206).

[106] For the two aspects, see Constantinesco, "La subsidiarité comme principe constitutionnel de l'intégration européenne" (1991) *Aussenwirtschaft* 439–459; Jacqué, "Centralisation et décentralisation dans les projets d'Union européenne" (1991) *Aussenwirtschaft* 469–483; Van Gerven, "De beginselen 'subsidiariteit, evenredigheid en samenwerking' in het Europese gemeenschapsrecht" (1991–1992) R.W. 1241–1246. For a somewhat critical view of the utility of the principle, see Pennings, "Is the Subsidiarity Principle Useful to Guide the European Integration Process?" (1993) Tilburg For.L.Rev. 153–163; Geelhoed, "Het subsidiariteitsbeginsel: een communautair principe?" (1991) S.E.W. 422–435.

which action may be taken.[107] It is above all pursuant to the latter idea that the process of European integration must respect the cultural and linguistic diversity of the Union and the regional identity of the Member States and come as close as possible to the citizen.[108] In order to achieve this, various amendments to the Treaties, on the one hand, enlarged Union competence to cover areas where a Union contribution appeared to be absolutely essential,[109] yet, on the other hand, safeguarded the powers of the Member States in those areas where a national contribution was required in some respect.[110]

In this sense, subsidiarity already permeated the original EEC Treaty,[111] both in the choice of powers which were conferred on the (predecessor to the) Union (common commercial policy, abolition of obstacles to free movement, common agricultural policy, common transport policy, etc. or else in the choice of areas in which the Union itself implemented its policies, such as competition policy or anti-dumping policy) and in the determination of the areas of competence left to the Member States (implementation of Union legislation by Member States: see para. 14–012; decentralised enforcement of Union law by national courts in cooperation with the Court of Justice: see para. 14–013; legislation by directives having to be transposed by the Member States: see para. 22–075). As a political principle, subsidiarity guides the development of the constitutional system and is therefore incapable of being enforced by a court within that system. As will be explained below, the position is different as far as the legal principle defined in Art. 5(3) TFEU is concerned.

The subsidiarity principle has a dual dimension in the Treaty provisions on social policy (see para. 11–044). Not only do those provisions reflect the subsidiary nature of Union action in relation to that of the Member States (Art. 153(1), (2) and (4) TFEU), they also give a role to management and labour in the formulation or implementation of measures at Union level (Art. 154 TFEU). Since Art. 5(3) TEU limits the action of the Union only vis-à-vis action

---

[107] For the origin of the subsidiarity principle, see Millon-Delsol, *L'etat subsidiaire. Ingérence et non-ingérence de l'Etat: le principe de subsidiarité aux fondements de l'histoire européenne* (Paris, Presses Universitaires de France, 1992), 232 pp.; Wilke and Wallace, *Subsidiarity: Approaches to Power-sharing in the European Community* (London, Royal Institute of International Affairs, 1990), 43 pp.; Adonis and Jones, "Subsidiarity and the European Community's Constitutional Future" (1991) *Staatswissenschaft und Staatspraxis* 179–196;

[108] Para. 7–006, *supra*.

[109] See, for example, economic and monetary union, para. 5–214 *et seq.* (a formulation of the subsidiarity principle was already contained in the Report of the Delors Committee; para. 5–218).

[110] See the wording of the new legal bases; para. 5–034. In a broader context, see Handoll, "The Protection of National Interests in the European Union" (1994) Ir.J.E.L. 221–246.

[111] See Berger, "Le principe de subsidiarité en droit communautaire" (1992) 79 Pet.Aff. 40–44; Kapteyn, "Community Law and the Principle of Subsidiarity" (1991) R.A.E. 35, at 38–39; for a somewhat different view, see Toth (n. 101, *supra*), at 1080–1086. For the role played by subsidiarity in the system of legal protection, see Chaltiel, "Le principe de subsidiarité dix ans après de traité de Maastricht" (2003) R.M.C.U.E. 365, at 370–371.

taken by the Member States, considerations of subsidiarity cannot detract from the Union's powers to adopt measures without the agreement of management and labour.

B. THE REQUIREMENTS OF SUBSIDIARITY

7–028　**Definition.** Wherever the Union does not possess exclusive competence, it may take action only,

> "*if* and *in so far* as the objectives of the proposed action cannot be suffi-ciently achieved by the Member States [. . .] but can rather, by reason of the scale or effects of the proposed action, be better achieved at Union level". (Art. 5(3), first subpara., TEU, emphasis supplied).

This definition tests Union action against both a decentralisation criterion and an efficiency criterion: the Union acts *only if* the proposed objectives cannot be suffi-ciently achieved by the Member States and if they can be *better* achieved by the Union.[112] Union action will conflict with the principle of subsidiarity only where it can be shown that the objective sought can be achieved just as much in all Member States either by individual action or by cooperation between the Member States concerned.[113] In this regard, it makes little difference whether the comparison with Union action is carried out at the level of the Member State or at the level of decen-tralised authorities: this is because in either case there will be a breach of the principle where the objective sought can be sufficiently achieved in all Member States and it is irrelevant by whose intervention or at what level of policy it is achieved within the Member States.[114] Since the Treaty of Lisbon, the Treaty for-mulation of the principle of subsidiarity explicitly refers to Member State action "either at central level or at regional and local level" (Art. 5(3), first subpara., TEU).

The initial Protocol on the application of the principles of subsidiarity and proportionality set out concrete guidelines for applying the principle of subsidiarity.[115] According to the protocol, the following issues needed to be

---

[112] Unlike the initial Protocol on the application of the principle of subsidiarity and proportionality, the Protocol introduced by the Lisbon Treaty (n. 105, *supra*) no longer specifies that Union action is to meet both aspects of the subsidiarity test. It should be noted that the expression "in so far as" makes Union action subject to an additional requirement of proportionality (see para. 7–039).

[113] However, the *acquis communautaire* would be affected if the Union had to justify its action against possible intergovernmental action on the part of all Member States: Lenaerts and van Ypersele, "Le principe de subsidiarité et son contexte: étude de l'article 3 B du traité CE" (1994) C.D.E. 13–30 and 35–44, at 45–57; Van Nuffel (see n. 30, *supra*), at 394–396.

[114] Van Nuffel, "The Protection of Member States' Regions through the Subsidiarity Principle" in Panara and De Becker (eds), *The Role of the Regions in European Governance* (Springer, Heidelberg, 2010).

[115] Protocol, annexed to the EC Treaty by the Treaty of Amsterdam, on the application of the princi-ples of subsidiarity and proportionality (n. 104, *supra*).

considered in examining whether the subsidiarity principle was satisfied: (1) whether the issue under consideration had transnational aspects which could not be satisfactorily regulated by action by Member States; (2) whether actions by Member States alone or lack of Community action would conflict with the requirements of the Treaty (such as the need to correct distortions of competition or avoid disguised restrictions on trade or strengthen economic and social cohesion) or would otherwise significantly damage Member States' interests; (3) whether action at Community level would produce clear benefits by reason of its scale or effects compared with action at the level of the Member States.[116] These guidelines were not taken over in the new Protocol on the application of the principles of subsidiarity and proportionality attached to the Treaties by the Treaty of Lisbon.

C. APPLICATION OF THE PRINCIPLE OF SUBSIDIARITY

Scope. Article 5(3), first subpara., TEU requires the Union to comply with the principle of subsidiarity in "areas which do not fall within its exclusive competence". This applies equally to the first measure which the Union adopts and to existing measures where they are tightened (e.g. where a recommendation or a communication is replaced by a binding measure) or made stricter (e.g. a regulation replacing a directive). The principle of subsidiarity is a dynamic concept which allows Union action to be expanded where circumstances so require and, conversely, to be restricted or discontinued where it is no longer justified.[117] Nevertheless, movement in either direction is constrained by the requirement for a legal basis and by the principle of proportionality: both an expansion of Union action and a restriction thereof must seek to achieve the objectives of the Treaties and be essential for achieving the intended aim.   **7–029**

In contrast, where the Union has exclusive competence, it does not have to take account of the principle of subsidiarity set out in Art. 5(3), although it does have to have regard to the principle of proportionality set out in Art. 5(4).[118]

Institutional implementation. The application of the principle of subsidiarity falls in the first place to the institutions of the Union, which must thereby observe the provisions of the Protocol on the application of the principles of subsidiarity and   **7–030**

---

[116] *Ibid.*, point 5, second para. (reiterating the guidelines set out in the European Council's overall approach—n. 102, *supra*—point I.18).

[117] See the original Protocol, annexed to the EC Treaty by the Treaty of Amsterdam, on the application of the principles of subsidiarity and proportionality (n. 104, *supra*), point 3.

[118] Para. 7–040, *infra*. Non-exclusive competences obtaining an "exclusive character" following their exercise by the Union do not remain outside the scope of the subsidiarity principle and do not constitute "exclusive competences" within the meaning of Art. 5(3), first subpara., TEU. If they did, the Union would be able, through its own action, to restrict the very principle which is intended to limit its action.

proportionality (Art. 5(3), second subpara., TEU). In exercising the powers conferred on it, each institution has to ensure constant respect for the principle of subsidiarity.[119] Just before the EU Treaty entered into effect, the European Parliament, the Council and the Commission concluded an Interinstitutional Agreement on procedures for implementing the principle of subsidiarity,[120] the thrust of which was incorporated in 1997 into the Protocol on the application of the principles of subsidiarity and proportionality. Since the Treaty of Lisbon, national parliaments play a major role in ensuring that the principle of subsidiarity is complied with. They are competent to monitor the application of that principle in accordance with the procedure set out in the new Protocol on the application of the principles of subsidiarity and proportionality (Art. 5(3), second subpara., TEU; see para. 7–031).

Before proposing legislative acts, the Commission must consult widely, except in cases of exceptional urgency. Such consultations must take into account the regional and local dimension of the action envisaged.[121] Any draft legislative act[122] must be justified with regard to the principles of subsidiarity and proportionality and should, therefore, contain a detailed statement making it possible to appraise its compliance with the principles of subsidiarity and proportionality.[123] The Commission is to report annually to the European Council, the European Parliament, the Council and the national parliaments on the application of Art. 5 TEU.[124]

After considering its pending proposals and existing legislation, the Commission decided in the early 1990s to withdraw some proposals and to make new proposals adapting existing legislation.[125] The Commission stated that it was prepared to withdraw certain initiatives after consulting interested parties[126] and hence interprets subsidiarity also as the political principle whereby public intervention is weighed against private initiative.

7–031   **Control by national parliaments.** The major change introduced by the new Protocol on the principles of subsidiarity and proportionality concerns the control

---

[119] Protocol on the application of the principles of subsidiarity and proportionality (n. 105, *supra*), Art. 1.

[120] (1993) 10 EC Bull. point 1.6.3; for the text of the Agreement, see point 2.2.2 (or 1993 O.J. C329/135).

[121] Protocol on the application of the principles of subsidiarity and proportionality (n. 105, *supra*), Art. 2.

[122] This term not only covers Commission proposals, but also refers to initiatives from a group of Member States, initiatives from the European Parliament, requests from the Court of Justice, recommendations from the European Central Bank and requests from the European Investment Bank for the adoption of a legislative act (Art. 3 of the Protocol).

[123] *Ibid.*, Art. 5. Accordingly, the reasons for concluding that a Union objective can be better achieved at Union level must be substantiated by qualitative and, wherever possible, quantitative indicators. (*Ibid.*).

[124] *Ibid.*, Art. 9, which further provides that this report will be forwarded to the Economic and Social Committee and the Committee of the Regions.

[125] See the Commission's answer of February 15, 1995 to question E-370/95 (Crampton), 1995 O.J. C175/38, and the lists of proposals which have already been withdrawn, [1995] O.J. C344/2, and [1997] O.J. C 2/2.

[126] (1992) 12 EC Bull. point I.23.

that national parliaments may exercise over the application of the principle of subsidiarity.[127]

First, any Commission proposal or other draft legislative act, as well as any position taken by the European Parliament and the Council in the course of the legislative process, will be sent to the national parliaments.[128] If the Commission proposes to base its action on the flexibility clause (Art. 352 TFEU [ex Art. 308 EC]), it must draw the national parliaments' attention specifically to the proposed use of that article (Art. 352(2) TFEU). Within eight weeks of the date of transmission of a draft legislative act, any national parliament (or any chamber of a national parliament) may send an opinion to the Presidents of the European Parliament, the Council and the Commission stating the reasons for which it considers that the draft in question does not comply with the principle of subsidiarity. If the draft legislative act concerns a matter for which, under national law, competence exists with regional parliaments with legislative powers, it will be for the national parliament to consult the regional parliaments concerned.[129] In this respect, Belgium has gone further by putting the parliaments of its autonomous regions ("Regions" and "Communities") on the same level as the chambers of the federal parliament for the application of the Protocol (see para. 14–010).

The Commission, the European Parliament and the Council must take account of the reasoned opinions issued by national parliaments. The draft legislative act must be reviewed where reasoned opinions on non-compliance with the principle of subsidiarity representing at least one-third of all the votes of the national parliaments (one-fourth in the case of a Commission proposal or an initiative initiating from a group of Member States relating to police cooperation or judicial cooperation in criminal matters).[130] After having reviewed its draft legislative act, the Commission (or another institution from which the draft act originated) may decide to maintain, amend or withdraw it, while giving its reasons for its decision.[131] This procedure has received the name "yellow card" after the football term for "warnings" issued by referees.

---

[127] See Barrett, "The king is dead, long live the king: the recasting by the Treaty of Lisbon of the provisions of the Constitutional Treaty concerning national parliaments" (2008) 33 E.L.Rev. 66–84; Kiiver, "The Treaty of Lisbon, the National Parliaments and the Principle of Subsidiarity" (2008) M.J.E.C.L. 77–83; Tans, "De oranje kaart: een nieuwe rol voor nationale parlementen?" (2007) R.W. 442–446; Cooper, "The watchdogs of subsidiarity: national parliaments and the logic of arguing in the EU" (2006) 44 J.C.M.S. 281–304; Wyatt, "Could a 'Yellow Card' for National Parliaments Strengthen Judicial as well as Political Policing of Subsidiarity?" (2006) C.Y.E.L.P. 1–17.

[128] Protocol on the application of the principles of subsidiarity and proportionality (n. 105, supra), Art. 4. See also Protocol (No. 1) on the role of National Parliaments in the European Union ([2010] O.J. C83/203), Art. 2.

[129] Ibid., Art. 6 (it is for each national parliament or each chamber of a national parliament to consult regional parliaments "where appropriate").

[130] Ibid., Art. 7(2), first subpara. (refers for the threshold of "one-fourth" to Art. 76 TFEU).

[131] Ibid., Art. 7(2), second subpara.

In the end, the Lisbon Treaty did not introduce the so-called "red card" procedure that some had proposed and according to which a two-third majority of the national parliaments would have forced the Commission to amend or even withdraw its proposal. With respect to matters falling under the ordinary legislative procedure, the Brussels European Council of June 2007 agreed however to introduce in the new Protocol on the application of the principles of subsidiarity and proportionality the possibility of having a legislative proposal being rejected, while leaving the final decision to discard such a proposal not to the national parliaments, but to the Union legislator itself. Under this so-called "orange card" procedure, the Commission must review a proposal made under the ordinary legislative procedure where reasoned opinions on non-compliance with the principle of subsidiarity represent at least a simple majority of the votes allocated to the national Parliaments. Again, the Commission may decide to maintain its proposal if it justifies this decision in a reasoned opinion, which is to be submitted to the Union legislator. However, if, by a majority of 55 per cent of the members of the Council or a majority of the votes cast in the European Parliament, the legislator is of the opinion that the proposal is not compatible with the principle of subsidiarity, the legislative proposal shall not be given further consideration.[132] For the purpose of calculating the threshold of one-third or one-fourth of the votes, every national parliament will have two votes, shared out on the basis of the national parliamentary system. In the case of a bicameral parliamentary system, each of the two chambers will have one vote.[133]

The introduction of this scrutiny mechanism for compliance with the principle of subsidiarity breaks with the approach put forward in the original Protocol on the application of the principles of subsidiarity and proportionality, according to which such scrutiny is not to take place in a prior or parallel decision-making procedure, but "as an integral part of the overall examination of Commission proposals".[134]

7–032   **Impact.** Judicial review of the validity of Union acts extends to compliance with the principle of subsidiarity.[135] A novel feature of the new protocol is that it makes

---

[132] *Ibid.*, Art. 7(3).

[133] *Ibid.*, Art. 7(1), second subpara.

[134] See the original Protocol on the application of the principles of subsidiarity and proportionality (n. 104, *supra*), point 11.

[135] See, for example, ECJ, Case C-377/98 *Netherlands v European Parliament and Council* [2001] E.C.R. I-7079, paras 30–33; ECJ, Case C-491/01 *British American Tobacco (Investments) and Imperial Tobacco* [2002] E.C.R. I-11453, paras 180–183; ECJ, Joined Cases C-154/04 and C-155/04 *Alliance for Natural Health* [2005] E.C.R. I-6451, paras 104–108, with a case note by Vandamme (2006) L.I.E.I. 305–318. See Van Nuffel, "The Protection of Member States' Regions through the Subsidiarity Principle", in Panara and De Becker (eds), *The Role of the Regions in European Governance* (Springer, Heidelberg, 2010); Timmermans, "Is het subsidiariteitsbeginsel vatbaar voor rechterlijke controle?" (2007) S.E.W. 224–230; Ritzer, "Die Kontrolle des Subsidiaritätsprinzips: Geltende Rechtlage und Reformperspektiven" (2006) EuR. 116–137; Chaltiel, "Le principe de subsidiarité dix ans après de traité de Maastricht" (2003) R.M.C.U.E. 365, at 368–370.

it clear that Member States may bring an action for annulment before the Court of Justice against a legislative act on grounds of infringement of the principle of subsidiarity on behalf of their national parliament or of one of its chambers.[136] The Committee of the Regions may also bring such an action against legislative acts where the Treaty on the Functioning of the European Union provides that it must be consulted.[137]

In theory, the principle of subsidiarity may appear to constitute an important limitation where the Union acts to achieve broadly framed objectives, such as the ones already contained in the original EEC Treaty.[138] In practice, however, the limitation placed on Union action by the principle of subsidiarity is not that important whenever it is considered whether such action affords "clear benefits" or is "better" than action at national level. This is because Union action is invariably tested against the objectives which the Union purports to achieve. If Union action is tested against objectives such as the achievement of uniform or coherent rules or the equal treatment of EU citizens or legal persons, it is obvious that Union action will be more efficient than individual action by Member States or voluntary coordination of national policies. In such cases, the objective sought by the Union or the matter dealt with is normally in itself such that national action would inevitably fall short (with the result that Union action is necessarily

---

[136] See Protocol on the application of the principles of subsidiarity and proportionality (n. 105, *supra*), Art. 8, first para. (refers to an action brought "in accordance with their legal order"). This possibility already existed before the entry into force of the Lisbon Treaty in so far as it was up to any Member State to determine the domestic authorities on behalf of which it brought an action before the Court. See Van Nuffel, "What's in a Member State? Central and decentralised authorities before the Community Courts" (2001) C.M.L.Rev. 871, at 879. As far as Belgium is concerned such action is possible not only on behalf of the chambers of the federal parliament, but also on behalf of the parliamentary assemblies of the Communities and the Regions (see the Declaration, annexed to the Lisbon Treaty, by the Kingdom of Belgium on national Parliaments, [2010] O.J. C83/355). See the discussion in Lenaerts and Cambien, "Regions and the European Courts: giving shape to the Regional Dimension of Member States" (2010) E.L.Rev. 609–635.

[137] *Ibid.*, Art. 8, second para. (see also para. 13–110, *infra*). This possibility exists irrespective of whether the action is brought to protect the prerogatives of the Committee, in contradistinction to actions brought under Art. 263, third para., TFEU.

[138] For a possible application in the field of *competition policy*, see Wesseling, "Subsidiarity in Community Antitrust Law: Setting the Right Agenda?" (1997) E.L.Rev. 35–54; Van den Bergh, "Economic Criteria for Applying the Subsidiarity Principle in the European Community: The Case of Competition Policy" (1996) Int'l Rev. of Law & Econ. 363–383; for *internal-market policy*, see Schmidhuber and Hitzler, "Binnenmarkt und Subsidiaritätsprinzip" (1993) Eu.Z.W. 8–10; for a possible application in the field of *social policy*, see Spicker, "The Principle of Subsidiarity and the Social Policy of the European Community" (1991) *Journal of European Social Policy* 3–14; for *environmental policy*, see Macrory, *Regulation, enforcement and governance in environmental law* (London, Cameron May, 2008), Ch. 21; Lenaerts, "The Principle of Subsidiarity and the Environment in the European Union: Keeping the Balance of Federalism" (1994) Fordham I.L.J. 846–895; Wils, "Subsidiarity and EC Environmental Policy: Taking People's Concerns Seriously" (1994) J.Env.L. 85–91.

"better").[139] Moreover, since, when considering Union action, the institutions make a judgement of complex practical and political circumstances, the courts will carry out a marginal review only of that judgement as it is set out in the statement of reasons of the act concerned.[140] The principle of subsidiarity therefore makes sense above all in so far as it compels consideration by the Union institutions of the necessity to take action at the stage of formulating proposals or in subsequent stages of the decision-making process. Various Treaty provisions already limit action on the part of the Union to encouraging and "if necessary" supporting and supplementing action on the part of the Member States.[141]

Where the application of the principle of subsidiarity leads to no action being taken by the Union, Member States are required in their action to comply with the general rules laid down in Art. 4(3) TEU, by taking all appropriate measures to ensure fulfilment of their obligations under the Treaties and by abstaining from any measure which could jeopardise the attainment of the Union's objectives.

The subsidiarity principle does not authorise Member States to avoid Union obligations.[142] Nor may the principle be interpreted as meaning that intervention by the Union authorities must be confined to what is strictly necessary where the result would be that private associations could adopt rules restricting the exercise of rights conferred on individuals by the Treaties.[143]

---

[139] See, for example, ECJ, Case C-377/98 *Netherlands v European Parliament and Council* [2001] E.C.R. I-7079, para. 32; ECJ, Case C-491/01 *British American Tobacco (Investments) and Imperial Tobacco* [2002] E.C.R. I-11453, paras 180–183; ECJ, Case C-103/01 *Commission v Germany* [2003] E.C.R. I-5369, para. 47; ECJ, Joined Cases C-154/04 and C-155/04 *Alliance for Natural Health* [2005] E.C.R. I-6451, paras 104–107, with a case note by Vandamme (2006) L.I.E.I. 305–318; ECJ (judgment of June 8, 2010), Case C-58/08 *Vodafone and Others*, not yet reported, paras 76–78. See already Van Nuffel, *De rechtsbescherming van nationale overheden in het Europees recht* (Deventer, Kluwer, 2000), at 364–388.

[140] See ECJ, Case C-233/94 *Germany v European Parliament and Council* [1997] E.C.R. I-2405, paras 22–29; ECJ, Case C-377/98 *Netherlands v European Parliament and Council* [2001] E.C.R. I-7079, para. 33; subsidiarity was considered summarily in ECJ, Case C-84/94 *United Kingdom v Council* [1996] E.C.R. I-5755, paras 80–81, with a case note by Van Nuffel (1997) Col.J.E.L. 298–309. For an exposition of this duty to provide a statement of reasons, see Lenaerts and van Ypersele (n. 27, *supra*), at 75–80, and Van Nuffel (n. 30, *supra*) at 412–424; for the duty to state grounds in general, see para. 22–065, *infra*. A call for more extensive judicial review is to be found in König and Lorz, "Stärkung des Subsidiaritätsprinzips" (2003) J.Z. 167–173. The Court of Justice has also used the principle of subsidiarity as an aid to interpretation; see ECJ, Case C-114/01 *AvestaPolarit Chrome Oy* [2003] E.C.R. I-8725, paras 56–57.

[141] See, *inter alia*, Arts 147 TFEU [*ex Art. 127*] (employment), Art. 165(1) TFEU [*ex Art. 149(1) EC*] (education); Art. 167(2) TFEU [*ex Art. 151(2) EC*] (culture) and Art. 168(2) TFEU [*ex Art. 152(1) EC*] (public health); paras 11–046—11–053, *infra*. See Lenaerts, "Subsidiarity and Community Competence in the Field of Education" (1994/95) Col.J.E.L. 1–28.

[142] See ECJ, Case C-11/95 *Commission v Belgium* [1996] E.C.R. I-4115, paras 51–53.

[143] ECJ, Case C-415/93 *Bosman* [1995] E.C.R. I-4921, para. 81.

IV. THE PRINCIPLE OF PROPORTIONALITY

A. ROLE PLAYED BY THE PRINCIPLE

Limit to the exercise of power. The principle of proportionality restricts the 7–033
authorities in the exercise of their powers by requiring a balance to be struck
between the means used and the intended aim (or result reached).[144] It is a general principle of law which affects the exercise of powers by Member States as
well as by the Union. In the case law, the principle of proportionality serves principally to assess the legality of an exercise of power where an admittedly legitimate aim is pursued, but at the same time other objectives deserving of protection
are damaged. The exercise of power in such a case will be regarded as lawful only
if it is appropriate to attain the intended aim and also indispensable in that alternative forms of exercise of power—which would inflict no or less damage on
other objectives worthy of protection—would not be capable of achieving the
intended aim. The principle is also applied in connection with the imposition of
sanctions (see para. 22–040, *infra*.).

Applications. Accordingly, it falls to the Court of Justice to adjudge whether 7–034
national measures which impede the free movement of goods, persons or services
or the freedom of establishment—central objectives of the internal market—can
be justified where they seek to attain objectives accepted by Union law. In this
connection, the Court of Justice will have regard in particular to whether the
national measures pursue their objectives in a proportional manner.[145] The
principle of proportionality is likewise in evidence in competition law when
the prohibition contained in Art. 101(1) TFEU [*ex Art. 81(1) EC*] is declared,
pursuant to Art. 101(3) of that Treaty, to be inapplicable to certain agreements
or concerted practices in so far as they impose only restrictions on competition
which are "indispensable" to the attainment of the objectives set out in

---

[144] For general discussions, see Tridimas, *The General Principles of EU Law* (Oxford, Oxford
University Press, 2007), Chs 3–5; Emiliou, *The Principle of Proportionality in European Law—A
Comparative Study* (London/The Hague, Kluwer, 1996), 288 pp; Bermann, "Proportionality
and Subsidiarity", in Barnard and Scott (eds), *The Law of the Single European Market*,
(Oxford/Portland, Hart, 2002), 75–100; Harbo, "The Function of the Proportionality Principle in
EU Law" (2010) E.L.J. 158–185; Jans, "Proportionality Revisited" (2000) L.I.E.I. 239–265;
Kischel, "Die Kontrolle der Verhältnismässigkeit durch den Europäischen Gerichtshof" (2000)
EuR. 380–402; de Búrca, "The Principle of Proportionality and its Application in EC Law"
(1993) Y.E.L. 105–150; Jans, "Evenredigheid: ja, maar waartussen?" (1992) S.E.W. 751–770;
Van Gerven, "Principe de proportionnalité, abus de droit et droits fondementaux" (1992) J.T.
305–309.
[145] Paras 9–036 and 9–044 (trade in goods), 9–065, 9–070 and 9–074 (movement of persons), 9–098
(freedom to supply services) and 9–106 (free movement of capital), *infra*.

Art. 101(3).[146] As far as the implementation of Union legislation is concerned, it follows from the principle of proportionality that whilst Member States may employ means which enable them effectively to attain the objectives pursued by their domestic laws, they must make sure that those means are the least detrimental to the objectives and principles laid down by the relevant Union legislation.[147]

In the same way, the Court tests the action of the Union against the principle of proportionality where the objective of the action conflicts with other Union objectives. It does so where the objectives of various Treaty articles[148] or aims defined within a given Treaty article[149] cannot be achieved concurrently. Some Treaty articles require the Union to take account of particular objectives irrespective of the field in which it is acting.[150] Since those Treaty articles do not provide for any ranking order of the various Union objectives, they certainly increase the importance of the principle of proportionality, which seeks to settle the conflict between them.

The principle of proportionality also guides the Court of Justice in resolving alleged conflicts between objectives of Union law and fundamental rights[151] or between procedural rights, for instance between providing confidential treatment for business secrets and the inter partes nature of court proceedings.[152]

---

[146] Article 101(3)(a) TFEU. See ECJ, Joined Cases 56 and 58/64 *Consten and Grundig v Commission* [1966] E.C.R. 299, at 347–350; ECJ, Case 258/78 *Nungesser v Commission* [1982] E.C.R. 2015, paras 76–78; CFI, Case T-66/89 *Publishers Association v Commission* [1992] E.C.R. II-1995, para. 98; CFI, Joined Cases T-39/92 and T-40/92 *CB and Europay v Commission* [1994] E.C.R. II-49, paras 111–114. With regard to the control of concentrations, see Schwarze, "Die Bedeutung des Grundsatzes der Verhältnismässigkeit bei der Behandlung von Verpflichtszusagen nach der europäischen Fusionskontrollverordnung" (2002) Eu.Z.W. 741–746.

[147] ECJ, Joined Cases C-286/94, C-340/95, C-401/95 and C-47/96 *Molenheide and Others* [1997] E.C.R. I-7281, paras 46–49.

[148] See, e.g., for a case in which the free movement of goods (Arts 28 to 30 [*now Arts 34 to 36 TFEU*]) had to be balanced against the aim of a directive adopted pursuant to Arts 37 and 94 [*now Arts 43 and 115 TFEU*] to protect agricultural products against harmful organisms, ECJ, Case 37/83 *Rewe-Zentrale* [1984] E.C.R. 1229, paras 18–20.

[149] See, for example, as regards the various objectives enumerated in Art. 39 TFEU [*ex Art. 33 EC*] (agricultural policy), ECJ, Case 5/73 *Balkan-Import-Export* [1973] E.C.R. 1091, para. 24; Case 29/77 *Roquette Frères* [1977] E.C.R. 1835, para. 30; ECJ, Case C-311/90 *Hierl* [1992] E.C.R. I-2061, para. 13; ECJ, Joined Cases C-133/93, C-300/93 and C-362/93 *Crispoltoni* [1994] E.C.R. I-4863, para. 32, and Case C-280/93 *Germany v Council* [1994] E.C.R. I-4973, paras 47–51.

[150] See para. 7–005, *supra*.

[151] For instance, the balancing of the right of property and effective enforcement of Union law obligations carried out by the Court of Justice in considering whether the sanction of forfeiture of security was proportional to the relevant infringement of agricultural law: ECJ, Case 181/84 *Man (Sugar)* [1985] E.C.R. 2889, paras 20–30; ECJ, Case C-199/90 *Italtrade* [1991] E.C.R. I-5545, paras 12–15; the balancing of the right of property and of freedom to pursue a trade or profession against a common organisation of the market: ECJ, Case 44/79 *Liselotte Hauer* [1979] E.C.R. 3727, para. 23; ECJ, Case 265/87 *Schräder* [1989] E.C.R. 2237, para. 15.

[152] See CFI (order of November 15, 1999), Joined Cases T-1/89 to T-4/89 and T-6/89 to T-15/89 *Rhône-Poulenc and Others v Commission* [1990] E.C.R. II-637, para. 22.

B. THE REQUIREMENTS OF PROPORTIONALITY

Requirements. As has already been mentioned, the principle of proportionality   7–035
requires action to be both "appropriate" to attain its objectives and not go beyond
what is necessary to achieve them ("indispensable").[153]

Appropriateness. Action is appropriate where it is capable of attaining the   7–036
intended objective. The Court of Justice leaves a measure of discretion to the
authority concerned and only considers whether it was not guilty of a manifest
error.[154] Accordingly, the Court does not replace the assessment of the authority
concerned by its own ex post facto assessment. Where it is asked to assess Union
legislation, it often considers that the area concerned involves political, economic
and social choices in which the Union legislator is called on to undertake complex assessments and where the Community legislature must thus be allowed a
broad discretion. Only if a measure adopted in this field is manifestly inappropriate in relation to the objective which the competent institutions are seeking to
pursue can the lawfulness of such a measure be affected.[155]

Indispensability. Action is indispensable where it cannot be replaced by   7–037
some alternative form of action which would have equal effectiveness (*effet utile*)
having regard to the intended aim and would be less detrimental to another aim or
interest protected by Union law. An appropriate measure may consequently not
entail needless adverse effects.[156] The Court of Justice respects the aim which the
authority seeks to achieve through its action and, as a rule, does not take account
of other measures which would not achieve it to a sufficient extent, even if such
measures would have no or less effect on a protected aim or interest. Consequently,
the Court generally does not weigh the detriment done to the aim or interest

---

[153] The second condition is also referred to as the requirement, when there is a choice between several appropriate measures, to have recourse to the least onerous (the "less restrictive alternative").
Sometimes, reference is made to a third condition, according to which "the disadvantages caused
must not be disproportionate to the aims pursued". On the (il)legitimacy of that third condition, see
para. 7–037, *infra*.

[154] ECJ, Case 40/72 *Schroeder v Germany* [1973] E.C.R. 125, para. 14. See also ECJ, Case 265/87
Schräder [1989] E.C.R. 2237, para. 22; ECJ, Joined Cases C-133/93, C-300/93 and C-362/93
Crispoltoni [1994] E.C.R. I-4863, paras 43–48, and Case C-280/93 *Germany v Council* [1994]
E.C.R. I-4973, paras 89–95.

[155] ECJ, Case C-84/94 *United Kingdom v Council* [1996] E.C.R. I-5755, para. 58; Case C-233/94
Germany v Parliament and Council [1997] E.C.R. I-2405, paras 55 and 56; Case C-157/96
National Farmers' Union and Others [1998] E.C.R. I-2211, para. 61; Case C-210/03 *Swedish
Match* [2004] E.C.R. I-11893, para. 48.

[156] See, e.g., ECJ, Joined Cases C-453/03, C-11/04, C-12/04 and C-194/04 *ABNA and Others* [2005]
E.C.R. I-10423, paras 76–88 (measures held to go further than necessary for the protection of public health to the detriment of economic interests of manufacturers). That condition is also referred
to as the requirement to opt for the "least onerous" or "less restrictive" alternative.

deserving of protection against the advantages of the action for the aim pursued, that is to say whether, on the whole, the disadvantages caused would be disproportionate to the aims pursued.[157] If it did so, the Court would be able to allow different aims to prevail over those which the authority concerned chose and so introduce its own hierarchy of legitimate aims.[158] There is only one area in which the Court takes the view that the aim chosen by the authority must yield to a higher objective. This is the field of fundamental rights, where the Court regards a measure as disproportionate to the intended aim if it impinges upon the "substance" of fundamental rights.[159]

C. APPLICATION OF THE PRINCIPLE OF PROPORTIONALITY

7–038 **Scope.** Article 5(4) TEU expresses the principle of proportionality as a limitation on action by the Union, the content and form of which "shall not exceed what is necessary to achieve the objectives of the Treaties". Accordingly, the Treaty makes clear that the principle of proportionality may restrict not only the substance but also the form of Union action. The first subpara. of Art. 5(3) TEU further specifies that principle with regard to the non-exclusive competence of the Union. Those two provisions constitute two expressions of the principle of proportionality, but, naturally, do not detract from the general application of the principle in Union law.

7–039 **Protecting national powers.** The first subpara. of Art. 5(3) TEU provides that the Union is to take action only "in so far as" the objectives of the proposed action cannot be sufficiently achieved by the Member States but can rather, by reason of the scale or effects of the proposed action, be better achieved at Union level. That provision embodies a specific application of the principle of proportionality with a view to protecting the residual powers of the Member States. Any Union action must be appropriate and indispensable to supplement the insufficient

---

[157] In the few cases in which the Court of Justice announced that it would assess whether the disadvantages were disproportionate to the aims pursued, it actually only tested whether the measures were appropriate and constantly confirmed the weighing of interests as conducted by the (Union or Member State) authority; see, e.g., ECJ, Case C-189/01 *Jippes and Others* [2001] E.C.R. I-5689, paras 80–100; ECJ (judgment of February 25, 2010), C-562/08 *Müller Fleisch*, not yet reported, paras 43–47; ECJ (judgment of June 8, 2010), Case C-58/08 *Vodafone and Others*, not yet reported, paras 53 and 69. See Van Nuffel (n. 30, *supra*), at 311–320.

[158] See, with regard to environment protection, Notaro, "The New Generation Case Law on Trade and Environment" (2000) E.L.Rev. 467, at 486–487.

[159] ECJ, Case 44/79 *Liselotte Hauer* [1979] E.C.R. 3727, paras 23 and 30; ECJ (judgment of March 9, 2010), Joined Cases C-379/08 and C-380/08 *Raffinerie Mediterranee (ERG) and Others*, not yet reported, paras 80 and 86 (para. 22–035, *infra*). For the problems raised by the overall balancing of interests, see Lenaerts and van Ypersele (n. 27, *supra*), at 56–60, and Van Nuffel (n. 30, *supra*), at 320–328.

capabilities of the Member States. Union action must first be "appropriate" to achieve the proposed objectives, which does not automatically follow from the fact that the Member States appear not to be capable. In addition, the action must be "indispensable" and therefore incapable of being replaced by measures which have less of an effect on the residual powers of the Member States. Where the Member States are in a position to achieve the contemplated objectives in part, the Union must encourage and support them and oblige them to do what they are capable of and, where necessary, take supplementary action where they fall short.

The original Protocol on the application of the principles of subsidiarity and proportionality contained detailed guidance in this regard. It stated that the principle required the form of Union action to be as simple as possible and preference to be given to directives over regulations and to framework directives over detailed measures.[160] It further provided that Union measures should leave as much scope for national decisions as possible and that well-established national arrangements and the organisation and working of Member States' legal systems should be respected. Lastly, it stated that, where appropriate and subject to the need for proper enforcement, Union measures should provide Member States with alternative ways to achieve the objectives of the measures.[161] The new protocol on the application of the principles of subsidiarity and proportionality no longer contains this concrete guidance. However, it requires draft legislative acts to contain an assessment of the proposal's financial impact and, in the case of a directive, of its implications for the rules to be put in place by Member States, including, where necessary, regional legislation.[162] Draft legislative acts should also take account of the need for any burden, whether financial or administrative, falling upon the Union, national governments, regional or local authorities, economic operators and citizens, to be minimised and commensurate with the objective to be achieved.[163]

Protecting legitimate interests. The first subpara. of Art. 5(4) TEU limits Union action to "what is necessary to achieve the objectives of the Treaties". However, action founded upon a legal basis afforded by the Treaties can hardly go beyond the objectives *of the Treaties* without at the same time exceeding the confines of the legal basis in question, which would mean that the action would be ultra vires. Rather, the principle of proportionality requires a given action not to go beyond what is necessary to achieve the objectives *of that action*.   **7–040**

---

[160] Protocol (No. 30), annexed to the EC Treaty, on the application of the principles of subsidiarity and proportionality, [1997] O.J. C340/105, point 6.

[161] *Ibid.*, point 7. For a case in which alternative ways of achieving the objectives of a particular measure (directive on working time) were weighed up, see ECJ, Case C-84/94 *United Kingdom v Council* [1996] E.C.R. I-5755, paras 50–66, with a case note by Van Nuffel (1997) Col.J.E.L. 298–309.

[162] Protocol on the application of the principles of subsidiarity and proportionality (n. 105, *supra*), Art. 5.

[163] *Ibid.*

In that sense, the principle, as it is expressed in Art. 5(4) TEU provides protection for Member States, regional and local authorities, trade and industry, and citizens against Union action involving obligations or burdens which are not proportionate to the proposed objective. Such legal subjects may plead infringement of Art. 5(4) TEU where the Union unreasonably affects their interests. In this respect, it must be remarked that Art. 4(2) TEU requires the Union to respect the "national identities [of the Member States], inherent in their fundamental structures, political and constitutional, inclusive of regional and local self-government" as well as,

> "their essential State functions, including those for ensuring the territorial integrity of the State, and for maintaining law and order and safeguarding national security".[164]

This clause does not prevent the Union from taking measures requiring the Member States to adapt their political and constitutional structures or the way in which they organise the essential functions of a State.[165] However, it certainly emphasises some elements of national sovereignty that the Union should not unnecessarily restrict.[166]

Even where the Union exercises exclusive powers, it must take account of Member States' potential to help to achieve the proposed objective. Although the actual principle of the exercise of Union powers in such a case does not have to be justified (the subsidiarity principle being inapplicable), Art. 5(4) TEU nevertheless imposes similar requirements in point of proportionality to Art. 5(3).

7–041 **Institutional implementation.** The institutions of the Union must apply the principle of proportionality in accordance with the Protocol on the application of the principles of subsidiarity and proportionality[167] (Art. 5(3), second subpara., TEU). Accordingly, each institution must ensure constant respect for the principle of proportionality.[168] Consequently, all draft legislative acts must be justified with regard to the principle of proportionality and, as mentioned above, contain a detailed statement making it possible to appraise compliance with the principle of proportionality.[169] The Commission is to report annually to the European

---

[164] Article 5(2) TEU, last sentence, adds that "In particular, national security remains the sole responsibility of each Member State".

[165] See, e.g. ECJ (judgment of March 9, 2010), Case C-518/07 *Commission v Germany* not yet reported, paras 52–55 (requirement for Member States to ensure that the national supervisory authority with regard to the processing of personal data is free from State scrutiny does not go further than necessary to achieve the objective of independence imposed by the Union legislation).

[166] Compare the equivalent protection of the Member States' "national identity" in Art. 6(3) EU, which, however, could not be enforced by the Court of Justice (para. 13–084, *infra*). See Van Nuffel (n. 30, *supra*), at 271 et seq.

[167] Protocol on the application of the principles of subsidiarity and proportionality (n. 105, *supra*).

[168] *Ibid.*, Art. 1.

[169] *Ibid.*, Art. 5.

Council, the European Parliament, the Council and the national parliaments on the application of Art. 5 TEU.[170] However, the Protocol does not set up any mechanism for the scrutiny by national parliaments of compliance with the principle of proportionality.

In its reports to the European Council on adjustment of existing legislation in the light of the principle of subsidiarity, the Commission has pointed to a number of proposals for legislation which, for reasons of proportionality, should be withdrawn or revised, and listed existing legislation which could be revised, simplified or repealed.[171] The intention to simplify legislation indicates how subsidiarity and proportionality fit into the process designed to make Union legislation more transparent (see para. 20–007 *et seq.*).

V. THE PRINCIPLE OF SINCERE COOPERATION

A. ROLE PLAYED BY THE PRINCIPLE

Definition. Pursuant to the principle of sincere cooperation, the Union and the   **7–042** Member States shall, in full mutual respect, assist each other in carrying out tasks which flow from the Treaties (Art. 4(3), first subpara., TEU [*ex Art. 10 EC*]).[172] Article 4(3) TEU requires Member States to,

> "take any appropriate measure, general or particular, to ensure fulfilment of the obligations arising out of the Treaties or resulting from the acts of the institutions of the Union"

and to "facilitate the achievement of the Union's tasks" (second and third subparas) and, at the same time, to "refrain from any measure which could jeopardise the attainment of the Union's objectives" (third subpara.). Accordingly, the principle of sincere cooperation (sometimes referred to as the duty of loyal cooperation or the duty to cooperate in good faith) is formulated in terms of a positive and a negative obligation, to which the Member States are subject in their dealings with the Union and as between themselves. Since the principle of sincere cooperation is an expression of Union solidarity,[173] it is not the same as the principle of international law that States are required to implement in good faith the treaties which they

---

[170] *Ibid.*, Art. 9, which further provides that this report will be forwarded to the European Economic and Social Committee and the Committee of the Regions.

[171] Para. 7–030, *supra.*

[172] See also Art. 192 EAEC.

[173] See ECJ, Joined Cases 6 and 11/69 *Commission v France* [1969] E.C.R. 523, para. 16.

conclude.[174] The principle of sincere cooperation is a reflection of the principle of "federal good faith" which is designed to secure mutual respect of the powers of the legislative, executive and judicial bodies of different levels of authority within a federal system and readiness to cooperate.[175] Article 4(3) TEU is binding on "all the authorities of Member States",[176] including, for matters within their jurisdiction, the courts[177] and decentralised authorities.[178]

Article 4(3) TEU does not have direct effect in itself, but it can be used as an additional argument where the Member State in question is alleged to have breached an unconditional and sufficiently precise obligation.[179] In such a case, the national court, as an institution of its Member State, has to refrain from applying the provisions of domestic law which prevent Union law from having its full effect (see para. 7–048).

7–043   **Scope.** Since it is chiefly the national authorities which have to implement Union law, most of the decided cases concerning the principle of sincere cooperation are concerned with the application of the principle to the Member States.

---

[174] See Constantinesco, "L'article 5 CEE, de la bonne foi à la loyauté communautaire", in Capotorti, Ehlermann, Frowein, Jacobs, Joliet, Koopmans and Kovar (eds), *Du droit international au droit de l'intégration. Liber amicorum P. Pescatore* (Baden-Baden, Nomos, 1987), at 97–114. For a general discussion, see Hatje, *Loyalität als Rechtsprinzip in der Europäischen Union* (Baden-Baden, Nomos, 2001), 118 pp.; Temple Lang "Article 10 EC—The most important 'general principle' of Community law" and Gormley, "Some Further Reflections on the Development of General Principles of Law within Article 10 EC", both in Bernitz, Nergelius and Cardner (eds), *General Principles of EC Law in a Process of Development* (The Hague, Kluwer Law International, 2008), 75–113 and 303–314, respectively; Temple Lang, "Developments, issues and new remedies—the duties of national authorities and courts under Article 10 of the EC Treaty" (2004) Fordham I.L.J. 1904–1939; Blanquet, *L'article 5 du traité CEE. Recherche sur les obligations de fidélité des Etats membres de la Communauté* (Paris, Librairie Générale de Droit et de Jurisprudence, 1994), 502 pp.

[175] Van Gerven with the collaboration of Gilliams, "Gemeenschapstrouw: goede trouw in E.G.-verband" (1989–90) R.W. 1158, at 1159. However, the Union principle does not alter the division of powers between the Union and the Member States. See Due, "Artikel 5 van het EEG-Verdrag. Een bepaling met een federaal karakter?" (1992) S.E.W. 355, at 366. For examples from Belgium, see Verhoeven, "The application in Belgium of the duties of loyalty and co-operation" (2000) S.E.W. 328–340.

[176] See, with respect to *ex Art. 10 EC*, ECJ, Case 80/86 *Kolpinghuis Nijmegen* [1987] E.C.R. 3969, para. 12.

[177] *Ibid.* See also the earlier case ECJ, Case 14/83 *Von Colson and Kamann* [1984] E.C.R. 1891, para. 26. For Art. 86 ECSC, see ECJ, Case C-341/94 *Allain* [1996] E.C.R. I-4631, para. 25.

[178] For municipal by-laws, see ECJ, Case 85/85 *Commission v Belgium* [1986] E.C.R. 1149, paras 22–23.

[179] See ECJ, Case 9/73 *Schlüter* [1973] E.C.R. 1135, para. 39, and ECJ, Case 10/73 *Rewe Zentral* [1973] E.C.R. 1175, para. 26; ECJ, Case 44/84 *Hurd* [1986] E.C.R. 29, paras 47–48; ECJ, Joined Cases C-72 and C-73/91 *Sloman Neptun* [1993] E.C.R. I-887, para. 28. *Cf.* Dauses, "Quelques réflexions sur la signification et la portée de l'article 5 du traité CEE", in Bieber and Ress (eds), *Die Dynamik des Europäischen Gemeinschaftsrechts/The Dynamics of EC-Law* (Baden-Baden, Nomos, 1987) 229, at 233–235.

Nevertheless, increasing activity on the part of the Union has made it clear that the Union institutions are also subject to the principle of sincere cooperation in their relations both with Member States and with each other.[180] Since the Lisbon Treaty, the Treaties explicitly provide that "[t]he institutions shall practice mutual sincere cooperation" (Art. 13(2) TEU). However, the adoption of a legislative measure by the Council cannot constitute a breach of the principle of sincere cooperation attaching to either the Council or the Member States, which defend their interests in that institution.[181]

B. THE REQUIREMENTS OF THE PRINCIPLE OF SINCERE COOPERATION

Twofold duty. The substance of the principle of sincere cooperation "depends in each individual case on the provisions of the Treaty or on the rules derived from its general scheme".[182] Where a provision of Union law contains a specific obligation for Member States, a finding that there has been a failure to fulfil the obligation in question may unquestionably be made.[183] Where, in contrast, there is no such obligation, a Member State's conduct may nonetheless constitute a breach of the principle of sincere cooperation. This is because the Court of Justice has gradually broadened its interpretation of the "obligations arising out of the Treaties or resulting from the acts of the institutions of the Union" and of the requirement not to "jeopardise the attainment of the Union's objectives" (Art. 4(3) TEU, also laid down in *ex Art. 10 EC*). The upshot is (1) ancillary obligations with which the Member States and the institutions must comply in implementing a specific provision of Union law or even independently of such implementation ("supplementary requirements" of the principle of sincere cooperation)[184] and (2) a prohibition on Member States or institutions to act where acting would constitute a misuse of powers ("derogatory requirements" of the principle of sincere cooperation).[185]

7–044

---

[180] ECJ, Case 230/81 *Luxembourg v European Parliament* [1983] E.C.R. 255, para. 37. See, inter alia, ECJ, Case 44/84 *Hurd* [1986] E.C.R. 29, para. 38, and ECJ, Case 52/84 *Commission v Belgium* [1986] E.C.R. 89, para. 16; ECJ, Case C-65/93 *European Parliament v Council* [1995] E.C.R. I-643, para. 23; ECJ, Case C-319/97 *Kortas* [1999] E.C.R. I-3143, para. 35; ECJ, Case C-29/99 *Commission v Council* [2002] E.C.R. I-11221, para. 69. See also Declaration (No. 3), annexed to the Treaty of Nice, on Art. 10 of the EC Treaty, [2001] O.J. C80/77.

[181] ECJ, Joined Cases C-63/90 and C-67/90 *Portugal and Spain v Council* [1992] E.C.R. I-5073, para. 53.

[182] ECJ, Case 78/70 *Deutsche Grammophon* [1971] E.C.R. 487, para. 5.

[183] See, for example, ECJ, Case C-48/89 *Commission v Italy* [1990] E.C.R. I-2425.

[184] Failure to comply with an undertaking to remedy an infringement of the Treaty itself constitutes a breach of the principle: ECJ, Case C-374/89 *Commission v Belgium* [1991] E.C.R. I-367, paras 12–15.

[185] *Cf.* Van Gerven with the collaboration of Gilliams (n. 175, *supra*), at 1160–1162.

1. Supplementary requirements

7–045   **Duty of care.** In the first place, Art. 4(3), second subpara., TEU puts the Member States under a duty to take all measures necessary to implement provisions of Union law (see para. 17–002 *et seq.*). In so doing, they have to lay down the necessary sanctions in so far as the actual Union provisions themselves do not provide for any.[186] In addition, the Member States are under a general duty of care in implementing Union law. They have to take all appropriate measures to guarantee the full scope and effect of Union law. They must also deal with any irregularities as quickly as possible.[187] The conduct of other Member States or apprehension of internal difficulties cannot justify a failure to apply Union law correctly.[188] Where the implementation of Union law raises special difficulties, the Member States should submit them to the Commission and work together with it in good faith with a view to overcoming the difficulties.[189] Where Member States wish to derogate from a harmonisation measure pursuant to Art. 114(4) and (5) TFEU [*ex Art. 95(4) and (5) EC*], the principle of sincere cooperation puts them under a duty to notify the derogating measures as soon as possible.[190] They are under a duty to facilitate the Commission's supervisory task and therefore have to provide it with all such information as it might request to that end.[191] In implementing the competition rules, the national courts and the Commission must collaborate with each other with a view to overcoming the problems arising

---

[186] For sanctions, see para. 17–005, *infra*.

[187] ECJ, Case C-34/89 *Italy v Commission* [1990] E.C.R. I-3603, para. 12; ECJ, Case C-28/89 *Germany v Commission* [1991] E.C.R. I-581, para. 31; ECJ, Case C-277/98 *France v Commission* [2001] E.C.R. I-8453, para. 40.

[188] ECJ, Case C-265/95 *Commission v France* [1997] E.C.R. I-6959, paras 55 and 63.

[189] ECJ, Case 52/84 *Commission v Belgium* [1986] E.C.R. 89, para. 16, at 105; ECJ, Case 94/87 *Commission v Germany* [1989] E.C.R. 175, para. 9, at 192; ECJ, Case C-217/88 *Commission v Germany* [1990] E.C.R. I-2879, para. 33. ECJ, Case C-75/97 *Commission v Belgium* [1999] E.C.R. I-3671, para. 88; ECJ, Case C-404/97 *Commission v Portugal* [2000] E.C.R. I-4897, para. 40; ECJ, Case C-261/99 *Commission v France* [2001] E.C.R. I-2537, para. 24; ECJ, Case 378/98 *Commission v Belgium* [2001] E.C.R. I-5107, para. 31; ECJ, Case C-499/99 *Commission v Spain* [2002] E.C.R. I-6031, para. 24. Where a Member State notifies difficulties in transposing a directive, no obligation can be inferred from Art. 4(3) TEU for the Commission to submit a proposal to amend the directive or to delay bringing an action for failure to fulfil obligations: ECJ, Case C-239/99 *Commission v Belgium* [2000] E.C.R. I-5657, paras 25–29.

[190] ECJ, Case C-319/97 *Kortas* [1999] E.C.R. I-3143, para. 35. For the correlative obligation on the Commission, see para. 5–053.

[191] ECJ, Case 96/81 *Commission v Netherlands* [1982] E.C.R. 1791, para. 7; ECJ, Case 240/86 *Commission v Greece* [1988] E.C.R. 1835, paras 25–28; ECJ, Case 272/86 *Commission v Greece* [1988] E.C.R. 4875, paras 30–32. See also ECJ, Case C-69/90 *Commission v Italy* [1991] E.C.R. I-6011, paras 11–15 (where a directive requires Member States to inform the Commission of implementing provisions adopted, a Member State must also notify the Commission of existing national provisions which allegedly already ensure full application of the directive in question).

and cooperate in the implementation of the investigation decision ordered by the Commission.[192]

In accordance with the principle of sincere cooperation, the national courts are entrusted with securing the legal protection which citizens derive from the direct effect of provisions of Union law.[193] The courts must also ensure that provisions of Union law not endowed with direct effect are given *effet utile*, since they must refrain from applying conflicting national provisions (see para. 7–048). Member States must make sure that procedural conditions applicable to claims seeking to assert rights derived from Union law are not less favourable than those relating to similar domestic claims (*principle of equivalence*) and are not such as in practice to make it impossible or excessively difficult to enforce those rights (*principle of effectiveness*).[194] As far as Member States' implementation of the legal instruments referred to in Art. 288 TFEU [*ex Art. 249 EC*] is concerned, Art. 4(3) TEU constitutes an additional ground for the duty of Member States to repeal national provisions incompatible with a Union regulation[195] and for the direct effect of non-implemented directives which are unconditional and sufficiently precise.[196] In particular, Art. 4(3) puts all national authorities, including the courts, under a duty to interpret national law in the light of the wording and purpose of Union directives.[197] More generally, the national courts must, as far as is at all possible, interpret national law in a way which accords with the requirements of Union law.[198]

The principle of sincere cooperation obliges all national authorities to remedy any unlawful consequences of an infringement of Union law (see para. 21–014). Although the principle of legal certainty precludes an administrative authority from going back on a decision which has become final when it subsequently becomes clear that it is based on a wrong interpretation of Union law, an administrative body which has the power to revise a decision which has become definitive may be obliged in certain circumstances to review that decision pursuant to the principle of sincere cooperation.[199] Where individuals suffer loss or damage

---

[192] ECJ, Case C-94/00 *Roquette Frères* [2002] E.C.R. I-9011, paras 91–94 (the competent national court must obtain the necessary information from the Commission or the national competition authority which the Commission must procure as rapidly as possible).

[193] ECJ, Case 33/76 *Rewe* [1976] E.C.R. 1989, para. 5, and ECJ, Case 45/76 *Comet* [1976] E.C.R. 2043, para. 12.

[194] *Rewe* (cited in preceding n.), para. 5; *Comet* (cited in the preceding n.), paras 13–16; ECJ, Case C-234/04 *Kapferer* [2006] E.C.R. I-2585, para. 22. See also para. 21–012, *infra*.

[195] ECJ, Case 74/86 *Commission v Germany* [1988] E.C.R. 2139, paras 10–12.

[196] See ECJ, Case 190/87 *Oberkreisdirektor des Kreises Borken and Others* [1988] E.C.R. 4689, paras 22–24.

[197] See ECJ, Case 14/83 *Von Colson and Kamann* [1984] E.C.R. 1891, para. 26; ECJ, Case C-106/89 *Marleasing* [1990] E.C.R. I-4135, para. 8 (interpretation of national law in the light of the wording and purpose of the directive, para. 22–087, *infra*).

[198] ECJ, Case C-262/97 *Engelbrecht* [2000] E.C.R. I-7321, para. 39 (see para. 21–007); ECJ Case C-115/08 *ČEZ* [2009] E.C.R. I-10265 (on Art. 192 EAEC).

[199] ECJ, Case C-453/00 *Kühne & Heitz* [2004] E.C.R. I-837, paras 20 to 28. For a critical comment, see Jans and de Graaf, "Bevoegdheid = verplichting?" (2004) N.T.E.R. 98–102.

as a result of breaches of Union law for which the State can be held responsible, it is inherent in the "system of the Treaties" and Art. 4(3) TEU that the Member State in question must allow a claim to be made against the public authorities.[200]

As regards legal protection against Union acts, the Member States are under a duty, together with the Union Courts, to establish a system of legal remedies and procedures which ensure respect for the right to effective judicial protection. In that context, in accordance with the principle of sincere cooperation, national courts are required, so far as possible, to interpret and apply national procedural rules governing the exercise of rights of action in a way that enables natural and legal persons to challenge before the courts the legality of any decision or other national measure relative to the application to them of a Union act of general application—which they cannot contest under Art. 263 TFEU [*ex Art. 230 EC*]—, by pleading the invalidity of such an act.[201]

7–046 **Duty to cooperate.** Article 4(3) TEU puts each Member State and the Commission under a duty of sincere cooperation with institutions of other Member States responsible for implementing Union law.[202] As a result of the obligation mutually to facilitate the implementation of Union law, Member States must recognise the equivalence of each other's product tests, diplomas and evidence of professional qualifications in the context of the free movement of goods, persons and services.[203]

Where the Union is empowered to conduct a particular policy but does not succeed in doing so on account of differences of opinion within the Council, the principle of sincere cooperation requires the Member States to take the necessary conservation measures, which they must notify to the Commission for its approval.[204] Such measures must also be notified to the other Member States.[205]

---

[200] ECJ, Joined Cases C-6/90 and C-9/90 *Francovich and Others* [1991] E.C.R. I-5357, paras 33–36; see also para. 21–014, *infra*.

[201] ECJ, Case C-50/00 P *Unión de Pequeños Agricultores v Council and Commission* [2002] E.C.R. I-6677, para. 42.

[202] ECJ, Case C-251/89 *Athanasopoulos and Others* [1991] E.C.R. I-2797, para. 57; ECJ, Case C-165/91 *Van Munster* [1994] E.C.R. I-4661, para. 32 (see para. 9–083, *infra*); ECJ, Case C-202/97 *Fitzwilliam Executive Search* [2000] E.C.R. I-883, paras 51–59; ECJ, Case C-178/97 *Banks and Others* [2000] E.C.R. I-2005, paras 38–45. Where a bilateral agreement between Member States is liable to impede the application of a provision of Union law, the Member States concerned are under a duty to assist each other in order to facilitate the application of the relevant provision: ECJ, Case 235/87 *Matteucci* [1988] E.C.R. 5589, paras 17–19.

[203] See with regard to the free movement of goods: ECJ, Case 25/88 *Wurmser and Others* [1989] E.C.R. 1105, para. 18 (para. 9–036, *infra*); with regard to the free movement of persons: ECJ, Case 71/76 *Thieffry* [1977] E.C.R. 765, paras 15–19; ECJ, Case C-340/89 *Vlassopoulou* [1991] E.C.R. I-2357, para. 14 (self-employed persons), and ECJ, Case 222/86 *Unectef v Heylens* [1987] E.C.R. 4097, para. 12 (workers) (para. 9–065, *infra*). For similar rulings concerning free movement of services, see para. 9–098, *infra*.

[204] See with regard to the conservation of fish stocks ECJ, Case 32/79 *Commission v United Kingdom* [1980] E.C.R. 2403, paras 10–15 and para. 25; ECJ, Case 804/79 *Commission v United Kingdom* [1981] E.C.R. 1045, para. 30 (para. 7–022, *supra*).

[205] ECJ, Case 141/78 *France v United Kingdom* [1979] E.C.R. 2923, paras 8–12.

They may only be temporary and provisional and must be abrogated as soon as Union measures are adopted.[206] The Member States are subject to obligations to cooperate in particular in the situation where the Commission has already submitted proposals to the Council.[207] In such case, the Member States, as "trustees of the common interest", may act only as part of the process of collaboration with the Commission (positive obligation) and may certainly not take any measures in spite of objections, reservations or conditions which might have been formulated by the Commission (negative obligation).[208]

The duty to cooperate further puts Member States under an obligation to consult the Union institutions where they propose adopting measures affecting the Staff Regulations of Union officials.[209]

Duties for institutions. Pursuant to the principle of sincere cooperation, the **7–047** Commission, for its part, has to display the necessary diligence where a Member State notifies the wish to derogate from a harmonisation measure under Art. 114(4) and (5) TFEU.[210] The institutions are also under a duty to collaborate with the Member States' judicial authorities. As far as the Court of Justice is concerned, that collaboration takes the form of the preliminary ruling procedure provided for in Art. 267 TFEU [*ex Art. 234 EC*]. Furthermore, every Union institution—especially the Commission in view of its duty of ensuring that Union law is applied—must give its active assistance to a national court conducting a preliminary judicial inquiry into breaches of a provision of Union law which makes a request for information concerning potential evidence of such breaches.[211] The duty to cooperate may also oblige institutions to take into account principles laid down in Union legislation, even where it is, strictly speaking, only applicable to the Member States and not to the institutions.[212]

In principle, the same mutual duties of sincere cooperation apply between the institutions as govern relations between the institutions and the Member States.[213] That is true in particular of decision-making procedures based on

---

[206] ECJ, Joined Cases 47–48/83 *Pluimveeslachterij Midden-Nederland and Van Miert* [1984] E.C.R. 1721, para. 23; ECJ, Case C-158/89 *Dietz-Matti* [1990] E.C.R. I-2013, para. 13.

[207] ECJ, Case 804/79 *Commission v United Kingdom* [1981] E.C.R. 1045, para. 28; ECJ, Case C-266/03 *Commission v Luxembourg* [2005] E.C.R. I-4805, paras 57–60; ECJ, Case C-433/03 *Commission v Germany* [2005] E.C.R. I-6985, paras 63–66. See also ECJ (judgment of April 20, 2010), Case C-246/07 *Commission v Sweden*, not yet reported, paras 71–75.

[208] *Ibid.*, paras 30–31. See also ECJ, Case 325/85 *Ireland v Commission* [1987] E.C.R. 5041, paras 15–16.

[209] ECJ, Case 186/85 *Commission v Belgium* [1987] E.C.R. 2029, para. 39.

[210] ECJ, Case C-319/97 *Kortas* [1999] E.C.R. I-3143, paras 35–36.

[211] ECJ, Case C-2/88 Imm. *Zwartveld and Others* [1990] E.C.R. I-3365, paras 17–22; ECJ, Case C-234/89 *Delimitis* [1991] E.C.R. I-935, para. 53. The Commission may refuse to provide information in order to avoid any interference with the functioning and independence of the Union or to safeguard its interests; see ECJ, Case C-275/00 *Frist and Franex* [2002] E.C.R. I-10943, para. 49.

[212] CST (judgment of April 30, 2009), Case F-65/07 *Aayhan and Others v European Parliament*, not yet reported.

[213] ECJ, Case 204/86 *Greece v Council* [1988] E.C.R. 5323, para. 16.

interinstitutional dialogue.[214] Where the Council is under a duty to consult the European Parliament, it should avail itself of all the openings afforded by the Treaties and the Parliament's Rules of Procedure in order to obtain the Parliament's prior opinion. In turn, the Parliament should comply with a justified request from the Council to deal with a particular proposal urgently (see para. 16–035). If the Parliament fails to do so, the Council is entitled to adopt the relevant act without awaiting the Parliament's opinion.[215] The Court of Justice has held that in such a case the

> "essential procedural requirement of Parliamentary consultation was not complied with because of the Parliament's failure to discharge its obligation to cooperate sincerely with the Council".[216]

Another example of an application of the principle of sincere cooperation is the obligation for the Council to ensure in approving an international agreement that such approval enables the other institutions and the Member States to comply with international law (see para. 25–059).

2. Derogatory requirements

7–048   **Respect for Union interest.** As has already been mentioned, Art. 4(3) TEU prohibits any measure which could jeopardise the attainment of the objectives of the Union. Accordingly, under that provision, Member States are precluded from reinforcing agreements in restraint of competition concluded by undertakings contrary to Art. 101 TFEU.[217] More generally, Member States must allow measures preventing Union rules from having full force and effect (*effet utile*) to be set aside. A national court which has to apply Union law must therefore have jurisdiction to do everything necessary to set aside provisions of (even constitutional) law which might prevent Union rules from having full effect.[218]

---

[214] ECJ, Case C-65/93 *European Parliament v Council* [1995] E.C.R. I-643, para. 23, with case notes by Heukels (1995) C.M.L.Rev. 1407–1426 and Van Nuffel (1995) Col.J.E.L. 504, at 511–515.

[215] *Ibid.*, para. 28.

[216] *Ibid.*

[217] See the judgments cited in the discussion of competition in para. 11–010, *infra*. However, such a requirement exists only where there is already a clear Union policy: ECJ, Case 229/83 *Leclerc* [1985] E.C.R. 1, para. 20.

[218] ECJ, Case C-213/89 *Factortame and Others* ("*Factortame I*") [1990] E.C.R. I-2433, para. 20 (setting aside the rule of the British Constitution to the effect that a court may not give interim relief against the Crown especially in the form of an order setting aside the application of an act of Parliament). See also the earlier case ECJ, Case 106/77 *Simmenthal* [1978] E.C.R. 629, para. 22, containing no express reference to Art. 5 EEC [*later Art. 10 EC*] (the national court has to refuse to apply any conflicting provision of national law of its own motion and does not have to await a ruling of its national Constitutional Court as required by its national legal system on the constitutionality of the domestic provision). See also the discussion of the primacy of Union law, paras 17–007—17–011. There is no obligation, however, to disapply a national provision where the issue before the national court

Article 4(3) TEU puts Member States under a duty to respect the division of competences between the Union and the Member States. Where a Union measure is adopted, conflicting national measures must be set aside pursuant to the principle of the primacy of Union law. The extent to which Member States' action is restricted depends on the scope of the Union measure (see para. 21–006). Member States must not exercise their powers (in particular in the field of international relations) in such a way as to affect the Union measure or alter its scope.[219] During the period for transposition of a directive, Member States must refrain from adopting measures which would jeopardise the achievement of what is provided for in the directive.[220] In situations in which Member States take action because the Union has failed to act, the principle of sincere cooperation requires them to refrain from adopting measures which do not have regard to the common interest. This applies to any action of Member States in areas which do not fall within the exclusive competence of the Union. The same is true *a fortiori* where Member States take action exceptionally in areas which do fall within the exclusive competence of the Union, e.g. during a transitional period[221] or where temporary conservation measures are necessary.[222]

Respect for institutional balance. Lastly, the principle of sincere cooperation 7–049 requires Member States to refrain from taking measures which might jeopardise the independence of the Union institutions and hence the institutional balance.[223] A Member State must avoid taking any measure which would result in officials and other servants of the Union directly or indirectly losing the benefit of the privileges and immunities to which they are entitled under the relevant Protocol.[224] Member States are also not entitled to adopt any measures which would result in a charge on the Union budget.[225]

---

concerns a situation which lies outside the scope of Union law: ECJ, Case C-264/96 *ICI* [1998] E.C.R. I-4695, paras 31–35.

[219] ECJ, Case 22/70 *Commission v Council* [1971] E.C.R. 263, para. 22 (AETR case); ECJ, Opinion 1/03 *New Lugano Convention on jurisdiction and the recognition and enforcement of judgments in civil and commercial matters* [2006] E.C.R. I-1145, para. 116. See also para. 25–058, *infra*, regarding limitations on the international action of the Member States.

[220] Para. 22–078, *infra*; for a general discussion of standstill obligations, see Meyring, "Europarechtliche Stillhalteverpflichtungen bei der nationalen Gesetzgebung" (2003) EuR. 949–959.

[221] See the fisheries policy during the transitional period provided for in Art. 102 of the 1972 Act of Accession: ECJ, Joined Cases 3, 4 and 6/76 *Kramer* [1976] E.C.R. 1279, paras 40–45; ECJ, Case 61/77 *Commission v Ireland* [1978] E.C.R. 417, paras 63–67. See also the judgments discussed above (see n. 204, *supra*): ECJ, Case 32/79 *Commission v United Kingdom* [1980] E.C.R. 2403, paras 10–15; ECJ, Case 141/78 *France v United Kingdom* [1979] E.C.R. 2923, paras 7–9.

[222] See the judgment on fisheries after the expiry of the transitional period: ECJ, Case 804/79 *Commission v United Kingdom* [1981] E.C.R. 1045, para. 30 (see ns. 204 and 207, *supra*, together with the discussion of powers in para. 7–022, *supra*).

[223] ECJ, Case 208/80 *Lord Bruce of Donington* [1981] E.C.R. 2205; ECJ, Case 230/81 *Luxembourg v European Parliament* [1983] E.C.R. 255. See also ECJ, Case C-345/95 *France v European Parliament* [1997] E.C.R. I-5215.

[224] ECJ, Case 85/85 *Commission v Belgium* [1986] E.C.R. 1149, paras 22–23.

[225] See the judgments concerning the European Schools, para. 13–125, *infra*.

VI. THE PRINCIPLE OF EQUAL TREATMENT

A. FIELD OF APPLICATION

7–050 **General principle of law.** The principle of equal treatment requires persons in the same situation to be treated in the same way. In other words, it requires that comparable situations must not be treated differently and that different situations must not be treated in the same way unless such treatment is objectively justified (prohibition of discrimination). It is a general principle of Union law,[226] which is enshrined in the Charter of Fundamental Rights of the European Union.[227] Moreover, it is one of the "values" on which the Union is founded (Art. 2 TEU, added by the Treaty of Lisbon). Among the Union's objectives, the fight against discrimination and the promotion of equality between women and men have a prominent place (Art. 3(3) TEU [*ex Art. 3(2) EC*]; see also Art. 157 TFEU [*ex Art. 141 EC*]). The principle of equal treatment further finds expression in the Treaties in the form of the general prohibition of discrimination on grounds of nationality (Art. 18 TFEU [*ex Art. 12 EC*]) and in the obligation incumbent on the Union to respect "the equality of Member States before the Treaties"[228] (Art. 4(2) TEU, introduced by the Treaty of Lisbon). Although the EAEC Treaty does not contain any explicit provision which corresponds to Art. 18 TFEU, the prohibition of discrimination on grounds of nationality is a general principle which is also applicable under the EAEC Treaty to situations coming within the scope of application of that Treaty.[229]

A number of Treaty provisions refer to the obligation to treat market participants in the same way.[230] For instance, the second subpara. of Art. 40(2) TFEU [*ex Art. 34(2) EC*] provides that the common organisation of the agricultural markets shall "exclude any discrimination between producers or consumers within the Union". The Court of Justice has declared that

---

[226] For a general discussion, see Tridimas, *The general principles of EU law* (Oxford, Oxford University Press, 2007), Ch. 2; Ellis, EU Anti-Discrimination Law (Oxford, Oxford University Press, 2005), 401 pp.; Lenaerts and Arts, "La personne et le principe de l'égalité en droit communautaire et dans la Convention européenne de sauvegarde des droits de l'homme et des libertés fondamentales" in *La personne humaine, sujet de droit* (Paris, Presses Universitaires de France, 1994), 101–134; Bell and Waddington, "Reflecting on equalities in European equality law" (2003) 28 E.L.Rev. 349–369; Demaret, "L'égalité de traitement" (1994) A.D. 165–208; Lenaerts, "L'égalité de traitement en droit communautaire: un principe unique aux apparences multiples" (1991) C.D.E. 3–41.

[227] Chapter III of the Charter, which deals with equality before the law (Art. 20), non-discrimination (Art. 21), cultural, religious and linguistic diversity (Art. 22), equality between men and women (Art. 23), the rights of the child (Art. 24), the rights of the elderly (Art. 25) and integration of persons with disabilities (Art. 26).

[228] See Lenaerts and Van Nuffel, "Advanced Integration and the Principle of Equality of Member States within the European Union", in Kaddous and Auer (eds), *Les principes fondamentaux de la Constitution européenne* (Helbing & Lichtenhahn/Bruylant/L.G.D.J., 2006), 245–276.

[229] ECJ, Case C-115/08 ČEZ (n. 198, *supra*), paras 87–98.

[230] See Art. 40(2), second subpara.; Art. 101(1)(d); Art. 102, second para., indent (c) TFEU.

"the prohibition of discrimination laid down in the aforesaid provision is merely a specific enunciation of the general principle of equality which is one of the fundamental principles of [Union] law [and] requires that similar situations shall not be treated differently unless differentiation is objectively justified."[231]

Scope. Within the scope of application of Union law, the principle of equal treatment is binding not only on Member States and individuals, but also on the institutions, which may not adopt any criteria in breach of that principle. The Court of Justice declared Art.73(2) of Reg. No. 1408/71 invalid because, for the purpose of determining the amount of family benefits for migrant workers with family members living in another Member State, it made a distinction between workers who were subject to French legislation and workers subject to the legislation of another Member State. Consequently, that provision was "not of such a nature as to secure the equal treatment laid down by Article 48 EEC [*now Art. 45 TFEU*]."[232] The Union institutions are to respect the principle of equal treatment not only in their legislative activity,[233] but also where they conclude international agreements[234] or where they implement Union legislation themselves, for example in the treatment of their own staff.[235] Furthermore, all Union acts must be interpreted in accordance with the principle of equal treatment.[236]

7–051

---

[231] ECJ, Joined Cases 117/76 and 16/77 *Ruckdeschel* [1977] E.C.R. 1753, para. 7. Where a common organisation of the market covers economic operators who are neither producers nor consumers, the prohibition of discrimination also applies to all other categories of operators subject to the common organisation: ECJ, Case C-280/93 *Germany v Council* [1994] E.C.R. I-4973, para. 68.

[232] ECJ, Case 41/84 *Pinna* [1986] E.C.R. 1, paras 22–25; for another provision of Regulation No. 1408/71 which was declared to be in breach of the principle of equal treatment enshrined in Art. 39 EC [*now Art. 45 TFEU*], see ECJ, Case 20/85 *Roviello* [1988] E.C.R. 2805, paras 14–18. For Regulation No 1408/71, see para. 9–082, *infra*.

[233] E.g. ECJ, Case 20/71 *Sabbatini v European Parliament* [1972] E.C.R. 345, para. 13.; ECJ, Case C-25/02 *Rinke* [2003] E.C.R. I-8349 paras 25–28 (prohibition of indirect discrimination on grounds of sex); ECJ, Case C-210/03 *Swedish Match* [2004] E.C.R. I-11893, paras 70–71 (different treatment of different tobacco products); ECJ, Case C-344/04 *IATA and ELFAA* [2006] E.C.R. I-403, paras 93–99 (different treatment of different means of transport); ECJ, Case C-127/07 *Arcelor Atlantique et Lorraine and Others* [2008] E.C.R. I-9895 (different treatment of different sectors of industry with regard to greenhouse gas emissions).

[234] ECJ, Case C-122/95 *Germany v Council* [1998] E.C.R. I-973, paras 59–72.

[235] Accordingly, the Council infringed the principle of equal treatment by applying the Staff Regulations differently with regard to institutions which were in the same situation: CFI, Case T-164/97 *Busaca and Others v Court of Auditors* [1998] E.C.R.-SC II-1699, paras 48–61 (upheld on appeal: ECJ, Case C-434/98 P *Council v Busaca and Court of Auditors* [2000] E.C.R. I-8577). The European Central Bank was found to have infringed the principle of equal treatment by granting an education allowance only to staff in receipt of expatriation allowance: CFI, Joined Cases T-94/01, T-125/01 and T-286/01 *Hirsch and Others v European Central Bank* [2003] E.C.R.-SC II-27, paras 45–72.

[236] ECJ, Joined Cases C-402/07 and C-432/07 *Sturgeon* [2009] E.C.R. I-10923, paras 48–61.

1. Prohibition of discrimination on grounds of the nationality of a Member State

7–052   **Discrimination on grounds of nationality.** The first para. of Art. 18 TFEU [*ex Art. 12 EC*] prohibits any discrimination on grounds of nationality "[w]ithin the scope of application of the Treaties" and "without prejudice to any special provisions contained therein".[237] In a situation governed by Union law,[238] a Member State must not discriminate, even indirectly, against nationals of other Member States. Thus, a Member State may not make the award of a right subject to the condition that the person concerned holds a residence permit or is a national of a country which has entered into a reciprocal agreement with that Member State.[239] However, Art. 18 does not prohibit differences in treatment between nationals of Member States and nationals of third countries.[240] Individuals too are subject to the prohibition of discrimination on grounds of nationality, in particular where a group or organisation exercises a certain power over individuals and is in a position to impose on them conditions which adversely affect the exercise of the fundamental freedoms guaranteed under the Treaties.[241]

  In some circumstances, however, a difference in treatment may be objectively justified, for example an obligation imposed only on non-residents to pay security in respect of infringements given the absence of international or Union instruments to ensure that a fine may if necessary be enforced in another Member State[242] or a residence requirement which places a Member State's own nationals at an advantage but is based on objective considerations that are independent of the nationality of the persons concerned and proportionate to the legitimate aim

---

[237] See Rossi, "Das Diskriminierungsverbot nach Art. 12 EGV" (2000) EuR. 197–217. Within the scope of application of the Treaties any discrimination on grounds of nationality is also prohibited by Art. 21(2) of the Charter of Fundamental Rights of the European Union.

[238] Before the Lisbon Treaty entered into force, Art. 12 EC applied only "within the scope of application of this Treaty", i.e. the scope of Community law, excluding the former second and third pillars. Nevertheless, the Court of Justice had already considered that the principle laid down in Art. 12 EC was applicable to measures adopted under the former third pillar where they infringed provisions of Community law, in particular the provisions on the freedom of movement and residence of citizens of the Union (ECJ, Case C-123/08 *Wolzenburg* [2009] E.C.R. I-9621, paras 44–47). Although the prohibition of discrimination on grounds of nationality within the scope of application of Union law is expressly laid down only in Art. 18 TFEU, it is a general principle which is also applicable under the EAEC Treaty: ECJ, Case C-115/08 *ČEZ* (n. 198, *supra*), paras 87–91.

[239] ECJ, Case 186/87 *Cowan* [1989] E.C.R. 195, para. 13.

[240] ECJ, Joined Cases C-22/08 and C-23/08 *Vatsouras and Koupatantze* [2009] E.C.R. I-4585, para. 52.

[241] ECJ, Case C-411/98 *Ferlini* [2000] E.C.R. I-8081, para. 50; see also ECJ, Case C-281/98 *Angonese* [2000] E.C.R. I-4139, paras 30–36.

[242] ECJ, Case C-224/00 *Commission v Italy* [2002] E.C.R. I-2965, paras 20–24.

of the national provisions.[243] Just as they cannot justify a barrier to the fundamental principles of free movement,[244] considerations that have been specifically addressed in Union harmonisation measures or aims of a purely economic nature cannot justify discrimination on grounds of nationality.[245]

Since the principle of non-discrimination also prohibits the treatment of different situations in the same way, individuals may rely on Art. 18 in order to contest a Member State's refusal to take account of their specific situation. Accordingly, a Member State must make it possible in its legislation on surnames for nationals having dual nationality of that State and of another Member State to bear the surname to which they are entitled according to the law of the second Member State.[246]

Independent application. Article 18 TFEU, which lays down the general principle of the prohibition of discrimination on grounds of nationality, applies independently only to situations governed by Union law in respect of which the Treaties lay down no specific prohibition of discrimination.[247] In fact, the words "special provisions" in Art. 18 refer to other Treaty provisions specifying the principle set forth in that article, such as the Treaty provisions on the free movement of goods, persons, services and capital which express the basic condition of the internal market, namely that all factors of production, irrespective of the nationality of persons[248] or the origin of goods,[249] services[250] and capital,[251] may participate in the market. It follows that whenever a situation is covered by one of the Treaty provisions on free movement, that situation must be considered on the basis of that specific provision and not of Art. 18 TFEU.[252]

7–053

Scope of application of the Treaties. Article 18 TFEU prohibits discrimination on grounds of nationality "within the scope of application of the Treaties". National legislation adopted in implementation of primary or secondary Union law clearly falls within the scope of application of the Treaties.[253] The ambit of the

7–054

---

[243] See ECJ, Case C-138/02 *Collins* [2004] E.C.R. I-2703, paras 65–73; ECJ, Case C-103/08 *Gottwald* [2009] E.C.R. I-9117, paras 31–40. See also ECJ (judgment of April 13, 2010), Case C-73/08 *Bressol and Others*, not yet reported, paras 62–81.

[244] See paras 9–041—9–042 (goods), 9–075—9–076 (persons) and 9–095—9–096 (services), *infra*.

[245] See ECJ, Case C-115/08 *ČEZ* (n. 198, *supra*), paras 109 and 110–136 (in the context of the EAEC Treaty).

[246] ECJ, Case C-148/02 *Garcia Avello* [2003] E.C.R. I-11613, paras 30–45.

[247] ECJ, Case C-193/94 *Skanavi and Chryssanthakopoulos* [1996] E.C.R. I-929, para. 20; ECJ, Case C-131/96 *Mora Romero* [1997] E.C.R. I-3659, para. 10.

[248] See Art. 37(1); Art. 45(2); Art. 49, second para.; Art. 92 and Art. 200(5) TFEU.

[249] See Art. 36, last sentence; Art. 95(1); Art. 110, first para. TFEU.

[250] See Art. 57, third para., and Art. 61 TFEU.

[251] See Art. 65(3) TFEU.

[252] See, e.g., ECJ, Case C-422/01 *Skandia and Ramstedt* [2003] E.C.R. I-6817, para. 61; ECJ, Case C-387/01 *Weigel and Weigel* [2004] I-0000, paras 57–59.

[253] E.g. ECJ, Case C-29/95 *Pastoors and Trans-Cap* [1997] E.C.R. I-285, paras 13–18.

Treaties also extends to certain international agreements concluded amongst the Member States in connection with the Treaties. They may not be implemented, therefore, under national law in a way that discriminates against nationals of other Member States.[254] In the case of the application of an agreement with third countries, the principle of equal treatment may even require a Member State to grant nationals of other Member States the benefits accruing from the agreement for its own nationals (see para. 22–049).

It follows from the case law that even when a particular matter falls within the competence of the Member States, Union law sets certain limits to their power and national legislative provisions

> "may not discriminate against persons to whom Union law gives the right to equal treatment or restrict the fundamental freedoms guaranteed by Union law."[255]

Accordingly, national legislative provisions are subject to the prohibition of discrimination laid down by Art. 18 where they fall within the scope of application of the Treaties by reason of their effects on intra-Union trade in goods and services or on free movement of persons, even where they do not as such restrict the free movement of goods, services or persons.[256] Thus, the Court declared in *Cowan* with regard to free movement of services that:

> "[W]hen [Union] law guarantees a natural person the freedom to go to another Member State the protection of that person from harm in the Member State in question, on the same basis as that of nationals and persons residing there, is a corollary of that freedom of movement. It follows that the prohibition of discrimination is applicable to recipients of services within the meaning of the Treaties as regards protection against the risk of assault and the right to obtain financial compensation provided for by national law when that risk materialises."[257]

---

[254] E.g. ECJ, Case C-28/04 *Tod's* [2005] E.C.R. I-05781, paras 20–27.

[255] E.g. ECJ, Case 186/87 *Cowan* [1989] E.C.R. 195, para. 19 (right to compensation of a person who is a victim of an offence, which comes under the French law of criminal procedure and, as a result, within the competence of the Member State). See also ECJ, Joined Cases C-92/92 and C-326/92 *Phil Collins and Others* [1993] E.C.R. I-5145, paras 19–28; ECJ, Case C-360/00 *Ricordi & Co Bühnen- und Musikverlag* [2002] E.C.R. I-5089, paras 24–34 (concerning copyrights and related rights); ECJ, Case C-43/95 *Data Delecta and Forsberg* [1996] E.C.R. I-4461, paras 10–22; ECJ, Case C-323/95 *Hayes* [1997] E.C.R. I-1711, paras 13–17; ECJ, Case C-122/96 *Saldanha and MTS* [1997] E.C.R. I-5325, paras 16–24 (concerning requirements to furnish security for costs); ECJ, Case C-224/02 *Pusa* [2004] E.C.R. I-5763, paras 22–35 (rules on enforcement for the recovery of debts).

[256] ECJ, Case C-323/95 *Hayes* [1997] E.C.R. I-1711, para. 16; ECJ, Case C-122/96 *Saldanha and MTS* [1997] E.C.R. I-5325, para. 20. However, there are limits to the scope of Union law, see ECJ, Case C-291/96 *Grado and Bashir* [1997] E.C.R. I-5531, paras 13–14.

[257] ECJ, Case 186/87 *Cowan* [1989] E.C.R. 195, para. 17. See also ECJ, Case C-164/07 *Wood* [2008] E.C.R. I-4143, paras 10–16 (workers from other Member States may not be excluded from entitlement to the right to obtain compensation for certain categories of losses).

The Court also ruled that nationals of a Member State who make use of their right to move to another Member State and reside there are in principle entitled, pursuant to Art. 18 TFEU, to treatment no less favourable than that accorded to nationals of the host State so far as concerns the use of languages which are spoken there.[258]

A disparity in treatment between Member States resulting simply from differences existing between their laws does not constitute discrimination within the meaning of Art. 18 TFEU, so long as the differences affect all persons subject to them in accordance with objective criteria and without regard to their nationality.[259] As regards matters of civil law which fall outside the scope of the Treaties, it is not contrary to Art. 18 for persons to be treated differently on grounds of their nationality as a result of the fact that the private international law of a Member State takes nationality as the connecting factor for determining the applicable substantive law.[260]

Combination with citizenship of the Union. Every citizen of the Union has the right not to suffer discrimination on grounds of nationality in all situations falling "within the scope of application of the Treaties". Such situations include those involving the exercise of the fundamental freedoms guaranteed by the Treaties, in particular the exercise of the right enjoyed by citizens of the Union to move and reside within the territory of the Member States (see Art. 21 TFEU [ex Art. 18 EC]).[261] Accordingly, a person can rely on the provisions of the Treaties if he or she, being a national of a Member State and thus a citizen of the Union, lawfully resides in the territory of another Member State.[262] Moreover, Art. 18 TFEU also applies where a family member of a citizen of the Union has made use of his or her right of free movement (as opposed to the citizen himself or herself), where this results in unequal treatment.[263]

7–055

---

[258] ECJ, Case C-274/96 *Bickel and Franz* [1998] E.C.R. I-7637, paras 13–31 (for the question of the justification under cultural policy, see para. 11–052, *infra*).

[259] See ECJ, Case C-177/94 *Perfili* [1996] E.C.R. I-161, para. 71.

[260] ECJ, Case C-430/97 *Johannes* [1999] E.C.R. I-3475, paras 26–29.

[261] ECJ, Case C-224/98 *D'Hoop* [2002] E.C.R. I-6191, para. 29; ECJ, Case C-148/02 *Garcia Avello* [2003] E.C.R. I-11613, para. 24; ECJ, Case C-224/02 *Pusa* [2004] E.C.R. I-5763, para. 17; ECJ, Case C-209/03 *Bidar* [2005] E.C.R. I-2119, para. 33; ECJ, Case C-524/06 *Huber* [2008] E.C.R. I-9705, para. 71. For a discussion, see Lenaerts, "Union citizenship and the principle of non-discrimination on grounds of nationality", in *Festskrift til Claus Gulmann—Liber Amicorum* (Copenhagen, Forlaget Thomson A/S, 2006) 289–309; Van Nuffel and Cambien, "De vrijheid van economisch niet-actieve EU-burgers om binnen de EU te reizen, te verblijven en te studeren" (2009) S.E.W. 144–154; White, "Free movement, equal treatment, and citizenship of the Union" (2005) 54 I.C.L.Q.885–906;.

[262] ECJ, Case C-85/96 *Martínez Sala* [1998] E.C.R. I-2691, para. 61. Lawful residence in the territory of another Member State suffices. It is not required that the citizen concerned has actually moved from one Member State to another: see ECJ, Case C-148/02 *Garcia Avello* [2003] E.C.R. I-11613, paras 13 and 27; ECJ, Case C-200/02 *Zhu and Chen* [2004] E.C.R. I-9925, para. 23–006).

[263] ECJ, Case C-403/03 *Schempp* [2005] E.C.R. I-6421, paras 22–25, with case notes by Panayi (2005) European Taxation 482–487 and Lutostanska (2006) 33 L.I.E.I. 335–345.

The exercise of the fundamental right to free movement enables citizens of the Union to claim equal treatment in a broad range of areas. Accordingly, a job-seeker in another Member State may claim equal treatment with regard to the grant of a financial benefit designed to facilitate access to the employment market in that Member State.[264] The Court also ruled that nationals of a Member State who, in accordance with Art. 21 TFEU, make use of their right to move to another Member State and reside there are in principle entitled to treatment no less favourable than that accorded to nationals of the host State so far as concerns the entitlement to a social benefit such as a child-raising allowance[265] or a minimum subsistence allowance.[266]

The Court of Justice likewise applies Art. 18 TFEU to the conditions governing access to education. Consequently, it is contrary to the principle of non-discrimination for a Member State to distinguish, as regards the level of educational fees, between students who are its nationals and students who are nationals of other Member States.[267] In *Gravier* the Court arrived at this conclusion by considering that the requirement to pay a fee in order to study cartoon art fell within the ambit of the "common vocational training policy" referred to in Art. 128 EEC. This case law was subsequently extended to university enrolment fees[268] and aspects related to access to education.[269] More recently, and in view of the introduction of citizenship of the Union,[270] the Court has held that assistance given to students for maintenance and for training, such as student grants or

---

[264] See ECJ, Case C-138/02 *Collins* [2004] E.C.R. I-2703, paras 54–64; case notes by Dougan (2005) E.J.Soc.Sec. 7–34; Oosterom-Staples (2005) 42 C.M.L.Rev. 205–223; Van Ooik and Schrauwen (2005) S.E.W. 40–46; Meulman and de Waele (2004) L.I.E.I. 275–288; Van der Mei (2004) E.J.M.L. 277–284; Niemann, (2004) EuR. 946–953.

[265] ECJ, Case C-85/96 *Martínez Sala* [1998] E.C.R. I-2691, para. 57.

[266] ECJ, Case C-184/99 *Grzelczyk* [2001] E.C.R. I-6193, paras 29–46; ECJ, Case C-456/02 *Trojani* [2004] E.C.R. I-7573. See Lenaerts, "Le développement de l'Union sociale européenne dans la jurisprudence de la Cour de justice" (2008) 9 ERA Forum 61–97; Giubboni, "Free movement of persons and European Solidarity", (2007) 13 E.L.J. 360–379; Ach, "La citoyenneté européenne au service d'une Europe Sociale" (2006) 14 J.T.D.E. 129–135; Lenaerts and Heremans, "Contours of a European social union in the case-law of the European Court of Justice" (2006) E.Const.L.Rev. 101–115; Hailbronner, "Unionsbürgerschaft und Zugang zu den Sozialsystemen" (2005) J.Z. 1138–1144.

[267] ECJ, Case 293/83 *Gravier* [1985] E.C.R. 593, paras 11–26.

[268] ECJ, Case 24/86 *Blaizot* [1988] E.C.R. 379, paras 10–24; ECJ, Case C-47/93 *Commission v Belgium* [1994] E.C.R. I-1593.

[269] Case C-357/89 *Raulin* [1992] E.C.R. I-1027, paras 35–43 (requirement to have a residence permit in order to be allowed to pursue higher studies); ECJ, Case 42/87 *Commission v Belgium* [1988] E.C.R. 5445, paras 7–9 (no State funding of educational establishments for students who are nationals of Member States other than Belgium and Luxembourg); ECJ, Case C-65/03 *Commission v Belgium* [2004] E.C.R. I-6427, paras 25–29, and ECJ, Case C-147/03 *Commission v Austria* [2005] E.C.R. I-5969, paras 31–35; ECJ (judgment of April 13, 2010), Case C-73/08 *Bressol and Others* (n. 243, *supra*), paras 40–46 (additional university entry requirements for students from other Member States).

[270] Students who move to another Member State to pursue studies make use of the right laid down in Art. 18 EC (see para. 5–009).

subsidised loans, also falls within the scope of the Treaties for the purposes of Art. 18 TFEU.[271]

A difference in treatment can be justified if it is based on objective considerations independent of the nationality of the persons concerned and is proportionate to the legitimate aim of the national provisions.[272] Accordingly, it is permissible for a Member State to ensure that the grant of assistance to cover the maintenance costs of students from other Member States does not become an unreasonable burden which could have consequences for the overall level of assistance which may be granted by that State,[273] for example by making entitlement conditional upon a condition of five years' continuous residence in that State.[274] However, since the provisions on citizenship of the Union necessarily imply a certain degree of financial solidarity with nationals of other Member States, Member States may not exclude nationals from other Member States altogether.[275] Accordingly, a discriminatory measure will not be justified where non-discriminatory measures could suffice in order to achieve the legitimate objective pursued.[276]

Combating discrimination. The second para. of Art. 18 TFEU empowers the European Parliament and the Council, acting under the ordinary legislative procedure, to adopt "rules designed to prohibit such discrimination". This means that the European Parliament and the Council may take the necessary measures to prohibit all forms of discrimination on grounds of nationality. The measures need not be confined to the right to equal treatment flowing from the first para. of Art. 18, but may also deal with ancillary aspects which ought to be settled in order to secure effective exercise of that right. The Court of Justice has held that Art. 18 was the only proper legal basis for the directive on students' right of

7–056

---

[271] ECJ, Case C-209/03 *Bidar* [2005] E.C.R. I-2119, paras 37–42. The Court thereby overruled earlier case law in which it held that such assistance fell outside the scope of the Treaty (ECJ, Case 39/86 *Lair* [1988] E.C.R. 3161, paras 11–16; ECJ, Case 197/86 *Brown* [1988] E.C.R. 3205, paras 14–19). For a discussion of the *Bidar* case, see Golynker (2006) E.L.Rev, 390–401; Brand (2005) 12 Col.J.E.L. 293–304; De Waele (2005) N.T.E.R. 122–127; Armbrecht, "Ausbildungsförderung für Studenten- Gleicher Zugang für Unionsbürger?" (2005) Z.Eu.S, 175–209; Dougan, "Fees, grants, loans and dole cheques: who covers the costs of migrant education within the EU?" (2005) C.M.L.Rev. 943–986. See also, Van der Mei, "Union citizenship and the 'de-nationalisation' of the Territorial Welfare State. Comments on Case C-456/02 Trojani and Case C-209/03 Bidar" (2005) E.J.M.L. 203–211.

[272] E.g. ECJ, Case C-224/98 *D'Hoop* [2002] E.C.R. I-6191, para. 36; ECJ, Case C-148/02 *Garcia Avello* [2003] E.C.R. I-11613, para. 31; ECJ, Case C-209/03 *Bidar* [2005] E.C.R. I-2119, para. 54; ECJ, Case C-524/06 *Huber* [2008] E.C.R. I-9705, para. 75.

[273] ECJ, Case C-209/03 *Bidar* [2005] E.C.R. I-2119, para. 56.

[274] ECJ, Case C-158/07 *Förster* E.C.R. [2008] E.C.R. I-8507, paras 48–55. This is confirmed by Art. 24(2) of Directive 2004/38 (see para. 5–009).

[275] ECJ, Case C-184/99 *Grzelczyk* [2001] E.C.R. I-6193, para. 44

[276] ECJ, Case C-147/03 *Commission v Austria* [2005] E.C.R. I-5969, paras 60–66; ECJ (judgment of April 13, 2010), Case C-73/08 *Bressol and Others* (n. 243, *supra*), paras 77–81.

residence on the ground that equal treatment in the matter of access to vocational training requires that students have the right to reside in the Member State where they have been admitted to vocational training.[277]

2. Prohibition of discrimination on grounds of sex/gender

7–057   **Sex and gender.** An important application of the prohibition of discrimination is the obligation that men and women must be treated equally.[278] The Court of Justice has referred to equal treatment of men and women as one of the fundamental human rights whose observance it has a duty to ensure.[279] The principle is also enshrined in Art. 23 of the Charter of Fundamental Rights of the European Union. The principle of equal treatment prohibits the Union and the Member States from discriminating on grounds of sex. This is also expressed in the Treaties in the form of the principle that male and female workers should receive equal pay for equal work or work of equal value (Art. 157(1) TFEU).[280]

Whenever there is evidence of discrimination, it is for the employer to prove that the practice at issue is justified by objective factors unrelated to any discrimination based on sex.[281] The justification given must be based on a legitimate

---

[277] ECJ, Case C-295/90 *European Parliament v Council* [1992] E.C.R. I-4193, paras 15–20.

[278] See Beveridge, "Gender, the Acquis and Beyond", in Dougan and Currie (eds), *50 Years of the European Treaties: Looking Back and Thinking Forward* (Oxford, Hart, 2009) 393–413; Hervey and O'Keeffe (eds), *Sex Equality Law in the European Union* (Chichester, John Wiley & Sons, 1996), 427 pp.; Masselot, "The state of gender equality law in the European Union" (2007) 13 E.L.J. 152–168; Millns, "Gender equality, citizenship and the EU's Constitutional Future" (2007) 13 E.L.J. 218–237; Hervey, "Thirty years of EU sex equality law: looking backwards, looking forwards" (2005) 12 M.J.E.C.L. 307–325; Jacqmain, "Egalité entre travailleurs féminins et masculins" (2000) J.T.D.E. 201–210; Mancini and O'Leary, "The New Frontiers of Sex Equality Law in the European Union" (1999) E.L.Rev. 331–353.

[279] ECJ, Case C-185/97 *Coote* [1998] E.C.R. I-5199, para. 23. For a survey of the case law, see Costello and Davies, "The Case Law of the Court of Justice in the Field of Sex Equality since 2000" (2006) C.M.L.Rev. 1567–1616; Pager, "Strictness vs. Discretion: The European Court of Justice's Variable Vision of Gender Equality" (2003) A.J.C.L. 553–609; Shaw "Gender and the European Court of Justice", in De Burca and Weiler (eds), *The European Court of Justice* (Oxford, Oxford University Press, 2001) 87–142.

[280] See the discussion of indirect discrimination, para. 7–063, *infra*, and the discussion of social policy, para. 5–236. For a blatant example, see ECJ, Case C-206/00 *Mouflin* [2001] E.C.R. I-10201, paras 28–31. Until the Treaty of Amsterdam, Art. 119 EC [*now Art. 157 TFEU*] referred only to "equal work"; however, the principle was already extended to "the same work" by Council Directive 75/117/EEC of February 10, 1975 on the approximation of the laws of the Member States relating to the application of the principle of equal pay for men and women, [1975] O.J. L45/19, now replaced by Directive 2006/54/EC of the European Parliament and of the Council of July 5, 2006 on the implementation of the principle of equal opportunities and equal treatment of men and women in matters of employment and occupation, [2006] O.J. L204/23.

[281] ECJ, Case 109/88 *Danfoss* [1989] E.C.R. 3199, paras 22 and 23; ECJ, Case C-33/89 *Kowalska* [1990] E.C.R. I-2591, para. 16; ECJ, Case C-243/95 *Hill and Stapleton* [1998] E.C.R. I-3739, para. 43; ECJ, Joined Cases C-4/02 and C-5/02 *Schönheit and Becker* [2003] E.C.R. I-12575, para. 71; ECJ, Case C-17/05 *Cadman* [2006] E.C.R. I-9583, paras 31 and 38–39.

objective and the means chosen to achieve that objective must be appropriate and necessary for that purpose.[282]

The Union law requirement for equal treatment of men and women applies to access to employment and, consequently, in principle also to military occupations.[283] However, the Member States' choices of military organisation for the defence of their territory or of their essential interests do not necessarily fall within Union law. Accordingly, Union law does not preclude compulsory military service being reserved to men.[284] As a result of the prohibition of discrimination on grounds of sex, a worker may not be discriminated against because he or she or his or her partner wishes to undergo a gender-reassignment operation or has undergone such an operation.[285] The Court of Justice considers, however, that discrimination on grounds of sexual orientation does not fall within the prohibition of discrimination on grounds of sex.[286]

In many areas, the Union law principle of equal treatment of men and women has prompted better protection for women against unjustified discrimination.[287] Article 3(3) TEU provides that, "the Union shall promote [. . .] equality, between men and women"[288] and Art. 10 TFEU (introduced by the Lisbon Treaty) states

---

[282] ECJ, Case 170/84 *Bilka* [1986] E.C.R. 1607, para. 37.

[283] ECJ, Case C-273/97 *Sirdar* [1999] E.C.R. I-7403, paras 11–29; ECJ, Case C-285/98 *Kreil* [2000] E.C.R. I-69, paras 15–32 (in spite of the constitutional ban on military service for women); the exclusion of women from service in special commando units may, however, be justified on the basis of Directive 76/207/EEC (n. 290, *infra*): *Sirdar*, paras 21–32.

[284] ECJ, Case C-186/01 *Dory* [2003] E.C.R. I-2479, paras 29–42 (see also para. 6–014, *infra*).

[285] ECJ, Case C-13/94 *P* [1996] E.C.R. I-2143, paras 13–24, with a case note by Brems (1996) Col.J.E.L. 339–345; ECJ, Case C-117/01 *K.B.* [2004] E.C.R. I-541, paras 30–34; ECJ, Case C-423/04 *Richards* [2006] E.C.R. I-3585, paras 27–31.

[286] ECJ, Case C-249/96 *Grant* [1998] E.C.R. I-621, paras 24–47, with a case note by McInnes (1999) C.M.L.Rev. 1043–1058. See also para. 5–064.

[287] The principle also opposes the discriminatory effects of legislation intended to protect women; see, inter alia, the case law rejecting a national ban on night work by women: ECJ, Case C-345/89 *Stoeckel* [1991] E.C.R. I-4047; ECJ, Case C-158/91 *Levy* [1993] E.C.R. I-4287; ECJ, Case C-203/03 *Commission v Austria* [2005] E.C.R. I-935, paras 42–50 and 69–75. See De Vos, "Le travail de nuit: La 'Realpolitik' de l'égalité!" (1993) J.T. 1–7 and, in addition, Foubert, *The legal protection of the pregnant worker in the European Community: sex equality, thoughts of social and economic policy and comparative leaps to the United States of America* (The Hague, Kluwer, 2002), 389 pp.; Caracciolo di Torella and Masselot, "Pregnancy, maternity and the organisation of family life: an attempt to classify the case law of the Court of Justice" (2001) E.L.Rev. 239–260; Masselot and Berthou, "La CJCE, le droit de la maternité et le principe de non-discrimination— vers une clarification?" (2000) C.D.E. 637–656.

[288] *Cf.* Council Recommendation 96/694/EC of December 2, 1996, adopted by the Council pursuant to Art. 235 EC [*now Art. 352 TFEU*], on the balanced participation of women and men in the decision-making process ([1996] O.J. L319/11); Commission Decision 2000/407/EC of June 19, 2000 relating to gender balance within the committees and expert groups established by it ([2000] O.J. L154/34); Regulation (EC) No. 806/2004 of the European Parliament and the Council of April 21, 2004 on promoting gender equality in development cooperation ([2004] O.J. L143/40).

that "In defining and implementing its policies and activities, the Union shall aim to combat discrimination based on sex". Equality between men and women with regard to labour market opportunities and treatment at work is also among the objectives of Union social policy (see Art. 153(1)(i) TFEU [*ex Art. 137(1)(i) EC*]).[289] Article 157(3) TFEU [*ex Art. 141(3) EC*] empowers the European Parliament and the Council, acting under the ordinary legislative procedure, to adopt measures to ensure the application of the principle of equal opportunities and equal treatment for men and women in matters of employment and occupation, including the principle of equal pay for equal work or work of equal value. The Community had already adopted directives to ensure men and women equal treatment as regards access to employment, vocational training, promotion and working conditions,[290] and in the field of social security.[291] Outside the context of the labour market, the Community has adopted directives on the basis of Art. 13 EC [*now Art. 19 TFEU*], for instance with regard to equal treatment between men and women in the access to and supply of goods and services.[292]

7–058   **Positive discrimination.** All this does not mean that the Member States are not entitled to take measures embodying "positive discrimination". The guarantee of equal access to employment and of equal promotion opportunities for men and women does not preclude measures to enhance equal opportunity for men and women which are intended, inter alia, to eliminate actual instances

---

[289] Article 137 EC took over the wording of Art. 2 of the Social Agreement (para. 11–043, *infra*), pursuant to which the Council adopted, on December 15, 1997, Directive 97/80/EC on the burden of proof in cases of discrimination based on sex, [1998] O.J. L14/6, now replaced by Directive 2006/54/EC (n. 280, *supra*).

[290] Council Directive 76/207/EEC of February 9, 1976 on the implementation of the principle of equal treatment for men and women as regards access to employment, vocational training and promotion, and working conditions, [1976] L39/40, now replaced by Directive 2006/54/EC (n. 280, *supra*). See also Council Directive 86/613/EEC of December 11, 1986 on the application of the principle of equal treatment between men and women engaged in an activity, including agriculture, in a self-employed capacity, and on the protection of self-employed women during pregnancy and motherhood, [1986] O.J. L359/56, now replaced by Directive 2010/41/EU of the European Parliament and of the Council of July 7, 2010 on the application of the principle of equal treatment between men and women engaged in an activity in a self-employed capacity, [2010] O.J. L180/1.

[291] Council Directive 79/7/EEC of December 19, 1978 on the progressive implementation of the principle of equal treatment for men and women in matters of social security, [1979] O.J. L6/24. See also Council Directive 86/378/EEC of July 24, 1986 on the implementation of the principle of equal treatment for men and women in occupational social security schemes, [1986] O.J. L225/40, now replaced by Directive 2006/54/EC (n. 280, *supra*). For a survey of the case law, see Cousins, "Equal Treatment and Social Security" (1994) E.L. Rev. 123–145.

[292] Council Directive 2004/113/EC of December 13, 2004 implementing the principle of equal treatment between men and women in the access to and supply of goods and services, [2004] O.J. L373/37. See Krois, "Directive 2004/113/EC on sexual equality in access to goods and services: progress or impasse in European sex discrimination law?" (2005) 12 Col.J.E.L. 323–338.

of inequality which affect women's opportunities.[293] However, this exception does not authorise a Member State to adopt or tolerate measures which guarantee absolute and unconditional priority for women in the matter of promotion or employment. Where both male and female candidates are equally qualified and where there are fewer women than men at the level of the relevant post, priority may be given to the promotion of female candidates if it is not excluded on account of one or more criteria specific to individual candidates—which may not be such as to discriminate against female candidates—to tilt the balance in favour of some male candidates.[294] Article 157(4) TFEU [*ex Art. 141(4) EC*] provides, with a view to ensuring full equality in practice between men and women in working life, that the principle of equal treatment shall not prevent any Member State from maintaining or adopting measures providing for specific advantages in order to make it easier for the underrepresented sex to pursue a vocational activity or to prevent or compensate for disadvantages in professional careers.

3. Other prohibited forms of discrimination

Forbidden grounds. In defining and implementing its policies and activities, the Union shall aim to combat discrimination based on sex, racial or ethnic

7–059

---

[293] Article 2(4) of Directive 76/207 (n. 290, *supra*). This applied where, in order to tackle the underrepresentation of women, a ministry reserved nursery places in principle for women employees: ECJ, Case C-476/99 *Lommers* [2002] E.C.R. I-2891, paras 31–50. This was not the case, however, where a measure entitled female employees with children alone to a service credit for the purpose of calculating their pensions: ECJ, Case C-366/99 *Griesmar* [2001] E.C.R. I-9383, paras 62–67 (the measure was in breach of the principle of equal pay and consequently discriminated against men).

[294] ECJ, Case C-409/95 *Marschall* [1997] E.C.R. I-6363, paras 21–35, with a case note by Brems (1998) Col.J.E.L. 668–675; ECJ, Case C-158/97 *Badeck and Others* [2000] E.C.R. I-1875, paras 13–67; ECJ, Case C-407/98 *Abrahamsson and Anderson* [2000] E.C.R. I-5539, paras 39–65; EFTA Court, Case E-1/02 *EFTA Surveillance Authority v Norway* [2003] EFTA Court Report 1, with a note by Tobler (2004) C.M.L.Rev. 245–260. In *Marschall* the Court qualified an earlier judgment according to which rules giving priority to equally-qualified female candidates for promotion or employment in sectors of public employment where they were underrepresented were precluded by Directive 76/207/EEC: ECJ, Case C-450/93 *Kalanke* [1995] E.C.R. I-3051, paras 15–24. That judgment came in for severe criticism, see Charpentier (1996), R.T.D.E. 281–303; De Schutter and Renauld (1996) J.T.T. 125–129; Moore (1996) E.L.Rev. 156–161; Prechal (1996) C.M.L.Rev. 1245–1259; Brems (1995/96) Col.J.E.L. 172–179; Loenen and Veldman (1995) N.J.B. 1521–1527. See also Caruso, "Limits of the Classic Method: Positive Action in the European Union After the New Equality Directives" (2003) Harv.I.L.J. 331–386; Hauquet, "*L'action* positive, instrument de l'égalité des chances entre hommes et femmes" (2001) R.T.D.E. 305–333; Barnard, "The Principle of Equality in the Community Context: *P., Grant, Kalanke* and *Marschall*: Four Uneasy Bedfellows?" (1998) Cambridge L.J. 352–373; Suhr, "Grenzen der Gleichbehandlung: Zur Vereinbarkeit von Frauenquoten mit dem Gemeinschaftsrecht" (1998) Eu.GR.Z. 121–128.

origin, religion or belief, disability, age or sexual orientation (Art. 10 TFEU).[295] Under Art. 19 TFEU [*ex Art. 13 EC*], introduced by the Amsterdam Treaty), the Council, acting unanimously in accordance with a special legislative procedure and after obtaining the consent of the European Parliament, is to take appropriate action within the limits of the powers conferred upon the Union by the Treaties to combat discrimination based on these grounds. Accordingly, the Council has adopted directives prohibiting discrimination on the basis of racial or ethnic origin[296] and a general framework for equal treatment in employment and occupation.[297] The purpose of the second directive is to combat any form of

---

[295] In addition, Art. 9 TEU proclaims the general principle of the equality of citizens of the Union before the Union's institutions, bodies, offices and agencies (principle of democratic equality).

[296] Council Directive 2000/43/EC of June 29, 2000 implementing the principle of equal treatment between persons irrespective of racial or ethnic origin, [2000] O.J. L180/22. For the scope of the notion of "direct discrimination" employed in Art. 2(2) of the Directive, see ECJ, Case C-54/07 *Feryn* [2008] E.C.R. I-5187, paras 21–28. See further, in general, Bell, *Racism and equality in the European Union* (Oxford, Oxford University Press, 2009), 227 pp.; Bell, "EU anti-racism policy; the leader of the pack?", in Meenan (ed.), *Equality Law in an Enlarged European Union. Understanding the Article 13 Directives* (Cambridge, Cambridge University Press, 2007) 145–176; Jones, "The Race Directive: Redefining Protection from Discrimination in EU Law" (2003) E.H.R.L.R. 515–526; Mahlmann, "Gleichheitsschutz und Privatautonomie—Probleme und Perspektiven der Umsetzung der Richtline 2000/43/EG gegen Diskriminierungen aufgrund von Rasse und etnischer Herkunft" (2002) Z.Eu.S. 407–425; Nickel, "Handlungsaufträge zur Bekämpfung von ethnischen Diskriminierungen in der neuen Gleichbehandlungsrichtlinie 2000/43/EC" (2001) N.J.W. 2668–2672; Sewandono, "De Rassenrichtlijn en de Algemene Wet gelijke behandeling" (2001) S.E.W. 218–226. For the origins of the directive, see Tyson, "The Negotiation of the European Community Directive on Racial Discrimination" (2001) E.J.M.L. 199–229. Pursuant to Arts 213 and 235 EC [*now Arts 337 and 352 TFEU*], the European Monitoring Centre on Racism and Xenophobia was set up in Vienna (para. 13–123, *infra*). See also the first para. of Art. 29 EU (on PJCC) and Council Framework Decision 2008/913/JHA of November 28, 2008 on combating certain forms and expressions of racism and xenophobia by means of criminal law, [2008] O.J. L328/55.

[297] Council Directive 2000/78/EC of November 27, 2000 establishing a general framework for equal treatment in employment and occupation, [2000] O.J. L303/16. See also Decision No. 1672/2006/EC of the European Parliament and of the Council of October 24, 2006 establishing a Community Programme for Employment and Social Solidarity—Progress, [2006] O.J. L315/1. For general considerations, see Bell and Waddington, "Reflecting on inequalities in European equality law" (2003) E.L.Rev. 349–369; Bayart, "De opmars van het discriminatierecht in de arbeidsverhoudingen" (2002) J.T.T. 309–329; Dollat, "Vers la reconnaissance généralisée du principe de l'égalité de traitement entre les personnes dans l'Union européenne" (2002) J.T.D.E. 57–64; Goldschmidt, "De hete adem van Europa. Implementatie van nieuw gelijke behandelingsrecht in Nederland" (2001) N.J.B. 983–990; Waddington and Bell, "More Equal than Others: Distinguishing European Union Equality Directives" (2001) C.M.L.Rev. 587–611.

discrimination on the grounds of religion or belief,[298] disability,[299] age[300] or sexual orientation[301] as regards employment and occupation. The Treaty of Nice made it possible for the European Parliament and the Council to adopt, under the ordinary legislative procedure, incentive measures, excluding any harmonisation of the laws and regulations of the Member States, to support action taken by the Member States (Art. 19(2) TFEU).[302] Where a person suffers discrimination outside that context on the basis of the specified (or other) criteria, he or she can bring an action on the basis of the general principle of equal treatment,[303]

---

[298] See Pitt, "Religion or Belief; aiming at the Right Target?", in Meenan (ed.), *Equality Law in an Enlarged European Union. Understanding the Article 13 Directives* (Cambridge, Cambridge University Press, 2007) 202–229.

[299] See ECJ, Case C-303/06 *Coleman* [2008] E.C.R. I-5603 (the prohibition of discrimination is not limited to employees who are themselves disabled, but also applies where less favourable treatment of an employee is based on the disability of his or her child). For Union competence with regard to the integration of persons with disabilities, see Quinn, "Disability discrimination law in the European Union, in Meenan (ed.), *Equality Law in an Enlarged European Union. Understanding the Article 13 Directives* (Cambridge, Cambridge University Press, 2007) 202–229; Whittle, "The Framework Directive for equal treatment in employment and occupation: an analysis from a disability rights perspective" (2002) E.L.Rev 303–326; Sarapas, "Les droits des personnes handicappées dans le domaine des transports européens" (2000) R.M.C.U.E. 395–406. See also Council Decision 2001/903/EC of December 3, 2001 on the European Year of People with Disabilities 2003, [2001] O.J. L335/15.

[300] See ECJ, Case C-411/05 *Palacios de la Villa* [2007] E.C.R. I-8531 (collective agreements providing for a compulsory retirement age held not to infringe Directive 2000/78); ECJ, Case C-88/08 *Hütter* [2009] E.C.R. I-5325 (national legislation not taking into account professional experience acquired before the age of 18 held to infringe Directive 2000/78); ECJ (judgments of January 12, 2010), Case C-229/08 *Wolf*, not yet reported, and C-341/08 *Petersen*, not yet reported (national legislation setting maximum age for recruitment of fireman and for practice as a dentist, respectively); ECJ (judgment of January 19, 2010), Case C-555/07 *Kücükdeveci*, not yet reported (national legislation on dismissal not taking into account a period of employment before the age of 25); CST (judgment of November 30, 2009), Case F-83/07 *Zangerl-Posselt v Commission*, not yet reported, paras 76–78 (recruitment condition for Union staff members held not to discriminate on grounds of age). See Jans, "The effect in national legal systems of the prohibition of discrimination on grounds of age as a general principle of Community Law" (2007) 34 L.I.E.I. 53–66; Meenan, "Reflecting on Age Discrimination and Rights of the Elderly in the European Union and the Council of Europe" (2007) M.J.E.C.L.39–82.

[301] See Fitzpatrick, "The 'mainstreaming' of sexual orientation into European equality law", in Meenan (ed.), *Equality Law in an Enlarged European Union. Understanding the Article 13 Directives* (Cambridge, Cambridge University Press, 2007) 313–341.

[302] See the Community action programme to promote organisations active at European level in the field of equality between men and women, established by Decision No. 848/2004/EC of the European Parliament and of the Council of April 29, 2004, [2004] L157 (republished with corrigendum: [2004] L195/7).

[303] See: ECJ, Case C-144/04 *Mangold* [2005] E.C.R. I-9981, paras 74–77 (age); ECJ, Case C-13/05 *Chacón Navas* [2006] E.C.R. I-6467, paras 55–56 (sickness and disability), with a case note by Waddington (2007) C.M.L.Rev. 487–499. See further Lenaerts, "Le respect des droits fondamentaux en tant que principe constitutionnel de l'Union européenne", in *Mélanges Michel Waelbroeck* (Brussels, Bruylant, 1999), I, 423–457. See also Art. 21(1) of the Charter of Fundamental Rights of the European Union, which, in addition to the grounds for discrimination mentioned in Art. 19 TFEU, prohibits discrimination on grounds of colour, social origin, genetic features, language, political or any other opinion, membership of a national minority, property and birth.

unless, as far as Union law is concerned, his or her situation contains no link with Union law.[304]

7–060   **Evolution.** Initially, the Union Courts did not regard unequal treatment of married couples and homosexual couples as prohibited discrimination. The Courts referred to the legislator's power to make societal choices connected with the assessment of such discrimination.[305] The Court of Justice did not consider that the situation of a married official was comparable to the same-sex partnerships recognised by some Member States. However, the case law may evolve further. According to the most recent Staff Regulations, Union officials in a non-marital relationship recognised by a Member State as a stable partnership who do not have legal access to marriage should be granted the same range of benefits as married couples.[306] For some benefits, this also extends to other kinds of non-marital partnerships recognised by a Member State.[307] Likewise, recent Union

---

[304] ECJ, Case C-427/06 *Bartsch* [2008] E.C.R. I-07245, paras 16–24. No such link arises from Art. 13 EC [*now Art. 19 TFEU*] taken on its own, or from Directive 2000/78 before the time-limit for its transposition had expired (*Ibid*). Such a link does, however, arise after the expiry of that time-limit, so that the primary law principle of non-discrimination on the ground of age can be relied upon between private parties, while Directive 2000/78 helps to flesh out the substance of that principle (ECJ, (judgment of January 19, 2010), Case C-555/07 *Kücükdeveci* (n. 300, *supra*), paras 20–27).

[305] ECJ, Case C-249/96 *Grant* [1998] E.C.R. I-621, para. 48; CFI, Case T-264/97 *D. v Council* [1999] E.C.R.-SC II-1, para. 32.: ECJ, Joined Cases C-122/99 P and C-125/99 P *D. and Sweden v Council* [2001] E.C.R. I-4319, paras 47–52; for a critical view, see Berthou and Masselot, "Le mariage, les partenariats et la CJCE: ménage à trois" (2000) C.D.E. 679–694. See further Zukaite, "Does the prohibition of same-sex marriages violate fundamental human rights and freedoms?" (2005) 2 *International Journal of Baltic Law* 1–23; Jessurun d'Oliveira, "Vrijheid van verkeer voor geregisteerde partners in de Europese Unie" (2001) N.J.B. 205–210; Guiguet, "Le droit communautaire et la reconnaissance des partenaires de même sexe" (1999) C.D.E. 537–567; Weyembergh, "Les droits des homosexuels devant le juge communautaire" (1998) J.T.D.E. 110–113.

[306] Council Regulation (EC, Euratom) No. 723/2004 of March 22, 2004 amending the Staff Regulations of officials of the European Communities and the Conditions of Employment of other servants of the European Communities, ([2004] O.J. L124/1) makes certain benefits formerly granted only to married couples available to an official who is registered as a stable non-marital partner, provided that the couple produces a legal document recognised as such by a Member State, or any competent authority of a Member State, acknowledging their status as non-marital partners, neither partner is in a marital relationship or in another non-marital partnership, the partners are not related in specified ways and the couple has no access to legal marriage in a Member State (Art. 1d(1) and Annex VII, Art. 1(2)(c)). See CST (judgment of October 14, 2010), Case F-86/09 *W v Commission*, not yet reported. For previous treatment of such a partnership in the same way as marriage, see the Commission's answers of October 15, 2001 to question P-2438/01 (Buitenweg), [2002] O.J. C93E/131, and of March 12, 2002 to question E-3261/01 (Swiebel), [2003] O.J. C28E/2, and Jessurun d'Oliveira, "De Europese Commissie erkent het Nederlands huwelijk" (2001) N.J.B. 2035–2040. *Cf.* the refusal to accord equal treatment in the Council's answer of December 17, 2001 to question E-1830/01 (Van der Laan), [2002] O.J. C115E/16.

[307] See CFI, Case T-58/08 P *Roodhuijzen* [2009] E.C.R. II-3797, paras 68–102 (on medical insurance). See also ECJ (judgment of April 15, 2010), Case C-485/08 P *Gualtieri v Commission*, not yet reported, paras 70–76 (marital status considered a relevant factor for determining amount of daily subsistence allowance).

legislation on the right of citizens of the Union and their family members to move and reside freely within the territory of the Member States includes among the "family members" of a citizen the registered partner if the legislation of the host Member State treats registered partnership as equivalent to marriage.[308] It is also contrary to the principle of equal treatment for the Union institutions to make the grant of an allowance for an official's children who have lost their other parent dependent upon the condition that the official was married to that other parent.[309]

B. CONTENT

1. Substantive discrimination

Definition. In Union law, the prohibition of discrimination does not only require equal treatment formally to be complied with, but also that no inequality is caused in practice. Where that occurs, there is substantive discrimination. According to the Court of Justice, it is specifically prohibited to treat "either similar situations differently or different situations identically".[310] In order to categorise cases as "similar" or "different", they must be considered in the light of the aims of the measure in question. Substantive discrimination will be tolerated only if the difference in treatment (or, conversely, the absence of differential treatment in the presence of differing cases) is justified.[311] In order for this to be so, the "unequal" treatment must be proportionate to the objective sought by the authority.[312] Often,

7–061

---

[308] Directive 2004/38/EC of the European Parliament and of the Council of April 29, 2004 on the right of the citizen of the Union and their family members to move and reside freely within the territory of the Member States, [2004] O.J. L158/77 (for that Directive, see paras 5–127 and 12–009).

[309] CFI, Case T-307/00 *C v Commission* [2003] E.C.R.—SC II-221, paras 48–56.

[310] ECJ, Case 13/63 *Italy v Commission* [1963] E.C.R. 165; see also ECJ, Case 8/82 *Wagner v Balm* [1983] E.C.R. 371, para. 18. For instances in which dissimilar situations required differing measures, see ECJ, Case 230/78 *Eridania* [1979] E.C.R. 2749, paras 18–19, at 2767–2768; CFI, Case T-47/91 *Auzat v Commission* [1992] E.C.R. II-2535 and Case T-75/91 *Scaramuzza v Commission* [1992] E.C.R. II-2557.

[311] ECJ, Joined Cases 117/76 and 16/77 *Ruckdeschel* [1977] E.C.R. 1753, para. 7. For a case in which unequal treatment arising out of uniform rules (establishment of a common organisation of the market in bananas) laid down for differing situations was justified by the aim of integrating the national markets, see ECJ, Case C-280/93 *Germany v Council* [1994] E.C.R. I-4973, para. 74; this judgment was criticised in Everling, "Will Europe Slip on Bananas? The Banana Judgment of the Court of Justice and National Courts" (1996) C.M.L.Rev. 401, at 415–416. For unequal treatment which is justified on grounds of environment protection, see para. 5–111.

[312] For different treatment which was objectively justified but not proportional, see ECJ, Case C-29/95 *Pastoors and Trans-Cap* [1997] E.C.R. I-285, paras 19–26;

the reason given in justification is considered together with the question whether the cases in question are similar or different.[313]

2. Direct and indirect discrimination

7–062 **Definitions.** Discrimination is direct where a measure employs a prohibited distinguishing criterion (e.g. nationality) or subjects different cases to formally similar rules. Indirect discrimination arises where, although not making use of an unlawful distinguishing criterion, a provision has effects coinciding with or approaching those of such a distinguishing criterion as a result of its use of other distinguishing criteria which are not as such prohibited.[314] Accordingly, the Court of Justice has held that:

> "[t]he rules regarding equality of treatment, both in the Treaty and in Article 7 of Regulation No 1612/68, forbid not only overt discrimination by reason of nationality but also all covert forms of discrimination which, by the application of other criteria of differentiation, lead in fact to the same result."[315]

Thus, for instance, the criterion of residence may in fact produce the same result as discrimination on grounds of nationality.[316] A measure will also be indirectly discriminatory where it distinguishes only formally between different cases, but in reality treats them the same.

7–063 **Indirect discrimination.** The Court of Justice has repeatedly had to consider cases of indirect sex discrimination, particularly when interpreting the "principle of equal pay for male and female workers for equal work or work of equal value" enshrined in Art. 157 TFEU [*ex Art. 141 EC*].[317] Thus, the question arose whether

---

[313] See, e.g. ECJ, Case 35/80 *Denkavit Nederland* [1981] E.C.R. 45, paras 16–17. Accordingly, it is possible to find that the principle of equality has been infringed where a difference in treatment does not have regard to the principle of proportionality: see ECJ, Case C-323/95 *Hayes* [1997] E.C.R. I-1711, paras 24–25.

[314] For a general discussion, see Garronne, "La discrimination indirecte en droit communautaire: vers une théorie générale" (1994) R.T.D.E. 425–449.

[315] ECJ, Case 152/73 *Sotgiu* [1974] E.C.R. 153, para. 11. See also ECJ, Case 41/84 *Pinna* [1986] E.C.R. 1, para. 23; ECJ, Case 33/88 *Allué and Others* [1989] E.C.R. 1591, paras 11–12. For an application under the EAEC Treaty, see ECJ, Case C-115/08 *ČEZ* (n. 198, *supra*), paras 95–97.

[316] See, for example, ECJ, Case C-29/95 *Pastoors and Trans-Cap* [1997] E.C.R. I-285, paras 17–18; ECJ, Case C-103/08 *Gottwald* (n. 243, *supra*), paras 27–28; ECJ (judgment of April 13, 2010), Case C-73/08 *Bressol and Others*, not yet reported, paras 44–46.

[317] See also para. 5–063. For this and other instances of indirect discrimination, see, for instance, Prechal, "Combating Indirect Discrimination in Community Law Context" (1993) L.I.E.I. 81–97; Adinolfi, "Indirect Discrimination on Grounds of Sex in Collective Labour Agreements" (1992) C.M.L.Rev. 637–645; Hervey, "Justification for Indirect Sex Discrimination in Employment: European Community and United Kingdom Law Compared" (1990) I.C.L.Q. 807–826.

a difference in the level of pay for work carried out part time and the same work carried out full time was capable of constituting discrimination where the category of part-time workers was exclusively or predominantly comprised of women. The Court of Justice held that different treatment was acceptable,

"in so far as the difference in pay between part-time work and full-time work is attributable to factors which are objectively justified and are in no way related to any discrimination based on sex."[318]

It is for the national court, which has jurisdiction to make findings of fact and interpret the national legislation, to determine whether a pay policy of a given employer or a statutory provision which in fact affects women more than men can be objectively justified. The measures chosen in the policy or provision must correspond to a real need on the part of the undertaking or a necessary aim of a national social policy and be in proportion to the objective pursued (that is to say, appropriate and indispensable in order to attain that objective).[319] Also in other circumstances in which a national or a Union measure is couched in neutral terms but women are in fact disadvantaged, it must be examined whether the criterion employed is justified by objective factors independent of any discrimination on grounds of sex.[320]

3. Reverse discrimination

Internal situations. The Union prohibition of discrimination cannot be applied to purely internal matters of a Member State which have no connection with a situation to which Union law applies. Accordingly, a national of a Member State may in principle rely on the provisions relating to the free movement of goods, persons, services and capital only in so far as he or she is not in a purely internal situation.[321] In such a situation, a Member State may adopt measures which treat its own nationals less favourably than nationals of other Member States. So a Member State may obviously treat its nationals differently from nationals of other Member States where it enacts legislation for vessels flying the national flag outside its territorial

7–064

---

[318] ECJ, Case 96/80 *Jenkins* [1981] E.C.R. 911, paras 11–12.

[319] See, by way of example, ECJ, Case 170/84 *Bilka* [1986] E.C.R. 1607, para. 36 (wages policy of an employer); ECJ, Case 171/88 *Rinner Kühn* [1989] E.C.R. 2743, paras 14–15 (national provision). The Court of Justice held that there was a justified national social policy objective in Case C-229/89 *Commission v Belgium* [1991] E.C.R. I-2205, paras 19–26. For the temporal effects of Art. 157 TFEU [*ex Art. 141 EC*], see para. 21–057, *infra*.

[320] ECJ, Case C-25/02 *Rinke* [2003] E.C.R. I-8349, paras 36–42.

[321] Compare the stricter requirement for a transborder situation for the application of the provisions on free movement of persons and services (see paras 9–057 and 9–088, *infra*) with the relatively ready acceptance of a transborder factor in applying the provisions on free movement of goods (see paras 5–088 and 5–100).

waters, since, under the rules of public international law, it may exercise its jurisdiction beyond territorial sea limits only over vessels flying its flag.[322] In a purely domestic situation falling outside the field of application of Union law, a Member State is also not debarred under that law from exercising "reverse discrimination" by treating its own subjects or national situations less favourably than nationals of other Member States or situations stemming from other Member States.[323] Any discrimination which this would cause must then be dealt with within the framework of the internal legal system of the State in question.[324] Even in such purely internal situations, national courts may have regard to provisions of Union law.[325]

7–065   **Free movement.** Such "reverse discrimination" is prohibited by Union law only where it threatens the aims of the Treaties. This will be the case in practice where a situation cannot be regarded as purely internal from the point of view of the Member State concerned. Thus, the fundamental freedoms relating to establishment and the provision of services do not admit of interpretation:

> "so as to exclude from the benefit of Union law a given Member State's own nationals when the latter, owing to the fact that they have lawfully resided on the territory of another Member State and have there acquired a trade qualification which is recognised by provisions of Union law, are, with regard to their State of origin, in a situation which may be assimilated to that of any other persons enjoying the rights and liberties guaranteed by the Treaty."[326]

When the Dutchman Knoors applied to the Netherlands authorities for an authorisation to carry on the trade of a plumber in his own country on the ground of the skills which he had acquired in Belgium, the Netherlands had to recognise those skills spursuant to Directive 64/427[327] relating to attainment of freedom of establishment

---

[322] ECJ, Case C-379/92 *Peralta* [1994] E.C.R. I-3453, para. 47.

[323] *Ibid.*, para. 27; ECJ, Case C-132/93 *Steen* [1994] E.C.R. I-2715, paras 8–11. Weyer, "Freier Wahrenverkehr, rein innerstaatliche Sachverhalte und umgekehrte Diskriminierung" (1998) EuR. 435–461; Münnich, "Art. 7 und Inländerdiskriminierung" (1992) Z.f.R.V. 92–100; See also Nicolaysen, 'Inländerdiskriminierung im Warenverkehr" (1991) EuR. 95–120.

[324] ECJ, Joined Cases C-45/96 and C-46/96 *Uecker and Jacquet* [1997] E.C.R. I-3171, para. 23 (which makes it clear that the introduction of citizenship of the Union makes no difference to this position). See also König, "Das Problem der Inländerdiskriminierung—Abschied von Reinheitsgebot, Nachtbackverbot und Meisterprüfung?" (1993) A.ö.R. 591–616.

[325] ECJ, Case C-212/06 *Government of the French Community and Walloon Government v Flemish Government* [2008] E.C.R. I-1683, paras 38–40. See also Judgment 11/2009 of January 21, 2009 of the Constitutional Court of Belgium (see the discussion by Van Elsuwege and Adam in (2009) E.Const.L.Rev. 327–339).

[326] ECJ, Case 115/78 *Knoors* [1979] E.C.R. 399, para. 24. See also para. 9–057, *infra.*

[327] Council Directive 64/427/EEC of July 7, 1964 laying down detailed provisions concerning transitional measures in respect of activities of self-employed persons in manufacturing and processing industries falling within ISIC Major Groups 23–40 (Industry and small craft industries), [1963–1964] O.J. English Spec. Ed. 148.

and freedom to provide services. There is no question of there being a purely internal situation where a national holds a professional diploma issued in another Member State, not even if the diploma is not actually recognised by a provision of Union law.[328] This also applies to nationals wishing to use a diploma which does not afford access to employment or self-employment, but nevertheless affords advantages for the exercise of a profession.[329] According to the Court of Justice, there is no question of there being an internal situation where a national can rely on a right to free movement against his own Member State.[330] EU nationals, as citizens of the Union, may not be disadvantaged simply because they have exercised their right to free movement, for example by studying in or moving to another Member State.[331] As a result of the increasing range of circumstances in which persons may derive rights from Union law with regard to the Member State of which they are nationals,[332] it will become more difficult for Member States to apply reverse discrimination.[333]

Circumvention. However, Union law does not allow a person to use free movement in order to evade the legislation of his or her Member State. A Member State may have a legitimate interest in preventing its nationals from wrongly evading the application of national legislation as regards training for a trade[334] or the manner of exercise of an activity, by means of facilities created under the Treaties.[335]   **7–066**

---

[328] ECJ, Case C-61/89 *Bouchoucha* [1990] E.C.R. I-3551, paras 11 and 14.

[329] See, for the use of an LLM degree, ECJ, Case C-19/92 *Kraus* [1993] E.C.R. I-1663, paras 17–18.

[330] ECJ, Case C-378/97 *Wijsenbeek* [1999] E.C.R. I-6207, paras 18–23.

[331] ECJ, Case C-224/98 *D'Hoop* [2002] E.C.R. I-6191, paras 27–35; ECJ, Case C-224/02 *Pusa* [2004] E.C.R. I-5763, para. 17; ECJ, Case C-520/04 *Turpeinen* [2006] E.C.R. I-10685, paras 20–23; ECJ, Case C-406/04 *De Cuyper* [2006] E.C.R. I-6947, para. 39; ECJ, Case C-192/05 *Tas-Hagen and Tas* [2006] E.C.R. I-10451, paras 30–32; ECJ, Case C-76/05 *Schwarz and Gootjes-Schwarz* [2007] E.C.R. I-6849, para. 93; ECJ, Joined Cases C-11/06 and C-12/06 *Morgan and Bucher* [2007] E.C.R. I-9161, para. 25; ECJ, Case C-499/06 *Nerkowska* [2008] E.C.R. I-3993, para. 32; ECJ, Case C-353/06 *Grunkin and Paul* [2008] E.C.R. I-7639 paras 21–28; ECJ, Case C-221/07 *Zablocka-Weyhermüller* [2008] E.C.R. I-9029 para. 35. See Tryfonidou, "Reverse Discrimination in Purely Internal Situations: An Incongruity in a Citizens' Europe" (2008) 35 L.I.E.I. 43–67; Staples, "Heeft omgekeerde discriminatie zijn langste tijd gehad?" (2002) N.T.E.R. 205–209.

[332] See, with regard to the free movement of workers, ECJ, Case C-281/98 *Angonese* [2000] E.C.R. I-4139 (discussed in para. 9–057, *infra*).

[333] See Papadopoulou, "Situations purement internes et droit communautaire: un instrument jurisprudentiel à double fonction ou une arme à double tranchant?" (2002) C.D.E. 95–129; De Beys, "Le droit européen est-il applicable aux situations purement internes? A propos des discriminations à rebours dans le marché unique" (2001) J.T.D.E. 137–144.

[334] ECJ, Case 115/78 *Knoors* [1979] E.C.R. 399, para. 25. That was the case in ECJ, Case C-61/89 *Bouchoucha* [1990] E.C.R. I-3551.

[335] ECJ, Case C-148/91 *Veronica Omroep Organisatie* [1993] E.C.R. I-487, paras 12–14; ECJ, Case C-23/93 *TV10* [1994] E.C.R. I-4795, paras 17–22, with a case note by Straetmans and Goemans (1995) Col.J.E.L. 319–331; ECJ, Case C-212/97 *Centros* [1999] E.C.R. I-1459, paras 23–30.

CHAPTER 8

THE CITIZENS OF THE UNION

Citizenship. Title II of the TEU ("Provisions on democratic principles") starts   **8–001**
out by stressing the principle of the equality of the Union's citizens, mentioning
at the same time Union citizenship as being additional to national citizenship
(Art. 9 TEU). In 1992, the Treaty on European Union introduced the idea of citizenship of the Union to make it clear that the European Union not only confers
rights on persons who are engaged in an economic activity, but on all persons who
have the nationality of a Member State. The Lisbon Treaty combined the provisions of the EC Treaty on non-discrimination with the ones on citizenship in Part
Two of the TFEU ("Non-discrimination and Citizenship of the Union").

I. CREATION OF CITIZENSHIP OF THE UNION

Steps towards citizenship. The idea of conferring certain rights on Member   **8–002**
State nationals as citizens of the supranational entity grew up in parallel with
proposals to bring together the various integration paths into a single European
Union (see paras 3–001—3–016).[1] At the instigation of the Paris Summit
(December 1974), the Tindemans Report on European Union (1975) considered
possible ways of strengthening the protection of citizens' rights and of making
European solidarity tangible by means of external signs.[2] Also on the instructions
of the Paris Summit, the Commission brought out reports on the feasibility of
introducing a uniform passport, establishing a passport union and conferring special rights on citizens of the Member States, inter alia, so as to allow them to vote
and stand as a candidate in municipal and, possibly also, regional elections and to
hold public office at those levels.[3]

---

[1] For a survey, see the Commission's communication to the European Parliament of June 24, 1988
entitled "A people's Europe" (1988) EC Bull. Suppl. 2. See also Condinazi, Lang and Nascimbene,
Citizenship of the Union and Freedom of Movement of Persons (Leiden & Boston, Martinus
Nijhoff, 2008) 265pp.
[2] (1976) EC Bull. Suppl. 1, 29–31. For the Paris Summit, see (1974) 12 EC Bull. point 1104, No. 13.
[3] Towards European citizenship, "A Passport Union" and "The granting of special rights", reports
presented by the Commission in implementation of points 10 and 11, respectively, of the final communiqué issued at the European Summit held in Paris on December 9 and 10, 1974, (1975) EC
Bull. Suppl. 7.

8–003 **Symbols of the Union.** Citizens did not start to become more involved in the integration process until the first direct elections to the European Parliament in 1979. In 1985, the Adonnino Committee set up by the European Council produced two reports containing further proposals on how to attain a people's Europe.[4] The proposals received a positive reception at the Milan European Council of June 28 and 29, 1985[5] and have since either largely been translated into measures securing free movement of persons and mobility for students or resulted in the conferral of new competences on the Union in the social and cultural spheres by the Single European Act and the EU Treaty.[6] As the Adonnino Committee had proposed, the Union's image and identity have been strengthened through the adoption of the flag and the anthem of the Council of Europe[7] and the introduction of a Union driving licence.[8] The Member States also agreed amongst themselves to introduce a passport of uniform pattern.[9] The flag and the anthem have developed into symbols of the European Union, together with the euro,[10] the motto "United in

---

[4] A People's Europe, Reports from the ad hoc Committee (1985) EC Bull. Suppl. 7 (reports of March 29–30, and June 28–29, 1985). For the Committee's terms of reference, see para. 3–005, *supra*.

[5] (1985) 6 EC Bull. point 1.4.8. In the *Erasmus* judgment, the Court of Justice referred to "achievement of a people's Europe" as one of the Union's general objectives: ECJ, Case 242/87 *Commission v Council* [1989] E.C.R. 1425, para. 29.

[6] See Schockweiler, "La dimension humaine et sociale de la Communauté européenne" (1993) 4 R.M.U.E. 11–45, especially at 14–35.

[7] The official flag of the Union is rectangular in form and blue in colour and has at its centre a circle of 12 five-pointed gold stars (the number twelve symbolises perfection and entirety and hence is not linked to the number of Member States; see the Commission's answer of November 22, 1993 to question No. E-1701/93 (Von Wechmar), [1994] O.J. C219/31); its anthem is the music of the Ode to Joy from the fourth movement of Beethoven's Ninth Symphony (both printed in (1986) 4 EC Bull. 52–53). See the request contained in the European Parliament's resolution of April 11, 1983 ([1983] O.J. C128/18), the approval of the Adonnino Committee's proposal by the European Council ((1985) 6 EC Bull. points 1.4.7 and 1.4.8), and the declaration of the Presidents of the Council and the other institutions ((1986) 4 EC Bull. point 2.1.8.1). See also Bieber, "Die Flagge in der EG", in Fiedler and Ress (eds), *Verfassungsrecht und Völkerrecht. Gedächtnisschrift für Wilhelm Karl Geck* (Cologne, Heymanns, 1989), 59–77. Further particulars of the flag as the European emblem may be found in CFI, Case T-127/02 *Concept—Anlagen u. Geräte nach "GMP" für Produktion u. Labor v Office of Harmonisation in the Internal Market* [2004] E.C.R. II-1113 (on the prohibition to register trade marks on account of their similarity to the European emblem).

[8] First Council Directive 80/1263/EEC of December 4, 1980 on the introduction of a Community driving licence, [1980] O.J. L375/1; Council Directive 91/439/EEC of July 29, 1991 on driving licences, [1991] O.J. L 237/1. See also para. 9–064, *supra*.

[9] See the resolutions adopted on June 23, 1981 and June 30, 1982 by the representatives of the governments of the Member States, meeting within the Council ([1981] O.J. C241/1, and [1982] O.J. C179/1, respectively), confirmed by the European Council at Fontainebleau on June 25 and 26, 1984 (1984) 6 EC Bull. points 1.1.9 and 3.5.1), on July 14, 1986 ([1986] O.J. C185/1) and on July 10, 1995 ([1995] C 200/1). See Denza, "Le passeport européen" (1982) R.M.C. 489–493.

[10] See Kaelberer, "The euro and European identity: symbols, power and the politics of European monetary union" (2004) 30 Rev.I.S. 161–178.

diversity" and May 9, as "Europe Day".[11] During the 2007 Intergovernmental Conference it was decided that the Treaties should not contain any explicit reference to these symbols, thereby departing from what was proposed in the European Constitution, which explicitly mentioned the symbols of the Union in Art. I-8.[12] For its part, the European Parliament included a reference to the Union's symbols in its Rules of Procedure (Rule 213).

Citizenship of the Union. The threads leading to the grant of political rights to Member State nationals were not woven together until it was decided to give such persons the status of "citizens of the Union". At Spain's instigation, the 1990–1991 Intergovernmental Conference decided to introduce citizenship of the Union concurrently with the establishment of the European Union.[13] The EU Treaty inserted "Part Two" of the EC Treaty on "Citizenship of the Union"[14] *[now replaced by Part II of the TFEU on "Non-discrimination and citizenship of the Union"].* Since, the introduction of citizenship has provided the justification for

8–004

---

[11] The celebration of May 9 refers to the day in 1950 on which Robert Schuman pronounced the declaration containing the proposal that led to the creation of the ECSC (see para. 1–006). For these symbols, see Favret, "L'Union européenne: 'l'unité dans la diversité'—Signification et pertinence d'une devise" (2003) R.T.D.E. 657–660; Röttinger, "Die Hoheitszeichen der Europäischen Union—ein paar vielleicht nicht nur theoretische Rechtsfragen" (2003) EuR. 1095–1108. On their impact, see Theiler, *Political symbolism and European integration* (Manchester, Manchester University Press, 2005), 192 pp.

[12] See, however, Declaration (No. 52), annexed to the Lisbon Treaty ([2010] O.J. C83/355), in which 16 of the Member States declare that these symbols will for them continue as symbols to express the sense of community of the people in the European Union and their allegiance to it.

[13] See Closa, "The Concept of Citizenship in the Treaty on European Union" (1992) C.M.L.Rev. 1137, at 1153–1157; Solbes Mira, "La citoyenneté européenne" (1991) R.M.C. 168–170. For the first worked-out proposal, see the text submitted to the Intergovernmental Conference by the Spanish delegation on September 24, 1990, reproduced in Laursen and Vanhoonacker (eds), *The Intergovernmental Conference on Political Union* (Maastricht, European Institute of Public Administration/Martinus Nijhoff, 1992), 328–332.

[14] For general discussions of citizenship of the Union, see, amongst others, Goudappel, *The Effects of EU Citizenship: Economic, Social and Political Rights in a Time of Constitutional Change* (Cambridge, Cambridge University Press, 2010), 250 pp.; Dollat, *La citoyenneté européenne: théorie et statuts* (Brussels, Bruylant, 2008), 698 pp.; Schönberger, *Unionsbürger; Europas föderales Bürgerrecht in vergleichender Sicht* (Tübingen, Mohr Siebeck 2005) 597 pp.; O'Leary, *The Evolving Concept of Community Citizenship. From the Free Movement of Persons to Union Citizenship* (The Hague, Kluwer Law International, 1996), 347 pp; the articles in the "Special issue: European Citizenship at Center-Stage" (2009) Col.J.E.L. Vol 15.2.; Calliess, "Der Unionsbürger: Status, Dogmatik und Dynamik" (2007) EuR. 7–42; Chiti, "Consequences of citizenship in Europe—are new layers of complexity emerging?" (2007) 19 E.Rev.Priv.L. 99–123; Dougan, "The Constitutional dimension to the case law on Union citizenship" (2006) E.L.Rev. 613–641; Kostakopoulou, "Ideas, Norms and European Citizenship: Explaining Institutional Change" (2005) Mod.L.Rev. 233–267; Reich, "The Constitutional Relevance of Citizenship and Free Movement in an Enlarged Union" (2005) E.L.J. 675–698; Oosterom-Staples and Vazquez Muñoz, "Burgerschap van de Unie" (2004) S.E.W. 494–506.

the Union, acting under Art. 308 EC *[now Art. 352 TFEU]*, to support organisations promoting "active European citizenship" (e.g. through the twinning of local authorities).[15]

II. DEFINITION OF CITIZENSHIP

8–005 **Nationality of Member State.** A citizen of the Union is defined as any person holding the nationality of a Member State (Art. 9 TEU and Art. 20(1) TFEU *[ex Art. 17(1) EC]*).[16] Accordingly, this includes persons having the nationality of a Member State who reside in one of the Overseas Countries and Territories referred to in Art. 355(3) TFEU *[ex Art. 299(3) EC]*.[17] Citizenship of the Union is additional to and does not replace national citizenship (Art. 9 TEU and Art. 20(1) TFEU).[18]

Since citizenship depends on a person's having the status of a national of a Member State, the Union differs fundamentally from federal States, in which nationality invariably falls within the jurisdiction of the federal authority.[19] Whether a person has the nationality of a Member State is to be determined solely by reference to the nationality rules of the Member State concerned.[20] This is

---

[15] See Council Decision of January 26, 2004 establishing a Community action programme to promote active European citizenship (civic participation), [2004] O.J. L30/6. In the preamble, reference is made to the call to bring citizens closer to the European design and the European institutions as formulated in the Declaration of Laeken (see para. 4–001, *supra*).

[16] The European Parliament used the same definition in its Declaration of fundamental rights and freedoms of April 12, 1989 ([1989] O.J. C120/51), Art. 25(3) of which states that a Community citizen shall be "any person possessing the nationality of one of the Member States".

[17] ECJ, Case C-300/04 *Eman and Sevinger* [2006] E.C.R. I-8055, paras 27–29. For the OCTs, see para. 12–007, *infra*. For the status under EU law of Dutch nationals from overseas territories, see Kochenov, "The Impact of European Citizenship on the Association of the Overseas Countries and Territories with the European Community" (2009) L.I.E.I. 239–256; Besselink, "Nederlands postkoloniaal kiesrecht: het Europees Parlement en de Tweede Kamer" (2007) N.T.E.R. 64–71; Staples, "Wie is burger van de Unie?" (2001) N.T.E.R. 109–112.

[18] The Treaty of Amsterdam added this provision to Art. 17 EC so as to make it absolutely clear that Union citizenship is complementary. The wording of the sentence inserted by the Amsterdam Treaty ("Citizenship of the Union complements and does not replace national citizenship") was slightly changed by the Treaty of Lisbon (see Art. 20(2) TFEU). See also Closa, "Citizenship of the Union and Nationality of Member States" (1995) C.M.L.Rev. 487–518.

[19] Schönberger, "European citizenship as federal citizenship. Some citizenship lessons of comparative federalism", (2007) 19 ERPL 61–81; Kovar and Simon, "La citoyenneté européenne" (1993) C.D.E. 285, at 294.

[20] This principle of international law was confirmed by Declaration (No. 2), annexed to the EU Treaty, on nationality of a Member State and the Decision of the Heads of State or Government, meeting within the European Council on December 11 and 12, 1992, concerning certain problems raised by Denmark on the Treaty on European Union (Section A, "Citizenship", [1992] O.J. C348/2). For the influence of the provisions on citizenship of the Union on national citizenship policies, see Rostek, "The impact of Union citizenship on national citizenship policies" (2007) 22 Tulane E. & Civ. L. F. 89–156.

because what underlies the bond of nationality is a "special relationship of allegiance to the State and reciprocity of rights and duties".[21] A declaration annexed to the EU Treaty authorised Member States to declare for information, who were to be considered their nationals for the purpose of application of Union law.[22] The Court of Justice considers itself bound by these declarations for the purpose of determining the scope of citizenship of the Union.[23] At the same time, the Court has made it clear that, when exercising their powers in the sphere of nationality, the Member States must have due regard to European Union law.[24] Consequently, the power of the Member States to lay down the conditions for the acquisition and loss of nationality is amenable to judicial review in so far as it affects the rights conferred by the Union on citizens of the Union.[25] Accordingly, a decision to withdraw nationality which leads to the loss for the individual concerned of his or her status of citizen of the Union may be reviewed in the light of the general principle of Union law, in particular the principle of proportionality.[26]

Where having the nationality of a Member State is a condition for enjoyment of a Union right, Union law requires Member States to recognise the nationality of another Member State without imposing any other condition (e.g. residence in

---

[21] ECJ, Case 149/79 *Commission v Belgium* [1980] E.C.R. 3881, para. 10.

[22] See Declaration No. 2 (cited in n. 20). Only two Member States made use of this possibility. See the declaration made upon signature of the EEC Treaty by the Government of the Federal Republic of Germany on the definition of the expression "German national" (mentioned in the final act to the EEC Treaty) and the declaration made on the accession of the United Kingdom by the British Government on the definition of the term "nationals", [1972] O.J. L73/196), replaced by a declaration of 1982, [1983] O.J. C23/1 (that declaration was reiterated, in slightly modified form, at the time of signature of the Treaty of Lisbon; see the Declaration (No. 63), annexed to the Lisbon Treaty, by the United Kingdom of Great Britain and Northern Ireland on the definition of the term "nationals", [2010] O.J. C83/358). See also Hailbronner, "Germany", in Bauböck, Ersbøll, Groenendijk and Waldrauch (eds), *Acquisition and loss of nationality: Policies and Trends in 15 European Countries. Volume 2: Country Analyses* (Amsterdam, Amsterdam University Press, 2006) 213–251; Simmonds, "The British Nationality Act 1981 and the Definition of the Term 'National' for Community Purposes" (1984) C.M.L.Rev. 675–686; Bleckmann, "German nationality within the meaning of the EEC Treaty" (1978) C.M.L.Rev. 435–446.

[23] ECJ, Case C-192/99 *Kaur* [2001] E.C.R. I-1237, paras 19–27; CFI, Case T-230/94 *Farrugia v Commission* [1996] E.C.R. II-195, paras 16–31. See Hall, "Determining the Scope ratione personae of European Citizenship: Customary International Law Prevails for Now" (2001) 28 L.I.E.I. 355–360.

[24] ECJ, Case C-369/90 *Micheletti and Others* [1992] E.C.R. I-4239, para. 10; ECJ, Case C-179/98 *Mesbah* [1999] E.C.R. I-7955, para. 29; ECJ, Case C-192/99 *Kaur* [2001] E.C.R. I-1237, para. 19; ECJ, Case C-200/02 *Zhu and Chen* [2004] E.C.R. I-9925, para. 37; ECJ (judgment of March 2, 2010), Case C-135/08 *Rottmann*, not yet reported, paras 39–45.

[25] ECJ, Case C-135/08 *Rottmann* (n. 24, *supra*), paras 46–48.

[26] ECJ, Case C-135/08 *Rottmann* (n. 24, *supra*), paras 50–59. Other general principles of Union law which Member States must, arguably, respect in this context are fundamental rights. See, already, Hall, "Loss of Union Citizenship in Breach of Fundamental Rights" (1996) E.L.Rev. 129–143.

the territory of the Member State whose nationality is relied on).[27] This means therefore that Member States must unconditionally accept the citizenship of the Union conferred by another Member State (through bestowal of the nationality of that State). In this way, Union law diverges from international law where a State may refuse to recognise the nationality of a person if it was granted contrary to international law and, in the case of a person having plural nationality (of two or more foreign States), may have regard to the "master" nationality.[28] A Member State cannot therefore preclude the application of Union law by relying, with regard to nationals of another Member States who are residing on their territory— and hence fall within the scope of application of Union law—, on the fact that the persons concerned also have the nationality of the Member State of residence.[29]

III. SUBSTANCE OF CITIZENSHIP

A. SURVEY

8–006 **Rights associated with citizenship.** Citizens of the Union enjoy the rights and are subject to the duties provided for in the Treaties (Art. 20(2) TFEU [ex Art. 17(2) EC]). Article 20(2) TFEU further sums up some of the rights associated with citizenship of the Union and provides that they have to be exercised in accordance with the conditions and limits defined by the Treaties and by the measures adopted thereunder. It concerns the rights which are laid down in Arts 21 to 24 TFEU (see the discussion in paras 8–008—8–014, *infra*). Those rights are vested in citizens of the Union in their capacity as nationals of a Member State

---

[27] ECJ, Case C-369/90 *Micheletti and Others* [1992] E.C.R. I-4239, paras 10–11 (on freedom of establishment), with a critical note by Jessurun d'Oliveira (1993) C.M.L.Rev. 623–637; ECJ, Case C-200/02 *Zhu and Chen* [2004] E.C.R. I-9925, para. 39, with case notes by Carlier (2005) C.M.L.Rev. 1121–1131, Hofstötter (2005) E.L.Rev. 548–558, Tryfonidou (2005) 11 E.Pub.L. 527–541, Vanvoorden (2005) 12 Col.J.E.L. 305–321. See also Kunoy, "A Union of national citizens: the origins of the Court's lack of avant-gardisme in the Chen case" (2006) C.M.L.Rev. 179–190. This is not the case where a Member State has to do with a worker who has both the nationality of that Member State and that of a third country with which the Union has concluded an association agreement: ECJ, Case C-179/98 *Mesbah* [1999] E.C.R. I-7955, paras 29–41.

[28] See Kovar and Simon (n. 19, *supra*), at 291–292, and especially Zimmermann, "Europäisches Gemeinschaftsrecht und Staatsangehörigkeit der Mitgliedstaaten unter besonderer Berücksichtigung der Probleme mehrfacher Staatsangehörigkeit" (1995) EuR. 54–70. The Court of Justice points out that the Hague Convention of April 12, 1930 on certain questions relating to the conflict of nationality laws (League of Nations Treaty Series, Vol. 179, p.89) does not impose an obligation but simply provides an option, in the case of dual nationality, for the contracting parties to give priority to their own nationality over any other: ECJ, Case C-148/02 *Garcia Avello* [2003] E.C.R. I-11613, para. 28.

[29] ECJ, Case C-148/02 *Garcia Avello* [2003] E.C.R. I-11613, para. 28; for a discussion of the case, see Verlinden (2005) 11 Col.J.E.L. 705–716; Iliopoulou (2004) 40 R.T.D.E. 559–579.

and therefore as Union citizens even if they are not in gainful employment or self-employed. Those articles not only codify rights recognised by Union law even before the EU Treaty entered into force (right to move and reside, right of petition), but also create rights of considerable political importance (right to vote and stand as a candidate in European and municipal elections; diplomatic protection; right to apply to the European Ombudsman).[30]

In the Charter of Fundamental Rights of the European Union, the rights of citizens of the Union are enshrined in the chapter entitled "Citizens' rights".[31] As in the case of the Treaties, the Charter extends some rights to natural and legal persons who reside or have their corporate seat in a Member State (access to documents and to the European Ombudsman and the right of petition) and reserves other rights to Union citizens (the right to vote and stand for election, diplomatic and consular protection). The other rights which the Charter confers only on citizens are the right to engage in work and to pursue a freely chosen or accepted occupation, to exercise the right of establishment and to provide services in any Member State and the right to move and reside freely within the territory of the Member States.[32]

The first paragraph of Art. 25 TFEU [ex Art. 22 EC] requires the Commission to report every three years on the application of the provisions on citizenship, taking into account the "development of the Union". In addition, the Council, acting unanimously in accordance with a special legislative procedure and after obtaining the consent of the European Parliament, may adopt provisions to strengthen or to add to the rights listed in Art. 20(2). Any provisions so adopted can only enter into force after approval by the Member States in accordance with their respective constitutional requirements (Art. 25, second para., TFEU; see para. 5–007).

Equal treatment. The rights associated with the status of Union citizen include the right enshrined in Art. 18 TFEU [ex Art. 12 EC] not to be discriminated against on grounds of nationality within the scope of application of the Treaties.[33] The Court has observed in this regard that: **8–007**

---

[30] For a survey, see Kadelbach, "Union Citizenship", in von Bogdandy and Bast, *Principles of European Constitutional Law* (Oxford, Hart, 2010) 443–478; Staeglich, "Rechte und Pflichten aus der Unionsbürgerschaft" (2004) Z.Eu.S. 485–531.

[31] See Arts 39 to 46 of the Charter. For the fact that citizenship confers rights on persons regardless of their economic activity, see ECJ, Case C-413/99 *Baumbast and R.* [2002] E.C.R. I-7091, paras 81–84.

[32] Charter, Art. 15(2) and Art. 45(1). Where nationals of third countries are authorised to work in the territories of the Member States, they are entitled to working conditions equivalent to those of citizens of the Union (Charter, Art. 15(3)); freedom of movement and residence may be granted, in accordance with the Treaty establishing the European Community, to nationals of third countries legally resident in the territory of a Member State (Charter, Art. 45(2)). Under the heading of "citizenship", the right to good administration is stated to be applicable to everyone (and hence not just to citizens) (Charter, Art. 41).

[33] E.g. ECJ, Case C-85/96 *Martínez Sala* [1998] E.C.R. I-2691, para. 62; case note by O'Leary (1999) E.L.Rev. 68–79. See the detailed discussion in paras 7–050 *et seq.*, *supra*.

"Union citizenship is destined to be the fundamental status of nationals of the Member States, enabling those who find themselves in the same situation to enjoy the same treatment in law irrespective of their nationality, subject to such exceptions as are expressly provided for".[34]

The strong link between the principle of non-discrimination and the provisions on citizenship of the Union was confirmed by the Treaty of Lisbon, which brought them together in Part II of the TFEU ("Non-discrimination and citizenship of the Union").[35]

B. FREE MOVEMENT AND RESIDENCE RIGHTS

8–008   **Free movement and residence.** Citizenship of the Union entails the right,

"to move and reside freely within the territory of the Member States, subject to the limitations and conditions laid down in the Treaties and by the measures adopted to give them effect" (Art. 21(1) TFEU [*ex Art. 18(1) EC*]).

As a result, the Treaties now explicitly enshrine the rights of free movement and residence conferred by secondary Union law in connection with the free movement of persons and services on qualifying persons and members of their families. Furthermore, it follows from Art. 21(1) TFEU that a national of a Member State who does not enjoy a right of residence as a result of other provisions of Union law may, simply by virtue of being a citizen of the Union, enjoy a right of residence directly pursuant to that article.[36] Article 21(1) does not, however, prevent Member States from imposing restrictions on the right of movement and residence pursuant to Arts 45(3), 52 and 62 TFEU [*ex Arts 39(3), 46 and 55 EC*]—i.e. in connection with the free movement of workers, self-employed persons and services—on grounds of public policy, public security or public health. In addition, Union legislation may make the exercise of the right of residence subject to still other conditions, provided that they can be reconciled with the wording of Art. 21(1) TFEU.

The fact that the right of residence is now derived directly from the Treaties has a number of important consequences. On the one hand, all restrictions and

---

[34] ECJ, Case C-184/99 *Grzelczyk* [2001] E.C.R. I-6193, para. 31.

[35] Part II contains both the provisions on European citizenship set out in *ex Arts 17 to 22 EC* [*now Arts 20 to 25 TFEU*] and the two general Treaty provisions on the principle of non-discrimination laid down in Arts 12 and 13 EC [*now Arts 18 and 19 TFEU*]. See also Art. 9 TEU which enshrines the principle of equality of Union citizens.

[36] See, e.g., ECJ, Case C-413/99 *Baumbast and R.* [2002] E.C.R. I-7091, para. 84, and ECJ Case C-456/02 *Trojani* [2004] E.C.R. I-7573, para. 31; ECJ, Case C-50/06 *Commission v The Netherlands* [2007] E.C.R. I-4383, para. 32.

conditions imposed by the Member States on that right must be applied having regard to the general principles of Union law, such as the principle of proportionality.[37] Accordingly, the Court of Justice held that the requirement for students to have sufficient resources in order to obtain the right to reside in another Member State cannot be interpreted as meaning that recourse to that Member State's social assistance system automatically entails the loss of this right of residence. The reason is that the right of residence for non-economically active citizens of the Union implies the existence of a certain degree of financial solidarity between nationals of a host Member State and nationals of other Member States.[38] Similarly, Member States may not impose requirements as to the origin of the resources which citizens of the Union must have in order to benefit from a right of residence.[39]

On the other hand, Art. 21 TFEU opposes national legislation which places at a disadvantage certain of the nationals of the Member State concerned simply because they have exercised their freedom to move and to reside in another Member State. Such a restriction can be justified only if it is based on objective considerations of public interest independent of the nationality of the persons concerned and proportionate to the legitimate objective of the national provisions.[40] The Court gives a wide interpretation to the "right of free movement and residence". Accordingly, pursuing studies in another Member State must be seen as an exercise of this right. It follows that national legislation which places at a disadvantage certain of the nationals of the Member State concerned simply because they study in another Member State constitutes a restriction on the freedoms conferred by Art. 21(1).[41] The Court has also held that Art. 21 TFEU precludes a Member State

---

[37] ECJ, Case C-413/99 *Baumbast and R.* [2002] E.C.R. I-7091, paras 85–94; CFI, Case T-66/95 *Kuchlenz-Winter v Commission* [1997] E.C.R. II-637, paras 47–48. As regards the latitude available to Member States in implementing the right of residence for the various categories of beneficiaries (and members of their families): ECJ, Case C-424/98 *Commission v Italy* [2000] E.C.R. I-4001, paras 20–48. See Scheuing, "Freizügigkeit als Unionsbürgerrecht" (2003) EuR. 744–792.

[38] ECJ, Case C-184/99 *Grzelczyk* [2001] E.C.R. I-6193, paras 37–46.

[39] ECJ, Case C-200/02 *Zhu and Chen* [2004] E.C.R. I-9925, paras 29–33; ECJ, Case C-408/03 *Commission v Belgium* [2006] E.C.R. I-2647, paras 38–52.

[40] ECJ, Case C-224/98 *D'Hoop* [2002] E.C.R. I-6191, paras 31–32; ECJ, Case C-224/02 *Pusa* [2004] E.C.R. I-5763, paras 19–20; ECJ, Case C-258/04 *Ioannidis* [2005] E.C.R. I-8275, paras 29–30; ECJ, Case C-406/04 *De Cuyper* [2006] E.C.R. I-6947, paras 39–40; ECJ, Case C-192/05 *Tas-Hagen and Tas* [2006] E.C.R. I-10451, paras 30–33 (see the case note by Martin (2007) E.J.M.L. 141–157); ECJ, Case C-499/06 *Nerkowska* [2008] E.C.R. I-3993, paras 32–34; ECJ, Case C-221/07 *Zablocka-Weyhermüller* [2008] E.C.R. I-9029, paras 34–37; ECJ, Case C-544/07 *Rüffler* [2009] E.C.R. I-3389, paras 74–75.

[41] ECJ, Case C-76/05 *Schwarz and Gootjes-Schwarz* [2007] E.C.R. I-6849, paras 90–94; ECJ, Case C-318/05 *Commission v Germany* [2007] E.C.R. I-6957, paras 126–132; ECJ, Joined Cases C-11/06 and C-12/06 *Morgan and Bucher* [2007] E.C.R. I-9161, paras 23–32.

from refusing to recognise a surname of one of its nationals determined in accordance with the legislation of another Member State and registered in that Member State, because such a refusal would result in numerous inconveniences for the citizen concerned, liable to hamper the exercise of his or her rights of free movement.[42] The end result is that, as is the case with the economic freedoms, Art. 21 prohibits not only discriminatory measures, but also measures which, despite the fact that they apply without distinction to nationals of all Member States, constitute a restriction of the right to move freely to and reside in another Member State.[43] However, Art. 21(1) TFEU offers no guarantee that moving to another Member State will always be neutral as regards social security[44] or taxation.[45]

Article 21(1) TFEU is framed sufficiently precisely and unconditionally so as to confer direct effect on the rights in question.[46]

8–009 **Implementing legislation.** The European Parliament and the Council may adopt provisions under the ordinary legislative procedure with a view to facilitating the exercise of the right to move and reside freely within the territory of the Member States. Such provisions may be adopted if "action by the Union should prove necessary to attain this objective and the Treaties have not provided the necessary powers" (Art. 21(2) TFEU).[47] Under the same circumstances, the Council may, acting unanimously after consulting the European Parliament, adopt measures concerning social security or social protection (Art. 21(3) TFEU) and concerning passports, identity cards, residence permits or any other such document (Art. 77(3) TFEU).

In April 2004, the various Union instruments dealing with the right of residence of citizens of the Union were simplified and merged in one Directive

---

[42] ECJ, Case C-353/06 *Grunkin and Paul* [2008] E.C.R. I-7639, paras 21–28; a first reference in the case was declared inadmissible by the Court because the body making the reference for a preliminary ruling could not be considered a court or tribunal for the purposes of Art. 234 EC [*now Art. 267 TFEU*] (ECJ, Case C-96/04 *Standesamt Stadt Niebüll* [2006] E.C.R. I-3561).

[43] ECJ, Case C-152/05 *Commission v Germany* [2008] E.C.R. I-39, paras 20–30. See Van Nuffel and Cambien, "De vrijheid van economisch niet-actieve EU-burgers om binnen de EU te reizen, te verblijven en te studeren" (2009) 57 S.E.W. 144–154.

[44] ECJ, Case C-208/07 *von Chamier-Glisczinski* [2009] E.C.R. I-6095, paras 83–87.

[45] ECJ, Case C-365/02 *Lindfors* [2004] E.C.R. I-7183, para. 34; ECJ, Case C-403/03 *Schempp* [2005] E.C.R. I-6421, paras 44–45 (see the case notes by Panayi (2005) European Taxation 482–487; Lutostanska (2006) 33 L.I.E.I. 335–345).

[46] ECJ, Case C-413/99 *Baumbast and R.* [2002] E.C.R. I-7091, paras 80–86. For the implications of the fact that the right of residence ensues directly from the Treaty, see Dougan and Spaventa, "Educating Rudy and the (non-)English Patient—A double-bill on residency rights under Article 18 EC" (2003) E.L.Rev. 699–712. For an application of Art. 18 together with Arts 39 and 42 EC [*now Arts 21, 45 and 48 TFEU*], see ECJ, Case C-135/99 *Elsen* [2000] E.C.R. I-10409, paras 33–36.

[47] Before the Treaty of Lisbon, it was provided that such Union action was not possible for "provisions on passports, identity cards, residence permits or any other such document" or for "provisions on social security or social protection" (see Art. 18(3) EC). That constraint was removed by the Treaty of Lisbon (see Arts 21(3) and 77(3) TFEU).

2004/38/EC of the European Parliament and of the Council on the right of citizens of the Union and their family members to move and reside freely within the territory of the Member States.[48]

Directive 2004/38 confers on Union citizens the right of residence on the territory of another Member State for a period of up to three months without any conditions or any formalities other than the requirement to hold a valid identity card or passport (Art. 6(1)). Union citizens and their family members enjoy this right as long as they do not become an unreasonable burden on the social assistance system of the host Member State (Art. 14(1)). Article 7(1) of the Directive grants the right of residence for a period of longer than three months to (a) Union citizens who are workers or self-employed persons in the host Member State, (b) all other Union citizens who have sufficient resources for themselves and their family members not to become a burden on the social assistance system of the host Member State during their period of residence and comprehensive sickness insurance cover in that State, (c) Union citizens following a course of study in the host Member State, if they have comprehensive sickness insurance cover in that State and assure the relevant authority that they have sufficient resources in the above sense, and (d) family members accompanying or joining a Union citizen who satisfies the conditions of Art. 7(1)(a), (b) or (c).[49] The right of residence for a period longer than three months exists as long as the Union citizens and their family members satisfy the conditions set out in Art. 7 of the Directive (Art. 14(2)). However, in line with the Court's judgment in *Grzelczyk*,[50] an expulsion measure should not be the automatic consequence of recourse to the social assistance system (see Art. 14(3)). The concept of the "social assistance system of the Member State" is a concept which has its own independent meaning in European Union law and cannot be defined by reference to concepts of national law.[51] It refers to assistance granted by the public authorities which compensates for a lack of stable, regular and sufficient resources.[52] The host Member State should examine whether it is a case of temporary difficulties and take into account the duration

---

[48] Directive 2004/38/EC of the European Parliament and of the Council of April 29, 2004 on the right of citizens of the Union and their family members to move and reside freely within the territory of the Member States amending Regulation (EEC) No. 1612/68 and repealing Directives 64/221/EEC, 68/360/EEC, 72/194/EEC, 73/148/EEC, 75/34/EEC, 75/35/EEC, 90/364/EEC, 90/365/EEC and 93/96/EEC, [2004] O.J. L158/77 (adopted on the basis of Arts 12, 18, 40, 44 and 52 EC [*now Arts 18, 21, 46, 52 and 59 TFEU*]). The Directive had to be implemented by April 30, 2006.

[49] A Union citizen who is no longer a worker or self-employed person is to retain that status in the circumstances listed in Art. 7(3) of the Directive. As far as persons satisfying the conditions set out in Art. 7(1)(c) are concerned, Art. 7(4) of the Directive limits qualifying "family members" to the spouse or registered partner and dependent children.

[50] ECJ, Case C-184/99 *Grzelczyk* [2001] E.C.R. I-6193, para. 43.

[51] See, e.g., in the context of Council Directive 2003/86/EC of September 22, 2003 on the right to family reunification, [2003] O.J. L251/12: ECJ (judgment of March 4, 2010), Case C-578/08 *Chakroun*, not yet reported, paras 45–51.

[52] *Ibid.*, paras 46 and 49.

of residence, the personal circumstances and the amount of aid granted in order to consider whether the beneficiary has become an unreasonable burden on its social assistance system and to proceed to his or her expulsion.[53] In no case—except on grounds of public policy or public security—should an expulsion measure be adopted against workers, self-employed persons or job-seekers with genuine chances of being engaged (Art. 14(4)). In the case of residence for periods longer than three months, a Member State may require Union citizens to register. A "residence card" will be issued only to family members who are not nationals of a Member State.[54] Furthermore, the directive grants Union citizens who have resided legally for a continuous period of five years in the host Member State the right of permanent residence there (Art. 16). The freedom of movement and residence of Union citizens and their family members may be restricted on grounds of public policy, public security and public health (Art. 27; see paras 9–70—9–71).

8–010   **Family members.** Directive 2004/38 extends the right of free movement and residence to family members of citizens of the Union, even if they do not have the nationality of a Member State.[55] Article 2(2) of the directive defines "family member" as: (a) the spouse; (b) the partner with whom the Union citizen has contracted a registered partnership, on the basis of the legislation of a Member State, if the legislation of the host Member State treats registered partnerships as equivalent to marriage and in accordance with the conditions laid down in the relevant legislation of the host Member State; (c) the direct descendants who are under the age of 21 or are dependants and those of the spouse or partner as defined in point (b); (d) the dependent direct relatives in the ascending line and those of the spouse or partner as defined in point (b).[56] According to the Court of Justice, the status of "dependent" family member is the result of a factual situation characterised by the fact that *material support* for that family member is provided by the Union national who has exercised his right of free movement or by his spouse.[57] Directive 2004/38 only applies to family members who "accompany or join"

---

[53] Recital 16 in the preamble to Directive 2004/38.

[54] Directive 2004/38, Arts 8 and 9.

[55] For a detailed overview of the rights granted to third-country family members by the various Community directives which were replaced by Directive 2004/38, see Barrett, "Family matters: European Community law and third-country family members" (2003) 40 C.M.L.Rev. 369–421.

[56] For the status of family members of migrant workers, see para. 9–062, *infra*. The category of ascendants also includes parents of a minor having the nationality of one of the Member States who are his or her primary carers, even though they are not "dependent" on their child but are instead in the opposite situation. Any other interpretation would deprive the child's right of residence as a citizen of the Union of effectiveness (ECJ, Case C-200/02 *Zhu and Chen* [2004] E.C.R. I-9925, paras 44–46).

[57] ECJ, Case 316/85 *Lebon* [1987] E.C.R. 2811, para. 22; ECJ, Case C-200/02 *Zhu and Chen* [2004] E.C.R. I-9925, para. 43. Proof of the need for material support may be adduced by any appropriate means, while a mere undertaking from the Union national or his or her spouse to support the family members concerned need not be regarded as establishing the existence of the family members' situation of real dependence (ECJ, Case C-1/05 *Jia* [2007] E.C.R. I-1. para. 43).

a citizen of the Union who moves to or resides in the host Member State (Art. 3(1) of the Directive). Article 3(1) is given a broad interpretation by the Court. Accordingly, in the case of a spouse of a citizen of the Union, the marriage need not have taken place before the latter moved to the host Member State.[58]

Equal Treatment. Subject to such specific provisions as are expressly provided for in the Treaties and secondary law, all Union citizens and their family members residing on the basis of Directive 2004/38 in the territory of the host Member State are to enjoy equal treatment with nationals of that Member State within the scope of the Treaties (Art. 24(1)). As such, the Directive contains a specific expression of the principle of equal treatment laid down in Art. 18 TFEU [*ex Art. 12 EC*] (see paras 7–052—7–054). Nonetheless, Directive 2004/38 does not require a Member State to confer entitlement to social assistance during the first three months of residence (or such longer period during which the citizen continues to seek employment with genuine chances of being engaged)[59] or, prior to the acquisition of the right of permanent residence, to grant maintenance aid for studies consisting of student grants or student loans to persons other than workers, self-employed persons, persons who retain such status and members of their families (Art. 24(2)).[60]   8–011

C. RIGHT TO PARTICIPATE IN MUNICIPAL AND EUROPEAN ELECTIONS

Right to participate in municipal and European elections. Among the new rights created when citizenship of the Union was introduced, those contained in Art. 22 TFEU [*ex Art. 19 EC*] are particularly important. That article proclaims that every citizen of the Union residing in a Member State of which he or she is not a national has the right to vote and to stand as a candidate in municipal and European Parliament elections in the Member State in which he or she resides, under the same conditions as nationals of that State (Art. 22(1) and (2)). These rights may be regarded as applications of the prohibition of discrimination on grounds of nationality in the exercise of political rights fostering the integration of Member State nationals who have made use of their right freely to reside in   8–012

---

[58] ECJ, Case C-127/08 *Metock and Others* [2008] E.C.R., paras 85–93; see the case note by Cambien (2009) Col.J.E.L. 321–341; ECJ (order of December 19, 2008), Case C-551/07 *Sahin* [2008] E.C.R. I-10453, paras 24–33.

[59] Benefits of a financial nature which, independently of their status under national law, are intended to facilitate access to the labour market cannot be regarded as constituting "social assistance" within the meaning of Art. 24(2) of Directive 2004/38: ECJ, Joined Cases C-22/08 and C-23/08 *Vatsouras and Koupatantze* [2009] E.C.R. I-4585, paras 44–45.

[60] See also ECJ, Case C-209/03 *Bidar* [2005] E.C.R. I-2119, paras 49–63; ECJ, Case C-158/07 *Förster* [2008] E.C.R. I-8507, paras 45–60.

other Member States.[61] Pursuant to Art. 19(2) EC *[now Art. 22(2) TFEU]*, which refers to "detailed arrangements" with regard to the right to vote and stand as a candidate in elections to the European Parliament, the Council adopted Directive 93/109 on December 6, 1993.[62] Then, acting under Art. 19(1) EC *[now Art. 22(1) TFEU]*, which provides for the adoption of "detailed arrangements" for the exercise of the right to vote and stand as a candidate in municipal elections, the Council adopted Directive 94/80 on December 19, 1994,[63] which lays down the arrangements for the participation of citizens of the Union in municipal elections in a Member State of which they are not nationals.

The two directives are designed to make the right to vote independent of nationality and require non-nationals to be subject to the same conditions, if any, as apply to nationals, in particular with regard to duration of residence and evidence of residence in the constituency. A voter is entitled to exercise the right to vote if he or she has expressed the wish to do so.[64] If voting is compulsory in the Member State of residence, Union nationals on the electoral roll are also obliged to vote;[65] once their names have been entered on the electoral roll, voters are to remain thereon under the same conditions as voters who are nationals.[66] Both directives provide for derogations for any Member State in which the proportion of Union citizens of voting age who reside in it but are not nationals of it exceeds 20 per cent (in practice, Luxembourg). In such a Member State, Union citizens having the nationality of another Member State may be made subject to specific residence conditions which do not apply to its own nationals.[67] At the same time,

---

[61] ECJ, Case C-145/04 *Spain v United Kingdom* [2006] E.C.R. I-7917, para. 66. At the same time, the direct relationship between the Union and its citizens is powerfully reflected by the fact that any given MEP is not necessarily elected solely by nationals of one particular Member State. This makes it legitimate for MEPs to carry out their mandate independently of their nationality; para. 13–019, *supra*. See also Pliakos, "La nature juridique de l'Union européenne" (1993) R.T.D.E. 187, at 194. See also the interesting points raised by Kochenov, Free Movement and Participation in the Parliamentary Elections in the Member State of Nationality: An Ignored Link?' (2009) M.J.E.C.L. 197–223.

[62] Council Directive 93/109/EC of December 6, 1993 laying down detailed arrangements for the exercise of the right to vote and stand as a candidate in elections to the European Parliament for citizens of the Union residing in a Member State of which they are not nationals, [1993] O.J. L329/34 (see also para. 13–018, *supra*). See the analysis by Shaw, *The transformation of citizenship in the European Union: electoral rights and the restructuring of political space* (Cambridge, Cambridge University Press), 398 pp.

[63] Council Directive 94/80/EC of December 19, 1994 laying down detailed arrangements for the exercise of the right to vote and to stand as a candidate in municipal elections by citizens of the Union residing in a Member State of which they are not nationals, [1994] O.J. L368/38. In a statement for the minutes, Spain declared that if the United Kingdom decided to extend the application of Directive 94/80 to Gibraltar, such application would be deemed to be without prejudice to Spain's position with regard to Gibraltar.

[64] Directive 93/109, Art. 8(1); Directive 94/80, Art. 7(1).

[65] Directive 93/109, Art. 8(2); Directive 94/80, Art. 7(2).

[66] Directive 93/109, Art. 9(4); Directive 94/80, Art. 8(3).

[67] Directive 93/109, Art. 14(1), first subpara.; Directive 94/80, Art. 12(1)(a) and (b).

measures may be taken with regard to the composition of lists of candidates in order to avoid polarisation between lists of national and non-national candidates.[68] In view of the specific features and balances linked to the fact that its Constitution provides for three different languages and a territorial division into regions and communities, Belgium is entitled to apply a similar specific residence condition in respect of voting in municipal elections in a limited number of local government units, the names of which are to be notified in advance.[69] The Commission has to report regularly on whether the reasons for the above-mentioned derogations still apply in the Member States concerned.[70] In the context of municipal elections a Member State may provide for one further reservation: it may provide that only its own nationals may hold the office of head, deputy or member of a municipal administration.[71]

---

[68] Directive 93/109, Art. 14(1), second subpara.; Directive 94/80, Art. 12(1)(c). That provision was incorporated despite criticism from the European Parliament to the effect that it was contrary to the spirit and the letter of the prohibition of discrimination enshrined in Art. 12 EC [now Art. 18 TFEU]: see point 5 of the resolution of November 17, 1993, [1993] O.J. C329/130. See Oliver, "Electoral Rights under Article 8b of the Treaty of Rome" (1996) C.M.L.Rev. 473, at 487.

[69] Directive 94/80, Art. 12(2). This is justified by the penultimate recital in the preamble. In a statement for the minutes, Belgium declared that it would apply that derogation only in "some of the local government units in which the number of [Union] voters [not of Belgian nationality] exceeded 20% of all voters where the Belgian Federal Government regarded the specific situation as justifying an exceptional derogation of that kind", [1994] O.J. L368/46. The European Parliament deplored the fact that it was not consulted on this derogation from the right to vote: resolution of April 5, 1995, [1995] O.J. C109/40. For the substance of this potential derogation, see Foubert, "Gemeentekiesrecht voor EU-burgers" (1998) T.B.P. 79–84. Belgium failed to implement the directive within the prescribed period: ECJ, Case C-323/97 *Commission v Belgium* [1998] E.C.R. I-4281. In the end, no use was made of this derogation.

[70] Directive 93/109, Art. 14(3); Directive 94/80, Art. 12(4). See the Commission's reports of January 7, 1998 on the application of Directive 93/109/EEC ((1998) 1/2 EU Bull. point 1.1.1.) and of November 22, 1999 on the application of Directive 94/80/EC ((1999) 11 EU Bull. Point 1.1.1.).

[71] Directive 94/80 allows Member States to provide that only their own nationals may hold the office of "elected head, deputy or member of the governing college of the executive of a basic local government unit" (Art. 5(3), first subpara) and to restrict the temporary or interim performance of such office to their own nationals (second subpara). In addition, Member States may also stipulate that Union citizens elected as members of a representative council shall take part in neither the designation of delegates who can vote in a parliamentary assembly nor the election of the members of such an assembly (Art. 5(4)). In Belgium, the derogation applies to *burgemeesters/bourgmestres* and *schepenen/échevins*. In France, Art. 88–3 of the Constitution, which was amended with a view to ratification of the EU Treaty, expressly excludes non-French citizens from holding the offices of "*maire*" or "*adjoint*" and from appointment to the electoral college which nominates members of the *Sénat* and from taking part in their election. See Kovar and Simon (n. 19, *supra*) and Oliver (n. 68, *supra*), at 494–496. For the position in the United Kingdom, see the Local Government Elections (Changes to the Franchise and Qualifications of Members) Regulations 1995.

D. DIPLOMATIC PROTECTION

8–013   **Diplomatic protection.** In the territory of third countries in which their Member State is not represented, Union citizens are entitled to protection by the diplomatic or consular authorities of any Member State on the same conditions as nationals of that State (Art. 23 TFEU [*ex Art. 20EC*]). Although diplomatic and consular missions in third countries coordinate their activities to some extent (see Art. 32 TEU), diplomatic and consular protection is among the powers which each Member State exercises with some freedom in regard to the policies pursued. Article 23 TFEU does not introduce any Union rules on diplomatic protection and does not confer any more rights to protection from another Member State on Union nationals than are enjoyed by nationals of that Member State. Article 23, first para., TFEU provides that the Member States are to "adopt the necessary provisions and start the international negotiations required to secure this protection".[72] The Council, acting in accordance with a special legislative procedure and after consulting the European Parliament, may adopt directives establishing the coordination and cooperation measures necessary to facilitate such protection (Art.23, second para., TFEU).[73]

E. CONTACTS WITH UNION INSTITUTIONS

8–014   **Contacts with Union institutions.** The second and third paras of Art. 24 TFEU [*ex Art. 21 EC*] give every Union citizen the right, respectively, to petition the European Parliament in accordance with Art. 227 TFEU [*ex Art. 194 EC*] and to apply to the European Ombudsman established under Art. 228 TFEU [*ex Art. 195 EC*]. Union citizens are entitled to exercise those rights even if they reside in a third country. The same rights likewise accrue to all other natural or legal persons residing or having their registered office in a Member State (see paras 13–118 and 13–005). Accordingly, any person, regardless of his or her political rights as a national of a Member State or a third country, who has been affected by a Union

---

[72] For the context of such provisions, see Kovar and Simon (n. 19, *supra*), at 312–315; for the existing "Guidelines for the protection of unrepresented EC nationals by EC missions in third countries", see the Commission's answer of May 4, 1994 to question No. E-822/94 (Kostopoulos), [1994] O.J. C362/50.

[73] This provision was introduced by the Treaty of Lisbon. Prior to that, the EC Treaty did not provide for any role to be played by Union institutions in this regard. As a result, the implementing rules were based on intergovernmental agreements and on the former Titles V and VI of the EU Treaty. See the Decisions of the representatives of the governments of the Member States, meeting within the Council, of December 19, 1995 regarding protection for citizens of the European Union by diplomatic and consular representations (Decision 95/553/EC, [1995] O.J. L314/73) and of June 25, 1996 on the establishment of an emergency travel document (Decision 96/409/CFSP, [1996] O.J. L168/4, adopted under Title V of the EU Treaty). See Szczekalla, "Die Pflicht der Gemeinschaft *und* der Mitgliedstaaten zum diplomatischen und konsularischen Schutz" (1999) EuR. 352–342.

institution, body, office or agency may have his or her situation reviewed by petitioning the European Parliament or making a complaint to the Ombudsman. Under Art. 15(3) TFEU [*ex Art. 255(1) EC*], any person also has a right of access to European Parliament, Council and Commission documents (see para. 13–167). Furthermore, the fourth para. of Art. 24 TFEU empowers any "citizen of the Union" to write to any of the institutions, bodies, offices or agencies in any of the Treaty languages and receive an answer in that language.[74] The Treaty of Lisbon introduced the right for a significant number of citizens to submit an initiative to the Commission (Art. 11(4) TEU and Art. 24, first para., TFEU; see para. 16–016).

---

[74] See para. 13–161, *infra*. Under Declaration (No. 4), annexed to the Treaty of Nice, the institutions of the Union, the European Economic and Social Committee, the Committee of the Regions and the European Ombudsman were to ensure that the reply to any written request by a citizen of the Union was made within a reasonable period.

CHAPTER 9

THE INTERNAL MARKET

Internal market. The establishment of an internal market remains one of the prin-   **9–001**
cipal tasks entrusted to the Union (Art. 3(3) TEU). The internal market is defined as,

> "an area without internal frontiers in which the free movement of goods,
> persons, services and capital is ensured in accordance with the provisions of
> the Treaties" (Art. 26(2) TFEU [*ex Art. 14 EC*]).

The functioning of the internal market is to be ensured in the sense that all practices
impeding the establishment of the internal market are to be eliminated as far as possible. Before the entry into force of the Lisbon Treaty, the EC Treaty referred in this
connection to the establishment of a "common market", a notion that was not defined
in the Treaty even though a number of provisions made reference thereto.[1] In 1986,
the Single European Act supplemented the task of establishing and ensuring the
common market with the aim of progressively establishing an "internal market" by
the end of 1992, defined as an "area without internal frontiers". At the same time,
the EC Treaty still referred to the "common market" as a frame of reference for the
compatibility of activities assessed under the Treaty provisions on competition and
State Aid.[2] The Lisbon Treaty has replaced the words "common market" throughout
by "internal market", which leaves the internal market as the sole expression of the
objective of market integration pursued by the Union.

I. THE ESTABLISHMENT OF THE INTERNAL MARKET

A. SCOPE OF THE INTERNAL MARKET

Market integration. The establishment of a common market was the most   **9–002**
important task entrusted to the Community by the EEC Treaty and, later, the EC
Treaty. The scope of the common market could be inferred from the list of tasks

---

[1] See para. 9–007, *infra*.
[2] See Arts 81–82 EC [*now Arts 101–102 TFEU*] and 87–88 EC [*now Arts 107–108 TFEU*], where
references to activities being held "(in)compatible with the common market" have been replaced
by references on activities being "(in)compatible with the internal market".

set out in Art. 3 EC and the provisions contained in Part Three of the EC Treaty. These tasks have not been substantially changed by the Lisbon Treaty, even though it did not take over the list of Art. 3 EC and replaced the term "common market" by "internal market".

9–003 **Negative integration.** The establishment of the internal market includes first the elimination, as between Member States, of obstacles to the free movement of goods, persons,[3] services and capital (Art. 26(2) TFEU [*ex Art. 3(1)(a) and (c) EC*]). Before the introduction in the Treaties of the concept of internal market, the Court of Justice already described the common market as involving,

> "the elimination of all obstacles to intra-Community trade in order to merge the national markets into a single market bringing about conditions as close as possible to those of a genuine internal market".[4]

As in the EC Treaty, the TFEU has broken down the objective of eliminating obstacles to trade into the free movement of goods (Part Three, Title II) and the free movement of persons, services and capital (Part Three, Title IV). The intention of the relevant provisions is that every market participant should be able to deploy his or her labour and capital, sell or buy goods and perform or receive services across the Union's "internal" frontiers without being impeded by national rules maintaining or reintroducing frontiers by means of trade restrictions. As the Treaty provisions on the free movement of goods, persons, services and capital come down to the enforcement of prohibitory provisions, they have been termed instruments of "negative integration".

Free movement of goods, including the abolition of customs duties as between the Member States, led to the introduction of a common customs tariff for goods coming from third countries. From the outset, the resulting customs union was set within the framework of a common commercial policy (see Art. 3(1)(b) EC). Free movement of persons did not directly give rise to any common policy on persons from non-Community countries wishing to enter the territory of the Member States. It was not until the Amsterdam Treaty that the Community was empowered to adopt "measures concerning the entry and movement of persons" (see Art. 3(1)(d) EC). This was subsequently developed into a more general competence to ensure the absence of internal border controls for persons and to frame a common policy on asylum, immigration and external border control (see para. 9–011).

9–004 **Positive integration.** From the outset, it was clear that in the agricultural and transport sectors the "common market" could not be attained by abolishing all

---

[3] "Free movement of persons" in this context refers to the free-movement provisions on economically active persons, namely workers and self-employed persons (see paras 9–046 *et seq., infra*). For the right of free movement of persons regardless of economic activity, see paras 8–008 *et seq., supra*).
[4] ECJ, Case 15/81 *Schul* [1982] E.C.R. 1409, para. 33.

national restrictions on trade between Member States. In all the Member States government had taken those sectors outside the mechanism of the free market, inter alia through guaranteed prices for agricultural products, investment in transport infrastructure and State operation of means of transport. Since the rules on the free movement of goods and services could not be declared to be applicable in full to those sectors, the market could be unified only by bringing national policies into alignment. Therefore, the EC Treaty and, nowadays, the TFEU provide for a common policy in the sphere of agriculture and fisheries and a common policy in the sphere of transport. As a result, the TFEU still contains, after the title on free movement of goods, a title on "agriculture and fisheries" (Title III of Part Three) and, after the title on free movement of persons, services and capital, a title on "transport" (Title VI of Part Three). Since these fields have developed into autonomous policy areas for the Union, they will be discussed amongst the other Union policies below (see paras 11–001—11–009). Nonetheless, the fact that, from the outset, the Treaties provided for powers to enact rules in these fields demonstrates that the establishment of the common/internal market does not constitute a purely negative form of integration, i.e. the enforcement of prohibitory provisions. It also requires the Union institutions to fulfil their Treaty obligations to act by laying down common policies.[5]

Undistorted competition. A third component of the internal market is constituted by the rules ensuring that competition is not distorted.[6] The EC Treaty expressly referred to a "system ensuring that competition in the internal market is not distorted" (see Art. 3(1)(g) EC). Whereas, for political reasons, this reference no longer features in the Treaties,[7] it is clear from the Protocol on the internal market and competition attached to them by the Lisbon Treaty that the internal market includes a system ensuring that competition is not distorted.[8] An internal market in which internal frontiers no longer impede free trade would not remain intact if the internal frontiers were to be retained or reintroduced by the action of undertakings or Member States. That could arise where an undertaking had a dominant position on a particular market, where undertakings formed cartels or where a Member State itself operated an undertaking or granted aid to its own undertakings. In order to obviate distortions of competition, Title VII of Part Three contains provisions applying to undertakings (Arts 101 to 105 TFEU [*ex Arts 81 to 85 EC*]) and provisions relating to public involvement in industry (Art. 106 TFEU [*ex Art. 86 EC*]) and State Aid to undertakings (Arts 108 to 109 TFEU [*ex Arts 87, 88 and 89 EC*]).

9–005

---

[5] For the Council's obligations with regard to the common transport policy, see ECJ, Case 13/83 *European Parliament v Council* [1985] E.C.R. 1513, para. 53 and paras 64–71 (see para. 11–008, *infra*).

[6] ECJ, Case 32/65 *Italy v Council and Commission* [1966] E.C.R. 389, at 405.

[7] See para. 7–007, *supra*.

[8] Protocol (No. 27), annexed to the TEU and TFEU, on the internal market and competition ([2010] O.J. C83/309).

The rules on competition will be discussed below amongst the Union's other internal policies (see paras 11–010—11–026). Indeed, the objective of ensuring that competition is not distorted in the internal market goes beyond the aim of integrating national markets to safeguard more generally the benefits of effective competition in terms of supply, prices and innovation.[9]

9–006 **Approximation of legislation.** Lastly, the Treaties foresaw that the common/internal market could not be attained merely by prohibiting trade restrictions, discrimination and distortions of competition. The unequal position of traders in the market is often ascribable to differences in national legislative or administrative provisions that are not as such incompatible with the provisions of the Treaties. Consequently, the Union's action includes the general task of positive integration (alongside the common agricultural and transport policies), which consists in approximating the laws of the Member States to the extent required for the functioning of the internal market (Arts 113 to 117 TFEU, *ex Arts 93 to 97 EC*). From the outset, it has also been possible for the Union to take supplementary action (Art. 352 TFEU, *ex Art. 308 EC*).

9–007 **Manifold references.** Since the term "common market" has now been replaced throughout the Treaties by "internal market", the TFEU continues to refer to the latter notion in various respects. In the same way as the common market, the internal market is still to be "established" while its functioning and development needs to be "ensured".[10] To that end, all practices impeding the establishment of the internal market are to be eliminated as far as possible[11] and the Union can intervene to assist where necessary.[12] Article 26(1) TFEU states that the Union is to adopt measures with the aim of establishing or ensuring the functioning of the internal market in accordance with the relevant Treaty provisions. As in the case of the "common market", the expression "internal market" also helps to define the (geographical) scope of the Union rules, in particular in the fields of competition and State Aid.[13]

---

[9] The market integration objective remains however fully relevant to the Union's competition rules, see ECJ, Joined Cases C-468/06 to C-478/06 *Sot. Lélos kai Sia EE and Others* [2008] E.C.R. I-07139, paras 65–66.

[10] See Arts 38(1) and (4); 108(1); 143(1), first subpara.; 144(1); 151, third para.; 309 and 347 TFEU [*ex Arts 32(1) and (4); 88(1); 119(1), first subpara.; 120(1); 136, third para.;267 and 297 EC*]. See also ex Arts 3(1)(h); 211 and 308 EC (with regard to the common market).

[11] See Arts 27, second para.; 101(1); 102, first para.; 107(1), (2) and (3) and 108(2) and (3) and TFEU [*ex Arts 15, second para.; 81(1); 82, first para.; 87(1), (2) and (3) and 88(2) and (3)*]. See also *ex Art. 134, third para., EC* (with regard to the common market).

[12] See Arts 114 and 115 TFEU [*ex Arts 95 and 94 EC*, with the latter referring to "the establishment or functioning of the common market"]. See also Art. 308 EC, which provided a legal basis for Union action "in the course of the operation of the common market".

[13] See Arts 101(1); 102, first para. and 104 TFEU [*ex Arts 81(1); 82, first para. and 84 EC*]. See also Arts 116, first para.; 346(1)(b) and 348, first para., TFEU [*ex Arts 96, first para.; 296(1)(b) and 298, first para., EC*].

B. FROM COMMON MARKET TO INTERNAL MARKET

Common market. According to Art. 8 EEC, the common market was to be estab-   **9–008**
lished over a transitional period of 12 years. That period could be extended in
certain circumstances to a maximum of 15 years. The Council decided that the first
of the three transitional stages had been completed on December 31, 1961.[14] The
second and third stages ended automatically, with the result that the transitional
period was over on December 31, 1969. Economic growth during the Community's
early years produced even quicker results: by means of the so-called "acceleration
decisions" of May 12, 1960 and May 15, 1962, the Member States introduced the
customs union earlier than had been anticipated.[15] By Council Decision of July 26,
1966, the customs union for industrial products was brought into being with effect
from July 1, 1968, one and a half years before the expiry of the transitional period
laid down by Art. 14 EEC.[16]

Nevertheless the Community did not succeed in achieving the common market
in all its component parts before the end of the transitional period. Technical complications and political sensitivities stood in the way of adopting measures to secure
the right of establishment and liberalise capital movements. The accession of
new Member States, budgetary disagreements and economic recession produced
euro-sclerosis, bringing the achievement of the common market to a standstill.
Admittedly, the Court of Justice had given a broad interpretation to the provisions
on free movement, but residual disparities between national legislation could be
harmonised only in so far as they directly affected the establishment or functioning of the common market, and this required a unanimous vote in the Council
(Art. 100 EEC).

White Paper. At the European Council held in Copenhagen in December 1982, the   **9–009**
Commission succeeded in persuading the Heads of State or Government that work
had to be carried out on "priority measures . . . to reinforce the internal market".[17]
At the European Council's request, the Commission adopted in June 1985 the

---

[14] Decision of the Council of January 14, 1962 concerning the transition to the second stage of the
transitional period, J.O. 164/62.

[15] Decision of May 12, 1960 of the representatives of the Member States of the European Economic
Community meeting within the Council on quickening the pace for achieving the objectives of the
Treaty, J.O. 1217/60; Decision of May 15, 1962 of the representatives of the Member States of the
European Economic Community meeting within the Council on quickening the pace for achieving
the objectives of the Treaty, J.O. 1284/62.

[16] Council Decision 66/532/EEC of July 26, 1966 concerning the abolition of customs duties and the
prohibition of quantitative restrictions as between Member States and the application of the common customs tariff duties to products not mentioned in Annex II [*now Annex I*] to the Treaty, J.O.
2971/66.

[17] (1982) 12 EC Bull. point 1.2.3.

White Paper entitled "Completing the internal market", setting out an extensive programme with a view to eliminating all the remaining barriers.[18] The White Paper classed the barriers in three categories: physical, technical and fiscal. The physical barriers encompassed frontier checks, which existed principally because of technical and fiscal differences as between Member States. According to the White Paper, if those differences disappeared, any frontier check would become superfluous, provided that ancillary measures were taken for the security of citizens, immigration and the control of drugs. Technical barriers were the result of the differing requirements to which Member States subjected products and services with a view to protecting, for instance, safety, health or the environment. Rather than harmonising these requirements, the Commission proposed fostering the equivalence and mutual recognition of national legislation. The Commission regarded the abolition of fiscal barriers as an important part of the internal market, but recognised that abolition was a controversial question. Consequently, the White Paper confined itself to proposing that efforts should be made towards mutual adjustment of national legislation. The White Paper announced some 300 measures (later reduced to 279 but expanded again in 1990 to 282 measures) to be adopted in accordance with a detailed timetable by no later than 1992 in order to abolish the barriers in question.

9–010　**Objective 1992.** The Single European Act added Arts 8a, 8b and 8c to the EEC Treaty, which committed the Union to adopting measures "with the aim of progressively establishing the internal market over a period expiring on 31 December 1992". It introduced in the EEC Treaty the definition of the "internal market" as,

> "an area without internal frontiers in which the free movement of goods, persons, services and capital is ensured in accordance with the provisions of the Treaties" (Art. 8a EEC, thereafter Art. 14(2) EC, now Art. 26(2) TFEU).

Moreover, the Single European Act conferred new powers to attain this goal by laying down harmonisation measures. Article 100a EEC (thereafter Art. 95 EC, now Art. 114 TFEU) empowered the Council to adopt by a qualified majority, and with participation of the European Parliament, measures for the,

> "approximation of the provisions laid down by law, regulation or administrative action in Member States which have as their object the establishment and functioning of the internal market" (see paras. 9–112—9–116).[19]

---

[18] Commission of the European Communities, *Completing the Internal Market: White Paper from the Commission to the European Council (Milan, June 28–29, 1985),* June 14, 1985, COM(85) 310 fin. The Milan European Council broadly welcomed the White Paper (1985) 6 EC Bull. point 1.2.5.

[19] The Single European Act made not only for more flexible decision-making but also for a greater role for the European Parliament by providing in Art.100a(1) EEC for the (new) procedure of cooperation with the Parliament. The EU Treaty maintained this trend by replacing the procedure provided for in Art. 100a [*later Art. 95*](1) EC by the new co-decision procedure. Article 95(2) EC did, however, preclude the application of Art. 95(1) to fiscal provisions, to those relating to the free movement of persons and to those relating to the rights and interests of employed persons.

The introduction of this legal basis went hand in hand with a new approach to harmonisation policy (see para. 9–111). The attainment of the internal market also included a drive for better knowledge of the activities of the Union and of Union law.[20]

From common and internal market to an area of freedom. At the time when the expression was first introduced into the Treaties, the "internal market" concentrated on ensuring, as between Member States, the free movement of goods, persons, services and capital and thus has a more limited scope than the pre-existing "common market".[21] Indeed, the White Paper which launched the internal market did not cover competition, agricultural or transport policy. At the same time, the definition of the internal market as an "area without internal frontiers" showed that the intended result was more ambitious than the establishment of a "common market", which merely set out to achieve "open" internal frontiers, but did not affect the relevance of those frontiers.[22] In contrast, the internal market "without internal frontiers" requires any formality imposed upon entry into the territory of a Member State from another Member State to be abolished. For this purpose the Union has been given the competence to ensure the absence of any internal border controls for persons and to frame a common policy on asylum, immigration and external border control (Arts 67(2) and 77 TFEU: see paras 10–012 *et seq.*). Furthermore, through the abolition of internal frontiers, the Treaties no longer seek to attain merely an open market but an "area". The use of this term makes it clear that integration is not confined to economic factors of production, but extends to the whole of life in society. The Amsterdam Treaty added the idea of the Union as "an area of freedom, security and justice" (Art. 2, fourth indent, EU).[23]

9–011

---

[20] On the ground that effective application of Union law is essential for the proper functioning of the internal market, Art. 95 EC [*now Art. 114 TFEU*] constituted the legal basis for, inter alia, Decision No. 1496/98/EC of the European Parliament and of the Council of June 22, 1998 establishing an action programme to improve awareness of Community law within the legal professions (Robert Schuman project), [1998] O.J. L196/24.

[21] For the debate on the relationship between the common market and the internal market, which has now become obsolete, see Mortelmans, "The Common Market, the Internal Market and the Single Market, What's in a Market" (1998) C.M.L.Rev. 101–136. For the meaning of the term "internal market", see also Gormley, "Competition and Free Movement: Is the Internal Market the Same as a Common Market?" (2002) E.Bus.L.Rev. 517–522; Müller-Graff, "Die Verdichtung des Binnenmarktsrechts zwischen Handlungsfreiheiten und Sozialgestaltung" (2002) EuR. Beiheft 1, 7–73; Dehousse and Demaret, "Marché unique, significations multiples" (1992) J.T. 137–141; Ehlermann, "The Internal Market Following the Single European Act" (1987) C.M.L.Rev. 361–404; Pescatore, "Some Critical Remarks on the 'Single European Act' " (1987) C.M.L.Rev. 9–18; Forwood and Clough, "The Single European Act and Free Movement—Legal Implications of the Provisions for the Completion of the Internal Market" (1986) E.L.Rev. 383–408; Steindorff, "Gemeinsamer Markt als Binnenmarkt" (1986) Z.H.R. 687–704.

[22] See, e.g., ECJ, Case 118/75 *Watson and Belmann* [1976] E.C.R. 1185, para. 17.

[23] Labayle, "Le Traité d'Amsterdam. Un espace de liberté, de sécurité et de justice" (1997) R.T.D.E. 813, at 824–825.

Article 3(2) TEU now explicitly states that the Union is to offer its citizens an "area of freedom, security and justice without internal frontiers". Accordingly, nationals of the Member States now enjoy a general right of free movement and residence, irrespective of any economic activity, as citizens of the Union (see the discussion in paras 8–008 *et seq.*). The directive on the right of citizens of the Union and their family members to move and reside freely within the territory of the Member States[24] is very significant in this regard.

II. THE TREATY PROVISIONS ON FREE MOVEMENT

9–012 **Four freedoms.** The foundations of the internal market are the Treaty provisions on the free movement of goods (Arts 28 to 37 TFEU [*ex Arts 23 to 31 EC*]) and the free movement of persons (workers and self-employed persons), services and capital (Arts 45 to 66 TFEU [*ex Arts 39 to 60 EC*]). The prohibition on Member States' discriminating against goods, persons, services and capital from other Member States is intended to secure the ability freely to deploy factors of production across frontiers. The Court of Justice also emphasises in its interpretation of the "four freedoms" the consumer's right freely to purchase goods and receive services in other Member States.[25] As far as goods are concerned, the rules on "free movement" encompass since the judgment in *Dassonville* (1974) not only the prohibition of discrimination but also a prohibition of other—even potential—barriers to free movement. The Court's case law has gradually extended that broad interpretation also to the rules on the supply of services and, subsequently, also to the rules on the movement of persons and capital.[26] At the same time, the Court has held, also in respect of the free movement of persons, services and capital, that a Member State may impose non-discriminatory restrictions on free movement only if they pursue an aim in the general interest and comply with the principle of proportionality. In other words, it has extended the *Cassis de Dijon* case law on free movement of goods to cover the other freedoms.[27] The

---

[24] Directive 2004/38/EC of the European Parliament and the Council of April 29, 2004 on the right of the citizens of the Union and their family members to move and reside freely within the territory of the Member States amending Regulation (EEC) No. 1612/68 and repealing Directives 64/221/EEC, 68/360/EEC, 72/194/EEC, 73/148/EEC, 75/34/EEC, 75/35/EEC, 90/364/EEC, 90/365/EEC and 93/96/EEC, [2004] O.J. L158/77.

[25] Paras 9–031 and 9–088, *infra*.

[26] *Cf.* paras 7–009 (goods) and 9–065 (persons), 9–092 (services) and 9–100 (capital).

[27] *Cf.* paras 9–039 *et seq.* (goods) and 9–074—9–078 (persons), 9–094—9–098 (services) and para. 5–185 (capital). For the convergence of the four freedoms, see Snell, "And Then There Were Two: Products and Citizens in Community Law", in Tridimas and Nebbia (eds), *European Union Law for the Twenty-First Century* (Vol II, Oxford, Hart Publishing, 2004) 49–72; Bernard, "Fitting the remaining pieces into the goods and persons jigsaw?" (2001) E.L.Rev. 35–59; Jarass, "Elemente einer Dogmatik der Grundfreiheiten II" (1995) EuR. 202–226 and (2000) EuR. 705–723. For the convergence of the four freedoms and competition law, see O'Loughlin, "EC Competition Rules and Free

provisions on the free movement of services which are provided across border without the provider or the recipient of the services moving are increasingly being interpreted in parallel with the provisions on free movement of goods.[28] As to the obligations flowing from the Treaties with regard to the treatment of providers of services from other Member States, they frequently match the obligations which apply in regard to employees or self-employed persons established from other Member States.[29] In order to promote free movement of goods and services, harmonisation is carried out of national provisions relating to the production and distribution of goods and services; the free movement of persons is further assisted by the harmonisation and mutual recognition of diplomas and professional rules.[30]

As such, the Treaty provisions on free movement impose obligations only on Member States; however, as far as the free movement of persons and services is concerned, the Court of Justice has made it clear that the prohibition of discrimination also entails obligations for private groups or organisations which exercise a degree of authority over individuals.[31]

From the outset, the Treaties supplemented the provisions on the free movement of goods within the Union by the Union's competence to determine, by means of a uniform customs policy and a common commercial policy, the conditions on which goods from third countries can enter into circulation in the Union.[32] Recent Treaty amendments have also given the Union competence (alongside the competence retained by the Member States in the relevant areas) to lay down rules on the entry of persons into the Union and on the conditions on which services and capital from third countries can be deployed within the Union.[33]

Applicable freedom. In certain situations a national measure will affect several freedoms at the same time. In such circumstances, it will have to be examined to   **9–013**

Movement Rules: An Examination of the Parallels and their Furtherance by the ECJ *Wouters* Decision" (2003) E.Comp.L.Rev. 62–69; Steinberg, "Zur Konvergenz der Grundfreiheiten auf der Tatbestands- und Rechtfertigungsebene" (2002) Eu.GR.Z. 13–25; Mortelmans, "Towards Convergence in the Application of the Rules on Free Movement and on Competition?" (2001) C.M.L.Rev. 613–649.

[28] For a joint application of trade in goods and trade in services, see ECJ, Case C-390/99 *Canal Satélite Digital* [2002] E.C.R. I-607, paras 39–41

[29] For the parallel treatment of two freedoms, see ECJ, Case C-439/99 *Commission v Italy* [2002] E.C.R. I-305, paras 35–41; ECJ, Case C-294/00 *Deutsche Paracelsus Schulen für Naturheilverfahren* [2002] E.C.R. I-6515, paras 38–52. To make the supply of services conditional upon the satisfaction of requirements which apply for establishment in a Member State is, however, a denial of the freedom to offer services in a Member State from an establishment in another Member State: para. 9–098, *infra*.

[30] For professional rules and diplomas, see paras 9–079—9–081, *infra*; for harmonisation, see also paras 9–108—9–116, *infra*.

[31] Paras 9–046 and 9–085, *infra*.

[32] Paras 9–016 and 9–028, *infra*.

[33] Paras 10–012—10–016, 9–099 and 9–107, *infra*.

what extent each of those freedoms is restricted, and whether, in the case at hand, one of the freedoms prevails over the others. If it is clear that, in the circumstances of the case, one of those freedoms is entirely secondary in relation to the other, the Court will, in principle, examine the contested measure in relation to the latter freedom only.[34] For example, the Court of Justice decided that a UK law prohibiting the importation of lottery advertisements and tickets was to be considered under the provisions on the freedom to provide services because the importation of these goods could not be considered independently of the lottery to which they related, and the latter was to be considered as a service within the meaning of Art. 57 TFEU [ex Art. 50 EC].[35] Likewise, national legislation which subjects holdings in undertakings established in other Member States to less favourable tax treatment than holdings in undertakings established in the Member State in question, may fall within both the provisions on freedom of establishment and on the free movement of capital,[36] unless it is clear that the legislation only applies to holdings that confer a definite influence over the company's decisions and therefore falls within the scope of the provisions on freedom of establishment only.[37]

A. FREE MOVEMENT OF GOODS

9–014 **Treaty rules.** In principle, the realisation of free movement of goods requires Member States to abolish all measures constituting a barrier to trade within the Union.[38] Abolition of restrictive national measures of a fiscal nature is the corollary of the establishment of a customs union, entailing the prohibition of duties on imports and exports and any charges having equivalent effect in trade between Member States (Art. 30 TFEU [ex Art. 25 EC]; see paras 9–016—9–024) and the setting-up of the Common Customs Tariff vis-à-vis third countries (Arts 31 and

---

[34] See, e.g., ECJ, Case C-390/99 *Canal Satélite Digital* [2002] E.C.R. I-607, paras 31; ECJ, Case C-71/02 *Karner* [2004] E.C.R. I-3025, para 46; ECJ, Case C-36/02 *Omega Spielhallen* [2004] E.C.R. I-9609, paras 26–27; ECJ, Case C-452/04 *Fidium Finanz* [2006] E.C.R. I-9521, paras 34 and 44–49, see the case note by O'Brien (2007) 44 C.M.L.Rev. 1483–1499.

[35] ECJ, Case C-275/92 *Schindler* [1994] E.C.R. I-1039, paras 21–25.

[36] ECJ, Case C-446/04 *Test Claimants in the FII Group Litigation* [2006] E.C.R. I-11753, paras 36 and 80.

[37] ECJ, Case C-196/04 *Cadbury Schweppes* [2006] E.C.R. I-7995, paras 31–33; ECJ, Case C-524/04 *Test Claimants in the Thin Cap Group Litigation* [2007] E.C.R. I-02107, paras 26–35; ECJ (Order of May 10, 2007), Case C-492/04 *Lasertec* [2007] E.C.R. I-3775, paras 19–25.

[38] For an exhaustive discussion of free movement of goods, see Oliver, *Free Movement of Goods in the European Community* (Oxford, Hart Publishing, 2010), 536 pp; Periin, *Free Movement of Goods and Limits of Regulatory Autonomy in the EU and WTO* (The Hague, T.M.C. Asser Press, 2008), 238 pp.; Barnard, *The Substantive Law of the EU: the Four Freedoms* (Oxford, Oxford University Press, 2007), at Part II; Gormley, *EU law of free movement of goods and customs union* (Oxford, Oxford University Press, 2007), 552 pp; Mayer, "Die Warenverkehrsfreiheit im Europarecht—Eine Rekonstruktion" (2003) EuR. 793–824.

32 TFEU [*ex Arts 26 and 27 EC*]; see para. 9–025).[39] Non-fiscal measures, namely quantitative restrictions on imports and exports and measures having equivalent effect, are prohibited by Arts 34–36 TFEU [*ex Arts 28 to 30 EC*],[40] which form the basis for a comprehensive body of case law (see paras 9–028— 9–045). For the sake of completeness, it should be noted that Art. 37 TFEU [*ex Art. 31 EC*] requires Member States to organise any State monopolies of a commercial character so as to preclude any discrimination between Member State nationals regarding conditions under which goods are procured and marketed.[41]

Since all the Treaty provisions laying down prohibitions have direct effect since the end of the transitional period,[42] individuals may enforce the free movement of goods vis-à-vis Member States. Those prohibitions are also binding on the institutions of the Union itself,[43] although the case law allows the Union a degree of discretion in balancing free movement of goods against other legitimate policy objectives.[44] In principle, restrictive measures agreed between individuals are not caught by those prohibitions.[45] Taken in conjunction with Art. 4(3) TEU [*ex Art. 10 EC*], however, the prohibiting provisions require Member States also to take all necessary and appropriate measures to eliminate barriers to free movement of goods the cause of which lies outside the sphere of the State.[46] The

---

[39] The Treaty of Amsterdam deleted from the chapter entitled "The Customs Union" the rules on the progressive abolition of customs duties between the Member States (the former Arts 13 to 17 EC) and on the establishment of the common customs tariff (the former Arts 18 to 27).

[40] The Treaty of Amsterdam amended the title of the chapter "Elimination of quantitative restrictions between Member States" to "Prohibition of quantitative restrictions between Member States" and repealed the transitional provisions (the former Arts 31 to 33 and 35 EC).

[41] ECJ, Case 59/75 *Manghera* [1976] E.C.R. 91; ECJ, Case C-347/88 *Commission v Greece* [1990] E.C.R. I-4747; ECJ, Case C-387/93 *Banchero* [1995] E.C.R. I-4663; ECJ, Case C-189/95 *Franzén* [1997] E.C.R. I-5909, paras 30–66; ECJ, Case C-438/02 *Hanner* [2005] E.C.R. I-4551, paras 32–49; ECJ, Case C-170/04 *Rosengren* [2007] E.C.R. I-4071, paras 17–26. In the event of an infringement of Art. 37, it is no longer possible to rely on the exception provided for in Art. 36; see ECJ, Case C-157/94 *Commission v Netherlands* [1997] E.C.R. I-5699, para. 24.

[42] See the discussion of the Treaty articles in paras 9–017, 9–018 and 9–028, *infra*.

[43] ECJ, Joined Cases 80 and 81/77 *Commissionaires Réunis* [1978] E.C.R. 927, para. 35; ECJ, Case C-108/01 *Consorzio del Prosciutto di Parma and Others* [2003] E.C.R. I-5121, paras 53–59.

[44] E.g., ECJ, Case 37/83 *Rewe-Zentrale* [1984] E.C.R. 1229, para. 20; ECJ, Case C-51/93 *Meyhui* [1994] E.C.R. I-3879, para. 21; ECJ, Case C-233/94 *Germany v European Parliament and Council* [1997] E.C.R. I-2405, para. 43. See Mortelmans, "The Relationship Between the Treaty Rules and Community Measures for the Establishment and Functioning of the Internal Market—Towards a Concordance Rule" (2002) C.M.L.Rev. 1303–1346.

[45] ECJ, Case C-159/00 *Sapod Audic* [2002] E.C.R. I-5031, para. 74. For the addressees of the prohibitions (and the question whether they may be individuals), see Mortelmans, "Excepties bij nontarifaire intracommunautaire belemmeringen: assimilatie in het nieuwe EG-Verdrag?" (1997) S.E.W. 182, at 185–186.

[46] ECJ, Case C-265/95 *Commission v France* [1997] E.C.R. I-6959, paras 30–32. (concerning acts taken by individuals against products from other Member States); ECJ, Case C-112/00 *Schmidberger* [2003] E.C.R. I-5659, paras 57–64 (individuals blocking traffic on the Brenner motorway). See also Ronkes Agerbeek (2004) E.L.Rev. 255–266; Jaeckel, "The duty to protect fundamental rights in the European Community" (2003) E.L.Rev. 508–527.

Council has specified this obligation in a regulation, under which the Commission is responsible for monitoring compliance.[47]

9–015 **Goods concerned.** Free movement of goods applies both to "products originating in Member States" and to "products coming from third countries which are in free circulation in Member States" (Art. 28(2) TFEU [*ex Art. 23(2) EC*]; see also Art. 29 TFEU [*ex Art. 24 EC*]).[48] The Court of Justice has defined "goods" as "products which can be valued in money and which are capable, as such, of forming the subject of commercial transactions".[49] As a result, the rules on free movement of goods are applicable, for example, to articles of artistic, historic, archaeological or ethnographic value[50] and even to non-recyclable waste.[51]

1. The customs union

9–016 **Customs union.** The abolition of customs duties as between Member States goes against the most-favoured nation clause enshrined in Article I of the General Agreement on Tariffs and Trade (GATT), which puts contracting parties under an obligation to accord any preferential treatment of any product originating in or destined for any other country to the like product originating in or destined for the territories of all other GATT countries. All Member States are contracting parties to GATT and the World Trade Organisation (WTO), which replaced the GATT in 1995 and took over the basic rules of the original General Agreement.[52] GATT accepts, however, as an exception to the most-favoured nation clause, the establishment of a customs union, which is defined as an area within which customs duties and other restrictive regulations of commerce are eliminated with respect to substantially all the trade between the constituent territories of the Member

---

[47] Council Regulation (EC) No. 2679/98 of December 7, 1998 on the functioning of the internal market in relation to the free movement of goods among the Member States, [1998] O.J. L337/8. See Gimeno Verdejo, "La réponse communautaire aux blocages des réseaux de transport: application et perspectives d'avenir du règlement n° 2679/98 en vue de la protection du marché intérieur" (2002) C.D.E. 45–93 ; Mattera, "Un instrument d'intervention rapide pour sauvegarder l'unicité du Marché intérieur: le règlement 2679/98. De nouveaux pouvoirs pour la 'Commission Prodi' " (1999) R.M.U.E. 9–33.

[48] ECJ, Case 41/76 *Donckerwolcke* [1976] E.C.R. 1921, paras 15–21; ECJ, Case 125/88 *Nijman* [1989] E.C.R. 3533, para. 11.

[49] ECJ, Case 7/68 *Commission v Italy* [1968] E.C.R. 423, at 428.

[50] *Ibid.* See Mattera, "La libre circulation des oeuvres d'art à l'intérieur de la Communauté et la protection des trésors nationaux ayant une valeur artistique, historique ou archéologique" (1993) 2 R.M.U.E. 9–31.

[51] ECJ, Case C-2/90 *Commission v Belgium* [1992] E.C.R. I-4431, paras 23–28, with a note by De Sadeleer (1993) C.D.E. 672–698; see also De Sadeleer, "La circulation des déchets et le Marché unique européen" (1994) 1 R.M.U.E. 71–116.

[52] For the General Agreement on Tariffs and Trade (GATT) and the World Trade Organisation, see para. 25–011 *et seq.*

States and in which substantially the same duties and other regulations of commerce are applied vis-à-vis third countries (GATT, Art. XXIV). GATT does impose conditions to the effect that the transitional period for achieving such a customs union must follow a schedule for the formation of the customs union within a reasonable length of time and that the customs union taken as a whole must not introduce higher duties for third States.[53] The EC Treaty set out a timetable for the stage-by-stage introduction of a customs union. Whenever Member States have acceded to the Union, a new transitional period has been laid down for the abolition of customs duties and charges having equivalent effect as between Member States. The culmination of the customs union envisaged by the Treaties is the establishment and uniform application of a common customs tariff vis-à-vis third countries.[54]

(a) *Prohibition of customs duties and charges having equivalent effect*

Customs duties. In trade in goods between Member States, customs duties on imports and exports and charges having equivalent effect are prohibited. This prohibition also applies to customs duties of a fiscal nature (Art. 30 TFEU [*ex Art. 25 EC*]).[55] It means that charges collected by a Member State where goods cross its border are prohibited. This embraces not only import and export duties, but also transit charges.[56] By Council decision of July 26, 1966 customs duties were completely abolished as from July 1, 1968.[57] The prohibition has had direct effect ever since the end of the transitional period.[58]

9–017

Charges having equivalent effect. Article 30 TFEU couples the ban on customs duties on imports and exports with a prohibition of charges having equivalent effect. The Court of Justice interprets that expression very broadly:

9–018

---

[53] For the significance of Art. XXIV of GATT for the customs union within the Union and free trade agreements with third countries, see Cremona, "Rhetoric and Reticence: EU External Commercial Policy in a Multilateral Context" (2001) C.M.L.Rev. 359–396.

[54] See also Art. 206 TFEU [*ex Art. 131 EC*], which stresses the positive contribution of the customs union to world trade. See Starink, "Veertig jaar EU-douane-unie" (1998) S.E.W. 241–252.

[55] The Amsterdam Treaty repealed the obligation to abolish existing duties (the former Arts 13 and 16 EC) and replaced the ban on the introduction of new duties or the increase of existing duties (stand-still provision) set out in the former Art. 12 EC by a straightforward prohibition of customs duties and charges having equivalent effect. For import duties, charges having equivalent effect and permitted charges, see Schön, "Die freie Warenverkehr, die Steuerhoheit der Mitgliedstaaten und der Systemgedanke im europäischen Steuerrecht" (2001) EuR. 216–233 and 341–362.

[56] ECJ, Case 266/81 *SIOT* [1983] E.C.R. 731, paras 16–19.

[57] Council Decision 66/532/EEC of July 26, 1966 abolishing customs duties and prohibiting quantitative restrictions as between Member States and applying the duties of the common customs tariff to products not mentioned in Annex II to the Treaty, J.O. 2971/66.

[58] ECJ, Case 26/62 *Van Gend & Loos* [1963] E.C.R. 1, at 13. The obligation to abolish existing charges having equivalent effect under the former Art. 13(2) EC (ECJ, Case 33/70 *SACE* [1970] E.C.R. 1213, paras 9–10) and the former Art. 16 EC (ECJ, Case 18/71 *Eunomia* [1971] E.C.R. 811, paras 6–7) have also been held to have direct effect.

"any pecuniary charge, however small and whatever its designation and mode of application, which is imposed unilaterally on domestic and foreign goods by reason of the fact that they cross a frontier, and which is not a customs duty in the strict sense, constitutes a charge having equivalent effect [. . .], even if it is not imposed for the benefit of the State, is not discriminatory or protective in effect or if the product on which the charge is imposed is not in competition with any domestic product".[59]

Charges collected on crossing "regional" borders within a Member State, such as taxes levied in a municipality of a Member State on goods which are transported across the territorial boundaries of that municipality[60] or contributions imposed by the authorities of an overseas territory on exports of goods,[61] are likewise prohibited, even where they are levied on goods coming from or destined for another region of the same Member State.[62] The prohibition of charges having an effect equivalent to customs duties also applies to charges levied by Member States on goods in transit through their territory, including those imported directly from third countries.[63]

Accordingly the Court has held the following to be contrary to the Treaties: a charge imposed to cover the cost of compiling statistics on movements of goods across frontiers[64]; pecuniary charges imposed on grounds of sanitary inspection of goods when they cross the frontier,[65] and charges imposed for compulsory quality controls on exports.[66] A Member State may not charge traders taking part in intra-Union trade the cost of inspections and administrative formalities carried out by customs offices.[67] Even if such a charge is imposed, not by virtue of a unilateral measure adopted by the authorities, but as a result of a series of private contracts, it will be caught by the prohibition laid down in Arts 28 and 30 TFEU.[68]

---

[59] ECJ, Joined Cases 2 and 3/69 *Sociaal Fonds voor de Diamantarbeiders* [1969] E.C.R. 211, para. 15/18, at 222.

[60] ECJ, Case C-72/03 *Carbonati Apuani* [2004] E.C.R. I-8027, paras 21–29. See also, ECJ, Case C-173/05 *Commission v Italy* [2007] E.C.R. I-4917, paras 35–44.

[61] ECJ, Case C-293/02 *Jersey Produce Marketing Organisation* [2005] E.C.R. I-9543, paras 61–67.

[62] ECJ, Case C-163/90 *Legros and Others* [1992] E.C.R. I-4625, paras 10–18; ECJ, Joined Cases C-363/93, C-407/93, C-408/93, C-409/93, C-410/93 and C-411/93 *Lancry and Others* [1994] E.C.R. I-3957, paras 25–32 (charge levied on imports); ECJ, Joined Cases C-485/93 and C-486/93 *Simitzi* [1995] E.C.R. I-2655, paras 10–22 (charges levied on imports and exports). See Graser, "Eine Wende im Bereich der Inländerdiskriminierung? Zur Entscheidung des EuGH in der Rechtssache *Lancry*" (1998) EuR. 571–579; Slotboom, "L'application du Traité CE au commerce intraétatique? Le cas de l'octroi de mer" (1996) C.D.E. 9–29.

[63] ECJ, Case C-173/05 *Commission v Italy* [2007] E.C.R. I-4917, paras 27–33.

[64] ECJ, Case 24/68 *Commission v Italy* [1969] E.C.R. 193, paras 14–17.

[65] ECJ, Case 29/72 *Marimex* [1972] E.C.R. 1309, para. 8; ECJ, Case 87/75 *Bresciani* [1976] E.C.R. 129, paras 4–9.

[66] ECJ, Case 63/74 *Cadsky* [1975] E.C.R. 281, paras 2–8.

[67] ECJ, Case 340/87 *Commission v Italy* [1989] E.C.R. 1483, para. 17.

[68] ECJ, Case C-16/94 *Dubois and Général Cargo Services* [1995] E.C.R. I-2421, paras 13–21.

(b) *Permissible charges*

Three types. The broad interpretation of "charges having equivalent effect"   **9–019**
reduces the number of permissible pecuniary charges on intra-Union trade
in goods to such an extent that only three types of charges satisfy the
Union-law test.

(1) Consideration for service rendered. In the first place, Member States may   **9–020**
charge for a service provided to the importer or exporter by the authorities ("consideration"). The Court of Justice has hedged this possibility about with strict
conditions. The consideration may not exceed either the value or the cost of the
service actually rendered to the importer or exporter and may be charged only in
"special cases". Administrative activity intended to maintain a system imposed in
the general interest (e.g. a phyto-sanitary or plant-health examination) cannot be
regarded as a service rendered to the importer or exporter such as to justify the
imposition of a pecuniary charge.[69] The Court of Justice accepted that the placing of goods, at the importer's request, in temporary storage in the special stores
of public warehouses constituted a service rendered to importers that could give
rise to the payment of charges commensurate with the service thus rendered. The
Court held, however, that when payment of storage charges was demanded solely
in connection with the completion of customs formalities, this constituted a
"charge having equivalent effect".[70]

(2) Charges forming part of Union regulation. Charges imposed for the pur-   **9–021**
poses of implementing a Union regulatory regime constitute a second exception
to the extensive prohibition of charges having equivalent effect. For instance, the
Court of Justice has held that certain charges imposed in connection with the
common agricultural policy[71] and fees charged for inspections required by a
Union directive[72] do not constitute charges having an effect equivalent to import
or export duties.

(3) Internal taxation. Thirdly, a charge may not be characterised as a charge   **9–022**
having equivalent effect if it forms part of a general system of internal taxation
applying systematically to categories of products according to objective criteria
applied without regard to the origin of the products. In that case the charge will
come within the scope of Art. 110 TFEU [*ex Art. 90 EC*] and will, therefore, have

---

[69] ECJ, Case 39/73 *Rewe-Zentralfinanz* [1973] E.C.R. 1039, para. 4.
[70] ECJ, Case 132/82 *Commission v Belgium* [1983] E.C.R. 1649, paras 10–14.
[71] ECJ, Case 106/81 *Kind v EEC* [1982] E.C.R. 2885, para. 21.
[72] ECJ, Case 46/76 *Bauhuis v Netherlands* [1977] E.C.R. 5, para. 31.

to comply with the requirements set by that provision.[73] As far as internal taxation is concerned, Art. 110 TFEU requires Member States not to impose directly or indirectly on products from other Member States any taxation in excess of that imposed on similar domestic products or impose internal taxation of such a nature as to afford protection to other domestic products. The criterion for testing whether a tax is caught by Art. 110 TFEU is therefore the discrimination or protection resulting therefrom.[74] The prohibition of discrimination also covers discrimination between national products which are processed and marketed on the domestic market and national products which are exported in an unprocessed state to other Member States.[75] The prohibition of discrimination applies to internal taxation "of any kind" (e.g. excise duty, VAT, registration charges, road fund taxes, etc.). Art. 110 TFEU has direct effect.[76]

9–023   **Identification of discrimination.** The application of Art. 110 TFEU requires a demarcation of the market for the national products with which the products imported (or to be exported) compete. It must therefore be considered which domestic products are similar or substitutable for the relevant imported products.[77] Then, it needs to be examined to what extent the taxation imposed on the products imported (or to be exported) discriminates against imported products or protects domestic products. The comparison ranges over all aspects of the imposition of the tax (determination of the basis of assessment, determination of rates, methods of collection of amounts due) and is not confined to a formal inquiry. Thus, the Court

---

[73] ECJ, Joined Cases C-393/04 and C-41/05 *Air Liquide Industries and Others* [2006] E.C.R. I-5293, paras 51 and 56; ECJ, Case C-206/06 *Essent Netwerk Noord* [2008] E.C.R. I-05497, para. 41; ECJ, Case C-221/06 *Stadtgemeinde Frohnleiten and Gemeindebetriebe Frohnleiten* [2007] E.C.R. I-9643, paras 30–73. See Schön, "Der freie Warenverkehr, die Steuerhoheit der Mitgliedstaaten und der Systemgedanke im europäischen Steuerrecht" (2001) EuR. 341–362. One and the same charge cannot be caught both by the provisions on charges having equivalent effect and by the prohibition of discriminatory internal taxation laid down in Art. 110 TFEU: ECJ, Case 94/74 *IGAV* [1975] E.C.R. 699, para. 12–13.

[74] ECJ, Joined Cases C-149/91 and C-150/91 *Sanders Adour and Guyomarc'h Orthez Nutrition animale* [1992] E.C.R. I-3899, para. 19. Article 110 TFEU does not preclude "reverse discrimination" arising where a Member State imposes internal taxation on its domestic products which is higher than that imposed on similar products imported from other Member States: ECJ, Case 86/78 *Peureux* [1979] E.C.R. 897, para. 32.

[75] ECJ, Case C-234/99 *Nygård* [2002] E.C.R. I-3657, para. 20.

[76] For the first para. of Art. 110 TFEU, see ECJ, Case 57/65 *Lütticke* [1966] E.C.R. 205, at 211; for the second para. of Art. 110, see ECJ, Case 27/65 *Fink Frucht* [1968] E.C.R. 223, at 232.

[77] See ECJ, Case 170/78 *Commission v United Kingdom* [1980] E.C.R. 417, paras 12–24, and [1983] E.C.R. 2265, paras 7–28; ECJ, Case 356/85 *Commission v Belgium* [1987] E.C.R. 3299, paras 9–21; ECJ, Case C-167/05 *Commission v Sweden* [2008] E.C.R. I-2127, paras 42–61 (consideration whether higher taxation on wine promoted the domestic consumption of beer). In the absence of similar or substitutable domestic products, the taxation is not in breach of Art. 110 TFEU: ECJ, Case 158/82 *Commission v Denmark* [1983] E.C.R. 3573, para. 22; ECJ, Case C-383/01 *De Danske Bilimportører* [2003] E.C.R. I-6065, paras 38–42.

of Justice held that a special French tax imposed on vehicles with a power rating of more than 16 fiscal horsepower which was higher than the differential tax charged on other vehicles was contrary to Art. 110 TFEU. The Court held that the power rating determining liability to the special tax had been fixed at a level such that only imported cars were subject to the special tax whereas French cars were liable to the distinctly more advantageous differential tax.[78] The Court held that the special tax discriminated against imported vehicles in favour of cars of domestic manufacture because it resulted in a much larger increase in taxation than passing from one category of car to another in the system of differential taxation.[79]

Burden offset or justified. For the purposes of the legal categorisation of a tax **9–024** which is imposed in accordance with the same criteria on domestic products and on products imported (or to be exported), it is necessary to take account of the destination of the proceeds of the taxation. Taxation is incompatible with Art. 110 TFEU and therefore prohibited where it discriminates against the product imported (or to be exported). This may be the case where the revenue from such taxation is intended to finance activities from which domestic products primarily benefit as a result of which the fiscal burden on domestic products is neutralised by the advantages which the charge is used to finance whilst the charge on the products imported (or to be exported) constitutes a net burden.[80] If the proceeds of the charge fully offset the burden borne by the domestic products, the burden is in fact borne exclusively by products imported (or to be exported) and the charge must be regarded as a charge having equivalent effect prohibited by the Treaties.[81] Within these limits, a Member State may differentiate a charge on the basis of objective criteria, such as the nature of the raw materials used or the production processes employed, provided that the differentiation pursues policy objectives which are compatible with Union law (e.g. environment protection).[82]

---

[78] ECJ, Case 112/84 *Humblot* [1985] E.C.R. 1367, para. 14.

[79] *Ibid.*, para. 15; *cf.* ECJ, Case C-113/94 *Casarin* [1995] E.C.R. I-4203, paras 17–26 (new French system of progressive taxation on motor vehicles held to be compatible with Art.110 TFEU); ECJ, Case C-421/97 *Tarantik* [1999] E.C.R. I-3633, paras 20–32; ECJ, Case C-265/99 *Commission v France* [2001] E.C.R. I-2305, paras 40–51. See also ECJ, Case C-345/93 *Fazenda Pública* [1995] E.C.R. I-479, paras 12–20; ECJ, Case C-393/98 *Gomes Valente* [2001] E.C.R. I-1327, paras 20–44.

[80] ECJ, Case 73/79 *Commission v Italy* [1980] E.C.R. 1533, paras 15–16 (discrimination against imported products); ECJ, Case C-234/99 *Nygård* [2002] E.C.R. I-3657, paras 21–22 (discrimination against products to be exported).

[81] ECJ, Joined Cases C-78/90–C-83/90 *Compagnie commerciale de l'Ouest and Others* [1992] E.C.R. I-1847, para. 27.

[82] ECJ, Case C-213/96 *Outokumpu* [1998]E.C.R. I-1777, paras 30–41. For the relationship between a discriminatory tax system and State Aid incompatible with the common market, see ECJ, Case C-234/99 *Nygård* [2002] E.C.R. I-3657, paras 50–65.

(c) *The Common Customs Tariff*

9–025 **Customs tariffs.** Further to the abolition of customs duties in intra-Union trade in goods, the Council adopted Regulation No. 950/68 on the basis of Arts 28 and 111 EEC, which introduced a Common Customs Tariff for goods from third countries as from July 1, 1968.[83] Art. 31 TFEU [*ex Art. 26 EC*] provides that the Council is to fix Common Customs Tariff duties. In the meantime, major changes have been made in the customs tariff, inter alia, as a result of bilateral agreements with third countries and the ratification of agreements reducing tariffs which have arisen in the multilateral trade negotiations under the auspices of the GATT. The legal basis for these "conventional" alterations to the Common Customs Tariff is to be found in the provisions concerning the common commercial policy (Art. 111 EEC during the transitional period, now Art. 207 TFEU). In pursuance of the Council regulations, the Commission has to draw up the customs tariff in force on the basis of a detailed nomenclature. The Commission has to adopt each year, by means of a regulation, the complete version of the nomenclature, together with the autonomous and conventional rates of duty in force.[84] The Union has exclusive competence with regard to the establishment of the customs union (see para. 7–023—7–025).

Alongside the general Common Customs Tariff, the Union also applies preferential tariffs in force under association agreements, free-trade agreements or general tariff preferences.[85]

9–026 **Customs legislation.** In order to secure uniform application of the common tariffs, it was necessary to harmonise the Member States' differing customs legislation. The Council has adopted directives and regulations pursuant to other Treaty provisions (Art. 115 TFEU [*ex Art. 94 EC*] and, as far as regulations are concerned, Art. 352 TFEU [*ex Art. 308 EC*] and/or the provisions concerning the common commercial policy) relating to such matters as determining the origin of goods, customs value, the various customs arrangements (bringing into free circulation, warehousing, inward and outward processing, temporary import/export, etc.), exemption from customs duties and payment of customs debt.[86]

---

[83] Regulation No. 950/68 (EEC) of the Council of June 28, 1968 on the Common Customs Tariff, [1968] O.J. English Spec. Ed. (I) 275; replaced by Council Regulation (EEC) No. 2658/87 of 23 July 1987 on the tariff and statistical nomenclature and on the Common Customs Tariff, [1987] O.J. L256.

[84] Article 12 of Regulation No 2658/87 (see preceding n.).

[85] Paras 25–009 and 25–010, *infra*.

[86] With effect from January 1, 1994, most of these rules have been replaced by Regulation (EEC) No. 2913/92 of October 12, 1992 establishing the Community Customs Code ([1992] O.J. L302/1), which the Council adopted on the basis of Arts 28, 100a and 113 EC [*now Arts 31, 114 and 207 TFEU*]. See also Lasok, *The Trade and Customs Law of the European Union* (The Hague, Kluwer Law International, 1998), 470 pp.

(d) Customs cooperation

Cooperation between customs authorities. Customs cooperation is one of the areas in which the Member States adopted joint actions[87] and drew up conventions[88] in the context of Title VI of the initial EU Treaty (cooperation in the fields of justice and home affairs) and where, as a result of the Treaty of Amsterdam, the Council could take action under Title VI of the EU Treaty (police and judicial cooperation in criminal matters) as well as under Art. 135 of the EC Treaty. Since the Lisbon Treaty, the European Parliament and the Council are to take measures in accordance with the ordinary legislative procedure in order to strengthen customs cooperation between the Member States and between the latter and the Commission (Art. 33 TFEU).

9–027

2. Prohibition of non-tariff restrictions

Non-tariff barriers. The GATT includes non-tariff barriers among the trade restrictions to be abolished in a customs union. In addition to the chapter on the customs union, Title II of Part Three of the Treaty on the Functioning of the European Union includes a chapter on prohibition of quantitative restrictions between Member States. Thus, Art. 34 TFEU [*ex Art. 28 EC*] prohibits "quantitative restrictions on imports and all measures having equivalent effect" and Art. 35 TFEU [*ex Art. 29 EC*] "quantitative restrictions on exports and all measures having equivalent effect". Article 36 TFEU [*ex Art. 30 EC*], however, permits such restrictions and measures where they are justified on grounds of public morality, public policy or public security; the protection of health and life of humans, animals or plants; the protection of national treasures possessing artistic, historic or archaeological value; or the protection of industrial and commercial property, provided that they do not constitute a means of arbitrary discrimination or a disguised restriction on trade between Member States. The provisions prohibiting quantitative restrictions and measures having equivalent effect have

9–028

---

[87] See, for instance, the Joint Actions adopted by the Council on November 29, 1996 (96/698/JHA) on cooperation between customs authorities and business organisations in combating drug trafficking ([1996] O.J. L322/3) and on June 9, 1997 (97/372/JHA) for the refining of targeting criteria, selection methods, etc., and collection of customs and police information ([1997] O.J. L159/1). See also the Council Resolutions of November 29, 1996 on the drawing up of police/customs agreements in the fight against drugs ([1996] O.J. C375/1) and of June 9, 1997 concerning a handbook for joint customs surveillance operations ([1997] O.J. C193/4).

[88] See the Convention of July 26, 1995 on the use of information technology for customs purposes ([1995] O.J. C316/34; for its provisional application between certain Member States, see [1995] O.J. C316/58), as supplemented by the Protocol of May 8, 2003 ([2003] O.J. L139/1) and the Convention of December 18, 1997 on mutual assistance and cooperation between customs administrations ([1998] O.J. C24/2; with an explanatory report in [1998] O.J. C189/1). A Protocol of November 29, 1996 drawn up on the basis of the former Art. K.3 of the EU Treaty confers jurisdiction on the Court of Justice to interpret, by way of preliminary rulings, the Convention on the use of information technology for customs purposes ([1997] O.J. C151/16) (para 23–015, *infra*).

direct effect.[89] Article 34 TFEU does not solely prohibit measures emanating from the State which, in themselves, create restrictions on trade between Member States, it may also apply where a Member State abstains from adopting the measures required in order to eliminate or prevent obstacles to the free movement of goods which are created by actions taken by individuals on its territory aimed at products originating in other Member States.[90] In such case, it has to be considered whether the Member State concerned can rely on the grounds which may be pleaded in justification of trade restrictions under Union law.[91]

The need to invoke these prohibitory provisions diminishes in practice where the national measures which might otherwise hinder trade in goods have been harmonised at Union level and made subject to a system of mutual recognition (see paras 9–108—9–116).

(a) *Prohibition of quantitative restrictions and measures having equivalent effect*

9–029   **Quantitative restrictions.** The Court of Justice has defined "quantitative restrictions" as "measures which amount to a total or partial restraint of, according to the circumstances, imports, exports or goods in transit".[92] These are measures which introduce a limitation depending upon the quantity or the value of the goods concerned. Since most trade "quotas" had already been abolished before the EEC Treaty entered into effect under the auspices of the OECD,[93] the prohibition of quantitative restrictions raises per se only a few problems.

9–030   **Measures having equivalent effect.** However, alongside quantitative restrictions, all measures having equivalent effect are also prohibited. This ancillary prohibition came to have great significance owing to its broad scope. The original interpretation given to that prohibition by the Commission[94] opened the way to a broad interpretation by the Court of Justice.

Indeed, in the 1974 judgment in *Dassonville*, the Court of Justice held that,

---

[89] For Art. 34 TFEU, see ECJ, Case 74/76 *Iannelli* [1977] E.C.R. 557, para. 13; for Art. 35 TFEU, see ECJ, Case 83/78 *Pigs Marketing Board* [1978] E.C.R. 2347, para. 66.

[90] ECJ, Case C-265/95 *Commission v France* [1997] E.C.R. I-6959, paras 30–32 (which refers to Member States' obligations under *ex Art. 10 EC* (the content of which was taken over by Art. 4(3) TFEU), see para. 7–045, *infra*).

[91] *Ibid.*, paras 33–66 (consideration of possible justificatory grounds and of the proportionality of the national measures which were in fact taken).

[92] ECJ, Case 2/73 *Geddo* [1973] E.C.R. 865, para. 7.

[93] On January 14, 1955 the Council of Ministers of the Organisation for European Economic Cooperation (now OECD, see para 1–003, *supra*) adopted, pursuant to Art. 4 of the OEEC Treaty, a Code with a list of products for which liberalisation was required to be achieved.

[94] Commission Directive 70/50/EEC of December 22, 1969 on the abolition of measures which have an effect equivalent to quantitative restrictions on imports and are not covered by other provisions adopted in pursuance of the EEC Treaty, [1970] O.J. English Spec. Ed. (I) 17.

"[a]ll trading rules enacted by Member States which are capable of hindering, directly or indirectly, actually or potentially, intra-Community trade are to be considered as measures having an effect equivalent to quantitative restrictions".[95]

In that case, the Court categorised as a measure having equivalent effect a Belgian provision prohibiting the import of Scotch whisky without a certificate of origin. Importers, such as Dassonville, which obtained the product from another Member State where it was in free circulation, found it less easy to get hold of that certificate than importers who obtained it directly from the country of origin. Thus, the Court of Justice interpreted the concept of measures having equivalent effect in the broadest possible manner. The test was no longer, as the Commission had suggested, the distinction made by the relevant national provision between domestic and imported products, but simply whether the measure directly or indirectly, actually or potentially, hindered the free movement of goods. Hence, once any link can be made between a national measure and the import of goods, the application of Art. 34 TFEU [*ex Art. 28 EC*] is not precluded on the sole ground that all the facts of the specific case are confined to a single Member State.[96] Nevertheless, it must be observed that in some cases the Court has held that the restrictions on trade in goods were too "uncertain and indirect" to hinder trade between Member States.[97]

The implications of *Dassonville*. That definition of "measures having equivalent effect" takes in a complete range of legislative and administrative measures which are applicable without distinction to domestic and imported products, yet have a—sometimes minimal—effect on potential sales of imported products and hence on the free movement of goods. Accordingly, the Court of Justice held that an unlawful measure having an effect equivalent to a quantitative restriction was involved in the case of a Belgian provision which, in order to protect consumers

9–031

---

[95] ECJ, Case 8/74 *Dassonville* [1974] E.C.R. 837, para. 5.
[96] ECJ, Joined Cases C-321-C-324/94 *Pistre and Others* [1997] E.C.R. I-2343, paras 44–45; ECJ, Case C-448/98 *Guimont* [2000] E.C.R. I-10663, paras 21–24. Only the application of the measure to imported products is prohibited: *Guimont*, paras 15–21. See Papadopoulou, "Situations purement internes et droit communautaire: un instrument jurisprudentiel à double fonction ou une arme à double tranchant?" (2002) C.D.E. 95–129; De Beys, "Le droit européen est-il applicable aux situations purement internes? A propos des discriminations à rebours dans le marché unique" (2001) J.T.D.E. 137–144.
[97] ECJ, Case C-69/88 *Krantz* [1990] E.C.R. I-583, para. 11; ECJ, Case C-93/92 *CMC Motorradcenter* [1993] E.C.R. I-5009, para. 12; ECJ, Case C-379/92 *Peralta* [1994] E.C.R. I-3453, para. 24; see to the same effect, ECJ, Case 155/80 *Oebel* [1981] E.C.R. 1993, paras 11–21; ECJ, Case 75/81 *Blesgen* [1982] E.C.R. 1211, para. 9; ECJ, Case 148/85 *Forest* [1986] E.C.R. 3499, para. 19; ECJ, Case C-23/89 *Quietlynn and Richards* [1990] E.C.R. I-3059, paras 10–11; ECJ, Joined Cases C-140/94, C-141/94 and C-142/94 *DIP and Others* [1995] E.C.R. I-3257, para. 29; ECJ, Case C-134/94 *Esso Española* [1995] E.C.R. I-4233, para. 24.

from confusing butter and margarine, provided that margarine could be marketed only in cubic form. Although the provision drew no distinction between domestic and imported products, it was nevertheless of such a nature as to render the marketing of imported products,

> "more difficult or more expensive either by barring them from certain channels of distribution or owing to the additional costs brought about by the necessity to package the products in question in special packs which comply with the requirements in force on the market of their destination".[98]

In principle, the same touchstone is used to assess national provisions governing import and export formalities, requirements to be fulfilled by products (such as requirements relating to the name, form, dimensions, weight, composition, presentation, labelling or packaging),[99] price rules, methods of sale and advertising,[100] conditions for public tenders and intellectual property rights. According to the Court, measures adopted by a Member State are to be regarded as measures having equivalent effect to quantitative restrictions where their object or effect is to treat products originating in other Member States less favourably or where they (otherwise) hinder the access of such products to the market of that Member State.[101] The Court also clarified that the latter is not normally the case for selling arrangements that apply to all traders operating within the national territory and that affect in the same manner, in law and in fact, the marketing of domestic products and of products originating from other Member States.[102] In contrast, requirements to be fulfilled by products lawfully manufactured and marketed in another Member State constitute measures of equivalent effect to quantitative restrictions even if those rules apply to all products alike.[103] Indeed, such requirements typically hinder the access to the market of the Member State concerned.

Accordingly, a national provision constitutes a measure having equivalent effect to a quantitative restriction where it discriminates against imported products or, at least, hinders the access to the market of the Member State concerned. This is the case of measures that do not affect trade in products imported or reimported through parallel channels in the same way as trade in products manufactured in the home market or imported into that market by approved distributors.[104]

---

[98] ECJ, Case 261/81 *Rau* [1982] E.C.R. 3961, para. 13.

[99] See the survey in Capelli, "La libre circulation des produits alimentaires à l'intérieur du marché commun" (1993) R.M.C.U.E. 790–811.

[100] But see para. 9–045, *infra*.

[101] ECJ, Case C-110/05 *Commission v Italy* [2009] E.C.R. I-519, para. 37; ECJ, Case C-142/05 *Mickelsson and Roos* [2009] E.C.R. I-4273, para. 24.

[102] Joined Cases C-267/91 and C-268/91 *Keck and Mithouard* [1993] E.C.R. I-6097, para. 17; ECJ, Case C-110/05 *Commission v Italy* [2009] E.C.R. I-519, para. 36. See para. 9–045, *infra*.

[103] ECJ, Case C-110/05 *Commission v Italy* [2009] E.C.R. I-519, paras 35 and 37; ECJ, Case C-142/05 *Mickelsson and Roos* (n. 101, *supra*), para. 24.

[104] ECJ, Case C-240/95 *Schmit* [1996] E.C.R. I-3179, paras 16–22.

A prohibition on the use of a certain product, even if applicable without distinction as regards its origin, has also been held to constitute a measure having equivalent effect to quantitative restrictions.[105] The Court of Justice considered the prohibition in Italian traffic regulations on using a motorcycle and a trailer together to constitute a measure having equivalent effect to a quantitative restriction to the extent that its effect is to hinder access to the Italian market for trailers which are specially designed for motorcycles and are lawfully produced and marketed in other Member States.[106] Indeed, a prohibition on the use of a product in a Member State has a considerable influence on the behaviour of consumers, which, in its turn, affects the access of that product to the market of that Member State.[107]

Free movement of goods concerns not only traders but also consumers. It requires that consumers resident in one Member State may travel freely to the territory of another Member State to shop under the same conditions as the local population and that businesses may direct advertising to consumers from other Member States.[108]

Export restrictions. Traditionally, in contradistinction to the broad interpretation of the concept of measures having effect equivalent to quantitative restrictions on imports (Art. 34 TFEU [*ex Art. 28 EC*]), the Court of Justice regarded as measures having equivalent effect to quantitative restrictions on exports (Art. 35 TFEU [*ex Art. 29 EC*]):   **9–032**

> "national measures which have as their specific object or effect the restriction of patterns of exports and thereby the establishment of a difference in treatment between the domestic trade of a Member State and its export trade in such a way as to provide a particular advantage for national production or for the domestic market of the State in question at the expense of the production or of the trade of other Member States".[109]

An example of such a restriction on exports is where a Member State requires wine protected by a designation of origin to be bottled in the region of

---

[105] ECJ, Case C-110/05 *Commission v Italy* [2009] E.C.R. I-519, paras 56–57; ECJ, Case C-142/05 *Mickelsson and Roos* (n. 101, *supra*), paras 26–28.

[106] ECJ, Case C-110/05 *Commission v Italy* [2009] E.C.R. I-519, para. 58.

[107] *Ibid.*, para. 56.

[108] ECJ, Case C-362/88 *GB-INNO-BM* [1990] E.C.R. I-667, para. 8 (consumers may not be deprived of access to advertising available in the country where purchases are made).

[109] ECJ, Case 15/79 *Groenveld* [1979] E.C.R. 3409, para. 7. Since the Treaty provisions on free movement of goods also apply to the Union institutions, Union measures may also constitute measures having equivalent effect: ECJ, Case C-469/00 *Ravil and Others* [2003] E.C.R. I-5053, paras 40–44, and ECJ, Case C-108/01 *Consorzio del Prosciutto di Parma and Others* [2003] E.C.R. I-5121, paras 54–59.

production.[110] Measures which are applicable without distinction to domestic and export trade were traditionally held to fall outside the scope of Art. 35 TFEU.[111]

In recent case law, however, the Court of Justice has shown itself prepared to adopt a broad interpretation of export restrictions, similar to the *Dassonville* interpretation of import restrictions. Accordingly, a Belgian prohibition on requiring from a consumer a deposit or payment before the expiry of a period for withdrawal was held to be contrary to Art. 35, even though it was applicable to all traders active in Belgium, since its actual impact was greater on exports than on the marketing of goods on the Belgian domestic market.[112] All the same, in this context too a measure will not qualify as a measure having equivalent effect to a quantitative restriction on exports where its effect on exports is too "uncertain and indirect".[113]

(b) *Exceptions*

9–033   **Survey.** The *Dassonville* definition of measures having equivalent effect brings within the prohibition set out in Art. 34 TFEU [*ex Art. 28 EC*] a whole series of national measures which pursue policy objectives in the general interest and thereby restrict trade. In so far as the policy in question cannot be justified on the basis of Art. 36 TFEU [*ex Art. 30 EC*], strict application of Art. 34 TFEU would make it impossible to pursue those goals. As a result, pending harmonisation of such national provisions—which would neutralise their effect of hampering trade—the Court of Justice has accepted in the *Cassis de Dijon* case law an additional exception which allows measures to be reconciled with Art. 34 TFEU where they protect legitimate interests in a reasonable manner (the rule of reason). It is for the Member State to prove that its measure which restricts trade (or its failure to prevent a restriction of trade) comes within one of the exceptions provided for in Art. 36 TFEU or that it is covered by the rule of reason.[114] In

---

[110] ECJ, Case C-388/95 *Belgium v Spain* [2000] E.C.R. I-3123, paras 36–42. For the justification identified by the Court of Justice in the good reputation of the wine in question, see Bianchi, "La mise en bouteille obligatoire des vins de qualité dans la région de production" (2001) R.M.C.U.E. 343–350.

[111] ECJ, Case 155/80 *Oebel* [1981] E.C.R. 1993, paras 15–16; ECJ, Case 237/82 *Jongeneel Kaas* [1984] E.C.R. 483, paras 22–27; ECJ, Case 15/83 *Denkavit Nederland* [1984] E.C.R. 2171, paras 16–18. For further applications, see ECJ, Case C-302/88 *Hennen Olie* [1990] E.C.R. I-4625, paras 17–18; ECJ, Case C-339/89 *Alsthom Atlantique* [1991] E.C.R. I-107, paras 13–16; ECJ, Case C-332/89 *Marchandise and Others* [1991] E.C.R. I-1027, paras 16–17; ECJ, Case C-47/90 *Delhaize Frères* [1992] E.C.R. I-3669, paras 11–27. For the distinction between this case law and that on Art. 34 TFEU, see Weatherill, "After *Keck*: Some Thoughts on How to Clarify the Clarification" (1996) C.M.L.Rev. 885, at 902–903; Roth, "Wettbewerb der Mitgliedstaaten oder Wettbewerb der Hersteller?" (1995) Z.H.W. 78–95;

[112] ECJ, Case C-205/07 *Gysbrechts* [2008] E.C.R. I-9947, paras 42–44.

[113] ECJ, Case C-412/97 *ED* [1999] E.C.R. I-3845, para. 11 (with a reference to the case law cited in n. 96).

[114] But see the view taken in Directive 70/50 (para. 9–030, *supra*) and the *Keck and Mithouard* case law on sales methods (para. 9–045, *infra*), where the burden of proof has to be discharged by the person arguing for protection of the free movement of goods.

addition, the Court of Justice has, by the judgment in *Keck and Mithouard*, taken all national provisions on methods of sale without discriminatory effects outside the scope of the *Dassonville* definition of measures having equivalent effect.[115]

(1) Article 36 TFEU

Grounds for justification. The exceptions provided for in Art. 36 TFEU [*ex Art. 30 EC*] relate to measures of a non-economic nature[116] and are strictly interpreted by the Court of Justice.[117] Only those interests listed in the Treaty article (protection of public morality, public policy, public security, health and life of humans, animals or plants, national treasures possessing artistic, historic or archaeological value, and industrial and commercial property) are capable of justifying a measure restricting trade.[118]   **9–034**

Absence of harmonisation. Article 36 TFEU does not amount to a constitutionally protected core of residuary powers of the Member States. A Member State may no longer justify a measure on the basis of Art. 36 TFEU where the national legislation intended to protect the specific interest concerned has been harmonised.[119] This explains, for instance, why it was not possible for the United Kingdom to rely on Art. 36 in respect of a ban on the export of calves, in view of a Union directive fully harmonising the measures necessary for the protection of the health of calves.[120]   **9–035**

---

[115] The consideration that such provisions have only a minimal impact on intra-Union trade (para. 9–045, *infra*) also underlies the judgments cited in n. 96, *supra*.

[116] ECJ, Case 7/61 *Commission v Italy* [1961] E.C.R. 317, at 329; ECJ, Case 238/82 *Duphar v Netherlands* [1984] E.C.R. 523, para. 23; ECJ, Case 288/83 *Commission v Ireland* [1985] E.C.R. 1761, para. 28. This does not mean that rules justified by objective circumstances may not also make it possible to achieve additional objectives of an economic nature sought by the Member State: ECJ, Case 72/83 *Campus Oil* [1984] E.C.R. 2727, para. 36.

[117] ECJ, Case 13/68 *Salgoil* [1968] E.C.R. 453, at 463.

[118] ECJ, Case 113/80 *Commission v Ireland* [1981] E.C.R. 1625, paras 7–8; ECJ, Case C-249/07 *Commission v Netherlands* [2008] E.C.R. I-174, paras 38–40. Article 36 TFEU can only be relied upon to justify measures restricting trade, not to justify derogations to secondary Union law (ECJ (judgment of March 4, 2010), Case C-197/08 *Commission v France*, not yet reported, para. 49; ECJ (judgment of March 4, 2010), Case C-198/08 *Commission v Austria*, not yet reportd, para. 38; ECJ (judgment of March 4, 2010), Case C-221/08 *Commission v Ireland*, not yet reported, para. 50).

[119] ECJ, Case 148/78 *Ratti* [1979] E.C.R. 1629, para. 36; ECJ, Case C-445/06 *Danske Slagterier* [2009] E.C.R. I-2119, para. 25. A harmonising directive precludes recourse to Art. 36 even if the directive itself does not lay down any Union procedure for monitoring compliance or any penalties: ECJ, Case C-5/94 *Hedley Lomas* [1996] E.C.R. I-2553, paras 18–20, with a case note by Van Calster (1996/97) Col.J.E.L. 132–145. Where harmonisation of national legislation has been carried out pursuant to Art. 114 TFEU, account must be taken of Art. 114(4) to (7); para. 9–115, *infra*.

[120] ECJ, Case C-1/96 *Compassion in World Farming* [1998] E.C.R. I-1251, paras 47–64; see Van Calster, "Export restrictions—a watershed for Article 30" (2000) E.L.Rev. 335–352.

9–036 **Proportionality.** In addition, the measure may not constitute "a means of arbitrary discrimination or a disguised restriction on trade between Member States". This means that the measure must be proportionate to the aim sought. The interest may not be capable of being as effectively protected by measures which do not restrict intra-Union trade so much.[121]

A Member State is not entitled unnecessarily to subject products to tests where the Member State in which they originated has already carried out tests which satisfy the requirements of health protection and the results are available.[122] In the absence of harmonisation, it is for the Member State to decide on the level of protection of human health and life they wish to ensure.[123] In the event that a Member State wishes to rely on Art. 36 in order to justify a measure restricting the free movement of goods, it must be able to show that the measure is based on a detailed assessment of the risk, based on the most recent reliable scientific data available. Where it proves to be impossible to determine with scientific certainty the existence or extent of the alleged risk to public health, a Member State may take protective measures on the basis of the precautionary principle without having to await full proof that the risk actually exists and is a major one.[124]

9–037 **Discrimination.** In the absence of harmonisation and if the national measure does not exceed what is necessary to attain one of the objectives listed in Art. 36 TFEU, that article will justify the measure, even if it embodies formal discrimination or has a discriminatory effect.

9–038 **Intellectual property.** The exception provided for in Art. 36 TFEU for the "protection of industrial and commercial property" (such as patents, designs, copyrights and trademarks) has obliged the Court of Justice to strike a balance between the principle of free movement of goods and protection of the rights in question. The Treaties do not affect the existence of exclusive rights recognised under national legislation with regard to industrial and commercial property (see Art. 345 TFEU [*ex Art. 295 EC*]), but do set limitations to the exercise of such rights. Article 36 only admits derogations from free movement of goods to the

---

[121] ECJ, Case 104/75 *De Peijper* [1976] E.C.R. 613, para. 17. For a very flexible application, see ECJ, Case C-320/93 *Ortscheit* [1994] E.C.R. I-5243, paras 17–20.

[122] ECJ, Case 272/80 *Frans-Nederlandse Maatschappij voor Biologische Produkten* [1981] E.C.R. 3277, paras 14–15; ECJ, Case 25/88 *Wurmser and Others* [1989] E.C.R. 1105, para. 18: "That rule is a particular application of a more general principle of mutual trust between the authorities of the Member States". See also ECJ, Case 373/92 *Commission v Belgium* [1993] E.C.R. I-3107, paras 8–10; ECJ, Case C-293/94 *Brandsma* [1996] E.C.R. I-3159, paras 10–13; ECJ, Case C-432/03 *Commission v Portugal* [2005] E.C.R. I-9665, para. 46.

[123] E.g., ECJ, Case C-95/01 *Greenham and Abel* [2004] E.C.R., I-01333, para. 37; ECJ (judgment of January 28, 2010), Case C-333/08 *Commission v France*, not yet reported, para. 85.

[124] ECJ, Case C-95/01 *Greenham and Abel* [2004] E.C.R. I-01333, paras 39–50; ECJ (judgment of January 28, 2010), Case C-333/08 *Commission v France*, not yet reported, para. 86–93. For the precautionary principle, see para. 22–040.

extent to which they are justified for the purpose of safeguarding rights which constitute the "specific subject-matter" of such property.[125]

The "exhaustion" doctrine expounded by the Court of Justice states that the owners of the right cannot rely on their exclusive right in order to prevent the importation and marketing of a product which has been marketed in another Member State by themselves, with their consent, or by a person economically or legally dependent on them.[126] Where a patentee is legally bound under national law or Union law to market his or her products in a Member State, he or she cannot be deemed to have given his or her consent to the marketing of the products concerned. He or she is therefore entitled to oppose importation and marketing of those products by a third party in the State where they are protected.[127] Putting a product on the market outside the European Economic Area does not entail exhaustion of the right to contest importation without consent.[128] It should be noted that Arts 36 and 345 TFEU do not reserve an exclusive power to the Member States to regulate the law on intellectual property and hence do not preclude harmonisation measures on the part of the Union.[129]

---

[125] For rights related to copyrights, see ECJ, Case 78/70 *Deutsche Grammophon* [1971] E.C.R. 487, paras 11–13; for trademarks, ECJ, Case 192/73 *Van Zuylen* [1974] E.C.R. 731, paras 7–10, reconsidered in ECJ, Case C-10/89 *Hag GF* [1990] E.C.R. I-3711, paras 10–20; ECJ, Case C-9/93 *IHT Internationale Heiztechnik and Danzinger* [1994] E.C.R. I-2789, paras 40–46; ECJ, Case 16/74 *Centrafarm* [1974] E.C.R. 1183, paras 7–8; ECJ, C-317/93 *Deutsche Renault* [1993] E.C.R. I-6227, paras 30–39; for patents, ECJ, Case 15/74 *Centrafarm* [1974] E.C.R. 1147, paras 8–9. For copyrights, see Joined Cases 55 and 57/80 *Musik-Vertrieb membran* [1981] E.C.R. 147, paras 11–13 (as regards free movement of services, see previously ECJ, Case 62/79 *Coditel* [1980] E.C.R. 881, paras 12–14); for designations and indications of origin, see ECJ, Case 12/74 *Commission v Germany* [1975] E.C.R. 181, paras 7–18; ECJ, Case C-3/91 *Exportur* [1992] E.C.R. I-5529, paras 23–38; ECJ, Case C-388/95 *Belgium v Spain* [2000] E.C.R. I-3123, paras 47–75; for designs, see ECJ, Case 53/87 *CICRA and Maxicar* [1988] E.C.R. 6039, para. 11, and ECJ, Case 238/87 *Volvo* [1988] E.C.R. 6211, para. 8.

[126] In addition to the judgments cited in the preceding n., see as regards patents: ECJ, Case 187/80 *Merck* [1981] E.C.R. 2063, paras 9–14; as regards trademarks: ECJ, Case 119/75 *Terrapin* [1976] E.C.R. 1039, paras 5–8 (also the right to a trade name); ECJ, Case 102/77 *Hoffmann-La Roche* [1978] E.C.R. 1139, paras 6–14; ECJ, Case 3/78 *Centrafarm* [1978] E.C.R. 1823, paras 7–22; ECJ, Joined Cases C-427/93, C-429/93 and C-436/93 *Bristol-Myers Squibb and Others* [1996] E.C.R. I-3457; ECJ, Joined Cases C-71/94, C-72/94 and C-73/94 *Eurim-Pharm* [1996] E.C.R. I-3603; ECJ, Case C-232/94 *MPA Pharma* [1996] E.C.R. I-3671; as regards copyrights: ECJ, Case 158/86 *Warner Brothers and Others* [1988] E.C.R. 2605, paras 1–19; with regard to designs, see ECJ, Case 144/81 *Keurkoop* [1982] E.C.R. 2853, paras 22–29.

[127] ECJ, Case 19/84 *Pharmon v Hoechst* [1985] E.C.R. 2281, paras 22–27 (compulsory licence); ECJ, Joined Cases C-267/95 and C-268/95 *Merck and Beecham* [1996] E.C.R. I-6285, paras 26–54.

[128] ECJ, Case C-355/96 *Silhouette International Schmied* [1998] E.C.R. I-4799, para. 26; ECJ, Case C-173/98 *Sebago and Maison Dubois* [1999] E.C.R. I-4103, para. 21; ECJ, Joined Cases C-414/99-C-416/99 *Zino Davidoff and Others* [2001] E.C.R. I-8691, paras 30–67; ECJ, Case C-479/04 *Laserdisken* [2006] E.C.R. I-8089, paras 17–27.

[129] ECJ, Case C-350/92 *Spain v Council* [1995] E.C.R. I-1985, paras 12–24. For Union harmonisation measures, see para. 9–108, *infra*.

(2) The rule of reason

9–039 **Cassis de Dijon.** In the leading *Cassis de Dijon* judgment of February 20, 1979, the Court of Justice opened the door to certain "reasonable" national measures in restraint of trade being regarded as compatible with Art. 34 TFEU [*ex Art. 28 EC*] on grounds other than those listed in Art. 36 TFEU [*ex Art. 30 EC*]. The Court had been called upon to rule on a provision of German law requiring various alcoholic beverages to have a minimum alcoholic strength. The requirement for fruit liqueurs to have a minimum of 25 per cent alcohol content prevented *Cassis de Dijon*, which contained only 15 to 20 per cent alcohol and was freely marketed in France, from being imported into Germany. The Court accepted that, in the absence of common rules, it was for Member States to "regulate all matters relating to the production and marketing of alcohol and alcoholic beverages on their own territory". The Court went on to state that:

> "[o]bstacles to movement within the Community resulting from disparities between the national laws relating to the marketing of the products in question must be accepted in so far as those provisions may be recognised as being necessary in order to satisfy mandatory requirements relating in particular to the effectiveness of fiscal supervision, the protection of public health, the fairness of commercial transactions and the defence of the consumer".[130]

9–040 **Four conditions.** In individual cases concerning the application of Art. 34 TFEU, the Court of Justice requires the given national measure invariably to satisfy four requirements.

9–041 **(1) Absence of harmonisation.** First, the Court allows a Member State to apply a measure restricting trade only in so far as there is no legislation at Union level. In fact, the rule of reason constitutes an exception to the prohibition of measures having equivalent effect pending the adoption of Union legislation. Once national legislation has been harmonised, a Member State may in principle no longer deviate from the Union rule.[131]

---

[130] ECJ, Case 120/78 *Rewe-Zentral* [1979] E.C.R. 649, para. 8. Later the Court of Justice was to refer to that case as follows (in Case 302/86 *Commission v Denmark* [1988] E.C.R. 4607, para. 6): "[I]n the absence of common rules relating to the marketing of the products in question, obstacles to free movement within the Community resulting from disparities between the national laws must be accepted in so far as such rules, applicable to domestic and imported products without distinction, may be recognised as being necessary in order to satisfy mandatory requirements recognised by Community law. Such rules must also be proportionate to the aim in view. If a Member State has a choice between various measures for achieving the same aim, it should choose the means which least restricts the free movement of goods." *Cf.* Art. 114 TFEU, which refers to "major needs".

[131] E.g., ECJ, Case C-221/00 *Commission v Austria* [2003] E.C.R. I-1007, para. 42. But see Art. 114(4) and (5) TFEU; para. 9–115, *infra*.

(2) Mandatory requirements. Next, the measure adopted by the Member State   **9–042**
must be justified by a "mandatory requirement" (*exigence impérative*) recognised
or to be recognised by the Court of Justice, such as protection of consumers,[132]
fairness of commercial transactions,[133] effectiveness of fiscal supervision,[134]
combating fraud,[135] completion of the internal market by establishing statistics on
the trading of goods between Member States,[136] protection of public health,[137]
protection of the environment,[138] road safety,[139] proper functioning of the public
telecommunications network,[140] protection of cultural works,[141] including the
protection of books as cultural objects,[142] and maintenance of press diversity with
a view to safeguarding freedom of expression.[143] This list is not exhaustive,
but may be supplemented by other non-economic policy aims in the general
interest.[144] A restriction of the free movement of goods may also be justified
on the ground of the need to protect fundamental rights, such as freedom of
expression and freedom of assembly.[145]

(3) Application without distinction. A Member State can comply with "manda-   **9–043**
tory requirements" only by means of a measure which is applicable without
distinction to domestic and imported products, even if it is indirectly discriminatory,[146] in particular where it will be more difficult for imported products than for
domestic products to conform to the measure or where the particular nature of the
imported products would have necessitated a derogating measure. In this way, the
Court of Justice had to consider whether the Belgian measure requiring margarine
to be packaged in cubes was justified[147] and, in *Cassis de Dijon*, the German minimum alcoholic strength requirement, which did not involve foreign products being

---

[132] ECJ, Case 27/80 *Fietje* [1980] E.C.R. 3839, paras 10–11.
[133] ECJ, Case 6/81 *Industrie Diensten Groep* [1982] E.C.R. 707, paras 7–9.
[134] Case 823/79 *Carciati* [1980] E.C.R. 2773, para. 9.
[135] See also ECJ, Case C-184/96 *Commission v France* [1998] E.C.R. I-6197, paras 23–37.
[136] ECJ, Case C-114/96 *Kieffer and Thill* [1997] E.C.R. I-3629, paras 29–31.
[137] ECJ, Case 120/78 *Rewe-Zentral* [1979] E.C.R. 649, paras 8–11.
[138] ECJ, Case 302/86 *Commission v Denmark* [1988] E.C.R. 4607, paras 7–9; ECJ, Case C-320/03 *Commission v Austria* [2005] E.C.R. I-9871, paras 71–84. See Notaro, "The New Generation Case Law on Trade and Environment" (2000) E.L.Rev. 467–491.
[139] ECJ, Case C-314/98 *Snellers Auto's* [2000] E.C.R. I-8633, para. 55.
[140] ECJ, Joined Cases C-388/00 and C-429/00 *Radiosistemi* [2002] E.C.R. I-5845, para. 44.
[141] ECJ, Joined Cases 60–61/84 *Cinéthèque* [1985] E.C.R. 2605, para. 23.
[142] ECJ, Case C-531/07 *LIBRO* [2009] E.C.R. I-3717, para. 34.
[143] ECJ, Case C-368/95 *Familiapress* [1997] E.C.R. I-3689, para. 18.
[144] A risk of seriously undermining the financial balance of the social security system may possibly constitute a mandatory requirement: ECJ, Case C-120/95 *Decker* [1998] E.C.R. I-1831, para. 39; ECJ, Case C-322/01 *Deutscher Apothekerverband* [2003] E.C.R. I-14887, para. 122, with a case note by Lang (2005) C.M.L.Rev. 189–204.
[145] ECJ, Case C-112/00 *Schmidberger* [2003] E.C.R. I-5659, para. 74.
[146] For this expression, see para. 7–062, *supra*.
[147] ECJ, Case 261/81 *Rau* [1982] E.C.R. 3961, paras 16–20 (see also para. 9–031, *supra*).

treated differently from domestic ones, but in practice kept foreign spirits off the German market.[148] Similarly, the Court was asked to rule on the compatibility with EU law of a deposit and return system for packaging of beer and soft drinks laying down the same rules for national producers and producers from other Member States.[149] A measure which makes a distinction between domestic and imported products and so directly discriminates against the latter may be tolerated only if it satisfies Art. 36 TFEU. Such a measure ceases to be discriminatory, however, where the distinction is due to particular characteristics of the product. Accordingly, before the harmonisation at Union level of the rules concerning shipments of waste, it was possible to justify preferential treatment for domestic, as opposed to imported waste, by the principle that environmental damage should as a matter of priority be remedied at source.[150] In such a case, the "non-discrimination" requirement is satisfied and the rule of reason may be applied.[151]

9–044   **(4) Proportionality.** Lastly, the national measure must be proportionate to the intended aim. If a Member State has a choice between different measures to attain the same objective it should choose the means which least restricts the free movement of goods.[152] Consequently, a national measure must not only be appropriate in order to achieve an aim in the general interest (which is regarded as a "mandatory requirement"), but it must also be indispensable in the sense that there are no less restrictive means available of achieving the intended aim.[153] In the *Cassis de Dijon* case, the Court of Justice accordingly held that it would go too far to

---

[148] Para. 9–039, *supra*. Another example is ECJ, Case 302/86 *Commission v Denmark* [1988] E.C.R. 4607, where what was at issue was a deposit-and-return system under which containers for beer and soft drinks not approved by a national agency might be used for only a maximum quantity of 3,000 hectolitres a year. Although the system did not distinguish between domestic and foreign producers, it impeded the import of drinks from other Member States in otherwise than approved containers. *Cf.* ECJ, Case C-237/94 *O'Flynn* [1996] E.C.R. I-2617, para. 18, in which the Court of Justice held that measures which are applicable without distinction in terms of nationality must be regarded as indirectly discriminatory if they can be more easily satisfied by national workers than by migrant workers or where there is a risk that they may operate to the particular detriment of migrant workers.

[149] ECJ, Case C-309/02 *Radlberger Getränkegesellschaft* [2004] E.C.R. I-11763, para. 60–69.

[150] ECJ, Case C-2/90 *Commission v Belgium* [1992] E.C.R. I-4431, para. 34; *cf.* ECJ, Case C-221/06 *Stadtgemeinde Frohnleiten and Gemeindebetriebe Frohnleiten* [2007] E.C.R. I-9643, paras 60–68.

[151] In some cases, the Court of Justice appears not to rule out a justification on grounds of "mandatory requirements" even in the case of discriminatory measures, e.g., ECJ, Case C-203/96 *Dusseldorp and Others* [1998] E.C.R. I-4075, paras 44–50; ECJ, Case C-389/96 *Aher-Waggon* [1998] E.C.R. I-4473, paras 18–19; ECJ, Case C-209/98 *Sydhavnens Sten & Grus* [2000] E.C.R. I-3473, paras 48–50 (environmental protection and public health); ECJ, Case C-531/07 *LIBRO* [2009] E.C.R. I-3717, paras 18–22 and 34 34 (obligation to sell imported books at fixed prices). See Notaro, "The New Generation Case Law on Trade and Environment" (2000) E.L.Rev. 467, at 489.

[152] See, e.g., ECJ, Case C-51/94 *Commission v Germany* [1995] E.C.R. I-3599, paras 32–37; ECJ, Case C-114/96 *Kieffer and Thill* [1997] E.C.R. I-3629, paras 31–38.

[153] See the discussion of the principle of proportionality, paras 7–035—7–036, *supra*.

"regard the mandatory fixing of minimum alcohol requirements as being an essential guarantee of the fairness of commercial transactions, since it is a simple matter to ensure that suitable information is conveyed to the purchaser by requiring the display of an indication of origin and of the alcohol content on the packaging of products".[154]

The Court further referred to reciprocal recognition of national provisions as a particular application of the principle of proportionality when it held that:

"[t]here is therefore no valid reason why, provided that they have been lawfully produced and marketed in one of the Member States, alcoholic beverages should not be introduced into any other Member State".[155]

A Member State wishing to apply a measure restricting trade must show that the aim sought by the measure is not already achieved by the legislation in force in the Member State from which the imported product originates. The burden of proof in fact requires the Member State to show why its own situation differs so much from that of other Member States as to necessitate a specific measure.[156] Accordingly, Art. 34 TFEU precludes a national rule which does not allow a trader to show that an imported product satisfied the prescribed requirements already in its State of origin.[157] However, the mere fact that one Member State imposes stricter rules than those applicable in other Member States does not mean that the former are ipso facto incompatible with Arts 34 and 36 TFEU.[158]

(3) Rules governing selling arrangements

Keck and Mithouard. The *Dassonville* interpretation of Art. 34 TFEU [*ex Art. 28 EC*] raised questions about the permissibility of national legislation relating to selling arrangements, which, although not intended to regulate trade in goods between Member States, nevertheless affect the volume of sales within the Member State concerned and hence also impede the sale of products from other Member States. In this way, the Court of Justice delivered a number of

9–045

---

[154] ECJ, Case 120/78 *Rewe-Zentral* [1979] E.C.R. 649, para. 13. The Court has also referred to labelling requirements as a less restrictive means of preventing confusion arising between butter and margarine than cubic packaging: ECJ, Case 261/81 *Rau* [1982] E.C.R. 3961, para. 17.

[155] *Rewe*, cited in the preceding n., para. 14.

[156] See Mattera, "L'Union européenne assure le respect des identités nationales, régionales et locales, en particulier par l'application et la mise en oeuvre du principe de la reconnaissance mutuelle" (2002) R.D.U.E. 217–239 and "L'article 30 du traité CEE, la jurisprudence 'cassis de Dijon' et le principe de la reconnaissance mutuelle" (1992) 4 R.M.U.E. 13–71.

[157] E.g., ECJ, Joined Cases C-388/00 and C-429/00 *Radiosistemi* [2002] E.C.R. I-5845, paras 44–46.

[158] ECJ (judgment of January 28, 2010), Case C-333/08 *Commission v France*, not yet reported, para. 105. For reliance by Member States on the protection of health and the life of persons, see also para 5–104 above.

controversial rulings on Sunday-trading legislation.[159] The question arose as to whether such indirect influence on free movement of goods sufficed in order for the legislation concerned to be regarded as unlawful measures having equivalent effect.[160]

> "In view of the increasing tendency of traders to invoke Article 30 [*now Art. 36 TFEU*] as a means of challenging any rules whose effect is to limit their commercial freedom even where such rules are not aimed at products from other Member States"

the Court considered in the judgment of November 24, 1993 in *Keck and Mithouard* that it was "necessary to re-examine and clarify its case law on this matter".[161] Within the class of measures applicable without distinction to domestic and imported products, the Court introduced a distinction between provisions laying down requirements which products have to satisfy and provisions restricting or prohibiting certain selling arrangements. The Court then declared that:

> "contrary to what has previously been decided, the application to products from other Member States of national provisions restricting or prohibiting certain selling arrangements is not such as to hinder directly or indirectly, actually or potentially, trade between Member States within the meaning of the *Dassonville* judgment . . ., so long as those provisions apply to all relevant traders operating within the national territory and so long as they affect in the same manner, in law and in fact, the marketing of domestic products and of those from other Member States".[162]

---

[159] See ECJ, Case C-145/88 *Torfaen Borough Council* [1989] E.C.R. I-3851; ECJ, Case C-312/89 *Conforama and Others* [1991] E.C.R. I-997 and Case C-332/89 *Marchandise and Others* [1991] E.C.R. I-1027; ECJ, Case C-169/91 *Council of the City of Stoke-on-Trent and Norwich City Council* [1992] E.C.R. I-6635.

[160] Some commentators advocated restricting the concept of "measures having equivalent effect": Steiner, "Drawing the Line: Uses and Abuses of Article 30 EEC" (1992) C.M.L.Rev. 749–774; Mortelmans, "Article 30 of the EEC Treaty and Legislation Relating to Market Circumstances: Time to Consider a New Definition?" (1991) C.M.L.Rev. 115–136; Van der Woude, "The Limits of Free Circulation: The Torfaen Borough Council Case" (1990) Leiden J.I.L. 57–63. Others argued for retaining its broad scope: Arnull, "What shall we do on Sunday?" (1991) E.L.Rev. 112–124; Gormley, "Recent Case Law on the Free Movement of Goods: Some Hot Potatoes" (1990) C.M.L.Rev. 825–857; See also the appraisal by Wils, "The Search for the Rule in Article 30 EEC: Much Ado About Nothing?" (1993) E.L.Rev. 475–492 and the survey of the debate by Straetmans, *Consument en markt* (Deurne, Kluwer, 1998) 323–326.

[161] Joined Cases C-267/91 and C-268/91 *Keck and Mithouard* [1993] E.C.R. I-6097, para. 14.

[162] *Ibid.*, para. 16 (in that case the Court considered that Art. 34 did not apply to a French provision imposing a blanket ban on resale at a loss; *ibid.*, para. 18). For some commentaries on the judgment, see the contributions by Rosas, Nicolaidis, Bernard and Regan, in Maduro and Azoulai (eds), *The Past and Future of EU Law* (Oxford, Hart Publishing, 2010) 433–473; Kovar, "Dassonville, Keck et les autres: de la mesure avant toute chose", (2006) 42 R.T.D.E. 213–247;

Accordingly, a measure governing selling arrangements which may affect trade between Member States, yet does not discriminate either "in law" or "in fact" against traders from other Member States, is no longer regarded as a measure having equivalent effect. In addition to the ban on selling at a loss or for a low margin,[163] the Court of Justice has accepted that "selling arrangements" cover, for example, rules relating to sales outlets,[164] making sales on rounds,[165] shop-opening hours,[166] advertising[167] and promotions.[168] Rules on packaging and labelling, for example, do not constitute selling arrangements.[169]

González Vaqué, "La jurisprudencia relativa al artículo 28 CE (antiguo artículo 30 TCE) sobre la libre circulación de mercancías después de *Keck y Mithouard*" (2000) G.J. 24–38; Picod, "La nouvelle approche de la Cour de justice en matière d'entraves aux échanges" (1998) R.T.D.E. 169–189; Becker, "Von 'Dassonville' über 'Cassis' zu 'Keck'—Der Begriff der Maßnahmen gleicher Wirkung in Art. 30 EGV" (1994) EuR. 162–174; Chalmers, "Repackaging the Internal Market: The Ramifications of the *Keck* Judgment" (1994) E.L.Rev. 385–403; Mattera, "De l'arrêt 'Dassonville' à l'arrêt 'Keck': l'obscure clarté d'une jurisprudence riche en principes novateurs et en contradictions" (1994) 1 R.M.U.E. 117–160; Poiares Maduro, "*Keck*: The End? The Beginning of the End? Or Just the End of the Beginning?" (1994) Ir.J.E.L. 30–43;.

[163] See, in addition to *Keck and Mithouard* (see preceding ns), ECJ, Case C-63/94 *Belgapom* [1995] E.C.R. I-2467, paras 8–15.

[164] ECJ, Case C-391/92 *Commission v Greece* [1995] E.C.R. I-1621, paras 9–21; ECJ, Case C-387/93 *Banchero* [1995] E.C.R. I-4663, paras 32–44; ECJ, Case C-189/95 *Franzén* [1997] E.C.R. I-5909, paras 69–72 (system of import licences); ECJ, Case C-322/01 *Deutscher Apothekerverband* [2003] E.C.R. I-14887, paras 68–76 (concerning a ban on mail order sales).

[165] ECJ, Case C-254/98 *TK-Heimdienst Sass* [2000] E.C.R. I-151, paras 24–37.

[166] ECJ, Joined Cases C-401/92 and C-402/92 *Tankstation 't Heukske and Boermans* [1994] E.C.R. I-2199, paras 10–12; ECJ, Joined Cases C-69/93 and C-258/93 *Punto Casa and PPV* [1994] E.C.R. I-2355, paras 12–14; ECJ, Joined Cases C-418-C-421/93, C-460-C-462/93, C-464/93, C-9-C-11/94, C-14–15/94, C-23–24/94 and C-332/94 *Semeraro Casa Uno and Others* [1996] E.C.R. I-2975, paras 9–28.

[167] ECJ, Case C-292/92 *Hünermund and Others* [1993] E.C.R. I-6787, paras 17–24; ECJ, Case C-320/93 *Ortscheit* [1994] E.C.R. I-5257, para. 9; ECJ, Case C-412/93 *Société d'Importation Leclerc-Siplec* [1995] E.C.R. I-179, paras 18–24; ECJ, Joined Cases C-34–36/95 *De Agostini and TV Shop* [1997] E.C.R. I-3843, paras 40–47; ECJ, Case C-405/98 *Gourmet International Products* [2001] E.C.R. I-1795, paras 18–25; ECJ, Case C-71/02 *Karner* [2004] E.C.R. I-3025. paras 38–39. Legislation imposing requirements with regard to the products themselves is not covered, see ECJ, Case C-315/92 *Verband Sozialer Wettbewerb* [1994] E.C.R. I-317, paras 17–24; ECJ, Case C-470/93 *Mars* [1995] E.C.R. I-1923, paras 11–14; see the case note by Ballon (1995) Col.J.E.L. 523–530; ECJ, Joined Cases C-158/04 and C-159/04 *Alfa Vita Vassilopoulos* [2006] E.C.R. I-8135, paras 17–18. See further ECJ, Case C-143/06 *Ludwigs—Apotheke* [2007] E.C.R. I-9623 (where a prohibition on advertising medicinal products was not assessed as a selling arrangement, presumably because it involved direct discrimination; see González Vaqué, "La sentencia 'Ludwigs-Apotheke' relativa a la publicidad de los medicamentos: ¿Dónde estás 'Keck y Mithouard'?" (2008) 25 Revista española de Derecho Europeo 67).

[168] This does not apply to rules relating to sales promotions which are liable to alter the content of the product: ECJ, Case C-368/95 *Familiapress* [1997] E.C.R. I-3689, paras 11–12, with a case note by Ballon (1998) Col.J.E.L. 172–178;

[169] E.g., ECJ, Case C-12/00 *Commission v Spain* [2003] E.C.R. I-459, para. 76.

By contrast, rules on selling arrangements which are liable to affect products from other Member States more than domestic products will not fall within the exception established by *Keck and Mithouard* and are to be considered as measures having equivalent effect within the meaning of Art. 34 TFEU.[170] The Court of Justice has held that a discriminatory effect ensues, for example, from a blanket prohibition on the advertising of alcoholic beverages, because such a ban is liable to impede access to the market by products from other Member States more than it impedes access by domestic products, with which consumers are instantly more familiar.[171] If it can be shown that a measure governing selling arrangements has discriminatory effects, it may still be justified in accordance with the *Cassis de Dijon* criteria in so far as it is applicable without distinction to domestic and imported products[172]; a formally discriminatory measure may be retained only under one of the exceptions provided for in Art. 36 TFEU.[173]

B. FREE MOVEMENT OF WORKERS AND SELF-EMPLOYED PERSONS

1. General scope

9–046   **Treaty rules.** The Treaty provisions on free movement of workers and self-employed persons—together referred to as the "free movement of persons"—seek to attain an optimum allocation of supply and demand in the Union market through complete movement of economic operators.[174] They are therefore

---

[170] E.g., ECJ, Case C-141/07 *Commission v Germany* [2008] E.C.R. I-6935, para. 34- 44; ECJ, Joined Cases C-158/04 and C-159/04 *Alfa Vita Vassilopoulos* [2006] E.C.R. I-8135, para. 20; ECJ, Case C-110/05 *Commission v Italy* [2009] E.C.R. I-519, paras 35–37; ECJ, Case C-142/05 *Mickelsson and Roos* (n. 101, *supra*), para. 24.

[171] ECJ, Case C-405/98 *Gourmet International Products* [2001] E.C.R. I-1795, paras 19–21. For the importance of "market access" as a criterion, see the commentary by Straetmans (2002) C.M.L.Rev. 1407–1421. For the notion of "market access", see Snell, "The Notion of Market Access: A Concept or a Slogan?" (2010) C.M.L.Rev 437–472.

[172] ECJ, Joined Cases C-34–36/95 *De Agostini and TV Shop* [1997] E.C.R. I-3843, paras 44–45; ECJ, Case C-441/04 *A-Punkt Schmuckhandels* [2006] E.C.R. I-2093, paras 25–29.

[173] See, for example, ECJ, Case C-320/93 *Ortscheidt* [1994] E.C.R. I-5243, paras 9–22; ECJ, Case C-189/95 *Franzén* [1997] E.C.R. I-5909, paras 69–7; ECJ, Case C-254/98 *TK-Heimdienst Sass* [2000] E.C.R. I-151, para. 36; ECJ, Case C-322/01 *Deutscher Apothekerverband* [2003] E.C.R. I-14887, paras 68–76.

[174] For general discussions, see Minderhoud en Trimikliniotis (eds), *Rethinking the free movement of workers; the European challenges ahead* (Nijmegen, Wolf Legal Publishers, 2009), 224 pp.; Barnard, *The substantive law of the EU: the four freedoms* (Oxford, Oxford University Press, 2007), at part III.; Weiss and Wooldridge, *Free movement of persons within the European Community* (The Hague, Kluwer Law International, 2007), 301 pp.; Carlier and Guild, *L'avenir de la libre circulation des personnes dans l'UE* (Brussels, Bruylant, 2006), 322 pp.; Rogers and Scannell, *Free movement of persons in the enlarged European Union* (London, Sweet & Maxwell, 2005), 685 pp.; Carrera, "What does free movement mean in theory and practice in an enlarged EU?" (2005) 11 E.L.J. 699–721.

intended to "facilitate the pursuit by [Union] citizens of occupational activities of all kinds throughout the [Union]".[175] The provisions preclude Member States from discriminating against or imposing restrictions on both workers (Art. 45 TFEU [*ex Art. 39 EC*]) and self-employed persons (Art. 49 TFEU [*ex Art. 43 EC*]) who are nationals of another Member State. The Treaties provide for exceptions on grounds of public policy, public security or public health (Art. 45(3) and 52 TFEU [*ex Art. 39(3) and Art. 46 EC*]) where the Union may adopt implementing regulations (Art. 45(3)(d)) or coordinating directives (Art. 52(2)), and also as regards employment in the public service (Art. 45(4) and 52 TFEU [*ex Art. 39(4) and Art. 45 EC*]). The provisions of the Treaties laying down prohibitions have direct effect,[176] not only vis-à-vis Member States in respect of action of public authorities, but also vis-à-vis associations or organisations not governed by public law in respect of acts resulting from the exercise of their legal autonomy creating obstacles to free movement of persons.[177] Accordingly, the prohibition of discrimination on grounds of nationality applies in cases where a group or organisation exercises a certain power over individuals and is in a position to impose on them conditions which adversely affect the exercise of the fundamental freedoms guaranteed under the Treaties.[178] Similarly, Art. 49 TFEU can be invoked against a trade union or a group of trade unions initiating collective action against a private undertaking in order to induce that undertaking to enter into a collective agreement, the terms of which are liable to deter it from exercising freedom of establishment.[179] The Court of Justice has held that the prohibition of discrimination enshrined in Art. 45 TFEU applies to an individual employer.[180] However, it

---

[175] ECJ, Case 143/87 *Stanton* [1988] E.C.R. 3877, para. 13, and ECJ, Joined Cases 154/87 and 155/87 *RSVZ* [1988] E.C.R. 3897, para. 13.

[176] See for Art. 45(1) to (3) TFEU, ECJ, Case 41/74 *Van Duyn* [1974] E.C.R. 1337, paras 5–7; see for Art. 49 TFEU, ECJ, Case 2/74 *Reyners* [1974] E.C.R. 631, para. 30.

[177] ECJ, Case 36/74 *Walrave* [1974] E.C.R. 1405, paras 15–23 (para. 21 states in general terms that "Article 48 [*now Article 45 TFEU*], relating to the abolition of any discrimination based on nationality as regards gainful employment, extends likewise to agreements and rules which do not emanate from public authorities"); ECJ, Case C-415/93 *Bosman* [1995] E.C.R. I-4921, paras 82–87; ECJ, Case C-94/07 *Raccanelli* [2008] E.C.R. I-5939, paras 40–46; ECJ (judgment of March 16, 2010), Case C-325/08 *Olympique Lyonnais*, not yet reported, paras 30–32.

[178] ECJ, Case C-411/98 *Ferlini* [2000] E.C.R. I-8081, para. 50 (concerning Art. 12 EC [*now Art. 18 TFEU*]).

[179] ECJ, Case C-438/05 *International Transport Workers' Federation and Finnish Seamen's Union* [2007] E.C.R. I-10779, paras 32–37 and 57–66; ECJ (judgment of July 15, 2010), Case C-271/08 *Commission v Germany*, not yet reported, paras 42–44. See Joerges, "Informal politics, formalised law and the social deficit of European Integration: reflections after the judgments of the ECJ in Viking and Laval" (2009) 15 E.L.J., 1–19; Prechal, "Viking/Laval en de grondslagen van het internemarktrecht" (2008) S.E.W. 425–440; Rodière, "Les arrets Viking et Laval, le droit de grève et le droit de négociation collective" (2008) 44 R.T.D.E. 47–66.

[180] ECJ, Case C-281/98 *Angonese* [2000] E.C.R. I-4139, paras 30–36; ECJ, Case C-94/07 *Raccanelli* [2008] E.C.R. I-5939, paras 45–46.

is not certain whether the prohibition of non-discriminatory restrictions can be invoked against individual private persons.[181]

9–047 **Legislation.** The Treaties give the Union the task of issuing directives or making regulations to facilitate free movement of workers (Art. 46 TFEU [*ex Art. 40 EC*]) and directives securing freedom of establishment (Art. 50(2) TFEU [*ex* Art. 44(2) EC]). As far as migrant workers and self-employed persons are concerned, Art. 48 TFEU [*ex Art. 42 EC*] contemplates ancillary measures in the social security field. As regards taking up and pursuing activities as self-employed persons, Art. 53 TFEU [*ex Art. 47 EC*] provides for directives for the mutual recognition of diplomas, certificates and other evidence of formal qualifications. The Treaty of Lisbon did not alter the rights that workers and self-employed persons may derive from the Treaties. It did however adapt, to a certain extent, the decision-making process by which the institutions are to facilitate free movement pursuant to the relevant Treaty provisions.

9–048 **Workers and self-employed persons.** As a result, workers and self-employed persons are subject to different Treaty rules. In view of the common objective of the free movement of persons and of the fact that Union legislation frequently confers identical rights on workers and the self-employed, both sets of rules will be discussed together.[182] Ultimately, these provisions give shape to the "fundamental right" of citizens to freedom to seek employment, to work, to exercise the right of establishment and to provide services in any Member State.[183]

2. Beneficiaries

9–049 **Survey.** The rules on free movement of workers and the right of establishment, respectively, apply to workers and self-employed persons who are nationals of a Member State and who find themselves in a situation warranting a connection with Union law.

(a) *Nationals of a Member State*

9–050 **Nationality.** Free movement of workers and the right of establishment apply in principle only to nationals of a Member State.[184] Each Member State determines

---

[181] For a critical view in a case note on the judgment in *Angonese*, see Körber (2000) EuR, 932, at 940–952; Stuyck (2001) S.E.W. 112–118; for a less critical view, see Van der Steen (2001) N.T.E.R. 4–9; Lengauer (2001) Z.f.RV. 57–65.

[182] See ECJ, Case C-107/94 *Asscher* [1996] E.C.R. I-3089, para. 29. See specifically as regards free movement of workers, Verschueren, *Internationale arbeidsmigratie* (Bruges, Die Keure, 1991), at 279–333; Martin, "Réflexions sur le champ d'application matériel de l'article 48 du Traité CE" (1993) C.D.E. 555–596.

[183] See Art. 15(2) of the Charter of Fundamental Rights of the European Union.

[184] See Art. 45(2) and Art. 49 TFEU: ECJ, Case 238/83 *Meade* [1984] E.C.R. 2631, para. 7.

the conditions on which a natural person acquires and loses nationality (for companies, see para. 9–056). A Member State must recognise the conferral of nationality by another Member State without imposing additional conditions (see para. 8–005). As a result, the scope of application of free movement of persons varies with every change in the nationality law of Member States.

Third-country nationals covered. Nevertheless, persons other than workers or self-employed persons having the nationality of a Member State enjoy the advantages of free movement.[185] Union legislation has extended enjoyment of certain rights to members of the families of employed persons,[186] self-employed persons[187] and other persons on whom Union law confers a right of residence,[188] regardless of their nationality. The rights of family members are generally limited to the Member State in respect of which the persons they accompany have exercised their right to free movement.[189] Agreements concluded with third countries have also conferred rights on nationals of third countries and members of their families (see para. 10–015).

    9–051

(b) *Qualifying workers*

Union definition. Article 45(2) TFEU prohibits "any discrimination based on nationality between workers of the Member States". Consequently, alongside each Member State's legislation on nationality, the concept of "worker" determines who qualifies for free movement of workers. The term "worker" employed in Arts 45 to 48 TFEU is a concept of Union law with an independent Union meaning. Indeed, if the definition of that term could be determined unilaterally by national law, it would be possible for each Member State to eliminate at will the protection afforded by the Treaties to certain categories of persons.[190] In view of the fact that the Treaties do not define the term "worker", the Court of Justice has clarified its scope by taking the view that it defines the field of application of one

    9–052

---

[185] For a survey, see Carlier, "Le droit d'entrée et de séjour des ressortissants des Etats membres" (1994) A.D. 143, at 147–160. Free movement also applies to workers (regardless of their nationality) of a provider of services established in a Member State, who must be able to move within the Union together with the provider of services: ECJ, Case C-113/89 *Rush Portuguesa* [1990] E.C.R. I-1417, para. 12; ECJ, Case C-43/93 *Van der Elst* [1994] E.C.R. I-3803, para. 21; ECJ, Case C-244/04 *Commission v Germany* [2006] E.C.R. I-885, paras 30–64.

[186] ECJ, Case 40/76 *Kermaschek v Bundesanstalt für Arbeit* [1976] E.C.R. 1669, para. 9. See Directive 68/360 and Regulations Nos 1612/68 and 1251/70; paras 9–059 and 9–062, *infra*. For a discussion, see Ziekow, "Der gemeinschaftsrechtliche Status der Familienangehörigen von Wanderarbeitnehmer" (1991) D.ö.V. 363–370.

[187] See Directives 73/148 and 75/34, since replaced by Directive 2004/38 (n. 24, *supra*).

[188] See para. 12–002.

[189] See, e.g., ECJ, Case C-10/05 *Mattern* [2006] E.C.R. I-3145, para. 28 (no right for a third country national married to an EU national to take up an activity as an employed person in a Member State other than the one in which his spouse pursues an economic activity).

[190] ECJ, Case 75/63 *Hoekstra (née Unger)* [1964] E.C.R. 177, at 184.

of the fundamental freedoms guaranteed by the Treaties and, as such, may not be interpreted restrictively.[191]

9–053   **Objective criteria.** The Court of Justice bases itself on objective criteria which distinguish the employment relationship by reference to the rights and duties of the persons concerned. The essential feature of an employment relationship is that

> "for a certain period of time a person performs services for and under the direction of another person in return for which he receives remuneration".[192]

This encompasses three separate criteria.

First of all, there needs to be the pursuit of real and genuine activity for remuneration, to the exclusion of activities on such a small scale as to be regarded as purely marginal and ancillary. The type of work is irrelevant, provided that an economic—that is, a remunerated—activity is involved.[193] Hence, the activities of professional or semi-professional sportsmen are covered by the provisions on the free movement of workers, with the exception of activities which are of sporting interest only, and therefore not of an economic nature.[194] By the same token, persons undergoing a traineeship will be considered workers if the training period is completed under the conditions of genuine and effective activity as an employed person.[195] The Court has further held that an official of the European Union (or of another international organisation) who is a national of a Member State other than that in which he or she is employed must be regarded as a migrant worker.[196] The duration of the work is not relevant: free movement of workers also covers persons carrying out genuine part-time work.[197]

Second, the person in question must perform services for and under the direction of another person. As in the case of the first criterion, this must be determined in each case on the basis of all the factors and circumstances characteris-

---

[191] ECJ, Case 53/81 *Levin* [1982] E.C.R. 1035, para. 13.

[192] ECJ, Case 66/85 *Lawrie-Blum* [1986] E.C.R. 2121, para. 17.

[193] ECJ, Case 196/87 *Steymann* [1988] E.C.R. 6159, paras 12–14 ((commercial) activities carried out by members of a community based on religion or another form of philosophy); ECJ, Case C-456/02 *Trojani* [2004] E.C.R. I-7573, paras 17–24 (performing jobs for the Salvation Army in return for board and lodging and some pocket money).

[194] ECJ, Case 36/74 *Walrave* [1974] E.C.R. 1405, paras 4–7; professional footballers: ECJ, Case 13/76 *Donà* [1976] E.C.R. 1333, para. 12, and ECJ, Case C-415/93 *Bosman* [1995] E.C.R. I-4921, paras 73–76 (paras 9–061 and 9–065, *infra*).

[195] ECJ, Case 66/85 *Lawrie-Blum* [1986] E.C.R. 2121, para. 19; ECJ, Case C-3/90 *Bernini* [1992] E.C.R. I-1071, para. 15; ECJ, Case C-109/04 *Kranemann* [2005] E.C.R. I-2421, paras 13–15.

[196] ECJ, Case C-411/98 *Ferlini* [2000] E.C.R. I-8081, para. 42.

[197] ECJ, Case 53/81 *Levin* [1982] E.C.R. 1035, para. 17; ECJ, Joined Cases C-22/08 and C-23/08 *Vatsouras and Koupatantze* [2008] E.C.R. I-4585, para. 29; ECJ (judgment of February 4, 2010), Case C-14/09 *Genc*, not yet reported, paras 26–28.

ing the arrangements between the parties, such as the sharing of the commercial risks of the business and the freedom for a person to choose his or her own working hours and to engage his or her own assistants.[198]

Third, the services must be performed in return for remuneration. Neither the origin of the funds from which the remuneration is paid, nor the limited amount of the remuneration can have any consequence in regard to whether or not the person is a worker for the purposes of Union law.[199] Hence, it is not necessary that the remuneration received in exchange for the work performed should cover the costs of subsistence of the person concerned (and his dependants). Thus, free movement of workers applies to employment relationships where the remuneration provided for genuine work is under the minimum subsistence level laid down in the Member State of employment,[200] even if the person concerned claims a supplementary benefit in the Member State concerned in order to supplement his or her remuneration.[201]

Job-seeker. Free movement of workers (especially in connection with unemployment insurance) applies only to persons who have already participated in the employment market by exercising an effective and genuine occupational activity which has conferred on them the status of workers within the EU meaning of that term.[202] The protection of free movement also extends to job-seekers in another Member State, but only as long as they are potential participants in the labour market. The principle of free movement of workers requires only that the legislation of a Member State give the persons concerned a reasonable time in which to apprise themselves, in the territory of the Member State concerned, of offers of employment corresponding to their occupational qualifications and to take, where appropriate, the necessary steps in order to be engaged. Job-seekers may, however, be required to leave the territory of that State if they have not found employment there after six months, unless the persons concerned provide evidence that

9–054

---

[198] ECJ, Case C-3/87 *Agegate* [1989] E.C.R. 4459, para. 36. The fact that a person is related by marriage to the director and sole owner of the undertaking does not mean that that person cannot be regarded as being a worker within the meaning of Art.45 TFEU if he or she pursues an effective and genuine activity in a relationship of subordination: ECJ, Case C-337/97 *Meeusen* [1999] E.C.R. I-3289, paras 14–16.

[199] ECJ, Case 53/81 *Levin* [1982] E.C.R. 1035, para.16; ECJ, Case 344/87 *Bettray* [1989] E.C.R. 1621, paras 15 and 16; and ECJ, Case C-188/00 *Kurz* [2002] E.C.R. I-10691, para. 32; ECJ, Joined Cases C-22/08 and C-23/08 *Vatsouras and Koupatantze* (n. 197, *supra*), paras. 27–28.

[200] ECJ, Case 53/81 *Levin* [1982] E.C.R. 1035, para. 15.

[201] ECJ, Case 139/85 *Kempf* [1986] E.C.R. 1741, para. 14.

[202] ECJ, Case C-278/94 *Commission v Belgium* [1996] E.C.R. I-4307, para. 40; ECJ, Case C-224/98 *D'Hoop* [2002] E.C.R. I-6191, para. 18. For the differing position of workers and job-seekers, see ECJ, Case C-138/02 *Collins* [2004] E.C.R. I-2703, paras 30–31. However, after exercising his or her rights of free movement, a job-seeking citizen of the Union may not suffer discrimination on grounds of nationality: *D'Hoop*, paras 27–40 (see para. 7–052).

they are continuing to seek employment and that they have genuine chances of being engaged.[203]

9–055 **Other beneficiaries.** Reliance may be made on the provisions relating to free movement of workers by others, in particular employers. In order to be truly effective, the right of workers to be engaged and employed without discrimination necessarily entails as a corollary the employer's entitlement to engage them in accordance with the rules governing freedom of movement for workers.[204] The Court of Justice has also held that a private-sector recruitment agency which represents a worker and seeks employment on his or her behalf may, in certain circumstances, rely on the rights directly granted to Union workers by Art. 45 TFEU.[205]

(c) *Self-employed persons and companies qualifying*

9–056 **Establishment.** The right of establishment relates to activities in another Member State not carried out by way of gainful employment. This means economic activities carried on by a person outside any relationship of subordination with regard to the conditions of work or remuneration and under his or her own personal responsibility.[206] "Establishment" of a natural or legal person within the meaning of the Treaties involves the actual pursuit of an economic activity through a fixed establishment in another Member State for an indefinite period.[207] If an occupational activity is not carried out in a lasting way, it may constitute the supply of a service (see para. 9–090). Both natural and legal persons enjoy the right of establishment. The first para. of Art. 49 TFEU refers to "freedom of establishment of nationals of a Member State in the territory of another Member State". For the purposes of the application of freedom of establishment, Art. 54 TFEU [*ex Art. 48 EC*] equates companies or firms

> "formed in accordance with the law of a Member State and having their registered office, central administration or principal place of business within the Union"

with natural persons who are nationals of Member States. Article 54 does not apply to "non-profit-making" companies or firms (see the second para. of that article).

---

[203] ECJ, Case C-292/89 *Antonissen* [1991] E.C.R. I-745, paras 16 and 22. Accordingly, a Member State cannot automatically oblige job-seekers to leave their territory after their time has expired: ECJ, Case C-344/95 *Commission v Belgium* [1997] E.C.R. I-1035, paras 12–18. For the reasonable time enjoyed by a Turkish national in order to seek work under the relevant Association Agreement, see ECJ, Case C-171/95 *Tetik* [1997] E.C.R. I-329, paras 27–48.

[204] ECJ, Case C-350/96 *Clean Car Autoservice* [1998] E.C.R. I-2521, paras 19–20.

[205] ECJ, Case C-208/05 *ITC* [2007] E.C.R. I-181, paras 22–28.

[206] ECJ, Case C-268/99 *Jany and Others* [2001] E.C.R. I-8615, paras 34–50 (definition applied to prostitution).

[207] ECJ, Case C-221/89 *Factortame II* [1991] E.C.R. I-3905, para. 20. See also para. 9–066 *et seq.*

(d) *Connection with Union law*

Transfrontier situation. A person may rely on the Treaty provisions on free movement of workers or the right of establishment only where his or her situation exhibits a genuine transfrontier factor. The Treaty provisions cannot be applied to situations wholly internal to a Member State.[208] For instance, a transfrontier situation exists where a person works, has worked or intends to work in the territory of a Member State other than the one in which he or she resides and/or of which he or she is a national.[209] The fact that an employment relationship is potentially of a transfrontier nature is insufficient to cause Union law to apply. When Moser, a German national, argued that the refusal of the *Land* of Baden-Württemberg to let him undertake teacher training on the ground that he was a member of the Communist Party made it impossible for him to apply for teaching posts in another Member State, the Court of Justice held that a purely hypothetical prospect of employment in another Member State did not establish a sufficient connection with Union law to justify the application of Art. 45 TFEU.[210]

9–057

A Member State is entitled to impose stricter requirements upon its own nationals than upon nationals of other Member States. Nevertheless, the Court of Justice explained in *Knoors* (see para. 7–065) that a Member State may not operate "reverse" discrimination against nationals who, by taking advantage of the facilities existing in the matter of freedom of movement and establishment, are in a situation which may be assimilated to that of any other person enjoying the rights and liberties guaranteed by the Treaties.[211] Any Union national who, irrespective of his or her place of residence or nationality, has worked in another Member State falls within the scope of free movement of workers or freedom of establishment.[212] In addition, the Court of Justice considered that an Italian who had studied in Austria could rely on the provisions relating to the free movement

---

[208] ECJ, Case 175/78 *Saunders* [1979] E.C.R. 1129, para. 11; ECJ, Case C-152/94 *Van Buynder* [1995] E.C.R. I-3981, paras 10–12; ECJ, Case C-134/94 *Esso Española* [1995] E.C.R. I-4223, paras 13–16; ECJ, Joined Cases C-225-C-227/95 *Kapasakalis and Others* [1998] E.C.R. I-4239, para. 22; ECJ, Case C-18/95 *Terhoeve* [1999] E.C.R. I-345, paras. 26; ECJ, Joined Cases C-95/99 to C-98/99 and C-180/99 *Khalil and Others* [2001] E.C.R. I-7413, para. 69; ECJ, Case C-208/05 *ITC* [2007] E.C.R. I-181, para. 29; ECJ, Case C-212/06 *Government of the French Community and Walloon Government v Flemish Government* [2008] E.C.R. I-1683, para. 33. See, with regard to the Union provisions governing the right of residence of nationals of other Member States and their spouses: ECJ, Joined Cases C-297/88 and C-197/89 *Dzodzi* [1990] E.C.R. I-3763, para. 28.

[209] ECJ, Case C-336/96 *Gilly* [1998] E.C.R. I-2793, para. 21; ECJ, Case C-227/03 *van Pommeren-Bourgondiën* [2005] E.C.R. I-6101, paras 40–44; ECJ, Case C-470/04 *N.* [2006] E.C.R. I-7409, para. 28.

[210] ECJ, Case 180/83 *Moser* [1984] E.C.R. 2539, para. 18.

[211] ECJ, Case 115/78 *Knoors* [1979] E.C.R. 399, paras 20 and 24.

[212] ECJ, Case C-419/92 *Scholz* [1994] E.C.R. I-505, para. 9. *Cf.* ECJ, Case C-19/92 *Kraus* [1993] E.C.R. I-1663, paras 16–22 (para. 9–065, *infra*); ECJ, Case C-443/93 *Vougioukas* [1995] E.C.R. I-4033, para. 38; ECJ, Case C-107/94 *Asscher* [1996] E.C.R. I-3089, paras 31–34; ECJ, Case C-18/95 *Terhoeve* [1999] E.C.R. I-345, paras 27–28. See also the discussion of reverse discrimination, para. 7–065, *supra*.

of workers as against an Italian employer who, as proof of knowledge of German, accepted only a certificate issued locally.[213] Similarly, the provisions on free movement of workers or freedom of establishment can be relied on by persons who move their residence to a Member State other than the one in which they pursue their occupational activity and who are treated less favourably than persons having their residence in the latter Member State.[214]

The applicability of the free movement of workers or the right of establishment is also important for the members of the family of such a worker or self-employed person. When a national who has availed himself or herself of the right of free movement or freedom of establishment returns to his or her country of origin, his or her family members must enjoy at least the same rights of entry and residence there as would be granted to him or her under Union law if the national in question chose to enter and reside in another Member State, even if the family members concerned are not nationals of a Member State.[215] The Court has also made it clear that a national who has made use of his or her right to free movement by establishing himself or herself in another Member State, has the right to be joined in that Member State by his or her family members, irrespective of the nationality of the latter. In this connection it is not required that these family members should have previously been legally resident in the territory of another Member State.[216] However, if the Union national in question himself or herself has never exercised the right to free movement within the Union, members of his or her family cannot necessarily rely on Union law.[217]

9–058   **Territorial aspects.** An employment relationship must exhibit not only a transfrontier element but also a sufficiently close link with the territory of the Union.[218] A national of a Member State who works for an undertaking of another

---

[213] ECJ, Case C-281/98 *Angonese* [2000] E.C.R. I-4139. See Stuyck (2001) S.E.W. 112–118, who criticises the judgment for failing to find that this was a purely internal situation.

[214] ECJ, Case C-152/03 *Ritter-Coulais* [2006] E.C.R. I-1711, paras 31–32 (workers); ECJ, Case C-212/05 *Hartmann* [2007] E.C.R. I-6303, paras 15–20 (workers); ECJ, Case C-470/04 *N.* [2006] E.C.R. I-7409, para. 28 (self-employed persons).

[215] ECJ, Case C-370/90 *Surinder Singh* [1992] E.C.R. I-4265, paras 21 and 23.

[216] ECJ, Case C-291/05 *Eind* [2007] E.C.R. I-10719, paras 41–44; ECJ, Case C-127/08 *Metock and Others* [2008] E.C.R. I-6241, with a case note by Cambien (2009) Col.J.E.L., 321–341. The latter case explicitly overturns *Akrich*, in which the Court of Justice had considered that in order to benefit from a right of residence under Union law, a national of a non-member country who was the spouse of a Union citizen had to be lawfully resident in a Member State before moving to the Member State in which a right of residence was claimed (ECJ, Case C-109/01 *Akrich* [2003] E.C.R. I-9607, paras 50–54). See also, ECJ, Case C-1/05 *Jia* [2007] E.C.R. I-1, paras 25–33, with a case note by Elsmore (2007) C.M.L.Rev. 787–801.

[217] ECJ, Joined Cases 35/82 and 36/82 *Morson and Jhanjan* [1982] E.C.R. 3723, paras 11–18; ECJ, Joined Cases C-64/96 and C-65/96 *Uecker and Jacquet* [1997] E.C.R. I-3171, paras 16–21; ECJ, Case C-127/08 *Metock and Others* [2008] E.C.R. I-6241, paras 76–79. See Seyr, "Das grenzüberschreitende Element in der Rechtsprechung des EuGH zur Unionsbürgerschaft" (2005) EuR. 667–675.

[218] See, for example, ECJ, Case C-248/96 *Grahame and Hollanders* [1997] E.C.R. I-6407, para. 36 (work in the territory of an overseas territory of a Member State).

Member State continues to enjoy the protection of Union law while working temporarily outside the Union, provided that he or she is working on behalf of the undertaking.[219] Union law is also applicable to a national of a Member State working for an embassy of another Member State in a third country as regards those aspects of his or her employment relationship which are governed by the law of the second Member State.[220]

3. Substance

(a) *Right to enter, leave and reside*

Entry and residence rights. Effective exercise of the right to obtain employment in another Member State is conditional upon the worker or the job-seeker being able readily to enter or leave the host country and reside there. This also applies to persons wishing to engage in self-employed activities in another Member State.

    The rights enshrined in Arts 45(3)(b), (c) and (d) and 49 TFEU have been enlarged upon in Directive 2004/38 of the European Parliament and of the Council,[221] which repeals previous directives on free movement of workers and self-employed persons[222] and replaces them with a uniform set of rules, which also applies to non-economically active citizens of the Union (see paras 8–008 *et seq.*).

    Persons qualifying for free movement (workers, self-employed persons and members of their families) may enter the territory of another Member State simply on production of a valid identity card or passport.[223] In view of the importance which the Union legislature attaches to the protection of family life, a third-country national married to an EU national may not be sent back because he or

9–059

---

[219] ECJ, Case 237/83 *Prodest* [1984] E.C.R. 3153, para. 7. See also ECJ, Case C-60/93 *Aldewereld* [1994] E.C.R. I-2991, paras 14–15 and 20–24.

[220] ECJ, Case C-214/94 *Boukhalfa* [1996] E.C.R. I-2253, paras 15–17. Consequently, the connection is not only with the territory but also with the law of a Member State, see the case note by Lhoest (1998) C.M.L.Rev. 247–267.

[221] See n. 24, *supra*. The Directive was adopted on the basis of Arts 12, 18, 40, 44 and 52 EC [*now Arts 18, 21, 46, 50 and 59 TFEU*].

[222] See in particular, with regard to the free movement of workers: Council Directive 68/360/EEC of October 15, 1968 on the abolition of restrictions on movement and residence for workers of Member States and their families, [1968] O.J. English Spec. Ed. (II) 485 (adopted on the basis of Art. 40 EC [*now Art. 46 TFEU*]). See, with regard to the freedom of establishment, Council Directive 73/148/EEC of May 21, 1973 on the abolition of restrictions on movement and residence within the Community for nationals of Member States with regard to establishment and the provision of services, [1973] O.J. L172/14 (adopted on the basis of Art. 44 and 52 EC [*now Arts 50 and 59 TFEU*]). See also Regulation (EEC) No. 1251/70 of the Commission of June 29, 1970 on the right of workers to remain in the territory of a Member State after having been employed in that State, [1970] O.J. English Spec. Ed. (II) 402; See also Council Directive 75/34/EEC of December 17, 1974 concerning the right of nationals of a Member State to remain in the territory of another Member State after having pursued therein an activity in a self-employed category, [1975] O.J. L14/10 (adopted on the basis of Art. 308 EC [*now Art. 352 TFEU*]).

[223] Directive 2004/38 (n. 24, *supra*), Art. 5(1).

she has no valid identity card, passport or visa, where the person in question is able to prove his or her identity and the conjugal ties.[224] A Member State may not require nationals of another Member State to present a valid identity card or passport in order to prove their nationality if it does not impose a general obligation on its own nationals to provide evidence of identity, and permits them to prove their identity by other means.[225] In the case of residence for periods longer than three months, a Member State may require Union citizens to register with the relevant authorities.[226]

The right of residence of a qualifying worker extends to his or her spouse or registered partner and their descendants who are under the age of 21 years or are dependants, as well as to dependent relations in the ascending line of the worker and his or her spouse or registered partner, irrespective of their nationality (Directive 2004/38, Art. 2; see para. 9–062). Workers and self-employed persons who have been employed in a Member State, and members of their families, are entitled to remain in the territory of that State (Art. 45(3)(d) TFEU and Directive 2004/38, Art. 17).

(b) *Prohibition of discriminatory and non-discriminatory obstacles*

9–060   **Content.** Article 45(2) TFEU [*ex Art. 39 EC*] provides that freedom of movement for workers is to entail

> "the abolition of any discrimination based on nationality between workers of the Member States as regards employment, remuneration and other conditions of work and employment".

In addition, the first para. of Art. 49 TFEU [*ex Art. 43 EC*] states that "restrictions on the freedom of establishment of nationals of a Member State in the territory of another Member State shall be prohibited". The Court of Justice has made it clear that the Treaties preclude, not only any form of discrimination in the exercise of free movement of workers (see paras 9–061—9–062) and the right of establishment (see paras 9–063—9–064), but also measures which are applicable without distinction

---

[224] ECJ, Case C-459/99 *MRAX* [2002] E.C.R. I-6591, paras 53–62. See also ECJ, Case C-68/89 *Commission v Netherlands* [1991] E.C.R. I-2637, para. 12. See also Directive 2004/38 (n. 24, *supra*), Art. 5(4).

[225] ECJ, Case C-215/03 *Oulane* [2005] E.C.R. I-1215, paras 28–35.

[226] Directive 2004/38 (n. 24, *supra*), Art. 8. According to Art. 4 of Directive 68/360, their right of residence in the host State was to be evidenced—but not determined—by production of a "Residence Permit for a National of a Member State of the EEC". See also *MRAX, ibid.*, paras 89–91 (a Member State cannot refuse a national of a non-member State who is married to an EU national a residence permit merely because that third-country national entered the territory unlawfully or because his or her visa expired before an application was made for a residence permit). For the prohibition on more extensive administrative obstacles in granting that right of residence, see ECJ, Case C-344/95 *Commission v Belgium* [1997] E.C.R. I-1033, paras 20–34.

to a Member State's own nationals and nationals from other Member States if they treat persons less favourably where they exercise their right of free movement or of establishment in a Member State other than their own (see para. 9–065).

Prohibited discrimination against workers. The Court of Justice considers that **9–061**
Art. 45(2) TFEU [*ex Art. 39(2) EC*] prohibits all direct or indirect discrimination[227] between nationals of a given Member State and nationals of other Member States.[228]

In some cases, the place of residence is held to be an unjustifiable criterion.[229] Accordingly, the Court of Justice has held that:

> "[e]ven though the criterion [applied by Luxembourg] of permanent residence in the national territory . . . in connection with obtaining any repayment of an overdeduction of tax applies irrespective of the nationality of the taxpayer concerned, there is a risk that it will work in particular against taxpayers who are nationals of other Member States. It is often such persons who will in the course of the year leave the country or take up residence there."[230]

Nevertheless, a Member State may, in principle, tax the income of a taxpayer who is employed in that State but has his residence elsewhere more heavily than the income of a "resident" with the same income. Generally, this will not involve any discrimination since there are objective differences between residents and non-residents justifying a difference in treatment, in particular as far as concerns taking account of the taxpayer's personal and family circumstances when making an assessment to tax.[231] This will result in unjustified discrimination, however, where a non-resident receives the major part of his income in the Member State in which he works and insufficient income in the State of his residence to enable his personal and family circumstances to be taken into account for taxation purposes.[232] Such discrimination may take place both against

---

[227] For these terms, see paras 7–061—7–063, *supra*.

[228] ECJ, Case 152/73 *Sotgiu* [1974] E.C.R. 153, paras 10–13; ECJ, Case 33/88 *Allué and Others* [1989] E.C.R. 1591, paras 11–12; ECJ, Case C-90/96 *Petrie and Others* [1997] E.C.R. I-6527, paras 53–56. Use of the criterion of nationality does not invariably constitute prohibited discrimination, see ECJ, Case C-336/96 *Gilly* [1998] E.C.R. I-2793, paras 30–34 (double taxation of frontier workers).

[229] See, e.g., ECJ, Case C-350/96 *Clean Car Autoservice* [1998] E.C.R. I-2521, paras 26–43.

[230] ECJ, Case C-175/88 *Biehl* [1990] E.C.R. I-1779, para. 14. See also ECJ, Case C-111/91 *Commission v Luxembourg* [1993] E.C.R. I-817, paras 9–10 and para. 23; ECJ, Case C-151/94 *Commission v Luxembourg* [1995] E.C.R. I-3685, paras 12–22.

[231] ECJ, Case C-279/93 *Schumacker* [1995] E.C.R. I-225, paras 30–35; ECJ, Case C-336/96 *Gilly* [1998] E.C.R. I-2793, paras 47–50; ECJ, Case C-391/97 *Gschwind* [1999] E.C.R. I-5451, paras 20–32.

[232] *Schumacker* (cited in the preceding n.), paras 36–47.

beneficiaries of free movement of workers and beneficiaries of freedom of establishment.[233]

Since free movement of workers holds good for all forms of gainful employment, discrimination on grounds of nationality is also prohibited in principle in professional sport. Nevertheless, the Court of Justice has accepted that foreign players may be excluded from certain matches for reasons of a non-economic nature which relate to the particular nature and context of such matches and are thus of sporting interest only, such as matches between national teams from different countries.[234] In *Bosman* the Court made it clear that nationality clauses are contrary to Art. 45 TFEU for matches between football clubs composed of professional players.[235]

9–062 **Equal treatment for migrant workers.** Council Regulation No. 1612/68 of October 15, 1968 defines the fundamental prohibition of discrimination with regard to migrant workers.[236] The regulation guarantees equal treatment within a given Member State of national workers and workers who are nationals of other Member States as regards all conditions of employment and work, in particular as regards remuneration, dismissal and, in the event of unemployment, reinstatement or re-employment (Art. 7(1)); social and tax advantages (Art. 7(2)); access to vocational training schools and retraining centres (Art. 7(3)); membership of

---

[233] ECJ, Case C-80/94 *Wielockx* [1995] E.C.R. I-2493, paras 20–27. See also the (unjustified) indirect discrimination in ECJ, Case C-107/94 *Asscher* [1996] E.C.R. I-3089, paras 37–49. See Lenaerts and Maselis, "Inkomstenbelasting en non-discriminatie in de Europese Unie", in *Liber Amicorum Jean-Pierre Lagae* (Diegem, Ced. Samson, 1998) 477–495; Weber, "In search of a new equilibrium between tax sovereignty and the freedom of movement within the EC" (2007) 35 *Intertax* 585–616; Wattel, "Red Herrings in Direct Tax Cases before the ECJ" (2004) L.I.E.I. 81–95; Farmer, "The Court's case law on taxation: a castle built on shifting sands?" (2003) *EC Tax Review* 75–81; Van Thiel, "Removal of income tax barriers to market integration in the European Union: litigation by the Community citizen instead of harmonisation by the Community legislature?" (2003) *EC Tax Review* 4–19; Vanistendael, "The compatibility of the basic economic freedoms with the sovereign national tax systems of the Member States" (2003) *EC Tax Review* 136–143; Vanistendael, "The Consequences of *Schumacker* and *Wielockx*: Two Steps Forward in the Tax Procession of Echternach" (1996) C.M.L.Rev. 255–269; Keeling and Shipwright, "Some Taxing Problems concerning Non-Discrimination and the EC Treaty" (1995) E.L.Rev. 580–597; for testing tax rules against the right of establishment, see also para. 9–069, *infra*.

[234] ECJ, Case 13/76 *Donà* [1976] E.C.R. 1333, paras 14–15.

[235] ECJ, Case C-415/93 *Bosman* [1995] E.C.R. I-4921, paras 127–137 (for the ruling on transfer fees, see para. 9–065, *infra*). Nationals of non-member countries can also invoke the prohibition of discrimination on the basis of association agreements concluded by the Union with third countries, see ECJ, Case C-438/00 *Kolpak* [2003] E.C.R. I-4135, paras 24–58 (concerning a Slovakian handball player), and Pautot, "La liberté de circulation des sportifs professionnels en Europe" (2001) R.M.C.U.E. 102–105. For the controversial case of *Bosman*, see Defalque (1996) J.T. 539–546; Hilf and Pache (1996) N.J.W. 1169–1177; Weatherill (1996) C.M.L.Rev. 991–1033; Van Nuffel (1996) Col.J.E.L. 345–359, and a number of articles in (1996) 1 R.M.C.U.E. For sport, see also para. 11–047, *infra*.

[236] Regulation (EEC) No. 1612/68 of the Council of October 15, 1968 on freedom of movement for workers within the Community, [1968] O.J. English Spec. Ed. (II) 475.

trade unions and the exercise of trade-union rights, including the right to vote (Art. 8(1)), and housing (Art. 9). The regulation confers on the worker's spouse and dependent children the right to take up any activity as an employed person.[237] In addition, migrant workers' children must be admitted to general educational, apprenticeship and vocational training courses under the same conditions as nationals of the host Member State (Art. 12).[238]

The Court of Justice has associated application of the requirement for equal treatment primarily with the expression "social and tax advantages" (Art. 7(2) of the regulation), defining it very broadly as all advantages:

> "which, whether or not linked to a contract of employment, are generally granted to national workers primarily because of their objective status of workers or by virtue of the mere fact of their residence on the national territory and the extension of which to workers who are nationals of other Member States therefore seems suitable to facilitate their mobility within the [Union]".[239]

Accordingly, the Court of Justice counted as a social advantage the migrant worker's right to use his or her own language—in proceedings not linked to his employment relationship—before the courts of the Member State in which he resided, on the ground that this played "an important role in the integration of a migrant worker and his family into the host country".[240] In the same spirit, Art. 7(2) of the Regulation puts a Member State which allows its nationals to obtain permission for foreign unmarried companions to reside with them under a duty to afford the same opportunity to nationals of another Member State.[241] Nevertheless, the Court of Justice has held that Member States are entitled to rely

---

[237] Regulation No. 1612/68, Art.11, now replaced by Art. 23 of Directive 2004/38 (see para. 9–059, *supra*).

[238] See ECJ (judgments of February 23, 2010), Case C-310/08 *Ibrahim*, not yet reported, and Case C-480/08 *Teixeira*, not yet reported (a migrant worker's children and the parent who is their primary carer can claim a right of residence in the host Member State on the sole basis of Art. 12 without such a right being conditional on their having sufficient resources and comprehensive sickness insurance cover in that Member State).

[239] ECJ, Case 207/78 *Even* [1979] E.C.R. 2019, para. 22. For the concept of "social advantages", see Ellis, "Social Advantages: A New Lease of Life?" (2003) C.M.L.Rev. 639, at 642–652.

[240] ECJ, Case 137/84 *Mutsch* [1985] E.C.R. 2681, paras 16–17. For the extension of this right to all persons who exercise their right of free movement, see ECJ, Case C-274/96 *Bickel and Franz* [1998] E.C.R. I-7637, paras 13–31 (see para. 7–054, *infra*).

[241] ECJ, Case 59/85 *Reed* [1986] E.C.R. 1283, paras 28–29. See also the fact that grant of funding for studying has been recognised as a social advantage, n. 275 to para. 11–048, *infra*. Other examples of "social advantages" are: a funeral payment (ECJ, Case C-237/94 *O'Flynn* [1996] E.C.R. I-2617, paras 17–30); unemployment benefits paid to young people who have just completed their studies ("tideover allowances") and are the dependants of workers resident in Belgium (ECJ, Case C-278/94 *Commission v Belgium* [1996] E.C.R. I-4307, paras 25–31); a benefit conditional on residence (ECJ, Case C-57/96 *Meints* [1997] E.C.R. I-6689, paras 44–48); the grant of a savings-pension bonus (ECJ, Case C-269/07 *Commission v Germany* [2009] E.C.R. I-7811, paras 37–47). See the note by Peers to *O'Flynn* and *Commission v Belgium* (1997) E.L.Rev. 157–165.

on any objective difference there may be between their own nationals and those of other Member States when they lay down the conditions under which leave to remain indefinitely in their territory is to be granted to the spouses of such persons.[242] However, the grant of a social advantage may not in principle be made dependent on the condition that the worker or members of his or her family dependent upon him be resident within the territory of the Member of State of employment.[243] Still, a Member State may restrict entitlement to certain social benefits to persons resident in its territory where this condition of residence is objectively justified and proportionate to the objective pursued.[244]

9–063   **Prohibited discrimination with respect to establishment.** As far as freedom of establishment is concerned, the Court of Justice held in *Reyners* that Art. 43 EC [*now Art. 49 TFEU*] constituted a particular embodiment of the general prohibition of discrimination on grounds of nationality and hence considered that

> "[a]fter the expiry of the transitional period the directives provided for by the Chapter on the right of establishment have become superfluous with regard to implementing the rule on nationality, since this is henceforth sanctioned by the Treaty itself with direct effect."[245]

Accordingly, Belgium had to allow Reyners, a Dutchman with a Belgian diploma of *docteur en droit*, to be inscribed on the roll of *avocats*. The Court referred to the transitional period, during which the Council had drawn up, pursuant to Art. 54 EEC, a General Programme for the Abolition of Restrictions on Freedom of Establishment, which advocated liberalisation of the rules on entry to and residence in other Member States by means of directives.[246] The General Programme went on to cite by way of restrictions to be abolished that access to self-employment might not be made subject to a period of prior residence or training in the host country and that the latter might not impose taxation or other financial burdens, such as the provision of security. Towards the end of the transitional period, the Council had not adopted all the necessary directives.[247] The Court of Justice, however, construed

---

[242] ECJ, Case C-356/98 *Kaba* [2000] E.C.R. I-2623, paras 31–34 (a Member State may require the spouse of a non-national to be resident for a longer period). For a critical commentary, see Peers, "Dazed and Confused: Family Members' Residence Rights and the Court of Justice" (2001) E.L.Rev. 76–83.

[243] ECJ, Case C-337/97 *Meeusen* [1999] E.C.R. I-3289, paras 21–25.

[244] ECJ, Case C-213/05 *Geven* [2007] E.C.R. I-6347, paras 26–30; ECJ, Case C-287/05 *Hendrix* [2007] E.C.R. I-6909, paras 50–58.

[245] ECJ, Case 2/74 *Reyners* [1974] E.C.R. 631, para. 30.

[246] General Programme for the Abolition of Restrictions on Freedom of Establishment, December 18, 1961, [1961] O.J. English Spec. Ed., Second Series, IX. Resolutions of the Council and of the Representatives of the Member States, p. 7.

[247] The Council adopted directives on the right of residence (n. 222, *supra*) and various others on agriculture, trade, industry and crafts (n. 363 to para. 5–145, *infra*), but did not, for example, adopt all the necessary directives on transport and the liberal professions.

the obligation to abolish restrictions on freedom of establishment "by progressive stages" (Art. 52 EEC) as having the same implications as the prohibition of discrimination laid down for workers in Art. 39 EC [now Art. 45 TFEU]. In the present version of this provision, Art. 49 TFEU consequently speaks of the "prohibition" of restrictions on freedom of establishment.[248]

Prohibited indirect discrimination. Article 49 TFEU [*ex Art. 43 EC*] also prohibits indirect discrimination, such as the refusal of the Paris Bar to admit a Belgian who held a Belgian diploma recognised by a French university as equivalent to the requisite French degree and had also fulfilled the French vocational training requirements for persons not holding a French diploma.[249] Article 49 TFEU prohibits any national rule which places nationals of another Member State in a less favourable situation than nationals of the State in question in the exercise of a self-employed activity. Accordingly, German legislation obliging a Greek hydrotherapist to have his name entered in the registers of civil status in a form modifying its pronunciation and thereby causing potential clients possibly to confuse him with other persons was held to be contrary to Art. 49 TFEU.[250] Freedom of establishment also means that self-employed persons from other Member States may not be discriminated against in the grant of social advantages to which they would be entitled under Regulation No. 1612/68 (see para. 9–062) if they were workers.[251]

9–064

Since national law can determine, inter alia, the nationality of companies from the place of their seat, indirect discrimination will arise where a Member State employs a criterion which is liable to work more particularly to the disadvantage of companies having their seat in other Member States.[252] Accordingly, the legislation of a Member State may not provide for a difference in treatment between taxpayers on the basis of the place where the company owned by those taxpayers employs a certain number of workers for a certain period of time.[253] Indirect

---

[248] In this way, the Amsterdam Treaty replaced the references to the abolition in progressive stages of the restrictions in question during the transitional period; at the same time, it removed the standstill provision set out in former Art. 53 EC (prohibition on Member States' introducing new restrictions) and the first para. of *former Art. 54 EC*, which referred to the General Programme.

[249] ECJ, Case 71/76 *Thieffry* [1977] E.C.R. 765, para. 19. For architects, see ECJ, Case 11/77 *Patrick* [1977] E.C.R. 1199, para. 18; for employees, see ECJ, Case 222/86 *Heylens* [1987] E.C.R. 4097, paras 11–12 (football trainer).

[250] ECJ, Case C-168/91 *Konstantinidis* [1993] E.C.R. I-1191, para. 17.

[251] ECJ, Case C-111/91 *Commission v Luxembourg* [1993] E.C.R. I-817, paras 16–18 and 33. ECJ, C-337/97 *Meeusen* [1999] E.C.R. I-3289, paras 26–30.

[252] ECJ, Case C-330/91 *Commerzbank* [1993] E.C.R. I-4017, paras 13–15 (residence for tax purposes); ECJ, Case C-101/94 *Commission v Italy* [1996] E.C.R. I-2691, paras 8–28 (corporate seat); ECJ, Case C-311/97 *Royal Bank of Scotland* [1999] E.C.R. I-2651, paras 28–31 (discrimination as compared with national companies in a like situation); ECJ, Joined Cases C-397/98 and C-410/98 *Metallgesellschaft and Others* [2001] E.C.R. I-1727, paras 37–76 (discrimination against subsidiaries of foreign companies as compared with subsidiaries of domestic companies).

[253] ECJ, Case C-464/05 *Geurts and Vogten* [2007] E.C.R. I-9325, paras 18–22; case note by Parisis (2008) J.T.D.E. 76–79.

discrimination also arises where a Member State directly awards a concession to an undertaking established in that Member State, because this works to the detriment of undertakings located in another Member State to which the concession may also be of interest.[254] The prohibition of direct or indirect discrimination on grounds of nationality must also be taken into account in registering vessels. Such grant of "nationality" to a vessel is a condition for the exercise of the right of establishment which cannot be made to depend on the nationality of the owners or charterers and, in the case of a company, on the nationality of the shareholders or directors, or on their place of residence or domicile.[255]

In the absence of any Union legislation on the matter, a Member State may impose certain administrative formalities in respect of the exercise of freedom of establishment, but any sanction for failing to comply with such a formality may not be so disproportionate to the gravity of the infringement as to become an obstacle to free movement of persons. Accordingly, where a person obtained a driving licence in a Member State and could have exchanged it for a driving licence issued by another Member State where he was established, but failed to do so within the time-limit prescribed, it is contrary to Art. 49 TFEU to treat that person as if he were driving without a licence, thereby incurring criminal penalties.[256]

The Court has held that it is a "corollary" of free movement of persons, in particular the right to pursue an employed or self-employed activity in another Member State and to reside there after having pursued such an activity, that there should be access to leisure activities available in that State. Consequently, French legislation under which only French nationals could register a leisure craft in France was held not to be compatible with free movement.[257] It clearly emerges

---

[254] ECJ, Case C-231/03 *Coname* [2005] E.C.R. I-7287, paras 17–20.

[255] ECJ, Case C-221/89 *Factortame II* [1991] E.C.R. I-3905, paras 22–33; the same form of words is to be found in ECJ, Case C-246/89 *Commission v United Kingdom* [1991] E.C.R. I-4585, paras 23–31; ECJ, Case C-93/89 *Commission v Ireland* [1991] E.C.R. I-4569, paras 10–11; ECJ, Case C-334/94 *Commission v France* [1996] E.C.R. I-1307, paras 12–19; ECJ, Case C-62/96 *Commission v Greece* [1997] E.C.R. I-6725, paras 17–18. More recently, the Court clarified that even a condition of having the nationality of one of the Member States or EEA States (as opposed to requiring the nationality of one specific Member State) is not compatible with Art. 43 EC [*now Art. 49 TFEU*] (ECJ, Case C-299/02 *Commission v Netherlands* [2004] E.C.R. I-9761, paras 19–26).

[256] ECJ, Case C-193/94 *Skanavi and Chryssanthakopoulos* [1996] E.C.R. I-929, paras 31–39. The restriction on Member States' power to impose criminal sanctions as a result of the free movement of persons does not apply, however, to a national of a third country who cannot rely on the rules governing free movement of persons: ECJ, Case C-230/97 *Awoyemi* [1998] E.C.R. I-6781, paras 28–30. Now Council Directive 91/439/EEC of July 29, 1991 on driving licences ([1991] O.J. L237/1, as amended most recently by Commission Directive 2009/112/EC of August 25, 2009, [2009] O.J. L 223/26, requires mutual recognition of driving licences and there is no need to exchange the driving licence issued by one Member State for the driving licence of the State of residence.

[257] ECJ, Case C-334/94 *Commission v France* [1996] E.C.R. I-1307, paras 21–23; ECJ, Case C-151/96 *Commission v Ireland* [1997] E.C.R. I-3327, paras 11–16; ECJ, Case C-62/96 *Commission v Greece* [1997] E.C.R. I-6725, paras 19–20.

from this case law that the Court of Justice treats the Treaty provisions on free movement of workers and freedom of establishment as having to be read together in governing free movement of persons.

Non-discriminatory obstacles. For a long time, it was assumed that the Treaty provisions on free movement of persons (workers and self-employed persons) did not preclude a restriction of the mobility of economic operators if the restriction applied without distinction to a State's own nationals and nationals of other Member States. The Court of Justice seemed not to recognise free movement of persons as having the same scope as free movement of goods and services.[258]

9–065

In the 1988 judgment in *Wolf*, the Court of Justice went further, however, by declaring incompatible with the principles of free movement of persons a national measure which both in law and in fact was applicable in the same way to nationals of the Member State in question and to nationals of other Member States but nevertheless restricted free movement of persons because it treated *all* Union nationals less favourably where they had been employed in the territory of more than one Member State.[259] Similarly, the Court considered that a Member State may not without due justification make the exercise of a profession dependent on the condition of having previously been established in a region of that Member State because such a condition is unfavourable to persons who have exercised their freedom of establishment by practising that profession in another Member State.[260] The 1993 judgment in *Kraus* took the further step of aligning the effect of the provisions on free movement of persons very closely with the rules on free movement of goods and services. The Court of Justice held that Arts 39 and 43 EC [*now Arts 45 and 49 TFEU*] preclude any national measure which, even though it is applicable without discrimination on grounds of nationality, is liable to hamper or to render less attractive the exercise by a national of any Member State of fundamental freedoms guaranteed by the Treaties.[261] Kraus, a German national, challenged a German provision requiring German nationals (and nationals of other Member States) to apply for authorisation in order to use an academic title of Master of Laws (LL.M.) obtained in another Member State. The Court of Justice held that this would accord with Arts 39 and 43 EC [*now Arts 45 and 49 TFEU*] only in so far as the obligation was proportionate to the aim of protecting

---

[258] For a description of how the case law developed, see Straetmans, *Consument en markt* (Deurne, Kluwer, 1998) 312–323; Daniele, "Non-Discriminatory Restrictions to the Free Movement of Persons" (1997) E.L.Rev. 191–200; Bernard, "Discrimination and Free Movement in EC Law" (1996) I.C.L.Q. 82–108; EuR. 145–162; Jarass, "Elemente einer Dogmatik der Grundfreiheiten" (1995) EuR. 202–226; Behrens, "Die Konvergenz der wirtschaftlichen Freiheiten im europäischen Gemeinschaftsrecht" (1992) EuR. 145.

[259] ECJ, Joined Cases 154–155/87 *Wolf and Others* [1988] E.C.R. 3897, paras 9–14. See also ECJ, Case 143/87 *Stanton* [1988] E.C.R. 3877, paras 9–14, delivered on the same date.

[260] ECJ, Case C-456/05 *Commission v Germany* [2007] E.C.R. I-10517.

[261] ECJ, Case C-19/92 *Kraus* [1993] E.C.R. 1663, para. 32; case notes by Roth (1993) C.M.L.Rev. 1251–1258, and Denys (1994) C.D.E. 638–662.

the public and intended solely to verify that the title was properly awarded.[262] It follows that the Treaty provisions on the free movement of workers and self-employed persons prohibit all measures that disadvantage nationals of a Member State who exercised their right to free movement through employment or other activities in another Member State or who intend to exercise that right.

Consequently, provisions which preclude or deter a national of a Member State from leaving the country in which he or she is pursuing an economic activity in order to exercise the right to freedom of movement constitute an obstacle to that freedom even if they apply without regard to the nationality of the worker concerned.[263] With regard to free movement of workers, the Court of Justice has held that such an obstacle exists only where a provision affects access of workers to the labour market.[264] In *Bosman* the Court of Justice declared an obstacle to free movement of workers transfer rules adopted by sports associations according to which, at the expiry of his contract, a professional footballer could be taken on by a new club only if it paid his old club a transfer fee.[265] With respect to the right of establishment, the Court likewise held that a restriction of that right may exist where a national measure has the effect of restricting access to the market of the Member State concerned.[266] That is the case for measures of a Member State that reserve the exercise of a self-employed activity to certain economic operators, such as allowing only pharmacists to operate pharmacies.[267] In this way, the Court's case law on the free movement of persons comes close to the case law on the free movement of goods, according to which a measure adopted by a Member State constitutes a "restriction" where it treats products originating in other Member States less favourably—through directly or indirectly discriminatory

---

[262] *Kraus*, cited in the preceding n., paras 32–38.

[263] ECJ, Case C-18/95 *Terhoeve* [1999] E.C.R. I-345, para. 39; ECJ, Case C-232/01 *Van Lent* [2003] E.C.R. I-11525, para. 16; ECJ, Case C-209/01 *Schilling and Fleck-Schilling* [2003] E.C.R. I-13389, para. 25; ECJ, Case C-464/02 *Commission v Denmark* [2005] E.C.R. I-7929, para. 35; ECJ, Case C-345/05 *Commission v Portugal* [2006] E.C.R. I-10633, para. 16; ECJ, Case C-104/06 *Commission v Sweden* [2007] E.C.R. I-671, para. 18; ECJ, Case C-522/04 *Commission v Belgium* [2007] E.C.R. I-5701, para. 65; ECJ, Case C-318/05 *Commission v Germany*, [2007] E.C.R. I-06957, para. 114.

[264] ECJ, Case C-190/98 *Graf* [2000] E.C.R. I-493, para. 23 (if not, there would only be a "too uncertain and indirect" possibility within the meaning of the case law on free movement of goods cited in n. 96: *ibid.*, para. 25). See Ranocher, "Grundfreiheiten und Spürbarkeitstheorie" (2001) Z.f.R.V. 95–107.

[265] ECJ, Case C-415/93 *Bosman* [1995] E.C.R. I-4921, paras 94–104 (for commentaries, see n. 235, *supra*). See also ECJ, Case C-325/08 *Olympique Lyonnais* (n. 177, supra) paras 27–37 (obligation for a young professional footballer to sign a contract at the end of his training period held to be a restriction on the free movement of workers).

[266] ECJ, Case C-442/02 *CaixaBank France* [2004] E.C.R. I-8961, paras 12–14, with a note by Spaventa (2005) C.M.L.Rev. 1151–1168; ECJ, Case C-518/06 *Commission v Italy* [2009] E.C.R. I-3491, paras 64–71; ECJ (judgment of March 11, 2010), Case C-384/08 *Attanasio Group*, not yet reported, paras 44–45.

[267] ECJ, Case C-531/06 *Commission v Italy* [2009] E.C.R. I-4103, paras 44–45.

provisions—or where it otherwise hinders access to the market of the Member State (see para. 9–031).[268]

Given that Arts 45 and 49 TFEU are applicable to the situation of a national of a Member State who is a worker or self-employed in a Member State other than the one in which he or she resides, those articles preclude Member States from enacting measures that deter nationals from taking up residence in another Member State, for example by refusing a subsidy for owner-occupied dwellings if the dwelling built or purchased is situated in the territory of another Member State.[269]

An obstacle to free movement of persons may be justified by pressing reasons of public interest, provided that it applies without distinction as to nationality, is appropriate and does not exceed what is necessary to attain its intended objective (see para. 9–074).

(c) *Primary and secondary right of establishment*

Definition of establishment. According to the second para. of Art. 49 TFEU [*ex Art. 43 EC*], freedom of establishment includes: **9–066**

> "the right to take up and pursue activities as self-employed persons and to set up and manage undertakings, in particular companies and firms within the meaning of the second para of Article 54, under the conditions laid down for its own nationals by the law of the country where such establishment is effected".

The term "establishment" is broadly construed in the case law so as to allow a Union national to participate, on a stable and continuous basis, in the economic life of a Member State other than his or her State of origin and to profit therefrom, so contributing to economic and social interpenetration within the Union in the sphere of activities as self-employed persons.[270] However, the substance of freedom of establishment is not the same in the case of natural persons as it is for legal persons.

Natural persons. As far as natural persons are concerned, freedom of establishment encompasses, alongside the right to create a first establishment in the territory of another Member State (the primary right of establishment), a second right of establishment in order to **9–067**

---

[268] See ECJ, Case C-456/05 *Commission v Germany* [2007] E.C.R. I-10517, paras 51–60 (authorisation to practice for psychotherapists dependent on whether they previously carried out activities under the national statutory sickness insurance system); ECJ, Case C-40/05 *Lyyski* [2007] E.C.R. I-99, paras 36–37 (training course open only to teachers employed in a school in the Member State concerned).

[269] ECJ, Case C-152/05 *Commission v Germany* [2008] E.C.R. I-39, paras 20–25.

[270] ECJ, Case C-55/94 *Gebhard* [1995] E.C.R. I-4165, para. 25, with case notes by Ballon (1996/97) Col.J.E.L. 145–151; Goffin (1996) C.D.E. 723–743; ECJ (judgment of September 8, 2010), Case C-409/06 *Winner Welten*, not yet reported, paras 45–47.

"set up and maintain, subject to observance of the professional rules of conduct, more than one place of work within the [Union]".[271]

Accordingly, a self-employed person may open a second office in another Member State or participate in setting up a company.[272] Article 49 TFEU provides that the prohibition of restrictions on the freedom of establishment is also to apply to restrictions on the "setting-up of agencies, branches or subsidiaries by nationals of any Member State established in the territory of any Member State".

9–068   **Companies.** Union law recognises a secondary right of establishment as far as concerns companies incorporated under the law of a Member State, but not the primary right to move their seat. Unlike natural persons, companies exist only by virtue of the law determining the conditions governing their formation and operation. Member States' legislation differs considerably in terms of the connection required to exist with the national territory when setting up a company under national law and with regard to changing that connection.[273] Hence, Art. 54 TFEU recognises three criteria for conferring the "nationality" of a Member State on a company (see para. 9–056).

In the absence of a single connecting factor imposed by Union law, the Member States thus have the power to define both the connecting factor required of a company if it is to be regarded as incorporated under the law of that Member State and, as such, capable of enjoying the right of establishment, and that required if the company is to be able subsequently to maintain that status.[274] Article 293 EC called on Member States to enter into negotiations with each other with a view to securing mutual recognition of companies and firms, the retention of legal personality in the event of the transfer of their seat from one country to another and the possibility of mergers between companies or firms governed by the laws of different countries, but no agreement to that effect ever entered into force.[275] However, the Council has created European corporate bodies, which, subject to certain conditions, can transfer their statutory seat to another Member

---

[271] ECJ, Case 107/83 *Klopp* [1984] E.C.R. 2971, para. 19.

[272] In *Klopp* (see preceding n.), the Court of Justice held that a lawyer was entitled to open a second set of chambers in another Member State. See also ECJ, Case C-55/94 *Gebhard* [1995] E.C.R. I-4165, para. 24; ECJ, Case C-53/95 *Kemmler* [1996] E.C.R. I-703, paras 10–14. See, with regard to auditors, ECJ, Case C-106/91 *Ramrath* [1992] E.C.R. I-3351, para. 22, and with regard to doctors, dentists and veterinary surgeons, ECJ, Case C-351/90 *Commission v Luxembourg* [1992] E.C.R. I-3945, para. 24.

[273] See Halbhuber, "National Doctrinal Structures and European Company Law" (2001) C.M.L.Rev. 1385–1420.

[274] ECJ, Case C-210/06 *Cartesio* [2008] E.C.R. I-9641, para. 110.

[275] Pursuant to Art. 220 EEC (renumbered into Art.293 EC), the Member States concluded the Brussels Convention of February 29, 1968 on the mutual recognition of companies and bodies corporate (see (1969) EC Bull. Suppl. 2), which has not entered into force. For a rather better unofficial English translation, see Stein, *Harmonisation of European Company Laws*, 1971.

State (see para. 9–079). In the absence of rules laid down by legislation or convention, the Court of Justice has held that Arts 49 and 54 TFEU do not confer on companies incorporated under the laws of a Member State a right to transfer their central management and control and their central administration to another Member State while retaining their status as companies incorporated under the legislation of the first Member State.[276] Indeed, the power of a Member State to define the connecting factor required of a company governed by its law includes the possibility not to permit such a company to retain that status if the company intends to reorganise itself in another Member State by moving its seat to the territory of the latter, thereby breaking the connecting factor required under the national law of the Member State of incorporation.[277] However, the Member State in which a company is incorporated may not, without due justification, prevent that company from converting itself into a company governed by the law of the Member State to which it transfers its central management and control.[278] Likewise, Arts 49 and 54 TFEU preclude requiring a company formed in one Member State to be re-incorporated in another Member State in order for it to retain legal capacity in that Member State.[279]

Secondary right of establishment. The upshot is that Union law confers only a   **9–069**
secondary right of establishment on companies incorporated under the laws of a Member State to set up agencies, branches and subsidiaries in other Member States.[280] According to the Court of Justice, it is inherent in the exercise of freedom of establishment that a national of a Member State who wishes to set up a company may choose to form it in the Member State whose rules of company law seem to him to be the least restrictive and then to set up branches in other Member States. The fact that a company is incorporated in a particular Member State in

---

[276] ECJ, Case 81/87 *Daily Mail and General Trust* [1988] E.C.R. 5483, para. 24; ECJ, Case C-210/06 *Cartesio* [2008] E.C.R. I-9641, para. 124.

[277] ECJ, Case C-210/06 *Cartesio* [2008] E.C.R. I-9641, paras 110.

[278] ECJ, Case C-210/06 *Cartesio* [2008] E.C.R. I-9641, paras 111–113.

[279] ECJ, Case C-208/00 *Überseering* [2002] E.C.R. I-9919, paras 52–94 (a Member State cannot deny a company legal capacity on the basis of the presumption that it has moved its actual centre of administration to its territory). See Ballarino, "Les règles de conflit sur les sociétés commerciales à l'épreuve du droit communautaire d'établissement" (2003) R.C.D.I.P. 373–402; Jonet, "Sociétés commerciales—La théorie du siège réel à l'épreuve de la liberté d'établissement" (2003) J.T.D.E. 33–37; Lombardo, "Conflict of Law Rules in Company Law after *Überseering*: An Economic and Comparative Analysis of the Allocation of Policy Competence in the European Union" (2003) E.Bus.Org.L.R. 301–336; Rammeloo, "The Long and Winding Road Towards Freedom of Establishment for Legal Persons in Europe" (2003) M.J.E.C.L. 169–196; Roth, "From Centros to Überseering: Free Movement of Companies, Private International Law, and Community Law" (2003) I.C.L.Q. 177–208. For a survey of the constraints which Union law places on the "emigration" and "immigration" of companies, see Wymeersch, "The Transfer of the Company's Seat in European Company Law" (2003) C.M.L.Rev. 661–695.

[280] See Roussos, "Realising the Free Movement of Companies" (2001) E.Bus.L.Rev. 7–25; Drury, "Migrating Companies" (1999) E.L.Rev. 354–372.

order to take advantage of more favourable legislative rules therefore does not in itself constitute an abuse of the right of establishment.[281] Consequently, a Member State cannot impose conditions on setting up a branch solely on the ground that the parent company does not conduct any business in the Member State in which it is established and pursues its activities only in the Member State where its branch is established.[282] Moreover, all restrictions imposed on grounds of imperative requirements in the general interest (e.g. in relation to combating fraud or protecting creditors) must satisfy the requirement of proportionality.[283]

The provisions concerning freedom of establishment prohibit the Member State of origin from hindering the establishment in another Member State of agencies, branches or subsidiaries of a company incorporated under its legislation.[284] Accordingly, Art. 49 TFEU precludes national legislation that confers tax advantages on parent companies whose subsidiaries are established in the same Member State, but not at all, or only under less favourable conditions, on parent companies with subsidiaries in other Member States.[285] Freedom of establishment is likewise restricted when a Member State subjects subsidiaries of foreign companies to a less favourable tax regime than subsidiaries of domestic companies.[286] Likewise, Art. 49 precludes national legislation which, in the case of companies established in that State belonging to a consortium, makes a form of tax relief subject to the requirement that the holding company's business must consist wholly or mainly of the

---

[281] ECJ, Case C-212/97 *Centros* [1999] E.C.R. I-1459, paras 18–27; ECJ, Case C-167/01 *Inspire Art* [2003] E.C.R. I-10155, paras 95–98 and 136–138; ECJ, Case C-196/04 *Cadbury Schweppes* [2006] E.C.R. I-7995, para. 37. However, in so far as such action does not conflict with freedom of establishment, a Member State is entitled to take measures designed to prevent certain of its nationals from attempting, under cover of the rights created by the Treaty, improperly to circumvent their national legislation: *Centros, ibid.*, paras 24–25; *Inspire Act, ibid.*, para. 136; *Cadbury Schweppes, ibid.*, para. 35.

[282] ECJ, Case C-212/97 *Centros* [1999] E.C.R. I-1459, para. 29; ECJ, Case C-167/01 *Inspire Art* [2003] E.C.R. I-10155.

[283] See, e.g., ECJ, Case C-212/97 *Centros* [1999] E.C.R. I-1459, paras 34–38; ECJ, Case C-167/01 *Inspire Art* [2003] E.C.R. I-10155, paras 133–134. See Behrens, "Reactions of Member State Courts to the *Centros* Ruling by the ECJ" (2001) E.Bus.Org.L.J. 159–174; Wouters, "Private International Law and Companies' Freedom of Establishment" (2001) E.Bus.Org.L.R. 101–139; Ebke "*Centros*—Some Realities and Some Mysteries" (2000) A.J.C.L. 623–660; Forsthoff, "Niederlassungsrecht für Gesellschaften nach dem *Centros*-Urteil des EuGH: Eine Bilanz" (2000) EuR. 167–196; De Wulf, "*Centros*: vrijheid van vestiging zonder *race to the bottom*" (1999) Ondernemingsrecht 318–324.

[284] ECJ, Case C-264/96 *ICI* [1998] E.C.R. I-4695, para. 21; ECJ, Case C-446/03 *Marks & Spencer* [2005] E.C.R. I-10837, para. 31; ECJ, Case C-196/04 *Cadbury Schweppes* [2006] E.C.R. I-7995, para. 42. See also ECJ, Case C-170/05 *Denkavit* [2006] E.C.R. I-11949, paras 20–30 (tax exemption of dividends paid to subsidiary conditional on the parent company being a resident of the Member State concerned).

[285] ECJ, Case C-200/98 *X and Y* [1999] E.C.R. I-8261; ECJ, Case C-251/98 *Baars* [2000] E.C.R. I-2787; ECJ, Case C-446/03 *Marks & Spencer* [2005] E.C.R. I-10837, paras 30–34.

[286] ECJ, Joined Cases C-397/98 and C-410/98 *Metallgesellschaft and Others* [2001] E.C.R. I-1727, paras 37–76; ECJ, C-231/05 *AA* [2007] E.C.R. I-6373, paras 30–43.

holding of shares in subsidiaries established in the Member State concerned.[287] The exercise of the freedom of establishment is also deterred by national rules that do not allow for the registration of mergers when some of the companies concerned are established in another Member State.[288] By the same token, it would run counter to Art. 49 to make the registration or operation with a view to carrying out an economic activity in a Member State of vessels owned by a legal person conditional on the seat of that legal person being located in that Member State. Such a condition would preclude the operation of such vessels by agencies, branches or subsidiaries of companies established in another Member State.[289]

4. Permitted restrictions

(a) *Restrictions on grounds of public policy, public security and public health*

Justificatory grounds. Under Art. 45(3) TFEU [*ex Art. 39(3) EC*], Member States   **9–070** may place limitations on the free movement of workers on grounds of public policy (*ordre public*), public security or public health. In some cases, individuals may also rely on these justificatory grounds.[290] Restrictions may also be imposed on freedom of establishment on the same grounds (Art. 52 TFEU [*ex Art. 46 EC*]). These concepts are further fleshed out in Directive 2004/38 of the European Parliament and of the Council, which codifies all existing Union legislation on the right of citizens of the Union to reside within the territory of the Member States.[291] The Directive makes it clear that a measure may only be justified on one of those grounds in so far as it is proportional to the aim pursued thereby.[292]

---

[287] ECJ, Case C-264/96 *ICI* [1998] E.C.R. I-4695, paras 22–30. See Travers, "Residence Restraints on the Transferability of Corporate Trading Losses and the Right of Establishment in Community Law" (1999) E.L.Rev. 403–425. For other tax rules held to be contrary to Art. 43 EC [*now Art. 49 TFEU*], see, for example, ECJ, Case C-254/97 *Baxter* [1999] E.C.R. I-4809 (tax deductibility of costs of research only if research carried out in the Member State); ECJ, Case C-141/99 *AMID* [2000] E.C.R. I-11619 (loss not capable of being set off against the profit made during previous years in so far as the profit came from a permanent establishment abroad).

[288] ECJ, Case C-411/03 *SEVIC Systems* [2005] E.C.R. I-10805, paras 20–23.

[289] ECJ, Case C-334/94 *Commission v France* [1996] E.C.R. I-1307, paras 16 and 19; see also ECJ, Case C-221/89 *Factortame II* [1991] E.C.R. I-3905, para. 35. See, with regard to aircraft, ECJ, Case C-203/98 *Commission v Belgium* [1999] E.C.R. I-4899.

[290] ECJ, Case C-415/93 *Bosman* [1995] E.C.R. I-4921, para. 86; ECJ, Case C-350/96 *Clean Car Autoservice* [1998] E.C.R. I-2521, para. 24.

[291] Directive 2004/38 (n. 24, *supra*), Art. 27(1). The Directive replaces Council Directive 64/221/EEC of February 25, 1964 on the coordination of special measures concerning the movement or residence of foreign nationals which are justified on grounds of public policy, public security or public health, [1963–1964] O.J. English Spec. Ed. (I) 117, which already allowed for exceptions on public policy, public security or public health grounds.

[292] *Ibid.*, Art. 27(2). This principle has been developed in the case law of the Court of Justice, see ECJ, Case C-101/94 *Commission v Italy* [1996] E.C.R. I-2691, paras 25–26; ECJ, Case C-294/00 *Deutsche Paracelsus Schulen für Naturheilverfahren* [2002] E.C.R. I-6515, paras 38–66.

9–071 **Genuine and serious threat.** The right of Member States to restrict freedom of movement for persons on grounds of public policy, public security or public health is not intended to exclude economic sectors or occupations from the application of that principle, but to allow Member States to refuse access to their territory or residence there to persons whose access or residence would in itself constitute a danger for public policy, public security or public health.[293] The rights associated with the citizenship of the Union require that any such derogation from the principle of free movement be interpreted strictly.[294] By virtue of Art. 45(3) TFEU a Member State may refuse to allow a worker who is a national of another Member State or his family members, regardless of their nationality, to enter its territory or reside therein only on the ground that his or her presence or conduct constitutes a genuine and sufficiently serious threat to the requirements of public policy,[295] affecting one of the fundamental interests of society.[296] Although Union law does not impose upon the Member States a uniform scale of values, it does not permit a Member State to apply an arbitrary distinction to the detriment of nationals of other Member States. In the 1974 judgment in the *Van Duyn* case, the Court of Justice had accepted that a Member State was entitled, on grounds of public policy, to prevent a national of another Member State from taking gainful employment within its territory with an organisation which it regarded as socially harmful, even though no similar restriction was placed on its own nationals.[297] In 1982, the Court of Justice held, however, that conduct on the part of nationals of other Member States is not a sufficiently serious threat where similar conduct by nationals of the Member State in question does not give rise to repressive measures or other genuine and effective measures intended to combat such conduct.[298] A genuine and sufficiently serious threat affecting one of the fundamental interests of society is also required where public policy or public security is invoked as the justification for limitations on freedom of establishment or to provide services, such as a rule that managers of an undertaking or the seat of an undertaking must be established in the Member State in question.[299]

---

[293] ECJ, Case 131/85 *Gül* [1986] E.C.R. 1573, para. 17; ECJ, Case C-114/97, *Commission v Spain* [1998] E.C.R. I-6717, para. 42; ECJ, Case C-405/01 *Colegio de Oficiales de la Marina Mercante Española* [2003] E.C.R. I-10391, para. 48, and ECJ, Case C-47/02 *Anker and Others* [2003] E.C.R. I-10447, para. 67.

[294] ECJ, Joined Cases C-482/01 and C-493/01 *Orfanopoulos and Others* [2004] E.C.R. I-5257, para. 65.

[295] ECJ, Case 36/75 *Rutili* [1975] E.C.R. 1291, para. 28. See now Directive 2004/38 (n. 24, *supra*), Art. 27(2), second subpara..

[296] ECJ, Case 30/77 *Bouchereau* [1977] E.C.R. 1999, para. 35. See now Directive 2004/38 (n. 24, *supra*), Art. 27(2), second subpara.

[297] ECJ, Case 41/74 *Van Duyn* [1974] E.C.R. 1337, paras 20–24.

[298] ECJ, Joined Cases 115 and 116/81 *Adoui and Cornuaille* [1982] E.C.R. 1665, para. 8; See also ECJ, Case 249/86 *Commission v Germany* [1989] E.C.R. 1263, paras 17–20; ECJ, Case C-363/89 *Roux* [1991] E.C.R. I-273, paras 29–31; ECJ, Case C-268/99 *Jany and Others* [2001] E.C.R. I-8615, paras 55–62; ECJ, Case C-100/01 *Oteiza Olazabal* [2002] E.C.R. I-10981, paras 27–45.

[299] ECJ, Case C-114/97 *Commission v Spain* [1998] E.C.R. I-6717, paras 44–47; ECJ, Case C-355/98 *Commission v Belgium* [2000] E.C.R. I-1221, paras 27–34.

Directive 2004/38 requires measures taken on grounds of public policy or public security to be "based exclusively on the personal conduct of the individual concerned".[300] Previous criminal convictions are not in themselves to constitute grounds for the taking of such measures.[301] Accordingly, a Member State may not refuse entry to a national of a third country who is the spouse of a Member State national on the ground that alerts for that person were entered in the Schengen Information System, without first verifying whether the presence of that person constitutes a genuine, present and sufficiently serious threat to one of the fundamental interests of society.[302] Moreover, for a person to be expelled, the "genuine threat" must in principle remain until the moment of his or her expulsion.[303] The directive formulates procedural requirements for the exercise of the public policy reservation by Member States.[304] In this way, the requirements and prohibitions laid down by the directive constitute a restriction of the Member State's residuary power in the sphere of public policy.[305]

(b) *Employment in the public service and exercise of public authority*

Public service. According to Art. 45(4) TFEU [*ex Art. 39(4) EC*], the provisions of that article do not apply to "employment in the public service". This exception applies only to posts   **9–072**

---

[300] Directive 2004/38 (n. 24, *supra*), Art.27(2), first subpara.; see previously Directive 64/221, Art. 3(1).

[301] Directive 2004/38 (n. 24, *supra*), Art.27(2), first subpara.; see previously Directive 64/221, Art. 3(2). Thus, automatic expulsion from the territory is not permitted in the case of nationals of other Member States found guilty on that territory of drug offences: ECJ, Case C-348/96 *Calfa* [1999] E.C.R. I-11, paras 16–29; ECJ, Joined Cases C-482/01 and C-493/01 *Orfanopoulos and Others* [2004] E.C.R. I-5257, paras 66–71. *Cf.* ECJ, Case C-340/97 *Nazli* [2000] E.C.R. I-957, paras 50–64 (the same applies to workers deriving rights from association agreements).

[302] ECJ, Case C-503/03 *Commission v Spain* [2006] E.C.R. I-1097, paras 41–59.

[303] ECJ, Joined Cases C-482/01 and C-493/01 *Orfanopoulos and Others* [2004] E.C.R. I-5257, paras 79 and 82; ECJ, Case C-136/03 *Dörr and Ünal*, [2005] E.C.R. I-4759, paras 41–43.

[304] Directive 2004/38 (n. 24, *supra*), Arts 30–33. See, previously, with respect to the procedural safeguards laid down by Directive 64/221: ECJ, Case 36/75 *Rutili* [1975] E.C.R. 1291, paras 33–39; ECJ, Case 30/77 *Bouchereau* [1977] E.C.R. 1999, paras 15–30; ECJ, Case 131/79 *Santillo* [1980] E.C.R. 1585, paras 11–19; ECJ, Joined Cases 115 and 116/81 *Adoui and Cornuaille* [1982] E.C.R. 1665, paras 14–19; ECJ, Joined Cases C-297/88 and C-197/89 *Dzodzi* [1990] E.C.R. I-3763, paras 57–69; ECJ, Case C-175/94 *Gallagher* [1995] E.C.R. I-4253, paras 1–26; ECJ, Joined Cases C-65/95 and C-111/95 *Shingara and Radiom* [1997] E.C.R. I-3343, paras 1–45; ECJ, Case C-357/98 *Nana Yaa Konadu Yiadom* [2000] E.C.R. I-9265, paras 17–43; ECJ, Case C-459/99 *MRAX* [2002] E.C.R. I-6591, paras 100–104.

[305] Peers, "National Security and European Law" (1996) Y.E.L. 363–404; Hubeau, "L'exception d'ordre public et la libre circulation des personnes en droit communautaire" (1981) C.D.E. 207–256. For further consideration of the development of the concept of "ordre public", see Chaltiel, "L'ordre public devant la Cour de justice des Communautés européennes" (2003) R.M.C.U.E. 120–123; Karydis, "L'ordre public dans l'ordre juridique communautaire: un concept à contenu variable" (2002) R.T.D.E. 1–26.

"which involve direct or indirect participation in the exercise of powers conferred by public law and duties designed to safeguard the general interests of the State or of other public authorities",

since such posts presume

"the existence of a special relationship of allegiance to the State and reciprocity of rights and duties which form the foundation of the bond of nationality".[306]

Other posts cannot be reserved for a Member State's own nationals, not even for considerations relating to the preservation of national identity.[307] Moreover, once a worker is admitted into the public service of a Member State, Art. 45(4) cannot be relied on by that Member State in order to restrict the rights which he or she derives from Art. 45(1) to (3) TFEU.[308]

This restrictive interpretation of the expression "public service" means that a large number of posts which do not involve the exercise of public authority, but where the employer is a public authority, are not taken outside the scope of the Treaties.[309] The legal categorisation of the employment relationship between the employee and the administration—that is to say, whether the relationship is governed by private or public law—is irrelevant for this purpose.[310] Accordingly, the Court of Justice has held that civil servants' and public employees' posts in public water, gas and electricity distribution services,[311] public-sector research,

---

[306] ECJ, Case 149/79 *Commission v Belgium* [1980] E.C.R. 3881, para. 10.

[307] ECJ, Case C-473/93 *Commission v Luxembourg* [1996] E.C.R. I-3207, para. 35 (there are less far-reaching means of protecting that interest recognised by Art. 6(3) EU [*see now Art. 4(2) TEU*]). For the impact of Union law on national civil-service law, see Kämmerer, "Europäisierung des öffentlichen Dienstrechts" (2001) EuR. 27–48.

[308] ECJ, Case 152/73 *Sotgiu* [1974] E.C.R. 153, para. 4; ECJ, Case C-392/05 *Alevizos* [2007] E.C.R. I-3505, para. 70.

[309] A number of guidelines were set out in the Commission communication on its action in respect of the application of Art. 48(4) EC [*now Art. 45(4) TFEU*]: [1988] O.J. C72/2; see Guillén and Fuentetaja, "Free Movement of Workers and Public Administration: The ECJ Doctrine on the Interpretation of the Scope of Article 39(4) EC" (1999) ERPL/REDP 1567–1593; Handoll, "Article 48(4) EEC and Non-National Access to Public Employment" (1988) E.L.Rev. 223–241.

[310] ECJ, Case 152/73 *Sotgiu* [1974] E.C.R. 153, paras 5–6. However, Art. 45(4) TFEU does not cover employment by a private natural or legal person: ECJ, Case C-283/99 *Commission v Italy* [2001] E.C.R. I-4363, para. 25.

[311] ECJ, Case C-473/93 *Commission v Luxembourg* [1996] E.C.R. I-3207, para. 31; Case C-173/94 *Commission v Belgium* [1996] E.C.R. I-3265, para. 17; Case C-290/94 *Commission v Greece* [1996] E.C.R. I-3285, para. 34. For an early case, see ECJ, Case 149/79 *Commission v Belgium* [1982] E.C.R. 1845, paras 8–9 (drivers and manual workers employed by railways).

254

education, health, postal and telecommunications services[312] and radio and television,[313] and some seamen's occupations,[314] private security posts[315] and members of an occupational guild[316] do not fall within the exception. Even where persons are granted powers conferred by public law, it is still necessary that such powers are exercised on a regular basis by their holders and do not represent a very minor part of their activities in order for them to fall within Art. 39(4).[317] The concept of "employment in the public service" does not encompass employment by a private natural or legal person, whatever the duties of the employee.[318]

Exercise of public authority. Nationals of a Member State have no right of establishment in another Member State in respect of "activities which in that State are connected, even occasionally, with the exercise of official authority" (Art. 51 TFEU [*ex Art. 45 EC*]). This exception is also interpreted restrictively by the Court of Justice. It relates only to activities which "taken on their own, constitute a direct and specific connection with the exercise of official authority" and

9–073

---

[312] ECJ, Cases C-473/93 and C-290/94, *ibid.* According to the Court of Justice, the following do *not* fall within the exception: various manual occupations, crèche nurses and children's nurses employed by local authorities (ECJ, Case 149/79 *Commission v Belgium* [1982] E.C.R. 1845, paras 8–9; although the exception was held to cover controllers, night watchmen and local authority architects); nurses in public hospitals (ECJ, Case 307/84 *Commission v France* [1986] E.C.R. 1725, para. 13); medical specialists working in the public service (ECJ, Case C-15/96 *Schöning-Kougebetopoulou* [1998] E.C.R. I-47, para. 13); directors and teachers in institutions specialising in supplementary instruction and music and dancing schools (ECJ, Case 147/86 *Commission v Greece* [1988] E.C.R. 1637, paras 19–21); foreign-language assistants at universities (ECJ, Case 33/88 *Allué and Others* [1989] E.C.R. 1591, para. 9); primary school teachers (ECJ, Case C-473/93 *Commission v Luxembourg* [1996] E.C.R. I-3207, paras 32–34); secondary school teachers (ECJ, Case C-4/91 *Bleis* [1991] E.C.R. I-5627, para. 7); trainee teachers (ECJ, Case 66/85 *Lawrie-Blum* [1986] E.C.R. 2121, paras 27–29) and researchers at a national research institution (Case 225/85 *Commission v Italy* [1987] E.C.R. 2625, para. 9; although the exception was held to cover posts involving management duties or advising the State).

[313] ECJ, Case C-290/94 *Commission v Greece* [1996] E.C.R. I-3285, para. 34 (which mentions also musicians in municipal and local orchestras and opera houses).

[314] ECJ, Case C-37/93 *Commission v Belgium* [1993] E.C.R. I-6295, paras 1–6. As far as masters and chief mates are concerned, the Court of Justice has since held that their powers conferred by public law were too incidental to warrant application of the exception: ECJ, Case C-405/01 *Colegio de Oficiales de la Marina Mercante Española* [2003] E.C.R. I-10391, paras 42 to 45, and ECJ, Case C-47/02 *Anker and Others* [2003] E.C.R. I-10447, paras 61 to 64.

[315] ECJ, Case C-114/97 *Commission v Spain* [1998] E.C.R. I-6717, para. 33; ECJ, Case C-355/99 *Commission v Belgium* [2000] E.C.R. I-1221, para. 26; ECJ, Case C-283/99 *Commission v Italy* [2001] E.C.R. I-4363, para. 20.

[316] ECJ, Case C-213/90 *ASTI* [1991] E.C.R. I-3507, paras 19–20; ECJ Case C-171/01 *Wählergruppe Gemeinsam* [2003] E.C.R. I-4301, paras 90–93.

[317] ECJ, Case C-405/01 *Colegio de Oficiales de la Marina Mercante Española* [2003] E.C.R. I-10391, para. 44, and ECJ, Case C-47/02 *Anker and Others* [2003] E.C.R. I-10447, para. 63.

[318] ECJ, Case C-109/04 *Kranemann* [2005] E.C.R. I-2421, para. 19; ECJ, Case C-345/08 *Pesla* (n. 324, *supra*), para. 29.

not the profession as such of which those activities form a part.[319] Consequently, the profession of a lawyer (*avocat*) cannot be reserved to nationals, since the most typical activities of that profession, such as consultation and legal assistance and representation and defence of parties in courts, cannot be regarded as participating in the exercise of official authority.[320] Sitting as a substitute judge, say, could certainly be restricted to nationals.[321] It is uncertain whether such a restriction could be placed on other legal professions, such as that of notary, which does not exist (or at least does not have the same connotations) in all Member States.[322] Moreover, the exception will not apply when the activities connected with the exercise of official authority are separable from the professional activity in question taken as a whole.[323] The exception does not apply to a legal trainee completing his training at a court as such a person will act in accordance with the instructions and under the supervision of a training principal.[324] Likewise, a private body cannot be regarded as participating in the exercise of official authority where it performs functions that are merely auxiliary and preparatory vis-à-vis an entity which itself exercises official authority.[325]

---

[319] ECJ, Case 2/74 *Reyners* [1974] E.C.R. 631, paras 45–46. The following activities have been held not to constitute the exercise of public authority: the establishment of institutions for supplementary instruction and vocational training schools and giving private lessons at home (ECJ, Case 147/86 *Commission v Greece* [1988] E.C.R. 1637, paras 8–10), the design, programming and operation of data-processing systems (ECJ, Case C-3/88 *Commission v Italy* [1989] E.C.R. 4035, para. 13), the activities of experts on traffic accidents (ECJ, Case C-306/89 *Commission v Greece* [1991] E.C.R. I-5863, para. 7), the post of "approved commissioner" with Belgian insurance undertakings (ECJ, Case C-42/92 *Thijssen* [1993] E.C.R. I-4047, paras 16–22), the concession for a lottery computerisation system (ECJ, Case C-272/91 *Commission v Italy* [1994] E.C.R. I-1409, paras 6–13), the activities of private security undertakings and their staff (ECJ, Case C-114/97 *Commission v Spain* [1998] E.C.R. I-6717, paras 34–39; ECJ, Case C-355/98 *Commission v Belgium* [2000] E.C.R. I-1221, para. 26; ECJ, Case C-283/99 *Commission v Italy* [2001] E.C.R. I-4363, para. 20), activities of advice and assistance in tax matters (ECJ, Case C-451/03 *Servizi Ausiliari Dottori Commercialisti* [2006] E.C.R. I-2941, paras 47–49) and the provision of public emergency services (ECJ (judgment of April 29, 2010), Case C-160/08 *Commission v Germany*, not yet reported, paras 80–86).

[320] *Reyners*, cited in the preceding n., para. 52.

[321] This is probably also true of (Bavarian) lay assessors according to the view taken by the Commission in its answer of September 5, 1996 to question No. E-1580/96 (Sakellariou), [1996] O.J. C356/61.

[322] See Schiller, "Freier Personenverkehr im Bereich der freiwilligen Gerichtsbarkeit?" (2004) EuR. 27–51; Demaret, "L'égalité de traitement" (1994) A.D. 165, at 203–204. The European Parliament considered that the notary's profession came within the exception; see the resolution of January 18, 1994 on the state and organisation of the profession of notary in the twelve Member States of the Community, [1994] O.J. C44/36, at point 4. See in this connection the actions brought by the Commission against Belgium on February 11, 2008 (Case C-47/08) and against France and Luxembourg on February 12, 2008 (Cases C-50/08 and C-51/08) ([2008] O.J. C128/18).

[323] ECJ, Case 2/74 *Reyners* [1974] E.C.R. 631, para. 47.

[324] ECJ, Case C-345/08 *Peśla* [2009] E.C.R. I-11677, paras 30 and 33.

[325] ECJ, Case C-393/05 *Commission v Austria* [2007] E.C.R. I-10195, paras 35–49; ECJ, Case C-404/05 *Commission v Germany* [2007] E.C.R. I-10239, paras 37–48; ECJ, Case C-438/08 *Commission v Portugal* [2009] E.C.R. I-10219, paras 36–37.

(c) Restrictions based on the rule of reason

Rule of reason. So long as the requirements for access to a given occupation have not been harmonised, Member States may themselves determine what knowledge and skills are needed in order to exercise it, and require diplomas or a professional qualification. The case law accepts that the obstacles to free movement of persons created by such requirements may be justified by public-interest requirements, provided that the restriction does not go beyond what is appropriate and indispensable in order to satisfy those requirements.[326] More generally, the Court of Justice declares—in terms similar to those employed in its case law on the movement of goods and services—that national measures liable to hinder or render less attractive the exercise of free movement of workers or self-employed persons may be compatible with the freedoms guaranteed by the Treaties if they satisfy the following conditions (rule of reason).[327]

9–074

(1) Absence of harmonisation. As was explained above, Member States can only invoke public-interest requirements to justify restrictions in matters that have not been harmonised at Union level.[328]

9–075

(2) Mandatory requirements. The measures must be justified by imperative requirements in the general interest. As regards measures governing the exercise of a professional activity, these may consist of rules relating to organisation, qualifications, professional ethics, supervision and liability[329] and with regard to the knowledge of languages required in order to exercise the professional activity.[330] More generally, however, obstacles to the free movement of persons may be justified to attain policy aims accepted by the case law in the areas of trade in goods and services, such as consumer protection,[331] protection of public

9–076

---

[326] See ECJ, Case 96/85 *Commission v France* [1986] E.C.R. 1475, para. 11 (self-employed persons); ECJ, Case C-204/90 *Bachmann* [1992] E.C.R. I-249, para. 28 (employees).

[327] For a list of the conditions, see ECJ, Case C-55/94 *Gebhard* [1995] E.C.R. I-4165, para. 37 (which refers to ECJ, Case C-19/92 *Kraus* [1993] E.C.R. I-1663, para. 32). See Tesauro, "The Community's Internal Market in the Light of the Recent Case-Law of the Court of Justice" (1995) Y.E.L. 1, at 7–10. Naturally, national measures must also comply with the fundamental rights of the persons concerned, see para. 22–026.

[328] ECJ, Case C-299/02 *Commission v Netherlands* [2004] E.C.R. I-9761, para. 17.

[329] ECJ, Case C-55/94 *Gebhard* [1995] E.C.R. I-4165, para. 35, following ECJ, Case 71/76 *Thieffry* [1977] E.C.R. 765, para. 12. See also ECJ, Case C-340/89 *Vlassopoulou* [1991] E.C.R. I-2357, para. 9 (ensuring that a person has the knowledge and skills required in order to pursue a particular occupation); ECJ, Case C-106/91 *Ramrath* [1992] E.C.R. I-3351, para. 35 (rules relating to the integrity and independence of auditors); ECJ, Case C-101/94 *Commission v Italy* [1996] E.C.R. I-2691, paras 19–24 (rules for the supervision of securities dealers); ECJ, Case C-19/92 *Kraus* [1993] E.C.R. I-1663, para. 35 (protection of the public against the unlawful use of academic titles).

[330] ECJ, Case C-424/97 *Haim* [2000] E.C.R. I-5123, paras 50–61.

[331] ECJ, Case C-204/90 *Bachmann* [1992] E.C.R. I-249, para. 16.

health,[332] road traffic safety[333] and the protection of victims of road traffic accidents,[334] effectiveness of fiscal controls,[335] the prevention of tax avoidance[336] and abusive practices[337] and the need to preserve the cohesion of the tax system[338] (but not avoiding loss of tax revenue[339] or administrative considerations,[340]) the need to avoid the risk of seriously undermining the financial balance of the social security system,[341] overriding requirements relating to the general interest, such as the protection of the interests of creditors, minority shareholders, employees or the taxation authorities[342] and the encouragement of employment,[343] including measures for the protection of jobs and conditions of employment of the members of a trade union[344] or the maintenance of employment in small and

---

[332] ECJ, Case 96/85 *Commission v France* [1986] E.C.R. I-1475, para. 10. It is for the Member States to determine the level of protection which they wish to afford to public health and the way in which that level is to be achieved. Since the level may vary from one Member State to another, Member States must be allowed discretion (ECJ, Case C-322/01 *Deutscher Apothekerverband* [2003] E.C.R. I-14887, para. 103; ECJ, Case C-169/07 *Hartlauer* [2009] E.C.R. I-1721, para. 30; ECJ, Case C-531/06 *Commission v Italy* [2009] E.C.R. ECJ, Case C-531/06 *Commission v Italy* [2009] E.C.R. I-4103, paras 44–45, para. 35; ECJ, Joined Cases C-171/07 and C-172/07 *Apothekerkammer des Saarlandes and Others* [2009] E.C.R. I-4171, para. 19); ECJ (judgment of June 1, 2010), Joined Cases C-570/07 and C-571/07 *Blanco Pérez and Chao Gómez*, not yet reported, para. 44.

[333] ECJ, Case C-246/00 *Commission v Netherlands* [2003] E.C.R. I-7485, para. 67.

[334] ECJ, Case C-518/06 *Commission v Italy* [2009] E.C.R. I-3491, para. 74.

[335] ECJ, Case C-204/90 *Bachmann* [1992] E.C.R. I-249, para. 18 (see also the parallel judgment of the same date, ECJ, Case C-300/90 *Commission v Belgium* [1992] E.C.R. I-305, para. 11); ECJ, Case C-264/96 *ICI* [1998] E.C.R. I-4695, para. 26.

[336] ECJ, Case C-446/03 *Marks & Spencer* [2005] E.C.R. I-10837, paras 49–56; ECJ, Case C-231/05 *Oy AA* [2007] E.C.R. I-6373, para. 58. In this context, the Court also referred to the need to safeguard the balanced allocation of the power to impose taxes between the Member States (ECJ, Case C-446/03 *Marks & Spencer* [2005] E.C.R. I-10837, paras 43–46), a ground of justification which needs to be assessed in conjunction with other grounds, such as the prevention of tax avoidance (see, e.g., ECJ, Case C-347/04 *Rewe Zentralfinanz* [2007] E.C.R. I-2647, paras 39–44 and ECJ, Case C-231/05 *Oy AA* [2007] E.C.R. I-6373, paras 51–56).

[337] ECJ, Case C-196/04 *Cadbury Schweppes* [2006] E.C.R. I-7995, paras 55–56.

[338] ECJ, Case C-204/90 *Bachmann* [1992] E.C.R. I-249, para. 21, and ECJ, Case C-300/90 *Commission v Belgium* [1992] E.C.R. I-305, para. 14 (where this ground was accepted as a justification); ECJ, Case C-264/96 *ICI* [1998] E.C.R. I-4695, para. 29 (where this ground was not accepted as a justification).

[339] ECJ, Case C-264/96 *ICI* [1998] E.C.R. I-4695, para. 28.

[340] ECJ, Case C-18/95 *Terhoeve* [1999] E.C.R. I-345, paras 44–45 (the aim of simplifying and coordinating the levying of taxes and contributions is not a justification).

[341] ECJ, Case C-158/96 *Kohll* [1998] E.C.R. I-1931, para 41; ECJ, Case C-208/05 *ITC* [2007] E.C.R. I-181, para. 43.

[342] ECJ, Case C-208/00 *Überseering* [2002] E.C.R. I-9919, para. 92.

[343] ECJ, Case C-208/05 *ITC* [2007] E.C.R. I-181, para. 39.

[344] ECJ, Case C-438/05 *International Transport Workers' Federation and Finnish Seamen's Union* [2007] E.C.R. I-10779, paras 77–89.

medium-sized undertakings in the event of succession,[345] the protection of an established right, such as the retention of patients following several years of professional activity,[346] maintaining or promoting the use of an official language,[347] preserving or improving the education system,[348] and, in view of the social importance of sport, maintaining a balance between football clubs and supporting the search for talent and the training of young players[349] and respecting fundamental rights.[350] Sometimes, the Court finds a restriction justified in the light of a number of imperative requirements, taken together.[351]

(3) Application without distinction. The measures must be applied in a non-discriminatory manner from the point of view of nationality (even if they are indirectly discriminatory).[352]

9–077

(4) Proportionality. Lastly, there is the requirement for proportionality: the measures must be appropriate for achieving the aim sought and must not exceed what is necessary in order to attain that aim. National measures are appropriate for securing attainment of the objective relied upon only if they genuinely reflect a concern to attain that objective in a consistent and systematic manner.[353] In

9–078

---

[345] ECJ, Case C-464/05 *Geurts and Vogten* [2007] E.C.R. I-9325, paras 25–26.

[346] ECJ, Case C-456/05 *Commission v Germany* [2007] E.C.R. I-10517, para. 63.

[347] ECJ, Case C-379/87 *Groener* [1989] E.C.R. 3967, para. 19; ECJ, Case C-222/07 *UTECA* [2009] E.C.R. I-1407, para. 27.

[348] ECJ, Case C-40/05 *Lyyski* [2007] E.C.R. I-99, paras 39–40.

[349] ECJ, Case C-415/93 *Bosman* [1995] E.C.R. I-4921, paras 106–110 (transfer fees not appropriate for achieving these aims); ECJ, Case C-325/08 *Olympique Lyonnais* (n. 177, *supra*), paras 39–48 (compensation for clubs must not go beyond what is necessary to encourage recruitment of young players and to fund those activities).

[350] ECJ, Case C-112/00 *Schmidberger* [2003] E.C.R. I-5659, paras 71–74 (the case concerns free movement of goods, but refers generally to "a fundamental freedom guaranteed by the Treaty"); ECJ, Case C-438/05 *International Transport Workers' Federation and Finnish Seamen's Union* [2007] E.C.R. I-10779, para. 45.

[351] ECJ, Case C-446/03 *Marks & Spencer* [2005] E.C.R. I-10837, paras 41–51, with a case note by Schiller (2006) EuR. 275–284; ECJ, Case C-231/05 *Oy AA* [2007] E.C.R. I-6373, paras 51–60.

[352] For this expression, see para. 7–062, *supra* and ECJ, Case C-451/03 *Servizi Ausiliari Dottori Commercialisti* [2006] E.C.R. I-2941, paras 36–37. Most instances which have arisen before the Court of Justice have been concerned with national measures which, albeit not making any distinction as to nationality, nevertheless place nationals of other Member States indirectly at a disadvantage. Sometimes the Court uses the expression "indirect discrimination" to denote more specifically the type of measures which cannot be justified in the case at issue, *cf.* ECJ, Case C-237/94 *O'Flynn* [1996] E.C.R. I-2617, paras 18–20.

[353] ECJ, Case C-106/91 *Ramrath* [1992] E.C.R. I-3351, paras 29–31; ECJ, Joined Cases C-338/04, C-359/04 and C-360/04 *Placanica and Others* [2007] E.C.R. I-1891, paras 53 and 58; ECJ, Case C-169/07 *Hartlauer* [2009] E.C.R. I-1721, para. 55; ECJ, Case C-42/07 *Liga Portuguesa de Futebol Profissional and Bwin International Ltd* [2009] E.C.R. I-7633, para. 61; ECJ, Case C-531/06 *Commission v Italy* [2009] E.C.R. ECJ, Case C-531/06 *Commission v Italy* [2009] E.C.R. I-4103, paras 44–45, para. 66.

order not to exceed what is necessary to attain such objective, in processing applications for recognition of foreign diplomas and vocational qualifications, the national authorities must inquire into the equivalence of the knowledge and qualifications obtained abroad (see para. 9–081). By the same token, the Court of Justice declared, with regard to a requirement to have a second language, that although the requirement for applicants to show that they had the requisite level of linguistic knowledge through possession of a diploma could be legitimate, the fact that it was impossible to submit proof of the required linguistic knowledge by means other than one particular diploma issued only in one particular province of a Member State must be considered disproportionate in relation to the aim in view.[354] Furthermore, a public body recruiting staff for posts or assessing seniority for personnel which takes account of previous employment in the public service may not make a distinction according to whether such employment was in the public service of the particular State or in the public service of another Member State.[355] Where the measure at issue constitutes an obstacle to free movement without being directly discriminatory, the assessment as to whether it is proportionate character may take the place of any inquiry into the existence of discrimination.[356] However, where a Member State subjects an economic activity to certain requirements, the fact that another Member State imposes less strict rules does not automatically mean that the first Member State's rules are disproportionate.[357]

It is up to the Member State which relies on an imperative requirement to justify a restriction to demonstrate that its rules are appropriate and necessary to attain the legitimate objective being pursued. However, that burden of proof is not so extensive that it requires the Member State to prove, positively, that no other conceivable measure could enable that objective to be attained under the same conditions.[358]

5. Harmonisation and recognition of professional rules

9–079   **Harmonisation.** Freedom of establishment is made more difficult by rules which differ from one Member State to another and are applicable without distinction to

---

[354] ECJ, Case C-281/98 *Angonese* [2000] E.C.R. I-4139, paras 37–46.

[355] ECJ, Case C-419/92 *Scholz* [1994] E.C.R. I-505, paras 11–12; ECJ, Case C-15/96 *Schöning-Kougebetopoulou* [1998] E.C.R. I-47, paras 21–28; ECJ, Case C-187/96 *Commission v Greece* [1998] E.C.R. I-1095, paras 17–23; Case C-195/98 *Österreichischer Gewerkschaftsbund—Gewerkschaft öffentlicher Dienst* [2000] E.C.R. I-10497, paras 33–51; ECJ, Case C-224/01 *Köbler* [2003] E.C.R. I-10239, paras 70–87.

[356] Huglo, "Droit d'établissment et libre prestation des services" (1993) R.T.D.E. 655, at 660–662. See also ECJ, Case C-111/91 *Commission v Luxembourg* [1993] E.C.R. I-817, paras 9–18, where proportionality was weighed in the balance in considering indirect discrimination.

[357] ECJ, Case C-108/96 *Mac Quen and Others* [2001] E.C.R. I-837, paras 33–34; ECJ, Case C-294/00 *Deutsche Paracelsus Schulen für Naturheilverfahren* [2002] E.C.R. I-6515, paras 44–50. See also the case law on the provision of services, para. 9–098, *infra*.

[358] ECJ, Case C-518/06 *Commission v Italy* [2009] E.C.R. I-3491, para. 84.

nationals and to subjects of other Member States. Article 50 TFEU [*ex Art. 44 EC*] makes provision for harmonisation of such rules. Accordingly, the Council adopted a series of directives pursuant to Art. 44(2)(g) EC [*now Art. 50(2)(g) TFEU*]—since the entry into force of the EU Treaty, acting with the European Parliament under what is now the ordinary legislative procedure—on the harmonisation of the law relating to the stock exchange[359] and company law.[360] In 2001

---

[359] The directives adopted by the Council pursuant to Art. 44 EC [*now Art. 50 TFEU*] have since been replaced by directives adopted by the European Parliament and the Council pursuant to Art. 95 EC [*now Art. 114 TFEU*] (in some cases in combination with Art. 44 EC [*now Art. 50 TFEU*]): Directive 2001/34/EC of May 28, 2001 on the admission of securities to official stock exchange listing and on information to be published on those securities, [2001] O.J. L184/1, Directive 2003/6/EC of January 28, 2003 on insider dealing and market manipulation (market abuse), [2003] O.J. L96/16 and Directive 2003/71/EC of November 4, 2003 on the prospectus to be published when securities are offered to the public or admitted to trading and amending Directive 2001/34/EC, [2003] O.J. L345/64; see also Directive 2004/25/EC of April 21, 2004 on takeover bids, [2004] O.J. L142/12, based on Art. 44 EC [*now Art. 50 TFEU*]. The Council has further adopted, on the basis of Art. 47(2) EC [*now Art. 53(1) TFEU*], Directive 85/611/EEC of December 20, 1985 (collective investment undertakings), [1985] L375/3, Directive 93/6/EEC of March 15, 1993 (capital adequacy of investments firms and credit institutions), [1993] O.J. L141/1, and Directive 2004/39/EC of April 21, 2004 (markets in financial instruments), [2004] O.J. L145/1. Further coordination of the securities markets has since been taking place in accordance with a new approach whereby the competent authorities consult with each other in a Committee of European Securities Regulators and a European Securities Committee; see Commission Decisions 2001/527/EC and 2001/528/EC of June 6, 2001, [2001] O.J. L191/43 and L191/45, respectively) and Vaccari, "Le processus Lamfalussy: une réussite pour la comitologie et un exemple de 'bonne gouvernance européenne' " (2005) R.D.U.E. 803–821; Janin, "Le premier cas pratique d'approche 'Lamfalussy'—Les mesures d'exécution de la directive sur les opérations d'initiés et les manipulations de marché (abus de marché)" (2003) R.M.C.U.E. 658–669; Moloney, "New Frontiers in EC Capital Markets Law: From Market Construction to Market Regulation" (2003) C.M.L.Rev. 809–843; Berger and Altemir Mergelina, "Un nouveau système de régulation communautaire des marchés de valeurs mobilières dans l'Union européenne" (2001) R.M.C.U.E. 529–534.

[360] See the First Directive (68/151/EEC) of March 9, 1968, [1968] O.J. English Spec. Ed. (I) 41; the Second Directive (77/91/EEC) of December 13, 1976 (formation and alteration of capital), [1977] O.J. L26/1; the Fourth Directive (78/660/EEC) of July 25, 1978 (annual accounts), [1978] O.J. L222/11; the Third Directive (78/855/EEC) of October 9, 1978 (mergers), [1978] O.J. L295/36; the Sixth Directive (82/891/EEC) of December 17, 1982 (division of companies), [1982] O.J. L378/47; the Seventh Directive (83/349/EEC) of June 13, 1983 (consolidated annual accounts), [1983] O.J. L193/1; the Eighth Directive (84/253/EEC) of April 10, 1984 (auditing), [1984] O.J. L126/20; the Eleventh Directive (89/666/EEC) of December 21, 1989 (disclosure requirements of branches of foreign companies), [1989] O.J. L395/36; the Twelfth Directive (89/667/EEC) of December 21, 1989 (single-member companies), [1989] O.J. L395/40. See also the directives adopted pursuant to Art. 94 EC [*now Art. 115 TFEU*], 90/434/EEC and 90/435/EEC of July 23, 1990 (tax treatment of mergers, divisions and parent/subsidiary companies, respectively), [1990] O.J. L25/1 and L25/6. See Dorresteijn, *European Corporate Law* (The Hague, Kluwer Law International, 2008), 328 pp.; Grundmann and Möslein, *European company law: organization, finance and capital markets* (Antwerp, Intersentia, 2007), 807 pp. For a general assessment, see Deakin, "Reflexive Governance and European Company Law" (2009) 15 E.L.J. 224–245; Grundmann, "The Structure of European Company Law: From Crisis to Boom" (2004) E.Bus.Org.L.R. 601–633; Winter, "EU Company Law on the Move" (2004) L.I.E.I. 97–114.

a European form of company, the Societas Europea (SE), was introduced under Art. 308 EC [*now Art. 352 TFEU*] which allows companies incorporated under the laws of different Member States to merge or to set up a holding company or a common subsidiary.[361] In 2003, the Council, acting under the same article of the Treaty, made it possible for natural or legal persons coming under the laws of different Member States to establish a European Cooperative Society (SCE).[362]

In order to "make it easier" for self-employed activities to be taken up and pursued, the Council (acting with the Parliament under the ordinary legislative procedure) is empowered to adopt directives for the mutual recognition of diplomas, certificates and other evidence of formal qualifications and for the coordination of provisions concerning the taking-up and pursuit of activities as self-employed persons (Art. 53(1)). Accordingly, some Council directives aim at ensuring that pursuit of an occupation in a Member State for a certain period is accepted as sufficient evidence that the person concerned has the knowledge and competence to carry on that occupation in another Member State.[363] In the banking and insurance sectors, directives have resulted in a substantial liberalisation of the right of establishment (on the basis of Art. 47 EC [*now Art. 53 TFEU*]) and of the supply

---

[361] Council Regulation (EC) No. 2157/2001 of October 8, 2001 on the Statute for a European company (SE), [2001] O.J. L294/1, as supplemented by Council Directive 2001/86/EC of October 8, 2001 with regard to the involvement of employees, [2001] O.J. L294/22. See McCahery, "Does the European company prevent the 'Delaware effect' " (2005) 11 E.L.J. 785–801; Edwards, "The European Company—Essential Tool or Reviscerated Dream?" (2003) C.M.L.Rev. 443–464; Blanquet, "Enfin la société européenne" (2001) R.D.U.E. 65–109, and "La société européenne n'est plus un mythe" (2001) R.D.I.D.C. 139–170; Fouassier, "Le statut de la 'société européenne': Un nouvel instrument juridique au service des entreprises" (2001) R.M.C.U.E. 85–88; Roelvink, "De Europese vennootschap na Nice" (2001) S.E.W. 162–165; Hopt, "The European Company (SE) under the Nice Compromise: Major Breakthrough or Small Coin for Europe?" (2000) Euredia 465–475.

[362] Council Regulation (EC) No. 1435/2003 of July 22, 2003 on the Statute for a European Cooperative Society (SCE), [2003] O.J. L207/1, as supplemented by Council Directive 2003/72/EC of July 22, 2003 with regard to the involvement of employees, [2003] O.J. L207/25. This regulation was validly adopted under Art. 308 EC [*now Art. 352 TFEU*]: see ECJ, Case C-436/03 *European Parliament v Council* [2006] E.C.R. I-3733, with a case note by Gutman (2006) 13 Col.J.E.L.147–187.

[363] See, for instance, Council Directive 64/427/EEC of July 7, 1964 laying down detailed provisions concerning transitional measures in respect of activities of self-employed persons in manufacturing and processing industries falling within ISIC Major Groups 23–40 (Industry and small craft industries), [1963–1964] O.J. English Spec. Ed. 148. See the judgment in *Knoors*, para. 7–065, *supra*. For an attempt at simplifying and amending these rules, see Directive 1999/42/EC of the European Parliament and of the Council of June 7, 1999 establishing a mechanism for the recognition of qualifications in respect of the professional activities covered by the Directives on liberalisation and transitional measures and supplementing the general systems for the recognition of qualifications, [1999] O.J. L201/77 (corrigendum in [2002] O.J. L23/48). See Fouassier, "Une tentative de simplification et d'amélioration de la législation communautaire: la directive 1999/42/CE relative à la reconnaissance mutuelle des qualifications professionnelles" (2000) R.M.C.U.E. 601–608.

of services[364] (on the basis of Art. 47 EC in conjunction with Art. 55 EC [*now Art. 62 TFEU*]).[365]

Mutual recognition of diplomas. In some sectors, the Council has adopted   **9–080** directives dealing with the mutual recognition of diplomas with a view to access to an occupation (not "academic" recognition) for both employed and self-employed persons (as a result of which Art. 40 EC [*now Art. 46 TFEU*] serves as the legal basis for these directives, alongside Art. 47(1) EC [*now Art. 53(1)*

---

[364] See also the discussion of free movement of services, paras 5–085—5–098, *infra*.

[365] See Directive 2000/12/EC of the European Parliament and of the Council of March 20, 2000 relating to the taking up and pursuit of the business of credit institutions, [2000] O.J. L126/1, codifying, inter alia, Directive 73/183/EEC of June 28, 1973, [1973] O.J. L194/1, and the coordinating directives, 77/780/EEC of December 12, 1977, [1977] O.J. L322/30, and Directive 89/646/EEC of December 15, 1989, [1989] O.J. L386/1. See Alpa, "The Harmonisation of the EC Law of Financial Markets in the Perspective of Consumer Protection" (2002) E.Bus.L.Rev. 523–540; Moreiro Gonzalez, "La codification de la réglementation communautaire relative à l'activité des établissements de credit et son exercice" (2001) R.T.D.E. 529–550; Garcia Collados, "La codification des directives bancaires" (2000) Euredia 313–319; Strivens, "The Liberalisation of Banking Services in the Community" (1992) C.M.L.Rev. 283–307. For the application of the rule of reason in this connection, see the Commission interpretative communication, Freedom to provide services and the interest of the general good in the Second Banking Directive, [1997] O.J. C209/6. See also Directive 94/19/EC of the European Parliament and the Council of May 30, 1994 on deposit-guarantee schemes, [1994] O.J. L135/5, and Directive 2000/46/EC of the European Parliament and of the Council of September 18, 2000 on the taking up, pursuit of and prudential supervision of the business of electronic money institutions, [2000] O.J. L275/39. For electronic commerce, see Roeges, "Quelques réflexions critiques sur le cadre légal pour la libre prestation de services bancaires et financiers" (2000) Euredia 149–156. A new approach is now being applied to coordinating supervision of the banking and insurance sectors (as for the securities industry: see n.359, *supra*), involving consultation through the Committee of European Banking Supervisors, the Committee of European Insurance and Occupational Pensions Supervisors, the European Banking Committee and the European Insurance and Occupational Pensions Committee, all of which were set up by Commission Decisions of November 5, 2003 ([2004] O.J. L3/28 to L3/36); see also Mogg, "Regulating Financial Services in Europe: A New Approach" (2002) Fordham I.L.J. 58–82. For the liberalisation of insurance, see, as regards establishment, the "first generation" coordination directives 73/239/EEC of July 24, 1973 (indemnity insurance), [1973] O.J. L228/3, and 79/267/EEC of March 5, 1979 (life assurance), [1979] O.J. L63/1; as regards the supply of services, the "second generation" coordinating directives 88/357/EEC of June 22, 1988 (indemnity insurance), [1988] O.J. L172/1, and 90/619/EEC of November 8, 1990 (life assurance), [1990] O.J. L330/50, and the "third generation" directives 92/49/EEC of June 18, 1992 (indemnity insurance), [1992] O.J. L228/1, and 92/96/EEC of November 10, 1992 (life assurance), [1992] O.J. L360/1. The provisions on life assurance were revised by Directive 2002/83/EC of the European Parliament and the Council of November 5, 2002, [2002] O.J. L345/1. See also Directive 2001/17/EC of the European Parliament and of the Council of March 19, 2001 on the reorganisation and winding-up of insurance undertakings, [2001] O.J. L110/28, and Directive 2002/92/EC of the European Parliament and of the Council of December 9, 2002 on insurance mediation, [2003] O.J. L9/3. The emergence of financial groups offering services and products in various financial sectors led to the need for appropriate supervision, resulting in Directive 2002/87/EC of the European Parliament and of the Council of December 16, 2002 on the supplementary supervision of credit institutions, insurance undertakings and investment firms in a financial conglomerate, [2003] O.J. L35/1.

TFEU]. They were aimed at medical and paramedical diplomas[366] and architects' diplomas.[367] Directive 89/48 of December 21, 1988, which introduced a general system for the recognition of higher-education diplomas awarded on completion of at least three years' professional education and training[368] marked the abandonment of the sectoral approach.

Those directives have now been replaced by Directive 2005/36/EC on the recognition of professional qualifications,[369] which had to be transposed by October 20, 2007 at the latest (Art. 63). Directive 2005/36 applies to nationals of a Member State wishing to pursue a regulated profession in a Member State, including those belonging to the liberal professions, other than that in which they obtained their professional qualifications, on either a self-employed or employed basis (Art. 1(2)). A profession must be regarded as regulated where access to, or pursuit of, the professional activity in question is governed by legal provisions requiring possession of certain professional qualifications.[370] The recognition of professional qualifications by the host Member State allows the beneficiary to gain access in that Member

---

[366] In the case of a number of medical and paramedical diplomas, each directive on mutual recognition was coupled with a directive coordinating the study curricula. Doctors: Directives 75/362/EEC and 75/363/EEC of June 16, 1975, [1975] O.J. L167/1 and L167/14, together with Directive 84/457/EEC of September 15, 1986 (training in general medical practice), which were repealed and replaced by (one) Directive 93/16/EEC of April 5, 1993, [1993] O.J. L165/1; nurses: Directives 77/452/EEC and 77/453/EEC of June 27, 1977, [1977] O.J. L176/1 and L176/8; dental practitioners: Directives 78/686/EEC and 78/687/EEC of July 25, 1978, [1978] O.J. L233/1 and L233/10; veterinary surgeons: Directives 78/1026/EEC and 78/1027/EEC of December 18, 1978, [1978] O.J. L362/1 and L362/7; midwives: Directives 80/154/EEC and 80/155/EEC of January 21, 1980, [1980] O.J. L33/1 and L33/8; pharmacists: Directives 85/432/EEC and 85/433/EEC of September 16, 1985, [1985] O.J. L253/34 and L253/37.

[367] Directive 85/384/EEC of June 10, 1985, [1985] O.J. L223/15.

[368] Council Directive 89/48/EEC of December 21, 1988 on a general system for the recognition of higher-education diplomas awarded on completion of professional education and training of at least three years' duration, [1989] O.J. L19/16, supplemented by Council Directive 92/51/EEC of June 18, 1992 on a second general system for the recognition of professional education and training, [1992] O.J. L209/25. For the difference between this and the sectoral approach based on minimum harmonisation of training, see ECJ, Case C-110/01 *Tennah-Durez* [2003] E.C.R. I-6239, paras 29–81. For a survey, see Pertek (ed.), *La reconnaissance des qualifications dans un espace européen des formations et des professions* (Brussels, Bruylant, 1998), 370 pp.; Obwexer and Happacher Brezinka, "The Recognition of Diplomas within the Internal Market" (2000/01) Eur.L.F. 377–386; Favret, "Le système général de reconnaissance des diplômes et des formations professionnelles en droit communautaire: l'esprit et la méthode. Règles actuelles et développements futurs" (1996) R.T.D.E. 259–280; Pertek, "Une dynamique de la reconnaissance des diplômes à des fins professionnelles et à des fins académiques: réalisations et nouvelles réflexions" (1996) R.M.U.E. 89–176.

[369] Directive 2005/36/EC of the European Parliament and of the Council of September 7, 2005 on the recognition of professional qualifications, [2005] O.J. L255/22.

[370] ECJ, Case C-313/01 *Morgenbesser* [2003] E.C.R. I-13467 (under Directive 89/48); ECJ (judgment of December 17, 2009), Case C-586/08 *Rubino*, not yet reported (under Directive 2005/36). Employment in the public service may also constitute a regulated profession where access thereto is dependent upon passing a final examination after at least three years' training: ECJ, Case C-285/01 *Burbaud* [2003] E.C.R. I-8219, paras 38–58 (this applies even where the final examination leads to an appointment to a permanent post without the award of a formal diploma).

State to the same profession for which he or she is qualified in the home Member State and to pursue it in the host Member State under the same conditions as its nationals (Art. 4). The Directive proceeds on the basis of the principles of minimum harmonisation and reciprocal recognition set out in the Commission's White Paper (see para. 9–111). In respect of certain activities related to industry, small craft industries and trade, it provides for automatic recognition of professional experience as sufficient proof of a professional qualification.[371] In respect of doctors, nurses responsible for general care, dental practitioners, veterinary surgeons, pharmacists and architects, the Directive provides for harmonised minimum training conditions. Qualifications that satisfy these conditions have to be automatically recognised by other Member States.[372] In respect of other professions, the Directive provides for a general system whereby Member States must recognise professional qualifications obtained in another Member State, but it allows the host Member State to require evidence of professional experience where the duration of the education and training in the other Member State is shorter, or completion of an adaptation period or aptitude test where the education and training received in the other Member State differs substantially in respect of the matters covered.[373] The Directive does not affect the operation of the specific directives concerning the provision of services by and the establishment of lawyers[374] because those directives do not concern the recognition of professional qualifications, but rather the recognition of the right to practise.[375] The recognition of professional qualifications for

---

[371] See Title III, Chapter II, of the Directive and Annex IV thereto.

[372] See Title III, Chapter III, of the Directive and Annex V thereto. Poland brought an unsuccesful action for annulment against a number of these provisions of the Directive (ECJ, Case C-460/05 *Poland v European Parliament and Council* [2007] E.C.R. I-102). Since a diploma obtained in a non-member country does not necessarily satisfy the harmonised minimum requirements, a Member State does not automatically have to recognise it—not even if other Member States do: ECJ, Case C-154/93 *Tawil-Albertini* [1994] E.C.R. I-451, paras 11–13.

[373] See Title III, Chapter I, of the Directive. However, where the fields of activity covered by a profession in a Member State greatly differ from those covered in the host Member State, the latter may be obliged to allow a holder of a diploma awarded in the first Member State partially to take up a profession (i.e. limited to those fields of activity covered in both Member States) without imposing compensatory measures (ECJ, Case C-330/03 *Colegio de Ingenieros* [2006] E.C.R. I-801, paras 35–39).

[374] Directive 98/5/EC of the European Parliament and of the Council of February 16, 1998 to facilitate practice of the profession of lawyer on a permanent basis in a Member State other than that in which the qualification was obtained, [1998] O.J. L77/36. The Court of Justice upheld the validity of that directive in Case C-168/98 *Luxembourg v European Parliament and Council* [2000] E.C.R. I-9131. See also the earlier Council Directive 77/249/EEC of March 22, 1977 to facilitate the effective exercise by lawyers of freedom to provide services, [1977] O.J. L78/17. See Pertek, "L'Europe des professions d'avocat après la directive 98/5 sur l'exercice permanent dans un autre Etat membre" (2001) R.M.C.U.E. 106–111; Dal and Defalque, "La directive 'établissement avocats' 98/5/CE du 16 février 1998" (1999) J.T. 693–695. See also Nascimbene, with the collaboration of Bergamini, *The Legal Profession in the European Union* (The Hague, Kluwer Law International, 2009), 247 pp.

[375] Directive 98/5 concerns only lawyers who are fully qualified to practise the profession of a lawyer in their Member State of origin (ECJ, Case C-313/01 *Morgenbesser* [2003] E.C.R. I-13467, para. 45).

lawyers for the purpose of immediate establishment under the professional title of the host Member State *is* covered by Directive 2005/36/EC.

9–081 **Comparison of qualifications.** The national authorities are generally obliged to examine to what extent the knowledge and qualifications attested by a diploma obtained in another Member State correspond to those required by its own rules.[376] The obligation to compare abilities already acquired with the knowledge and qualifications required by the national rules also applies with regard to persons in possession of a diploma in an area for which a directive on the mutual recognition of diplomas has been adopted but who, nevertheless, cannot rely on the automatic recognition introduced by the directive in question.[377] If the diplomas correspond only partially, the national authorities in question are entitled to require the person to prove that he or she has acquired the knowledge and qualifications which are lacking.[378] In the case of the profession of a lawyer, a Member State may thus carry out a comparative examination of diplomas taking account of the differences identified between the legal system of the Member State of origin and that of the host Member State.[379]

The mutual-recognition directives ensure admission to the selection and recruitment procedures for a regulated profession, but do not themselves afford any right to be recruited.[380] However, it is contrary to the Treaty provisions on free movement of persons for a recruitment procedure to require a person to pass an examination giving access to training organised by the State where that procedure does not enable account to be taken of qualifications that a candidate has already obtained in another Member State by completing such training.[381]

---

[376] ECJ, Case 222/86 *Heylens* [1987] E.C.R. 4097, paras 10–13 (access to gainful employment, as a football trainer); ECJ, Case C-340/89 *Vlassopoulou* [1991] E.C.R. I-2357, paras 9–21 (access to self-employment, as a lawyer). See also ECJ, Case C-19/92 *Kraus* [1993] E.C.R. I-1663, paras 32–38 (authorisation required in order to use the title LL.M. obtained in another Member State, para. 9–065, *supra*).

[377] See ECJ, Case C-238/98 *Hocsman* [2000] E.C.R. I-6623, para. 23 (diploma obtained in a non-member country); ECJ, Case C-31/00 *Dreessen* [2002] E.C.R. I-663, para. 28 (the diploma fell outside the scope of the directive); ECJ, Case C-313/01 *Morgenbesser* [2003] E.C.R. I-13467, paras 54–61 (diploma of *maîtrise en droit* does not give access to the Bar and, therefore, does not constitute a diploma, certificate or other evidence of formal qualifications within the meaning of Directive 89/48). See also ECJ, Case C-232/99 *Commission v Spain* [2002] E.C.R. I-4235, paras 18–41.

[378] ECJ, Case C-340/89 *Vlassopoulou* [1991] E.C.R. I-2357, paras 16–23, in which the Court of Justice applied the principles of Directive 89/48 to facts dating back to before the end of the period prescribed for implementing the directive. See, to the same effect, ECJ, Case C-234/97 *Fernández de Bobadilla* [1999] E.C.R. I-4773; ECJ, Case C-313/01 *Morgenbesser* [2003] E.C.R. I-13467, paras 62–72.

[379] ECJ, Case C-340/89 *Vlassopoulou* [1991] E.C.R. I-2357, para. 18; ECJ, Case C-345/08 *Peśla* (n. 324, *supra*), paras 42–48.

[380] The fact that a person has been successful in a recruitment examination in one Member State does not entitle that person to be recruited in another Member State: ECJ, Case C-285/01 *Burbaud* [2003] E.C.R. I-8219, paras 85–93.

[381] *Ibid.*, paras 94–112.

6. Social security and the free movement of persons

Coordination of social security systems. Article 48 TFEU [*ex Art. 42 EC*] **9–082** requires the Union legislation to adopt such measures in the field of social security as are necessary to provide freedom of movement for employed and self-employed migrant workers and their dependants. The article refers to arrangements to secure for them aggregation of all periods taken into account under the laws of the several countries for acquiring benefits and payment of benefits to persons resident in the territories of Member States. Such arrangements were been laid down in Regulation No. 1408/71 of June 14, 1971,[382] which has been replaced by Regulation No. 883/2004 of April 29, 2004.[383] Article 42 EC only covered migrant workers and their dependants. The Treaty of Lisbon extended the scope of application of the Treaty provisions for "migrant workers and their dependants" to "employed and self-employed migrant workers and their dependants". However, acting on the basis of Art. 308 EC [*now Art. 352 TFEU*], the Council had already extended the scope of Regulation No. 1408/71 to cover self-employed persons and members of their families,[384] students and special schemes for civil servants.[385] Regulation No. 883/2204, which was also been adopted on the basis of Art. 42 and Art. 308 EC [*now Art. 48* and *Art. 352 TFEU*], likewise applies to all nationals of a Member State, stateless persons and refugees resident in the territory of a Member State who are or have been subject to the social security legislation of one or more Member States, as well as to the members of their families and to their survivors.[386]

---

[382] Regulation (EEC) No. 1408/71 of the Council of June 14, 1971 on the application of social security schemes to employed persons and their families moving within the Community, [1971] O.J. English Spec. Ed. (II) 416, and the implementing Council Regulation No. 574/72 of March 21, 1972, [1972] O.J. English Spec. Ed. (I) 159. These regulations had been codified by Council Regulation (EC) No. 118/97 of December 2, 1996, [1997] O.J. L28/1.

[383] Regulation (EC) No. 883/2004 of the European Parliament and the Council of April 29, 2004 on the coordination of social security systems, [2004] O.J. L166/1; republished with *corrigendum*: [2004] O.J. L200/1. See Pennings, "The European Commission Proposal to Simplify Regulation 1408/71" (2001) Eur.J.Soc.Sec. 45–60.

[384] Council Regulation (EEC) No. 1390/81 of May 12, 1981, [1981] O.J. L143/1.

[385] Council Regulation (EC) No. 1606/98 of June 29, 1998, [1998] O.J. L209/1, and Council Regulation (EC) No. 307/1999 of February 8, 1999, [1999] O.J. L38/1. Civil servants' supplementary pension rights are covered by Council Directive 98/49/EC of June 29, 1998 on safeguarding the supplementary pension rights of employed and self-employed persons moving within the Community, [1998] O.J. L209/46. See also the extension of Regulations Nos 1408/71 and 574/72 pursuant to Art.63(4) EC to nationals of third countries legally resident in the territory of the Member States: Council Regulation (EC) No. 859/2003 of May 14, 2003, [2003] O.J. L124/1.

[386] See also the extension of Regulations Nos 883/2004 and 987/2009 pursuant to Art. 79(2)(b) TFEU to nationals of third countries legally resident in the territory of the Member States: Regulation (EU) No. 1231/2010 of 27 November 2010 of the European Parliament and the Council, [2010] O.J. L344/1. As to Regulation No. 1408/71, the Court of Justice held that stateless persons and refugees also fell within that regulation in view of the international obligations incumbent on Member States to treat stateless persons and refugees in the same way as their own nationals for the purposes of social security: ECJ, Joined Cases C-95/99 to C-98/99 and C-180/99 *Khalil and Others* [2001] E.C.R. I-7413, paras 39–58. See Baquero Cruz, "Khalil e.a.: Les réfugiés et les apatrides face au droit communautaire" (2002) C.D.E. 501–516.

According to this regulation, these persons retain rights which they have acquired in one Member State, with benefits being paid elsewhere in the Union.[387] The Regulation also entitles them to enjoy the same benefits as nationals of the host State (Art. 4 of Regulation No. 883/2004; see previously Art. 3(1) of Regulation No. 1408/71). Acceptance of an employment relationship in another Member State therefore has no (or only minimal) adverse effect on the social security status of the worker concerned. The Regulation enshrines the principle that a worker is to be subject to the legislation of a single Member State only, and indicates by means of a number of conflict-of-law rules what legislation is to be applicable (Title II of Regulation No. 883/2004). Title III of the Regulation sets out specific provisions relating to different sorts of benefits, namely: sickness, maternity and equivalent paternity benefits, benefits in respect of accidents at work and occupational diseases, death grants, invalidity benefits, old-age and survivors' pensions, unemployment benefits, pre-retirement benefits, family benefits and special non-contributory cash benefits. However, the Court held, as regards Regulation No. 1408/71, that it did not apply to situations which are confined in all respects within a single Member State.[388]

Article 48 TFEU requires the European Parliament and the Council to adopt measures in accordance with the ordinary legislative procedure. The Treaty of Lisbon removed in this connection the requirement for the Council to act unanimously throughout the procedure. However, it introduced a safeguard clause according to which any Member State which considers that a draft legislative act would affect important aspects of its social security system or the financial balance of that system, may request that the matter be referred to the European Council (Art. 48, second para., TFEU).[389] In that event, the European Council can either refer the draft back to the Council or take no action or request the Commission to submit a new proposal.

---

[387] As a sample of the extensive case law on the content of entitlements acquired and the calculation thereof, see ECJ, Case 21/75 *Petroni* [1975] E.C.R. 1149, paras 10–21 (pensions); ECJ, Case 320/82 *D'Amario* [1983] E.C.R. 3811, paras 4–10 (orphans' benefits); ECJ, Case 242/83 *Patteri* [1984] E.C.R. 3171, paras 7–11 (family allowances); ECJ, Case C-131/96 *Mora Romero* [1997] E.C.R. I-3659, paras 27–36 (legislation providing for payment of orphan's benefit to be extended for a period equal to the duration of military service also has to be applied where the military service was carried out by a national of another Member State in that State).

[388] ECJ, Joined Cases C-95/99 to C-98/99 and C-180/99 *Khalil and Others* [2001] E.C.R. I-7413, paras 39–58. For a critical view, see Mavridis, "La sécurité sociale et les promesses des droits fondamentaux dans l'Union européenne" (2002) C.D.E. 643–677.

[389] See also Declaration (No. 23), annexed to the Lisbon Treaty, on the second para. of Art. 48 of the Treaty on the Functioning of the European Union, [2010] O.J. C83/346 (recalling that the European Council acts by consensus). This possibility of having the matter referred to the European Council is similar to the "alarm bell" procedure which applies in the field of judicial cooperation in criminal matters, except for the fact that Art.48 does not provide that, where it is not possible to find agreement on a new draft directive, Member States wishing to proceed with enhanced cooperation on the basis of that draft, will be authorised to do so (see para. 16–033, *infra*).

Facilitating free movement. The Court of Justice has held that even if the Union **9–083**
legislation has not carried out any coordination in respect of a social security
scheme, Arts 39 to 42 EC [now Arts 45 to 48 TFEU] require social security benefits to which a worker is entitled under that system not to be affected as a result
of the fact that the work was performed in another Member State (or of the fact
that the worker moved his or her residence to another Member State[390]). Where the
adverse effects experienced by a worker can be overcome without Union coordination measures, the national authorities may have to apply the rules of Regulation
No. 883/2004 by analogy. This was the case where national legislation provided
that only periods of employment completed in national public hospitals might be
recognised as pensionable because the fact that comparable periods completed in
public hospitals in other Member States might not be recognised as such dissuaded
workers from exercising their right to freedom of movement and discriminated
against workers who had exercised that right.[391] Where a social security entitlement of a migrant worker falls under two different statutory schemes (e.g. a right
to a pension after being employed in two Member States), the application of one
set of national rules to a migrant worker may give rise to unforeseen consequences,
hardly compatible with Arts 45 to 48 TFEU. According to the Court of Justice, the
national authorities should ascertain whether their legislation can be applied liter-
ally to migrant workers, in exactly the same way as to non-migrant workers, without causing migrant workers to lose a social security advantage.[392] In addition, the
national court concerned should interpret its own legislation in the light of the aims
of those articles and, as far as possible, prevent its interpretation from being such
as to discourage a migrant worker from actually exercising his or her right to freedom of movement.[393] Where it is impossible to apply national law in conformity
with Union law in this way, the national court must fully apply Union law and disapply any provision which would lead to a result contrary to Union law.[394]

Reimbursement of costs. Article 48 TFEU leaves in being differences between the **9–084**
Member States' social security systems and hence in the rights of persons working

---

[390] See, e.g., ECJ, Case C-396/05 *Habelt and Others* [2007] E.C.R. I-11895, para. 78; ECJ, Case
C-228/07 *Petersen* [2008] E.C.R. I-6989, paras 54–55.
[391] ECJ, Case C-443/93 *Vougioukas* [1995] E.C.R. I-4033, paras 39–42. For a case in which it was
held that the negative consequences of working in another Member State could be overcome only
by recourse to coordination measures adopted by the Council, see ECJ, Case C-360/97 *Nijhuis*
[1999] E.C.R. I-1919, paras 28–32.
[392] ECJ, Case C-165/91 *Van Munster* [1994] E.C.R. I-4661, para. 33; ECJ, Case C-202/97 *Fitzwilliam
Executive Search* [2000] E.C.R. I-883, paras 51–59; ECJ, Case C-178/97 *Banks and Others* [2000]
E.C.R. I-2005, paras 38–45; ECJ, Case C-3/08 *Leyman* [2009] E.C.R. I-9085, paras 40–50. If the
national authorities cannot reach agreement on the applicable national legislation, they must initiate proceedings under Art. 227 EC [*now Art. 259 TFEU*]: *Fitzwilliam Executive Search*, para. 58,
and *Banks and Others*, para. 45. See Van Zeben and Donders, "Coordination of Social Security:
Developments in the Area of Posting" (2001) Eur.J.Soc.Sec. 107–116.
[393] *Van Munster*, cited in the preceding n., para. 34.
[394] ECJ, Case C-262/97 *Engelbrecht* [2000] E.C.R. I-7321, para. 40.

in the Member States. Subject to the limits imposed by free movement of goods, persons, services and capital, the Member States still have the power to determine the conditions under which a person may become affiliated to a social security scheme and entitled to social security benefits. It is clear that rules making reimbursement of costs incurred for medical products or medical care in another Member State dependent on prior authorisation constitute an obstacle to the free movement of goods or the freedom to provide services, respectively. The Court of Justice has held that such a requirement for prior authorisation could not be justified with regard to reimbursement of costs for medical products or non-hospital care.[395] However, with regard to reimbursement of costs for hospital treatment, as well as for other treatment involving the use of major medical equipment, a requirement of prior authorisation could in certain circumstances be justified by the need to safeguard the financial balance of the social security system.[396]

C. FREEDOM TO PROVIDE OF SERVICES

9–085   **Treaty rules.** Under Art. 56 TFEU [*ex Art. 49 EC*], restrictions on freedom to provide services within the Union are prohibited within the framework of the provisions set out thereafter.[397] Article 62 TFEU [*ex Art. 55 EC*] states that

---

[395] ECJ, Case C-120/95 *Decker* [1998] E.C.R. I-1831 (medical products); ECJ, Case C-158/96 *Kohll* [1998] E.C.R. I-1931 (dental treatment as an outpatient); ECJ, Case C-385/99 *Müller-Fauré and van Riet* [2003] E.C.R. I-4509, paras 93–108 (non-hospital services). For *Decker* and *Kohll*, see Van Raepenbusch (1998) C.D.E. 683–697; for *Müller-Fauré*, see Flear (2004) C.M.L.Rev. 209–233.

[396] ECJ, Case C-157/99 *Smits and Peerbooms* [2001] E.C.R. I-5473 and ECJ, Case C-385/99 *Müller-Fauré and van Riet* [2003] E.C.R. I-4509, paras 66–92; ECJ, Case C-372/04 *Watts* [2006] E.C.R. I-4325; ECJ, Case C-169/07 *Hartlauer* [2009] E.C.R. I-1721, para. 47; ECJ, Case C-444/05 *Stamatelaki* [2007] E.C.R. I-3185; ECJ (judgment of October 5, 2010), Case C-173/09 *Elchinov*, not yet reported, (hospital treatment); ECJ (judgment of October 5, 2010), Case C-512/08 *Commission v France*, not yet reported, paras 34–42 (use of major medical equipment). However, where an insured person has been authorised to receive hospital treatment in another Member State, the Court of Justice has held that a limitation of reimbursement of that treatment to the lower level applicable in that State is incompatible with freedom to provide services (ECJ, Case C-368/98 *Vanbraekel and Others* [2001] E.C.R. I-5363). Such a limitation does not have a restrictive effect of the free provision on services where a person received unscheduled hospital treatment during a temporary stay in another Member State: ECJ (judgment of June 15, 2010), Case C-211/08 *Commission v Spain*, not yet reported, paras 55–80 (the restrictive effect was held to be "too uncertain and indirect": *ibid.*, para. 72). See Cousins, "Patient Mobility and National Health Systems" (2007) L.I.E.I. 183–193; Van Nuffel, "Patients' free movement rights and cross-border access to healthcare", (2005) 12 M.J.E.C.L. 253–270; Nowak, "Zur grundfreiheitlichen Inanspruchnahme von Gesundheitsleistungen im europäischen Binnenmarkt" (2003) EuR. 644–656; Hatzopoulos, "Killing National Health and Insurance Systems but Healing Patients? The European Market for Health Care Services after the Judgments of the ECJ in Vanbraekel and Peerbooms" (2002) C.M.L.Rev. 683–729.

[397] Before the simplification carried out by the Amsterdam Treaty, the EC Treaty debarred Member States from introducing any new restrictions (former Art. 62 EC) and existing restrictions had to be gradually abolished over a transitional period (former Art. 59, first para., EC). Just as in the case of freedom of establishment, the provision of services was to be liberalised on the basis of a general programme and implementing directives (former Art. 63, first para., EC).

Arts 51 to 54 [*ex Arts 45 to 48 EC*] are to apply to services. Consequently, free movement of services is subject to the same exceptions as the provisions on free movement of workers and self-employed persons with regard to the exercise of public authority (Art. 51 TFEU; see para. 9–073) and public policy, public security and public health (Art. 52 TFEU; see para. 9–070), and is to be facilitated by the mutual recognition of diplomas, certificates and other evidence of formal qualifications and by further coordinating directives (Art. 53 TFEU; see paras 9–079—9–081). Just as in the case of the provisions on free movement of workers and self-employed persons, the provisions on the free movement of services not only apply to the action of public authorities but extend also to associations or organisations not governed by public law where they lay down collective rules in the exercise of their legal autonomy.[398] Where it concerns similar situations, the case law interprets the provisions on free movement of services and free movement of goods in a parallel manner, in particular where services are provided across border without the provider or the recipient moving.

1. Definition and beneficiaries

Services. The first para. of Art. 57 TFEU [*ex Art. 50 EC*] regards as "services" those which are

> "normally provided for remuneration, in so far as they are not governed by the provisions relating to freedom of movement for goods, capital and persons".

What is therefore covered is activities, for instance of an industrial or commercial character, of craftsmen or of the professions (see Art. 57, second para), which "normally" yield an economic consideration or "remuneration".[399] Consequently, services which are normally remunerated, but sporadically provided free of charge, are not excluded. Services do not necessarily have to be paid for by the person for whom they are performed,[400] although they do have to be paid for primarily with private money. Accordingly, tuition provided in an educational institution which is principally funded by the State does not constitute a service within the meaning of the Treaties.[401] However, the Court has held that courses given by

9–086

---

[398] ECJ, Joined Cases C-51/96 and C-191/97 *Deliège* [2000] E.C.R. I-2549, para. 47 (referring to the judgments in *Walrave* and *Bosman*, see para. 9–046); ECJ, Case C-519/04 P *Meca-Medina and Majcen v Commission* [2006] E.C.R. I-6991, para. 24; ECJ, Case C-341/05 *Laval un Partneri* [2007] E.C.R. I-11767, para. 98. See Wernsmann, "Bindung Privater an Diskriminierungsverbote durch Gemeinschaftsrecht" (2005) J.Z. 224–233. The prohibition on restriction on freedom of services also applies against measures adopted by the Union institutions: ECJ (judgment of October 26, 2010), Case C-97/09 *Schmeltz*, not yet reported, paras 48–77.

[399] ECJ, Joined Cases C-51/96 and C-191/97 *Deliège* [2000] E.C.R. I-2549, paras 49–59 (public and private sponsoring as remuneration for sporting activities).

[400] ECJ, Case 352/85 *Bond van Adverteerders and Others* [1988] E.C.R. 2085, para. 16.

[401] ECJ, Case C-109/92 *Wirth* [1993] E.C.R. I-6447, paras 15–19.

educational establishments essentially financed by private funds constitute services within the meaning of Art. 57 TFEU, even if the private funding is not provided principally by the pupils or their parents.[402] Medical treatment in or outside a hospital which is paid directly by a sickness insurance fund on a flat-rate basis does constitute a service.[403] An activity will be regarded as a service, even if it is strictly regulated or even forbidden in some Member States. Accordingly, medical termination of pregnancy which is prohibited in one Member State constitutes a service when lawfully carried out in another Member State.[404] National legislation requiring profits from such an activity (e.g. a lottery) to be paid to the State or used for specific ends, does not cause that activity to lose its economic character.[405]

9–087 **Residuary nature.** Article 57 regards as "services" only activities not falling under the other freedoms. Thus, the transmission of television signals is a service, but the material, sound recordings, films, apparatus and other products used for the diffusion of television signals are subject to the rules relating to freedom of movement for goods.[406] Nevertheless, Art. 57 does not establish any order of precedence between the freedom to provide services and the other fundamental freedoms: the notion of "services" covers services which are not governed by other freedoms, in order to ensure that all economic activity falls within the scope of the fundamental freedoms.[407]

---

[402] ECJ, Case C-76/05 *Schwarz and Gootjes-Schwarz* [2007] E.C.R. I-6849, paras 40–41; ECJ (judgment of May 20, 2010), Case C-56/09 *Zanotti*, not yet reported, paras 30–33.

[403] ECJ, Case C-157/99 *Smits and Peerbooms* [2001] E.C.R. I-5473, paras 56–59 and the case law cited in n. 392; ECJ, Case C-372/04 *Watts* [2006] E.C.R. I-4325, para. 89.

[404] ECJ, Case C-159/90 *Society for the Protection of Unborn Children Ireland* [1991] E.C.R. I-4685, paras 18–21 (also known as the *Grogan* case). Article 40.3.3. of the Irish Constitution prohibits abortion. In order to safeguard that prohibition, a Protocol (No. 17) was appended to the Treaties, declaring that nothing in the Treaties shall affect the application in Ireland of that provision of its Constitution ([1992] O.J. C224/130, see now Protocol No. 35, [2010] C83/321). Following the turmoil caused by the application of this prohibition in February 1992, the Irish Government secured the adoption by the Contracting Parties as an annex to the EU Treaty of a Declaration, made in Guimarâes on May 1, 1992, in which they give the following "legal interpretation" of the Protocol: "[I]t was and is their intention that the Protocol shall not limit freedom to travel between Member States or, in accordance with conditions which may be laid down, in conformity with Community law, by Irish legislation, to obtain or make available in Ireland information relating to services lawfully available in Member States". As a result of a referendum held on November 25, 1992, Art. 40.3.3 of the Constitution was amended by the addition of particulars recognising the freedom to travel to another Member State and to obtain and disseminate information regarding lawful abortion elsewhere. See Murphy, "Maastricht: Implementation in Ireland" (1994) E.L.Rev. 94–104; Curtin, note to the *Grogan* judgment of the Court of Justice (1992) C.M.L.Rev. 583–603. Since then, Protocol No. 7 on abortion in Malta, annexed to the 2003 Act of Accession, specifies that nothing in the Treaties shall affect the application in the territory of Malta of national legislation relating to abortion, [2003] O.J. L236/947).

[405] ECJ, Case C-275/92 *Schindler* [1994] E.C.R. I-1039, paras 31–35.

[406] ECJ, Case 155/73 *Sacchi* [1974] E.C.R. 409, paras 6–7.

[407] ECJ, Case C-452/04 *Fidium Finanz* [2006] E.C.R. I-9521, paras 31–33.

Service providers and recipients. According to Art. 56 TFEU [*ex Art. 49 EC*],   **9–088**
the beneficiaries of free movement of services are

> "nationals of Member States who are established in a Member State other
> than that of the person for whom the services are intended".

The provider of the service (not the recipient) must be a national of a Member
State (or a company or firm formed in accordance with the law of a Member
State; see Art. 55 TFEU in conjunction with Art. 62 TFEU) and established in a
Member State.[408] Freedom to provide services may be relied upon not only by the
provider and recipient of services, but also in certain circumstances by the
employees of the service provider.[409]

Transfrontier element. The transfrontier element mentioned in Art.56 TFEU is   **9–089**
that the provider and recipient of the service must be established in different
Member States. Nevertheless, in practice the transfrontier element also assumes
other forms. The Treaty refers only to the situation in which a provider of services "temporarily pursue[s] his activity in the Member State where the service is
provided" (Art. 57, third para.). However, the Court of Justice has regarded "the
freedom for the recipients of services to go to another Member State in order to
receive a service there" as a natural corollary of the provision of services "which
fulfils the objective of liberalising all gainful activity not covered by the free
movement of goods, persons and capital".[410] Consequently, tourists, persons
receiving medical treatment and persons travelling for the purpose of education
or business may invoke freedom to provide services.[411] In this connection, the
provider and the recipient of the service do not necessarily have to be established
in different Member States. Where a travel agent takes tourists from its own
country to another Member State and makes use of a guide who may be
established in another Member State or in its own country, the rules on freedom
to provide services are applicable in either case, since services are being provided
in a Member State other than the one in which the provider of the services is

---

[408] ECJ, Case C-290/04 *Scorpio Konzertproduktionen* [2006] E.C.R. I-9461, paras 66–68 (the
provisions on the freedom to provide services are not applicable to providers of services who are
nationals of non-member countries, even if they are established within the Union and an
intra-Union provision of services is concerned).

[409] ECJ, Joined Cases C-317/01 and C-369/01 *Abatay and Others* [2003] E.C.R. I-12301, para. 106.

[410] ECJ, Joined Cases 286/82 and 26/83 *Luisi and Carbone* [1984] E.C.R. 377, paras 10 and 16.

[411] *Ibid.*, para. 16. As regards tourists, see, ECJ, Case 186/87 *Cowan* [1989] E.C.R. 195, paras 15–17;
ECJ, Case C-45/93 *Commission v Spain* [1994] E.C.R. I-911, paras 5–10; Tichadou, "Der Schutz
des Touristen in der Rechtsprechung des Europäischen Gerichtshofs" (2002) Z.Eu.S. 299–319;
Van der Woude and Mead, "Free Movement of the Tourist in Community Law" (1988) C.M.L.Rev.
117. As regards medical activities, see ECJ, Case C-159/90 *Society for the Protection of Unborn
Children Ireland* [1991] E.C.R. I-4685, para. 18.

established.[412] This is because both the provider and the recipient of the service move from their Member State to another. In the case of maritime transport between Member States, the service is provided on behalf of persons who may or may not be established in another Member State, but the service is offered in either case—at least in part—on the territory of another Member State.[413] This is a sufficient transfrontier element in itself.

In addition, the rules on free movement of services apply where the provider of the service and the recipient remain in the countries where they are established and only the service crosses the border. Thus, the transmission of television signals across a frontier falls under the free movement of services both as regards the service provided by cable network operators relaying television programmes sent out by broadcasters in other Member States and as regards the service provided by the broadcasters transmitting advertisements to the public in another Member State on behalf of advertisers established in that State.[414] Another case to which those rules apply is that of a service offered by a service provider over the telephone or the Internet to potential recipients in another Member State without the provider leaving the Member State where he or she is established.[415]

However, the Treaty provisions on freedom to provide services cannot be applied to activities which are confined in all respects within a single Member State.[416] Freedom to provide services may be relied upon by an undertaking as against the Member State in which it is established if the services are provided for persons established in another Member State.[417] The same applies to intermediaries established in the Member State of the potential recipients of the services who make it easier for a supplier of services to offer his or her services across borders.[418]

---

[412] ECJ, Case C-154/89 *Commission v France* [1991] E.C.R. I-659, para. 11; ECJ, Case C-180/89 *Commission v Italy* [1991] E.C.R. I-709, para. 10; ECJ, Case C-198/89 *Commission v Greece* [1991] E.C.R. I-727, para. 11.

[413] ECJ, Case C-381/93 *Commission v France* [1994] E.C.R. I-5145, paras 14–15.

[414] ECJ, Case 352/85 *Bond van Adverteerders and Others* [1988] E.C.R. 2085, paras 14–15. See also ECJ, Joined Cases C-34–36/95 *De Agostini and TV Shop* [1997] E.C.R. I-3843, para. 29, with a case note by Verhoeven (1997/98) Col.J.E.L. 479–491. For advertising, see also para. 9–045, *supra*.

[415] ECJ, Case C-384/93 *Alpine Investments* [1995] E.C.R. I-1141, paras 20–22 (services offered by telephone); ECJ, Case C-243/01 *Gambelli and Others* [2003] E.C.R. I-13031, paras 53–54 (services offered on the Internet).

[416] ECJ, Joined Cases C-29-C-35/94 *Aubertin* [1995] E.C.R. I-301, para. 9.

[417] ECJ, Case C-384/93 *Alpine Investments* [1995] E.C.R. I-1141, paras 29–31, with case notes by Hatzopoulos (1995) C.M.L.Rev. 1427–1445 and Straetmans (1995/96) Col.J.E.L. 154–164. See also ECJ, Case C-224/97 *Ciola* [1999] E.C.R. I-2517, paras 10–13; ECJ, Case C-60/00 *Carpenter* [2002] E.C.R. I-6279, para. 29. For the cross-border nature of services, see Straetmans, *Consument en markt* (Deurne, Kluwer, 1998), 296–303.

[418] ECJ, Case C-243/01 *Gambelli and Others* [2003] E.C.R. I-13031, para. 58.

Temporary nature. Where the provider of the service goes to the Member State   **9–090**
of the recipient of the service, freedom to provide services differs from freedom
of establishment by reason of its temporary nature. Free movement of services
cannot be relied upon where a national of a Member State goes to reside in the
territory of another Member State and establishes his principal residence there in
order to provide or receive services there for an indefinite period.[419] The temporary nature of the activities in question has to be determined in the light, not only
of the duration of the provision of the service, but also of its regularity, periodic-
ity or continuity. A provider of services within the meaning of the Treaties may
equip himself or herself with some form of infrastructure in the host Member
State (including an office, chambers or consulting rooms) in so far as such infrastructure is necessary for the purposes of performing the services in question.[420]
Services within the meaning of the Treaties may cover services which a business
established in a Member State supplies with a greater or lesser degree of frequency or regularity, even over an extended period, to persons established in one
or more other Member States, for example the giving of advice or information for
remuneration. The Court holds that the Treaties do not afford a means of
determining, in an abstract manner, the duration or frequency beyond which the
supply of a service in another Member State can no longer be regarded as the
provision of services within the meaning of the Treaties.[421]

2. Substance of the freedom to provide services

Prohibited discrimination. Direct effect attaches to the principle of non-   **9–091**
discrimination enshrined in the first para. of Art. 56 TFEU and the third para. of
Art. 57 TFEU,

> "in so far as they seek to abolish any discrimination against a person
> providing a service by reason of his nationality or of the fact that he
> resides in a Member State other than that in which the service is to be
> provided".[422]

---

[419] ECJ, Case 196/87 *Steymann* [1988] E.C.R. 6159, para. 17; ECJ, Case C-70/95 *Sodemare and
Others* [1997] E.C.R. I-3395, paras 38–40.

[420] ECJ, Case C-55/94 *Gebhard* [1995] E.C.R. I-4165, para. 27. See with regard to lawyers, ECJ, Case
C-145/99 *Commission v Italy* [2002] E.C.R. I-2235, paras 22–23. In 1986 the Court still held that
an insurance company which maintains a "permanent presence" in another Member State cannot
rely on the freedom to provide services "even if that presence does not take the form of a branch
or agency, but consists merely of an office managed by the undertaking's own staff or by a person
who is independent but authorised to act on a permanent basis for the undertaking, as would be the
case with an agency": ECJ, Case 205/84 *Commission v Germany* [1986] E.C.R. 3755, para. 21.

[421] ECJ, Case C-215/01 *Schnitzer* [2003] E.C.R. I-14847, paras 30 and 31; ECJ, Case C-171/02
Commission v Portugal [2004] E.C.R. I-5645, paras 26–27.

[422] ECJ, Case 33/74 *Van Binsbergen* [1974] E.C.R. 1299, para. 27.

The Court of Justice recognised the direct effect of the corresponding provisions of the EC Treaty after a transitional period, in which the Council adopted, just as in the case of freedom of establishment, a General Programme for the abolition of restrictions on entry, exit and residence imposed on nationals established in one Member State who wish to receive or provide services in another Member State. The Council adopted legislation pursuant to that programme.[423] Under these rules, persons providing or receiving services have a right of residence of equal duration to the period during which the services are provided.[424]

In *Van Binsbergen*, the Court of Justice held that the Netherlands could not restrict the right to represent parties in legal proceedings to persons established in that country. This was because freedom to provide services prohibited all restrictions

"imposed on the person providing the service by reason in particular of his nationality or of the fact that he does not habitually reside in the State where the service is provided, which do not apply to persons established within the national territory or which may prevent or otherwise obstruct the activities of the person providing the service".[425]

Thus, the Treaty provisions on freedom to provide services preclude making the supply of services conditional upon obtaining a prior authorisation or licence, unless this can be justified objectively (see para. 9–093 *et seq.*). An obligation that a particular activity may be carried out only under a contract of employment likewise constitutes a restriction on trade in services, for which the Member State concerned must provide justification.[426] Trade in services is also restricted where a service provider is required to have a particular legal form or status or to conduct his or her business on an exclusive basis and there is a prohibition of pursuing profit.[427] This is because such requirements often discriminate indirectly against service providers from other Member States. More generally, the Court of Justice will investigate whether different tax treatment of residents and non-residents constitutes indirect discrimination against service providers established

---

[423] General Programme for the Abolition of Restrictions on Freedom to Provide Services, [1962] O.J. English Spec. Ed., Second Series, IX. Resolutions of the Council and of the Representatives of the Member States, p.3, adopted on the basis of the former Art. 63 EC, and see Council Directive 73/148/EEC of May 21, 1973 on the abolition of restrictions on movement and residence within the Community for nationals of Member States with regard to establishment and the provision of services, [1973] O.J. L172/14 (see also para. 9–059, *supra*).

[424] Article 4(2) Directive 73/148/EEC. These rules have been replaced by the general system of residence rights for Union citizens laid down in Directive 2004/38/EC (n. 24, *supra*), see para. 8–008, *supra*.

[425] ECJ, Case 33/74 *Van Binsbergen* [1974] E.C.R. 1299, para. 10.

[426] ECJ, Case C-398/95 *SETTG* [1997] E.C.R. I-3091, paras 14–19.

[427] ECJ, Case C-439/99 *Commission v Italy* [2002] E.C.R. I-305, para. 32.

abroad.[428] Similarly, it has been held, for example, that the freedom to supply services as a lawyer is impeded where, if a party was successful in a dispute in which he or she was represented by a lawyer established in another Member State, that party cannot obtain reimbursement, from the unsuccessful party, of the fees of the lawyer practising before the court seised with whom, under national law, the lawyer from another Member State had to work in conjunction.[429] Equal treatment of nationals of other Member States wishing to pursue activities other than those of an employed person extends so far that they must have the same right as nationals of the host State to purchase or lease housing built or renovated with the help of public funds and to obtain reduced-rate mortgage loans.[430] Providers of services (in the same way as self-employed persons) must be able to take part in legal and economic transactions locally in the same way as nationals of the host State, even as regards aspects which are not directly connected with their occupational activities. Accordingly, persons who go to another Member State where they intend or are likely to receive services are likewise entitled in principle to treatment no less favourable than that accorded to nationals of the host State as regards the right to protection against criminal offences and the right to use in court proceedings the languages spoken there (see para. 7–054).

Non-discriminatory obstacles. In more recent case law, the Court of Justice has made it clear that freedom to provide services does not require only the abolition of all overt and covert[431] discrimination against the provider of the services by reason of his nationality or the place at which he is established,   **9–092**

> "but also the abolition of any restriction, even if it applies without distinction to national providers of services and to those of other Member States, when it is liable to prohibit or otherwise impede the activities of a provider of services established in another Member State where he lawfully provides similar services".[432]

In this way, in 1991 the Court applied *Dassonville* (1974), which was concerned with free movement of goods (see para. 9–030), to freedom to provide services: national legislation which, although applicable irrespective of the nationality of

---

[428] See, for example, ECJ, Case C-234/01 *Gerritse* [2003] E.C.R. I-5933, paras 23–55; ECJ, Case C-169/08 *Regione Sardegna* [2009] E.C.R. I-10821 (see also para. 9–064, *supra*) on the right of establishment.

[429] ECJ, Case C-289/02 *AMOK Verlags* [2003] E.C.R. I-15059, paras 36–39.

[430] ECJ, Case 63/86 *Commission v Italy* [1988] E.C.R. 29, paras 16–20.

[431] ECJ, Joined Cases 62 and 63/81 *Seco* [1982] E.C.R. 223, para. 8.

[432] ECJ, Case C-76/90 *Säger* [1991] E.C.R. I-4221, para. 12. For the prohibition of restrictive conditions imposed on members of staff of a provider of services who are not nationals of a Member State, see the judgments cited in n. 185, *supra*.

the provider of services, has the effect of making the provision of services between Member States more difficult than the provision of services purely within one Member State, no longer withstands the test of Union law.[433] For this reason, the Court has held that national measures applicable to all market operators are contrary to freedom to provide services where they restrict market access for undertakings from other Member States.[434] By the same token, the Court of Justice held that a municipal tax on satellite dishes was contrary to freedom to supply services because it constituted a charge on the reception of broadcasts from foreign operators and therefore impeded the activities of foreign operators more than those of operators established in the Member State in question.[435] Conversely, a tax on mobile and personal communications infrastructures was held not to infringe Art. 56 since foreign operators were not, either in fact or in law, affected more adversely by it than national operators.[436] Article 56 also precludes legislation which makes it more difficult to *receive* services from service providers established in another Member State. Accordingly, Art. 56 precludes a Member State from enacting tax legislation which provides for tax relief for schooling costs incurred in private schools established in that Member State, but not for school fees paid to private schools established in other Member States. Such legislation discourages taxpayers resident in the Member State concerned from sending their children to schools established in another Member State, and also hinders the offering of education by these schools to children of taxpayers resident in that Member State.[437] As mentioned above, national legislation which deters persons with social security cover in a Member State from seeking medical treatment from service providers established in another Member State, constitutes, both for them and for the service providers, a restriction on the freedom to provide services (see para. 9–084). In certain cases, however, the possible restrictive effects of national legislation may be too "uncertain and indirect" to be regarded as hindering the free provision of services.[438]

---

[433] See also ECJ, Case C-381/93 *Commission v France* [1994] E.C.R. I-5145, paras 17–21.

[434] ECJ, Case C-518/06 *Commission v Italy* [2009] E.C.R. I-3491, paras 64–71.

[435] ECJ, Case C-17/00 *De Coster* [2001] E.C.R. I-9445, paras 31–35. See, similarly, ECJ, Case C-250/06 *United Pan-Europe Communications Belgium and Others* [2007] E.C.R. I-11135, paras 28–38 (obligation for cable operators to broadcast certain domestic broadcasters). See, likewise, ECJ, Joined Cases C-94/04 and C-202/04 *Cipolla and Others* [2006] E.C.R. I-11421, paras 55–70 (prohibition of derogation, by agreement, from the minimum fees set for court services and services reserved to lawyers).

[436] ECJ, Joined Cases C-544/03 and C-545/03 *Mobistar and Belgacom Mobile* [2005] E.C.R. I-7723, paras 26–35.

[437] ECJ, Case C-76/05 *Schwarz and Gootjes-Schwarz* [2007] E.C.R. I-6849, paras 64–67; ECJ, Case C-318/05 *Commission v Germany* [2007] E.C.R. I-6957, paras 77–81.

[438] ECJ (judgment of June 15, 2010), Case C-211/08 *Commission v Spain*, not yet reported, paras 55–80 (see n. 396, *supra*). See the corresponding case law with respect to the free movement of goods (para. 9–030, *supra*) and the free movement of persons (see para. 9–065, *supra*).

3. Permitted restrictions on freedom to provide services

(a) *Restrictions on grounds of public policy, public security and public health*

Justificatory grounds. A Member State may impose restrictions on freedom to   **9–093**
provide services which are dependent on the origin of the service and hence discriminate only on the basis of the derogating provisions of Art. 51 TFEU [*ex
Art. 45 EC*] (public authority; see para. 9–073) and Art. 52 TFEU [*ex Art. 46 EC*]
(public policy, public security and public health; see paras 9–070—9–071).[439]
Objectives of an economic nature cannot constitute public policy grounds.[440]

Restrictions must be limited to what is necessary in order to protect the interests which they seek to safeguard (principle of proportionality). This was held not
to be the case with the general prohibition in the Netherlands on distributing radio
and television programmes broadcast from other Member States containing
advertisements intended for the public in that country or subtitled in Dutch.
Although in the final analysis the aim of the rule in question was not to secure for
a public foundation all the revenue from advertising, but to safeguard the non-
commercial and, thereby, pluralistic nature of the Netherlands broadcasting system, that objective could be achieved by means of a less restrictive measure, such
as making the advertising restrictions imposed on national broadcasters generally
applicable.[441] An example of a restriction which can be justified on grounds of
public policy is the German prohibition on the commercial exploitation of games
simulating acts of homicide. According to the Court of Justice, this prohibition
did not go beyond what was necessary for the protection of human dignity,
guaranteed by the German Constitution.[442]

(b) *Restrictions based on the rule of reason*

Rule of reason. In *Van Binsbergen*, the Court of Justice held that: **9–094**

"taking into account the particular nature of the services to be provided, specific requirements imposed on the person providing the service cannot be considered incompatible with the Treaties where they have as their purpose the
application of professional rules justified by the general good—in particular
rules relating to organisation, qualifications, professional ethics, supervision

---

[439] See, for instance, ECJ, Case C-484/93 *Svensson and Gustavsson* [1995] E.C.R. I-3955, paras 12
and 15; ECJ, Case C-341/05 *Laval un Partneri* [2007] E.C.R. I-11767, paras 115–119; ECJ, Case
C-153/08 *Commission v Spain* [2009] E.C.R. I-9735, paras 36–37.
[440] ECJ, Case C-211/91 *Commission v Belgium* [1992] E.C.R. I-6757, paras 9–11; ECJ, Case C-17/92
Distribuidores Cinematográficos [1993] E.C.R. I-2239, paras 16–21; ECJ, Case C-224/97 *Ciola*
[1999] E.C.R. I-2517, paras 15–17; ECJ, Case C-388/01 *Commission v Italy* [2003] E.C.R. I-721,
paras 18–19.
[441] ECJ, Case 352/85 *Bond van Adverteerders and Others* [1988] E.C.R. 2085, paras 34–37. See
also ECJ, Case C-11/95 *Commission v Belgium* [1996] E.C.R. I-4115, para. 92.
[442] ECJ, Case C-36/02 *Omega Spielhallen* [2004] E.C.R. I-9609, paras 29–39.

and liability—which are binding upon any person established in the State in which the service is provided, where the person providing the service would escape from the ambit of those rules being established in another Member State".[443]

Following the *Cassis de Dijon* line of cases on free movement of goods (see paras 9–039—9–044), the Court has formulated conditions for allowing exceptions in respect of freedom to provide services on the basis of a rule of reason.[444] The distinction drawn in *Keck and Mithouard* with regard to selling arrangements does not apply, particularly where access to the market in services in another Member State is restricted.[445]

9–095   **(1) Absence of harmonisation.** An obstacle to the freedom to provide services created by national rules may only be justified in the absence of Union harmonisation measures in the field.[446] Accordingly, with regard to services that fall within the scope of Directive 2006/1123 (the "Services Directive"),[447] Member States may not make access to or exercise of a service subject to compliance with any requirements which do not respect the principles of non-discrimination and proportionality and are justified for reasons of public policy, public security, public health or the protection of the environment.[448]

9–096   **(2) Public-interest requirements.** Secondly, the restrictions must be justified in the public interest, which does not necessarily relate to the protection of the

---

[443] ECJ, Case 33/74 *Van Binsbergen* [1974] E.C.R. 1299, para. 12.

[444] ECJ, Case 205/84 *Commission v Germany* [1986] E.C.R. 3755, paras 27–29; ECJ, Case C-154/89 *Commission v France* [1991] E.C.R. I-659, paras 14–15; ECJ, Case C-180/89 *Commission v Italy* [1991] E.C.R. I-709, paras 17–18; ECJ, Case C-198/89 *Commission v Greece* [1991] E.C.R. I-727, paras 18–19; ECJ, Case C-288/89 *Collectieve Antennevoorziening Gouda* [1991] E.C.R. I-4007, paras 13–15; ECJ, Case C-353/89 *Commission v Netherlands* [1991] E.C.R. I-4069, paras 17–19. See also the commentaries cited in n. 258, *supra*, and Becker, "Vorraussetzungen und Grenzen der Dienstleistungsfreiheit" (1996) N.J.W. 179–181.

[445] ECJ, Case C-384/93 *Alpine Investments* [1995] E.C.R. I-1141, paras 32–39 (for commentaries, see n. 417, *supra*); see also with regard to access to the employment market, ECJ, Case C-415/93 *Bosman* [1995] E.C.R. I-4921, paras 102–103. As explained above, however, even in the context of the free movement of goods, a specific regime for selling arrangements normally may not embody measures adopted by a Member State that restrict access to the market: see para. 9–045, *supra*.

[446] ECJ, Case C-243/01 *Gambelli and Others* [2003] E.C.R. I-13031, paras 64–65; ECJ, Case C-429/02 *Bacardi France* [2004] E.C.R. I-6613, para. 32.

[447] Directive 2006/123/EC of the European Parliament and of the Council of December 12, 2006 on services in the internal market, [2006] O.J. L376/36. See Mulder, "Aangenomen dienstenrichtlijn: sociale dumping of het dumpen van socialisme?" (2008) S.E.W. 2–9; Peglow, "La libre prestation de services dans la directive n° 2006/123/CE. Réflexion sur l'insertion de la directive dans le droit communautaire existant" (2008) 44 R.T.D.E. 67–118; Drijber, "Van democratie en bureaucratie: de Dienstenrichtlijn is erdoor" (2007) N.T.E.R. 1–7; Simon, "La directive "services": quelle contribution au marché intérieur?" (2007) 15 J.T.D.E. 33–43.

[448] *Ibid.*, Art. 16, third para.

occupation as such, but can also be designed to secure protection for the recipient of the service,[449] consumer protection,[450] protection of employees[451] (for instance against possible social dumping,[452]) protection of investors' confidence in the domestic financial markets,[453] fair trading,[454] the maintenance of order in society,[455] combating fraud,[456] protection of creditors or safeguarding the sound administration of justice in relation to the provision of litigation services on a professional basis,[457] ensuring the effectiveness of the supervision of taxation and cohesion of the tax system[458] and the financial balance of the social security system[459] including maintaining a balanced medical service open to all,[460] road safety,[461] protection of intellectual property,[462] ensuring the provision of reliable medicinal products of good quality,[463] promotion of research and development,[464] conservation of the national historical and artistic heritage,[465] proper appreciation of places and things of historical interest and the widest possible dissemination of knowledge of a country's artistic and cultural heritage,[466] maintaining or promoting the use of an official language,[467] the maintenance of a certain level of (television) programme quality,[468] cultural policy intended to safeguard the freedom

---

[449] ECJ, Joined Cases 110–111/78 *Van Wesemael* [1979] E.C.R. 35, para. 28.

[450] ECJ, Case 205/84 *Commission v Germany* [1986] E.C.R. 3755, paras 30–33.

[451] ECJ, Case 279/80 *Webb* [1981] E.C.R. 3305, paras 18–19; ECJ, Joined Cases 62 and 63/81 *Seco* [1982] E.C.R. 223, para. 14.

[452] ECJ, Case C-341/05 *Laval un Partneri* [2007] E.C.R. I-11767, para. 103.

[453] ECJ, Case C-384/93 *Alpine Investments* [1995] E.C.R. I-1141, paras 42–44.

[454] ECJ, Joined Cases C-34–36/95 *De Agostini and TV Shop* [1997] E.C.R. I-3843, para. 53.

[455] ECJ, Case 15/78 *Société Générale Alsacienne de Banque* [1978] E.C.R. 1971, para. 5; ECJ, Case C-275/92 *Schindler* [1994] E.C.R. I-1039, paras 57–58. This includes, for example, the prevention of both fraud and incitement to squander money on gaming; see ECJ, Case C-243/01 *Gambelli and Others* [2003] E.C.R. I-13031, para. 67; ECJ, Joined Cases C-338/04, C-359/04 and C-360/04 *Placanica and Others* [2007] I-1891, para. 46.

[456] ECJ, Case C-275/92 *Schindler* [1994] E.C.R. I-1039, paras 60–63.

[457] ECJ, Case C-3/95 *Reisebüro Broede* [1996] E.C.R. I-6511, para. 36.

[458] ECJ, Case C-204/90 *Bachmann* [1992] E.C.R. I-249, para. 33; ECJ, Case C-150/04 *Commission v Denmark* [2007] E.C.R. I-1163, paras 65–74.

[459] ECJ, Case C-158/96 *Kohll* [1998] E.C.R. I-1931, para. 41.

[460] This objective may also fall within the public health derogation provided for in Art. 52: *ibid*, paras 50–51; ECJ, Case C-157/99 *Smits and Peerbooms* [2001] E.C.R. I-5473, paras 73–74; ECJ, Case C-444/05 *Stamatelaki* [2007] E.C.R. I-3185, para. 31.

[461] ECJ, Case C-55/93 *Van Schaik* [1994] E.C.R. I-4837, para. 19.

[462] ECJ, Case 62/79 *Coditel v Ciné Vog Films* [1980] E.C.R. 881, para. 15.

[463] ECJ (judgment of June 1, 2010), Joined Cases C-570/07 and C-571/07 *Blanco Pérez and Chao Gómez*, not yet reported, paras 64–66.

[464] ECJ, Case C-39/04 *Laboratoires Fournier* [2005] E.C.R. I-2057, para. 23.

[465] ECJ, Case C-180/89 *Commission v Italy* [1991] E.C.R. I-709, para. 20.

[466] ECJ, Case C-154/89 *Commission v France* [1991] E.C.R. I-659, para. 17; ECJ, Case C-198/89 *Commission v Greece* [1991] E.C.R. I-727, para. 21.

[467] ECJ, Case C-222/07 *UTECA* [2009] E.C.R. I-1407, para. 27.

[468] ECJ, Case C-288/89 *Collectieve Antennevoorziening Gouda* [1991] E.C.R. I-4007, para. 27; ECJ, Case C-6/98 *ARD* [1999] E.C.R. I-7599, para. 50.

of expression of the different social, cultural, religious, philosophical or linguistic components of a State or region,[469] promoting teaching, research and development[470] and respecting fundamental rights generally.[471] "Maintaining industrial peace" as a means of preventing labour disputes from having any adverse effects on an economic sector is not acceptable as a public-interest ground.[472] Neither can a Member State rely on the need to ensure tax revenue.[473] Aims of a purely economic nature cannot constitute overriding reasons in the general interest.[474]

9–097 **(3) Application without distinction.** Thirdly—and in contradistinction to Arts 51 and 52 TFEU—the restrictions on trade in services must apply without distinction to all providers of services, regardless of the origin of the services and of the nationality of the service providers or of the Member State in which they are established (even if the restrictions discriminate indirectly).[475] A directly discriminatory restriction on the freedom to provide or receive services can be justified only by the expressly derogatory provisions of Arts 51 and 52 TFEU.[476]

9–098 **(4) Proportionality.** Finally, restrictions placed on freedom to provide services must be "objectively justified" by the need to comply with such objectives in the public interest, that is, they must be suitable for securing the attainment of the interest pursued and not go beyond what is necessary in order to attain it.[477] The restrictions must be suitable for achieving those objectives, which implies that they

---

[469] ECJ, Case C-288/89 *Collectieve Antennevoorziening Gouda* [1991] E.C.R. I-4007, paras 22–23; and ECJ, Case C-353/89 *Commission v Netherlands* [1991] E.C.R. I-4069, para. 30 (both judgments were prompted by the Dutch Media Law; see also ECJ, Case C-148/91 *Veronica Omroep Organisatie* [1993] E.C.R. I-487; ECJ, Case C-23/93 *TV10* [1994] E.C.R. I-4795); ECJ, Case C-250/06 *United Pan-Europe Communications Belgium and Others* [2007] E.C.R. I-11135, paras 40–42 (with respect to must-carry obligations imposed on a Brussels cable operator).

[470] ECJ, Case C-281/06 *Jundt* [2007] E.C.R. I-12231, paras 56–58.

[471] ECJ, Case C-112/00 *Schmidberger* [2003] E.C.R. I-5659, paras 71–74 (the case concerns free movement of goods, but refers generally to "a fundamental freedom guaranteed by the Treaty"); ECJ, Case C-36/02 *Omega Spielhallen* [2004] E.C.R. I-9609, paras 32–35, with a case note by Bulterman and Kranenborg (2006) E.L.Rev. 93–101.

[472] ECJ, Case C-398/95 *SETTG* [1997] E.C.R. I-3091, para. 23 (referring to *Collectieve Antennevoorziening Gouda* (n. 444, *supra*), in which economic aims were held to be incapable of constituting a justificatory ground under Art. 46 [*now Art. 52 TFEU*]).

[473] E.g., ECJ, Case C-243/01 *Gambelli and Others* [2003] E.C.R. I-13031, para. 61.

[474] ECJ, Case C-388/01 *Commission v Italy* [2003] E.C.R. I-721, para. 21.

[475] ECJ, Case C-490/04 *Commission v Germany* [2007] E.C.R. I-6095, para. 86. In some cases however, the Court seems to require the absence of even indirect discrimination: ECJ, Case C-234/03 *Contse* [2005] E.C.R. I-9315, paras 37–38.

[476] ECJ, Case C-153/08 *Commission v Spain* (n. 439, *supra*), paras 37–38; ECJ (judgment of January 21, 2010), Case C-546/07 *Commission v Germany*, not yet reported, paras 47–48.

[477] ECJ, Joined Cases 110 and 111/78 *Van Wesemael* [1979] E.C.R. 35, para. 29.

have to genuinely reflect a concern to attain these objectives in a consistent and systematic manner.[478] Accordingly, a Member State may not rely on public policy in order to restrict the organisation of gaming when it is at the same time encouraging consumers to participate in games of chance.[479] Furthermore, restrictions may be imposed only if the public interest is not already protected by the rules of the State of establishment of the provider of services and the same result cannot be obtained by less restrictive rules.[480] The obligation imposed on foreign undertakings employing workers in Germany to have certain documents relating to the employment relationship translated into German and to keep them during the posted workers' stay could be objectively justified according to the Court since, in the absence of these requirements, it would become extremely difficult or even impossible for the competent authorities to carry out the monitoring necessary to ensure compliance with the national provisions regarding worker protection.[481]

For the assessment of proportionality, the same principle of mutual recognition applies as with regard to the other freedoms. Accordingly, the Court of Justice has held that social legislation designed to protect an interest which is already similarly protected in the Member State in which the provider of services is established, for instance as a result of the implementation of a directive,[482] conflicts with free movement of services.[483] In the context of road safety, a Member State may subject a service provider who is already subject to technical inspections in another Member State to additional testing only if the first Member State subjects domestic service providers to the same inspections in the same circumstances.[484] For the same reasons, a Member State may not impose unnecessary requirements when it places restrictions upon the possibility to receive a service in another Member State, for example in connection with the reimbursement of medical treatment received abroad.[485] All the same, in view of the particular characteristics of

---

[478] ECJ, Case C-42/07 *Liga Portuguesa de Futebol Profissional and Bwin International* (n. 353, *supra*), para. 38; ECJ, Case C-169/08 *Regione Sardegna* (n. 428, *supra*), para. 42.

[479] ECJ, Case C-243/01 *Gambelli and Others* [2003] E.C.R. I-13031, paras 67–69.

[480] ECJ, Case C-154/89 *Commission v France* [1991] E.C.R. I-659, para. 15. See, with regard to the imposition of a minimum wage, ECJ, Case C-165/98 *Mazzoleni* [2001] E.C.R. I-2189, paras 25–39.

[481] ECJ, Case C-490/04 *Commission v Germany* [2007] E.C.R. I-6095, paras 69–80.

[482] ECJ, Case C-341/05 *Laval un Partneri* [2007] E.C.R. I-11767, paras 107–110.

[483] ECJ, Case 279/80 *Webb* [1981] E.C.R. 3305, paras 18–20. ECJ, Case C-272/94 *Guiot* [1996] E.C.R. I-1905, paras 9–2; ECJ, Joined Cases C-369/96 and C-376/96 *Arblade and Others* [1999] E.C.R. I-8453, paras 32–80; see also Joined Cases C-49/98, C-50/98, C-52/98 to C-54/98 and C-68/98 to C-71/98 *Finalarte Sociedade de Construçao Civil and Others* [2001] E.C.R. I-7831, paras 28–83; ECJ, Case C-279/00 *Commission v Italy* [2002] E.C.R. I-1425, paras 19–25 and 33–35; ECJ, Case C-244/04 *Commission v Germany* [2006] E.C.R. I-885, paras 44–51. See Giesen, "Posting: Social Protection of Workers vs. Fundamental Freedoms?" (2003) C.M.L.Rev. 143–158.

[484] ECJ, Case C-451/99 *Cura Anlagen* [2002] E.C.R. I-3193, para. 46.

[485] ECJ, Case C-158/96 *Kohll* [1998] E.C.R. I-1931, para. 35; ECJ; ECJ, Case C-157/99 *Smits and Peerbooms* [2001] E.C.R. I-5473, paras 45 and 62–69; ECJ, Case C-8/02 *Leichtle* [2004] E.C.R. I-2641. paras 27–51; ECJ, Case C-444/05 *Stamatelaki* [2007] E.C.R. I-3185, paras 26–28 and 34–37.

the sector involving games of chance via the Internet, the principle of mutual recognition does not apply automatically.[486] The fact that less strict provisions apply in one Member State than in another does not signify in itself that provisions in force in the latter Member State are disproportionate and hence incompatible with Union law.[487]

A requirement for prior authorisation or permission may constitute a justified restriction on freedom to provide services where national rules on the receipt or performance of the relevant services have not (yet) been harmonised. A prior authorisation scheme must, in any event, be based on objective, non-discriminatory criteria which are known in advance.[488] Such a prior administrative authorisation scheme must likewise be based on a procedural system which is easily accessible and capable of ensuring that a request for authorisation will be dealt with objectively and impartially within a reasonable time and refusals to grant authorisation must also be capable of being challenged in legal proceedings.[489] Provided that it is objectively justified, a Member State may impose on service providers a requirement to have a particular legal form or status. The requirement to have a permanent establishment in the territory of the Member State is the "very negation of that freedom" and can therefore be accepted only if it is "indispensable for attaining the objective pursued".[490]

9–099   Provision of services and establishment. A Member State may not make the provision of services in its territory subject to compliance with all the conditions required for establishment. This would deprive the right freely to provide services of all practical effectiveness.[491] The Treaties do not require a provider also to

---

[486] ECJ, Case C-42/07 *Liga Portuguesa de Futebol Profissional and Bwin International* (n. 353, *supra*), paras 68–72. Accordingly, a Member State may take the view that the fact that an operator of services in this sector is already subject to statutory conditions and control in the Member State in which it is established, cannot be regarded as amounting to a sufficient assurance that national consumers will be protected against the risks of fraud and crime, in the light of the difficulties liable to be encountered in such a context by the authorities of the Member State of establishment in assessing the professional qualities and integrity of operators (*ibid.*).

[487] ECJ, Case C-384/93 *Alpine Investments* [1995] E.C.R. I-1141, para. 51; ECJ, Case C-3/95 *Reisebüro Broede* [1996] E.C.R. I-6511, para. 42.

[488] ECJ, Case C-205/99 *Analir and Others* [2001] E.C.R. I-1271, para. 38; ECJ, Case C-157/99 *Smits and Peerbooms* [2001] E.C.R. I-5473, para. 90.

[489] ECJ, Case C-157/99 *Smits and Peerbooms* [2001] E.C.R. I-5473, para. 90.

[490] ECJ, Case 205/84 *Commission v Germany* [1986] E.C.R. 3755, para. 52; ECJ, Case C-101/94 *Commission v Italy* [1996] E.C.R. I-2691, para. 31; ECJ, Case C-439/99 *Commission v Italy* [2002] E.C.R. I-305, para. 30. The Court of Justice accepted a requirement for a permanent establishment for example in Case C-204/90 *Bachmann* [1992] E.C.R. I-249, paras 32–33.

[491] ECJ, Case C-154/89 *Commission v France* [1991] E.C.R. I-659, para. 12; ECJ, Case C-76/90 *Säger* [1991] E.C.R. I-4221, para. 13.

offer services in the Member State in which it is established.[492] If, however, providers of services direct their activities entirely or principally towards the territory of a neighbouring State for the purpose of avoiding its professional rules of conduct, the Member State concerned may apply its rules relating to the right of establishment and not to the provision of services.[493] Accordingly, a Member State may prohibit national undertakings from participating in undertakings established in another Member State from which they provide services which would frustrate national legislation,[494] or subject such providers of services to the same conditions as providers established on its own territory.[495] A Member State may not prohibit altogether the provision of certain services by operators established in other Member States, as that would be tantamount to abolishing the freedom to provide services.[496] However, a domestic prohibition on the provision of particular services may make it necessary to ban the same services provided from other Member States.[497]

D. FREE MOVEMENT OF CAPITAL AND PAYMENTS

1. Definition and substance

Context. Article 63 TFEU [*ex Art. 56 EC*] prohibits all restrictions on the movement of capital and payments between Member States and between Member States and third countries. That prohibition is part of the chapter which, since the beginning of the second stage of economic and monetary union (January 1, 1994), has replaced the former Arts 67 to 73 EEC. The prohibitive provision of Art. 63 TFEU has direct effect.[498]

9–100

Capital movement. Free movement of capital constitutes a necessary support for the freedoms discussed above: a transaction in goods or services or establishment in another Member State will often require investment necessitating a capital movement to another Member State. Nevertheless, the EEC Treaty provided only for the

9–101

---

[492] ECJ, Case C-56/96 *VT4* [1997] E.C.R. I-3143, para. 22.

[493] ECJ, Case 33/74 *Van Binsbergen* [1974] E.C.R. 1299, para. 13; see also ECJ, Case 115/78 *Knoors* [1979] E.C.R. 399, para. 25 (para. 7–066, *supra*).

[494] ECJ, Case C-148/91 *Veronica Omroep Organisatie* [1993] E.C.R. I-487, paras 12–14.

[495] ECJ, Case C-23/93 *TV10* [1994] E.C.R. I-4795, paras 20–22.

[496] ECJ, Case C-211/91 *Commission v Belgium* [1992] E.C.R. I-6757, para. 12; ECJ, Case C-11/95 *Commission v Belgium* [1996] E.C.R. I-4115, para. 65.

[497] ECJ, Case C-275/92 *Schindler* [1994] E.C.R. I-1039, paras 61–62. See also ECJ, Case 15/78 *Société Générale Alsacienne de Banque* [1978] E.C.R. 1971, para. 5.

[498] ECJ, Joined Cases C-163/94, C-165/94 and C-250/94 *Sanz de Lera and Others* [1995] E.C.R. I-4821, paras 40–48 (Art.56(1) EC in conjunction with Arts 57 and 58(1)(b) EC [*now Arts 63(1), 64 and 65(1)(b) TFEU*]. For a survey of the case law, see Flynn, "Coming of Age: The Free Movement of Capital Case Law 1993–2002" (2002) C.M.L.Rev. 773–805.

gradual abolition over a transitional period of restrictions on capital movements and of discrimination on grounds of nationality or place of establishment/investment. National policy on capital movements is intermeshed with Member States' economic and monetary policies and could be liberalised only when the economic policy options of the Member States were more attuned to each other. Article 67(1) EEC required liberalisation "to the extent necessary to ensure the proper functioning of the common market". The Court of Justice made it clear that restrictions on capital movements, unlike those on the free movement of goods and services and on the right of establishment, could not be regarded as having been abolished at the end of the transitional period.[499] Consequently, Art. 67 and the stand-still provision of Art. 71 EEC were not held to have direct effect. This was because it was still open to the Council to adopt on the basis of Art. 69 EEC "the necessary directives for the progressive implementation of the provisions of Article 67". Following the adoption of a first directive on May 11, 1960, the Council introduced a gradual liberalisation of the various categories of capital movements, culminating in the general liberalisation requirement laid down by Directive 88/361 of June 24, 1988, which entered into force on July 1, 1990.[500]

Article 56 EC [*now Art. 63 TFEU*] went further than the directive in that it also liberalised in principle capital movements with third countries.[501] The prohibition of restrictions on movements of capital aims at more than eliminating discrimination based on nationality on the financial markets and precludes all rules which make free movement of capital illusory by preventing market participants from investing in other Member States or by rendering it difficult for undertakings to raise capital in another Member State.[502] Accordingly, national measures dissuading nationals of the Member State in question from taking out loans or making investments in other

---

[499] ECJ, Case 203/80 *Casati* [1981] E.C.R. 2595, paras 10–13.

[500] Council Directive 88/361/EEC of June 24, 1988 for the implementation of [*the former*] Art. 67 of the Treaty, [1988] O.J. L178/5. The directive allowed Spain, Portugal, Greece and Ireland a longer transitional period (Art. 5, Art. 6(2) and Annexes II and III). Member States may still adopt protective measures in respect of certain capital movements, but only with the Commission's authorisation and for a maximum six-month period (Art. 3). The first steps towards liberalisation were taken with the First Council Directive of May 11, 1960 for the implementation of [*the former*] Art. 67 of the Treaty, [1959–1962] O.J. English Spec. Ed. 49, and the Second Council Directive (63/21/EEC) of December 18, 1962 adding to and amending the First Directive for the implementation of [*the former*] Art. 67 of the Treaty, [1963–1964] O.J. English Spec. Ed. 5. No further steps were taken until the programme for achieving the internal market. See Louis, "La libre circulation des capitaux", in Aussant, Fornasier, Louis, Séché and Van Raepenbusch, *Commentaire Mégret— Le droit de la CEE. 3. Libre circulation des personnes, des services et des capitaux. Transports* (Brussels, Editions de l'Université de Bruxelles, 1990), 171–189.

[501] Article 7(1) of Directive 88/361 contains only a commitment on the part of the Member States to endeavour to achieve this end.

[502] ECJ, Case C-35/98 *Verkooijen* [2000] E.C.R. I-4071, paras 34–35.

Member States[503] or making direct foreign investment dependent on authorisation[504] are incompatible with the free movement of capital. Even if such measures apply without distinction to both residents and non-residents, they are prohibited if they are liable to deter investors from making investments in another Member State and, consequenly, affect access to the market.[505]

Although the Treaties do not define the term "movement of capital", it is settled case law that, inasmuch as Art. 63 TFEU substantially reproduces the content of Art. 1 of Directive 88/361, the nomenclature of capital movements annexed thereto retains an indicative value for the purposes of defining the term "movement of capital", subject to the qualification, contained in the introduction to the nomenclature, that the list set out therein is not exhaustive.[506] Accordingly, the "movement of capital" does not only cover investments and loans, but also inheritances[507] and deduction for tax purposes of gifts in money or in kind.[508]

Movement of payments. Free movement of payments relates to transfers of foreign exchange as consideration for a transaction and not, as in the case of capital movements, to investment of the funds in question.[509] Article 106(1) EEC required Member States to liberalise payments connected with the movement of goods, persons, services or capital to the extent that the underlying transactions   **9–102**

---

[503] ECJ, Case C-484/93 *Svensson and Gustavsson* [1995] E.C.R. I-3955, paras 9–10; ECJ, Case C-222/97 *Trummer and Mayer* [1999] E.C.R. I-1661, para. 26; ECJ, Case C-439/97 *Sandoz* [1999] E.C.R. I-7041, para. 19. See also ECJ, Case C-478/98 *Commission v Belgium* [2000] E.C.R. I-7587, para. 20 (prohibition of acquisition of securities for loans issued abroad); ECJ, Case C-367/98 *Commission v Portugal* [2001] E.C.R. I-4731, paras 45–46; ECJ, Case C-483/99 *Commission v France* [2002] E.C.R. I-4781, paras 40–42 ("golden shares"; requirement for approval of the acquisition of holdings in privatised companies); ECJ, Case C-98/01 *Commission v United Kingdom* [2003] E.C.R. I-4641, paras 38–50; ECJ, Joined Cases C-282/04 and C-283/04 *Commission v Netherlands* [2006] E.C.R. I-9141, paras 18–31 (restriction on the possibility of buying voting shares in a privatised company); ECJ, Case C-319/02 *Manninen* [2004] E.C.R. I-7477, paras 20–23; ECJ, Case C-292/04 *Meilicke and Others* [2007] E.C.R. I-1835, paras 20–24 (tax credit not applicable to dividends from companies established in other Member States); ECJ, Case C-112/05 *Commission v Germany* [2007] E.C.R. I-8995, paras 38–56 ("Volkswagen"; capping of shareholders' voting rights).
[504] ECJ, Joined Cases C-163/94, C-165/94 and C-250/94 *Sanz de Lera and Others* [1995] E.C.R. I-4821, paras 24–25; ECJ, Case C-302/97 *Konle* [1999] E.C.R. I-3099, paras 23 and 38–39; ECJ, Case C-54/99 *Eglise de scientologie* [2000] E.C.R. I-1335, para. 14.
[505] ECJ (judgment of July 8, 2010), Case C-171/08 *Commission v Portugal*, not yet reported, para. 67 (see, to the same effect, the case law with respect to the free movement of goods and persons: paras. 9–031, 9–045 and 9–065, *supra*).
[506] E.g. ECJ, Case C-222/97 *Trummer and Mayer* [1999] E.C.R. I-1661, para. 21; Joined Cases C-515/99, C-519/99 to C-524/99 and C-526/99 to C-540/99 *Reisch and Others* [2002] E.C.R. I-2157, para. 30; ECJ, Case C-376/03 *D.* [2005] E.C.R. I-5821, para. 24; ECJ, Case C-513/03 *van Hilten-van der Heijden* [2006] E.C.R. I-1957, para. 39.
[507] ECJ, Case C-513/03 *van Hilten-van der Heijden* [2006] E.C.R. I-1957, paras 40–42.
[508] ECJ, Case C-318/07 *Persche* [2009] E.C.R. I-359, paras 24–30.
[509] ECJ, Joined Cases 286/82 and 26/83 *Luisi and Carbone* [1984] E.C.R. 377, para. 21.

had been liberalised.[510] Accordingly, the attainment of free movement of goods, persons and services entailed liberalisation of the resultant payments. Consequently, until such time as capital movements were liberalised, it was important to distinguish in financial transactions between capital movements and payments.[511] Since January 1, 1994, all payments have been liberalised in currencies of Member States, in euros (ECUs) or in currencies of third countries.

2. Permitted restrictions on the free movement of capital and payments

9–103 **Permitted restrictions.** Restrictions on the free movement of capital may be justified on grounds of general interest, including the grounds for exceptions set out in Art. 65 TFEU [*ex Art. 58 EC*] and other mandatory requirements.[512] Besides, in certain circumstances, restrictions may be imposed on capital movements (Arts 64 and 66 TFEU [*ex Arts 57 and 59 EC*]) or on capital movements and payments (Art. 75 TFEU [*ex Art. 60 EC*]) to or from third countries. Furthermore, the provisions of the Chapter of the Treaty on capital and payments are stated to be without prejudice to the applicability of restrictions on the right of establishment which are compatible with the Treaties (Art. 65(2) TFEU).[513]

9–104 **Explicit justificatory grounds.** Article 65(1) b) TFEU allows the Member States to take "all requisite measures" (i) to prevent infringements of national law and regulations, in particular in the tax field and in regard to the prudential supervision of financial institutions, (ii) to lay down procedures for the declaration of capital movements for the purposes of administrative or statistical information and (iii) to take measures justified on grounds of public policy or public security.[514] Moreover,

---

[510] Article 106(1) EEC was in force until January 1, 1994 as the former Art. 73h EC. For current payments connected with the movement of capital, see the former Art. 67(2) EEC.

[511] ECJ, Joined Cases 286/82 and 26/83 *Luisi and Carbone* [1984] E.C.R. 377, paras 33–34.

[512] Moreover, Protocol (No. 32) annexed to the Treaties on the acquisition of property in Denmark by the EU Treaty ([1992] O.J. C224/104, now [2010] O.J. C83/318) and Protocol No. 6, annexed to the 2003 Act of Accession, on the acquisition of secondary residences in Malta, ([2003] O.J. L236/947) allow these Member States to maintain in force restrictions on the acquisition and holding of immovable property for secondary residence purposes. In the case of Malta, this applies to nationals of the Member States who have not legally resided in that State for at least five years.

[513] For the relationship between free movement of capital, the right of establishment and freedom to supply services, see Landsmeer, "Het kapitaalverkeer en overige vrijheden" (2001) S.E.W. 434–439.

[514] See ECJ, Case C-439/97 *Sandoz* [1999] E.C.R. I-7041, paras 24–37; ECJ, Case C-54/99 *Eglise de scientologie* [2000] E.C.R. I-1335, para. 19; ECJ, Case C-423/98 *Albore* [2000] E.C.R. I-5965, paras 17–25; ECJ, Case C-478/98 *Commission v Belgium* [2000] E.C.R. I-7587, paras 37–38. For restrictions on capital movements in connection with public security, in particular in order to secure energy supplies in a crisis, *cf.* ECJ, Case C-367/98 *Commission v Portugal* [2002] E.C.R. I-4731, paras 52–54, and ECJ, Case C-483/99 *Commission v France* [2002] E.C.R. I-4781, paras 47–54 (requirement for the approval of the acquisition of holdings in privatised companies held to be in breach of free movement of capital) with ECJ, Case C-503/99 *Commission v Belgium* [2002] E.C.R. I-4809, paras 46–55 (more specifically defined restriction held not to be in breach of free movement of capital).

Art. 65(1) (a) contains a general exception for provisions of tax law which justifiably

> "distinguish between taxpayers who are not in the same situation with regard to their place of residence or with regard to the place where their capital is invested".[515]

However, that article cannot be interpreted as meaning that any tax legislation making a distinction between taxpayers by reference to the place where they invest their capital is automatically compatible with the Treaties.[516] A distinction contained in national tax provisions is compatible with Union law only if it concerns situations which are not objectively comparable[517] or if it can be justified by overriding reasons in the general interest, in particular in relation to the cohesion of the tax system.[518] Accordingly, Member State legislation, designed to prevent double taxation, which provides for a tax benefit in relation to dividends paid to persons subject to income tax in that State may not exclude from this benefit dividends paid by companies established in other Member States.[519] Conversely, it is not incompatible with EU law for a Member State to deny non-resident taxpayers who hold the major part of their wealth in the State where they are resident entitlement to the allowances which it grants to resident taxpayers.[520] Article 65 also does not preclude a Member State from subjecting dividends from shares in companies established in the territory of that State and dividends from shares in companies established in another Member State to the same uniform rate of taxation even in the absence of rules to avoid double taxation.[521]

Rule of reason. The Court of Justice is further prepared to inquire into whether a **9–105** restriction on capital movements can be justified on grounds of general interest other than those mentioned in Art. 65(1) TFEU. Accordingly, restrictions are held to be permissible provided that they are not applied in a discriminatory manner and do not exceed what is necessary in order to achieve an objective in the general

---

[515] Declaration (No. 7), annexed to the EU Treaty, on Art. 73d EC [*now Art. 65 TFEU*] made it clear that Member States are entitled to apply the derogation in respect of capital movements and payments between Member States only as far as provisions in force at the end of 1993 are concerned.

[516] ECJ, Case C-319/02 *Manninen* [2004] E.C.R. I-7477, para. 28.

[517] ECJ, Case C-279/93 *Schumacker* [1995] E.C.R. I-225.

[518] ECJ, Case C-204/90 *Bachmann v Belgian State* [1992] E.C.R. I-249; ECJ, Case C-300/90 *Commission v Belgium* [1992] E.C.R. I-305; ECJ, Case C-35/98 *Verkooijen* [2000] E.C.R. I-4071, para. 43; ECJ, Case C-315/02 *Lenz* [2004] E.C.R. I-7063, paras 34–39; ECJ, Case C-379/05 *Amurta* [2007] E.C.R. I-9569, paras 42–56.

[519] ECJ, Case C-319/02 *Manninen* [2004] E.C.R. I-7477. See, in the same vein, ECJ, Case C-446/04 *Test Claimants in the FII Group Litigation* [2006] E.C.R. I-11753; ECJ, Case C-292/04 *Meilicke and Others* [2007] E.C.R. I-1835.

[520] ECJ, Case C-376/03 *D.* [2005] E.C.R. I-5821, paras 25–43.

[521] ECJ, Case C-513/04 *Kerckhaert and Morres* [2006] E.C.R. I-10967.

interest (rule of reason),[522] such as for instance the need to preserve the cohesion of the tax system,[523] objectives in connection with town and country planning[524] and public housing policy,[525] objectives connected with the carrying on of the activities of agricultural and forestry holdings[526] and preservation of jobs in such holdings in cases of inheritance[527] or the objective of maintaining or promoting the use of an official language.[528] Economic grounds cannot afford a valid justification.[529]

9–106 **Proportionality.** A parallel may be drawn with the requirement of proportionality applying to permissible derogations from free movement of goods and services, since the

> "measures and procedures referred to in Article 65(1) and (2) shall not constitute a means of arbitrary discrimination or a disguised restriction on the free movement of capital and payments" (Art. 65(3); *cf.* Art. 36).

Accordingly, France could not deny foreign companies the benefit of a tax exemption enjoyed by companies established in France on the sole ground that the information needed by the French authorities effectively to combat tax evasion could not be obtained from the competent authorities of other Member States involved since it would have been possible to request that the necessary documentary evidence be provided by the taxpayer himself.[530] Similarly, on grounds of public policy (e.g. preventing illegal activities such as tax evasion, money laundering, drug trafficking or terrorism), a Member State may make the export of foreign currency conditional on a prior declaration, but not on prior authorisation, which would make capital movements conditional upon the consent of the

---

[522] E.g. ECJ, Case C-367/98 *Commission v Portugal* [2002] E.C.R. I-4731, para. 49, ECJ, Case C-483/99 *Commission v France* [2002] E.C.R. I-4708, para. 45, and ECJ, Case C-503/99 *Commission v Belgium* [2002] E.C.R. I-4809, para. 45.

[523] See ECJ, Case C-35/98 *Verkooijen* [2000] E.C.R. I-4071, paras 43.

[524] See ECJ, Case C-302/97 *Konle* [1999] E.C.R. I-3099, paras 36–49; ECJ, Joined Cases C-515/99, C-519–524/99, C-526–540/99 *Reisch and Others* [2002] E.C.R. I-2157, para. 34; ECJ, Case C-300/01 *Salzmann* [2003] E.C.R. I-4899, para. 42. See Glöckner, "Grundverkehrsbeschränkungen und Europarecht" (2000) EuR. 592–622.

[525] ECJ, Case C-567/07 *Woningstichting Sint Servatius* [2009] E.C.R. I-9021, para. 30 (this aim was not, by contrast, accepted as a public-policy ground within the meaning of Art. 65 TFEU [ex *Art. 58 EC*]: *ibid*, para. 28).

[526] ECJ, Case C-370/05 *Festersen* [2007] E.C.R. I-1129, paras 27–28.

[527] ECJ, Case C-256/06 *Jäger* [2008] E.C.R. I-123, para. 50.

[528] ECJ, Case C-222/07 *UTECA* [2009] E.C.R. I-1407, para. 27.

[529] ECJ, Case C-367/98 *Commission v Portugal* [2002] E.C.R. I-4731, para. 52.

[530] ECJ, Case C-451/05 *ELISA* [2007] E.C.R. I-8251, paras 94–96; ECJ, Case C-318/07 *Persche* [2009] E.C.R. I-359, paras 53–69. For a general discussion of the impact of the provisions on free movement of capital on the competence of the Member States in the field of direct taxation, see Dahlberg, *Direct Taxation in Relation to the Freedom of Establishment and the Free Movement of Capital* (The Hague, Kluwer Law International, 2005), 363 pp.

administrative authorities.[531] Prior authorisation for foreign investment cannot be regarded as a proportionate measure where the same objective can be achieved by prior notification and the associated possibilities for supervision and imposing sanctions.[532] In any event, any authorisation system must be based on objective, non-discriminatory criteria which are known in advance to the undertakings concerned, and all persons affected by a restrictive measure of that type must have a legal remedy available to them.[533]

Movement to and from third countries. Movement of capital to or from third countries takes place in a different legal context than between Member States. It follows that a Member State may be able to justify a restriction on the movement of capital to or from third countries for a particular reason in circumstances where that reason would not constitute a valid justification for a restriction on capital movements between Member States.[534] For instance, where the legislation of a Member State makes the grant of a tax advantage dependent on satisfying requirements compliance with which can be verified only by obtaining information from the competent authorities of a third country, it is, in principle, legitimate for that Member State to refuse to grant that advantage if—in particular, because that third country is not under any contractual obligation to provide information—it proves impossible to obtain such information from that country.[535] As far as capital movements to and from third countries are concerned, restrictions existing on December 31, 1993[536] under national or Union law in respect of direct investment (including investment in real estate), establishment, the provision of financial services or the admission of securities to capital markets may continue to be applied (Art. 64(1) TFEU [*ex Art. 57(1) EC*]). In order to secure compliance with such restrictions, Member States are entitled to verify the nature and reality of the transactions and transfers in question by means of a prior declaration.[537] The European

9–107

---

[531] ECJ, Joined Cases C-163/94, C-165/94 and C-250/94 *Sanz de Lera and Others* [1995] E.C.R. I-4821, paras 23–30. This was already the case under Directive 88/361: ECJ, Joined Cases C-358/93 and C-416/93 *Bordessa and Others* [1995] E.C.R. I-361, paras 16–31.

[532] E.g. ECJ, Joined Cases C-515/99, C-519–524/99, C-526–540/99 *Reisch and Others* [2002] E.C.R. I-2157, paras 35–39.

[533] ECJ, Case C-367/98 *Commission v Portugal* [2002] E.C.R. I-4731, para. 50; ECJ, Case C-483/99 *Commission v France* [2002] E.C.R. I-4781, para. 45, and ECJ, Case C-503/99 *Commission v Belgium* [2002] E.C.R. I-4809, para. 46.

[534] ECJ, Case C-446/04 *Test Claimants in the FII Group Litigation* [2006] E.C.R. I-11753, para. 171; ECJ, Case C-101/05 *A* [2007] E.C.R. I-11531, paras 36–37.

[535] *Ibid.*, paras 58–63.

[536] As far as Bulgaria, Estonia and Hungary are concerned, the date is December 31, 1999 (see Art. 64(1)).

[537] ECJ, Joined Cases C-163/94, C-165/94 and C-250/94 *Sanz de Lera and Others* [1995] E.C.R. I-4821, paras 37–38. See also Ståhl, "Free movement of capital between Member States and third countries" (2004) *EC Tax Review* 47–56. For a complete picture of the framework for investments from non-member countries, see Vadcar, "Un cadre communautaire pour l'investissement?" (2001) R.M.C.U.E 332–342.

Parliament and the Council, acting in accordance with the ordinary legislative procedure, may adopt measures on such capital movements (Art. 64(2)). Moreover, the Council may unanimously, and after consulting the European Parliament, adopt measures which constitute new restrictions on such capital movements (Art. 64(3) TFEU[538]). In addition, the Council may take such safeguard measures as are strictly necessary where,

> "in exceptional circumstances, movements of capital to or from third countries cause, or threaten to cause, serious difficulties for the operation of economic and monetary union" (Art. 66 TFEU [*ex Art. 59 EC*]).

The European Central Bank must be consulted and the measures may not go on for more than six months. Article 75(1) TFEU defines the Union's power to take economic sanctions in the sphere of capital movements and payments for the purpose of preventing and combating terrorism and related activities. The European Parliament and the Council, acting in accordance with the ordinary legislative procedure are to define a framework for such measures, which is to be implemented by the Council (Art. 75 TFEU).

III. HARMONISATION OF NATIONAL LEGISLATION

9–108   **Legal bases for harmonisation.** Specific Treaty provisions empower the Union to bring divergent national laws more in line with each other, even though they are completely compatible with Union law, where the disparities between the legislation affect the competitive position of the market participants concerned or lead to irregularities amongst consumers.[539] Thus, the Treaties supplement the provisions on free movement of goods, persons, services and capital by providing a legal basis for harmonisation, coordination, approximation and mutual recognition of national legislation or administrative provisions.[540] In some cases,

---

[538] In the absence of such measures, the Commission or the Council may decide that restrictive tax measures adopted by a Member State concerning one or more third countries are to be considered compatible with the Treaties in so far as they are justified by one of the objectives of the Union and compatible with the proper functioning of the internal market. The Council is to act unanimously on application by a Member State (Art. 65(4) TFEU).

[539] Andenas and Andersen (eds), *The Theory and Practice of Harmonisation* (Cheltenham, Edward Elgar Press, forthcoming); Slot, "Harmonisation" (1996) E.L.Rev. 378–397; Vignes, "Le rapprochement des législations", in Calleja, Vignes and Wägenbaur, *Commentaire Mégret. Le droit de la CEE. 5. Dispositions fiscales. Rapprochement des législations* (Brussels, Editions de l'Université de Bruxelles, 1993), 299–379; for the political implications, see Dougan, "Minimum harmonisation and the internal market" (2000) C.M.L.Rev. 853–885.

[540] With regard to the free movement of goods, see Art. 113 TFEU [*ex Art. 93 EC*] (indirect taxation); as regards free movement of persons and services, see Arts 46 and 48, Art.50, in particular para. 2(g), and Arts 52, 53 and 59 TFEU [ex *Arts 40, 42, 46, 47 and 52 EC*]. For the free movement of capital, see the former Art. 70 EC in its original version.

harmonisation of national legislation is necessary where the Union intends to pursue a policy of its own.[541] In addition, Arts 114 to 118 TFEU [*ex Arts 94 to 97 EC*] afford general bases for powers for "approximation of legislation", together with the supplementary legal basis of Art. 352 TFEU [*ex Art. 308 EC*].[542]

The Treaty of Lisbon preserved these general bases for harmonisation virtually in full, whilst enlarging their scope somewhat. Indeed, some of the changes that the Treaty of Lisbon introduced in specific policy areas result in an extension of the Union's powers to harmonise national law.[543] Besides, the conferral on the Union of specific powers in the fields of intellectual property, tourism, civil protection, and energy makes it less necessary to have recourse to the "flexibility clause" of Art. 352 TFEU.[544] In addition, the Treaty of Lisbon enables the Member States to set up "open methods of coordination" with the Commission in various policy areas. Where there is an open method of coordination, the Member States are encouraged to submit national policies to periodic monitoring and evaluation against guidelines and indicators established in common.[545] In some cases, this voluntary coordination of national policies can make formal harmonisation unnecessary.[546]

A. THE IMPACT OF UNION HARMONISATION MEASURES

Expanding Union law. As a result of the harmonisation of national legislation, Union law penetrates into areas which do not form a direct part of the Union's

9–109

---

[541] See, for instance, Arts 40 and 41 TFEU relating to agriculture; Art. 91 TFEU relating to transport; Art. 121 TFEU for the coordination of Union economic policy; Art. 153 TFEU as regards social policy.

[542] Paras 7–018—7–019, *supra*. Before the Treaty of Lisbon, the Treaties also provided for the possibility for the Member States to conclude agreements between themselves which could lead to the approximation of laws (see Art. 293 EC). The Lisbon Treaty no longer provides for this possibility.

[543] See, for example, the extended powers with respect to coordination of national social security law (see para. 9–082, *supra*), immigration laws (see para. 10–014, *infra*), and criminal law (see paras 10–021 and 10–022, *infra*).

[544] See, with respect to intellectual property rights, Art. 118 TFEU (entailing the power to provide uniform protection of intellectual property rights throughout the Union and to set up centralised Union-wide authorisation, coordination and supervision arrangements). See with respect to energy, tourism, civil protection and administrative cooperation, Arts 194–197 TFEU (these articles, however, explicitly exclude harmonisation measures).

[545] See Art. 156, second para., TFEU [*ex Art. 140 EC*] (on social policy, see also para. 11–043, *infra*); Art. 168(2), second para. TFEU [*ex Art. 152 EC*] (on public health); Art. 173, second para. TFEU [*ex Art. 157 EC*] (on industrial policy); Art. 181, second para., TFEU [*ex Art. 165 EC*] (on research and technological development). Compare the formal coordination of national economic policies on the basis of *ex Art. 99 EC* and of national employment policies on the basis of Art. 128 EC (see para. 11–046, *infra*).

[546] For this method, see de Búrca, "The constitutional challenge of new governance in the European Union" (2003) E.L.Rev. 814–839.

competence.[547] Thus the Member States had to adapt their administrative rules to suit directives coordinating national procedures for the award of public works contracts[548] and the relevant review procedures[549] in order to guarantee free movement of goods, persons and services in connection with the award of public contracts.[550] In addition, the Union has adopted rules for the coordination of national law on intellectual property[551] and has introduced Community intellec-

---

[547] See Usher, "Maastricht and English Law" (1993) Stat.L.Rev. 27, at 35–39.

[548] See Directive 2004/18/EC of the European Parliament and of the Council of March 31, 2004 on the coordination of procedures for the award of public works contracts, public supply contracts and public service contracts, [2004] O.J. L134/114), adopted pursuant to *ex Arts 47(2), 55* and *95 EC [now Arts 53(1), 62 and 114 TFEU]* and replacing previous Council Directives on public works contracts (93/37/EEC of June 14, 1993, [1993] O.J. L199/54), public supply contracts (93/36/EEC of June 14, 1993, [1993] O.J. L199/1) and public service contracts (92/50/EEC of June 18, 1992, [1992] O.J. L209/1). Since the water, energy, transport and telecommunications sectors do not invariably come under public law, the Council adopted specific directives relating to them; see, most recently, Directive 2004/17/EC of the European Parliament and of the Council of March 31, 2004 coordinating the procurement procedures of entities operating in the water, energy, transport and postal services sectors ([2004] O.J. L134/1). Purchasing by the telecommunications sector is no longer covered in view of the liberalisation of this sector and the resultant opening to competition (see recital 5 in the preamble to Directive 2004/17).

[549] See the Council directives adopted pursuant to Art. 100a EC [*now Art. 114 TFEU*]: Directive 89/665/EEC of December 21, 1989 on the application of review procedures to the award of public supply and public works contracts, [1989] O.J. L395/33, and, specifically as regards the sectors referred to in the preceding n., Directive 92/13/EEC of February 25, 1992 on the application of Community rules on procurement procedures, [1992] O.J. L76/14.

[550] Bovis, "Developing public procurement regulation: jurisprudence and its influence on law making" (2006) C.M.L.Rev. 461–495; Bovis, "Public procurement in the European Union: lessons from the past and insights to the future" (2005) Col.J.E.L. 53–123; Bovis, "The new public procurement regime of the European Union: a critical analyis of policy, law and jurisprudence" (2005) E.L.Rev. 607–630; Arrowsmith, "An assessment of the new legislative package on public procurement" (2004) C.M.L.Rev. 1277–1325. For the review procedures, see Boyenga-Bofala, "L'impact des directives-recours sur l'organisation des voies de droit internes et les modalités d'exercice par le juge administratif français de son office" (2002) R.T.D.E. 499–525. See also the Commission interpretative communications on concessions under Community law, [2000] C121/2) and on the possibilities for integrating environmental considerations and social considerations into public procurement ([2001] O.J. C333/12 and C333/17, respectively).

[551] Council Directive 87/54/EEC of December 16, 1986 on the legal protection of topographies of semiconductor products, [1987] O.J. L24/36; Council Directive 91/250/EEC of May 14, 1991 on the legal protection of computer programs, [1991] O.J. L122/42; Council Directive 93/83/EEC of September 27, 1993 on the coordination of certain rules concerning copyright and rights related to copyright applicable to satellite broadcasting and cable retransmission, [1993] O.J. L248/15; Directive 96/9/EC of the European Parliament and of the Council of March 11, 1996 on the legal protection of databases, [1996] O.J. L77/20; Directive 98/44/EC of the European Parliament and of the Council of July 6, 1998 on the legal protection of biotechnological inventions, [1998] O.J. L213/13; Directive 98/71/EC of the European Parliament and of the Council of October 13, 1998 on the legal protection of designs, [1998] O.J. L289/28; Directive 2001/29/EC of the European Parliament and of the Council of May 22, 2001 on the harmonisation of certain aspects of copyright and related rights in the information society, [2001] O.J. L167/10; Directive 2001/84/EC of the European Parliament and of the Council of September 27, 2001 on the resale right for the

tual property rights.[552] Furthermore, there was harmonisation in the fields of tourism and civil protection, even before the Treaties provided for a specific competence in these fields (see now Arts 194 and 196 TFEU).[553] As a result of its action to protect tourists and other consumers, in particular with regard to financial services (see paras 9–079 and 11–054), and its action with respect to judicial collaboration in civil matters (see para. 10–016), the Union is becoming involved in increasing areas of private law, such as the law of contractual and non-contractual liability and family law.[554]

---

benefit of the author of an original work of art, [2001] O.J. L275/32; Directive 2006/115/EC of the European Parliament and of the Council of December 12, 2006 on rental right and lending right and on certain rights related to copyright in the field of intellectual property, [2006] O.J. L376/28 (repealing Directive 92/100); Directive 2006/116/EC of the European Parliament and of the Council of December 12, 2006 on the term of protection of copyright and certain related rights, [2006] O.J. L372/12; Directive 2008/95/EC of the European Parliament and of the Council of October 22, 2008 to approximate the laws of the Member States relating to trade marks, [2008] O.J. L299/25 (repealing Directive 89/104/EEC)

[552] See, pursuant to Art. 308 EC [*now Art. 352 TFEU*], Council Regulation (EC) 40/94 of December 20, 1993 on the Community trade mark ([1994] O.J. L11/1); Council Regulation (EC) No. 2100/94 of July 27, 1994 on Community plant variety rights ([1994] O.J. L227/1; now replaced by Council Regulation (EC) No. 207/2009 of 26 February 2009, [2009] O.J. L78/1) and Council Regulation (EC) No. 6/2002 of December 12, 2001 on Community designs ([2002] O.J. L3/1). See also, pursuant to Art. 100a *EEC* [*later Art. 95 EC, now Art. 114 TFEU*], Council Regulation (EEC) No. 1768/92 of June 18, 1992 concerning the creation of a supplementary protection certificate for medicinal products ([1992] O.J. L182/1) (for the Union's competence: ECJ, Case C-350/92 *Spain v Council* [1995] E.C.R. I-1985, paras 25–41); Regulation (EC) No. 1610/96 of the European Parliament and of the Council of July 23, 1996 concerning the creation of a supplementary protection certificate for plant protection products ([1996] O.J. L198/30) and Directive 2004/48/EC of the European Parliament and of the Council on the enforcement of intellectual property rights ([2004] O.J. L157/45; republished with corrigendum: [2004] O.J. L195/16). The rules adopted under Art. 308 EC can, since the Lisbon Treaty, be adopted under Art. 118 TFEU, which makes provision for the creation of European intellectual property rights. For further particulars, see Tritton, *Intellectual Property in Europe* (London, Sweet & Maxwell, 2008), 1275 pp.; Leistner, "Harmonization of intellectual property law in Europe: the European Court of Justice's trade mark case law 2004–2007" (2008) 45 C.M.L.Rev. 69–91.

[553] See, for instance, the Community action plan to assist tourism, Council Decision 92/421/EEC of July 31, 1992 ([1992] O.J. L231/26). The EC Treaty did not confer a specific competence to take action in these fields, although they were mentioned as one of the policy spheres listed in *ex Art. 3 EC*. Even before that, the Council adopted on December 22, 1986 a decision (86/664/EEC) establishing a consultation and cooperation procedure in the field of tourism ([1986] O.J. L384/52) and resolutions on standardised information in existing hotels (86/665/EEC, [1986] O.J. L384/54) and fire safety in existing hotels (86/666/EEC, [1986] O.J. L384/60). See Guyot, "Le droit européen du tourisme" (2008) J.T.D.E. 101–111.

[554] See the Communications from the Commission to the Council and the European Parliament on European contract law, [2001] O.J. C255/1, and on a more coherent European contract law—An action plan, [2003] O.J. C63/1 and the more recent Commission documents available at the Commission's website: *http://ec.europa.eu/consumers/rights/contract_law_en.htm* [Accessed December 5, 2010]. See, most recently, the Green Paper from the Commission on policy options for progress towards a European Contract Law for consumers and businesses, COM (2010) 348. For a selection of the general literature with further citations therein, see Gutman, The Constitutionality of European Contract Law. Comparative Reflections with the United States (PhD dissertation, Katholieke Universiteit Leuven, 2010); Schulze (ed.), *Common Frame of Reference*

Because of the primacy of Union law, once legislation has been harmonised, it can no longer be amended or replaced by national rules. In policy areas where this influence on national law is not desired, the Treaties have expressly precluded any power to harmonise on the part of the Union.[555] In view of the political implications of harmonisation, disputes often arise with regard to the proper legal basis for the relevant Union legislation, with general legal bases or specific Treaty provisions being argued for, depending on the different voting procedures in the Council or the input of the European Parliament (see paras 7–014—7–016).

9–110 **Minimum harmonisation.** In some cases, a harmonisation measure allows the Member States to adopt or maintain stricter rules in its national legislation than those required by the harmonisation itself. Where the harmonisation measure does not expressly so provide, it has to be inferred from the wording, purpose and structure of the measure to what extent complete harmonisation is intended (*maximum harmonisation*) or whether it leaves the Member States any margin to deviate from a requirement or a level of protection laid down by the measure (*minimum harmonisation*).[556]

---

and Existing EC Contract Law (Munich, Sellier, 2009), 313 pp.; Boele-Woelki and Grosheide (eds), *The Future of European Contract Law: Essays in Honour of Ewoud Hondius* (The Hague, Kluwer Law International, 2007), 434 pp.; Grundmann and Stuyck (eds), An Academic Green Paper on European Contract Law (The Hague, Kluwer Law International, 2002), 432 pp. and, with particular regard to developments concerning EU consumer contract law, Howells and Schulze (eds), *Modernising and Harmonising Consumer Contract Law* (Munich, Sellier, 2009), 322 pp. Discussion is under way on the utility of a wider ranging harmonisation of private law. For a selection of the general literature, see Micklitz and Cafaggi (eds), *European Private Law after the Common Frame of Reference* (Cheltenham, Edward Elgar, 2010), 288 pp.; Cafaggi and Muir Watt (eds), Making European Private Law: Governance Design (Cheltenham, Edward Elgar, 2008), 355 pp.; Andenas, Diaz Alabart, Markesinis, Micklitz and Pasquini, *Liber Amicorum Guido Alpa: Private Law Beyond the National Systems* (London, British Institute of International and Comparative Law, 2007), 1112 pp.; Hartkamp, Hesselink et al., Towards a European Civil Code (The Hague, Kluwer Law International, 2004), 847 pp. For the influence of the case law of the Court of Justice on family law, see Lenaerts, "La portée de la jurisprudence de la Cour de justice des Communautés européennes en matière de droit de la famille et des personnes" (2008) *Revue trimestrielle de droit familial* 637–656.

[555] See para. 7–014, *supra*.

[556] See, e.g., with regard to liability for defective products: ECJ, Case C-52/00 *Commission v France* [2002] E.C.R. I-3827, paras 13–24, ECJ, Case C-154/00 *Commission v Greece* [2002] E.C.R. I-3879, paras 9–20, and ECJ, Case C-183/00 *González Sanchez* [2002] E.C.R. I-3901, paras 23–34; ECJ, Case C-402/03 *Skov* [2006] E.C.R. I-199, paras 22–45; ECJ, Case C-470/03 *A.G.M.-COS.MET* [2007] E.C.R. I-2749, paras 50–54. See also ECJ, Case C-445/06 *Danske Slagterier* [2009] E.C.R. I-2119, paras 23–25; with respect to the Directive on unfair commercial practices: ECJ (judgment of January 14, 2010), Case C-304/08 *Zentrale zur Bekämpfung unlauteren Wettbewerbs*, not yet reported, para. 41. For the differing intensity of harmonisation, see Weatherill, "Supply of and demand for internal market regulation: strategies, preferences and interpretation" in Nic Shuibhne (ed), *Regulating the Internal Market* (Cheltenham, Edward Elgar 2006) 29–60; Rott, "Minimum Harmonisation for the Completion of the Internal Market? The Example of Consumer Sales Law" (2003) C.M.L.Rev. 1107–1135; Kurcz, "Harmonisation by means of Directives—never-ending story?" (2001) E.Bus.L.Rev. 287–307.

New approach to harmonisation. Harmonisation of national legislation   **9–111**
becomes protracted where unanimity has to be achieved on detailed rules. Since
the 1980s, a major part of harmonisation has taken a new approach: only minimum requirements are harmonised, after which the Member States must recognise each other's legislation. That approach links up with the *Cassis de Dijon* case
law, which prohibits Member States, in the absence of harmonisation, from
imposing restrictions on the marketing of products which are lawfully marketed
in another Member State, unless such restrictions are necessary in order to
protect "mandatory [or overriding] requirements" (see para. 9–044).

As early as 1985, the Council advocated laying down by directive only the
fundamental safety standards for products and leaving it to other bodies (e.g.
standardisation institutes) to specify them in technical standards. Every administration would then have to accept that products complying with those technical
standards also complied with the basic safety standards.[557] Likewise, in its White
Paper on completing the internal market, the Commission put forward a "new
strategy", whereby harmonisation designed to eliminate technical barriers would
be limited to requirements for which the mutual recognition of national legislation alone did not produce a satisfactory result (see also paras 9–079—9–081).[558]
The Union also seeks to forestall measures restricting trade. Union information
procedures require Member States to notify any draft technical regulations and
standards to the Commission and to take account of any observations submitted
by the Commission or other Member States.[559]

---

[557] Council Resolution of May 7, 1985 on a new approach to technical harmonisation and standards,
[1985] O.J. C136/1. The following standardisation bodies operate at European level: CEN
(European Committee for Standardisation), Cenelec (European Committee for the Coordination of
Electrical Standards) and ETSI (European Telecommunications Standards Institute); see also the
Council resolutions of October 28, 1999 on the role of standardisation in Europe and on mutual
recognition, [2000] O.J. C141/1 and C141/5, respectively. See also Ehricke, "Dynamische
Verweise in EG-Richtlinien auf Regelungen privater Normungsgremien" (2002) Eu.Z.W.
746–753; Andrieu, "La normalisation européenne, instrument de cohésion—quelques points de
repère" (1992) R.M.C.U.E. 627–630; MacMillan, "La 'certification', la reconnaisance mutuelle et
le marché unique" (1991) 2 R.M.U.E. 181–211; Waelbroeck, "L'harmonisation des règles et
normes techniques dans la CEE" (1988) C.D.E. 243–275.

[558] Commission of the European Communities, *Completing the internal market: Commission white
paper for the European Council (Milan, June 28–29, 1985)*, June 14, 1985, COM(85) 310 fin, 19,
s. 65.

[559] See Directive 98/34/EC of the European Parliament and of the Council of June 22, 1998 laying
down a procedure for the provision of information in the field of technical standards and regulations and of rules on Information Society services, [1998] O.J. L 204/37 (as amended by Directive
98/48/EC of the European Parliament and the Council of July 20, 1998, [1998] O.J. L217/18),
replacing Council Directive 83/189/EEC of March 28, 1983 for the provision of information in the
field of technical standards and regulations, [1983] O.J. L109/8. For the inapplicability of non-
notified provisions, see n. to para. 21–008, *infra*.

B. HARMONISATION UNDER ARTS 114 AND 115 TFEU

9–112 **Harmonisation within the internal market.** "Approximation of laws, regulations and administrative provisions" of the Member States may be based on Art. 114(1) TFEU [*ex Art. 95(1) EC*] where they "have as their object the establishment and functioning of the internal market" or on Art. 115 TFEU [*ex Art. 94 EC*] where they "directly affect the establishment or functioning of the internal market".[560] The manner in which the decision is taken to effect such approximation of national legislation differs sharply: under Art. 114 TFEU, the Council and the European Parliament decide in accordance with the ordinary legislative procedure, which requires only a qualified majority in the Council; under Art. 115 TFEU, the Council is to act unanimously after consulting the European Parliament. The legal instruments differ also: only directives may be issued under Art. 115 TFEU, whereas Art. 114 TFEU authorises the adoption of any "measures". Although preference was to be given to directives under Art. 114,[561] the Council could impose harmonisation of national legislation also by regulation.[562] In addition, Art. 114—and not Art. 115—allows Member States to maintain or introduce national provisions derogating from a Union harmonisation measure.[563]

9–113 **Scope of application of Art. 114.** The first para of Art. 114 TFEU [*ex Art. 95 EC*] applies "for the achievement of the objectives set out in Article 26" "[s]ave where otherwise provided in the Treaties". The provision has a broad sphere of application as a result of the definition of the internal market set out in Art. 26 TFEU (see para. 9–001). Nevertheless, it does not confer a general power on the Union to regulate the internal market. The application of Art. 114 is not triggered by a mere finding of disparities between national rules. In the judgment by which the Court of Justice annulled the tobacco advertising directive, the Court held that the measures referred to in Art. 95 EC [*now Art. 114 TFEU*] must genuinely have as their object the improvement of the conditions for the establishment and

---

[560] Before the entry into force of the Lisbon Treaty, Art. 94 EC referred in this connection to the "establishment or functioning of the *common* market", while Art. 95(1) EC already referred to the "establishment or functioning of the *internal* market". For this difference in terminology, see para. 9–011, *supra*.

[561] See the declaration annexed to the Single European Act that the Commission shall give preference to the use of the instrument of a directive in its proposals pursuant to Art. 95(1) [*now Art. 114(1) TFEU*] if harmonisation involves the amendment of legislative provisions in one or more Member States.

[562] Depending on the harmonising instrument, Union legislation itself gives rise to obligations on individuals (regulations) or does so only after it has been transposed into national law (directives); see ECJ, Case C-91/92 *Faccini Dori* [1994] E.C.R. I-3325, para. 24 (concerning Directive 85/577/EEC, n. 310 to para. 11–054, *infra*). See also para. 22–084, *infra*.

[563] Para. 9–115, *infra*.

functioning of the internal market.[564] Where such a measure has the aim of preventing the emergence of future obstacles to trade resulting from multifarious development of national laws, the emergence of such obstacles must be likely and the measure in question must be designed to prevent them.[565] In addition, in assessing the legality of a measure adopted on the basis of Art. 114, the Court of Justice verifies whether the distortion of competition which the measure purports to eliminate is appreciable.[566] Article 114 cannot be used as a legal basis for measures which leave unchanged the different laws of the Member States already in existence and cannot be regarded as aiming to approximate the national laws.[567]

A number of Treaty articles explicitly preclude the power to harmonise on the part of the Union, for instance with regard to public health (see Art. 168(5) TFEU).[568] In that case, it is not possible for the Union legislator to use other articles of the Treaty, Art. 114 in particular, as a legal basis in order to circumvent the express exclusion of harmonisation. However, provided that the conditions for recourse to Art. 114 as a legal basis are fulfilled, the Union legislator cannot be prevented from relying on that legal basis on the ground that public health protection is a decisive factor in the choices to be made.[569] Where obstacles to trade are existent or likely to emerge in the future, Art. 114 enables the Union legislator to adopt not only measures requiring the Member States to authorise the marketing of certain products, but also measures that oblige them to subject such an authorisation to certain conditions, or even provisionally or definitively to prohibit the marketing of the products concerned.[570] By the expression "measures for the approximation" Art. 114 TFEU confers on the Union legislature a discretion

---

[564] ECJ, Case C-376/98 *Germany v European Parliament and Council* [2000] E.C.R. I-8419, paras 83–84 (for commentaries, see n. 46 to para. 7–012, *supra*). In the aftermath of the judgment a new Directive on Tobacco Advertising was adopted, which was more limited in scope. The Court rejected Germany's action for the annulment of that new directive (ECJ, Case C-380/03 *Germany v European Parliament and Council* [2006] E.C.R. I-11573). See also ECJ (judgment of March 9, 2010), Case C-518/07 *Commission v Germany*, not yet reported, paras 49–51 (independence of supervisory authority for processing of personal data held to contribute to the free movement of data).

[565] *Ibid.*, para. 86; ECJ, Case C-377/98 *Netherlands v European Parliament and Council* [2001] E.C.R. I-7079, paras 15–18; ECJ, Case C-491/01 *British American Tobacco (Investments) and Imperial Tobacco* [2002] E.C.R. I-11453, paras 60–61; ECJ (judgment of June 8, 2010), Case C-58/08 *Vodafone and Others*, not yet reported, paras 33–48.

[566] ECJ, Case C-376/98 *Germany v European Parliament and Council* [2000] E.C.R. I-8419, para. 106. For limits on the power to harmonise, see Selmayr, Kamann and Ahlers, "Die Binnenmarktkompetenz der Europäischen Gemeinschaft" (2003) E.W.S. 49–61; Möstl, "Grenzen an der Rechtsangleichung im europäischen Binnenmarkt" (2002) EuR. 318–350.

[567] ECJ, Case C-436/03 *European Parliament v Council* [2006] E.C.R. I-3733, paras 40–45.

[568] See para. 7–014, *supra*.

[569] ECJ, Case C-376/98 *Germany v European Parliament and Council* [2000] E.C.R. I-8419, paras 79 and 88.

[570] ECJ, Case C-434/02 *Arnold André* [2004] E.C.R. I-11825, paras 34–35; ECJ, Case C-210/03 *Swedish Match* [2004] E.C.R. I-11893, paras 33–34; ECJ, Joined Cases C-154/04 and C-155/04 *Alliance for Natural Health* [2005] E.C.R. I-6451, paras 32–38.

as regards the harmonisation technique most appropriate for achieving the desired result, in particular in fields which are characterised by complex technical features.[571] The addressees of the measures adopted on the basis of Art. 114 are not necessarily the individual Member States. The legislature may provide for the establishment of a Union body responsible for contributing to the implementation of a process of harmonisation if the tasks conferred on such a body are closely linked to the subject-matter of the acts approximating the laws, regulations and administrative provisions of the Member States.[572]

By the same token, the Court has held that *ex-Art. 95 EC* could not be used as a legal basis for measures which predominantly relate to PJCC. Accordingly, the Court annulled a Council decision on the conclusion of an international agreement providing for the processing of passenger data for the purpose of safeguarding public security and for law-enforcement purposes, even though the initial collection of those data took place in the course of an activity which fell within the scope of (then) Community law.[573] By contrast, *ex Art. 95 EC* was held to constitute the appropriate legal basis for a directive on the processing of personal data which was directed essentially at service providers and did not contain any rules governing the activities of public authorities for law-enforcement purposes.[574]

Finally, it is clear from the very wording of Art. 114(1) that it applies only if the Treaties do not otherwise provide. It follows that, if the Treaties contain a more specific provision that is capable of constituting the legal basis for the measure in question, that measure must be founded on such provision.[575]

---

[571] ECJ, Case C-66/04 *United Kingdom v European Parliament and Council* [2005] E.C.R. I-10553, paras 45–46, with a case note by Gutman (2006) 13 Col.J.E.L.147–187.

[572] ECJ, Case C-217/04 *United Kingdom v European Parliament and Council* [2006] E.C.R. I-3771, paras 44–45, see the notes by Randazzo (2007) C.M.L.Rev. 155–169 and Gutman (2006) 13 Col.J.E.L.147–187.

[573] ECJ, Joined Cases C-317/04 and C-318/04 *European Parliament v Council and Commission* [2006] E.C.R. I-4721. After the annulment, a new agreement was concluded on the basis of *ex Arts 24 and 38 EU*; see the Agreement between the European Union and the United States of America on the processing and transfer of Passenger Name Record (PNR) data by air carriers to the United States Department of Homeland Security (DHS) (2007 PNR Agreement), which provisionally applies as of the date of its signature (see Council Decision 2007/551/CFSP/JHA of July 23, 2007, [2007] O.J. L204/16). For a detailed discussion of the original agreement, see the House of Lords European Union Committee 21st Report of Session 2006–2007, available at *http://www.publications.parliament.uk/* [Accessed December 10, 2010]; see also de Hert and de Schutter, "International Transfers of Data in the Field of JHA: The Lessons of Europol, PNR and Swift", in Martenczuk and van Thiel (eds), *Justice, Liberty, Security: New Challenges for the External Relations of the European Union* (Brussels, VUBpress, 2009) 303–340; Mendez, "Passenger name record agreements. European Court of Justice" (2007) E.Const.L.Rev. 127–147; Adam, "L'échange de données à caractère personnel entre l'Union européenne et les Etats-Unis" (2006) 42 R.T.D.E. 411–437.

[574] ECJ, Case C-301/06 *Ireland v European Parliament and Council* [2009] E.C.R. I-593, paras 56–93.

[575] ECJ, Case C-338/01 *Commission v Council* [2004] E.C.R. I-4829, paras 59–60; ECJ, Case C-533/03 *Commission v Council* [2006] E.C.R. I-1025, paras 44–46; see the case note by O'Brien (2007) 44 C.M.L.Rev. 1483–1499.

Scope of application of Art. 115. Article 115 TFEU [*ex Art. 94 EC*] is relevant **9–114** above all for the three areas which Art. 114(2) excludes from the application of Art. 114(1). However, the practical significance of Art. 115 is not so great given that harmonisation may be carried out in these areas also on the basis of other Treaty articles. The first category listed in Art. 114(2) consists of "fiscal provisions". This covers all areas and aspects of taxation, whether substantive rules or procedural rules, including arrangements for the collection of such taxes.[576] In this field, Art. 115 is relevant primarily to harmonisation of direct taxation[577] since indirect taxation may be harmonised pursuant to Art. 113 TFEU [*ex Art. 93 EC*] (the procedure is the same as for Art. 115 TFEU).[578] During the negotiations leading to the adoption of the Constitution, it was proposed, as regards harmonisation of indirect taxation, to enable the Council to take a decision by qualified majority on matters relating to administrative cooperation or combating tax fraud and tax evasion and, as far as direct taxation was concerned, to introduce a specific power for the harmonisation of company taxation subject to the same conditions.[579] The

---

[576] ECJ, Case C-338/01 *Commission v Council* [2004] E.C.R. I-4829, paras 63–67; ECJ, Case C-533/03 *Commission v Council* [2006] E.C.R. I-1025, para. 47.

[577] E.g. Council Directive 2003/48/EC of June 3, 2003 on taxation of savings income in the form of interest payments, [2003] O.J. L157/38. Article 94 EC [*now Art. 115 TFEU*] was also the legal basis for the conclusion of international agreements providing for measures equivalent to those laid down in that directive between the European Union and Switzerland, Liechtenstein, San Marino and Monaco (see [2004] O.J. L385/28, [2004] O.J. L379/83, [2004] O.J. L381/32 and [2005] O.J. L19/35 respectively). See Dassesse, "The EU Directive 'on taxation of savings': the provisional end of a long journey?" (2004) *EC Tax Review* 41–46; Malherbe and Hermand, "La nouvelle directive du 3 juin 2003 sur la fiscalité de l'épargne: éléments d'actualité" (2004) J.T. 145–150; Berlin, "La fiscalité de l'épargne dans l'Union européenne. Histoire d'une harmonisation en voie de disparition" (2003) J.T.D.E. 162–168. For the competence to harmonise tax, see Lenaerts, " 'United in Diversity': also *In Fiscalibus*?", in Hinnekens and Hinnekens (eds), *A Vision of Taxes within and outside European Borders"—Festschrift in honor of Prof. Dr. Frans Vanistendael* (The Hague, Kluwer Law International, 2008) 617–634; Hrehorovska, "Tax harmonisation in the European Union", (2007) 34 *Intertax* 158–166; Lenaerts and Bernardeau, "L'encadrement communautaire de la fiscalité directe" (2007) C.D.E. 19–109; Laule, "Harmonisierung der Steuern in Europa" (2002) Z.Eu.S. 381–405; Vanistendael, "Memorandum on the taxing powers of the European Union" (2002) *EC Tax Review* 120–129. For the toilsome harmonisation of direct taxation, see also the Conclusions of the ECOFIN Council Meeting on December 1, 1997 concerning taxation policy and the annexed Resolution of the Council and the Representatives of the Governments of the Member States, meeting within the Council of December 1, 1997 on a code of conduct for business taxation—Taxation of savings, together with the Annex on taxation of savings, [1998] O.J. C2/1 and Bratton and McCahery, "Tax Coordination and Tax Competition in the European Union: Evaluating the Code of Conduct on Business Taxation" (2001) C.M.L.Rev. 677–718. See further Lenaerts, *Die direkte Besteuerung in der EU* (Baden-Baden, Nomos, 2007), 151 pp., and Lenaerts, "Die Entwicklung der Rechtsprechung des Gerichtshofs der Europäischen Gemeinschaften auf dem Gebiet der direkten Besteuerung" (2009) EuR 728–748.

[578] For an example, see Council Regulation (EC) No. 2073/2004 of November 16, 2004 on administrative cooperation in the field of excise duties, [2004] O.J. L359/1.

[579] See Arts III-62(2) and 63 of the draft EU Constitution. In both cases, it would have been up to the Council, acting unanimously on a proposal from the Commission, to determine whether the measures concerned relate to administrative cooperation or combating tax fraud or tax evasion.

proposals were rejected by the 2003 Intergovernmental Conference and were not taken up in the Treaty of Lisbon. The second excluded category listed in Art. 114(2) is provisions "relating to the free movement of persons". This refers above all to aspects of free movement of persons who are not economically active. Indeed, as regards persons coming under the rules on workers, self-employed persons, providers of services or recipients of services, national provisions may be harmonised under specific articles of the Treaties.[580] The third category is provisions "relating to the rights and interests of employed persons", in respect of which specific articles likewise permit harmonisation in some cases.[581]

9–115 **Authorised derogations.** Harmonisation of national legislation decided by the Council acting by a qualified majority vote constitutes a threat to Member States where their legislation is based on a higher degree of protection than that afforded in most Member States. Accordingly, Art. 114(3) TFEU [*ex Art. 95(3) EC*] provides that, in its proposals concerning health, safety, environmental protection and consumer protection, the Commission is to take as its base a high level of protection, taking into account in particular any new development based on scientific facts.[582] In the event that the Commission adopts the high level of protection of a Member State, that State may prevent the Council from setting a lower level.[583] In addition, a harmonising measure may embody a safeguard clause authorising Member States to take provisional measures on one or more of the grounds listed in Art. 36 TFEU [*ex Art. 30 EC*] (Art. 114(10) TFEU).[584]

Lastly, there are the exceptional provisions set out in Art. 114(4) and (5) TFEU, which enable a Member State to apply national provisions when the European Parliament and the Council, or the Commission have adopted a harmonisation measure. In the first place, a Member State may maintain existing measures which it deems necessary on grounds of major needs referred to in Art. 36 TFEU or relating to the protection of the environment or the working environment (Art. 114(4) TFEU). Accordingly, a Member State may base an application to maintain its already existing national provisions on an assessment of the risk to public health different from that accepted by the Union legislature when it adopted the harmon-

---

[580] See n. 540, *supra*.

[581] See Art. 153(2) TFEU [ex *Art. 137(2) EC*], para. 11–044, *infra*.

[582] According to Declaration (No. 22) annexed to the Treaty of Amsterdam, account must also be taken of the needs of persons with a disability ([1997] O.J. C340/135).

[583] This is because the Council may only amend a Commission proposal by a unanimous vote (Art. 293(1) TFEU). See also the requirement for a high level of Union protection in Art. 168(1), first subpara. TFEU (public health), Art. 169(1), first subpara. TFEU (consumer protection) and Art. 191(2) TFEU, first subpara. (the environment).

[584] See De Sadeleer, "Procedures for Derogations from the Principle of Approximation of Laws under Article 95 EC" (2003) C.M.L.Rev. 889–915 and "Les clauses de sauvegarde prévues à l'article 95 du traité CE" (2002) R.T.D.E. 53, at 55–57.

isation measure from which the national provisions derogate. To that end, it must prove that those national provisions ensure a level of health protection which is higher than the Union harmonisation measure and that they do not go beyond what is necessary to attain that objective.[585] Next, on grounds of a problem specific to a Member State arising after the adoption of the harmonisation measure, the Member State concerned may apply (new) national provisions based on new scientific evidence relating to the protection of the environment or the working environment (Art. 114(5) TFEU). In this particular instance, grounds other than protection of the environment or the working environment cannot justify a derogation.[586] In both instances, the Member State has to notify the Commission of the provisions maintained or introduced and of the grounds for maintaining or introducing them.[587] Within six months of notification, the Commission is to approve or reject the national provisions after having verified whether or not they are a

"means of arbitrary discrimination or a disguised restriction on trade between Member States and whether or not they . . . constitute an obstacle to the functioning of the internal market" (Art. 114(6)).[588]

The Commission is not required to formally hear the notifying Member State before it takes its decision.[589] In the absence of a decision by the Commission, the

---

[585] ECJ, Case C-3/00 *Denmark v Commission* [2003] E.C.R. I-2643, paras 63–65.

[586] For the difference between those two situations, see ECJ Case C-512/99 *Germany v Commission* [2003] E.C.R. I-845, para. 41; ECJ, Case C-3/00 *Denmark v Commission* [2003] E.C.R. I-2643, paras 57–62.

[587] By analogy with the third sentence of Art. 108(3) TFEU (see para. 11–024, *infra*), it follows from Art. 114(5) that the Member State is debarred from applying "proposed measures" which deviate from the harmonisation measure. See Barents, "Het Verdrag van Amsterdam en het Europees gemeenschapsrecht" (1997) S.E.W. 351, at 354. Paras 4 to 9 of ex Art. 95 EC [*now Art. 114 TFEU*] were added by the Treaty of Amsterdam to specify para. 4 of the former Art. 100a EC, see De Sadeleer "Les clauses de sauvegarde prévues à l'article 95 du traité CE" (2002) R.T.D.E. 53, at 58–73; Bähr and Albin, "The 'Environmental Guarantee' on the Rise? The Amended Article 95 after the Revision through the Treaty of Amsterdam" (2000) E.J.L.Ref. 119–134.

[588] See, e.g., the series of decisions of October 26, 1999 ([1999] O.J. L329) by which the Commission approved national provisions on the marketing and use of creosote (notified by the Netherlands, Germany, Sweden and Denmark) but not national provisions on the use of sulphites, nitrites and nitrates in foodstuffs (notified by Denmark) and concerning mineral wool (notified by Germany). See Verheyen, "Article 95 EC Treaty in practice: The European Commission decisions on creosote, sulphite, nitrates and nitrites" (2000) R.E.C.I.E.L. 71–75. The action brought by Denmark against the decision addressed to that Member State resulted in its partial annulment: ECJ, Case C-3/00 *Denmark v Commission* [2003] E.C.R. I-2643 (as regards nitrites and nitrates); Germany's action against the decision addressed to that Member State was declared unfounded: ECJ, Case C-512/99 *Germany v Commission* [2003] E.C.R. I-845.

[589] ECJ, Joined Cases C-439/05 P and C-454/05 P *Land Oberösterreich* [2007] E.C.R. I-7141, paras 28–45.

national provisions in question are deemed to have been approved.[590] Rejection or approval constitutes a Commission decision against which an action will lie (e.g. where the national provisions confirmed are considered not to be proportional to the major needs referred to in Art. 114(4)).[591]

When a Member State is authorised to maintain or introduce national provisions derogating from a harmonisation measure, the Commission is to examine immediately whether to propose an adaptation to that measure (Art. 114(7)). In the event that the Commission or a Member State considers that another Member State is making improper use of the powcers conferred by Art. 114, it may bring the matter directly before the Court of Justice by way of derogation from the procedure laid down in Arts 258 and 259 TFEU (*former Arts 226 and 227 EC*) (Art. 114(9)). Such misuse would be present if a Member State continued to apply the diverging national provisions after the Commission had rejected them or if it went beyond the limits of the approval granted by the Commission.

In some areas, approximation of national legislation is not sufficient to attain a single market. As a result, the Council may empower the Commission, in a harmonising measure adopted pursuant to Art. 114(1), to adopt a decision requiring Member States to take temporary measures where the objectives sought by the harmonising measure can be ensured only by supplementary action at Union level.[592]

9–116   **Distortion of trade.** Where a difference between national laws affects the conditions of competition in such a way as to give rise to "distortion", the procedures laid down in Art. 114 or 115 TFEU do not have to be followed. In that event, the

---

[590] In the pre-Amsterdam Treaty version, Art. 100a EC referred in general terms to provisions which a Member State wished to "apply" and the Commission could "confirm". Pursuant thereto, on August 2, 1991 the Federal Republic of Germany notified the Commission of its decision to apply a stricter ban on pentachlorophenol (PCP) than that embodied in Council Directive 91/713/EEC of March 21, 1991 amending Directive 76/769/EEC relating to the marketing and use of certain dangerous substances and preparations, [1991] O.J. L85/34, which Germany had voted against in the Council. On December 2, 1992, the Commission adopted a decision "confirming" the national provisions, [1992] O.J. C334/8. On an application from France, the Court of Justice annulled that decision for failure to satisfy the obligation to state the reasons on which it was based (Art. 253 EC [*now Art. 296 TFEU*]) by judgment of May 17, 1994 in ECJ Case C-41/93 *France v Commission* [1994] E.C.R. I-1829, paras 31–37. By Decision 94/783/EC of September 14, 1994, the Commission re-confirmed the derogation granted to Germany, [1994] O.J. L316/43. The former Art. 100a(4) EC did not contain any time within which the Commission had to take a decision. Failure by the Commission to react to a notification made by a Member State constituted a breach of the principle of sincere cooperation, but did not affect the applicability of the directive in question: ECJ, Case C-319/97 *Kortas* [1999] E.C.R. I-3143, paras 33–38.

[591] However, a mere opinion adopted by the Commission on the scope of a certain harmonisation measure does not constitute an action that can be challenged by a Member State: CFI, Case T-234/04 *Netherlands v Commission* [2007] E.C.R. II-4589, paras 47–73.

[592] ECJ, Case C-359/92 *Germany v Council* [1994] E.C.R. I-3681, paras 30–37 (accordingly, the Court of Justice rejected the action brought by Germany for annulment of Council Directive 92/59/EEC of June 29, 1992 on general product safety ([1992] O.J. L228/24), which has since been replaced; for the new directive, see n. 310 to para. 11–054, *infra*).

European Parliament and the Council, acting in accordance with the ordinary legislative procedure, may issue the "necessary directives" or "other appropriate measures" pursuant to Art. 116 TFEU [*ex Art. 96 EC*]. In order to avoid an amendment of national legislation giving rise to distortion, the Commission is to make recommendations to the Member State concerned (Art. 117 TFEU [*ex Art. 97 EC*]).[593]

In practice, national measures impeding trade in goods in non-harmonised areas often prompt the Commission to bring proceedings before the Court of Justice or national courts to make references for preliminary rulings in connection with the obligations arising under Art. 34 TFEU. In order to deal with such problems more expeditiously, the Union has introduced a procedure obliging Member States to notify the Commission of measures constituting an obstacle to trade.[594] Where a Union measure has carried out an exhaustive harmonisation of the grounds on which obstacles to trade may be justified, any national measure relating thereto must be assessed in the light of the provisions of that harmonising measure and not of Arts 34 and 36 TFEU.[595]

---

[593] After such distortion has arisen, the Council is not entitled to apply Art. 116 to the other Member States in order to require them to amend their own legislation or to apply it in favour of a Member State which has caused distortion detrimental only to itself (Art. 117(2)). For a general discussion, see Van Grinsven, "Het distorsiebegrip bij voortschrijdende Europese integratie" (1991) S.E.W. 173–193.

[594] Decision No. 3052/95/EC of the European Parliament and of the Council of December 13, 1995 establishing a procedure for the exchange of information on national measures derogating from the principle of the free movement of goods, [1995] O.J. L321/1 (adopted on the basis of Art. 95 EC [*now Art. 114 TFEU*]).

[595] ECJ, Case C-221/00 *Commission v Austria* [2003] E.C.R. I-1007, para. 42 (see paras 9–135— 9–136, *supra*).

CHAPTER 10

AREA OF FREEDOM,
SECURITY AND JUSTICE

Area of Freedom, Security and Justice. In Title V of Part Three of the TFEU,   **10–001**
the Lisbon Treaty brought together the fields previously covered by Title IV of
the EC Treaty (visa, asylum, immigration and judicial cooperation in civil matters) and by Title VI of the EU Treaty (the "third pillar" of the EU: police and
judicial cooperation in criminal matters). Through its policy in these fields, the
Union is to ensure an,

> "area of freedom, security and justice with respect for fundamental rights
> and the different legal systems and traditions of the Member States"
> (Art. 67(1) TFEU).

In principle, the Union's action will take shape through legislation adopted by the
European Parliament and the Council in accordance with the ordinary legislative
procedure. However, some institutional arrangements enable the Member States'
governments to exercise a measure of control over policy-making.[1] The Union's
action in the area of freedom, security and justice will be amenable in full to judicial review by the Court of Justice. In order to appreciate the significance of the
changes introduced by the Lisbon Treaty in this area, it is necessary to set out the
steps by which the Member States have gradually agreed to have recourse to
supranational decision-making in matters such as the entry and residence of
third-country nationals, police cooperation and judicial cooperation in civil and
criminal matters.

---

[1] For example, some sensitive matters will still be decided by the Council acting unanimously after
consulting the European Parliament or, in some cases, after obtaining the consent of the European
Parliament (see para. 16–034, *infra*); an "alarm bell procedure" allows discussions on measures
affecting fundamental aspects of a Member State's criminal justice system to be referred to the
European Council (see para. 16–033, *infra*); the right of initiative is conferred not only on the
Commission but also on (a group of at least a quarter of) the Member States (see para. 16–015,
infra). For a recent example, see the initiative of January 22, 2010 of the Kingdom of Belgium, the
Republic of Bulgaria, the Republic of Estonia, the Kingdom of Spain, the French Republic, the
Italian Republic, the Republic of Hungary, the Republic of Poland, the Portuguese Republic,
Romania, the Republic of Finland and the Kingdom of Sweden for a Directive of the European
Parliament and of the Council on the European Protection Order (2010/0802 (COD)).

I. The Gradual Integration of Member States' Action in Matters of Justice and Home Affairs

A. Policies with Respect to Border Checks and Free Movement of Nationals of Third Countries

10–002 **Checks at internal and external borders.** The establishment of an internal market "without internal frontiers" required any formality imposed upon entry into the territory of a Member State from another Member State to be abolished (see paras 9–001 *et seq.*). From January 1, 1993 checks at internal borders in principle disappeared, but the Court of Justice made it clear that so long as the rules on the crossing of external borders had not been harmonised, the Member States retained the right to carry out identity checks at internal borders; it had indeed to be possible to establish the nationality of persons, even of nationals of Member States.[2] The expiry of the date of December 31, 1992 prescribed by Art. 14 EC [*now Art. 26 TFEU*] therefore did not automatically entail an obligation for the Member States to abolish all identity checks at the internal borders.[3] There was protracted discussion as to whether the Community was competent to adopt measures relating to third-country nationals' access to and residence in the territory of the Member States. Despite the adoption of some Community measures in this field,[4] certain Member States denied that the Community was generally empowered to adopt the necessary measures of cooperation in the fields of police and judicial cooperation to accompany the complete liberalisation of movements of persons.[5]

10–003 **Treaty on European Union.** The EU Treaty did not settle the debate with regard to Community competence, but conferred express Community powers with regard to policy on visas (former Arts 100c and 100d EC), whilst also bringing

---

[2] ECJ, Case C-378/97 *Wijsenbeek* [1999] E.C.R. I-6207, paras 39–43. The Court added, however, that Member States were not entitled to prescribe a disproportionate penalty for failure to comply with the obligation to produce an identity document; *ibid.*, para. 44.

[3] *Ibid.*, para. 40.

[4] The Commission White Paper proposed that directives should be adopted to align national law on weapons and drugs and for the coordination of provisions relating to the status of nationals of third countries, the law relating to asylum, the status of refugees, national visa policy and extradition. Nevertheless, Community measures were adopted only on weapons and drugs.

[5] For this debate, see Timmermans, "Free Movement of Persons and the Division of Powers Between the Community and its Member States", in Schermers, Flinterman, Kellermann, Van Haersolte and Van de Meent (eds), *Free Movement of Persons in Europe. Legal Problems and Experiences* (Dordrecht, Martinus Nijhoff, 1993) 352–368; O'Keeffe, "The Free Movement of Persons and the Single Market" (1992) E.L.Rev. 3–19; Plender, "Competence, European Community Law and Nationals of Non-Member States" (1990) I.C.L.Q. 559–610. For interesting reservations about the link made between migration and security, see Huysmans, "The European Union and the Securitisation of Migration" (2000) J.C.M.S. 751–777.

the question within the ambit of cooperation in the field of justice and home affairs (JHA cooperation), the initial "third pillar" of the EU (see para. 3–013). JHA cooperation contemplated primarily such police and judicial cooperation as was necessary to accompany the liberalisation of the movement of persons in the internal market.[6] In the meantime, most Member States applied common rules in the context of the Schengen Convention with regard to controls at the external borders and the grant of visas for extended stays of no more than three months (the Schengen *acquis*; see para. 2–011). Outside the Schengen and JHA arrangements, the conditions for an extended stay on the part of nationals of non-Community countries and asylum policy remained largely determined by each of the Member States themselves.[7]

The European Parliament sought to infer from Art. 14 EC an obligation on the Community to act and repeatedly urged the Commission to put forward proposals for Community rules.[8] In August 1995 the Commission submitted proposals for directives on various aspects of free movement of persons.[9] Ultimately, the Commission's proposals were not adopted, but the Intergovernmental Conference of 1996–1997 elected by means of the Amsterdam Treaty to take over the "Schengen *acquis*" as EU legislation.

Treaty of Amsterdam. As a result of the incorporation of Title IV into the EC Treaty, the Treaty of Amsterdam brought this discussion to a close. Title IV of the EC Treaty empowered the Community to adopt measures relating to the whole policy field of aliens in order to establish progressively "an area of freedom, security and justice" (Art. 61 EC, reiterating the objective added by the Amsterdam

10–004

---

[6] See Labayle, "La coopération européenne en matière de justice et d'affaires intérieures et la Conférence intergouvernementale" (1997) R.T.D.E. 1–35; Den Boer, "Police Cooperation in the TEU: Tiger in a Trojan Horse?" (1995) C.M.L.Rev. 555–578; Lepoivre, "Le domaine de la justice et des affaires intérieures dans la perspective de la Conférence intergouvernementale" (1995) C.D.E. 323–349; O'Keeffe, "Recasting the Third Pillar" (1995) C.M.L.Rev. 893–920. Compare Vignes, "Plaidoyer pour le IIIème pilier" (1996) R.M.C.U.E. 273–281, with Dehousse and Van den Hende, "Plaidoyer pour la réforme du troisième pilier" (1996) R.M.C.U.E. 714–718.

[7] See, for instance, O'Keeffe, "The Emergence of a European Immigration Policy" (1995) E.L.Rev. 20–36; Hailbronner, "Perspectives of a Harmonisation of the Law of Asylum after the Maastricht Summit" (1992) C.M.L.Rev. 917–939. The draft Convention on the crossing of external borders of the Member States (para. 2–010, *supra*) failed to be signed.

[8] The Commission elected to await the outcome of the intergovernmental initiatives, whereupon on November 18, 1993 the Parliament brought an action against the Commission for failure to act, ([1994] O.J. C1/12). As a result of the submission of proposals for directives (see following n.), the proceedings were held to be no longer to any purpose: ECJ (order of July 11, 1996), Case C-445/93 *European Parliament v Commission*, not reported.

[9] For the proposals based on Art. 94 EC [*now Art. 115 EC*], see [1995] O.J. C289/16, and C306/5, and [1997] O.J. C139/6 and C140/21; for proposals based on Arts 40, 44(2) and 52(2) EC [*now Arts 46, 50(2) and 59(2) TFEU*], see [1995] O.J. C307/18. See in this connection the editorial "Legislating Free Movement: An Over-ambitious Commission Package?" (1996) C.M.L.Rev. 1–5.

Treaty to Art. 2, fourth indent, EU).[10] This included measures to permit the abolition of border checks at the internal borders and directly related flanking measures with respect to external border controls, asylum and immigration (Arts 61, 62 and 63 EC).

By empowering the Community to adopt flanking measures with respect to the abolition of border controls on persons and measures to achieve a Community policy at its external borders with regard to entry into and residence in the territory of the Union for third-country nationals, the achievements of the Schengen cooperation could be integrated into Community law. That part of the "Schengen *acquis*" which could not be so integrated was incorporated as Union law in the context of police and judicial cooperation in criminal matters (PJCC, the revised "third pillar" or Title VI of the EU Treaty, see para. 10–006).[11] Accordingly, the procedural framework for the development of the Schengen information system was laid down in decisions adopted in parallel on the basis of Title IV of the EC Treaty and Title VI of the EU Treaty.[12]

The 1996–1997 Intergovernmental Conference succeeded in agreeing on this Community power by simultaneously confirming in a Protocol annexed to the EC Treaty and the EU Treaty the right of the United Kingdom and Ireland to carry out border controls on travellers.[13] Under protocols annexed to the EC Treaty and

---

[10] See Wollenschläger, " 'Das Asyl- und Einwanderungsrecht der EU" (2001) Eu.GR.Z. 354–364; Pollet, "The Amsterdam Treaty and Immigration and Asylum Policies: A Legal Analysis" (2000) R.A.E. 57–80; Hailbronner, "European Immigration and Asylum Law under the Amsterdam Treaty" (1998) C.M.L.Rev. 1047–1067; Hailbronner and Thiery, "Amsterdam— Vergemeinschaftlichung der Sachbereiche Freier Personenverkehr, Asylrecht und Einwanderung sowie Überführung des Schengen-Besitzstands auf EU-Ebene" (1998) EuR. 583–615; Peers, "Building Fortress Europe: The Development of EU Migration Law" (1998) C.M.L.Rev. 1235–1272. See also Bell, "Mainstreaming Equality Norms into European Union Asylum law" (2001) E.L.Rev. 20, at 30–34. For discussions of Community powers in connection with JHA cooperation, see Bribosia, "Liberté, sécurité et justice: l'imbroglio d'un nouvel espace" (1998) 1 R.M.U.E. 27–54; Harings, "Die Zusammenarbeit in den Bereichen Justiz und Inneres" (1998) EuR. Beiheft 2, 81–97; Donner, "De derde pijler en de Amsterdamse doolhof" (1997) S.E.W. 370–378; Labayle, "Le Traité d'Amsterdam. Un espace de liberté, de sécurité et de justice" (1997) R.T.D.E. 813–881. On December 3, 1998, the Council adopted an Action Plan on how best to implement the provisions of the Amsterdam Treaty on an area of freedom, security and justice, [1999] O.J. C19/1. In this connection, the European Council called for a common European asylum and migration policy, facilitated access to courts, enhanced mutual recognition of judicial decisions and judgments, greater convergence of civil law and the combating of crime through prevention and cooperation: Conclusions of the European Council held in Tampere on October 15 and 16, 1999 (1999) 10 EU.Bull point 1.6.1.

[11] See Protocol (No. 2), annexed to the EU Treaty and the EC Treaty by the Amsterdam Treaty, integrating the Schengen *acquis* into the framework of the European Union; para. 10–010, *infra*.

[12] See para. 10–010, *infra*.

[13] Protocol (No. 3), annexed to the EU Treaty and the EC Treaty by the Amsterdam Treaty, on the application of certain aspects of Art. 14 of the Treaty establishing the European Community to the United Kingdom and Ireland (n. 151, *infra*).

the EU Treaty,[14] the Schengen *acquis* was not to apply to the United Kingdom and Ireland and those two Member States, together with Denmark, did not, in principle, take part in further Community action under Title IV of the EC Treaty (see paras 10–028—10–029).

For a period of five years after the entry into force of the Treaty of Amsterdam,[15] the Council was to act unanimously, on proposals from the Commission or on the initiative of a Member State, after consulting the European Parliament; since January 1, 2005, the co-decision procedure applied in most cases (see Art. 67 EC).

Particular rules. Measures adopted under Title IV of the EC Treaty had a number of particular characteristics as compared with other measures of Community law. First of all, measures adopted by the Council concerning refugees and displaced persons and immigration policy did not prevent any Member State from maintaining or introducing in the areas concerned national provisions which were compatible with the EC Treaty and with international agreements (Art. 63, second para., EC). At first sight, this appeared to authorise Member States to retain or adopt provisions potentially deviating from measures adopted by the Council in the same fields, provided that they respected "this Treaty" and "international agreements". However, that interpretation was hard to square with the primacy which Council measures ought to enjoy as Community law. This problem was avoided as far as checks on persons at external borders were concerned, since a protocol confirmed the Member States' power to conclude agreements with third countries "as long as they respect Community law and other relevant international agreements".[16] The reference to Community law covered all measures adopted by the Council in the field. These Treaty provisions were to be construed as not precluding all powers of the Member States in the areas covered by Title IV of the EC Treaty and as therefore conferring non-exclusive competence on the Community, without however authorising the Member States to deviate from measures adopted by the Council. The Lisbon Treaty eliminated the provision of Art. 63, second para., EC, but preserved the protocol authorising Member States to conclude international agreements with regard to the crossing of external borders.[17]

10–005

---

[14] See Protocol (No. 4), annexed to the EU Treaty and the EC Treaty by the Amsterdam Treaty, on the position of the United Kingdom and Ireland (n. 155, *infra*) and Protocol (No. 5), annexed to the EU Treaty and the EC Treaty, on the position of Denmark (n. 140, *infra*).

[15] The five-year period did not apply to measures adopted under Art. 63(2)(b), (3)(a) or (4) (Art. 63, third para., EC).

[16] Protocol (No. 31), annexed to the EC Treaty by the Amsterdam Treaty, on external relations of the Member States with regard to the crossing of external borders, [1997] O.J. C340/108. This was confirmed as regards Art. 63(3)(a) EC by Declaration (No. 18), annexed to the Amsterdam Treaty, [1997] O.J. C340/134.

[17] See Protocol (No. 23), annexed to the TEU and TFEU, on external relations of the Member States with regard to the crossing of external borders, [2010] O.J. C83/304.

Furthermore, the EC Treaty declared that Title IV did not affect the exercise of the responsibilities incumbent upon Member States with regard to the maintenance of law and order and the safeguarding of internal security (Art. 64(1) EC). These policy aspects were also excluded from the jurisdiction of the Court of Justice with regard to measures or decisions taken pursuant to Art. 62(1) EC (Art. 68(2) EC).[18] The Lisbon Treaty kept only the first clause (now Art. 72 TFEU).

Lastly, the Court's jurisdiction to give preliminary rulings was limited to references emanating from courts ruling at last instance as far as the provisions of Title IV of the EC Treaty were concerned (see para. 13–084). This limitation also disappeared with the entry into force of the Lisbon Treaty.

B. POLICIES WITH RESPECT TO JUDICIAL AND POLICE COOPERATION

10–006   **From JHA to PJCC.** Until the entry into force of the Lisbon Treaty, Title VI of the EU Treaty provided the framework for police and judicial cooperation in criminal matters between Member States. Initially, Title VI of the EU Treaty covered all "cooperation in the fields of justice and home affairs" (JHA), which encompassed also measures with respect to asylum and immigration as well as judicial cooperation in civil matters.[19] The Treaty of Amsterdam retained in Title VI of the EU Treaty only the areas of police cooperation and judicial cooperation in criminal matters (PJCC).[20]

If a comparison is made with the procedure which applied to JHA cooperation, it stands out that in the case of PJCC the Council did not invariably have to decide by a unanimous vote and the Commission (alongside the Member States) could

---

[18] I.e. measures relating to the elimination of controls on persons at internal borders. See Peers, "National Security and European Law" (1996) Y.E.L. 363, at 398–403.

[19] These matters were also the subject of intergovernmental cooperation between the Member States before the EU Treaty entered into force (see paras 2–009—2–011). See further Müller-Graff, "The Legal Base of the Third Pillar and its Position in the Framework of the Union Treaty" (1994) C.M.L.Rev. 493–503.

[20] The Amsterdam Treaty conferred competence on the Community to adopt measures with respect to visas, asylum, immigration and other areas connected with free movement of persons (Arts 61 to 69 EC; see para. 10–012 et seq.), customs cooperation (Art. 135 EC; see para. 9–027) and countering fraud (Art. 280 EC; see para. 13–128). Nevertheless, even after the Amsterdam Treaty, the— less precise—abbreviation "JHA" was used for decisions adopted pursuant to Title VI of the EU Treaty. For a discussion of the PJCC provisions, see Monar, "Justice and Home Affairs in the Treaty of Amsterdam: Reform at the Price of Fragmentation" (1998) E.L.R. 320–335; Margue, "La coopération européenne en matière de lutte contre la criminalité organisée dans le contexte du traité d'Amsterdam" (1997) 3 R.M.U.E. 91–117; Peers, *EU Justice and Home Affairs Law* (Oxford, Oxford University Press, 2006), 588 pp.; Anderson and Apap, *Police and Justice Co-operation and the New European Borders* (The Hague, Kluwer Law International, 2002), 303 pp. For the implementation of these provisions in the various legal orders of the Member States, see Moore and Chiavario (eds), *Police and Judicial Co-operation in the European Union* (Cambridge, Cambridge University Press, 2004), 397 pp.

put forward initiatives in all areas.[21] The Council was always to consult the European Parliament before adopting a framework decision or a decision and before establishing a convention or an implementing measure.[22] Article 35 EU conferred on the Court of Justice jurisdiction to give rulings on the validity and interpretation of framework decisions, decisions and implementing measures and on the interpretation of conventions in so far as the Member State concerned accepted the Court's jurisdiction.[23]

Article 42 EU provided that action in areas referred to in Art. 29 EU could be brought within the scope of Title IV of the EC Treaty. In the event that this was done, the Council was to determine the relevant voting conditions.[24] However, no such decision was taken.

Scope and objectives of PJCC. Pursuant to Title VI of the EU Treaty, the Union acted in various ways in order to prevent and combat crime, organised or otherwise, in particular terrorism, trafficking in persons and offences against children, illicit drug trafficking and illicit arms trafficking, corruption and fraud (see Art. 29, second para., EU).[25] Article 29, first para., EU further mentioned preventing and combating racism and xenophobia as a means of achieving the Union's objective of "providing citizens with a high level of safety within an area of freedom, security and justice". At the Tampere European Council of October 15 and 16, 1999 an inventory was made of the actions needed to make the "area of freedom, security and justice" a reality.[26] In criminal matters, this required

10–007

---

[21] In the case of JHA cooperation, the Commission was not entitled to take the initiative in proposing a common position, a joint action or a draft convention on judicial cooperation in the fields of criminal matters, customs cooperation or police cooperation.

[22] In the case of JHA cooperation, the Parliament was merely regularly informed and consulted.

[23] Article 35(1), (2) and (3) EU. Subject to certain conditions, Member States and the Commission could submit a dispute to the Court of Justice and bring before it an application for annulment of PJCC framework decisions and decisions. For the jurisdiction of the Court of Justice in the sphere of PJCC, see para. 13–085, *infra*.

[24] The Council was to adopt such a decision by a unanimous vote on the initiative of the Commission or a Member State, after consulting the European Parliament, and to recommend the Member States to adopt it in accordance with their respective constitutional requirements.

[25] Mitsilegas, "Defining organised crime in the European Union: the limits of European criminal law in an area of 'freedom, security and justice' " (2001) E.L.Rev. 565–581; Margue, "La coopération en matière de prévention et de lutte contre le crime dans le cadre du nouveau troisième pilier" (2000) R.D.U.E. 729–747.

[26] The principles of the Tampere Programme were further developed in the Hague Programme adopted by the Hague European Council of November 4 and 5, 2004. See the Council and Commission Action Plan implementing the Hague Programme on strengthening freedom, security and justice in the European Union, [2005] O.J. C198/1. For an appraisal, see Genson, "Un nouveau programme pluriannuel pour consolider l'espace de liberté, de sécurité et de justice. Le programme de la Haye (2005–2010)" (2005) R.M.C.U.E. 172–176. This programme has been replaced by the Stockholm Programme adopted by the European Council on December 10–11, 2009 (Council document 17024/09) and see the Commission's Action Plan Implementing the Stockholm Programme, proposed on April 20, 2010 (COM(2010) 171 final).

harmonisation of national legislation, mutual recognition of judicial decisions and improvement of the mechanisms of judicial and international cooperation. As a result, the European Union became the pre-eminent forum for bringing Member States' criminal law policy closer together and for making a start with European criminal law.[27] In the same way as Title IV of the EC Treaty, the EU Treaty specified however that it was not to affect the exercise of the responsibilities incumbent upon Member States with regard to the maintenance of law and order and the safeguarding of internal security (see Art. 33 EU—a limitation which is preserved in Art. 72 TFEU).

C. ABANDONMENT OF THE "THIRD PILLAR" WITH THE TREATY OF LISBON

10–008   **Area of freedom, security and justice.** The Treaty of Lisbon conjoined the powers of the Union in the field of police and judicial cooperation in criminal matters with the competences contained in Title IV of the EC Treaty under the single new Treaty title "Area of freedom, security and justice" (Title V of the TFEU). This title brings together all competences of the Union with regard to border checks, asylum, immigration, judicial cooperation in civil and criminal matters and police cooperation.

In all those areas, legislation is enacted, in principle, under the ordinary legislative procedure, whereas action by the Union and the Member States is fully sub8ect to judicial review by the Court of Justice.[28] For the competences previously based on Title IV of the EC Treaty, this means that the "particular rules" discussed in para. 10–005 have disappeared, except for the reservation with regard to the exercise of the responsibilities incumbent upon Member States with regard to maintaining law and order and safeguarding internal security.[29] Also, as

---

[27] See also Barents, "De denationalisering van het strafrecht" (2006) S.E.W. 358–374; Guild, "Crime and the EU's Constitutional Future in an Area of Freedom, Security and Justice" (2004) E.L.J. 218–234; von Bubnoff, "Institutionelle Kriminalitätsbekämpfung in der EU—Schritte auf dem Weg zu einem europäischen Ermittlungs- und Strafverfolgungsraum" (2002) Z.Eu.S. 185–237; Harding, "Exploring the intersection of European law and national criminal law" (2000) E.L.Rev. 374–390. See also, for the possibility to harmonise national criminal law by measures adopted under the former first pillar, para. 7–017, *supra*.

[28] See Hinarejos, "The Lisbon Treaty Versus Standing Still: A View from the Third Pillar" (2009) E.Const.L.Rev. 99–116; Ladenburger, "Police and Criminal Law in the Treaty of Lisbon. A new dimension for the Community Method" (2008) E.Const.L.Rev. 20–40. Before the Lisbon treaty, the Court of Justice already played a role of capital importance in the development of the area of freedom, security and justice, see Lenaerts, "The Contribution of the European Court of Justice to the Area of Freedom, Security and Justice" (2010) I.C.L.Q. 1–47.

[29] See Art. 72 TFEU. Article 73 TFEU mentions the possibility for the Member States to organise between themselves and under their responsibility such forms of cooperation and coordination as they deem appropriate between the competent departments of their administrations responsible for safeguarding national security.

far as police and judicial cooperation in criminal matters is concerned, the specific institutional arrangements of the former third pillar have disappeared. Some sensitive matters, however, are still decided by the Council acting unanimously after consulting the European Parliament or, in some cases, after obtaining the consent of the European Parliament.

At the substantive level, the Lisbon Treaty further enlarged the competence of the Union as regards policies on border checks, asylum and immigration.[30] The same is true as far as judicial cooperation in civil matters is concerned. It is noteworthy in that connection that the EU's competence regarding mutual recognition and execution of judgments and decisions in extrajudicial cases is no longer limited to "civil and commercial cases".[31] The Lisbon Treaty also significantly extended the Union's power to take action in the field of judicial cooperation in criminal matters in so far as it enabled the Union to lay down measures aimed at harmonising not only the definition of certain types of criminal offences and 2anctions, but also aspects of criminal procedure.[32]

General provisions. Chapter 1 of Title V of the TFEU sets out the "general provisions" on the area of freedom, justice and security. Article 67 TFEU mentions several fields of action in this connection. First of all, the Union is to ensure the absence of internal border controls for persons and to frame a common policy on asylum, immigration and external border control, based on solidarity between Member States which is fair towards third-country nationals (Art. 67(2) TFEU).[33] Secondly, the Union is to facilitate access to justice, in particular through the principle of mutual recognition of judicial and extrajudicial decisions in civil matters (Art. 67(4) TFEU). Lastly, the Union endeavours to ensure a high level of security through measures to prevent and combat crime, racism and xenophobia, and through measures for coordination and cooperation between police and judicial authorities and other competent authorities, as well as through the mutual recognition of judgments in criminal matters and, if necessary, through the approximation of criminal laws (Art. 67(3) TFEU).

10–009

The Council may take measures in order to secure cooperation between departments of the administrations of the Member States responsible for the areas covered by Title V of the TFEU and between those departments and the

---

[30] For an overview, see Peers, "Legislative Update: EU Immigration and Asylum Competence and Decision-Making in the Treaty of Lisbon" 10 (2008) 219–247.

[31] Brousse, "Le Traité de Lisbonne et le droit international privé" (2010) *Journal du droit international* 3–34.

[32] For a discussion, see Herlin-Karnell, "The Treaty of Lisbon and the Criminal Law: Anything New Under the Sun?" (2008) E.J.L.Ref. 321–337; Peers, "EU Criminal law and the Treaty of Lisbon" (2008) E.L.Rev. 2008 507–529.

[33] See also Art. 80 TFEU, which specifies that the Union's policies in this connection are to be governed by the principles of solidarity and fair sharing of responsibility (which includes the financial implications) between the Member States (Art. 80 TFEU).

Commission.[34] The Council acts by a qualified majority on a proposal from the Commission[35] after consulting the European Parliament (Art. 74 TFEU [ex Art. 66 EC]).

D. INCORPORATION OF THE SCHENGEN *ACQUIS*

10–010 **Incorporation.** The provisions of Title IV of the EC Treaty provided the Community with a legal basis for transposing the Schengen obligations into Community law. The Amsterdam Treaty attached a protocol to the EU Treaty and the EC Treaty, which empowered the Member States involved in the Schengen cooperation (the United Kingdom and Ireland are not participating; see para. 2–011) to integrate the whole of that cooperation within the framework of the European Union[36]: existing provisions or decisions had to be converted and developed as Community law under Title IV of the EC Treaty or as "Union law" under Title VI of the EU Treaty. The Protocol declared the Schengen *acquis* (including decisions of the Executive Committee) applicable from the date of entry into force of the Treaty of Amsterdam (Art. 2(1), first subpara., of the Protocol). Pursuant to the Schengen Protocol, the Council determined for each provision or decision of the Schengen *acquis* the (Community or non-Community) legal basis.[37] Depending upon the choice of legal basis, the Court of

---

[34] See Council Decision 2002/463/EC of June 13, 2002 adopting an action programme for administrative cooperation in the fields of external borders, visas, asylum and immigration (ARGO programme), [2002] O.J. L161/11 (following on from the Odysseus programme introduced by Council Joint Action 98/244/JHA of March 19, 1998, [1998] O.J. L99/2) and Council Regulation (EC) No. 377/2004 of February 19, 2004 on the creation of an immigration liaison officers network, [2004] L64/1 (not applicable to Denmark). See also Council Decision 2001/470/EC of May 28, 2001 establishing a European Judicial Network in civil and commercial matters, [2001] O.J. L174/25 (amended by Decision No. 568/2009/EC of the European Parliament and of the Council of June 18, 2009, [2009] O.J. L168/35) and Council Regulation (EC) No. 2424/2001 of December 6, 2001 on the development of the second generation Schengen Information System (SIS II), [2001] O.J. L328/4 (not applicable to Denmark). See further Council Decision 2006/688/EC of October 5, 2006 on the establishment of a mutual information mechanism concerning Member States' measures in the areas of asylum and immigration, [2006] O.J. L283/40.

[35] As far as PJCC is concerned, the Council may also act on the initiative of a quarter of the Member States (see Art. 76 TFEU, to which Art. 74 TFEU refers).

[36] Protocol (No. 2), annexed to the EU Treaty and EC Treaty, integrating the Schengen *acquis* into the framework of the European Union, [1997] O.J. C340/93.

[37] Council Decision 1999/436/EC of May 20, 1999 determining, in conformity with the relevant provisions of the Treaty establishing the European Community and the Treaty on European Union, the legal basis for each of the provisions or decisions which constitute the Schengen *acquis*, [1999] O.J. L176/17. To this end, the Council had to list the provisions which form part of the Schengen *acquis*, see Council Decision 1999/435/EC of May 20, 1999 concerning the definition of the Schengen *acquis* for the purpose of determining, in conformity with the relevant provisions of the Treaty establishing the European Community and the Treaty on European Union, the legal basis for each of the provisions or decisions which constitute the *acquis*, [1999] O.J. L176/1 (it names those provisions for which it is unnecessary or inappropriate to determine a legal basis) and the publication of those provisions in [2000] O.J. L239 (corrigendum in Council Decision 2000/645/EC of

Justice had the jurisdiction conferred upon it by either the EC Treaty or the EU Treaty (Art. 2(1), second and third subparas, of the Protocol).[38] Schengen cooperation was further continued, moreover, on the basis of the provisions of Title IV of the EC Treaty and Title VI of the EU Treaty (PJCC), as appropriate.[39]

Further development. Since the entry into force of the Lisbon Treaty, the **10–011** Schengen *acquis* is to be further developed on the basis of the provisions of Title V of Part Three of the TFEU, in accordance with the modified Schengen Protocol attached to the Treaties.[40] The Schengen countries can consult personal data relating to nationals of other States through the central Schengen Information System, of which a newer version (SIS II) was developed in 2001.[41] The Council takes the place of the Executive Committee (Schengen Protocol, Art. 2). Denmark, in common with the United Kingdom and Ireland, is in a special position (see paras 10–028 and 10–029). New Member States have to accept the Schengen *acquis* in full in any event as part of the Union *acquis* (Schengen Protocol, Art. 7). As a result, the provisions of the Schengen *acquis* became binding on all the Member States which acceded on May 1, 2004 and January 1, 2007. Since

---

October 17, 2000, [2000] O.J. L272/24). For the extension of PJCC provisions to Iceland and Norway, see, for example, n. 45, *infra*. See, in this regard, Den Boer, "Not Merely a Matter of Moving House: Police Co-operation from Schengen to the TEU" (2000) M.J.E.C.L. 336–357; Kuijper, "Some Legal Problems Associated with the Communitarisation of Policy on Visas, Asylum and Immigration Under the Amsterdam Treaty and Incorporation of the Schengen Acquis" (2000) C.M.L.Rev. 345, at 346–350.

[38] So long as the Council had not taken such measures, the Schengen provisions and decisions were to be regarded as acts based on Title VI of the EU Treaty (Art. 2(1), fourth subpara., of the Protocol).

[39] As a result the Council, acting under Art. 63 EC, amended Art. 18 of the 1990 Schengen Convention by Regulation (EC) No. 1091/2001 of May 28, 2001, [2001] O.J. L150/4 and supplemented Art. 26 of that Convention (relating to carriers' obligation to return third-country nationals) by means of Directive 2001/51/EC of June 28, 2001, [2001] O.J. L187/45. Further, acting under Arts 32 and 34 of the EU Treaty, the Council amended Art. 40(1) and (7) of the Schengen Convention by Decision 2003/725/JHA (so as to extend cross-border surveillance), [2003] O.J. L260/37.

[40] Protocol (No. 19), annexed to the TEU and TFEU, integrating the Schengen *acquis* into the framework of the European Union, [2010] O.J. C83/290.

[41] This second-generation Schengen Information System is based on the dual EU/EC legal basis of Council Decision 2001/886/JHA of December 6, 2001 and Council Regulation (EC) No. 2424/2001 of December 6, 2001 ([2001] O.J. L328/1 and L328/4, respectively); amended by Council Decision 2006/1007/JHA and Council Regulation (EC) No. 1988/2006 ([2006] O.J. L411178 and L411/1, respectively); for its implementation, see Regulation (EC) No. 1987/2006 of the European Parliament and of the Council of December 20, 2006 [2006] O.J. L381/4. This also applies to the related system for the exchange of information between the national "Sirene offices" in accordance with the "Sirene Manual"; see the procedures for amending the Sirene Manual laid down in Council Regulation (EC) No. 378/2004 of February 19, 2004 and Council Decision 2004/201/JHA of February 19, 2004 ([2004] O.J. L64/5 and L64/45, respectively). See Peers, "Key Legislative Developments on Migration in the European Union: SIS II" E.J.M.L. 10 (2008) 77–104.

accession the bulk of the existing rules (in particular on visa and asylum policy) has been in force; the remainder of the *acquis* (including the elimination of checks on persons at the internal borders) becomes applicable when the Member States concerned meet the necessary conditions.[42] At present, this is so for all the Member States concerned, with the exception of Cyprus, Bulgaria and Romania.[43]

Iceland and Norway, which were associated with the Schengen cooperation, continue to be associated with the implementation of the Schengen *acquis* and its further development in accordance with procedures agreed by those States and the Council on May 18, 1999.[44] The same is true for Switzerland, which has been associated by way of an international agreement and to which the Schengen *acquis* has been extended as from December 12, 2008.[45] Liechtenstein has

---

[42] See Schengen Protocol (n. 41, *supra*; see also para. 19–003, *infra*), Art. 2, which refers to Art. 3 of the 2003 Act of Accession and Art. 4 of the 2005 Act of Accession. Articles 3 and 4 of the 2003 Act of Accession and the 2005 Act of Accession, respectively, refer to the acts listed in Annex to the Act; Arts 3(2) and 4(2) of those Acts provide that the provisions not so listed, while binding on the new Member States, shall only apply in a new Member State pursuant to a Council decision to that effect after verification in accordance with the applicable Schengen evaluation procedures that the necessary conditions have been met. The 2005 Act of Accession provided for temporary assistance for Bulgaria and Romania to finance investment for the purposes of carrying out checks at the new external frontiers of the Union (see Art. 32).

[43] Council Decision 2007/801/EC of December 6, 2007 on the full application of the provisions of the Schengen *acquis* in the Czech Republic, the Republic of Estonia, the Republic of Latvia, the Republic of Lithuania, the Republic of Hungary, the Republic of Malta, the Republic of Poland, the Republic of Slovenia and the Slovak Republic, [2007] O.J. L323/34.

[44] Agreement with the Republic of Iceland and the Kingdom of Norway concerning the latters' association with the implementation, application and development of the Schengen *acquis*, [1999] O.J. L176/35 (corrigendum for certain language versions in [2000] O.J. L58/31). For provisions implementing that agreement, see Council Decision 1999/437/EC of May 17, 1999, [1999] O.J. L176/31. The Council concluded a further agreement with Iceland and Norway on June 30, 1999 on the establishment of rights and obligations between Ireland and the United Kingdom of Great Britain and Northern Ireland, on the one hand, and the Republic of Iceland and the Kingdom of Norway, on the other, in areas of the Schengen *acquis* which apply to these States, [2000] O.J. L15/2. See Den Boer, "Not Merely a Matter of Moving House: Police Co-operation from Schengen to the TEU" (2000) M.J.E.C.L. 336, at 350–351; Kuijper, "Some Legal Problems Associated with the Communitarisation of Policy on Visas, Asylum and Immigration Under the Amsterdam Treaty and Incorporation of the Schengen Acquis" (2000) C.M.L.Rev. 345, at 350–354. The Schengen *acquis* entered into effect for the Nordic countries on March 25, 2001: Council Decision 2000/777/EC of December 1, 2000 on the application of the Schengen *acquis* in Denmark, Finland and Sweden, and in Iceland and Norway, [2000] O.J. L309/24.

[45] See Art. 15(1) of the Agreement between the European Union, the European Community and the Swiss Confederation on the Swiss Confederation's association with the implementation, application and development of the Schengen *acquis*, [2008] O.J. L53/52, on the basis of which the Council adopted Council Decision 2008/903/EC of November 27, 2008 on the full application of the provisions of the Schengen *acquis* in the Swiss Confederation, [2008] O.J. L327/15.

acceded to that same international agreement and will therefore also accede to the Schengen area when the agreement enters into force.[46]

II. POLICIES ON BORDER CHECKS, ASYLUM AND MIGRATION WITH RESPECT TO THIRD-COUNTRY NATIONALS

A. BORDER CHECKS AND VISA POLICY

Border checks and visa policy. In the Member States which have taken over the **10–012** Schengen *acquis*, border checks at the internal borders have in principle been abolished.[47] Pursuant to Art. 77(1) TFEU [*ex Art. 62 EC*], the Union is to develop a policy with a view to ensuring the absence of any controls on persons, whatever their nationality, when crossing internal borders. The necessary measures are laid down by the European Parliament and the Council, acting in accordance with the ordinary legislative procedure (Art. 77(1)(a) and (2)(e) TFEU).

As regards the external borders of the Union, the European Parliament and the Council, acting in accordance with the ordinary legislative procedure, further adopt measures for carrying out checks on persons and the efficient monitoring of the crossing of external borders (Art. 77(1)(b) and (2)(a) to (c) TFEU). Such measures concern the checks to which persons crossing external borders are subject,[48] the common policy on visas and other short-stay residence permits and the conditions under which nationals of third countries have the freedom to travel within the Union for a short period.[49] This Treaty competence does not affect, however, the Member States' competence concerning the geographical demarcation of their

---

[46] Protocol between the European Union, the European Community, the Swiss Confederation and the Principality of Liechtenstein on the accession of the Principality of Liechtenstein to the agreement between the European Union, the European Community and the Swiss Confederation on the Swiss Confederation's association with the implementation, application and development of the Schengen *acquis*; see Council Decision 2008/261/EC of February 28, 2008 on the signature, on behalf of the European Community, and on the provisional application of certain provisions of this protocol, [2008] O.J.L83/3.

[47] For the possibility of introducing temporary border checks, see Groenendijk, "Reinstatement of Controls at the Internal Borders of Europe; Why and Against Whom?" (2004) E.L.J. 150–170.

[48] See Regulation (EC) No. 562/2006 of the European Parliament and of the Council of March 15, 2006 establishing a Community Code on the rules governing the movement of persons across borders (Schengen Borders Code), [2006] O.J. L105/1. See also Regulation (EC) No. 1931/2006 of the European Parliament and of the Council of December 20, 2006 laying down rules on local border traffic at the external land borders of the Member States and amending the provisions of the Schengen Convention, [2006] O.J. L405/1. A protocol to the Treaties specifies that such measures "shall be without prejudice to the competence of the Member States to negotiate or conclude agreements with third countries as long as they respect Union law and relevant international agreements" (Protocol (No. 23), annexed to the TEU and TFEU, on external relations of the Member States with regard to the crossing of external borders ([2010] O.J. C83/304))

[49] See formerly Art. 62(2)(b) EC. These rules cover matters for which the Community already had competence under the former Arts 100c and 100d EC (Maastricht version).

borders (Art. 77(4) TFEU). Union measures concerning short-term visas include: (i) the list of third countries whose nationals must be in possession of visas when crossing the external borders and those whose nationals are exempt from that requirement[50]; (ii) the procedures and conditions for issuing visas by Member States[51]; (iii) a uniform format for visas[52] and (iv) rules on a uniform visa.[53] As a result of the integration of the Schengen *acquis*, the criteria agreed for the grant of short-term visas between the Schengen States apply within the Union in this regard. In the sphere of visa applications and border surveillance, the Council initially granted itself implementing powers in order to amend provisions of the incorporated Schengen *acquis*.[54] More recently,

---

[50] See Council Regulation (EC) No. 539/2001 of March 15, 2001 listing the third countries whose nationals must be in possession of visas when crossing the external borders and those whose nationals are exempt from that requirement, [2001] O.J. L81/1, as amended, most recently, by Council Regulation (EC) No. 1932/2006 of December 21, 2006, [2006] O.J. L405/23 (this regulation, however, does not apply to Ireland and the United Kingdom). See also Peers, "The Visa Regulation: Free Movement Blocked Indefinitely" (1996) E.L.Rev. 150–155; Hailbronner, "Visa Regulations and Third-Country Nationals in EC Law" (1994) C.M.L.Rev. 969–995. See further Martenczuk, "Visa Policy and EU External Relations", in Martenczuk and van Thiel (eds), *Justice, Liberty, Security: New Challenges for the External Relations of the European Union* (Brussels, VUBpress, 2009), 21–52.

[51] See Regulation (EC) No. 810/2009 of the European Parliament and of the Council of July 13, 2009 establishing a Community Code on Visas (Visa Code), [2009] O.J. L243/1 (not binding on Denmark, Ireland and the United Kingdom). The Visa Code also allows for special arrangements, such as the ones adopted with regard to the issuing of visas for members of the Olympic family taking part in the 2004 Olympic or Paralympic Summer Games in Athens and the 2006 Olympic and/or Paralympic Winter Games in Turin, see Regulation (EC) No. 1295/2003 of July 15, 2003, [2003] O.J. L183/1, and Regulation (EC) No. 2046/2005 of the European Parliament and of the Council of December 14, 2005, [2005] O.J. L334/1, respectively. See Peers, "Legislative Update, EC Immigration and Asylum Law: The New Visa Code" 12 (2010) E.J.M.L. 105–131.

[52] See Council Regulation (EC) No. 1683/95 of May 29, 1995—adopted under the former Art. 100c(1) EC—laying down a uniform format for visas, [1995] O.J. L164/1, as amended, pursuant to Art. 62 EC, most recently, by Council Regulation (EC) No. 856/2008 of July 24, 2008, [2008] O.J. L235/1 (not binding on Ireland).

[53] See the Council Communication "Common Consular Instructions on Visas for the Diplomatic Missions and Consular Posts", [2005] O.J. C326/1. For the specific situation of third-country nationals who have to travel through one or more Member States in order to move between two non-contiguous parts of their countries (as in the case of Russians, who have to travel through Lithuania in order to reach Kaliningrad), see the specific Facilitated Transit Document and the Facilitated Rail Transit Document governed by Council Regulations (EC) Nos 693/2003 and 694/2003 of April 14, 2003, [2003] O.J. L99/8 and L99/15 (not binding on Denmark, Ireland and the United Kingdom). See Potemkina, "Some Ramifications of Enlargement on the EU-Russia Relations and the Schengen Regime" (2003) E.J.M.L. 229–247.

[54] See Council Regulations (EC) No. 789/2001 of April 24, 2001 reserving to the Council implementing powers with regard to certain detailed provisions and practical procedures for examining visa applications and (EC) No. 790/2001 of April 24, 2001 reserving to the Council implementing powers with regard to certain detailed provisions and practical procedures for carrying out border checks and surveillance, [2001] O.J. L116/2 and L116/5, respectively). The Commission's action for annulment against the latter regulation on the ground that the Council had infringed Art. 202 EC and Art. 1 of the Comitology Decision (see para. 17–012, *infra*) was dismissed (ECJ, Case C-257/01 *Commission v Council* [2005] E.C.R. I-345).

however, the Commission has been empowered to implement the relevant Union legislation.[55]

The Lisbon Treaty introduced the competence for the Council, acting unanimously after consulting the European Parliament, to adopt provisions concerning passports, identity cards, residence permits or any other such document where necessary to facilitate the right of Union citizens to move and reside freely within the territory of the Member States (e.g. with respect to their family members) (Art. 77(3) TFEU).[56] Another innovation is the competence of the European Parliament and the Council, acting in accordance with the ordinary legislative procedure, to adopt the necessary measures for the gradual establishment of an integrated management system for external borders (Art. 77(1)(c) and (2)(d) TFEU). Even before the Lisbon Treaty, the Council had set up an Agency (Frontex) to facilitate and coordinate cooperation between Member States on the management of their external borders.[57]

B. ASYLUM AND OTHER INTERNATIONAL REGIMES OF PROTECTION

Common policy. As far as asylum is concerned, the Amsterdam Treaty had granted the Community powers only to establish "minimum standards" with respect to the categorisation of refugees and the granting and withdrawal of refugee status. The Lisbon Treaty has now conferred on the Union competence to set up a common European asylum system. Pursuant to Art. 78(1) TFEU, the Union is indeed to develop a common policy on asylum, subsidiary protection and temporary protection with a view to offering appropriate status to any third-country national requiring international protection and ensuring compliance with the principle of *non-refoulement*.[58]

10–013

European asylum policy must be in accordance with the Geneva Convention of July 28, 1951 and the Protocol of January 31, 1967 relating to the status of

---

[55] See the Schengen Borders Code (Regulation No. 562/2006, see n. 49 above) and the Visa Code (Regulation No. 810/2009, see n. 52, *supra*), which repealed Council Regulations No. 790/2001 and No. 789/2001, respectively.

[56] This provision applies only "if the Treaties have not provided the necessary powers".

[57] Council Regulation (EC) No. 2007/2004 of October 26, 2004 establishing a European Agency for the Management of Operational Cooperation at the External Borders of the Member States of the European Union, [2004] O.J. L349/1. Frontex has its seat in Warsaw (Poland), see Council Decision 2005/358/EC of April 26, 2005, [2005] O.J. L114/13. See Fischer-Lescano, "Europäisches Grenzkontrollregime. Rechtsrahmen der europäischen Grenzschutzagentur FRONTEX" (2007) Z.a.öRV. 1219–1276.

[58] The principle of *non-refoulement* is a principle of international law according to which no refugee may be expelled or returned to territories where his or her life or freedom would be threatened (see, e.g., Art. 33(1) of the Geneva Convention relating to the Status of Refugees, n. 59, *infra*).

refugees, and other relevant treaties[59] (Art. 78(1) TFEU). The right to asylum, together with protection in the event of removal, expulsion or extradition, is also enshrined in the Charter of Fundamental Rights of the European Union.[60] For all legal and practical purposes in relation to asylum matters, Member States are to be regarded as constituting safe countries of origin; according to a protocol annexed to the Treaties, in principle applications for asylum made by a national of a Member State will be regarded as inadmissible for processing by another Member State or admitted only in expressly stated cases.[61]

---

[59] Geneva Convention relating to the Status of Refugees, signed on July 28, 1951 (*TS* 39 (1954); Cmd. 9171), which has been ratified by all the Member States of the European Union. See ECJ (judgment of March 2, 2010), Joined Cases C-175/08, C-176/08, C-178/08 and C-179/08 *Salahadin Abdulla and Others*, not yet reported, paras 51–53 (duty to respect the Geneva Convention). According to Declaration (No. 17), annexed to the Amsterdam Treaty, on Art. 63 of the Treaty establishing the European Community, [1997] O.J. C340/134), consultations are to be established with the United Nations High Commissioner for Refugees and other relevant international organisations on matters relating to asylum policy. So as to ensure harmonised application of Art. 1 of the Geneva Convention, the Council defined a Joint Position (96/196/JHA) on March 4, 1996 on the definition of the term "refugee", [1996] O.J. L63/2. For an analysis of the substance of policy on asylum, see Ferguson Sidorenko, *The common European asylum system: background, current state of affairs, future direction* (The Hague, T.M.C. Asser Press, 2007), 241 pp.; Peers and Rogers, *EU immigration and asylum law: text and commentary* (Leyden, Martinus Nijhoff, 2006), 1025 pp.; Lynskey, "Complementing and completing the Common European Asylum System: a legal analysis of the emerging extraterritorial elements of EU refugee protection policy" (2006) E.L.Rev. 230–250; Guild, "Seeking asylum: storm clouds between international commitments and EU legislative measures" (2004) E.L.Rev. 198–218; Harvey, "The Right to Seek Asylum in the European Union" (2004) E.H.R.L.R. 17–36.

[60] Article 18 (referring to the Geneva Convention and the Protocol) and Art. 19 of the Charter of Fundamental Rights of the European Union. See Peers, "Immigration, Asylum and the European Union Charter of Fundamental Rights" (2001) E.J.M.L. 141–169.

[61] Sole Art. of Protocol (No. 24), annexed to the TEU and TFEU, on asylum for nationals of Member States of the European Union, [2010] O.J. C83/305 (replacing Protocol (No. 29), annexed to the EC Treaty by the Amsterdam Treaty, [1997] O.J. C340/103), which mentions, alongside cases where the Member State avails itself of Art. 15 ECHR (derogation in the event of war or other public emergency) and the procedure referred to in Art. 7 TEU (see para. 6–017, *supra*), the case in which a Member State so decides "unilaterally in respect of the application of a national of another Member State", in which event the Council is to be informed and the application "shall be dealt with on the basis of the presumption that it is manifestly unfounded without affecting in any way, whatever the cases may be, the decision-making power of the Member State". What prompted this protocol was Spain's unhappiness with Belgium's refusal to surrender suspected Basque terrorists who had asked to be recognised as refugees. According to a declaration (No. 48), annexed to the Amsterdam Treaty, on Protocol (No. 29), the Protocol does not prejudice the right of each Member State to take the organisational measures it deems necessary to fulfil its obligations under the Geneva Convention of July 28, 1951 relating to the status of refugees, [1997] O.J. C340/141. For the tense relationship between the Protocol and the Geneva Convention, see the Commission's answer of December 8, 1997 to question No. E-3441/97 (Van Dijk), [1998] O.J. C174/58 (the Commission considered it "unfortunate" that the Protocol was included in the Amsterdam Treaty, but was pleased to note that the Protocol nevertheless sought to respect the objectives of the Geneva Convention) See Bribosia and Weyembergh, "Le citoyen européen privé du droit d'asile?" (1997) J.T.D.E. 204–206. Belgium made a unilateral declaration on the Protocol in which it stated that it would carry out an "individual examination" of any asylum request made by a national of another Member State, [1997] O.J. C340/144.

Pursuant to Art. 78(2) TFEU [*ex Art. 63(1) and (2), EC*] the European Parliament and the Council, acting in accordance with the ordinary legislative procedure, are to set up the common European asylum system. They are to lay down, first of all, a uniform status of asylum for nationals of third countries, valid throughout the Union and a uniform status of subsidiary protection for such nationals who, without obtaining European asylum, are in need of international protection[62] (Art. 78(2)(a) and (b) TFEU). They must also establish a common system of temporary protection for displaced persons in the event of a massive inflow,[63] common procedures for the granting and withdrawing of uniform asylum or subsidiary protection status[64] and criteria and mechanisms for determining which Member State is responsible for considering an application for asylum or subsidiary protection (Art. 78(2)(c) to (e) TFEU). In order to determine which State is to be responsible for examining applications for asylum in a given case, the Member States established the Dublin Convention in 1990, which entered into effect in 1997.[65] Pursuant to Art. 63(1)(a) EC [*now Art. 78(2)(e) TFEU*], that convention has been replaced since September 1, 2003 by a regulation which determines the Member State responsible for examining an asylum application lodged in one of the Member States by a third-country national.[66] Acting under the same

---

[62] See Council Directive 2004/83/EC of April 29, 2004 on minimum standards for the qualification and status of third-country nationals or stateless persons as refugees or as persons who otherwise need international protection and the content of the protection granted, [2004] O.J. L304/12 (not applicable in Denmark).

[63] Council Directive 2001/55/EC of July 20, 2001 on minimum standards for giving temporary protection in the event of a mass influx of displaced persons and on measures promoting a balance of efforts between Member States in receiving such persons and bearing the consequences thereof, [2001] O.J. L212/12 (this directive does not apply to Denmark or Ireland); Van Selm, "Temporarily Protecting Displaced Persons or Offering the Possibility to Start a New Life in the European Union" (2001) E.J.M.L. 23–35. See also Decision No. 537/2007/EC of the European Parliament and of the Council of May 23, 2007 establishing the European Refugee Fund for the period 2008 to 2013 as part of the General programme "Solidarity and Management of Migration Flows", O.J. 2007, L144/1 (Denmark alone did not participate in the Fund).

[64] Council Directive 2005/85/EC of December 1, 2005 on minimum standards on procedures in Member States for granting and withdrawing refugee status, [2005] O.J. L326/13.

[65] Convention determining the State responsible for examining applications for asylum lodged in one of the Member States of the European Communities; for the text see (1990) 6 EC Bull. point 2.2.2 or [1997] O.J. C254/1 (for its entry into effect on September 1, 1997, see the notice in [1997] O.J. L242/63).

[66] Council Regulation (EC) No. 343/2003 of February 18, 2003 establishing the criteria and mechanisms for determining the Member State responsible for examining an asylum application lodged in one of the Member States by a third-country national, [2003] O.J. L50/1 (not binding on Denmark—but nevertheless applicable in Denmark by virtue of the Agreement concluded between the European Community and the Kingdom of Denmark extending to Denmark the provisions of Council Regulation (EC) No. 343/2003 establishing the criteria and mechanisms for determining the Member State responsible for examining an asylum application lodged in one of the Member States by a third-country national and Council Regulation (EC) No. 2725/2000 concerning the establishment of "Eurodac" for the comparison of fingerprints for the effective application of the Dublin Convention, [2006] O.J. L66/38, approved on behalf of the Community by Council Decision 2006/188/EC of February 21, 2006, [2006] O.J. L66/37).

legal basis, the Council has adopted a system for the identification of asylum seekers.[67] Furthermore, the European Parliament and the Council must lay down standards concerning the conditions for the reception of applicants for asylum or subsidiary protection (Art. 78(2)(f) TFEU). The minimum standards for the reception of asylum seekers are designed to ensure them a dignified standard of living and comparable living conditions in all Member States.[68] Lastly, the European Parliament and the Council must ensure partnership and cooperation with third countries for the purpose of managing inflows of people applying for asylum or subsidiary or temporary protection (Art. 78(2)(g) TFEU).

In the event of one or more Member States being confronted with an emergency situation characterised by a sudden inflow of nationals of third countries, the Council may, acting by a qualified majority on a proposal from the Commission and after consulting the European Parliament, adopt provisional measures for the benefit of the Member States concerned (Art. 78(3) TFEU [*ex Art. 64(2) EC*]). In this respect, it should be mentioned that, by virtue of Art. 80 TFEU, the Union's policies in the area of border checks, asylum and immigration are to be governed by the principle of solidarity and fair sharing of responsibility (including the financial implications) between the Member States.

C. IMMIGRATION POLICY

10–014 **Immigration.** With respect to immigration, the Lisbon Treaty has embedded the previous Community competences in a "common immigration policy" aimed at ensuring, at all stages, the efficient management of migration flows, fair treatment of third-country nationals residing legally in Member States, and the prevention of, and enhanced measures to combat, illegal immigration and trafficking in human beings (Art. 79(1) TFEU).

The European Parliament and the Council, acting in accordance with the ordinary legislative procedure, are to adopt measures on conditions of entry and residence and standards for the issue by Member States of long-term visas and residence permits, including those for the purpose of family reunification,[69]

---

[67] Council Regulation (EC) No. 2725/2000 of December 11, 2000 concerning the establishment of "Eurodac" for the comparison of fingerprints for the effective application of the Dublin Convention, [2000] O.J. L316/1 (not binding on Denmark—but nevertheless applicable in Denmark by virtue of the agreement mentioned in the preceding n.). See Bell, "Mainstreaming Equality Norms into European Union Asylum law" (2001) E.L.Rev. 20, at 26–28; Peers, "Key Legislative Developments on Migration in the European Union" (2001) E.J.M.L. 231, at 235–236.

[68] Council Directive 2003/9/EC of January 27, 2003 laying down minimum standards for the reception of asylum seekers, [2003] O.J. L31/18 (not binding on Denmark and Ireland).

[69] See Council Regulation (EC) No. 1030/2002 of June 13, 2002 laying down a uniform format for residence permits for third-country nationals, [2002] O.J. L157/1 (as amended by Council Regulation No. 380/2008 of April 18, 2008, [2008] O.J. L115/1; not binding on Ireland or Denmark); Council Directive 2003/86/EC of September 22, 2003 on the right to family reunification, [2003] O.J.

and on illegal immigration and unauthorised residence, including removal and repa-triation of persons residing without authorisation.[70] They are further to adopt meas-ures defining the rights of third-country nationals residing legally in a Member State, including the conditions governing freedom of movement and of residence in other Member States[71] and measures for combating trafficking in persons, in par-ticular women and children (Art. 79(2) TFEU [*ex Art. 63(3) and (4) EC*]).[72]

In accordance with Directive 2003/109 a Member State is to grant long-term resident status to third-country nationals who have resided legally and continu-ously within its territory during the previous five years and have sufficient

---

L251/12 (not binding on Denmark, Ireland or the United Kingdom) and Council Directive 2003/109/EC of November 25, 2003 concerning the status of third-country nationals who are long-term residents, [2004] O.J. L16/44 (not binding on Denmark, Ireland or the United Kingdom); Council Directive 2005/71/EC of October 12, 2005 on a specific procedure for admitting third-country nationals for the purposes of scientific research, [2005] O.J. L289/15 (not binding on Denmark or the United Kingdom); Council Directive 2009/50/EC of May 25, 2009 on the conditions of entry and residence of third-country nationals for the purposes of highly qualified employment, [2009] O.J. L155/17 (the so-called "Blue card" Directive; not binding on Denmark or the United Kingdom). With regard to Directive 2003/86, see ECJ, Case C-540/03, *European Parliament v Council* [2006] E.C.R. I-5769 (action for annulment of the Directive, rejected by the ECJ; see also para. 13–013, *infra*), with a case note by Bultermann (2008) 45 C.M.L.Rev. 245–259. See further Peers, "Family Reunion and Community Law", in Walker (ed.) *Europe's Area of Freedom, Security and Justice* (Oxford, Oxford University Press, 2004) 143–97; Peers, "Legislative Update: EC Immigration and Asylum Law Attracting and Deterring Labour Migration: The Blue Card and Employer Sanctions Directives" (2009) 11 E.J.M.L. 387–426; Groenendijk, "Family reunification as a right under Community law" (2006) E.J.M.L. 215–230; Groenendijk and Guild, "Converging Criteria: Creating an Area of Security of Residence for Europe's Third Country Nationals" (2001) E.J.M.L. 37–59.

[70] See Council Directive 2001/40/EC of May 28, 2001 on the mutual recognition of decisions on the expulsion of third country nationals, [2001] O.J. L149/34, and, by way of compensation for the financial imbalances resulting from the application of this directive, Council Decision 2004/191/EC of February 23, 2004, [2004] O.J. L60/55 (neither the directive nor the decision applies to Ireland and Denmark); see also Council Directive 2002/90/EC of November 28, 2002 defining the facilitation of unauthorised entry, transit and residence, [2002] L328/17 (this directive does not apply to Denmark) and Council Regulation (EC) No. 377/2004 of February 19, 2004 on the creation of an immigration liaison officers' network, [2004] O.J. L64/1 (this regulation does not apply to Denmark); Directive 2008/115/EC of the European Parliament and of the Council of December 16, 2008 on common standards and procedures in Member States for returning illegally staying third-country nationals, [2008] O.J. L348/98 (not binding on Denmark, Ireland or the United Kingdom). See Acosta, "The Good, the Bad and the Ugly in EU Migration Law: Is the European Parliament Becoming Bad and Ugly? (The Adoption of Directive 2008/15: The Returns Directive) 2009 E.J.M.L. 19–39.

[71] On this basis, the application of Regulations Nos 1408/71 and 574/72 on the coordination of social security systems has been extended to third-country nationals legally residing in the territory of the Member States. This remains true after the replacement of Regulation No. 1408/71 by Regulation No. 883/2004 (see para. 9–082): see Art. 90(1)(a) of the latter regulation.

[72] See Askola, "Violence against women, trafficking and migration in the European Union" (2007) 13 E.L.J. 204–217.

---

resources and sickness insurance cover for themselves and their dependants.[73] The status may be refused on grounds of public policy or public security.[74] Stricter conditions apply with respect to the right of a long-term resident to reside in the territory of Member States other than the one which granted him or her long-term resident status, for a period exceeding three months.[75] Subject to certain conditions, long-term residents are to enjoy equal treatment with nationals of the host State as regards access to employment and self-employed activities, conditions of employment and working conditions, education and vocational training, recognition of professional diplomas, certificates and other qualifications, social security, tax benefits, access to goods and services and the supply of goods and services made available to the public, and freedom of association.[76]

In addition, the European Parliament and the Council, acting in accordance with the ordinary legislative procedure, may establish measures to provide incentives and support for the action of Member States with a view to promoting the integration of third-country nationals residing legally in their territories, but without carrying out any harmonisation of the laws and regulations of Member States (Art. 79(4) TFEU). It will be up to the Member States to determine the number of third-country nationals who may be admitted to their territory in order to seek work (Art. 79(5) TFEU). Furthermore, the Union may cooperate with third countries for the readmission to their countries of origin or provenance of third-country nationals who do not or who no longer fulfil the conditions for entry, presence or residence in the territory of one of the Member States (Arts 78(2)(g) and 79(3) TFEU).

D. RIGHTS DERIVED FROM AGREEMENTS WITH THIRD COUNTRIES

10–015   **Agreements with third countries.** Third-country nationals may also obtain certain rights where the Union concludes an agreement with their country which confers rights on them.[77] In this way, the association agreements with the

---

[73] Council Directive 2003/109/EC (n. 70, *supra*), Arts 4 and 5. For a critical analysis of the directive, see Boelaert-Suominen, "Non-EU Nationals and Council Directive 2003/109/EC on the Status of Third-Country Nationals who are Long-term Residents: Five Paces Forward and Possibly Three Paces Back" (2005) C.M.L.Rev. 1011–1052.

[74] Council Directive 2003/109/EC (n. 70, *supra*), Art. 6(1).

[75] *Ibid.*, Arts 14–23.

[76] *Ibid.*, Art. 11(1). According to Art. 11(3), Member States may retain restrictions to access to employment or self-employed activities where these activities are reserved to nationals, EU or EEA citizens. Whereas Art. 11(1) also mentions social assistance and social protection, Art. 11(4) allows Member States to limit equal treatment in these fields to core benefits.

[77] Hedemann-Robinson, "An Overview of Recent Legal Developments at Community Level in Relation to Third Country Nationals Resident within the European Union, with Particular Reference to the Case Law of the European Court of Justice" (2001) C.M.L.Rev. 525–586.

Maghreb countries and some decisions of the EU-Turkey Association Council[78] confer on nationals of those countries who are lawfully employed in the Member States the right to be treated in the same way as their own nationals as regards conditions of employment, remuneration and social security.[79] However, nationals of the third countries concerned do not as a result obtain the right to free movement within the Union.[80] According to the Charter of Fundamental Rights of the European Union, nationals of third countries who are authorised to work in the territories of the Member States are entitled to working conditions equivalent to those of the citizens of the Union.[81]

III. JUDICIAL COOPERATION IN CIVIL MATTERS

Scope. The Union is to develop judicial cooperation in civil matters having cross-border implications, including the adoption of harmonisation measures. Judicial cooperation in civil matters is based on the principle of mutual recognition of judgments and of decisions in extrajudicial cases (Art. 81(1) TFEU [*see ex Arts 61(c) and 65 EC*]). **10–016**

---

[78] For these association agreements and decisions, see para. 25–021, *infra*. For a general discussion, see Kellerman, "The rights of non-Member State nationals under the EU association agreements" (2008) E.For.Aff.Rev. 339–382; Peers, "EU Migration Law and Association Agreements", in Martenczuk and van Thiel (n. 51, *supra*) 53–88.

[79] This also applies to resident family members who qualify for benefit under the legislation of a Member State: ECJ, Case C-18/90 *Kziber* [1991] E.C.R. I-199, para. 28; ECJ, Case C-126/95 *Hallouzi-Choho* [1996] E.C.R. I-4807, paras 21–40; ECJ, Case C-179/98 *Mesbah* [1999] E.C.R. I-7955, paras 42–48 (Cooperation Agreement with Morocco); ECJ, Case C-103/94 *Krid* [1995] E.C.R. I-719, paras 21–24; ECJ, Case C-113/97 *Babahenini* [1998] E.C.R. I-183, paras 19–31 (Cooperation Agreement with Algeria). However, the agreement with Morocco embodies more limited rights than the agreement with Turkey, which is supplemented by association decisions: ECJ, Case C-416/96 *El-Yassini* [1999] E.C.R. I-1209, paras 33–67. For examples of rights arising under Decisions 2/76 and 1/80 of the EEC-Turkey Association Council, see ECJ, Case C-192/89 *Sevince* [1990] E.C.R. I-3461, paras 27–33; ECJ, Case C-237/91 *Kus* [1994] E.C.R. I-6781, paras 11–36; ECJ, Case C-188/00 *Kurz* [2002] E.C.R. I-10691, paras 26–70; ECJ, Case C-171/01 *Wählergruppe Gemeinsam* [2003] E.C.R. I-4301, paras 68–94. For Decision 3/80, see, e.g., ECJ, Case C-277/94 *Taflan-Met* [1996] E.C.R. I-4085; ECJ, Case C-262/96 *Sürül* [1999] E.C.R. I-2685, paras 75–105; ECJ, Joined Cases C-102/98 and C-211/98 *Kocak and Örs* [2000] E.C.R. I-1287, paras 32–55; ECJ, Case C-275/02 *Ayaz* [2004] E.C.R. I-8765, paras 34–48; ECJ, Case C-383/03 *Dogan* [2005] E.C.R. I-6237, paras 13–25; ECJ, Case C-337/07 *Altun* [2008] E.C.R. I-10323, paras 19–64. For Art. 41(1) of the Additional Protocol to the agreement with Turkey (on establishment and services), see ECJ, Case C-37/98 *Savas* [2000] E.C.R. I-2927, paras 56–71; ECJ, Joined Cases C-317/01 and C-369/01 *Abatay and Others* [2003] E.C.R. I-12301, paras 58–117. With regard to the direct effect of such provisions, see para. 22–046, *infra*.

[80] E.g. ECJ, Case C-179/98 *Mesbah* [1999] E.C.R. I-7955, para. 356. See also Tezcan, "Le droit du travail et le droit de séjour des travailleurs turcs dans l'Union européenne à la lumière des arrêts récents de la Cour de justice des Communautés européennes" (2001) R.M.C.U.E. 117–128; Stangos, "La jurisprudence récente de la Cour de justice des Communautés européennes concernant les travailleurs migrants, ressortissants de pays tiers" (2000) R.A.E. 107–117.

[81] Charter of Fundamental Rights of the European Union, Art. 15(3). *Cf.* para. 9–048, *supra*.

The Treaty of Amsterdam introduced this competence with regard to private (international) law, while limiting it to measures "necessary for the proper functioning of the internal market".[82]

With the entry into force of the Lisbon Treaty, the latter limitation disappeared, although Art. 81(2) TFEU specifies that the measures are to be adopted "particularly when necessary for the proper functioning of the internal market". Although private law is primarily within the competence of the Member States, the Union legislation adopts measures pursuant to Art. 81 TFEU which restrict national policy options and, just as in other Union policy areas, may in some cases preclude any parallel exercise of competence by the Member States.[83]

Since the entry into force of the Treaty of Nice, the European Parliament and the Council are to take measures in this context in accordance with the ordinary legislative procedure (formerly the co-decision procedure), with the exception of aspects relating to family law. For measures concerning family law with cross-border implications, the Council acts by unanimous vote on a proposal from the Commission after consulting the European Parliament (Art. 81(3), first subpara.,

---

[82] See Art. 65 EC. For general discussions, see Basedow, "The Communitarisation of Private International Law" (2009) (73)3 RabelsZ 455–664; Remien, "European Private International Law, the European Community and its Emerging Area of Freedom, Security and Justice" (2001) C.M.L.Rev. 53–86; Basedow, "The Communitarisation of the Conflict of Laws under the Treaty of Amsterdam" (2000) C.M.L.Rev. 687–708. For the relationship with the Hague Conference on Private International Law and the question whether Art. 65 EC [*now Art. 81 TFEU*] implies the power to conclude agreements with third countries, see Wagner, "Die Haager Konferenz für internationales Privatrecht zehn Jahre nach der Vergemeinschaftlichung der Gesetzgebungskompetenz in der justiziellen Zusammenarbeit in Zivilsachen—mit einem Rückblick auf die Verhandlungen zum Haager Gerichtsstandsübereinkommen" (2009) (73)2 RabelsZ 215–240; Traest, "Development of a European Private International Law and the Hague Conference" (2003) Yearbook of Private International Law 223–259; Kotuby, "External Competence of the European Community in the Hague Conference on Private International Law: Community Harmonisation and Worldwide Unification" (2001) N.I.L.R. 1–30;.

[83] See, e.g., Regulation No. 1347/2000 (n. 92, *infra*) and Regulation No. 44/2001 (n. 89, *infra*) preclude any parallel competence on the part of the Member States within the meaning of the *AETR* case law (see para. 7–024, *supra*), which confers an "exclusive nature" on the Union in the relevant areas. This means that the Member States may no longer act internationally in the fields covered by these regulations without the authorisation of the Union. See Council Decision 2003/882/EC of November 27, 2003 authorising the Member States which are Contracting Parties to the Paris Convention of July 29, 1960 on Third Party Liability in the Field of Nuclear Energy to sign, in the interest of the European Community, the Protocol amending that Convention, [2003] O.J. L338/30 and see Regulation (EC) No. 662/2009 of the European Parliament and of the Council establishing a procedure for the negotiation and conclusion of agreements between Member States and third countries on particular matters concerning the law applicable to contractual and non-contractual obligations, [2009] O.J. L200/25, and Council Regulation (EC) No. 664/2009 of July 7, 2009 establishing a procedure for the negotiation and conclusion of agreements between Member States and third countries concerning jurisdiction, recognition and enforcement of judgments and decisions in matrimonial matters, matters of parental responsibility and matters relating to maintenance obligations, and the law applicable to matters relating to maintenance obligations, [2009] O.J. L200/46. See also ECJ, Opinion 1/03 on the Community's exclusive competence to conclude the Lugano Convention (n. 91, *infra*).

TFEU). However, the Council, acting unanimously on a proposal from the Commission after consulting the European Parliament, may adopt a decision determining those aspects of family law with cross-border implications which may be the subject of acts adopted by the ordinary legislative procedure. National parliaments must be notified of any such proposal. If a national Parliament opposes the measure within six months of its notification, it cannot be adopted (Art. 81(3), second and third subparas, TFEU)

Cross-border actions. What is involved is, first, measures aimed at ensuring the mutual recognition and enforcement between Member States of judgments and of decisions in extrajudicial cases,[84] the cross-border service of judicial and extrajudicial documents and cooperation in the taking of evidence (Art. 81(2)(a), (b) and (d) TFEU [ex Art. 65(a) EC]). In these areas, regulations have been adopted on the basis of the EC Treaty to replace and build upon agreements concluded as between the Member States under Art. 293 EC or outside the Community framework which the Court of Justice had jurisdiction to interpret.[85]   **10–017**

For the purpose of the taking of evidence in civil and commercial matters, a Council regulation has introduced a system of cooperation between the courts of the Member States.[86] As far as cross-border service of documents is concerned, a regulation has replaced the convention concluded by the Member States in the context of cooperation in the fields of justice and home affairs.[87] Moreover, as regards recognition and enforcement of judgments, Regulation No. 44/2001 has been adopted to deal with the recognition and enforcement of judicial decisions in civil and commercial matters while laying down common rules as to

---

[84] Before the Lisbon Treaty, this competence was limited to "the recognition and enforcement of decisions in civil and commercial cases, including decisions in extrajudicial cases" (Art. 65(a), third indent, EC).

[85] See paras 23–014—23–015. See also Van Houtte and Pertegás Sender (eds), *Het nieuwe Europese IPR: van verdrag naar verordening* (Antwerp, Intersentia, 2001), 303 pp; Traest, "Internationaal privaatrecht in verordeningen: een verdere stap in de ontwikkeling van Europees internationaal privaatrecht" (2000–2001) A.J.T. 537–564.

[86] Council Regulation (EC) No. 1206/2001 of May 28, 2001 on the cooperation between the courts of the Member States in the taking of evidence in civil or commercial matters, [2001] O.J. L174/1; Van het Kaar, "De Europese Bewijsverordening wordt op 1 januari 2004 van kracht" (2003) N.T.E.R. 287–291; Mougenot, "Le règlement européen sur l'obtention des preuves" (2002) J.T. 17–21; Berger, "Die EG-Verordnung über die Zusammenarbeit der Gerichte auf dem Gebiet der Beweisaufnahme in Zivil- und Handelssachen (EuBVO)" (2001) IPRax. 522–527.

[87] Regulation (EC) No. 1393/2007 of the European Parliament and of the Council of November 13, 2007 on the service in the Member States of judicial and extrajudicial documents in civil or commercial matters, [2007] O.J. L324/79 (replacing Council Regulation (EC) No. 1348/2000 of May 29, 2000, [2000] O.J. L160/37). See Ekelmans, "Le règlement 1348/2000 relatif à la signification et à la notification des actes judiciaires et extrajudiciaires" (2001) J.T. 481–488; Heß, "Die Zustellung von Schriftstücken im europäischen Justizraum" (2001) N.J.W. 15–23. See, formerly, the Convention of May 26, 1997 on the service in the Member States of the European Union of judicial and extrajudicial documents in civil or commercial matters, [1997] O.J. C261/26 (explanatory report in [1997] O.J. C261/26).

jurisdiction.[88] That regulation took over from the Brussels Convention (or "Brussels I"), which the Member States concluded as long ago as 1968 pursuant to Art. 220 [*later Art. 293*] EC.[89] The arrangements laid down in Regulation No. 44/2001 were extended to Iceland, Norway and Switzerland by virtue of the Lugano Convention.[90] Similar regulations have been adopted on jurisdiction and the recognition and enforcement of judgments in matrimonial matters and in matters of parental responsibility[91] and on jurisdiction, applicable law and

---

[88] Council Regulation (EC) No. 44/2001 of December 22, 2000 on jurisdiction and the recognition and enforcement of judgments in civil and commercial matters, [2001] O.J. L12/1; Stradler, "From the Brussels Convention to Regulation 44/2001: cornerstones of a European law of civil procedure" (2005) C.M.L.Rev. 1637–1661; Piltz, "Vom EuGVÜ zur Brüssel-I-Verordnung" (2002) N.J.W. 789–794; Droz and Gaudemet-Tallon, "La transformation de la Convention de Bruxelles du 27 septembre 1968 en Règlement du Conseil concernant la compétence judiciaire, la reconnaissance et l'exécution des décisions en matière civile et commerciale" (2001) R.C.D.I.P. 601–652.

[89] Brussels Convention of September 27, 1968 on jurisdiction and the enforcement of judgments in civil and commercial matters (Accession Convention for Denmark, Ireland and the United Kingdom: [1978] O.J. L304/77), implemented in the United Kingdom by the Civil Jurisdiction and Judgments Act 1982; see the consolidated text of the Convention in [1998] O.J. C27/1. See Briggs and Rees, *Civil Jurisdiction and Judgments* (London, Lloyd's of London Press, 1997), 472 pp; Van Houtte and Pertegás Sender (eds), *Europese IPR-verdragen* (Leuven, Acco, 1997), 410 pp. For its interpretation by the Court of Justice, see para. 23–014, *infra*. Interpretation provided by the Court in respect of the provisions of the Brussels Convention is also valid for those of Regulation No. 44/2001 whenever the provisions of those instruments may be regarded as equivalent (ECJ (judgment of May 4, 2010), Case C-533/08 *TNT Express Nederland*, not yet reported, para. 36).

[90] Convention on jurisdiction and the enforcement of judgments in civil and commercial matters (the Lugano Convention, constituting a de facto extension of the territorial scope of the Brussels Convention of September 27, 1968), [1988] O.J. L319/9. In 2007 a new, revised Lugano Convention was signed by the European Communities, Denmark, Iceland and Norway: Convention on jurisdiction and the recognition and enforcement of judgments in civil and commercial matters ([2007] O.J. L339/3), which entered into force on January 1, 2010 between the EU, Denmark and Norway ([2010] O.J. L140/1). That Convention is currently open for ratification. For the Community's exclusive competence to conclude that Convention, see ECJ, Opinion 1/03, *Competence of the Community to conclude the new Lugano Convention on jurisdiction and the recognition and enforcement of judgments in civil and commercial matters*, [2006] E.C.R. I-1145. See the case notes by Kruger (2006) Col.J.E.L. 189–199 and Lavranos (2006) C.M.L.Rev. 1087–1100 and Schroeter in (2006) *GPR* 203 *et seq.*

[91] Council Regulation (EC) No. 2201/2003 of November 27, 2003 concerning jurisdiction and the recognition and enforcement of judgments in matrimonial matters and the matters of parental responsibility, [2003] O.J. L338/1: "Brussels IIa" or "Brussels IIbis" Regulation), which replaced Council Regulation (EC) No. 1347/2000 of May 29, 2000 on jurisdiction and the recognition and enforcement of judgments in matrimonial matters and in matters of parental responsibility for children of both spouses, [2000] O.J. L160/19; *corrigendum* in [2000] O.J. C219/6: "Brussels II"). See the contributions in Mankowski and Magnus (eds), *Brussels IIbis Regulation* (Munich, Sellier, *forthcoming*), 300 pp.; McEleavy, "The Brussels II Regulation: How the European Community has Moved into Family Law" (2002) I.C.L.Q. 883–908; Ancel and Muir Watt, "La désunion européenne: le Règlement dit 'Bruxelles II' " (2001) R.C.D.I.P. 403–457; Kohler, "Internationales Verfahrensrecht für Ehesachen in der Europäischen Union: Die Verordnung 'Brüssel II' " (2001) N.J.W. 10–15; Watté and Boularbah, "Les nouvelles règles de conflits de juridictions en matière de désunion des époux. Le règlement communautaire 'Bruxelles II' " (2001) J.T. 369–378.

recognition and enforcement of decisions and cooperation in matters relating to maintenance obligations.[92] The former regulation replaced a convention concluded by the Member States in the context of cooperation in the fields of justice and home affairs with regard to judicial decisions in matrimonial matters ("Brussels II").[93] Another regulation has laid down rules on jurisdiction and the applicable law with regard to cross-border insolvency proceedings and the recognition of judgments delivered on the basis of such proceedings.[94] By means of a regulation, the possibility has been created for a judgment on uncontested claims to be certified as a European Enforcement Order, allowing the judgment to be recognised and enforced in another Member State without any intermediate proceedings needing to be brought in that State.[95] The recognition and enforcement of orders freezing property or evidence in criminal matters are the subject of Council decisions adopted in the context of police and judicial cooperation in criminal matters (see para. 10–021).

None of these regulations, however, apply to Denmark. In order to make Regulation No. 44/2001 applicable in Denmark the Council had recourse to a special technique: an international agreement was concluded between the Community and Denmark which provides for the application of the provisions of that regulation and its implementing measures to relations between the

---

[92] Council Regulation (EC) No. 4/2009 of December 18, 2008 on jurisdiction, applicable law, recognition and enforcement of decisions and cooperation in matters relating to maintenance obligations, [2009] O.J. L7/1. See also Council Decision 2009/941/EC of November 30, 2009 on the conclusion by the European Community of the Hague Protocol of November 23, 2007 on the Law Applicable to Maintenance Obligations, [2009] O.J. L331/17. For a commentary, see Beaumont, "International Family Law in Europe—the Maintenance Project, the Hague Conference and the EC: A Triumph of Reverse Subsidiarity" (2009) (73) 3 RabelsZ 509–546.3

[93] Convention of May 28, 1998 on jurisdiction and the recognition and enforcement of judgments in matrimonial matters (Second Brussels Convention, [1998] O.J. C221/2). For its interpretation by the Court of Justice, see para. 23–015, *infra*.

[94] Council Regulation (EC) No. 1346/2000 of May 29, 2000 on insolvency proceedings, [2000] O.J. L160/1 (not applicable to Denmark). See Bariatti, "Recent Case-Law Concerning Jurisdiction and the Recognition of Judgments under the European Insolvency Rules" (2009) (73) 3 RabelsZ 629–659; Bos, "The European Insolvency Regulation and the Harmonisation of Private International Law in Europe" (2003) N.I.L.Rev. 31–57; Bureau, "La fin d'un îlot de résistance— Le règlement du Conseil relatif aux procédures d'insolvabilité" (2002) R.C.D.I.P. 613–679. A convention on insolvency proceedings was adopted on November 23, 1995 but did not enter into force since it was not signed by all Member States.

[95] Regulation (EC) No. 805/2004 of the European Parliament and of the Council of April 21, 2004 creating a European Enforcement Order for uncontested claims, [2004] O.J. L143/15. See also, in this connection, Regulation (EC) No. 1896/2006 of the European Parliament and of the Council of December 12, 2006 creating a European order for payment procedure, [2006] O.J. L399/1; Regulation (EC) No. 861/2007 of the European Parliament and of the Council of July 11, 2007 establishing a European Small Claims Procedure, [2007] O.J. L199/1. None of these regulations are applicable to Denmark.

Community and Denmark.[96] The same technique was used in order to render the provisions of the regulation on the service of documents and its implementing measures applicable in relations between the Community and Denmark.[97] Denmark also signed the new Lugano Convention as an independent contracting party, after taking part in the negotiations.

Where the Union has not harmonised a particular area or introduced a system of reciprocal recognition, the Treaty provisions on free movement of persons may require national authorities to accept certificates and analogous documents relative to personal status issued by the competent authorities of the other Member States, unless their accuracy is seriously undermined by concrete evidence relating to the individual case in question. This will be the case in particular where workers have to prove facts set out in registers of civil status (in their Member State of origin) in order to assert entitlements to social security benefits in another Member State.[98]

10–018 **Conflict of laws.** In addition, the Council is to take measures to ensure the compatibility of the rules applicable in the Member States concerning conflict of laws and of jurisdiction (Art. 81(2)(c) TFEU [*ex Art. 65(b) EC*]). Apart from rules on jurisdiction, this relates to instruments such as the Rome Convention concluded by the Member States in 1980 on the law applicable to contractual obligations.[99] The Rome Convention has since been replaced by a regulation on the law

---

[96] Agreement between the European Community and the Kingdom of Denmark on jurisdiction and the recognition and enforcement of judgments in civil and commercial matters, [2005] O.J. L299/62, approved on behalf of the Community by Council Decision 2006/325/EC of April 27, 2006, [2006] O.J. L120/22 (as amended by Council Decision 2009/943 of November 30, 2009, [2009] L 331/26). For its entry into force, see [2007] O.J. L94/70.

[97] Agreement between the European Community and the Kingdom of Denmark on the service of judicial and extrajudicial documents in civil or commercial matters, [2005] O.J. L300/55, approved on behalf of the Community by Council Decision 2006/326/EC of April 27, 2006, [2006] O.J. L120/23 (as amended by Council Decision 2009/942 of November 30, 2009, [2009] L 331/24). For its entry into force, see [2007] O.J. L94/70.

[98] ECJ, Case C-336/94 *Dafeki* [1997] E.C.R. I-6761, paras 8–21.

[99] Rome Convention of June 19, 1980 on the law applicable to contractual obligations [1980] O.J. L266/1; see the consolidated version in [2005] O.J. C334/1). For this Convention, see Van Houtte and Pertegás Sender (eds), *Europese IPR-verdragen* (Leuven, Acco, 1997), 189–320 pp.; Plender, *The European Contracts Convention* (London, Sweet & Maxwell, 1991), 351 pp; Martigny, "Internationales Vertragsrecht im Schatten des Europäischen Gemeinschaftsrechts" (2001) Z.Eu.P. 308–366. For the harmonisation of the rules of private international law, see also Jayme and Kohler, "Europäisches Kollisionsrecht 2001: Anerkennungsprinzip statt IPR" (2001) IPRax. 501–514; for the extent to which Union law influences the application of national conflicts rules, see Wilderspin and Lewis, "Les relations entre le droit communautaire et les règles de conflits de lois des Etats membres" (2002) R.C.D.I.P. 1–37.

applicable to contractual obligations.[100] Likewise, a regulation has been adopted on the law applicable to non-contractual obligations (Rome II).[101] The European Union has acceded to the Hague Conference on Private International Law, and hence has become a member of that conference alongside the Member States.[102]

Civil procedure. Lastly, Art. 81(2)(f) TFEU [*ex Art. 65(c) EC*] provides for measures to eliminate obstacles to the good functioning of civil proceedings, if necessary by promoting the compatibility of the rules on civil procedure applicable in the Member States. Since the Lisbon Treaty, the Union has obtained express competences to enact measures aimed at ensuring effective access to justice and the development of alternative methods of dispute settlement (Art. 81(2)(e) and (g) TFEU). Even before, the Union laid down minimum standards for legal aid in cross-border disputes for persons without sufficient financial means[103] and facilitated the use of mediation as a method of settling disputes in civil and commercial matters.[104]   **10–019**

European judicial network. Pursuant to Art. 81(2)(h) TFEU, the Union is to support the training of the judiciary and judicial staff. Even before the Lisbon Treaty added this provision, the Council had already established a European judicial network in civil and commercial matters and other forms of collaboration   **10–020**

---

[100] Regulation (EC) No. 593/2008 of the European Parliament and of the Council of June 17, 2008 on the law applicable to contractual obligations (Rome I), [2008] O.J. L177/6 (not applicable to Denmark; corrigendum in [2009] O.J. L309/87).

[101] Regulation (EC) No. 864/2007 of the European Parliament and of the Council of July 11, 2007 on the law applicable to non-contractual obligations (Rome II), [2007] O.J. L199/40 (not applicable to Denmark). See Kadner Graziano, "Das auf ausservertragliche Schuldverhältnisse anzuwendbare Recht nach Inkrafttreten der Rom-II-Verordnung" (2009) 73 RabelsZ 1–77 and Von Hein, "Of Older Siblings and Distant Cousins: The Contribution of the Rome II Regulation to the Communitarisation of Private International Law" (2009) 73 RabelsZ 461–508; Francq, "Le règlement Rome II concernant la loi applicable aux obligations non contractuelles. Entre droit communautaire et droit international privé" (2008) J.T.D.E. 289–296.

[102] See Council Decision 2006/719/EC of October 5, 2006 on the accession of the Community to the Hague Conference on Private International Law, [2006] O.J. L297/1. See Boele-Woelki and van Ooik, "Exclusieve externe bevoegdheden van de EG inzake het Internationaal Privaatrecht" (2006) N.T.E.R. 194–201; Traest, "Harmonisation du droit international privé: relation entre la Communauté européenne et la Conférence de La Haye" (2003) R.D.Unif. 499–507.

[103] Council Directive 2003/8/EC of January 27, 2003 to improve access to justice in cross-border disputes by establishing minimum common rules relating to legal aid for such disputes, [2003] O.J. L26/41 (the directive does not apply to Denmark).

[104] Directive 2008/52/EC of the European Parliament and of the Council of May 21, 2008 on certain aspects of mediation in civil and commercial matters, [2008] O.J. L136/3 (the Directive does not apply to Denmark).

between legal practitioners on the basis of its competence to eliminate obstacles to judicial cooperation in civil matters.[105]

IV. JUDICIAL COOPERATION IN CRIMINAL MATTERS

10–021 **Aspects of criminal procedure.** As in the case of judicial cooperation in civil matters, judicial cooperation in criminal matters is based on the principle of mutual recognition of judgments and judicial decisions (Art. 82(1) TFEU).[106] The Lisbon Treaty conferred on the Union competence to adopt measures to (i) lay down rules and procedures for ensuring recognition throughout the Union of judgments and judicial decisions, (ii) prevent and settle conflicts of jurisdiction between Member States and (iii) facilitate cooperation between national judicial or equivalent authorities in relation to proceedings in criminal matters and the enforcement of decisions (Art. 82(1) TFEU). The necessary measures to that end are to be adopted by the European Parliament and the Council under the ordinary legislative procedure. In this connection, they may adopt directives establishing minimum rules concerning the mutual admissibility of evidence, the rights of individuals in criminal procedure, the rights of victims of crime and such other specific aspects of criminal procedure as are identified in advance by the Council, acting unanimously after obtaining the consent of the European Parliament (Art. 82(2) TFEU). Such minimum rules may be adopted only

> "[t]o the extent necessary to facilitate mutual recognition of judgments and judicial decisions and police and judicial cooperation in criminal matters having a cross-border dimension"

and must take into account the differences between the legal traditions and systems of the Member States (Art. 82(2) TFEU).[107] As in the case of judicial

---

[105] Council Decision 2001/470/EC of May 28, 2001 establishing a European Judicial Network in civil and commercial matters, [2001] O.J. L174/25 (adopted on the basis of Art. 61(c) and (d) and Art. 66 EC; not applicable to Denmark; the decision has been amended by Decision No. 568/2009/EC of the European Parliament and of the Council of June 18, 2009, [2009] O.J. L168/35). Council Regulation (EC) No. 743/2002 of April 25, 2002 established a general Community framework of activities to facilitate the implementation of judicial cooperation in civil matters, [2002] O.J. L115/1 (not applicable to Denmark). See also the European Judicial Training Network (*http://www.ejtn.net* [Accessed November 6, 2010]), a non-profit making international organisation which promotes training programmes with a European dimension for members of the judiciary in Europe.

[106] For a critical view of the principle of mutual recognition in criminal matters, see Alegre and Leaf, "Mutual Recognition in European Judicial Cooperation: A Step Too Far Too Soon? Case Study— the European Arrest Warrant" (2004) E.L.J. 200–217; Peers, "Mutual Recognition and Criminal Law in the European Union: Has the Council Got it Wrong?" (2004) C.M.L.Rev. 5–36.

[107] Article 82(2) TFEU makes it plain that the adoption of such rules does not prevent Member States from maintaining or introducing a higher level of protection for individuals. For a first example, see Directive 2010/64/EU of the European Parliament and the Council of 20 October 2010 on the right to interpretation and translation in criminal proceedings, [2010] O.J. L280/1.

cooperation in civil matters, the Union may adopt measures to support the training of the judiciary and judicial staff (Art. 82(1), second subpara., sub (c), TFEU).

A special "alarm bell procedure" applies to decision-making under Art. 82(1) and (2) TFEU where a member of the Council considers that a draft directive would affect fundamental aspects of its criminal justice system (Art. 82(3) TFEU; see para. 19–008).

Before the Lisbon Treaty, measures in this field were adopted, first, within the framework of JHA cooperation, mainly in the form of conventions between the Member States[108] and, since the Treaty of Amsterdam, in the form of framework decisions adopted under Art. 31 EU. The framework decision on the European arrest warrant[109] is especially noteworthy in this context. It replaced the system of formal extradition between Member States[110] by a system of surrender between judicial authorities of sentenced or suspected persons. The European arrest warrant was the first concrete measure in the field of criminal law implementing the principle of mutual recognition, a principle referred to by the Tampere

---

[108] See, for example, the Convention of May 29, 2000 on Mutual Assistance in Criminal Matters between the Member States of the European Union established by Council Act of the same date in accordance with Art. 34 of the EU Treaty, [2000] O.J. C197/1; for the explanatory report, see [2000] O.J. C379/7 and the protocol to this convention of October 16, 2001, [2001] O.J. C326/1 (for the explanatory report, see [2002] O.J. C257/1). Both parts have been extended to Iceland and Norway; see the agreement concluded by the European Union with those States to that end on December 19, 2003, approved by Council Decision 2004/79/EC of December 17, 2003, [2004] O.J. L26/1). See Denza, "The 2000 Convention on Mutual Assistance in Criminal Matters" (2003) C.M.L.Rev. 1047–1074.

[109] Council Framework Decision 2002/584/JHA of June 13, 2002 on the European arrest warrant and the surrender procedures between Member States, [2002] O.J. L190/1). See further the Agreement between the European Union and the Republic of Iceland and the Kingdom of Norway on the surrender procedure between the Member States of the European Union and Iceland and Norway, concluded on behalf of the Community by Council Decision 2006/697/EC of June 27, 2006, [2006] O.J. L292/1. See Wouters and Naert, "Of Arrest Warrants, Terrorist Offences and Extradition Deals: An Appraisal of the EU's Main Criminal Law Measures against Terrorism after '11 September' " (2004) C.M.L.Rev. 909–935. The validity of national measures implementing Framework Decision 2002/584/JHA was contested before a number of national constitutional courts, in particular in Germany, Cyprus, the Czech Republic and Poland (see paras 21–029, 21–046, 21–047 and 21–051, *infra*). In several Member States, the Constitution was adapted to allow for its implementation; see, for example, Fichera, "The European Arrest Warrant and the Sovereign State: a Marriage of convenience" (2009) 15 E.L.J. 70–97; Deen-Racsmany, "The European arrest Warrant and the Surrender of nationals revisited: the lessons of constitutional challenges", (2006) E.J.C.C.L. & C.J. 271–306; Monjal, "La décision-cadre instaurant le mandat d'arrêt européen et l'ordre juridique français: la constitutionnalité du droit dérivé de l'Union européenne sous contrôle du Conseil d'Etat" (2003) R.D.U.E. 109–187. For the the validity of this framework decision, see ECJ, Case C-303/05 *Advocaten voor de Wereld* [2007] E.C.R. I-3633.

[110] See the Convention of March 10, 1995, adopted on the basis of the former Art. K.3 of the EU Treaty, on simplified extradition procedure between the Member States of the European Union, [1995] O.J. C78/2) and the Convention of September 27, 1996 relating to extradition between the Member States of the European Union, [1996] O.J. C313/12 (for the explanatory report, see [1997] O.J. C191/13.

European Council as the "cornerstone" of judicial cooperation. More recently, the Council has adopted framework decisions on the execution of orders freezing property or evidence[111] and on the application of the principle of mutual recognition to financial penalties,[112] criminal judgments imposing custodial sentences[113] and decisions on supervision measures as an alternative to provisional detention[114] as well as on the exchange of information extracted from the criminal record[115] and the creation of a European evidence warrant.[116] In addition, it has adopted a framework decision to foster the application of the principle of mutual recognition to decisions rendered in the absence of the person concerned at the trial.[117] The Council has also adopted measures with a view to improving the standing of victims of crime in criminal proceedings[118] and on prevention and settlement of conflicts of exercise of jurisdiction in criminal proceedings.[119]

---

[111] Council Framework Decision 2003/577/JHA of July 22, 2003 on the execution in the European Union of orders freezing property or evidence, [2003] O.J. L196/45.

[112] Council Framework Decision 2005/214/JHA of February 24, 2005 on the application of the principle of mutual recognition to financial penalties, [2005] O.J. L76/16.

[113] Council Framework Decision 2008/909/JHA of November 27, 2008 on the application of the principle of mutual recognition to judgments in criminal matters imposing custodial sentences or measures involving deprivation of liberty for the purpose of their enforcement in the European Union, [2008] O.J. L327/27.

[114] Council Framework Decision 2009/829/JHA of October 23, 2009 on the application, between Member States of the European Union, of the principle of mutual recognition to decisions on supervision measures as an alternative to provisional detention, [2009] O.J. L294/20.

[115] Council Framework Decision 2009/315/JHA of February 26, 2009 on the organisation and content of the exchange of information extracted from the criminal record between Member States, [2009] O.J. L93/23 (replacing Council Decision 2005/876/JHA of November 21, 2005, [2005] O.J. L322/33). Further arrangements are laid down in Council Decision 2009/316/JHA of April 6, 2009, [2009] O.J. L93/33.

[116] Council Framework Decision 2008/978/JHA of December 18, 2008 on the European evidence warrant for the purpose of obtaining objects, documents and data for use in proceedings in criminal matters, [2008] O.J. L350/72. For the protection of personal data processed within the framework of PJCC, see Council Framework Decision 2008/977/JHA of November 27, 2008, [2008] O.J. L350/60.

[117] Council Framework Decision 2009/299/JHA of February 26, 2009 amending Framework Decisions 2002/584/JHA, 2005/214/JHA, 2006/783/JHA, 2008/909/JHA and 2008/947/JHA, thereby enhancing the procedural rights of persons and fostering the application of the principle of mutual recognition to decisions rendered in the absence of the person concerned at the trial, [2009] O.J. L81/24.

[118] Council Framework Decision 2001/220/JHA of March 15, 2001 on the standing of victims in criminal proceedings, [2001] O.J. L82/1. In order to ensure access to compensation to crime victims in cross-border situations, the Council adopted Directive 2004/80/EC of April 29, 2004, [2004] O.J. L261/15 pursuant to Art. 308 EC [now Art. 352 TFEU]. See Blanc, "Vers un statut communautaire de la victime? A propos de la directive 2004/80/CE du Conseil du avril 29, 2004 relative à l'indemnisation des victimes de la criminalité" (2006) R.M.C.U.E. 195–201.

[119] Council Framework Decision 2009/948/JHA of November 30, 2009 on prevention and settlement of conflicts of exercise of jurisdiction in criminal proceedings, [2009] O.J. L328/42.

Definition of criminal offences and sanctions. Article 83(1), first subpara.,   **10–022**
TFEU enables the European Parliament and the Council, acting in accordance
with the ordinary legislative procedure, to adopt directives establishing minimum
rules on the definition of criminal offences and sanctions in the area of

> "particularly serious crime with a cross-border dimension resulting from the
> nature or impact of such offences or from a special need to combat them on
> a common basis."

The offences in question are terrorism, trafficking in human beings and sexual
exploitation of women and children, illegal drug trafficking, illegal arms trafficking, money laundering, corruption, counterfeiting of means of payment, computer
crime and organised crime, as well as other areas of crime to be identified by the
Council, acting unanimously after obtaining the consent of the European
Parliament (Art. 83(1) TFEU, second and third subparas).

Before the Lisbon Treaty, this competence was more limited in scope, since
Art. 31(e) EU referred to the progressive adoption of measures establishing minimum rules relating to the constituent elements of criminal acts and to penalties in
the fields of organised crime, terrorism and illicit drug trafficking. On that basis,
for example, the Council defined crimes in the areas of fraud and forgery, corruption, trafficking in human beings, sexual exploitation and illicit drug trafficking.[120]

---

[120] See Council Decision 2000/375/JHA of May 29, 2000 to combat child pornography on the
Internet, [2000] O.J. L138/1; Council Framework Decision 2000/383/JHA of May 29, 2000 on
increasing protection by criminal penalties and other sanctions against counterfeiting in connection with the introduction of the euro, [2000] O.J. L140/1; Council Framework Decision
2001/413/JHA of May 28, 2001 combating fraud and counterfeiting of non-cash means of payment, [2001] O.J. L149/1; Council Framework Decision 2001/500/JHA of June 26, 2001 on
money laundering, the identification, tracing, freezing, seizing and confiscation of instrumentali-
ties and the proceeds of crime, [2001] O.J. L182/1; Council Framework Decision 2002/629/JHA
of July 19, 2002 on combating trafficking in human beings, [2002] O.J. L203/1; Council
Framework Decision 2002/946/JHA of November 28, 2002 on the strengthening of the penal
framework to prevent the facilitation of unauthorised entry, transit and residence, [2002] O.J.
L328/1; Council Framework Decision 2003/568/JHA of July 22, 2003 on combating corruption in
the private sector, [2003] O.J. L192/54; Council Framework Decision 2004/68/JHA of December
22, 2003 on combating the sexual exploitation of children and child pornography, [2004] O.J.
L13/44; and Council Framework Decision 2004/757/JHA of October 25, 2004 laying down minimum provisions on the constituent elements of criminal acts and penalties in the field of illicit drug
trafficking, [2004] O.J. L335/8. For commentaries, see Obokata, "EU Council Framework
Decision on Combating Trafficking in Human Beings: A Critical Appraisal" (2003) C.M.L.Rev.
917–936. See also to this effect the definition of "fraud" in the Convention on the protection of the
European Communities' financial interests, para. 13–151, *infra*, the Convention of June 17, 1998,
drawn up on the basis of the former Art. K.3 of the EU Treaty, on driving disqualifications, [1998]
O.J. C216/2, and the Joint Actions adopted by the Council on the basis of the former Art. K.3 of
the EU Treaty on making it a criminal offence to participate in a criminal organisation
(98/733/JHA of December 21, 1998, [1998] O.J. L351/1) and on corruption in the private sector
(98/742/JHA of December 22, 1998, [1998] O.J. L358/2).

Following the terrorist attacks of September 11, 2001, the Council adopted measures to ensure that any assistance to acts of terrorism would be criminal offences.[121]

In addition, the Union will be empowered to accompany its harmonisation measures by minimum rules with regard to the definition of criminal offences and sanctions in the area concerned. If it proves essential in order to ensure the effective implementation of a Union policy, a directive may be established to this end in accordance with the same procedure as was used to adopt the harmonisation measure (Art. 83(2) TFEU).[122] This competence was introduced by the Treaty of Lisbon. Even before that, the Court of Justice had already held that a Community harmonisation measure could require the Member States to introduce effective, proportionate and dissuasive criminal penalties in order to ensure that the rules which it lays down are fully effective.[123] At the same time, the Court held that Community measures could not determine the type and level of the criminal penalties to be applied.[124]

A special "alarm bell procedure" applies to decision-making under Art. 83(1) and (2) TFEU where a member of the Council considers that a draft directive would affect fundamental aspects of its criminal justice system (Art. 83(3) TFEU; see para. 19–008).

10–023   **Crime prevention.** The European Parliament and the Council, acting in accordance with the ordinary legislative procedure, may establish measures to promote and support the action of Member States in the field of crime prevention. These

---

[121] Council Framework Decision 2002/475/JHA of June 13, 2002 on combating terrorism, [2002] O.J. L164/3, which builds on Council Common Position 2001/930/JHA of December 27, 2001 on combating terrorism, [2001] O.J. L344/90. See Margue, "Les initiatives menées par l'Union dans la lutte antiterroriste dans le cadre du troisième pilier (Justice et afffaires intérieures)" (2002) R.D.U.E. 261–281; Dubois, "The Attacks of 11 September: EU-US Cooperation Against Terrorism in the Field of Justice and Home Affairs" (2000) E.For.Aff.Rev. 317–335.

[122] However, since such directives fall within the area of PJCC, the parallel right of initiative for the Member States must be taken into account (see Art. 76 TFEU, to which Art. 83(2) TFEU refers).

[123] ECJ, Case C-176/03 *Commission v Council* [2005] ECR I-7879, para. 48. Given the availability of a Community legal basis, the Court held that it was contrary to Art. 47 EU for the Council to lay down on the basis of Title VI of the EU Treaty the sanctions necessary to enforce infringements of a Community harmonisation measure. Hence, the Court annulled Council Framework Decision 2003/80/JHA of January 27, 2003 on the protection of the environment through criminal law, [2003] O.J. L29/55. See likewise ECJ, Case C-440/05 *Commission v Council* [2007] E.C.R. I-9097 (annulment of Council Framework Decision 2005/667/JHA of July 12, 2005 to strengthen the criminal-law framework for the enforcement of the law against ship-source pollution, [2005] O.J. L255/164). Following the annulment of those framework decisions, Directive 2008/99/EC of the European Parliament and of the Council of November 19, 2008 on the protection of the environment through criminal law, [2008] O.J. L328/28 and Directive 2009/123/EC of the European Parliament and of the Council of October 21, 2009 amending Directive 2005/35/EC on ship-source pollution and on the introduction of penalties for infringements, [2009] O.J. L280/52 were adopted on the basis of Arts 175(1) and 80(2) of the EC Treaty, respectively.

[124] ECJ, Case C-440/05 *Commission v Council* [2007] E.C.R. I-9097, paras 70–71.

measures may not, however, extend to approximation of Member States' legislative and regulatory provisions (Art. 84 TFEU).

Eurojust. The Union also promotes cooperation between national authorities   **10–024**
through Eurojust. Eurojust is a unit composed of prosecutors, magistrates or police
officers seconded from each Member State to facilitate the coordination of national
prosecution authorities and support criminal investigations into organised crime.[125]
As a result, Eurojust constitutes the embryonic beginnings of a genuine European
public prosecutor's office (see para. 10–052). It has its seat in The Hague. Since the
entry into force of the Lisbon Treaty, its mission is to support and strengthen coordination and cooperation between national investigating and prosecuting authorities,

> "in relation to serious crime affecting two or more Member States or requiring a prosecution on common bases, on the basis of operations conducted and information supplied by the Member States' authorities and by Europol"
> (Art. 85(1), first subpara., TFEU).

Eurojust's structure, operation, field of action and tasks are now to be determined
by the European Parliament and the Council by means of regulations adopted in
accordance with the ordinary legislative procedure (Art. 85(1), second subpara.,
TFEU).[126] Eurojust has in particular the task of strengthening judicial cooperation, including through resolution of conflicts of jurisdiction and by close cooperation with the European Judicial Network.[127]

European Public Prosecutor. Since the Lisbon Treaty, the Treaties not only provide   **10–025**
for measures relating to the operation, scope of action and tasks of Eurojust but also
hold out the prospect of setting up a European Public Prosecutor's Office in order
to combat crimes affecting the Union's financial interests (Art. 86(1) TFEU).[128]

---

[125] Council Decision 2002/187/JHA of February 28, 2002 setting up Eurojust with a view to reinforcing the fight against serious crime, [2002] O.J. L63/1), pursuant to Declaration (No. 2) annexed to the Nice Treaty, on Art. 31(2) of the EU Treaty, [2001] O.J. C80/77. Until Eurojust was set up, a Provisional Judicial Cooperation Unit operated by virtue of Council Decision 2000/799/JHA of December 14, 2000, [2000] O.J. L324/2.

[126] These regulations must determine arrangements for involving the European Parliament and national Parliaments in the evaluation of Eurojust's activities (Art. 85(1), third subpara., TFEU).

[127] See Art. 85(1), second subpara., sub (c), TFEU. The European Judicial Network in criminal matters was set up by the Council by Joint Action 98/428/JHA of June 29, 1998, [1998] O.J. L191/4, now replaced by Council Decision 2008/976/JHA of December 16, 2008 on the European Judicial Network, [2008] O.J. L348/130.

[128] For earlier debate on this matter, see Fijnaut and Groenhuijsen, "Een Europees openbaar ministerie: kanttekeningen bij het Groenboek" (2002) N.J.B. 1234–1241; Veldt, "Een Europees Openbaar Ministerie: de oplossing voor de EU-fraude?" (2001) J.J.B. 666–671; Van Gerven, "Constitutional Conditions for a Public Prosecutor's Office at the European Level" (2000) E.J.C.C.L. & C.J. 296–318.

The European Public Prosecutor's Office may be established by the Council, acting unanimously after obtaining the consent of the European Parliament.[129] The European Public Prosecutor's Office will be responsible for investigating, prosecuting and bringing to judgment the perpetrators of offences against the Union's financial interests and their accomplices. In relation to those offences the European Public Prosecutor's Office will act as prosecutor in the competent courts of the Member States (Art. 86(2) TFEU).[130] In 2003 the Convention on the Future of Europe had proposed to confer on the European Public Prosecutor's Office powers with respect to other "serious crimes having a cross-border dimension". However, in 2007 the Intergovernmental Conference agreed only on a clause leaving it to the European Council to determine whether its powers should be extended to include serious crimes affecting more than one Member State (Art. 86(4) TFEU). In this connection, the European Council is to act unanimously after obtaining the consent of the European Parliament and after consulting the Commission (ibid.).

V. POLICE COOPERATION

10–026 **Police cooperation.** Article 87(1) TFEU [ex Art. 30(1) TEU] provides for police cooperation involving all the Member States' competent authorities, including police, customs and other specialised law enforcement services in relation to the prevention, detection and investigation of criminal offences, both directly and through the European Police Office (Europol).[131] To that purpose, the European Parliament and the Council, acting in accordance with the ordinary legislative procedure, may establish measures concerning:

    (a) the collection, storage, processing, analysis and exchange of relevant information[132];

---

[129] In the case of disagreement between the Members of the Council, special arrangements apply whereby a group of Member States may proceed on the basis of enhanced cooperation (Art. 86(1), second and third subparas, TFEU; see para. 19–008, infra).

[130] The regulations setting up the European Public Prosecutor's Office must determine the general rules applicable to it, the conditions governing the performance of its functions, the rules of procedure applicable to its activities, as well as those governing the admissibility of evidence, and the rules applicable to the judicial review of procedural measures taken by it in the performance of its functions (Art. 86(3) TFEU).

[131] See Heckler, "Europäisches Verwaltungskooperationsrecht am Beispiel der grenzüberschreitenden polizeilichen Zusammenarbeit" (2001) EuR 826–845.

[132] E.g. Council Decision 2000/261/JHA of March 27, 2000 on the improved exchange of information to combat counterfeit travel documents, [2000] O.J. L81/1; Council Decision 2000/642/JHA of October 17, 2000 concerning arrangements for cooperation between financial intelligence units of the Member States in respect of exchanging information, [2000] O.J. L271/4; Council Decision 2001/886/JHA of December 6, 2001 on the second-generation Schengen Information System, [2001] O.J. L328/1; Council Decision 2002/348/JHA of April 25, 2002 concerning security in connection with football matches with an international dimension, [2002] O.J. L121/1.

(b) support for the training of staff, and cooperation on the exchange of staff, equipment and research into crime-detection and

(c) common investigative techniques in relation to the detection of serious forms of organised crime[133] (Art. 87(2) TFEU).

National police training institutions work together within the framework of the European Police College (CEPOL), established at Bramshill (United Kingdom).[134] In addition, the Council, acting unanimously after consulting the European Parliament, may establish measures concerning operational cooperation between the different law enforcement authorities.[135] Special arrangements apply in the case of disagreement between the Member States (Art. 87(3) TFEU; see para. 19–008).

It is also for the Council, acting unanimously after consulting the European Parliament, to determine the conditions and limitations under which national judicial and law enforcement authorities may operate in the territory of another Member State, in liaison and agreement with the authorities of that State (Art. 89 TFEU [*ex Art. 32 EC*]).

Europol. The European Police Office (Europol) was established by a convention concluded between the Member States pursuant to the former Art. K.3 of the EU Treaty, which entered into force on October 1, 1998 (Europol Convention),[136] the provisions of which have been replaced, as from January 1, 2010 onwards, by a Council decision (Europol Council Decision).[137]

10–027

---

[133] See Council Decisions of February 12, 2007 establishing the Specific Programme Prevention of and Fight against Crime and the Specific Programme "Criminal Justice", [2007] O.J. L58/7 and L58/13, respectively, which coordinate for the period 2007 to 2013 existing exchange, training and cooperation programmes for legal practitioners and other legal occupations and for law enforcement authorities.

[134] Council Decision 2005/681/JHA of September 20, 2005 establishing the European Police College (CEPOL) and repealing Decision 2000/820/JHA, [2005] O.J. L256/63.

[135] See Council Framework Decision 2002/465/JHA of June 13, 2002 on joint investigation teams, [2002] O.J. L162/1, and Council Decision 2002/956/JHA of November 28, 2002 setting up a European Network for the Protection of Public Figures, [2002] O.J. L333/1.

[136] Convention of July 26, 1995 on the establishment of a European Police Office (Europol Convention), [1995] O.J. C316/1. For the interpretation by the Court of Justice of the Europol Convention, see para. 23–015, *infra*. Europol started work on June 1, 1999; see the notice in [1999] C185/1. In anticipation of the establishment of Europol, the Member States set up a Europol Drugs Unit (EDU) in 1993 ((1993) 6 EC Bull. point 1.4.19). Its mandate was laid down by Joint Action 95/73/JHA of March 10, 1995, [1995] O.J. L62/1) and extended by Joint Action 96/748/JHA of December 16, 1996, [1996] O.J. L342/4. See Subhan, "L'Union européenne et la lutte contre la drogue" (1999) R.M.C.U.E. 196–201.

[137] Council Decision of April 6, 2009 establishing the European Police Office (Europol), [2009] O.J. L121/37. According to Art. 1(2) of that decision, "Europol, as referred to in this Decision, shall be regarded as the legal successor of Europol, as established by the Europol Convention".

In common with Eurojust, Europol has its seat in The Hague. Its mission is to support and strengthen action by the Member States' police authorities and other law enforcement services and their mutual cooperation in preventing and combating serious crime affecting two or more Member States, terrorism and forms of crime which affect a common interest covered by a Union policy (Art. 88(1) TFEU).[138] Europol's structure, operation, field of action and tasks are now to be laid down in regulations adopted in accordance with the ordinary legislative procedure by the European Parliament and the Council. These regulations must also lay down specific procedures for scrutiny of Europol's activities by the European Parliament and the national parliaments (Art. 88(2) TFEU).

Operational actions by Europol are possible solely in liaison and in agreement with the authorities of the Member State concerned. In this sphere, the competent national authorities have the exclusive responsibility to apply coercive measures (Art. 88(3) TFEU).

VI. EXCEPTIONAL STATUS OF DENMARK, IRELAND AND THE UNITED KINGDOM

10–028 **Denmark.** Denmark is bound by the Schengen *acquis* and so has agreed to the elimination of checks on persons at the internal borders and to the arrangements regarding checks at the external borders and entry for a short stay. However, in the negotiations leading up to the Treaty of Amsterdam, it obtained the right—laid down in a separate protocol—not to participate in any measure in the field of visas, asylum, immigration and judicial cooperation in civil matters. Denmark did not take part in the further adoption by the Council of measures pursuant to Title IV of the EC Treaty, was not bound by such measures (or by decisions of the Court of Justice interpreting them), and was not to bear the financial consequences ensuing therefrom.[139] Moreover, the part of the Schengen *acquis* that was subsequently incorporated into Community law had binding force in Denmark merely as rules of international law, not as Community law.[140] With respect to

---

[138] See the Council Decision establishing Europol, Art.3. See Barbé, "L'Union européenne face au blanchiment du produit du crime" (2001) R.M.C.U.E. 161–163; Weyembergh, "L'Union européenne et la lutte contre la traite des êtres humains" (2000) C.D.E. 215–251. For the operation of Europol, see Ellermann, "Von Sammler zu Jäger—Europol auf dem Weg zu einem 'europäischen FBI'?" (2002) Z.Eu.S. 561–585; for the relationship between Eurojust and Europol, see Berthelet and Chevallier-Govers, "Quelle relation entre Europol et Eurojust? Rapport d'égalité ou rapport d'autorité?" (2001) R.M.C.U.E. 468–474.

[139] Articles 1 to 3 of Protocol (No. 20), annexed to the EU Treaty and the EC Treaty, on the position of Denmark, [1997] O.J. C340/101.

[140] According to Art. 3, first para., of the initial Schengen Protocol (n. 37, *supra*), the parts of the Schengen *acquis* that had been determined to have their legal basis in Title IV of the EC Treaty did not create any new rights or obligations for that country vis-à-vis the other Schengen States as before that determination.

police and judicial cooperation in criminal matters, however, Denmark had no specific status.[141]

In the negotiations leading up to the Lisbon Treaty, Denmark obtained an extension of its opt-out. Although it continues to be bound by the Schengen *acquis*, it does not participate in the adoption of measures in the area of freedom, security and justice as it is not bound by Title V of Part Three of the TFEU.[142] The only exception is that Denmark participates in the measures determining the third countries whose nationals must be in possession of a visa when crossing the external borders of the Member States, or relating to a uniform format for visas.[143] This means that, apart from this exception, Denmark will not be bound by any of the provisions of Title V of Part Three of the TFEU nor by measures adopted pursuant to that Title (or by decisions of the Court of Justice interpreting them), and is not to bear the financial consequences ensuing therefrom.[144] It follows that this now includes measures of police and judicial cooperation in criminal matters. However, the protocol provides that acts of the Union in the field of police and judicial cooperation in criminal matters adopted before the entry into force of the Treaty of Lisbon which are amended "shall continue to be binding upon and applicable to Denmark unchanged".[145]

Denmark does not have the right to participate in acts adopted under Title V of Part Three of the TFEU where it wishes to do so. However, the Union has already concluded international agreements with Denmark regarding the application of specific measures as between Denmark and the other Member States.[146] Denmark

---

[141] The second para. of Art. 3 of the initial Schengen Protocol (n. 36, *supra*) provided that Denmark continued to have the "same rights and obligations" as the other signatories with regard to those parts of the Schengen *acquis* that were determined to have their legal basis in Title VI of the EU Treaty. This covered, among other things, the judicial review provided for by Art. 35 EU.

[142] Articles 1 and 2 of Protocol (No. 22), annexed to the TEU and TFEU by the Lisbon Treaty, on the position of Denmark, ([2010] O.J. C83/299. Denmark may relinquish its separate status by informing the other Member States: *ibid.*, Art. 7. For the special decision-making procedure, see 19–002 *et seq., infra.*

[143] Protocol (No. 22) on the position of Denmark (preceding n.), Art. 6. See, e.g., the participation of Denmark in the adoption of Council Regulation (EC) No. 539/2001 of March 15, 2001 (n. 51, *supra*).

[144] *Ibid.*, Arts 2 and 3. Denmark will also not be bound by the Union's data protection rules with respect to activities of police and judicial cooperation in criminal matters: *ibid.*, Art. 2a.

[145] Protocol (No. 22) on the position of Denmark (n. 142, *supra*), Art. 2. It should be recalled, moreover, that, pursuant to Art. 9 of Protocol (No. 36), annexed to the TEU, TFEU and EAEC Treaty, on transitional provisions ([2010] O.J. C83/322), the legal effects of Union acts adopted on the basis of the EU Treaty prior to the entry into force of the Lisbon Treaty, are to be preserved until those acts are repealed, annulled or amended in implementation of the current Treaties (see also para. 10–029, *infra*).

[146] This technique was used, for instance, to allow Denmark to participate in the adoption and application of the Regulation which replaces the Dublin Convention and the "Eurodac" system for the identification of asylum seekers (ns 66 and 67, *supra*) and to allow for its participation in Regulation No. 44/2001 ("Brussels I") and the regulation on service of documents (ns 90 and 97, *supra*).

may also decide to implement in national law a Council decision to build upon the Schengen *acquis*. If it decides to do so, its decision will create "an obligation under international law" between Denmark and the other participating Member States.[147] The upshot will be that a given act of the Union institutions will be binding for all the Member States concerned, but, as far as Denmark is concerned, not as Union law. Similarly, where Denmark formally participates, pursuant to an international agreement, in the implementation of an act adopted under Title V of Part Three of the TFEU, that agreement merely creates an obligation under international law.

Finally, the Lisbon Treaty has granted Denmark the option of abandoning its general opt-out, either as such[148] or else in favour of a system under which it—in common with Ireland and the United Kingdom—has the possibility to notify to the other Member States its intention to participate in one or another proposed measures in the area of freedom, security and justice.[149]

10–029   **Ireland and United Kingdom.** Unlike Denmark, Ireland and the United Kingdom are not Schengen States and are not bound by the Schengen *acquis* following its integration into the framework of the European Union. Under a separate protocol to the Treaties—first annexed by the Treaty of Amsterdam and subsequently, slightly adjusted, by the Lisbon Treaty—the United Kingdom retains the right to conduct controls on persons at its frontiers in order to verify that persons purportedly having the right to enter the United Kingdom do in fact have such a right and to determine whether or not to grant other persons permission to enter the country.[150] Since the United Kingdom and Ireland have arrangements between themselves relating to the movement of persons between their territories ("the Common Travel Area"), Ireland also has the right to carry out such controls as long as the arrangements are maintained.[151] The other Member States are entitled to exercise controls on persons seeking to enter their territories from the United Kingdom or Ireland.

It follows from the Schengen Protocol that both the United Kingdom and Ireland may request the Council to take part in specific provisions of the Schengen *acquis*—which they did and which was accepted by the

---

[147] Protocol (No. 22) on the position of Denmark (n. 142, *supra*), Art. 2.

[148] Protocol (No. 22) on the position of Denmark (n. 142, *supra*), Art. 2.

[149] If it exercises this latter option, all the Schengen *acquis* and measures adopted to build upon this *acquis*, which until then have been binding on Denmark as obligations under international law, "shall be binding upon Denmark as Union law" six months after the date on which the notification takes effect (Protocol (No. 22) on the position of Denmark (n. 142, *supra*), Art. 8).

[150] Article 1 of Protocol (No. 20), annexed to the TEU and TFEU, on the application of certain aspects of Art. 26 of the TFEU to the United Kingdom and to Ireland ([2010] O.J. C83/293) (replacing Protocol (No. 3), annexed to the EU Treaty and the EC Treaty by the Amsterdam Treaty, [1997] O.J. C340/97), which states that nothing in Arts 26 and 77 TFEU or in any other Treaty provisions shall prejudice the right of the United Kingdom to adopt or exercise such controls.

[151] *Ibid.*, Art. 2. See Ryan, "The Common Travel Area between Britain and Ireland" (2001) Mod.L.Rev. 855–874.

Council.[152] These Member States are entitled to take part in the adoption of measures that build upon the Schengen *acquis* if they notify the Council within a reasonable period of their wish to do so.[153] However, where one or both of these Member States notify their wish not to take part in the adoption of an act building on provisions of the Schengen *acquis*, the Council may determine whether it should reverse the decision which authorised the Member State concerned in the first place to take part in those provisions (see para. 19–003).

Pursuant to yet another protocol to the Treaties (Protocol (No. 21)), however, the United Kingdom and Ireland do not in principle take part in the adoption of measures based on Title V of Part Three of the TFEU; they are not bound by such measures (or by decisions of the Court of Justice relating thereto) and they do not bear the financial consequences of such measures.[154] Before the entry into force of the Lisbon Treaty, that arrangement only concerned measures adopted in the field of visa, asylum, immigration and judicial cooperation in civil matters; since then it concerns the whole area of freedom, security and justice, including police and judicial cooperation in criminal matters. If the United Kingdom or Ireland so wishes, it may notify the President of the Council of its intention to take part in the adoption and application of a proposed measure.[155] The same regime applies

---

[152] Schengen Protocol (see n. 40, *supra*), Art. 4. They do not have the right to participate in the adoption of measures that build upon specific provisions of the Schengen *acquis* if they are not taking part in the latter provisions (Schengen Protocol, Art. 5): ECJ, Case C-77/05 *United Kingdom v Council* [2007] E.C.R. I-11459, paras 54–68, with a case note by Rijpma (2008) C.M.L.Rev. 835–852; ECJ, Case C-137/05 *United Kingdom v Council* [2007] E.C.R. I-11593, paras 49–56. For the participation of the United Kingdom in part of the Schengen *acquis*, see Council Decision 2000/365/EC of May 29, 2000, [2000] O.J. L131/43 and Council Decision 2004/926/EC of December 22, 2004, [2004] O.J. L395/70; for the participation of Ireland, see Council Decision 2002/192/EC of February 28, 2002, [2002] O.J. L64/20—which includes a virtually identical list of Schengen measures). As a result of that decision, a number of decisions are also binding on Ireland, even though that State, unlike the United Kingdom, did not take part in their adoption, e.g. Directive 2001/51/EC (n. 39, *supra*) and Council Regulation (EC) No. 2424/2001 of December 6, 2001 on the Schengen Information System (n. 35, *supra*). Neither the United Kingdom nor Ireland participated in the adoption of, for instance, Council Regulation (EC) No. 539/2001 of March 15, 2001 listing the third countries whose nationals must be in possession of visas when crossing the external borders and those whose nationals are exempt from that requirement (n. 50, *supra*), with the result that they are free to draw up their own lists.

[153] Schengen Protocol (see n. 40, *supra*), Art. 5(1).

[154] Articles 1, 2 and 5 of Protocol (No. 21), annexed to the TEU and the TFEU, on the position of the United Kingdom and Ireland in respect of the Area of Freedom, Security and Justice ([2010] O.J. C83/295) (replacing Protocol (No. 4), annexed by the Amsterdam Treaty to the EU Treaty and the EC Treaty, [1997] O.J. C340/99). Ireland may notify the Council that it no longer wishes to be covered by this Protocol: *ibid.*, Art. 8.

[155] *Ibid.*, Art. 3. E.g. the notification given by the United Kingdom (and not Ireland) that it would participate in Regulation No. 1030/2002 (n. 69, *supra;* see recital 14 in the preamble thereto) and the notification given by Ireland and the United Kingdom that they would participate in Regulation No. 343/2003 (n. 66, *supra*; see recital 17 in the preamble thereto). For the decision-making procedure and for the possibility of accepting a measure, even after it has been adopted, under the "enhanced cooperation" procedure, see para. 19–003, *infra*.

to measures pursuant to Title V of Part Three of the TFEU that amend a measure to which the United Kingdom or Ireland are bound.[156] However, for Ireland, the opt-in arrangement does not apply to restrictive measures imposed pursuant to Art. 75 TFEU on natural and legal persons, groups or non-State entities.[157]

As regards the measures that the Union adopted before the entry into force of the Lisbon Treaty on the basis of the EU Treaty (that is to say, principally, measures of police and judicial cooperation in criminal matters), it already follows from Protocol (No. 36) on transitional provisions attached to the Treaties by the Lisbon Treaty that the legal effects of these measures will be preserved until those acts are repealed, annulled or amended in implementation of the present Treaties (see paras 4–014 and 4–015). Moreover, with regard to acts adopted in the field of police and judicial cooperation in criminal matters prior to the entry into force of the Lisbon Treaty ("PJCC acts"), the same Protocol provides for reduced powers for the Commission and the Court of Justice during a transitional period of five years: the Commission cannot enforce the application of such acts by bringing infringement actions under Art. 258 TFEU and the Court of Justice has only the powers that were attributed to it by Title VI of the EU Treaty before December 1, 2009, that is to say the powers conferred under Art. 35 EU.[158] For the United Kingdom and Ireland (as well as Denmark), that means that, until December 1, 2014, national courts cannot refer questions on the interpretation of validity of PJCC acts to the Court of Justice.[159]

Curiously, as far as the United Kingdom is concerned, Protocol (No. 36) affords that Member State the possibility, at the expiry of that five year transitional period, of not accepting the supervisory powers of the Commission and the Court with respect to pre-Lisbon PJCC acts. At the latest six months before the expiry of that transitional period, the United Kingdom may notify to the Council that it does not accept the powers of these institutions with respect to such acts.[160] In that case, all such pre-Lisbon PJCC acts shall cease to apply to it as from the date of expiry of the transitional period.[161] The Council, acting by a qualified

---

[156] Article 4a of Protocol (No. 21) on the position of the United Kingdom and Ireland in respect of the Area of Freedom, Security and Justice (n. 154, *supra*).

[157] Article 9 of Protocol (No. 21) on the position of the United Kingdom and Ireland in respect of the Area of Freedom, Security and Justice (n. 154, *supra*). According to the Declaration (No. 65), annexed to the Lisbon Treaty, by the United Kingdom on Art. 75 TFEU ([2010] O.J. C83/359), that Member State intends to make use of Art. 3 of the Protocol on the position of the United Kingdom and Ireland in order to take part in the adoption of proposals based on Art. 75 TFEU.

[158] Article 10(1) of Protocol (No. 36), annexed to the TEU, TFEU and EAEC Treaty, on Transitional Provisions, [2010] O.J. C83/322. However, where such PJCC acts are amended, the reduction in powers of both the Commission and the Court no longer applies with respect to the amended act and for those Member States to which that amended act applies: *ibid.*, Art. 10(2).

[159] This is because those Member States did not make a declaration, pursuant to Art. 35(2) EU, accepting the jurisdiction of the Court of Justice to rule on such matters.

[160] Article 10(4), first subpara., of Protocol (No. 36), annexed by the Lisbon Treaty to the TEU, TFEU and EAEC Treaty, on Transitional Provisions.

[161] However, this will not apply with respect to amended acts which are applicable to the United Kingdom (*ibid.*).

majority—without the participation of the United Kingdom—on a proposal from the Commission, is to determine the necessary consequential and transitional arrangements.[162] Still, at any time afterwards, the United Kingdom may notify the Council of its wish to participate in acts which have ceased to apply to it. In that case, the relevant provisions of the Schengen Protocol or Protocol (No. 21), as the case may be, will apply, with the full powers of the relevant institutions (including the jurisdiction of the Court of Justice).[163]

---

[162] *Ibid.*, Art. 10(4), second subpara. The Council, acting by a qualified majority on a proposal from the Commission, may also adopt a decision determining that the United Kingdom shall bear the direct financial consequences, if any, necessarily and unavoidably incurred as a result of the cessation of its participation in those acts. *Ibid.*, Art. 10(4), third subpara.

[163] *Ibid.*, Art. 10(5), which stresses that "[w]hen acting under the relevant Protocols, the Union institutions and the United Kingdom shall seek to re-establish the widest possible measure of participation of the United Kingdom in the *acquis* of the Union in the area of freedom, security and justice without seriously affecting the practical operability of the various parts thereof, while respecting their coherence".

CHAPTER 11

OTHER AREAS OF UNION POLICY

I. AGRICULTURE AND FISHERIES

Common agricultural policy. The internal market extends to agriculture,   **11–001**
fisheries and trade in agricultural products (Art. 38(1) TFEU [*ex Art. 32(1) EC*]).
The operation and development of the internal market for agricultural products
must be accompanied by the establishment of a common agricultural policy
(CAP) (Art. 38(4) TFEU).[1] The common agricultural policy relates to,

"the products of the soil, of stockfarming and of fisheries and products of
first-stage processing directly related to these products",

as listed in "Annex I" to the TFEU (Art. 38(1) and (3) TFEU).[2] Article 38(2) TFEU
provides that the rules laid down for the establishment of the internal market are
to apply to agricultural products, save as otherwise provided in Arts 39 to 44.
Article 42 TFEU [*ex Art. 36 EC*] lays down that the rules on competition are to apply
to production of and trade in agricultural products only to the extent determined
by the Council, which made it necessary for the Council to adopt an implementing
regulation.[3] Both national organisations of agricultural markets and the common

---

[1] For an exhaustive discussion of the CAP, see Skogstad and Verdun, *The common agricultural policy:
policy dynamics in a changing context (special issue of the Journal of European Integration)*
(Routledge, 2009) 176 pp.; McMahon, *EU agricultural law* (Oxford, Oxford University Press, 2008),
515 pp.; Bianchi, *La politique agricole commune (PAC): Toute la PAC, rien d'autre que la PAC!*
(Brussels, Bruylant, 2006), 639 pp.; Usher, *EC Agricultural Law* (Oxford, Oxford University Press,
2002), 207 pp.; Barents, *The Agricultural Law of the EC* (Deventer, Kluwer, 1994), 417 pp.; Van Rijn,
"De ontwikkelingen in het Europees landbouwrecht" (2009) T.Agr.R. 316–324.

[2] "Annex II" until the Treaty of Amsterdam.

[3] Council Regulation (EC) No. 1184/2006 of July 24, 2006 applying certain rules of competition to the
production of, and trade in, certain agricultural products, [2006] O.J. L214/7, as amended and supplemented by Arts 175 to 182 and 200 of Council Regulation (EC) No. 1234/2007 of October 22, 2007
(see n. 12, *infra*). Council Regulation No. 1184/2006 replaced Council Regulation No. 26 applying certain rules of competition to production of and trade in agricultural products, [1959–1962] O.J. English
Spec. Ed. 129. For the application of EU competition law, see, for example, ECJ, Joined Cases
C-319/93, C-40/94 and C-224/94 *Dijkstra and Others* [1995] E.C.R. I-4471, paras 15–24; for an application of national competition law, see ECJ, Case C-137/00 *Milk Marque and National Farmers'
Union* [2003] E.C.R. I-7975, paras 57–67. For the priority enjoyed by agriculture over the objectives
in respect of competition, see ECJ, Case C-280/93 *Germany v Council* [1994] E.C.R. I-4973,
paras 59–61, and the discussion in Dony, "L'affaire des bananes" (1995) C.D.E. 461, at 470–471.

organisations of the markets by which the Union replaces them must adapt themselves to the rules on free trade and free competition within the internal market.[4] Accordingly, additional aid to the agricultural sector is subject to the rules on State Aid set forth in Arts 107, 108 and 109 TFEU [*ex Arts 87, 88 and 89 EC*].[5]

11–002 **Objectives.** The objectives of the common agricultural policy are listed in Art. 39(1) TFEU [*ex Art. 33(1) EC*]:

    (a) increased agricultural productivity;

    (b) a fair standard of living of the agricultural community;

    (c) stable markets;

    (d) secured supplies; and

    (e) reasonable prices.

Over the years, the emphasis has gradually shifted from helping to make good the shortfall in satisfying the Union's own needs to concern to maintain farmers' incomes, overproduction notwithstanding. Together with the objectives set in other policy spheres,[6] agricultural policy is to take account of the particular nature of agricultural activity, the need to effect the necessary adjustments by degrees and the close links between the sector and the economy as a whole (Art. 39(2) TFEU). Every measure cannot invariably take all the objectives into account. Hence, measures adopted under the common agricultural policy must be based on a balance of interests which has to be in accordance with the principle of proportionality.[7]

---

[4] ECJ, Case 48/74 *Charmasson* [1974] E.C.R. 1383, paras 6–20 (national organisation of agricultural markets); ECJ, Joined Cases 80 and 81/77 *Commissionaires Réunis* [1978] E.C.R. 927, paras 22–38 (common organisation of the market).

[5] Dehousse and Ghilain, "Les règles de concurrence sur les aides d'Etat dans le secteur de l'agriculture" (2000) Stud. Dipl. 41–58.

[6] E.g. environmental protection (Art. 11 TFEU [*ex Art. 6 EC*]), public health (Art. 168(1), first subpara., TFEU [*ex Art. 152(1)*, first para., EC]) and economic and social cohesion (Arts 174 and 175, first para., TFEU [*ex Arts 158 and 159, first para., EC*]). See in this connection, Bianchi, "La politique agricole commune au lendemain du traité d'Amsterdam" (2001) R.T.D.E. 371–395; Gencarelli, "La politique agricole commune et les autres politiques communautaires: la nouvelle frontière" (2001) R.D.U.E. 173–188. For environment protection, see also Jack, *Agriculture and EU Environmental Law* (Farnham, Ashgate Publishing, 2009), 273 pp.; Rosso Grossman, *Agriculture and the Polluter Pays Principle* (London, British Institute of International and Comparative Law, 2009), 392 pp.; Born, "La conservation de la biodiversité dans la politique agricole commune" (2001) C.D.E. 341–401.

[7] For the requisite weighing of interests, see ECJ, Case 68/86 *United Kingdom v Council* [1988] E.C.R. 855, paras 10–14; ECJ, Case C-122/94 *Commission v Council* [1996] E.C.R. I-881, paras 23–25; for the necessary proportionality in achieving the objectives, see para. 7–034, *supra*. For a number of case studies, see Barents, "De commautaire maatregelen ter bestrijding van mond- en klauwzeer" (2001) N.T.E.R. 169–177; Mortelmans and Van Ooik, "De Europese aanpak van mond- en klauwzeer en de rechtmatigheid van het preventieve vaccinatieverbod" (2001) A.Ae. 911–927; Dehousse and Lewalle, "La crise de la dioxine: un révélateur des faiblesses de la réglementation alimentaire nationale" (2000) Stud. Dipl. 5–27.

Instruments. Since the entry into force of the Lisbon Treaty, the European Parliament and the Council, acting in accordance with the ordinary legislative procedure and after consulting the Economic and Social Committee, establish the common organisation of agricultural markets and the other provisions necessary for the pursuit of the objectives of the common agricultural policy and the common fisheries policy.[8] Measures on fixing prices, levies, aid and quantitative limitations and on the fixing and allocation of fishing opportunities are adopted by the Council, on a proposal from the Commission (Art. 43 (2) and (3) TFEU).

11–003

The common agricultural policy is made up primarily of the common organisations of the markets and rural development actions. Under Art. 40(3) TFEU [*ex Art. 34(3) EC*], the European Agricultural Guidance and Guarantee Fund was set up,[9] of which the Guarantee Section funds the common organisations of the markets and actions underpinning rural development and the Guidance Section other rural development actions ("structural policy").[10]

Market organisations. The Council has adopted common organisations of the market for most agricultural products by means of some twenty basic regulations,[11]

11–004

---

[8] Before the Lisbon Treaty, the Council acted after consulting the European Parliament. See Bianchi, "Une PAC 'dénaturée', 'délaissée' et 'malmenée'? Plaidoyer en faveur d'une politique agricole moderne dans le projet de Constitution européenne" (2004) R.T.D.E. 71–95.

[9] See Regulation (EC) No. 25 of the Council of April 4, 1962 on the financing of the common agricultural policy, [1959–1962] O.J. English Spec. Ed. (I) 118, and Regulation (EC) No. 729/70 of the Council of April 21, 1970 on the financing of the common agricultural policy, [1970] O.J. English Spec. Ed. (I) 218 (before the Treaty of Amsterdam, para. 3 was numbered 4).

[10] For the present rules, see Council Regulation (EC) No. 1290/2005 of June 21, 2005 on the financing of the common agricultural policy, [2005] O.J. L209/1, as amended by Council Regulation (EC) No. 13/2009 of December 18, 2008, [2009] O.J. L5/1. See also the provisions on economic and social cohesion, para. 11–055, *infra*.

[11] See the Council Regulations (EC) on the establishment of a common organisation of the market in live trees and other plants, bulbs, roots and the like, cut flowers and ornamental foliage (Regulation No. 234/68 of February 27, 1968, [1968] O.J. English Spec. Ed. (I) 26, certain products listed in Annex I to the Treaty (Regulation No. 827/68 of June 28, 1968, [1968] O.J. English Spec. Ed. (I) 209), pigmeat (Regulation No. 2759/75 of October 29, 1975, [1975] O.J. L282/1), eggs (Regulation No. 2771/75 of October 29, 1975, [1975] O.J. L282/49), poultrymeat (Regulation No. 2777/75 of October 29, 1975, [1975] O.J. L282/77), raw tobacco (Regulation No. 2075/92 of June 30, 1992, [1992] O.J. L215/70), bananas (Regulation No. 404/93 of February 13, 1993, [1993] O.J. L47/1), processed fruit and vegetable products (Regulation No. 2201/96 of October 28, 1996, [1996] O.J. L297/29), beef and veal (Regulation No. 1254/1999 of May 17, 1999, [1999] O.J. L160/21), milk and milk products (Regulation No. 1225/1999 of May 17, 1999, [1999] O.J. L160/48), flax and hemp (Regulation No. 1673/2000 of July 27, 2000, [2000] O.J. L193/16), sheepmeat and goatmeat (Regulation No. 2529/2001 of December 19, 2001, [2001] O.J. L341/3), cereals (Regulation No. 1784/2003 of September 29, 2003, [2003] O.J. L270/78), rice (Regulation No. 1785/2003 of September 29, 2003, [2003] O.J. L270/96), dried fodder (Regulation No. 1786/2003 of September 29, 2003, [2003] O.J. L270/114), olive oil and table olives (Regulation No. 865/2004 of April 29, 2004, [2004] O.J. L161, republished with *corrigendum*: [2004] O.J. L203/37), hops (Regulation No. 1952/2005 of November 23, 2005, [2005] O.J. L314/1), seeds (Regulation No. 1947/2005 of

which were replaced, for reasons of simplification, by a single regulation.[12] The management of the common organisations is delegated to the Commission. Of the forms of market organisation provided for in Art. 40(1) TFEU [*ex Art. 34(1) EC*], the Union has invariably opted for "a European market organisation" (indent (c)).[13] Every common market organisation (CMO) proceeds on the basis of the principles of a unified market (free movement of agricultural products and uniform prices), "Union preference" (utmost self-sufficiency) and financial solidarity within the Union (the Union manages and distributes agricultural expenditure).

There are, however, large differences in terms of the methods of market organisation. Since a high level of prices guarantees producers' income, most of the market organisations have provided for price intervention. In order to eliminate the competitive advantage of producers from non-Union countries, the Union imposes import duties and other import levies to cover the difference between the world market price and a "threshold price". Producers exporting surplus products outside the Union are entitled to additional "export refunds". Within the Union market, supply and demand determine the price of a given product, but at the same time it has a "target price" (sometimes known as a "reference" or "guide" price). If the market price deviates from the target price to such an extent as to reach the "intervention price", intervention agencies may or must buy in the product. The uniform agricultural prices are expressed in euro. To prevent any loss of income owing to exchange-rate fluctuations for producers from Member States not belonging to the euro zone, the new agrimonetary system provides for such loss of income to be replaced by direct aid.[14]

As long as the agricultural policy made the income support of farmers depend on the quantities produced, this encouraged structural surpluses (butter, cereals, beef and wine), constituting a heavy burden on the Union budget, which no longer resulted in increased incomes. Accordingly, in May 1992 the Council set in train a reform of the common agricultural policy, something which the Commission had been proposing for some time.[15] The Union has been lowering farm prices towards

---

November 23, 2005, [2005] O.J. L312/1), sugar (Regulation No. 318/2006 of February 20, 2006, [2006] O.J. L58/1), fruit and vegetables (Regulation No. 1182/2007 of September 26, 2007, [2007] O.J. L273/1) and wine (Regulation No. 479/2008 of April 29, 2008, [2008] O.J. L148/1).

[12] Council Regulation (EC) No. 1234/2007 of October 22, 2007 establishing a common organisation of agricultural markets and on specific provisions for certain agricultural products (Single CMO Regulation), [2007] O.J. L299/1. Since the fruit and vegetables and wine sectors were the subject of policy reforms, the substantive provisions of the common market organisation in those sectors have not been incorporated in the Single CMO Regulation.

[13] The other forms provided for in Art. 34(1) are "common rules on competition" and "compulsory coordination of the various national market organisations".

[14] Council Regulation (EC) No. 2799/98 of December 15, 1998 establishing agrimonetary arrangements for the euro, [1998] O.J. L349/1. For the period before the introduction of the euro, see Council Regulation (EC) No. 3813/92 of December 28, 1992 on the unit of account and the conversion rates to be applied for the purposes of the common agricultural policy, [1992] O.J. L 387/1.

[15] Blumann, "La réforme de la PAC" (1993) R.T.D.E. 247–298; Viscardini Dona, "La politique agricole commune et sa réforme" (1992) R.M.U.E. 13–48.

world market prices. This is accompanied by increasing direct income support for farmers, which is no longer calculated on the basis of production and dependent on restrictions of the acreage in use or herd size.

The 2003 reform of the CAP introduced a new system of direct payments to farmers, under which aid is no longer linked to production ("decoupling"). The most important system of direct payments is the single payment scheme.[16] Member States may base that single payment on the payments that an individual farmer received during a reference period or on the sum of payments received during the reference period by all farmers of a given region, divided by the number of eligible hectares declared by the individual farmer. To receive direct payments, farmers must meet certain standards concerning public, animal and plant health, the environment and animal welfare and keep their land in good agricultural and environmental condition.[17] Since these reforms of the CAP, the income support of farmers has been transferred from the common market organisations to the new system of direct payments to farmers.

In addition to market intervention and income support, the common agricultural policy also makes provision for general quality standards, including the protection of geographical indications and designations of origin[18] and the labelling of organic products,[19] and measures to protect animal welfare.[20]

Where an agricultural product comes under a common organisation of the market, the only action open to Member States is to adopt measures implementing the agricultural policy. In some cases, Union legislation leaves a measure of discretion to Member States.[21]

---

[16] Council Regulation (EC) No. 73/2009 of January 19, 2009 establishing common rules for direct support schemes for farmers under the common agricultural policy and establishing certain support schemes for farmers, [2009] O.J. L30/16, which replaced Regulation (EC) No. 1782/2003 of September 29, 2003 establishing common rules for direct support schemes under the common agricultural policy and establishing certain support schemes, [2003] O.J. L270/1.

[17] These are called the "cross compliance" obligations. For an application, see ECJ, Case C-428/07 *Horvath* [2009] E.C.R. I-6355.

[18] Council Regulation (EC) No. 510/2006 of March 20, 2006 on the protection of geographical indications and designations of origin for agricultural products and foodstuffs, [2006] O.J. L93/12. For an application, see ECJ (judgment of September 8, 2009), Case C-478/07 *Budějovický Budvar*, not yet reported.

[19] Council Regulation (EC) No. 834/2007 of June 28, 2007 on organic production and labelling of organic products and repealing Regulation (EC) No. 2092/91, [2007] O.J. L189/1. For an application of the latter regulation, see ECJ, Case C-393/05 *Commission v Austria* [2007] E.C.R. I-10195 and ECJ, Case C-404/05 *Commission v Germany* [2007] E.C.R. I-10239.

[20] E.g., Council Directives 2008/119/EC and 2008/120/EC of December 18, 2008 laying down minimum standards for the protection of calves and pigs, respectively (Codified versions), [2009] O.J. L10/7 and L47/5.

[21] Sometimes, for example, the Member State can choose the method of calculation or determine the level of premiums within a set "bracket". Moreover, structural policy is based on initiatives emanating from Member States.

11–005 **Structural policy.** Structural policy consists, among other things, of measures for the modernisation and expansion of agricultural holdings, aid upon the cessation of farming and, since the Single European Act, support for the least-favoured regions.[22] Among the measures for rural development, the reformed agricultural policy emphasises environmental measures, afforestation of agricultural land and structural improvements through early retirement, while seeking at the same time to improve the safety and quality of foodstuffs. The Union confines itself to making a financial contribution to the cost of programmes submitted by Member States and regions.[23]

11–006 **Fisheries.** Fishery measures form part of the common agricultural policy.[24] The power conferred by Art. 102 of the 1972 Act of Accession to determine conditions for fishing with a view to ensuring protection of the fishing grounds and conservation of the biological resources of the sea, falls within the exclusive competence of the Union (see paras 7–021). In 1983 a common fisheries policy was established. It was reformed at the end of 2002. Its most important aim is to preserve fish stocks, for the purpose of which catch quotas and specific preservation measures have been laid down.[25] At the same time, it has to ensure the viability of the fishery industry and create a fair standard of living for those who depend on fishing activities. The Union therefore is pursuing a common structural policy for the fishery sector,[26] whilst a common organisation of the market in fishery products is in operation.[27]

II. TRANSPORT

11–007 **Common transport policy.** Article 90 TFEU [*ex Art. 70 EC*] requires Member States to pursue the objectives of the Treaties within the framework of a common transport policy.[28] The provisions of the Title of the TFEU headed "Transport" apply

---

[22] See Gonzales, "Het EG-landbouwstructuurbeleid: integrerend onderdeel van het gemeenschappelijk landbouwbeleid?" (1997) S.E.W. 7–19.

[23] Council Regulation (EC) No. 1257/1999 of May 17, 1999 on support for rural development from the European Agricultural Guidance and Guarantee Fund (EAGGF) and amending and repealing certain Regulations, [1999] O.J. L160/80.

[24] For a critical analysis, see Wakefield, "Fisheries: A failure of values" (2009) C.M.L.Rev. 431–470.

[25] See Council Regulation (EC) No. 2371/2002 of December 20, 2002 on the conservation and sustainable exploitation of fisheries resources under the Common Fisheries Policy, [2002] O.J. L358/59.

[26] See Council Regulation (EC) No. 1198/2006 of July 27, 2006 on the European Fisheries Fund, [2006] O.J. L223/1.

[27] Council Regulation (EC) No. 104/2000 of December 17, 1999 on the common organisation of the markets in fishery and aquaculture products, [2000] O.J. L17/22.

[28] For an exhaustive discussion, see Greaves, *EC Transport Law* (London, Longman, 2000), 162 pp.; Tromm, *Juridische aspecten van het communautair vervoerbeleid* (The Hague, T.M.C. Asser Institute, 1990), 534 pp. and, for air transport, Kassim and Handley, *Air Transport and the European Union: Europeanisation and its Limits* (Basingstoke, Palgrave Macmillan, 2010), 332 pp. See also Kaeding, *Better regulation in the European Union: lost in translation or full steam ahead: the transposition of EU transport directives across Member States* (Amsterdam, Amsterdam University Press, 2007), 244 pp.

to transport by rail, road and inland waterway (Art. 100 (1) TFEU; *ex Art. 80(1) EC*). This is not automatically so as regards sea and air transport. First, the Council had to decide whether, to what extent and by what procedure appropriate provisions were to be laid down [*ex Art. 80(2) EC*]. Now, the European Parliament and the Council, acting in accordance with the ordinary legislative procedure, have to lay down the appropriate provisions. The Economic and Social Committee and the Committee of the Regions need to be consulted (Art. 100(2) TFEU).[29]

Actions in the transport sector come under the general rules of the Treaties, especially the rules on the establishment of the internal market, unless the Treaties provide otherwise.[30] Accordingly, Art. 58(1) TFEU [*ex Art. 51(1) EC*] provides that freedom to provide services in the field of transport shall be governed by the provisions of the Title relating to transport. This has not prevented freedom to supply services from being introduced for transport between Member States and third countries and within Member States (*cabotage*). The Treaty rules on competition also apply in the transport sector.[31]

Instruments. In the context of the common transport policy, the European Parliament and the Council are empowered to adopt, under the ordinary legislative

11–008

---

[29] Article 80(2) EC required the Council to act by qualified majority and in accordance with the general decision-making procedure applicable to transport, which became the co-decision procedure with the Treaty of Amsterdam. For the application of freedom to provide services to maritime transport between Member States and between Member States and third countries, see Council Regulation (EC) No. 4055/86 of December 22, 1986, [1986] O.J. L378/1; for maritime transport within Member States (maritime cabotage), see Council Regulation (EC) No. 3577/92 of December 7, 1992, [1992] O.J. L364/7. For the application of freedom to supply services in air transport, see most recently Regulation (EC) No. 1008/2008 of the European Parliament and of the Council of September 24, 2008 on common rules for the operation of air services in the Community, [2008] O.J. L293/3, which replaced the Council Regulations of July 23, 1992 on licensing of air carriers (Regulation (EC) No. 2407/92, [1992] O.J. L240/1), on access for Community air carriers to intra-Community air routes (Regulation (EC) No. 2408/92, [1992] O.J. L240/8) and on fares and rates for air services (Regulation (EC) No. 2409/92, [1992] O.J. L240/15). For the extent to which Union action places limits on the differential treatment of sea transport to non-Union and Union ports, see ECJ, Case C-435/00 *Geha Naftiliaki EPE and Others* [2002] E.C.R. I-10615, paras 21–22.

[30] ECJ, Case 167/73 *Commission v France* [1974] E.C.R. 359, paras 24–28.

[31] See ECJ, Case 156/77 *Commission v Belgium* [1978] E.C.R. 1881, para. 10 (application of rules relating to State Aid); ECJ, Joined Cases 209–213/84 *Asjes and Others* [1986] E.C.R. 1425, paras 35–42 (application of Arts 81 to 86). During an initial period, however, the Council adopted specific legislation to prevent the transport sector from being subject to the general rules for the implementation of competition law laid down in Regulation No. 17/62, now replaced by Regulation No. 1/2003 (see n. 57, *infra*). Now, these general rules also apply to the transport sector, see Council Regulation (EC) No. 411/2004 of February 26, 2004, [2004] O.J. L 68/1 (air transport) and Council Regulation (EC) No. 1419/2006 of September 25, 2006, [2006] O.J. L269/1 (maritime transport), even though some specific rules continue to apply to transport by rail, road and inland waterway, see Council Regulation (EC) No. 169/2009 of February 26, 2009, [2009] O.J. L61/1. With regard to rules relating to State Aid, see also Bovis, "The application of State Aid rules to the European Union Transport sectors" (2005) Col.J.E.L 557–604.

procedure, any measures which they deem appropriate, inter alia in relation to international transport, the conditions under which non-resident carriers may operate transport services and transport safety, while taking account of "the distinctive features of transport" (Art. 91(1) TFEU [*ex Art. 71(1) EC*]; see also Art. 94 TFEU [*ex Art. 74 EC*]). In a 1985 judgment, the Court of Justice held that there was not yet a coherent set of rules which might be regarded as a common transport policy. Yet it did not regard this as a failure to act on the part of the Council, on the ground that that institution had a discretion, for example, to decide whether action in the transport sector must first deal with relations between the railways and the public authorities or with competition between road and rail.[32] In contrast, the Council had failed to fulfil its obligations in the fields of international transport and of the conditions under which non-resident carriers might operate transport services in a Member State, since those obligations were sufficiently well-defined in the Treaty.[33] Since then, the Council has phased in a Union licensing system for carriage of goods by road to replace the system of national quotas.[34] Alongside this, there has been a gradual liberalisation of domestic goods and passenger transport (*cabotage*).[35]

The achievement of the common transport policy, also for sea and air transport, goes hand in hand with the abolition of frontier controls between Member States and harmonisation of technical and social rules.

11–009 **Non-discrimination.** Member States may not introduce any provisions which are less favourable for carriers of other Member States (Art. 92 TFEU [*ex Art. 72 EC*]).[36] The Treaties debar carriers from discriminating on grounds of the country of origin or of destination of the goods transported and empower the Council to introduce checks on the part of the Union (Art. 95(1) and (3) TFEU [*ex Art. 75(1) and (3)*], respectively).[37] The Member States are debarred from imposing rates and conditions involving any element of support or protection in the interest of one or

---

[32] ECJ, Case 13/83 *European Parliament v Council* [1985] E.C.R. 1513, paras 46–50.

[33] *Ibid.*, paras 64–68.

[34] See, in particular, Council Regulation (EC) No. 881/92 of March 26, 1992 on access to the market in the carriage of goods by road within the Community to or from the territory of a Member State or passing across the territory of one or more Member States, [1992] O.J. L95/1.

[35] For the determination of the conditions under which non-resident carriers may transport goods or passengers by inland waterway in a Member State in which they are not established, see Council Regulation (EC) No. 3921/91 of December 16, 1991, [1991] O.J. L373/1, and Council Regulation (EC) No. 1356/96 of July 8, 1996, [1996] O.J. L175/7; the equivalent regulations for road passenger services and road haulage services are Council Regulation (EC) No. 12/98 of December 11, 1997, [1998] O.J. L4/10, and Council Regulation (EC) No. 3118/93 of October 25, 1993, [1993] O.J. L279/1.

[36] Article 76 EC [*now Art. 96 TFEU*] may be relied upon to contest any amendment to national legislative provisions and also any change in an administrative practice which may disadvantage carriers from other Member States: ECJ, Joined Cases C-184/91 and C-221/91 *Oorburg and van Messem* [1993] E.C.R. I-1633, paras 12–15.

[37] Regulation No. 11 concerning the abolition of discrimination in transport rates and conditions, in implementation of Art. 79 [*later Art. 75(3)*] of the Treaty establishing the European Economic Community, [1959–1962] O.J. English Spec. Ed. 60.

more particular undertakings or industries, unless authorised by the Commission (Art. 96(1) TFEU [*ex Art. 76(1) EC*]). The Commission may authorise such rates and conditions provided that they comply with Art. 96(2) TFEU [*ex Art. 76(2) EC*]. For the rest, aid measures are caught by the rules set out in Arts 107, 108 and 109 TFEU [*ex Arts 87, 88 and 89 EC*] (see para. 11–019), unless they can be justified under Art. 93 TFEU [*ex Art. 73 EC*] on the ground that they meet the needs of coordination of transport or they represent reimbursement for the discharge of certain obligations inherent in the concept of a public service.

III. COMPETITION

Undertakings and Member States. The Union is based on an open market economy with free competition, "favouring an efficient allocation of resources" (Arts 119(1) and (2), 120 and 127(1) TFEU [*ex Arts 98 and 105(1) EC*]).[38] The "rules on competition" comprise rules prohibiting distortion of competition by undertakings (Arts 101–106 TFEU [*ex Arts 81 to 86 EC*]) and rules restricting State Aid granted to undertakings (Arts 107, 108 and 109 TFEU [*ex Arts 87, 88 and 89 EC*]). A brief overview of the scope of these rules is set out below.[39] The Treaty of Lisbon did not alter these rules in any significant way.[40]

    11–010

Although Arts 101 and 102 TFEU are directed at undertakings, the third subpara. of Art. 4(3) TEU (which replaces *ex Art. 10 EC*] requires Member States to abstain from any measure which could detract from the effectiveness of those provisions. This is the case, for example, where a Member State requires or favours the adoption of agreements contrary to Art. 101 TFEU or reinforces their effects or deprives

---

[38] Unlike Art. 3(g), of the EC Treaty, the provisions on the objectives and values of the Union in the TEU do not refer to "a system ensuring that competition in the internal market is not distorted". However, Protocol (No. 27), annexed to the TEU and TFEU, on the internal market and competition, clearly states that "the internal market as set out in Article 3 TFEU includes a system ensuring that competition is not distorted" ([2010] O.J. C83/309). See Steenbergen, "Het mededingingsbeleid en het Verdrag van Lissabon" (2008) S.E.W. 136–143.

[39] For further information on EU competition law, see, among other works, Van Bael and Bellis, *Competition Law of the European Community* (The Hague, Kluwer Law International, 2010), 1674 pp.; Whish, *Competition Law*, (Oxford, Oxford University Press, 2009), 1006 pp.; Roth and Rose (eds), *Bellamy & Child, European Community Law of Competition*, (Oxford, Oxford University Press, 2008), 1679 pp.; Faull and Nikpay, *The EC Law of Competition* (Oxford, Oxford University Press, 2007), 1844 pp.; Jones and Sufrin, *EC Competition Law: text, cases and materials* (Oxford, Oxford University Press, 2007), 1418 pp.; Korah, *An introductory guide to EC competition law and practice* (Oxford, Hart Publishing, 2007), 539 pp. See also, Lenaerts, "Some Thoughts on Evidence and Procedure in European Community Competition Law" (2007) Fordham I.L.J. 1463–1495.

[40] For the changes, see mainly Art. 14 TFEU (on services of general economic interest, para. 11–017, *infra*) and Arts 105(3) and 108(4) TFEU, which confirm the Council's present practice of determining the categories of agreements or aid measures, respectively, in respect of which the Commission may grant a "block exemption" (see paras 11–014 and 11–019, *infra*).

its own legislation of its official character by delegating to private traders the responsibility for taking decisions affecting the economic sphere.[41] Consequently, it has been held that a Member State infringed Arts 4(3) TEU and 101 TFEU by obliging the national council of customs agents to set a uniform tariff for all customs agents.[42] In such a case, the national authorities must disapply the provisions conflicting with Art. 101 or 102 TFEU.[43] If those provisions preclude the possibility of competition, no penalties may be imposed on the undertakings concerned in respect of the period preceding the finding of an infringement of Arts 101 or 102 TFEU. But penalties may be imposed for any future conduct in breach of the competition rules. If, however, the national provisions merely encourage or make it easier for undertakings to engage in autonomous anti-competitive conduct, those undertakings have themselves to bear the consequences of the infringement of Arts 101 and 102 TFEU.[44]

11–011   **Concept of an "undertaking".** In competition law, the concept of an undertaking encompasses every entity engaged in an economic activity, regardless of the legal status of the entity and the way in which it is financed.[45] The same criteria apply to an "association of undertakings" within the meaning of Art. 101(1) TFEU.[46] These criteria are not fulfilled in the case of an institution charged with the management of a social security system on the basis of the principle of solidarity[47] or

---

[41] ECJ, Case 13/77 *INNO* [1977] E.C.R. 2115, paras 30–33; ECJ, Joined Cases 209–213/84 *Asjes* [1986] E.C.R. 1425, paras 70–77; ECJ, Case 311/85 *Vereniging van Vlaamse Reisbureaus* [1987] E.C.R. 3801, para. 10; ECJ, Case 267/86 *Van Eycke* [1988] E.C.R. 4769, para. 16; ECJ, Case C-2/91 *Meng* [1993] E.C.R. I-5751, para. 14; ECJ, Case C-185/91 *Reiff* [1993] E.C.R. I-5801, para. 14; ECJ, Case C-245/91 *Ohra* [1993] E.C.R. I-5851, para. 10; ECJ, Case C-35/99 *Arduino* [2002] E.C.R. I-1529, para. 35; ECJ, Case C-198/01 *Consorzio Industrie Fiammiferi* [2003] E.C.R. I-8055, para. 46; ECJ, Joined Cases C-94/04 and C-202/04 *Cipolla and Others* [2006] E.C.R. I-11421, paras 46–47; ECJ, Case C-446/05 *Doulamis* [2008] E.C.R. I-1377, paras 19–20.

[42] ECJ, Case C-35/96 *Commission v Italy* [1998] E.C.R. I-3851, paras 33–60. See also Ballarino and Bellodi, "Contraintes étatiques en matière de concurrence" (2003) R.D.U.E. 555–589; Schwarze, "Der Staat als Adressat des europäischen Wettbewerbsrechts" (2000) Eu.Z.W. 613–627.

[43] ECJ, Case C-198/01 *Consorzio Industrie Fiammiferi* [2003] E.C.R. I-8055, paras 48–51.

[44] *Ibid.*, paras 52–57.

[45] For the definition of the term "undertaking", see ECJ, Case C-41/90 *Höfner and Elser* [1991] E.C.R. I-1979, paras 21–22; ECJ, Case C-244/94 *Fédération française des sociétés d'assurance and Others* [1995] E.C.R. I-4013, paras 14–22; ECJ, Case C-343/95 *Diego Calì & Figli* [1997] E.C.R. I-1547, paras 16–25; ECJ, Case C-205/03 P *FENIN v Commission* [2006] E.C.R. I-6295, paras 25–27. For *FENIN*, see Krajewski and Farley, "Non-economic activities in upstream and downstream markets and the scope of competition law after FENIN" (2007) E.L.Rev. 111–124.

[46] ECJ, Case C-309/99 *Wouters and Others* [2002] E.C.R. I-1577, paras 56–71 (where a Bar association was regarded as being an "association of undertakings").

[47] ECJ, Joined Cases C-159/91 and C-160/91 *Poucet and Pistre* [1993] E.C.R. I-637, paras 17–20; ECJ, Case C-218/00 *Cisal di Battistello Veneziano* [2002] E.C.R. I-691, paras 31–46; ECJ, Joined Cases C-264/01, C-306/01, C-354/01 and C-355/01 *AOK Bundesverband and Others* [2004] E.C.R. I-2493, paras 47–65; see the note by Drijber (2005) C.M.L.Rev. 523–533; ECJ, Case C-350/07 *Kattner Stahlbau* [2009] E.C.R. I-1513, para. 34.

of an organisation entrusted by Member States with the exercise of powers which are typically those of a public authority, such as the control and supervision of air space.[48]

A. Rules for Undertakings

1. Article 101 TFEU

Prohibited agreements. Article 101(1) TFEU prohibits **11–012**

> "all agreements between undertakings, decisions by associations of undertakings and concerted practices which may affect trade between Member States and which have as their object or effect the prevention, restriction or distortion of competition within the internal market".[49]

The prohibited agreements, decisions or concerted practices, of which Art. 101(1) TFEU lists some examples, cover both horizontal "agreements" between competitors and vertical "agreements" between producers, suppliers and customers. In order to be caught by the prohibition, the agreements must also affect trade between Member States.[50] This does not mean that the undertakings concerned have to operate in different Member States: intra-Union trade may also be adversely affected where the agreement is between undertakings from one Member State[51] or even between undertakings from non-Union countries where they implement the agreement in the Union.[52]

Agreements between undertakings or decisions of an association of undertakings fall outside the prohibition laid down in Art. 101(1) TFEU where they pursue legitimate objectives—such as rules relating to professional ethics or to the fair conduct of sports—and where the consequential effects restrictive of competition are inherent in the pursuit of those objectives.[53] Agreements concluded in

---

[48] ECJ, Case C-364/92 *Eurocontrol* [1994] E.C.R. I-43, paras 18–31; ECJ, Case C-113/07 P *SELEX* [2009] E.C.R. I-2207, paras 66–80.

[49] For the distinction between "agreements between undertakings", "decisions by associations of undertakings" and "concerted practices", see, inter alia, CFI, Case T-1/89 *Rhône-Poulenc v Commission* [1991] E.C.R. II-867, paras 118–128. *Cf.* Pais Antunes, "Agreements and Concerted Practices under EEC Competition Law: Is the Distinction Relevant?" (1992) Y.E.L. 57–77.

[50] See ECJ, Joined Cases C-295/04 to C-298/04 *Manfredi* [2006] E.C.R. I-6619, paras 40–51; Commission Notice—Guidelines on the effect on trade concept contained in Arts 81 and 82 of the Treaty, [2004] O.J. C 101/81.

[51] ECJ, Case 8/72 *Cementhandelaren v Commission* [1972] E.C.R. 977, paras 26–31.

[52] ECJ, Joined Cases 89, 104, 114, 116–177 and 125–129/85 *Åhlström v Commission* [1988] E.C.R. 5193, paras 16–17.

[53] ECJ, Case C-309/99 *Wouters and Others* [2002] E.C.R. I-1577, para. 97; ECJ, Case C-519/04 P *Meca-Medina and Majcen v Commission* [2006] E.C.R. I-6991, paras 42–47.

the context of collective negotiations between management and labour to improve conditions of work and employment are also not caught by Art. 101 TFEU.[54]

Prohibited agreements or decisions are automatically void (Art. 101(2) TFEU), which means that they have no validity retroactively or vis-à-vis third parties. Nevertheless, the prohibition is not absolute in that Art. 101(3) TFEU affords an opportunity for Art. 101(1) TFEU to be declared inapplicable. To that end, that provision requires the agreement, decision or concerted practice in question to have beneficial effects (it must contribute to improving the production or distribution of goods or promote technical or economic progress, while giving consumers a share of the benefit), not to impose disproportionate restrictions on the undertakings concerned and afford some opportunity for competition.

11–013   **Decentralised enforcement.** The prohibition set out in Art. 101 TFEU has direct effect and may therefore be relied upon before national courts, which are to consider whether an agreement, decision or concerted practice within the meaning of Art. 101(1) TFEU satisfies the requirements of Art. 101(3) TFEU.[55] Compensation may be claimed before the national courts for loss caused by a prohibited agreement, even by an individual who was party to the agreement.[56] The Treaties also require

---

[54] ECJ, Case C-67/96 *Albany* [1999] E.C.R. I-5751, paras 53–60 (see also the judgments of the same date in ECJ, Joined Cases C-115-C-117/97 *Brentjens' Handelsonderneming and Others* [1999] E.C.R. I-6025 and ECJ, C-219/97 *Drijvende Bokken* [1999] E.C.R. I-6121); ECJ, Case C-222/98 *van der Woude* [2000] E.C.R. I-7111, paras 24–27. However, Art. 81 EC [now Art. 101 TFEU] does cover collective agreements between self-employed persons or members of a liberal profession: ECJ, Joined Cases C-180-C-184/98 *Pavlov and Others* [2000] E.C.R. I-6451, paras 67–70; ECJ, Case C-309/99 *Wouters and Others* [2002] E.C.R. I-1577, paras 44–71. See O'Loughlin, "EC Competition Rules and Free Movement Rules: An Examination of the Parallels and their Furtherance by the ECJ *Wouters* Decision" (2003) E.Comp.L.Rev. 62–69; Boni and Manzini, "National Social Legislation and EC Antitrust Law" (2001) World Comp. 239–255; Evju, "Collective Agreements and Competition Law. The *Albany* Puzzle, and *van der Woude*" (2001) Int'l J.Comp.Lab.L.Ind.Rel. 165–184; Van den Bergh and Camesasca, "Irreconcilable Principles? The Court of Justice Exempts Collective Labour Agreements from the Wrath of Antitrust" (2000) E.L.Rev. 492–508.

[55] For the direct effect of Art. 101(1) TFEU, see ECJ, Case 127/73 *BRT* [1974] E.C.R. 51, para. 16. Articles 1 to 6 of Regulation No. 1/2003 (see below) confirm the direct effect of Art. 101(3) TFEU, which, before May 1, 2004, was precluded by the fact that the Commission had been granted exclusive competence to apply Art. 81(3) (Art.9 of Regulation No. 17/62; see also below).

[56] ECJ, Case C-453/99 *Courage* [2001] E.C.R. I-6297, paras 17–28. However, a Member State may debar a party from relying on its own unlawful actions to obtain damages where it is established that that party bears significant responsibility for the distortion of competition: *ibid.*, paras 29–36; ECJ, Joined Cases C-295/04 to C-298/04 *Manfredi* [2006] E.C.R. I-6619. See Oosterhuis, "Manfredi: respect voor deze rechter" (2007) N.T.E.R. 33–39; Riley, "Damages in EC antitrust actions: who pays the piper?" (2007) E.L.Rev. 748–761; Reich, "The "Courage" Doctrine: Encouraging or Discouraging Compensation for Antitrust Injuries?" (2005) C.M.L.Rev. 35–66; Andreangeli, "*Courage Ltd v Crehan* and the Enforcement of Article 81 EC before National Courts" (2004) E.Comp.L.Rev. 758–764; Mäsch, "Private Ansprüche bei Verstößen gegen das europäische Kartellverbot—*Courage* und die Folgen" (2003) EuR. 825–846; Komninos, "New Prospects for Private Enforcement of EC Competition Law: *Courage v Crehan* and the Community Right to Damages" (2002) C.M.L.Rev. 447–487. See further the Commission's White Paper on Damages actions for breach of the EC antitrust rules, available at *http://ec.europa.eu/competition/antitrust/actionsdamages/* [Accessed December 6, 2010].

the Commission and the national competition authorities to supervise compliance with the competition rules (Arts 104 and 105 TFEU; *ex Arts 84 and 85 EC*]. That supervision is carried out in accordance with provisions adopted by the Council pursuant to Art. 103 TFEU [*ex Art. 83 EC*]. Of those provisions, Regulation No. 1/2003 is of prime importance because of its general scope.[57] Originally, only the Commission was empowered to apply Art. 101(3) TFEU and undertakings had to notify all agreements conflicting with Art. 101(1) TFEU to it in order to have the prohibition declared inapplicable or, in the event that this was not possible, to avoid the imposition of a fine.[58] With effect from May 1, 2004, Regulation No. 1/2003 abolished the notification system. Undertakings must henceforth work out for them selves whether their agreements conflict with Art. 101 TFEU and the whole of that article (including as a result para. 3) may be applied by the national courts and the national competition authorities.[59] Responsibility for supervising compliance with Art. 101 TFEU is vested primarily in the national courts and the national competition authorities in order that the Commission can concentrate on investigating the most serious infringements.[60]

The national competition authorities, together with the Commission, form the "European Network of Competition Authorities".[61] They are to inform the

---

[57] Council Regulation (EC) No. 1/2003 of December 16, 2002 on the implementation of the rules on competition laid down in Arts 81 and 82 of the Treaty, [2003] O.J. L1/1. Regulation No. 1/2003 is generally applicable unless a separate implementing regulation has been adopted for a particular sector (see for the transport sector, para. 11–007, *supra*).

[58] This system was set up by Regulation No. 17: First Regulation implementing Arts 85 and 86 [*thereafter Arts 81 and 82*] of the Treaty, [1959–1962] O.J. English Spec. Ed. 87.

[59] See, however, the Commission Notices on informal guidance relating to novel questions concerning Arts 81 and 82 of the EC Treaty that arise in individual cases (guidance letters) and on the handling of complaints by the Commission under Arts 81 and 82 of the EC Treaty ([2004] O.J. C101/78 and C101/65, respectively). Moreover, where the EU public interest so requires, the Commission, acting on its own initiative, may by decision find that Art. 81 of the Treaty is not applicable to an agreement; see Art. 10 of Regulation No. 1/2003.

[60] See Gilliams, "Modernisation: From Policy to Practice" (2003) E.L.Rev. 451–474; Lavagne, "La réforme du droit des ententes—Le règlement du 13 décembre 2002" (2003) R.M.C.U.E. 526–529; Nyssens, "Le règlement 1/2003 CE: vers une décentralisation et privatisation du droit de la concurrence" (2003) T.B.H. 286–294; Paulis and Gauer, "La réforme des règles d'application des articles 81 et 82 du Traité" (2003) J.T.D.E. 65–73; Venit, "Brave New World: The Modernisation and Decentralisation of Enforcement under Articles 81 and 82 of the EC Treaty" (2003) C.M.L.Rev. 545–580. The debate which culminated in this "decentralisation" started with the White Paper on modernisation of the rules implementing Arts 81 and 82 of the EC Treaty, [1999] O.J. C132/1. Compare the critical observations in Möschel, "Guest Editorial: Change of Policy in European Competition Law" (2000) C.M.L.Rev. 495–499 with Ehlermann, "The Modernisation of EC Antitrust Policy: A Legal and Cultural Revolution" (2000) C.M.L.Rev. 537–590 and the commentaries in (2001) C.D.E. 134–236. For the extent to which national authorities continue to have the power to apply national competition law, see Art. 3 of Regulation No. 1/2003. For the openings for arbitrators, see Komninos, "Arbitration and the Modernisation of European Competition Law Enforcement" (2001) World Comp. 211–238.

[61] A division of work is set out in the Joint Statement of the Council and the Commission on the functioning of the Network of Competition Authorities, entered in the Council minutes upon the adoption of Regulation No. 1/2003 (document No. 15435/EDD, available on the Internet at

Commission of the steps they take in investigating infringements of Art. 101 TFEU (and Art. 102 TFEU) and exchange information amongst themselves and with the Commission.[62] Once the Commission has initiated a procedure of its own, the national competition authorities are relieved of their competence to apply Arts 101 and 102 TFEU.[63] This does not apply to national courts before which reliance is made on Art. 101 or 102 TFEU. Where the Commission has initiated a procedure itself, the national court must, however, avoid taking a decision which would conflict with the decision contemplated by the Commission.[64] The national court may, if necessary, stay proceedings and enter into consultations with the Commission.[65] Where the Commission has taken a decision, the national court may not take a decision conflicting with that of the Commission.[66] Where an action for annulment has been brought against the Commission decision, it is for the national court to decide whether it should stay proceedings until a definitive decision has been given by the Union Court.[67]

11–014   **Investigation by the Commission.** In order to track down infringements of Arts 101 and 102 TFEU, Regulation No. 1/2003 confers broad powers of investigation on the Commission, including the power to inspect business premises (Arts 17 to 21). Acting under Regulation No. 1/2003, the Commission may make a finding that there has been an infringement of Art. 101 or Art. 102 TFEU and require the

---

http://register.consilium.eu.int/pdf/en/02/st15/15435-a1en2.pdf). See also Brammer, "Concurrent jurisdiction under regulation 1/2003 and the issue of case allocation" (2005) C.M.L.Rev. 1383–1424; Smits, "The European Competition Network: Selected Aspects" (2005) L.I.E.I. 175–192; Böge and Scheidgen, "Das neue Netzwerk der Wettbewerbsbehörden in der Europäischen Union" (2002) E.W.S. 201–206.

[62] See Arts 11, 12 and 13 of Regulation No. 1/2003 and the Commission Notice on cooperation within the Network of Competition Authorities, [2004] O.J. C101/43. See Dekeyser and De Smijter, "The exchange of evidence within the ECN and how it contributes to the European co-operation and co-ordination in cartel cases" (2005) L.I.E.I. 161–174. Only where the national competition authority constitutes a "court or tribunal of a Member State" may it refer a question to the Court of Justice for a preliminary ruling under Art. 267 TFEU [*ex Art. 234*]; see Komninos, "Article 234 EC and National Competition Authorities in the Era of Decentralisation" (2004) E.L.Rev. 106–114.

[63] Regulation No. 1/2003, Art. 11(6).

[64] Regulation No. 1/2003, Art. 16(1), and the Commission Notice on the cooperation between the Commission and the courts of the EU Member States in the application of Arts 81 and 82 EC, [2004] O.J. C101/54. See Lenaerts and Gerard, "Decentralisation of EC Competition Law Enforcement: Judges in the Frontline" (2004) World Comp. 313–350.

[65] ECJ, Case C-234/89 *Delimitis* [1991] E.C.R. I-935, paras 43–55. The national court may also make a reference to the Court of Justice for a preliminary ruling: ECJ, Case 127/73 *BRT* [1974] E.C.R. 51, paras 20–23; ECJ, Joined Cases C-319/93, C-40/94 and C-224/94 *Dijkstra and Others* [1995] E.C.R. I-4471, paras 25–36.

[66] Regulation No. 1/2003, Art. 16(1).

[67] ECJ, Case C-344/98 *Masterfoods and HB Ice Cream* [2000] E.C.R. I-11369, paras 45–60. If it has doubts as to the validity of the Commission decision, the national court may always make a reference for a preliminary ruling to the Court of Justice: *ibid.*, para. 57. See Fierstra (2001) N.T.E.R. 159–163; O'Keefe (2001) E.L.Rev. 301–311; Malferrari (2001) EuR. 605–616.

undertakings concerned to bring it to an end (Art. 7(1)). The Commission may also impose fines or periodic penalty payments (Regulation No. 1/2003, Arts 23 and 24).[68] During the procedure, hearings of interested parties take place in accordance with Art. 27 of Regulation No. 1/2003 and detailed implementing rules drawn up by the Commission.[69] Article 31 of Regulation No. 1/2003 confers on the Court of Justice (the General Court) unlimited jurisdiction to review decisions whereby the Commission has fixed a fine or periodic penalty payment.

The Council empowered the Commission to grant exemptions by regulation in respect of categories of agreements.[70] The Treaty of Lisbon explicitly empowers the Commission to do so (Art. 105(3) TFEU). If an agreement satisfies the requirements for "block exemption", as it is termed, the undertakings concerned may, under the regulation, rely directly on exemption from the prohibition set out in Art. 101 TFEU.[71] In order to simplify compliance with Art. 101 TFEU, the Commission has clarified in guidelines in what circumstances vertical agreements (between producer, supplier or buyer) and horizontal agreements (between competitors), in its view, do not have an appreciable effect on competition or

---

[68] For the setting of fines, see the Commission's guidelines in [2006] O.J. C210/2. See Völcker, "Rough justice? An analysis of the European Commission's new fining guidelines" (2007) C.M.L.Rev. 1285–1320; Wils, "The European Commission's 2006 guidelines on antitrust fines: a legal and economic analysis" (2007) World Comp. 197–229. See also the Commission Notice on immunity from fines and reduction of fines in cartel cases, [2006] O.J. C298/17.

[69] See Commission Regulation (EC) No. 773/2004 of April 7, 2004 relating to the conduct of proceedings by the Commission pursuant to Arts 81 and 82 of the EC Treaty, [2004] O.J. L123/18.

[70] For the Council's authorisation, see Regulation No. 19/65/EEC of the Council of March 2, 1965 on application of Art. 85 [now Art. 81](3) of the Treaty to certain categories of agreements and concerted practices, [1965–1966] O.J. English Spec. Ed. 36, as amended by Council Regulation (EC) No. 1215/1999, [1999] O.J. L148/1, and Regulation (EC) No. 2821/71 of the Council of December 20, 1971 on application of Art. 85 [now Art. 81](3) of the Treaty to categories of agreements, decisions and concerted practices ([1971] O.J. English Spec. Ed. (III) 1032). For authorisations for individual sectors, see Council Regulation No. 1534/91 of May 31, 1991 (insurance sector), [1991] O.J. L143/1, Council Regulations (EC) Nos 4056/86 and 479/92 (sea transport and liner shipping companies, respectively ([1986] O.J. L378/13, and [1992] O.J. L55/3) and Council Regulation (EC) No. 3976/87 of December 14, 1987 (air transport), [1987] O.J. L374/9.

[71] The Commission has drawn up block exemptions for agreements in Regulation (EU) No. 1217/2010 of December 14, 2010, [2010] O.J. L335/36 (research and development agreements), Regulation (EU) No. 1218/2010 of December 14, 2010, [2010] O.J. L335/43 (specialisation agreements), Regulation (EU) No. 330/2010 of April 20, 2010, [2010] O.J. L102/1 (vertical agreements in general), Regulation (EU) No. 461/2010 of May 27, 2010, [2010] O.J. L129/52 (agreements in the motor vehicle sector), Regulation (EU) No. 267/2010 of March 24, 2010 [2010] O.J. L83/1 (insurance), Regulation (EC) No. 906/2009, [2009] O.J. L256/31 (liner shipping companies) and Regulation (EC) No. 772/2004 of April 27, 2004, [2004] O.J. L123/11 (technology transfer agreements). See Schuermans and Teerlinck, "A New Block Exemption for the Insurance Sector" (2004) Euredia 81–109. On the previous block exemption for vertical agreements (Regulation (EC) No. 2790/1999 of December 22, 1999, [1999] O.J. L336/21), see Whish, "Regulation 2790/99: The Commission's 'New Style' Block Exemption for Vertical Agreements" (2000) C.M.L.Rev. 887–924.

satisfy the requirements of Art. 101(3) TFEU.[72] In addition, the Commission publishes policy statements concerning categories of agreements in respect of which it does not consider it necessary to take action.[73]

2. Article 102 TFEU

11-015   **Abuse of dominant position.** Article 102 TFEU prohibits one or more undertakings from abusing a dominant position within the internal market or in a substantial part of it in so far as it may affect trade between Member States. In common with the prohibition laid down by Art. 101 TFEU, the corresponding provision of Art. 102 TFEU has direct effect[74] and is subject to supervision by the national courts, the national competition authorities and the Commission in accordance with the provisions of Regulation No.1/2003.

A dominant position is determined by defining the relevant market both from the geographic point of view and from the standpoint of the product and by evaluating the market power (not solely market share) of the undertaking or undertakings.[75] Article 102 TFEU lists some instances of prohibited abuse of a dominant position (including limiting of production, markets or technological development or "tying" the conclusion of contracts to the acceptance by parties of supplementary obligations without necessary connection with the subject of the contracts).[76]

Article 102 TFEU also applies where an undertaking holding a dominant position on a particular market has such freedom of conduct on a neighbouring but separate market compared with the other economic operators on that market that, even without its holding a dominant position there, it bears a special responsibility to maintain genuine undistorted competition.[77]

---

[72] See, accompanying the block exemptions listed in the preceding note, the Guidelines on the applicability of Art. 101 TFEU to horizontal cooperation agreements [2011] O.J. C11/1, on Vertical Restraints ([2010] O.J. C1301/1) and on the application of Art. 81 of the EC Treaty to technology transfer agreements ([2004] O.J. C101/2). In addition, see the guidelines mentioned in n. 50, *supra*, and the Commission's Notice—Guidelines on the application of Art. 81(3) of the Treaty, [2004] O.J. C101/97. For the latter, see Bourgeois, "Guidelines on the application of article 81(3) of the EC Treaty or how to restrict a restriction" (2005) L.I.E.I. 111–121.

[73] See, for instance, the Commission Notice on agreements of minor importance which do not appreciably restrict competition under Art.81(1) of the Treaty establishing the European Community (*de minimis*), [2001] O.J. C368/13.

[74] ECJ, Case 155/73 *Sacchi* [1974] E.C.R. 409, para. 18.

[75] ECJ, Case 22/76 *United Brands V Commission* [1978] E.C.R. 207, paras 10–129; CFI, Case T-51/89 *Tetra Pak v Commission* [1990] E.C.R. II-309. See the Commission Notice on the definition of relevant market for the purposes of Community competition law, [1997] O.J. C372/5.

[76] For examples, see CFI, Case T-228/97 *Irish Sugar v Commission* [1999] E.C.R. II-2969; CFI, Case T-203/01 *Michelin v Commission* [2003] E.C.R. II-4071; CFI, Case T-201/04 *Microsoft v Commission* [2007] E.C.R. II-3601. See also the Commission's Guidance on its enforcement priorities in applying Art.82 EC to exclusionary conduct by dominant undertakings, [2009] O.J. C45/7.

[77] CFI, Case T-83/91 *Tetra Pak v Commission* [1994] E.C.R. II-755, paras 112–122, as upheld by ECJ, Case C-333/94 P *Tetra Pak v Commission* [1996] E.C.R. I-5951.

3. Control of concentrations

Merger control. Initially, supervision of mergers or concentrations of undertakings was confined to the Commission's control of compliance with Art. 102 TFEU, since the Court of Justice held that an undertaking abuses its dominant position if it strengthens its position in such a way that the degree of dominance reached substantially fetters competition, i.e. with the result that only undertakings remain in the market whose behaviour depends on the dominant one.[78] Ever since September 21, 1990, all concentrations of undertakings with a Union dimension have been subject to the obligatory prior notification and control introduced by Regulation No. 4064/89,[79] which has been replaced with effect from May 1, 2004 by Regulation No. 139/2004.[80]

    11–016

The Union dimension is determined by means of thresholds in terms of the aggregate worldwide turnover of the undertakings concerned and the aggregate Union-wide turnover of the two largest undertakings concerned (Regulation No. 139/2004, Art. 1(2)). The requirement for a Union dimension is also satisfied where a concentration meets—lower—thresholds which have a significant impact in at least three Member States (Regulation No. 139/2004, Art. 1(3)).[81] In accordance with these criteria, the concentration regulation may also be applied to undertakings which are not established in a Member State and carry out their production activities outside the Union.[82] Following notification, the Commission must reach a decision on the compatibility of the concentration with the internal market within the time-limits fixed by Regulation No. 139/2004. Concentrations which would significantly impede effective competition, in the internal market or in a substantial part of it, in particular as a result of the creation or strengthening

---

[78] ECJ, Case 6/72 *Europemballage and Continental Can v Commission* [1973] E.C.R. 215, para. 26.

[79] Council Regulation (EC) No. 4064/89 of December 21, 1989 on the control of concentrations between undertakings, [1989] O.J. L395/1.

[80] Council Regulation (EC) No. 139/2004 of January 20, 2004 on the control of concentrations between undertakings (the EC Merger Regulation), [2004] O.J. L24/1. See Van Gerven and Snels, "The New ECMR: Procedural Improvements" (2005) L.I.E.I. 193–208; Brunet and Girgenson, "La double réforme du contrôle communautaire des concentrations" (2004) R.T.D.E. 1–31; González Díaz, "The Reform of European Merger Control: *Quid Novi Sub Sole?*" (2004) World Comp. 177–199. See also, more generally, Furse, *The Law of Merger Control in the EC and the UK* (Oxford, Hart Publishing, 2007), 518 pp.; Cook and Kerse, *E.C. Merger Control* (London, Sweet & Maxwell, 2005), 631pp.; Navarro, Font, Folguera and Briones, *Merger Control in the European Union* (Oxford, Oxford University Press, 2005), 742 pp.

[81] For the notifications, time limits and hearings of parties concerned and third parties, see Commission Regulation (EC) No. 802/2004 of April 7, 2004 implementing Council Regulation (EC) No. 139/2004 on the control of concentrations between undertakings, [2004] O.J. L133/1.

[82] See CFI, Case T-102/96 *Gencor v Commission* [1999] E.C.R. II-753, paras 78–88 (concerning the same thresholds in Regulation No. 4064/89). Under international law, it must be foreseeable that a proposed concentration will have an immediate and substantial effect in the Union: *ibid.*, paras 90–101. See in this regard Slot (2001) C.M.L.Rev. 1573–1586; Ryngaert, *Jurisdiction over Antitrust Violations in International Law* (Antwerp, Intersentia, 2008), 230 pp.

of a dominant position, are declared incompatible with the internal market and may not be put into effect.[83]

4. Public undertakings and services of general interest

11–017   **Special or exclusive rights.** Under EU competition law, Member States may establish or operate publicly-owned undertakings ("public undertakings") or grant undertakings special or exclusive rights.[84] According to Art. 106(1) TFEU [*ex Art. 86(1) EC*], such undertakings have to comply with the rules of the Treaties, including the principle of equality and the competition rules.[85] The establishment or operation of public undertakings carrying out economic activities will therefore be incompatible with the Treaties where the undertakings have exclusive rights such that their exercise must be regarded as the abuse of a dominant position and that abuse is liable to affect trade between Member States.[86] Accordingly, the Court of Justice has held that Art. 106(1) is infringed by a Member State which grants a monopoly to public placement offices where those offices are unable to satisfy demand on the employment market, placement of employees by private companies is rendered impossible and the placement activities in question could extend to the nationals or the territory of other Member States.[87] The creation of a dominant position through the grant of an exclusive right within the meaning of

---

[83] Regulation No. 139/2004, Art. 2(3) and Art. 8(3), which still refers to compatibility with the "common market". Under Regulation No. 4064/89, only concentrations which created or strengthened a dominant position were incompatible with the common market. See also the Commission's Guidelines on the assessment of horizontal and non-horizontal mergers under the Council Regulation on the control of concentrations between undertakings ([2004] O.J. C31/5 and [2008] O.J. C265/6, respectively), the consolidated Jurisdictional Notice under Council Regulation (EC) No. 139/2004 ([2008] O.J. C95/1) and the Commission notices on acceptable remedies ([2008] O.J. C267/1) and on restrictions directly related and necessary to concentrations ([2005] O.J. C56/24). As regards the substantive control which the Commission has to carry out in relation to concentrations, see ECJ, Joined Cases C-68/94 and C-30/95 *France and Others v Commission* [1998] E.C.R. I-1375, paras 90–250; ECJ, Case C-12/03 P *Commission v Tetra Laval* [2005] E.C.R. I-987 and ECJ, Case C-413/06 P *Bertelsmann and Sony Corporation of America* [2008] E.C.R. I-4951; see also Bailey, "Standard of Proof in EC Merger Proceedings: A Common Law Perspective" (2003) C.M.L.Rev. 845–888. For the application of the principle of proportionality, see n. 146 to para. 7–034.

[84] For a survey of the status of public undertakings, see Szyszczak, *The regulation of the state in competitive markets in the EU* (Oxford, Hart Publishing, 2007), 293 pp.; Buendía Sierra, *Exclusive rights and state monopolies under EC law* (Oxford, Clarendon, 1999), 458 pp.; Blum and Logue, *State Monopolies under EC Law* (Chichester, Wiley, 1998), 402 pp.; Weiss, "Öffentliche Unternehmen und EGV" (2003) EuR. 165–190; Burgi, "Die öffentlichen Unternehmen im Gefüge des primären Gemeinschaftsrechts" (1997) EuR. 261–290.

[85] Article 106(1) refers to Art. 18 TFEU.

[86] An undertaking with a statutory monopoly may be regarded as occupying a dominant position within the meaning of Art. 102 TFEU and the territory of the Member State covered by that monopoly may constitute a substantial part of the internal market: ECJ, Case 311/84 *CBEM* [1985] E.C.R. 3261, para. 16.

[87] ECJ, Case C-55/96 *Job Centre* [1997] E.C.R. I-7119, para. 38.

Art. 106(1) is not as such incompatible with Art. 102 TFEU.[88] A Member State is in breach of the prohibitions set out in those two provisions only if the undertaking in question, merely by exercising the exclusive right granted to it, cannot avoid abusing its dominant position[89] or where the grant of exclusive rights is liable to create a situation in which the undertaking concerned is led to infringe Art. 102 TFEU.[90] An exclusive right which restricts the freedom of establishment of nationals of another Member State will be contrary to Arts 49 and 106 TFEU where that restriction is not appropriate and necessary to satisfy requirements of overriding public interest.[91]

Derogations from the rules on free trade and competition are possible only on the basis of the exceptions provided for in Art. 106(2) TFEU for undertakings entrusted with the operation of services of general economic interest or having the character of a revenue-producing monopoly.[92] Examples arise in the fields of transport, (tele)communications, postal services, energy and other utilities as well as for certain entities implementing social security schemes. The exceptions apply in so far as the application of the Treaty rules would obstruct the performance, in law or in fact, of the particular tasks assigned to the undertakings in question[93] and to the extent that the development of trade is not affected contrary to the interests of the Union.[94] The national court has to determine whether the conduct of a public undertaking contrary to Treaty provisions may be justified under Art. 106(2) TFEU.[95] Consequently, the provisions of Art. 106(1) and (2) have direct effect.

---

[88] ECJ, Case 311/84 *CBEM* [1985] E.C.R. 3261, para. 17.

[89] ECJ, Case C-41/90 *Höfner and Elser* [1991] E.C.R. I-1979, para. 29.

[90] ECJ, Case C-260/89 *ERT* [1991] E.C.R. I-2925, paras 37–38; see also ECJ, Case C-320/91 *Corbeau* [1993] E.C.R. I-2533, paras 9–12, and the case note by Hancher in (1994) C.M.L.Rev. 105–122. For the determination of abuse and adverse effects on trade between Member States, see also ECJ, Case C-179/90 *Merci convenzionali porto di Genova* [1991] E.C.R. I-5889, paras 14–22; ECJ, Case C-18/88 *GB-INNO-BM* [1991] E.C.R. 5941, paras 17–27; ECJ, Case C-163/96 *Raso and Others* [1998] E.C.R. I-533, paras 25–33.

[91] CFI, Case T-266/97 *VTM v Commission* [1999] E.C.R. II-2329, paras 105–123.

[92] ECJ, Case 155/73 *Sacchi* [1974] E.C.R. 409, para. 13; ECJ (judgment of April 20, 2010), Case C-265/08 *Federutility and Others*, not yet reported, paras 27–47 (derogation from the competition rules); ECJ, Case C-157/94 *Commission v Netherlands* [1997] E.C.R. I-5699, para. 32; ECJ, Case C-158/94 *Commission v Italy* [1997] E.C.R. I-5789, para. 43; ECJ, Case C-159/94 *Commission v France* [1997] E.C.R. I-5815, para. 49 (derogation from Art. 37 TFEU). See Kovar, "Droit communautaire et service public: esprit d'orthodoxie ou pensée laïcisée" (1996) R.T.D.E. 215–242 and 493–533.

[93] ECJ, Case C-320/91 *Corbeau* [1993] E.C.R. I-2533, paras 13–20; ECJ, Case C-67/96 *Albany* [1999] E.C.R. I-5751, paras 53–60; ECJ, Case C-340/99 *TNT Traco* [2001] E.C.R. I-4109, paras 54–58; ECJ, Case C-475/99 *Firma Ambulanz Glöckner* [2001] E.C.R. I-8089, paras 55–56.

[94] For a discussion of this exception and its relationship with grounds justifying restrictions on free movement, see Wachsmann and Berrod, "Les critères de justification des monopoles: un premier bilan après l'affaire *Corbeau*" (1994) R.T.D.E. 39–61.

[95] ECJ, Case 66/86 *Ahmed Saeed Flugreisen and Others* [1989] E.C.R. 803, paras 53–56; ECJ, Case C-260/89 *ERT* [1991] E.C.R. I-2925, para. 34.

The Treaty of Amsterdam emphasised the role played by services of general interest, yet without associating this with any limitation on the application of the competition rules. Thus, it introduced Art. 16 EC [now Art. 14 TFEU] according to which the Union and the Member States are to take care that such services operate on the basis of principles and conditions which enable them to fulfil their missions "[w]ithout prejudice to Article 4 [TEU] or Articles 93, 106 and 107 [TFEU]",

> "given the place occupied by services of general economic interest in the shared values of the Union as well as their role in promoting social and territorial cohesion".[96]

Since the entry into force of the Lisbon Treaty, the European Parliament and the Council, acting by means of regulations in accordance with the ordinary legislative procedure, are competent to establish these principles and set these conditions without prejudice to the competence of Member States to commission and to fund such services (Art. 14 TFEU).[97] As far as the public service remit of broadcasting organisations is concerned, a protocol to the Treaties confirms that the Member States have competence to provide for the public funding of public service broadcasting.[98]

11–018   Liberalisation. Article 106(3) TFEU empowers the Commission to address directives or decisions to the Member States. As a result, the Commission may act individually by decision against public undertakings and Member States

---

[96] Article 93 TFEU is concerned with State Aid in respect of transport, Art. 107 TFEU with State Aid generally (see also para. 11–019 *et seq., infra*). See Napolitano, "Towards a European Legal order for services of general economic interest", (2005) 11 E.Pub.L. 565–581; Schwintowski, "The common good, public subsistence and the functions of public undertakings in the European internal market" (2003) E.Bus.Org.L.R. 353–382; Rojanski, "L'Union européenne et les services d'intérêt général" (2002) R.D.U.E. 735–773; Frenz, "Dienste von allgemeinem wirtschaftlichen Interesse" (2000) EuR. 901–925; Rodrigues, "Les services publics et le traité d'Amsterdam. Genèse et portée juridique du projet de nouvel article 16 du traité CE" (1998) R.M.C.U.E. 37–46. Declaration (No. 13), annexed to the Amsterdam Treaty, confirmed that Art. 16 was to be implemented with full respect for the jurisprudence of the Court of Justice, inter alia as regards the principles of equality of treatment, quality and continuity of public services ([1997] O.J. C340/133). Declaration (No. 37), annexed to the Amsterdam Treaty, was concerned with services of general economic interest provided by public credit institutions existing in Germany ([1997] O.J. C340/138). See also the Communication from the Commission, "Services of general interest in Europe", [2001] O.J. C17/4.

[97] See further Protocol (No. 26), annexed to the TEU and TFEU, on Services of General Interest, [2010] O.J. C83/308.

[98] Protocol (No. 29), annexed to the TEU and TFEU, on the system of public broadcasting in the Member States, [2010] O.J C83/312. See also the Resolution of the Council and of the representatives of the Governments of the Member States, meeting within the Council, of January 25, 1999 concerning public service broadcasting, [1999] O.J. C30/1.

(alongside its supervisory powers under Art. 258 TFEU),[99] but may also issue general rules specifying the Member States' Treaty obligations by directives.[100] On this basis the Commission has adopted directives for the liberalisation of sectors of the economy which in most Member States were the province of publicly-owned corporations or monopoly undertakings, such as telecommunications and energy.[101] In parallel with these liberalisation measures, the European Parliament and the Council have adopted harmonisation directives pursuant to Art. 114 TFEU [*ex Art. 95 EC*] which especially emphasise opening up non-discriminatory access to infrastructure, for instance in telecommunications.[102]

---

[99] ECJ, Joined Cases C-48/90 and C-66/90 *Netherlands and Others v Commission* [1992] E.C.R. I-565, paras 27–37. See also Lenaerts, Arts and Maselis, *Procedural Law of the European Union*, (3rd edn, London, Sweet & Maxwell, 2011) Ch.5.

[100] For the Commission's discretion, see ECJ, Case C-141/02 P *Commission v T-Mobile Austria* [2005] ECR I-1283, paras 66–69, with a case note by Castillo de la Torre (2005) C.M.L.Rev. 1751–1763; CFI, Case T-32/93 *Ladbroke Racing v Commission* [1994] E.C.R. II-1015, paras 36, 37 and 38 and 44; for the first application of Art. 86(3) of the EC Treaty [*now Art. 106 TFEU*], see Commission Directive 80/723/EEC of June 25, 1980 on the transparency of financial relations between Member States and public undertakings, [1980] O.J. L195/35, now replaced by Commission Directive 2006/111/EC of November 16, 2006 on the transparency of financial relations between Member States and public undertakings as well as on financial transparency within certain undertakings, [2006] O.J. L318/17.

[101] See Directive 88/301/EEC of May 16, 1988 on competition in the markets in telecommunications terminal equipment, [1988] O.J. L131/73 and Directive 90/388/EEC of June 28, 1990 on competition in the markets for telecommunications services, [1990] O.J. L192/10), since replaced by Directive 2002/77/EC of September 16, 2002 on competition in the markets for electronic communications networks and services, [2002] O.J. L249/21. The Commission's competence was confirmed by the Court of Justice following actions for annulment brought by Member States: ECJ, Joined Cases 188–190/80 *France, Italy and United Kingdom v Commission* [1982] E.C.R. 2545 (Directive 80/723/EEC); ECJ, Case C-202/88 *France v Commission* [1991] E.C.R. I-1223, para. 14 (Directive 88/301/EEC); ECJ, Joined Cases C-271/90, C-281/90 and C-289/90 *Spain and Others v Commission* [1992] E.C.R. I-5833 (Directive 90/388/EEC). As regards the Commission's competence, see Hocepied, "Les directives article 90, paragraphe 3: une espèce juridique en voie de disparition?" (1994) 2 R.A.E. 49–63. For the energy sector, see Fiquet, "Vers une réconciliation entre l'Europe et les services publics: l'exemple de l'électricité" and Lombart, "Le service public du gaz sous les feux de l'actualité juridique" (1998) A.J.D.A. 864–872 and 873–883, respectively.

[102] See, for example, the directives of the European Parliament and of the Council of March 7, 2002 on a common regulatory framework for electronic communications networks and services: Directive 2002/21/EC (framework) and Directive 2002/19/EC (access), Directive 2002/20/EC (authorisation) and Directive 2002/22/EC (universal service), [2002] O.J. L108/33, L108/7, L108/21 and L108/51, respectively. For "open network provision" or OPN, see, inter alia, Council Directive 90/387/EEC of June 28, 1990, [1990] O.J. L192/1. See Garzaniti, *Telecommunications, Broadcasting and the Internet: EU Competition Law and Regulation* (London, Sweet & Maxwell, 2010), 1216 pp.; Bavasso, "Electronic Communications: A New Paradigm for European Regulation" (2004) C.M.L.Rev. 87–118; De Streil, Queck and Vernet, "Le nouveau cadre réglementaire européen des réseaux et services de communications électroniques (2002) C.D.E. 243–341; Franzius, "Strukturmodelle des europäischen Telekommuikationsrechts" (2002) EuR. 660–690; for universal service, seeKarayannis, "Le service universel de télécommunications en droit communautaire: entre intervention publique et concurrence" (2002) C.D.E. 315–375. For the relationship between liberalisation

B. STATE AID

11–019   **Prohibited aid.** Free competition in the internal market requires a prohibition in principle of aid funded out of the public purse which distorts or threatens to distort competition by favouring certain undertakings or the production of certain goods and adversely affects trade between Member States (Art. 107(1) TFEU).[103] By way of exception, the Treaties list three types of aid which are, by operation of law, compatible with the internal market (Art. 107(2) TFEU) and refers to other types of aid measures which *may* be compatible with the internal market[104] (Art. 107(3) TFEU). Even where aid is compatible with the internal market, it may not be "misused" (Art. 108(2) TFEU; *ex* Art. 88(2) EC]. Pursuant to Art. 109 TFEU [*ex Art. 89 EC*], the Council, acting by a regulation, empowered the Commission to grant exemptions for certain categories of aid.[105] The Commission has implemented the regulation through a number of "block exemptions" concerning aid granted in various sectors.[106] Moreover, pursuant to the same regulation, it has declared that aid not exceeding 200,000 over any period of three years (100,000 for undertakings active in the road transport sector) does not affect trade between Member States and/or does not distort competition.[107]

---

of the markets and the privatisation carried out by the Member States, see Verhoeven, "Privatisation and EC Law: Is the European Commission 'neutral' with respect to Public versus Private Ownership of Companies?" (1996) I.C.L.Q. 861–887; Edward and Hoskins, "Article 90: Deregulation and EC Law. Reflections arising from the XVI Fide Conference" (1995) C.M.L.Rev. 157–186.

[103] For further particulars, see Quigley, *European State Aid Law* (Oxford, Hart, 2008), 450 pp.; Hancher, Ottervanger and Slot, *EC State Aids* (London, Sweet & Maxwell, 2006) 909 pp.; Biondi, Eeckhout and Flynn (eds), *The Law of State Aid in the European Union* (Oxford, Oxford University Press, 2004), 389 pp.; Evans, *EC Law of State Aid* (Oxford, Clarendon Press, 1997), 484 pp. With regard to the definition of State Aid, see, for instance, Bacon, "The Concept of State Aid: The Developing Jurisprudence in the European and UK Courts" (2003) E.Comp.L.Rev. 54–61; Ross, "State Aids and National Courts: Definitions and Other Problems—A Case of Premature Emancipation?" (2000) C.M.L.Rev. 401–423.

[104] This list may be supplemented by the Council on a proposal from the Commission (Art. 107(3)(e) TFEU).

[105] Council Regulation (EC) No. 994/98 of May 7, 1998 on the application of Arts 92 and 93 of the Treaty establishing the European Community [*now Arts 107 and 108 TFEU*] to certain categories of horizontal State Aid, [1998] O.J. L142/1

[106] Since the Treaty of Lisbon, the Treaty explicitly empowers the Commission to do so (see Art. 108(4) TFEU). See Regulation (EC) No. 800/2008 of August 6, 2008, [2008] O.J. L214/3 (general block exemption regulation). See also Regulation (EC) No. 1857/2006 of December 15, 2006, [2006] O.J. L358/3 (aid to SMEs in the agricultural sector) and Regulation (EC) No. 736/2008 of July 22, 2008, [2008] O.J. L201/16 (aid to SMEs in the fisheries sector).

[107] Commission Regulation (EC) No. 1998/2006 of December 15, 2006 on the application of Arts 87 and 88 of the Treaty to *de minimis* aid, [2006] O.J. L379/5. Different rules apply in the case of *de minimis* aid in the sector of agricultural production (see Commission Regulation (EC) No. 1535/2007 of December 20, 2007, [2007] O.J. L337/35) and in the fisheries sector (see Commission Regulation (EC) No. 875/2007 of July 24, 2007, [2007] O.J. L193/6). See Sevinga, "De de-minimissteunverordening: enkele belangrijke vernieuwingen" (2007) N.T.E.R. 60–63.

Concept of State Aid. According to the Court of Justice, Art. 107(1) lays down **11–020** four conditions.[108] First of all, the aid should be granted by a Member State or through State resources. As a result, an economic benefit for an undertaking is in the nature of aid only if it can be imputed to the State and is directly or indirectly paid out of public funds.[109] Consequently, Art. 107(1) covers not only aid granted directly by the State, but also aid granted by public or private bodies designated or established by the State.[110] Moreover, in order to qualify as State Aid, a measure must constitute a burden on State resources.[111] Secondly, the measure must confer an advantage on the recipient. This must be interpreted in broad terms. The aid concept covers not only positive benefits, such as subsidies, loans and public shareholdings, but also interventions which, in various forms, mitigate the charges which are normally included in the budget of an undertaking and which, without therefore being subsidies in the strict meaning of the word, are similar in character and have the same effect.[112] Moreover, a general measure must not be involved, but a benefit which, by displaying a degree of selectivity, is such as to favour "certain undertakings or the production of certain goods".[113] Aid measures adopted by a regional authority of a Member State which are applicable only in the territory of the region concerned will constitute selective measures unless the region has sufficiently autonomous powers so as to constitute the appropriate framework of reference for the assessment of the measures.[114] Where the public authorities

---

[108] E.g. ECJ, Case C-172/03 *Heiser* [2005] E.C.R. I-1627, para. 27; ECJ, Case C-237/04 *Enirisorse* [2006] E.C.R. I-2843, para. 39; ECJ, Case C-169/08 *Regione Sardegna* [2009] E.C.R. I-10821, para. 52. See Winter, "Re(de)fining the Notion of State Aid in Article 87(1) of the EC Treaty" (2004) C.M.L.Rev. 475–504.

[109] ECJ, Case C-345/02 *Pearle and Others* [2004] E.C.R. I-7139, para. 35.

[110] See, in particular, ECJ, Case C-379/98 *PreussenElektra* [2001] E.C.R. I-2099, paras 57–66; ECJ, Case C-482/99 *France v Commission* [2002] E.C.R. I-4397, paras 50–59.

[111] ECJ, Joined Cases C-72/91 and C-73/91 *Sloman Neptun* [1993] E.C.R. I-887, para. 21; ECJ, Case C-345/02 *Pearle and Others* [2004] E.C.R. I-7139, para. 36.

[112] ECJ, Case 30/59 *De Gezamenlijke Steenkolenmijnen in Limburg v High Authority* [1961] E.C.R. 1, at 40; ECJ, Case C-387/92 *Banco Exterior de España* [1994] E.C.R. I-877, para. 13; ECJ, Case C-39/94 *SFEI and Others* [1996] E.C.R. I-3547, paras 57–62; ECJ, Joined Cases C-393/04 and C-41/05 *Air Liquide Industries and Others* [2006] E.C.R. I-5293, para. 29; ECJ, Case C-237/04 *Enirisorse* [2006] E.C.R. I-2843, para. 42.

[113] E.g. ECJ, Case C-241/94 *France v Commission* [1996] E.C.R. I-4551, paras 22–40; ECJ, Case C-143/99 *Adria-Wien Pipeline and Wietersdorfer & Peggauer Zementwerke* [2001] E.C.R. I-8365, para. 34; ECJ, Case C-409/00 *Spain v Commission* [2003] E.C.R. I-1487, para. 47; ECJ, Case C-308/01 *GIL Insurance and Others* [2004] E.C.R. I-4777, para. 68; ECJ, Case C-172/03 *Heiser* [2005] E.C.R. I-1627, para. 40. See Gonen, "Steun of geen steun, een kwestie van (onder meer) selectiviteit" (2007) N.T.E.R. 14–22; Kurcz, "Can general measures be . . . selective? Some thoughts on the interpretation of a State Aid definition" (2007) C.M.L.Rev. 159–182; Nicolaides, "Developments in fiscal aid: new interpretations and new problems with the concept of selectivity", (2007) E.St.A.L.Q. 43–49. See also Lenaerts, "State Aid and Direct Taxation" in Kanninen, Korjus and Rosas (eds), *EU Competition Law in Context: Essays in Honour of Virpi Tiili* (Oxford, Hart Publishing, 2009) 291–306.

[114] ECJ, Case C-88/03 *Portugal v Commission* [2006] E.C.R. I-7115, paras 52–85 (case note by Winter (2007) C.M.L.Rev. 183–198); ECJ, Joined Cases C-428/06, C-429/06, C-430/06, C-431/06, C-432/06, C-433/06 and C-434/06 *Unión General de Trabajadores de la Rioja* [2008] E.C.R. I-6747,

intervene as shareholders, creditors or contractors vis-à-vis an undertaking, that public intervention will constitute State Aid only where in similar circumstances a private shareholder, creditor or contractor, would not have so intervened.[115] Thirdly, the measure must result in a distortion of competition or threaten to distort competition. According to the Court of Justice, this will be the case where the measure enables an undertaking to reduce its costs and therefore strengthens its competitive position compared with other undertakings.[116] Lastly, the aid measure must affect intra-Union trade. Intra-Union trade is considered to be affected where the aid strengthens the position of an undertaking compared with other undertakings competing in intra-Union trade.[117]

11–021 **Services of general economic interest.** Compensation for services performed by an undertaking in discharging public-service obligations does not constitute aid within the meaning of Art. 107 TFEU.[118] The following conditions apply: (1) the recipient undertaking must actually have clearly defined public-service obligations to discharge; (2) the parameters on the basis of which the compensation is calculated must be established in advance in an objective and transparent manner; (3) the compensation cannot exceed what is necessary to cover all or part of the costs incurred in the discharge of public-service obligations, taking into account the relevant receipts and a reasonable profit for discharging those obligations; (4) where the undertaking which is to discharge public-service obligations in a specific case is not chosen pursuant to a public procurement procedure which would allow for the selection of the tenderer capable of providing those services at the least cost to the community, the level of compensation needed must be determined on the

---

paras 45–143. See also ECJ, Case C-169/08 *Regione Sardegna* (n. 109, *supra*) paras 59–64. For a discussion, See Lenaerts and Cambien, "Regions and the European Courts: giving shape to the Regional Dimension of Member States" (2010) E.L.Rev.; Greaves, "Autonomous regions, taxation and EC state-aid rules" (2009) 34 E.L.Rev. 779–793.

[115] ECJ, Case 234/84 *Commission v Belgium* [1986] E.C.R. 2263, para. 14, and ECJ, Case 40/85 *Commission v Belgium* [1986] E.C.R. 2321, para. 13. See Karydis, "Le principe de l'opérateur économique privé', critère de qualification des mesures étatiques, en tant qu'aides d'Etat, au sens de l'article 87§1 du traité CE" (2003) R.T.D.E. 389–413. However, the Court has specified, in relation to undertakings entrusted with services of a general economic interest such as the French postal services, that "in the absence of any possibility of comparing the situation of [such an undertaking] with that of a private group of undertakings not operating in a reserved sector, 'normal market conditions', which are necessarily hypothetical, must be assessed by reference to the objective and verifiable elements available" (ECJ, Joined Cases C-341/06 P and C-342/06 P *Chronopost* [2008] E.C.R. I-4777, para. 148, referring to ECJ, Joined Cases C-83/01 P, C-93/01 P and C-94/01 P *Chronopost* [2003] E.C.R. I-6993, para. 38).

[116] ECJ, Case 730/79 *Philip Morris v Commission* [1980] E.C.R. 2671, para. 11; ECJ, Case 259/85 *France v Commission* [1987] E.C.R. I-4393, para. 24.

[117] ECJ, Case 730/79 *Philip Morris v Commission* [1980] E.C.R. 2671, para. 11; CFI, Case T-214/95 *Vlaams Gewest v Commission* [1998] E.C.R. II-717, para. 50.

[118] ECJ, Case 53/00 *Ferring* [2001] E.C.R. I-9067, para. 27; ECJ, Case C-280/00 *Altmark Trans and Regierungspräsident Magdeburg* [2003] E.C.R. I-7747, para. 87.

basis of an analysis of the costs which a typical well run undertaking would have incurred in discharging those obligations.[119] Measures that fulfil these criteria do not constitute State Aid, and Member States are not under a duty to notify them. Public-service compensation that does not meet these criteria will constitute State Aid if the other conditions of Art. 107 TFEU are met. However, the Commission has specified that such aid may still be covered by Art. 106(2) TFEU, and will, under certain conditions, be exempt from the duty of notification set out in Art. 108(3) TFEU.[120]

Centralised supervision. All State Aid which falls within the prohibition set out in Art. 107(1) TFEU is subject to the supervision of the Commission in accordance with the procedure codified in Regulation No. 659/1999.[121] For the purposes of the Commission's supervision of State Aid, the rules differ depending on whether existing aid or aid which Member States wish to introduce or to alter is concerned.[122] In both cases, it is for the Commission alone to determine whether an aid measure is compatible with the internal market, subject to review by the General Court and the Court of Justice.[123] In this connection, the Commission has a broad discretion and this limits, but does not eliminate, the room for judicial review.[124] The Commission has indicated in a number of communications the

11–022

---

[119] *Altmark Trans and Regierungspräsident Magdeburg*, paras 88–94. For this question, see Bracq (2004) R.T.D.E. 33–70; Louis and Vallery (2004) World Comp. 53–74; van Marissing (2004) S.E.W. 325–330; Drijber and Sanen-Siebenga (2003) N.T.E.R. 253–258; Leibenath (2003) EuR. 1052–1066; Nicolaides (2003) E.Comp.L.Rev. 561–573; Thouvenin and Lorieux (2003) R.M.C.U.E. 633–641.

[120] See Commission Decision 2005/842/EC of November 28, 2005 on the application of Art. 86(2) of the EC Treaty to State Aid in the form of public service compensation granted to certain undertakings entrusted with the operation of services of general economic interest, [2005] O.J. L312/67 (adopted on the basis of Art. 86(3) of the EC Treaty). The Commission has also fleshed out the conditions under which State Aid which does not fall within the scope of that decision, and hence must be notified, can be justified under Art. 86(2): see the Community framework for State Aid in the form of public service compensation, [2005] O.J. C297/4. For these measures, see Renzulli, "Services of general economic interest: the post-Altmark scenario" (2008) E.Pub.L. 399–431; De Beys, "Aide d'Etat et financement des services publics. Un bilan après l'adoption du paquet post-Altmark" (2006) J.T.D.E. 1–10; Hancher and Evans, "Altmark als katalysator: het Commissiepakket met alle antwoorden rond Staatssteun en diensten van algemeen economisch belang?" (2006) N.T.E.R. 153–159.

[121] Council Regulation (EC) No. 659/1999 of March 22, 1999 laying down detailed rules for the application of Art. 93 of the EC Treaty [*now Art. 108 TFEU*], [1999] O.J. L83/1. See Rivas Andrés and Gutiérrez Gisbert, "Un comentario crítico al Reglamento procedimental en materia de ayudas de Estado" (2000) G.J. 40–58; Sinnaeve and Slot, "The New Regulation on State Aid Procedures" (1999) C.M.L.Rev. 1153–1194.

[122] As far as the States are concerned which acceded on May 1, 2004 and on January 1, 2007, "existing aid" on accession is defined in Annex IV to the 2003 Act of Accession pursuant to Art. 22 of that Act, [2003] O.J. L236/797) and in Annex V to the 2005 Act of Accession pursuant to Art. 21 of that Act ([2005] O.J. L157/268), respectively.

[123] ECJ, Case 78/76 *Steinike und Weinlig* [1977] E.C.R. 595, para. 9.

[124] CFI, Joined Cases T-371/94 and T-394/94 *British Airways v Commission* [1998] E.C.R. II-2405.

conditions under which it regards aid for particular regions or activities as being compatible with the internal market.[125] Accordingly, in the context of the financial and economic crisis that broke out in autumn 2008, the Commission adopted a temporary framework under which Member States were allowed to grant aid to companies experiencing difficulties in obtaining financing.[126] A national court may rule on whether or not action by a public authority constitutes State Aid and whether or not it was granted in accordance with the applicable procedural rules, but has no jurisdiction to rule on whether an aid measure is compatible or incompatible with the internal market.[127]

11–023   **Existing aid.** Existing systems of aid are kept under constant review by the Commission. In this connection, the Commission is to propose any appropriate measures required by the progressive development or the functioning of the internal market (Art. 108(1) TFEU). If the Member State concerned does not accept the proposed modification, the Commission initiates the formal inter partes investigation procedure (by notice published in the *Official Journal*) which culminates in a decision by which the Commission determines either that the measure—subject, where appropriate, to certain conditions—is not aid or is compatible with the internal market or that the measure is incompatible with the internal market.[128] If the Commission finds that existing aid is incompatible with the internal market having regard to Art. 107 TFEU or that such aid is being misused, it is to decide that the Member State concerned must abolish or alter the aid within such time as the Commission shall determine (Art. 108(2), first subpara., TFEU). An action may be brought directly before the Court of Justice, by way of derogation from Arts 258 and 259 TFEU [*ex Arts 226 and 227 EC*], by the Commission or any interested Member State against a Member State in breach of that obligation (Art. 108(2), second subpara., TFEU).

11–024   **New aid.** There is a procedure for new aid without which no aid may be regarded as lawful. Any plans to grant or alter aid must be notified to the Commission in time

---

[125] For the Commission's communications and guidelines, in particular for aid for regional development, employment, research and development, protection of the environment, rescue and restructuring of firms in difficulty, see the link "State Aid" on the website of the Commission's DG Competition (*http://ec.europa.eu/dgs/competition/* [Accessed December 8, 2010]).

[126] Communication from the Commission—Temporary framework for State Aid measures to support access to finance in the current financial and economic crisis, adopted on December 17, 2008, [2009] O.J. C16/1.

[127] ECJ, Case 78/76 *Steinike & Weinlig v Germany* [1977] E.C.R. 595, paras 10–15; ECJ, Case C-44/93 *Namur-Les Assurances du Crédit* [1994] E.C.R. I-3829, para. 17, at I-3871. For the distribution of tasks as between the national courts and the Commission, see the Commission Notice on the enforcement of State Aid by national courts, [2009] O.J. C85/1 and Struys and Abbott, "The role of national courts in State Aid litigation" (2003) E.L.Rev. 172–189.

[128] Regulation No. 659/1999 (para. 121, *supra*), Art. 7 in conjunction with Art. 19(2).

for it to submit its comments (Art. 108(3) TFEU).[129] If, after an initial examination, the Commission should find that the notified measure is not aid or that no doubts are raised as to its compatibility with the internal market, it adopts a decision to that effect.[130] If, in contrast, the Commission should consider that the measure notified raises doubts as to its compatibility with the internal market, it must initiate without delay the inter partes procedure provided for by Art. 108(2).[131] If it does so, the Member State concerned is debarred under the last sentence of Art. 108(3) from putting its proposed measure into effect until the procedure has resulted in a final decision by which the Commission finds that the measure is not aid or is compatible with the internal market. In assessing the compatibility with the internal market, the Commission must apply the rules in force at the time when it gives its decision.[132] If the Commission determines in its final decision that the measure is aid incompatible with the internal market, the measure may not be put into effect.[133] Pending a final decision, a proposed aid measure may be implemented only if the Commission, after being informed of it, fails to carry out the examination involving interested parties and sufficient time has elapsed for the preliminary examination, provided that the Member State gives the Commission prior notice—after which the aid measure comes under the rules relating to existing aid.[134]

An aid measure which is put into effect in infringement of the obligations arising from Art. 108(3) EC is unlawful aid.[135] A Commission decision finding such a measure to be compatible with the internal market does not have the effect of regularising it retroactively.[136] Since the last sentence of Art. 108(3) has direct

---

[129] The obligation to notify the Commission does not apply to categories of aid covered by a "block exemption"; see para. 11–014, *supra*. Compulsory notification forms have been laid down in Commission Regulation (EC) No. 794/2004 of April 21, 2004 implementing Council Regulation (EC) No. 659/1999, [2004] O.J. L140/1.

[130] Regulation No. 659/1999 (para. 121, *supra*), Art. 4(2) and (3). Such a decision may be challenged by interested parties before the European Courts (ECJ, Case C-367/95 P *Commission v Sytraval and Brink's France* [1998] E.C.R. I-1719, paras 33–49).

[131] Article 108(3) TFEU and Regulation No. 659/1999, Art. 4(4). For that obligation, see, for instance, ECJ, Case C-294/90 *British Aerospace and Rover v Commission* [1992] E.C.R. I-493, paras 10–15; ECJ, Case C-225/91 *Matra v Commission* [1993] E.C.R. I-3203, para. 33.

[132] ECJ, Case C-334/07 P *Commission v Freistaat Sachsen* [2008] E.C.R. I-9465, paras 52–54. However, where the legal rules under which a Member State notified proposed aid change before the Commission takes its decision, the Commission must ask the interested parties to express their views on the compatibility of that aid with those rules (*ibid.*, para. 56).

[133] Regulation No. 659/1999, Art. 7(5).

[134] ECJ, Case 120/73 *Lorenz* [1973] E.C.R. 1471, para. 4. For this first investigation, which the Commission has two months to carry out (Regulation No. 659/1999, Art. 4(6)), see ECJ, Case C-99/98 *Austria v Commission* [2001] E.C.R. I-1101, paras 34–37.

[135] Regulation No. 659/1999, Art. 1(f). See, e.g., ECJ, Joined Cases C-266/04 to C-270/04, C-276/04 and C-321/04 to C-325/04 *Distribution Casino France and Others* [2005] E.C.R. I-9481, para. 30.

[136] ECJ, Case C-354/90 *FNCE* [1991] E.C.R. I-5505, para. 16; ECJ, Joined Cases C-261/01 and C-262/01 *van Calster and Others* [2003] E.C.R. I-12249, para. 63 (case note by Van de Gronden (2004) S.E.W. 341–347); ECJ, Case C-368/04 *Transalpine Ölleitung in Österreich* [2006] E.C.R. I-9957, paras 40–42 (case note by Retter (2007) E.St.A.L.Q. 129–137).

effect,[137] the national courts are empowered to determine whether a measure which has not been notified to the Commission nevertheless has to be regarded as a new aid measure which, in the absence of notification, must be considered to be unlawful (even if it subsequently transpires that the aid is compatible with the internal market).[138] By the same token, a national court may consider whether (non-notified) aid falls within the categories of aid measures which are exempted by the Commission. If the measure does not satisfy the requirements for exemption, the national court may find in an appropriate case only that the duty to notify has been infringed; it cannot itself rule on the compatibility of the aid with the internal market. If the national court entertains doubts about the categorisation of the measure at issue it may seek clarification from the Commission or request the Court of Justice for a preliminary ruling on the interpretation of Art. 107 TFEU.[139] Since compatible aid alone may be implemented, the implementation of planned aid is to be deferred until the doubts as to its compatibility have been resolved by a Commission decision.[140]

11–025 **Intervention by the Council.** Under the third subparagraph of Art. 108(2) TFEU, a Member State may apply to the Council, which may declare existing or proposed aid compatible with the internal market by a unanimous vote "if such a decision is justified by exceptional circumstances".[141] If the Commission has initiated the inter partes procedure, the fact that the State concerned has made its application to the Council will have the effect of suspending that procedure for a period of three months (Art. 108(2), third and fourth subparas, TFEU). Where that period has expired, the Council is no longer competent to adopt a decision in relation to the aid concerned. If the Member State concerned has made no application to the Council before the Commission declares the aid in question incompatible with the internal

---

[137] ECJ, Case 6/64 *Costa* [1964] E.C.R. 585, at 596.

[138] ECJ, Case 78/76 *Steinike und Weinlig* [1977] E.C.R. 595, para. 14; ECJ, Case C-44/93 *Namur-Les Assurances du Crédit* [1994] E.C.R. I-3829, para. 16; ECJ, Case C-295/97 *Industrie Aeronautique e Meccaniche Rinaldo Piaggio* [1999] E.C.R. I-3735, paras 44–50.

[139] ECJ, Case C-39/94 *SFEI and Others* [1996] E.C.R. I-3547, para. 50–51.

[140] If the national court considers it necessary in order to safeguard the interests of the parties, it may order interim relief, such as suspension of the measures at issue (ECJ, Case C-39/94 *SFEI and Others* [1996] E.C.R. I-3547, para. 52), order non-notified aid which has already been disbursed to be repaid (*ibid.*, para. 70) or order the placement of the funds on a blocked account so that they do not remain at the disposal of the recipient (ECJ (judgment of March 11, 2010), Case C-1/09 *CELF* ("*CELF II*"), not yet reported, para. 37). A national court before which an application has been brought for repayment of unlawful aid may not stay the proceedings until the Commission has ruled on the compatibility of the aid: *CELF II*, paras 28–40.

[141] ECJ, Case C-110/02 *Commission v Council* [2004] E.C.R. I-6333, para. 24. For the broad discretion of the Council in this connection, see ECJ, Case C-122/94 *Commission v Council* [1996] E.C.R. I-881, paras 7–25. See, e.g., Council Decisions 2002/361/EC, 2002/362/EC and 2002/363/EC of May 3, 2002 on the granting of a national aid in favour of road transport undertakings by the authorities of the Netherlands, Italy and France, respectively, [2002] O.J. L131/12, L131/14 and L131/15.

market and thereby closes the inter partes procedure, the Council is no longer authorised to declare such aid compatible with the internal market.[142] In addition, the Council cannot validly declare compatible with the internal market an aid measure allocating to the beneficiaries of an unlawful aid which a Commission decision has previously declared incompatible with the internal market, an amount designed to compensate for the repayments which they are required to make pursuant to that decision.[143]

Repayment of unlawfully granted aid. The Commission will require unlawfully granted aid that is incompatible with the internal market to be repaid; the procedures for recovering it are left to national law.[144]   **11–026**

The national courts must in principle order all appropriate measures, in accordance with their national law, for the recovery of unlawfully granted aid. An undertaking to which aid has been granted cannot resist the recovery of aid by claiming that it had a legitimate expectation that it was lawful if the procedure laid down in Art. 108 TFEU was not complied with when the aid was granted.[145] Similarly, an undertaking cannot resist recovery by invoking rules of national law precluding the recovery of State Aid granted in breach of EU law. Such rules are incompatible with EU law and have to be dissapplied.[146] However, there may be exceptional circumstances in which it would be inappropriate to order repayment of the aid.[147]

---

[142] ECJ, Case C-110/02 *Commission v Council* [2004] E.C.R. I-6333, paras 28–36; ECJ, Case C-399/03 *Commission v Council* [2006] E.C.R. I-5629, paras 23–37; ECJ, Case C-119/05 *Lucchini* [2007] E.C.R. I-06199, paras 59–63, see the case note by Hatje (2007) EuR. 654–659.

[143] ECJ, Case C-110/02 *Commission v Council* [2004] E.C.R. I-6333, paras 37–50.

[144] See the Commission Notice "Towards an effective implementation of Commission decisions ordering Member States to recover unlawful and incompatible State Aid", [2007] C 272/4. See Karpenschif, "La récupération des aides nationales versées en violation du droit communautaire à l'aune du règlement n° 659/1999: du mythe à la réalité?" (2001) R.T.D.E. 551–596; Priess, "Recovery of Illegal State Aid: An Overview of Recent Developments in the Case Law" (1996) C.M.L.Rev. 69–91.

[145] ECJ, Case C-5/89 *Commission v Germany* [1990] E.C.R. I-3437, para. 14; ECJ, Case C-169/95 *Spain v Commission* [1997] E.C.R. I-135, paras 51–54; ECJ, Case C-24/95 *Alcan Deutschland* [1997] E.C.R. I-1591, paras 22–54; ECJ, Case C-199/06 *CELF* ("*CELF I*") [2008] E.C.R. I-469, paras 66–68. For defences of Member States and recipients of aid, see Montaldo and Medina Palomino, "Aides d'Etat et moyens de défense des entreprises" (1991) 4 R.M.C.U.E 11–48.

[146] ECJ, Case C-119/05 *Lucchini* [2007] E.C.R. I-06199, paras 59–63.

[147] E.g. ECJ, Case C-39/94 *SFEI and Others* [1996] E.C.R. I-3547, para. 70. See also Art. 14 of Regulation No. 659/1999, which provides that recovery of aid is not required if this would be contrary to a general principle of Community law. For an exceptional case in which recovery of unlawful State Aid was held to have become impossible, see ECJ, Case C-301/87 *France v Commission* [1990] E.C.R. I-307. The fact that the Commission has adopted decisions declaring unlawful aid to be compatible with the internal market which were subsequently annulled by the Union courts, is not, in itself, capable of constituting an exceptional circumstance that would limit the obligation to repay that aid: ECJ (judgment of March 11, 2010), Case C-1/09 *CELF* ("*CELF II*"), not yet reported, paras 41–55.

However, where the Commission has adopted a positive decision declaring the aid to be compatible with the internal market, EU law does not impose an obligation of full recovery of the unlawful aid, even in the absence of exceptional circumstances. In such a situation, pursuant to EU law, the national court must order the aid recipient to pay interest in respect of the period of unlawfulness. Within the framework of its domestic law, it may, if appropriate, also order the recovery of the unlawful aid, without prejudice to the Member State's right subsequently to re-implement it. It may also be required to uphold claims for compensation for damage caused by reason of the unlawful nature of the aid.[148]

A Member State and an undertaking in receipt of the aid are entitled to challenge a Commission decision on aid measures in proceedings before the General Court (Art. 263 TFEU; *ex Art. 230 EC*).[149] Once the time-limit laid down has expired, the validity of the decision may no longer be called in to question by the Member State concerned (e.g. in infringement proceedings before the Court of Justice under the second subpara. of Art. 108(2)).[150] Nor may it be challenged in the national court by the recipient of the aid who has been notified of the decision by the Member State (e.g. after steps have been taken to recover the unlawful aid).[151]

IV. ECONOMIC AND MONETARY POLICY

11–027 **EMU.** Article 3(4) TEU proclaims that the Union shall establish an economic and monetary union whose currency is the euro. Article 119 TFEU [*ex Art. 4 EC*] provides a definition of the economic and monetary union which the Union is to establish. The economic aspect is described as

> "an economic policy which is based on the close coordination of Member States' economic policies, on the internal market and on the definition of common objectives, and conducted in accordance with the principle of an open market economy with free competition" (Art. 119(1) TFEU).

Although that policy is conducted by action on the part of the Member States and the Union, the definition shows that any economic policy must square with the free

---

[148] ECJ, Case C-199/06 *CELF* ("*CELF I*") [2008] E.C.R. I-469, paras 46 and 52–53; ECJ, Case C-384/07 *Wienstrom* [2008] E.C.R. I-10393, paras 27–29. See Adriaanse, "Effectieve handhaving van het Staatssteunrecht ondermijnd?" (2008) N.T.E.R. 308–317.

[149] ECJ, Case 730/79 *Philip Morris v Commission* [1980] E.C.R. 2671, para. 5. For other interested parties entitled to contest Commission decisions relating to State Aid, see ECJ, Case C-367/95 P *Commission v Sytraval and Brink's France* [1998] E.C.R. I-1719, paras 33–49; Lenaerts, Arts and Maselis, *Procedural Law of the European Union* (3rd edn, London, Sweet & Maxwell, 2012) Ch. 7; Winter, "The Rights of Complainants in State Aid Cases: Judicial Review of Commission Decisions Adopted under Article 88 (*ex* 93) EC" (1999) C.M.L.Rev. 521–568.

[150] ECJ, Case 156/77 *Commission v Belgium* [1978] E.C.R. 1881, paras 21–24; ECJ, Case C-183/91 *Commission v Greece* [1993] E.C.R. I-3131, para. 10.

[151] ECJ, Case C-188/92 *TWD Textilwerke Deggendorf* [1994] E.C.R. I-833, paras 17–26.

movement of goods, persons, services and capital and with general objectives, such as economic and social cohesion, and competition policy. The monetary policy includes,

> "a single currency, the euro, and the definition and conduct of a single monetary policy and exchange-rate policy the primary objective of both of which shall be to maintain price stability and, without prejudice to this objective, to support the general economic policies in the Union, in accordance with the principle of an open market economy with free competition" (Art. 119(2) TFEU).

Unlike economic policy, monetary policy entails a definitive transfer of powers from the national level to the Union.[152] Article 119(3) TFEU underlines the guiding principles of EMU: stable prices, sound public finances and monetary conditions and a sustainable balance of payments.

In Title VIII of Part Three of the TFEU, economic and monetary union is dealt with in separate chapters on economic policy and monetary policy (Chs 1 and 2) and on the institutional framework of EMU (Ch. 3).[153] Chapter 4, which was introduced by the Lisbon Treaty, contains provisions specific to the Member States who have adopted the euro. The transitional provisions set out in Ch. 5 deal with the procedure and criteria for determining which Member States were to take part in the third stage of EMU as from January 1, 1999 or at a later date.

A. Preparation of Economic and Monetary Union

Coordination of economic and monetary policies. Under the original EEC Treaty, **11–028** the maintenance of stable prices, sound public finances and monetary conditions and

---

[152] In Protocol (No. 15), annexed to the TEU and the TFEU, on certain provisions relating to the United Kingdom of Great Britain and Northern Ireland ([2010] O.J. C83/284), the United Kingdom retained the right not to move to the third stage as a result of which Art.119(2) TFEU does not apply to it (para. 11–042, *infra*).

[153] For a general discussion of the Treaty provisions relating to EMU (in addition to paras 13–096—13–100, *infra*, on the European Central Bank), see Andenas and others (eds), *European Economic and Monetary Union: The Institutional Framework* (London, Kluwer Law International, 1997), 565 pp.; Slot, "The Institutional Provisions of the EMU", in Curtin and Heukels (eds), *Institutional Dynamics of European Integration. Essays in Honour of Henry G. Schermers*, Vol. II (Dordrecht, Martinus Nijhoff, 1994), 229–249; Louis, "The Economic and Monetary Union: Law and Institutions" (2004) C.M.L.Rev. 575–608; Seidel, "Konstitutionelle Schwächen der Währungsunion" (2001) EuR. 861–878; Lardoux, "L'Union économique et monétaire: génèse, mise en place, perspectives" (1998) R.M.C.U.E. 429–436; Partsch, "De quelques questions juridiques relatives au passage à la troisième phase de l'Union économique et monétaire et au fonctionnement de celle-ci" (1998) R.T.D.E. 35–74; Pipkorn, "Legal Arrangements in the Treaty of Maastricht for the Effectiveness of the Economic and Monetary Union" (1994) C.M.L.Rev. 263–291. For the changes introduced by the Lisbon Treaty, see Amtenbrink, "Economisch recht en het Verdrag van Lissabon II: Europese Economische en Monetaire Unie" (2008) S.E.W. 389–394.

a sustainable balance of payments was left to national economic policy, which Member States were to coordinate in close cooperation with the institutions of the Community "to the extent necessary to attain the objectives of this Treaty".[154] Member States were to regard their conjunctural and monetary policies as "a matter of common concern".[155]

A first plan for enlarging the economic and monetary powers of the Community and ultimately achieving economic and monetary union was adopted as long ago as 1970 in the report of the Werner Committee, which was never completely implemented (see para. 2–006). On the basis of a resolution of the European Council of December 5, 1978, the European Monetary System was started and, subsequently, the ECU was introduced as the unit of account for the exchange rate mechanism and as a means of settling transactions between the Community and the Member States (see para. 2–007).

It soon became clear, above all in the course of the implementation of the internal-market programme,[156] that the progressive integration of the markets of the Member States necessitated a greater degree of coordination at Community level of the Member States' economic and monetary policies. The elimination of internal frontiers for movements of goods, persons, services and capital rendered the economies of the Member States so dependent on each other that any national economic policy decision had a direct cross-frontier effect. Thus, a Member State could not pursue a policy of stimulating its own economy if expenditure stimuli only gave rise to increased imports from other Member States, resulting in a balance-of-payments deficit.[157] Furthermore, the internal market accentuated existing regional and structural disequilibria within the Union, especially differences in production costs, price stability and budget deficits. The disequilibria brought strong pressure to bear on Member States' exchange rates.

This prompted further steps to be taken in the coordination of economic and monetary policies. A high degree of coordination of economic policies by the Union was likely to result in uniform growth within the Member States and at the same time might decrease the pressure on Member States' monetary policies. A monetary union would make fixed exchange rates possible and eliminate the economic cost of uncertain exchange rates. Liberalisation of capital movements and integration of financial markets would make it impossible for many Member States to pursue an independent monetary policy. Consequently, effective supervision of

---

[154] See Art. 12(1) EEC.

[155] Art. 103(1) EEC and Art. 107(1) EEC, respectively.

[156] See VerLoren van Themaat, "Some Preliminary Observations on the Intergovernmental Conferences: The Relations Between the Concepts of a Common Market, a Monetary Union, an Economic Union, a Political Union and Sovereignty" (1991) C.M.L.Rev. 291–318; Louis, "A Monetary Union for Tomorrow?" (1989) C.M.L.Rev. 301–326.

[157] For an example, see the policy of the French Mauroy administration in 1981 to 1982, referred to by Lauwaars and Timmermans, *Europees recht in kort bestek* (Deventer, W.E.J. Tjeenk Willink, 1999), 305 pp.

the currency and of financial and capital markets had to be ensured at Union level. It followed that economic union and monetary union were to be achieved in parallel. On the one hand, a centralised monetary policy could not be pursued in the presence of sharply divergent national economies. On the other hand, monetary policy constituted one of the available instruments for intervening in the economy.

Single European Act. The Single European Act contained a reference to economic and monetary union.[158] At the monetary level, the EEC Treaty merely adverted to existing cooperation within the framework of the European Monetary System and in developing the ECU.[159] Article 102a(2) of the EEC Treaty did, however, announce a formal amendment of the Treaty "in so far as further development in the field of economic and monetary policy necessitates institutional changes". **11–029**

B. INTRODUCTION OF ECONOMIC AND MONETARY UNION

Delors Committee. The European Council held in Hanover on June 27 and 28, 1988 set up a committee under the chairmanship of the President of the Commission, Jacques Delors, with the task of studying and proposing concrete stages leading towards economic and monetary union.[160] The Delors Committee proposed that economic and monetary union should be attained in three stages.[161] According to the Committee, a single currency was not strictly necessary to monetary union, but commended itself for its economic, psychological and political advantages. A single currency would reinforce the irreversible nature of EMU, facilitate Community monetary policy, avoid transaction costs in exchanging currencies and, provided that stability was ensured, have more weight internationally than the individual currencies of the Member States.[162] **11–030**

First stage. On the basis of the Report of the Delors Committee, the Madrid European Council decided in June 1989 that the first stage of EMU should start **11–031**

---

[158] The title of the new Ch. 1 ("Cooperation in economic and monetary policy") of Title II ("Economic policy") of the EEC Treaty (Art. 102a) included in brackets the words "economic and monetary union". According to the Court of Justice, it appeared therefrom that the Community aimed at integration which would result in economic and monetary union: ECJ, Opinion 1/91 *Draft Agreement between the Community, on the one hand, and the countries of the European Free Trade Association, on the other, relating to the creation of the European Economic Area* [1991] E.C.R. I-6079, para. 17.

[159] The ECU developed into a parallel currency which was used above all on financial markets for the issue of bonds and gradually introduced itself into banking transactions.

[160] (1988) 6 EC Bull. point 3.4.1.

[161] Committee for the Study of Economic and Monetary Union, *Report on Economic and Monetary Union in the European Community* (Luxembourg, Official Publications Office of the European Communities), 1989 [hereinafter "Report of the Delors Committee"]; also published in *Europe*, doc. 1550/1551, April 20, 1989.

[162] Report of the Delors Committee, s.23. See also Gnos, "La transition vers l'Union économique et monétaire" (1992) R.M.C.U.E. 621–626.

on July 1, 1990.[163] The first stage of EMU comprised, on the economic level, achieving the internal market (free movement of persons, goods, services and capital), reinforcing the Community's regional and structural policies[164] and introducing new procedures for supervising national economic policies, incorporating specific rules for coordinating budgetary policy (which were to become binding only in the final stage).[165] On the monetary level, the initial stage required the complete liberalisation of capital transactions.[166] All Member States had to join the European Monetary System,[167] all barriers to the private use of the ECU were to disappear and the Committee of Central-Bank Governors was to obtain additional consultative powers.[168]

11–032 **Second stage.** The EU Treaty made the necessary changes to the EC Treaty to make the second and third stages of EMU possible. Denmark and the United Kingdom obtained exceptional status in the EU Treaty, as a result of which they are free to decide whether or not to accede to the third stage of the EMU (see para. 11–042). Other Member States are in principle required to accede to the third stage of the EMU as soon as they fulfil all the conditions laid down in the Treaties. The second stage began on January 1, 1994 (see *Art. 116(1) EC*). Capital and payments movements were liberalised and the economic policies of the Member States and the Community had to comply with the supervisory procedure and rules laid down in the Treaty, albeit without any binding sanctions.[169] Each Member State prepared the status of its central bank for the third stage (see

---

[163] (1989) 6 EC Bull. point 1.1.11. See the Report of the Delors Committee, s.43.

[164] See, inter alia, the reform of the structural funds effected by Council Regulation (EC) No. 2052/88 of June 24, 1988 on the tasks of the Structural Funds and their effectiveness and on the coordination of their activities between themselves and with the operations of the European Investment Bank and the other existing financial instruments, [1988] O.J. L185/9.

[165] Council Decision 90/141/EEC of March 12, 1990 on the attainment of progressive convergence of economic policies and performance during stage one of economic and monetary union, [1990] O.J. L78/23.

[166] Council Directive 88/361/EEC of June 24, 1988 for the implementation of [the former] Art. 67 of the Treaty, [1988] O.J. L178/5; para. 9–101, *supra*.

[167] However, not all Member States were participating in the exchange rate mechanism. At the start of the EMS, all the then Member States, with the exception of the United Kingdom took part. The Spanish peseta was accepted into the exchange rate system in July 1989, the pound sterling in October 1990 and the Portuguese escudo in April 1999. Following financial turbulence in September 1992, the pound sterling and the Italian lira suspended their participation in the mechanism. The Austrian schilling acceded on January 9, 1995, the Finnish markka on October 14, 1996 and the Greek drachma on March 16, 1998; the Italian lira re-entered the exchange rate mechanism on November 25, 1996. The Swedish krona never joined the mechanism. The Member States which did not participate in the exchange rate mechanism had acceded to the agreements with regard to the EMS.

[168] Council Decision 90/142/EEC of March 12, 1990 amending Decision 64/300/EEC (see the discussion of the Committee of Central-Bank Governors; para. 2–007, *supra*), [1990] O.J. L78/25.

[169] See the Council measures mentioned in paras 11–034—11–035 and 11–038, *infra*.

Art. 116(5) EC). Monetary policy remained for the time being in the hands of the Member States, but the currency composition of the ECU was frozen (see *Art. 118 EC*).[170] The European Monetary Institute (EMI) monitored the operation of the EMS, organised consultations between the central banks and prepared the instruments for the third stage of EMU (see *Art. 117 EC*). As from June 1, 1998, the EMI was replaced by the European Central Bank, which was set up in anticipation of the third stage (see *Art. 123(1) and (2) EC*).[171] The national governments decided at the European Council held in Madrid on December 15 and 16, 1995 that the term "ECU" used in the EC Treaty to refer to the European currency unit was a generic term. They agreed to call the European currency unit the "euro" and to interpret all Treaty provisions mentioning the ECU as referring to the euro.[172]

Third stage. On January 1, 1999 the third stage started as between the eleven Member States which satisfied the conditions for the adoption of a single currency.[173] Before July 1, 1998, the Council had to decide which States fulfilled the conditions for the adoption of a single currency (See Art. 140(1) and (2) TFEU [*ex Art. 121(1) and (2) EC*]). The situation in a given Member State had to be assessed primarily by reference to four convergence criteria, more closely formulated in a Protocol:

11–033

(1) a rate of inflation not exceeding by more than 1.5 percentage points that of the three best performing Member States in terms of price stability;

(2) a deficit which was not excessive within the meaning of Art. 104;

(3) the normal fluctuation margins of the EMS had to have been complied with for at least the preceding two years and

---

[170] See Vissol, "L'écu dans la phase de transition vers UEM" (1994) R.M.C.U.E. 425–436.

[171] See Decision 98/345/EC taken by common accord of the Governments of the Member States adopting the single currency at the level of Heads of State or Government of May 26, 1998 appointing the President, the Vice-President and the other members of the Executive Board of the European Central Bank, [1998] O.J. L154/33.

[172] Conclusions of the Presidency (1995) 12 EU Bull. point I.3. An action was brought against the Commission on the ground that it had used the term "euro" when the Treaty referred to ECUs, but it was declared inadmissible on the ground that it was directed against a proposal for legislation: CFI (order of May 15, 1997), Case T-175/96 *Berthu v Commission* [1997] E.C.R. II-811.

[173] To do this, the Council, meeting in the special composition of the Heads of State or Government, had to decide by a qualified majority by no later than December 31, 1996. In December 1996 the Council found that there was not a majority of Member States which fulfilled the conditions. Under Art. 121(4) of the EC Treaty, the third stage was then to start automatically on January 1, 1999 as between the Member States fulfilling the conditions, regardless as to their number. See Council Decision 96/736/EC of December 13, 1996 in accordance with Art. 109j of the Treaty establishing the European Community, on entry into the third stage of economic and monetary union, [1996] O.J. L335/48.

(4) the average long-term interest rate must not have exceeded by more than 2 percentage points than that of the three best performing Member States in terms of price stability.[174]

On May 3, 1998 the Council held by decision that Austria, Belgium, Germany, Finland, France, Ireland, Italy, Luxembourg, the Netherlands, Spain and Portugal fulfilled the conditions for the adoption of the single currency on January 1, 1999.[175] The United Kingdom and Denmark were not subjected to assessment in view of their having notified the intention not to move to the third stage.[176] Greece and Sweden did not fulfil the conditions. As for Sweden, this was the result of a political decision not to introduce the required changes in its legislation; as in Denmark and the United Kingdom, the political will is lacking to introduce the euro.[177] On December 31, 1998 the Council fixed the conversion rates between the euro and the currencies of the eleven participating Member States in accordance with *ex Art. 123(4) EC*.[178] A similar decision was taken in 2000 with regard to the Greek currency,[179] since by then Greece fulfilled the criteria for adoption of the euro; as from January 1, 2001, Greece has taken part in the third stage of EMU.[180]

Although the participating currencies were replaced by the euro as of January 1, 1999, the use of the euro was confined to transfer payments. From January 1, 2002, euro-denominated banknotes and coins were brought into circulation. National banknotes continued to circulate as legal tender for a short transitional period and

---

[174] First subpara. of Art. 140(1) TFEU and Protocol (No. 13), introduced by the EU Treaty and now annexed to the TEU and TFEU, on the convergence criteria ([2010] O.J. C83/281).

[175] Article 1 of Council Decision 98/317/EC of May 3, 1998 in accordance with Art. 109j [*now Art. 121*](4) of the EC Treaty, [1998] O.J. L139/30, by which the Council, meeting in the composition of the Heads of State or Government, adopted the identically worded recommendation drawn up that weekend and submitted to the European Parliament for its opinion: Council Recommendation 98/316/EC of May 1, 1998 in accordance with Art. 109j [*now Art. 121*](2) of the Treaty, [1998] O.J. L139/21. For a commentary on the May 1998 decisions, see Smits, "Het begin van de muntunie: besluitvorming en regelgeving" (1999) S.E.W. 2–21 and the editorial "The Birth of the Euro" (1998) C.M.L.Rev. 585–594.

[176] See recitals 4 to 7 in the preamble to Decision 98/317/EC, *ibid.*

[177] On September 14, 2003 the Swedish people came out against the introduction of the single currency in a referendum in which 56.1 per cent voted against ((2003) 9 EU Bull. point 1.3.2).

[178] Council Regulation (EC) No. 2866/98 of December 31, 1998 on the conversion rates between the euro and the currencies of the Member States adopting the euro, [1998] O.J. L359/1 (for the ECB's opinion of the same date on the Commission's proposal, see [1998] O.J. C142/1). Under the regulation, conversion rates (to six significant figures) were adopted as one euro expressed in terms of each of the national currencies of the participating countries (1 euro = 13.7603 Austrian schillings; 40.3399 Belgian francs; 5.94573 Finnish markkas; 6.55957 French francs; 1.95583 Deutsche Mark; 0.787564 Irish pounds; 1936.27 Italian lira; 40.3399 Luxembourg francs; 2.20371 Dutch guilders; 200.482 Portuguese escudo, and 166.386 Spanish pesetas).

[179] Council Regulation (EC) No. 1478/2000 of June 19, 2000, [2000] O.J. L167/1 (1 euro = 340.750 Greek drachmas).

[180] The Council decided on June 19, 2000 to abrogate the derogation with regard to Greece with effect from January 1, 2001; see Council Decision 2000/427/EC of June 19, 2000, [2000] O.J. L167/19.

had to be completely replaced by the euro in all participating States by no later than six months afterwards.[181] The 2003 and 2005 Acts of Accession conferred on the 12 Member States which acceded in 2004 and 2007 the status of Member State with a derogation,[182] which means that they have to introduce the euro as soon as they fulfil the conditions (see para. 11–041).[183] Since then, four of these have acceded to the third stage and have replaced their former national currency by the euro: Slovenia (as from January 1, 2007,[184]) Cyprus and Malta (as from January 1, 2008)[185] and Slovakia (as from January 1, 2009).[186] On January 1, 2011 Estonia introduced the euro as 17th Member State.[187] The euro is also the currency of a number of third countries (see para. 11–040, *infra*).

---

[181] In accordance with the scenario approved by the European Council in Madrid on December 15 and 16, 1995 ((1995) EU Bull. 12, points I.3 and I.49). For the transitional provisions on the 2002 cash changeover, see Guideline ECB/2001/1 of the ECB of January 10, 2001, [2001] O.J. L55/80. For the status of the euro, see Koppenol-Laforce, "De euro: enkele (internationaal) privaatrechtelijke aspecten" (November 2000) *Mededelingen van de Nederlandse vereniging voor internationaal recht*, 1–67; Ruiz Ruiz, "L'introduction de l'euro et la continuité des contrats sur les obligations pécuniaires" (2000) R.T.D.E. 705–726; Block, "Les incidences du passage à l'euro en procédure civile" (1999) J.T. 97–105; Usher, "Legal Background of the Euro" (1999) S.E.W. 12–23; Botter, Van Kuijk, Van Olffen and Verdam, "Invoering van de euro in de verschillende lidstaten" (1998) T.V.V.S. 361–367; Malferrari, "Le statut juridique de l'euro dans la perspective du droit allemand, européen et international" (1998) C.D.E. 509–560; Sunt, "Juridische aspecten van de invoering van de euro" (1998–99) R.W. 761–778. See also Denters, "Volkenrechtelijke aspecten van de introductie van de euro" (November 2000) *Mededelingen van de Nederlandse vereniging voor internationaal recht*, 69–114.

[182] Act of Accession 2003, Art. 4; Act of Accession 2005, Art. 5.

[183] For a discussion, see Angeloni, "Monetary integration of the new EU Member states: what sets the pace of Euro adoption" (2007) J.C.M.S. 367–409; Fatur, "What Challenges do the Central European and Mediteranian States Face in Trying to Join the Third Stage of European Monetary Union?" (2005) 28 Fordham I.L.J. 145–192.

[184] See Council Decision 2006/495/EC of July 11, 2006 in accordance with Art. 122(2) of the EC Treaty on the adoption by Slovenia of the single currency on January 1, 2007, [2006] O.J. L195/25. For the conversion rate, see Council Regulation (EC) No. 1086/2006 of July 11, 2006, [2006] O.J. L195/1 (1 euro = 239.640 Slovenian tolars).

[185] See Council Decision 2007/504/EC of July 10, 2007 in accordance with Art. 122(2) of the EC Treaty on the adoption by Malta of the single currency on January 1, 2008, [2007] O.J. L186/32 and Council Decision 2007/503/EC of July 10, 2007 in accordance with Art. 122(2) of the EC Treaty on the adoption by Cyprus of the single currency on January 1, 2008, [2007] O.J. L186/29. For the conversion rates, see Council Regulation (EC) No. 1134/2007 of July 10, 2007, [2007] O.J. L256/1 (1 euro = 0.429300 Maltese liras) and Council Regulation (EC) No. 1135/2007 of July 10, 2007, [2007] O.J. L256/2 (1 euro = 0.585274 Cyprus pounds).

[186] Council Decision 2008/608/EC of July 8, 2008 in accordance with Art. 122(2) of the EC Treaty on the adoption by Slovakia of the single currency on January 1, 2009, [2008] O.J. L195/24. For the conversion rates, see Council Regulation (EC) No. 694/2008 of July 8, 2008, [2008] O.J. L195/3 (1 euro = 30.1260 Slovak korunas).

[187] Council Decision 2010/416/EU of July 13, 2010 in accordance with Art. 140(2) TFEU on the adoption by Estonia of the euro on January 1, 2011, [2010] O.J. L 196/24. For the conversion rate, see Council Regulation (EU) No. 671/2010 of July 13, 2010, [2010] O.J. L196/4 (1 euro = 15.6466 Estonian kroons).

C. Economic Policy

11–034   **Economic guidelines.** Member State's economic policies must contribute to the achievement of the objectives of the Union as defined in Art. 3 TEU (Art. 120 TFEU [*ex Art. 98 EC*]). Article 122 TFEU [*ex Art. 100 EC*] empowers the Council, on a proposal from the Commission and in a spirit of solidarity between Member States, to "decide upon the measures appropriate to the economic situation". Article 122(2) TFEU allows the Council, in accordance with the same procedure, to grant Union financial assistance to a Member State in difficulties or seriously threatened with severe difficulties caused by exceptional occurrences beyond its control—which was the basis for the Union to establish in May 2010 a European financial stabilisation mechanism in response to the international financial crisis and the deterioration of the borrowing conditions of Greece and other Member States.[188] Although the economic policy may thus require direct intervention on the part of the Union, it still consists primarily of measures of the Member States, which are to regard their economic policies as a matter of common concern and to coordinate them within the Council (Art. 121(1) TFEU [*ex Art. 99(1) EC*]).[189] To this end, the Council is to adopt "broad guidelines" in accordance with a procedure whereby the Council, acting on a recommendation from the Commission, submits draft guidelines to the European Council and, subsequently, on the basis of the latter's conclusion, is to adopt a recommendation setting out the broad guidelines. The Council has to inform the European Parliament of its recommendations (Art. 121(2) TFEU).[190]

11–035   **Stability and growth pact.** The Member States' economic policies are to be coordinated by means of multilateral surveillance of economic developments in each of the Member States and in the Union and of their consistency with the broad guidelines. Economic policy coordination also affects the Member States which are not taking part in the third stage of EMU. This is intended to secure sustained convergence of the economic performance of the Member States. For the purpose of multilateral surveillance, Member States are obliged to forward information to the Commission about important measures taken by them in the field of their economic policy and such other information as they deem necessary. Pursuant to a stability and growth pact agreed in 1997 and updated in

---

[188] Councl Regulation (EU) No. 407/2010 of May 11, 2010 establishing a European financial stabilisation mechanism, [2010] O.J. L118/1.

[189] Louis, "The Eurogroup and Economic Policy Co-ordination" (2001–2002) Euredia 19–43.

[190] See, e.g., the broad guidelines for the economic policies of the Member States and the Union adopted by Council recommendations of June 26, 2003 ([2003] O.J. L195/1), July 12, 2005 ([2005] O.J. L205/28), May 14, 2008 ([2008] O.J. L137/13) and July 13, 2010 ([2010] O.J. L191/28). See Buzelay, "De la coordination des politiques économiques nationales au sein de l'Union européenne" (2003) R.M.C.U.E. 235–241.

2005,[191] the Member States have to show each year by means of stability or convergence programmes that their budgetary situation provides an adequate basis for price stability and sustainable growth or that they are taking adjustment measures to that end.[192] The Commission is to report to the Council, which has regularly to assess the situation (Art. 121(3) TFEU [*ex Art. 99(3) EC*]). In 2005, it was agreed that the Commission would issue policy advice to encourage Member States to stick to previously defined medium-term budgetary objectives.[193] The President of the Council and the Commission have to report to the European Parliament on the results of multilateral surveillance (Art. 121(5) TFEU [*ex Art. 99(4) EC*]).

In the event that the economic policies of a Member State are not consistent with the broad guidelines or they risk jeopardising the proper functioning of EMU, the Commission may address a warning to the Member State concerned. The Council, on a recommendation from the Commission, may make the necessary— secret—recommendations to the Member State concerned. The Council may, on a proposal from the Commission, decide to make its recommendation public (Art. 121(4), first subpara.),[194] in which case the President of the Council may be

---

[191] The stability and growth pact, on which the European Council reached agreement in Dublin as long ago as December 1996 (see (1996) 12 EU Bull. point I.3), was elaborated on by Regulation No. 1466/97 on the strengthening of the surveillance of budgetary positions and the surveillance and coordination of economic policies, [1997] O.J. L209/1 (as amended by Council Regulation No. 1055/2005 of June 27, 2005, [2005] O.J. L174/1) and Council Regulation (EC) No. 1467/97 of July 7, 1997 on speeding up and clarifying the implementation of the excessive deficit procedure, [1997] O.J. L209/6 (as modified by Council Regulation No. 1056/2005 of June 27, 2005, [2005] O.J. L174/5) and the Resolution of the Amsterdam European Council of June 17, 1997 on the stability and growth pact, [1997] O.J. C236/1. For an assessment, see Amtenbrink and De Haan, "Reforming the Stability and Growth pact" (2006) E.L.Rev. 402–413; Louis, "The Review of the Stability and Growth Pact" (2006) C.M.L.Rev. 85–106; Heipertz, "The Stability and Growth Pact—theorizing a Case in European Integration" (2005) J.C.M.S. 985–1008; Amtenbrink and De Haan, "Economic Governance in the European Union: Fiscal Policy Discipline Versus Flexibility" (2003) C.M.L.Rev. 1075–1106.

[192] See Council Regulation (EC) No. 1466/97, which requires Member States taking part in EMU to submit a stability programme and the others a convergence programme and to regularly update these programmes. These programmes are examined by the Council, which delivers an opinion (see Art. 5 of the regulation).

[193] See the report of the ECOFIN Council of March 20, 2005 on "Improving the implementation of the Stability and Growth Pact, which was endorsed by the European Council in its conclusions of 22 March 2005 (the so-called "Code of Conduct"). Pursuant to the power to issue recommendations conferred by Art. 211 of the EC Treaty (provision repealed by the Lisbon Treaty), the Commission adopted recommendations with policy advice on the economic and budgetary policy on May 28, 2008 with respect to France (document SEC(2008) 1942/3) and on June 12, 2008 with respect to Romania (document C(2008) 2563).

[194] See Council Recommendation 2010/190/EU to Greece of February 16, 2010 with a view to ending the inconsistency with the broad guidelines of the economic policies in Greece and removing the risk of jeopardising the proper functioning of the economic and monetary union ([2010] O.J. L83/65) and Council Recommendation 2001/191/EC of February 12, 2001 with a view to ending the inconsistency with the broad guidelines of the economic policies in Ireland ([2001] O.J.

invited to appear before the competent committee of the European Parliament (Art. 121(5), second sentence). The Council is to act without taking into account the vote of the Member State concerned (Art. 121(4), second subpara.).

11–036 **Prohibitions.** The Treaties impose specific prohibitions in regard to economic policy. They are contained in Art. 123(1), Art. 124 and Art. 125(1) TFEU [*ex Art. 101(1), Art. 102(1) and Art. 103(1) EC*] (see para. 11–037), which have been in force for the Union and the Member States since the second stage entered into effect, and in Art. 126 TFEU [*ex Art. 104 EC*] (see para. 11–038).

11–037 **No bail out.** Article 123(1) TFEU prohibits monetary financing of Union institutions, bodies, offices or agencies, central governments, regional, local or other public authorities, other bodies governed by public law or public undertakings of the Member States, with the result that neither the European Central Bank (ECB) nor the national central banks may grant them credit or overdraft facilities or purchase their debt instruments directly from them.[195] Article 124 TFEU precludes the same entities from having privileged access to financial institutions, unless this is based on prudential considerations. Article 125(1) TFEU declares that neither the Union nor a particular Member State may be made liable for the commitments of any (other) Member State (the "no bail out" rule).[196]

11–038 **Excessive deficits.** Article 126(1) TFEU provides that the Member States are to avoid excessive government deficits. The Commission is to monitor the development of the budgetary situation and of the stock of government debt in the Member States having regard, inter alia, to the ratio of government deficit and government debt, respectively, to gross domestic product. Those ratios may not exceed reference values specified in a Protocol annexed to the Treaties (Art. 126(2) TFEU): the planned or actual government deficit may not exceed 3 per cent of gross domestic

---

L69/22), each accompanied by a Council Decision of the same date making that recommendation public; see further Council Recommendation of January 21, 2003 with a view to giving early warning to France in order to prevent the occurrence of an excessive deficit ([2003] O.J. L34/18). See also, as regards the stability and growth pact, Art. 6 of Council Regulation (EC) No. 1466/97 of July 7, 1997 (n. 191, *supra*).

[195] This does not prevent central banks from supplying publicly owned credit institutions with liquidity in the same way as private credit institutions (Art. 123(2) TFEU [*ex Art. 101(2) EC*]).

[196] The Council is entitled to lay down definitions for the purpose of the application of these prohibitory provisions. Thus, on December 13, 1993, the Council adopted Regulation (EC) No. 3604/93, pursuant to Art. 104a [*now Art. 102 TFEU*], specifying definitions for the application of the prohibition of privileged access referred to in Art. 104a [*now Art. 102*] of the Treaty, [1993] O.J. L332/4, and Regulation (EC) No. 3603/93, pursuant to Art. 104b(2) [*now Art. 103(2) TFEU*], specifying definitions for the application of the prohibitions referred to in Arts 104 and 104b(1) [*now Arts 101 and 103(1) TFEU*] of the Treaty, [1993] O.J. L332/1, as amended by Council Regulation (EC) No. 475/2000 of February 28, 2000, [2000] O.J. L58/1.

product and government debt may not exceed 60 per cent of gross domestic product.[197]

In the event that a Member State does not satisfy a given criterion or the Commission considers that there is a risk of an excessive deficit, the Commission is to prepare a report, on which the Economic and Financial Committee formulates an opinion. Where appropriate, the Commission is to address an opinion to the Member State concerned and to inform the Council accordingly (Art. 126(3) to (5)). After hearing any observations from the Member State concerned and deciding whether an excessive deficit exists, the Council makes recommendations (which are not made public) to the Member State (Art. 126(6) and (7)). Since the introduction of the euro, excessive deficits have been found for all Member States, except Estonia, Luxembourg and Sweden.[198] Any Member State is at liberty to publish a

---

[197] Protocol (No. 12), introduced by the EU Treaty and now annexed to the TEU and TFEU, on the excessive deficit procedure, [2010] O.J. C83/279. Article 126(2)(a) TFEU allows the reference values to be overshot where the deficit or debt is declining and comes close thereto. In assessing government deficit, the Commission takes account of all relevant factors, including the ratio between the deficit and investment expenditure and the medium-term economic and budgetary situation (Art. 126(3), first subpara., TFEU). For clarifications of the terms employed in Art. 126, see Art. 2 of Council Regulation (EC) No. 1467/97 of July 7, 1997 (n. 191, *supra*).

[198] Excessive deficits were found, inter alia, on November 5, 2002 for Portugal (Decision 2002/923/EC, [2002] O.J. L322/30), on January 21, 2003 for Germany (Decision 2003/89/EC, [2003] O.J. L34/16), on June 3, 2003 for France (Decision 2003/487/EC, [2003] O.J. L165/29), on July 5, 2004 for Greece (Decision 2004/917/EC, [2004] O.J. L389/25), Hungary (Decision 2004/918/EC, [2004] O.J. L389/27), Slovakia (Decision 2005/182/EC, [2005] O.J. L62/16), Poland (Decision 2005/183/EC, [2005] O.J. L62/18), Cyprus (Decision 2005/184/EC, [2005] O.J. L62/19), the Czech Republic (Decision 2005/185/EC, [2005] O.J. L62/20) and Malta (Decision 2005/186/EC, [2005] O.J. L62/21), on July 28, 2005 for Italy (Decision 2005/695/EC, [2005] O.J. L266/57), on September 20, 2005 for Portugal (Decision 2005/730/EC, [2005] O.J. L274/91) on January 24, 2006 for the United Kingdom (Decision 2006/125/EC, [2006] O.J. L51/14) and on July 8, 2008 for Poland (Decision 2007/738, [2008] O.J. L238/5). The Council also sent on the same date to each of those States, pursuant to Art. 104(7) of the EC Treaty, a recommendation on how to remedy the situation (the recommendations may be found on the website of the Commission's DG for Economic and Financial Affairs). On July 11, 2006 the Council abrogated the decision on the existence of an excessive deficit in Cyprus (Decision 2006/627/EC, [2006] O.J. L256/13), on June 5, 2007 in respect of Malta and Greece (Decisions 2007/464/EC and 2007/465/EC, [2007] O.J. L176/19), on October 9, 2007 in respect of the United Kingdom (Decision 2007/738/EC, [2007] O.J. L300/49), on June 3, 2008 in respect of Italy, Portugal, Slovakia and the Czech Republic (Decisions 2008/560, 2008/561, 2008/562, 2008/263, [2008] O.J. L181/39) and on July 8, 2008 in respect of Poland (Decision 2008/622/EC, [2008] O.J. L200/22). Since the outbreak of the financial and economic crisis, excessive deficits have again been found, on July 8, 2008, for the United Kingdom (Decision 2008/713/EC, [2008] O.J. L238/5), on April 27, 2009 for France, Greece, Ireland and Spain (Decisions 2009/414, 2009/415, 2009/416 and 2009/417, [2009] O.J. L135/19), on July 7, 2009 for Latvia, Lithuania, Malta, Poland and Romania, on December 2, 2009 for Austria, Belgium, the Czech Republic, Germany, Italy, the Netherlands, Portugal, Slovakia and Slovenia and on July 13, 2010 for Bulgaria, Cyprus, Denmark and Finland (Decisions 2010/401, 2010/407, 2010/408 and 2010/422/EU, [2010] O.J. L186/30, L189/15, L189/17 and L199/26).

recommendation concerning it.[199] Where it establishes that there has been no effective action in response to its recommendations within the period laid down, the Council may make its recommendations public (Art. 126(8)).[200]

If a Member State persists in failing to put into practice the Council's recommendations, the Council may give it notice to take remedial measures within a specified time-limit (Art. 126(9)).[201] As long as a Member State fails to comply therewith, the Council may decide to apply

> "one or more of the following measures:—to require the Member State concerned to publish additional information, to be specified by the Council, before issuing bonds and securities;—to invite the European Investment Bank to reconsider its lending policy towards the Member State concerned;—to require the Member State concerned to make a non-interest-bearing deposit of an appropriate size with the Union until the excessive deficit has, in the view of the Council, been corrected;—to impose fines of an appropriate size" (Art. 126(11); the President of the Council is to inform the European Parliament of the decisions taken).[202]

---

[199] See, e.g., Council Decision 2010/182/EU of February 16, 2010 giving notice to Greece to take measures for the deficit reduction judged necessary in order to remedy the situation of excessive deficit ([2010] O.J. L3/13) as revised by Council Decision 2010/320/EU of May 10, 2010 addressed to Greece with a view to reinforcing and deepening fiscal surveillance and giving notice to Greece to take measures for the deficit reduction judged necessary in order to remedy the situation of excessive deficit ([2010] O.J. L145/6); Council Decision 2006/344/EC of March 14, 2006 giving notice to Germany to take measures for the deficit reduction judged necessary in order to remedy the situation of excessive deficit ([2006] O.J. L126/20). On November 25, 2003 the Council did not take up the Commission's recommendation to address a recommendation to France and Germany, but evaluated in "conclusions" the measures taken by those Member States. The "conclusions" were however annulled by ECJ, Case C-27/04 *Commission v Council* [2004] E.C.R. I-6649 (see ns 206 and 210 and accompanying text, *infra*).

[200] See, e.g., Council Decision of January 18, 2005 establishing whether effective action has been taken by the Hellenic Republic in response to recommendations of the Council in accordance with Art.104(7) of that Treaty, [2005] O.J. L107/24; Council Decisions of November 28, 2006 and July 10, 2007 establishing that the actions taken by Poland and the Czech Republic respectively are proving to be inadequate ([2006] O.J L 414/81 and [2007] O.J. L260/13 respectively).

[201] See, e.g., Council Decision 2006/344/EC of March 14, 2006 giving notice to Germany to take measures for the deficit reduction judged necessary in order to remedy the situation of excessive deficit, [2006] O.J. L126/20). On November 25, 2003 the Council did not take up the Commission's recommendation to address a recommendation to France and Germany. The Council evaluated in "conclusions" the measures taken by those Member States. The "conclusions" were annulled by ECJ, Case C-27/04 *Commission v Council* [2004] E.C.R. I-6649 (see ns 206 and 210 and accompanying text, *infra*).

[202] Once the deficit has been corrected, the Council is to abrogate its decisions; where public recommendations have been made, a public statement has to be given (Art. 104(12)). By the same token, the Council published the decisions abrogating decisions finding an excessive deficit.

Pursuant to the stability and growth pact, the Council has laid down strict time-limits for this procedure.[203] It has also determined that the sanction which it would apply for an excessive deficit would be to require the offending Member State to make a non-interest-bearing deposit with the Commission. The deposit would be converted into a fine if the excessive deficit was not corrected within two years.[204] Member States not taking part in the third stage of EMU are not subject to any sanctions for excessive general government deficits (see para. 11–041).

The right of the Commission or a Member State to bring an action against a Member State under Arts 258 and 259 TFEU [*ex Arts 226 and 227 EC*] may not be exercised within the framework of paras 1 to 9 of Art. 126 TFEU (Art. 126(10) TFEU). That right may, however, be exercised in order judicially to enforce sanctions imposed under Art. 126(11) TFEU.

The Council takes the decisions referred to in paras 8 to 12 of Art. 126 TFEU on a recommendation from the Commission.[205] This means that the Council may adopt a decision different from that recommended by the Commission but cannot subsequently modify its decision without a fresh recommendation from the Commission.[206] The Council adopts the decisions mentioned in paras 6 to 9 and 11 and 12 of Art. 126 by a special majority, excluding the votes of the representative of the Member State concerned.[207] Further provisions on the implementation of the procedure described in Art. 126 are set out in the Protocol on the excessive deficit procedure, to which reference has already been made (Art. 126(14))[208] and in the stability and growth pact as elaborated by the Council.[209] The Council cannot have recourse to an alternative procedure, for example in order to adopt a measure that would not be the very decision envisaged at a given

---

[203] Council Regulation (EC) No. 1467/97 of July 7, 1997 (n. 191, *supra*), Arts 3 to 8.

[204] *Ibid.*, Arts 11 to 16.

[205] Article 126(6) and (13) TFEU. Already in 2004, the IGC failed to agree on the Convention's proposal to have both the Council decision as to whether an excessive deficit exists and the Council recommendation addressed to the Member State concerned adopted on a "proposal" from the Commission (see the initial version of Art. III-76(6) of the draft EU Constitution).

[206] ECJ, Case C-27/04 *Commission v Council* [2004] E.C.R. I-6649, paras 91–92 (annulment of Council "conclusions" that modified a Council recommendation without a recommendation from the Commission and not in accordance with the voting rules prescribed).

[207] A qualified majority of the other members of the Council is to be defined in accordance with Art. 238(3)(a) TFEU (Art. 226(13), third subpara., TFEU).

[208] See n. 197, *supra*. The Council, acting unanimously on a proposal from the Commission and after consulting the European Parliament and the ECB, may replace the said Protocol (Art. 126(14), second subpara., TFEU). The Council is entitled to lay down detailed rules and definitions for the application of the Protocol (Art. 126(14), third subpara., TFEU), see, e.g., Council Regulation (EC) No. 479/2009 of May 25, 2009 on the application of the Protocol on the excessive deficit procedure annexed to the Treaty establishing the European Community, [2009] O.J. L145/1.

[209] See Council Regulation (EC) No. 1467/97 of July 7, 1997 (n. 191, *supra*), adopted pursuant to Art. 104(14) of the EC Treaty [*now Art. 126(14) TFEU*].

stage or that would be adopted in conditions different from those required by the applicable provisions.[210]

D. MONETARY POLICY

11–039 **Price stability.** Monetary policy in the Member States participating in EMU is fully determined by the European System of Central Banks (Eurosystem or ESCB), a network of central banks, each possessing legal personality: the European Central Bank (ECB), which has legal personality by virtue of Art. 282 TFEU, and the central banks of the Member States, established under national law. The primary objective of the ESCB is to maintain price stability and it is to support the general economic policies in the Union with a view to contributing to the achievement of the objectives of the Union as laid down in Art. 3 TEU, in accordance with the principles prescribed for economic policy (Art. 127(1) TFEU [*ex Art. 105(1) EC*]; see Art. 120 TFEU [*ex Art. 98 EC*]).[211] Both the ECB and the national central banks operate within the ESCB completely independently of the national or Union political authorities.[212]

11–040 **Monetary policy.** The ESCB's four "basic tasks" are:

(1) to define and implement the monetary policy of the Union;

(2) to conduct foreign exchange operations;

(3) to hold and manage the official foreign reserves of the Member States, without prejudice to the governments of the Member States holding and managing working balances in foreign exchange; and

(4) to promote the smooth operation of payment systems (Art. 127(2) and (3) TFEU). The Statute of the ESCB defines the "monetary functions and operations of the ESCB".[213]

---

[210] ECJ, Case C-27/04 *Commission v Council* [2004] E.C.R. I-6649, paras 81–97 (Council "conclusions" annulled in so far as they contained a decision to hold the excessive deficit procedure in abeyance and a decision modifying the recommendation previously adopted by the Council).

[211] See Herdegen, "Price Stability and Budgetary Restraints in the Economic and Monetary Union: The Law as Guardian of Economic Wisdom" (1998) C.M.L.Rev. 9–32.

[212] Article 130 TFEU [*ex Art. 108 EC*] and the Statute of the ECB, see para. 13–097. Each Member State has to ensure that its national legislation is compatible with the Treaty and the Statute of the ESCB (Art. 130 TFEU [*ex Art. 109 EC*]; see the provisions with regard to the term of office of the Governor of a national central bank (ESCB Statute, Art. 14.2) and special functions of national central banks (ESCB Statute, Art. 14.4, and Protocol (No. 17), annexed to the TFEU, on Denmark ([2010] O.J. C83/288), which authorises the National Bank of Denmark to continue to carry out its existing tasks concerning those parts of the Kingdom of Denmark which are not part of the Union).

[213] Protocol (No. 4), introduced by the EU Treaty and now annexed to the TEU and TFEU, on the Statute of the European System of Central Banks and of the European Central Bank ([2010] O.J. C83/230), Arts 17 to 24.

The ECB draws up the necessary guidelines for the conduct of the common monetary policy, with which the national central banks have to comply.[214] In so far as it is necessary for the performance of its tasks, the ECB may adopt regulations and decisions, make recommendations and deliver opinions.[215] In its fields of competence, the ECB must be consulted on any proposed Union or draft national legislation[216] and may itself submit opinions to the appropriate authorities (Art. 127(4) TFEU). It has certain reporting obligations.[217]

The ECB is also responsible for developing an exchange rate system for the euro in relation to non-Union currencies. The Council takes its decisions in this connection, on a recommendation from the ECB or after consulting it (following a recommendation from the Commission), "in an endeavour to reach a consensus consistent with the objective of price stability".[218] Accordingly, the Council adopted rules entitling Monaco, San Marino, the Vatican City and certain overseas territories to use the euro as their currency unit.[219] Some non-Union

---

[214] For the monetary policy instruments and procedures of the Eurosystem, see Guideline ECB/2000/7 of the European Central Bank of August 31, 2000, [2000] O.J. L310/1. For the ECB's role within the ESCB, see Weiss, "Kompetenzverteilung in der Währungspolitik und Außenvertretung des Euro" (2002) EuR. 165–191; Seidel, "Im Kompetenzkonflikt: Europäisches System der Zentralbanken (ESZB) versus EZB" (2000) Eu.Z.W. 552–554.

[215] E.g., with regard to credit institutions, Regulation (EC) No. 1745/2003 of the European Central Bank of September 12, 2003 on the application of minimum reserves, [2003] O.J. L250/1.

[216] The obligation to consult applies to legislation relating to specific functions exercised by the ECB in the EU framework for which, by virtue of the high degree of expertise that it enjoys, the ECB is particularly well placed to play a useful role in the legislative process envisaged: ECJ, Case C-11/00 *Commission v European Central Bank* [2003] E.C.R. I-7147, paras 110–111 (no obligation in the case of legislation on combating fraud). The national authorities' obligation to consult the ECB has been fleshed out, in accordance with Art. 105(4) [*now Art. 127(4) TFEU*], by Council Decision 98/415/EC of June 29, 1998 on the consultation of the European Central Bank by national authorities regarding draft legislative provisions, [1998] O.J. L189/42.

[217] See Art. 284(3) TFEU [*ex Art. 113(3) EC*]; ESCB Statute, Art. 15.

[218] The Council is empowered to conclude agreements on an exchange-rate system for the euro in relation to currencies of third States (Art. 219(1) TFEU [*ex Art. 111(1) EC*]). The Council decides by a unanimous vote on a recommendation from the ECB or the Commission after consulting the ECB and the European Parliament. The Council may, acting by a qualified majority on a recommendation from the ECB or from the Commission, and after consulting the ECB in an endeavour to reach a consensus consistent with the objective of price stability, adopt, adjust or abandon the central rates of the ecu within the exchange-rate system. The European Parliament is only informed after the event (*ibid.*). For policy with regard to the currencies of the Member States not taking part in the third stage of EMU, see para. 11–041, *infra*.

[219] See the monetary agreements concluded by Italy on behalf of the Community with San Marino and the Vatican City, [2001] O.J. C209/1, and C299/1, respectively (the latter was replaced by a new agreement of December 17, 2009) and by France on behalf of the Community with Monaco, [2002] O.J. L142/59. Under Council Decision 1999/95/EC of December 31, 1998, [1999] O.J. L30/29, the euro is the currency unit of Saint-Pierre-et-Miquelon and Mayotte, which at present have the status of French overseas communities (COM) (see para. 25–017, *supra*). When Cyprus joined the Eurozone, the euro also became the official currency in the Sovereign Base Areas of Akrotiri and Dhekelia. See the authorisations given by the Council to Portugal and France to

countries have de facto adopted the euro, without any formal agreement with the Union.[220]

The ESCB is also to be responsible for contributing to the smooth conduct of policies pursued by the competent authorities relating to the prudential supervision of credit institutions and the stability of the financial system (Art. 127(5)). The Council, acting by means of regulations in accordance with a special legislative procedure, may unanimously, and after consulting the European Parliament and the European Central Bank, confer on the ECB specific tasks concerning policies relating to the prudential supervision of credit institutions and other financial institutions (but not insurance undertakings) (Art. 127(6) TFEU).

The ECB has the exclusive right to authorise the issue of banknotes within the Member States participating in the third stage of EMU. The ECB and the national central banks may issue such notes. They are the only banknotes to have the status of legal tender within the participating Member States (Art. 128(1) TFEU [*ex Art. 106(1) EC*]).[221] The ECB and the central banks of the participating Member States put banknotes denominated in euro into circulation as from January 1, 2002.[222] The participating Member States have issued euro and cent coins from that date.[223] Only the Member States are authorised to issue coins. However, the volume of coins issued must be approved by the ECB (Art. 128(2) TFEU). Pursuant to Art. 128(2), the Council has harmonised the denominations and technical specifications of euro coins.[224] Accordingly, all euro coins have one common face and

---

conclude agreements with regard to the Cape Verde escudo and with regard to the CFA and Comorian franc, respectively, securing parity between the euro and those currencies: Decision 98/683/EC of November 23, 1998, [1998] O.J. L320/58 and Decision 98/744/EC of December 21, 1998, [1998] O.J. L358/111.

[220] This is the case with Kosovo and Montenegro, where the euro succeeded the German mark which had previously been the de facto currency in these areas. Andorra also uses the euro; the Commission has been authorised to conclude an agreement with Andorra (see Council Decision 2004/548/EC of May 11, 2004, [2004] O.J. L244/47) and negotiations have been opened (see Council Decision 2004/750/EC of October 21, 2004, [2004] O.J. L332/15); however, no agreement has been concluded so far. For the use of the euro as the domestic means of payment in countries not belonging to the EU, see Stumpf, "The introduction of the euro to States and territories outside the European Union" (2003) E.L.Rev. 283–292, and the Commission's answer of March 18, 2002 to question E-0088/02 (Meijer), [2002] O.J. C309E/9.

[221] See the Decision ECB/2003/4 of the European Central Bank of March 20, 2003 on the denominations, specifications, reproduction, exchange and withdrawal of euro banknotes, [2003] O.J. L78/16 and Decision ECB/2001/15 of the ECB of December 6, 2001 on the issue of euro banknotes, [2001] L337/52.

[222] Article 10 of Council Regulation (EC) No. 974/98 of May 3, 1998 on the introduction of the euro, [1998] O.J. L139/1. Banknotes are denominated in the range 5 euros to 500 euros.

[223] *Ibid.*, Art. 11.

[224] Council Regulation (EC) No. 975/98 of May 3, 1998 on denominations and technical specifications of euro coins intended for circulation, [1998] O.J. L139/6 (the text of which had already been determined, see the Annex to the Council Resolution of January 19, 1998 on denominations and technical specifications of euro coins intended for circulation, [1998] O.J. C35/5).

one face with a national design.[225] Pursuant to the third subpara. of Art. 123(4) EC, the Council was to take the measures necessary for the introduction of the euro.[226] In this way, it adopted the necessary measures to protect the euro against counterfeiting.[227]

E. POSITION OF MEMBER STATES NOT BELONGING TO THE EURO ZONE

Derogations. Member States not fulfilling the requisite conditions for adoption of a single currency fall under a derogating system, conduct their own monetary policies, retain their own currencies and will not take part in the Council's international monetary action. Major rules in force for the third stage of EMU do not apply to them (see the list in Art. 139(2) TFEU). For instance, they cannot have sanctions imposed upon them by the Council on account of excessive budget deficits; they are not subject to decisions of the ECB (and their undertakings are not liable to have fines or periodic penalty payments imposed on them by the ECB), and they are not entitled to vote for members of the Executive Board of the ECB. Accordingly, they are not able to vote in the Council or the ECB when decisions are taken in this connection (see para. 19–004). Nevertheless, they must avoid excessive deficits (Art. 126(1) TFEU) and submit an annual convergence programme to this end.[228] In order to foster convergence of their economies

11–041

---

[225] Photographs of the common face and the national faces together with a description of their designs may be found in the Commission communication: "The visual characteristics of the euro coins", [2001] O.J. C373/1. As from 2007, new common faces were introduced in view of the enlargement of the EU: see Commission communication: "New common sides of euro circulation coins", [2006] O.J. C225/7. See further Commission recommendation of June 3, 2005 on common guidelines for the national sides of euro circulation coins ([2005] O.J. L186/1).

[226] See Servais, Vigneron and Ruggeri, "Le Traité de Nice. Son impact sur l'Union économique et monétaire" (2000) Euredia 477, at 483. In order to make cross-border payments cheaper with the introduction of the euro, the European Parliament and the Council adopted on December 19, 2001, pursuant to Art. 95 EC [*now Art. 114 TFEU*], Regulation (EC) No. 2560/2001 on cross-border payments in euro, [2001] O.J. L344/13. See Allix, "Le règlement sur les paiements transfrontaliers en euros: les bases de l'espace unique de paiement" (2002) R.D.U.E. 485–511.

[227] Since the euro has to enjoy the same protection in the other Member States, the Council has extended those measures to the other Member States on the basis of Art. 308 EC [*now Art. 352 TFEU*], see Council Regulation (EC) No. 1338/2001 and extending Regulation (EC) No. 1339/2001 both of June 28, 2001 ([2001] O.J. L181/6 and L181/11) and the "Pericles" action programme establishing an exchange, assistance and training programme for the protection of the euro against counterfeiting, established by Council Decision 2001/923/EC and extending Decision 2001/924/EC of December 17, 2001 ([2001] O.J. L339/50 and L339/55). For cooperation between the European and national central banks, Europol and Eurojust, see Council Decision 2001/887/JHA of December 6, 2001 on the protection of the euro against counterfeiting, [2001] O.J. L329/1 and the Agreement of December 13, 2001 between the European Police Office (Europol) and the European Central Bank (ECB), [2002] O.J. C23/11; for the Counterfeit Monitoring System (CMS), see Decision 2001/912/EC of the European Central Bank of November 8, 2001, [2001] O.J. L337/49. See also Van den Berghe, "Valsemunterij en de euro" (2002) S.E.W. 3–10.

[228] Para. 11–035, *supra*.

and to obtain support for their monetary policies, these Member States may voluntarily take part in an exchange rate mechanism ("ERM II" or "EMS 2"), linking their currencies with the euro.[229]

At least every two years or at the request of a Member State with a derogation, the Commission and the ECB are to report to the Council, which is to decide which Member States with a derogation have fulfilled the necessary conditions in the meantime (Art. 140(1) TFEU). The Council will sit in its normal composition when taking that decision, but it must first consult the European Parliament and have the matter discussed in the European Council. It is to act on a proposal from the Commission after receiving, within 6 months of that proposal, a recommendation of a qualified majority of those among its members representing Member States whose currency is the euro. Member States with a derogation will take part in the decision, which requires a qualified majority (Art. 140(2) and 238(3)(a) TFEU)).

In the event that the Council abrogates the derogation of a Member State, it is to adopt, by a unanimous vote of the Member States without a derogation and the Member State concerned, the rate at which the euro is to be substituted for its currency, and the necessary accompanying measures (Art. 140(3) TFEU [*ex Art. 123(5) EC*]).

11–042 **United Kingdom and Denmark.** The United Kingdom and Denmark are covered by special protocols.[230] Those Member States enjoy a measure of latitude as to whether or not they take part in the third stage of EMU, even if they do fulfil the requisite conditions.

By giving notice that it did not intend to take part in the third stage[231] Denmark was granted an exemption, resulting in its obtaining the status of a Member State with a derogation in the third stage. Unlike other Member States with a derogation, the exemption may be abrogated only at Denmark's request, in which case

---

[229] See the Resolution of the Amsterdam European Council of June 16, 1997 on the establishment of an exchange rate mechanism in the third stage of economic and monetary union, [1997] O.J. C236/5, as effectuated by the Agreement of September 1, 1998 between the European Central Bank and the national central banks of the Member States outside the euro area laying down the operating procedures for an exchange rate mechanism in stage three of Economic and Monetary Union, [1998] O.J. C345/6 (amended in view of the accession of ten new Member States by an Agreement of April 29, 2004, [2004] O.J. C135/3).

[230] Protocol (No. 15), introduced by the EU Treaty and now annexed to the TEU and TFEU, on certain provisions relating to the United Kingdom of Great Britain and Northern Ireland (n. 152, *supra*); Protocol (No. 16), introduced by the EU Treaty and now annexed to the TEU and TFEU, on certain provisions relating to Denmark ([2010] O.J. C83/287). See Vigneron and Mollica, "La différenciation dans l'union économique et monétaire—Dispositions juridiques et processus décisionnel" (2000) Euredia 197–231.

[231] Section B of the Decision of the Heads of State and Government, meeting within the European Council on December 11 and 12, 1992, concerning certain problems raised by Denmark on the Treaty on European Union, [1992] O.J. C348/2.

the procedure set out in Art. 140 TFEU will be followed.[232] In a referendum held on September 28, 2000, 53.1 per cent of Danes voted against the introduction of the common currency.[233]

The United Kingdom also notified the Council that it did not intend to enter the third stage. That country not only retains its monetary powers, it also does not have to subscribe to the actual objective of monetary union (Art. 119(2) TFEU) or to a number of essential obligations which Member States with a derogation accept completely in the third stage: the United Kingdom will only have to "endeavour" to overcome excessive government deficits,[234] will not have to consult the ECB on draft monetary/economic legislation and would not have to remove political control from the Bank of England (although it has in fact done so).[235] The Protocol also authorises the United Kingdom so long as it does not participate in the third stage to continue not to comply with the prohibition of monetary financing of public authorities laid down in Art. 123 TFEU [*ex Art. 101 EC*].[236] If the United Kingdom gives notice that it wishes to take part in EMU, the Council is to decide on its request in accordance with the procedure laid down in Art. 140(1) and (2) TFEU and adopt the necessary measures pursuant to Art. 140(3) TFEU.[237]

V. SOCIAL POLICY AND EMPLOYMENT

Social policy. The harmonisation of national legislation which the Union has carried out pursuant to specific or general Treaty provisions in order to realise the internal market, has often affected Member States' social policy.[238] The third para. of Art. 151 TFEU [*ex Art. 136 EC*] reflects the Member States' belief that social progress will ensue

11–043

---

[232] See Protocol (No. 16) on certain provisions relating to Denmark (n. 230, *supra*). As a result of Section E of the December 1992 decision, Denmark may "at any time" inform other Member States that it no longer wishes to avail itself of all or part of that decision, upon which Denmark will "apply in full all relevant measures then in force taken within the framework of the European Union".

[233] *Europe*, September 30, 2000, p. 4.

[234] However, the obligations of the stability and growth pact continue to be applicable: see the third and fourth recitals in the preambles to Regulations (EC) Nos 1466/97 and 1467/97 (n. 191, *supra*).

[235] See the list of articles of the Treaty and the Statute of the ESCB in Arts 4 to 7 of Protocol (No. 15) on certain provisions relating to the United Kingdom of Great Britain and Northern Ireland (n. 152, *supra*). For the independence of the Bank of England, see the Bank of England Act 1997.

[236] Article 10 of Protocol (No. 15) on certain provisions relating to the United Kingdom of Great Britain and Northern Ireland (n. 152, *supra*), which refers to the "ways and means" facility with the Bank of England.

[237] Article 9(a) and (c) of Protocol (No. 15) on certain provisions relating to the United Kingdom of Great Britain and Northern Ireland relating to the United Kingdom (n. 152, *supra*). An act of Parliament is required before the United Kingdom government may give such notice; see the European Communities (Amendment) Act 1993 (reproduced in Denza, "La ratification du traité de Maastricht par le Royaume Uni" (1994) R.M.C.U.E. 172, at 180).

[238] See Art. 39(1)(b) TFEU [*ex Art. 33(1)(b) EC*] (agriculture); Arts 46 and 48 TFEU [*ex Arts 40 and 42 EC*] (free movement of workers); Art. 166 TFEU [*ex Art. 150 EC*] (vocational training).

"not only from the functioning of the internal market, which will favour the harmonisation of social systems, but also from the procedures provided for in the Treaties and from the approximation of provisions laid down by law, regulation or administrative action".

Harmonisation measures touching on social rights have been adopted pursuant to Arts 114, 115 and 352 TFEU [*ex Arts 95, 94 and 308 EC*].[239] In addition, the Union has had the possibility from the outset of pursuing its own social policy and this was widened by the addition of a special "social" harmonisation power in Art. 118a EEC, which allowed the Council to set out minimum requirements with a view to improving the working environment and protecting workers' health and safety[240].

The Heads of State or Government of eleven Member States (not including the United Kingdom) concluded on December 9, 1989 the Charter of Fundamental Social Rights of Workers.[241] At the 1990–1991 Intergovernmental Conference, the United Kingdom alone opposed the incorporation into the EC Treaty of broader objectives and instruments for the purpose of giving effect to the Charter. The other Member States agreed on more extensive powers to be exercised using the Community's institutions pursuant to a protocol annexed to the EC Treaty and in accordance with an agreement which they concluded (the "Social Agreement").[242] Depending upon the objective and content of the proposed action and the expected standpoint of the United Kingdom, the Community therefore based its social policy either on the EC Treaty or on the Social Agreement. In the

---

[239] See, for example, the directives on equal treatment of men and women (all listed in ns 290–292 to para. 7–057, *supra*), adopted pursuant to Art. 100 EC [*now Art. 115 TFEU*] (Directive 75/117), Art. 235 EC [*now Art. 352 TFEU*] (Directives 76/207 and 79/7) or both articles (Directives 86/613 and 86/378). For directives adopted on the basis of Art. 100 EC, see also Council Directive 98/59/EC of July 20, 1998 on the approximation of the laws of the Member States relating to collective redundancies, [1998] O.J. L225/16 and those cited in n. 247 to para. 11–044, *infra*.

[240] For the scope of Art.118a and the review in the light of that provision of Council Directive 93/104/EC of November 23, 1993 concerning certain aspects of the organisation of working time, ([1993] O.J. L307/18), see ECJ, Case C-84/94 *United Kingdom v Council* [1996] E.C.R. I-5755, paras 11–45, with a case note by Van Nuffel (1997) Col.J.E.L. 298–309; see also Banks, "L'article 118 A—Element dynamique de la politique communautaire" (1993) C.D.E. 537–554.

[241] (1989) 12 EC Bull. point 1.1.10; the text may be found in Commission of the European Communities, *Social Europe*, 1/90; see also Blanpain and Engels, *European Labour Law* (The Hague, Kluwer Law International, 1998), at 441–448; Hepple, "The Implementation of the Community Charter of Fundamental Social Rights" (1991) M.L.R. 643–654; Watson, "The Community Social Charter" (1991) C.M.L.Rev. 37–68; Bercusson, "The European Community's Charter of Fundamental Social Rights of Workers" (1990) M.L.R. 624–642.

[242] See Protocol (No. 14) on social policy, annexed by the EU Treaty to the EC Treaty, [1992] O.J. C224/126 and the Agreement on social policy concluded between the Member States of the European Community with the exception of the United Kingdom of Great Britain and Northern Ireland, [1992] O.J. C224/127. The Social Agreement was accepted as it stood by the Member States which joined the Community in 1995. For the construction brought about by the Social Protocol and the Social Agreement, see para. 12–013, *infra*.

Treaty of Amsterdam, the United Kingdom agreed to incorporate the broader powers provided for by the Social Agreement in the EC Treaty as the new Arts 136 to 143 EC (and to repeal the Social Agreement and the Social Protocol.[243]) At the same time, the Contracting Parties emphasised the promotion of employment as a prime objective of the Community and added a new title to the EC Treaty for the coordination of national employment policies.[244] Consequently, the current Treaties contain titles on employment (Arts 151 to 159 TFEU), while emphasising a high level of employment, social progress and social protection as objectives of the Union (see Art. 3(3) TEU and Art. 9 TFEU). Various fundamental social rights have now been recognised in the chapter on "solidarity" of the Charter of Fundamental Rights of the European Union.[245]

Minimum harmonisation. As objectives of the social policy of the Union and the Member States, the first para. of Art. 151 TFEU [*ex Art. 136 EC*] refers to the promotion of employment, the steady improvement of living and working conditions, proper social protection, dialogue between management and labour, the development of human resources, lasting high employment and the combating of exclusion.[246] The Union and the Member States are to take account of the diverse forms of national practices, in particular in the field of contractual relations, and

11–044

---

[243] Treaty of Amsterdam, Art. 2(58).

[244] For a general discussion of Union social policy, see Bercusson, *European labour law* (Cambridge, Cambridge University Press, 2009), 752 pp.; Watson, *EU social and employment law: policy and practice in an enlarged Europe* (Oxford, Oxford University Press, 2009), 538 pp.; Barnard, *EC Employment* Law (Oxford, Oxford University Press, 2006), 936 pp.; de Búrca (ed.), *EU law and the welfare state: in search of solidarity (Collected courses of the Academy of European law)* (Oxford, Oxford University Press, 2005), 250 pp.; Lenaerts and Foubert, "De plaats van de sociale politiek in het Europees Gemeenschapsrecht", in *Liber Amicorum Prof. Dr. Roger Blanpain* (Bruges, Die Keure, 1998), 15–36.

[245] See workers' right to information and consultation within the undertaking (Art. 27), the right of collective bargaining and action (Art. 28), the right of access to placement services (Art. 29), the right to protection in the event of unjustified dismissal (Art. 30), the right to fair and just working conditions, including the right to paid leave (Art. 31), the prohibition of child labour and protection of young people at work (Art. 32), the right to family and professional life, including the right to be paid maternity leave and to parental leave (Art. 33), and entitlement to social security and social assistance (Art. 34). See Lenaerts, "La solidarité ou le chapitre IV de la Charte des droits fondamentaux de l'Union européenne" (2010) R.T.D.H. 217–236; Ashiagbor, "Economic and Social Rights in the European Charter of Fundamental Rights" (2004) E.H.R.L.R. 62–72; McGlynn, "Families and the European Union Charter of Fundamental Rights: progressive change or entrenching the status quo?" (2001) E.L.Rev. 582–598; De Schutter, "La contribution de la Charte des droits fondamentaux de l'Union européenne à la garantie des droits sociaux dans l'ordre juridique communautaire" (2000) R.U.D.H. 33–47.

[246] Article 151, first para., TFEU. The former Art. 117 EC referred only to improving the standard of living and working conditions, although a high level of employment and social protection was already mentioned in the former Art. 2 of the EC Treaty. For a practical expression of these objectives, see the European Social Agenda approved by the European Council of December 7–9, 2000 in Nice, [2001] O.J. C157/4.

the need to maintain the competitiveness of the Union economy (Art. 151, second para., TFEU).

In order to support and complement Member States' activities, the European Parliament and the Council are to adopt directives embodying minimum requirements relating to:

(a) improvement of the working environment (with a view to protecting workers' health and safety);

(b) working conditions;

(c) social security and social protection of workers;

(d) protection of workers where their employment contract is terminated;

(e) the information and consultation of workers;

(f) representation and collective defence of the interests of workers and employers;

(g) conditions of employment for third-country nationals legally residing in Union territory;

(h) the integration of persons excluded from the labour market; and

(i) equality between men and women with regard to labour market opportunities and treatment at work (Art. 153(1) and (2), first subpara., indent (b) TFEU [see *ex Art. 137 EC*]).

Such directives are to avoid holding back the creation and development of small and medium-sized undertakings (Art. 153(2)(b)). In this way, directives have been adopted requiring Union-scale undertakings and groups of undertakings to introduce a European Works Council or an information and consultation procedure and establishing a general framework for informing and consulting employees.[247] The

---

[247] Council Directive 94/45/EC of September 22, 1994 on the establishment of a European Works Council or a procedure in Community-scale undertakings and Community-scale groups of undertakings for the purposes of informing and consulting employees, [1994] O.J. L254/64 (which will be replaced in 2011 by Directive 2009/38/EC of the European Parliament and of the Council of May 6, 2009, [2009] O.J. L122/28); Directive 2002/14/EC of the European Parliament and of the Council of March 11, 2002 establishing a general framework for informing and consulting employees in the European Community, [2002] O.J. L80/219. See Blanpain, *European works councils the European directive 2009/38/EC of 6 May 2009" (special issue of the Bulletin of comparative labour relations)* (Deventer, Kluwer, 2009), 286 pp.; Rojot, Le Flanchec and Voynnet-Fourboul, "European Collective Bargaining, New Prospects or Much Ado about Little?" (2001) Int'l J. Comp.Lab.L. Ind. Rel. 345–370; Pélissier, "Le droit à l'information et à la consultation des travailleurs" (1997) R.M.C.U.E. 203–212. These directives were adopted pursuant to Art. 2(2) of the Social Agreement, which was the basis of Art. 137 EC [now Art. 153 TFEU]. This was also the case with Council Directive 97/80/EC of December 15, 1997 on the burden of proof in cases of discrimination based on sex, [1998] O.J. L14/6; Council Directive 96/34/EC of June 3, 1996 on the framework agreement on

European Parliament and the Council may also adopt measures designed to encourage cooperation between Member States in these areas and also with a view to combating social exclusion and modernising systems of social protection, without proceeding to any harmonisation of national laws or regulations (Art. 153(2), first subpara., indent (a)).[248]

Such directives and other measures are not to affect the right of Member States to define the fundamental principles of their social security systems and must not significantly affect the financial equilibrium of those systems.[249] In addition, those measures do not prevent any Member State from maintaining or introducing more stringent protective measures (Art. 153(4)). In principle, the European Parliament and the Council adopt the directives and other measures in question under the ordinary legislative procedure; in cases (c), (d), (f) and (g) the Council has to act unanimously after consulting the European Parliament. However, the Treaties provide that the Council, acting unanimously on a proposal from the Commission, after consulting the European Parliament, may decide to render the ordinary legislative procedure applicable to cases (d), (f) and (g) (Art. 153(2), second subpara.). In some cases, Art. 153 is inapplicable, namely in the case of pay, the right of association, the right to strike and the right to impose lock-outs (Art. 153(5)). However, the fact that the Union does not have competence to regulate these areas does not mean that they fall outside the scope of the provisions on the four freedoms. Hence, collective action which hinders the exercise of one of those freedoms will only be in accordance with Union law if it can be objectively justified.[250] Furthermore, the

---

parental leave concluded by UNICE, CEEP and the ETUC, [1996] O.J. L145/4; Council Directive 97/81/EC of December 15, 1997 concerning the Framework Agreement on part-time work concluded by UNICE, CEEP and the ETUC, [1998] O.J. L14/9. These directives have been extended to cover the United Kingdom pursuant to Art. 100 EC [*now Art. 115 TFEU*] by Council Directive 97/74/EC of December 15, 1997, [1998] O.J. L10/22 (for Directive 94/45/EC); Council Directive 97/75/EC of December 15, 1997, [1998] O.J. L10/24 (for Directive 96/34/EC); Council Directive 98/23/EC of April 7, 1998, [1998] O.J. L131/10 (for Directive 97/81/EC) and Council Directive 98/52/EC of July 13, 1998, [1998] O.J. L205/66 (for Directive 97/80/EC). For a more recent measure, see Directive 2008/104/EC of the European Parliament and of the Council of November 19, 2008 on temporary agency work, [2008] O.J. L327/9.

[248] See the Community action programme to encourage cooperation between Member States to combat social exclusion, adopted by Decision No. 50/2002/EC of the European Parliament and of the Council of December 7, 2001, [2002] O.J. L10/1, and Schoukens, "How the European Union Keeps the Social Welfare Debate on Track: A Lawyer's View of the EU Instruments Aimed at Combating Social Exclusion" (2002) E.J.Soc.Sec. 117–150.

[249] Article 153(4) TFEU. However, that does not preclude the Union from laying down legislation concerning social protection on the basis of other Treaty provisions that does not significantly affect Member States' social security schemes. See ECJ (judgment of January 14, 2010), C-343/08 *Commission v Czech Republic*, not yet reported, paras 65–68.

[250] ECJ, Case C-438/05 *International Transport Workers' Federation and Finnish Seamen's Union* [2007] E.C.R. I-10779, paras 39–41; ECJ, Case C-341/05 *Laval un Partneri* [2007] E.C.R. I-11767, paras 86–88.

Court has held that, in establishing the constituent parts of pay and the level of those constituent parts, the competent national bodies must ensure that the principle of non-discrimination is guaranteed.[251]

The Treaties encourage management and labour themselves to conclude agreements at Union level and they may be charged with the implementation of directives adopted by the Council (see paras 16–043—16–044). The Commission is charged to promote dialogue between management and labour at European level (Art. 154(1) TFEU [ex Art. 138(1) EC]) and to encourage cooperation between the Member States by making studies, delivering opinions and arranging consultations on a variety of subjects (Art. 156 TFEU (Art. 140 EC]).[252]

The task of the European Social Fund is to render the employment of workers easier, to increase their geographical and occupational mobility and to facilitate their adaptation to industrial changes and changes in production systems, in particular through vocational training and retraining (Art. 162 TFEU [ex Art. 146 EC]; see also Art. 166 TFEU [ex Art. 150 EC] as regards vocational training).[253] The European Parliament and the Council adopt implementing decisions relating to the Fund (Art. 164 TFEU [ex Art. 148 EC]); it is administered by the Commission, assisted by a committee composed of representatives of governments, trade unions and employers' associations (Art. 163 TFEU [ex Art. 147 EC]).[254] The European Parliament and the Council established the European Globalisation Adjustment Fund to provide support and show solidarity to workers made redundant as a result of major structural changes in world trade patterns due to globalisation.[255]

11–045 **Equal treatment.** Article 157 TFEU [ex Art. 141 EC] puts Member States under a duty to ensure the application of the principle that men and women should receive equal pay for equal work or work of equal value.[256] That principle has

---

[251] ECJ, Case C-268/06 Impact [2008] E.C.R. I-2483, paras 126–130.

[252] The Council set up, pursuant to Art. 235 EC [now Art. 352 TFEU], a European Foundation for the Improvement of Living and Working Conditions (Council Regulation (EC) No. 1365/75 of May 26, 1975, [1975] O.J. L139/1) and a European Agency for Safety and Health at Work (Council Regulation (EC) No. 2062/94 of July 18, 1994, [1994] O.J. L216/1), which principally carry out studies and exchange information between Member States.

[253] Council Decision 83/516/EEC of October 17, 1983 on the tasks of the European Social Fund, [1983] O.J. L289/38.

[254] See Regulation (EC) No. 1081/2006 of the European Parliament and of the Council of July 5, 2006 on the European Social Fund [2006], O.J. L210/12.

[255] Regulation (EC) No. 1927/2006 of the European Parliament and of the Council of December 20, 2006, [2006] O.J. L48/82.

[256] For an assesment of the Union's policy, see Prechal, "Equality of Treatment, Non-Discrimination and Social Policy: Achievements in Three Themes" (2004) 41 C.M.L.Rev. 533–551.

direct effect.[257] Through the many questions which national courts have referred for preliminary rulings, the Court of Justice has given a broad interpretation to the term "pay" and has clarified several instances of direct and indirect discrimination.[258] The Union also pursues a general policy on equal opportunities for men and women (see para. 7–057).

Employment. In order to achieve the objective of a high level of employment, the Member States and the Union are to work towards a coordinated strategy for employment and particularly for promoting a skilled and adaptable workforce and labour markets responsive to economic change (Art. 145 TFEU [*ex Art. 125 EC*]).[259] The Member States are to regard promoting employment as a matter of common concern "having regard to national practices related to the responsibilities of management and labour". Their employment policies are to be consistent with the broad guidelines of their economic policies (see para. 11–034) and they are to coordinate their action in this respect within the Council (Art. 146(1) and (2) TFEU [*ex Art. 126(1) and (2) EC*]). To this end, the Council is to draw up separate "guidelines" each year as the culmination of a procedure in which the Council and the Commission submit a joint annual report to the European Council on the employment situation, on the basis of which the latter is to adopt conclusions. The conclusions are to be used in turn as the basis for the guidelines, which are to be adopted by the Council by a qualified majority on a proposal from the Commission and after consulting the European Parliament and the advisory Employment Committee (Art. 148(1) and (2) TFEU [*ex Art. 128(1) and (2) EC*]).[260]

11–046

---

[257] ECJ, Case 43/75 *Defrenne* [1976] E.C.R. 445, paras 24 and 40. See the discussion of the principle of equal treatment in paras 7–057 and 7–063, *supra*. In the light of the recognition of the principle of non-discrimination as a fundamental right, the original economic aim pursued by that provision of the Treaty, namely the elimination of distortions of competition between undertakings established in different Member States, is secondary to the social aim pursued by it; see ECJ, Case C-50/96 *Schröder* [2000] E.C.R. I-743, paras 53–57, and ECJ, Joined Cases C-270/97 and C-271/97 *Sievers and Schrage* [2000] E.C.R. I-929, paras 53–57.

[258] Para. 7–063, *supra*. For the temporal effect of Art. 141 EC [*now Art. 157 TFEU*] following the judgments in *Defrenne* and *Barber*, see para. 22–113, *infra*.

[259] See Raveaud, "The European employment strategy: towards more and better jobs?" (2007) 45 J.C.M.S. 411–434; Euzéby, "La Communauté européenne face au défi de l'emploi" (2001) R.M.C.U.E. 185–192; Szyszczak, "The New Paradigm for Social Policy: A Virtuous Circle?" (2001) C.M.L.Rev. 1125–1170; Kenner, "Employment and Macroeconomics in the EC Treaty: A Legal and Political Symbiosis?" (2000) M.J.E.C.L. 375–397; Martin, "Le traité d'Amsterdam inaugure-t-il une politique communautaire de l'emploi?" (2000) R.T.D.E. 47–65; Martinelli, "La stratégie européenne en faveur de l'emploi" (1998) 1 R.M.U.E. 55–75.

[260] See the guidelines for Member States' employment policies for the year 2000 (Council Decision of March 13, 2000, [2000] O.J. L72/15), for 2001 (Council Decision of January 19, 2001, [2001] O.J. L22/18), for 2002 (Council Decision of February 18, 2002, [2002] O.J. L60/60), for 2003 (Council Decision of July 22, 2003, [2003] O.J. L197/13), for 2004 (Council Decision of October 4, 2004, [2004] O.J. L326/45), for 2005 (Council Decision 2005/600/EC, [2005] O.J. L205/21), for 2006 (Council Decision 2006/544/EC, [2006] O.J. L215/26), for 2007 (Council Decision 2007/491/EC, [2007] O.J. L183/25), and for 2008 (Council Decision 2008/618/EC, [2008] O.J. L198/47).

Article 148(2) provides that these social guidelines have to be consistent with the broad economic-policy guidelines adopted pursuant to Art. 121(2) TFEU, which, however, provides for less of a say on the part of the other institutions.[261] On the basis of annual reports furnished by the Member States, the Council is to carry out an examination of the implementation of national employment policies in the light of the employment guidelines. This so-called "open method of coordination" results in exposing national policies to peer review with the aim of learning from examples of "best practices".[262] If the Council considers it appropriate, it may, by a qualified majority, make recommendations to the Member States on the basis of a recommendation of the Commission (Art. 148(4)).[263]

Union employment policy sets out primarily to complement national policies and encourage cooperation. Accordingly, Art. 147(1) TFEU [ex Art. 127(1) EC] provides that the competences of the Member States are to be respected.[264] Article 149 TFEU [ex Art. 129 EC] empowers the European Parliament and the Council, acting under the ordinary legislative procedure, to adopt "incentive measures" designed to encourage cooperation between Member States and to support their action in the field of employment, but makes no provision for harmonisation of national administrative and statutory provisions.[265] In addition, the Union has to take the objective of a high level of employment into consideration in the formulation and implementation of other Union policies and activities (Art. 147(2) TFEU [ex Art. 127(2) EC]).

---

[261] Thus, under Art. 121 TFEU (ex Art. 99 EC] the European Council adopts conclusions, not on the basis of a joint report of the Council and the Commission, but in the light of a report drawn up by the Council acting on a recommendation from the Commission; moreover, other institutions are not consulted—the European Parliament is only informed after the event: para. 11–034, supra).

[262] See Senden and Tahtah, "Reguleringsintensiteit en regelgevingsinstrumentarium in het Europees Gemeenschapsrecht. Over de relatie tussen wetgeving, soft law en de open methode van coördinatie" (2008) S.E.W. 43–57; Lodge, "Comparing non-hierarchical governance in action: the open method of co-ordination in pensions and information society" (2007) J.C.M.S. 343–365; Ashiagbor, "Soft Harmonisation: The 'Open Method of Coordination' in the European Employment Strategy" (2004) E.Pub.L. 305–332.

[263] See the Council Recommendations on the implementation of Member States' employment policies of February 14, 2000 ([2000] O.J. L52/32), January 19, 2001, ([2001] O.J. L22/27), February 18, 2002 ([2002] O.J. L60/70), July 22, 2003 ([2003] O.J. L197/22) and July 12, 2005 ([2005] O.J. L205/21). See also the Council Recommendation of May 14, 2008 on the 2008 update of the broad guidelines for the economic policies of the Member States and the Community and on the implementation of Member States' employment policies, [2008] O.J. L139/57.

[264] This does not preclude Union competence under other Treaty provisions; see, for e.g., before the introduction of Title VIII of the EC Treaty, the decision taken by the Council pursuant to Art. 308 EC [now Art. 352 TFEU] on February 23, 1998 on Community activities concerning analysis, research and cooperation in the field of employment, [1998] O.J. L63/26 (which further refers in its preamble to the new title on employment to be incorporated by the Amsterdam Treaty).

[265] See, e.g., Decision No. 1672/2006/EC of the European Parliament and of the Council of October 24, 2006 establishing a Community Programme for Employment and Social Solidarity—Progress, [2006] O.J. L315/1.

VI. EDUCATION, VOCATIONAL TRAINING, YOUTH AND SPORT

Union competence. The Union is empowered to adopt measures to supplement   **11–047**
Member States' policy in the field of education and vocational training.[266] Articles
149 and 150 EC *[now replaced by Arts 165 and 166 TFEU]* were introduced by the
EU Treaty to replace Art. 128 EEC, which provided only for "a common vocational
training policy".[267] The Court of Justice paved the way for an actual educational
policy for the Community, first by construing the expression "vocational training" in
Art. 128 EEC as covering most educational curricula[268] and secondly by regarding
also Community action programmes requiring cooperation between the Member
States as "an application of a common policy".[269] The addition of Art. 149 EC made
recourse to the provisions on vocational training unnecessary for educational questions which, according to the case law of the Court of Justice, could be regarded as
"vocational training". Since the entry into force of the Lisbon Treaty, the Union's
competence in the fields of education, vocational training, youth and—now also—
sport is limited to carrying out actions to "support, coordinate or supplement"
Member States' action (see para 7–025).

Education. As far as education is concerned, Art. 165(1) TFEU refers to the   **11–048**
Union contributing to the development of quality education by encouraging cooperation between Member States and supporting and supplementing their action.
The preamble to the TFEU also lists access to education and its continuous updat-
ing as means of promoting the highest possible level of knowledge of the peoples
of the Union. The list of Union tasks set out in Art. 165(2) TFEU mentions primarily language teaching and trans-frontier aspects of education and work with
young people. The various action programmes set up with the aim of encouraging the mobility of students and teachers, in particular the Erasmus programme

---

[266] For a survey of this power, see Moutsios, "The European Union and its Education Policy", in Kotthoff
and Moutsios (eds), *Education Policies in Europe: Economy, Citizenship, Diversity* (Münster,
Waxmann Verlag, 2007), 15–26; Bache, "The europeanization of higher education: markets, politics
or learning?" (2006) 44 J.C.M.S. 231–248; Kilian, "Die Europäisierung des Hochschulraumes"
(2006) 5 J.Z. 209–243; Frazier, "L'éducation et l'Union européenne" (1997) R.M.C.U.E. 476–491;
Lenaerts, "Education in European Community Law after 'Maastricht' " (1994) C.M.L.Rev. 7–41;. For
international powers (Arts 165 and 166(1) and (3) TFEU), see para. 25–057, *infra*.

[267] Admittedly, the Council adopted positions in the form of "resolutions" or "conclusions" of the
"Council and the Ministers of Education, meeting within the Council". For the previous powers of the
Union in the sphere of education, see De Witte (ed.), *European Community Law of Education* (Baden-
Baden, Nomos, 1989), 159 pp.; De Witte, "The Scope of Community Powers in Education and Culture
in the Light of Subsequent Practice", in Bieber and Ress (eds), *Die Dynamik des Europäischen
Gemeinschaftsrechts/ The Dynamics of EC-Law* (Baden-Baden, Nomos, 1987), at 261–281.

[268] ECJ, Case 293/83 *Gravier* [1985] E.C.R. 593, paras 19–31 (para. 7–055, *supra*); ECJ, Case 24/86
Blaizot [1988] E.C.R. 379, paras 15–21; ECJ, Case 263/86 *Humbel* [1988] E.C.R. 5365, paras 8–20.

[269] ECJ, Case 242/87 *Commission v Council* [1989] E.C.R. 1425. See also the interpretation of the
principle of non-discrimination contained in Art. 7 EEC in conjunction with Art. 128 EEC: ECJ,
Case 295/90 *European Parliament v Council* [1992] E.C.R. I-4193, paras 15–20.

for higher education,[270] are very significant in this regard. Together with the Comenius programme (school education), the Grundtvig programme (adult education) and the Leonardo da Vinci programme (vocational training), the Erasmus programme became part of the "Lifelong Learning" programme as from 2007.[271]

In this connection, the Treaties make it clear what boundaries have to be drawn for Union action. First, the Union has to respect the Member States' responsibility for the content of teaching and the organisation of educational systems and their cultural and linguistic diversity (Art. 165(1); see also para. 5–242). This does not do away with the Member States' obligation to comply with Union law, in particular the Treaty provisions on free movement and the principle of non-discrimination on grounds of nationality.[272] Secondly, the Union's action is to consist of (a) "incentive measures" which the European Parliament and the Council adopt by means of the ordinary legislative procedure, "excluding any harmonisation of the laws and regulations of the Member States",[273] and (b) "recommendations" adopted by the Council by a qualified majority vote on a proposal from the Commission (Art. 165(4)).[274] It is noteworthy that all of the Member States are now coordinating their

---

[270] See Council Decision 87/327/EEC of June 15, 1987 adopting the European Community Action Scheme for the Mobility of University Students (Erasmus), [1987] O.J. L166/20 adopted on the basis of Arts 128 and 235 EEC and replaced by Decision 89/663/EEC of December 14, 1989, based on Art. 128 EEC, [1989] O.J. L395/23; see the discussion of its legal basis. It was continued by the "Socrates" programme, adopted by the European Parliament and the Council on the basis of Arts 149 and 150 EC [*now Arts 165 and 166 TFEU*]: Decision 819/95/EC of March 14, 1995, [1995] O.J. L87/10 (see the joint statement by the European Parliament, the Council and the Commission, [1995] O.J. L132/18) and extended until 2006 by Decision 253/2000/EC of the European Parliament and of the Council of January 24, 2000, [2000] O.J. L28/1. See also the "Erasmus Mundus" programme for the enhancement of quality in higher education and the promotion of intercultural understanding through cooperation with third countries, established for 2004–2008 by Decision No. 2317/2003/EC of the European Parliament and of the Council of December 5, 2003, [2003] O.J. L345/1, and for 2009–2013 by Decision No. 1298/2008/EC of the European Parliament and of the Council of December 16, 2008, [2008] O.J. L340/83.

[271] Decision No. 1720/2006/EC of the European Parliament and of the Council of November 15, 2006 establishing an action programme in the field of lifelong learning, [2006] O.J. L327/45.

[272] See ECJ (judgment of April 13, 2010), Case C-73/08 *Bressol and Others*, not yet reported, para. 28.

[273] See Decision No. 1031/2000/EC of the European Parliament and of the Council of April 13, 2000 establishing the "Youth" Community action programme, [2000] O.J. L117/1, amended by Decision No. 786/2004/EC of the European Parliament and of the Council of April 21, 2004, [2004] O.J. L138/7. See also Decision No. 1719/2006/EC of the European Parliament and of the Council of November 15, 2006 establishing the Youth in Action programme for the period 2007 to 2013, [2006] O.J. L327/30. For the exclusion of harmonisation, see Hablitzel, "Harmonisierungsverbot und Subsidiaritätsprinzip im Europäischen Bildungsrecht" (2002) D.ö.V. 407–414.

[274] E.g. the Recommendation of the European Parliament and of the Council of July 10, 2001 on mobility within the Community for students, persons undergoing training, volunteers, teachers and trainers, [2001] O.J. L215/30. See also Pertek and Sleiman, "Les étudiants et la Communauté: l'esquisse d'un statut de l'étudiant en mobilité" (1998) R.M.C.U.E. 306–321. See also the Commission Recommendation of March 11, 2002 on a common European format for curricula vitae (CVs), [2002] O.J. L79/66, based on Arts 149, 150 and 211 EC.

higher-education policy pursuant to the Sorbonne and Bologna declarations of intent and hence have agreed on a de facto harmonisation of their education systems outside the framework of the European Union.[275] In the creation of the "European Higher Education Area" with three cycles (Bachelor, Master, PhD), the Bologna process builds on experience gained within the framework of the Erasmus programme with respect to the European Credit Transfer and Accumulation System (ECTS). Through its participation in the Bologna process, the Commission ensures coordination with the Union's education policy, in particular with respect to the recognition of qualifications for education and training.[276] In addition, the Union has long been tackling aspects of education in the context of its policy on equal educational opportunities for migrant workers' children (Art. 46 TFEU [*ex Art. 40 EC*])[277] and mutual recognition of diplomas (Art. 53 TFEU [*ex Art. 47 EC*]).[278]

Sport. The Treaty of Lisbon extended the Union's competence under the Title "education, vocational training and youth" to cover sport.[279] Union action in this field is to aim at developing the European dimension in sport, by promoting fairness and openness in sporting competitions and cooperation between bodies responsible for sports, and by protecting the physical and moral integrity of sportsmen and sportswomen, especially the youngest sportsmen and sportswomen (Art. 165(2) last indent TFEU). In order to achieve those objectives, the Union has at its disposal the same instruments as it has for its education policy (Arts 165(3) and (4)).[280] While contributing to the promotion of European sporting issues, the

11–049

---

[275] See the references to the Bologna process on the website of the European Commission's Directorate-General for Education and Culture. For a detailed discussion, see Terry, "The Bologna process and its impact in Europe: it's so much more than degree changes" (2008) 41 *Vanderbilt Journal of Transnational Law* 107–227. See also Garben, "The Bologna Process from a European Law Perspective" (2010) E.L.J. 186–210; Pertek, "L'action communautaire en matière d'éducation et le processus de Bologne" (2004) J.T.D.E. 65–70; Verbruggen, "De Bolognaverklaring kritisch getoest aan het Europees onderwijsbeleid" (2003) S.E.W. 199–212.

[276] Recommendation of the European Parliament and of the Council of April 23, 2008 on the establishment of the European Qualifications Framework for lifelong learning, [2008] O.J. C111/1.

[277] See Art. 12 of Regulation (EEC) No. 1612/68 of the Council of October 15, 1968 on freedom of movement for workers within the Community, [1968] O.J. English Spec. Ed. (II) 475. As long ago as 1974 the Court of Justice held that, although the determination of the conditions for admission to education is a matter of national law, Union law requires that they must be applied without discrimination between national workers' children and those of migrant workers: ECJ, Case 9/74 *Casagrande* [1974] E.C.R. 773, para. 14. See also the case law according to which a grant awarded for maintenance and training with a view to the pursuit of university studies leading to a professional qualification constitutes a "social advantage" within the meaning of Art.7(2) of Regulation No. 1612/68: ECJ, Case 39/86 *Lair* [1988] E.C.R. 3161, para. 28. As regards the principle of non-discrimination on grounds of nationality as applied to such grants, see para. 7–055, *supra*.

[278] Paras 9–079—9–081, *supra*.

[279] Rangeon, "Le Traité de Lisbonne: acte de naissance d'une politique européenne du sport?" (2010) R.M.C.U.E. 302–309.

[280] See the Commision's White Paper on sport of July 11, 2007, COM(2007)391 final.

Union is to take account of "the specific nature of sport, its structures based on voluntary activity and its social and educational function" (Art. 165(1) TFEU). This does not mean that the sports sector is to be protected from the application of the Treaty rules on free movement and competition.[281]

11–050 **Vocational training.** As far as vocational training is concerned, the Union pursues a policy of its own, although it is designed to support and supplement the action of the Member States, which remain responsible for the content and organisation of such training (Art. 166(1) TFEU). The European Parliament and the Council adopt measures, "excluding any harmonisation of the laws and regulations of the Member States", by the ordinary legislative procedure (Art. 166(4)).[282] As long ago as 1975, the Council set up under Art. 308 EC [*now Art. 352 TFEU*] a European Centre for the Development of Vocational Training (Cedefop) to promote and coordinate vocational training in the Member States.[283]

VII. CULTURE

11–051 **Incentive measures.** The Union's powers in the cultural field (introduced by the EU Treaty), in common with those in the sphere of education, are conceived as supplementary (see also Art. 6 TFEU), that is, as contributing to the flowering of the

---

[281] For the application of the Treaty provisions on the free movement of persons and competition, see paras 9–061 and 9–065 and para. 11–013, *supra*. In assessing the proportionality of arrangements concerning sports, the "specific characteristics" of sports and the "social and educational function" mentioned in Art. 165(1) TFEU need to be taken into account: ECJ (judgment of March 16, 2010), Case C-325/08 *Olympique Lyonnais*, not yet reported, paras 40–45. See also Vermeersch, *Europese spelregels voor sport: overzicht van het Europees sportbeleid in wording en de toepassing van het Europees recht op sport* (Antwerpen, Maklu, 2009), 542 pp.; Bogusz, Cygan, and Szyszczak (eds), *The regulation of sport in the European Union* (Cheltenham, Elgar, 2007), 234 pp.; Weatherill (ed.), *European Sports Law: Collected Papers* (Leyden, T.M.C. Asser Press, 2007), 396 pp.; Barani, "The role of the European Court of Justice as a political actor in the integration process: the case of sport regulation after the Bosman ruling" (2005) J.C.E.R. 42–58; Dubey and Dupont, "Droit européen et sport: Portrait d'une cohabitation" (2002) J.T.D.E. 1–15. Declaration (No. 29), annexed to the Amsterdam Treaty, [1997] O.J. C340/136 had already emphasised the "social significance of sport, in particular its role in forging identity and bringing people together". The Intergovernmental Conference of 1997 therefore called on the bodies of the European Union to "listen to" sports associations when important questions affecting sport are at issue (*ibid.*).

[282] See the "Leonardo da Vinci" Action Programme established for the period 2000–2006 by Council Decision 1999/382/EC of April 26, 1999, [1999] O.J. L 146/33, which, as from 2007, was integrated into the EU's "Lifelong Learning" programme (see n. 271 *supra*). See also the training programme for professionals in the European audiovisual programme industry (MEDIA-Training), established by Decision No. 163/2001/EC of the European Parliament and of the Council of January 19, 2001, [2001] O.J. L 26/1, and amended by Decision No. 786/2004/EC of the European Parliament and of the Council of April 21, 2004, [2004] O.J. L138/7.

[283] Council Regulation (EC) No. 337/75 of February 10, 1975 establishing a European Centre for the Development of Vocational Training, [1975] O.J. L39/1.

cultures of the Member States, whilst emphasising the common cultural heritage yet respecting national and regional diversity (Art. 167(1) TFEU [*ex Art. 151(1)*]).[284] Art. 167(2) TFEU enumerates the areas in which the European Parliament and the Council may adopt, under the ordinary legislative procedure, incentive measures,[285] excluding any harmonisation of the laws and regulations of the Member States, and the Council may adopt recommendations (Art. 167(5) TFEU).[286] The Union is to take cultural aspects into account in its action in other spheres, in particular in order to respect and to promote the diversity of its cultures (Art. 167(4) TFEU).[287]

---

[284] See Ward, *The European Union and the culture industries: regulation and the public interest* (London, Ashgate, 2008), 264 pp.; Craufurd Smith (ed.), *Culture and European Union Law* (Oxford, Oxford University Press, 2004), 458 pp.; Albers, *Europees Gemeenschapsrecht en cultuur: eenheid en verscheidenheid* (Deventer, Kluwer, 1999), 460 pp.; Nettesheim, "Das Kulturverfassungsrecht der Europäischen Union" (2002) J.Z. 157–166. For the incorporation of the competence in respect of culture by the EU Treaty, see Niedobitek (trans. Benn and Bray), *The Cultural Dimension in EC Law* (London/The Hague, Kluwer Law International, 1997), 344 pp.; Cornu, *Compétences culturelles en Europe et principle de subsidiarité* (Brussels, Bruylant, 1993), 231 pp.; Loman, Mortelmans, Post and Watson, *Culture and Community law: Before and After Maastricht* (Deventer, Kluwer, 1992), 258 pp.; Missir di Lusignano, "Communauté et culture" (1994) R.M.C.U.E. 181–194; Niedobitek, "Die kulturelle Dimension im Vertrag über die Europäische Union" (1995) EuR. 349–376.

[285] See Decision No. 1855/2006/EC of the European Parliament and of the Council of December 12, 2006 establishing the Culture Programme (2007–2013), [2006] O.J. L372/2, which follows on Decision No. 508/2000/EC of the European Parliament and of the Council of February 14, 2000 establishing the Culture 2000 programme, [2000] O.J. L63/1), which constituted the framework for the period 2000–2006 for the cultural policy formerly implemented through the following programmes: Kaleidoscope (Decision No. 719/96/EC of the European Parliament and of the Council of March 29, 1996 establishing a programme to support artistic and cultural activities having a European dimension, [1996] O.J. L99/20), Ariane (Decision No. 2085/97/EC of the European Parliament and of the Council of October 6, 1997 establishing a programme of support, including translation, in the field of books and reading, [1997] O.J. L291/26) and Raphael (Decision No. 2228/97/EC of the European Parliament and of the Council of October 13, 1997 establishing a Community action programme in the field of cultural heritage, [1997] O.J. L 305/31). See also Decision No. 1622/2006/EC of the European Parliament and of the Council of October 24, 2006 establishing a Community action for the European Capital of Culture event for the years 2007 to 2019, [2006] O.J. L304/1; Decision No. 1904/2006/EC of the European Parliament and of the Council of December 12, 2006 establishing for the period 2007 to 2013 the programme Europe for Citizens to promote active European citizenship, [2006] O.J. L378/32.

[286] In view of the need for the free expression of culture, the Union's action is not restricted to cultural expressions with a European dimension, see Britz, "Die Freiheit der Kunst in der europäischen Kulturpolitik" (2004) EuR. 1–26.

[287] See also the Council Resolution of January 20, 1997 on the integration of cultural aspects into Community actions, [1997] O.J. C36/4, and the resolution of the European Parliament relating thereto of January 30, 1997, [1997] O.J. C55/37. For an argument in favour of a broad interpretation, see Cunningham, "In Defence of Member State Culture: The Unrealised Potential of Article 151(4) of the EC Treaty and the Consequences for EC Cultural Policy" (2001) Cornell I.L.J. 119–163. Article 107(3)(d) TFEU mentions the promotion of culture and heritage conservation as a possible justification for State Aid (see para. 11–019 *et seq.*). See also Protocol (No. 29), introduced by the Amsterdam Treaty and now annexed to the TEU and TFEU, on the system of public broadcasting in the Member States, para. 11–017, *supra*.

11–052   **Cultural diversity.** Union action in the cultural field is to remain complementary on the ground that each Member State wishes to conduct its own cultural policy with its own emphases. Accordingly, the conferral of clearly circumscribed powers on the Union in regard to both culture and education also operates as a protection under Treaty law of the "national identities" of the Member States (see Art. 4(2) TEU).

For some time now, the Court of Justice has recognised cultural aims as overriding or mandatory requirements in view of which Member States may place reasonable restrictions on the free movement of goods, persons and services.[288] Accordingly, the Court of Justice accepted the fact that Ireland required a Dutch lecturer to have a certificate of knowledge of Irish in order to teach art full time in Ireland, even though the teaching was conducted essentially in English.[289] This was not precluded by free movement of workers. The Court of Justice held that the EC Treaty,

> "does not prohibit the adoption of a policy for the protection and promotion of a language of a Member State which is both the national language and the first official language"

and recognised the importance of education for the implementation of such a policy,

> "provided that the level of knowledge required is not disproportionate in relation to the objective pursued".[290]

Likewise, the Court accepted the objective pursued by a Member State to promote its official languages by means of an obligation to invest in films in one of these languages, even though such a measure may constitute an advantage for undertakings established in that Member State.[291] Moreover, protection of an ethno-cultural minority (such as German-speakers in northern Italy) constitutes a legitimate aim, provided that it is not pursued in a disproportionate manner.[292] As far as the use of

---

[288] See, for instance, paras 9–042 (goods), 9–174 (persons) and 9–194 (services), *supra*; Karydis, "Le juge communautaire et la préservation de l'identité culturelle nationale" (1994) R.T.D.E. 551–560. However, the Court has clarified that Art. 151 EC [*now Art. 167 TFEU*] in itself is not to be regarded as a provision inserting into Union law a justification for national measures liable to hinder intra-Union trade (ECJ, Case C-531/07 *LIBRO* [2009] E.C.R. I-3717, para. 151).

[289] ECJ, Case C-379/87 *Groener* [1989] E.C.R. 3967;

[290] *Groener*, paras 19–21.

[291] ECJ, Case C-222/07 *UTECA* [2009] E.C.R. I-1407, paras 25–36.

[292] ECJ, Case C-274/96 *Bickel and Franz* [1998] E.C.R. I-7637, paras 23–30 (discrimination where nationals of other Member States who do not reside in the Member State concerned are precluded from the right conferred on the minority to use their language in judicial proceedings); ECJ, Case C-281/98 *Angonese* [2000] E.C.R. I-4139, paras 37–45 (discrimination where proof of bilingualism is conditional upon possession of a language diploma that may be obtained only in the national territory). For the situation of minorities under Union law, see also von Arnauld, "Minderheitenschutz im Recht der Europäischen Union" (2004) A.Völkerr. 111–141; Hilpold, "Minderheiten im Unionsrecht" (2001) A.Völkerr. 432–471.

languages in product labelling is concerned, such policy considerations did not initially prevail. The Court considered that a requirement to use the official language or languages in the part of the country in which the products were marketed was compatible with free movement of goods only in so far as a particular statement in the language or languages in question was necessary in order to ensure that the consumer was adequately informed.[293] Where a directive provides that the Member States are to ensure that particulars about foodstuffs provided on labelling must appear "in a language easily understood by purchasers", the Court held that this does not mean that Member States may make use of the language or languages of the linguistic region compulsory, even if they do not preclude inclusion of the relevant particulars also in other languages.[294] The directive in question was subsequently amended in order to allow the Member States to impose such an obligation.[295] The question remains, however, as to whether, in the absence of Union legislation on the matter, the principle of free movement of goods may limit the Member States' power to regulate the use of languages. In view of the respect for national and regional diversity required by the Treaties, national and regional authorities may most probably impose reasonable limitations on free movement (of goods) also in order to protect language and culture.[296] However, this consideration in itself does not authorise a Member State from deviating from harmonisation measures adopted by the Union.[297]

---

[293] ECJ, Case C-369/89 *Piageme* [1991] E.C.R. I-2971, paras 14–16 (a rule allowing only the official language or languages of the Member State to be used on labelling is incompatible with free movement of goods); ECJ, Case C-51/93 *Meyhui* [1994] E.C.R. I-3879, paras 18–21 (an obligation to use a particular language or languages will be lawful if a clearly specified definition in that language or languages is necessary for the protection of consumers), case note by Temmink (1995) S.E.W. 615–620.

[294] ECJ, Case C-85/94 *Piageme and Others* [1995] E.C.R. I-2955, paras 14–21, with a case note by Verbruggen (1995/96) Col.J.E.L. 164–171; ECJ, Case C-366/98 *Geffroy and Casino France* [2000] E.C.R. I-6579, paras 24–28. The Court took the view that the national court has to determine in each individual case whether the compulsory particulars given in a language other than the language mainly used in the Member State or region concerned can be easily understood by consumers in that State or region: *Piageme and Others*, paras 28–30; ECJ, Case C-385/96 *Goerres* [1998] E.C.R. I-4431, paras 16–25. See also Candela Soriano "Les exigences linguistiques: une entrave légitime à la libre circulation?" (2002) C.D.E. 9–44.

[295] Directive 97/4/EC of the European Parliament and of the Council of January 27, 1997 amending Directive 79/112/EEC on the approximation of the laws of the Member States relating to the labelling, presentation and advertising of foodstuffs, [1997] O.J. L 43/21 (replaced by Directive 2000/13/EC of the European Parliament and of the Council of March 20, 2000, [2000] O.J. L109/29).

[296] See Pieter Van Nuffel, note to the first *Piageme* judgment (n. 293, *supra*) (1992) S.E.W. 397, at 400. The free movement of goods remains for the present the chief concern: see ECJ, Case C-33/97 *Colim and Bigg's Continent Noord* [1999] E.C.R. I-3175, paras 36–42 (a measure requiring the use of a language which consumers can readily understand must not exclude the possible use of other means of informing them and must be restricted to the information made mandatory by the Member State concerned) and the Commission's answer of June 15, 2000 to question E-0614/00 (Staes), [2001] O.J. C46E/19. To place this in the broader context of the protection of national values vis-à-vis Union law, see De Witte, "Community Law and National Constitutional Values" (1992) 2 L.I.E.I. 1, at 15–18.

[297] See, for example, ECJ, Case C-11/95 *Commission v Belgium* [1996] E.C.R. I-4115, para. 50.

On the other hand, the requirement to take account of diversity in and as between the Member States means that the Union has to take account in its educational and cultural policies also of the special characteristics of regions and geographical and cultural minorities.[298]

VIII. Public Health

11–053   **Health policy.** Before the EU Treaty added to the EC Treaty Title XIII on "Public health", the Council had already adopted a number of measures to protect public health, principally on the basis of Art. 100a (para. 3 of which required the Commission to take as its base a high level of protection of public health) and Art. 235 of the EEC Treaty.[299] Thus the Council set up pursuant to that provision of the EEC Treaty a European Monitoring Centre for Drugs and Drug Addiction, which provides and processes information.[300] The Council and the Ministers of Public Health, meeting in the Council, agreed on common positions in the form of "resolutions" and "conclusions".

The present title of the TFEU on public health sees Union action as complementing national policies and as directed towards improving public health, preventing human illness and diseases, and obviating sources of danger to physical and mental health (Art. 168 (1), second subpara., TFEU; [*ex Art. 152(1), second subpara., EC*]).[301] Such action is to cover promotion of research and health information and education and monitoring, early warning of and combating serious cross-border threats to health. The Union is to encourage cooperation between the Member States,

---

[298] See, for instance, the concern for minority languages in the Socrates and Ariane programmes (see n. 270, *supra*) and the suggestions made by the European Parliament in its resolution of February 9, 1994 on cultural and linguistic minorities in the European Communities, [1994] O.J. C61/110. Linguistic diversity is also covered by Union industrial policy; see ECJ, Case C-42/97 *European Parliament v Council* [1999] E.C.R. I-869. See further Donders, "The Protection of Cultural Rights in Europe: None of the EU's Business?" (2003) M.J.C.E.L. 117–147.

[299] See, inter alia, Council Directive 89/105/EEC of December 21, 1988 relating to the transparency of measures regulating the prices of medicinal products for human use and their inclusion in the scope of national health insurance systems, [1989] O.J. L40/8 and Council Directive 89/107/EEC of December 21, 1988 on the approximation of the laws of the Member States concerning food additives authorised for use in foodstuffs intended for human consumption, [1989] O.J. L40/27, replaced—pursuant to Art. 152 EC—by Regulation (EC) No. 1920/2006 of the European Parliament and of the Council of December 12, 2006, [2006] O.J. L376/1.

[300] Regulation (EC) No. 302/93 of February 8, 1993, [1993] O.J. L36/1.

[301] See Davies, "The community's internal market-based competence to regulate healthcare: scope, strategies and consequences" (2007) 14 M.J.E.C.L. 215–238; Hatzopoulos, "Is it healthy to have an EU health law?" (2005) E.L.Rev. 697–710; Sander, "Europäischer Gesundheidsschutz als primärrechtliche Aufgabe und grundrechtliche Gewährleistung" (2005) Z.Eu.S. 253–271; Hervey, "Mapping the Contours of European Union Health Law and Policy" (2002) E.Publ.L. 69–105; Hervey, "Community and National Competence in Health after *Tobacco Advertising*" (2001) C.M.L.Rev. 1421–1446; Van Schwanenflügel, "Gesundheit in Europa" (1998) EuR. 210–21.

in particular so as to improve the complementarity of their health services in cross-border areas (Art. 168(2), first subpara., TFEU).

In liaison with the Commission, the Member States are to coordinate among themselves their health policies and programmes. In this connection, the Lisbon Treaty introduced in the area of public health a similar method of coordination to that previously implemented in the area of employment (see para. 11–046). Under this so-called "open method of coordination", the Commission takes initiatives to establish guidelines and indicators, organise the exchange of "best practice" and prepare for periodic monitoring and evaluation (Art. 168(2) TFEU). Without conferring any direct powers on the Union, that method exposes Member States to peer review, which may eventually persuade them to adapt their policies.

The Treaty of Lisbon included the field of public health among the areas where the Union has competence only to carry out actions to support, coordinate or supplement the actions of the Member States (Art. 6(a) TFEU). However, the Treaties make an exception for "common safety concerns in public health matters", which are, for the aspects defined by the TFEU, included within the general category of the Union's shared competences (Art. 4(2)(k) TFEU). Accordingly, the European Parliament and the Council may adopt harmonisation measures in a number of fields to meet common safety concerns (Art. 168(4) TFEU). This applies to:

(a) measures setting high standards of quality and safety of organs and substances of human origin, blood and blood derivatives (although Member States are not precluded from maintaining or introducing more stringent measures);

(b) measures in the veterinary and phytosanitary fields which have as their direct object the protection of public health and

(c) measures setting high standards of quality and safety for medicinal products and devices for medical use.[302]

This concerns largely the same substantive matters in respect of which the European Parliament and the Council were already entitled to adopt harmonisation measures under the EC Treaty ever since the Amsterdam Treaty.[303] In this way, the Union has harmonised foodstuffs legislation and set up the European Food Safety Authority with the task of providing scientific advice and scientific and technical support for the Union's legislation and policies in all fields which have a direct or indirect impact on food safety.[304] Pursuant to that power, the Union also established a European

---

[302] Measures adopted under (a) must not affect national provisions on the donation or medical use of organs and blood (Art. 168(7) TFEU).

[303] Compare Art. 168(4) TFEU with Art.152(4)(a) and (b) EC.

[304] Regulation (EC) No. 178/2002 of the European Parliament and of the Council of January 28, 2002 laying down the general principles and requirements of food law, establishing the European Food Safety Authority and laying down procedures in matters of food safety, [2002] O.J. L31/1 (adopted

Medicines Agency and a European Centre for disease prevention and control.[305] In other fields, the European Parliament and the Council are to adopt "incentive measures"[306] under the ordinary legislative procedure "excluding any harmonisation of the laws and regulations of the Member States" (Art. 168(5) TFEU). The Council may also adopt recommendations by a qualified majority vote on a proposal from the Commission (Art. 168(6) TFEU).[307]

In taking such action, the Union must fully respect the responsibilities of the Member States for the definition of their health policy and for the organisation and delivery of health services and medical care (Art. 168(7)). These responsibilities include both the management of health services and medical care and the allocation of the resources assigned to them (*ibid.*). However, in the organisation of their public health and social security systems, the Member States must comply with Union law, in particular the provisions of the Treaties on the freedoms of movement, which prohibit the Member States from introducing or maintaining unjustified restrictions on the exercise of those freedoms in the healthcare sector.[308] Nonetheless, in assessing whether Member States comply with Union law, account must be taken of the fact that a Member State may determine the level of protection which it wishes to afford to public health and the way in which that level is to be achieved.[309] Since the level of protection may vary from one Member State to the other, Member States must be allowed the necessary discretion.[310]

Under Art. 168(1) all Union policies and activities are to ensure a high level of protection of human health. Consequently, the Union may adopt under Arts 113 and 114 TFEU [*ex Arts 93 and 95 EC*] measures which are designed to eliminate

on the basis of Arts 37, 95, 133 and 152(4)(b) EC [*now Arts 31, 114, 207 and 168(4)(b) TFEU*]). See Beurdeley, "La sécurité alimentaire au sein de l'Union européenne: un concept en gestation" (2002) R.M.C.U.E. 89–103; Dehousse, Engelstadt and Gevers, "La sécurité alimentaire et le principe de la précaution" (2000) Stud. Dipl. 95–112.

[305] Regulation (EC) No. 726/2004 of the European Parliament and of the Council of March 31, 2004 laying down Community procedures for the authorisation and supervision of medicinal products for human and veterinary use and establishing a European Medicines Agency, [2004] O.J. L136/1; Regulation (EC) No. 851/2004 of the European Parliament and of the Council of April 21, 2004 establishing a European Centre for disease prevention and control, [2004] O.J. L142/1.

[306] See, e.g., Decision No. 1350/2007/EC of the European Parliament and of the Council of October 23, 2007 establishing a second programme of Community action in the field of health (2008–2013), [2007] O.J. L301/3.

[307] E.g. Council Recommendation of June 5, 2001 on the drinking of alcohol by young people, in particular children and adolescents, [2001] O.J. L161/38.

[308] ECJ, Case C-372/04 *Watts* [2006] ECR I-4325, paras 92 and 146; ECJ, Case C-531/06 *Commission v Italy* [2009] E.C.R. I-4103, paras 35 and 36.

[309] ECJ, Case C-169/07 *Hartlauer* [2009] E.C.R. I-1721, para. 30; ECJ, Joined Cases C-171/07 and C-172/07 *Apothekerkammer des Saarlandes* [2009] E.C.R. I-4171, paras 18–19; ECJ (judgment of January 12, 2010), Case C-341/08 *Petersen*, not yet reported, para. 51; ECJ (judgment of June 1, 2010), Joined Cases C-570/07 and C-571/07 *Blanco Pérez and Chao Gómez*, not yet reported, paras 43–44.

[310] *Ibid.*

obstacles to the functioning of the internal market and, at the same time, have an eye to the protection of public health.[311]

IX. CONSUMER PROTECTION

Consumer policy. In order to promote the interests of consumers and to ensure a high level of consumer protection, the Union is to contribute to protecting the health, safety and economic interests of consumers, as well as to promoting their right to information, education and to organise themselves in order to safeguard their interests (Art. 169(1) TFEU [*ex Art. 153(1) EC*]).[312] The means employed are harmonising measures adopted pursuant to Art. 114 TFEU [*ex Art. 95 EC*][313]

11–054

[311] See ECJ (judgment of March 4, 2010), Case C-197/08 *Commission v France*, not yet reported, paras 51–52 (protection of public health taken into account in the adoption of fiscal legislation with respect to tobacco products); ECJ, Case C-376/98 *Germany v European Parliament and Council* [2000] E.C.R. I-8419, para. 88 (by which, however, a general prohibition of all forms of tobacco advertising and sponsoring, even where the tobacco product was not named, was annulled on the ground that Arts 47(2), 55 and 95 EC did not afford a sufficient legal basis). See Hervey, "Up in Smoke? Community (anti-)tobacco law and policy" (2001) E.L.Rev. 101–125. Articles 47(2), 55 and 95 EC [*now Arts 53, 62 and 114 TFEU*] were used as the legal basis for an adapted tobacco advertising ban in Directive 2003/33/EC of the European Parliament and the Council of May 26, 2003, [2003] O.J. L152/16. The action for annulment brought by Germany against this second directive was dismissed by the Court (ECJ, Case C-380/03 *Germany v European Parliament and Council* [2006] E.C.R. I-11573). Other examples are Directives 2001/82/EC and 2001/83/EC of the European Parliament and of the Council of November 6, 2001 on the Community code relating to veterinary medicinal products and on the Community code relating to medicinal products for human use ([2001] O.J. L311/1 and L311/67, respectively). See also the Council resolution of November 18, 1999 on ensuring health protection in all Community policies and activities, [2000] O.J. C86/3.

[312] For general discussions, see, for instance, Micklitz, Reich and Rott, *Understanding EU Consumer Law* (Antwerp, Intersentia, 2009), 378 pp.; Weatherill, *EU Consumer Law and Policy* (Cheltenham, Edward Elgar, 2005), 253 pp.; De Witte and Vermeersch, *Europees consumenten-recht* (Antwerpen, Maklu, 2004), 290 pp.; Howells and Wilhelmsson, "EC Consumer Law: Has it Come of Age?" (2003) E.L.Rev. 370–388; Stuyck, "European Consumer Law after the Treaty of Amsterdam: Consumer Policy in or Beyond the Internal Market?" (2000) C.M.L.Rev. 367–400.

[313] See Directive 97/7/EC of the European Parliament and of the Council of May 20, 1997 on the protection of consumers in respect of distance contracts, [1997] O.J. L144/19; Directive 98/27/EC of the European Parliament and the Council of May 19, 1998 on injunctions for the protection of consumers' interests, [1998] O.J. L166/5; Directive 1999/44/EC of the European Parliament and of the Council of May 25, 1999 on certain aspects of the sale of consumer goods and associated guarantees, [1999] O.J. L171/12; Directive 2000/31/EC of the European Parliament and of the Council of June 8, 2000 on certain legal aspects of information society services, in particular electronic commerce, in the Internal Market ("Directive on electronic commerce"), [2000] O.J. L178/1; Directive 2001/95/EC of the European Parliament and of the Council of December 3, 2001 on general product safety, [2002] O.J. L11/4; Directive 2005/29/EC of the European Parliament and of the Council of May 11, 2005 concerning unfair business-to-consumer commercial practices in the internal market ("Unfair Commercial Practices Directive"), [2005] O.J. L149/22; Directive 2006/114/EC of the European Parliament and of the Council of December 12, 2006 concerning misleading and comparative advertising, [2006] O.J. L376/21; Directive 2008/48/EC of the

and measures supporting, supplementing and monitoring the policy pursued by the Member States, which the European Parliament and the Council are to adopt under the ordinary legislative procedure (Art. 169(2) and (3) TFEU).[314] As far as this second type of measure is concerned, Member States may maintain or introduce more stringent measures, provided that they are compatible with the Treaties and that the Commission is notified of them (Art. 169(4) TFEU). However, the same is not necessarily true of measures adopted on the basis of Art. 114 or 115 TFEU [*ex Art. 95 or 94 EC*] with respect to which the question whether they lay down complete or merely minimum harmonisation is to be determined for each individual measure on the basis of its wording, purpose and structure.[315] Consumer protection requirements must be taken into account in defining and implementing other Union policies and activities (Art. 12 TFEU [*ex Art. 153(2) EC*]).

X. ECONOMIC, SOCIAL AND TERRITORIAL COHESION AND TRANS-EUROPEAN NETWORKS

11–055   **Regional policies.** Economic, social and territorial cohesion[316] aims to reduce disparities between the levels of development of the various regions and the backwardness of the least-favoured regions or islands (Art. 174 TFEU [*ex Art. 158 EC*]). The Single European Act incorporated into the EC Treaty a title

---

European Parliament and of the Council of April 23, 2008 on credit agreements for consumers, [2008] O.J. L133/66. For the role of the directive on electronic commerce in the context of other Union legislation, see Walden, "Regulating electronic commerce: Europe in the global E-conomy" (2001) E.L.Rev. 529–547. For Directive 2005/29/EC, see Abbamonte, "The unfair commercial practices directive: an example of the new European consumer protection approach" (2006) Col.J.E.L 695–713. Directives were adopted on the basis of Art. 100a EEC even before specific competence was introduced in the matter of consumer protection: see, for instance, Council Directive 93/13/EEC of April 5, 1993 on unfair terms in consumer contracts, [1993] O.J. L95/29. See also the directives adopted by the Council pursuant to Art. 100 EEC on liability for defective products (Directive 85/374/EEC of July 25, 1985, [1985] O.J. L210/29, extended by Directive 1999/34/EC of the European Parliament and of the Council of May 10, 1999, [1999] O.J. L141/20) and protection of the consumer in respect of contracts negotiated away from business premises (Directive 85/577/EEC of December 20, 1985, [1985] O.J. L372/31).

[314] See Decision No. 1926/2006/EC of the European Parliament and of the Council of December 18, 2006 establishing a programme of Community action in the field of consumer policy (2007–2013), [2006] O.J. L404/39. Prior to the Amsterdam Treaty, Art. 129a of the EC Treaty referred to "specific action", see Directive 98/6/EC of the European Parliament and of the Council of February 16, 1998 on consumer protection in the indication of the prices of products offered to consumers, [1998] O.J. L80/27 (*corrigendum* in [1998] O.J. L190/86), which was adopted on the basis of that provision.

[315] See para. 9–110, *supra*.

[316] Before the Lisbon Treaty, the EC Treaty referred to "Economic and social cohesion".

on economic and social cohesion; since the EU Treaty, cohesion has constituted an express objective for the Union (Art. 3(3) TEU).[317]

The Union grants aid through the Structural Funds (the European Agricultural Guidance and Guarantee Fund, Guidance Section,[318] the European Social Fund[319] and the European Regional Development Fund,[320]) the European Investment Bank[321] and other financial instruments (Art. 175, first para., TFEU [*ex Art. 159, first para., EC*]). The European Parliament and the Council, acting in accordance with the ordinary legislative procedure, are responsible for defining the tasks, priority objectives and the organisation of the Structural Funds, which may involve grouping the Funds, and for laying down the general rules for coordinating the Funds with one another and with the other financial instruments[322] (Art. 177, first para., TFEU [*ex Art. 161, first para., EC*]). The Council radically reformed the existing funds in 1988.[323] A new reform was carried out in 1999 with a view to preparing for the accession of the new Member States (Agenda 2000),[324] and again

---

[317] For a survey, see Molle, *European Cohesion Policy* (Abingdon, Routledge, 2007), 347 pp.; Evans, *The EU Structural Funds* (Oxford, Oxford University Press, 1999), 348 pp.; Comijs, *Europese structuurfondsen* (Deventer, Kluwer, 1998), 319 pp.; Bandarra, "La politique de cohésion dans l'union européenne et l'élargissement" (2006) R.M.C.U.E. 177–188; David, "Territorialer Zusammenhalt: Kompetenzzuwachs für die Raumordnung auf europäischer Ebene oder neues Kompetenzfeld?" (2003) D.ö.V. 146–155; Mestre and Petit, "La cohésion économique et sociale après le Traité sur l'Union européenne" (1995) C.D.E. 207–243; Kenner, "Economic and Social Cohesion—The Rocky Road Ahead" (1994) 1 L.I.E.I. 1–37.

[318] Para. 11–002, *supra*.

[319] Para. 11–044, *supra*.

[320] According to Art. 176 TFEU [*ex Art. 160 EC*], that fund is intended to help redress regional imbalances through participation in the development and structural adjustment of regions whose development is lagging behind and in the conversion of declining industrial regions. The European Parliament and the Council adopt implementing decisions relating to the Fund by the ordinary legislative procedure (Art. 178, first para., TFEU [*ex Art. 162, first para., EC*]). See Regulation (EC) No. 1080/2006 of the European Parliament and of the Council of July 5, 2006 on the European Regional Development Fund, [2006] O.J. L210/1.

[321] Paras 13–116—13–117, *infra*.

[322] E.g. the European Fisheries Fund, see Council Regulation (EC) No. 1198/2006 of July 27, 2006, [2006] O.J. L223/1, replacing the Financial Instrument for Fisheries Guidance, see Council Regulation (EC) No. 1263/1999 of June 21, 1999, [1999] O.J. L161/54.

[323] Council Regulation (EC) No. 2052/88 of June 24, 1988 on the tasks of the Structural Funds and their effectiveness and on coordination of their activities between themselves and with the operations of the European Investment Bank and the other existing financial instruments, [1988] O.J. L185/9. The regulation classified the tasks of the various financial instruments by reference to five objectives, which were increased to six by Protocol No. 6 to the 1994 Act of Accession. See Célimène, "La réforme de l'action des fonds structurels européens" (1991) A.J.D.A. 251–266.

[324] Council Regulation (EC) No. 1260/1999 of June 21, 1999 laying down general provisions on the Structural Funds, [1999] O.J. L161/1. Its principal aims were: (1) promoting the development and structural adjustment of regions whose development is lagging behind; (2) supporting the economic and social conversion of areas facing structural difficulties; (3) supporting the adaptation and modernisation of policies and systems of education, training and employment.

in 2006.[325] In addition, the Cohesion Fund[326] provides a financial contribution to projects in the fields of the environment and trans-European networks in the area of transport infrastructure (Art. 177, second para., TFEU), but only in Member States fulfilling the criteria set out in a Protocol annexed to the Treaties.[327] The Commission reports every three years on progress made towards achieving economic and social cohesion.

If "specific actions" prove necessary outside the Funds, the European Parliament and the Council may adopt them under the ordinary legislative procedure (Art. 175, third para., TFEU). In this way, a Solidarity Fund has been set up which can provide rapid assistance to Member States in the event of a major natural disaster.[328] In order to overcome the obstacles hindering cross-border and interregional cooperation, the Union has provided for the creation of "European groupings of territorial cooperation" (EGTC), invested with legal personality and allowing national, regional and local authorities to carry out specific actions of territorial cooperation.[329]

11–056   **Trans-European networks.** Since the EU Treaty, the Treaty provisions on "trans-European networks" have supplemented the existing Union competence to promote economic, social and territorial cohesion. The Union is to contribute to the

---

[325] Council Regulation (EC) No. 1083/2006 of July 11, 2006 laying down general provisions on the European Regional Development Fund (ERDF), the European Social Fund (ESF) and the Cohesion Fund, [2006] O.J. L210/25. The three Funds contribute to the principal objective of convergence with the aim of speeding up the convergence of the least-developed Member States and regions by improving conditions for growth and employment; the ERDF and ESF also contribute to the objective of regional competitiveness and employment; finally, the EDRF also contributes to the objective of European territorial cooperation with the aim of strengthening transnational and interregional cooperation.

[326] Council Regulation (EC) No. 1084/2006 of July 11, 2006 establishing a Cohesion Fund, [2006] O.J. L210/79 (replacing Council Regulation (EC) No. 1164/94 of May 16, 1994 establishing a Cohesion Fund, [1994] O.J. L130/1).

[327] Protocol (No. 28), introduced by the EU Treaty and now annexed to the TEU and TFEU, on economic, social and territorial cohesion ([2010] O.J. C83/311) requires the Member State concerned to have a per capita GNP of less than 90 per cent of the Union average (which, up to 2004, limited qualifying Member States to Greece, Ireland, Portugal and Spain and, at present, to Bulgaria, Cyprus, the Czech Republic, Estonia, Greece, Hungary, Latvia, Lithuania, Malta, Poland, Portugal, Romania, Slovakia and Slovenia) and to have a programme for the fulfilment of the economic convergence criteria set out in Art. 126 TFEU.

[328] See Council Regulation (EC) No. 2012/2002 of November 11, 2002 establishing the European Union Solidarity Fund, [2002] O.J. L311/3. This regulation is based on the third para. of Art. 159 EC [*now Art. 175 TFEU*] and Art. 308 EC [*now Art. 352 TFEU*] so as to make the regulation also applicable to candidate countries. For the financing of the fund, see the Interinstitutional Agreement of November 7, 2002 between the European Parliament, the Council and the Commission, [2002] O.J. C283/1 supplementing the Interinstitutional Agreement of May 6, 1999 (see para. 13–139).

[329] Regulation (EC) No. 1082/2006 of the European Parliament and of the Council of July 5, 2006 on a European grouping of territorial cooperation (EGTC), O.J. 2006, L210/19.

development of infrastructure networks in the areas of transport, telecommunications and energy by promoting the interconnection and "interoperability" of national networks and access to those networks.[330] Importance is attached to linking island, landlocked and peripheral regions with the central regions of the Union. The intention behind Union action is to help to attain the objectives of the single market and economic and social cohesion in such a way that not only economic operators, but also communities and citizens, benefit (Art. 170 TFEU [*ex Art. 154 EC*]). Member States are to coordinate their policies among themselves, in liaison with the Commission (Art. 171(2) TFEU [*ex Art. 155(2) EC*]). The European Parliament and the Council are to adopt guidelines covering the objectives, priorities and broad lines of measures envisaged, identifying projects of common interest.[331] In addition, the Union is to adopt such (harmonisation) measures as may prove necessary to ensure the interoperability of networks (Art. 171(1) TFEU), for example by arranging for a "*.eu*" domain on the Internet[332] or by ensuring the interoperability of the European rail system.[333] Article 171 TFEU constitutes, together with Art. 172 TFEU [*ex Art. 156 EC*], the specific legal basis for such measures, even where they also cover objectives pursued by the single market.[334] The Union may also support projects of common interest financially supported by Member States and contribute through the Cohesion Fund (para. 5–247, *infra*) to the financing of projects (Art. 171(1) TFEU).[335] The guidelines and measures are drawn up under the ordinary legislative procedure (Art. 172, first para., TFEU). Guidelines and projects of common interest which relate to the territory of a Member State require the approval of the Member State concerned (Art. 172, second para., TFEU).

---

[330] Roggenkamp, "Transeuropese netwerken. Op weg naar een communautair infrastructuurbeleid?" (1998) S.E.W. 416–423.

[331] See the Decisions of the European Parliament and of the Council laying down guidelines for trans-European energy networks (Decision No. 1364/2006/EC of September 6, 2006, [2006] O.J. L262/1), for the development of the trans-European transport network (Decision No. 884/2004/EC of April 29, 2004, [2004] O.J. L201/1) and for trans-European telecommunications networks (Decision No. 1336/97/EC of June 17, 1997, [1997] O.J. L183/12). The guidelines need not necessarily have been preceded by a separate measure adopted beforehand: ECJ, Case C-22/96 *European Parliament v Council* [1998] E.C.R. I-3231, para. 34.

[332] Regulation (EC) No. 733/2002 of the European Parliament and of the Council of April 22, 2002 on the implementation of the *.eu* Top Level Domain, [2002] O.J. L113/1.

[333] See Directive 2008/57/EC of the European Parliament and of the Council of June 17, 2008 on the interoperability of the rail system within the Community, [2008] O.J. L191/1.

[334] ECJ, Case C-271/94 *European Parliament v Council* [1996] E.C.R. I-1689, paras 13–35 (annulment of a decision based on Art. 308 EC [*now Art.352 TFEU*]; the decision was subsequently replaced by a decision based on Art. 156 EC, [1996] O.J. L327/34).

[335] For general rules for the granting of Union financial aid in the field of trans-European networks, see Regulation (EC) No. 67/2010 of the European Parliament and the Council of November 30, 2009, [2010] O.J. L27/20.

XI. INDUSTRY

11–057 **Competitiveness.** Article 173(1) TFEU [*ex Art. 157(1) EC*] lists aims for fostering competitiveness of the Union's industry. The Member States are to address
their policies to this, where necessary coordinating their action, possibly at the initiative of the Commission (Art. 173(2) TFEU). The Lisbon Treaty also introduced
here the "open method of coordination", according to which the Commission may
take initiatives to establish guidelines and indicators, organise the exchange of
"best practice" and prepare for periodic monitoring and evaluation. The Union
endeavours to attain the objectives of improving the competitiveness of the
Union's industry by means of policies and action based on other provisions of the
Treaties.[336] The addition (by the EU Treaty) of a title "Industry" in the Treaties did
not confer on the Union competence to conduct its own industrial policy, but
enabled the European Parliament and the Council to adopt, under the ordinary legislative procedure, "specific measures" in support of action taken in the Member
States (Art. 173(3), first subpara.).[337] Union action in this field may not lead to the
harmonisation of the laws and regulations of the Member States (Art. 173(3), first
subpara., TFEU). Moreover, any Union measure may in no event lead to a
distortion of competition or contain tax provisions or provisions relating to the
rights and interests of employed persons (Art. 157(3), second subpara.). The provisions on industry are thus among the areas where the Union may "carry out
actions to support, coordinate or supplement the actions of the Member States"
(see para. 7–025).

XII. RESEARCH AND TECHNOLOGICAL DEVELOPMENT AND SPACE

11–058 **Union support.** Although the Union has long been providing support for research
and technological development, for instance by means of measures based on
Art. 308 EC [*now Art. 352 TFEU*], the title "Research and technological development" was introduced for the first time into the Treaties by the Single European
Act. The Treaty of Lisbon supplemented these provisions by a legal basis which
allows the Union to draw up a European space policy (Art. 189 TFEU).

---

[336] See Commission of the European Communities, *European Industrial Policy for the Nineties* (1991)
EC Bull. Suppl. 3. For an overview, see Nicolaides, *Industrial Policy in the European Community*
(Maastricht, European Institute of Public Administration, 1993), 134 pp.

[337] See Decision 1639/2006/EC of the European Parliament and of the Council of October 24,
2006 establishing a Competitiveness and Innovation Framework Programme (2007 to 2013),
[2006] O.J. L310/15; Decision No. 1718/2006/EC of the European Parliament and of the Council
of November 15, 2006 concerning the implementation of a programme of support for the European
audiovisual sector (MEDIA 2007), [2006] O.J. L327/12; Decision No. 456/2005/EC of the
European Parliament and of the Council of March 9, 2005 establishing a multiannual Community
programme to make digital content in Europe more accessible, usable and exploitable, [2005]
O.J. L79/1.

Title XIV deals with the Union's activities in this field with the objective of strengthening its scientific and technological bases by achieving a European research area in which researchers, scientific knowledge and technology circulate freely, and encouraging it to become more competitive, including in its industry, while promoting all the research activities deemed necessary by virtue of other Chapters of the Treaties. (Art. 179 TFEU [ex Art. 163 EC]).[338] Action by the Union is simply to complement activities undertaken by Member States. It is to cover programmes fostering cooperation between undertakings, research centres and universities, together with international cooperation, disseminating and optimising the results of research and stimulating the training and mobility of researchers (Art. 180 TFEU [ex Art. 164 EC]).

The Commission is empowered to take any useful initiative to promote coordination of national policies and Union policy (Art. 181 TFEU [ex Art. 165 EC]). Again, the Commission is to encourage peer review amongst Member States through the so-called "open method of coordination", according to which the Commission may take initiatives to establish guidelines and indicators, organise the exchange of "best practice" and prepare for periodic monitoring and evaluation (Art. 181(2)TFEU). The European Parliament and the Council, acting under the ordinary legislative procedure, are to adopt multiannual framework programmes setting out all the activities of the Union (Art. 182(1) TFEU [ex Art. 166(1) EC]).[339] The Council, acting in accordance with a special legislative procedure and after consulting the European Parliament, may then adopt specific programmes for the implementation of the framework programmes (Art. 182(3) and (4) TFEU). Other procedures apply where implementation is carried out by means of supplementary programmes in which only some Member States take part,[340] Union participation,[341] international cooperation[342] or the creation of joint undertakings by the Union.[343]

The European Parliament and the Council, acting in accordance with the ordinary legislative procedure, are to establish the necessary measures to draw up a European space policy, which may take the form of a European space programme. The Union's measures are to promote joint initiatives, support research and technological development and coordinate the efforts needed for the exploration and exploitation of space (Art. 189(1) and (2) TFEU).

The Union's competence for research and technological development and space is not included among the areas where the Union may take only "coordinating,

---

[338] See Commission of the European Communities, *Research after Maastricht: a balance sheet, a strategy* (1992) EC Bull. Suppl. 2.

[339] See Decision 1982/2006/EC of the European Parliament and of the Council of December 18, 2006 concerning the Seventh Framework Programme of the European Community for research, technological development and demonstration activities (2007–2013), [2006] O.J. L412/1. See Dévoué, "La coordination des politiques de recherche-développement: le cas européen" (2002) R.M.C.U.E. 688–695.

[340] Articles 184 and 188, second para., TFEU [ex Art. 168 and Art. 172, second para., EC].

[341] Articles 185 and 188, second para., TFEU [ex Art. 169 and Art. 172, second para., EC].

[342] Article 186 TFEU [ex Art. 170 EC] (see also para. 25–054, infra).

[343] Articles 187 and 188, first para., TFEU [ex Art. 171 and Art. 172, first para., EC] (para. 13–123, infra).

complementary or supporting action". However, it follows from Art. 4(3) TFEU that it was not the intention of the Treaty of Lisbon that the exercise by the Union of its powers should prevent the Member States from pursuing their own policy (see para. 7–024, *supra*). Measures adopted with regard to the establishment of European space policy may not in any event lead to the harmonisation of the laws and regulations of the Member States (Art. 189(2) TFEU).

XIII. ENVIRONMENT

11–059 **Sustainable development.** Ever since the Single European Act, the Union has had express powers in regard to environment policy under the title of the Treaties headed "Environment".[344] The aim of the Union's policy is to preserve, protect and improve the quality of the environment, protect human health, ensure prudent and rational use of natural resources, and promote an international approach to regional or worldwide environmental problems, and in particular combating climate change (Art. 191(1) TFEU [*ex Art. 174(1) EC*]. In this connection, the Union cooperates with third countries and with the competent international organisations.[345] The policy aims at a high level of protection taking account of the diversity of situations in the various regions of the Union (Art. 191(2), first subpara.).[346] The Treaties list

---

[344] For a discussion of environment policy, see Jans and Vedder, *European Environmental Law* (Groningen, Europa Law Publishing, 2008), 496 pp.; Krämer, *EC Environmental Law* (London, Sweet & Maxwell, 2007), 513 pp.; Lee, *EU Environmental Law: Challenges, Change and Decision-making* (Oxford, Hart Publishing, 2005), 275 pp. For the formal recognition of environmental protection as a Union objective, see para. 7–003, *supra*, and the action programmes adopted in 1973 ([1973] O.J. C112), 1977 ([1977] O.J. C139), 1983 ([1983] O.J. C46), 1987 ([1987] O.J. C328) and 1993 ([1993] O.J. C138/1) in the form of a declaration or resolution of the Council and representatives of the Member State Governments, meeting in the Council. As early as April 2, 1979, the Council adopted, pursuant to Art. 235 EC [*now Art. 352 TFEU*], Directive 79/409/EEC on the conservation of wild birds, [1979] O.J. L103/1. For the development of Union powers, see Scheuing, "Regulierung und Marktfreiheit im Europäischen Umweltrecht" (2001) EuR. 1–26; Van Calster and Deketelaere, "Amsterdam, the Intergovernmental Conference and Greening the EC Treaty" (1998) E.Env.L.Rev. 12–25; Lenaerts, "The Principle of Subsidiarity and the Environment in the European Union: Keeping the Balance of Federalism" (1994) Fordham I.L.J. 846–895. For a study of the real impact of environmental concerns, see Jans, "Environmental spill-overs into general community law" (2008) 31 Fordham I.L.J. 1360–1386; Bär and Klasing, "Fit for Enlargement? Environmental Policy after Nice" (2001) E.Env.L.Rev. 212–220; Stetter, "Maastricht, Amsterdam and Nice: the Environmental Lobby and Greening the Treaties" (2001) E.Env.L.Rev. 150–159.

[345] Article 191(4) TFEU; para. 25–054, *infra*.

[346] Under Art. 191(3) TFEU, the Union is to take account, inter alia, of environmental conditions in the various regions and the balanced development of the regions, together with the economic and social development of the Union as a whole. In order to be able to take available scientific and technological data into consideration, the European Environment Agency collects all useful environmental data and supplies them to the Commission and the Member States, in particular through the Environment Information and Observation Network: Regulation (EC) No. 401/2009 of the European Parliament and of the Council of April 23, 2009, [2009] O.J. L126/13.

the principles on which the Union's environment policy is based as follows: the precautionary principle; the principle of preventive action; environmental damage to be rectified as a priority at source; "the polluter should pay".[347] Environmental requirements must be integrated into Union policies in other spheres, in particular with a view to promoting sustainable development (Art. 11 TFEU [*ex Art. 6 EC*]).[348]

Environment policy. The European Parliament and the Council, acting under the ordinary legislative procedure, are to decide what action is to be taken by the Union in order to achieve the objectives of the environment policy (Art. 192(1) TFEU [*ex Art. 175(1) EC*]).[349] A powerful example is the scheme for greenhouse gas emission

11–060

---

[347] See De Sadeleer, *Les principes du pollueur-payeur, de prévention et de précaution* (Brussels, Brulant, 1999), 437 pp.; Bleeker, "Does the Polluter Pay? The Polluter-Pays Principle in the Case Law of the European Court of Justice" (2009) E.En.Env.L.Rev. 289–306; Cheyne, "The precautionary principle in EC and WTO Law: searching for a common understanding" (2006) E.Env.L.Rev. 257–277; Vandekerckhove, "The Polluter Pays Principle in the European Community" (1993) Y.E.L. 201–262. For the principle that environmental damage should be rectified at source and the polluter-pays principle: ECJ, Case C-293/97 *Standley, Metson and Others* [1999] E.C.R. I-2603, paras 51–53 (testing Union law against these principles); ECJ, Joined Cases C-175/98 and C-177/98 *Lirussi and Bizarro* [1999] E.C.R. I-6881, para. 51; ECJ, Case C-318/98 *Fornasar and Others* [2000] E.C.R. I-4785, para. 38; ECJ, Case C-188/07 *Commune de Mesquer* [2008] E.C.R. I-4501, paras 64–89; ECJ (judgment of March 9, 2010), Case C-378/08 *Raffinerie Mediterranee (ERG) and Others*, not yet reported, paras 52–70 (interpretation of Union law in the light of those principles). As established in Art. 191 TFEU, the polluter pays principle is directed at action at Union level and cannot be relied upon in order to exclude the application of national legislation in an area for which there is no Union legislation that covers the situation in question: *Raffinerie Mediterranee (ERG) and Others*, para. 46. For the precautionary principle, see para. 22–040. Article 191(3) TFEU refers to the process of weighing potential benefits and costs which must take place before the Union takes any decision in this field.

[348] See London, "Droit communautaire de l'environnement—Interaction environnement et santé: état des lieux" (2001) R.T.D.E. 139–154. According to Declaration (No. 12), annexed to the Treaty of Amsterdam ([1997] O.J. C340/133), the Commission undertakes to prepare environmental impact assessment studies when making proposals which may have significant environmental implications.

[349] See, for example, Regulation (EC) No. 1655/2000 of the European Parliament and of the Council of July 17, 2000 concerning the Financial Instrument for the Environment (LIFE), [2000] O.J. L192/1 (now replaced by Regulation (EC) No. 614/2007 of the European Parliament and of the Council of May 23, 2007 concerning the Financial Instrument for the Environment (LIFE+), [2007] O.J. L149/1); Directive 2001/42/EC of the European Parliament and of the Council of June 27, 2001 on the assessment of the effects of certain plans and programmes on the environment, [2001] O.J. L197/30; Decision 1411/2001/EC of the European Parliament and of the Council of June 27, 2001 on a Community framework for cooperation to promote sustainable urban development, [2001] O.J. L191/1; Directive 2004/35/EC of the European Parliament and of the Council of April 21, 2004 on environmental liability with regard to the prevention and remedying of environmental damage, [2004] O.J. L143/56; Directive 2006/44/EC of the European Parliament and of the Council of September 6, 2006 on the quality of fresh waters needing protection or improvement in order to support fish life, [2006] O.J. L264/20. Each successive amendment of the Treaty altered the procedure laid down in Art. 175(1). In the version embodied in the EEC Treaty, all environmental measures required a Council decision taken by a unanimous vote after consultation of the European Parliament. After the EU Treaty, the cooperation procedure was applied, which was replaced by the co-decision procedure as a result of the Treaty of Amsterdam.

trading set up by the Union to fulfil the commitments of the Union and its Member States under the Kyoto Protocol to the United Nations Framework Convention on Climate Change, to reduce greenhouse gas emissions.[350] In the case of a number of matters, the Council is to take its decisions unanimously in accordance with a special legislative procedure and after consulting the European Parliament (Art. 192(2)).[351] In addition, the European Parliament and the Council are to adopt general action programmes in accordance with the ordinary legislative procedure (Art. 192(3) TFEU).[352] In principle, it is for the Member States to finance and implement the environment policy (Art. 192(4) TFEU). If a measure based on Art. 192(1) TFEU involves disproportionate costs for a given Member State, the Council may apply a temporary derogation or provide for financial support from the Cohesion Fund (Art. 192(5) TFEU). Member States wishing to maintain or introduce more stringent measures may do so provided that they are compatible with the Treaties and notified to the Commission (Art. 193 TFEU [*ex Art. 176 EC*]).[353] At the same time, harmonisation measures are to include a safeguard clause allowing Member States to take provisional measures for non-economic environmental reasons, subject to a procedure of inspection by the Union (Art. 191(2), second subpara., TFEU).

---

[350] Directive 2003/87/EC of the European Parliament and of the Council of October 13, 2003 establishing a scheme for greenhouse gas emission allowance trading within the Community, [2003] O.J. L275/32. Under the EU Emissions Trading Scheme, Member States are required to draw up national allocation plans for each trading period setting out how many emission rights ("allowances") each installation will receive each year. Companies that keep their emissions below the level of their allowances can sell their excess allowances; those facing difficulty in remaining within their allowance limit can take measures to reduce their emissions and/or buy extra allowances on the market. See on this Directive: ECJ, Case C-127/07 *Arcelor Atlantique et Lorraine and Others* [2008] E.C.R. I-9895.

[351] These are: (a) provisions primarily of a fiscal nature; (b) measures affecting:—town and country planning,—quantitative management of water resources or affecting, directly or indirectly, the availability of those resources,—land use, with the exception of waste management; (c) measures significantly affecting a Member State's choice between different energy sources and the general structure of its energy supply. The extension of the expression "quantitative management of water resources" by the Treaty of Nice accords with the way in which the Court of Justice confined the areas under (b) to measures relating to the management of limited resources in its quantitative aspects: ECJ, Case C-36/98 *Spain v Council* [2001] E.C.R. I-779, paras 50–53. However, the Council may define (by a unanimous vote) such of those matters as may be decided on under the ordinary legislative procedure (Art. 192(2), second subpara., TFEU). Article 192(2) TFEU applies "without prejudice to Article 114", which may serve as the legal basis for Union measures intended (in part) to protect the environment (para. 7–014, *supra*).

[352] See Decision 1600/2002/EC of the European Parliament and of the Council of July 22, 2002 laying down the Sixth Community Environment Action Programme 2002–2012, [2002] O.J. L242/1. The measures necessary for the implementation of general action programmes are to be adopted by the procedure laid down in para. 1 or 2 of Art. 192 TFEU, depending on the case (Art. 192(3), second subpara., TFEU).

[353] For a general discussion of the Member States' discretion, see Somsen, "Discretion in European Community Environmental Law: An Analysis of ECJ Case Law" (2003) C.M.L.Rev. 1413–1453.

XIV. ENERGY

Energy. In a sense, energy has been a central feature of European integration from   **11–061**
the outset: coal in the ECSC Treaty and nuclear energy in the EAEC Treaty. The
EC Treaty did not, however, confer on the Community any specific competence to
lay down the "measures in the [sphere] of energy" mentioned in Art. 3 of that
Treaty (see para. 7–005). Nevertheless, national energy policies have been affected
by numerous Union measures in the fields of agriculture, transport and the environment and national energy markets have been harmonised and liberalised as part
of the establishment of the internal market.[354]

The Treaty of Lisbon for the first time endowed the Union with express powers in
the field of energy. Union action is to ensure the functioning of the energy market,
to ensure security of energy supply in the Union,[355] to promote energy efficiency and
saving and the development of new and renewable forms of energy and to promote
the interconnection of energy networks (Art. 194(1) TFEU). In order to achieve
those objectives, the European Parliament and the Council, acting in accordance
with the ordinary legislative procedure, are to establish the necessary measures.[356]
Such measures may not, however, affect the Member States' right to determine the
conditions for exploiting their energy resources, their choice between different
energy sources or the general structure of their energy supply (Art. 194(2), second
subpara., TFEU).

XV. TOURISM AND CIVIL PROTECTION

Tourism and civil protection. Before the Lisbon Treaty, the Treaties referred to   **11–062**
measures in the sphere of civil protection and tourism (see Art. 3(u) EC] without
containing any specific competence to lay down such measures (see para. 7–005).
Nevertheless, various aspects of tourism had been the subject of harmonisation

---

[354] For this liberalisation, see para. 11–018, *supra*. See for energy, Council Decision 1999/21/EC,
Euratom of December 14, 1998 adopting a multiannual framework programme for actions in the
energy sector (1998–2002) and connected measures, [1999] O.J. L7/16, together with specific programmes adopted on the basis of Art. 308 of the EC Treaty [*now Art. 352 TFEU*]. For the relationship between EC and EAEC powers, see Trüe, "Legislative competences of Euratom and the
European Community in the energy sector: the 'Nuclear Package' of the Commission" (2003)
E.L.Rev. 664–685. See Cameron, "The internal market in energy: harnessing the new regulatory
regime" (2005) E.L.Rev. 631–648.

[355] See Baumann, "Europe's Way to Energy Security: The Outer Dimension of Energy Security: From
Power Politics to Energy Governance" (2010) E.For.Aff.Rev. 77–95; Haghigi, "Energy Security
and the Division of Competences Between the European Community and its Member States"
(2008) 14 E.L.J. 461–482.

[356] Where these measures are primarily of a fiscal nature, they are to be adopted by the Council in
accordance with a special legislative procedure, that it to say, unanimously after consulting the
European Parliament (Art. 194(3)).

measures adopted on the basis of Arts 114 and 352 TFEU [*ex Arts 95 and 308 EC*] (see para. 9–109). As for civil protection, the Council had used Art. 308 EC as the legal basis for setting up a mechanism for cooperation between the Member States and likewise for civil protection assistance interventions.[357]

The Treaty of Lisbon conferred on the Union an express power to lay down measures with respect to the tourism sector, in particular to promote the competitiveness of undertakings in that sector (Art. 195 TFEU). It also created a specific competence for civil protection, which enables the Union to encourage cooperation between the Member States with a view to improving the effectiveness of systems for preventing and protecting against natural or man-made disasters (Art. 196 TFEU). It is up to the European Parliament and the Council, acting in accordance with the ordinary legislative procedure, to establish the necessary measures (Arts 195(2) and 196(2) TFEU). In the same way as civil protection, tourism is regarded as an area where the Union is competent to support, coordinate or supplement the actions of the Member States, with the result that any harmonisation of the laws and regulations of the Member States is ruled out (see para. 7–025).

XVI. ADMINISTRATIVE COOPERATION

11–063 **Implementing Union law.** Effective implementation of Union law by the Member States is essential for the proper functioning of the Union and is therefore regarded as being a matter of common interest. The Lisbon Treaty introduced a legal basis which enables the Union to support Member States' efforts to improve their administrative capacity to implement Union law (Art. 197 TFEU). In this connection, Art. 197(2) mentions facilitating the exchange of information and exchanges of civil servants and supporting training schemes. The European Parliament and the Council, acting by means of regulations in accordance with the ordinary legislative procedure, are to establish the necessary measures (Art. 197(2) TFEU). Again, this power is regarded as a competence to support, coordinate or supplement Member States' action, whereby any harmonisation of the laws and regulations of the Member States is excluded (Arts 6(g) and 197(2) TFEU).

XVII. IMPLEMENTATION OF THE SOLIDARITY CLAUSE

11–064 **Solidarity clause.** In the wake of the attacks of March 11, 2004 in Madrid, the Heads of State or Government of the Member States adopted a declaration on

---

[357] See Council Decision 1999/847/EC of December 9, 1999 establishing a Community action programme in the field of civil protection, [1999] O.J. L327/53 and Council Decision 2007/162 (EC, Euratom) of March 5, 2007 establishing a Civil Protection Financial Instrument, [2007] O.J. L71/9 (replacing Council Decision 2001/792, [2001] O.J. L297/7).

combating terrorism[358] which referred to the solidarity clause then contained in Art. I-43 of the EU Constitution, which was later taken over by Art. 222 TFEU. Pursuant to that clause, the Union and the Member States are to act jointly in a spirit of solidarity if a Member State is the victim of a terrorist attack or of a natural or man-made disaster. To that end the Member States are to coordinate between themselves in the Council. The Council may have recourse to the structures developed under the common security and defence policy.[359] The Union is to mobilise "all the instruments at its disposal, including the military resources made available by the Member States".[360] The Council, acting by qualified majority on a joint proposal by the Commission and the High Representative of the Union for Foreign Affairs and Security Policy, is to define the arrangements for the implementation of the solidarity clause. The European Parliament will then be informed.[361] The Lisbon Treaty incorporated Art. 222 TFEU on the solidarity clause in Part Five of the TFEU on the Union's external action. However, it is clear that actions taken to prevent terrorist threats, to protect democratic institutions and the civilian population and to assist a Member State in the event of a terrorist attack or natural or man-made disaster (see Art. 222(1) TFEU) would also have an "internal" Union component.

---

[358] See the Declaration annexed to the Conclusions of the European Council held in Brussels on March 25 and 26, 2004 (referring to then Art. I-42 of the draft EU Constitution).

[359] Article 222(1) and (2) TFEU.

[360] Article 222(1) TFEU.

[361] The Council is to decide unanimously where its decision has defence implications: Art. 222(3), first subpara., TFEU, in conjunction with Art. 31(1) TEU.

CHAPTER 12

LIMITS AND EXCEPTIONS TO THE APPLICATION OF THE TREATIES

I. PERSONAL SCOPE OF THE TREATIES

Personal scope. The scope *ratione personae* of the Treaties covers, generally speaking, all who come under the jurisdiction of the Member States. As far as free movement is concerned, originally the Treaties conferred rights only on Member State nationals who were engaged in an economic activity. However, Union legislation and case law have extended enjoyment of a number of those rights to Member State nationals who are not engaged in an economic activity (and even to nationals of third countries who are dependants of nationals of Member States (see para 9–051)). Moreover, since the introduction of citizenship of the Union, the Treaties confer residence and other rights on all nationals of the Member States as citizens of the Union (see paras 8–006 *et seq.*). More generally, legislative acts adopted by the Union institutions in the various policy areas confer rights and obligations on all natural and legal persons who come within their scope of application, often without any consideration of nationality. Such persons may invoke Union law in domestic courts against other persons or against authorities of their own or another Member State.[1]

12–001

Third-country nationals. Traditionally, nationals of third countries did not enjoy any uniform status under Union law which determined their access to the territory of the Member States, their rights of residence and the activities they were allowed to carry on there. However, as a result of the abolition of checks carried out on persons at the Union's internal borders, the Member States had to agree on uniform rules on third-country nationals entering and residing in their territory. Since the Treaty of Amsterdam, the Union has initiated a common policy in the field of visas, asylum and immigration pursuant to Title IV of the EC Treaty and, since

12–002

---

[1] However, where persons invoke the Treaty provisions on free movement of persons, they may not normally rely on such provisions against authorities in their own State (that is to say, where there is a "purely internal situation") unless, in exercising free movement, they find themselves in a situation equivalent to that of a national of another Member State: paras 7–064—7–066, *supra*.

the Lisbon Treaty, this policy is based on the provisions on the area of freedom, security and justice of Title V of Part Three of the TFEU (see para. 10–003 *et seq.*). In this way, third-country nationals are subject to common rules as to entry to and residence in the territories of the Member States. However, some Member States do not take part in the adoption of those rules and are not bound by them.[2] In addition, nationals from third countries may enjoy tributary rights of free movement which accrue to them as members of a Union national's family.[3] Finally, some nationals of third countries are entitled to assert rights in these respects by virtue of conventions concluded between their countries and the Union.

Nationals of third countries may enforce the rights which they derive from Union law before the Court of Justice and the General Court on the same terms as citizens of the Union.[4] Third-country nationals with the right of residence in a Member State are entitled to have access to documents of the Union institutions and to petition the European Parliament or to make a complaint to the European Ombudsman (see paras 8–013 and 8–014).

II. TEMPORAL SCOPE OF THE TREATIES

A. ENTRY INTO FORCE OF THE TREATIES

12–003 **Entry into force.** Each of the Treaties stipulates the conditions and time of its entry into force. The entry into force of the ECSC, EEC, EAEC and EU Treaties was conditional upon their ratification by all the Contracting Parties in accordance with their respective constitutional requirements and the deposit of the instruments of ratification.[5] Ratification by all Member States was also a requirement for the entry into force of Treaties amending those Treaties (see para. 5–003) and of Treaties governing the accession of new Member States (see para. 6–011). Each Treaty specified the exact day following the deposit of the last instrument of

---

[2] See the special position of Denmark, para. 10–128, *supra*, and the exceptional status of Ireland and the United Kingdom, para. 10–129, *supra*.

[3] Paras 9–051 and 10–015, *supra*. For the extent to which nationals of third countries might rely on more rights than EU nationals, see Weiss, "Gibt es eine EU-Inländerdiskriminierung? Zur Kollision von Gemeinschaftsrecht mit Welthandelsrecht und Assoziationsrecht" (1999) EuR. 499–516.

[4] Article 263, fourth para., TFEU [*ex Art. 230, fourth para., EC*] and Art. 265, third para., TFEU [*ex Art. 232, third para., EC*] refer to "any natural or legal person".

[5] Article 99 ECSC; Art. 247 EEC; Art. 224 EAEC; Single European Act, Art. 33; EU Treaty, Art. 52; Treaty of Amsterdam, Art. 14; Treaty of Nice, Art. 12; Treaty of Lisbon, Art. 6. The ECSC Treaty provided for the instruments of ratification to be lodged with the French Government; the instruments of ratification of the subsequent Treaties were to be lodged with the Italian Government.

ratification on which it is to enter into force.[6] Unless otherwise provided, such a Treaty will apply to the future effects of situations arising prior to the date on which it entered into force.[7] Accordingly, the Court has held that, where the Act concerning the conditions of accession of a Member State contains no specific conditions with regard to the application of a provision of the Treaties, that provision must be regarded as being immediately applicable and binding on that Member State from the date of its accession, with the result that it applies to the future effects of situations arising prior to that new Member State's accession.[8] However, in order to ensure observance of the principles of legal certainty and the

---

[6] The same day under Art. 99 ECSC (namely July 23, 1952); the first day of the following month under Art. 247 EEC, Art. 224 EAEC (since the Benelux countries deposited their instruments of ratification last on December 13, 1957, this was January 1, 1958) and Art. 33 of the Single European Act. The Treaty of Amsterdam entered into force under Art. 14 on the first day of the second month following the deposit of the instrument of ratification by the last signatory State (namely May 1, 1999). The same arrangements applied to the Treaty of Nice by virtue of Art. 12 thereof (entry into force on February 1, 2003). Article 52(2) of the EU Treaty fixed an earliest date for its entry into force (January 1, 1993), failing which it was to enter into force on the first day of the month following the deposit of the instrument of ratification by the last State to do so (this proved to be November 1, 1993). The Treaty of Lisbon adopted the same system in Art. 6(2), fixing the earliest date of entry into force as January 1, 2009, failing which it was to enter into force on the first day of the month following the deposit of the last instrument of ratification (which proved to be December 1, 2009). The Accession Treaties also laid down a fixed (earliest) date for their entry into force: January 1, 1973 in the second para. of Art. 2 of the Accession Treaty of January 22, 1972 ([1972] O.J. English Spec. Ed. (I) (March 27) 5); January 1, 1981 in the second para. of Art. 2 of the Accession Treaty of May 28, 1979 ([1979] O.J. L291/9); January 1, 1986 in the first subpara. of Art. 2(2) of the Accession Treaty of June 12, 1985 ([1985] O.J. L302/9); January 1, 1995 in the first subpara. of Art. 2(2) of the Accession Treaty of June 24, 1994 ([1994] O.J. C241/13); May 1, 2004 in Art. 2(2) of the Accession Treaty of April 16, 2003 ([2003] O.J. L236/17); January 1, 2007 in Art. 4(2) of the Accession Treaty of April 25, 2005 ([2005] O.J. L157/11). For the complete references for the Accession Treaties, see paras 6–001—6–007, *supra*.
[7] ECJ, Case C-122/96 *Saldanha and MTS* [1997] E.C.R. I-5325, para. 14; ECJ, Case C-321/97 *Andersson and Andersson* [1999] E.C.R. I-3551, paras 35–46; ECJ, Case C-512/99 *Germany v Commission* [2003] E.C.R. I-845, para. 46. For the resolution of intermediate temporal problems (in particular in connection with the entry into force of Accession Treaties, see Kaleda, "Immediate Effects of Community Law in the New Member States: Is There a Place for a Consistent Doctrine?" (2004) E.L.J. 102–122). For applications in the case law, see ECJ, Case C-366/05 *Optimus* [2007] E.C.R. I-4985; ECJ, Case C-414/07 *Magoora* [2008] E.C.R. I-10921.
[8] ECJ, Case C-122/96 *Saldanha and MTS* [1997] E.C.R. I-5325, para. 14; ECJ, Case C-162/00 *Pokrzeptowicz-Meyer* [2002] E.C.R. I-1049, para. 50; ECJ, Case C-441/08 *Elektrownia Patnów* [2009] E.C.R. I-10799, para. 32. As regards Accession Treaties, the Court considers that the Act of Accession of a new Member State is based essentially on the general principle that the provisions of Community law apply *ab initio* and *in toto* to that State, derogations being allowed only in so far as they are expressly laid down by transitional provisions: ECJ, Case C-420/07 *Apostolides* [2009] E.C.R. I-3571, para. 33. However, the Court has jurisdiction to interpret the provisions of the Treaties as regards their application in a new Member State only with effect from the date of that State's accession to the Union: ECJ, Case C-302/04 *Ynos* [2006] E.C.R. I-371, para. 36; ECJ (judgment of April 15, 2010), Case C-96/08 *CIBA*, not yet reported, para. 14.

protection of legitimate expectations, the substantive rules of Community law must be interpreted as applying to situations existing before their entry into force only in so far as it follows clearly from their terms, objectives or general scheme that such effect must be given to them.[9] As regards procedural rules, they are generally held to be of immediate application.[10] Where a Treaty (or a protocol thereto) makes it necessary to adopt implementing measures, the principle of good administration requires the preliminary work leading to the adoption of those measures to be started before the entry into force of the Treaty, in order for them to be applicable from a date as close as possible to that of the entry into force of the Treaty.[11]

B. Duration of the Treaties

12–004 **Limited validity of the ECSC Treaty.** Only the ECSC Treaty was concluded for a specific period: it expired on July 23, 2002 (ECSC Treaty, Art.97). This is because the Contracting Parties regarded the ECSC as a provisional first step towards European integration (see para. 1–006). Since the tasks of the ECSC could be taken over by the EC, the ECSC Treaty was not extended.[12] As from July 24, 2002, the sectors previously covered by the ECSC Treaty became subject to the EC Treaty (now TFEU).[13] The succession of the legal framework of the EC Treaty (*lex generalis*) to that of the ECSC Treaty (*lex specialis*) was held to be part of the unity and continuity of the Community legal order.[14] The continuity of the Community legal order and the objectives which govern its functioning—notably in the field of competition—thus required that, in so far as the European Community succeeded the ECSC, it was to ensure compliance with the rights and obligations which applied *eo tempore* to both Member States and individuals under the ECSC Treaty. However, in conformity with the principles

---

[9] ECJ, Case C-162/00 *Pokrzeptowicz-Meyer* [2002] E.C.R. I-1049, para. 49; ECJ, Case C-441/08 *Elektrownia Patnów* (n. 8, *supra*) para. 33. See also CFI, Case T-348/04 *SIDE v Commission* [2008] E.C.R. II-625, paras 50–56; CFI, Case T-24/07 *ThyssenKrupp Stainless v Commission* [2009] E.C.R. II-2309, para. 85.

[10] Joined Cases 212/80 to 217/80 *Salumi and Others* [1981] E.C.R. 2735, para. 9; Case C-61/98 *De Haan* [1999] E.C.R. I-5003, para. 13; CFI, Case T-334/07 *Denka International v Commission* [2009] E.C.R. II-4025, para. 45.

[11] CFI, Joined Cases T-164/99, T-37/00 and T-38/00 *Leroy and Others v Council* [2001] E.C.R. II-1819, para. 82.

[12] See the Resolution of the Council of the European Union and the representatives of the governments of the Member States, meeting within the Council of July 20, 1998 concerning the expiry of the Treaty establishing the European Coal and Steel Community, [1998] O.J. C247/5.

[13] See, e.g., the Communication from the Commission concerning certain aspects of the treatment of competition cases resulting from the expiry of the ECSC Treaty, [2002] O.J. C152/5.

[14] CFI (judgment of July 1, 2009), Case T-24/07 *ThyssenKrupp Stainless v Commission* [2009] E.C.R. II-2309, paras 80–84.

governing the temporal application of the law, situations that were definitively established before the expiry of the ESCS Treaty had to be assessed under the substantive provisions of the ECSC Treaty even if, after the expiry of that Treaty, such assessment was to be carried out on the basis of the procedural provisions laid down under the EC Treaty.[15]

Unlimited period. The subsequent Treaties were concluded for an unlimited period (EEC Treaty, Art. 240, and EAEC Treaty, Art. 208; see also EU Treaty, Art. 51 [*now Art. 53 TEU*], Treaty of Amsterdam, Art. 13, Treaty of Nice, Art. 11, and Treaty of Lisbon, Art. 3).[16] The fact that a Union, having its own institutions and powers, was established for an unlimited duration demonstrates that the Member States intended to create a new legal order, which binds both their subjects and themselves.[17] In order to bring about the abrogation of the Treaties and, with them, the Union, the Member States may not rely unconditionally on the rule of international law that a treaty may be terminated if the parties conclude a subsequent treaty between them.[18] It appears to be contrary to Union law for the Member States simply to bring an end to European integration by means of an amendment to the Treaties or in some other manner.[19]   **12–005**

III. TERRITORIAL SCOPE OF THE TREATIES

Jurisdiction of Member States. The territorial scope of the Treaties is defined by Art. 52(1) TEU, which declares the Treaties to be applicable to all of the Member States, which are listed therein.[20] The upshot is that the territorial field of application of the Treaties is constituted by the EU Member States. Under international law, the Treaties therefore apply to all areas which are under the sovereignty or within the jurisdiction of the Member States. As far as Union legislation on checks at external borders is concerned, the Treaties expressly confirm that the Union's competence in that area is not to affect the competence of the   **12–006**

---

[15] *Ibid.*, paras 85–89; see also CFI, Case T-405/06 *ArcelorMittal Luxembourg and Others v Commission* [2009] E.C.R. II-771, paras 59–69.

[16] The TEU and TFEU also expressly state that they are concluded for an unlimited period (see Art. 53 TEU [*ex Art. 51 EU*] and Art. 356 TFEU [*ex Art. 312 EC*]).

[17] ECJ, Case 6/64 *Costa* [1964] E.C.R. 585, at 593 (para. 1–024, *supra*).

[18] For this rule, see Art. 54 of the 1969 Vienna Convention (para. 22–055, *infra*).

[19] This question is directly related to the possible substantive limitations on amending the Treaties, para. 5–011, *infra*.

[20] Article 52 was introduced by the Treaty of Lisbon. Before that, the EU Treaty did not define its territorial scope, but simply employed the expression "Member States". In contrast, Art. 299(1) of the EC Treaty (now repealed) declared that the EC Treaty was applicable to all the Member States, which were listed therein. For the EAEC Treaty, see Art. 198 EAEC.

Member States concerning the geographical demarcation, in accordance with international law, of their borders (Art. 77(4) TFEU). The territorial scope of the Treaties is further specified in Art. 355 TFEU, which contains provisions on territories with a special status under EU law, such as the Member States' overseas territories (see also Art. 51(2) TEU; see the discussion in para. 25–017).[21]

The application of the Treaties extends to the airspace and maritime waters which come under the sovereignty or within the jurisdiction of the Member States, territorial waters and, in so far as the Member State concerned lays claim to it, the fishing zone or exclusive economic zone, together with the continental shelf.[22] The Union itself accepted the international rules adopted in 1982 in the Convention on the Law of the Sea.[23] As long as the territory of Cyprus is partitioned, the *acquis communatunaire* applies, according to a protocol annexed to

---

[21] For a general discussion, see Ziller, "Flexibility in the geographical scope of EU law: diversity and differentiation in the application of substantive law on member states' territories", in De Búrca and Scott (eds), *Constitutional change in the EU—From Uniformity to Flexibility?* (Oxford, Hart Publishing, 2000), at 113–131; Ziller, "The European Union and the Territorial Scope of European Territories" (2007) 38 V.U.W.L.R. 51–62; Groux, " 'Territorialité' et droit communautaire" (1987) R.T.D.E. 5–33.

[22] Most Member States limit their territorial waters to 12 nautical miles from the baseline, except for Greece (6 nautical miles). In accordance with the Council Resolution of November 3, 1976, [1981] O.J. C105/1, the Member States concerned have set their fishing zone or an exclusive economic zone in the North Sea and the North Atlantic Ocean at 200 nautical miles. See Scovazzi, "La liberté de navigation dans la zone économique exclusive confrontée à l'attitude des Etats membres de la CEE en matière de prévention de la pollution", in Lebullenger and Le Morvan (eds), *La Communauté européenne et la mer* (Paris, Economica, 1990), 307–315. Where a State has exclusive rights over the continental shelf in respect of the exploration and the exploitation of the natural resources of the sea-bed and subsoil of the shelf, it also has exclusive fishing rights in an exclusive economic zone (*cf.* Arts 77–81 and 55–73 of the Convention on the Law of the Sea, see following n.). For the contested general application of Union law to the continental shelf, see Van der Mensbrugghe, "La CEE et le plateau continental des Etats membres", in *Mélanges F. Dehousse* (Paris/Brussels, Nathan/Labor, 1979), Vol. II, at 311–317; Michael, "L'application du droit communautaire au plateau continental des Etats membres et ses conséquences" (1983) R.M.C. 82–90. For the limitations imposed by customary international law on Union competence, see ECJ, Case C-286/90 *Poulsen and Diva Navigation* [1992] ECR I-6019, paras 21–34; for its competence in respect of the conservation of the fishery resources of the high seas, see *ibid.*, paras 9–11, and ECJ, Case C-405/92 *Mondiet* [1993] E.C.R. I-6133, paras 12–15; ECJ, Case C-25/94 *Commission v Council* [1996] E.C.R. I-1469, para. 44.

[23] United Nations Convention on the Law of the Sea, signed at Montego Bay on December 10, 1982, which was ratified by the Community (together with the Agreement of July 28, 1994 relating to the implementation of Part XI thereof) by Council Decision 98/392/EC of March 23, 1998, [1998] O.J. L179/1. See Garzón Clariana, "L'Union européenne et la Convention de 1982 sur le droit de la mer" (1995) B.T.I.R. 36–45. Nonetheless, the nature and the broad logic of the Convention prevent the Court of Justice from being able to assess the validity of a Union measure in the light of that Convention: ECJ, Case C-308/06 *Intertanko and Others* [2008] E.C.R. I-4057, paras 53–65.

the 2003 Act of Accession, only to those (southern) areas in which the Government of the Republic of Cyprus exercises effective control.[24] Within that framework, the Treaties apply to legal relationships which can be located "within the territory of the Union", by reason of the place where they are entered into or of the place where they take effect[25] or by reason of a sufficiently close link with the law of a Member State and thus the relevant rules of Union law.[26]

Territories with specific status. The Treaties provide for certain overseas territories to have a special status. As far as the French overseas departments (Guadeloupe, French Guiana, Martinique and Réunion),[27] Saint-Barthélemy and

12–007

---

[24] Article 1 of Protocol (No. 10) on Cyprus, annexed to the 2003 Act of Accession, suspends the application of the *acquis* in those areas of the Republic of Cyprus in which the Government of the Republic of Cyprus does not exercise effective control. This does not preclude application of Union rules on the recognition of judgments to those delivered by courts located in the southern area, but concerning land situated in the northern area (ECJ, Case C-420/07 *Apostolides* [2009] E.C.R. I-3571, paras 32–39). See Skoutaris, "The application of the acquis communautaire in the areas not under the effective control of the republic of Cyprus: the green line regulation" (2008) 45 C.M.L.Rev. 727–755; Bilge, "La situation juridique de Chypre dans ses deux composantes par rapport au droit communautaire" (2006) R.M.C.U.E. 586–591; Yakemtchouk, "Chypre: la réunification avortée" (2004) R.M.C.U.E. 239–296; Berramdane, "Chypre entre adhésion à l'Union européenne et réunification" (2003) R.D.U.E. 87–108; Klebes-Pelissier, "L'adhésion de la République de Chypre à l'Union européenne" (2003) R.T.D.E. 441–469. See para. 12–008 for the procedure for bringing this exceptional regime to an end.

[25] See ECJ, Case 36/74 *Walrave* [1974] E.C.R. 1405, para. 28; ECJ, Case 237/83 *Prodest* [1984] E.C.R. 3153, paras 6–7 (para. 9–058, *supra*); ECJ, Joined Cases 89, 104, 114, 116–117 and 125–129/85 *Åhlström v Commission* [1988] E.C.R. 5193, paras 16–17 (para. 11–012, *supra*); CFI, T-102/96 *Gencor v Commission* [1999] E.C.R. II-753, paras 89–108 (para. 11–016, *supra*).

[26] ECJ, Case C-214/94 *Boukhalfa* [1996] E.C.R. I-2253, para. 15 (para. 9–058, *supra*). For a definition of the legal subjects of the Union, see also Vanhamme, *Volkenrechtelijke beginselen in het Europees recht* (Groningen, Europa Law Publishing, 2001), at 131–148.

[27] The term "overseas departments" (*départements d'outre-mer* or DOM), which appeared in Art. 299(2) of the EC Treaty, no longer appears in Arts 349 and 355(2) TFEU. For these territories (not to be confused with the "overseas communities" (*collectivités d'outre-mer*), before 2003 "overseas territories" or *territoires d'outre-mer*, TOM), see Faberon and Ziller, *Droit des collectivités d'outre-mer* (Paris, LGDJ, 2007), 546 pp.; Gautron, "Le statut communautaire des DOM et des PTOM" (2006) R.A.E. 385–393; Omarjee, "Le traité d'Amsterdam et l'avenir de la politique de différenciation en faveur des départements français d'outre-mer" (1998) R.T.D.E. 515–533; Puissochet, "Aux confins de la Communauté européenne: les régions ultrapériphériques", in Rodriguez-Iglesias, Due, Schintgen and Elsen (eds), *Mélanges en hommage à Fernand Schockweiler* (Baden-Baden, Nomos, 1999), 491–509; Brial, "La place des régions ultrapériphériques au sein de l'Union européenne" (1998) C.D.E. 639–659. Initially, the EC Treaty was to be fully applicable to the French *départements d'outre mer* (DOM) only after two years; see, inter alia, ECJ, Case 148/77 *Hansen* [1978] E.C.R. 1787, paras 7–10. The third subparagraph of the former Art. 227(2) EC authorised the Council to determine specific conditions of application without derogating from the Treaty provisions mentioned in the first subparagraph of that provision.

Saint-Martin,[28] the Azores, Madeira and the Canary Islands[29] are concerned, the provisions of the Treaties apply in principle, although the Council may adopt specific measures making the application of the Treaties subject to certain conditions in view of the structural social and economic situation of those areas (Art. 349 and Art. 355(1) TFEU [*ex Art. 299(2) EC*]).

Part Four of the TFEU (Arts 198 to 204 TFEU [*ex Arts 182 to 188 EC*]) contains special association arrangements for the overseas countries and territories ("OCTs") listed in Annex II to the Treaties (Art. 355(2) TFEU [*ex Art. 299(3) EC*]).[30] However, most of the countries and territories listed in the original annex to the EEC Treaty have since become parties, as independent States, to the ACP-EC Conventions (see para. 25–024). In 1984, an amendment to the Treaties caused them not to apply to Greenland as from February 1, 1985.[31] In accordance

---

Consequently, the Council was not empowered to authorise France to collect charges in a DOM—contrary to "free movement of goods" mentioned in the first subparagraph—on products coming from other French departments (ECJ, Joined Cases C-363/93 and C-407/93 to C-411/93 *Lancry* [1994] E.C.R. I-3957, paras 36–38), but this did not prevent the Council from authorising exemptions from those charges subject to strict conditions (ECJ, Case C-212/96 *Chevassus-Marche* [1998] E.C.R. I-743, paras 1–54). For other decisions, see the Commission's answer of February 4, 1985 to question 1839/84 (Poniatowski), [1985] O.J. C263/1.

[28] The Lisbon Treaty added Saint-Barthélemy and Saint Martin to the territories listed in Art. 299(2) EC. Both territories were formerly part of a French overseas department (Guadeloupe), but constitute, since 2007, separate overseas communities. However, unlike the other French overseas communities, they were not mentioned in Annex II to the Treaties. Consequently, their status under Union law did not change with the Lisbon Treaty. However, as from January 1, 2012, Saint-Barthélemy ceases to be an outermost region of the Union and shall have the status of overseas country or territory referred to in Part Four of TFEU pursuant to European Council Decision 2010/718/EU of October 29, 2010 amending the status with regard to the European Union of the island of Saint-Barthélemy, [2010] O.J. L325/4.

[29] With regard to the Canary Islands, see Council Regulation (EEC) No. 1911/91 of June 26, 1991 on the application of the provisions of Community law to the Canary Islands, [1991] O.J. L171/1. For an application, see ECJ (Order of April 16, 2008), Case C-186/07 *Club Náutico de Gran Canaria* [2008] E.C.R. I-60, para. 18 (common system of VAT not applicable to the Canary Islands). The derogation provided for in Art. 25 of the 1985 Act of Accession and Protocol No. 2 thereto applied to the Canary Islands, just as it applied to Ceuta and Melilla. See ECJ, Case C-45/94 *Ayuntamiento de Ceuta* [1995] E.C.R. I-4385, paras 14–21 and 42.

[30] For the list of those areas, see para. 25–017, *infra*. For the purposes of the application of certain provisions of Union legislation, work performed in such an area may be equated with work carried out in the territory of the Member State concerned: ECJ, Case C-248/96 *Grahame and Hollanders* [1997] E.C.R. I-6407, para. 36 (see para. 9–058, *infra*). The second subparagraph of Art. 355(2) TFEU [*ex Art. 299(3) EC*] excludes countries and territories having special relations with the United Kingdom which are not listed in Annex II; this referred only to Hong Kong.

[31] Treaty of March 13, 1984 amending, with regard to Greenland, the Treaties establishing the European Communities, [1985] O.J. L29/1. In a referendum held on February 23, 1982, the people of Greenland expressed the desire to leave the Community, whereupon the Danish Government applied to have the Treaty amended. However, Greenland remains part of Denmark and therefore falls by virtue of Arts 2, 3 and 4 of that Treaty under the association arrangements provided for in Part Four of the TFEU. For the specific legal regime governing the relationship between the EC and Greenland, see Decision 2006/526/EC of July 17, 2006 on relations between the European

with a Protocol to the EEC Treaty, the Netherlands declared that the EEC Treaty was not applicable to Surinam and the Netherlands Antilles—territories which since have become independent or listed in Annex II fall under the association arrangements.[32]

The Treaties are also stated to be applicable to European territories for whose external relations a Member State is responsible,[33] which boils down in practice to Gibraltar.[34] The 1972 Act of Accession provided that major areas of Community law should not apply to Gibraltar,[35] in particular free movement of goods and harmonisation measures adopted for that purpose.[36] The other provisions of the Treaties fully apply.[37]

The Treaties exclude the Faroe Islands[38] from their scope and provide for special arrangements for the Åland Islands (located between Sweden and

---

Community on the one hand, and Greenland and the Kingdom of Denmark on the other, [2006] O.J. L208/28. See also the Fisheries Partnership Agreement between the European Community and the Government of Denmark and the Home Rule Government of Greenland, concluded on behalf of the Community by Council Decision 2006/1006/EC of December 21, 2006, [2006] O.J. L411/27.

[32] Surinam, which became independent on June 16, 1976, has acceded to the ACP-EC Convention. The association arrangements provided for in Part Four of the EEC Treaty (now Part Four TFEU) apply to the Netherlands Antilles by virtue of the Convention of November 13, 1962 amending Part Four of the EEC Treaty, [1964] O.J. 2414 and the countries of the former Netherlands Antilles which have since January 1, 1986 (Aruba) and October 10, 2010 (Curaçao and Sint Maarten)—like the Netherlands— the status of an autonomous "country" within the Kingdom of the Netherlands. See the Rijkswet van 7 september 2010 tot wijziging van het Statuut voor het Koninkrijk der Nederlanden in verband met de wijziging van der staatkundige hoedanigheid van de eilandgebieden van de Nederlandse Antillen, *Stb.* 333. With respect to voting right for the elections to the European Parliament, see ECJ, Case C-300/04 *Eman and Sevinger* [2006] E.C.R. I-8055 (see para. 13–018, *infra*).

[33] Article 355(3) TFEU [*ex Art. 229(4) EC*]; Art. 198, second para., EAEC. Before the entry into force of the Lisbon Treaty, the EU Treaty (in contrast to the EC Treaty) was not stated to be applicable to territories for the foreign relations of which a Member State is responsible. Acts adopted pursuant to the EU Treaty were, therefore, where appropriate, expressly declared to be applicable to Gibraltar. See, e.g., Council Decision 2003/642/JHA of July 22, 2003 concerning the application to Gibraltar of the Convention on the fight against corruption involving officials of the European Communities or officials of Member States of the European Union, [2003] O.J. L226/27.

[34] The Treaties expressly exclude other territories, which could qualify (e.g. the Channel Islands and the Isle of Man; see n. 41, *infra*). Nor are they considered to apply to Andorra (for the EC-Andorra Agreement, see para. 25–009, *infra*).

[35] See Art. 28 (exclusion of measures relating to certain agricultural products and to the harmonisation of turnover tax) and Annex I(I) (customs legislation) of the 1972 Act of Accession.

[36] ECJ, Case C-30/01 *Commission v United Kingdom* [2003] E.C.R. I-9481, paras 47–59 (this follows from Gibraltar's exclusion from the customs territory of the Union).

[37] ECJ, Case C-349/03 *Commission v United Kingdom* [2005] E.C.R. I-7321, paras 40–54 (provisions on VAT and excise duties), with a case note by Stanley (2007) C.M.L.Rev. 195–203; CFI, Joined Cases T-195/01 and T-207/01 *Government of Gibraltar v Commission* [2002] E.C.R. II-2309, para. 12. With respect to voting right for the elections to the European Parliament, see ECJ, Case C-145/04 *Spain v United Kingdom* [2006] E.C.R. I-7917 (see para. 13–018, *infra*). Gibraltar is now no longer excluded from the scope of the elections for the European Parliament (see para. 13–018, *infra*).

[38] Article 355(5)(a) TFEU [*ex Art. 299(6)(a) EC*], and Art. 198, fourth para., EAEC, indent (a). The EU Treaty had removed from those articles Denmark's option, which was open to it until the end of 1975 but never exercised, to declare the Treaties applicable to the Faroe Islands.

Finland),[39] the UK Sovereign Base Areas in Cyprus (Akrotiri and Dhekelia),[40] and the Channel Islands and the Isle of Man, which are Crown dependencies, but not part of the United Kingdom.[41]

12–008   **Change in territorial jurisdiction.** Apart from those specific arrangements for particular areas, the application of the Treaties coincides with the territorial jurisdiction of the Member States under international law. Union law is automatically applicable to areas acquired by a Member State as a result of a change in its frontiers and it deals with territories ceded by a Member State in the same way as it would with a third country. Such changes do not require any amendment of the Treaties,[42] but consultation as between the Member States is advisable.[43] Accordingly, the European Council decided that it was unnecessary to amend the Treaties when the *Länder* of the former German Democratic Republic acceded to the Federal Republic of Germany on October 3, 1990 and therefore to the Communities.[44] The Council adopted a number of adjusting and transitional

---

[39] Article 355(4) TFEU [*ex Art. 299(5) EC*], and Art. 198, third para., EAEC, provide that the Treaties are applicable to the Åland Islands in accordance with the provisions of Protocol No. 2 to the 1994 Act of Accession (see [1995] O.J. L75/18).

[40] Article 355(5)(b) TFEU [*ex Art. 299(6)(b) EC*], as amended by Protocol No. 3 to the 2003 Act of Accession, [2003] O.J. L236/940 provides that the Treaty is to apply to the "United Kingdom Sovereign Base Areas of Akrotiri and Dhekelia in Cyprus" only to the extent necessary to ensure the implementation of the exceptional arrangements set out in that protocol. After Cyprus became independent in 1960, the United Kingdom has continued to maintain two military bases in southern Cyprus; see the Commission's Opinion on Cyprus's application to accede (1993) EC Bull. Suppl. 5, 12.

[41] Article 355(5)(c) TFEU [*ex Art. 299(6)(c) EC*], and Art. 198, fourth para., indent (c), EAEC. The Treaties apply to the Channel Islands and the Isle of Man only to the extent necessary to ensure the implementation of the special arrangements for those islands set out in Protocol No. 3 to the 1972 Act of Accession. See ECJ, Case C-171/96 *Pereira Roque* [1998] E.C.R. I-4605, paras 34–58; ECJ, Case C-293/02 *Jersey Produce Marketing Organisation* [2005] E.C.R. I-09543, paras 35–41. See further Sutton, "Jersey's changing constitutional relationship with Europe" (2005) 9 *The Jersey Law Review* 1.

[42] The Community accepted the independence of Algeria in 1962 without amending Art. 227(2) EEC, which treated that country as a French overseas department. The EU Treaty deleted the reference to Algeria. The transfer of the Saar to the Federal Republic of Germany necessitated an amendment to the Treaties, since Germany sought a change in the allocation of votes (n. 31 to para. 5–010, *supra*).

[43] For the general obligation to consult other Member States, see Ehlermann, "Mitgliedschaft in der Europäischen Gemeinschaft—Rechtsproblem der Erweiterung, der Mitgliedschaft und der Verkleinerung" (1984) EuR. 113, at 118–119.

[44] See the conclusions of the Dublin European Council of April 28, 1990 (1990) 4 EC Bull. point I.5. Under the Protocol annexed to the EEC Treaty on German internal trade and connected problems, the FRG was entitled to regard trade with the GDR as part of German internal trade. Nevertheless, the GDR did not form part of the Community and goods from the GDR were not regarded as originating in the FRG: ECJ, Case 14/74 *Norddeutsches Vieh- und Fleischkontor* [1974] E.C.R. 899, para. 6.

measures in the light of German reunification.[45] A similar solution is foreseen for Cyprus in the event that a settlement is found for bringing the partition of the island to an end. By means of a protocol annexed to the 2003 Act of Accession, the Council, acting unanimously, is then to decide on the adaptations to the terms concerning the accession of Cyprus with regard to the Turkish Cypriot Community.[46]

The territorial field of application of the Treaties also adjusts itself where a Member State changes the status of a territory under its sovereignty.[47] Nevertheless, in some of these cases the Member States have revised the Treaties.[48] This not only ensures acceptance on the part of the Member States, but also provides a democratic foundation for the acceptance into the Union, or the loss, of what is often a substantial population. To ensure involvement of other Member States in changes in the status of overseas Danish, French or Netherlands territories, the Treaty of Lisbon enabled the European Council, on the initiative

---

[45] See the package of legislation adopted by the Council on October 4, 1990, [1990] O.J. L353; Westlake, "The Community Express Service: The Rapid Passage of Emergency Legislation on German Unification" (1991) C.M.L.Rev. 599–614. See also Drobnig, "Die Eingliederung der ehemaligen DDR in die Europäischen Gemeinschaften" (1991) Z.f.R.V. 321–332; Grabitz, "L'unité allemande et l'intégration européenne" (1991) C.D.E. 423–441; Glaesner, "Les problèmes de droit communautaire soulevés par l'unification allemande" (1990) R.M.C. 647–654; Jacqué, "L'unification de l'Allemagne et la Communauté européenne" (1990) R.G.D.I.P. 997–1018.

[46] Protocol (No. 10) on Cyprus annexed to the 2003 Act of Accession, Art. 4. After the rejection of the proposed plan for reunification, on the eve of accession, the Council laid down measures to facilitate trade and other links between the northern and southern areas of the island, whilst ensuring that appropriate standards of protection were maintained as to the security of the European Union with regard to illegal immigration, threats to public order and public health. See Council Regulation (EC) No. 866/2004 of April 29, 2004 on a regime under Art. 2 of Protocol No. 10 of the Act of Accession, [2004] O.J. L161/128 (republished with *corrigendum*: [2004] O.J. L206/51; most recently amended by Council Regulation No. 587/2008 of June 16, 2008, [2008] O.J. L163/1). For the extraordinary elections of the representatives in the European Parliament to be held in the whole of Cyprus in the event of a settlement of the Cyprus problem, see Council Decision 2004/511/EC of June 10, 2004 concerning the representation of the people of Cyprus in the European Parliament in the case of a settlement of the Cyprus problem, [2004] O.J. L211/22. See further, Rumelili, "Transforming conflicts on EU borders: the case of Greek-Turkish relations" (2007) 45 J.C.M.S. 105–126.

[47] In 1976 France granted Saint-Pierre-et-Miquelon, which were associated with the Community as *territoires d'outre mer* (TOM), the status of *départements d'outre mer* (DOM) by Law No. 76–664 of July 19, 1976. As a result, the islands became part of the Community by virtue of Art. 227(2) EEC. Similarly, they left the Community in 1985 when, by Law No. 85–595 of June 11, 1985, the islands resumed the status of TOMs.

[48] See the Convention on the Netherlands Antilles (n. 32, *supra*), by which the Member States sought to introduce in a Protocol to the EEC Treaty special arrangements for imports of petroleum products refined in the Netherlands Antilles ([1964] J.O. 2416; now Protocol (No. 31) annexed to the TEU and TFEU, [2010] O.J. C83/315), and the Treaty on the withdrawal of Greenland (n. 31, *supra*).

of the Member State concerned, to adopt a decision amending the status, with regard to the Union, of those countries and territories (Art. 355(6) TFEU)— which has been done for the French island of Saint-Barthélemy.[49]

Where a new State wishes to join the Union, this can occur only in accordance with the accession procedure laid down in Art. 49 TEU (see para. 6–008).

12–009   **Acts with specific territorial scope.** Acts of the Union institutions in principle cover the same geographical field of application as the Treaty on which they are based. Member States' extension of their exclusive fishing zones to 200 miles off their North Sea and North Atlantic coasts therefore resulted in a commensurate extension of the field of application of Union measures relating to a structural policy for the fishing industry.[50] Nevertheless, Union legislation often defines its own field of application. For instance, customs law does not apply to certain areas coming under the jurisdiction of a Member State.[51] However, the fact that particular areas have an exceptional status under the Treaties does not mean that the Court of Justice has no jurisdiction to give preliminary rulings on questions referred by courts in those areas, even though Union law is only partially in force there.[52] Conversely, secondary Union law may also be applicable in areas which do not belong to the Member States. For instance, Monaco comes within the customs territory of the Union,[53] other Union acts are declared by agreement to be applicable to Monaco[54] and Union legislation on euro banknotes and coins applies in Monaco, San Marino, the Vatican City and some other areas which have obtained by agreement the right to use the euro as their currency unit.[55] As

---

[49] This concerns the territories listed in Arts 355(1) and (2). The European Council is to act unanimously after consulting the Commission: for Saint-Barthélemy, see n. 28 *supra*.

[50] ECJ, Case 61/77 *Commission v Ireland* [1978] E.C.R. 417, paras 45–50. See also ECJ, Joined Cases 3, 4 and 6/76 *Kramer* [1976] E.C.R. 1279, paras 30–33.

[51] For the customs territory of the Union, see Art.3 of Council Regulation (EEC) No. 2913/92 of October 12, 1992 establishing the Community Customs Code, [1992] O.J. L302/1, most recently amended by Commission Regulation (EC) No. 414/2009 of April 30, 2009, [2009] O.J. L125/6 (see para. 9–026, *supra*).

[52] ECJ, Joined Cases C-100/89 and C-101/89 *Kaefer and Procacci* [1990] E.C.R. I-4647, paras 8–10 (Polynesia, a *territoire d'outre mer*); ECJ, Case C-355/89 *Barr and Montrose Holdings* [1991] E.C.R. I-3479, paras 6–10 (Isle of Man).

[53] Under Art. 3(2) of Regulation No. 2913/92 (see n. 86 to para. 9–026), the Principality of Monaco, as its territory is defined in a bilateral convention signed with France, forms part of the customs territory. Before a customs agreement was signed with the EC (para. 25–009, *infra*), San Marino also belonged to the customs territory of the Community. The Vatican City and Andorra do not belong to the customs territory (but see the EC-Andorra Agreement, see para. 25–009, *infra*).

[54] See the Agreement on the application of certain Community acts on the territory of the Principality of Monaco, approved by Council Decision 2003/885/EC of November 17, 2003, [2003] O.J. L332/41.

[55] See para. 11–040, *supra*. On the monetary level, special relations existed between France and Monaco and between Italy and San Marino and the Vatican City. On behalf of the Union, France and Italy conducted the respective negotiations as a result of which those three States obtained the right to use the euro as their currency unit.

a result of agreements with third countries, a substantial part of Union law also applies in third countries, in particular the States belonging to the European Economic Area (see paras 25–029 *et seq.*).

Extraterritorial effects. The application of Union law sometimes depends on factors situated outside the territorial jurisdiction of the Member States. That is generally the case with independent or conventional measures of Union commercial policy. Union measures may impose obligations—even on non-Union undertakings—having to be complied with outside the territory of the Union.[56] Union competition policy may be applied to undertakings which are established outside the Union and not incorporated under the laws of one of the Member States but which act in the Union (see paras 11–012 and 11–016).   **12–010**

IV. EXCEPTIONS TO THE APPLICATION OF THE TREATIES

A. SAFEGUARD CLAUSES

Internal or external security. Various articles of the Treaties empower the Commission to authorise a Member State temporarily not to comply in full with its Union obligations.[57] Articles 346 to 348 TFEU [*ex Arts 296 to 298 EC*] allow the Member States themselves to deviate from their general Treaty obligations on grounds of internal or external security.[58] Articles 346 and 347 TFEU authorise a Member State to take unilateral measures where "the essential interests of its security" are at stake (Art. 346(1) TFEU) or,   **12–011**

> "in the event of serious internal disturbances affecting the maintenance of law and order, in the event of war, serious international tension constituting a threat of war or in order to carry out obligations entered into by the Member State for the purpose of maintaining peace and international security" (Art. 347 TFEU).

---

[56] See, for example, ECJ, Case C-177/95 *Ebony Maritime and Loten Navigation* [1997] E.C.R. I-1111, paras 15–27 (sanction imposed in respect of the conduct of vessels on the high seas— conduct giving good reason to believe that a breach of sanctions imposed on Yugoslavia might result—irrespective of whether the vessels were flying the flag of a Member State).

[57] See Art. 114(6) TFEU [*ex Art. 95(6) EC*]; Art. 143(3) TFEU [*ex Art. 119(3) EC*]; Art. 348, first para., TFEU [*ex Art. 298, first para., EC*]. See Mortelmans, "Excepties bij non-tarifaire intracommunautaire belemmeringen: assimilatie in het nieuwe EG-Verdrag?" (1997) S.E.W. 182 at 185–186.

[58] See Trybus, "The Limits of European Community Competence for Defence" (2004) E.For.Aff.Rev. 189–217 and "The EC Treaty as an Instrument of European Defence Integration: Judicial Scrutiny of Defence and Security Exceptions" (2002) C.M.L.Rev. 1347–1372; Peers, "National Security and European Law" (1996) Y.E.L. 363, at 379–387. However, those provisions do not authorise any derogation from the principles of liberty, democracy and respect for human rights and fundamental freedoms (ECJ, Joined Cases C-402/05 P and C-415/05 P *Kadi and Al Barakaat International Foundation* [2008] E.C.R. I-6351, paras 302–303).

In such a situation, a Member State may withhold information which it would otherwise be bound to provide (Art. 346(1)(a) TFEU) or take such measures as it considers necessary which are connected with the production of or trade in weapons, munitions and war material (Art. 346(1)(b) TFEU). The Council adopted a list, by a unanimous vote, of the products to which Art. 346 TFEU applies.[59] One example of the effects of this exceptional provision is that where a Member State adopts an aid measure in favour of activities relating to products appearing on that list, the Commission cannot initiate an investigation procedure under Art. 108 TFEU [ex Art. 88 EC].[60] No similar exceptions exist under the EAEC Treaty. In fact, the Court has held that activities falling within the military sphere fall outside the scope of that Treaty.[61]

Just as in the case of the exceptions provided for in the TFEU with regard to the free movement of goods, persons, services and capital (see Arts 25, 45(3) and (4), 51–52 and 65 TFEU [ex Arts 30, 39(3) and (4), 45–46 and 58 EC]), Arts 346 and 347 TFEU must be strictly construed.[62] These articles leave Member States free to a degree to estimate themselves whether there is a risk to security and to what extent the risk justifies departing from the obligations laid down by the Treaty. However, a Member State which seeks to rely on those exceptions is to furnish evidence that the exemptions in question are proportionate to the alleged risk to security.[63] In this connection, the Court has held that the confidentiality obligation by which Union and national officials are bound in the implementation of the Union customs system is capable of protecting the essential security interests of

---

[59] The list was published as the Council's answer of September 27, 2001 to question E-1324/01 (Staes), [2001] O.J. C364E/85; a detailed list was published in connection with a CFSP Code of Conduct for Weapons Exports; see now the common list of military equipment covered by the European Union code of conduct on arms export, adopted by the Council on February 23, 2009, [2009] O.J. C65/1. See Trybus, *European Defence Procurement* (The Hague, Kluwer Law International, 1999), 331 pp.; Vincentelli-Meria, "Vers une normalisation de l'application de l'article 296 du TCE dans le secteur des industries d'armement" (2001) R.M.C.U.E 96–101. The export regime adopted by the Council on "dual-use goods" (civil and military use) expressly provides that it does not affect Art. 296 EC [now Art. 346 TFEU]: Art. 26 of Regulation No. 428/2009 of May 5, 2009 setting up a Community regime for the control of exports, transfer, brokering and transit of dual-use items, [2009] O.J. L134/1.

[60] See CFI, Case T-26/01 *Fiocchi munizioni v Commission* [2003] E.C.R. II-3951, paras 58–59.

[61] ECJ, Case C-61/03 *Commission v United Kingdom* [2005] E.C.R. I-2477, paras 35–45.

[62] ECJ, Case 13/68 *Salgoil* [1968] E.C.R. 453, at 463; Case 222/84 *Johnston* [1986] E.C.R. 1651, paras 25–26; ECJ, Case C-414/97 *Commission v Spain* [1999] E.C.R. I-5585, para. 21; ECJ, Case C-337/05 *Commission v Italy* [2008] E.C.R. I-2173, paras 42–52; ECJ, Case C-157/06 *Commission v Italy* [2008] E.C.R. I-7313, paras 22–33; ECJ, Case C-284/05 *Commission v Finland* [2009] E.C.R. I-11705, para. 46.

[63] Trybus, "The EC Treaty as an Instrument of European Defence Integration: Judicial Scrutiny of Defence and Security Exceptions" (2002) C.M.L.Rev. 1347, at 1364–1369. According to the Court of Justice, the Member State must prove that reliance on Art. 346 TFEU is necessary to protect the essential interests of its security: ECJ, Case C-414/97 *Commission v Spain* [1999] E.C.R. I-5585, para. 22; ECJ, Case C-284/05 *Commission v Finland* (n. 62, *supra*), paras 47–49.

Member States.[64] Article 347 TFEU refers to Member States consulting each other with a view to taking steps together to prevent the functioning of the common market being affected by a measure which a Member State feels itself called upon to take. The consultation with other Member States may make unilateral national measures unnecessary should the outcome of the consultation be a decision to adopt a Union measure.[65] If the national measures have the effect of distorting the conditions of competition, the Commission, together with the State concerned, will examine how these measures can be adjusted to the rules laid down in the Treaty (Art. 348, first para., TFEU).[66] In the event that the Member State makes "improper use" of the powers provided for in Arts 346 and 347 TFEU, the Commission[67] or any Member State may bring the matter directly before the Court of Justice, by way of derogation from the procedure laid down in Arts 258 and 259 TFEU [*ex Arts 226 and 227 EC*]. The Court is to give its ruling *in camera* (Art. 348, second para., TFEU). Pending its decision on the substance, the Court of Justice may make an order prescribing interim measures.[68] The procedure provided for in Art. 348, second paragraph, TFEU is applicable only where "improper use" of the powers provided for in Arts 346 and 347 TFEU is alleged, and does not prevent the Commission from bringing an action against a Member State under Art. 258 TFEU for failure to fulfil other Treaty obligations.[69]

---

[64] ECJ, Case C-284/05 *Commission v Finland* (n. 62, *supra*), para. 51; see also the parallel cases of the same date: Case C-294/05 *Commission v Sweden* [2009] E.C.R. I-11777; Case C-372/05 *Commission v Germany* [2009] E.C.R. I-11801; Case C-387/05 *Commission v Italy*, not yet reported; Case C-409/05 *Commission v Greece* not yet reported; Case C-461/05 *Commission v Denmark* not yet reported; Case C-239/06 *Commission v Italy*, not yet reported, and ECJ (judgment of March 4, 2010), Case C-38/06 *Commission v Portugal*, not yet reported.

[65] See Gilsdorf (n. 72, *infra*), at 21; Koutrakos, "Is Article 297 EC a 'Reserve of Sovereignty'?" (2000) C.M.L.Rev. 1339–1362. For the application of Art. 347 TFEU in the case of economic sanctions, see para. 25–049, *infra*.

[66] This will be the case, for example, where a national aid measure benefits activities connected with products not on the Council's list of April 15, 1958 or having a "dual use": CFI, Case T-26/01 *Fiocchi munizioni v Commission* [2003] E.C.R. II-3951, para. 63. For the Commission's powers in this connection, see *ibid.*, paras 74–75.

[67] In this connection, the Commission has to look after the Union's interests, not those of third countries: ECJ (order of June 29, 1994), Case C-120/94 R *Commission v Greece* [1994] E.C.R. I-3037, paras 99–101.

[68] *Ibid.*, paras 38–45 (with a case note by Vanhamme (1994/95) Col.J.E.L. 134–139). In this first application of Art. 298 EC [*now Art. 348 TFEU*], the Commission accused Greece of having infringed rules of the common commercial policy without being in one of the situations for which Art. 297 EC [*now Art. 347 TFEU*] provided for exceptions, by imposing a ban on imports and trade in products from the former Yugoslav Republic of Macedonia. The Court of Justice did not have to rule on the substance, since the Commission discontinued the proceedings in view of the conclusion of an agreement between Greece and Macedonia; see ECJ (order of 19 March 1996), Case C-120/94 *Commission v Greece* [1996] E.C.R. I-1513. Advocate-General F.G. Jacobs took the view that Greece had not abused the then Art.297 EC: *ibid.*, at I-1525–1533; see also Peers (n. 58, *supra*), at 384–387.

[69] ECJ, Case C-372/05 *Commission v Germany* (n. 64, *supra*), paras 28–30.

The derogations laid down in Arts 346–348 TFEU do not take away from the Union any substantive competence to deal with security aspects in a Union act. Moreover, a measure taken on grounds of public security does not necessarily fall outside the scope of Union law. Accordingly, decisions taken by the Member States with regard to the organisation of their armed forces are not outside the application of Union law, notably where it is a question of respecting the principle of the equal treatment of men and women in employment relationships, in particular with regard to access to military occupations.[70] Nevertheless, the Court of Justice makes an exception for the application of Union law to decisions of Member States relating to military organisation whose aim is the defence of their territory or of their essential interests.[71] Where the Union itself has laid down rules, however, it may be hard for a Member State to invoke exceptional circumstances.[72]

12–012 **Transitional derogations.** During the transitional period which was provided for in the EEC Treaty, a Member State could apply to the Commission for authorisation to take protective measures if difficulties arose which were serious and liable to persist in any sector of the economy or which could bring about serious deterioration in the economic situation of a given area.[73] Every Accession Treaty provides for a transitional period during which similar protective measures can be taken at the request of an acceding Member State.[74]

B. DIFFERENTIATED INTEGRATION

12–013 **Differentiated integration.** In some circumstances the application of Union law may lead to difficulties in certain Member States or parts of Member States. In

---

[70] ECJ, Case C-273/97 *Sirdar* [1999] E.C.R. I-7403, para. 19, and ECJ, Case C-285/98 *Kreil* [2000] E.C.R. I-69, para. 16.

[71] ECJ, Case C-186/01 *Dory* [2003] E.C.R. I-2479, paras 35–42 (Germany's decision to ensure its defence in part by compulsory military service limited to men is the expression of a choice of military organisation to which Union law is not applicable). For critical observations, see Trybus (2003) C.M.L.Rev. 1269–1280; for a somewhat favourable view, see Koutrakos (2003) Mod.L.Rev. 759–768; Anagnostaras (2003) E.L.Rev. 713–722; Dietrich (2003) D.ö.V. 883–889.

[72] See ECJ, Case C-124/95 *Centro-Com* [1997] E.C.R. I-81, para. 46 (where exceptions to the Union export regime were relied on; see para. 25–007, *infra*). See also Gilsdorf, "Les réserves de sécurité du traité CEE, à la lumière du traité sur l'Union européenne" (1994) R.M.C.U.E. 17, at 18–19 and 23–25, where it is argued that a CFSP joint action may also raise the hurdles which a Member State must overcome in order to invoke such safeguard clauses.

[73] Article 226(1) EEC; for applications, see ECJ, Case 13/63 *Italy v Commission* [1963] E.C.R. 165, at 175–179; ECJ, Joined Cases 73 and 74/63 *Handelsvereniging Rotterdam* [1964] E.C.R. 1, at 11–14; ECJ, Case 37/70 *Rewe-Zentrale* [1971] E.C.R. 23, paras 2–19; ECJ, Case 72/72 *Einfuhr-und Vorratsstelle Getreide* [1973] E.C.R. 377, paras 4–20.

[74] See Art. 135 of the 1972 Act of Accession; Art. 130 of the 1979 Act of Accession; Art. 379 of the 1985 Act of Accession; Art. 152 of the 1994 Act of Accession; Art. 37 of the 2003 Act of Accession; Art. 36 of the 2005 Act of Accession. See Garcia-Duran Huet, "Le traité d'Athènes, un traité d'adhésion comme les autres?" (2004) R.M.C.U.E. 290–292; Van Haersolte, "Het Toetredingsverdrag 2003 (alias het Verdrag van Athene)" (2003) N.T.D.E. 301, at 308–310.

order to avoid or resolve such difficulties, provisions of Union law sometimes contain exceptions for certain Member States, which must respect the principles of equal treatment and proportionality.[75] As a result, the process of European integration is not needlessly hampered on account of difficulties in one or more Member States. It has been accepted that as long as all Member States fully subscribe to the objectives of the integration process, Member States struggling with generally acknowledged difficulties may be authorised temporarily not to take part in Union policy in certain areas, whilst the other Member States provide support in order to enable the Member State or States concerned to get to grips with the situation.[76] Such "differentiated integration" can be traced back to the transitional arrangements applied on the accession of Member States (see para. 6–010) and the derogations granted to Member States not fulfilling the criteria for entry to the third stage of EMU (see para. 11–041). The technique is also frequently invoked in connection with the possible accession of new Member States which are not yet in a position to implement all the Union obligations.[77]

In addition, the Member States have accepted forms of integration whereby some Member States may permanently withdraw from the realisation of intended objectives.[78] The EU Treaty allowed Denmark and the United Kingdom to opt out from participating in the third stage of EMU (see para. 11–042). The United Kingdom, Ireland and Denmark have the right not to take part in Union measures adopted pursuant to Title V of Part Three of the TFEU (see paras 10–028—10–029). The Lisbon Treaty also granted the United Kingdom the possibility not to accept the full powers of the Commission and the Court of Justice with respect

---

[75] For the principle of equal treatment, see ECJ, Case 153/73 *Holtz & Willemsen v Council and Commission* [1974] E.C.R. 675, paras 13–14, and para. 7–050, *supra*; for the principle of proportionality, see para. 7–035 *et seq*. See also Lenaerts and Van Nuffel, "Advanced Integration and the Principle of Equality of Member States Within the European Union", in Kaddous and Auer (eds), *Les principes fondamentaux de la Constitution européenne* (Helbing & Lichtenhahn/Bruylant/L.G.D.J., 2006), 245–276; Andersen, "Differentiated integration: what is it and how much can the EU accommodate" (2006) 28 *European Integration* 313–330.

[76] See already the Tindemans Report on European Union (1976) EC Bull. Suppl. 1, 22 (new approach proposed to economic and monetary policy); Ehlermann, "How Flexible is Community Law? An Unusual Approach to the Concept of 'Two Speeds'" (1984) Michigan L.Rev. 1274–1293; Langeheine, "Abgestufte Integration" (1983) EuR. 227–280; Grabitz and Langeheine, "Legal Problems Related to a Proposed 'Two-Tier System' of Integration within the Community" (1981) C.M.L.Rev. 33–48.

[77] See, inter alia, Fastenrath, "Die Struktur der erweiterten Europäischen Union" and Lautenschlager, "Die Struktur der erweiterten Europäischen Union" (1994) EuR. Beiheft 1, 101–126 and 127–146, respectively (and the discussion at 147–150, *ibid.*). For the problems associated with differentiated integration, see Ehlermann, "Différenciation accrue ou uniformité renforcée?" (1995) 3 R.M.U.E. 191–218; Maillet, "Convergence et géométrie variable; l'organisation du fonctionnement de l'Union européenne diversifiée est à repenser" (1995) R.M.C.U.E. 145–159.

[78] For some critical comments, see Curtin, "The Constitutional Structure of the Union: A Europe of Bits and Pieces" (1993) C.M.L.Rev. 17, at 51–52; Whiteford, "Social Policy After Maastricht" (1993) E.L.Rev. 216–217 (concerning the Social Agreement).

to acts adopted on the basis of the former Title VI of the EU Treaty on the expiry of the five-year period during which those acts preserve the status they had before the Lisbon Treaty entered into force (see para. 10–029). By virtue of a protocol, Denmark is not to participate in the elaboration and implementation of the European Security and Defence Policy (ESDP), and in particular in CFSP measures which have defence implications (see para. 25–046). Where decision-making is confined to particular Member States, the voting requirements in the European Council and the Council have to be adjusted, but the other institutions and bodies of the Union retain their usual composition and mode of operation (see para. 19–001). Consequently, the Court of Justice can rule in its normal composition on disputes concerning the validity and interpretation of Union acts adopted in this way.[79] In so far as the exceptional status of the Member State concerned stems from a political decision on its part not to collaborate with the other Member States in the field in question, it may become involved simply by intimating the wish to do so.[80]

Often, the organisation of differentiated integration leads to complex legal arrangements. That was the case with the system (now abrogated) through which the EU Treaty allowed the Member States in 1993 to develop social policies on the basis of new Treaty provisions without the participation of the United Kingdom, which did not accept the conferral of these powers on the (then) Community. In order to provide the United Kingdom with an opt-out vis-à-vis the social policy which the other Member States wished to pursue, the EU Treaty created a legal structure whereby a protocol to the EC Treaty (signed by all the Member States) authorised the Member States, with the exception of the United Kingdom, to "have recourse to the institutions, procedures and mechanisms of the Treaty" for the purpose of taking and applying the acts and decisions required for giving effect to the "Agreement on Social Policy" annexed to the protocol, which was concluded only between those Member States (the "Social Protocol" and the "Social Agreement").[81] Under the more extensive powers provided for in the

---

[79] *Cf.* Koenig, "Die Europäische Sozialunion als Bewährungsprobe der supranationalen Gerichtsbarkeit" (1994) EuR. 175–195 (concerning the Social Agreement). In principle, courts in the Member States with an opt-out which would be concerned with applying the acts in question might refer questions to the Court of Justice for a preliminary ruling on their validity and interpretation and the States enjoying an opt-out could bring actions for the annulment of such measures. See Curtin (n. 78, *supra*), at 60.

[80] This is the case with Denmark and its exceptional position on defence policy and Title V of Part Three of the TFEU (see para. 10–028, *supra*); the same is true of Ireland as regards Title V of Part Three of the TFEU (see para. 10–029, *supra*). In the negotiations, the United Kingdom did not consider it necessary to press for such an option. As far as participation in EMU is concerned, however, the Member States which have opted out have to satisfy the requisite criteria if they should wish to participate; see paras 11–041—11–042, *supra*.

[81] See Watson, "Social Policy After Maastricht" (1993) C.M.L.Rev. 481–513; Schuster, "Rechtsfragen der Maastrichter Vereinbarungen zur Sozialpolitik" (1992) Eu.Z.W. 178–187; Whiteford (n. 78, *supra*), at 202–222.

Figure 1: Differentiated integration among European States

		EEA (para. 25–029)	Euro (para. 11–033)	Schengen-acquis (para. 10–011)		ESDP (para. 25–046)	EU accession negotiation (para. 6–013)
				Integration existing acquis	Further development acquis		
EU Member States	Austria	X	X	X	X	X	
	Belgium	X	X	X	X	X	
	Bulgaria	X		X	X	X	
	Cyprus	X	X	X	X	X	
	Czech Rep.	X		X	X	X	
	Denmark	X	(opt-out)	X	(opt-in)		
	Estonia	X	X	X	X	X	
	Finland	X	X	X	X	X	
	France	X	X	X	X	X	
	Germany	X	X	X	X	X	
	Greece	X	X	X	X	X	
	Hungary	X		X	X	X	
	Ireland	X	X	(opt-in)		X	
	Italy	X	X	X	X	X	
	Latvia	X		X	X	X	
	Lithuania	X		X	X	X	
	Luxembourg	X	X	X	X	X	
	Malta	X	X	X	X	X	
	Netherlands	X	X	X	X	X	
	Poland	X		X	X	X	
	Portugal	X	X	X	X	X	
	Romania	X		X	X	X	
	Slovak Rep.	X	X	X	X	X	
	Slovenia	X	X	X	X	X	
	Spain	X	X	X	X	X	
	Sweden	X		X	X	X	
	UK	X	(opt-out)	(opt-in)		X	
Candidate Member States	Croatia						X
	FYROM						X
	Turkey						X
EFTA	Iceland	X		X	X		
	Liechtenstein	X					
	Norway	X		X	X		
	Switzerland			X	X		

Social Agreement, the other Member States then adopted directives—using Community institutions and procedures—which had the same legal force as other Community directives for all the Member States with the exception of the United Kingdom.[82] At the 1996 Intergovernmental Conference, the (new) British government accepted the incorporation of the more extensive powers enshrined in the Social Agreement into the EC Treaty as a result of the Treaty of Amsterdam (see para. 11–043). Following the European Council held in Amsterdam on June 16 and 17, 1997, the United Kingdom was already involved in discussion of the directives which were still to be adopted pursuant to the Social Agreement.[83] In addition, the Council adopted directives on the basis of Art. 100 EC [*later Art. 94 EC, now Art. 115 TFEU*], which extended the directives adopted pursuant to the Social Agreement to the United Kingdom.[84] Having amended the Treaty provisions on social policy, the Treaty of Amsterdam then abrogated the Social Protocol and the Social Agreement.

---

[82] For the directives adopted pursuant to the Social Agreement, see n. 245 to para. 11–044, *supra*. Those directives have the same status as other directives, see, e.g., the interpretation in ECJ, Case C-366/99 *Griesmar* [2001] E.C.R. I-9383, paras 62–67.

[83] (1997) 6 EU Bull. point I.8; for the first occasion, see the Social Affairs Council held on June 27, 1997 (*Europe* Nos 7004–7006 of June 27, 28 and 30, 1997, at p. 8).

[84] See the directives mentioned in n. 245 to para. 11–044, *supra*. According to the preamble of each of these directives, the fact that the directive was not applicable to the United Kingdom had a direct effect on the functioning of the internal market and the implementation of the directive in all the Member States was to improve the operation of the internal market.

Part III

THE ACTORS OF THE EUROPEAN UNION

CHAPTER 13

THE INSTITUTIONS AND BODIES OF THE UNION

Institutional framework. The Union is served by a single institutional frame-   **13–001**
work (Art. 13(1) TEU). The "institutions" of the Union in the strict sense are the
European Parliament, the European Council, the Council, the European
Commission, the Court of Justice of the European Union, the European Central
Bank (ECB) and the Court of Auditors (Art. 13(1) TEU; Art. 3(1), first subpara,
EAEC). The European Council and the European Central Bank have had this
status only since the Lisbon Treaty. Except for the ECB, which has legal personality in accordance with Art. 282(3) TFEU,[1] the Union's institutions do not
have legal personality, but act on behalf of the Union.[2] The European Parliament,
the Council and the Commission are assisted by a European Economic and
Social Committee and a Committee of the Regions (Art. 13(4) TEU). Other advisory or consultative committees sometimes have a specific role to play (see para.
13–114).

The Treaties established another body which carries out its duties as a legal
person in its own right: the European Investment Bank (EIB; Arts 308 and 309
TFEU). In addition, the Union has a number of other bodies, offices and agencies,
established by or pursuant to the Treaties and with or without legal personality. In
common with acts of the EIB, their acts are subject to judicial review by the Court
of Justice of the European Union in the same way as those of the institutions.[3]

In so far as the Treaties or the statutes annexed to them do not regulate their
operation and establishment, Union institutions, bodies, offices and agencies have
the power to organise their internal operation.

---

[1] See also Art. 9.1 of Protocol (No. 4), annexed to the TEU and TFEU, on the Statute of the European
System of Central Banks and of the European Central Bank [ESCB Statute], [2010] O.J. C83/230.
[2] For the position of the Union in the legal systems of the Member States, see para. 13–126, *infra*,
and at international level, see para. 24–002 *et seq.*
[3] See Arts 263, 267 and 277 TFEU. Compare ECJ, Case 294/83 *Les Verts v European Parliament*
[1986] E.C.R. 1339, para. 23; ECJ, Case C-15/00 *Commission v European Investment Bank* [2003]
I-7281, para. 75.

13–002 **Institutions.** As noted above, seven bodies have the status of "institutions"[4] and, as a result, special legal status. The powers, composition and manner of operation of each institution are governed by the Treaties. The most important characteristics of every institution—with the exception of the ECB and the Court of Auditors—are set out in Title III of the TEU. Provisions relating to the ECB and the Court of Auditors and detailed provisions on the other institutions are set out in the TFEU. The institutions act within the limits of the powers conferred on them by the Treaties, and in conformity with the procedures, conditions and objectives set out therein (Art. 13(2) TEU). They are to operate in mutual sincere cooperation (*ibid*). An overview will be given below of each institution's powers, composition, operation and internal organisation. First, the four "political institutions" (European Parliament, European Council, Council and European Commission) will be discussed, next the three other institutions (Court of Justice of the European Union, European Central Bank and Court of Auditors).

I. POLITICAL INSTITUTIONS OF THE UNION

A. THE EUROPEAN PARLIAMENT

13–003 **Representative assembly.** The European Parliament[5] was originally established as the "Common Assembly" of the ECSC[6] and as the "Assembly" of the EEC and the EAEC, which the Convention on certain institutions common to the European Communities (see para. 1–016) merged as long ago as 1957 into a single Assembly for the three Communities. It was not long before the Assembly started to refer to itself as the "European Parliament".[7] The title "European Parliament" did not gain general acceptance until the Single European Act provided that the institutions of the European Communities were to be "henceforth designated as referred to hereafter" (Single European Act, Art. 3(1)).[8] Since then, the title has been used in all acts and was systematically introduced into other Treaty provisions by the EU Treaty.

---

[4] See ECJ (order of March 17, 2004), Case C-176/03 *Commission v Council*, not reported (the European Economic and Social Committee does not constitute an "institution" entitled to be joined in proceedings before the Court of Justice pursuant to Art. 40 of the ECJ Statute).

[5] See in general Corbett, Jacobs and Shackleton, *The European Parliament* (London, Harper, 2007), 416 pp. For the website of the European Parliament, see *http://www.europarl.europa.eu/* [Accessed December 8, 2010].

[6] Within the institutional framework of the ECSC Treaty, the European Parliament played the modest role of supervising the High Authority (Art. 20 ECSC).

[7] Resolutions of March 20, 1958, [April 20, 1958] J.O. 6 ("European Parliamentary Assembly") and of March 30, 1962, [1962] J.O. 1045 ("European Parliament").

[8] See Bieber, Pantalis and Schoo, "Implications of the Single Act for the European Parliament" (1986) C.M.L.Rev. 767, at 770–772.

1. Powers

(a) *Nature*

Overview. According to Art. 14(1) TEU, the European Parliament exercises, jointly with the Council, legislative and budgetary functions and exercises, in addition, functions of political control and consultation as laid down in the Treaties. Accordingly, the European Parliament's powers are (1) to take part in Union decision-making, (2) to adopt the EU budget in cooperation with the Council, (3) to supervise other institutions and bodies of the Union and (4) to advise. A brief analysis follows of these powers on the basis of which the European Parliament secures at Union level respect for the fundamental democratic principle that "the peoples should take part in the exercise of power through the intermediary of a representative assembly".[9] It will become clear that, in respect of decision-making and budgetary powers, the various Treaty amendments have gradually placed the European Parliament on a virtually equal footing with the Council.

13–004

Voice of citizens. The European Parliament's role does not lie only in giving political expression to the will of the democratic majority within the Union, it also gives citizens of the Union and other persons affected by action taken by the Union a means of making their views known on the policy which is being conducted.

13–005

In the first place, Members of the European Parliament ("MEPs") may be informed of problems personally. Secondly, citizens of the Union and any natural or legal person residing or having its registered office in a Member State have the right to petition the European Parliament (Arts 24, second para., and 227 TFEU [*ex Arts 21 and 194 EC*]).[10] Beneficiaries of the right may,

---

[9] ECJ, Case 138/79 *Roquette Frères v Council* [1980] E.C.R. 3333, para. 33, and ECJ, Case 139/79 *Maïzena v Council* [1980] E.C.R. 3393, para. 34; ECJ, Case C-300/89 *Commission v Council* [1991] E.C.R. I-2867, para. 20. For the (growing) say of the European Parliament in decision-making, see also para. 16–011 *et seq.*

[10] That right is now also confirmed in Art. 44 of the Charter of Fundamental Rights of the European Union. The Rules of Procedure of the European Parliament govern the right of petition. See further Guckelberger, "Das Petitionsrecht zum Europäischen Parlament sowie das Recht zur Anrufung des Europäischen Bürgerbeauftragten im Europa der Bürger" (2003) D.ö.V. 829–838; Maniatis, "Le règlement des pétitions au Parlement européen" (2002) R.D.U.E. 133–145; Baviera, "Les pétitions au Parlement européen et le médiateur européen" (2001) R.M.C.U.E. 129–135; Marias, "The Right to Petition the European Parliament after Maastricht" (1994) E.L.Rev. 169–183; Pliakos, "Les conditions d'exercice du droit de pétition" (1993) C.D.E. 317–350. *Cf.* Art. 44 of the Charter of Fundamental Rights; see Holdscheidt, "Die Ausgestaltung des Petitionsrechts in der EU-Grundrechtecharta" (2002) EuR. 441–448. The introduction of Art. 194 EC by the EU Treaty transformed a "custom" into a right of petition protected by the Treaties. See previously the exchanges of letters between the European Parliament, the Council and the Commission of the European Communities of April 12, 1989 on the right to petition, [1989] O.J. C120/90.

"address, individually or in association with other citizens or persons, a petition to Parliament on a matter which comes within the European Union's fields of activity and which affects him, her or it directly".[11]

Lastly, persons qualifying to exercise the right of petition under the Treaties may also submit complaints of maladministration in the activities of Union institutions, bodies, offices or agencies to the European Ombudsman, who is closely connected with the European Parliament (Art. 228 TFEU [*ex Art. 195 EC*]; see para. 13–118).

As the voice of the citizens of the Union, the European Parliament represents their interests in the exercise of its various powers.

(b) *Survey of powers*

(1) *Participation in decision-making*

13–006   **Co-legislator.** The Court of Justice has held that participation of the European Parliament in Union decision-making is an essential procedural requirement with which other institutions must comply, failing which the act adopted may be annulled.[12] The Lisbon Treaty introduced the "ordinary legislative procedure" pursuant to which the European Parliament and the Council act on an equal footing (see para. 16–022). Consequently, the European Parliament can now be said to have fully-fledged legislative powers, which it exercises jointly with the Council. Even before the Lisbon Treaty, the European Parliament had sufficient decision-making and supervisory powers to constitute part of the Union's "legislature" for the purposes of Art. 3 of Protocol No. 1 to the ECHR.[13]

All the same, the European Parliament still has no right of initiative. The European Parliament may, acting by a majority of its Members, request the

---

[11] Rules of Procedure, Rule 201(1). The responsible parliamentary committee decides whether a given petition is admissible (EP Rules of Procedure, Rule 201(7) and (8)). The formal requirements for the admissibility of a petition are that it must show each petitioner's name, nationality and permanent address and must be written in one of the official languages (or a translation drawn up in an official language must be attached) (EP Rules of Procedure, Rule 201(2) and (5)). Article 194 EC did not cover the non-Community matters dealt with in Titles V and VI of the EU Treaty, but the European Parliament decided to entertain petitions in those fields, pursuant to its power of internal organisation.

[12] See ECJ, Case 138/79 *Roquette Frères* [1980] E.C.R. 3333 and Case 139/79 *Maïzena* [1980] E.C.R. 3393 (n. 9, *supra*) on breaches of the right to be consulted.

[13] Judgment of the European Court of Human Rights of February 18, 1999 in Case No. 24833/94 *Matthews v United Kingdom*. *Cf.* the joint dissenting opinion relying on Dashwood, "The Limits of European Community Powers" (1996) E.L.Rev. 113, at 127, "the Community has no legislature only a legislative process in which the different political institutions have different parts to play" (see the dissenting opinion, paras 4–7). See also the judgment of June 30, 2009 of the *Bundesverfassungsgericht* (discussed in Chapter 21).

Commission to submit any appropriate proposal on matters on which it considers that a Union act is required for the purpose of implementing the Treaties (Art. 225 TFEU [*ex Art. 192, second para., EC*]), but this does not amount to a genuine right to initiate legislation (see para. 16–021). Neither does the European Parliament have a decisive say in the ordinary procedure for amending the Treaties; the role of "constituent assembly" in this connection falls to the Member States.[14] However, the Lisbon Treaty significantly boosted the European Parliament's role in the revision procedure and, moreover, introduced simplified revision procedures which do not require national ratification (see para. 5–007 *et seq.*).

External relations. As far as the Union's external relations are concerned, it was only as a result of the Single European Act and, subsequently, the EU Treaty that the European Parliament was given significant powers in this field, in particular in connection with the conclusion by the Community of international agreements. Since the Single European Act entered into force, the European Parliament has to give its consent to association agreements (Arts 300(3), second subpara., and 310 EC [*now Arts 218(6) and 217 TFEU*]) and to the accession of new Member States to the Union (Art. 237 EEC, replaced by Art. 49 EU [*now Art. 49 TEU*]) and since the EU Treaty it has to give its consent to international agreements establishing a specific institutional framework or having important budgetary implications for the Union (Art. 300(3), second subpara., EC [*now Art. 218(6) TFEU*]). The Lisbon Treaty extended the requirement for the European Parliament to give its consent to the agreement whereby the Union is to accede to the European Convention for the Protection of Human Rights and Fundamental Freedoms and to agreements covering fields to which either the ordinary legislative procedure applies or the special legislative procedure where the consent of the European Parliament is required (Art. 218(6) TFEU).[15] **13–007**

   In addition, the European Parliament is consulted on the conclusion of all other international agreements, with the exception of those coming under the CFSP (Art. 218(6) TFEU). In decision-making with regard to the CFSP, the European Parliament has only an (unenforceable) right to be consulted on "the main aspects and the basic choices".[16] Since the Treaty of Nice, the European Parliament may also obtain the opinion of the Court of Justice as to whether an international agreement envisaged is compatible with the Treaties (Art. 218(11) TFEU [*ex Art. 300(6) EC*]).

---

[14] Article 48(2) to (5) TEU. See para 5–004 *et seq.*

[15] This last category replaces the more narrowly phrased category of "agreements entailing amendment of an act adopted under the co-decision procedure", introduced by the EU Treaty.

[16] See Art. 36, first para., TEU [*ex Art. 21, first para., EU*]. Article 225 TFEU [*Art. 192, second subpara., EC*] does not apply to decision-making in connection with the CFSP (Art. 24(1), second subpara., TEU). For the limited role of the European Parliament in PJCC matters before the entry into force of the Lisbon Treaty, see Arts 39(1) EU and 41(1) EU.

(2) Budgetary authority

13–008   **Finances.** Ever since the First Treaty on Budgetary Provisions, the European Parliament and the Council have together formed the budgetary authority of what is now the Union (for the adoption of the budget, see para. 13–141 *et seq.*). The European Parliament has the final say over all categories of expenditure[17] and may also reject the budget in its entirety. It has made use of these powers on several occasions in order to assert its views in respect of the most diverse policy matters.

These powers also enable the European Parliament to increase its limited say in decision-making with regard to the CFSP where action of the Union is charged to the EU budget.[18]

The European Parliament's power to give a discharge to the Commission in respect of the implementation of the budget reinforces the European Parliament's supervision of the Commission.

(3) Supervision of other institutions and bodies

13–009   **Supervision of the Commission.** Since the EU Treaty entered into force, the European Parliament has to approve the Members of the Commission proposed for nomination; since the Lisbon Treaty, the Parliament has first to elect by a majority of its component members the person whom the European Council, acting by a qualified majority, proposes to appoint as President of the Commission, after which the Council may select, in agreement with the President-elect and on the basis of suggestions made by Member States, the other persons whom it proposes for appointment as members of the Commission (see para. 13–069). The Commission is subject as a body to a vote of consent by the European Parliament, after which it is appointed by the European Council, acting by a qualified majority (Art. 17(7) TEU).

The Commission is politically answerable to the European Parliament. This is reflected in the first place in the European Parliament's right to put oral or written questions to the Commission (Art. 230, second para., TFEU [*ex Art. 197, third para., EC*]). Oral questions are placed on the agenda for a Parliamentary sitting and must be referred to the Commission at least a week beforehand.[19] The Commission is obliged to have one of its Members answer them. Written questions must be answered within six weeks and the answers are published together with the questions.[20] Question time is held at each part-session, at which a

---

[17] Before the Lisbon Treaty, this was true only in respect of non-compulsory expenditure (para. 13–141, *infra*).

[18] Para.13–128, *infra*.

[19] EP Rules of Procedure, Rule 115(1) and (2).

[20] EP Rules of Procedure, Rule 117. They are published in the *Official Journal* (Part C). Questions requiring an immediate answer but no detailed research (priority questions) should be answered within three weeks, other questions within six: Rule 117(4) and (5).

Member of the Commission briefly answers questions submitted in advance and two concise supplementary questions.[21]

Besides, the European Parliament has the right to pass a motion of censure on the activities of the Commission (Art. 234 TFEU [*ex Art. 201 EC*]). Such a motion may be submitted by a tenth of its Members.[22] However, a vote cannot—publicly—be held on such a motion until at least three days after it has been submitted. In order for a motion to be carried, it must obtain a two-thirds majority of the votes cast, representing a majority of MEPs. If such a motion is carried, the Members of the Commission have to resign as a body. Pending their replacement, they continue to deal with current business only. Owing to the onerous requirement for a majority and the collective nature of the sanction, this method of control has to be kept in reserve for genuinely exceptional situations.[23] So far, the European Parliament has held ten votes on motions of censure, but a motion has never been carried.[24] On January 14, 1999, the European Parliament failed by a relatively narrow margin to obtain the necessary majority to pass a motion of censure against the Santer Commission. In the result, the Parliament proposed that a committee of independent experts be set up under the auspices of the Parliament and the Commission to examine the way in which the Commission detected and dealt with fraud, mismanagement and nepotism and to review Commission practices in the awarding of financial contracts. The committee submitted its first report to the President of the Commission on allegations regarding fraud, mismanagement and nepotism in the European Commission on March 15, 1999. Thereupon the Santer Commission decided to resign as a body (see para. 13–073). Following the collective resignation of the Commission, a discussion

---

[21] Rule 116 and the guidelines on the conduct of question time set out in Annex II to the EP Rules of Procedure.

[22] EP Rules of Procedure, Rule 107(1).

[23] Lenaerts, "Some Reflections on the Separation of Powers in the European Community" (1991) C.M.L.Rev. 11, at 23. In a 1988 judgment the Court of Justice referred to the motion of censure as a means available to the European Parliament to put political pressure on the Commission to defend the Parliament's prerogatives: ECJ, Case 302/87 *European Parliament v Council* [1988] ECR 5638, para. 12. In a 1990 judgment, the Court of Justice qualified its earlier judgment and held that the Parliament was entitled to bring an action for annulment to safeguard its prerogatives, in order, *inter alia*, that it should not be dependent on compelling the Commission to act: ECJ, Case C-70/88 *European Parliament v Council* [1990] ECR I-2041, para. 19 (for these judgments, see n. 52, *infra*).

[24] See Debates of the European Parliament, [1972] O.J. C-156/8 and C156/52 (motion withdrawn without being put to a vote); [1976] O.J. C204/12 (no majority); 1976, 210, p. 287 (motion withdrawn without being put to a vote); [1977] O.J. C-215/63 (no majority); [1990] O.J. C-386/85 and C-386/316 (no majority); [1991] O.J. C240/167 (no majority); [1993] O.J. C21/30 and C21/124 (no majority); [1997] O.J. C85/103 (following a report of a committee of inquiry on "mad cow disease": no majority); [1999] O.J. C104/97 (following allegations of fraud, mismanagement and nepotism made against individual Commissioners of the Santer Commission: no majority); *Europe*, No. 8699, May 5, 2004, p. 7 (following allegations of mismanagement in Eurostat: no majority) and [2005] O.J. C117E/8 (following allegations of a conflict of interests made against Commission President Barroso: no majority).

was initiated as to the possibility of compelling individual Commissioners to resign.[25] In a framework agreement concluded between the Commission and the European Parliament, the Commission accepted that, where the European Parliament expresses lack of confidence in a Member of the Commission, the President of the Commission will either request that Member to resign or to explain his or her decision not to do so to the European Parliament.[26] The Treaties now also provide that a member of the Commission has to resign if the President so requests (Art. 17(6) TEU; see para 13–073). The possibility of a motion of censure being carried against the Commission, together with the vote of consent in the process of appointment of the Commission, constitutes the cornerstone of the Commission's political accountability to the European Parliament.[27]

Lastly, the Commission is required to draw up an annual report on the activities of the European Union and other reports for presentation to the European Parliament.[28] The Commission is also under a duty to submit a number of reports to the European Parliament and to give it hearings in connection with the latter institution's supervision of the implementation of the budget.[29] At the request of the President of the European Parliament, the Commission is to provide all information necessary for the exercise of the European Parliament's supervisory tasks.[30]

13–010   **Relations with the Council and the European Council.** The Treaties do not confer any general power of supervision on the European Parliament as far as the Council is concerned. The reason for this is that members of the Council are accountable to their national parliaments (Art. 10(2) TEU). The third para. of Art. 230 TFEU [*ex Art. 197 EC*] merely provides for the Council to be "heard by the European Parliament in accordance with the conditions laid down by the

---

[25] See the resolution of the European Parliament of March 23, 1999 on the resignation of the Commission and the appointment of a new Commission, [1999] O.J. C177/19.

[26] Framework Agreement of May 26, 2005 on relations between the European Parliament and the Commission, [2006] O.J. C117E/125 (annexed to the Rules of Procedure of the European Parliament), point 3, (see n. 26, *supra*) replacing the Framework Agreement of May 26, 2005.

[27] For a critical discussion, see Raworth, "A Timid Step Forwards: Maastricht and the Democratisation of the European Community" (1994) E.L.Rev. 16, at 31–32.

[28] For the general report, see Arts 233 and 249(2) TFEU [*ex Arts 200 and 212 EC*] and Art. 125 EAEC. See also Art. 161 TFEU [*ex Art. 145 EC*], which requires a separate chapter on social developments to be included. There are other reports as well; see n. 282, *infra*.

[29] Article 318 TFEU [*ex Art. 275 EC*] (see para. 13–147, *infra*) and Art. 319 TFEU [*ex Art. 276 EC*] (see para 13–150, *infra*).

[30] For the procedures, see Annex II (Forwarding of confidential information to the European Parliament) to the framework agreement of October 20, 2010 on relations between Parliament and the Commission, [2006] O.J. C117E/125 replaced by the Framework Agreement of October 20, 2010 on relations between the European Parliament and the Commission, [2010] O.J. L304/47, point 5. That agreement does not limit the right of Members of Parliament to put questions to the Commission, see CFI (order of January 17, 2002), Case T-236/00 *Stauner and Others v European Parliament and Commission* [2002] ECR II-135, paras 59–62. For criticism of the Council, see Rodriques, "La paix des braves? A propos du nouvel accord-cadre 'Commission-Parlement européen' " (2000) R.M.C.U.E. 590, at 592.

Council in its Rules of Procedure".[31] Nevertheless, members of the Council customarily came before the European Parliament in order to answer questions. In 1973 the Council converted that practice into an obligation,[32] which was subsequently extended to cover matters relating to European Political Cooperation (EPC).[33] The EU Treaty codified the right to put questions on the CFSP.[34]

The European Parliament has adopted rules governing written and oral questions put to the Council during question time in much the same manner as questions put to the Commission.[35]

In addition, the President of the Council has a number of obligations to provide information to the European Parliament.[36] Since the Lisbon Treaty, the obligation to inform the European Parliament in matters of CFSP has been transferred to the High Representative, who has regularly to consult the European Parliament on the main aspects and the basic choices of the CFSP and the common security and defence policy and inform it of how those policies evolve (Art. 36, first para., TEU).[37]

The President of the European Council has to present a report to the European Parliament after each of the meetings of the European Council.[38]

Relations with other institutions and bodies. The supervision exercised indirectly by the European Parliament over other institutions and bodies takes the   **13–011**

---

[31] See Council Rules of Procedure, Art. 26.

[32] See the letter from the President of the Council of March 6, 1973 on the introduction of question time ((1973) 3 EC Bull. point 2402) and the communication from the Council to the European Parliament of October 16, 1973 ((1973) 34 EP Bull.); see also the Solemn Declaration of Stuttgart, June 19, 1983 (1986) 6 EC Bull. point 1.6.1., under 2.3.3.

[33] See the decision of the Ministers for Foreign Affairs, meeting within the framework of European Political Cooperation, of February 28, 1986 (1986) 1 EPC Bulletin point I.86, at 108 (document No. 86/090).

[34] Article 31, second para., TEU [*ex Art. 21, second para., EU*]. See also, for PJCC prior to the Lisbon Treaty: Art. 39(3) EU.

[35] Para. 13–009, *supra*. Questions for oral answer must, however, be submitted to the Council at least one week before the sitting. No time-limits are prescribed for questions on matters coming under the common security and defence policy and the Council must reply with sufficient promptness to keep the Parliament properly informed (EP Rules of Procedure, Rule 115(2) and (3)).

[36] The President of the Council reports on multilateral economic surveillance, just as the Commission does, and may be invited to appear before the competent parliamentary committee if the Council has made its recommendations public (Art. 121(4) and (5) TFEU [*ex Art. 99(4) EC*]). He or she is to inform the Parliament of any decision of the Council taken where a Member State fails to comply with measures for deficit reduction (Art. 126(11) TFEU [*ex Art. 104(11) EC*]).

[37] See also Rule 96(1) and (2) of the EP Rules of Procedure. Rule 96(4) provides that the Council and/or the High Representative are to be invited to every plenary debate that involves foreign, security or defence policy. As far as concerns the European Parliament's access to sensitive information in the field of security and defence policy, the rules laid down in the Interinstitutional Agreement between the European Parliament and the Council of November 20, 2002 apply (see para. 15–004, *infra*).

[38] Article 15(6)(d) TEU.

form of its right to appoint the European Ombudsman and its right to be consulted on the appointment of Members of the Court of Auditors, Members of the Executive Board of the ECB and the Director of OLAF.[39] The European Parliament further has the right to obtain information from the Court of Auditors by way of assistance in exercising its powers of control over the budget[40] and to have an annual report from the ECB.[41] The competent committee of the European Parliament is also entitled to hold hearings of the President of the ECB and of the other members of its Executive Board.[42]

13–012　**Inquiries.** Lastly, the European Parliament's right of supervision extends to the right to hold inquiries into alleged contraventions of Union law or maladministration in its implementation (Art. 226 TFEU [*ex Art. 193, first para., EC*]). Complaints relating thereto may arrive at the European Parliament inter alia in the form of information from other institutions or bodies, petitions or complaints made to the European Ombudsman.[43] Even the conduct of national authorities in implementing Union law may be the subject of an inquiry by the European Parliament.[44]

The European Parliament may organise hearings, dispatch MEPs to establish the facts of the situation *in situ* and request the Commission to submit documents, supply information and grant it access to its facilities.[45] Where the European Parliament deems it appropriate, it may refer the matter in question to the

---

[39] See the further discussion of these Union bodies in paras 13–098, 13–103, 13–119 and 13–122, *infra*. The European Parliament expressed a wish to be involved in the appointment of Members of the Court of Justice and asked for arrangements to be made for its (former) Committee on Legal Affairs and Citizens' Rights to meet with prospective Members of the Court prior to their appointment: resolution of February 9, 1994 ([1994] O.J. C61/126). Since the entry into force of the Lisbon Treaty, a panel has to give its opinion on the suitability of candidates for appointment at the Court. That panel includes one member proposed by the European Parliament (see para. 13–091, *infra*).

[40] Articles 287(1) and (4) and 319(1) TFEU [*ex Arts 248(1) and (4) and 276(1) EC*] (paras 13–149—13–150, *infra*).

[41] Article 284(3), first subpara., TFEU [*ex Art. 113(3), first subpara., EC*].

[42] Article 284(3), second subpara., TFEU [*ex Art. 113(3), second subpara., EC*]. See also Rules 113 and 118 of the EP Rules of Procedure (Rule 118 provides for the possibility of putting written questions to the ECB).

[43] See the right of petition provided for in Art. 227 TFEU [*ex Art. 194 EC*] (para. 13–005, *supra*) and the regulations governing the European Ombudsman provided for by Art. 228 TFEU [*ex Art. 195 EC*] (para. 13–118, *infra*). The right of petition entails a corresponding obligation on the Parliament to accept petitions satisfying the admissibility requirements and to deal with them effectively. See Pliakos (n. 10, *supra*), at 335–337.

[44] The European Parliament has no right to conduct an inquiry where "the alleged facts are being examined before a court and while the case is still subject to legal proceedings" (Art. 226, first para., TFEU [*ex Art. 193, first para., EC*]). The European Ombudsman is not entitled to carry out an inquiry where "the alleged facts are or have been the subject of legal proceedings" (Art. 228, second subpara., TFEU [*ex Art. 195(1), second subpara., EC*]).

[45] See EP Rules of Procedure, Rule 202(3) and (4) on the examination of petitions.

European Ombudsman.[46] At the request of a quarter of its Members, the European Parliament may set up a temporary committee of inquiry. In this connection, the EU Treaty took over the procedure already in use.[47] Agreement was not reached between the European Parliament, the Council and the Commission on how the Parliament's right of inquiry was to be exercised until April 1995.[48] The European Parliament determines the composition and the rules of procedure of committees of inquiry.[49]

In any event, the Member States are under a duty to cooperate with any inquiries which the European Parliament is entitled to carry out.[50]

Legal proceedings. The European Parliament may bring proceedings before the Court of Justice for the annulment of acts of the European Council, the Council, the Commission or the ECB.[51] The Parliament may also bring an action in the Court of Justice for failure to act against the European Council, the Council, the Commission or the ECB.[52] However, the prerogatives which it exercises in connection with the

13–013

---

[46] EP Rules of Procedure, Rule 201(12).

[47] Rule 185 of the EP Rules of Procedure.

[48] Decision 95/167/EC, Euratom, ECSC of the European Parliament, the Council and the Commission of April 19, 1995 on the detailed provisions governing the exercise of the European Parliament's right of inquiry, [1995] O.J. L113/2, appended to the EP Rules of Procedure as Annex IX.

[49] *Ibid.*, Art. 2(1), second subpara. See Rules 185 and 186 of the EP Rules of Procedure. The European Parliament set up a committee of inquiry to consider allegations of offences committed or of maladministration under the Community transit system ([1996] O.J. C7/1; identical version in C17/47) and in connection with bovine spongiform encephalopathy (BSE or "mad cow disease") ([1996] O.J. C239/1). For the recommendations made by those committees, see (1997) 3 EU Bull. point 2.2.1 and (1997) 1/2 EU Bull. point 2.2.1, respectively. See also Blanquet, "Le contrôle parlementaire européen sur la crise de la 'vache folle' " (1998) R.M.C.U.E. 457–470; Beckedorf, "Das Untersuchungsrecht des Europäischen Parlaments. Eine erste Bestandsaufnahme nach zwei parlamentarischen Untersuchungen" (1997) EuR. 237–260. See also the Committee of Inquiry into the crisis of the Equitable Life Assurance Society ([2006] O.J. L186/58).

[50] See Art. 4(3) TEU [*ex Art. 10 EC*]. For cooperation with the examination of complaints, see the works cited in n. 10, *supra*. However, before the Lisbon Treaty, the powers of inquiry conferred by Arts 193 to 195 EC [*now Arts 226 to 228 TFEU*] did not apply to action pursuant to the CFSP (see Art. 28(1) EU).

[51] The Nice Treaty abolished the requirement that an action brought by the European Parliament must seek to safeguard its prerogatives. Subject to that condition, the EU Treaty had codified in Art. 230 EC [*now Art. 263 TFEU*] the European Parliament's right to bring proceedings as recognised by the Court of Justice: see ECJ, Case C-70/88 *European Parliament v Council* [1990] E.C.R. I-2041, paras 11–31. That right was not embodied in Art.173 EEC and had not been accepted in an earlier judgment of the Court of Justice: ECJ, Case 302/87 *European Parliament v Council* [1988] E.C.R. 05615, paras 8–28. A first example of an action not brought to safeguard prerogatives was the Parliament's application for the annulment of a number of provisions of Council Directive 2003/86/EC of September 22, 2003 on the right to family reunification (see para. 10–012, *supra*), which was rejected by the ECJ in ECJ, Case C-540/03, *European Parliament v Council* [2006] E.C.R. I-5769.

[52] Article 265, first para., TFEU [*ex Art. 232, first para., EC*]. See ECJ, Case 13/83 *European Parliament v Council* [1985] E.C.R. 1513, paras 13–19.

common foreign and security policy (CFSP) may not be enforced by bringing proceedings in the Court of Justice.[53]

(4) *Provision of advice*

13–014 **Resolutions.** Finally, the European Parliament is entitled to give advice on any question concerning the Union and to adopt resolutions on such questions.[54] Even where the power to act lies with other institutions or with national governments, the European Parliament is entitled to "invite them to act".[55]

2. Composition

13–015 **Representatives of the citizens.** Until the Lisbon Treaty, the European Parliament was considered to consist of "representatives of the peoples of the States brought together in the Community" (Art. 189 EC). Now, the European Parliament consists of "representatives of the Union's citizens" (Art. 14(2) TEU). Since 1979, MEPs have been elected by direct universal suffrage. This gives the institution a democratic legitimacy which others lack. MEPs are elected for a five-year term by direct universal suffrage (Art. 14(3) TEU). Since they represent citizens directly and not their Member States, they form a genuine supranational institution. This means that all MEPs may participate in debates and decision-making even in policy areas in which not all Member States of the Union participate.[56]

13–016 **Number of MEPs.** Article 14(2), first subpara., TEU provides that the representation of citizens is to be degressively proportional to the size of the population of the Member States, with a minimum of six and a maximum of ninety-six members per Member State. The precise composition is to be determined by the European Council, acting unanimously on the initiative of the European Parliament and with its consent (Art. 14(2), second subpara., TEU). Before the Lisbon Treaty, the allocation of parliamentary seats to the various Member States was laid down in the Treaties itself, and was amended upon each accession of new Member States and following German reunification.[57] In order to ensure the

---

[53] Article 275 TFEU. Before the Lisbon Treaty, Art. 35 EU provided, as far as PJCC was concerned, that the Court of Justice had jurisdiction to give preliminary rulings on the validity and interpretation of acts of the Union, but the European Parliament was not given the right to contest the legality of such acts by bringing an action in the Court (Art. 35(6) EU conferred such a right only on the Member States and the Commission).

[54] ECJ, Case 230/81 *Luxembourg v European Parliament* [1983] E.C.R. 255, para. 39.

[55] *Ibid.* (with regard to national governments).

[56] Resolution of the European Parliament of January 19, 1994, [1994] O.J. C44/88.

[57] Article 190 EC, last amended by Art. 9(2) of the 2005 Act of Accession. Initially, the allocation of seats was laid down in Art. 2 of the Act on the direct election of the European Parliament (now repealed), as amended by Art. 10 of the Acts of Accession of 1979 ([1979] O.J. L291/17) and 1985 ([1985] O.J. L302/23), by Council Decision of February 1, 1993 ([1993] O.J. L33/15) and by

efficient functioning of the European Parliament, the Treaty of Amsterdam fixed the maximum number of MEPs at 700, which the Treaty of Nice however raised again to 732 and the 2003 and 2005 Acts of Accession to 736.[58] For the 2004–2009 electoral term, the European Parliament initially existed of 732 members,[59] and after the accession of Bulgaria and Romania in 2007, by way of provisional derogation from the maximum number of MEPs, of 785 members.[60]

The Treaty of Lisbon fixed the maximum number of MEPS at 750, plus the President (see Art. 14(2) TEU) and left the precise composition to be determined by the European Council. The new composition was agreed during the final negotiations of the 2007 Intergovernmental Conference; Italy's request to have an additional seat was accommodated eventually by not taking the seat of the President of the European Parliament into account for the purposes of calculating the maximum number of representatives of 750.[61] According to a draft decision on the composition of the European Parliament, which the European Council committed itself to approve,[62] Germany was to have 96 seats, France 74, the United Kingdom and Italy 73 each, Spain 54, Poland 51, Romania 33, the Netherlands 26, Belgium, the Czech Republic, Greece, Hungary and Portugal 22 each, Sweden 20, Austria 19, Bulgaria 18, Denmark, Finland and Slovakia 13

Art.11 of the 1994 Act of Accession (as amended by Council Decision of January 1, 1995, [1995] O.J. L1/1). The Treaty of Amsterdam incorporated the distribution of seats set out in the Act in Art. 190 EC. Note that before the 1994 elections, the new German Länder were represented by only 18 observers. See also ECJ, Case C-25/92 *Miethke v European Parliament* [1993] E.C.R. I-473.

[58] Article 189, second para., EC. For the short period in 2004 between the date of accession and the beginning of the new parliamentary term, transitional arrangements were provided for whereby the new Member States were represented in the European Parliament by members of their national parliaments (see the 2003 Act of Accession, Art. 25). During that period, the European Parliament had 788 members: this is because the new Member States had the number of seats laid down for the 2004–2009 parliamentary term, whereas the fifteen existing Member States still had the (larger) number of representatives allocated to them by Art. 190 EC before the accession: Germany 99 representatives (the same), but France, Italy and the United Kingdom 87 each, Spain 64, the Netherlands 31, Belgium, Greece and Portugal 25 each, Sweden 22, Austria 21, Denmark and Finland 16 each, Ireland 15; Luxembourg already had 6 representatives. In Protocol (No. 10) on the enlargement of the European Union, annexed to the EU Treaty and EC Treaty by the Nice Treaty, [2001] O.J. C80/49, it had already been agreed to reduce the total number of representatives for the fifteen Member States, whilst at the same time a new distribution was laid down for the number of representatives per Member State.

[59] Germany had 99 seats, France, Italy and the United Kingdom 78 each, Poland and Spain 54 each, the Netherlands 27, Belgium, the Czech Republic, Greece, Hungary and Portugal 24 each, Sweden 19, Austria 18, Denmark, Finland and Slovakia 14 each, Ireland and Lithuania 13 each, Latvia 9, Slovenia 7, Cyprus, Estonia and Luxembourg 6 each, and Malta 5.

[60] 18 seats were allocated to Bulgaria and 35 to Romania; see 2005 Act of Accession, Art. 24.

[61] See Declaration (No. 4), annexed to the Lisbon Treaty, on the composition of the European Parliament, [2010] O.J. C83/337.

[62] See Declaration (No. 5), annexed to the Lisbon Treaty, on the political agreement by the European Council concerning the draft Decision on the composition of the European Parliament, [2010] O.J. C83/337.

each, Ireland and Lithuania 12 each, Latvia 9, Slovenia 7, Cyprus, Estonia and Luxembourg and Malta 6 each.[63] It was envisaged that these arrangements would be in place in time before the 2009 European Parliament elections.[64] However, since the Treaty of Lisbon had not entered into force at the time the 2009 elections took place, the number of representatives for each Member State was determined in accordance with Art. 190(2) EC, as amended by the 2005 Act of Accession (see para. 13–016). Accordingly, for the 2009–2014 electoral term the European Parliament has 736 members: Germany has 99 seats, France, Italy and the United Kingdom 72 each, Poland and Spain 50 each, Romania 33, the Netherlands 25, Belgium, the Czech Republic, Greece, Hungary and Portugal 22 each, Sweden 18, Bulgaria and Austria 17, Denmark, Finland and Slovakia 13 each, Ireland and Lithuania 12 each, Latvia 8, Slovenia 7, Cyprus, Estonia and Luxembourg 6 each, and Malta 5. In order to allow the European Parliament to have the number of representatives agreed upon during the 2007 Intergovernmental Conference even before 2014, the Spanish Presidency submitted a proposal for an amendment of the Protocol on transitional provisions. A special Intergovernmental Conference has been convened to agree on that amendment, which would add 18 members to the Parliament for the remainder of the 2009–2014 term, thereby temporarily derogating from the maximum number laid down in Art. 14(2) TEU.[65]

13–017   **Direct elections.** Initially, the Parliament consisted of delegates designated by the respective national parliaments from among their members.[66] Nevertheless, the EEC Treaty itself looked forward to the direct election of the Parliament in accordance with a uniform procedure in all Member States. The Treaty required the

---

[63] European Parliament resolution of October 11, 2007 on the composition of the European Parliament (2007/2169(INI)), as approved by the European Council (Presidency Conclusions December 14, 2007; Council document 16616/1/07, point 5). The draft decision of the European Parliament allocated 72 seats to Italy; this was raised to 73 by the European Council in accordance with Declaration (No. 4) (n. 61, *supra*).

[64] See Art. 2 of Protocol (No. 36), annexed to the TEU, TFEU and EAEC Treaty, on transitional provisions ([2010] O.J. C83/322), which makes it clear that the Treaty of Lisbon did not change anything as far as concerns the composition of the Parliament for the 2004–2009 period.

[65] See the Protocol amending the Protocol on transitional provisions ([2010] O.J. (263/1), according to which. Spain would thus obtain 4 extra seats, Austria, France and Sweden each 2 extra, and Bulgaria, Italy, Latvia, Malta, the Netherlands, Poland, Slovenia and the United Kingdom each 1 extra. European Council Decision 2010/350/EU of June 17, 2010 on the examination by a conference of representatives of the governments of the Member States of the amendments to the Treaties proposed by the Spanish Government concerning the composition of the European Parliament and not to convene a Convention, [2010] O.J. L160/5. The amendment will enter into force only after being ratified in all of the Member States.

[66] Article 138(1) EEC. The choice which Art. 21 ECSC left to each Member State to have members of the Assembly directly elected or designated by the national parliaments was abolished when in 1958 the Assembly merged into the Common Assembly of the three Communities, constituted in accordance with Art. 138 EEC.

European Parliament to draw up "proposals" to this end, after which the Council, acting unanimously and—since the EU Treaty—with the assent of the Parliament, which was to act by a majority of its component Members, was to lay down the necessary provisions. Those provisions were then to be recommended to the Member States for adoption in accordance with their respective constitutional requirements. This is still the procedure set out in Art. 223(1) TFEU. Using this procedure, the Council adopted the Decision of September 20, 1976 and the Act annexed thereto concerning the election of the representatives of the Assembly by direct universal suffrage.[67] The Act did not set out a uniform procedure for elections, but did apportion the number of seats among the Member States and determine the term of office of MEPs. The Council was to determine the period for the first elections.[68] Since then, elections have always been held in the period starting on a Thursday morning and ending on the following Sunday evening corresponding to the same period five years before,[69] except where the Council decided to hold the elections (not more than one month) later or earlier.[70]

The 1976 Act was amended in 2002, after the Treaty of Amsterdam had weakened the aim of Art. 190 EC to the extent that elections by direct universal suffrage were to take place in accordance with a uniform procedure in all Member States or "in accordance with principles common to all Member States". The amendments which the Council made to the Act on direct elections on the basis of a draft submitted by the European Parliament[71] entered into force after they

---

[67] Decision 76/787/ECSC, EEC, Euratom of the representatives of the Member States meeting in the Council relating to the Act concerning the election of the representatives of the Assembly by direct universal suffrage, [1976] O.J. L278/1. The European Parliament had regard to the first draft convention of May 17, 1960 ([1960] O.J. 834) in drawing up the Patijn draft convention of January 14, 1975, [1975] O.J. C32/15. Pursuant to the second subpara. of para. 3 of Art. 190 EC and Art. 108 EAEC, the Act declared that paras 1 and 2 of those articles had lapsed, without, however, introducing the "uniform procedure" referred to in para. 3, first subpara.

[68] Council Decision 78/639/Euratom, ECSC, EEC of July 25, 1978, [1978] O.J. L205/75, prescribed the period June 7–10, 1979.

[69] Such as from June 10 to 13, 2004. Voting took place on the Thursday in two Member States (the Netherlands and the United Kingdom), on the Friday in Ireland, on the Saturday in Latvia and Malta, Cyprus and Slovakia, on the Friday and the Saturday in the Czech Republic, on the Saturday and the Sunday in Italy and on a Sunday in the rest of the Union.

[70] See the periods June 14 to 17, 1984 (Council Decision 83/285/EEC, Euratom, ECSC of June 2, 1983, [1983] O.J. L155/11) and June 15 to 18, 1989 (Council Decision 88/435/ECSC, EEC, Euratom of July 26, 1988, [1988] O.J. L210/25). In 1994 the elections were held on June 9 and 12 and in 2009 they were held from June 4 to 7. Special elections were organised in Bulgaria on May 20, 2007 and in Romania on November 25, 2007 in view of the accession of these two countries to the I on January 1, 2007.

[71] Council Decision 2002/772/EC, Euratom of June 25, 2002 and September 23, 2002 amending the Act concerning the election of the representatives of the European Parliament by direct universal suffrage, annexed to Decision 76/787/ECSC, EEC, Euratom, [2002] O.J. L283/1 (*corrigendum* to certain language versions in [2004] O.J. L64/48). In referring to the Act hereinafter, use will consistently be made of the new numbering introduced by that decision. Earlier drafts of the European

had been approved by the Member States in accordance with their constitutional provisions.[72] The amended Act provides that members of the European Parliament are to be elected on the basis of proportional representation, using the list system or the single transferable vote (Act, Art. 1(1)). Member States may opt for a preferential list system (Act, Art. 1(2)), may establish constituencies or other subdivisions for elections (Art. 2) and may set a minimum threshold for the distribution of seats (Art. 3) and ceilings for candidates' election expenses (Art. 4).[73] The rules on the election period remained virtually unchanged.[74] Subject to the provisions of the Act, the electoral procedure is to be governed in each Member State by its national provisions, which, however, may not affect the essentially proportional nature of the voting system.[75] Accordingly, the European Parliament must "take note" of the results officially declared by the Member States, although it may review the credentials of members of the European Parliament (Act, Art. 12).[76]

13–018   **Right to participate in elections.** Neither Art. 223 TFEU nor the 1976 Act defines expressly and precisely who are to be entitled to the right to vote and to stand as a candidate in elections to the European Parliament. The definition of the

---

Parliament were less successful; see the draft of March 10, 1982 ([1982] O.J. C87/61) and the resolutions of October 10, 1991 ([1992] O.J. C280/141) and March 10, 1993 ([1993] O.J. C115/121), as a result of which it was held unnecessary to proceed to judgment in proceedings brought against the European Parliament for failure to fulfil its Treaty obligations: ECJ (order of June 10, 1993), Case C-41/92 *The Liberal Democrats v European Parliament* [1993] E.C.R. I-3153. For the Council's reaction, see the Council's answer of January 17, 1997 to question E-2205/96 (De Vries), [1997] O.J. C83/8. See also De Vries, "La procédure électorale uniforme du Parlement européen: un pas pour rapprocher l'Europe des citoyens" (1996) R.M.C.U.E. 417–421.

[72] See Art. 3 of Decision 2002/772/EC. Article 14 of the Act (there was a corresponding provision also in the original version) empowers the Council to adopt any necessary implementing measures unanimously, in accordance with an unusual procedure: the Council acts on a proposal from the Parliament, after consulting the Commission, and after endeavouring to reach agreement with the Parliament in a conciliation committee consisting of the Council and representatives of the Parliament.

[73] In the absence of a uniform election procedure, there are also no uniform rules on the reimbursement of election expenses: see Joliet and Keeling, "The Reimbursement of Election Expenses: A Forgotten Dispute" (1994) E.L.Rev. 243–267.

[74] Act, Arts 10 and 11 (Art. 11(2) allows the Council to set the election period two months earlier or one month later than the normal period).

[75] Act, Art. 8. Usually in Member States where there is no obligation to go to the polls, the turnout for elections to the European Parliament is low. For ideas to improve this situation, see Lodge, "Making the Election of the European Parliament Distinctive: Towards E-Uniform Election Procedure" (2000) E. J. L. Ref. 191–215.

[76] This power does not amount to a general power to review the official declaration, but must be given a limited scope (ECJ, Joined Cases C-393/07 and C-9/08 *Italy and Donnici v European Parliament* [2009] E.C.R. I-3679, paras 50–73). See also ECJ, Case C-208/03 P *Le Pen* [2005] E.C.R. I-06051, paras 43–58 (the European Parliament is under a duty to "take note" of a communication from a Member State that a MEP is disqualified as a result of a criminal conviction).

persons entitled to vote and to stand as a candidate in elections to the European Parliament falls within the competence of each Member State in compliance with Union law, and the principle of equal treatment in particular. Consequently, Member States could validly choose to grant the right to vote and to stand as a candidate to certain persons who have close links to them, other than their own nationals or citizens of the Union resident in their territory.[77] However, the Netherlands could not without infringing the principle of equal treatment deny the right to vote and stand as a candidate to Dutch nationals resident in the Netherlands Antilles or Aruba while at the same time granting this right to Dutch nationals resident in a third country.[78]

Article 22 TFEU [*ex Art. 19 EC*] applies the principle of non-discrimination on grounds of nationality to the exercise of the right to vote and stand as a candidate in elections to the European Parliament, by providing that every citizen of the Union residing in a Member State of which he is not a national is to have this right in the Member State in which he resides, under the same conditions as nationals of that State. The detailed arrangements surrounding this right are laid down in Council Directive 93/109/EC of December 6, 1993, which was adopted pursuant to Art. 19(2) EC [*now Art. 22(2) TFEU*].[79] A person having the right to vote may exercise it either in the Member State of residence or in his or her home Member State; a person eligible to stand as a candidate may do so in only one Member State (Directive 93/109, Art. 4). If a Member State requires candidates to have been nationals for a certain minimum period, Union citizens are deemed to satisfy that condition if they have been nationals of a Member State for that period (Directive 93/109, Art. 3). Where nationals of the Member State in question are required to have spent a certain minimum period as a resident in the electoral territory of that State in order to be able to vote or stand for election, Union citizens satisfy that condition if they have resided for an equivalent period in other

---

[77] ECJ, Case C-145/04 *Spain v United Kingdom* [2006] E.C.R. I-7917. It should be noted, however, that this judgment was given "in the current state of Community law" (see para. 78 of the judgment), which included, at the time, the definition of the European Parliament as composed of "representatives of the peoples of the States brought together in the Community" and not of "representatives of the Union's citizens" (see para. 13–015). In response to the ruling of the European Court of Human Rights in *Matthews* (see para. 22–029, *infra*), the United Kingdom in fact gave Commonwealth citizens residing in Gibraltar the right to vote in the 2004 elections for the European Parliament (see European Parliament (Representation) Act 2003).

[78] ECJ, Case C-300/04 *Eman and Sevinger* [2006] E.C.R. I-8055, paras 40–61.

[79] Council Directive 93/109/EC of December 6, 1993 laying down detailed arrangements for the exercise of the right to vote and stand as a candidate in elections to the European Parliament for citizens of the Union residing in a Member State of which they are not nationals, [1993] O.J. L329/34, implemented in the United Kingdom by the European Parliamentary Elections (Changes to the Franchise and Qualification of Representatives) Regulations 1994, amending the European Parliamentary Elections Act 1978. For a discussion of this right to stand and vote (and its application for the first time in 1994), see Oliver, "Electoral Rights under Article 8b [*later Article 19*] of the Treaty of Rome" (1996) C.M.L.Rev. 473–498.

Member States. Nevertheless, this does not apply in the case of a Member State which imposes specific conditions as to length of residence in a given constituency or locality (Directive 93/109, Art. 5). Where, in a given Member State, the proportion of Union citizens of voting age who reside in it but are not nationals of it exceeds 20 per cent of the total number of Union citizens residing there who are of voting age, the directive authorises the Member State in question to restrict non-nationals' right to vote and stand in elections to those who have been resident in that State for a specified minimum period (Directive 93/109, Art. 14; implemented by Luxembourg).[80] As far as the right to stand for election is concerned, account must be taken of the restrictions which national criminal law may impose in relation to eligibility.

13–019 **Conditions for exercise of office.** MEPs are to vote on an individual and personal basis, are not bound by any instructions and do not receive a binding mandate (Act on the Direct Election of the European Parliament, Art. 6(1)).[81] The European Parliament is to lay down the regulations and general conditions governing the performance of the duties of its Members after consulting the Commission and with the approval of the Council, acting by a qualified majority, except for the tax arrangements for Members or former Members, for which unanimity is required (Art. 223(2) TFEU [ex Art. 190(5) EC]).[82] The Act provides only that the holding of a number of offices is incompatible with being an MEP: member of the Government of a Member State; member of another Union institution (for the ECB: of the Board of Directors); member of the European Economic and Social Committee or the Committee of the Regions; member of committees or other bodies set up to manage Union funds or to carry out a permanent direct administrative task; European Ombudsman; member of the Board of Directors or Management Committee of the EIB, or active official or servant of the Union (Act, Art. 7(1)).[83] Originally, the Act expressly provided that an

[80] Luxembourg requires nationals of other Member States to have resided in its territory for at least five of the last six years in order to be able to vote and for at least ten of the last twelve years in order to be able to stand as a candidate: see the law of January 28, 1994, *JO du Grand-Duché de Luxembourg*, January 31, 1994.
[81] See Böttger, "Die Rechtsstellung des Abgeordneten des Europäischen Parlaments" (2002) EuR. 898–916.
[82] See the Statute for Members of the European Parliament, adopted by Decision 2005/684/EC, Euratom of the European Parliament of September 28, 2005, [2005] O.J. L262/1 and implemented by Decision of the Bureau of May 19, and July 9, 2008, [2009] O.J. C159.
[83] Since members of a government of a federated State or of a devolved legislative body may represent that Member State in the Council since the EU Treaty entered into force, holding such an office would also appear to be incompatible with membership of the European Parliament. According to the Memorandum of Understanding between the United Kingdom Government, the Scottish Ministers, the Welsh Ministers and the Northern Ireland Executive Committee of March 2010 and the Concordat on coordination of European Union policy issues, Ministers of the devolved administrations are able to participate in Council meetings and speak for the United Kingdom. Hence it

MEP might also be a member of a national parliament.[84] With effect from the election of the European Parliament in 2004, the capacity of MEP is incompatible with the office of national member of parliament (Act, Art. 7(2), which provided for temporary exceptions for Ireland and the United Kingdom[85]). It should be noted that national rules may prescribe other incompatibilities.[86] Members of the European Parliament enjoy privileged free movement and may not be the subject of proceedings in respect of opinions which they express in the performance of their duties.[87] During the session of the European Parliament, MEPs enjoy

---

would appear that holding such office is incompatible with being an MEP (but not mere membership of the Scottish Parliament, National Assembly for Wales and the Northern Ireland Assembly: see Scotland Act 1998, s.15 (and s.82(1)(b) on reduction of Members' remuneration to take account of remuneration as an MEP), Government of Wales Act 2006, s.16 (and s.21(1)(b) on remuneration) and Northern Ireland Act 1998, s.36 (and s.47(b) on remuneration). Moreover, Art. 305, third para., TFEU [ex Art. 263, fourth para., EC] provides that membership of the Committee of the Regions is incompatible with being an MEP.

[84] In this context, the question arose as to whether a Member State could prohibit such a dual mandate. See, e.g., Art. 42 of the Belgian Law of March 23, 1989 on elections to the European Parliament, *Belgisch Staatsblad/Moniteur belge*, March 5, 1989 (as amended by laws of July 16, 1993 and April 11, 1994, *Belgisch Staatsblad/Moniteur belge*, July 20, 1993 and April 16, 1994). As to whether a Member State was entitled to prohibit dual mandates, see question 2102/86 (De Gucht), [1987] O.J. C112/45.

[85] See now, the European Parliament (House of Lords Disqualification) Regulations 2008 (SI 2008/1647), which make provision for a life peer who is elected to the office of member of the European Parliament to be disqualified from sitting and voting in the House of Lords for the duration of his of her membership of the European Parliament. Taking effect from the 2009 European Parliamentary elections, this allows a life peer to be elected and serve as a member of the European Parliament, without breaching the prohibition on dual mandates.

[86] Paragraph 5 of Sch. 1 to the European Parliamentary Elections Act 1978 provides that a person is disqualified for the office of MEP if he or she is disqualified, whether under the House of Commons Disqualification Act 1975 or otherwise, for membership of the House of Commons, or if he or she is a Lord of Appeal in Ordinary. However, by virtue of subpara. 3 and in contradistinction to the position with regard to the House of Commons, peers, members of the clergy, holders of an office mentioned in s. 4 of the House of Commons Disqualification Act 1975 (stewardship of the Chiltern Hundreds, etc.) and holders of an office described in Part II or Part III of Sch. 1 to that Act, provided they are designated by the Secretary of State as non-disqualifying offices in relation to the European Parliament, may stand for election to the European Parliament. But see the preceding n.

[87] Protocol (No. 7), annexed to the TEU, TFEU and EAEC Treaty, on Privileges and Immunities ([2010] O.J. C83/266), Arts 7 and 8 of the Chapter formerly entitled "Members of the Assembly" also apply to directly elected Members of the European Parliament, as confirmed by Art. 6(2) of the Act on the Direct Election of the European Parliament (para. 13–015, *supra*). For the scope of MEPs' privileged free movement under Art. 7 of the Protocol, see ECJ, Case 208/80 *Bruce of Donington* [1981] ECR 2205, para. 14, and CFI, Case T-345/05 *Mote* [2008] E.C.R. II-2849, paras 47–51. For the scope of the immunity for opinions expressed in the performance of their duties, which has to be established on the basis of Union law alone, and the Parliament's right to defend immunity under Rule 7 of its Rules of Procedure, see ECJ, Joined Cases C-200/07 and C-201/07 *Marra* [2008] E.C.R. I-7929, paras 24–45; see also EGC (March 19, 2010), Case T-42/06 *Gollnisch v European Parliament*, not yet reported. It should be noted that, in contradistinction to the immunities conferred by Art. 9 of the Protocol, the immunity conferred by Art. 8 cannot be waived by the Parliament (see *Marra*, para. 44).

immunity from any measure of detention and legal proceedings in other Member States and the immunities accorded to Members of the national parliament in their own Member State. This parliamentary immunity may not be claimed if an MEP is found in the act of committing an offence and may be waived by the European Parliament.[88]

3. Operation

13–020 Rules of Procedure. In so far as the Treaties do not provide otherwise, the European Parliament operates in accordance with its Rules of Procedure, adopted by a majority of its members (Art. 232, first para., TFEU [*ex Art. 199, first para., EC*]).[89] Pursuant to the power to determine its own internal organisation, the Parliament is entitled to "adopt appropriate measures to ensure the due functioning and conduct of its proceedings".[90] Its annual "session" meets on the second Tuesday in March (Art. 299, first para., TFEU [*ex Art. 196, first para., EC*]) and lasts in practice until the session of the following year or until the first meeting of a newly elected Parliament.[91] The session includes monthly meetings of committees and political groups and plenary sessions (sometimes referred to as "sittings").[92] If the Parliament does not close the session earlier, there will be no need to hold an extraordinary session (Art. 229, second para., TFEU [*ex Art. 196, second para., EC*]) and MEPs enjoy the immunities conferred upon them for the whole of the year.[93]

The Commission is entitled to attend meetings.[94] Members of the Commission, the Council and the European Council may make statements to the European Parliament.[95] For its part, the Commission ensures that the responsible

---

[88] Protocol (No. 7) on Privileges and Immunities, Art.9, and EP Rules of Procedure, Rules 5 to 7. For the possibility of invoking immunity in connection with an investigation carried out by the Community Anti-Fraud Office OLAF (n. 325, *supra*), see CFI (order of the President of May 2, 2000), Case T-17/00 R *Rothley and Others v European Parliament* [2000] E.C.R. II-2085; as upheld by ECJ, Case C-167/02 P *Rothley and Others v European Parliament* [2004] E.C.R. I-03149. See Thym, "Europaabgeordnete gegen Europaparlement—der erste Akt des Streits um OLAF" (2000) EuR. 990–998. For another example, see CFI, Case T-345/05 *Mote* [2008] E.C.R. II-2849.

[89] Rules of Procedure of the European Parliament [EP Rules of Procedure] of December 2009.

[90] ECJ, Case 230/81 *Luxembourg v European Parliament* [1983] E.C.R. 255, para. 38.

[91] The newly elected Parliament meets for the first time on the first Tuesday in the month after the end of the election period (Act on the Direct Election of the European Parliament, Art. 11(3)).

[92] See EP Rules of Procedure, Rule 133.

[93] ECJ, Case 101/63 *Wagner* [1964] E.C.R. 195; ECJ, Case 149/85 *Wybot* [1986] E.C.R. 2391, paras 15–27. For the immunity of MEPs, see para. 13–156, *infra*.

[94] Article 230, first para., TFEU [*ex Art. 197, second para., EC*].

[95] Article 230, second and third para., TFEU [*ex Art. 197, third and fourth para., EC*] and EP Rules of Procedure, Rule 110(1). See also points 45–50 of the Framework Agreement of October 20, 2010 (n. 26, *supra*), which provide that Commissioners may also be heard at their request in a parliamentary committee.

Commissioner is present at the plenary session or in committee when the European Parliament requests his or her presence.[96]

Seat. Meetings of the European Parliament are held in accordance with the provisions of the Treaties. Pursuant to Art. 289 EC [*now Art. 341 TFEU*], the governments of the Member States have determined in the First Decision on the Seats of the Institutions of December 12, 1992 that the European Parliament has its seat in Strasbourg, where the twelve periods of monthly plenary sessions, including the budget session, are to be held (no session is held in Strasbourg in August, but two in September). Additional plenary sessions are to be held in Brussels, where the parliamentary committees also meet. The general secretariat and its departments have remained in Luxembourg.[97] By requiring that the European Parliament should meet in principle every month in Strasbourg, the governments endorsed that institution's previous practice. In determining its internal organisation, the Parliament must respect the national governments' competence to determine its seat. Only if the European Parliament holds its twelve ordinary part sessions, including the budgetary part session, in Strasbourg may it hold additional part sessions in Brussels.[98] By incorporating the Decision on the Seats of the Institutions into the Protocol on the location of the seats of the institutions and of certain bodies and departments of the European Communities and of Europol[99] (Protocol on Seats, see para. 13–153), the Treaty of Amsterdam gave these rules the status of Treaty law.

13–021

Proceedings. Before each part-session (i.e. the meeting convened as a rule each month and divided into daily sittings) the European Parliament draws up its

13–022

---

[96] Points 45–50 of the Framework Agreement of October 20, 2010 (n. 26, *supra.*) and point 8 of the Interinstitutional Agreement of December 16, 2003 on better law-making, [2003] O.J. C321/1. For that commitment, see also the Commission's answer of February 8, 1990 to question No. 1207/89 (McMahon), [1990] O.J. C125/44.

[97] Article 1(a) of the First Decision on the Seats of the Institutions of December 12, 1992, para. 13–153, *infra*.

[98] The Court of Justice annulled the European Parliament's vote to hold only eleven part-sessions in Strasbourg in 1996 on the ground that it infringed the First Decision on the Seats of the Institutions: ECJ, Case C-345/95 *France v European Parliament* [1997] E.C.R. I-5215, paras 13–35. An action brought against a similar vote relating to the calendar of part sessions for 1997 (Case C-267/96 *France v European Parliament*, lodged on August 5, 1996, [1996] O.J. C269/21) was removed from the register following the judgment in Case C-345/95 (order of December 19, 1997, [1998] O.J. C94/17). The Court held that the constraints as regards the organisation of parliamentary work imposed by the Decision on the Seats of the Institutions did not conflict with the Parliament's power of internal organisation (Case C-345/95, *ibid.*, paras 30–32). See also para. 13–160, *infra*.

[99] See now Protocol (No. 6), annexed to the TEU, TFEU and EAEC Treaty, on the location of the seats of the institutions and of certain bodies, offices, agencies and departments of the European Union, [2010] O.J. C83/265.

agenda.[100] Save as otherwise provided in the Treaties, the European Parliament acts by an absolute majority of the votes cast (Art. 231, first para., TFEU [*ex Art. 198, first para., EC*]). A number of Treaty articles require it to act by a majority of its component Members[101] and/or by two-thirds of the votes cast.[102] The Parliament is quorate when one-third of its component Members is present in the Chamber (EP Rules of Procedure, Rule 155(2)). Debates in the house are public (EP Rules of Procedure, Rule 103(2)). MEPs prepare decisions to be adopted at the plenary session in parliamentary committees.[103]

In the ordinary legislative procedure, a delegation from the European Parliament may meet with members of the Council or their representatives in a Conciliation Committee, which is presided over jointly by the Presidents of the Parliament and the Council.[104] The two delegations have the same number of members, equal to the number of members of the Council. The European Parliament delegation consists of three Members appointed by the political groups as permanent members of successive delegations for a period of twelve months and other Members appointed for each particular conciliation case, preferably from among the members of the committees concerned.[105]

4. Internal organisation

13–023 **Internal bodies.** The European Parliament elects a President and a Bureau from among its Members (Art. 14(4) TEU [*ex Art. 197, first para., EC*]). The Bureau

---

[100] EP Rules of Procedure, Rule 137(1). The draft agenda drawn up by the Conference of Presidents (para. 13–024, *infra*) may be amended at that time at the proposal of a committee, a political group or at least 40 MEPs (*ibid.*).

[101] See Arts 223(1), second para.; 225; 229, second para.; 232, first para.; 234, second para.; 294(7)(b) and (c); 314(4)(c) and (7) (b) and (c) TFEU and Arts 17(7), 48(7), fourth subpara., and 49 TEU.

[102] Two-thirds majority of the votes cast, representing a majority of the component Members: Art. 234, second para., TFEU; Art. 354, fourth para., TFEU. Other, different majorities are laid down in the Rules of Procedure.

[103] Twenty standing committees have been set up pursuant to Rule 183 of the EP Rules of Procedure, as amended. For temporary committees of inquiry, see para. 13–012, *supra*. For the manner of operation of these committees, see Mamadouh and Raunio, "The Committee System: Powers, Appointments and Report Allocation" (2003) J.C.M.S. 335–351.

[104] See Art. 294 TFEU [*ex Art. 251 EC*] (para. 16–022 *et seq.*, *infra*).

[105] See EP Rules of Procedure, Rule 68(3) (which provides that the chairman and the rapporteur of the committee responsible in each particular case are members of the delegation in any event). Meetings are held alternately in the premises of the Parliament and those of the Council and are chaired alternately by one of the two co-chairmen. The secretariat of the Conciliation Committee is provided jointly by the General Secretariats of the Council and the Parliament, in collaboration with the General Secretariat of the Commission. See the Joint Declaration of the European Parliament, the Council and the Commission on practical arrangements for the new co-decision procedure (Art. 251 of the Treaty establishing the European Community), [1999] O.J. C148/1. For Interinstitutional negotiations in legislative procedures and first—and second—reading agreements in the ordinary legislative procedure, see EP Rules of Procedure, Rules 70–71, and Annex XX, Code of conduct for negotiating in the context of the ordinary legislative procedures.

consists of the President and the Vice-Presidents of Parliament, together with the Quaestors sitting in an advisory capacity (EP Rules of Procedure, Rule 22). The President, Vice-Presidents and Quaestors are elected in that order by MEPs for a term of office of two and a half years (see EP Rules of Procedure, Rules 12–17). The President presides over parliamentary proceedings and represents the Parliament in its relations with the outside world (EP Rules of Procedure, Rule 20). The Rules of Procedure entrust the Bureau with financial, administrative and organisational tasks (EP Rules of Procedure, Rule 23); the Quaestors are responsible for purely administrative and financial matters (EP Rules of Procedure, Rule 26). The Bureau appoints a Secretary-General to head the Secretariat (see EP Rules of Procedure, Rule 207). The Secretariat has a staff of around 5,000 and is divided into a legal service and 10 directorates-general.[106]

Political groups and parties. Most MEPs belong to political groups; the remainder are referred to as non-attached.[107] A political group must have members from at least one-quarter of the Member States and at least 25 members.[108] A political group can only be set up on the basis of political affinity.[109] The President of the Parliament exercises certain powers together with the chairmen of the political groups as the Conference of Presidents.[110]

13–024

In some political groups, the members have underpinned their political cooperation by forming a European political party.[111] The European Parliament and the Council, acting in accordance with the ordinary legislative procedure, lay down the regulations governing political parties at European level and in particular the rules

---

[106] The Secretariat had 5093 permanent posts and 126 temporary posts as at December 2009. See Commission of the European Union, *General Report on the Activities of the European Union 2009*, Brussels, 2010, at 96.

[107] EP Rules of Procedure, Rules 30, 31, 32 and 33.

[108] EP Rules of Procedure, Rule 30(2). See further Nessler, "Die Fraktion im Europäischen Parlament" (1997) EuR. 311–320.

[109] EP Rules of Procedure, Rule 30. This requirement ensues from social and political circumstances peculiar to parliamentary democracies and from the specific features and responsibilities of the European Parliament: CFI, Joined Cases T-222/99, T-327/99 and T-329/99 *Martinez and Others v European Parliament* [2001] E.C.R. II-2823, paras 145–148, confirmed on the merits by ECJ (order of November 11, 2003), Case C-488/01 P *Martinez v European Parliament* [2003] E.C.R. I-13355, and set aside, as to the admissibility of the action brought by a political party, by ECJ, Case C-486/01 P *Front National v European Parliament* [2004] E.C.R. I-6289. This does not preclude members of a group in their day-to-day conduct from expressing different political opinions on any particular subject: CFI, *ibid.*, paras 80–94.

[110] See EP Rules of Procedure, Rule 24. The Conference replaced the enlarged Bureau, consisting of the members of the Bureau and the presidents of the political groups.

[111] See the Party of European Socialists (PES) (established in 1974), the European Liberal Democrat and Reform Party (ELDR) and the European People's Party (EPP) (both set up in 1976), the European Green Party, European Free Alliance, Party of the European Left and European Democratic Party (all set up in 2004) and the EUDemocrats (set up in 2005).

regarding their funding (Art. 224 TFEU).[112] According to the relevant regulation, a political party at European level must be represented, in at least one quarter of the Member States, by Members of the European Parliament or members of the national or regional Parliaments or must have received, in at least one quarter of the Member States, 3 per cent or more of the votes cast in each of those Member States at the most recent European Parliament elections.[113] In addition, it must have participated in elections to the European Parliament, or have expressed the intention to do so.[114] Article 10(4) TEU [*ex Art. 191, first para., EC*] declares that political parties at European level "contribute to forming European political awareness and to expressing the will of citizens of the Union".[115] However, so far the existence of European political parties has not prevented political debate at European level from attracting less attention from public opinion than national political discussions. European elections tend all too soon to be dragged in the wake of national issues and it is often hard to regard them as being any indication of voters' views on future European policy choices.

B. THE EUROPEAN COUNCIL

13–025 **Union institution.** The European Council obtained the status of an "institution" only upon the entry into force of the Lisbon Treaty. As long ago as 1974, the Heads of State or Government of the Member States started meeting a few times a year at "summit conferences" (see para. 2–005). Article 2 of the Single European Act enshrined this meeting in the Treaties under the name of the "European Council".[116] That new organ was deliberately not given any legal status in the Community Treaties so as to prevent the institutional balance between Community institutions from being upset by an intergovernmental and politically

---

[112] Regulation (EC) No. 2004/2003 of the European Parliament and of the Council of November 4, 2003 on the regulations governing political parties at European level and the rules regarding their funding, [2003] O.J. L297/1, as amended by Regulation (EC) No. 1524/2007 of December 18, 2007, [2007] O.J. L343/5. Implementing rules have been laid down by Decision of the Bureau of the European Parliament of March 29, 2004, [2008] O.J. C252/1. See von Arnim, "The New EU Party Financing Regulation" (2005) 30 E.L.Rev. 273–284.

[113] Regulation No. 2004/2003, Art. 3.

[114] *Ibid.*

[115] See also Art. 12(2) of the Charter of Fundamental Rights of the European Union. See also Bieber, "Les perspectives d'un statut pour les partis politiques européens" (1999) R.T.D.E. 349–362; Huber, "Die politischen Parteien als Partizipationsinstrument auf Unionsebene" (1999) EuR. 579–596; Stentzel, "Der normative Gehalt des Art.138a EGV—Rechtlicher Grundstein eines europäischen Parteiensystems?" (1997) EuR. 174–191; Tsatsos, "Europäische politische Parteien? Erste Überlegungen zur Auslegung des Parteienartikels des Maastrichter Vertrages—Art.138a EGV" (1994) Eu.GR.Z. 45–53.

[116] For a detailed discussion of the European Council, see Werts, *The European Council* (London, Harper, 2008), 280 pp.; Taulegne, *Le Conseil européen* (Paris, Presses Universitaires de France, 1993), 504 pp.; Glaesner, "Der Europäische Rat" (1994) EuR. 22–34.

higher-ranking organ. The EU Treaty conferred on the European Council the task of providing "the Union with the necessary impetus for its development" and of defining "the general political guidelines" (Art. 4, first para., EU). In addition, the European Council obtained some specific tasks, in particular in the context of the CFSP. Whereas the Treaty of Lisbon included the European Council among the "institutions" of the Union (Art. 13(1) TEU), it has been at pains not to involve that institution in the normal course of legislative proceedings.

1. Powers

Initial powers. When they started to meet in 1974, the Heads of State or Government delicately stated that the arrangements regarding the European Council did not in any way affect the rules and procedures laid down in the Community Treaties.[117] Although the European Council was initially not involved in the Community decision-making process and did not take legally binding decisions, it was clear that, on the political level, the institutionalisation of the meetings of the Heads of State or Government did pose a threat to the position of the Commission and the Council. The subjects on which the European Council was to confer were initially prepared by national civil servants, whilst the Commission was involved in the meetings only passively, even so far as Community matters were concerned.[118] The Council's role was also weakened in that, at the political level, crucial decisions which that institution was empowered to take by a majority vote were often left to the European Council, which had to find a consensus. The trend became even clearer after 1987 when decision-making in the Council was no longer by consensus, as a result of the 1966 "Luxembourg Compromise".[119]

13–026

As mentioned above, the EU Treaty conferred on the European Council the task of providing "the Union with the necessary impetus for its development" and of defining "the general political guidelines" (Art. 4, first para., EU). In addition, the European Council obtained some specific tasks in the context of the Communities' decision-making process[120] and in the context of the CFSP.[121] As regards CFSP, the Treaty of Amsterdam institutionalised the practice of having politically sensitive discussions, issues being transferred from the Council to the European

---

[117] Communiqué of the Heads of State or Government meeting in Paris on December 9 and 10, 1974 (n. 140, *supra*), (3).

[118] From 1985 onwards, the Commission itself began to take more initiatives within the European Council. See the discussion in Werts (n. 116, *supra*).

[119] See the discussion of the operation of the Council, para. 13–047, *infra*.

[120] It was to discuss a conclusion on the broad lines of the economic policies of the Member States and the Community (Art. 99(2) EC) and to adopt conclusions on the employment situation in the Community (Art. 128(1) EC).

[121] The European Council was to define the principles of and general guidelines for the common foreign and security policy and could decide on the progressive framing of a common defence policy, which might lead to a common defence (Arts 13(1)–(2) and 17(1) EU).

Council. As regards the CFSP, it provided that a vote was not to be taken if a member of the Council declared that, for important and stated reasons of national policy, it intended to oppose a measure which would otherwise be adopted by a qualified majority; the Council, acting by a qualified majority, would then request that the matter be referred to the European Council for decision by unanimity.[122] The Lisbon Treaty further developed the European Council's tasks.

13–027   **High-level steering and conciliation.** According to Art. 15(1) TEU, the European Council's tasks remain to provide the Union with the necessary impetus for its development and to define the general political directions and priorities of the Union.

More specifically, the European Council defines the strategic guidelines for legislative and operational planning within the area of freedom, security and justice (Art. 68 TFEU) and adopts conclusions on the broad lines of the economic policies of the Member States and Union (Art. 121(2) TFEU) and on the employment situation in the Union (Art. 148(1) TFEU).[123] In addition, the European Council is to identify the strategic interests and objectives of the Union's external action (Arts 22(1) and 26(1) TEU). It regularly assesses the threats facing the Union in order to enable the Union and its Member States to take effective action (Art. 222(4) TFEU). The CFSP is the only field where the European Council is responsible not only for determining the objectives and defining the general guidelines, but also—together with the Council—for defining and implementing that policy.[124]

In addition, the European Council continues to play the role of political arbitrator in certain fields where the Council has the power to adopt measures by qualified majority and where a member of the Council intends to oppose the adoption of a measure for important political reasons or because it would affect fundamental aspects of national systems for social security or criminal justice.[125]

---

[122] Article 23(2), second subpara., EU (CFSP) and Art. 27c, second para. (enhanced cooperation in connection with the CFSP).

[123] As was the case even before the Lisbon Treaty, the European Council receives reports from the Council on the guidelines of the economic policies of the Member States and of the Union (Art. 121 TFEU), from the Council and the Commission on the employment situation in the Union and on the implementation of the guidelines for employment (Art. 148(1) and (5) TFEU), from the European Central Bank on the activities of the European System of Central Banks and monetary policy (Art. 284(3), first subpara., TFEU) and from the Commission on the application of Art. 5 TEU (Art. 9 of Protocol (No. 2), annexed to the TEU and TFEU, on the application of the principles of subsidiarity and proportionality, [2010] O.J. C83/206). See already Martenczuk, "Der Europäische Rat und die Wirtschafts- und Währungsunion" (1998) EuR. 151–177.

[124] See Arts 24(1), 26(1) and 32 TEU.

[125] See Art. 31(2), second subpara., TEU (opposition against CFSP decision for "vital and stated reasons of national policy"); Art. 48 TFEU (opposition against a social security measures that would affect "important aspects of its social security system" or "the financial balance of that system"); Arts 82(3) and 83(3) TFEU (opposition against certain PJCC measures that would affect "fundamental aspects of its criminal justice system"). See also Arts 86(1), second subpara., and 87(3) TFEU (opposition against certain PJCC measures by a group of at least nine Member States).

In such a case, that member of the Council may request the measure to be referred to the European Council, which will then try to find a consensus on the proposed measure.

There is no intention that the European Council should involve itself with the legislative work carried out by the Council jointly with the European Parliament. To this end, the Treaties stress that the European Council "shall not exercise legislative functions" (Art. 15(1) TEU). In practice, however, the compromises reached by the European Council in sensitive cases may lead to detailed guidelines that do not leave much latitude to the Council and the Parliament if they do not want to upset a political agreement which has been attained.[126]

Status of decisions. Since the entry into force of the Lisbon Treaty, it is clear that decisions of the European Council may have binding effects. According to Art. 263, first para., TFEU, acts of the European Council intended to produce legal effects vis-à-vis third parties are subject to review by the Court of Justice.

13–028

Before the Lisbon Treaty, the interventions of the European Council in matters coming within the sphere of the Communities, did not lead to binding measures of Community law. Although, in theory, the European Council could act as the Council (since it was composed of a representative at ministerial level of each Member State,[127]) it never applied the decision-making procedures laid down in the Treaties. Where appropriate, decisions of the European Council were transformed by Community institutions into decisions of Community law.[128] Since the incorporation of the European Council into the EU Treaty did not change the powers conferred on the institutions by the Community Treaties,[129] the "impetus" and "guidelines" which the European Council was to give since 1993, could not

---

[126] See Editorial Comments "An ever mighty European Council—Some recent institutional developments" (2009) C.M.L.Rev. 1383–1393.

[127] To that effect, the procedural rules laid down in the Treaties had to be complied with, in particular a vote on the basis of a Commission proposal, having regard to the prerogatives of the European Parliament.

[128] Admittedly the European Council held in Milan on June 29, 1985 adopted by a majority vote against a minority the decision to initiate the procedure provided for in Art. 236 EEC and to consult the Parliament on amending the Treaty. In so doing, it disregarded the Council's Rules of Procedure, which provide that an agenda item must be already on the agenda before a decision can be taken. However, the formal decision was taken by the Council, after consulting the Parliament, in July 1985. See De Ruyt, *L'Acte unique européen* (Brussels, Editions de l'Université de Bruxelles, 1987), at 62.

[129] Article 47 EU. See Curtin, "The Constitutional Structure of the Union: A Europe of Bits and Pieces" (1993) C.M.L.Rev. 17, at 27; VerLoren van Themaat, "De constitutionele problematiek van een Europese politieke Unie" (1991) S.E.W. 436, at 442.

be legally binding on the Community institutions.[130] A decision of the European Council therefore did not prevent a Member State from taking up the matter again within the Council. This was also the case where, in the context of the CFSP, the Council took decisions "on the basis of the general guidelines adopted by the European Council" or implemented common strategies decided on by the European Council.[131] Nevertheless, it was clear in practice that, in all these cases, the Council only gave legal effect to what the European Council had decided on the political level. Also in the sphere of economic and monetary policy, some European Council resolutions embodied in practice determinative policy choices which directed the action of the Community institutions and the Member States.[132] Moreover, CFSP action on the part of the European Council had legal effects inasmuch as whenever the European Council had decided on a common strategy, the Council could implement it by a qualified majority vote.[133] Still, most decisions of the European Council took the form of "resolutions" of a non-binding nature.[134]

---

[130] That also applied where the Council was to adopt the broad guidelines of the economic policies of the Member States and the Community and the guidelines for employment policy "on the basis of" the European Council's conclusions (Arts 99(2) and 128(2) EC). Although, in view of its composition, the Council would normally have been of the same view as the European Council, it was not under a legal obligation to be so. See Everling, "Reflections on the Structure of the European Union" (1992) C.M.L.Rev. 1053, at 1062.

[131] See Art. 13(2) and (3) EU.

[132] See the resolutions of the European Council of June 16, 1997 on the establishment of an exchange-rate mechanism in the third stage of economic and monetary union ([1997] O.J. C236/5), of June 17, 1997 on the Stability and Growth Pact ([1997] O.J. C236/1), of December 13, 1997 on economic policy coordination in Stage 3 of EMU and on Treaty Arts 109 and 109b [later Arts 111 and 113] EC ([1998] O.J. C35/1) and of January 19, 1998 on denominations and technical specifications of euro coins intended for circulation ([1998] O.J. C35/5). The scenario for the changeover to the single currency approved by the European Council on December 15 and 16, 1995 at Madrid also turned out to be of major importance ((1995) 12 EU Bull. points I-3 and I.49).

[133] Article 13(2) EU. See Timmermans, "Het Verdrag van Amsterdam. Enkele inleidende kanttekeningen" (1997) S.E.W. 344, at 347.

[134] The decision that the European Council meeting in Edinburgh on December 11 and 12, 1992 took concerning certain problems raised by Denmark on the Treaty on European Union (para. 3–010, supra) had certain legal effects and was therefore entitled "decision of the Heads of State or Government, meeting within the European Council". See Curtin and van Ooik, "De bijzondere positie van Denemarken in de Europese Unie" (1993) S.E.W. 675, at 677–678. Likewise, the decision of the European Council held on June 18 and 19, 2009 in Brussels to address the (presumed) concerns of the Irish people expressed in the negative referendum on the Lisbon Treaty (para. 4–008, supra) took the form of a "Decision of the Heads of State or Government of the 27 Member States of the EU, meeting within the European Council". Whereas the European Council, in its conclusions, refers to that decision as "legally binding", it also provided that, at the time of the conclusion of the next accession Treaty, the provisions of that Decision would be set out in a Protocol to be attached to the TEU and TFEU. In contrast, the European Council meeting held on October 29 and 30, 2009 in Brussels that paved the way for the Czech Republic to ratify the Lisbon Treaty limited itself to agreeing on the text of a Protocol that was to be attached to the TEU and TFEU at the time of the conclusion of the next accession Treaty.

Constituent decisions. On some occasions, the European Council is called upon   **13–029** to take decisions as a "constituent authority".

First, there is the case where the European Council intervenes in the ordinary revision procedure for the amendment of the Treaties provided for by Art. 48 TEU (see para. 5–003 *et seq.*) or takes decisions under the simplified revision procedure to amend certain provisions of Part Three of the TFEU (Art. 48(6) TEU; see para. 5–007). The European Council also acts as a constituent authority in so far as it may decide, in respect of certain provisions of the Treaties, to replace a special legislative procedure by the ordinary legislative procedure and voting by unanimity by qualified majority voting (see, e.g., Arts 31(3) and 48(7) TEU and 312(2) TFEU).[135] In the course of the progressive framing of a common Union defence policy, the European Council, acting unanimously, may decide to establish a common defence for the Union. In that event, it is to recommend to the Member States the adoption of the relevant decisions in accordance with their respective constitutional requirements (Art. 42(2), first subpara., TEU).

Secondly, the European Council is to lay down a number of important institutional arrangements to complement the Treaty provisions on the institutions, concerning such matters as the composition of the European Parliament (Art. 14(2), second subpara., TEU), the list of Council configurations and their Presidency (Arts 16(6) and (9) TEU and 236 TFEU) and the rotation system for members of the Commission (Arts 17(5) TEU and 244 TFEU). The European Council also proposes to the European Parliament a candidate for President of the Commission and appoints the Commission (Art. 17(7) TEU). It also appoints the High Representative of the Union for Foreign Affairs and Security Policy (Art. 18(1) TEU) and the members of the executive board of the ECB (Art. 283(2), second subpara., TFEU).[136]

In its role of "constituent authority", the European Council further determines the conditions for the accession of a Member State (Art. 49, first para., TEU) and has to be notified by Member States that wish to withdraw from the Union of their intention to do so (Art. 50(2) TEU).[137] Further, the European Council may amend

---

[135] The European Council acts unanimously after obtaining the consent of the European Parliament, given by a majority of its component members; no national parliament is to oppose the decision. For another possibility of Treaty amendment by the European Council, see Art. 86(4) TFEU (which enables the European Council, acting unanimously after obtaining the consent of the European Parliament and consulting the Commission, to extend the powers of the European Public Prosecutor's Office); see para. 5–009, *supra*.

[136] Before the Lisbon Treaty, the President of the Commission was nominated by the Council meeting in the composition of the Heads of State or Government, whereas the President and the other members of the Commission were appointed by the Council (see Art. 214(2) EC). The members of the executive board of the ECB were appointed by the governments of the Member States at the level of the Heads of State or Government (Art. 112(2)(b) EC).

[137] The Union negotiates and concludes an agreement with the State concerned, setting out the arrangements for its withdrawal, in the light of the guidelines provided by the European Council (Art. 50(2) TEU). The Treaties will normally cease to apply to the State in question from the date of entry into force of the withdrawal agreement or, failing that, two years after the notification to the European Council of the intention to withdraw, but the European Council, in agreement with the Member State concerned, may decide to extend this period (Art. 50(3) TEU).

the status under Union law of a Danish, French or Netherlands overseas territory (Art. 355(6) TFEU). Lastly, it is the European Council which is to determine the existence of a serious and persistent breach by a Member State of the values referred to in Art. 2 TEU, which may lead to the suspension of certain Treaty rights of the Member State in question (see Art. 7(2) TEU).

Finally, it should be mentioned that although the European Council does not have the right to bring an action for annulment against acts of other institutions, it does have the right to bring actions for failure to act in the Court of Justice (Art. 265 TFEU).

2. Composition

13–030   **Composition.** The European Council consists of the Heads of State or Government of the Member States, together with its President and the President of the Commission (Art. 15(2) TEU). The High Representative of the Union for Foreign Affairs and Security Policy is entitled to take part in the work of the European Council (Art. 15(2) TEU). The members of the European Council may decide to be assisted by a Minister or, in the case of the President of the Commission, by a Member of the European Commission (Art. 15(3) TEU). Before the Lisbon Treaty, the European Council consisted of the Heads of State or Government of the Member States and the President of the Commission, assisted by the Ministers of Foreign Affairs of the Member States and a Member of the Commission (Art. 4, second para., EU).[138]

13–031   **President of the European Council.** Initially, the European Council met under the chairmanship of the Head of State or Government of the Member State which held the Presidency of the Council (Art. 4, second para., EU). Since the Lisbon Treaty, the European Council has a full time president, who is elected by the European Council, by a qualified majority, for a term of two and a half years, renewable once (Art. 15(5) TEU).[139] In the event of an impediment or serious

---

[138] See the Solemn Declaration of Stuttgart, June 19, 1983 (1983) 6 EC Bull. point 2.1.1 and Art. 2 of the Single European Act. It was agreed, however, that the President of the European Council was to invite the Economic and Finance Ministers to participate in European Council meetings when the European Council was discussing matters relating to economic and monetary union (See Declaration (No. 4) of the signatories of the EU Treaty on Part Three, Title VI [*later Title VII*], of the Treaty establishing the European Community).

[139] Declaration (No. 6), annexed to the Lisbon Treaty, states that in choosing the persons called upon to hold the offices of President of the European Council, President of the Commission and High Representative of the Union for Foreign Affairs and Security Policy "due account is to be taken of the need to respect the geographical and demographic diversity of the Union and its Member States" (Declaration (No. 6) on Art. 15(5) and (6), Art. 17(6) and (7) and Art. 18 of the Treaty on European Union), [2010] O.J. C83/338). The first President elected was Herman Van Rompuy (see European Council Decision 2009/879/EU of December 1, 2009 electing the President of the European Council, [2009] O.J. L315/48).

misconduct, the European Council can end the President's term of office in accordance with the same procedure (*ibid.*). In that event, and in the case of an impediment because of illness and in the event of his or her death, the President of the European Council will be replaced, where necessary until the election of his or her successor, by the member of the European Council representing the Member State holding the six-monthly Presidency of the Council (European Council, Rules of Procedure, Art. 2(4)).

The President of the European Council may not hold a national mandate (Art. 15(6) TEU). The President's tasks are to:

(a) chair the European Council and drive forward its work;

(b) ensure the preparation and continuity of the work of the European Council in cooperation with the President of the Commission, and on the basis of the work of the General Affairs Council; and

(c) endeavour to facilitate cohesion and consensus within the European Council.

In addition, the President of the European Council ensures, at his level and in that capacity, the external representation of the Union on issues concerning its common foreign and security policy, without prejudice to the powers of the High Representative of the Union for Foreign Affairs and Security Policy (Art. 15(6) TEU).

3. Operation

Rules of procedure. The European Council operates in accordance with the Rules of Procedure which it adopted pursuant to Art. 235(3) TFEU by a simple majority.[140]   **13–032**

Meetings. The European Council meets twice every six months, convened by its President.[141] Special meetings may be convened by the President when the situation so requires (Art. 15(3) TEU). At the latest one year before the beginning of   **13–033**

---

[140] See European Council Decision 2009/882/EU of December 1, 2009 adopting its Rules of Procedure, [2009] O.J. L315/51. For earlier rules of procedure, see Annex I to the Conclusions of the European Council held on June 21 and 22, 2002 in Seville ((2002) 6 EU Bull. point I.27); before then, see the Communiqué of the Heads of State or Government meeting in Paris on December 9 and 10, 1974 (1974) 12 EC Bull. point 1104(3); Decision of the European Council meeting in London (1977) 6 EC Bull. point 2.3.1; Solemn Declaration of Stuttgart (n. 32, *supra*), point 1.6.1.

[141] Ordinary meetings of the European Council last for a maximum of two days, unless the European Council or the General Affairs Council, on the initiative of the President of the European Council, decides otherwise (European Council Rules of Procedure, Art. 4(1)).

a six-month period, in close cooperation with the Member State which will hold the Presidency of the Council during that six-month period, the President of the European Council makes known the dates which he or she envisages for the meetings of the European Council during that six-month period (European Council Rules of Procedure, Art. 1(1)).

Meetings of the European Council are not public (European Council Rules of Procedure, Art. 4(3)). Where the European Council adopts a decision, it may decide, in accordance with the voting arrangement applicable for the adoption of that decision, to make public the results of votes, as well as the statements in its minutes and the items in those minutes relating to the adoption of that decision.[142]

13–034 **Seat.** The European Council meets in Brussels. In exceptional circumstances, the President of the European Council, with the agreement of the General Affairs Council or the Committee of Permanent Representatives, acting unanimously, may decide that a meeting of the European Council will be held elsewhere.[143] Before the Lisbon Treaty, the Member State presiding over the Council was responsible for organising European Council meetings. Each Member State presiding over the Council used to organise meetings of the European Council in its own territory. From 2002 onwards, one European Council meeting per Presidency was to be held in Brussels. As from the accession of new Member States in 2004, all European Council meetings were to be held in Brussels.[144]

13–035 **Decision-making.** The European Council takes its decisions by consensus "[e]xcept where the Treaties provide otherwise" (Art. 15(4) TEU).[145] Some Treaty articles require the European Council to take decisions unanimously.[146] Abstentions by members present in person or represented do not prevent the adoption of such decisions (Art. 235(1), third subpara., TFEU). In other cases, the European Council may take decisions by a qualified majority.[147] For qualified majority voting, the

---

[142] In such case, the explanations of the vote given when the vote was taken are also made public at the request of the member of the European Council concerned, "with due regard for these Rules of Procedure, legal certainty and the interests of the European Council" (European Council Rules of Procedure, Art. 10(1)).

[143] European Council Rules of Procedure, Art. 1(2).

[144] See Declaration (No. 22), annexed to the Nice Treaty, on the venue for European Councils ([2001] O.J. C80/85), according to which this would be the case "when the Union comprises 18 members".

[145] Before the Lisbon Treaty, the European Council invariably took its decisions by consensus.

[146] See, e.g., Art. 7(2) TEU; Art. 14(2), second subpara., TEU; Art. 17(5) TEU; Art. 22(1), third subpara., TEU; Art. 24(1), second subpara., TEU; Art. 31(3) TEU; Art. 42(2) TEU; Art. 48(6), second subpara., TEU; Art. 48(7), fourth subpara., TEU; Art. 50(3) TEU; Art. 86(4) TFEU; 312(2), second subpara., TFEU; Art. 355(6) TFEU.

[147] See, e.g., Art. 17(7), first and third subparas, TEU; Art. 18 TEU and Art. 236 TFEU; Art. 283(2), second subpara.

same arrangements apply as in the Council (Art. 235(1), second subpara., TFEU, which refers to Art. 16(4) TEU and 238(2) TFEU; see paras 13–052 *et seq.*, *infra*). The European Council acts by a simple majority for procedural questions and for the adoption of its Rules of Procedure (Art. 235(3) TFEU).[148]

When a vote is held in the European Council, neither its President nor the President of the Commission may vote. Members may vote on behalf of no more than one other member (Art. 235(1), first and second subparas, TFEU). The voting procedure is opened by the President, on his or her own initiative, or on the initiative of a member of the European Council, provided that a majority of the members of the European Council so decides (European Council Rules of Procedure, Art. 6(2)). The presence of two-thirds of the members of the European Council is required to enable the European Council to vote. The President of the European Council and the President of the Commission do not count towards the quorum (European Council Rules of Procedure, Art. 6(3)).

Decisions of the European Council on an urgent matter may be adopted by a written vote where the President of the European Council proposes to use that procedure. Written votes may be used where all members of the European Council having the right to vote agree to that procedure (European Council Rules of Procedure, Art. 7).

Relations with the European Parliament. The President of the European Council has to present a report to the European Parliament after each of the meetings of the European Council (Art. 15(6)(d) TEU). The member of the European Council representing the Member State holding the Presidency of the Council presents to the European Parliament the priorities of its Presidency and the results achieved during the six-month period (European Council Rules of Procedure, Art. 5). Initially, the European Parliament obtained information about the activities of the European Council only on the occasion of the report which the Minister of Foreign Affairs of the Member State holding the Presidency of the Council and the President of the Commission made before the Parliament at the end of each Presidency. Starting in 1981, the Head of State or Government occupying the Presidency of the European Council came before Parliament to report, initially half-yearly, subsequently after every European Council.[149]

The European Council has the right to be heard by the European Parliament (Art. 230, third subpara., TFEU). It is represented before the European Parliament by its President (European Council Rules of Procedure, Art. 5). The President of the European Parliament may be invited to be heard by the European Council (Art. 235(2) TFEU).

13–036

---

[148] For another case of decisions where the European Council decides by a simple majority, see Art. 48(3), first and second subparas, TEU (ordinary revision procedure).

[149] Werts (n. 116, *supra*). See also the Solemn Declaration of Stuttgart (n. 32, *supra*), point 2.1.4.

4. Internal organisation

13–037   **General Secretariat.** At the administrative level, the European Council and its President are assisted by the General Secretariat of the Council, under the authority of its Secretary-General (Art. 235(4) TFEU and European Council Rules of Procedure, Art. 13(1)). The Secretary-General of the Council attends the meetings of the European Council and takes all the measures necessary for the organisation of proceedings (European Council Rules of Procedure, Art. 13(2)).

C. THE COUNCIL

13–038   **Designation.** As a result of Art. 1 of the Merger Treaty, this institution, as the "Council of the European Communities", replaced the Special Council of Ministers of the ECSC, the Council of the EEC and the Council of the EAEC. Following the entry into force of the EU Treaty, the Council[150] decided that henceforth it would be known as the "Council of the European Union".[151] Since the Lisbon Treaty, the Treaties refer only to the "Council" (Art. 13(1) TEU).

1. Powers

13–039   **Survey.** According to Art. 16(1) TEU, the Council, jointly with the European Parliament, exercises legislative and budgetary functions and carries out policy-making and coordinating functions as laid down in the Treaties (see *ex Art. 202 EC*). The Council's decision-making power also extends to the Union's external action. It may also exercise implementing powers. Moreover, the Council takes decisions as to the nomination of members of other Union bodies.

(a) *Decision-making*

13–040   **Policy choices.** Union decision-making is carried out virtually always via the Council, which adopts most legislation on the basis of a Commission proposal, together with the European Parliament. Together with the European Parliament, the Council makes the policy choices intended to attain the objectives set out in the Treaties. In many cases, the Council has to assess complex economic situations and has a discretion as to what priorities should be given to these policies,[152] the actual aim of any given action and the suitability of its action in order to achieve that aim,[153] the nature and scope of such action and, to a certain extent,

---

[150] See in general Westlake, *The Council of the European Union* (London, Harper, 1999), 417 pp. For the Council's website, see *http://www.consilium.europa.eu/* [Accessed December 7, 2010].

[151] Decision 93/591/EU, Euratom, ECSC, EC of November 8, 1993, [1993] O.J. L281/18 (*corrigendum* L285, p. 41). The Merger Treaty was repealed by Art. 9 of the Treaty of Amsterdam.

[152] See, e.g., ECJ, Case 13/83 *European Parliament v Council* [1985] E.C.R. 1513, para. 50.

[153] Paras 7–012 and 7–036, respectively, *supra*.

the determination of basic data.[154] In addition, the Council decides on the general budget of the Union together with the European Parliament. As far as external action is concerned, the Council concludes international agreements negotiated by the Commission or the High Representative on behalf of the Union. The Council and the Commission, assisted by the High Representative, are responsible for ensuring the consistency between the different areas of the Union's external action and between these and its other policies (Art. 21(3), second sub-para., TEU). Decision-making in connection with the CFSP falls almost entirely to the Council.

(b) Coordination

Coordination. The Council carries out coordinating functions as laid down in the Treaties (Art. 16(1) TEU) and may adopt non-binding measures vis-à-vis the Member States to bring national policies and Union action into line with each other. The Treaties give the Council a specific power to coordinate the Member States' economic policies and it may impose sanctions in this connection.[155] Also as regards the CFSP, Member States' policies are coordinated in the European Council and the Council (Art. 32 TEU [ex Art. 16 EU]).[156]

13–041

(c) Implementation

Implementing powers. Implementation of legislative acts falls, in principle, to the Commission. However, in duly justified specific cases, the power to adopt implementing acts may be conferred on the Council (Art. 291(2) TFEU; see para. 17–010). The Council is also responsible for implementing the CFSP, together with the High Representative.[157] The Treaties confer certain implementing powers expressly on the Council, in particular with regard to economic monitoring (Art. 121(3) TFEU [ex Art. 99(3) EC] and Art. 126 TFEU [ex Art. 104 EC]).

13–042

(d) Relationship to other institutions and bodies

Appointments and other prerogatives. Because it is made up of representatives of the Member States, the Council has a number of prerogatives which enable it to influence, to some extent, the operation of the other institutions, with the exception of the European Parliament.[158] Thus, the Council is to propose candidates for appointment to the Commission and appoints the members of the Court

13–043

---

[154] ECJ, Case 138/79 *Roquette Frères v Council* [1980] E.C.R. 3333, paras 25–26.

[155] Article 121 TFEU [ex Art. 99 EC] (paras 11–034—11–035, *supra*) and Art. 126(9) and (11) TFEU [ex Art. 104(9) and (11) EC] (para. 11–038, *supra*).

[156] See also, with regard to PJCC before the entry into force of the Lisbon Treaty, Art. 34(1) EU.

[157] Article 291(2) TFEU, which refers to Arts 24 and 26 TEU.

[158] Even though, since the Treaty of Amsterdam, the Council has to approve the "regulations and general conditions governing the performance of the duties" of the Members of the European Parliament (Art. 223(2) TFEU [ex Art. 190(5) EC]).

of Auditors,[159] may alter the number of Advocates General at the Court of Justice,[160] and determines the emoluments of most members of the institutions, except for the European Parliament.[161] The Council also appoints members of other bodies or determines their exact composition[162] and adopts the rules governing their organisation.[163] The Council is further entitled to exercise some control over the activities of the Commission: it can ask it to carry out studies and make proposals[164] and participates in controlling the Commission's implementation of the budget.[165] The Council is entitled to consult the Court of Auditors, the European Economic and Social Committee and the Committee of the Regions.[166] It is also entitled to an annual report from the ECB[167] and may monitor its policy by having its President attend meetings of the ECB's Governing Council.[168]

Lastly, the Council has the right to bring actions for annulment or for failure to act in the Court of Justice.[169]

2. Composition

13–044 **Configurations.** The Council consists of a representative of each Member State at ministerial level, who may commit the government of the Member State in question and cast its vote (Art. 16(2) TEU [*ex Art. 203, first para., EC*]). Each Member State itself determines the person of ministerial rank who is to represent it.

Depending on the subject-matter under discussion, the Council is to meet in various "configurations" (Art. 16(6) TEU). The list of Council configurations is

---

[159] Article 17(7) TEU and Art. 286(2) TFEU [*ex Art. 247(3) EC*].

[160] Article 252 TFEU [*ex Art. 222, first para., EC*].

[161] Article 243 TFEU [*ex Art. 210 EC*]. See, e.g., the Council decisions of December 1, 2009 laying down the conditions of employment of the President of the European Council, of the High Representative of the Union for Foreign Affairs and Security Policy and of the Secretary-General of the Council of the European Union ([2009] O.J. L322/35, L322/36 and L322/38). In addition, the Council has to approve amendments to the Statute of the Court of Justice, the Rules of Procedure established by the Court of Justice and the General Court (Art. 253, sixth para., TFEU [*ex Art. 223, sixth para., EC*]; Art. 254, fifth para., TFEU [*ex Art. 224, fifth para., EC*] and Art. 281, second para., TFEU [*ex Art. 245, second para., EC*]) and the Rules of Procedure of the Court of Auditors (Art. 287(4), fifth subpara., TFEU [*ex Art. 248(4), fifth subpara., EC*]).

[162] This applies, inter alia, to the European Economic and Social Committee (para. 13–108, *infra*) and the Committee of the Regions (para. 13–112, *infra*).

[163] See also Art. 242 TFEU [*ex Art. 209 EC*] (para. 13–115, *infra*).

[164] Article 241 TFEU [*ex Art. 208 EC*]; Art. 122 EAEC (para. 16–021, *infra*).

[165] Para. 13–150, *infra*.

[166] Article 287(4), second subpara. TFEU [*ex Art. 248(4), second subpara., EC*]; Art. 304 TFEU [*ex Art. 262 EC*]; Art. 307 TFEU [*ex Art. 265 EC*].

[167] Article 284(3) TFEU [*ex Art. 113(3) EC*].

[168] Article 284(1) TFEU [*ex Art. 113(1) EC*]. The President of the Council may submit a motion for deliberation, *ibid*.

[169] Article 263, second para., TFEU [*ex Art. 230, second para., EC*]; Art. 265, first para., TFEU [*ex Art. 232, first para., EC*].

to be adopted by the European Council by a qualified majority (Art. 236(a) TFEU).[170] However, two Council configurations are established by the Treaties themselves: the General Affairs Council and the Foreign Affairs Council (Art. 16(6) TEU). The General Affairs Council has the task of ensuring consistency in the work of the different Council configurations and of preparing and ensuring the follow-up meetings of the European Council, in liaison with the President of the European Council and the Commission (Art. 16(6), second subpara., TFEU).[171] It is responsible for the overall coordination of policies, institutional and administrative questions, horizontal dossiers which affect several of the Union's policies and any dossier entrusted to it by the European Council. The Foreign Affairs Council is to elaborate the Union's external action on the basis of strategic guidelines laid down by the European Council and ensure that the Union's action is consistent (Art. 16(6), third subpara., TFEU). It is responsible for the whole of the European Union's external action, namely the common foreign and security policy, the common security and the defence policy, common commercial policy, development cooperation and humanitarian aid (Art. 16(6), third subpara., TFEU).[172] In the General Affairs Council, each Member State is represented by the Minister or State Secretary of its choice.[173] Sometimes, the General Affairs Council meets together with another configuration (a "jumbo" Council) or specialised configurations ("Special Councils") meet jointly.

Alongside the General Affairs Council and the Foreign Affairs Council, there are at present eight configurations of the Council:

---

[170] Before the Lisbon Treaty, the list of configurations was adopted by the Council itself, in its General Affairs and External Relations configuration. This "practice" was laid down for the first time when the Council Rules of Procedure were amended on June 5, 2000 ([2002] O.J. L230/7), and confirmed in the Council Rules of Procedure of July 22, 2002, which reduced the number of configurations (for the earlier more extensive list, see [2000] O.J. C174/2) and transformed the long-standing General Affairs Council into the General Affairs and External Relations Council. The Lisbon Treaty split that configuration into separate Council configurations. Article 4 of Protocol (No. 36) on transitional provisions (n. 64, *supra*) provides that until the entry into force of the European Council decision adopted under Art. 16(6), first subpara., TEU, the list of Council configurations, in addition to the General Affairs and the Foreign Affairs Councils, should be established by the General Affairs Council, acting by a simple majority. See Decision of the Council (General Affairs) 2009/878/EU of December 1, 2009 ([2009] O.J. L315/46), and European Council Decision 2010/594/EU of September 16, 2010 ([2010] O.J. L263/12) which adapted the list of Council configurations set out in Annex I to the Council Rules of Procedure.

[171] See also Art. 3 of European Council Decision 2009/881 (n. 184, *infra*) and Art. 2(2) and (4) of the Council's Rules of Procedure.

[172] See also Art. 2(5) of the Council Rules of Procedure.

[173] See Annex I to the Council Rules of Procedure. In practice, it is generally the Member States' Ministers of Foreign Affairs or Ministers or State Secretaries responsible for European Affairs. See Gomez and Peterson, "The EU's Impossibly Busy Foreign Ministers: 'No One is in Control' " (2001) E.For.Aff.Rev. 53–74.

(1) Economic and Financial Affairs (ECOFIN);

(2) Justice and Home Affairs;

(3) Employment, Social Policy, Health and Consumer Affairs;

(4) Competitiveness (Internal Market, Industry and Research);

(5) Transport, Telecommunications and Energy;

(6) Agriculture and Fisheries;

(7) Environment; and

(8) Education, Youth, Culture and Sport.[174]

Since the EU Treaty, the General Affairs Council has surrendered some of its coordinating influence. This is because, as far as matters relating to Economic and Monetary Union are concerned, the 1991 Intergovernmental Conference put the emphasis on the ECOFIN Council.[175] Meetings of the ECOFIN Council attended only by representatives of Member States whose currency is the euro constitute the "Euro Group" or "Euro Council" (see para. 19–004).[176] In addition, increasing reliance was placed on decisions taken by the Council in the configuration of the Heads of State or Government.[177] In practice, meetings of this configuration of the Council generally coincided with those of the "European Council", although legally there was a difference: unlike the European Council, the Council meeting in the composition of the Heads of State or Government had to apply the Council's operating rules and did not include the President of the Commission, even though the latter attended its meetings. The EU Treaty introduced this composition for some decisions relating to EMU.[178] The Treaties of

---

[174] See the list in Annex I to the Council Rules of Procedure.

[175] See the declarations adopted when the EU Treaty was signed: Declaration (No. 3) on Part Three, Titles III and VI [*later Titles III and VII*], of the EC Treaty and Declaration (No. 4) on Part Three, Title VI [*later Title VII*], of the EC Treaty. Under Art. 2(2) of the Council Rules of Procedure, tasks are to be assigned to the General Affairs Council "having regard to operating rules for the Economic and Monetary Union".

[176] The procedures in the Council are adapted thereto. See Art. 16 of the Council Rules of Procedure and the annex thereto.

[177] See Mayer, "Nationale Regierungsstrukturen und europäische Integration" (2002) Eu.GR.Z. 111–124; Martenczuk, "Der Europäische Rat und die Wirtschafts- und Währungsunion" (1998) EuR. 151, at 175–176.

[178] See Art. 121(2), (3) and (4) EC (decision on entry into the third stage of EMU) and Art. 122(2) EC (discussion of which Member States with a derogation may take part in EMU). For the application of these provisions, see Council Decision 96/736/EC of December 13, 1996 in accordance with Art. 109j [*later Art. 121*](3) of the Treaty establishing the European Community, on entry into the third stage of economic and monetary union, [1996] O.J. L335/48.

Amsterdam and Nice conferred on the Council in the configuration of the Heads of State or Government the power to take some major constitutional decisions.[179] Since the Lisbon Treaty, these decisions are taken by the European Council (see para. 13–029), which has replaced the "Council meeting in the composition of the Heads of State and Government" throughout.

Representatives at ministerial level. Before the EU Treaty entered into force, each government had to delegate "one of its members" to the Council.[180] However, in federal Member States, such as Germany and Belgium, the federal government shares powers with the governments of the federated states or regions. At the insistence of those Member States, the EU Treaty altered the composition of the Council so as to allow members of government of federated states or regions to represent their Member State in the Council. Article 16(2) TEU now provides that each Member State is represented by a representative at ministerial level, who may commit the government of the Member State in question and cast its vote. Since each Member State has only one representative in the Council, a federal Member State has to determine who is delegated to the Council and how that representative is to defend as one view in the Council may be conflicting views within the Member State.[181] The composition of the Council as it is defined in Art. 16(2) TEU also confirms the practice whereby a Member State is represented by junior ministers who under domestic law do not form part of the government, but are nevertheless deemed to be of "ministerial level".

13–045

Presidency of the Council. Since the Lisbon Treaty, the Council configurations are chaired by representatives of the Member States on the basis of equal rotation, the conditions of which are established by the European Council by a qualified majority (Arts 16(9) TEU and 236(b) TFEU). The only exception is the Foreign Affairs Council, which is chaired by the High Representative for Foreign Affairs and Security Policy (Art. 18(3) TEU, see para. 13–070).[182] The 2007

13–046

---

[179] See Art. 214(2), first subpara., EC (nomination of the President of the Commission) and Art. 7(2) EU (determination of the existence of a serious and persistent breach by a Member State of principles mentioned in Art. 6(1) EU). See also Art. 10.6 of the ESCB Statute (see para. 13–099, *infra*). For a critical commentary, see Dashwood, "The Constitution of the European Union after Nice: law-making procedures" (2001) E.L.Rev. 215, at 234–236.

[180] Merger Treaty, Art. 2, first para., repealed by Art. 50 of the EU Treaty.

[181] Para. 14–016, *infra*. When the Council decides by a qualified majority and each Member State has more than one vote, the number of votes cast is always expressed as a single block. If a single view cannot be reached within a Member State, its representative may abstain. For the various effects of abstention, see para 13–050, *infra*.

[182] Moreover, the informal meetings of the Ministers of the Member States whose currency is the euro (the "Euro Group") are chaired by a president elected for a period of two and a half years, by a majority of the Member States. See Art. 2 of Protocol (No. 14), annexed to the TEU and the TFEU, on the Euro Group ([2010] O.J. C83/283).

Intergovernmental Conference agreed that the Presidency of the Council, with the exception of the Foreign Affairs configuration, would be held by pre-established groups of three Member States for a period of 18 months.[183] For this purpose the European Council adopted a Decision,[184] which was further implemented by a Decision of the Council.[185] In order to make up such groups of Member States, account is to be taken of "their diversity and geographical balance within the Union".[186] It was decided to keep the order for the rotation of the Council presidency established in 2007[187] and to divide the resulting list into groups of three Member States.[188] Each member of the group in turn chairs for a six-month period all configurations of the Council, with the exception of the Foreign Affairs configuration, while being assisted by the other members of the group. However, members of the team may decide alternative arrangements among themselves.[189] Accordingly, Spain, Belgium and Hungary hold the Presidency of the Council for the periods January–June 2010, July–December 2010 and January–June 2011, respectively. The same applies as regards the period July 2011–December 2012 for Poland, Denmark and Cyprus, the period January 2013–June 2014 for Ireland, Lithuania and Greece and the period July 2014–December 2015 for Italy, Latvia and Luxembourg.[190]

Before the Lisbon Treaty, each Member State occupied the Presidency of the Council in rotation for a period of six months.[191] The EC Treaty required the

---

[183] See Declaration (No. 9), annexed to the Lisbon Treaty, on Art. 16(9) of the Treaty on European Union concerning the European Council decision on the exercise of the Presidency of the Council, [2010] O.J. C83/341, which set out a Draft European Council Decision on the exercise of the Presidency of the Council in an annex.

[184] European Council Decision 2009/881/EU of December 1, 2009 on the exercise of the Presidency of the Council, [2009] O.J. L315/50, by which the European Council adopted the Decision set out in the Annex to Declaration (No. 9) (see previous n.).

[185] Council Decision 2009/908/EU of December 1, 2009 laying down measures for the implementation of the European Council Decision on the exercise of the Presidency of the Council, and on the chairmanship of preparatory bodies of the Council, [2009] O.J. L322/28 (corrigendum: [2009] O.J. L344/56).

[186] Article 1(1) of European Council Decision 2009/881 (n. 184, supra) and Art. 2 of Council Decision 2009/908 (n. 185, supra).

[187] See Council Decision (2007/5/EC, Euratom) of January 1, 2007 determining the order in which the office of President of the Council shall be held, [2007] O.J. L1/11.

[188] Article 1 of Council Decision 2009/908 (n. 185, supra).

[189] Article 1(2) of European Council Decision 2009/881 (n. 184, supra) and Art. 20(2) of the Council Rules of Procedure.

[190] Annex I of Council Decision 2009/908 (n. 185, supra). Furthermore, that annex lists the Netherlands, Slovakia and Malta (January 2016–June 2017), the United Kingdom, Estonia and Bulgaria (July 2017–December 2018) and Austria, Romania and Finland (January 2019–June 2020). Article 3 of the Council Decision states that "[t]he order in which the Member States will hold the Presidency as from July 1, 2020 shall be decided by the Council before July 1, 2017".

[191] See Hummer and Obwexer, "Die 'EU-Präsidentschaft' " (1999) EuR. 401–451.

Council to determine the order by unanimous vote.[192] In order to ensure continuity in the Council's activities the Presidency was assisted by the next Member State to hold the Presidency.[193] Even before, there was the practice of the "troika", whereby the previous and the next President of the Council assisted the holder of the office for the time being.[194] The EU Treaty formally enshrined this practice for the purposes of the external representation of the Union and the implementation of the CFSP.[195] In order to ensure that the troika had sufficient weight internationally, the order of succession of the Member States was constructed in such a way that the troika virtually always included one "large" Member State.[196] The Treaty of Amsterdam departed from this practice by entrusting the international representation of the Union to the Presidency, assisted by a High Representative for the CFSP (EU Treaty, Art. 18(3)).[197] Since the Lisbon Treaty, it is no longer for the Council's Presidency to represent the Union externally as this task has been conferred both upon the Commission and the new High Representative for Foreign Affairs and Security Policy, who also presides the Foreign Affairs Council.

3. Operation

Rules of Procedure. The Council operates in accordance with the provisions of the Treaties and the Rules of Procedure which it adopts pursuant to Art. 240(3)   **13–047**

---

[192] See the second para. of Art. 203 EC (as amended by Art. 12 of the 1994 Act of Accession); Council Decision (2007/5/EC, Euratom) of January 1, 2007 determining the order in which the office of President of the Council shall be held, [2007] O.J. L1/11, Art. 1(1). The Council, acting unanimously on a proposal from the Member State concerned, could decide that a Member State would hold the Presidency during a period other than that resulting from the above order (Art. 1(2)). Under a similar provision in the previous Council Decision, the order of the Presidencies of Germany and Finland was reversed for 2006–2007 at their request by Council Decision (2002/105/EC, ECSC, Euratom) of January 28, 2002, [2002] O.J. L39/17. Before Art. 12 of the 1994 Act of Accession entered into force, Art. 203, second para., EC laid down a cycle determined by the alphabetical order of the names of the Member States in their respective languages. In the subsequent cycle, the same list was taken but the order of each pair of Member States on the list was inverted.

[193] Article 18(4) EU.

[194] For the first occurrence of this, see the London report on European Political Cooperation (1981) EC Bull. Suppl. 3, 14–18, especially point 10.

[195] Article J.5(3) of the original EU Treaty.

[196] See Council Decision 95/2/EC, Euratom, ECSC of 1 January 1995 determining the order in which the office of President of the Council shall be held ([1995] O.J. L1/220), as agreed at the European Council held in Brussels on December 12 and 13, 1993 ((1993) 12 EC Bull. point I.18, 17–18), upon entry into force of the 1994 Accession Treaty.

[197] Javier Solana was appointed first Secretary-General of the Council, High Representative for the CFSP; see the Council Decision of September 13, 1999, [1999] O.J. L284/33. He remained in office until December 31, 2009 (see Council Decision of October 29, 2009 ([2009] O.J. L283/57).

TFEU.[198] The Council is not entitled to depart from its Rules of Procedure without formally amending them.[199] The President convenes the Council on his or her own initiative or at the request of one of its members or the Commission (Art. 237 TFEU). Dates for meetings of the Council are made known to the Member States before the beginning of each sixth-month period (Council Rules of Procedure, Art. 1(2)). Where a rapid decision is required in matters coming under the CFSP, the High Representative may convene an extraordinary Council meeting within 48 hours or, in an emergency, at even shorter notice (Art. 30(2) TEU). Meetings take place in Brussels, except in April, June and October, when the Council meets in Luxembourg, or, if the Council or the Coreper (see para. 13–056) so decides by a unanimous vote, elsewhere.[200] The Commission is invited to take part in Council meetings, unless the Council decides by a majority vote to deliberate in its absence. The same applies to the European Central Bank (Council Rules of Procedure, Art. 5(2)). Members of the Council and the Commission may be accompanied by civil servants (Council Rules of Procedure, Art. 5(3)). Exceptionally, a representative of other bodies may be invited to a meeting concerning matters falling within the remit of the body in question. The Treaties confer this right on the President of the ECB (Art. 284(2) TFEU).

13–048   **Public nature of deliberations.** The Council meets in public when it deliberates and votes on a draft legislative act (Art. 16(8) TEU and 15(2) TFEU; Council Rules of Procedure, Art. 5(1)). In order to make this possible, each Council meeting is divided into two parts, dealing respectively with deliberations on legislative acts and non-legislative activities (Art. 16(8) TEU).[201]

Legislative deliberations are open to the public, and documents submitted to the Council in relation thereto and the Council minutes relating to legislative deliberations are made public. Besides, the Council publishes the results of its votes, together with explanations of votes by members of the Council or their representatives on the Conciliation Committee provided for under the ordinary legislative procedure, statements in the minutes and items relating to the

---

[198] See the current Rules of Procedure, adopted by Council Decision 2009/937/EU of December 1, 2009, [2009] O.J. L325/35, replacing the Rules of September 15, 2006, [2006] O.J. L285/47, and the previous versions of March 22, 2004 ([2004] O.J. L106/22), July 22, 2002 ([2002] O.J. L230/7), June 5, 2000 ([2000] O.J. L149/21), May 31, 1999 ([1999] O.J. L147/13), December 6, 1993 ([1993] O.J. L304/1; *corrigendum* [1994] O.J. L71/26; amended by [1995] O.J. L31/14 and [1998] O.J. L337/40) and of July 24, 1979 ([1979] O.J. L268/1, as amended on July 20, 1987 ([1987] O.J. L291/27).

[199] ECJ, Case 68/86 *United Kingdom v Council* [1988] E.C.R. 855, para. 48. Non-compliance with the Rules of Procedure may constitute an infringement of an essential procedural requirement within the meaning of Art. 263, second para., TFEU (*United Kingdom v Council*, para. 49).

[200] Sole Art., para. (b), of the Protocol on Seats, para. 13–153, *infra*, and Art. 1(3) of the Council Rules of Procedure.

[201] Council Rules of Procedure, Arts 3(6) and 7(1).

Conciliation Committee meeting (Council Rules of Procedure, Art. 7(2) and (4)). Public access is secured by relaying the Council meeting to another room by audiovisual means and by posting a recorded version on the Council's website (Council Rules of Procedure, Art. 7(3)).[202]

The Council's first deliberations on important new non-legislative proposals are also open to the public where they relate to the adoption of rules which are legally binding in or for the Member States, by means of regulations, directives or decisions.[203] The same is true for subsequent Council deliberations on such proposals where the Presidency of the Council so decides, unless the Council or Coreper decides otherwise (Council Rules of Procedure, Art. 8(1)). In these cases, the Council publishes the results of votes and explanations of votes by Council members, as well as the statements in the Council minutes and the items in those minutes relating to the adoption of such acts (Council Rules of Procedure, Art. 9(1)). Policy debates on the Council's or the Commission's operational programme and, where the Council or Coreper so decides by a qualified majority vote, debates on important issues affecting the interests of the European Union and its citizens are also open to the public (Council Rules of Procedure, Art. 8(2) and (3)). At the request of a member of the Council, results of votes, explanations of votes and the statements in the Council minutes may also be published when the Council adopts a decision in the field of CFSP and in all other cases (Council Rules of Procedure, Art. 9(2)(c)).[204]

In all those cases, results of votes and declarations of vote may be consulted on the Internet; the minutes are available from the Council's website.[205] The Council adopts the necessary rules on security to cover matters where secrecy is required.[206]

---

[202] See already the Council's answer of May 8, 1996 to question E-1095/96 (Moorhouse), [1996] O.J. C385/6.

[203] Article 8(1), first subpara., of the Council Rules of Procedure makes an exception for internal measures, administrative or budgetary acts, acts concerning interinstitutional or international relations or non-binding acts (such as conclusions, recommendations or resolutions). The Presidency is to identify which new proposals are important and the Council or Coreper may decide otherwise, whenever appropriate (*ibid.*).

[204] In the case of action pursuant to Title V of the EU Treaty, the Council must so decide by a unanimous vote (Council Rules of Procedure, Art. 9(2) (a)). Explanations of votes are made public at the request of the Council members concerned "with due regard for these Rules of Procedure, legal certainty and the interests of the Council"; a Council decision is also required to make public statements entered in the Council minutes and items in those minutes (Council Rules of Procedure, Art. 9(2), second and third subparas).

[205] For the Council website, see n. 150, *supra*.

[206] Article 24 of the Council Rules of Procedure, as implemented by Council Decision 2001/264/EC of March 19, 2001, [2001] O.J. L101/1 (as amended, most recently, by Council Decision 2007/438/EC of June 18, 2007, [2007] O.J. L164/24).

13–049   **Vote.** A valid vote may be held in the Council if a majority of the members of the Council who are, under the Treaties, entitled to vote are present (Council Rules of Procedure, Art. 11(4)).[207] Although a Member State may be represented by persons other than ministers (e.g. by its Permanent Representative; see para. 13–156), such a representative may not vote. The right to vote may be delegated only to another member of the Council (Art. 239 TFEU [*ex Art. 206 EC*]; Council Rules of Procedure, Art. 11(3)). Members of the Council vote in the order in which the Member States hold the Presidency (Council Rules of Procedure, Art. 11(2)).

13–050   **Three types of majorities.** As far as voting in the Council is concerned, there exist, alongside specific rules, three types of majorities which have to be attained depending on the Treaty article serving as the legal basis for the act to be adopted.[208] First, if the article in question does not specify that the Council has to vote by a particular majority, the act has to be adopted by a qualified majority (Art. 16(3) TEU).[209] In that case, or where the Treaty article in question expressly requires a qualified majority, a particular majority of the Member States representing at least a certain percentage of the population of the Union must vote in favour (see para. 13–052). Second, where a Treaty article requires the Council to act by a simple majority, it has to act by a majority of its component members (Art. 238(1) TFEU [*ex Art. 205(1) EC*]). Third, where the Treaty article serving as the legal basis requires the Council to vote unanimously, the act cannot be adopted if any Member State votes against.[210] The effect of abstentions differs depending on whether a decision is to be taken by qualified or simple majority or by unanimity. While abstentions make it more difficult to achieve a qualified or simple majority, they do not prevent a decision from being adopted by unanimous vote, since they are not regarded as votes cast against the proposal where a unanimous vote is required (Art. 238(4) TFEU [*ex Art. 205(3) EC*]).[211]

13–051   **Increased importance of (qualified) majority voting.** For a long time the rules on (qualified) majority voting laid down by the Treaties did not reflect reality. In

---

[207] Decisions taken under Art. 322 TFEU (decisions on expenditure for enhanced cooperation) must, however, be taken by a unanimous vote of all the members.

[208] For special requirements as to majorities, see para. 16–009, *infra*, where Union decision-making is discussed. For matters in relation to which not all Member States take part in decision-making, the voting right of the Member State concerned is suspended and the requirement for unanimity or a particular majority vote is amended accordingly; see paras 19–002, 19–004 and 19–009, *infra*.

[209] Before the Lisbon Treaty, Art. 205 EC required a simple majority in such a case.

[210] Unanimity is required for numerous Union decisions of a general nature (para. 16–009, *infra*) and for some decisions taken at the request of the Court of Justice (Art. 252, first para., TFEU [*ex Art. 222, first para., EC*]) or at the request of the EIB (Art. 308, third para., TFEU [*ex Art. 266, third para., EC*]). In principle, unanimity is required for decisions taken in connection with the CFSP (see Art. 31, first subpara., TFEU [*ex Art. 23(1), first subpara., EU*]). The same applied for PJCC prior to the entry into force of the Lisbon Treaty (see Art. 34(2) EU).

[211] This is also the rule for votes on matters relating to the CFSP. The same applied to PJCC prior to the entry into force of the Lisbon Treaty (see Art. 41(1) EU (which referred to Art. 205(3) EC)).

July 1965 the Community was struck by a serious crisis when France refused to take part in Council meetings (the "empty chair" policy) and complained about majority voting on Council decisions bearing on fundamental policy choices, even though the Treaty allowed this to take place with regard to matters such as agricultural policy after the second stage of the transitional period (January 1, 1966). In order to break out of the impasse, the Council, meeting on January 17 and 18, and January 28 and 29, 1966 adopted the so-called "Luxembourg Compromise", in which the Member States declared, inter alia, that where—in cases where acts could be adopted by a majority vote on a proposal from the Commission—"very important interests" of one or more of the partners were at stake, the members of the Council would try within a reasonable time-limit to find a solution acceptable to all of them "while respecting their mutual interests and those of the Community, in accordance with Article 2 of the Treaty".[212] Subsequently, delegations to the Council found that there were differences of opinion as to what had to be done when divergent views could not be reconciled fully. Although the "Compromise" did not renounce the principle of majority voting, it did find a practice whereby almost all Council acts, with the exception of budgetary measures, had to be adopted by a unanimous vote. This practice became further entrenched following the accession of the United Kingdom, which attached constitutional importance to the Compromise, since it was partly on the strength of it that Britain joined the Community. Nevertheless, it proved possible from time to time for acts to be adopted against the will of a minority.[213]

As a result of the Single European Act, the number of Treaty articles prescribing a vote by qualified majority increased dramatically. Accordingly, it appeared essential to rein in the previous practice. The Council succeeded in so doing by means of an amendment to its Rules of Procedure adopted on 20 July 1987.[214] As a result, the President is required, at the request of a member of the Council or of the Commission, to open a voting procedure, provided that a majority of the Council's members so decides (see Council Rules of Procedure, Art. 11(1), second subpara.). This means that negotiations must be continued in the Council only if fourteen Member States object to a vote being held. Once the Commission is persuaded that a given proposal has the support of a certain majority, it can call for a vote and get the proposal adopted.

This rule was not affected by the political decision taken by the Council when it determined the weighted votes to be given to the new Member States which were to join the Union on January 1, 1995. This so-called "Ioannina Compromise" applied when a certain number of Member States, not as such

---

[212] Luxembourg Compromise, Part B, s. 1 (1966) 3 Bull. CE 10.

[213] Thus, in May 1982 the farm prices were determined for the first time by a qualified majority vote. For the practical significance of the "Compromise", see Vasey, "Decision-making in the Agriculture Council and the 'Luxembourg Compromise'" (1988) C.M.L.Rev. 725–732; see the Council's answer of June 3, 1996 to question No. E-0317/96 (Moorhouse), [1996] O.J. C217/22; *corrigendum*: [1996] O.J. C345/117).

[214] For that decision see n. 198, *supra*.

constituting a blocking minority, indicated their intention to oppose the adoption by the Council of a decision by qualified majority.[215] In such case, the Council would "do all in its power" to reach an agreed solution which could be adopted by a majority larger than that required for qualified majority voting. The arrangements set out in the Ioannina Compromise were not adapted however to the changes made to the voting procedure by the Treaty of Nice and the 2003 Act of Accession and could therefore no longer be applied as from May 1, 2004. However, the 2007 Intergovernmental Conference agreed on arrangements that were clearly inspired by the Ioannina Compromise (see para. 13–054).

13–052 **Changes in the "qualified majority" threshold.** Initially, where the Council was to act by a "qualified" majority, the Treaties allotted to each Member State a specific number of votes—depending on the country's population size, but corrected to give more weight to the smaller Member States[216]—and required a specific number of those votes to be cast in favour.[217] The allocation of votes among the Member States was adjusted with a view to the accession of ten new Member States by a Protocol on the enlargement of the Union annexed to the EC Treaty by the Treaty of Nice, and subsequently by the Acts of Accession of 2003 and 2005.[218]

---

[215] Council Decision of March 29, 1994 concerning the taking of a Decision by a qualified majority by the Council ([1994] O.J. C105/1, adapted because only three new Member States acceded to the Union on January 1, 1995, [1995] O.J. C1). For a comparison with the Luxembourg Compromise, see "Editorial Comments: the Ioannina Compromise—Towards a Wider and Weaker European Union?" (1994) C.M.L.Rev. 453–457. See also De l'Ecotais (n. 216, *supra*), at 324–327. For the significance of a "right of veto", see also Van Nuffel, *De rechtsbescherming van nationale overheden in het Europees recht* (Deventer, Kluwer, 2000), at 453–458.

[216] The final allocation of votes was not based on objective criteria, but reflected the influence in decision-making which the Member States in fact allow each other: De l'Ecotais, "La pondération des voix au Conseil de ministres de la Communauté européenne" (1996) R.M.C.U.E. 388–393 and 617–620 and (1997) R.M.C.U.E. 324–327. See also Bangemann, "Le vote majoritaire pour l'Union européenne élargie" (1995) 3 R.M.U.E. 175–180; Vignes, "Le calcul de la majorité qualifiée, un casse-tête pour 1996" (1994) R.M.C.U.E. 561–563.

[217] Before May 1, 2004, France, Germany, Italy and the United Kingdom each had 10 votes, Spain 8, Belgium, Greece, the Netherlands and Portugal 5 each, Austria and Sweden 4 each, Denmark, Finland and Ireland 3 each, and Luxembourg 2. There was a qualified majority if the Commission proposal received 62 out of the 87 weighted votes or 71.26 per cent (hence the blocking minority consisted of 26 votes). Where the Council did not vote on a Commission proposal, there was already a dual requirement in order to attain a qualified majority: 62 weighted votes in favour out of 87, which had to be cast by at least 10 out of 15 members.

[218] See Art. 205(1) EC as amended by Art.12 of the 2003 Act of Accession and Art. 10 of the 2005 Act of Accession. Protocol (No. 10), annexed by the Nice Treaty to the EU Treaty and the Community Treaties, on the enlargement of the European Union ([2001] O.J. C80/49) already determined the number of votes for the fifteen existing Member States; as regards the number of votes for the new Member States, the Protocol referred to Declaration (No. 20), annexed to the Nice Treaty, on the enlargement of the European Union ([2001] O.J. C80/80), which was adjusted by the European Council held in Brussels on October 24 and 25, 2002 to take account of the fact that Bulgaria and Romania would not be acceding in 2004. See also Declaration (No. 21), annexed to the Nice Treaty, on the qualified majority threshold and the number of votes for a blocking minority in an enlarged Union.

When the Treaty of Nice was approved, agreement was reached on a more complex decision-making system that required differing thresholds to be met in order to attain a "qualified" majority.[219]

That system has been amended again by the Lisbon Treaty, which took over some, but not all, of the amendments that had earlier been proposed by the Convention on the future of Europe and the Constitution for Europe. The 2003 Convention had proposed to abandon the initial method for calculating the qualified majority laid down in Art. 205 EC (based on the attainment of a specific number of weighted votes) and retain only the two additional conditions introduced in that article by the Treaty of Nice—albeit in a slightly adapted version (that is to say, a majority of the Member States representing 60 per cent of the total population of the Union). Starting from that proposal, the 2003 Intergovernmental Conference laid down in the Constitution for Europe a system based on higher majority thresholds. This system has been preserved in the Lisbon Treaty, although it will not enter into force until November 1, 2014 (Art. 16(4) TEU).[220] Until October 31, 2014, the arrangements existing since the Treaty of Nice are kept in place, in accordance with the Protocol on transitional provisions annexed to the Treaties (Art. 16(5) TEU).[221] In accordance with that Protocol, further transitional provisions will apply between November 1, 2014 and March 31, 2017 (Art. 16(5) TEU). During that period, when an act is to be adopted by qualified majority, a member of the Council may still request that a decision be adopted under the previously existing system for qualified majority votes.[222]

Qualified majority until October 2014. Until October 31, 2014, in the case of acts of the Council (and the European Council) requiring a qualified majority, each Member State has a weighted vote. In order to obtain a qualified majority, a particular number of votes must be obtained and, at the same time, a majority of the Member States representing at least 62 per cent of the population of the Union must vote in favour (Protocol on transitional provisions, Art. 3(3)). France, Germany, Italy and the United Kingdom each have 29 votes, Spain and Poland 27, Romania 14, the Netherlands 13, Belgium, the Czech Republic, Greece, Hungary and Portugal 12 each, Austria, Bulgaria and Sweden 10 each, Denmark, Finland, Ireland, Lithuania and Slovakia 7 each, Cyprus, Estonia, Latvia, Luxembourg and Slovenia 4 each and Malta 3. A qualified majority is attained where the Commission proposal obtains 255 out of 345 weighted votes (or 73.91 per cent)

13–053

---

[219] Article 3(1) of Protocol (No. 10) on the enlargement of the European Union (n. 218, *supra*) announced that this system would take effect on January 1, 2005. However, that article was repealed by Art. 12(2) of the 2003 Act of Accession, which introduced the system of differing majority thresholds with effect from November 1, 2004.

[220] See Van den Bogaert, "Qualified majority voting in the Council: first reflections on the new rules" (2008) 15 M.J.E.C.L. 97–108.

[221] Protocol (No. 36) on transitional provisions (n. 64, *supra*), Art. 3(3).

[222] Protocol (No. 36) on transitional provisions (n. 64, *supra*), Art. 3(2).

and, at the same time, the majority of the members of the Council vote in favour.[223] This means that at least 14 Member States must vote in favour and that a 91-vote minority can block the adoption of the act. Where the Council does not vote on a Commission proposal, a qualified majority consists of 255 weighted votes in favour out of 345, which must be cast by at least two-thirds of the members.[224] In any case, a member of the Council may request verification that the Member States constituting the qualified majority represent at least 62 per cent of the total population of the Union. If that condition is shown not to have been met, the decision in question shall not be adopted.[225] To that end, the Council updates every year, as at January 1, the population figures of all the Member States contained in Annex III to its Rules of Procedure.[226]

Special arrangements apply in areas where not all Member States participate in decision-making. In such cases, a qualified majority requires the same percentage of the weighted votes and the same proportion of the number of Member States, but only the participating Member States are taken into account.[227] This means that, where the Council decides on a proposal from the Commission, a qualified majority is attained where the Commission proposal obtains 73.91 per cent of the weighted votes of the participating Member States and a majority of the participating members of the Council vote in favour. Where the Council does not vote on a Commission proposal, a qualified majority requires 73.91 per cent of the weighted votes of the participating Member States, which must be cast by at least two-thirds of the participating members of the Council. In any case, a member of the Council may request verification that the Member States constituting the qualified majority represent at least 62 per cent of the population of the participating Member States.

13–054 **Qualified majority after October 2014.** As explained above, the new voting arrangements introduced by the Lisbon Treaty will apply as from November 1, 2014. Under the new system, all decisions taken by a qualified majority will require at least 55 per cent of the members of the Council, comprising at least fifteen of them and representing Member States making up at least 65 per cent of the population of the Union (Art. 16(4), first subpara., TEU). Decisions which the

---

[223] Article 3(3), second and third subparas, of Protocol (No. 36) on transitional provisions (n. 64, *supra*); see Art. 205(2) EC.

[224] *Ibid.* The stricter requirement in terms of the majority required reflects the fact that a Commission proposal has already weighed up the interests of, inter alia, the smaller Member States, see De l'Ecotais (n. 216, *supra*), at 392–393.

[225] Article 3(3), fourth subpara., of Protocol (No. 36) on transitional provisions (n. 64, *supra*); see Art. 205(4) EC.

[226] Article 2(2) of Annex III to the Council Rules of Procedure. See, most recently, Council Decision 2010/795/EU of December 14, 2010 amending the Council's Rules of Procedure, [2010] O.J. L338/47 (applicable from January 1, 2011 to December 31, 2011).

[227] Article 3(4) of Protocol (No. 36) on transitional provisions. (n. 64, *supra*)

Council is to take by a qualified majority and not on the basis of a proposal from the Commission or from the High Representative of the Union for Foreign Affairs and Security Policy will need to be approved by at least 72 per cent of the members of the Council representing Member States comprising at least 65 per cent of the population of the Union (Art. 238(2) TFEU). In addition, in both instances, a blocking minority is to include at least four members of the Council, failing which the qualified majority will be deemed to have been attained (Art. 16(4) TEU).

It proved impossible to agree on the new method for calculating the qualified majority without at the same time providing that the adoption of an act by a qualified majority will be delayed if a certain number of Member States, which do not, as such, constitute a blocking minority, express their opposition. Those special arrangements can be found in a declaration attached to the Lisbon Treaty which set out a "draft" decision[228] that was formally adopted by the Council on the date of signature of the Lisbon Treaty.[229] Its provisions entered into force together with the Lisbon Treaty and are to be applied from November 1, 2014 onwards. The decision provides that if members of the Council, representing at least three-quarters of the population or of the number of Member States necessary to constitute a blocking minority, indicate their opposition to the Council adopting an act by a qualified majority, the Council is to "discuss" the issue.[230] As from April 1, 2017, the same rule will apply, but already where members of the Council, representing at least 55 per cent of the population or of the number of Member States necessary to constitute a blocking minority, indicate their opposition to the adoption of an act by a qualified majority.[231]

In much the same way as the 1994 Ioannina Compromise (see para. 13–051), the Council will then be required to "do all in its power" to reach within a reasonable time and without prejudicing obligatory time-limits a "satisfactory solution" to address "concerns" raised by the members of the Council who indicated their opposition.[232] Poland had asked the Intergovernmental Conference of 2007 to include these arrangements in the Treaties themselves. The IGC did not, however, acceded to this request, deciding that the arrangements would be laid down in a decision to be adopted by the Council. At the same time, however, a protocol was added to the Treaties which provides that that decision cannot be amended or

---

[228] See Declaration (No. 7), annexed to the Lisbon Treaty, on Art. 16(4) TEU and Art. 238(2) TFEU, and the annexed "draft decision of the Council" ([2010] O.J. C83/338).

[229] Council Decision 2009/857/EU of December 13, 2007 relating to the implementation of Art. 9C(4) TEU and Art. 205(2) TFEU between November 1, 2014 and March 31, 2017 on the one hand, and as from April 1, 2017 on the other, [2009] O.J. L314/73.

[230] *Ibid.*, Art. 1.

[231] *Ibid.*, Art. 4.

[232] *Ibid.*, Arts 2 and 4. It will be up to the President of the Council, with the assistance of the Commission, to undertake any initiative necessary to "facilitate a wider basis of agreement in the Council": *ibid.*, Arts 3 and 5.

abrogated by the Council without a preliminary deliberation in the European Council, acting by consensus.[233]

Special arrangements apply in areas where not all Member States participate in decision-making.[234] In such cases, a qualified majority will require at least 55 per cent of the members of the Council representing the participating Member States, comprising at least 65 per cent of the population of these States. A blocking minority must include at least the minimum number of Council members representing more than 35 per cent of the population of the participating Member States, plus one member (Art. 238(3)(a) TFEU). Decisions which the Council are to take by a qualified majority and not on the basis of a proposal from the Commission or from the High Representative of the Union for Foreign Affairs and Security Policy will need to be approved by at least 72 per cent of the members of the Council representing the participating Member States, comprising at least 65 per cent of the population of these States (Art. 238(3)(b) TFEU).

13–055 **"A" and "B" items.** In practice, the Council does not have to take a formal vote on many acts, since the decision is prepared by the national delegations and the Commission in working parties and in the Committee of Permanent Representatives (Coreper; see para. 13–056). All matters on which Coreper has already reached agreement appear on the agenda for Council meetings as "A" items. The Council approves them without further ado unless a member requests that the particular item be subjected to further discussion (Council Rules of Procedure, Art. 3(6) and (8)). In that event, the agenda item in question is generally sent back to Coreper. Matters on which Coreper has not reached agreement but which are nevertheless up for decision may be placed on the agenda as "B" items by a member of the Council or the Commission. The Council then endeavours to reach agreement or to get a sufficient majority behind the proposal, after which it may be sent back to Coreper to be finalised. It then comes back on the agenda for the Council meeting for approval as an "A" item. Urgent matters may be dealt with

---

[233] Protocol (No. 9), annexed to the TEU and TFEU, on the decision of the Council relating to the implementation of Art. 16(4) of the Treaty on European Union and Art. 238(2) of the Treaty on the Functioning of the European Union between November 1, 2014 and March 31, 2017 on the one hand, and as from April 1, 2017 on the other, [2010] O.J. C83/274.

[234] See the reference to Art. 238(3) TFEU in Art. 46(3), third subpara., and (4), third subpara., TEU (permanent structured cooperation in the framework of the common security and defence policy); Art. 50(4), second subpara., TEU (arrangements relating to the withdrawal of a Member State); Art. 121(4), third subpara., TFEU (recommendations to a Member State regarding its economic policy); Art. 126(13), third subpara., TFEU (excessive government deficits); Art. 136(2), second subpara., TFEU, Art. 138(3), second subpara., TFEU, Art. 139(4), second subpara., TFEU and Art. 140(2), third subpara., TFEU (certain decisions relating to the eurozone); Art. 330, third para., TFEU (enhanced cooperation); Art. 354, second and third paras, TFEU (suspension of Treaty rights).

by a written vote.[235] That procedure is also used for routine matters.[236] The formal vote on an act takes place in the Council, not in the working party or in Coreper. The latter only carry out the preparatory work and determine whether or not there is a consensus or a sufficient majority. If there is no consensus or an insufficient majority, the Council has to cut the Gordian knot.[237]

4. Internal organisation

Coreper. The Committee of Permanent Representatives of the Governments of the Member States (Coreper) prepares the work of the Council and carries out tasks assigned to it by that institution (Art. 16(7) TEU and Art. 240(1) TFEU [*ex Art. 207(1) EC*]).[238] Each Member State delegates to it a Permanent Representative, who has the status of an ambassador based in Brussels, together with a Deputy Permanent Representative, who has the diplomatic rank of minister. The Permanent Representatives head the Member States' Permanent Representations to the European Union, which are in continual contact with the ministries in their respective Member States. Coreper has two parts, which are not in a hierarchical relationship. Part I consists of the Deputy Permanent Representatives. It deals chiefly with matters concerning the internal market and

13–056

---

[235] The Council or Coreper decides by a unanimous vote whether to take advantage of this possibility; if the President proposes recourse to written votes, such a vote may take place if all Member States agree (Council Rules of Procedure, Art. 12(1), first subpara.). The Commission's agreement is required to the use of that procedure where the written vote is on a matter brought before the Council by that institution (Council Rules of Procedure, Art. 12(1), second subpara.). For the purposes of implementing the CFSP, there exists a simplified written procedure which makes use of COREU (*correspondance européenne*), a confidential communications network linking the national Foreign Ministries, the Commission and the Council's General Secretariat (Council Rules of Procedure, Art. 12(2)(d)). Under that procedure, a proposal made by the Presidency is deemed adopted if no member of the Council objects within a period laid down by the Presidency.

[236] See De Zwaan, *The Permanent Representatives Committee: Its Role in European Decision-making* (Amsterdam, Elsevier, 1995), 340 pp., who also describes in detail the use of the "A" and "B" item procedures; Hayes-Renshaw, "When and why the EU Council of Ministers votes explicitly" (2006) 44 J.C.M.S., 161–194.

[237] So as to preserve efficient decision-taking with delegations of 25 Member States around the table, the Council adopted on March 22, 2004 "Working methods for an enlarged Council", [2004] O.J. L106/42 (see now Annex V to the Council Rules of Procedure, "Council working methods"). They call upon delegations to avoid pointless presentations and keep their interventions brief, substantive and to the point (see points 6–13). For an inquiry into the decisive nature of the final vote in the Council, see Van Schendelen, " 'De Raad beslist'. Beslist de Raad?" (1995) S.E.W. 706–721. For a survey by Member State of abstentions and votes cast against, see the Council's answer of June 26, 2000 to question E-917/00 (Huhne), [2001] O.J. C26E/131.

[238] For this Committee, usually known as "Coreper", an abbreviation of *Comité des représentants permanents*, see Hayes-Renshaw, Lequesne and Mayor Lopez, "The Permanent Representations of the Member States to the European Communities" (1989) J.C.M.S. 119–137; De Zwaan (n. 236, *supra*).

technical and economic questions. Part II, which comprises the Permanent Representatives themselves, discusses general issues and questions of foreign policy. A special committee discharges Coreper's tasks in the field of agricultural policy.[239]

Coreper is an auxiliary body and cannot exercise the decision-making powers conferred by the Treaties on the Council.[240] In this context, Coreper is to ensure consistency of the Union's policies and actions and see to it that the principles of legality, subsidiarity, proportionality and providing reasons for acts are respected, together with the rules establishing the powers of Union institutions, bodies, offices and agencies, the budgetary provisions and the rules on procedure, transparency and the quality of drafting.[241] In the cases mentioned in Art. 19(7) of the Council's Rules of Procedure, Coreper is entitled to adopt procedural decisions (Art. 240(1) TFEU).

13–057 **Working groups.** Various committees and working parties, consisting of national civil servants and representatives of the Commission, operate under the auspices of Coreper.[242] Some working parties are brought together on an ad hoc basis, others are permanent. The first discussions of Commission proposals for legislation generally take place within these working groups. They report to Coreper, which in turn refers the matters on to the Council.[243] Member States may choose to delegate representatives of decentralised governments, to the extent that they are competent to represent the Member State.

13–058 **Preparatory committees.** The Treaties expressly entrust a number of committees with the task of preparing the work of the Council, without prejudice to Coreper's general competence. As far as financial and monetary questions are concerned, the Economic and Financial Committee does the preparatory work for the Council (Art.134(2), second indent, TFEU [*ex Art. 114(2), third indent, EC*]; see para. 13–144). For the purposes of promoting coordination of employment and social policies, the advisory Employment and Social Protection Committees

---

[239] Article 5(4) of the Decision of May 12, 1960 of the representatives of the Member States of the European Economic Community meeting within the Council on quickening the pace for achieving the objectives of the Treaty, [1960] J.O. 1217, and the Council Decision of July 20, 1960 setting up the committee (1960) 5 EC Bull. 74–75.

[240] ECJ, Case C-25/94 *Commission v Council* [1996] E.C.R. I-1469, paras 25–28.

[241] Council Rules of Procedure, Art. 19(1).

[242] See, inter alia, the "207 Committee" (previously "133 Committee") set up pursuant to Art. 207 TFEU [*ex Art. 133 EC*]; the Committee on Cultural Affairs set up by Resolution of the Council of the Ministers responsible for cultural affairs meeting within the Council of May 27, 1988 ([1988] O.J. C197/1) and the Financial Services Committee set up by Council Decision 2003/165/EC of February 18, 2003 ([2003] O.J. L67/17).

[243] See Council Rules of Procedure, Arts 19(3) and 21. In the case of agricultural affairs, reports are made to the Special Agriculture Committee.

contribute to the preparation of Council proceedings (Arts 150 and 160 TFEU [*ex Arts 130 and 144 EC*]; see para. 13–144). As for the area of freedom, security and justice, a standing Committee facilitates coordination of the Member States' competent authorities (Art. 71 TEU [*ex Art. 36(1) EU*]).[244] For advice on the implementation of the CFSP, the Council has a Political and Security Committee (Art. 38, first para., TFEU [*ex Art. 25, first para., EU*]) consisting of the "Political Directors" from the Member States or their deputies.[245] This committee plays a central role in European security and defence policy, including crisis management. It exercises, under the responsibility of the Council and the High Representative, political control and strategic direction of crisis management operations and may be authorised, for the purpose and for the duration of a crisis management operation, to take the relevant decisions (Art. 38, second and third paras, TEU [*ex Art. 25, second and third paras, EC*]; see para. 18–007).

Presidency of committees and groups. Since the Lisbon Treaty, Coreper is chaired by the Permanent Representative or the Deputy Permanent Representative of the Member State holding the Presidency of the General Affairs Council; the various committees and working parties are chaired by a delegate of the Member State chairing the relevant Council configuration, unless the Council decides otherwise.[246] The Political and Security Committee and various other preparatory bodies of the Foreign Affairs Configuration are chaired by a representative of the High Representative for Foreign Affairs and Security

13–059

---

[244] Council Decision 2010/131/EU of February 25, 2010 on setting up the Standing Committee on operational coordination on internal security, [2010] O.J. L52/50. Before the Lisbon Treaty, this "coordinating committee" dealt with technical aspects of policy relating to PJCC, whilst the broader political and institutional implications were left to Coreper. See the Council's answer of March 17, 1994 to question E-3815/93 (Van Outrive), [1994] O.J. C102/26. The original Art. K.4 of the EU Treaty created this committee (known as the "K.4 Committee"). The K.4 Committee replaced the Coordinators' Group (para. 2–010, *supra*), which was wound up after the EU Treaty entered into effect. For a discussion of the previous organisation plan for JHA cooperation within the Council, see Lepoivre, "Le domaine de la justice et des affaires intérieures dans la perspective de la Conférence intergouvernementale de 1996" (1995) C.D.E. 323, at 339–340 and 349.

[245] Council Decision 2001/78/CFSP of January 22, 2001 setting up the Political and Security Committee, [2001] O.J. L27/1. The Political and Security Committee is assisted by the Committee for civilian aspects of crisis management (set up by Council Decision 2000/354/CFSP of May 22, 2000, [2000] O.J. L127/1) and by the Military Committee of the European Union (set up by Council Decision 2001/79/CFSP of January 22, 2001, [2001] O.J. L127/4). See also para. 18–003, *infra*. For a brief period, there was an Interim Political and Security Committee (Council Decision 2000/143/CFSP of February 14, 2000, [2000] O.J. L49/1) and an Interim Military Body (Council Decision 2000/144/CFSP of February 14, 2000, [2000] O.J. L49/2). See Juncos and Reynolds, "The Political and Security Committee: governing in the shadow" (2007) E.For.Aff.Rev. 127–147.

[246] See Art. 2 of European Council Decision 2009/881/EU of December 1, 2009 on the exercise of the Presidency of the Council ([2009] O.J. L315/50), and Art. 19(4) of the Council Rules of Procedure of the same date.

Policy.[247] Some other Council preparatory bodies are chaired by a fixed, elected chair,[248] or by the General Secretariat of the Council.[249] This complex arrangement for the Presidency of committees and groups was set up upon the entry into force of the Lisbon Treaty, and replaces the previous system whereby Coreper and all committees and working parties were chaired by representatives of the same Member State, namely the Member State holding the Presidency of all Council configurations for a six-month period. The previous system enabled the Member State holding the Presidency to make an impression on Council policy through its diplomats and civil servants during that period. As explained above, the Lisbon Treaty still requires each Member State to chair for a six-month period the Council configurations, except for the Foreign Affairs Council, but organises this by groups of three Member States that may decide alternative arrangements among themselves on the Presidency of Council configurations. Moreover, the Foreign Affairs Council is now chaired by the High Representative for Foreign Affairs and Security Policy (see para. 13–046). Consequently, with respect to the external affairs of the Union, it is no longer for the Member State holding the Presidency to set the political agenda. In all other matters, the Member State holding the Presidency—or, if an arrangement has been made to this end, another Member State from the same group of three Member States—is to take all necessary steps to have work advanced between meetings of Coreper, working parties or committees, for example, by organising bilateral consultations and by requesting the delegations of the Member States to take a position on specific proposals for amendment of the documents discussed.[250] Finally, it should be mentioned that the Commission is represented, not only at Council meetings, but also on Coreper and the working parties.[251] As a result, it plays a dynamic role in the legislative process (see para. 16–020).

---

[247] *Ibid.* The list of preparatory bodies chaired either by the six-monthly Presidency (e.g. preparatory bodies in the area of trade and development, such as the "207 Committee") or by a representative of the High Representative (e.g., several CFSP preparatory bodies) is set out in Annex II ("Chairmanship of the preparatory bodies of the Foreign Affairs Council") to Council Decision 2009/908/EU of December 1, 2009 laying down measures for the implementation of the European Council Decision on the exercise of the Presidency of the Council, and on the chairmanship of preparatory bodies of the Council ([2009] O.J. L322/28, *corrigendum*: [2009] O.J. L344/56).

[248] See Art. 5 and Annex III ("Chairpersons of Council preparatory bodies with a fixed chair") of Council Decision 2009/908/EU (see previous n.), that mentions, inter alia, the Economic and Financial Committee, the Employment Committee and the Social Protection Committee.

[249] *Ibid.* (mentioning, inter alia, the Security Committee and the Working Party on Codification of Legislation).

[250] See also the tasks entrusted to the Presidency in so far as the preparation for meetings is concerned in Annex V of the Council Rules of Procedure ("Council working methods", n. 237, *supra*).

[251] See Ponzano, "Les relations entre le Coreper et la Commission européenne" (2000)1 *Il Diritto dell'Unione Europea* 23–38.

General Secretariat. The Council's administrative structure is its General   **13–060**
Secretariat (Art. 240(2) TFEU [*Art. 207(2) EC*]),[252] which is based in Brussels.
The Secretary-General is responsible for running the General Secretariat.[253] The
General Secretariat is divided into eight Directorates-General (A to I) and a legal
service. It employs about around 3,500 staff.[254] The General Secretariat organises
meetings of the Council, Coreper and the working parties, translates and distributes documents, assists the President and deals with the Council's relations with
the other institutions.[255]

D. THE EUROPEAN COMMISSION

Designation. As a result of Art. 9 of the Merger Treaty, the "Commission of   **13–061**
the European Communities" replaced the High Authority of the ECSC, the
Commission of the EEC and the Commission of the EAEC. Ever since the entry
into force of the EU Treaty, the Commission[256] has referred to itself by the short
title of the "European Commission".[257] Even though that is now the official designation of that institution (see Art. 13(1) TEU), the Treaties also use the shorter
"Commission".

1. Powers

Survey. Article 17(1) unequivocally declares that the Commission is the Union   **13–062**
institution which promotes the general interest of the Union and takes appropriate
initiatives to that end. Article 17(1) TEU further sets out a detailed description of
the roles played by that institution, in particular in monitoring the application of
the law and initiating legislation, together with its budgetary powers, executive
powers and powers of representation.[258] The Commission is also responsible for
initiating the Union's annual and multiannual programming with a view to achieving interinstitutional agreements. Its supervisory powers, participation in decision-
making and implementing powers are fleshed out in other Treaty articles, together
with powers with regard to the Union's external relations policy. As far as CFSP
action on the part of the Union is concerned, the Commission has virtually no

---

[252] See also Art. 23 of the Council Rules of Procedure.

[253] The Secretary-General is appointed by the Council (Art. 240(2), first subpara., TFEU). See
Council Decision of December 1, 2009 appointing the Secretary-General of the Council of the
European Union ([2009] O.J. L322/37).

[254] As at December 2009, the Council had 3476 established posts and 36 temporary posts: *General
Report on the Activities of the European Union 2009* (n. 106, *supra*), at 96.

[255] See Egger, *Das Generalsekretariat des Rates der EU* (Baden-Baden, Nomos, 1994), 359 pp.

[256] See, in general, Spence and Edwards, *The European Commission* (London, Harper, 2006), 592
pp. For the Commission's website, see *http://ec.europa.eu/* [Accessed December 7, 2010].

[257] *Europe*, No. 6130, 8/9 November 1993, 7.

[258] Before the Lisbon Treaty, Art. 211 EC listed the tasks which the Commission was to carry out "in
order to ensure the proper functioning and development of the common market".

supervisory power, its participation in decision-making is limited and, apart from the implementation of the budget, has only such tasks of implementation and representation as the Council delegates to it.

(a) *Supervision*

13–063 **Guardian of the Treaties.** The Commission ensures that the provisions of the Treaties and the measures taken pursuant thereto by the institutions are applied (see Art. 17(1) TEU). It therefore checks that the other institutions, bodies and agencies, the Member States and natural and legal persons comply with Union law.[259] To this end it receives information in the shape of informal or formal complaints and information with which it has to be provided pursuant to specific provisions.[260] Where Union provisions so provide (e.g., with regard to competition law), the Commission is obliged to respond to complaints from natural or legal persons.[261] In the event of failure to comply with Union law on the part of national authorities, citizens may submit a complaint to the Commission.[262] However, there is no formal procedure obliging the Commission to take any action in response to citizens' complaints.[263]

In order to perform its tasks, the Commission also has the right—under Art. 337 TFEU [*ex Art. 284 EC*]—to collect any information and carry out any checks required within the limits and under conditions laid down by the Council.[264] It falls

---

[259] For a survey, see Van Rijn, "The Investigative and Supervisory Powers of the Commission", in Curtin and Heukels (eds), *Institutional Dynamics of European Integration. Essays in Honour of Henry G. Schermers*, Vol. II (Dordrecht, Martinus Nijhoff, 1994), 409–421. For some critical comment, see Palacio Vallelersundi, "La Commission dans son rôle de gardienne des Traités" (2001) R.D.U.E. 901–907.

[260] See the annual reports of the Court of Auditors (Art. 287(4), first subpara., TFEU) and of the ECB (Art. 284(3) TFEU). See the obligations to provide information imposed on the Member States by, inter alia, Arts 108(3); 114(5) and (8); 121(3), second subpara.; 140(2); 148(3) and 193. As far as natural and legal persons are concerned, see, inter alia, the obligation to notify certain concentrations of undertakings; para. 11–016, *supra*.

[261] See the complaints relating to breaches of Arts 101 and 102 TFEU [*ex Arts 81 and 82 EC*] under Art. 7 of Regulation No. 1/2003 (para. 11–013, *supra*); as for other formal complaints, there are in particular the questions put by members of the European Parliament (para. 13–009, *supra*).

[262] A standard form is to be found in [1999] O.J. C119/5. The Commission undertakes to comply with the rules set out in the annex to the Commission communication to the European Parliament and the European Ombudsman on relations with the complainant in respect of infringements of Community law ([2002] O.J. C166/3). See Harden, "A quel avenir la mise en application centralisée du droit communautaire peut-elle s'attendre?" (2002) R.D.U.E. 461–483.

[263] See the discussion of the action for failure to fulfil obligations (Art. 258 TFEU) in Lenaerts, Arts and Maselis, *Procedural Law of the European Union*, (3rd edn, London, Sweet & Maxwell, 2011), Ch. 5. The European Ombudsman has argued for a more extensive right to complain, see Söderman, "Le citoyen, l'Etat de droit et le principe de transparence" (2001) R.D.U.E. 889–900.

[264] See, e.g., Council Regulation (EC) No. 405/2003 of February 27, 2003 concerning Community monitoring of imports of hard coal originating in third countries, [2003] O.J. L62/1 (based on Art. 284 EC [*now Art. 337 TFEU*]).

to the European Parliament and the Council, acting under the ordinary legislative procedure, to adopt measures for the production of statistics necessary for the performance of the activities of the Union (Art. 338(1) TFEU [*Art. 285(1) EC*]).[265]

In the event that the Commission finds that the European Parliament, the Council or certain bodies, offices or agencies have infringed Union law, it may bring an action for annulment or for failure to act in the Court of Justice (Arts 263 and 265 TFEU [*Arts 230 and 232 EC*]).[266]

If a Member State fails to fulfil its obligations, the Commission puts it on notice, giving it the opportunity to rectify matters and submit any observations. If necessary, it will then deliver a reasoned opinion, with which the Member State has to comply within a specified period (Art. 258 TFEU [*ex Art. 226 EC*]).[267] Exceptionally, the Commission may even summon a Member State directly before the Court of Justice.[268] If the Court of Justice finds that the Member State has infringed Union law, the Member State is required to take the necessary measures to comply with the Court's judgment, failing which the Commission may bring the case before the Court, after giving the Member State concerned the opportunity to submit its observations, and ask the Court to order payment of a lump sum or a penalty payment (Art. 260(1) and (2) TFEU [*ex Art. 228 EC*]).[269] The Court is competent to impose both a lump sum and a penalty payment.[270] Where the Commission brings an action against a Member State for failure to fulfil its obligation to notify measures transposing a directive adopted under a legislative procedure, the Commission may obtain the imposition of a lump sum

---

[265] See, e.g., Regulation (EC) No. 223/2009 of the European Parliament and of the Council of March 11, 2009 on European statistics, [2009] O.J. L87/164. The production of Union statistics must not entail excessive burdens on economic operators, see Art. 338(2) TFEU [*ex Art. 285(2) EC*].

[266] The Commission can also bring an action against the ECB (Arts 263, third para., and 265, fourth para., TFEU) and against decisions of the Board of Governors and the Board of Directors of the EIB (Art. 271(b) and (c) TFEU).

[267] The Treaties preclude such supervision in connection with the obligation (in the third stage of EMU) to avoid excessive government deficits (Art. 126(10) TFEU [*ex Art. 104(10) EC*]).

[268] See the direct remedies provided for in Arts 114(9) and 348, second para., TFEU [*ex Arts 95(9) and 298, second para., EC*] and the procedure related to Art. 258 TFEU provided for in Art. 108(2) [*ex Art. 88(2) EC*].

[268] It is for the Commission to provide the Court, in the course of these proceedings, with the information necessary to determine the extent to which a Member State has complied with a judgment declaring it to be in breach of its obligations (ECJ, Case C-387/97 *Commission v Greece* [2000] E.C.R. I-5047, para. 73; ECJ, Case C-119/04 *Commission v Italy* [2006] E.C.R. I-6885, para. 41). The Lisbon Treaty simplified the procedure whereby the Commission can bring a second action before the Court of Justice. Under Art. 228 EC, the Commission could only bring such an action after delivering a second reasoned opinion laying down a time-limit for the Member State concerned to comply with the Court's judgment.

[270] ECJ, Case C-304/02 *Commission v France* [2005] E.C.R. I-6263, paras 80–86. See Clément-Wilz, "Une nouvelle interprétation de l'article 228-2 CE favorisée par le dialogue entre la Cour et son Avocat général" (2005) C.D.E. 725–748.

or penalty payment when it brings its initial action based on Art. 258 TFEU (Art. 260(3) TFEU, introduced by the Lisbon Treaty). The Commission determines the amount of the sanction sought in the light of the required deterrent effect and the seriousness and duration of the infringement.[271] As far as the Court of Justice is concerned, the suggested sanctions are a "useful point of reference", but not binding on the Court, except with the aforementioned setting of Art. 260(3) TFEU where the lump sum or penalty payment imposed by the Court or the Member State concerned may not exceed the amount specified by the Commission.[272] Whilst a penalty payment is likely to encourage the Member State in breach to put an end as soon as possible to the infringement found, the imposition of a lump sum is prompted more by the assessment of the consequences for private and public interests of the failure by the Member State concerned to comply with its obligations.[273] An order imposing a penalty payment and/or a lump sum is not intended to compensate for any damage which may have been caused by the Member State concerned, but to place it under economic pressure which induces it to put an end to the infringement that has been established. The financial penalties imposed must therefore be decided upon according to the degree of persuasion needed for the Member State in question to alter its conduct.[274] According to the Court, the basic criteria which must be taken into account in order to ensure that penalty payments have coercive force are, in principle, the duration of the infringement, its degree of seriousness and the ability of the Member State to pay. In applying those criteria, regard should be had in particular to the effects of failure to comply on private and public interests and to the urgency of getting the Member State concerned to fulfil its obligations.[275]

In certain circumstances, the Commission is entitled to impose fines on natural or legal persons for infringements of competition law.[276]

---

[271] For the position adopted by the Commission, see the Communication from the Commission—Application of Art. 228 of the EC Treaty, SEC(2005)1658 of December 13, 2005, replacing the previous Commission communications: [1996] O.J. C242/6, and [1997] O.J. C63/2.

[272] ECJ, Case C-387/97 *Commission v Greece* [2000] E.C.R. I-5047, para. 89; ECJ, Case C-304/02 *Commission v France* [2005] E.C.R. I-6263, para. 103; ECJ, Case C-121/07 *Commission v France* [2008] E.C.R., para. 61; ECJ, Case C-109/08 *Commission v Greece* [2009] E.C.R. I-4657, para. 27. See Hilson (2001) Env.L.Rev. 131–138; Härtel, "Durchsetzbarkeit von Zwangsgeld-Urteilen des EuGH gegen Mitgliedstaaten" (2001) EuR. 617–630.

[273] ECJ, Case C-304/02 *Commission v France* [2005] E.C.R. I-6263, para. 82; ECJ, Case C-568/07 *Commission v Greece* [2009] E.C.R. I-4505, para. 45.

[274] ECJ, Case C-304/02 *Commission v France* [2005] E.C.R. I-6263, para. 91; ECJ, Case C-177/04 *Commission v France* [2006] E.C.R. I-2461, para. 60.

[275] ECJ, Case C-387/97 *Commission v Greece* [2000] E.C.R. I-5047, para. 92.; ECJ, Case C-304/02 *Commission v France* [2005] E.C.R. I-6263, para. 104; ECJ, Case C-177/04 *Commission v France* [2006] E.C.R. I-2461, para. 62.

[276] Paras 11–014—11–016, *supra*.

CFSP. The Treaties do not give the Commission the task of supervising that the obligations entered into under the CFSP are complied with (see para. 18–006).[277]

(b) *Participation in decision-making*

Decision-making. In some cases, the Commission has the power to take decisions with regard to Union matters. That decision-making power consists mainly[278] of means whereby the Commission, as the guardian of Union law, assesses whether Member States have complied with their Treaty obligations and permits them in appropriate cases to deviate from their obligations[279] or takes steps for the purpose of coordinating Member States' policies.[280] What is more important is the Commission's virtually exclusive right to initiate legislation in all the fields of competence of the Union, except for PJCC, where it shares this right with the Member States, and the CFSP, where it has no right of initiative (see para. 16–015). In this connection, the Treaties explicitly state that the Union's legislative acts can be adopted only on the basis of a Commission proposal, except where the Treaties provide otherwise (Art. 17(2) TEU). At the same time, it is the Commission which submits the draft EU budget (Art. 314(2) TFEU [*ex Art. 272(2) EC*]; see para. 13–142). In view of its decisive role in the decision-making process, the Commission may take part in sessions of the European Parliament (see para. 13–022) and in meetings of the Council (see para. 13–047). Furthermore, the Treaties empower the Commission to formulate recommendations (Art. 292 TFEU) or deliver opinions on various matters dealt with in the Treaties.[281]

---

[277] Before the Lisbon Treaty, the same applied to PJCC. The only power that the Commission had in this respect was the right to bring an action for annulment against PJCC framework decisions and decisions of the Council (Art. 35(6) EU).

[278] See, however, the powers to adopt acts of a general nature provided for, inter alia, in Arts 45(3)(d) and 106(3) TFEU (para. 11–017, *supra*).

[279] For the power to grant derogations, see para. 11–022, *supra*. See also the supervision provided for in Arts 96(2) and 108(1) and (2) TFEU (para. 11–017, *supra*).

[280] See Articles 168(2); 171(2); 173(2); 181(2) and 210(2) TFEU. As far as social provisions are concerned, see its task of promoting dialogue between management and labour (Art. 154 TFEU) and its power to organise consultations between the Member States (Art. 156 TFEU).

[281] See also the recommendations provided for in, inter alia, Arts 60, second para.; 97, third para.; 117(1); 143(1), first subpara., TFEU and opinions addressed to Member States (Art. 156 TFEU); for recommendations and opinions addressed to the Council, see para. 16–015, *infra*. Before the Lisbon Treaty, Art. 211, second indent, EC empowered the Commission more generally to formulate recommendations or deliver opinions on matters dealt with in the Treaty if it expressly so provided or if the Commission considered it necessary. For an application, see the Commission Recommendation of July 12, 2004 on the transposition into national law of Directives affecting the internal market, [2005] O.J. L98/47.

Besides, the Commission draws up numerous reports in pursuance of its duty to keep other institutions informed[282] and on its own initiative,[283] and is entitled to consult the Court of Auditors, the European Economic and Social Committee and the Committee of the Regions.[284]

(c) *Implementation*

13–066 **Implementing powers.** The Commission has extensive powers of implementation. First, it is, in principle, the institution competent for adopting "implementing acts" where legally binding Union acts need to be implemented under uniform conditions (see Art. 291(2) TFEU; see para. 17–010). The Commission has to act in accordance with the rules and general principles laid down by the European Parliament and the Council (Art. 291(3) TFEU; see para. 17–012). Second, the Commission adopts "delegated acts" where it has been so authorised by a legislative act (see Art. 290 TFEU; see para. 17–009). In any event, the Commission has the task of implementing the EU budget (Art. 317 TFEU [*ex Art. 274 EC*]; see para. 13–147).

(d) *Representation*

13–067 **Representation.** The Commission represents the Union in legal transactions within each Member State (Art. 335 TFEU [*ex Art. 282 EC*]; see para. 13–126) and, as a rule, also in international transactions (Art. 17(1) TEU; see para. 24–007). However, in areas coming under the CFSP, the Union is represented by the High

---

[282] Alongside the General Report on the Activities of the European Union intended for the European Parliament (n. 106, *supra*), the Commission also makes three-yearly reports to the European Parliament, the Council and the European Economic and Social Committee on non-discrimination and citizenship (Art. 23, first para., TFEU) and economic and social cohesion (Art. 175, second para., TFEU: the latter report is also to be forwarded to the Committee of the Regions); an annual report to the European Parliament and the Council on social policy (Art. 159 TFEU: the latter report is also to be forwarded to the European Economic and Social Committee), on research and technological development (Art. 190 TFEU) and on measures taken for countering fraud (Art. 325 TFEU); reports to the European Parliament on particular social problems (Arts 159 and 161, second para., TFEU) and on the results of multilateral economic surveillance (Art. 121(5) TFEU) and a number of reports to the Council on matters relating to Economic and Monetary Union (Arts 121(3), first subpara.; 126(3), first subpara. and 140(1), first subpara. TFEU; see also former Arts 116(2)(b) and 122(2) EC). See, in addition, the annual report for the European Council, the European Parliament, the Council and national parliaments on the application of Art. 5 TEU (Art. 9 of Protocol (No. 2), annexed to the TEU and TFEU, on the application of the principles of subsidiarity and proportionality, [2010] O.J. C83/206; that report is also to be sent to the Committee of the Regions and the European Economic and Social Committee). The Commission, together with the Council, also produces an annual report on the employment situation in the Union (Art. 148(5) TFEU).

[283] The Commission has committed itself to issuing annual reports on competition policy, the application of Union law and the completion of the internal market.

[284] Articles 287(4), second subpara.; 304 and 307 TFEU.

Representative of the Union for Foreign Affairs and Security Policy, who is to be assisted by the European External Action Service (see para. 24–009 *et seq.*).

2. Composition

Number of Commissioners. The present Commission has twenty-seven Members (often referred to as "Commissioners"), including the President and the High Representative of the Union for Foreign Affairs and Security Policy. This is because, since May 1, 2004, the rule applies that each Member State will have one of its nationals as a Member of the Commission (Art. 17(4) TEU [*ex Art. 213(1) EC*[285]]).[286] Before, the rule was that the Commission included at least one national of each of the Member States, but could not include more than two nationals of any given country. In practice, the five large Member States were entitled to two Members each and the small countries to one.[287] The Council could alter the number of Members of the Commission by unanimous vote.[288]

13–068

The Treaty of Nice introduced the present system while stating that, "when the Union consists of 27 Member States", a system would be introduced whereby the number of Members of the Commission would be smaller than the number of Member States.[289] Accordingly, after the accession of the twenty-seventh Member State, the Council was under a duty to lay down the arrangements to

---

[285] As amended by Art. 4(1) of Protocol (No.10) on the enlargement of the European Union (n. 218, *supra*). The date of January 1, 2005 mentioned by the Protocol was changed to November 1, 2004 by Art. 45(2)(d) of the 2003 Act of Accession.

[286] Article 246, third para., TFEU [*ex Art. 215, second para., EC*] provides for an exception thereto in the event that the Council should decide unanimously not to fill a vacancy.

[287] Originally, the High Authority of the ECSC and the Commission of the EEC had nine Members and the Commission of the EAEC had five. With the Merger Treaty, the number of Members of the single Commission came to nine (after a transitional period when it had fourteen Members: Merger Treaty, Art. 32). Since then the number of Members has been increased to thirteen (Council Decision of January 1, 1973, [1973] O.J. L2/28), to fourteen (1979 Act of Accession, Art. 15, [1979] O.J. L291), to seventeen (1985 Act of Accession, Art. 15, [1985] O.J. L302) and to twenty (1994 Act of Accession, Art. 16, as amended by Council Decision of January 1, 1995, [1995] O.J. L1/4). As a result of Art. 42(2)(a) of the 2003 Act of Accession, the Commission has been enlarged by one Member for each new Member State. Between May 1 and October 30, 2004 the Commission had 30 Members.

[288] Article 213(1), third subpara., EC. See, for example, the Council Decision of January 1, 1973, n. 286, *supra*. See Temple Lang, "How Much Do the Smaller Member States Need the European Commission? The Role of the Commission in a Changing Europe" (2002) C.M.L.Rev. 315–335.

[289] Article 4 of Protocol (No. 10) on the enlargement of the European Union (n. 218, *supra*), which heralded further amendments to Art. 213(1) EC and further provided how the Council had to determine the number of Members of the Commission and the system of rotation. For reservations, see Bradley, "Institutional design in the Treaty of Nice" (2001) C.M.L.Rev. 1095, at 1117–1119; Georgopoulos and Lefèvre, "La Commission après le traité de Nice: métamorphose ou continuité?" (2001) R.T.D.E. 597, at 600–602.

establish a rotation system whereby a smaller number of Commissioners would be chosen among the Member States.

Meanwhile, a proposal for reducing the number of Commissioners was put forward by the 2003 Convention, which proposed that the Commission would consist of a President, the Union Minister for Foreign Affairs and thirteen "European Commissioners" selected on the basis of a system of equal rotation between the Member States. In addition, the Commission would have comprised non-voting "Commissioners", coming from the Member States that would not have one of their nationals selected as European Commissioner. Several Member States insisted, however, on preserving the right for each Member State to have one of its nationals appointed as a full member of the Commission. The EU Constitution struck a compromise, which has largely been taken over by the Treaty of Lisbon.

Under this compromise, the first Commission appointed after the entry into force of the Treaty of Lisbon consists of one national of each Member State, including its President and the High Representative of the Union for Foreign Affairs and Security Policy, who is one of its Vice-Presidents (Art. 17(4) TEU). Again, under this compromise, as from November 1, 2014, the Commission would consist of a number of members, including its President and the High Representative, corresponding to two-thirds of the number of Member States, unless the European Council, acting unanimously, decided to alter this figure. The members of the Commission would be selected on the basis of a system of strictly equal rotation between the Member States as regards the determination of, the sequence of and the time spent by their nationals as Members of the Commission.[290] Each Commission would have to be so composed as to reflect satisfactorily the demographic and geographical range of all the Member States (Art. 17(5) TEU and Art. 244 TFEU). The precise arrangements were to be adopted by the European Council, acting unanimously (Art. 244 TFEU).

However, in order to accommodate the concerns of the Irish people after the 2008 negative referendum on the Lisbon Treaty, the European Council of December 11 and 12, 2008 agreed that, after the entry into force of the Lisbon Treaty, a decision will be taken "in accordance with the necessary legal procedures" to ensure that the Commission continues to include one national of each Member State (see para. 4–008). Before November 2014, the European Council is therefore to decide, in accordance with Art. 17(5) TFEU, that the Commission will continue to consist of a number of members equal to the number of Member States.

13–069   **Appointment.** Commissioners have to be chosen on the ground of their general competence and European commitment from persons whose independence is beyond doubt (Art. 17(3), second subpara., TEU [*Art. 213(1), first subpara.,*

---

[290] Consequently, the difference between the total number of terms of office held by nationals of any given pair of Member States could never be more than one (Art. 244(a) TFEU).

EC]). Since the Lisbon Treaty, Commissioners are appointed by the European Council, acting by a qualified majority. Before, they were appointed by the Member State Governments "by common accord" and, since the Treaty of Nice, by the Council by a qualified majority vote. The European Parliament's say in the appointment of the President and Members of the Commission has been gradually increased.[291]

The European Council, acting by a qualified majority, proposes a candidate for the Presidency who will then have to be elected by the European Parliament (Art. 17(7), first subpara., TEU).[292] The proposal must take the elections to the European Parliament into account and be adopted after appropriate consultations (*ibid.*).[293] The Council, acting by a qualified majority and in common accord with the President-elect, is to adopt the list of the other persons whom it proposes for

---

[291] The European Parliament pressed for a say in the appointment of the Commission ever since the early days of the Community: see the resolution of June 27, 1963, [1963] J.O. 1916. As long ago as 1983, the European Council decided in the Solemn Declaration of Stuttgart (n. 32, *supra*) that, before appointing the President of the Commission, the Member State governments would seek the opinion of the enlarged Bureau of the European Parliament and that, after the Members of the Commission had been appointed, the European Parliament would vote on the Commission's proposed programme (point 2.3.5). See Louis, "La désignation de la Commission et ses problèmes", in Louis and Waelbroeck (eds), *La Commission au coeur du système institutionnel des Communautés européennes* (Brussels, Editions de l'Université de Bruxelles, 1989), at 9–23. The EU Treaty added the obligation for the Parliament to be *consulted* on the person whom the governments wished to appoint as President; at the same time, the national governments had to nominate the other persons whom they wished to appoint as Members of the Commission *in consultation with* the nominee for President and the appointment of the President and Members of the Commission as a body depended on the European Parliament's approval. So, Jacques Santer was nominated in the Decision of the representatives of the Governments of the Member States of July 26, 1994 ([1994] O.J. L203/20) which was only adopted after the European Parliament had delivered its opinion on July 21, 1994 (even though the governments had already agreed on the person to be appointed on July 15, 1994 at an extraordinary meeting of the European Council in Brussels). The Treaty of Amsterdam made the appointment of the President depend upon the *approval* of the European Parliament and required the governments to reach *agreement* with the nominee President on the other persons whom they intended to appoint as Commissioners. Lastly, the Nice Treaty introduced a qualified majority vote for the nomination of the President and the appointment of the President and Members of the Commission and replaced "governments of the Member States" by "the Council". As far as the Members from the new Member States appointed on May 1, 2004 were concerned, a simplified procedure was applied whereby the Members were appointed by the Council, acting by qualified majority and by common accord with the President of the Commission (2003 Act of Accession, Art. 45(2)(a)).

[292] See, for instance, Council Decision 2009/532/EC, meeting in the composition of Heads of State or Government of July 9, 2009 nominating the person it intends to appoint as President of the Commission for the period 2009–2014, [2009] O.J. L179/61.

[293] Declaration (No. 6), annexed to the Lisbon Treaty ([2010] O.J. C83/338), states that in choosing the persons called upon to hold the office of President of the Commission (and also the persons to be appointed as President of the European Council and High Representative of the Union for Foreign Affairs and Security Policy) "due account is to be taken of the need to respect the geographical and demographic diversity of the Union and its Member States" (see n. 139, *supra*).

appointment as Members of the Commission, on the basis of the suggestions made by Member States (Art. 17(7), second subpara., TEU). Pursuant to its Rules of Procedure, the European Parliament requests the nominee for President and, subsequently, the nominees for the various posts of Commissioners to appear before the appropriate committees according to their prospective fields of responsibility. This occurs at public hearings where each nominee is invited to make a statement and answer questions.[294] The very prospect of a negative vote in Parliament may induce the Council, in accord with the President-elect of the Commission, to adapt a new list of persons proposed for appointment.[295] Next, the President, the High Representative and the other Members of the Commission are submitted collectively to a vote of consent by the European Parliament. On the basis of that consent, the Commission is appointed by the European Council, acting by a qualified majority (Art. 17(7), third subpara., TEU).

The President of the Commission appoints Vice-Presidents, other than the High Representative, from among its Members (Art. 17(6)(c) TEU [ex Art. 217(3) EC]).[296]

13–070 **High Representative of the Union.** As was explained earlier, the EU Constitution created the function of "Union Minister of Foreign Affairs", which was taken over by the 2007 Intergovernmetnal Conference, under the title "High Representative of the Union for Foreign Affairs and Security Policy". The High Representative of the Union for Foreign Affairs and Security Policy is part of the College of Commissioners, as one of the Commission's Vice-Presidents, but his or her status is somewhat singular owing to his or her dual role. On the one hand, the High Representative conducts the Union's common foreign and security policy, including its common security and defence policy, as mandated by the Council. On the other hand, he or she is responsible within the Commission for handling external relations and for coordinating other aspects of the Union's external action (Art. 18(2) and (4) TEU). As befits this dual role, the High Representative is appointed by the European Council, acting by a qualified majority, with the agreement of the President of the Commission, and is also submitted, together with the President and the other Members of the Commission, to a vote of consent by the European Parliament (Arts 17(7) and

---

[294] EP Rules of Procedure, Rules 105(1) and 106(1)–(2).

[295] See the replacement on January 22, 2010 of the first list adopted by the Council on December 4, 2009 ([2009] O.J. L321/51) by a new list ([2010] O.J. L20/5) in which the candidate proposed initially by the Bulgarian government was replaced by Ms Kristalina Georgieva. See also the earlier instance in which Rocco Buttiglione withdrew his candidacy and was replaced by Franco Frattini in 2004.

[296] The Nice Treaty amended Art. 217 EC, which, since the EU Treaty, provided that the President could appoint one or two Vice-Presidents. Prior to that, Art. 14 of the Merger Treaty provided that the President and six Vice-Presidents were to be appointed by the Member State governments from amongst the Members of the Commission.

18(1) TEU).[297] This dual role also explains why, as far as the CFSP is concerned, the High Representative is answerable to the European Council, which may end his or her tenure by the same procedure by which he or she is appointed. In contrast, when the High Representative carries out the tasks entrusted to him or her as a Member of the Commission, he or she will be bound by Commission procedures (Art. 18(1) and (4) TEU).[298]

Term of office. The EU Treaty increased Commissioners' (renewable) term of office from four to five years (Art. 17(3) TEU [*ex Art. 214(1) EC*]), with the result that it is the same as that of the European Parliament. This means that the legislative work needs to be interrupted only once every five years when the membership of the institutions changes. This association of the term of office of Members of the Commission with the election of the European Parliament enables the political outcome of the elections to be reflected to some extent in the composition of the Commission. So long as the European Council has not appointed new Members to the Commission at the end of its term of office, the old Commission remains in office, but its powers are limited to dealing with current business.[299] This occurred with the first Barroso Commission, whose term ended on October 31, 2009. The appointment of a new Commission was delayed in view of the Treaty obligation, introduced by the Nice Treaty, to reduce the number of the Commissioners and of the pending ratification of the Lisbon Treaty.[300]

13–071

---

[297] In choosing the person called upon to hold the offices of High Representative "due account is to be taken of the need to respect the geographical and demographic diversity of the Union and its Member States": Declaration (No. 6), annexed to the Lisbon Treaty, see n. 139, *supra*. The first High Representative appointed was Baroness Catherine Ashton of Upholland, initially in the first Barroso Commission for its remaining term (European Council Decision 209/880/EU taken with the agreement of the President of the Commission of December 1, 2009 appointing the High Representative of the Union for Foreign Affairs and Security Policy, [2009] O.J. L315/49) and thereafter in the second Barroso Commission (European Council Decision 209/950/EU taken with the agreement of the President of the Commission of December 4, 2009 appointing the High Representative of the Union for Foreign Affairs and Security Policy, [2009] O.J. L328/69).

[298] Article 18(4) TEU provides that the High Representative is bound by Commission procedures "to the extent that this is consistent with paragraphs 2 and 3". Likewise, where the President of the Commission requests the High Representative to resign, he or she will have to do so "in accordance with the procedure set out in Article 18(1)" (Art. 17(6) TEU). Where a motion of censure is carried and the Commission is to resign as a body, the High Representative is under a duty only to "resign from the duties that he or she carries out in the Commission" (Art. 17(8) TEU).

[299] This was the view taken by the Commission's Legal Service, see *Europe*, No. 6396, January 12, 1995, 6.

[300] The second Barroso Commission was appointed by European Council Decision 2010/80/EU of February 9, 2010, [2010] O.J. L38/7. A similar situation occurred after the expiry of the term of office of the Commission presided over by Jacques Delors on January 6, 1995 because the European Parliament wished to pronounce on the nominated President (Santer) and other Members of the Commission at its first plenary session which MEPs from the Member States which acceded on January 1, 1995 were to attend. After it was approved by the European Parliament on January 18, 1995, the Santer Commission was appointed by decision of the representatives of the

13–072 **Independence.** In carrying out its responsibilities, the Commission must be completely independent (Art. 17(3), third subpara., TEU [*ex Art. 213(2), first subpara., EC*]). This applies in the first place to the Commission as an institution, which has to weigh the different interests of groups and Member States against the general interest of the Union. As far as individual Members of the Commission are concerned, this means that they may not seek or take instructions from any government or any other institution, body, office or entity, that they may not in principle engage in any other gainful or other occupation and that they must take care in accepting certain appointments or benefits even after they have ceased to hold office (Arts 17(3), third subpara., TEU and 245, second para., TFEU). The Member States also undertake to respect the independence of Members of the Commission (Art. 245 TFEU [*ex Art. 213(2), EC*]). In point of fact, they are entitled to assert their national interests in the Council.[301]

Having regard to the importance of the responsibilities assigned to them, it is important that the Members of the Commission observe the highest standards of conduct. Hence, it is their duty to ensure that the general interest of the Union takes precedence at all times, not only over national interests, but also over personal interest.[302] When entering upon their duties they give a solemn undertaking that they will respect these obligations. This is done at a solemn sitting of the Court of Justice. In the event of a breach of these obligations, the Commission itself and the Council may apply directly to the Court of Justice (Art. 245(2), second subpara., TFEU [*ex Art. 213(2) second and third subpara., EC*]), after the person concerned has been informed in sufficient time of the complaints made against him or her and after he or she has had the opportunity of being heard.[303] If the Court finds that a breach of a certain degree of gravity has been committed, it may impose a penalty, such as compulsory retirement or the deprivation in whole or in part of the right to a pension or other benefits in its stead (Arts 245, second para., and 247 TFEU). This procedure was used for the first time when the Council brought an action against Martin Bangemann, a former Member of the

---

Governments of the Member States of January 23, 1995, [1995] O.J. L19/51. Likewise, after the expiry of the term of office of the Commission presided over by Romano Prodi on October 31, 2004, that Commission stayed into office until the appointment on November 22, 2004 of the (first) Commission presided over by José Manuel Barroso by Council Decision 2004/780/EC, Euratom of November 19, 2004, [2004] O.J. L344/33.

[301] For problems arising in practice, see, e.g., the Commission's answers of September 13, 1996 to question E-1776/96 (Schreiner), [1996] O.J. C385/36, and of December 4, 1996 to question E-2837/96 (Wiebenga), [1997] O.J. C72/84. According to the Commission, Members of the Commission are politicians carrying out a political function, who, while honouring the obligations imposed by this function, remain free to express their personal opinions quite independently and on their own responsibility: see the answer of February 7, 2000 to questions E-2459/99, E-2600/99 and E-2628/99, [2000] O.J. C255E/139.

[302] ECJ, Case C-432/04 *Commission v Cresson* [2006] E.C.R. I-6387, paras 70–71.

[303] *Ibid.*, paras 103–109.

Commission who resigned in order to take up an appointment with a company active in the sector for which he had been competent.[304] However, the application was withdrawn after Mr Bangemann gave an assurance that he would not take up any appointment with any undertaking in the sector for a certain period.[305] In contrast, the Court had to give judgment on an application brought against former Commissioner Edith Cresson for appointing a close acquaintance as her "personal adviser", in dubious circumstances. The Court held that she had acted in breach of the obligations arising from her office as a Member of the Commission.[306]

Voluntary or compulsory retirement. Apart from formal replacement, or death, a Member of the Commission gives up his or her duties on voluntary or compulsory retirement. Compulsory retirement takes place where the European Parliament decides for political reasons to pass a motion of censure requiring the Commission to resign as a body (Art. 234 TFEU [*ex Art. 201 EC*]; see para. 13–009) or where the Court of Justice compulsorily retires a Member of the Commission on an application by the Council or the Commission on the ground that he or she no longer fulfils the conditions required for the performance of his or her duties or if he or she has been guilty of serious misconduct (Art. 247 TFEU). A Member of the Commission also has to resign if the President so requests (Art. 17(6), second subpara., TEU [*ex Art. 217(4) EC*]).[307] As far as the High Representative is concerned, the President's request has to be confirmed by the European Council, acting by a qualified majority (Arts 17(6), second subpara., and Art. 18(1) TEU). In each of these cases, the Council, by common accord with the President of the Commission and after consulting the European

13–073

---

[304] See the Council Decision of July 9, 1999 ([1999] O.J. L192/55; for the application thereof, see Case C-290/99 *Council v Bangemann*, [1999] O.J. C314/2); see also the resolution of the European Parliament of July 22, 1999 ([1999] O.J. C301/34).

[305] See the Council Decision of December 17, 1999 on the settlement of the Bangemann case, [2000] O.J. L16/73, which was subject to the proviso that Mr Bangemann would withdraw his action against the Council Decision of July 9, 1999 (Case T-208/99, [1999] O.J. C314/14). See also CFI, Joined Cases T-227/99 and T-134/00 *Kvaerner Warnow Werft v Commission* [2002] E.C.R. II-1205, paras 47–60 (validity of a Commission decision unaffected by the fact that Mr Bangemann had taken leave of absence after his announcement that he had accepted an appointment outside the Commission before the Council's decision not to replace him) and ECJ, Case C-334/99 *Germany v Commission* [2003] E.C.R. I-1139, paras 17–27 (following the Commission's decision to grant Mr Bangemann "leave of absence" until the Council decided whether to replace him, the composition of the Commission was lawful, since that decision had no influence on Mr Bangemann's status as Member of the Commission).

[306] ECJ, Case C-432/04 *Commission v Cresson* [2006] E.C.R. I-6387, paras 70–71.

[307] Before the Lisbon Treaty, Art. 217(4) EC required the President to obtain the approval of the College before requesting a member of the Commission to resign. See Coutron, "Le principe de la collégialité au sein de la Commission européenne après le Traité de Nice" (2003) R.T.D.E. 247, at 263–265.

Parliament, appoints a replacement (a new member of the same nationality) by a qualified majority vote or decides, unanimously on a proposal from the President of the Commission, that the vacancy is not to be filled (Art. 246, second and third paras, TFEU).[308] However, the High Representative must be replaced by the European Council, acting by a qualified majority and with the agreement of the President (Art. 18(1) TEU and Art. 246, fifth para., TFEU). Where the President has to be replaced, the procedure laid down in Art. 17(7) TEU has to be applied (see Art. 246, fourth para., TFEU).

In the event that the Commission as a body is made to resign by the European Parliament, the Commission, including the High Representative, remains in office and continues to deal with current business until it is replaced (Art. 234 TFEU). The same is true where all Members of the Commission voluntarily resign (Art. 246, sixth para., TFEU). That was different before the Lisbon Treaty, since the Treaties merely provided that in the case of voluntary resignation, the resigning Members of the Commission remained in office until such time as they were replaced (see Art. 215, fourth para., EC).[309] Nevertheless, the Members of the Commission who resigned as a body on March 16, 1999 declared that, although under the Treaties their powers were not limited in the circumstances (voluntary resignation), they had decided to exercise their powers in a restrictive manner until such time as they were replaced, that is to say, they would deal with current and urgent business, and comply with their institutional and legal obligations, but not take fresh political initiatives.[310]

3. Operation

13–074 **Rules of Procedure.** The Commission has to act collectively in accordance with the Treaties and its Rules of Procedure, adopted pursuant to Art. 249(1) TFEU

---

[308] E.g., if the Commission's term of office is coming to an end, the Council may take a unanimous decision under Art. 246, third para., TFEU that there is no need to fill the vacancy. See, for example, Council Decision 1999/493/EC, ECSC, Euratom of July 9, 1999 on the composition of the Commission, [1999] O.J. L192/53.

[309] Therefore, after their decision of March 16, 1999 to resign as a body, the Commission's powers were not confined to dealing with current business: CFI, Case T-219/99 *British Airways v Commission* [2003] E.C.R. II-05917, paras 46–56. In an earlier case, the Court of First Instance [*now the General Court*] did not rule on whether or not the Commission's powers were limited after March 16, 1999: CFI, Joined Cases T-228/99 and T-233/99 *Westdeutsche Landesbank Girozentrale v Commission* [2003] E.C.R. II-435, paras 94–100 (a decision by which the Commission declared State Aid incompatible with the common market falls in any event under the heading of "current business").

[310] Press communiqué of March 17, 1999, doc. IP/99/186. See Rodrigues, "Quelques réflexions juridiques à propos de la démission de la Commission européenne—de la responsabilité des institutions communautaires comme 'manifestation ultime de la démocratie'?" (1999) R.M.C.U.E. 472–483; Tomkins, "Responsibility and Resignation in the European Commission" (1999) Mod.L.Rev. 744–765.

[*ex Art. 218(2) EC*].[311] It works under the political guidance of its President, who is to decide on its internal organisation in order to ensure that it acts consistently, efficiently and as a collegiate body (Art. 17(6)(b) TFEU [*ex Art. 217(1) EC*]).[312] The President of the Commission convenes the Commission to meet at least once a week (Commission Rules of Procedure, Art. 5). Its meetings are not public and its discussions are confidential (Commission Rules of Procedure, Art. 9). The Secretary-General and the President's Head of Cabinet attend its meetings and other persons may be heard (Commission Rules of Procedure, Art. 10).

Collective responsibility. The Commission acts by a majority of its Members   **13–075**
(Art. 250, first para., TFEU [*ex Art. 219, first para., EC*]). It is quorate if a majority of its Members is present (Art. 250, second para., TFEU and Commission Rules of Procedure, Art. 7). However, decisions may be taken by means of a written procedure whereby a proposal made by one or more Members is deemed to have been adopted if no Member enters a reservation within a specified period or asks that the proposal be discussed at a meeting.[313] The fact that Commissioners participate equally in decision-making is indicative of the collegiate nature of the Commission, which means that

> "decisions should be the subject of a collective deliberation and that all the Members of the college of Commissioners bear collective responsibility on the political level for all decisions adopted".[314]

In a framework agreement between the European Parliament and the Commission, it is stated, however, that, without prejudice to the principle of Commission collegiality, each Member of the Commission is to take political responsibility for action in the field for which he or she is responsible.[315]

---

[311] The present Rules of Procedure were adopted by the Commission on November 29, 2000 ([2000] O.J. L55/60), and most recently amended on February 24, 2010 (see [2010] O.J. L55/60). Previous versions date from September 18, 1999 ([1999] O.J. L252/41) and February 17, 1993 ([1993] O.J. L230/16, adopted pursuant to Art. 16 of the Merger Treaty) and January 31, 1963 (provisionally retained after the Merger Treaty entered into force by decision of July 6, 1967, [1967] J.O. 147/1). The provisions on security (Commission Decision of November 29, 2001, [2001] O.J. L317/1), the detailed rules on public access to documents (Commission Decision of December 5, 2001, [2001] O.J. L345/94) and the provisions on document management (Commission Decision of January 23, 2002, [2002] O.J. L21/23) are annexed to the Rules of Procedure.

[312] See Karagiannis, "Le Président de la Commission" (2000) C.D.E. 9, at 36–55.

[313] Commission Rules of Procedure, Art. 12. According to that article, the procedure in question may be employed only if the departments involved are in agreement and the proposal has been approved by the Commission's Legal Service.

[314] ECJ, Case 5/85 *AKZO Chemie v Commission* [1986] E.C.R. 2585, para. 30. For the principle of collegiality, see also Mistò, "La collégialité de la Commission européenne" (2003) R.D.U.E. 189–255; Coutron (n. 307, *supra*), at 247–266.

[315] Framework agreement on relations between Parliament and the Commission of October 20, 2010 (n. 26, *supra*), point 4. See also Mehde, "Responsibility and Accountability in the European Commission" (2003) C.M.L.Rev. 423–442.

Provided that the principle of collective responsibility is fully respected, the Commission may empower one or more of its Members to take management or administrative measures on its behalf and subject to such restrictions and conditions as it shall impose.[316] The Commission may likewise instruct one or more of its Members, with the President's agreement, to adopt the definitive text of any instrument or of a proposal for submission to other institutions if the substance of the act or proposal has already been determined.[317] Accordingly, the Commission may authorise one of its Members to amend a proposal before the Council in a particular way.[318] Where the Commission itself takes the final decision, the principle of collective responsibility requires that the operative part of that final decision and its statement of reasons should be adopted in its definitive written form by the

---

[316] Commission Rules of Procedure, Art. 13(1). According to the Court of Justice, the system of delegation of authority remains within the Commission's power of internal organisation since the Commission does not thereby divest itself of powers (the decisions may still be the subject of judicial review as Commission decisions and the Commission may always reserve certain decisions for itself) and the procedure is necessary for the sound functioning of the Commission's decision-making power: ECJ, Case 5/85 *AKZO Chemie v Commission* [1986] E.C.R. 2585, paras 35–37; ECJ, Joined Cases 97–99/87 *Dow Chemica Ibérica and Others v Commission* [1989] E.C.R. 3165, para. 58; CFI, Joined Cases T-300/05 and T-316/05 *Cyprus v Commission*, [2009] E.C.R. II-192*, summ. pub., paras 211–215 (on the notion of "management and administrative measures": paras 216–224). See the earlier recognition of the delegation of the power of signature for management and administrative measures: ECJ, Case 48/69 *ICI v Commission* [1972] E.C.R. 619, paras 12–14, and ECJ, Case 52/69 *Geigy v Commission* [1972] E.C.R. 787, para. 5; ECJ, Case 8/72 *Cementhandelaren v Commission* [1972] E.C.R. 977, paras 11–13; ECJ, Joined Cases 43 and 63/82 *VBVB and VBBB v Commission* [1984] E.C.R. 19, paras 12–14. No management or administrative measure constitutes a decision finding an infringement of Art. 81(1) EC [*now Art. 101(1) TFEU*] in the authentic language: CFI, Joined Cases T-79/89, T-84/89, T-85/89, T-86/89, T-89/89, T-91/89, T-92/89, T-94/89, T-96/89, T-98/89, T-102/89 and T-104/89 *BASF and Others v Commission* [1992] E.C.R. II-315, paras 57–59; ECJ, Case C-137/92 P *Commission v BASF and Others* [1994] E.C.R. I-2555, paras 62–65; CFI, Joined Cases T-80/89, T-81/89, T-83/89, T-87/89, T-88/89, T-90/89, T-93/89, T-95/89, T-97/89, T-99/89, T-100/89, T-101/89, T-103/89, T-105/89, T-107/89 and T-112/89 *BASF and Others v Commission* [1995] E.C.R. II-729, paras 96–102. With regard to State Aid, see CFI, Case T-435/93 *ASPEC and Others v Commission* [1995] E.C.R. II-1281, paras 100–104, and CFI, Case T-442/93 *AAC and Others v Commission* [1995] E.C.R. II-1329, paras 81–95. Neither does a decision to issue a reasoned opinion or to commence infringement proceedings before the Court of Justice constitute a measure of administration or management: ECJ, Case C-191/95 *Commission v Germany* [1998] E.C.R. I-5449, paras 33–37. Powers conferred by delegation may be subdelegated to the Directors-General and Heads of Department unless this is expressly prohibited in the empowering decision (Commission Rules of Procedure, Art. 13(3)).

[317] Commission Rules of Procedure, Art. 13(2) taking over Art. 11 of the 1993 Rules of Procedure, as amended following the judgment of the Court of First Instance [*now the General Court*] of February 27, 1992 in *BASF and Others v Commission* (n. 316, *supra*) and again following the judgment of the Court of Justice of June 15, 1994 in *Commission v BASF and Others* (*ibid*; for the amendment, see [1995] O.J. L97/82). For the application of the new rule, see CFI, Joined Cases T-427/04 and T-17/05 *France and France Télécom v Commission* [2009] E.C.R. II-4315, paras 119–129.

[318] ECJ, Case C-445/00 *Austria v Council*[2003] E.C.R. I-8549, paras 40–42.

Commission as a body, which means that only simple corrections of spelling and grammar may be made to the text of an act after its formal adoption.[319] Since 2001, the Commission may, provided that the principle of collective responsibility is fully respected, delegate the adoption of management or administrative measures to the Directors-General and Heads of Department, acting on its behalf and subject to such restrictions and conditions as it shall impose.[320]

4. Internal organisation

Directorates-General. The President of the Commission decides on its internal organisation and lays down guidelines within which the Commission is to work (Art. 17(6)(a) and (b) TEU).[321] He or she structures the responsibilities incumbent upon the Commission, allocates them among its Members and may reshuffle the allocation of those responsibilities during the Commission's term of office (Art. 248 TFEU [*ex Art. 217(2) EC*]). Accordingly, the President assigns to Members of the Commission special fields of activity with regard to which they are specifically responsible for the preparation of Commission work and the implementation of its decisions.[322] The President of the Commission is to notify the European Parliament immediately of any decision concerning the allocation of responsibilities to any of the Members of the Commission.[323] The Members of the Commission are to carry out the duties devolved upon them by the President under his or her authority

13–076

---

[319] ECJ, Case C-137/92 P *Commission v BASF and Others* [1994] E.C.R. I-2555, paras 66–70. The Court of Justice mitigated these formal requirements as regards decisions to issue a reasoned opinion or to commence infringement proceedings. Such decisions must be the subject of collective deliberation by the college of Commissioners; accordingly, the information on which they are based must be available to the Members of the college; however, the college itself does not have to decide formally on "the wording of the acts which give effect to those decisions and put them into final form": ECJ, Case C-191/95 *Commission v Germany* [1998] E.C.R. I-5449, paras 41–48. See also ECJ, Case C-272/97 *Commission v Germany* [1999] E.C.R. I-2175, paras 16–22; ECJ, Case C-198/97 *Commission v Germany* [1999] E.C.R. I-3257, paras 19–22; ECJ, Case C-1/00 *Commission v France* [2001] E.C.R. I-9989, paras 79–86.

[320] Commission Rules of Procedure, Art. 14. However, in the absence of such delegation, a decision taken by a Director-General will be vitiated by a lack of powers and may be annulled by the Court (see CFI, Case T-33/01 *Infront v Commission* [2005] E.C.R. II-5897, paras 173–178; the appeal against this judgment was dismissed: ECJ, Case C-125/06 P *Commission v Infront* [2008] E.C.R. I-1451).

[321] For more details on the Commission's internal organisation, see the relevant chapters of Spence and Edwards, *The European Commission* (London, John Harper, 2006), 592 pp.

[322] Commission Rules of Procedure, Art. 2, second subpara. Commissioners have their own *cabinets* (private offices) and give policy directions to one or more directorates-general (or certain directorates) and other departments. See also Georgopoulos and Lefèvre (n. 289, *supra*), at 602–608. The hierarchical link between a Commissioner and the administration is not legally determined; see Mehde (n. 315, *supra*), at 429–433.

[323] Point 7 of the Framework Agreement of October 20, 2010 on relations between the European Parliament and the Commission, [2010] O.J. L304/47.

(Art. 248 TFEU). The Commission's administrative services consist of Directorates-General and equivalent departments (Commission Rules of Procedure, Art. 21). The Directorates-General (DGs), which are subdivided into directorates, each deal with a specific area of policy under the leadership of a Director-General.[324] Other departments include the Secretariat General, the Legal Service and a number of offices.[325] The different Departments closely cooperate in the preparation and implementation of Commission decisions and must consult each other before submitting a document to the Commission (Commission Rules of Procedure, Art. 23(1) to (3)). The Legal Service must in any event be consulted on all drafts or proposals for legal instruments and on all documents which may have legal implications (Commission Rules of Procedure, Art. 23(4)). The Commission's seat is in Brussels, but a number of its departments are established in Luxembourg.[326] With more than 24,000 officials, the Commission constitutes the largest of the institutions.[327]

---

[324] For internal policy: DG Agriculture and Rural Development (AGRI), DG Climate Action (CLIMA), DG Competition (COMP), DG Economic and Financial Affairs (ECFIN), DG Education and Culture (EAC), DG Employment, Social Affairs and Equal Opportunities (EMPL), DG Energy (ENER), DG Enterprise and Industry (ENTR), DG Environment (ENV), DG Maritime Affairs and Fisheries (MARE), DG Mobility and Transport (MOVE), DG Health and Consumers (SANCO), DG Information Society and Media (INFSO), DG Internal Market and Services (MARKT), DG Justice (JUSTICE), DG Home Affairs (HOME), DG Regional Policy (REGIO), DG Research (RTD) and DG Taxation and Customs Union (TAXUD). For external relations: DG Development and Cooperation (DEVCO), DG Enlargement (ELARG), DG Humanitarian Aid (ECHO) and DG Trade (TRADE). For general services: DG Communication (COMM), DG Budget (BUDG), DG Human Resources and Security (HR), DG Informatics (DIGIT), DG for Interpretation (SCIC) and DG for Translation (DGT). In external actions, the Commission also relies on the European External Action Service (see para. 13–121). For more information, see the Commission's website: *http://ec.europa.eu/dgs_en.htm* [Accessed December 9, 2010].

[325] Such as the Internal Audit Service (IAS), the Bureau of European Policy Advisors (BEPA), The Foreign Policy Instruments Service (FPIS), the Joint Research Centre (JRC), the Offices for infrastructure and logistics in Brussels (OIB) and Luxembourg (OIL), the Statistical Office (Eurostat), the European Anti-Fraud Office (OLAF) and the Paymaster Office (PMO). See also, on an inter-institutional basis, the Publications Office (OP) and the European Personnel Selection Office (EPSO) (see para. 13–122, *infra*).

[326] See the sole Art., para. (c), of the Protocol on Seats (para. 13–153, *infra*), which refers, as regards the departments to remain in Luxembourg, to the list in the Decision on Provisional Location of April 8, 1965 (para. 13–152, *infra*). See also ECJ, Case C-137/92 P *Commission v BASF and Others* [1994] E.C.R. I-2555, paras 41–42 (for the purpose of the extension of procedural time-limits on account of distance, the Commission has its "habitual residence" in Brussels).

[327] As at December 2009, the Commission had 20,018 permanent administrative posts and 366 temporary administrative posts, and 3827 permanent research posts. There were also 1883 permanent posts and 115 temporary posts for offices attached to the Commission: *General Report on the Activities of the European Union 2009* (n. 106, *supra*), at 96.

II. OTHER INSTITUTIONS OF THE UNION

A. THE COURT OF JUSTICE OF THE EUROPEAN UNION

Establishment. When the EEC Treaty and the EAEC Treaty entered into force, one **13–077** institution, the Court of Justice of the European Communities,[328] took the place of the existing Court of Justice of the ECSC. The Court of Justice exercised jurisdiction in accordance with each of the three Community Treaties and the protocols on the Statute of the Court appended thereto. By means of a new Protocol on the Statute of the Court of Justice, the Treaty of Nice introduced a single Statute for the Court of Justice.[329] From September 1, 1989 on, the institution known as the Court of Justice consisted of two independent courts, one bearing that name, the other entitled the Court of First Instance.[330] Since the Lisbon Treaty, the "Court of Justice of the European Union" is made up not only of the Court of Justice itself and the General Court (the new name given by the Lisbon Treaty to the former Court of First Instance) but also of "specialised courts" (Art. 19(1), first subpara. TEU).

"Specialised courts" took the place of the so-called "judicial panels", which since the Treaty of Nice could be attached to the Court of First Instance (now the General Court) to exercise judicial competence in certain specific areas (see former Art. 220, second para., EC). To this end, the European Parliament and the Council, acting in accordance with the ordinary legislative procedure, have to adopt a regulation, either on a proposal from the Commission after consultation of the Court of Justice or at the request of the Court of Justice after consultation

---

[328] For the website of the Court of Justice of the European Union, see *http://curia.europa.eu/* [Accessed December 9, 2010].

[329] See now Protocol (No. 3), annexed to the TEU, TFEU and the EAEC Treaty, on the Statute of the Court of Justice of the European Union, [2010] O.J. C83/210, which replaced Protocol (No. 6) on the Statute of the Court of Justice, annexed to the EU Treaty, the EC Treaty and the EAEC Treaty ([2001] O.J. C80/53). The provisions of the Statute have the same normative force as Treaty articles (see Art. 51 TEU and Art. 207 EAEC), although the European Parliament and the Council, acting in accordance with the ordinary legislative procedure and at the request of the Court of Justice and after consultation of the Commission, or on a proposal from the Commission and after consultation of the Court of Justice, may amend the provisions of the Statute (with the exception of Title I and Art. 64: see Art. 281 TFEU). The Statute annexed by the Nice Treaty replaced Council Decision 88/591/ECSC, EEC, Euratom of October 24, 1988 establishing a Court of First Instance of the European Communities and the respective Protocols relating to the Statute of the Court of Justice which were annexed to the EC Treaty, the EAEC Treaty and the ECSC Treaty, with the exception of a number of provisions remaining in force for the Court of Justice and the Court of First Instance in matters relating to the ECSC (Nice Treaty, Arts 7 to 10).

[330] Council Decision 88/591/ECSC, EEC, Euratom of October 24, 1988 establishing a Court of First Instance of the European Communities [hereinafter: CFI Decision], [1988] O.J. L319/1, and L241 (republished as amended by *corrigenda* in [1989] O.J. C215/1). By that decision, the Council, acting unanimously at the request of the Court of Justice and after consulting the Commission and the European Parliament, established a Court of First Instance of the European Communities pursuant to Art. 32d ECSC, Art. 168a EEC and Art. 140a EAEC. The EU Treaty rooted the existence of the Court of First Instance in the EC Treaty itself (see former Art. 225(1) EC).

of the Commission, which lays down the rules on the organisation of the specialised court and the extent of the jurisdiction conferred upon it (Art. 257, first and second paras, TFEU [*ex Art. 225a, first and second paras, EC*][331]). At present, only one specialised court has been established, namely the European Union Civil Service Tribunal.[332]

Unless the Statute of the Court of Justice or the regulation establishing the specialised court provides otherwise, the provisions of the Treaties relating to the Court of Justice are to apply to the General Court and the specialised courts.[333]

1. Jurisdiction

13–078   **Decentralised enforcement of Union law.** The Court of Justice of the European Union ensures that in the interpretation and application of the Treaties the law is observed (Art. 19(1), first subpara., TEU [*ex Art. 220 EC and Art. 136 EAEC*]). This does not mean that the Court of Justice, the General Court and the specialised courts automatically hear and determine all disputes whose outcome depends on the correct application of Union law. The founding fathers of the Communities and the Union opted for a system under which enforcement of Community and Union law was left in principle to the national courts. Since the Lisbon Treaty, the Treaties explicitly state that Member States must provide remedies sufficient to ensure effective legal protection in the fields covered by Union law (Art. 19(1), second subpara., TEU).

A dispute relating to Union law may be brought before the European Courts only if this is permitted under one of the procedures prescribed by the Treaties.[334] When interpreting the provisions with respect to these procedures, the Court of Justice has to respect the limits to the jurisdiction conferred on it by the Treaties.[335] The Court of Justice has interpreted its own jurisdiction only exceptionally in a

---

[331] Article 225a EC required the Council to take a decision acting unanimously on a proposal from the Commission and after consulting the European Parliament and the Court of Justice or at the request of the Court of Justice and after consulting the European Parliament and the Commission.

[332] Council Decision (2004/752/EC, Euratom) of November 2, 2004 establishing the European Union Civil Service Tribunal, [2004] O.J. L333/7. See also Declaration (No. 16), annexed to the Nice Treaty, which called upon the Court of Justice and the Commission "to prepare as swiftly as possible a draft decision establishing a judicial panel which has jurisdiction to deliver judgments at first instance on disputes between the Community and its servants" ([2001] O.J. C80/80). For a discussion, see Kraemer, "The European Union Civil Service Tribunal: A New Community Court Examined After Four Years of Operation" (2009) C.M.L.Rev. 1873–1913. See also Lenaerts, "The future organisation of the European Courts", in Demaret, Govaere and Hanf (eds), *European Legal Dynamics/Dynamiques Juridiques Européennes* (Brussels, PIE-Peter Lang, 2007) 129–145.

[333] See Arts 254, sixth para., and 257, sixth para., TFEU [*ex Arts 224, sixth para., and Art. 225a, sixth para., EC*]

[334] See ECJ, Case 66/76 *CFDT v Council* [1977] E.C.R. 305, para. 8.

[335] ECJ, Case C-50/00 P *Unión de Pequeños Agricultores v Council and Commission* [2002] E.C.R. I-6677, paras 44–45.

manner exceeding the literal scope of a given procedure, inter alia in order to fill a lacuna in the system of legal protection or to secure the coherence of the Union's legal order.[336]

Dual purpose. According to Art. 19(3) TEU, the Court of Justice of the European Union: 13–079

(a) rules on actions brought by a Member State, an institution or a natural or legal person;

(b) gives preliminary rulings, at the request of courts or tribunals of the Member States, on the interpretation of Union law or the validity of acts adopted by the institutions; and

(c) rules in other cases provided for in the Treaties.

The procedures provided for in the Treaties in fact enable the Court of Justice of the European Union to carry out a four-fold task.[337] The Court decides:

(1) disputes between institutions, bodies, agencies and offices of the Union;

(2) disputes between the Union and its Member States;

(3) disputes between the Member States; and

(4) disputes between natural or legal persons and the Union.

These procedures serve a dual purpose. On the one hand, they enable the Court,

---

[336] See ECJ, Case 294/83 *Les Verts v European Parliament* [1986] E.C.R. 1339, paras 23–25, and ECJ, Case C-70/88 *European Parliament v Council* [1990] E.C.R. I-2041, paras 11–27 (recognition of the fact that the Parliament may be a defendant or an applicant in proceedings, respectively, despite the wording of Art. 173 EEC, for the sake of institutional balance; para. 15–010, *infra*); ECJ, Case C-2/88 Imm. *Zwartveld and Others* [1990] E.C.R. I-3365, paras 15–26 (interpretation of the privileges and immunities of the Communities in the light of the duty of sincere cooperation within the meaning of Art. 10 EC, para. 7–047, *supra*); ECJ, Case 314/85 *Foto-Frost* [1987] E.C.R. 4199, paras 12–17 (where it was held that national courts have no power to declare Community acts invalid in spite of the limitation of the obligation to make references for preliminary rulings to national courts of last instance); ECJ, Case C-47/07 P *Masdar v Commission* [2008] E.C.R. I-09761, paras 49–50 (interpretation of the Treaty provisions on actions for damages against the Community so as to also include actions for unjust enrichment). See Lenaerts, "The Legal Protection of Private Parties under the EC Treaty: A Coherent and Complete System of Judicial Review?", in *Scritti in onore di Giuseppe Federico Mancini* (Milan, Dott. A. Giuffrè Editore, 1998), II, 591–623; Lenaerts, "The rule of law and the coherence of the judicial system of the European Union" (2007) C.M.L.Rev. 1–35.

[337] For further details, see Lenaerts, Arts and Maselis, *Procedural Law of the European Union* (3rd edn, London, Sweet & Maxwell, 2012); Lenaerts, "La systématique des voies de recours dans l'ordre juridique de l'Union européenne", in *Mélanges en hommage à Georges Vandersanden. Promenades au sein du droit européen* (Brussels, Bruylant, 2008), 257–282.

together with the national courts, to see to it that Union law is correctly interpreted and applied in the Member States. On the other, they seek to guarantee judicial redress against Union institutions and bodies, agencies and offices for individuals, Member States or (other) institutions that are affected by acts of the Union.

13–080 **(1) Disputes between institutions bodies, agencies and offices.** First, the Court decides disputes between Union institutions, bodies, offices and agencies, both directly following the bringing of an action for annulment or of an action for failure to act, and indirectly pursuant to other procedures. The European Parliament, the Council, the Commission and—if the action seeks to safeguard their prerogatives— the Court of Auditors, the ECB and the Committee of the Regions are entitled to bring an action for annulment under Art. 263 TFEU [*ex Art. 230 EC*]. Using that procedure, they can challenge legislative acts, acts of the Council, the Commission and the European Central Bank (if the contested act is not a recommendation or an opinion), acts of the European Parliament and the European Council (only if the contested act has legal effects on third parties) and acts of the bodies, offices or agencies of the Union (if the contested act is intended to produce legal effects on third parties).[338] The institutions may bring an action for failure to act under Art. 265 TFEU [*ex Art. 232 EC*] against the European Parliament, the European Council, the Council, the Commission or the ECB or against the bodies, offices or agencies of the Union.[339] A dispute between institutions, bodies, offices and agencies may be raised incidentally where they intervene in proceedings[340] or submit observations to the Court of Justice where a national court has put a question for a preliminary ruling on the validity of an act of the institutions, bodies, offices or agencies[341] or where the Court of Justice gives an opinion on a proposed international agreement pursuant to Art. 218(11) TFEU [*ex Art. 300(6) EC*].

---

[338] This possibility was introduced by the Lisbon Treaty. However, even before the Lisbon Treaty, the Court of First Instance (now the General Court) had already accepted that it could review the acts of certain independent bodies with legal effects vis-à-vis third parties (see CFI, Case T-411/06 *Sogelma v European Agency for Reconstruction* [2008] E.C.R. II-2771, paras 33–57). The acts setting up bodies, offices and agencies of the Union may lay down specific conditions and arrangements concerning such actions (Art. 263, fifth para., TFEU). The Commission is further entitled to bring proceedings against acts of the Board of Governors or the Board of Directors of the EIB (Art. 271(b) and (c) TFEU [*ex Art. 237(b) and (c) EC*]). In this way, the Commission may bring proceedings against all acts adopted by the EIB falling within the sphere of competence of the Board of Governors, even if the act in question was adopted by another organ: ECJ, Case C-15/00 *Commission v European Investment Bank* [2003] E.C.R. I-7281, paras 73–74.

[339] This possibility was introduced by the Lisbon Treaty.

[340] ECJ Statute, Art. 40. Institutions, bodies, offices and agencies may intervene, inter alia, in order to defend an act adopted by them against which an objection of illegality has been raised (Art. 277 TFEU [*ex Art. 241 EC*]).

[341] ECJ Statute, Art. 23.

(2) Disputes between the Union and Member States. Secondly, the Court **13–081** determines disputes between the Union and the Member States. The Commission may bring an action against a Member State which has failed to fulfil its Treaty obligations in accordance with the procedure set out in Arts 258 and 260 TFEU [*ex Arts 226 and 228 EC*].[342] A Member State may bring an action for annulment against any act mentioned in the preceding paragraph or an action for failure to act against the European Parliament, the European Council, the Council, the Commission and the ECB or against the bodies, offices and agencies of the Union. Equally, a dispute between the Union and a Member State may be raised before the Court of Justice indirectly, given that Member States have the same right as the institutions to intervene or to submit observations in pending cases (they tend especially to submit observations in connection with requests for preliminary rulings on the interpretation of Union law from which it may ensue that national law is in breach of Union law).[343]

(3) Disputes between Member States. The Court also has to hear and determine **13–082** cases between Member States, but this is a fairly rare occurrence. A Member State may bring an alleged infringement of the Treaties by another Member State before the Court of Justice (Art. 259 TFEU [*ex Art. 227 EC*]). Member States may also bring a dispute before the Court of Justice under a special agreement (Art. 273 TFEU [*ex Art. 239*]). In addition, disputes between Member States may be determined indirectly in all the aforementioned procedures. Art. 344 TFEU [*ex Art. 292 EC*] provides that Member States may not submit a dispute concerning the interpretation or application of the Treaties to any method of settlement other than those provided for therein. Given this exclusive jurisdiction of the Court of Justice, a Member State may not bring proceedings against another Member State for non-compliance with Union law before an international tribunal.[344]

(4) Disputes between natural or legal persons and Union. The Union Courts **13–083** afford legal protection to natural and legal persons where a national court or tribunal makes a reference for a preliminary ruling on the interpretation of the

---

[342] See also Arts 108(2), second subpara., Art. 114(9) and 348 TFEU [*ex Art. 88(2), second subpara., 95(9) and 298 EC*]. The Board of Directors of the EIB and the Board of the ECB have the same powers in respect of the fulfilment of obligations by Member States under the EIB Statute or the Treaties and the ESCB Statute: see Art. 271(a) and (d) TFEU [*ex Art. 237(a) and (d) EC*], respectively.

[343] See Granger, "When governments go to Luxembourg . . .: the influence of governments on the Court of Justice" (2004) E.L.Rev. 3–31. See also the procedure set out in Art. 218(11) TFEU.

[344] ECJ, Case C-459/03 *Commission v Ireland* [2006] E.C.R. I-4635 (concerning proceedings brought by Ireland against the United Kingdom in the International Tribunal for the Law of the Sea). See the case note by Lavranos (2006) *European Current Law* 11–15 and Lavranos, "The scope of the exclusive jurisdiction of the Court of Justice" (2007) E.L.Rev. 83–94. A dispute between Member States may be brought before an international tribunal only where the dispute relates to rights and obligations which do not flow from the Treaties. See, e.g., the proceedings brought by Germany against Italy (for failing to respect its jurisdictional immunity as a sovereign State) before the International Court of Justice (see the website: *www.icj-cji.org* [Accessed December 9, 2010]).

Treaties or on the validity or interpretation of acts of the institutions, bodies, offices or agencies of the Union (Art. 267 TFEU [*ex Art. 234 EC*]) or where such persons bring an action against an institution, body, agency or office of the Union. Natural or legal persons may bring an action for annulment against binding acts which are addressed to them or of direct (and individual) concern[345] to them under Art. 263, fourth para., TFEU [*ex Art. 230, fourth para., EC*] or may bring an action for failure to act under Art. 265, third para., TFEU [*ex Art. 232, third para., EC*]. In this way, the Treaties seek to establish a complete system of legal remedies and procedures to permit the Union Courts to review the legality of measures adopted by the Union institutions and bodies.[346] Where natural or legal persons cannot, by reason of the conditions for admissibility laid down in the fourth para. of Art. 263 TFEU, directly challenge Union measures of general application, they are able, depending on the case, either indirectly to plead the invalidity of such acts before the Union Courts by way of an objection of illegality (Art. 277 TFEU [*ex Art. 241 EC*]) or to do so before the national courts and ask them, since those courts have no jurisdiction themselves to declare those measures invalid,[347] to make a reference to the Court of Justice for a preliminary ruling on validity. In addition, the Union Courts determine damages claims brought against the Union (Arts 268 and 340 TFEU [*Arts 235 and 288 EC*]), disputes between the Union and its officials and other servants (Art. 270 TFEU [*ex Art. 236 EC*]) and disputes submitted to it pursuant to an arbitration clause (Art. 272 TFEU [*ex Art. 238 EC*]). Some provisions establishing Union bodies and agencies confer jurisdiction on the Court of Justice of the European Union to hear and determine disputes pursuant to an arbitration clause contained in a contract concluded by the body or agency in question and disputes relating to the non-contractual liability of that body or agency.[348] In future, the Court of Justice of the European Union may also obtain jurisdiction to hear and determine disputes as between individuals with regard to European intellectual property rights.[349]

---

[345] Since the entry into force of the Lisbon Treaty, individual concern is no longer required in the case of regulatory acts which are of direct concern to the applicant and do not entail implementing measures (Art. 263, fourth para., TFEU). For a discussion of the changes introduced by the Lisbon Treaty, see Lenaerts, "Le traité de Lisbonne et la protection juridictionnelle des particuliers en droit de l'Union" (2009) C.D.E. 711–745.

[346] ECJ, Case 294/83 *Les Verts v European Parliament* [1986] E.C.R. 1339, para. 23; ECJ, Case C-50/00 P *Unión de Pequeños Agricultores v Council and Commission* [2002] E.C.R. I-6677, paras 40–42; ECJ, Case C-491/01 *British American Tobacco (Investments) and Imperial Tobacco* [2003] E.C.R. I-11453, para. 39; ECJ, Case C-263/02 P *Commission v Jégo-Quéré* [2004] E.C.R. I-3425, paras 29–32.

[347] ECJ, Case 314/85 *Foto-Frost* [1987] E.C.R. 4199, para. 20 (n. 336, *supra*); ECJ, Case C-461/03 *Gaston Schul Douane-expediteur* [2005] E.C.R. I-10513, para. 17.

[348] See, e.g., ESCB Statute, Arts 35.3 and 35.4.

[349] To this end, the Council, acting unanimously on a proposal from the Commission and after consulting the European Parliament, has to adopt provisions to confer jurisdiction on the Court of Justice and the Member States have to adopt them in accordance with their respective constitutional requirements (Art. 262 TFEU [*ex Art. 229a EC*]).

Fields of limited jurisdiction. The Court of Justice of the European Union   **13–084**
exercises its powers in respect of disputes which come within the scope of the
provisions of the Treaties. However, during a transitional period, the Court's
jurisdiction remains subject to certain limits in matters of police and judicial
cooperation in criminal matters (PJCC, see para. 13–085) and it has only very
limited jurisdiction in the fields covered by the common foreign and security policy (CFSP; see para. 13–086).

Area of freedom, security and justice. Before the entry into force of the Lisbon   **13–085**
Treaty, the Court's jurisdiction was limited as regards both matters falling under
Title IV of Part Three of the EC Treaty (visas, asylum, immigration and other
policies related to free movement of persons, which included judicial cooperation
in civil matters) and matters of police and judicial cooperation in criminal
matters (PJCC).[350]

The Court of Justice now has full jurisdiction over all matters falling under Title
V of Part Three of the TFEU (which incorporates both the provisions previously
contained in Title IV of the EC Treaty and the Union's powers in the field of PJCC).
However, as regards PJCC, the Lisbon Treaty has not done away with the clause
according to which the Court has no jurisdiction to review the validity or proportionality of operations carried out by the police or other law-enforcement services
of a Member State or the exercise of the responsibilities incumbent upon Member
States with regard to the maintenance of law and order and the safeguarding of
internal security (Art. 276 TFEU).[351]

As regards Ch. 2 (policies on border checks, asylum and immigration) and
Ch. 3 (judicial cooperation in civil matters) of Title V on the area of freedom, security and justice, the Lisbon Treaty has done away with the limit on the Court's
jurisdiction which was imposed by Art. 68(1) EC, according to which in those
matters the Court of Justice had jurisdiction to give preliminary rulings in these
matters only on questions referred by a national court or tribunal against whose
decisions there was no judicial remedy under national law.[352] The possibility for

---

[350] See Knapp, "Die Garantie des effektiven Rechtsschutzes durch den EuGH im 'Raum der Freiheit,
der Sicherheit und des Rechts' " (2001) D.ö.V. 12–21; Arnull, "Les incidences du traité
d'Amsterdam sur la Cour de justice des Communautés européennes" (2000) R.A.E 223–230;
Fennelly, " 'The Area of Freedom, Security and Justice' and the European Court of Justice—A
Personal View" (2000) I.C.L.Q. 1, at 4–8. See also, Lenaerts, "The Contribution of the European
Court of Justice to the Area of Freedom, Security and Justice" (2010) I.C.L.Q. 1–47.

[351] See, previously, Art. 35(5) EU. However, there is no trace in the TFEU of Art. 68(2) EC, according to which, as regards measures or decisions taken to ensure the absence of controls on persons
crossing internal borders, the Court of Justice had no jurisdiction to rule on any measure or decision relating to the maintenance of law and order and the safeguarding of internal security.

[352] Consequently, in this context the EC Treaty precluded preliminary references from "inferior"
courts; see ECJ (order of March 18, 2004), Case C-45/03 *Dem'Yanenko*, not reported; ECJ (order
of 31 March 2004), Case C-51/03 *Georgescu* [2004] E.C.R. I-3203; ECJ (order of 10 June 2004),
Case C-555/03 *Warbecq* [2004] E.C.R. I-6041.

the Council, the Commission or any Member State to request the Court of Justice to give a ruling on a question of interpretation of Title IV or of acts of the institutions based thereon has also disappeared.[353]

As regards Ch. 4 (judicial cooperation in criminal matters) and Ch. 5 (police cooperation), the Court's jurisdiction was subject to even more limits. Those limits will however remain valid until November 30, 2014 pursuant to Protocol (No. 36) on transitional provisions (see para. 4–014) in respect of PJCC acts adopted on the basis of the EU Treaty before the entry into force of the Lisbon Treaty (see paras 23–002 *et seq.*). Consequently, the boundaries to the Court's jurisdiction set out in Art. 35 EU[354] will still apply with respect to acts based on Title VI of the EU Treaty which were adopted before December 1, 2009.[355]

First, Art. 35(1) to (3) EU recognises the Court's jurisdiction to give preliminary rulings only in so far as a Member State accepts the Court's jurisdiction

> "to give preliminary rulings on the validity and interpretation of framework decisions and decisions, the interpretation of conventions and the validity and interpretation of measures implementing them".

In the declaration through which Member States accept the Court's jurisdiction, they are to determine whether only those courts or tribunals against whose decisions there is no judicial remedy[356] or any national court or tribunal may request a preliminary ruling[357] (Art. 35(3) EU). Given the extended applicability of the

---

[353] Article 68(3) EC. No such request was ever made. The resultant preliminary ruling would not have applied to judgments of national courts or tribunals which had become res judicata (Art. 68(3) EC).

[354] Before the introduction of Art. 35 EU by the Treaty of Amsterdam, judicial review by the Court of Justice in the (non-Community) field of police and judicial cooperation in criminal matters existed only in so far as the Council had conferred jurisdiction on the Court in conventions concluded under the initial Title VI of the EU Treaty (cooperation in the fields of justice and home affairs) to rule on disputes between Member States or between Member States and the Commission concerning the interpretation and application of the convention in question and had enabled Member States to opt to confer jurisdiction on the Court to give preliminary rulings on the interpretation of conventions at the request of a national court (see para. 23–012, *infra*).

[355] However, pursuant to Art. 10 of Protocol (No. 36) on transitional provisions (n. 64, *supra*), the limits to the Court's jurisdiction fall away when such a PJCC act is amended (see para. 4–014, *supra*).

[356] Spain has accepted the jurisdiction of the Court of Justice under this condition, see [1999] O.J. L114/56. This was initially also the case with Hungary (see [2005] O.J. L327/19). However, in 2008 it opted for the other regime (see the declaration cited in next n.).

[357] A declaration to this effect has been made by Austria, Belgium, Finland, Germany, Greece, Italy, Luxembourg, the Netherlands, Portugal and Sweden (see [1999] O.J. L114/56), France (*J.O.R.F.* No. 165 of July 19, 2000, p. 11073, and [2005] O.J. L327/19), the Czech Republic (Declaration (No. 26) annexed to the 2003 Act of Accession on Art. 35 of the EU Treaty, [2003] O.J. L236/980), Hungary, Latvia, Lithuania and Slovenia (see [2008] O.J. L70/23 and C69/1) and Cyprus and Romania (see [2010] O.J. L56/14). When making such a declaration, Member States may reserve the right to make provisions in their national law to the effect that, where a question is raised in a case before a national court or tribunal against whose decision there is no judicial remedy under national law, that court or tribunal will be *required* to refer the matter to the Court of Justice:

system set out in Art. 35(1)–(3) EU, Member States may make such a declaration even after the entry into force of the Lisbon Treaty.[358] At present, there are eight Member States whose courts and tribunals may not make a reference to the Court of Justice on these matters (Bulgaria, Denmark, Estonia, Ireland, Malta, Poland, the Slovak Republic and the United Kingdom). Secondly, Art. 35 EU confers on the Court, jurisdiction to review the legality of framework decisions and decisions in actions brought by a Member State or the Commission, to rule on any dispute between Member States regarding the interpretation or the application of PJCC acts,[359] and to rule on any dispute between Member States and the Commission regarding the interpretation or the application of PJCC conventions (Art. 35(6) and (7) EU). As far as the United Kingdom is concerned, under Protocol (No. 36) it may elect not to accept the Court's jurisdiction over pre-Lisbon PJCC acts even after November 30, 2014 (see para. 10–029).

Jurisdiction in the field of the CFSP. Even after the entry into force of the Lisbon Treaty, the Court of Justice has no jurisdiction with respect to the provisions of the Treaties relating to the common foreign and security policy (CFSP) and acts adopted on the basis of those provisions (Art. 24(1), second subpara., TEU and Art. 275, first para., TFEU).[360] In this field, the Treaties confer on the Court of Justice jurisdiction only (i) to rule on actions for annulment brought by natural or legal persons against decisions of the Council providing for restrictive measures against natural and legal persons[361] and (ii) to ensure that implementation of the CFSP does not affect the application of Union powers in other areas (Art. 275, second para., TFEU and Art. 40 TEU).[362]

13–086

Declaration (No. 10) on Art. 35 of the Treaty on European Union, [1997] O.J. C340/133. In their declarations, Austria, Belgium, the Czech Republic, France, Germany, Italy, Luxembourg, the Netherlands, Romania, Slovenia and Spain reserved that right, *ibid*. See Fennelly (n. 350, *supra*), at 8–12; Knapp (n. 350, *supra*), at 13–14. The German law in fact obliges a court whose decision is not amenable to appeal to make a reference for a preliminary ruling; see the opinion of Advocate-General Ruiz-Jarabo Colomer in ECJ, Joined Cases C-187/01 and C-385/01 *Gözütok and Brügge* [2003] ECR I-1345, point 32.

[358] See the declarations made by Cyprus and Romania ([2010] O.J. L56/14).

[359] Article 35(7) refers in some language versions to *decisions* "adopted under Article 34(2)"; it is clear from the other versions, however, that all acts referred to in Art. 34(2) are meant and not only "decisions". In order for the Court to have this power, the Council must have failed in settling the dispute within six months of its being referred to that institution by one of its members (Art. 35(7), second sentence, EU).

[360] See also the Report of March 15, 2004 on "the Future Role of the European Court of Justice" of the House of Lords' European Union Committee (HLP 46, 6th report of the session 2003–04); Louis, "La fonction juridictionnelle de Nice à Rome" (2003) J.T.D.E. 257–263.

[361] Article 275, second para. TFEU. For the restrictive measures in question, see para. 25–051, *infra*.

[362] See, before the entry into force of the Lisbon Treaty, ECJ, Case C-91/05 *Commission v Council* [2008] E.C.R. I-3651.

13–087   **Jurisdiction under conventions.** The Court of Justice also has jurisdiction to give preliminary rulings at the request of national courts and tribunals on the interpretation of conventions which the Member States have concluded amongst themselves where a protocol to the convention confers jurisdiction on the Court (see para. 22–110). Examples are the Brussels I or Judgments Convention and the Rome Convention on the law applicable to contractual obligations, which have now been replaced by regulations.[363]

13–088   **Jurisdiction of the General Court.** Since October 31, 1989, part of the jurisdiction of the Court of Justice has been transferred to the Court of First Instance, which has been renamed the General Court by the Lisbon Treaty.[364] The Court of First Instance was set up in order to lighten the Court of Justice's case-load and to assign specific tasks to each of the two courts, thereby improving the quality of judicial review.[365] This reordering of jurisdiction was also intended to allow the Court of Justice to concentrate on its function as the highest court guaranteeing the unity and consistency of Union law.[366] Initially, the General Court ruled only on actions brought by natural and legal persons against Community institutions and bodies. The Treaty of Nice not only allowed for the creation of specialised judicial panels but also enlarged the jurisdiction of the General Court.[367]

---

[363] See para. 10–017. For the limited scope of the Court's jurisdiction under the Brussels Convention, see ECJ (Order of March 22, 2002), Case C-24/02 *Marseille Fret* [2002] E.C.R. I-3383.

[364] There has been an incremental transfer of jurisdiction, first by Art. 3 of the CFI Decision ([1988] O.J. L319/1, which came into force as a result of Art. 13 on October 31, 1989), as amended by Council Decision 93/350 of June 8, 1993 ([1993] O.J. L144/21, which took effect on August 1, 1993), by Council Decision 94/149 of March 7, 1994 ([1994] O.J. L66/29, which entered into force on March 15, 1994) and Decision 1999/291/EC, ECSC, Euratom of April 26, 1999 ([1999] O.J. L114/52, which entered into force on May 16, 1999). The CFI Decision was repealed on the entry into force on February 1, 2003 of a new ECJ Statute (n. 329, *supra*).

[365] See Lenaerts, "Le Tribunal de première instance des Communautés européennes: regard sur une décennie d'activités et sur l'apport du double degré d'instance au droit communautaire" (2000) C.D.E. 323–411.

[366] For further discussion of the jurisdiction of the courts, see Lenaerts, Arts and Maselis, *Procedural Law of the European Union* (3rd edn, London, Sweet & Maxwell, 2012).

[367] For the changes to the judicial system, see Tizzano, "La Cour de justice après Nice: le transfert de compétences au Tribunal de première instance" (2002) R.D.U.E. 665–685; Lenaerts and Desomer, "Het Verdrag van Nice en het 'post-Nice'-debat over de toekomst van de Europese Unie" (2001–2002) R.W. 73, at 78–81; Craig, "The Jurisdiction of the Community Courts Reconsidered" (2001) Tex. Int'l L.J. 555–586; Johnston, "Judicial Reform and the Treaty of Nice" (2001) C.M.L.Rev. 499–523; Fierstra, "Een nieuw toekomstperspectief voor het Hof van Justitie: de tussenstand na het Verdrag van Nice" (2001) N.T.E.R. 95–103; Kapteyn, "De rechterlijke organisatie van de Europese Unie en de Intergouvernementele Conferentie 2000" (2001) N.J.B. 1–6; Lenz, "Die Gerichtsbarkeit in der Europäischen Gemeinschaft nach dem Vertrag von Nizza" (2001) Eu.GR.Z. 433–441; Lipp, "Europäische Justizreform" (2001) N.J.W. 2657–2663; Ruiz-Jarabo Colomer, "La réforme de la Cour de justice opérée par le traité de Nice et sa mise en oeuvre" (2001) R.T.D.E. 705–725; Tambou, "Le système juridictionnel communautaire revu et corrigé par le traité de Nice" (2001) R.M.C.U.E. 164–170; Dubos, "Quel avenir pour le Tribunal de première instance après le traité de Nice?" (2000) R.A.E. 426–440.

According to Art. 256(1) TFEU [*ex Art. 225(1) EC*], the General Court has juris-diction over all actions against institutions, bodies, agencies and offices with the exception of those assigned to a specialised court[368] and those reserved in the Statute for the Court of Justice. Article 256(3) TFEU adds that the General Court has jurisdiction to hear and determine questions referred for a preliminary ruling in specific areas laid down by the Statute.[369] Consequently, the exact jurisdiction of the Court of Justice and of the General Court can only be determined by refer-ence to Art. 51 of the Statute of the Court of Justice of the European Union.[370]

At present, only the Court of Justice has jurisdiction to give preliminary rul-ings, since the Statute does not confer any jurisdiction on the General Court in this regard. Jurisdiction is further reserved to the Court of Justice in respect of actions brought by an institution insofar as actions brought against an act of or failure to act by the European Parliament, the Council, by both those institutions acting jointly, or the Commission or the ECB[371] are concerned. Lastly, the Court of Justice has exclusive jurisdiction over actions brought by a Member State against an act of or failure to act by the European Parliament or the Council (with the exception of certain Council acts of a clearly executive nature), by both insti-tutions acting jointly, or by the Commission under the first para. of Art. 331 TFEU [*ex Art. 11a EC*] (on enhanced cooperation).[372] This means that, alongside all actions brought by natural and legal persons against Union institutions, bod-ies, agencies and offices, the General Court will hear all actions brought by Member States against all acts of or failures to act by the Commission (with the one exception mentioned), acts of or failures to act by the Council in the cases mentioned above, as well as against acts of or failures to act by any Union body, office or agency. Besides, the General Court has jurisdiction to hear and deter-mine actions or proceedings brought against decisions of the specialised courts (Art. 256(2) TFEU [*ex Art. 225 (2) EC*]).

There is a right of appeal to the Court of Justice against decisions of the General Court on points of law only (Art. 256(1), second subpara., TFEU), except where the General Court hears and determines actions or proceedings brought

---

[368] At present, this has to be understood as referring to the Civil Service Tribunal (see para. 13–077).
[369] The article adds, however, that when the General Court considers that the case requires a decision of principle likely to affect the unity or consistency of Union law, it may refer the case to the Court of Justice for a ruling (Art. 256(3), second subpara., TFEU).
[370] ECJ Statute, Art. 51.
[371] ECJ Statute, Art. 51, second para. (referring, more precisely, to actions "brought by an institution of the Union against an act of or failure to act by the European Parliament, the Council, both those institutions acting jointly, or the Commission, or brought by an institution of the Union against an act of or failure to act by the European Central Bank").
[372] ECJ Statute, Art. 51, first para. The Council decisions against which actions are not reserved to the Court of Justice are "decisions taken by the Council under the third subpara. of Article 108(2) TFEU; acts of the Council adopted pursuant to a Council regulation concerning measures to protect trade within the meaning of Article 207 TFEU; acts of the Council by which the Council exercises implementing powers in accordance with the second para. of Article 291 TFEU".

against decisions of specialised courts or where it gives preliminary rulings (for which it has no jurisdiction as yet). In the last two cases, its decisions may be subject to review by the Court of Justice only exceptionally, namely where there is a serious risk of the unity or consistency of Union law being affected.[373]

13–089 **Jurisdiction of the Civil Service Tribunal.** The Civil Service Tribunal exercises the jurisdiction previously exercised by the Court of First Instance (now the General Court) in staff matters. It has jurisdiction in disputes between the Union and its servants (see Art. 270 TFEU [*ex Art. 236 EC*]), including disputes between bodies or agencies and their servants in respect of which jurisdiction is conferred on the Court of Justice of the European Union.[374] There is a right of appeal to the General Court against decisions of the Civil Service Tribunal, limited to points of law.[375]

2. Composition

13–090 **Judges and Advocates General.** The Court of Justice consists of one Judge for each Member State (since January 1, 2007 twenty-seven in all), assisted by Advocates General and a Registrar (Art. 19(2) TEU and Arts 252, first para., and 253, fifth para., TFEU). Until the changes made by the Treaty of Nice, the EC Treaty provided for a fixed number of Judges, but it did not allocate them among the Member States.[376] The General Court has at least one Judge for each Member State (since January 1, 2007 twenty-seven in all) and a Registrar. No Advocates General are appointed to the General Court, but the Statute may provide for that Court to be assisted by Advocates General (Art. 19(2), second subpara., TEU and

---

[373] Article 260(2), second subpara., and (3), third subpara., TFEU. This may occur where the First Advocate-General puts this proposition to the Court of Justice within one month of delivery of the decision by the General Court: ECJ Statute, Art. 62. For an example, see ECJ (decision of June 24, 2009), Case C-197/09 RX-II *M v EMEA*, not yet reported.

[374] Annex I to the Statute of the Court of Justice, Art. 1.

[375] Annex I to the Statute of the Court of Justice, Arts 9 and 11.

[376] Where there was an even number of Member States, the Court of Justice generally had one Judge more than the number of Member States in order to ensure that the Court might sit with an uneven number of Judges (as required by Art. 17 of the Statute of the Court of Justice). In order to have an uneven number, the accession of four Member States in 1973 was to have increased the original number of 7 Judges to 11 (1972 Act of Accession, Art. 17; [1972] O.J. L73), but this number was reduced to 9 when Norway decided not to join the Community (Art. 4 of the Council Decision of January 1, 1973, [1973] O.J. L2). Following the accession of Greece, the Court of Justice had at first 10 Judges (Art. 16 of the 1979 Act of Accession, [1979] O.J. L291, and Council Decision of December 22, 1980, [1980] O.J. L380/6). Subsequently, the Council increased the number to 11 by Decision of March 31, 1981 ([1981] O.J. L100/20). After the accession of Portugal and Spain there were thirteen Judges (Art. 17 of the 1985 Act of Accession, [1985] O.J. L302). After the accession of Austria, Sweden and Finland, the Court of Justice had fifteen Judges. The accession of Member States in 2004 and 2007 brought the number up to 25 and 27, respectively.

Art. 254, first and fourth paras, TFEU).[377] The Treaties do not require Members of the Court of Justice or the General Court to be nationals of a Member State.

The Advocates General, "acting with complete impartiality and independence", assist the Court of Justice by making, in open court, reasoned submissions prior to the Court's deliberations.[378] The number of Advocates General, which is currently fixed at eight, may be increased by the Council, acting unanimously, if the Court of Justice so requests (Art. 252, first para., TFEU). The Treaties do not allocate the number of Advocates-General among the Member States. According to an established practice, one comes from each of the five largest Member States and the other three come in turn from the remaining Member States.[379] However, during the 2007 Intergovernmental Conference, Poland asked to have a permanent Advocate-General. To accommodate this demand, a declaration annexed to the Lisbon Treaty states that, if the Court so requests, the Council will increase the number of

---

[377] Article 49 of the Statute of the Court of Justice nevertheless retains the existing rule that one of the Members of the General Court may be called upon to perform the task of an Advocate-General. For the impact of Advocates General, see Ritter, "A new look at the role and impact of Advocates-General collectively and individually" (2006) 12 Colum. J. Eur. L. 751–774.

[378] Article 252, second para., TFEU. The Court of Justice considers that the fact that the parties may not submit observations in response to the Advocate-General's opinion is not in conflict with Art. 6 of the ECHR: ECJ (order of February 4, 2000), Case C-17/98 *Emesa Sugar* [2000] E.C.R. I-665, paras 10–18; rightly criticised in Benoît-Rohmer, "L'affaire *Emesa Sugar*: l'institution de l'avocat general de la Cour de justice des Communautés européennes à l'épreuve de la jurisprudence *Vermeulen* de la Cour européenne des droits de l'homme" (2001) C.D.E. 403–426; Maes, "Is drie keer tegenspraak voor het EHRM geen scheepsrecht voor het H.v.J.?" (2001) T.B.P. 179–184; Lawson (2000) C.M.L.Rev. 983–990. Initially, it appeared that the European Court of Human Rights took another view: see the judgment of June 7, 2001 in *Kress v France* (2001) S.E.W. 440–444, with a case note by Lawson; (2001) R.T.D.E. 809–819, with a case note by Benoît-Rohmer. However, when recently invited to assess the ECJ's system, the European Court of Human Rights did not see any problem as parties have the right to ask for the oral procedure to be re-opened: decision of January 20, 2009 in *PO Kokkelvisserij v The Netherlands*, No. 13645/05, with a case note by Vande Heyning (2009) C.M.L.Rev. 2117–2125.

[379] Upon the accession of new Member States in 1973, the original number of Advocates-General was raised from two to four (Art. 1 of the Council Decision of January 1, 1973, [1973] O.J. L2/29) and divided among the four largest Member States. Following the accession of Greece, a fifth such post was created (Council Decision of March 30, 1981, [1981] O.J. L100/21), which was to go to one of the smaller Member States. Their number was increased to six after the accession of Portugal and Spain (Art. 18 of the 1985 Act of Accession, [1985] O.J. L302). Article 20 of the 1994 Act of Accession provided for eight Advocates-General ([1994] O.J. C241/25). As agreed in a Joint Declaration annexed to the Act of Accession (*ibid.*, at p. 381), the accession of an uneven number of new Member States (following Norway's decision not to accede) resulted in the "thirteenth Judge" being made into a ninth Advocate-General for the remainder of his term of office (i.e. until October 6, 2000). See the Joint Declaration on Art. 31 of the Decision adjusting the instruments concerning the accession of the new Member States to the European Union ([1995] O.J. L1/221). The 2003 and 2005 Acts of Accession made no changes in the number of Advocates-General. According to a Joint Declaration on the Court of Justice of the European Communities ([2003] O.J. L236/971), the new Member States were to be integrated into the existing system for the appointment of Advocates-General.

Advocates-General by three, to eleven instead of eight. The other Member States will then continue to appoint an Advocate-General under the present rotation system, although it will involve the rotation of five Advocates-General rather than three.[380]

13–091   **Appointment.** The Judges and Advocates General of the Court of Justice and the Judges of the General Court are appointed by common accord of the governments of the Member States for a six-year term.[381] Membership is partially renewed every three years, although retiring Members are eligible for reappointment (Art. 19(2), third subpara., TEU and Arts 253 and 254 TFEU [*ex Arts 223 and 224 EC*]).[382] Since the Lisbon Treaty, appointment takes place after obtaining the opinion of a panel on the suitability of the candidates to perform the duties of Judge or Advocate-General.[383] That panel is composed of seven persons chosen from among former members of the Court of Justice and the General Court, members of national supreme courts and lawyers of recognised competence, one of whom is to be proposed by the European Parliament. To that end, the Council, on the initiative of the President of the Court of Justice, adopts a decision establishing the panel's operating rules and a decision appointing its members (Art. 255 TFEU).[384] The panel hears the candidates in private and issues a reasoned opinion, which is forwarded to the Governments of the Member States.[385]

Members of the specialised courts are appointed by the Council, acting unanimously (Art. 257 TFEU [*ex Art. 225a, fourth para., EC*]).[386]

13–092   **Conditions for appointment.** Judges and Advocates General of the Court of Justice and Judges of the General Court as well as Judges of the specialised courts are

---

[380] Declaration (No. 38), annexed to the Lisbon Treaty, on Art. 252 of the TFEU regarding the number of Advocates General in the Court of Justice, [2010] O.J. C83/350.

[381] For the fact that the Council as an institution is not involved in appointing members of the Court, see the Council's answer of December 20, 1995 to question P-2529/95 (Vandemeulebroecke), [1996] O.J. C56/24.

[382] See ECJ Statute, Art. 9 (for the Court of Justice).

[383] See, for the first time, the Decision of the Representatives of the Governments of the Member States of June 2, 2010 appointing a judge to the Court of Justice, [2010] O.J. 137/3.

[384] See Council Decision 2010/124/EU of February 25, 2010 relating to the operating rules of the panel provided for in Art. 255 of the TFEU, [2010] O.J. L50/18. Its members are appointed by taking into account "a balanced membership of the panel, both in geographical terms and in terms of representation of the legal systems of the Member States", see Council Decision 2010/125/EU of February 25, 2010 appointing the members of the panel, [2010] O.J. L50/20.

[385] See Arts 7 and 8 of the operating rules for the panel, as annexed to Council Decision 2010/124/EU. Such a hearing is not held where it is proposed to reappoint a sitting Judge or Advocate-General (*ibid.*, Art. 7).

[386] Members of the Civil Service Tribunal are appointed by the Council after consulting a committee consisting of former members of the Court of Justice and the Court of First Instance (*now the General Court*) and lawyers of recognised competence (Annex I to the ECJ Statute, Art. 3). For the operating rules of that committee, see Council Decision 2005/49/EC, Euratom of January 18, 2005, [2005] O.J. L21/13. For its members, see, most recently, Council Decision 2009/69/EC of December 18, 2008, [2009] O.J. L24/11.

"chosen from persons whose independence is beyond doubt". The Treaties further require Judges and Advocates General of the Court of Justice to "possess the qualifications required for appointment to the highest judicial offices in their respective countries" or to be "jurisconsults of recognised competence" (Art. 19(3) TEU and Art. 253, first para., TFEU [*ex Art. 223, first para., EC*]); Judges of the General Court must "possess the ability required for appointment to high judicial office" (Art. 19(3) TEU and Art. 254, second para., TFEU [*ex Art. 224, second para., EC*]); Judges of specialised courts must "possess the ability required for appointment to judicial office" (Art. 257 TFEU [*ex Art. 225a, fourth para., EC*]).

Duties. Before taking up their duties, each Judge and Advocate-General has to take up an oath in open court to perform his or her duties impartially and conscientiously and to preserve the secrecy of the deliberations of the Court (ECJ Statute, Arts 2 and 8).[387] Members may not hold any political or administrative office and are subject to the same requirements as Members of the Commission as regards engaging in any other occupation and the acceptance of appointments and benefits. A Judge or Advocate-General may be deprived of his or her office only if, in the unanimous opinion of the other Judges and Advocates-General, he or she no longer fulfils the requisite conditions or meets the obligations arising from his or her office (ECJ Statute, Arts 6 and 8). If the office of Judge or Advocate-General becomes vacant before the end of the term of office as a result of death or voluntary or compulsory retirement, the successor is appointed for the remainder of his or her predecessor's term of office (ECJ Statute, Art. 7). **13–093**

3. Procedure

Rules of Procedure. The Court of Justice operates in accordance with the procedure laid down in the Treaties, the Statute and the Rules of Procedure, which the Court itself adopts but has to submit to the Council for its approval.[388] Procedure before the General Court is determined by the Statute of the Court of Justice of the European Union and by its Rules of Procedure, which, under Art. 254, fifth para., TFEU, it establishes in agreement with the Court of Justice. Those Rules also have to be approved by the Council.[389] The procedure of the specialised courts is based on the Statute of the Court of Justice and on their own Rules of **13–094**

---

[387] See also the Code of Conduct of the Court of Justice, [2007] O.J. C223/1.
[388] Article 253, sixth para., TFEU. The consolidated text of the Rules of Procedure of the Court of Justice [ECJ Rules of Procedure] can be found on the website of the Court of Justice of the European Union: *http://curia.europa.eu/* [Accessed December 9, 2010]. For procedure before the Court, see Lenaerts, Arts and Maselis, *Procedural Law of the European Union* (3rd edn, London, Sweet & Maxwell, 2012), Chs 23 to 25.
[389] Article 254, fifth para., TFEU. See Arts 47 to 62b of the ECJ Statute and the consolidated text of the Rules of Procedure of the General Court, which can be found on the Court's website: *http://curia.europa.eu/* [Accessed December 9, 2010]. See Lenaerts, Arts and Maselis, *Procedural Law of the European Union* (3rd edn, London, Sweet & Maxwell, 2012), Chs 23 to 25.

Procedure, which, under Art. 257, fifth para., TFEU, they are to establish in agreement with the Court of Justice.[390] Those rules have to be approved by the Council.

4. Internal organisation

13–095 **Chambers.** Both in the Court of Justice and in the General Court, the Judges elect their President from among their number for a term of three years. The President may be re-elected. Both Courts appoint their Registrar and lay down the rules governing his or her service (Arts 253, third and fourth paras, and Art. 254, third and fourth paras, TFEU). The Court of Justice sits in Chambers of three or five Judges or in a Grand Chamber (thirteen Judges) or, exceptionally, as a full Court.[391] Decisions of the full Court are valid only if 15 judges are sitting.[392] The General Court sits in Chambers of three or five Judges. In certain cases it may sit as a full Court or in a Grand Chamber (thirteen judges) or be constituted by a single Judge.[393] The Judges and Advocates General are assisted by law clerks, known as legal secretaries or *référendaires*.[394] The Court of Justice, the General Court and the Civil Service Tribunal employ some 2,000 staff.[395] When the Court of Justice was established by the ECSC Treaty, its seat was fixed in Luxembourg,[396] which is also where the General Court and the Civil Service Tribunal are based.[397]

---

[390] For the Civil Service Tribunal, see the consolidated text of the Rules of Procedure, which can be found on the Court's website: *http://curia.europa.eu/* [Accessed December 9, 2010]. Lenaerts, Arts and Maselis, *Procedural Law of the European Union* (3rd edn, London, Sweet & Maxwell, 2012), Chs 23 to 25.

[391] Article 251 TFEU [*ex Art. 221 EC*] and ECJ Statute, Arts 16 and 17.

[392] ECJ Statute, Art. 17, fourth para.. The Grand Chamber is presided over by the President of the Court and consists of the Presidents of the Chambers of five Judges, the Judge Rapporteur and such Judges as are necessary to bring the number to thirteen (ECJ Rules of Procedure, Art.11b).

[393] ECJ Statute, Art. 50; General Court, Rules of Procedure, Arts 10 and 11.

[394] See Erniquin, "Les référendaires attachés aux juridictions supérieures" (2003) J.T. 717–729; Kennedy, "Beyond Principals and Agents—Seeing Courts as Organizations by Comparing *Référendaires* at the European Court of Justice and Law Clerks at the U.S. Supreme Court" (2000) *Comparative Political Studies* 593–625. For their recruitment, see also CFI, Case T-406/04 *Bonnet v Court of Justice* [2006] E.C.R. II-A-2-01097.

[395] As at December 2009, the Court of Justice had a total of 1493 permanent posts and 438 temporary posts: *General Report on the Activities of the European Union 2009* (n. 106, *supra*), at 96.

[396] Para. 13–152, *infra*.

[397] Sole Art, para. (d), of the Protocol on Seats (para. 13–153, *infra*). Article 3 of the Decision on Provisional Location of April 8, 1965 (para. 13–152, *infra*) itself provided that existing and future judicial and quasi-judicial bodies set up under the Community Treaties should have their seat in Luxembourg. See also the Declaration to the Decision of October 29, 1993 (n. 622 to para. 13–154, *infra*). In a unilateral declaration by Luxembourg, of which the Conference took note in signing the Nice Treaty ([2001] O.J. C80/87), that Member State undertook not to claim the seat of the Boards of Appeal of the Office for Harmonisation in the Internal Market (trade marks and designs), even if those Boards were to become judicial panels within the meaning of Art. 220 EC.

B. The European Central Bank

Union Institution. The European Central Bank (ECB)[398] is a Union institution   **13–096**
with legal personality.[399] It performs the tasks entrusted to it by the Treaties
within the European System of Central Banks, which has managed Economic and
Monetary Union (EMU) since the start of its third stage (January 1, 1999) for the
Member States which adopted the euro as their currency unit.

On June 1, 1998 the ECB took over the tasks which the EC Treaty had entrusted
to the European Monetary Institute (EMI), an independent body with legal personality, since the start of the second stage of EMU. The EMI itself had replaced
the Committee of Governors of the central banks and the European Monetary
Cooperation Fund.[400] Since, prior to the third stage of EMU, monetary policy
remained in the hands of the Member States, national central banks constituted the
members of the EMI and the EMI was directed and managed by a Council,
consisting of a President and the governors of the national central banks.[401] The
EMI operated in accordance with its Statute, adopted in the form of a Protocol
annexed to the EC Treaty,[402] and its Rules of Procedure, which the Council of
the EMI adopted independently. The EMI's seat was established at Frankfurt by
the national governments at the level of Heads of State or Government.[403]

1. Powers

Tasks. Together with the national central banks of the Member States whose   **13–097**
currency is the euro, the ECB conducts the Union's monetary policy (Art. 282(1)
TFEU). Under Art. 130 TFEU [*ex Art. 108 EC*], the ECB—just like the national
central banks—exercises its powers and carries out its tasks and duties com-

---

[398] For the ECB website, see *http://www.ecb.int/* [Accessed December 9, 2010].

[399] Article 282(2) TFEU. Before the Lisbon Treaty the ECB was not a Union institution, but an inde-
pendent Community body, see ECJ, Case C-11/00 *Commission v European Central Bank* [2003]
E.C.R. I-7147, paras 89–96. See, in general, Zilioli and Selmayer, *The Law of the European
Central Bank* (Oxford, Hart Publishing, 2001), 268 pp.

[400] See Art. 117(1), first subpara., and (2), fifth indent., EC. All the assets and liabilities of the
European Monetary Cooperation Fund passed automatically to the EMI. Under Art. 123(2) EC,
the assets and liabilities of the EMI were transferred to the ECB, which liquidated the EMI.

[401] Article 117(1), first subpara., EC; Louis, "L'Institut monétaire européen", in *Reflets et
Perspectives de la vie économique* (Brussels, Recherche et diffusion économiques, 1993),
285–299; Slot, "The Institutional Provisions of the EMU", in *Institutional Dynamics of European
Integration. Essays in Honour of Henry G. Schermers* (n. 259, *supra*) 229–249. Baron A.
Lamfalussy was appointed President of the EMI (from the start of the second stage of EMU—
January 1, 1994 until June 30, 1997). He was followed by W.F. Duisenberg (July 1, 1997 until the
start of the ECB).

[402] Article 117(1), third subpara., EC and Protocol (No. 19), annexed to the EC Treaty, on the Statute
of the European Monetary Institute (EMI Statute), [1992] O.J. C224/115.

[403] See EMI Statute, Art. 13, and the Second Decision on the Seats of the Institutions of October 29,
1993, para. 13–154, *infra*.

pletely independently of the political authorities of the Union and the Member States or any other body. That independence does not mean that the ECB is separated entirely from the Union but seeks to shield the ECB from political influences in exercising the specific tasks attributed to it.[404] The Statute of the European System of Central Banks (ESCB) governs the financial and administrative independence of the ECB.[405] That statute is set out in a Protocol annexed to the Treaties, together with that of the ECB.[406] The ECB ensures that it and the national central banks (of Member States whose currency is the euro) carry out the tasks which the TFEU confers on the ESCB (see para. 11–040).[407] The ECB is entitled to impose fines and periodic penalty payments on undertakings for failure to comply with obligations imposed by its regulations and decisions (Art. 132(3) TFEU [ex Art. 110(3) EC]).[408] In addition, the ECB supervises the national central banks to make sure that they comply with their obligations and may bring a central bank before the Court of Justice if it finds that there has been an infringement (Art. 271(d) TFEU [ex Art. 237(d) EC]).[409] The central bank concerned is under a duty to take the necessary measures to comply with the Court's judgment finding that it has failed to fulfil its obligations, but cannot be fined if it persists in the infringement.[410]

---

[404] ECJ, Case C-11/00 Commission v European Central Bank [2003] E.C.R. I-7147, paras 134–135. For the substance of that independence, see ibid., paras 130–132. See also Lavranos, "The limited, functional independence of the ECB" (2004) E.L.Rev. 115–123; Elderson and Weenink, "The European Central Bank redefined? A landmark judgment of the European Court of Justice" (2003) Euredia 273–301.

[405] See, inter alia, Art.27 (independent audit of accounts), Art. 28 (capital of the ECB) and Art. 36 (staff) of the ESCB Statute.

[406] Article 129(2) TFEU [ex Art. 107(4) EC] and Protocol (No.4), annexed to the TEU and TFEU, on the Statute of the European System of Central Banks and of the European Central Bank [ESCB Statute], [2010] O.J. C83/230 (replacing the Protocol annexed to the EC Treaty, [1992] O.J. C224/104). Notwithstanding the status of that Protocol as part of the Treaties (Art. 51 TEU), some of its articles may be amended by the European Parliament and the Council, acting in accordance with the ordinary legislative procedure. They act either on a recommendation from the ECB and after consulting the Commission or on a proposal from the Commission and after consulting the ECB (Art. 129(3) TFEU [ex Art. 107(5) EC] and ESCB Statute, Art. 40).

[407] ESCB Statute, Art. 9.2.

[408] The ECB exercises this power within the limits and under the conditions laid down in Council Regulation (EC) No. 2532/98 of November 23, 1998 concerning the powers of the European Central Bank to impose sanctions, [1998] O.J. L318/4. For the applicable infringement procedure, see European Central Bank Regulation (EC) No. 2157/1999 of September 23, 1999, [1999] O.J. L264/21. See Fernández Martín and Texieira, "The imposition of sanctions by the European Central Bank" (2000) E.L.Rev. 391–407.

[409] Article 271(d) TFEU confers on the Council of the ECB the same powers as are conferred on the Commission by Art. 258 TFEU. See also ESCB Statute, Art. 35.6 and Gaiser, "Gerichtliche Kontrolle im Europäischen System der Zentralbanken" (2002) EuR. 517, at 520–523. Remarkably, Art. 14.2 of the ESCB Statute makes provision for proceedings to be brought in the Court of Justice against a decision relieving a governor of a central bank from his or her office by the Governing Council of the ECB or by the governor concerned. See Gaiser, ibid., at 523–524.

[410] Compare Art. 271(d), last sentence, TFEU with Art. 260 TFEU. See Slot (n. 401, supra), at 246.

2. Composition

Organisation. The decision-making bodies of the ECB govern the ESCB   **13–098**
(Art. 282(2) TFEU [*ex Art. 107(3) EC*]). Accordingly, the ECB's Governing
Council is made up of the governors of the central banks of Member States whose
currency is the euro and the members of the ECB's Executive Board. The Executive
Board consists of the President, the Vice-President and four members (Art. 283(1)
and (2) TFEU). The European Council, acting by a qualified majority, appoints the
Executive Board for a non-renewable eight-year term on a recommendation from
the Council, after consulting the European Parliament and the ECB's Governing
Council.[411] Member States with a derogation have no voting rights.[412] Candidates
for office must be nationals of Member States without a derogation and of recognised standing and professional experience in monetary or banking matters (see Arts
139(2)(h) and second subpara., and Art. 283(2) TFEU). Before their appointment,
the European Parliament invites the nominees for President, Vice-President and
other Executive Board Members of the ECB to make a statement before the committee responsible and answer questions put by MEPs.[413] Board members perform
their duties on a full-time basis and may be compulsorily retired only by the Court
of Justice on application by the Governing Council or the Executive Board.[414]

The Governing Council formulates the Union's monetary policy; the Executive
Board implements that policy and gives the necessary directions to the national
central banks.[415] The Executive Board is responsible for the preparation of meetings of the Governing Council and for current business of the ECB.[416] As a
rule, the President represents the ECB externally.[417] To the extent deemed possible and appropriate, the ECB has recourse to the national central banks to carry
out operations forming part of the ESCB's tasks.[418]

---

[411] See the first Decision (98/345/EC) taken by common accord of the Governments of the Member
States adopting the single currency at the level of Heads of State or Government of May 26, 1998
appointing the President, the Vice-President and the other members of the Executive Board of the
European Central Bank, [1998] O.J. L154/33. Willem ("Wim") Duisenberg was appointed President;
after he stepped down in 2003, he was replaced by Jean Claude Trichet, see Decision 2003/767/EC
taken by common accord, at the level of Heads of State or Government, by the Governments of the
Member States having the euro as their currency of October 16, 2003, [2003] O.J. L277/16.

[412] See Art. 139(2)(h) and (4) TFEU

[413] EP Rules of Procedure, Rule 109(1) and (5). If the Parliament's opinion on a nominee is negative,
it will request the Council to submit a new nomination: Rule 109(4).

[414] ESCB Statute, Arts 11.1 and 11.4. Art.11.4 makes it possible for a Board member to be retired (as
in the case of a Member of the Commission) if he or she no longer fulfils the conditions required
for the performance of his or her duties or if he or she has been guilty of serious misconduct. The
Code of Conduct for the members of the Governing Council may be found in [2002] O.J. C123/9.

[415] ESCB Statute, Art. 12.1, first and second subparas. The second subpara. also provides that the
Governing Council may delegate powers to the Board.

[416] *Ibid.*, Arts 11.6 and 12.2.

[417] *Ibid.*, Art. 13.2.

[418] *Ibid.*, Art. 12.1, third subpara.

As long as there are Member States with a derogation, the governors of the central banks of all the Member States, together with the President and Vice-President of the ECB, will have certain responsibilities as the General Council of the ECB (Art. 141(1) TFEU [*ex Art. 123(3) EC*]).[419]

3. Operation

13–099   **Operation.** The EMI's seat at Frankfurt has been taken over by the ECB.[420] In principle, both the Governing Council and the Executive Board take their decisions by a simple majority vote, although in some cases the Governing Council has to act by a qualified majority of votes weighted according to the national central banks' shares in the ECB's subscribed capital.[421] The operation of the Governing Council may be amended by the European Council by a unanimous vote, subject to ratification by the Member States in accordance with their respective constitutional requirements. In this way, a system was introduced on the accession of the new Member States in 2004 to the effect that not all governors of Central Banks would have the same voting rights.[422] Depending on the size of the share of their Member State in the aggregate GDP of the Member States which have adopted the euro and in the total aggregated balance sheet of the monetary financial institutions of those Member States, the national central banks are allocated to groups within which the right to vote rotates.[423] The national central banks are the only shareholders of the ECB.[424] The key for subscription to shares in the ECB takes account of each Member State's share of the population of the Union and of its GDP.[425]

---

[419] For those responsibilities, see ESCB Statute, Art. 46.

[420] Second Decision on the Seats of the Institutions of October 29, 1993, taken over by the Protocol on Seats, Sole Art, para. (i); para. 13–154, *infra*. See ESCB Statute, Art. 37, and Heim, "The European Central Bank: Was it not bound to go to Luxembourg?" (1994) E.L.Rev. 48–55.

[421] For the Governing Council, see ESCB Statute, Arts 10.2 and 10.3 (qualified majority); for the Executive Board, see ESCB Statute, Art. 11.5.

[422] See Art. 40(2) ESCB Statute and Decision 2003/223/EC of the Council meeting in the composition of the Heads of State or Government of March 21, 2003 on an amendment to Art. 10.2 of the Statute of the European System of Central Banks and of the European Central Bank, [2003] O.J. L83/66.

[423] ESCB Statute, Art. 10(2). According to that article, the rotation system is to be implemented as from the date on which the number of members of the Governing Council (i.e. governors of national central banks and members of the Executive Board) exceeds 21. This happened upon the adoption of the euro by Slovakia (see para. 11–033). However, the ECB decided to postpone the start of the rotation system until the number of *governors* in the Governing Council exceeded 18; see Decision ECB/2008/29 of December 18, 2008, [2009] O.J. L3/4. See Krauskopf and Steven, "The Institutional Framework of the European System of Central Banks: Legal Issues in the Practice of the First Ten Years of its Existence" (2009) C.M.L.Rev. 1143–1176.

[424] ESCB Statute, Art. 28.2.

[425] *Ibid.*, Art. 29.1. For the most recent subscription key, see Decision ECB/2008/23 of the European Central Bank of December 12, 2008 ([2009] O.J. L21/66); for the measures necessary for the paying-up of the capital of the ECB, see most recently Decision ECB/2008/24 of the ECB of December 12, 2008 ([2009] O.J. L21/69—for participating Member States) and Decision ECB/2008/28 of December 12, 2008 ([2009] O.J. L21/81—for non-participating Member States).

4. Internal organisation

Rules of Procedure. The internal organisation of the ECB is determined by its   **13–100**
Rules of Procedure, adopted by the Governing Council.[426] The proceedings are
confidential.[427] The President of the Council and a Member of the Commission
may take part, without any voting rights, in meetings of the Governing Council;
moreover, the President of the Council may submit a motion for deliberation
(Art. 284(1) TFEU [*ex Art. 113(1) EC*]).

C. THE COURT OF AUDITORS

History. The Court of Auditors[428] was brought into being by the Second Treaty on   **13–101**
Budgetary Provisions of July 22, 1975, which established the present budgetary
procedure.[429] At the request of the Commission and the European Parliament, the
Member States set up the Court of Auditors as an independent supervisory body.[430]
That body took over the task which the ECSC Treaty conferred on auditors and the
EEC Treaty and the EAEC Treaty on an Audit Board, which the Merger Treaty
also made responsible for the ECSC budget.[431] The EU Treaty put the Court of
Auditors on an equal footing with the other institutions.[432] On December 9, 1993,
the Court decided to take the name of "European Court of Auditors".[433]

See also Art.30 of the ESCB Statute as regards the transfer of foreign reserve assets to the ECB
and Arts 26 and 27 as regards financial accounts and auditing. For permitted increases in the
ECB's capital, see Council Regulation (EC) No. 1009/2000 of May 8, 2000, [2000] O.J. L115/1.

[426] ESCB Statute, Art.12.3 and the ECB's Rules of Procedure adopted pursuant thereto on February
19, 2004 ([2004] O.J. L80/33), as amended by Decision ECB/2009/5 of March 19, 2009 ([2009]
O.J. L100/10). The Rules of Procedure of the Executive Board of the ECB were adopted by ECB
Decision of October 12, 1999 ([1999] O.J. L314/34). For the Rules of Procedure of the General
Council of the ECB of June 17, 2004, see [2004] O.J. L230/61.

[427] ESCB Statute, Art.10.4. Under this provision, the Governing Council may decide, however, to
make the outcome of its deliberations public.

[428] For the website of the Court of Auditors, see *http://eca.europa.eu/* [Accessed December 9, 2010].

[429] Treaty of July 22, 1975 amending certain financial provisions of the Treaties establishing the
European Communities and of the Treaty establishing a Single Council and a Single Commission
of the European Communities, [1977] O.J. L359/1 (para. 13–141, *infra*).

[430] See Art. 4(3) and Art. 206 EEC and Art. 3(3) and Art. 180 EAEC (before the EU Treaty).

[431] Article 78 ECSC, Art.206 EEC and Art. 180 EAEC were replaced as a result of the Merger Treaty
by Arts 78e to 78g ECSC, Arts 206 to 206b EEC and Arts 180 to 180b EAEC, which have since
been amended or repealed.

[432] See Art. 7(1) EC [*see now Art. 13(1) TEU*]. The EU Treaty renumbered the provisions relating to
the Court of Auditors as Arts 246 to 248 EC [*see now Arts 285 to 287 TFEU*]. The Court of
Auditors was already equated in fact to an institution before as regards the status of its Members,
officials and other servants.

[433] (1993) 12 EC Bull. point 1.7.41. For a survey, see O'Keeffe, "The Court of Auditors", in
Institutional Dynamics of European Integration. Essays in Honour of Henry G. Schermers (n. 259,
supra), at 177–194; Engwirda and Moonen, "De Europese Rekenkamer: positie, bevoegdheden en
toekomstperspectief" (2000) S.E.W. 246–257; Inghelram, "The European Court of Auditors:
Current Legal Issues" (2000) C.M.L.Rev. 129–146; Kok, "The Court of Auditors of the European
Communities: 'The Other European Court in Luxembourg' " (1989) C.M.L.Rev. 345–367.

1. Powers

13–102 **External audit.** The Court of Auditors examines the accounts of all revenue and expenditure of the Union. The external audit of the budget which it carries out results in an annual report which is forwarded to all the institutions and published (Art. 287 TFEU [*ex Art. 248 EC*]; see para. 13–149). In addition, the Court may submit observations, particularly in the form of special reports, on specific questions (Art. 287(4), second subpara., TFEU). It transmits such special reports to the institution or body concerned and to the European Parliament and the Council; it may publish them.[434] The Court of Auditors may also deliver opinions at the request of one of the other Union institutions[435] and is consulted on legislation relating to the budget and accounts.[436] The Court of Auditors also assists the European Parliament and the Council in supervising and implementing the budget (see para. 13–149).

2. Composition

13–103 **Appointment.** The Court of Auditors consists of one national from each Member State (Art. 285, second para., TFEU).[437] Members of the Court of Auditors are appointed by the Council by a qualified majority vote (following the Treaty of Nice), after consulting the European Parliament (Art. 286(2) TFEU [*ex Art. 247(3) EC*]). Prospective Members must belong or have belonged in their respective countries to external audit bodies or be especially qualified for that office. Their independence must be beyond doubt (Art. 286(1) TFEU [*ex Art. 247(2) EC*]). Before their appointment, candidates nominated as Members are invited by the European Parliament to make a statement before the committee responsible and answer questions put by MEPs.[438] The Members are appointed for a renewable six-year term (Art. 286(2) TFEU).

---

[434] See Financial Regulation (n. 440, *infra*), Art. 144(1).

[435] Article 287(4), second subpara., TFEU [*ex Art. 248(4), second subpara., EC*]. Under Art. 144(2) of the Financial Regulation, it may publish the opinion after consulting the institution concerned.

[436] Article 322 TFEU [*ex Art. 279 EC*].

[437] Before the Nice Treaty, Art. 247 EC provided for a fixed number of Members. Thus, the original membership of nine was increased following the accession of new Member States to 10 (Art. 18 of the 1979 Act of Accession, [1979] O.J. L291), 12 (Art. 20 of the 1985 Act of Accession, [1985] O.J. L302) and 15 (Art. 22 of the 1994 Act of Accession, as amended by Council Decision of January 1, 1995, [1995] O.J. L1/4). As a result of Art. 47 of the 2003 Act of Accession, ten new Members joined the existing fifteen on May 1, 2004.

[438] EP Rules of Procedure, Rule 108(1). If the Parliament's opinion on an individual nomination is negative, it will request the Council to submit a new nomination: Rule 108(4). In May 2004, negative opinions on two candidates prompted one candidate to withdraw his candidacy but did not prevent the other candidate from being appointed: *Europe*, No. 8700, May 6, 2004, p. 8.

Independence. As in the case of Commissioners, Members of the Court of   **13–104**
Auditors have to be completely independent in the performance of their duties in
the general interests of the Union (Art. 285 TFEU). They are subject to the same
rules with regard to occupations incompatible with their office and their professional duties as Commissioners (see Art. 286(3) and (4) TFEU). When they take
up office they solemnly undertake to respect those obligations.[439] The independence of the Court of Auditors is made clear by the fact that its Members may not
be removed before the end of their term of office except at the request of the
Court of Auditors itself if the Court of Justice finds that the Member concerned
no longer fulfils the requisite conditions or meets the obligations arising from his
or her office (See Art. 286(5) and (6) TFEU).

3. Operation

Rules of Procedure. The Court of Auditors acts collectively in accordance with   **13–105**
the Treaties, the Financial Regulation[440] and its Rules of Procedure, which it
draws up subject to the approval of the Council.[441] It may establish internal chambers in order to adopt certain categories of reports or opinions (Art. 287(4), third
subpara., TFEU). The Members of the Court of Auditors elect from among their
number a President to serve a three-year term (Art. 286(2), second subpara.,
TFEU). He or she convenes and chairs meetings of the Court, which are not open
to the public.[442] The Court adopts its reports and opinions by a majority of its
Members.[443] For the purposes of carrying out its auditing duties, the Court of
Auditors forms Chambers which share out their respective responsibilities and
have the task of preparing the deliberations of the Court.[444]

4. Internal organisation

Staff. The Court of Auditors has been based in Luxembourg since it was first set   **13–106**
up.[445] A Secretary-General appointed by the Court of Auditors itself is responsible

---

[439] As in the case of Members of the Commission, they take an oath, at a solemn sitting of the Court
of Justice.

[440] Financial Regulation of June 25, 2002 applicable to the general budget of the European
Communities, [2002] O.J. L248/1 (para. 13–129, *infra*).

[441] Article 287(4), fifth subpara., TFEU [*ex Art. 248(4), fifth subpara., EC*]. Before the Nice Treaty
added this legal basis to the Treaties, the Court of Auditors used to adopt its Rules of Procedure on
the basis of its powers of internal organisation. See at present the Rules of Procedure of March 11,
2010 [2010] O.J. L103/1. For the collective nature of the Court of Auditors, see Art. 1 of the Rules.

[442] See Arts 20 and 22 of the Rules of Procedure of the Court of Auditors.

[443] Article 25 of the Rules of Procedure. The Court of Auditors determines which decisions are to be
adopted by a majority of the Members of the Court; other decisions are to be taken by a majority
vote of the Members present (Art.25(2) and (3)), possibly by a written procedure (Art. 25(5)).

[444] Rules of Procedure, Art. 10.

[445] Decision of the Representatives of the Governments of the Member States of April 5, 1977 on the
provisional location of the Court of Auditors, [1977] O.J. L104/40, as confirmed by the Protocol
on Seats, Sole Art., para. (e), para. 13–153, *infra*.

for its secretariat and for personnel policy and administration.[446] The Court of Auditors has a staff of around 800, employed in its administrative departments and audit groups.[447]

III. OTHER BODIES OF THE EUROPEAN UNION

A. ADVISORY BODIES

1. The European Economic and Social Committee

13–107   **Advisory tasks.** The Treaties make provision for committees advising on Union decision-making in which representative interest groups may make their views known. In this way, the ECSC Treaty set up a Consultative Committee consisting of producers, workers, consumers and dealers in order to assist the High Authority. The EC and EAEC Treaties created the Economic and Social Committee[448] in order to advise the Council, the Commission and—since the Lisbon Treaty—the European Parliament (Art. 13(4) TEU). This committee consists of representatives of organisations of employers, of the employed, and of other parties representative of civil society, notably in socioeconomic, civic, professional and cultural areas (Art. 300(2) TFEU).[449] The Treaties list the matters in respect of which an opinion has to be sought from the Committee before a decision is taken.[450] In addition to obligatory consultation, the Commission and the Council may also request an opinion if they consider it desirable. The

---

[446] Article 13 of the Rules of Procedure.

[447] See the website of the EU: *http://europa.eu/institutions/inst/auditors/index_en.htm* [Accessed December 9, 2010].

[448] The Treaties refer to the "Economic and Social Committee" without the adjective "European". However, the Committee has consistently used the name "European Economic and Social Committee" as its official desigation. See the website of the European Economic and Social Committee, see *http://eesc.europa.eu/* [Accessed December 9, 2010].

[449] See also Arts 3(2) and Art. 165 EAEC. The nature of the composition of the European Economic and Social Committee must be reviewed at regular intervals by the Council to take account of economic, social and demographic developments within the Union. The Council is to adopt decisions to that end, on a proposal from the Commission (Art. 300(5) TFEU).

[450] See the obligation for the European Parliament and the Council in Arts 43(2); 46; 50; 59(1); 91(1); 95(3), first subpara.; 113; 114(1); 115; 148(2); 149, first para.; 153(2), second subpara.; 156, third para.; 157(3); 164; 165(4); 166(4); 168(4); 169(3); 172, first para.; 173(3), first subpara.; 175, third para.; 177, first para.; 178, first para.; 182(1) and (4); 188, first and second paras; 199(1), (2) and (3) and 194(2) TFEU. See in the EAEC Treaty the obligation for the Commission to consult laid down in Art. 9, first para.; Art. 31, first para.; Art. 32, first para.; Art. 40; Art. 41, second para.; Art. 96, second para.; and Art. 98, second para. See also Ferté and Roncin, "Quel avenir pour le Comité économique et social européen?" (2001) R.M.C.U.E. 52–59.

Committee may also deliver opinions on its own initiative (Art. 304, first para., TFEU).[451]

Composition. The European Economic and Social Committee may have no more than 350 members (at present it has 344). Since the Lisbon Treaty, the exact composition of the Committee is to be determined by the Council, acting unanimously on a proposal from the Commission (Art. 301, second para., TFEU).[452]   **13–108**

Members are appointed by the Council by a qualified majority vote on proposals from the Member States (Art. 302(1) TFEU). The Council is to consult the Commission and may obtain the opinion of European bodies which are representative of the various economic and social sectors and of civil society to which the Union's activities are of concern (Art. 302(2) TFEU). Members are appointed for a renewable five-year term (Art. 302(1) TFEU).[453] Because members are appointed personally, in principle—just like MEPs—they may not be bound by any mandatory instructions, but must be completely independent in the performance of their duties, in the Union's general interest, just like Members of the Commission or the Court of Auditors (Art. 300(4) TFEU).

Operation. The European Economic and Social Committee adopts its own rules of procedure.[454] Twice during their term of office, the Members of the Committee are to elect a President and a Bureau, which is required to reflect the sectors represented on the Committee itself.[455] The Chairman convenes the Committee at the request of the European Parliament, the Council, the Commission or its Bureau.[456]   **13–109**

---

[451] The EU Treaty introduced this possibility in Art. 262, first para., EC, although the Committee's Rules of Procedure already provided for it. The Commission submits its three-yearly report on economic and social cohesion to the European Economic and Social Committee (Art. 175, second para., TFEU [ex Art. 159, second para., EC]).

[452] Before the Lisbon Treaty, the Treaties allocated each Member State a number of members (Art. 258, first and second paras, EC, most recently amended by Art. 12 of the 2005 Act of Accession). In Declaration (No. 20), annexed to the Nice Treaty, on the enlargement of the European Union ([2001] O.J. C80/80), the then Member States determined the composition of the European Economic and Social Committee for the candidate States (with the exception of Turkey) to be adopted by common position during the accession negotiations. Under Art. 7 of Protocol (No. 36) on transitional provisions (n. 64, *supra*), this allocation is to remain in place until the entry into effect of a Council Decision adopted under Art. 301 TFEU.

[453] The Lisbon Treaty extended this term from four to five years and, accordingly, brought it into line with that of Members of the European Parliament.

[454] See the Rules of Procedure adopted pursuant to the second para. of Art. 303 TFEU [ex Art. 260 EC] (which, since the EU Treaty, no longer have to be approved by the Council); the latest consolidated version was adopted on July 14, 2010 ([2010] O.J. L324/52).

[455] Article 303, first para., TFEU [ex Art. 260, first para., EC] and ESC Rules of Procedure, Rule 3.

[456] Article 303, third para., TFEU., and ESC Rules of Procedure, Rule 29. Under that article, the Committee may be convened on a proposal from its Bureau, with the approval of the majority of its members.

The Committee has set up specialist sections for the principal fields covered by the Treaties.[457] The seat of the European Economic and Social Committee is in Brussels.[458] It has a staff of about 800 officials.[459]

2. The Committee of the Regions

13–110   **Advisory tasks.** Since the entry into force of the EU Treaty, representatives of regional and local bodies also have a right to be consulted in the decision-making process.[460] The EU Treaty established a Committee of the Regions,[461] which, in the same way as the European Economic and Social Committee, is entitled to be consulted by the European Parliament, the Council and the Commission where the Treaties so provide[462] and may issue an opinion on its own initiative where it considers such action appropriate (Art. 307, first and fourth paras, TFEU). The Committee of the Regions may also be consulted by the European Parliament, the Council or the Commission in all other cases, in particular those which concern cross-border cooperation, in which one of those institutions considers it appropriate (Art. 307, first para., TFEU). The Committee is informed of every request for an opinion made to the European Economic and Social Committee with a view to

---

[457] The Committee sets up its sections at the inaugural session following each renewal (ESC Rules of Procedure, Rule 14).

[458] Sole Art., para. (f), of Protocol (No. 6), annexed to the TEU, TFEU and EAEC Treaty, on the location of the seats of the institutions and of certain bodies, offices, agencies and departments of the European Union, [2010] O.J. C83/265. The ECSC Consultative Committee was based in Luxembourg.

[459] As at December 2009, the Committee had 643 permanent posts and 146 temporary posts: *General Report on the Activities of the European Union 2009* (n. 106, *supra*), at 96.

[460] By Decision of June 24, 1988 ([1988] O.J. L247/23), the Commission set up a Consultative Council of Regional and Local Authorities, which was wound up after the Committee of the Regions started its work (Commission Decision of April 21, 1994, [1994] O.J. L103/28).

[461] Piattoni, "The Committee of the Regions: Multi-Level Governance after Enlargement", in Best, Christiansen and Settembri (eds), *The Institutions of the Enlarged European Union: Continuity and Change* (Cheltenham, Edward Elgar, 2008), 162–182; Domorenok, "The Committee of the Regions: in Search of Identity" (2009) 19 *Regional and Federal Studies*, 143–163; Christiansen and Lintner, "The Committee of the Regions after 10 Years: Lessons from the Past and Challenges for the Future" (2005) *Eipascope* 7–13; Kottmann, "Europe and the regions: sub-national entity representation at Community level" (2001) E.L.Rev. 159–176; Wiedmann, "Der Ausschuss der Regionen nach dem Vertrag von Amsterdam" (1999) EuR. 49–86; Ingelaere, "Het Comité van de Regio's" (1995) S.E.W. 383–398; Bassot, "Le Comité des Régions—Régions françaises et Länder allemands face à un nouvel organe communautaire" (1993) R.M.C.U.E. 729–739; Wuermeling, "Das Ende der 'Länderblindheit': Der Ausschuß der Regionen nach dem neuen EG-Vertrag" (1993) EuR. 196–206. For the website of the Committee of the Regions, see *http://www.cor.europa.eu/* [Accessed December 9, 2010].

[462] See Arts 91(1); 148(2); 149, first para.; 153(2), second subpara.; 164; 165(4), first indent; 166(4); 167(5), first indent; 168(4); 172, first and third paras; 175, third para., 161, first and second paras; 178, first para.; 192(1), (2) and (3) TFEU.

its delivering an opinion on the matter if it considers that specific regional aspects are involved (Art. 307, third para., TFEU).[463]

Locus standi. The Lisbon Treaty conferred on the Committee of the Regions **13–111**
locus standi to bring an action for annulment for the purpose of protecting its prerogatives[464] or to denounce an infringement of the principle of subsidiarity.[465] It is not altogether clear whether actions should be brought in the Court of Justice or in the General Court. In favour of the latter Court's jurisdiction pleads the fact that Art. 51 of the Statute of the Court of Justice of the European Union reserves to the Court of Justice only actions for annulment brought by an institution of the Union, which the Committee of the Regions clearly is not (Art. 13 TEU). Yet, the purpose of the said reservation of jurisdiction to the Court of Justice was to have it judged as a constitutional court would do, all litigation of an interinstitutional character. If this functional reading of Art. 51 of the Statute were to prevail, the Committee of the Regions would have to bring its actions for annulment in the Court of Justice.

Composition. The Committee of the Regions may have no more than 350 mem- **13–112**
bers (at present it has 344). Since the Lisbon Treaty, the Council is to determine the exact composition of the Committee, using the same procedure as with respect to the European Economic and Social Committee (Art. 305, second para., TFEU).[466] The members consist of representatives of regional and local bodies who either hold a regional or local authority electoral mandate or are politically accountable to an

---

[463] Conversely, every act requiring an opinion of the Committee of the Regions is also submitted to the European Economic and Social Committee for its opinion (except as regards culture) and to the European Parliament. The Committee of the Regions also receives the three-yearly report on economic and social cohesion provided for in Art. 175, second para., TFEU.

[464] Article 263, third para., TFEU.

[465] See Art. 263, third para., TFEU and Art. 8 of Protocol (No. 2), annexed to the TEU and TFEU, on the application of the principles of subsidiarity and proportionality ([2010] O.J. C83/206), by virtue of which the Committee can bring an action under Art. 263 TFEU on grounds of infringement of the principle of subsidiarity—irrespective of whether or not such action is intended to protect its prerogatives—in respect of legislative acts for the adoption of which the TFEU provides that it be consulted. See also the Opinion of the Committee of the Regions on Guidelines for the application and monitoring of the subsidiarity and proportionality principles, [2006] O.J. C115/35.

[466] Before the Lisbon Treaty, Art. 263, third para., EC explicitly distributed the members among the Member States in the same way as the members of the European Economic and Social Committee. See the most recent amendment in Art. 13 of the 2005 Act of Accession. In Declaration (No. 20), annexed to the Nice Treaty, on the enlargement of the European Union (n. 218, *supra*), the then Member States determined the composition of the Committee of the Regions for the candidate States (with the exception of Turkey) to be adopted by common position during the accession negotiations. In accordance with Art. 8 of Protocol (No. 36) on transitional provisions (n. 64 *supra*), this allocation remains in place until the entry into effect of a Council Decision adopted under Art. 305 TFEU.

elected assembly (Art. 300(3) TFEU).[467] The members of the Committee are appointed by the Council by a qualified majority vote in accordance with the proposals made by each Member State, together with an equal number of alternate members (Art. 305, third para., TFEU [*ex Art. 263, fourth para., EC*]). Consequently, the Member States themselves decide which domestic levels of administration they wish to have represented on the Committee, one of the reasons being that the status and powers of regional and local bodies differ greatly from one Member State to another.[468] As in the case of their counterparts at the European Economic and Social Committee, members of the Committee of the Regions are appointed for a renewable five-year term,[469] may not be bound by any mandatory instructions and have to be completely independent in the performance of their duties in the Union's general interest (Art. 300(4) and 305, second para., TFEU).

13–113   **Operation.** The Committee of the Regions adopts its own rules of procedure.[470] Twice during their term of office, the members are to elect a President, who convenes it on his or her own initiative or at the request of the European Parliament, the Council or the Commission (Art. 306 TFEU).[471]

The Committee of the Regions shares certain services with the European Economic and Social Committee.[472] As a result, the Committee of the Regions is also based in Brussels.[473]

3. Other committees

13–114   **Consultative bodies.** In a number of policy areas, the Treaties involve national civil servants, representatives of interest groups and independent experts in the decision-making process by means of committees created for that purpose. Pursuant to Art. 242 TFEU [*ex Art. 209 EC*], the Council adopts the rules governing committees

---

[467] The requirement that the proposed members must have an electoral mandate was introduced by the Nice Treaty. Before, each Member State decided whether to put forward (indirectly) elected representatives. The nature of the composition of the Committee must be reviewed at regular intervals by the Council to take account of economic, social and demographic developments within the Union. The Council is to adopt decisions to that end, on a proposal from the Commission (Art. 300(5) TFEU).

[468] For the Belgian representation, see Ingelaere (n. 461, *supra*), at 387; for the Netherlands, see Hessel and Mortelmans, *Het recht van de Europese Gemeenschappen en de decentrale overheden in Nederland* (Deventer, Tjeenk Willink, 1997), 67 pp.

[469] The Lisbon Treaty extended this term from four to five years and, accordingly, brought it into line with that of Members of the European Parliament.

[470] Rules of Procedure adopted by the Committee of the Regions on December 3, 2009, [2010] O.J. L6/14, replacing previous versions.

[471] The President has to convene the Plenary Assembly at least once every three months and is under a duty to hold an extraordinary meeting if requested by at least a quarter of the members (Rules of Procedure, Rule 14).

[472] As at December 2009, the Committee had 465 permanent and 37 temporary posts: *General Report on the Activities of the European Union 2009* (n. 106, *supra*), at 96.

[473] Sole Art., para. (g), of the Protocol on Seats, para. 13–153, *infra*.

provided for in the Treaties (by a simple majority vote) after receiving the opinion of the Commission. Examples are the Advisory Committee on Transport, consisting of experts designated by the national governments, attached to the Commission (Art. 99 TFEU [*ex Art. 79 EC*]) and the Committee of the European Social Fund, composed of representatives of governments, trade unions and employers' associations and presided over by a member of the Commission, which assists the Commission in administering the Fund (Art. 163 TFEU [*ex Art. 147 EC*]).[474] The Treaty of Amsterdam created the Employment Committee, to which each Member State and the Commission appoint two members (Art. 150 TFEU [*ex Art. 130 EC*]).[475] That committee consults management and labour in order to perform its task of formulating opinions and contributing (together with Coreper) to the preparation of Council proceedings (see para. 13–058). A similar task has been conferred on the Social Protection Committee, enshrined in the Treaties by the Treaty of Nice, to which each Member State and the Commission appoint two members (Art. 160 TFEU [*ex Art. 144 EC*]).

An important role is played by the Economic and Financial Committee, which keeps under review the economic and financial situation of the Member States and the Union and reports in particular on financial relations with third countries and international institutions (Art. 134(2), second indent TFEU [*ex Art. 114(2), second indent, EC*]).[476] It reports on these matters to the Council and the Commission and advises those institutions at their request or on its own initiative. It prepares (together with Coreper) certain Council proceedings, reports to the Council and the Commission on free movement of capital and freedom of payments and carries out such other advisory and preparatory tasks as the Council should entrust to it (Art. 134(2), third and fourth indents, TFEU). The Committee also keeps under review the monetary and financial situation and the general payments system of Member States with a derogation (Art. 114(4) TFEU). The Member States, the Commission and the ECB each appoint no more than two members of the Committee (Art. 134(2), second subpara., TFEU).[477]

---

[474] Rules of the Transport Committee, adopted by the Council on September 15, 1958, [1952–1958] O.J. English Spec. Ed. 72; Rules of the Committee of the European Social Fund, adopted by the Council on August 25, 1960, [1959–1962] O.J. English Spec. Ed. 65.

[475] Council Decision 2000/98/EC of January 24, 2000 establishing the Employment Committee, [2000] O.J. L29/21.

[476] Statutes of the Economic and Financial Committee as revised by the Council on June 18, 2003, [2003] O.J. L158/58. This committee is the successor of the Monetary Committee, which kept under review the monetary and financial situation of the Member States and the Community and advised the Council and the Commission (see Art. 114(1) EC). Under Art. 6 of the Decision on Provisional Location of April 8, 1965 (para. 13–152, *infra*), the Committee was to meet in Brussels and Luxembourg.

[477] The two members appointed by the Member States comprise one senior official from the administration and one from the national central bank, see Council Decision 98/743/EC of December 21, 1998 on the detailed provisions concerning the composition of the Economic and Financial Committee, [1998] O.J. L358/109. The members of the national central banks do not attend all meetings; see Art. 4 of the Statute of the Economic and Financial Committee.

13–115   **Other committees.** A number of Union acts have set up advisory committees, the Council being deemed to have the power to determine their rules by virtue of Art. 242 TFEU. This also applies to the committees which supervise the Commission's implementing powers under the various comitology procedures (see para. 17–012). Each such committee consists of representatives of the Member States and one representative of the Commission. Just as in the case of committees created by the Treaties, the Commission pays for the costs of these committee meetings out of its budget.[478]

B. THE EUROPEAN INVESTMENT BANK

13–116   **Tasks.** The European Investment Bank[479] (EIB) is an independent Union body endowed with legal personality.[480] Its task is to finance, by recourse to the capital market and utilising its own resources, private and public investment projects fostering the balanced and steady development of the Union (Art. 309 TFEU [*ex Art. 267 EC*]). Together with the Structural Funds and other financial instruments, the EIB seeks in this way to promote economic, social and territorial cohesion within the Union.[481] In addition, as part of the Union's development policy, it may finance projects to be carried out in non-Union countries.[482]

13–117   **Operation.** The members of the EIB are the Member States (Art. 308, second para., TFEU), each subscribing fixed amounts of its capital.[483] General directives for the EIB's credit policy and important decisions such as increases in capital are adopted by the Board of Governors, which consists of ministers designated by the Member States (in practice, the Finance Ministers).[484] The Board of Governors approves the Bank's Rules of Procedure[485] and therefore has the power to

---

[478] See the list of some four hundred committees in Final adoption of the general budget for the European Union for the financial year 2004, [2004] O.J. C105 (II) 1391.

[479] For the website of the EIB, see *http://www.eib.org/* [Accessed December 9, 2010].

[480] See Arts 308 and 309 TFEU [*ex Arts 266 and 267 EC*], and Protocol (No. 5), annexed to the TEU and TFEU, on the Statute of the European Investment Bank [EIB Statute] ([2010] O.J. C83/251). For the EIB as a Union body, see ECJ, Case 110/75 *Mills v European Investment Bank* [1976] E.C.R. 955, paras 7–14, and ECJ, Case C-15/00 *Commission v European Investment Bank* [2003] E.C.R. I-7281, para. 75; for the extent of its financial and institutional independence, see ECJ, Case 85/86 *Commission v European Investment Bank* [1988] E.C.R. 1281, paras 28–30; ECJ, Case C-370/89 *SGEEM v European Investment Bank* [1992] E.C.R. I-6211, paras 12–17; ECJ, Case C-15/00 *Commission v European Investment Bank* [2003] E.C.R. I-7281, paras 101–110. For further details, see Dunnett, "The European Investment Bank: Autonomous Instrument of Common Policy?" (1994) C.M.L.Rev. 721–763.

[481] For economic and social cohesion, see Art. 175 TFEU (para. 11–055, *supra*); see also Arts 170 and 171 TFEU on Trans-European Networks.

[482] See EIB Statute, Art. 16(1).

[483] *Ibid.*, Arts 4 and 5.

[484] *Ibid.*, Art. 7(1) and (2).

[485] *Ibid.*, Art. 7(3)(h).

organise internal matters and is authorised to take the appropriate measures in order to ensure the internal operation of the EIB in conformity with the interests of its good administration.[486] The Board of Directors takes decisions in respect of granting loans and guarantees and raising loans.[487] It also ensures that Member States fulfil their obligations under the EIB Statute.[488] The Board of Directors consists of 28 directors, of whom the Member States and the Commission nominate one each. They are then appointed by the Board of Governors for a five-year term.[489] The Board of Directors generally takes its decisions by at least one-third of the members with voting rights representing at least 50 per cent of the capital; where a qualified majority is required, 18 votes in favour and 68 per cent of the capital are needed.[490] Responsibility for the current business of the Bank lies with the Management Committee, which consists of a President and eight Vice-Presidents, who are appointed for a six-year term by the Board of Governors on a proposal from the Board of Directors.[491] Members of the Board of Directors and of the Management Committee perform their duties in complete independence and may be dismissed only by the Board of Governors.[492] The European Investment Bank has its seat in Luxembourg.[493]

C. THE EUROPEAN OMBUDSMAN

Task. The European Ombudsman,[494] introduced by the EU Treaty, looks into complaints of maladministration in the activities of Union institutions, bodies, offices or agencies, with the exception of the Court of Justice of the European Union acting in its judicial role (Art. 228 TFEU).[495] According to the

13–118

---

[486] ECJ, Case C-15/00 *Commission v European Investment Bank* [2003] E.C.R. I-7281, paras 67–81.

[487] *Ibid.*, Art. 9(1).

[488] Article 271(a) TFEU, which gives the Board of Directors the same powers as are enjoyed by the Commission under Art. 258 TFEU.

[489] EIB Statute, Art. 9(2).

[490] *Ibid.*, Art. 10.

[491] *Ibid.*, Art. 11.

[492] *Ibid.*, Art. 9(2), last subpara., Art. 9(3) and Art. 11(8). Members of the Management Committee may be retired only on a proposal from the Board of Directors (EIB Statute, Art. 11(2)).

[493] Protocol on Seats, Sole Art., para. (h). See Art. 5 of the Decision on Provisional Location of April 8, 1965 (n. 695, *infra*).

[494] For the Ombudsman's website, see *http://www.ombudsman.europa.eu/* [Accessed December 9, 2010].

[495] Marias, *The European Ombudsman* (Maastricht, European Institute of Public Administration, 1994), 150 pp.; Pliakos, "Le médiateur de l'Union européenne" (1994) C.D.E. 563–606; Pierucci, "Le médiateur européen" (1993) R.M.C.U.E. 818–822. Before the Lisbon Treaty, Arts 28(1) and 41(1) EU precluded the exercise of the powers of investigation provided for in Art. 193 EC [*now Art. 226 TFEU*] in connection with action pursuant to the CFSP and PJCC, respectively. Nevertheless, there was nothing to prevent the Ombudsman from investigating a complaint concerning the activities of Union institutions and bodies which fell outside the ambit of the Community Treaties. The Ombudsman took the view that he could rule on a refusal by the Council to give a citizen access to documents, regardless of the subject-matter, see European Ombudsman, *Annual Report 1997*, Luxembourg, Office for Official Publications of the EC, at 23–24.

Ombudsman, there is "maladministration" if a public authority fails to observe a rule or principle which is binding on it.[496] The regulations and general conditions governing the performance of the European Ombudsman's duties are laid down by the European Parliament in accordance with a special procedure, under which the Commission delivers an opinion and the Council grants its approval by a qualified majority (Art. 228(4) TFEU).[497]

13–119 Appointment. The European Parliament elects the European Ombudsman for the duration of his or her term of office (Art. 228(2) TFEU).[498] The Ombudsman may be dismissed by the Court of Justice only at the request of the European Parliament.[499] He or she has to be completely independent in the performance of his or her duties, which are to be carried out on a full-time basis.[500] The Ombudsman is assisted by his or her own secretariat, established at Strasbourg.[501] The Ombudsman's seat is that of the European Parliament.[502]

13–120 Inquiries. The European Ombudsman conducts inquiries into maladministration by Union institutions, bodies, offices or agencies, either on his or her own initiative or on the basis of complaints submitted to him or her directly or through an MEP.[503] Such a complaint may be made by any citizen of the Union or any

---

[496] See the 1997 Annual Report (n. 495, *supra*), at p. 22. For the broad interpretation given to this expression in practice, see recent annual reports and Yeng-Seng, "Premier bilan de l'activité du médiateur européen: d'une politique des petits pas à une pratique consolidée" (2003) R.M.C.U.E. 326, at 329–330.

[497] Decision of the European Parliament of March 9, 1994 on the regulations and general conditions governing the performance of the Ombudsman's duties, [1994] O.J. L113/15, as amended by Decision of the European Parliament of June 18, 2008, [2008] O.J. L189/25 [Ombudsman Regulations], appended to the EP Rules of Procedure as Annex XI. See also Rules 204 to 206 of the EP Rules of Procedure. On July 8, 2002, the European Ombudsman issued new implementing provisions, which are also published in Annex XI to the EP Rules of Procedure.

[498] The Ombudsman has to be a Union citizen, have full civil and political rights, offer every guarantee of independence and meet the conditions required for the exercise of the highest judicial office in his or her country or have the acknowledged competence and experience to undertake the duties of Ombudsman (Ombudsman Regulations, Art. 6(2)). Since the responsible parliamentary committee was unable to reach agreement on the first candidate to be approved by the plenary session, the EP Rules of Procedure were amended so as to enable several nominations to be put forward (see now Rule 204). The plenary session then chooses between them. For the appointment procedure, see CFI, Case T-146/95 *Bernardi v European Parliament* [1996] E.C.R. II-769 (action for annulment held to be unfounded).

[499] The Ombudsman may be dismissed if he or she no longer fulfils the conditions required for the performance of his or her duties or if he or she is guilty of serious misconduct (Art. 228(2), second subpara., TFEU).

[500] Article 228(3) TFEU; Ombudsman Regulations, Art. 9 and Art. 10(1).

[501] Ombudsman Regulations, Art. 11(1).

[502] Ombudsman Regulations, Art. 13.

[503] Article 228(1), second subpara., TFEU. See Yeng-Seng (n. 496, *supra*), at 331–332.

natural or legal person residing or having its registered office in a Member State.[504] The Ombudsman will not investigate a complaint if the facts have been known to the complainant for more than two years[505] or if the facts are or have been the subject of legal proceedings.[506] This means that a complainant must decide whether to bring judicial proceedings or to bring a complaint before the Ombudsman (which does not cause time for bringing judicial proceedings to stop running).[507]

The Ombudsman's first task is to try to seek a solution with the institution or body concerned.[508] If the Ombudsman finds that there has been maladministration, he or she informs the institution concerned—which then has three months to inform him or her of its views—and may make recommendations for resolving the matter.[509] At this point, the Ombudsman forwards a report to the European Parliament and to the institution concerned. The Ombudsman keeps the complainant informed of the outcome of the inquiries[510] and also reports to the responsible committee of the European Parliament.[511] If necessary, the European Parliament will be in the best position to take the requisite steps, since it also receives an annual report from the Ombudsman on the outcome of his or her inquiries.[512]

Union institutions and bodies must supply any information requested and give access to any documents in their possession, subject to compliance with the security rules of the institution or body concerned.[513] The Ombudsman may not

---

[504] Article 228(1), first subpara., TFEU. Naturally, other persons may place facts before the European Ombudsman in order to induce him or her to carry out an inquiry on his or her own initiative. "The European Ombudsman. How to complain" is set out in [1996] O.J. C157/1, and on the Internet ([1998] O.J. C44/14).

[505] Ombudsman Regulations, Art. 2(4).

[506] Article 228(1), second subpara., TFEU. In addition, prior to making a complaint the appropriate administrative approaches must have been made to the institution or body concerned (Ombudsman Regulations, Art. 2(4)). An official or other servant of the Communities may make a complaint concerning work relationships with a Community institution or body only if all the possibilities for the submission of internal administrative requests and complaints under the Staff Regulations have been exhausted and the relevant time-limits have expired (Ombudsman Regulations, Art. 2(8)).

[507] CFI, Case T-209/00 *Lamberts v European Ombudsman* [2002] E.C.R. II-2203, paras 65–66, upheld by ECJ, Case C-234/02 P *European Ombudsman v Lamberts* [2004] E.C.R. I-02803.

[508] Ombudsman Regulations, Art. 3(5).

[509] Article 228(1), second subpara., TFEU and Ombudsman Regulations, Art. 3(6). For the Ombudsman's discretion to close a case or to reach a friendly settlement, see ECJ, Case C-234/02 P *European Ombudsman v Lamberts* [2004] E.C.R. I-02803, para. 82, and judgment upheld thereby: CFI, Case T-209/00 *Lamberts v European Ombudsman* [2002] E.C.R. II-2203, paras 78–85.

[510] Ombudsman Regulations, Art. 3(7).

[511] EP Rules of Procedure, Rule 205(3). It is not possible to bring an action for failure to act against the Ombudsman on account of his or her refusal to initiate an inquiry, see CFI (order of May 22, 2000), Case T-103/99 *Associazione delle cantine sociali Venete v European Ombudsman and the European Parliament* [2000] E.C.R. II-4165.

[512] Article 228(1), third para., TFEU. For recent annual reports, see the website cited in n. 494, *supra* (for earlier reports, see [1998] O.J. C380/11 (1997), [1999] O.J. C300/1 (1998) and [2000] O.J. C260/1 (1999)).

[513] Ombudsman Regulations, Art. 3(3).

divulge information or documents obtained in the course of inquiries.[514] The national authorities must provide the Ombudsman with any information requested which may help to clarify instances of maladministration by Union institutions or bodies unless provision of the said information is precluded by national law.[515] Provided that he or she complies with the applicable national law, the Ombudsman may cooperate with similar authorities in Member States.[516]

D. OTHER UNION BODIES

13–121 **European External Action Service.** The Lisbon Treaty provided for the establishment of a European External Action Service (EEAS) to assist the High Representative of the Union for Foreign Affairs and Security Policy in his or her various tasks of conducting the CFSP, chairing the Foreign Affairs Council, fulfilling the responsibilities in external relations incumbent on it within the Commission and coordinating the Union's external action. The Council is to determine the organisation and functioning of the EEAS, on a proposal from the High Representative after consulting the European Parliament and after obtaining the consent of the Commission (Art. 27(3) TEU).[517] Before the Lisbon Treaty, the external action of the Communities relied mainly on the administrative support provided by the relevant Commission's Directorates General, including the Commission delegations (see para. 24–006), whereas in CFSP matters the Presidency of the Council was to rely on the General Secretariat of the Council and the diplomatic services of the Member States. Together with the creation of the function of High Representative of the Union for Foreign Affairs and Security Policy, the Lisbon Treaty introduced with the EEAS an integrated external actions service, which is to comprise officials from relevant departments of the General Secretariat of the Council and of the Commission as well as staff seconded from national diplomatic services (Art. 27(3) TEU).[518] The EEAS consists of a central

---

[514] *Ibid.*, Art. 4(1). If he or she learns of facts which he or she considers might relate to criminal law, the competent national authorities must be notified. The Ombudsman must inform the institution with authority over the official or other servant and may do so if he or she discovers facts calling into question the conduct of the staff member from the disciplinary point of view (Ombudsman Regulations, Art. 4(2)).

[515] *Ibid.*, Art. 3(3).

[516] *Ibid.*, Art. 5.

[517] See Council Decision 2010/427/EU of July 26, 2010 establishing the organisation and the functioning of the European External Action Service, [2010] O.J. L201/30.

[518] All staff members of the EEAS are covered by the Staff Regulations and the Conditions of Employment of Other Servants and have the same rights and obligations, regardless whether they are officials of the European Union or temporary agents coming from the diplomatic services of the Member States: *ibid.*, Art. 6(7). They are to carry out their duties solely with the interests of the Union in mind and are not to seek or take instructions from any government, authority, organisation or person outside the EEAS or any body or person other than the High Representative: *ibid.*, Art. 6(2).

administration in Brussels and of the Union delegations in third countries and at international organisations (see para. 24–006). The EEAS is a functionally autonomous body, separate from the Commission and the Council's General Secretariat, under the authority of the High Representative.[519] The EEAS is also to assist the Commission and the President of the European Council and may extend appropriate support to the other Union institutions and bodies. Although it does not have legal personality, the EEAS is endowed "with the legal capacity necessary to perform its tasks".[520] The day-to-day administration of the EEAS is to be ensured by an Executive Secretary-General.[521]

Separate offices. In order effectively to carry out certain tasks, various other sectors of the administration have a degree of independence.[522] Examples, on an interinstitutional footing,[523] are the Publications Office of the European Union (OP),[524] the European Personnel Selection Office (EPSO),[525] the European Administrative School[526] and, for those answerable to the Commission, the Statistical Office (Eurostat),[527] the Office for the administration and payment of

13–122

---

[519] *Ibid.*, Art. 1(2).

[520] *Ibid.*

[521] *Ibid.*, Art. 4.

[522] For the legitimacy of such bodies, see Curtin, "Holding (Quasi-)autonomous EU administrative actors to public account" (2007) 13 E.L.J. 523–541.

[523] See, generally, Hummer, "From 'interinstitutional agreements' to 'interinstitutional agencies/ offices' " (2007) 13 E.L.J. 47–74.

[524] Decision of the European Parliament, the Council, the Commission, the Court of Justice, the Court of Auditors, the European Economic and Social Committee and the Committee of the Regions of June 26, 2009, [2009] O.J. L168/41 (formerly known as the "Office for Official Publications of the European Communities", see Decision 2000/459/EC, ECSC, Euratom of the European Parliament, the Council, the Commission, the Court of Justice, the Court of Auditors, the Economic and Social Committee and the Committee of the Regions of July 20, 2000, [2000] O.J. L183/12). The Office is based in Luxembourg as a result of Art. 8 of the Decision on Provisional Location (para. 13–152, *infra*).

[525] Decision 2002/620/EC of the European Parliament, the Council, the Commission, the Court of Justice, the Court of Auditors, the Economic and Social Committee, the Committee of the Regions and the European Ombudsman of July 25, 2002, [2002] O.J. L197/53; for its operation and internal organisation, see Decision 2002/621/EC of the Secretaries-General of those institutions and committees and of the Representative of the European Ombudsman of July 25, 2002, [2002] O.J. L197/56.

[526] Decision 2005/118/EC of the European Parliament, the Council, the Commission, the Court of Justice, the Court of Auditors, the European Economic and Social Committee, the Committee of the Regions and the Ombudsman of January 26, 2005 setting up a European Administrative School, [2005] O.J. L37/14.

[527] Based in Luxembourg as a result of Art. 9(a) of the Decision on Provisional Location; see now the Protocol on Seats, Sole Art., para. (c) (para. 13–152, *infra*). For the role played by Eurostat in the production of Community statistics, see the Commission's decision of April 21, 1997, [1997] O.J. L112/56.

individual entitlements,[528] the Offices for infrastructure and logistics[529] and the Office for Veterinary and Plant-Health Inspection and Control.[530] The European Anti-Fraud Office (OLAF) set up by the Commission carries out powers of investigation in complete independence.[531] The European Data-Protection Supervisor, introduced pursuant to Art. 286 EC [*now Art. 16 TFEU*], also operates completely independently (see para. 13–169). Article 8 EAEC provides for the establishment by the Commission of a Joint Nuclear Research Centre, which has evolved towards a general research-based organisation active in various fields (JRC).[532] Contrary to what their titles might suggest, the Union "Funds" are not separate bodies, but operate as normal administrative departments of the Commission.[533]

It is also worth mentioning at this juncture that a number of international agreements concluded by the Union—Association Agreements especially—have created joint consultative bodies and joint decision-making bodies.[534]

13–123 **Independent legal persons.** Some Union bodies take the form of separate legal persons under the name of agencies, foundations, centres or offices. They have a

---

[528] Established by the Commission by decision of November 6, 2002, [2003] O.J. L183/30. This "Paymaster Office" (PMO) is responsible for determining, calculating and paying pecuniary entitlements of staff of the Union.

[529] The Commission established these offices in Brussels (OIB) and Luxembourg (OIL) by decisions of November 6, 2002, [2003] O.J. L183/35 and L183/40, respectively.

[530] The Commission approved the establishment of the Office by Decision of December 18, 1991: (1991) 12 EC Bull. point 1.2.201. The "Food and Veterinary Office" (FVO) is part of the Directorate-General for Health and Consumers and based in Grange (Ireland). The Second Decision on the Seats of the Institutions of October 29, 1993 (para. 13–154, *infra*) provided that its seat was to be determined by the Irish Government.

[531] Commission Decision 1999/352/EC, ECSC, Euratom of April 28, 1999 establishing the European Anti-fraud Office (OLAF), [1999] O.J. L136/20 (para. 13–163, *infra*). The Director of OLAF is appointed by the Commission, after consulting the European Parliament and the Council: Art. 5(1) of Decision 1999/352 and Art. 12(2) of Regulation (EC) No. 1073/1999 of the European Parliament and of the Council of May 25, 1999 concerning investigations conducted by the European Anti-Fraud Office (OLAF), [1999] O.J. L136/1. The members of OLAF's Supervisory Committee are appointed by common accord of the European Parliament, the Council and the Commission: Art. 11(2) of Regulation No. 1073/1999. See Kuhl and Spitzer, "Das Europäische Amt für Betrugsbekämpfung (OLAF)" (2000) EuR. 671–685. For the Rules of Procedure adopted by OLAF's Supervisory Committee on November 17, 1999, see [2000] O.J. L41/12.

[532] See Commission Decision 96/282/Euratom of April 10, 1996 on the reorganisation of the Joint Research Centre, [1996] O.J. L107/12. The JRC has institutes located in Petten (Netherlands), Karlsruhe (Germany), Ispra (Italy), Seville (Spain) and Geel (Belgium).

[533] European Social Fund: DG Employment and Social Affairs (see also Art. 162 TFEU); European Agricultural Guidance and Guarantee Fund (EAGGF or FEOGA): DG Agriculture and Rural Development; European Development Fund (EDF): the EuropeAid Cooperation Office; European Regional Development Fund (ERDF) and Cohesion Fund: DG Regional Policy.

[534] For further details, see paras 25–009 and 25–020, *infra*. Admittedly, such bodies are not "Union" bodies as such, but their decisions may sometimes be enforced as part of Union law: see para. 22–046, *infra*.

measure of independence in regard to their budgets and personnel policies. Their special status does not prevent their acts from being subject in many cases to the Commission's administrative supervision and invariably subject to judicial review (see para. 17–022).

Some bodies are explicitly referred to by the Treaties. The EAEC Treaty established a Supply Agency, which has legal personality and financial autonomy and operates under the Commission's supervision (Arts 52 to 56 EAEC).[535] Article 45 EAEC and Art. 187 TFEU [ex Art. 171 EC] make it possible to set up joint undertakings for research and development.[536] In addition, pursuant to the Protocol on the Statute of the EIB, the EIB's Board of Governors has set up a European Investment Fund.[537]

On a more general note, the Union is entitled to set up an independent body whenever this squares with action pursuant to a specific Treaty article or Art. 352 TFEU [ex Art. 308 EC] (see paras 17–020—17–021).[538] In this way, it has created the European Centre for the Development of Vocational Training (Cedefop),[539] the European Foundation for the Improvement of Living and Working Conditions (EUROFOUND)[540] and the European Agency for

---

[535] For the statute of the Agency, see Council Decision 2008/114 (EC, Euratom) of February 12, 2008, [2008] O.J. L41/15.

[536] See, e.g., the Joint European Torus (JET) joint undertaking set up by Council Decision of May 30, 1978 at Culham, [1978] O.J. L151/10 (for the United Kingdom, see European Community (Definition of Treaties) (No. 5) (Joint European Torus) Order 1978). The undertaking's statutes are appended to that decision. Not all members of JET's staff are officials of the EAEC: see ECJ, Joined Cases 271/83, 15, 36, 113, 158 and 203/84 and 13/85 Ainsworth v Commission and Council [1987] E.C.R. 167, paras 19–23. On the legal status of JET staff members, see further: CFI, Case T-45/01 Sanders and Others v Commission [2007] E.C.R. II-2665, CFI, Case T-144/02 Eagle and Others [2007] E.C.R. II-2721. See also the Galileo Joint Undertaking (on satellite radio-navigation), set up by Council Regulation (EC) No. 876/2002 of May 21, 2002, [2002] O.J. L138/1 whose statutes are annexed to that regulation and the European Joint Undertaking for ITER and the Development of Fusion Energy (Fusion for Energy), set up by Council Decision 2007/198/Euratom of March 27, 2007 ([2007] O.J. L90/8), which has its seat in Barcelona.

[537] Statutes of the European Investment Fund, adopted on June 14, 1994 and June 19, 2000, amended by the general meeting, [2001] O.J. C225/2. Shareholders in the Fund are the European Union, the European Investment Bank and a group of financial institutions.

[538] On the increased use of these powers, see van Ooik, "De wonderbaarlijke vermenigvuldiging van Europese agentschappen. Verklaring, analyse, perspectief" (2006) S.E.W. 102–111.

[539] Council Regulation (EEC) No. 337/75 of February 10, 1975, [1975] O.J. L39/1 (para. 11–050, supra), as amended by Council Regulation (EC) No. 2051/2004 of October 25, 2004, [2004] O.J. L355/1. For its nature as a Community body, see ECJ, Case 16/81 Alaimo v Commission [1982] E.C.R. 1559, paras 7–12, at 1566–1567. As agreed when the seats of various new bodies were allocated on October 29, 1993, the Council moved the Centre's seat from Berlin to Thessaloniki: Council Regulation (EC) No. 1131/94 of May 16, 1994, [1994] O.J. L127/1.

[540] Council Regulation (EEC) No. 1365/75 of May 26, 1975, [1975] O.J. L139/1, as amended by Council Regulation (EC) No. 1111/2005 of June 24, 2005, [2005] O.J. L184/1 (see ns to para. 11–044, supra). Its seat is in Ireland (Art. 4(2)), more specifically in Dublin.

Cooperation.[541] A series of bodies were able to start operation once the Member States decided on the location of their seats on October 29, 1993[542]: the European Environmental Agency (EEA)[543]; the European Training Foundation (ETF)[544]; the European Monitoring Centre for Drugs and Drug Addiction (EMCDDA)[545]; the European Medicines Agency (EMEA)[546]; the European Office for Harmonisation in the Internal Market (Trade Marks and Designs) (OHIM)[547]; and the European Agency for Safety and Health at Work (EU-OSHA).[548] In addition, the Council set up a Community Plant Variety Office (CPVO),[549] a Translation Centre for Bodies

---

[541] Council Regulation (EEC) No. 3245/81 of October 26, 1981, [1981] O.J. L328/1. The Agency should deal with personnel policy and recruitment as regards staff which the Community makes available as part of its financial and technical cooperation with developing countries but has never become operational.

[542] By the Second Decision on the Seats of the Institutions of October 29, 1993, para. 13–154, *infra*. The regulations setting up these bodies provided that they were to enter into force on the day following the date on which the competent authorities took a decision as to where they were to be based. They therefore entered into force on October 30, 1993 (see the notice in [1994] O.J. L294/29).

[543] Council Regulation (EEC) No. 1210/90 of May 7, 1990, [1990] O.J. L120/1. The Agency's seat is in the Copenhagen area.

[544] Council Regulation (EEC) No. 1360/90 of May 7, 1990, [1990] O.J. L131/1, as amended on several occasions (para. 11–050, *supra*). Its seat is at Turin.

[545] Council Regulation (EEC) No. 302/93 of February 8, 1993, [1993] O.J. L36/1. The Centre's seat is at Lisbon.

[546] Regulation (EC) No. 726/2004 of the European Parliament and of the Council of March 31, 2004 laying down Community procedures for the authorisation and supervision of medicinal products for human and veterinary use and establishing a European Medicines Agency, [2004] O.J. L136/1, replacing Council Regulation (EEC) No. 2309/93 of July 22, 1993, [1993] O.J. L214/1 (which had established the European Agency for the Evaluation of Medicinal Products, the name of which was changed to European Medicines Agency by Regulation 726/2004). The Agency's seat is in London.

[547] Council Regulation (EC) No. 40/94 of December 20, 1993 on the Community trade mark, [1994] O.J. L11/1. The Office is responsible for organising procedures for applying for and using the Community trade mark and the Community design. It has a Board of Appeal, against whose decisions an action may be brought in the General Court. The Second Decision on the Seats of the Institutions of October 29, 1993 provided that the Office was to have its seat in Spain. The Spanish Government decided that it was to be located in Alicante. See the declaration of the Council and the Commission annexed to the regulation, [1994] O.J. L11/36.

[548] Council Regulation (EC) No. 2062/94 of July 18, 1994, [1994] O.J. L216/1. Pursuant to the Second Decision on the Seats of the Institutions of October 29, 1993, the Spanish Government determined that its seat would be at Bilbao: see the declaration of the Council and the Commission annexed to the regulation.

[549] Council Regulation (EC) No. 2100/94 of July 27, 1994 on Community plant variety rights, [1994] O.J. L227/1, as amended by Council Regulation (EC) No. 2506/95 of October 25, 1995, [1995] O.J. L258/3 (introduction of a procedure before the General Court against decisions of Boards of Appeal by analogy with the appeal procedures in respect of the Community trade mark). The Office is responsible for organising procedures relating to applications for and the use of Community plant variety rights. The Office is based in Angers (France): see the Decision taken by common accord of the representatives of the governments of the Member States of December 6, 1996, [1996] O.J. C36/1.

of the European Union (CdT),[550] a European Union Agency for Fundamental Rights (FRA)[551] and the European Agency for Reconstruction.[552] In 2002, the European Parliament and the Council further established the European Food Safety Authority (EFSA),[553] the European Maritime Safety Agency (EMSA) and the European Aviation Safety Agency (EASA).[554] The locations of these three agencies were not determined until December 13, 2003 by the Third Decision on Seats, which also decided on the locations of the European Network

---

[550] Council Regulation (EC) No. 2965/94 of November 28, 1994, [1994] O.J. L314/1, as amended by Council Regulation (EC) No. 2610/95 of October 30, 1995, [1995] O.J. L268/1. The Centre, which is based in Luxembourg, provides translation services for the aforementioned bodies and for institutions and bodies of the Union which have their own translation services should they wish to make use of the Centre's services. For the implementing provisions necessary to ensure the confidentiality of certain activities of the Translation Centre, see [1999] O.J. C295/3.

[551] Council Regulation (EC) No. 168/2007 of February 15, 2007 establishing a European Union Agency for Fundamental Rights, [2007] O.J. L53/1. The seat of the Agency is in Vienna (*ibid*, Art. 23 (5)). The Agency was established as the successor to the European Monitoring Centre on Racism and Xenophobia (established by Council Regulation (EC) No. 1035/97 of June 2, 1997, [1997] O.J. L151/1), which also had its seat in Vienna. See von Bogdandy and van Bernstoff, "The EU Fundamental Rights Agency within the European and international human rights architecture: the legal framework and some unsettled issues in a new field of administrative law" (2009) C.M.L.Rev. 1035–1068; De Schutter, "L'agence de droit fondamentaux" (2007) 15 J.T.D.E. 97–102; Verhagen and Timmermans, "Grondrechtenagentschap. Quis custodiet ipsos custodes?" (2007) N.J.B. 1055–1057; Howard, "The European Union Agency for fundamental rights" (2006) E.H.R.L.R. 445–455; and the contributions in Alston and De Schutter (eds), *Monitoring Fundamental Rights in the EU. The contribution of the fundamental rights agency* (Oxford, Hart Publishing, 2005), 282 pp. See further the Agreement between the European Community and the Council of Europe on cooperation between the European Union Agency for Fundamental Rights and the Council of Europe ([2008] O.J. L186/7).

[552] Council Regulation (EC) No. 2454/1999 of November 15, 1999 ([1999] O.J. L299/1), as amended by Council Regulation (EC) No. 2667/2000 of December 5, 2000 on the European Agency for Reconstruction ([2000] O.J. L306/7). The Agency's operational centre was located at Pristina, its seat in Thessaloniki. It was operational until December 31, 2008 in accordance with Council Regulation (EC) No. 1756/2006 of November 28, 2006, [2006] O.J. L332/18.

[553] Regulation (EC) No. 178/2002 of the European Parliament and of the Council of January 28, 2002 laying down the general principles and requirements of food law, establishing the European Food Safety Authority and laying down procedures in matters of food safety, [2002] O.J. L31/1 (see para. 11–053). After operating provisionally in Brussels, the Authority's seat was established in Parma (Italy) by the Third Decision on Seats. See Vos, "Naar een Europese FDA? De nieuwe Europese Autoriteit voor Voedselveiligheid" (2003) N.T.E.R. 177–181; Petit, "L'autorité alimentaire de sécurité des aliments (A.E.S.A.) et la nouvelle approche alimentaire communautaire" (2002) J.T.D.E. 209–214.

[554] Regulation (EC) No. 1406/2002 of the European Parliament and of the Council of June 27, 2002 establishing a European Maritime Safety Agency, [2002] O.J. L208/1, and Regulation (EC) No. 1592/2002 of the European Parliament and of the Council of July 15, 2002 on common rules in the field of civil aviation and establishing a European Aviation Safety Agency, [2002] O.J. L240/1, now replaced by Regulation (EC) No. 216/2008 of February 20, 2008, [2008] O.J. L79/1. The Maritime Safety Agency has its seat in Lisbon, the Aviation Agency in Cologne (see the Third Decision on Seats).

and Information Security Agency (ENISA),[555] the European Centre for Disease Prevention and Control (ECDC)[556] and the European Railway Agency (ERA).[557] Bodies that were established more recently include the Community Fisheries Control Agency (CFCA),[558] the European Agency for the Management of Operational Cooperation at the External Borders (FRONTEX),[559] the European Chemicals Agency (ECHA),[560] the European Institute for Gender Equality (GSA),[561] the European Global Navigation Satellite System (GNSS) Authority (GSA),[562] the European Institute of Innovation and Technology

---

[555] Regulation (EC) No. 460/2004 of the European Parliament and of the Council of March 10, 2004 establishing the European Network and Information Security Agency, [2004] O.J. L77/1, as amended by Regulation (EC) No. 1007/2008 of the European Parliament and of the Council of September 24, 2008 amending Regulation (EC) No. 460/2004 establishing the European Network and Information Security Agency, as regards its duration, [2008] O.J. L293/1. It has its seat in Heraklion.

[556] Regulation (EC) No. 851/2004 of the European Parliament and of the Council of April 21, 2004 establishing a European Centre for disease prevention and control, [2004] O.J. L142/1. It has its seat in Stockholm (see the Third Decision on Seats).

[557] Regulation (EC) No. 881/2004 of the European Parliament and of the Council of April 29, 2004 establishing a European Railway Agency (Agency Regulation), [2004] O.J. L164/1 (republished with *corrigendum*: [2004] O.J. L220/3). It has its seat in Lille-Valenciennes (see the Third Decision on Seats).

[558] Council Regulation (EC) No. 768/2005 of April 26, 2005 establishing a Community Fisheries Control Agency and amending Regulation (EEC) No. 2847/93 establishing a control system applicable to the common fisheries policy, [2005] O.J. L128/1. The Agency has its seat in Vigo (*ibid.*, Art. 18(4)).

[559] Council Regulation (EC) No. 2007/2004 of October 26, 2004 establishing a European Agency for the Management of Operational Cooperation at the External Borders of the Member States of the European Union, [2004] O.J. L349/1. The Agency has its seat in Warsaw (see Council Decision of April 26, 2005 designating the seat of the European Agency for the Management of Operational Cooperation at the External Borders of the Member States of the European Union, [2005] O.J. L114/13).

[560] Regulation (EC) No. 1907/2006 of the European Parliament and of the Council of December 18, 2006 concerning the Registration, Evaluation, Authorisation and Restriction of Chemicals (REACH), establishing a European Chemicals Agency, amending Directive 1999/45/EC and repealing Council Regulation (EEC) No. 793/93 and Commission Regulation (EC) No. 1488/94 as well as Council Directive 76/769/EEC and Commission Directives 91/155/EEC, 93/67/EEC, 93/105/EC and 2000/21/EC, [2006] O.J. L396/1. The Agency has its seat in Helsinki (see the Third Decision on Seats).

[561] Regulation (EC) No. 1922/2006 of the European Parliament and of the Council of December 20, 2006 on establishing a European Institute for Gender Equality, [2006] O.J. L403/9. The Institute has its seat in Vilnius (see Decision 2006/966/EC taken by common agreement between the representatives of the Governments of Member States of December 11, 2006 on the location of the seat of the European Institute for Gender Equality, [2006] O.J. L403/61), where it opened its offices on December 16, 2009 after being provisionally located in Brussels.

[562] Regulation (EU) No. 912/2010 of the European Parliament and of the Council of September 22, 2010, [2010] O.J. L276/11, replacing Council Regulation (EC) No. 1321/2004 of July 12, 2004 on the establishment of structures for the management of the European satellite radio-navigation programmes, [2004] O.J. L246/1. The agency has its seat in Prague (see Decision of the Representatives of the Governments of the Member States of December 10, 2010 [2010] O.J. L342/15).

(EIT),[563] the Agency for the Cooperation of Energy Regulators,[564] the Office of the Body of European Regulators for Electronic Communications (BEREC)[565] and the European Asylum Support Office.[566] As part of the accession process, candidate countries may be authorised to participate in Union agencies.[567]

In addition, for the purposes of managing Union programmes, the Commission may set up executive agencies with legal personality.[568] Accordingly, the Commission is now assisted by a number of "executive agencies".[569]

CFSP and PJCC bodies. A number of bodies have been set up in connection with the CFSP and PJCC, mostly under the non-Community provisions of the EU Treaty, before the entry into force of the Lisbon Treaty. The EU Treaty set up two committees, which prepare the Council's work in the areas of the CFSP and PJCC, respectively: the Political and Security Committee and the Coordinating Committee (see para. 13–058).

13–124

---

[563] Regulation (EC) No. 294/2008 of the European Parliament and of the Council of March 11, 2008 establishing the European Institute of Innovation and Technology, [2008] O.J. L97/1. The Institute has its seat in Budapest (see Decision 2008/634/EC taken by common agreement between the Representatives of the Governments of the Member States of June 18, 2008, [2008] O.J. L206/16).

[564] Regulation (EC) No. 713/2009 of the European Parliament and of the Council of July 13, 2009 establishing an Agency for the Cooperation of Energy Regulators [2009] O.J. L211/1. The Agency has its seat in Ljubljana (see Decision 2009/913/EU taken by common agreement between the Representatives of the Governments of the Member States of December 7, 2009 ([2009] O.J. L322/39)).

[565] Regulation (EC) No. 1211/2009 of the European Parliament and of the Council of November 25, 2009 establishing the Body of European Regulators for Electronic Communications, [2009] O.J. L337/1. The Office has its seat in Riga (see Decision 2010/349/EU taken by common agreement between the Representatives of the Governments of the Member States of May 31, 2010 ([2010] O.J. L156/12)).

[566] Regulation (EU) No. 439/2010 of the European Parliament and the Council of May 19, 2010 establishing a European Asylum Support Office, [2010] O.J. L 132/11. The agency has its seat in Valletta Harbour (see Decision of the Representatives of the Governments of the Member States, meeting within the Council, of February 25, 2010, [2010] O.J. L324/47).

[567] See, e.g., the agreements on the participation of each of the candidate countries in the European Environment Agency and the European environment information and observation network, [2001] O.J. L213.

[568] On the basis of Council Regulation (EC) No. 58/2003 of December 19, 2002 laying down the statute for executive agencies to be entrusted with certain tasks in the management of Community programmes, [2003] O.J. L11/1.

[569] See the Education, Audiovisual and Culture Executive Agency (EACEA, see Commission Decision 2009/336/EC of April 20, 2009, [2009] O.J. L101/26), the European Research Council Executive Agency (ERC, see Commission Decision 2008/37/EC of December 14, 2007, [2008] O.J. L9/15), the Executive Agency for Health and Consumers (EAHC, see Commission Decision 2008/544/EC of June 20, 2008, [2008] O.J. L173/27), the Research Executive Agency (REA, see Commission Decision 2008/46/EC of December 14, 2007, [2008] O.J. L11/9), the Executive Agency for Competitiveness and Innovation (EACI, see Commission Decision 2007/372/EC of May 31, 2007, [2007] O.J. L140/52) and the Transeuropean Transport Network Executive Agency (TEN-T; see Commission Decision 2007/60/EC of October 26, 2006, [2007] O.J. L32/88).

Under the CFSP, a number of bodies have been set up with legal personality pursuant to Art. 14 EU [*now Art. 28 TEU*]. These include an Institute for Security Studies (ISS)[570] and a European Union Satellite Centre (EUSC),[571] which have taken over structures already existing within the framework of the Western European Union (WEU), as well as a European Defence Agency (EDA).[572]

The provisions of the EU Treaty on cooperation in the fields of justice and home affairs envisaged the creation of a European Police Office (Europol). Europol was ultimately set up by a convention concluded between the Member States,[573] although the convention was replaced as from January 1, 2010 by a Council Decision.[574] At present, Europol carries out tasks in the context of PJCC as provided for in Art. 88 TFEU (see para. 10–020). Europol has legal personality.[575] Each Member State, as well as the Commission, has a representative on its Management Board with one vote. The Management Board acts, in principle, by a majority of two-thirds of its members.[576] A Director is responsible for day-to-day administration and for representing Europol.[577] The Second Decision on the Seats of the Institutions of October 29, 1993 provided that Europol and the existing Europol Drugs Unit were to have their seat at The Hague.[578] Legal personality has also been conferred on the European Police College (see para. 10–020).

The Treaty of Nice amended the JHA provisions of the EU Treaty so as to attribute tasks to Eurojust, an entity which was set up by the Council as a body with legal personality even before the Treaty of Nice entered into force.[579] Its tasks are now set out in Art. 85 TFEU. Eurojust is composed of one national member seconded by each Member State in accordance with its legal system,

---

[570] Council Joint Action 2001/554/CFSP of July 20, 2001 on the establishment of a European Union Institute for Security Studies, [2001] O.J. L200/1. The institute has its seat in Paris.

[571] Council Joint Action 2001/555/CFSP of July 20, 2001 on the establishment of a European Union Satellite Centre, [2001] O.J. L200/5. The centre is established at Torrejón de Ardoz (Spain). Denmark is not taking part in those activities of the centre which have implications for defence policy.

[572] Council Joint Action 2004/551/CFSP of July 12, 2004 on the establishment of the European Defence Agency, [2004] O.J. L245/17. The Agency has its seat in Brussels. Denmark is not bound by this Joint Action.

[573] Convention of July 26, 1995, based on the former Art. K.3 of the Treaty on European Union, on the establishment of a European Police Office (Europol Convention), [1995] O.J. C316/2, as amended by Council Act of November 28, 2002 ([2002] O.J. C312/1) and Council Act of November 27, 2003 ([2004] O.J. C2/1).

[574] Council Decision 2009/371/JHA of April 6, 2009 establishing the European Police Office (Europol), [2009] O.J. L121/37. See Roland and Buyssens, "La transformation d'Europol en agence de l'Union—Regards sur un nouveau cadre juridique" (2009) R.M.CU.E. 83–87.

[575] *Ibid.*, Art. 2(1).

[576] *Ibid.* Art. 31(1) and (8). Under the Europol Convention, virtually all its decisions had to be taken unanimously.

[577] *Ibid.*, Art. 38. For the internal organisation of Europol, see Gless, "Kontrolle über Europol und seine Bedienstete" (1998) EuR. 748–766.

[578] See the Protocol on Seats, Sole Art., para. (j) and Art. 1 of Council Decision 2009/371.

[579] Council Decision 2002/187/JHA of February 28, 2002 setting up Eurojust with a view to reinforcing the fight against serious crime ([2002] O.J. L63/1). See now Art. 85 TFEU [*ex Art. 31 EU*].

being a prosecutor, judge or police officer of equivalent competence.[580] The national members form a college under the chairmanship of a member chosen from amongst their number. Each national member has one vote and votes are taken in accordance with the rules of procedure.[581] As in the case of Europol, the Commission is to be fully associated with the work of Eurojust and the daily management is ensured by an Administrative Director.[582] The seat of Eurojust is likewise located at The Hague.[583] Since the Treaty of Lisbon, the Treaties envisage, moreover, the establishment of a European Public Prosecutor's Office from Eurojust (Art. 86 TFEU; see para. 10–025).

Connected bodies. The Member States have also, by convention, set up a number of bodies which fall outside the framework of the Treaties, yet are closely connected with them. These are the European University Institute in Florence[584] and the various European Schools.[585] The Union is represented in the management of those bodies and the EU budget covers costs not paid by the Member States.[586] As a result of the latter aspect, a Member State which acts in breach of the Statute of the European Schools thereby producing a burden on the EU budget, also infringes Art. 4(3) TEU.[587]

13–125

---

[580] *Ibid.*, Art. 2.

[581] *Ibid.*, Arts 10, 28 and 29. For the Rules of Procedure of May 30, 2002, see [2002] O.J. C286/1.

[582] *Ibid.*, Art. 11.

[583] See Art. 1(c) of the Third Decision on Seats (para. 13–154, *infra*). From the outset, it carried out its activities in that city on a provisional basis in accordance with recital 17 in the preamble to the decision establishing Eurojust.

[584] Convention of April 19, 1972 setting up a European University Institute, [1976] O.J. C29/1 [the Convention]. Article 9 EAEC, which provides for the establishment of "an institution of university status", has never been implemented.

[585] See the establishment of a European School in Luxembourg by the Statute of the European School of April 12, 1957 and in other places of work of institutions and bodies by the Protocol on the establishment of European Schools of April 13, 1962 adopted pursuant to that Statute. For the United Kingdom, see the European Communities (European Schools) Order 1972, the European Communities (Definition of Treaties) (European School) Order 1990 and the European Communities (Privileges of the European School) Order 1990. The 1962 protocol has been replaced by the Convention of June 21, 1994 defining the Statute of the European Schools, [1994] O.J. L212/3 [the Statute] (this convention was concluded between the Member States and the three Communities; it was ratified on behalf of the EC and the EAEC by a Council decision of June 17, 1994 pursuant to Art. 235 EC [*now Art. 352 TFEU*] and Art. 203 EAEC and on behalf of the ECSC by a Commission decision based on the first para. of Art. 95 ECSC).

[586] See the representative of the Union on the High Council of the European University Institute (Convention, Art. 6(3); the representative does not have voting rights) and the Union representative on the Board of Governors of the European Schools (Statute, Art. 8(1); that representative does have the right to vote) and the Union's contribution towards operating costs (provided for in Art. 19(2) of the Convention and Art. 25(2) of the Statute).

[587] ECJ, Case 44/84 *Hurd* [1986] E.C.R. 29, paras 36–45; ECJ, Case C-6/89 *Commission v Belgium* [1990] E.C.R. I-1595 (para. 7–049, *supra*). *Cf.* ECJ (judgment of September 30, 2010), Case C-132/09 *Commission v Belgium*, not yet reported.

IV. Administrative Organisation

A. The position of the Union under the domestic legal systems of the Member States

13–126 **Legal personality and legal capacity.** The Treaties confer legal personality on the Union (Art. 47 TEU). Before the Lisbon Treaty, the Treaties conferred legal personality on each of the Communities (Art. 281 EC; Art. 184 EAEC; see also Art. 6 ECSC), but not on the European Union, although the latter was widely considered to have functional legal personality (see para. 24–002). Under Art. 1, third para., TEU, the European Union replaces and succeeds the European Community. The European Atomic Energy Community continues to exist as an entity with its own legal personality (see para. 4–009). The fact that the Union has legal personality means in the first place that the Union is a subject of international law (see para. 24–002). Secondly, it enjoys the most extensive legal capacity accorded to legal persons governed by public law[588] under the laws of the Member States, in particular to acquire or dispose of property and to be a party to legal proceedings (Art. 335 TFEU).[589]

The fact that the Union has legal capacity and the capacity to enter into transactions means that it may also sue and be sued. Thus, the Union may appear before the national courts, except in disputes which, under the Treaties, have to be brought before the Court of Justice. In this way, the Union Courts have exclusive jurisdiction to entertain damages claims for non-contractual liability based on the second para. of Art. 340 TFEU.[590] Since the national courts have no jurisdiction to entertain such claims, they are likewise not entitled to prescribe, with regard to one of the institutions, any interim measure or measure of inquiry (e.g., commissioning an expert report) whose purpose is to establish the role of that institution in the events which allegedly caused damage.[591]

The ECB and any body, office or agency of the Union with legal personality in its own right takes part in domestic legal transactions in the Member States independently. It may participate in legal proceedings before the competent national courts, provided that the disputes do not come within the jurisdiction of the Court of Justice.[592] Thus disputes based on non-contractual liability are generally

---

[588] See ECJ, Joined Cases 43/59, 45/59 and 48/59 *Von Lachmüller and Others v Commission* [1960] E.C.R. 463, at 472; ECJ, Case 44/59 *Fiddelaar v Commission* [1960] E.C.R. 535, at 543.

[589] See also Art. 185 EAEC.

[590] In addition to the jurisdiction of the Court of Justice to entertain claims for damage caused by Union institutions or the ECB or their servants (non-contractual liability: Arts 268 and 340 TFEU), there are also staff disputes (Art. 270 TFEU) and disputes brought before the Court pursuant to arbitration clauses (Art. 272 TFEU). See in this connection Lenaerts, Arts and Maselis, *Procedural Law of the European Union* (3rd edn, London, Sweet & Maxwell, 2012), Chs 11, 16 and 17.

[591] ECJ, Case C-275/00 *Frist and Franex* [2002] E.C.R. I-10943, paras 43–48.

[592] See, e.g., ESCB Statute, Art. 35; EIB Statute, Art. 27.

governed by the system of liability determined by the second para. of Art. 340 TFEU.[593]

Representation of the Union. In the domestic legal systems of the Member States, the Union is, in principle, represented by the Commission. However, it may also be represented by each of the institutions, by virtue of their administrative autonomy, in matters relating to their respective operation (Art. 335 TFEU[594]). In principle, the Commission is thus empowered to act before the national courts, but it may authorise another institution to do so.[595]   **13–127**

Privileges and immunities. In common with other international organisations, the Union enjoys privileges and immunities with a view to its being able to carry out its tasks undisturbed. These privileges and immunities—enshrined in a Protocol appended to the Treaties in accordance with Art. 343 TFEU[596]—have a purely functional character: they are intended to avoid any interference with the functioning and independence of the Union.[597]   **13–128**

In addition to conferring privileges and immunities on members of the institutions and on officials and other servants of the Union,[598] the Protocol provides that the Union's premises, buildings and archives are inviolable, exempt from search, requisition, confiscation or appropriation and not to be the subject of any administrative or legal measure of constraint without the authorisation of the Court of Justice (Arts 1 and 2). As far as garnishee orders are concerned, the jurisdiction of the Court of Justice is confined to considering whether such a measure is likely to interfere with the proper functioning and the independence of the European Union.[599] For the rest, the garnishee procedure is governed by the applicable

---

[593] See, e.g., Art. 35.3 of the ESCB Statute and Art. 21(2) of Regulation No. 58/2003 (n. 568, *supra*).

[594] Before the Lisbon Treaty, Art. 282 EC stated that the Community was to be represented by the Commission. In practice, however, the other institutions also engaged in domestic legal transactions, in particular pursuant to their power to engage in expenditure authorised under the budget (see para. 13–147).

[595] For details of the Commission's involvement in legal proceedings, see the Commission's answer of July 11, 1988 to question 2/88 (Dury), [1989] O.J. C24/10.

[596] See now Protocol (No. 7), annexed to the TEU, TFEU and EAEC Treaty, on the Privileges and Immunities of the European Union, [2010] O.J. C83/266, which replaced Protocol (No. 36), appended by the Member States to the EC Treaty in accordance with Art. 291 EC, on the Privileges and Immunities of the European Communities (enacted in the United Kingdom by the European Communities Act 1972). Article 291 EC took over the wording of Art. 28 of the Merger Treaty as a result of the simplification introduced by the Amsterdam Treaty. See Schmidt, "Le Protocole sur les privilèges et immunités des Communautés européennes" (1991) C.D.E. 67–99.

[597] ECJ, Case C-2/88 Imm. *Zwartveld and Others* [1990] E.C.R. I-3365, paras 19–20.

[598] For the status of members of the institutions, see paras 13–156—13–157, *infra*; for the status of officials and other servants of the Union, see paras 13–158—13–159, *infra*.

[599] ECJ (order of June 17, 1987), Case 1/87 SA *Universal Tankship* [1987] E.C.R. 2807, para. 3; ECJ, Case 1/88 SA *Générale de Banque v Commission* [1989] E.C.R. 857, para. 15 (the case numbers include the initials SA for the French "*saisie-arrêt*").

national law. In addition, the Union is exempt from direct taxes (Art. 3, first para.) and from customs duties and restrictions on imports and exports (Art. 4). Under bilateral arrangements with Member States, appropriate measures are to be taken to remit or refund indirect taxes paid on purchases made by the Union for its official use (see Art. 3, second para.). This includes all types of purchase, including obtaining a supply of services, which are necessary for the accomplishment of the Union's task, but it is required that the indirect taxes should be included in the purchase price.[600] This exemption does not apply to taxes levied on parties contracting with the Union, even when such tax is passed on to the Union.[601]

In order to secure their independence, the ECB, the EIB and other Union bodies with legal personality are also covered by the Protocol on Privileges and Immunities.[602] As a result of their connection with the Union, the ECB and the EIB do not have the same status as other similar international organisations.[603]

As far as Europol[604] and bodies set up in connection with the CFSP[605] are concerned, the necessary privileges and immunities have been laid down in an agreement concluded between the Member States. This also applies to the military and civilian personnel whom the Member States make available for CFSP activities of the European Union.[606]

B. THE BUDGET OF THE UNION

13–129   **General budget.** Each year a general budget is drawn up,[607] which since 1994 has been entitled the "general budget of the European Union". This is done in

---

[600] ECJ, Case C-199/05 *European Community v Belgian State* [2006] E.C.R. I-10485, paras 31–44.

[601] ECJ, Case C-437/04 *Commission v Belgium* [2007] E.C.R. I-2513, paras 48–63.

[602] For the EIB and the ECB, see Art. 343 TFEU, and Arts 21 and 22 of the Protocol and Art. 39 of the ESCB Statute. For the executive agencies set up pursuant to Regulation No. 58/2003 (n. 568, *supra*), see Art. 17 of that regulation. As far as other bodies and agencies are concerned, see the regulations establishing them referred to in para. 13–125, *supra*.

[603] See Schermers (1988) C.M.L.Rev. 617, at 625–626 (note to ECJ, Case 85/86 *Commission v European Investment Bank* [1988] E.C.R. 1281 concerning the tax levied on EIB salaries which should accrue to the Communities, para. 13–158, *infra*).

[604] Protocol of June 19, 1997 on the privileges and immunities of Europol, the members of its organs, the deputy directors and employees of Europol ([1997] O.J. C221/2), drawn up, on the basis of the former Art. K.3 of the EU Treaty and Art. 41 of the Europol Convention (n. 573, *supra*), to be adopted by the Member States in accordance with their respective constitutional requirements. At present, Art. 51(1) of Council Decision 2009/371/JHA (see n. 574, *supra*) makes the Protocol on the Privileges and Immunities applicable. For a critical view, see Ellermann, "Von Sammler zu Jäger—Europol auf dem Weg zu einem 'europäischen FBI'?" (2002) Z.Eu.S. 561, at 580–582.

[605] For the European Institute for Security Studies, see Art. 15 of Council Joint Action 2001/554/CFSP of July 20, 2001 (n. 570, *supra*); for the Satellite Centre, see Art. 16 of Council Joint Action 2001/555/CFSP of July 20, 2001 (n. 571, *supra*); for the European Defence Agency, see Art. 26 of Council Joint Action 2004/551/CFSP of July 12, 2004 (n. 572, *supra*).

[606] See the agreement between the EU Member States of November 17, 2003, [2003] O.J. C321/6.

[607] See Art. 9(6) of the Amsterdam Treaty which took over Art. 20(1) of the Merger Treaty.

accordance with specific Treaty articles and with the Financial Regulation which the Council adopted pursuant to Art. 279 EC [*now Art. 322 TFEU*].[608] The European Parliament and the Council work together in drawing up the budget, thereby constituting together the "budgetary authority".

1. Content of the budget

(a) *General principles*

Scope of the budget. In principle, all items of revenue and expenditure for each financial year are to be included in estimates and shown in the budget (Art. 310 TFEU). Both administrative expenditure and operating expenditure are charged to the general budget.[609] However, in the case of the CFSP the Council may decide, by unanimous vote, that operating expenditure will not be charged to the general budget.[610] Operational expenditure arising from operations having military or defence implications is always borne by the Member States (Art. 41(2), first sub-para., TEU). Where expenditure is charged to the Member States, it is allocated in accordance with the GNP scale, unless the Council decides otherwise by a unanimous vote (Art. 41(2), second subpara., TEU).[611] Member States which have abstained by formal declaration from CFSP decisions under the second subpara. of Art. 31(1) are not obliged to contribute to the financing of operations having

13–130

---

[608] Financial Regulation applicable to the general budget of the European Communities, as most recently laid down by Council Regulation (EC, Euratom) No. 1605/2002 of June 25, 2002, [2002] O.J. L248/1 (*corrigendum* in [2003] O.J. L25/43). For general discussions of this subject, see Lindner, *Conflict and change in EU budgetary politics* (Abingdon, Routledge, 2006), 265 pp.; Walder, *The Budgetary Procedure of the European Economic Community* (Vienna, Böhlau, 1992), 122 pp.; Strasser, *The Finances of Europe* (Luxembourg, Office for Official Publications of the EC, 1991), 439 pp.; Van Craeyenest and Saarilahti, "Le nouveau règlement financier applicable au budget général de l'Union européenne: un maillon essentiel dans la réforme de la Commission" (2004) R.M.C.U.E. 30–51;

[609] The distinction between these two types of expenditure dates back to the ECSC: since the ECSC financed its expenditure out of levies on the coal and steel sectors, its budget was divided into administrative expenditure, which came under the general budget, and operating expenditure, which was covered by a separate budget.

[610] See Art. 41(2) TEU. Administrative expenditure is always charged to the general budget (Art. 41(1) TEU). That system already existed before the Lisbon Treaty (see Art. 41(3) EU). See also the interinstitutional agreement concluded by the European Parliament, the Council and the Commission on July 16, 1997 on provisions regarding the financing of the CFSP (1997) 7/8 EU Bull. point 2.3.1; para. 13–139, *infra*. Initially, the EU Treaty determined, as far as the CFSP (and JHA cooperation) was concerned, that operational expenditure could be charged to the EU budget *only if* the Council so decided by unanimous vote. In practice, the Council decided virtually always that it should be so charged with the result that in fact operational expenditure was invariably charged to the budget unless the Council decided otherwise.

[611] Reference is made to the GNP scale in Art. 23 of Council Decision 2008/975/CFSP of December 18, 2008 establishing a mechanism to administer the financing of the common costs of European Union operations having military or defence implications (Athena), [2008] O.J. L345/96.

military or defence implications (Art. 41(2), second subpara., TEU).[612] Furthermore, Member States are only obliged to pay their share of the institutions' administrative costs in some instances in which the Treaties authorise them not to take part in the operations in question.[613]

13–131   **Separate budgets.** A further exception to the "unity" of the budget is loans incurred or made by the Union and the activities of the European Central Bank,[614] the European Investment Bank,[615] the Supply Agency and the EAEC Joint Undertakings.[616] Bodies and agencies having legal personality in their own right have their own budgets, which may be mentioned in the general budget as an explanation for the subsidy granted to such bodies and agencies by the Commission.[617] This is also true of Europol and, partially, of Eurojust.[618] However, the CFSP bodies have their own budget, financed by contributions from the Member States.[619] Since the Financial Regulation provides for consultation of the European Parliament on the determination of Union expenditure, the Parliament exercises supervision to make sure that such expenditure is actually incorporated in the budget.[620] In the case of other expenditure assumed by the

---

[612] This applies in any case to Denmark under Art. 5 of the Protocol (No. 22), annexed to the TEU and TFEU, on the position of Denmark, [2010] O.J. C83/299. See, e.g., the exception for Denmark Council Decision 2008/975/CFSP of December 18, 2008 (n. 611, *supra*) and in respect of the Member States' contributions for the satellite centre: Art. 12(3) of Council Joint Action 2001/555/CFSP of July 20, 2001 (n. 571, *supra*).

[613] Thus, there is no obligation for Member States to contribute towards the financing of expenditure in respect of enhanced cooperation if they do not participate therein, with the exception of the administrative costs entailed for the institutions, unless the Council, acting unanimously, decides otherwise (Art. 332 TFEU). By the same token, Art. 5 of Protocol (No. 21), annexed to the TEU and TFEU, on the position of the United Kingdom and Ireland in respect of the Area of Freedom, Security and Justice ([2010] O.J. C83/295) provides that a Member State not bound by a measure adopted pursuant to Title V of Part Three of the TFEU is to bear no financial consequences of that measure other than administrative costs entailed for the institutions, unless the Council unanimously decides otherwise.

[614] ESCB Statute, Arts 26 and 27.

[615] See EIB Statute, Art. 7(3)(f) and Art. 12.

[616] Article 171(2) and (3) EAEC.

[617] See the acts establishing those bodies and agencies mentioned in paras 13–123—13–125, *supra*, as amended by the Council on July 22, 2003 ([2003] O.J. L245); for the executive agencies set up pursuant to Regulation No. 58/2003 (n. 568, *supra*), see Art.12 of that regulation.

[618] For Europol, see Art. 42 of Council Decision 2009/371/JHA (n. 574, *supra*). Initially, pursuant to Art. 35 of the Europol Convention (n. 573, *supra*), Europol had its own budget financed by contributions from the Member States. For Eurojust, see Art. 34 and recital 4 of Council Decision 2002/187/JHA (n. 579, *supra*), as supplemented by the Council on July 22, 2003 ([2003] O.J. L245/44).

[619] For the European Union Institute for Security Studies and the European Union Satellite Centre, see Art. 11 of Joint Action 2001/554/CFSP (n. 570, *supra*) and Art. 12 of Joint Action 2001/555/CFSP (n. 571, *supra*); for the European Defence Agency, see Art. 13 of Joint Action 2004/551/CFSP (n. 572, *supra*).

[620] See ECJ, Case C-316/91 *European Parliament v Council* [1994] E.C.R. I-625, paras 16–19.

Member States, such as expenditure of the European Development Fund, the States operate by mutual agreement and there is nothing to prevent them from using procedural steps drawing on the rules applicable to Union expenditure and from associating the Union institutions with the procedure thus set up.[621]

Structure of the budget. In accordance with the annual nature of the budget, it contains the revenue resulting from the amounts collected during the financial year[622] and the expenditure authorised for the financial year in question.[623] The financial year runs from January 1, to December 31.[624] The general budget of the Union is published annually in a voluminous issue of the *Official Journal*. The expenditure of Union institutions is set out in separate sections of the budget.[625] The revenue and expenditure of other bodies are fully covered by the budgetary sections of the Commission.[626] Under the chapters of each section, expenditure is grouped into items according to its nature or purpose and subdivided in accordance with the Financial Regulation.[627] The budget is drawn up in euros,[628] even though the financial transactions are not necessarily carried out in that currency.

13–132

Budgetary principles. The budget is otherwise constructed in accordance with the classical rules governing public finances. Revenue is to be used without distinction to finance all expenditure entered in the budget (the so-called universality principle).[629] In addition, revenue and expenditure may not be adjusted against each other.[630] Expenditure must be carried out in accordance with the classification into budget items approved by the budgetary authority (the so-called principle of specialisation). Accordingly, any transfer of appropriations from one title to another and from one chapter to another is subject in principle to the budgetary authority's

13–133

---

[621] *Ibid.*, paras 38–42. For the European Development Fund, see paras 25–017 and 25–026, *infra*. The European Parliament considers that the EDF should be incorporated into the Union budget: see its resolution of July 12, 1995, [1995] O.J. C249/68.

[622] Financial Regulation, Art. 8(1).

[623] Under the first para. of Art. 316 TFEU, the Financial Regulation provides for exceptions for unexpended appropriations.

[624] Article 313 TFEU.

[625] See Art. 316, third para., TFEU [*ex Art. 271, fourth para., EC*], as elaborated in Arts 40 to 45 of the Financial Regulation, which provides for separate sections for all institutions and, by virtue of Art. 1 of the Financial Regulation, also for the European Economic and Social Committee, the Committee of the Regions, the European Ombudsman and the Data-Protection Supervisor.

[626] Financial Regulation, Arts 171 to 176.

[627] Article 316, second para., TFEU.

[628] Article 320 TFEU; Financial Regulation, Art. 16.

[629] Article 6 of the Sixth Decision on Own Resources (para. 13–134, *infra*) and Art. 17 of the Financial Regulation. Exceptions to that principle are contained in Art. 18 of the Financial Regulation.

[630] Financial Regulation, Art. 17. Exceptions to that principle are contained in Art. 20 of the Financial Regulation.

approval.[631] Lastly, the Treaties require the budget to be in balance as to revenue and expenditure.[632] If at the end of the financial year, there is a shortfall or a surplus of revenue over expenditure, the deficit or the surplus is carried over to the subsequent year's budget.[633]

(b) *Revenue*

13–134   **Own resources.** The revenue side of the budget covers the Union's own resources. The ECSC operated from the outset with its own resources, consisting of levies on the production of coal and steel. In common with most international organisations, the EEC and the EAEC initially only had financial contributions from the Member States, although the Treaties put the Commission under a duty to investigate a system of own resources.[634] Such a system eventually resulted from the First Decision on Own Resources of April 21, 1970.[635] Since that system meant that considerable financial resources were taken outside the scope of national supervision, its adoption was coupled with the grant of budgetary powers to the European Parliament. To this end, the First Treaty on Budgetary Provisions of April 22, 1970 amended the Communities' budgetary procedure.[636] The system was adjusted by the consecutive "Decisions on Own Resources",[637] which, in accordance with Art. 269 EC [the former *Art. 201 EEC; now Art. 311 TFEU*], were adopted by the Council on a proposal from the Commission after consulting the European

---

[631] Financial Regulation, Art. 24. Nevertheless, the Financial Regulation provides for a degree of flexibility of management so as to permit the assignment of financial and administrative means by purpose ("activity based budgeting"); see Arts 22 and 23 of the Financial Regulation.

[632] Article 310(1), third para., TFEU.

[633] Financial Regulation, Art. 15. That budgetary principle, which is also expressed in Art. 7 of the Sixth Decision on Own Resources, takes priority over the provision of the First Decision on Own Resources according to which a percentage of the VAT basis of assessment is to accrue to the Community as own resources. Where a surplus in revenue is carried over in full to the next financial year this increases the revenue for that financial year, which means that a lower rate may be applied to the VAT basis of assessment: ECJ, Case C-284/90 *Council v European Parliament* [1992] E.C.R. I-2277, para. 31; note by Van den Bossche (1994) C.M.L.Rev. 653–668.

[634] See Art. 201 EEC, and Art. 173 EAEC (old version).

[635] Council Decision 70/243/ECSC/EEC/Euratom of April 21, 1970 on the replacement of financial contributions from Member States by the Communities' own resources, [1970] O.J. English Spec. Ed. (I) 224.

[636] Treaty of April 22, 1970 amending Certain Budgetary Provisions of the Treaties establishing the European Communities and of the Treaty establishing a Single Council and a Single Commission of the European Communities; for the text in English, see Treaties establishing the European Communities (Luxembourg, Office for Official Publications of the EC, 1978), at 855.

[637] See Council Decision 85/257 of May 7, 1985 on the system of the Communities' own resources, [1985] O.J. L128/15 (Second Decision on Own Resources); Council Decision 88/376 of June 24, 1988 on the system of the Communities' own resources. (Third Decision on Own Resources); Council Decision 94/728 of October 31, 1994 on the system of the Communities' own resources, [1994] O.J. L293/9 (Fourth Decision on Own Resources); Council Decision 2000/597/EC, Euratom of September 29, 2000 on the system of the Communities' own resources, [2000] O.J. L253/42 (Fifth Decision on Own Resources).

Parliament and then adopted by the Member States in accordance with their respective constitutional requirements. The most recent arrangements are laid down in the Sixth Decision on Own Resources of June 7, 2007.[638]

Article 311, second para., TFEU provides that, without prejudice to other revenue, the budget is to be financed wholly from own resources. Implementing measures for the Union's own resources system are laid down by the Council, acting by a qualified majority after obtaining the consent of the European Parliament (Art. 311, fourth para., TFEU).

Revenue sources. The Union's own resources consist of three sources of revenue:

13–135

(1) levies, Common Customs Tariff duties, anti-dumping duties and other duties established within the framework of trade with third countries as well as contributions and other duties provided for within the framework of the common organisation of the markets in sugar;

(2) the application of a uniform rate to the VAT assessment base; and

(3) the application of a rate to be determined pursuant to the budgetary procedure to the sum of all the Member States' gross national income (GNI).[639]

The first of these sources is to be collected by the Member States, which may retain a predetermined percentage (25 per cent) of the amounts collected by way of collection costs.[640]

Correction mechanism. Unlike the first "traditional" source of income, the second source was not introduced until after the Sixth VAT Directive of May 17, 1977 harmonised the VAT basis of assessment throughout the Community.[641] The VAT assessment basis to be taken into account for each Member State may not exceed 50 per cent of the gross national income (GNI) of that State.[642] The maximum rate applied to the VAT assessment base was to be reduced from 1 per cent

13–136

---

[638] Council Decision 2007/436/EC, Euratom of June 7, 2007 on the system of the European Communities' own resources, [2007] O.J. L163/17.

[639] Sixth Decision on Own-Resources, Art. 2(1).

[640] Sixth Decision on Own-Resources, Arts 2(3) and 8. See ECJ, Case C-392/02 *Commission v Denmark* [2005] E.C.R. I-9811, paras 54–69 (Member States must establish the Communities' own resources as soon as their customs authorities are in a position to calculate the amount of duties arising from a customs debt and determine the debtor).

[641] Sixth Council Directive (77/388/EEC) of May 17, 1977 on the harmonisation of the laws of the Member States relating to turnover taxes—Common system of value added tax: uniform basis of assessment, [1977] O.J. L145/1, now replaced by Council Directive 2006/112/EC of November 28, 2006 on the common system of value added tax, [2006] O.J. L347/1.

[642] Sixth Decision on Own-Resources, Art. 2(1)b.

in 2001 to 0.75 per cent in 2002, to 0.50 per cent in 2004 and to 0.30 per cent in 2007.[643] After the United Kingdom repeatedly complained that it was paying much more into the budget than the Communities spent in that country, a hard-won compromise was reached by the European Council meeting at Fontainebleau on June 25 and 26, 1984 whereby the British VAT contribution was reduced and the contributions of other Member States increased, although Germany benefited by a more advantageous regime as it refused to finance the concession to the United Kingdom in full. The "correction of budgetary imbalances" was incorporated in the Second Decision on Own Resources, subsequently extended and amended by the Fifth Decision on Own Resources so as to diminish the share of Community financing, not only for Germany, but also for Austria, the Netherlands and Sweden. The third category of own resources was introduced by the Third Decision on Own Resources in order to cope with rising expenditure on the part of the Communities. The rate of the contribution is determined under the budgetary procedure in the light of revenue from all other sources and of the expenditure anticipated in the financial year. The correction mechanism also applies to this category of own resources. The total amount of own resources assigned to the Communities was fixed by the Sixth Decision on own resources at 1.24 per cent of the sum of all the Member States' GNIs; in case of significant changes in the GNIs, this ceiling can be recalculated by the Commission in accordance with a formula laid down in the decision.[644]

13–137   **Other revenue.** In addition, there is miscellaneous revenue, such as the proceeds of the Union tax on officials' salaries,[645] the fines imposed by the Commission for contraventions of the competition rules[646] and the lump sums and penalty payments which may be imposed on the Member States in application of Art. 260 TFEU [*ex Art. 228 EC*].

(c) *Expenditure*

13–138   **Compulsory and non-compulsory expenditure.** Traditionally, the Communities' expenditure was divided into compulsory and non-compulsory expenditure. Compulsory expenditure was expenditure necessarily resulting from the Treaties or from acts adopted in accordance therewith. All other expenditure was non-compulsory. The distinction was important in so far as the European Parliament had the last word on non-compulsory expenditure (see Art. 272(6) EC; see

---

[643] Sixth Decision on Own-Resources, Art. 2(4).

[644] Sixth Decision on Own Resources, Art. 3.

[645] See Art. 12 of the Protocol on Privileges and Immunities, the regulations on the emoluments of members of the institutions, the Staff Regulations and the Rules applicable to other servants and Regulation No. 260/68 on the tax for the benefit of the European Communities, para. 13–158, *infra*.

[646] See, inter alia, Arts 17 and 18 of Regulation No. 11/60, Arts 23 and 24 of Regulation No. 1/2003 and Arts 14 and 15 of Regulation No. 139/2004 (paras 11–014—11–016, *supra*).

para. 13–141 *et seq.*). This gave the Parliament a say in matters over which it would not otherwise have much influence, for instance where the Union charged action under the CFSP or PJCC to the EU budget. Given the political stake, the Parliament and the Council were often at loggerheads about the classification of expenditure.

However, the Lisbon Treaty introduced a new procedure for the adoption of the budget, which gives the European Parliament a final say over all expenditure. Consequently, the distinction between compulsory and non-compulsory expenditure is now only of historical interest.

As regards the distinction between compulsory and non-compulsory expenditure, the European Parliament, the Council and the Commission set out in a Joint Declaration of June 30, 1982 a classification of expenditure and a procedure for reaching agreement on the classification of new budget items.[647] As far as expenditure under the CFSP is concerned, the European Parliament and the Council decided on June 16, 1997 to classify such expenditure as non-compulsory expenditure.[648] These agreements were incorporated in the Interinstitutional Agreements subsequently concluded between the European Parliament, the Council and the Commission.[649] For CFSP expenditure, the European Parliament and the Council were to secure each year agreement on the amount and its distribution within the relevant budget chapter. In the absence of agreement, the amount contained in the previous budget for the CFSP was to be taken over unless the Commission proposed a lower amount.[650] The constraints resulting from the financial perspective adopted (see para. 13–139) made the distinction between compulsory and non-compulsory expenditure less important in practical terms. Nevertheless, disputes arose between the institutions from time to time in connection with the classification of budgetary expenditure.[651]

Budgetary discipline. In order to keep expenditure under control, the European Council decided in 1988 to impose strict budgetary discipline. The practical upshot of this was a Council Decision and an Interinstitutional Agreement between the European Parliament, the Council and the Commission.[652] Together

13–139

---

[647] Joint Declaration by the European Parliament, the Council and the Commission of June 30, 1982 on various measures to improve the budgetary procedure, [1982] O.J. C194/1.

[648] Interinstitutional Agreement of July 16, 1997 on the financing of the CFSP (1997) 7/8 EU Bull. point 2.3.1; see also [1997] O.J. C286/80, point B. This applies both to administrative and policy expenditure.

[649] See, most recently, the interinstitutional Agreement of May 17, 2006 between the European Parliament, the Council and the Commission on budgetary discipline and sound financial management, [2006] O.J. C139/1.

[650] *Ibid.*, point 42.

[651] See ECJ, Case C-41/95 *Council v European Parliament* [1995] ECR I-4411, paras 1–31.

[652] Interinstitutional Agreement of June 29, 1988 on budgetary discipline and improvement of the budgetary procedure, [1988] O.J. L185/33; Council Decision 88/377/EEC of June 24, 1988 on budgetary discipline, [1988] O.J. L185/29.

with every new Decision on Own Resources, the Council adopted a decision or regulation on budgetary discipline.[653] Likewise, interinstitutional agreements have been concluded between the European Parliament, the Council and the Commission to ensure budgetary discipline and to lay down the financial perspectives on which the European Council had reached a political agreement.[654] The most recent interinstitutional agreement, of May 17, 2006, contains the financial perspectives for 2007–2013.[655] Apart from technical adjustments, the financial perspective may be revised only by agreement between the European Parliament and the Council on a proposal from the Commission.[656] Such interinstitutional agreements facilitate decision-making, but do not affect the respective budgetary powers of the institutions as laid down in the Treaties.[657]

The Treaty of Lisbon replaced the system of multiannual financial perspectives by a system of multiannual financial frameworks, established for a period of at least five years (Art. 312 TFEU). The Council is to adopt a regulation laying down this financial framework, acting unanimously after obtaining the consent of the European Parliament, which requires a majority of its component members. The regulation laying down the multiannual financial framework will replace the major part of the existing Interinstitutional Agreement, so that the new Interinstitutional Agreement to be concluded will remain relevant for interinstitutional purposes

---

[653] Council Decision 94/729/EC of October 31, 1994 on budgetary discipline, [1994] O.J. L293/14; Council Regulation (EC) No. 2040/2000 of September 26, 2000 on budgetary discipline, [2000] O.J. L244/27, repealed by Council Regulation (EC) No. 1248/2007 of October 22, 2007, [2007] O.J. L282/3. For the first application of Regulation No. 2040/2000, see Grossir, "La procédure budgétaire pour 2001: un long fleuve tranquille?" (2001) R.M.C.U.E. 374–396.

[654] See Interinstitutional Agreement of June 29, 1988 on budgetary discipline and improvement of the budgetary procedure, [1988] O.J. L185/33; Interinstitutional Agreement of October 29, 1993 on budgetary discipline and improvement of the budgetary procedure, [1993] O.J. C331/1; Interinstitutional Agreement of May 6, 1999 between the European Parliament, the Council and the Commission on budgetary discipline and improvement of the budgetary procedure, [1999] O.J. C172/1. See Chevalier, "L'accord interinstitutionnel du 6 mai 1999 et les perspectives financiers 2000–2006: de nouvelles ambitions pour l'Union européenne" (2000) R.M.C.U.E. 441–460 and 524–532; Godet, "Le nouveau 'code de procédure budgétaire' de l'Union européenne" (2000) R.T.D.E. 273–298. The 1999 agreement was supplemented by, inter alia, the Interinstitutional Agreement of November 7, 2002 between the European Parliament, the Council and the Commission on the financing of the European Union Solidarity Fund ([2003] O.J. C283/1) and the Interinstitutional Agreement of February 28, 2002 on the financing of the Convention on the future of the European Union ([2002] O.J. C54/1; extended by Interinstitutional Agreement of December 12, 2002, [2002] O.J. C320/1).

[655] Interinstitutional Agreement of May 17, 2006 between the European Parliament, the Council and the Commission on budgetary discipline and sound financial management, [2006] O.J. C139/1.

[656] Ibid., points 21–24. See, e.g., Decision 2009/407/EC of the European Parliament and of the Council of May 6, 2009 amending the Interinstitutional Agreement of May 17, 2006 on budgetary discipline and sound financial management as regards the multiannual financial framework (2007 to 2013), [2009] O.J. L132/8.

[657] Ibid., point 3.

only.[658] The European Council, acting unanimously, may adopt a decision allowing the Council to lay down the financial framework by a qualified majority (Art. 312(2) TFEU). The financial framework determines the amounts of the annual ceilings on commitment appropriations by category of expenditure[659] and the amount of the annual ceiling on payment appropriations. It is further to lay down any other provisions required for the annual budgetary procedure to run smoothly (Art. 312(3) TFEU). The Union's annual budget must comply with the multiannual financial framework (Art. 312(1), third subpara., TFEU). In addition, the European Parliament, the Council and the Commission are to ensure that the financial means are made available to allow the Union to fulfil its legal obligations in respect of third parties (Art. 323 TFEU).

Limits on expenditure. With a view to maintaining budgetary discipline, Art. 310(4) TFEU debars the Union from adopting any act which is likely to have appreciable implications for the budget without providing an assurance that the expenditure arising from such an act is capable of being financed out of the Union's own resources and in compliance with the multiannual financial framework referred to in Art. 312 TFEU.

13–140

2. Adoption of the budget

Procedure. Article 314 TFEU, introduced by the Lisbon Treaty, governs the procedure for adopting the budget. It replaces the unwieldy procedure provided for in Art. 272 EC.[660] Under that provision the budget was adopted in stages, with the Council placing drafts before the European Parliament on two occasions. After the first reading by the Parliament, the Council already had the last word on compulsory expenditure. The Parliament took the definitive decision on non-compulsory expenditure in the second reading. Moreover, if the Parliament was dissatisfied with the Council's final decision on compulsory expenditure, it could reject the draft budget and ask for a new draft to be submitted. Owing to the fact that the budget has to be in balance, that decision indeed affected the amount of leeway the Parliament had with regard to non-compulsory expenditure.[661]

13–141

---

[658] See the Commission proposal of March 3, 2010 for a regulation laying down the multiannual framework for the years 2007–2013, COM(2010)72 fin.

[659] The categories of expenditure, limited in number, must correspond to the Union's major sectors of activity (Art. 312(3) TFEU).

[660] For the origins of this provision, see the Treaty of April 22, 1970 amending Certain Budgetary Provisions (n. 636, *supra*) [First Treaty on Budgetary Provisions]; and the Treaty of July 22, 1975 amending Certain Budgetary Provisions of the Treaties establishing the European Communities and of the Treaty establishing a Single Council and a Single Commission of the European Communities [Second Treaty on Budgetary Provisions], [1977] O.J. L359/1.

[661] The Parliament has used this power on three occasions, see the resolutions of the European Parliament of December 13, 1979 ([1980] O.J. C4/37), December 16, 1982 ([1983] O.J. C13/67) and December 13, 1984 ([1985] O.J. C12/90).

The new procedure introduced by the Lisbon Treaty is significantly less cumbersome. Under Art. 314 TFEU, the draft budget is established by the Commission and subject to one reading only by the Council and the European Parliament. Since the procedure for the adoption of the budget no longer distinguishes between compulsory and non-compulsory expenditure, the European Parliament thus has the final say over all expenditure. However, the budget must remain within the limits of the multiannual financial framework established by the Council (see para. 13–139). The Presidents of the European Parliament, the Council and the Commission take all the necessary steps to promote consultation and the reconciliation of the positions of the institutions (Art. 324 TFEU). In the past, the interinstitutional agreements have provided for tripartite dialogue ("trilogue") between the Commission, the Parliament and the Council even before the Commission establishes the preliminary draft budget and likewise before and after the European Parliament's (first) reading of the budget.[662]

13–142   **Draft budget.** Each institution, with the exception of the ECB, draws up estimates of its expenditure for the following year before July 1.[663] The Commission consolidates these estimates in a draft budget. The draft budget containing an estimate of revenue and expenditure must be placed before the European Parliament and the Council no later than September 1 of the year preceding the year in which the budget is to be implemented (Art. 314(1) and (2), first subpara., TFEU). At that stage, the Council adopts its position on the draft budget and forwards it, before October 1 of the same year, to the European Parliament, informing the latter in full of the reasons which led it to adopt its position. If the European Parliament, within forty-two days of this communication, approves the position of the Council or does not take any decision, the budget stands as finally adopted (Art. 314(3) and (4)(a) and (b) TFEU).

If the European Parliament, by a majority of its component members, adopts amendments, the amended draft is forwarded to the Council and the Commission. In that case, the President of the European Parliament, in agreement with the President of the Council, must convene a meeting of the Conciliation Committee, except where the Council, within ten days of the draft being forwarded, informs the European Parliament that it has approved all its amendments (Art. 314(4)(c) TFEU).

13–143   **Conciliation Committee.** The Conciliation Committee in this context is modelled on the conciliation committee which may be convened in the course of the ordinary legislative procedure (see para. 16–029). It is composed of the members

---

[662] See the interinstitutional collaboration in the budgetary sector provided for in Annex II to the Interinstitutional Agreement of May 17, 2006 (n. 649, *supra*).

[663] Under Art. 39 of the Financial Regulation, the Commission and the budgetary authority may agree to bring forward certain dates in the procedure provided that this does not have the effect of reducing or delaying the periods allowed for considering the relevant texts.

of the Council (or their representatives) and an equal number of members representing the European Parliament. The Conciliation Committee attempts to reach agreement on a joint text within twenty-one days of its being convened, on the basis of the positions of the European Parliament and the Council. Agreement requires a qualified majority of the members of the Council (or their representatives) and a majority of the representatives of the European Parliament. The Commission takes part in the Conciliation Committee's proceedings and takes all the necessary initiatives with a view to reconciling the positions of the European Parliament and the Council (Art. 314(5) TFEU).

If, within the fixed deadline, the Conciliation Committee does not approve a joint text, the Commission is to submit a new draft budget (Art. 314(8) TFEU). If it reaches agreement within this deadline, the joint text is to be approved by the European Parliament (acting by a simple majority) and the Council (acting by qualified majority) within a period of fourteen days of that agreement (Art. 314(6) TFEU). The European Parliament needs a majority of its component members to reject the joint text. If the European Parliament rejects it, the Commission is to submit a new draft budget. It must also do so where the Council or the European Parliament rejects the joint text and the other institution fails to take a decision (Art. 314(7)(b) and (c) TFEU).

If both institutions approve the text or fail to take a decision, or if one of the institutions approves the text while the other one fails to take a decision, the budget is definitively adopted in accordance with the joint text (Art. 314(7)(a) TFEU). If the European Parliament approves the joint text whilst the Council rejects it, the European Parliament may, within fourteen days from the date of the rejection, and acting by a majority of its component members and three-fifths of the votes cast, decide to confirm all or some of its amendments. If it fails to reach this special majority, the position agreed in the Conciliation Committee on the budget heading which is the subject of the amendment is retained (Art. 314(7)(d) TFEU).

Constraints. In exercising their decision-making powers under this procedure, **13–144** the institutions need to take account of the constraints imposed upon their powers by the Treaties and the acts adopted thereunder. In particular, they have to maintain a balance between expenditure and revenue (Art. 314(10) TFEU).[664] The Commission, for its part, may amend the draft budget at all times during the procedure, but only until such time as the Conciliation Committee is convened (Art. 314(2), second subpara., TFEU).

Adoption of budget. When the procedure provided for in Art. 314 TFEU has **13–145** been completed, the President of the European Parliament declares that the

---

[664] Infringement of the principle that the budget must be in equilibrium constitutes a ground for annulling the act of the President of the Parliament declaring that the budget has been finally adopted. See ECJ, Case C-284/90 *Council v European Parliament* [1992] E.C.R. I-2277, paras 32–33 (n. 633, *supra*).

budget has been definitively adopted (Art. 314(9) TFEU). That declaration endows the budget with binding force vis-à-vis the institutions and the Member States.[665]

13–146 **Amending budget.** If, in the event of unavoidable, exceptional or unforeseen circumstances, expenditure or revenue is not in accordance with the estimates, the Council decides on whether it is necessary to adopt an amending budget.[666] The amending budget is adopted in accordance with the procedure laid down in Art. 314 TFEU.[667]

Article 315 TFEU deals with the situation where the budget has not yet been voted at the beginning of the financial year. In that event, the Commission may in principle undertake monthly expenditure of one-twelfth of the relevant budgetary appropriations for the preceding financial year, provided that the monthly expenditure does not exceed one-twelfth of the appropriations provided for in the draft budget.[668]

3. Implementation of the budget

13–147 **Implementation of expenditure.** The Commission implements the budget in cooperation with the Member States on its own responsibility and within the limits of the appropriations, having regard to the principles of sound financial management (Art. 317, first para., TFEU). Its power to implement the budget is separate from its power to implement legislative measures (see para. 17–008 *et seq.*).[669] Consequently, any implementation of expenditure by the Commission presupposes, in addition to the entry of the relevant appropriation in the budget, the prior adoption of a legally binding Union act providing a legal basis for its action, except in cases provided for by the Financial Regulation (Art. 310(3) TFEU). Prior adoption of such a "basic act" is not required where expenditure is being implemented for non-significant Union action.[670] Such action is defined in

---

[665] ECJ, Case 34/86 *Council v European Parliament* [1986] E.C.R. 2155, para. 8.
[666] Financial Regulation, Art. 37. Prior to the Financial Regulation of June 25, 2002, there was a formal distinction between amending and supplementary budgets, but this was abolished as it served no practical purpose.
[667] Financial Regulation, Art. 37. See, e.g., Amending Budgets Nos 1 to 10 of the European Union for the financial year 2009, [2009] O.J. L99, L157, L174, L293 and L326 and [2010] O.J. L78.
[668] Article 315, first para., TFEU in conjunction with Art. 13(2) of the Financial Regulation. The Council may decide to authorise an increase in the "provisional twelfths". However, the European Parliament may decide to reduce this expenditure (Art. 315, second, third and fourth paras, TFEU).
[669] ECJ, Case 16/88 *Commission v Council* [1989] E.C.R. 3457, paras 16–19.
[670] See ECJ (order of the President of September 24, 1996), Joined Cases C-239/96 R and C-240/96 R *United Kingdom v Commission* [1996] E.C.R. I-4475, paras 41–46; ECJ, Case C-106/96 *United Kingdom v Commission* [1998] E.C.R. I-2729, paras 21–37 (annulment of a Commission decision to carry out expenditure for which the Council had not adopted a basic act).

the Financial Regulation on the basis of the Interinstitutional Agreement concluded between the European Parliament, the Council and the Commission on October 13, 1998.[671]

The Commission confers the necessary powers to implement their own sections of the budget on the European Economic and Social Committee, the Committee of the Regions, the European Ombudsman and the European Data-protection Supervisor (Art. 317, second para., TFEU; Financial Regulation, Art. 50). Nevertheless, it retains responsibility for financial management, even where the implementation of the budget is entrusted to national authorities or to the Union and the Member States jointly. On the basis of the information provided to it by the institutions by March 1 each year, the Commission draws up annual accounts for the Union, a financial statement of assets and liabilities and an evaluation report on budgetary and financial management and forwards them to the European Parliament, the Council and the Court of Auditors (Art. 318 TFEU; Financial Regulation, Arts 121 to 128).

4. Budgetary control

Internal audit. The uptake and utilisation of Union funds is subject to internal and external controls. Each institution entrusts authorising officers with implementing revenue and expenditure in accordance with the principles of sound financial management. The authorising officers are responsible for ensuring that the requirements of legality and regularity are complied with and introduce appropriate procedures for management and internal audit.[672] An internal auditor is charged with verifying the proper operation of budgetary implementation systems and procedures and reporting to his or her institution thereon.[673]   **13–148**

External audit. The external controls are carried out in the first instance by the Court of Auditors and subsequently by the European Parliament, working together with the Council. The Court of Auditors examines the accounts of all revenue and expenditure of the Union. It examines not only the general budget, but also the accounts of all bodies, offices or agencies set up by the Union in so far as the relevant constituent instrument does not preclude such examination   **13–149**

---

[671] Interinstitutional Agreement on legal bases and implementation of the budget ([1998] O.J. C344/1; see also (1998) 7/8 EU Bull. point 1.6.1), as taken over in Art. 49 of the Financial Regulation. Such expenditure concerns appropriations for pilot schemes, preparatory actions and specific or indefinite actions carried out by the Commission by virtue of its prerogatives (other than the right of initiative) and appropriations intended for the internal administration of each institution.

[672] Article 322(b) TFEU; Financial Regulation, Arts 59 and 60.

[673] Financial Regulation, Arts 85 and 86. For the changes in terms of internal audits, see Craig, "The constitutionalisation of Community administration" (2003) E.L.Rev. 840, at 845–846.

(Art. 287(1), first subpara., TFEU).[674] The purpose of the audit is to establish that all revenue has been received and all expenditure incurred in a lawful and proper manner having regard to financial regulations and the substantive provisions on the basis of which the operations were carried out.[675] The Court of Auditors also verifies that the financial management has been sound[676] and accordingly that resources have been utilised efficiently.[677] In particular, the Court is to report on any cases of irregularity.[678]

The external audit is carried out after operations have been performed, but does not have to wait until the accounts for the relevant financial year have been closed (Art. 287(2) TFEU). The Court of Auditors is entitled to have access to all necessary decisions and information, which Union institutions, any bodies managing revenue or expenditure on behalf of the Union, any natural or legal person in receipt of payments from the budget and national audit bodies or the relevant national departments are under a duty to provide on request. Where necessary, it will carry out its inspections on the spot in Union institutions and on the premises of the aforementioned bodies and natural or legal persons. Where investigations are carried out in Member States, the Court of Auditors works in liaison with national audit bodies or competent departments, provided that they wish to take part in the audit. The Court and the national audit bodies are to cooperate in a spirit of trust while maintaining their independence.[679]

After the close of each financial year, the Court of Auditors draws up an annual report which is forwarded to the other institutions and published, together with their replies to the Court's observations, in the *Official Journal* (Art. 287(4), first subpara., TFEU). Persons mentioned in reports also have the right to be heard.[680]

13–150   **Discharge.** The European Parliament is empowered to give a discharge to the Commission in respect of the implementation of the budget; it acts on a recommendation from the Council, acting by qualified majority. The European

---

[674] Article 12 of the EIB Statute set up a special committee to verify the Bank's operations and accounts. However, the Court of Auditors does examine expenditure of Union funds carried out by the EIB on the Commission's instructions. Article 287(3), third subpara., TFEU refers to the Court of Auditors' right of access to information held by the EIB, which is to be governed by an agreement between the Court of Auditors, the EIB and the Commission.

[675] See Article 287(2) TFEU and Financial Regulation, Art. 140(1).

[676] Article 287(2), first subpara., TFEU.

[677] For the methods which the Court of Auditors has developed against a background of different auditing traditions in the Member States, see O'Keeffe (n. 433, *supra*), at 186–191.

[678] Article 287(2), first subpara., TFEU

[679] Article 287(3) TFEU. See, in this connection, Flizot, "Les rapports entre la Cour des comptes européenne et les institutions supérieures de contrôle des Etats membres. Quelle application du principe du subsidiarité?" (2002) R.M.C.U.E. 112–121.

[680] See ECJ, Case C-315/99 P *Ismeri Europa v Court of Auditors* [2001] E.C.R. I-5281, paras 27–35, and the discussion by Inghelram in (2001) C.D.E. 707–728.

Parliament decides by a majority of the votes cast.[681] The Council and the European Parliament take their decisions in the light of the accounts and the financial statement and the evaluation report submitted by the Commission,[682] the annual report of the Court of Auditors,[683] the statement of the Court of Auditors of assurance as to the reliability of the accounts and the legality and regularity of the underlying transactions[684] and any relevant special reports of that institution (Art. 319(1) TFEU).

The EU Treaty reinforced the accountability of the Commission. Before giving a discharge to that institution, the European Parliament may ask the Commission to give evidence with regard to the execution of expenditure or the operation of financial control systems and to provide any necessary information (Art. 319(2) TFEU). As in the case of the Council's recommendation, the decision giving discharge may be accompanied by observations on the implementation of the budget. The Commission has to take all appropriate steps to act on those observations and to report to the European Parliament and the Council on measures taken (Art. 319(3) TFEU). The discharge is a decision which formally closes the accounts. Although it has no effect on the Commission's legal position, the Parliament's refusal to discharge it in full or in part is a powerful political signal.[685] Nevertheless, the Commission may be dismissed only if a motion of censure is passed by the Parliament (see para. 13–009).

Combating fraud. More than half of Union resources are utilised by national authorities, for which the Commission has set up control systems in a number of policy areas. Under Art. 325 TFEU, the Union and the Member States are to counter fraud and any other illegal activities affecting the financial interests of the   **13–151**

---

[681] See Art. 5 of the Procedure for the consideration and adoption of decisions on the granting of discharge in Annex VI to the EP Rules of Procedure.

[682] See Art. 318 TFEU.

[683] Article 287(4), first subpara., TFEU.

[684] Article 287(1), second subpara., TFEU. The statement is submitted to the European Parliament and the Council and published in the *Official Journal*.

[685] The European Parliament refused to give the Commission a discharge for the 1982 financial year ([1984] O.J. C337/23; subsequently, discharge was given for purposes of closure of the accounts by resolution of March 15, 1985, [1985] O.J. C94/153) and the 1996 financial year (resolution of May 4, 1999, [1999] O.J. C279/115: the reasons, which were adopted on December 17, 1998, are appended thereto). See Beurdeley, "Les motifs du refus de décharge relatif au budget général de l'Union européenne" (2000) R.M.C.U.E. 696–702). It provisionally refused to give a discharge in respect of the 1990 financial year (resolution of October 27, 1993, [1993] O.J. C315/89) and for the 1992 financial year (see the resolution of April 21, 1994, [1994] O.J. C128/322; discharge was granted by decision of April 5, 1995, [1995] O.J. L141/51; see also [1995] O.J. C109/51). The grant of a discharge was also postponed for the 1997 financial year, see the resolution of May 4, 1999, [1999] O.J. C279/119 (discharge was granted by decision of January 19, 2000, [2000] O.J. L45/36) and for the 1998 financial year, see the resolution of April 13, 2000, [2000] O.J. C40/381 (discharge was granted by resolution of July 6, 2000, A5-0190/2000).

Union through deterrent measures affording effective protection in the Member States and in all the Union's institutions, bodies, offices and agencies.[686]

The investigative duties conferred on the Commission by Union legislation are now performed by the European Anti-Fraud Office (OLAF, see para. 13–122), which may undertake both internal investigations in Union institutions and bodies and external investigations in the Member States.[687] Protection of the Union's financial interests signifies combating fraud and other irregularities at all levels at which those interests are liable to be affected, both within the Member States and at the level of the Union institutions and bodies.[688] As far as combating fraud at the Union level is concerned, Union bodies may not introduce their own systems to prevent and combat fraud in place of the general power of investigation vested in OLAF by Union legislation.[689]

Since the Union has no criminal jurisdiction, the prosecution of financial fraud is left principally to the Member States. The Member States are under a duty to coordinate their action aimed at protecting the Union's financial interests against fraud and to take the same measures to counter fraud affecting those financial interests as they take in respect of their own financial interests (Art. 325(2) and

---

[686] See White, *Protection of the Financial Interests of the European Communities: The Fight against Fraud and Corruption* (Deventer, Kluwer Law International, 1998), 244 pp.

[687] See Regulation (EC) No. 1073/1999 adopted by the European Parliament and the Council on May 25, 1999 under Art. 280 EC [now Art. 325 TFEU] concerning investigations conducted by the European Anti-Fraud Office (OLAF) ([1999] O.J. L136/1) and the Interinstitutional Agreement of May 25, 1999 between the European Parliament, the Council and the Commission concerning internal investigations by the European Anti-Fraud Office (OLAF) ([1999] O.J. L136/15). For the terms and conditions for internal investigations in relation to the prevention of fraud, corruption and any illegal activity detrimental to the Union's interests, see amongst others, Council Decision 1999/394/EC, Euratom of May 25, 1999 ([1999] O.J. L149/36), the Commission Decision of June 2, 1999 ([1999] O.J. L149/57) and the Decision of the European Parliament of November 18, 1999 appended as Annex XI to the EP Rules of Procedure, [2003] O.J. L61/112. See Trasca, "La place de l'Office Européen de Lutte Antifraude dans la répression de la fraude au budget communautaire" (2008) 44 C.D.E. 7–82; Combeaud, "L'Olaf et les autorités judiciaires: quelle répression contre la fraude communautaire?" (2001) R.M.C.U.E. 695–702. See also n. 88 with regard to the discussion as to whether Members of the European Parliament may invoke parliamentary immunity in the context of an OLAF investigation.

[688] ECJ, Case C-11/00 *Commission v European Central Bank* [2003] E.C.R. I-7147, paras 103–104, and ECJ, Case C-15/00 *Commission v European Investment Bank* [2003] E.C.R. I-7281, paras 134–135.

[689] According to the Court of Justice, the expression "financial interests of the Community" covers the use by the ECB and the EIB of their own resources, even though they are managed autonomously: ECJ, Case C-11/00 *Commission v European Central Bank* [2003] E.C.R. I-7147, paras 89–97, and ECJ, Case C-15/00 *Commission v European Investment Bank* [2003] E.C.R. I-7281, paras 120–136. The fact that these bodies are subject to Union legislation on combating fraud does not detract from their functional independence: see para. 17–024. See also Marchegiani, "La BEI et l'OLAF, un conflit de nature constitutionnelle" (2000) R.M.C.U.E. 690–695. For a critical analysis, see Goebel, "Court of Justice oversight over the European Central Bank: delimiting the ECB's constitutional autonomy and independence in the Olaf judgment" (2006) 29 Fordham I.L.J. 610–654.

(3) TFEU). In order to make combating fraud more effective, common legal rules have been created for all areas covered by Union policies which are applicable to the administrative penalties provided for by Union law.[690] Under Art. 325(4) TFEU, the European Parliament and the Council are to adopt, in accordance with the ordinary legislative procedure, after consulting the Court of Auditors, the necessary measures in the field of the prevention of and the fight against fraud affecting the Union's financial interests.[691] As has already been mentioned, this covers the fight against fraud at both the Union and the national levels.

Before the Lisbon Treaty, such measures could not concern the application of national criminal law or the national administration of justice.[692] National provisions of criminal law were harmonised through conventions established by the Council pursuant to Title VI of the EU Treaty (PJCC) in which general rules and a common definition of fraud were formulated.[693]

C. THE SEATS OF THE INSTITUTIONS AND BODIES

Provisional locations. Article 341 TFEU [*ex Art. 289 EC*] puts the national governments under a duty to determine the seat of the institutions of the Union by common accord (see also Art. 189 EAEC).[694] However, it was a long time before the definitive locations were determined. When the ECSC Treaty entered into force, the Foreign Ministers agreed that the High Authority and the Court of

13–152

---

[690] Council Regulation (EC, Euratom) No. 2988/95 of December 18, 1995 on the protection of the European Communities' financial interests, [1995] O.J. L312/1. See Wolfgang and Ulrich, "Schutz der finanziellen Interessen der Europäischen Gemeinschaften" (1998) EuR. 616–647; Lenaerts, "Sanktionen der Gemeinschaftsorgane gegenüber natürlichen und juristischen Personen" (1997) EuR. 17–46; Michiels, "Nieuwe instrumenten ter bescherming van de financiële belangen van de Europese Gemeenschappen" (1996) S.E.W. 362–371.

[691] See, e.g., Decision No. 804/2004/EC of the European Parliament and of the Council of April 21, 2004 establishing a Community action programme to promote activities in the field of the protection of the Community's financial interests (Hercule programme), [2004] O.J. L143/9.

[692] Article 280(4) EC. See Veldt Foglia, "(Nog) geen strafrecht in de Eerste Pijler?" (2002) S.E.W. 162–169.

[693] Convention of July 26, 1995 on the protection of the Communities' financial interests, [1995] O.J. C316/48 (explanatory report in [1997] O.J. C191/1). When consulted by the Council, the European Parliament came out against the Commission's proposal for this convention on the ground that the matter would be better dealt with by a directive based on Arts 95 and 280 EC, see the resolution of March 15, 1995, [1995] O.J. C89/82. See further the additional protocols to the above Convention of September 27, 1996 ([1996] O.J. C313/2; explanatory report in [1998] O.J. C11/5) and June 19, 1997 ([1997] O.J. C221/11). See Korte, "Der Schutz der finanziellen Interessen der Europäischen Gemeinschaften mit den Mitteln des Strafrechts—Das 'Zweite Protokol'" (1998) N.J.W. 1464–1466. See also the Convention drawn up on the basis of the former Art.K.3 of the EU Treaty on the fight against corruption involving officials of the European Communities or officials of Member States of the European Union (adopted by Council Act of May 26, 1997, [1997] O.J. C195/1). For the interpretation by the Court of Justice of these conventions and the protocols thereto, see para. 23–013, *infra*.

[694] ECJ, Case 230/81 *Luxembourg v European Parliament* [1983] E.C.R. 255, para. 35.

Justice would start work in Luxembourg and that the Assembly would hold its first session at Strasbourg, where the Council of Europe hemicycle was available. The Council met in Luxembourg, where the departments of the institutions, including the secretariat of the Assembly, were located. Following the entry into force of the EEC and EAEC Treaties, the two Commissions held their meetings in Brussels on grounds of convenience. The EEC and EAEC Councils also met in Brussels, followed by the committees of the Assembly, which continued to operate in Strasbourg and Luxembourg.

Concurrently with the establishment by the Merger Treaty of a single Council and a single Commission, the representatives of the national governments adopted the Decision on Provisional Location of April 8, 1965 pursuant to the power conferred by that Treaty to settle "certain problems peculiar to the Grand Duchy of Luxembourg".[695] The Decision declared that Luxembourg, Brussels and Strasbourg were to remain the provisional places of work of the institutions of the Communities (Art. 1). As far as the institutions were concerned, the decision provided that during the months of April, June and October, the Council would hold its sessions in Luxembourg (Art. 2), that the Court of Justice would remain in Luxembourg (Art. 3) and that the General Secretariat of the Assembly and its departments would remain in Luxembourg (Art. 4), together with certain departments of the Commission (Arts 5–9). Since the governments were unable to reach agreement on the seats of the institutions,[696] the institutions remained free to determine their internal organisation within the confines of the decision. Thus, the European Parliament was entitled to decide to hold its plenary sessions in Strasbourg, meetings of political groups and parliamentary committees in Brussels—with the gradual transfer of some members of staff required for this purpose[697]—and special or additional plenary sessions in Brussels during the weeks when the political groups and parliamentary committees met.[698]

---

[695] Decision of the Representatives of the Governments of the Member States on the provisional location of certain institutions and departments of the Communities (*Treaties establishing the European Communities*, 1978, Office for Official Publications, Luxembourg, at 837), adopted pursuant to Art. 37 of the Merger Treaty.

[696] On June 30, 1981 a Conference of Representatives of the Governments convened for this purpose in 1980 merely confirmed the Member States' power and maintained the status quo (as agreed at the European Council held in Maastricht on March 23 and 24, 1981; (1981) 3 EC Bull. point 1.1.8).

[697] ECJ, Case 230/81 *Luxembourg v European Parliament* [1983] E.C.R. 255, paras 37–58; ECJ, Joined Cases C-213/88 and C-39/89 *Luxembourg v European Parliament* [1991] E.C.R. I-5643, paras 35–38, 42–44 and 54–58. The division of staff must not be such, however, as to mean that the secretariat is no longer based in Luxembourg: ECJ, Case 108/83 *Luxembourg v European Parliament* [1984] E.C.R. 1945, para. 31. See Neville Brown, "The Grand Duchy Fights Again: Comment on Joined Cases C-213/88 and C-39/89" (1993) C.M.L.Rev. 599–611.

[698] ECJ, Joined Cases 358/85 and 51/86 *France v European Parliament* [1988] E.C.R. 4821, paras 29–41.

Seats of institutions. By the First Decision on the Seat of the Institutions of   **13–153**
December 12, 1992,[699] the national governments at last acted upon Art. 289
EC [*now Art. 341 TFEU*].[700] The decision fixed a seat for each institution
without altering the status quo: the European Parliament was to have its seat
in Strasbourg, but was to continue to work in Brussels and Luxembourg (see
para. 13–021); the Council was to have its seat in Brussels, but to continue to hold
its meetings in April, June and October in Luxembourg; the Commission was
to have its seat in Brussels, but its departments located in Luxembourg were to
remain there; the Court of Justice, the Court of First Instance [*now the General
Court*] and the Court of Auditors were to continue to have their seats in
Luxembourg. The Treaty of Amsterdam enshrined those arrangements in a
Protocol annexed to the Treaties (the "Protocol on Seats", which was taken over
by the Lisbon Treaty),[701] which means that they can only be changed by means
of the procedure for amending the Treaties. Consequently, the Union institutions
have no common seat and indeed most of them have more than one place of
work.[702] Above all the fact that the European Parliament is obliged to meet in
Strasbourg, whilst the institutions with which it collaborates institutionally operate principally in Brussels, makes for needless costs and inconvenience for all
those concerned.

Seats of other bodies. A decision of the national governments was required to fix   **13–154**
the seats of the EIB, the EMI and the ECB. In order to determine the locations of
other bodies, it is sufficient for a decision to be taken of the same legal nature as the
one which set up the body in question or, failing this, a decision taken by the body
itself pursuant to its power to determine its internal organisation.[703] Nevertheless,
the Member States often have recourse to Art. 341 TFEU [*ex Art. 289 EC*] to fix
the seat of such a body, even though it is not an "institution". Accordingly, by the
Decision on Provisional Location of April 8, 1965 the national governments did fix

---

[699] Decision of December 12, 1992 taken by common agreement between the Representatives of the
Governments of the Member States on the location of the seats of the institutions and of certain
bodies and departments of the European Communities, [1992] O.J. C341/1.
[700] ECJ, Case C-345/95 *France v European Parliament* [1997] E.C.R. I-5215, para. 23.
[701] Protocol (No. 6), annexed to the TEU, the TFEU and the EAEC Treaty, on the location of the seats
of the institutions and of certain bodies, offices, agencies and departments of the European Union,
[2010] O.J. C83/265 (which replaces Protocol (No. 8), annexed to the EU Treaty and the
Community Treaties, on the location of the seats of the institutions and of certain bodies and
departments of the European Communities and Europol, [1997] O.J. C340/112).
[702] Although the European Parliament argued that this practice was contrary to Arts 10, 199 and 289
EC [*now Arts 4(3) TEU and 232 and 341 TFEU*] (see the position taken by the Parliament on April
20, 1993, [1993] O.J. C150/26), the Court of Justice endorsed maintaining several places of work
for that institution in ECJ, Case C-345/95 *France v European Parliament* [1997] E.C.R. I-5215.
[703] See, e.g., the regulation establishing the European Agency for Reconstruction, para. 13–123,
supra.

the working places of a number of bodies and departments. By the same token, the Heads of State or Government, acting under Art. 289 EC [*now Art. 341 TFEU*], fixed the definitive location of certain bodies and departments by, inter alia, the First Decision on the Seat of the Institutions of December 12, 1992,[704] the Second Decision on the Seat of the Institutions of October 29, 1993[705] and the Third Decision on Seats of December 13, 2003.[706] The executive agencies responsible for managing Union programmes on behalf of the Commission are established where the Commission has its seat.[707]

D. STATUS OF MEMBERS OF INSTITUTIONS AND BODIES

13–155   **Independent status.** Apart from the members of the European Council and the Council, the status of members of the institutions in performing their duties is one of independence. Following their appointment by the national governments, the European Council or the Council, they cannot be compelled to stand down except by the Court of Justice acting at the request of their particular institution.[708] Members of the European Parliament are answerable only to the electorate in

---

[704] See n. 699, *supra*. The Decision fixed the seat of the Economic and Social Committee at Brussels and the seats of the Court of Auditors (at that time still not an "institution") and of the European Investment Bank in Luxembourg (Art. 1(e) to (g)).

[705] Decision of October 29, 1993 taken by common agreement between the Representatives of the Governments of the Member States, meeting at Head of State and Government level, on the location of the seats of certain bodies and departments of the European Communities and of Europol, [1993] O.J. C323/1. See the bodies and departments mentioned in para. 13–123, *supra*. See also the Decision by common accord of the representatives of the Governments of the Member States of December 6, 1996 determining the seat of the Community Plant Variety Office ([1996] O.J. C36/1). However, in determining the seat of the European Monitoring Centre on Racism and Xenophobia, the representatives of the national governments based their decision of June 2, 1997 ([1997] O.J. C194/4), not on Art. 289 EC, but simply on the regulation establishing that body (para. 13–123, *supra*).

[706] Decision 2004/97/EC, Euratom taken by common agreement between the Representatives of the Member States, meeting at Head of State or Government level, of December 13, 2003 on the location of the seats of certain offices and agencies of the European Union, [2004] O.J. L29/15. See the bodies and agencies mentioned in para. 13–123. See also, based on Art. 289 EC, the decisions taken by common agreement between the representatives of the governments of Member States on the location of the seat of the European Institute for Gender Equality (Decision 2006/966/EC, n. 561, *supra*), of the European Institute of Innovation and Technology (Decision 2008/634/EC, n. 563, *supra*) and of the Office of the Body of European Regulators for Electronic Communications (Decision 2010/349/EU, n. 565, *supra*).

[707] Article 5 of Regulation No. 58/2003 (n. 568, *supra*).

[708] For the Court of Justice and the General Court, see para. 13–093, *supra*; for the ECB, see para. 13–098, *supra*; for the Court of Auditors, see para. 13–104, *supra*. The Council may also request that a Member of the Commission be compulsorily retired (para. 13–073, *supra*); the Commission may be made to resign as a body if the European Parliament passes a motion of censure (para. 13–009, *supra*).

their constituencies. Members of the other three political institutions are answerable to parliamentary assemblies: the Heads of State or Government sitting in the European Council to their national parliament or to their citizens; Ministers who sit in the Council to their national or regional parliaments; Members of the Commission collectively to the European Parliament, which gives its consent to their appointment.[709] The executive board members of the ECB, who are appointed by the European Council, acting by a qualified majority, also have an independent status.[710] As in the case of the European Ombudsman (appointed by the European Parliament) and the European Data-Protection Supervisor (appointed by the European Parliament and the Council), they may be compelled to retire only by the Court of Justice.[711]

Duties and immunities. Members of the institutions are under a duty not to disclose information of the kind covered by the obligation of professional secrecy laid down by Art. 339 TFEU [*ex Art. 287 EC*]. Members of the European Parliament, the Council, the Commission, the Court of Justice of the European Union, the ECB and the Court of Auditors enjoy the privileges and immunities which the Protocol on Privileges and Immunities confers on officials and other servants of the Union in respect of the performance of their official duties.[712] The Protocol on Privileges and Immunities also applies to the European Ombudsman, the EIB, the European Data-Protection Supervisor and the other Union bodies and agencies with legal personality.[713] Members of advisory bodies enjoy privileges and immunities in the performance of their duties and during their travel to and from the place of meeting.[714]   **13–156**

Financial status. The Council, acting by a qualified majority, is empowered to determine the salaries, allowances and pensions of the President of the European   **13–157**

---

[709] For the particular position of the President of the European Council and the High Representative, see paras 13–031 and 13–070, *supra*.

[710] Article 283(2), second subpara., TFEU.

[711] Paras 13–119 and 13–123, *supra*. As regards the European Data-Protection Supervisor, an application to this effect may be made not only by the European Parliament, but also by the Council or the Commission: Regulation (EC) No. 45/2001, Art. 42(6) (n. 812, *infra*).

[712] For representatives of the Member States sitting in the European Council or the Council, see Art. 10; for the President of the European Council and Members of the Commission, see Art. 19; for the Court of Justice of the European Union, see Art. 20; for the ECB, see Arts 22 and 39 of the ESCB Statute; for the Court of Auditors, see Art. 286(8) TFEU [*ex Art. 247(9) EC*].

[713] For the European Ombudsman, see Ombudsman Regulations, Art. 10(3); for the EIB and the ECB, see Arts 21 and 22 of the Protocol on Privileges and Immunities and Art. 39 of the ESCB Statute. For the (Assistant) Data-Protection Supervisor, see Art. 42(7) and (8) of Regulation (EC) No. 45/2001 (n. 812, *infra*). See also the regulations establishing the other bodies and agencies with legal personality, para. 13–123, *supra*.

[714] Protocol on Privileges and Immunities, Art. 10, second para.

Council, the Secretary-General of the Council, Members of the Commission, the Court of Justice of the European Union[715] and the Court of Auditors.[716] The payments are subject only to a tax for the benefit of the Union.[717] This is also the case with the salary of Members of the European Parliament, which has been fixed by the European Parliament in the Statute for MEPs.[718] Before that Statute was adopted, the Member States fixed their MEPs' remuneration whereas MEPs received lump-sum expenses paid by the Union. In order not to impair the internal functioning of the European Parliament and MEPs' privileged free movement, Member States could not tax those expenses.[719]

Bodies and agencies having legal personality in their own right fix the salaries of members of their management boards.[720] The European Ombudsman has the same financial status as Members of the Court of Justice.[721] Any payments made instead of remuneration to members of advisory bodies are determined by the Council pursuant to Art. 243 TFEU.[722]

E. STATUS OF OFFICIALS AND OTHER SERVANTS

13–158 **Staff Regulations.** The institutions and bodies of the European Union employ more than 38,000 officials. Under Art. 336 TFEU [*ex Art. 283 EC*], the European Parliament and the Council, acting by means of regulations in accordance with

---

[715] Article 243 TFEU [*ex Art. 210 EC*; before the EU Treaty: Art. 6 of the Merger Treaty]. See Regulation No. 422/67/EEC, No. 5/67/Euratom of the Council of July 25, 1967 determining the emoluments of the President and Members of the Commission and of the President, Judges, Advocates General and Registrar of the Court of Justice, [1967] O.J. English Spec. Ed. 199, as amended, inter alia, by Council Regulation (EC, Euratom) No. 202/2005 of January 18, 2005, [2005] O.J. L33/1.

[716] Article 286(7) TFEU. See Council Regulation (EEC/Euratom/ECSC) No. 2290/77 of October 18, 1977 determining the emoluments of members of the Court of Auditors, [1977] O.J. L268/1.

[717] See also para. 13–158, *infra*.

[718] See Arts 9 to 12 of the Statute for Members of the European Parliament, adopted by Decision 2005/684/EC, Euratom (see n. 82, *supra*). But a number of Member States have taken advantage of Art. 12(3), which provides that the fact that an MEP's salary is subject to tax for the benefit of the Communities is "without prejudice to the Member States' power to make the salary subject to national tax law provisions, provided that any double taxation is avoided". The Statute introduced the uniform payment of MEPs and a system of reimbursement of travel costs actually incurred, together with a flat rate for other expenses. *Ibid.*, Art. 20.

[719] ECJ, Case 208/80 *Lord Bruce of Donington* [1981] E.C.R. 2205, paras 15–20. The lump sum paid in respect of expenses could be subject to national tax if it were to be shown that it was excessively high and in reality constituted disguised remuneration, a question which would be a matter of Union law alone: *ibid.* para. 21.

[720] See, e.g., ESCB Statute, Art. 11.3 (Executive Board of the ECB); EIB Statute, Art. 11(5) (Management Committee).

[721] Ombudsman Regulations, Art. 10(2).

[722] See Art. 301, third para., TFEU, as regards the European Economic and Social Committee.

the ordinary legislative procedure on a proposal from the Commission and after consulting with the other institutions concerned, are to lay down the Staff Regulations of officials of the European Union and the Conditions of Employment of other servants of the Union.[723] The latter set of rules consists of special rules applying to staff who do not have the status of Union officials.[724]

The Staff Regulations and the Conditions of Employment of Other Servants apply to the institutions, the European Economic and Social Committee, the Committee of the Regions, the European Ombudsman, the European Data-Protection Supervisor and all bodies to which the Staff Regulations apply under the Union acts establishing them.[725] Some Union bodies may adopt their own staff regulations,[726] but in any case the Civil Service Tribunal has jurisdiction to hear and determine any disputes.[727] More often, however, the decision setting up a new body or agency provides that the Staff Regulations and Conditions of

---

[723] Regulation (EEC, Euratom, ECSC) No. 259/68 of the Council of February 29, 1968 laying down the Staff Regulations of Officials and the Conditions of Employment of Other Servants of the European Communities and instituting special measures temporarily applicable to officials of the Commission, [1968] O.J. English Spec. Ed. (I) 30 [Staff Regulations; Conditions of Employment of Other Servants].

[724] The Conditions of Employment of Other Servants apply to temporary staff, auxiliary staff, contract staff, local staff and special advisers. The executive agencies responsible for managing Union programmes operate partly with officials of the institutions and partly with contract staff (Art. 17 of Regulation No. 58/2003 (n. 568, supra)). National civil servants seconded to the European External Action Service under Art. 27(3) TEU will have the status of temporary staff under a Title of the Conditions of Employment (COM(2010) 309 final): see Art. 6 of Council Decision 2010/427/EU of July 26, 2010 establishing the organisation and the functioning of the European External Action Service, [2010] O.J. L201/30.

[725] Staff Regulations, Art. 1 to 1b; Conditions of Employment of Other Servants, Art. 6.

[726] See the independence in staff matters granted by EIB Statute, Art. 11(7), and ESCB Statute, Art. 36.1. The contractual employment relationship between the ECB and its staff does not prevent the ECB from adjusting the employment relationship in the interests of the service: CFI, Joined Cases T-178/00 and T-341/00 Pflugradt v European Central Bank [2002] E.C.R. II-4035, paras 48–54.

[727] See ESCB Statute, Art. 36.2 (see CFI, Case T-333/99 X v European Central Bank [2001] E.C.R. II-3021, paras 36–44) and the conditions of employment drawn up for the staff of the European Training Foundation (see Art. 14 of the regulation establishing that body, para. 13–123, supra), the European Foundation for the Improvement of Living and Working Conditions (Art. 44 of Council Regulation (ECSC, EEC, Euratom) No. 1860/76 of June 29, 1976, [1976] O.J. L214/24) and the European Agency for Cooperation (Art. 18(1), second subpara., of the regulation setting up the agency, para. 13–123, supra); for the EIB, see ECJ, Case 110/75 Mills v European Investment Bank [1976] E.C.R. 955, paras 5–18. As regards the character of a "Union body", see ECJ, Case 16/81 Alaimo v Commission [1982] E.C.R. 1559, paras 7–12 (where it was accepted that the European Centre for the Development of Vocational Training was such a body) and CFI (order of December 16, 1994), Case T-177/94 Altmann and Others v Commission [1994] E.C.R. II-1245, paras 41–44 (where it was held that the JET Joint Undertaking (n. 536, supra) was not part of the Union; this does not preclude Union legal protection for JET officials: CFI, Joined Cases T-177/94 and T-377/94 Altmann and Others v Commission [1996] E.C.R. II-2041, and CFI, Case T-99/95 Stott v Commission [1996] E.C.R. II-2227).

Employment of Other Servants are to apply to it.[728] This also applies to Eurojust[729] and—recently—to Europol,[730] but not to CFSP bodies, where the Council lays down specific staff regulations.[731]

13–159 **Status.** Formerly, officials' posts were classified in four categories (A (LA in the case of the language service), B, C, D) in descending order of rank (for instance A 1 to A 8).[732] Since May 1, 2004, the established staff is organised in two function groups: administrators (AD), corresponding to administrative, advisory, linguistic and scientific duties, and assistants (AST), corresponding to executive, technical and clerical duties.[733] Within each function group, officials are classified in grades

---

[728] This is true of the European Ombudsman's secretariat (Ombudsman Regulations, Art. 11(2)) and, by virtue of the regulations establishing them (for the references see para. 13–123, *supra*), the secretariat of the European Data Protection Supervisor (Art. 43), the European Centre for the Development of Vocational Training (Art. 13), the European Office for Harmonisation in the Internal Market (Art. 112(1)), the European Environment Agency (Art. 17, first para.), the European Monitoring Centre for Drugs and Drug Addiction (Art. 15, first para.), the European Medicines Agency (Art. 75), the European Training Foundation (Art. 14), the European Agency for Health and Safety at Work (Art. 20), the Community Plant Variety Office (Art. 31), the Translation Centre (Art. 17(1)), the European Agency for Reconstruction (Art. 10), the European Food Safety Authority (Art. 48), the European Maritime Safety Agency (Art. 6), the European Aviation Safety Agency (Art. 29), the European Network and Information Security Agency (Art. 19), the European Centre for Disease Prevention and Control (Art. 29), the European Railway Agency (Art. 24), the European Union Agency for Fundamental Rights (Art. 24), the Community Fisheries Control Agency (Art. 19), the European Agency for the Management of Operational Cooperation at the External Borders (Art. 17), the European Chemicals Agency (Art. 103), the European Institute for Gender Equality (Art. 13), the European Global Navigation Satellite System (GNSS) Authority (Art. 16), the Agency for the Cooperation of Energy Regulators (Art. 28), the Office of the Body of European Regulators for Electronic Communications (Art. 10) and the European Asylum Support Office (Art. 38).

[729] See Art. 30 of Council Decision 2002/187/JHA (n. 579, *supra*).

[730] See Art. 39 of Council Decision 2009/371/JHA (n. 574, *supra*). Before, the Council determined the staff regulations pursuant to Art. 30(3) of the Europol Convention (n. 573, *supra*), see the Council Decision of December 3, 1998, [1999] O.J. C26/23. For the transitional regime, see Art. 57 of Council Decision 2009/371/JHA.

[731] For the European Union Institute for Security Studies and the European Union Satellite Centre, see Arts 7 and 8 of Joint Action 2001/554/CFSP (n. 570, *supra*) and Art. 9 of Joint Action 2001/555/CFSP, which confer the status of contract staff on its personnel. For its staff regulations, see [2005] O.J. L235/1 and [2009] O.J. L276/2, respectively. For the European Defence Agency, see Art. 11 of Joint Action 2004/551/CFSP (n. 572, *supra*); for is staff regulations, see [2004] O.J. L310/09.

[732] Under the former system, Category A (eight grades) comprised staff engaged in administrative and advisory duties; category B (five grades) executive duties; category C (five grades) clerical duties; category D (five grades) manual or service duties; LA (6 grades) translating and interpreting, and each grade was divided into a number of salary steps. The system of salary steps still applies under the revised Staff Regulations.

[733] See Council Regulation (EC, Euratom) No. 723/2004 of March 22, 2004 amending the Staff Regulations of officials of the European Communities and the Conditions of Employment of other servants of the European Communities, [2004] O.J. L124/1.

in ascending hierarchical order.[734] In this way, a Director-General (AD 16 or AD 15), possibly assisted by a Deputy Director-General, will have under him or her Directorates run by Directors (AD 15 or AD 14). In turn, each Directorate is divided into administrative units in which administrators work under Heads of Unit (AD 14 to AD 9). Each administration has one or more appointing authorities. In principle, officials are appointed following an open competition.[735] Normally, only nationals of Member States are recruited, the aim being to achieve the broadest possible geographical basis.[736]

Officials are obliged to carry out their duties and conduct themselves solely with the interests of the Union in mind.[737] Officials must refrain from any unauthorised disclosure of information received in the line of duty, even after they have left the service, unless that information has already been made public or is accessible to the public.[738] They enjoy certain privileges and immunities in this connection.[739] Since those privileges and immunities are conferred on officials solely in the interests of the Union, each institution is required to waive the immunity of an official or other servant wherever it considers that such waiver is not contrary to the Union's interests (Protocol on Privileges and Immunities, Art. 17). Article 12 of the Protocol provides that officials and other servants are to be exempt from national taxes on salaries, wages and emoluments paid to them by the Union and have to pay a tax for the benefit of the Union on their Union salaries.[740] This tax is intended to secure the independent operation of the Union and to place staff from different Member States on an equal footing.[741] Anyone deriving rights from the Staff Regulations

---

[734] See Art. 5 of the amended Staff Regulations. In order to be recruited in function group AD it is necessary to have a university degree or equivalent professional experience; for function group AST, the requirement is for a diploma of post-secondary education or a diploma of secondary education and appropriate professional experience of at least three years.

[735] *Ibid.*, Art. 29(1). A different procedure may be employed for the recruitment of senior officials (Directors-General or their equivalent in grade AD 16 or AD 15 and Directors or their equivalent in grade AD 15 or AD 14) and, in exceptional cases, also for recruitment to posts which require special qualifications (Art. 29(2)). Recruitment has recently been entrusted to the European Personnel Selection Office (see para. 13–122). See *www.europa.eu/epso* [Accessed December 9, 2010].

[736] *Ibid.*, Art. 27. Under Art. 28(a), an official may be appointed only if "he is a national of one of the Member States of the [Union], unless an exception is authorised by the appointing authority, and enjoys his full rights as a citizen".

[737] *Ibid.*, Art. 11.

[738] *Ibid.*, Art. 17; see also Art. 339 TFEU [*ex Art. 287 EC*].

[739] Protocol on Privileges and Immunities (para. 13–128, *supra*).

[740] See Regulation (EEC, Euratom, ECSC) No. 260/68 of the Council of February 29, 1968 laying down the conditions and procedure for applying the tax for the benefit of the European Communities, [1968] O.J. English Spec. Ed. (I) 37. It does not empower the Union to make freelance interpreters subject to Union tax: CFI, Joined Cases T-202/96 and T-204/96 *Von Löwis and Alvarez-Cotera v Commission* [1998] E.C.R. II-2829, paras 51–58. This exemption from national tax is to be distinguished from the fiscal immunity enjoyed by the Union itself, under specific conditions: ECJ, Case C-437/04 *Commission v Belgium* [2007] E.C.R. I-2513, paras 50–59.

[741] ECJ, Case 85/86 *Commission v European Investment Bank* [1988] E.C.R. 1281, para. 23.

(for instance, dependants, persons taking part in open competitions) may bring proceedings in the Civil Service Tribunal after submitting a complaint to the appointing authority which has been rejected expressly or by implication.[742] Officials and other staff are to act in accordance with such codes of conduct as the institutions and bodies shall determine.[743]

F. RULES GOVERNING LANGUAGES

13–160 **Treaty languages.** When the EEC and EAEC Treaties were signed, it was provided that the text in each official language of the Contracting Parties was equally authentic (Art. 248 EEC; Art. 225 EAEC). As a result of the successive accession treaties, authentic Bulgarian, Czech, Danish, English, Estonian, Finnish, Greek, Hungarian, Irish, Latvian, Lithuanian, Maltese, Polish, Portuguese, Romanian, Slovak, Slovenian, Spanish and Swedish texts of the EEC and EAEC Treaties and of the amending and supplementing treaties came into being alongside the Dutch, French, German and Italian texts.[744] All subsequent amending treaties provide that the text in each Treaty language is equally authentic.[745] As a result, the Treaties on which the Union is based exist in 23 authentic languages. Only the French text of the ECSC Treaty was authentic (Art. 100 ECSC Treaty), but there were official translations in the other Treaty languages.[746]

---

[742] See Staff Regulations, Art. 90 (administrative procedure) and Art. 91 (appeal to the Court of Justice). For further particulars, see Lenaerts, Arts and Maselis, *Procedural Law of the European Union*, (3rd edn, London, Sweet & Maxwell, 2012), Ch.16.

[743] E.g. the Codes of Conduct of officials and other servants of the European Parliament ([2000] O.J. C97/1), of the General Secretariat of the Council ([2001] O.J. C189/1), of the Commission ([2000] O.J. L267/63), of the European Central Bank ([2001] O.J. C76/12), of the European Investment Bank ([2001] O.J. C17/26), of the Community Plant Variety Office ([2000] O.J. C371/14), of the European Environment Agency ([2000] O.J. L216/15) and of the European Foundation for the Improvement of Living and Working Conditions ([2000] O.J. L316/69). Codes of Conduct for the Court of Auditors, the European Training Foundation, the European Agency for the Evaluation of Medicinal Products and the Translation Centre for the Bodies of the European Union may be found on their websites. See Martinez Soria, "Die Kodizes für gute Verwaltungspraxis" (2001) EuR. 682–705.

[744] Article 55 TEU [*see ex Art. 314 EC*], and Art. 225 EAEC, as most recently amended by the second para. of Art. 60 of the 2005 Act of Accession. In 1984, Letzeburgisch, which is not a Treaty language, became an official language of the Grand Duchy of Luxembourg (alongside French and German).

[745] See Single European Act, Art. 34; EU Treaty, Art. 53; Amsterdam Treaty, Art. 15; Nice Treaty, Art. 13; Lisbon Treaty, Art. 7. It is noted that the language regime for intergovernmental conferences is determined by the participating States; see, e.g., the Commission's answer of December 20, 2002 to question P-3442/02 (Dehousse), [2003] O.J. C110E/213.

[746] The Decisions of Accession to the ECSC were authentic in all versions (i.e. in the Treaty languages at the time of accession). 1972, 1979 and 1985 Decisions of Accession (ns to para. 6–002—6–004), Art. 3.

Official languages of the Union. The rules governing the languages of the institutions are determined by the Council, acting unanimously, without prejudice to the Statute of the Court of Justice (Art. 342 TFEU [*ex Art. 290 EC*]; Art. 190 EAEC). In Art. 1 of Regulation No. 1, the Council declares the twenty-three languages to be official languages and working languages of the Union.[747] A Member State or one of its nationals may write to Union institutions in any Union language and the reply has to be drawn up in the same language (Art. 2 of Regulation No. 1).[748] Documents sent by a Union institution to a Member State or to one of its nationals must be drafted in the official language of that State (Art. 3) and, where the Member State has more than one official language, the language to be used is to be governed by the general rules of its law, if the Member State so requests (Art. 8). An irregularity in this respect is a ground for annulment only if, were it not for that irregularity, the procedure could have led to a different result.[749]

Regulations and other documents of general application must be drafted in all the official languages (Art. 4) and the *Official Journal* must be published in all official languages (Art. 5). As a result, the principle that all language versions are equally authentic also applies to secondary Union law. In order to secure legal certainty, all existing acts which are translated into a new official language upon

13–161

---

[747] Regulation No. 1 determining the languages to be used by the European Economic Community, [1952–1958] O.J. English Spec. Ed. 59, as amended upon the accession of each new Member State (referring now in Art.1 to languages "of the Union"). Irish has been included in the list only since 2007 (see Council Regulation (EC) No. 920/2005 of June 13, 2005, [2005] L156/3, which provides for a transitional period during which the institutions are not bound to translate all acts into Irish). See also Schilling, "Beyond Multilingualism: On Different Approaches to the Handling of Diverging Language Versions of a Community Law" (2010) E.L.J. 47–66; Vanhamme, "L'équivalence des langues dans le marché intérieur: l'apport de la Cour de justice" (2007) C.D.E. 359–380; Schübel-Pfister, "Enjeux et perspectives du multilinguisme dans l'Union européenne: après l'élargissement, la 'babélisation' " (2005) R.M.C.U.E. 325–333; Yvon, "Sprachenvielfalt und europäische Einheit— Zur Reform des Sprachenregimes der Europäischen Union" (2003) EuR. 681–695. The "language policy" of the European Union should also be concerned with the clarity of the communication, see Aziz, "Mainstreaming the Duty of Clarity and Transparency as part of the Good Administrative Practice in the EU" (2004) E.L.J. 282–295; see also para. 20–021, *infra*.

[748] See also Art. 24, fourth para., TFEU [*ex Art. 21, third para., EC*], proclaiming the right of every citizen of the Union to write to any of the institutions, the European Economic and Social Committee, the Committee of the Regions and the European Ombudsman in one of the Treaty languages and have an answer in the same language (para. 8–014, *infra*).

[749] ECJ, Joined Cases C-465/02 and C-466/02 *Germany and Denmark v Commission* [2005] E.C.R. I-9115, para. 37; CFI, Case T-219/04 *Spain v Commission* [2007] E.C.R. II-1323, para. 35. Where versions of an instrument in other, non-authentic languages are also sent to the person concerned, this does not affect its legality: ECJ, Joined Cases 40–48, 54–56, 111 and 113–114/73 *Suiker Unie and Others v Commission* [1975] E.C.R. 1663, paras 114–115. Whereas procedural documents, such as a decision and a statement of objections defining the institution's position must be sent to their addressee in the language of the case, annexes thereto which do not emanate from the institution must be regarded as supporting documentation and must be brought to the addressee's attention as they are: CFI, Case T-77/92 *Parker Pen v Commission* [1994] E.C.R. II-549, paras 70–74; CFI, Case T-148/89 *Tréfilunion v Commission* [1995] E.C.R. II-1063, paras 19–21.

the accession of a new Member State are also authentic as from the date of accession.[750] In principle, all the authentic language versions have the same weight and it makes no difference what proportion of the population of the Union the language in question represents.[751] As a result of the need for uniform interpretation of Union law, texts are not considered in isolation, but in cases of doubt are interpreted and applied in the light of the other authentic language versions.[752] Accordingly, the wording used in one language version of a Union provision cannot serve as the sole basis for the interpretation of that provision, or be made to override the other language versions in that regard.[753] For the sake of legal certainty, the words of a given version of a text should be given their natural and usual meaning and points at issue should, if possible, be resolved without giving preference to any one of the versions.[754] In the case of divergence between versions, the provision in question must be interpreted by reference to the purpose and general scheme of the rules of which it forms a part.[755] Individual decisions do not necessarily have to be drawn up in all the official languages. Even if an individual decision is published in the *Official Journal* and is therefore translated into all the languages for the information of citizens, only the language used in the relevant procedure will be authentic and will be used to interpret that decision.[756]

---

[750] See 1972 Act of Accession, Art. 155; 1979 Act of Accession, Art. 147; 1985 Act of Accession, Art. 397; 1994 Act of Accession, Art. 170; 2003 Act of Accession, Art. 58, 2005 Act of Accession, Art. 58. Acts which have not been published in the official language of a Member State in the *Official Journal* cannot be enforced against individuals in that Member State (ECJ, Case C-161/06 *Skoma-Lux* [2007] E.C.R. I-10841, paras 32–50). See Lasinki-Sulecki, "Late publication of EC Law in languages of new member states and its effects: obligations on individuals following the Court's Judgment in Skoma-Lux" (2008) 45 C.M.L.Rev. 705–725.

[751] ECJ, Case C-296/95 *EMU Tobacco and Others* [1998] E.C.R. I-1605, para. 36.

[752] ECJ, Case 19/67 *Bestuur van de Sociale Verzekeringsbank* [1967] E.C.R. 345, at 354. For an example, see ECJ, Case C-327/91 *France v Commission* [1994] E.C.R. I-3641, para. 35; see also the (somewhat amusing) question No. 1896/92 (McCubbin) and the Commission's answer of September 3, 1993, [1994] O.J. C251/1.

[753] ECJ, Joined Cases C-261/08 and C-348/08 *Zurita García and Choque Cabrera* [2009] E.C.R. I-10143, para. 55.

[754] ECJ, Case 80/76 *Kerry Milk* [1977] E.C.R. 425, para. 11; CFI, Case T-42/89 *Yorck von Wartenburg v European Parliament* [1990] E.C.R. II-31, paras 16–18, and CFI, Case T-42/89 OPPO *European Parliament v Yorck von Wartenburg* [1990] E.C.R. II-299, paras 10–13. See also Sevón, "Languages in the Court of Justice of the European Communities" (1998) Riv.D.E. 533–546 and Van Calster, "The EU's Tower of Babel—The Interpretation by the Court of Justice of Equally Authentic Texts Drafted in More than One Official Language" (1997) Y.E.L. 363–393.

[755] ECJ, Case 30/77 *Bouchereau* [1977] E.C.R. 1999, para. 14; see, more recently, ECJ, Case C-72/95 *Kraaijeveld* [1996] E.C.R. I-5403, paras 28–31; ECJ, Joined Cases C-267/95 and C-268/95 *Merck and Beecham* [1996] E.C.R. I-6285, paras 21–24; ECJ, Case C-257/00 *Givane and Others* [2003] E.C.R. I-345, paras 29–50; ECJ, Case C-428/02 *Fonden Marselisborg Lystbådehavn* [2005] E.C.R. I-1527, paras 41–47; ECJ (judgment of April 29, 2010), Case C-340/08 *M and Others*, not yet reported, paras 38–69.

[756] ECJ, Case C-361/01 P *Kik v Office for Harmonisation in the Internal Market* [2003] E.C.R. I-8283, para. 87, with a case note by Shuibhne (2004) 41 C.M.L.Rev. 1093–1111.

Other official languages of the Member States. In 2005, the Council considered   **13–162**
that, as part of the efforts being made to bring the Union closer to all its citizens,
the richness of its linguistic diversity had to be taken more into consideration. It
was considered that allowing citizens the possibility of using additional languages
in their relations with the Union institutions would be an important factor in
strengthening their identification with the European Union's political project.
Accordingly, since 2005, the Council may authorise the official use of languages
other than the languages referred to in Regulation No. 1 whose status is recognised
by the Constitution of a Member State on all or part of its territory or the use of
which as a national language is authorised by law.[757] For this purpose, Member
States are to conclude administrative arrangements with the Council, and possibly
other Union institutions and bodies, which will allow a Member State to use one
of these other languages in the Council and in other institutions and bodies. The
direct or indirect costs associated with implementation of these arrangements are
to be borne by the requesting Member State. Administrative arrangements may
also provide for translation in one of these languages of acts adopted by the
European Parliament and the Council under the ordinary legislative procedure.
However, such translations will not have the status of law. Finally, a Member State
can provide for a right of its citizens to communicate with Union institutions or
bodies in one of these languages; the Member State in question will then be
responsible for translations into or from one of the official languages of the Union.
In an administrative arrangement with the Council, Spain has committed itself
to enable the use of Basque, Catalan and Galician in the aforementioned situations.[758] Since the entry into force of the Lisbon Treaty, the Treaties explicitly
provide that they may be translated into any other languages as determined by
Member States among those which, in accordance with their constitutional order,
enjoy official status in all or part of their territory.[759]

Linguistic regime in the Court of Justice. For the rules on the use of languages   **13–163**
before the Court of Justice, Art. 7 of Regulation No. 1 refers to the ECJ Rules of
Procedure.[760] The Rules of Procedure of the Court of Justice and the General Court
provide that any of the Treaty languages may be used as the language of the case,

---

[757] Council Conclusion of June 13, 2005 on the official use of additional languages within the Council
and possibly other institutions and bodies of the European Union, [2005] O.J. C148/1.

[758] Administrative arrangement between the Kingdom of Spain and the Council of the European
Union, [2006] O.J. C40/2. See, similarly, as far as the United Kingdom is concerned, the
Administrative arrangement between the Government of the United Kingdom of Great Britain and
Northern Ireland and the Council of the European Union, [2008] O.J. C194/7.

[759] Article 55(2) of the TEU; Art. 358 TFEU.

[760] Following on from Art. 342 TFEU [*ex Art. 290 EC*], which refers as regards the rules governing
languages to the Statute of the Court of Justice, Art. 64 of that Statute states that until the rules
governing the language arrangements applicable at the Court of Justice and the General Court have
been adopted in the Statute, the provisions of the Rules of Procedure of the Court of Justice and
of the General Court governing language arrangements are to continue to apply.

which is to be chosen by the applicant.[761] However, where the defendant is a Member State or a national of a particular Member State, the applicant must opt for the official language (or one of the official languages) of that State.[762] Nevertheless, at the joint request of the parties or at the request of one of the parties (provided that it is not a [Union] institution), and after the opposite party and the Advocate-General have been heard, the Court may authorise an official language other than the language of the case to be used.[763] Questions referred for a preliminary ruling are dealt with in the language of the court which made the reference.[764]

Although in principle all documents are translated into the language of the case and the parties plead in that language, the Rules of Procedure provide for exceptions. Member States are entitled to use their official language (at their election) and the President may conduct the hearing in a language other than the language of the case. By the same token, Judges and Advocates-General may put questions in another official language and the latter generally deliver their Opinions in their native tongue.[765] Witnesses and experts may be authorised to use another language, even a language other than one of the Treaty languages.[766] In order to avoid the use of interpreters, the two Courts use French as their working language. Judgments, orders intended for publication and Opinions (of the Court or Advocates-General) are reported in all official languages.[767] The texts of documents drawn up in the language of the case or in any other language authorised by the Court are authentic.[768]

13–164   **Linguistic regime in other institutions.** Article 6 of Regulation No. 1 provides that the Union institutions may stipulate in their rules of procedure which of the official languages are to be used in specific cases. Thus, the European Parliament works on the basis that each Member is entitled to use his or her official language

---

[761] ECJ Rules of Procedure, Art. 29(1); General Court Rules of Procedure, Art. 35(1). Pursuant to Art. 29 of the Rules of Procedure of the Civil Service Tribunal, the provisions of the Rules of Procedure of the General Court governing language arrangements apply to that Tribunal.

[762] ECJ Rules of Procedure, Art. 29(2)(a). This situation may arise where the Court of Justice adjudicates pursuant to an arbitration clause contained in a contract concluded with Union institutions or bodies (Art. 272 TFEU).

[763] ECJ Rules of Procedure, Art. 29(2)(b) and (c); General Court Rules of Procedure, Art. 35(2).

[764] ECJ Rules of Procedure, Art. 29(2), second subpara.

[765] The Registrar arranges for translation into the language of the case (ECJ Rules of Procedure, Art. 29(3) to (5); General Court Rules of Procedure, Art. 35(3) to (5)).

[766] ECJ Rules of Procedure, Art. 29(4); General Court Rules of Procedure, Art. 35(4).

[767] ECJ Rules of Procedure, Art. 30(2); General Court Rules of Procedure, Art. 36(2). Since January 1, 1994 an exception has been made for staff cases, where the judgment is generally published only in the language of the case. See the introduction to the source material. For a discussion, see Mulders, "Translation at the Court of Justice of the European Communities", in Prechal and van Roermund (eds), *The Coherence of EU Law* (Oxford, Oxford University Press, 2008), at 45–61.

[768] ECJ Rules of Procedure, Art. 31; General Court Rules of Procedure, Art. 37.

and provides that documents are to be drawn up in and speeches interpreted into all the official languages.[769] Consequently, knowledge of languages is not required in order to stand for election to the European Parliament.[770] Speeches in Parliament may also be interpreted into any other language the Bureau may consider necessary. Interpretation is provided in committee and delegation meetings for the official languages used and requested by the members.[771] An exception to the normal rule on the use of languages is made for recommendations within the framework of the CFSP.[772] In other institutions, it is not practicable for all the official languages to be on an equal footing as working languages. The European Council and the Council deliberate and take decisions,

> "only on the basis of documents and drafts drawn up in the languages specified in the rules in force governing languages",

but may decide otherwise by unanimous vote on grounds of urgency.[773] As far as CFSP is concerned, meetings at official level and exchanges of information among Member States are conducted in English and French.[774] In practice, English and French are chiefly used for communications within the Council, the exception being meetings of the Council itself. The Commission has to annex instruments adopted by it at a meeting in the authentic language or languages to the minutes of the meeting at which they were adopted.[775] In the case of instruments of general application, this means translation is required in all the official languages of the Union; in other cases, translation in the language or languages of those to whom they are addressed suffices. In the Court of Auditors, reports, opinions, observations and statements of assurance must be drafted in all the official languages.[776] Whilst these rules on the use of languages are complied with,

---

[769] EP Rules of Procedure, Rule 146; see the resolution of the European Parliament of May 6, 1994 on the right to use one's own language, [1994] O.J. C205/528.

[770] Resolution of the European Parliament of October 14, 1982 on multilingualism of the European Community, [1982] O.J. C292/96.

[771] EP Rules of Procedure, Rule 146(2) and (3).

[772] EP Rules of Procedure, Rule 97(3).

[773] European Council Rules of Procedure, Art. 9(1); Council Rules of Procedure, Art. 14(1).

[774] See Declaration (No. 29) annexed to the initial EU Treaty. See also the Council's answer of October 8, 2000 to question E-1212/01 (Marchiani), [2002] O.J. C40E/25. The previous EPC practice continues to apply to the simplified written procedure (COREU). This consists in using only English and French as working languages: see the answer of the Presidency of November 6, 1985 to Question No. 1673/84 (Formigoni) (1985) 2 EPC Bulletin doc. 85/242, 140.

[775] Commission Rules of Procedure, Art. 17(1). Instruments adopted by the written procedure, the empowerment procedure, the delegation procedure and by way of subdelegation (para. 13–075, *supra*) are to be attached, in the authentic language or languages, in such a way that they cannot be separated, to a day note recorded in the minutes (Commission Rules of Procedure, Art. 17(2)—(5)).

[776] Rules of Procedure of the Court of Auditors, Art. 28(1).

in practice French, English and (to a lesser extent) German are used as working languages within the administration.[777]

13–165 **Linguistic regime in other bodies.** The Treaties do not contain any provision on the use of languages by other bodies and agencies of the Union, which means that their power of internal organisation is not restricted in this respect. The Council has made the rules governing the use of languages by the institutions applicable when setting up certain bodies.[778] Those rules also apply in Europol and Eurojust.[779] In Regulation No. 40/94 establishing the Office for Harmonisation in the Internal Market (trade-marks and designs) and its successor Regulation No. 207/2009, the Council broke away from the principle that all the official

---

[777] For discussions of the language regime, under which English is increasingly obtaining the upper hand, see de Witte, "Language Law of the European Union: Protecting or Eroding Linguistic Diversity?", in Craufurd Smith (ed.), *Culture and European Union Law* (Oxford, Oxford University Press, 2004) 205–242. Fenet, "Diversité linguistique et construction européenne" (2001) R.T.D.E. 235–269; Oppermann, "Reform der Sprachenregelung?" (2001) N.J.W. 2663–2668. While the Commission may validly decide which languages are used in specific cases and is not required to publish vacancy notices in all the official languages, a Commission decision under which the external publication of vacancy notices for senior management posts in the *Official Journal* is made only in English, French and German infringes the principle of non-discrimination as laid down in Art. 1(d) of the Staff Regulations (CFI, Case T-185/05 *Italy v Commission* [2008] E.C.R. II-3207, paras 127–152). Nonetheless, Regulation No. 1 does not apply to the contracts between the institutions and their staff, see EGC (judgment of September 13, 2010), Joined Cases T-156/07 and T-232/07 *Spain v Commission*, and Joined Cases T-166/07 and T-285/07 *Italy v Commission*, not yet reported. See also CST (judgment of October 21, 2009), Case F-33/08 *V v Commission*, not yet reported, paras 170 and 173.

[778] See the regulations establishing the European Centre for the Development of Vocational Training (Art. 15), the European Foundation for the Improvement of Living and Working Conditions (Art. 19), the European Agency for Health and Safety at Work (Art. 17), the Community Plant Variety Office (Art. 34(1)), the European Maritime Safety Agency (Art. 9), the European Network and Information Security Agency (Art. 22), the European Union Agency for Fundamental Rights (Art. 25), Community Fisheries Control Agency (Art. 22), the European Agency for the Management of Operational Cooperation at the External Borders (Art. 27), the European Chemicals Agency (Art. 104), the European Institute for Gender Equality (Art. 16), the European Global Navigation Satellite System Supervisory Authority (Art. 18), the Agency for the Cooperation of Energy Regulators (Art. 33) and the European Asylum Support Office (Art. 41). The regulation establishing the European Training Foundation provides that the governing board is to determine the rules governing the languages of the Foundation "taking into account the need to ensure access to, and participation in, the work of the Foundation by all interested parties" (Art. 5(5)). In the case of the European Agency for Reconstruction, the regulation establishing it provided only that the Governing Board shall determine by unanimous decision the "rules governing the languages used by the Agency" (Art. 4(8); similar arrangements apply in the European Railways Agency (Art. 35(1)), where the Management Board/Administrative Board is to decide on the linguistic arrangements for the Agency by a unanimous vote.

[779] Article 47 of Council Decision 2009/371/JHA (n. 574, *supra*) and Art. 31 of Council Decision 2002/187/JHA (n. 579, *supra*). Spain considered that these rules had been broken by the establishment of English and French as de facto working languages and brought an action against notices of vacancy requiring knowledge of those languages, which was, however, declared inadmissible (ECJ, Case C-160/03 *Spain v Eurojust* [2005] E.C.R. I-2077).

languages are on an equal footing by providing that only English, French, German, Italian and Spanish are to be the languages of the Office.[780] The Office arranges for the translation of trade-mark applications submitted in other official languages of the Union (Regulation No. 207/2009, Art. 119(3), second subpara.). In proceedings before the Office, so long as the applicant is the sole party to proceedings before the Office, the language used for filing the application for registration remains the language of proceedings (Art. 119(4)) and all documents necessary for dealing with the application will be drawn up in that language.[781] In opposition, revocation or invalidity proceedings, the language of the proceedings is such language of the Office as the applicant chooses (Art. 119(3), first subpara., and (5)), unless the parties agree to use another official language (Art. 119(7)).[782] Applications for the registration of designs are subject to similar rules.[783] The Court of Justice has held that the choice to limit the languages to those which are most widely known in the European Union is an appropriate and proportionate linguistic solution to the difficulties arising where parties with different languages cannot agree on the language to be used. In so far as direct proceedings between the Office and the applicant can be conducted in the language of the applicant, the rules on use of languages in the Office are therefore not in breach of the principle of equal treatment.[784] The second para. of Art. 118 TFEU on the creation of European intellectual property rights, testifies to the sensitivity of the language issue, whereas the rights may be created under the ordinary legislative procedure, the language arrangements are to be established by the Council, under a special legislative procedure, whereby the Council has to act unanimously (after consulting the European Parliament).

G. TRANSPARENCY AND ACCESS TO DOCUMENTS

Transparency. The Treaties stress that decisions by the Union are taken "as openly as possible" (Art. 1, second para., and 10(3) TEU; Art. 15(1) TFEU). **13–166**

---

[780] Article 119(2) of Council Regulation (EC) No. 207/2009 of February 26, 2009 on the Community trade mark ([2009] O.J. L78/1), replacing Art. 115(2) of Council Regulation (EC) No. 40/94 of December 20, 1993 on the Community trade mark, [1994] O.J. L11/1. Cf. the equality of official languages in dealings with the Community Plant Variety Office (Art. 34(2) and (3) of Regulation (EC) No. 2100/94). See Gundel, "Zur Sprachenregelung bei den EG-Agenturen—Abschied auf Raten von der Regel der 'Allsprachigkeit' der Gemeinschaft im Verkehr mit dem Bürger?" (2001) EuR. 776–783.

[781] CFI, Case T-120/99 *Kik v Office for Harmonisation in the Internal Market* [2001] E.C.R. II-2235, para. 61, as upheld by ECJ, Case C-361/01 P *Kik v Office for Harmonisation in the Internal Market* [2003] E.C.R.I-08283, paras 44–49.

[782] See also General Court Rules of Procedure, Art. 131, for the language regime applicable to disputes relating to intellectual property rights.

[783] Article 98 of Council Regulation (EC) No. 6/2002 of December 12, 2001 on Community designs, [2002] O.J. L3/1).

[784] CFI, Case T-120/99 *Kik v Office for Harmonisation in the Internal Market* [2001] E.C.R. II-2235, paras 62–63, as upheld by ECJ, Case C-361/01 P *Kik v Office for Harmonisation in the Internal Market* [2003] E.C.R.I-8283, paras 82–96.

Openness of decision-making applies as regards the operation of the European Parliament and, to a lesser extent, of the European Council, the Council and the Commission (see paras 22–007—22–008). As far as officials of Union institutions are concerned, the 2004 reform of the Staff Regulations has replaced the general duty of confidentiality by a prohibition of the unauthorised disclosure of information received in the line of duty unless that information has already been made public or is accessible to the public (see para. 13–158).

13–167   **Access to documents.** Since 1991 the debate on the need for the Union to be "transparent" has concentrated on citizens' ability to have access to documents issued by the institutions or in their possession.[785] As a result of the Treaty of Amsterdam, access to documents was enshrined in Treaty law (see Art. 255 EC). At present, Art. 15(3) TFEU gives any citizen of the Union and any natural or legal person residing or having its registered office in a Member State a right of access to documents of the Union institutions, bodies, offices and agencies. General principles and limits on grounds of public or private interest governing this right of access are determined in Regulation No. 1049/2001 of the European Parliament and the Council,[786] which also applies to bodies with legal personality established pursuant to the Treaties.[787] The Regulation builds upon the access

---

[785] See Declaration (No. 17) to the EU Treaty on the right of access to information and the Birmingham Declaration of October 16, 1992—A Community close to its citizens (1992) 10 EC Bull. point I.8 (see para. 20–017). For a general discussion, see Harden, "Citizenship and Information" (2001) E.Publ.L 165–193; Curtin, "Citizens' fundamental right of access to EU information: an evolving digital *passepartout?*" (2000) C.M.L.Rev.7–41; Bradley, "La transparence de l'Union européenne: une évidence ou un trompe l'oeil?" (1999) C.D.E. 283–360.

[786] Regulation (EC) No. 1049/2001 of the European Parliament and of the Council of May 30, 2001 regarding public access to European Parliament, Council and Commission documents, [2001] O.J. L145/43. See Kranenborg, "Access to documents and data protection in the European Union: on the public nature of personal data" (2008) 45 C.M.L.Rev. 1079–114; Bartelt and Zeitler, "Zugang zu Dokumenten der EU" (2003) EuR. 487–503; De Leeuw, "The Regulation on public access to European Parliament, Council and Commission documents in the European Union: are citizens better off?" (2003) E.L.Rev. 324–348; Schauss, "L'accès du citoyen aux documents des institutions communautaires" (2003) J.T.D.E. 1–8; Schram, "Openbaarheid van Europese bestuursdocumenten" (2003) N.J.Wb. 581–592; Wägenbaur, "Der Zugang zu EU-Dokumenten—Transparenz zum Anfassen" (2001) Eu.Z.W. 680–685. When the European Parliament, the Council and the Commission act in pursuance of the EAEC Treaty, they should draw guidance from the regulation; see recital 5 in the preamble to the regulation and Declaration (No. 41), annexed to the Amsterdam Treaty on the provisions relating to transparency, access to documents and the fight against fraud, [1997] O.J. C340/140. For the importance of the right of access to documents, see the earlier case, ECJ, C-58/94 *Netherlands v Council* [1996] E.C.R. I-2169, paras 34–37. Since Art. 255 EC [*now Art. 15(3) TFEU*] requires further implementing measures, that article does not have direct effect: CFI, Case T-191/99 *Petrie and Others v Commission* [2001] E.C.R. II-3677, paras 34–35. With regard to EFTA countries, see Decision of the Standing Committee of the EFTA States No. 3/2005/SC of June 9, 2005 on public access to EFTA documents, [2006] O.J. L98/80.

[787] See the amendments made by the Council to this effect on July 22, 2003 in the various regulations establishing such bodies ([2003] O.J. L245).

to documents regulated by the Council and the Commission by a joint code of conduct and internal decisions,[788] on which the Union Courts have repeatedly had occasion to rule, in particular in order to determine whether, in exercising their discretion, the institutions had genuinely balanced the interests of citizens in gaining access to their documents against any interest of their own in maintaining the confidentiality of their deliberations.[789] Regulation No. 1049/2001 applies to all documents held by an institution, that is to say, documents drawn up or received by it and in its possession, in all areas of activity of the European Union.[790] If a document has already been released and is easily accessible, it is sufficient for the institution to inform the applicant how to obtain the requested document.[791] Other documents must in principle also be disclosed upon request, but the regulation provides for a number of exceptions in this regard (see para. 13–168). The regulation requires each institution or body to keep a register and also provides for special treatment for sensitive documents.[792]

Each institution, body, office or agency is to ensure that its proceedings are transparent and must elaborate in its own rules of procedure specific provisions regarding access to its documents, in accordance with the limits laid down in the regulations of

---

[788] Code of Conduct of December 6, 1993 concerning public access to Council and Commission documents, [1993] O.J. L340/41 (*corrigendum* in [1993] O.J. L23/34); Council Decision 93/731/EC of December 20, 1993 ([1993] O.J. L340/43), Council Decision 2001/320/EC of April 9, 2001 ([2001] O.J. L111/29) and Commission Decision 94/90/ECSC, EC, Euratom of February 8, 1994 ([1994] O.J. L46/58).

[789] See, e.g., CFI, Case T-194/94 *Carvel and Guardian Newspapers v Council* [1995] ECR II-2765, paras 62–80; CFI, Case T-105/95 *WWF UK v Commission* [1997] ECR II-313, para. 59; ECJ, Case C-353/99 P *Council v Hautala* [2001] ECR I-9565, paras 21–31. For the obligation to state the reason for which access is refused, see, in particular, CFI, Case T-105/95 *WWF UK v Commission* [1997] ECR II-313, paras 66–78; CFI, Case T-124/96 *Interporc v Commission* [1998] ECR II-231, paras 46–57; CFI, Case T-174/95 *Svenska Journalistförbundet v Council* [1998] ECR II-2289, paras 109–127 (annulment of insufficiently reasoned decisions); for confirmation that Decision 93/731 also applied to Council documents relating to non-Community activities, see CFI, Case T-174/95 *Svenska Journalistförbundet v Council* [1998] ECR II-2289, paras 81–86.

[790] Article 2(3) of Regulation No. 1049/2001. Under the former rules, access to a document of which the institution itself was not the originator had to be sought from its author, see CFI, Case T-92/98 *Interporc v Commission* [1999] E.C.R. II-3521, paras 65–72, upheld by ECJ, Case C-41/00 P *Interporc v Commission* [2003] E.C.R. I-2125, paras 34–59; see the note by de Leeuw (2005) 42 C.M.L.Rev. 261–280. The public's right of access to documents does not imply a duty on the part of the institution to reply to any request for information from an individual: CFI (order of October 27, 1999), Case T-106/99 *Meyer v Commission* [1999] E.C.R. II-3273, para. 35.

[791] Regulation No. 1049/2001, Art. 10(2). See also CFI (order of October 27, 1999), Case T-106/99 *Meyer v Commission* [1999] E.C.R. II-3273, para. 39 (access to documents is not applicable where the documents have already been published in the *Official Journal*).

[792] Article 9 of Regulation No. 1049/2001 provides for the classification of documents as "top secret", "secret" or "confidential".

the European Parliament and of the Council.[793] The European Parliament and the Council must ensure publication of the documents relating to the legislative procedures under the terms laid down by these regulations (Art. 15(3), fifth subpara., TFEU). However, the right of access to documents applies with regard to the Court of Justice, the ECB and the EIB only to the extent that they are exercising administrative tasks (Art. 15(3), fourth subpara., TFEU).[794]

13–168 **Refusal of access.** Under Regulation No. 1049/2001, a person requesting access to documents is not required to justify his request (Art. 6(1)) and therefore he or she does not have to demonstrate any interest in having access to the documents.[795] Regulation No. 1049/2001 provides that the institutions and bodies are to refuse access to a document so as to protect certain interests, namely (a) the public interest as regards public security, defence and military matters, international relations or the financial, monetary or economic policy of the Union or a Member State[796] and (b) privacy and the integrity of the individual[797] (Art. 4(1)). Unless there is an overriding public interest in disclosure, access to a document is also to be refused where disclosure would undermine the protection of (a) commercial interests of a natural or legal person,[798] including intellectual property,

---

[793] See Art. 15(3), third subpara., TFEU [*ex Art. 255(3) EC*]. For the implementation thereof, see Art. 104 of the EP Rules of Procedure and the Decision of the Bureau of the European Parliament of November 28, 2001 ([2001] O.J. C374/1; consolidated version in [2005] O.J. C289/6); Council Decision 2001/840/EC adding as Annex III (now Annex II) to the Rules of Procedure specific provisions regarding public access to Council documents ([2001] O.J. L313/40); the provisions appended as an annex to the Rules of Procedure adopted by the Commission by Decision of December 5, 2001 ([2001] O.J. L345/94); Decision No. 12/2005 of the Court of Auditors of the European Communities of March 10, 2005 regarding public access to Court of Auditors documents, [2009] O.J. C67/1; Decision 2003/603/EC of the European Economic and Social Committee of July 1, 2003 ([2003] O.J. L205/19), Decision No. 64/2003 of the Committee of the Regions of February 11, 2003 ([2003] O.J. L160/96); and the rules for access to Europol documents ([2007] O.J. C72/37). See Driessen, "The Council of the European Union and access to documents" (2005) E.L.Rev. 675–696.

[794] See the rules on public access to documents of the European Central Bank ([2004] O.J. L80/42) and of the European Investment Bank ([2002] O.J. C292/10).

[795] CFI, Case T-124/96 *Interporc v Commission* [1998] E.C.R. II-231, para. 48; CFI, Joined Cases T-391/03 and T-70/04 *Franchet and Byk* [2006] E.C.R. II-2023, para. 82.

[796] The Union legislature enjoys a broad discretion in applying the public interest exceptions of Art. 4(1)(a) (ECJ, Case C-266/05 P *Sison v Council* [2007] E.C.R. I-1233, paras 32–36).

[797] See ECJ (judgment of June 29, 2010), Case C-28/08 P *Commission v Bavarian Lager*, not yet reported (where access is requested to documents including personal data, application should be made of Regulation No. 45/2001, n. 812, *infra*). On the exceptions to the right of access to document, see Adamski, "How Wide is "The Widest Possible"? Judicial Interpretation of the Exceptions to the Right of Access to Official Documents Revisited" (2009) C.M.L.Rev. 521–549.

[798] See EGC (judgment of January 19, 2010), Joined Cases T-355/04 and T-446/04, *Co-Frutta v Commission*, not yet reported, paras 99–107 and 122–140; EGC (judgment of June 9, 2010), Case T-237/05, *Editions Odile Jacob v Commission*, not yet reported, paras 109–129.

(b) court proceedings[799] and legal advice[800] or (c) the purpose of inspections, investigations and audits[801] (Regulation No. 1049/2001, Art. 4(2)). An institution or body may also refuse access to internal and preparatory documents if disclosure of the document would seriously undermine the institution's decision-making process, unless there is an overriding public interest in disclosure (Regulation

---

[799] This exception covers the pleadings or other documents lodged, internal documents concerning the investigation of the case, and correspondence concerning the case between the Directorate-General concerned and the Legal Service or a lawyers' office. The purpose of this exception is to ensure both the protection of work done within the Commission and confidentiality and the safeguarding of professional privilege for lawyers: CFI, Case T-92/98 *Interporc v Commission* [1999] E.C.R. II-3521, paras 40–42 (holding that the exception for court proceedings cannot enable the Commission to escape from its obligation to disclose documents which were drawn up in connection with a purely administrative matter). No access should be given to an institution's pleadings before the Court of Justice while proceedings are still pending: see ECJ (judgment of September 21, 2010), Joined Cases C-514/07P, C-528/07P and C-532/07P *Sweden v Commission*, not yet reported. Where the Commission has received a request for access to documents which it has supplied to a national court in the context of its cooperation with national courts in applying competition law, it must verify whether their disclosure would constitute an infringement of national law. In the event of doubt, it must consult the national court and refuse access only if that court objects to disclosure of the documents: ECJ, Joined Cases C-174/98 P and C-189/98 P *The Netherlands and Van der Wal v Commission* [2000] E.C.R. I-1, paras 20–33. See also CFI, Joined Cases T-391/03 and T-70/04 *Franchet and Byk* [2006] E.C.R. II-2023, paras 88–103.

[800] This exception protects an institution's interest in seeking legal advice and receiving frank, objective and comprehensive advice: ECJ, Joined Cases C-39/05 P and C-52/05 P *Sweden and Turco v Council* [2007] E.C.R. I-4723, paras 42–43. For the protection of internal legal advice in administrative proceedings, see CFI Case T-403/05 *My Travel v Commission* [2008] E.C.R. II-2027, paras 122–128, and EGC (judgment of June 9, 2010), Case T-237/05 *Editions Odile Jacob v Commission*, not yet reported, paras 156–161 (access to opinion of the Commission's legal service may be refused to preserve the freedom of the legal service to express its views and its ability effectively to defend before the Union judicature, on an equal footing with the representatives of other parties, the Commission's definitive position and the internal decision-making process of that institution); CFI (order of the President of March 3, 1998), T-610/97 R *Carlsen v Council* [1998] E.C.R. II-485, paras 43–53 (access may be refused on account of the maintenance of legal certainty and stability of Union law). However, disclosure of documents containing the advice of an institution's legal service on legal questions arising when legislative initiatives are being debated increases the transparency and openness of the legislative process and strengthens the democratic right of European citizens to scrutinise the information which has formed the basis of a legislative act. Consequently, Regulation No. 1049/2001 imposes, in principle, an obligation to disclose the opinions of the Council's legal service relating to a legislative process: ECJ, Joined Cases C-39/05 P and C-52/05 P *Sweden and Turco v Council* [2007] E.C.R. I-4723, paras 40–68.

[801] This exception applies only where disclosure of the documents in question may endanger the completion of inspections, investigations or audits: CFI, Joined Cases T-391/03 and T-70/04 *Franchet and Byk* [2006] E.C.R. II-2023, para. 109; EGC (judgment of June 9, 2010), Case T-237/05, *Editions Odile Jacob v Commission*, not yet reported, paras 72–76. Acts of investigation may remain covered by the exception as long as the investigation continues, even if the particular inspection which gave rise to the report to which access is sought is completed: CFI, Case T-20/99 *Denkavit Nederland v Commission* [2000] E.C.R. II-3011, para. 48. In the context of State Aid, a general presumption applies that disclosure of documents in the administrative file to persons others than those which have access to the file, in principle undermines the protection of the

No. 1049/2001, Art. 4(3)).[802] Accordingly, an institution cannot refuse to grant access to documents pertaining to its deliberations merely on the basis that they contain information relating to positions taken by representatives of the Member States.[803] Those exceptions apply only where the risk of the public interest being undermined is reasonably foreseeable and not purely hypothetical.[804] In any event, exceptions must be applied strictly.[805]

Under the regulation, a Member State may request the Commission or the Council not to disclose a document originating from that Member State without its prior consent.[806] If a Member State makes such a request, it is obliged to state reasons for that objection by reference to the exceptions mentioned in Regulation No. 1049/2001; where it fails to do so, the institution requested must consider for its part whether one of these exceptions applies. If the Member State concerned has reasoned its objection against the disclosure of the documents at stake, the institution requested must refuse disclosure, while setting out the reasons relied on by that Member State.[807]

Where a document includes items of information falling within one of the grounds for refusing access, the principle of proportionality requires the institutions or bodies to consider granting access to the items for which those exceptions do not

---

objective of the investigation: ECJ (judgment of June 29, 2010), Case C-139/07 P *Commission v Technische Glaswerke Ilmenau*, not yet reported, paras 55–62. In the context of infringement proceedings under Art. 226 EC [*now Art. 258 TFEU*], the General Court held that access to documents relating to the investigation must be refused in order to prevent a breach of confidentiality affecting the proper functioning of such proceedings: CFI, Case T-105/95 *WWF UK v Commission* [1997] E.C.R. II-313, para. 63; CFI, Case T-309/97 *The Bavarian Lager Company v Commission* [1999] E.C.R. II-3217, paras 45–46 (refusal during the inspection and investigation stage); CFI, Case T-191/99 *Petrie and Others v Commission* [2001] E.C.R. II-3677, paras 67–69 (refusal after institution of proceedings in the Court of Justice); cf. ECJ (judgment of September 21, 2010), Joined Cases C-514/07 P, C-528/07 P and C-532/07 P *Sweden v API and Commission*, not yet reported, para 118–222 (no refusal after judgement has been delivered). For criticism of the lack of access to the finding of an infringement and the reasoned opinion, see Krämer, "Access to Letters of Formal Notice and Reasoned Opinions in Environmental Law Matters" (2003) E.Env.L.Rev. 197–203.

[802] See CFI, Case T-403/05 *MyTravel v Commission* [2008] E.C.R. II-2027, paras 42–68 (disclosure of an internal report held to seriously undermine the decision-making freedom of the Commission—appeal pending: C-506/08 P); CFI, Joined Cases T-391/03 and T-70/04 *Franchet and Byk* [2006] E.C.R. II-2023, paras 135–139 (the right to a fair hearing invoked by the applicants as an overriding interest is not an overriding public interest justifying disclosure of the requested documents).

[803] CFI, Case T-111/00 *British American Tobacco International v Commission* [2001] E.C.R. II-2997, paras 52–57.

[804] CFI, Case T-211/00 *Kuijer v Council* [2002] ECR II-485, paras 56–70 (adverse reports about human rights in third countries are not necessarily prejudicial to the Union's relations with those countries); ECJ, Joined Cases C-39/05 P and C-52/05 P *Sweden and Turco v Council* [2008] E.C.R. I-4723, paras 40–43.

[805] E.g., CFI, Case T-264/04 *WWF European Policy Programme* [2007] E.C.R. II-911, para. 39.

[806] Regulation No. 1049/2001, Art. 4(5).

[807] ECJ, Case C-64/05 P *Sweden v Commission and Others* [2007] E.C.R. I-11389.

apply.[808] Within 15 working days of receipt of a written application, the institution or body must either grant access or refuse it totally or partially. If an application for access is refused or unanswered, the applicant must seek, by means of a confirmatory application, a formal refusal, against which an action for annulment will lie and/or a complaint may be made to the European Ombudsman.[809]

In principle, the exceptions relating to access to documents apply for a maximum period of 30 years. In the case of documents covered by the exceptions relating to privacy or commercial interests and in the case of sensitive documents, the exceptions may, if necessary, continue to apply after this period.[810] Subject to these limitations, documents of historical or administrative value of the institutions and bodies may be consulted after the expiry of the 30-year period in the institutions' historical archives.[811]

H. PROTECTION OF PERSONAL DATA

European Data-Protection Supervisor. Everyone has the right to the protection of personal data concerning them (Art. 16(1) TFEU). The rules with regard to the processing of personal data by Union institutions, bodies, offices and agencies, and by the Member States when carrying out activities which fall within the scope of Union law, and the rules relating to the free movement of such data are adopted by the European Parliament and the Council, acting in accordance with the ordinary legislative procedure (Art. 16(2), first subpara., TFEU).[812] An independent

13–169

---

[808] ECJ, Case C-353/99 P *Council v Hautala* [2001] E.C.R. I-9565, paras 21–31, upholding CFI, Case T-14/98 *Hautala v Council* [1999] E.C.R. II-2489, paras 75–88, and ECJ, Case C-353/01 P *Mattila v Council and Commission* [2004] E.C.R. I-1073, paras 29–32.

[809] Regulation No. 1049/2001, Arts 6, 7 and 8. A person may also make a new demand for access relating to documents to which he has previously been denied access. Such an application requires the institution concerned to examine whether the earlier refusal of access remains justified in the light of any change in the legal or factual situation which has taken place in the meantime: ECJ (judgment of January 26, 2010), Case C-362/08 P *Internationaler Hilfsfonds v Commission* [2010] E.C.R. nr, para. 57.

[810] Regulation No. 1049/2001, Art. 4(7).

[811] See Council Regulation (EEC, Euratom) No. 354/83 of February 1, 1983 concerning the opening to the public of the historical archives of the European Economic Community and the European Atomic Energy Community ([1983] O.J. L43/1), as radically amended by Council Regulation (EC, Euratom) No. 1700/2003 of September 22, 2003 ([2003] O.J. L243/1). See the introduction to the source material.

[812] See the harmonisation of national law effected on the basis of Art. 95 EC [*now Art. 114 TFEU*] by Directive 95/46/EC of the European Parliament and of the Council of October 24, 1995 on the protection of individuals with regard to the processing of personal data and on the free movement of such data ([1995] O.J. L281/31) and Directive 2002/58/EC of the European Parliament and of the Council of July 12, 2002 concerning the processing of personal data and the protection of privacy in the electronic communications sector (Directive on privacy and electronic communications) ([2002] O.J. L201/37) as well as, with regard to Union institutions and bodies, Regulation (EC) No. 45/2001 of the European Parliament and of the Council of December 18, 2000 on the protection of individuals with regard to the processing of personal data by the Community institutions

supervisory body, the European Data-Protection Supervisor, monitors compliance with this legislation.[813] The European Parliament and the Council appoint by common accord the European Data-Protection Supervisor, who is to act completely independently, assisted by a secretariat.[814]

Special rules apply to the protection of personal data in the field of the CFSP. The Council is to adopt a decision laying down the rules relating to the protection of individuals with regard to the processing of personal data by the Member States when carrying out activities falling within the scope of the CFSP (Art. 39 TEU and Art. 16 (2), second subpara., TFEU).

---

and bodies and on the free movement of such data, adopted on the basis of Art. 286 EC [*now Art. 16 TFEU*] ([2001] O.J. L8/1). See Maiani, "Le cadre réglementaire des traitements de données personnelles effectués au sein de l'Union européenne" (2002) R.T.D.E. 283–309; Feral, "Un pas supplémentaire vers la reconnaissance et la protection d'un droit fondamental dans l'Union européenne: le règlement (CE) n° 45/2001" (2001) R.M.C.U.E. 475–485; Brühann, "La protection des données à caractère personnel et la Communauté européenne" (1999) R.M.C.U.E. 328–341.

[813] Articles 41 *et seq.* of Regulation No. 45/2001 (n. 812, *supra*); see also the obligation to this effect in Art. 8 of the Charter of Fundamental Rights of the European Union. For an assessment, see Hijmans, "The European Data Protection Supervisor: the institutions of the EC controlled by an independent authority" (2006) C.M.L.Rev. 1313–1342.

[814] For the regulations governing the duties of the Brussels-based European Data-Protection Supervisor and the appointment procedure, see also Decision No. 1247/2002/EC of the European Parliament, the Council and the Commission of July 1, 2002, [2002] O.J. L183/1. The website is at *http://www.edps.europa.eu/* [Accessed December 9, 2010].

CHAPTER 14

THE MEMBER STATES OF THE UNION

National authorities. After the establishment of the European Communities and, more recently, the European Union, the national authorities remain continuously involved in the adoption, implementation and enforcement of decisions, both within the institutions of the Union and as a result of the exercise of their own functions. As will be explained below, this is true of the parliamentary, executive and judicial authorities of the Member States, at national or even at regional level. The Union is to respect the "fundamental structures, political and constitutional, inclusive of regional and self-government" as part of the "national identities" of the Member States (Art. 4(2) TEU). In order to emphasise the multiple democratic foundations of the Union, the Lisbon Treaty has also introduced a reference in the Treaties to the particular role of national parliaments, which "contribute actively to the good functioning of the Union" (Art. 12 TEU). Article 12 TEU specifies a number of ways in which national parliaments make that contribution, either through their participation in constituent decisions of the Union or through their involvement in the Union's decision-making and in the implementation of Union acts.[1]

14–001

I. THE MEMBER STATES AS CONSTITUENT AUTHORITY

Requirement for ratification. The Treaties on which the Union is founded were concluded by representatives of the national governments. In each Member State, the Parliament has to approve the Treaties (sometimes after a referendum) before the government can deposit the instrument of ratification. Moreover, amendments

14–002

---

[1] Article 12 TEU refers to national parliaments' contributions (a) through being informed by the institutions of the Union and having draft legislative acts of the Union forwarded to them; (b) by seeing to it that the principle of subsidiarity is respected; (c) by taking part, within the framework of the area of freedom, security and justice, in the evaluation mechanisms for the implementation of the Union policies in that area; (d) by taking part in the revision procedures of the Treaties; (e) by being notified of applications for accession to the Union; and (f) by taking part in inter-parliamentary cooperation between national parliaments and with the European Parliament. For a detailed overview on how different national parliaments exercise their new powers under the Lisbon Treaty, see the Thirteenth Bi-annual Report *Developments in European Union Procedures and Practices Relevant to Parliamentary Scrutiny* prepared by the COSAC Secretariat in May 2010 (available on the website *http://www.cosac.eu* [Accessed December 10, 2010]).

to the Treaties are determined by common accord of the representatives of the governments of the Member States or are decided unanimously by the European Council and do not enter into force until they have been ratified by all Member States "in accordance with their respective constitutional requirements",[2] except for the simplified revision procedure laid down in Art. 48(7) TEU under which a national parliament can make known its opposition to a draft amendment initiated by the European Council within six months. The Treaties also prescribe the procedure of ratification in accordance with national constitutional requirements for a number of decisions with "constitutional" status at Union level.[3] It is then for each Member State's constitutional order to determine who is to decide on membership of the Union and on the related transfer of national powers.[4]

14–003 **Domestic organisation of ratification.** Since the subject-matter of the decision is the outcome of negotiations between the national governments, the decision is confined to approval or rejection and there is no possibility of making any changes. If a Member State rejects the proposed text, that text may be amended only by common accord between the national governments and whether it is ultimately adopted depends on it being approved in all the Member States. A Member State is at liberty to frame its constitutional law in such a way that the government has to consult the national parliament before approving the proposed text[5] or—conversely—that certain "constituent" decisions are deemed to have been already approved by a government act.[6] By the same token, a Member State

---

[2] Article 48(2) to (6) TEU. See the discussion of the entry into effect of the Treaties and of amending Treaties (para. 12–003, *infra*); see also the procedure for acceding to the Union (Art. 49 TEU; para. 6–011, *supra*). See also Albi and Ziller (eds), *The European Constitution and national constitutions: ratification and beyond* (The Hague, Kluwer, 2006), 328 pp.

[3] These include the acts on the direct election of the European Parliament and the Union's own resources (see para. 5–007, *supra*).

[4] That determination relates to the question in which (direct or representative) manner, by which (legislative or executive) body and at which (national or possibly devolved) level the decision is taken. For the question as to whether Union law subjects that ultimate right of decision of the Member States (*Kompetenz-Kompetenz*) to formal and substantive constraints, see paras 5–010—5–011, *supra*.

[5] See Lepka and Terrebus, "Les ratifications nationales, manifestations d'un projet politique européen—la face cachée du Traité d'Amsterdam" (2003) R.T.D.E. 365, at 382–386. Generally, the national parliament has at most the right to be informed during the negotiations and to have cognisance of the draft Treaty before it is signed. See Art. 168 of the Belgian Constitution and the commentary by Ingelaere, "De Europeesrechtlijke raakvlakken van de nieuwe wetgeving inzake de internationale bevoegdheid van de Belgische Gemeenschappen en Gewesten" (1994) S.E.W. 67, at 79–81; Louis and Alen, "La Constitution et la participation à la Communauté européenne" (1994) B.T.I.R. 81, at 84.

[6] Thus under United Kingdom constitutional law, the government may ratify Treaties without parliamentary approval being needed. However, under the European Parliamentary Elections Act 1978, an act of Parliament is required in order to ratify any Treaty which confers additional powers on the European Parliament: Denza, "La ratification du Traité de Maastricht par le Royaume-Uni" (1994) R.M.C.U.E. 172, at 173. Regarding the Lisbon Treaty, see the UK European Union

may make ratification of a Treaty amendment dependent upon the approval of all the federated States or regions competent to that end.[7] In practice, some Member States hold a referendum which has to have a favourable outcome before constituent acts, such as Treaty amendments, can be ratified.[8] Applicant Member States have in many cases held a referendum on the Treaty by which they acceded to the Union[9] and likewise Member States not wishing to take a major decision with regard to the activities of the Union without the express approval of the people.[10] Accordingly, France has made the future accession of Member States dependent upon the positive outcome of a referendum.[11]

The Treaties leave Member States the freedom to organise the involvement of their citizens or national parliaments in constituent decisions, such as Treaty amendments or the accession of new Member States. Nonetheless, Art. 48 TEU associates national parliaments with some aspects of the revision

---

(Amendment) Act, 2008. See also *R. (on the application of Wheeler) v Office of the Prime Minister* [2008] EWHC 1409 (Admin); where the High Court rejected a claim that the Lisbon Treaty could not be ratified without holding a referendum. In so doing, the High Court found that the promise of the UK government to hold a referendum for the ratification of the Constitutional Treaty did not give rise to legitimate expectations regarding the Lisbon Treaty. For a commentary on this case, see Tucker (2009) L.Q.R. 233–238. In 2010, the incoming British Government promised to introduce a European Union Bill, which would mean that a referendum would have to be held to approve any future treaties handing over new powers to the EU.

[7] This was the case in Belgium as regards the ratification of the EU Treaty (para. 3–010, *supra*), the Treaty of Amsterdam (para. 3–020, *supra*), the Treaty of Nice (para. 3–024, *supra*) and the Lisbon Treaty. This does not mean of itself that the regions are part of the "constituent authority" at Union level. If the national government ratifies a Treaty amendment without awaiting the requisite approvals, the Member State will be bound as a party to the Treaty. For the involvement of decentralised bodies in the negotiations resulting in the Treaty of Nice, see Wiedmann, "Der Vertrag von Nizza—Genesis einer Reform" (2001) EuR. 185, at 196–202.

[8] In this way, referendums were held to approve the Single European Act (para. 3–006, *supra*), the EU Treaty (para. 3–010, *supra*), the Treaty of Amsterdam (para. 3–020, *supra*), the Treaty of Nice (para. 3–024, *supra*) and the Lisbon Treaty (*supra*, para. 4–008). In some cases, the decision to ratify a Treaty was subjected to a referendum; in others, the referendum related to the amendment to the Constitution which was required in order to ratify the relevant Treaty; see Lepka and Terrebus (n. 5, *supra*), at 378–382.

[9] Paras 6–001—6–007, *supra*.

[10] See the referendum held in Italy on June 18, 1989 on the status of Italian Members of the European Parliament and the referendums held in Denmark on September 28, 2002 and in Sweden on September 14, 2003 on the introduction of the single currency (paras 11–033 and 11–042, *supra*). For a study of the various referendums, see Mendez and Mendez, "Referendums and European integration: beyond the Lisbon vote" (2010) Pub. L. 223–23; Roberts-Thomson, "EU Treaty referendums and the European Union" (2001) *European Integration* 105–137.

[11] See Art. 88–5 of the French Constitution. However, the holding of a referendum will not be constitutionally mandated where a three-fifths majority in both the *Sénat* and the *Assemblée Nationale* supports accession. In the past, France has held a referendum for the purposes of the enlargement of the EU. See the referendum held on April 23, 1972 on the accession of Denmark, Ireland and the United Kingdom to the European Communities.

procedure[12] and Art. 49 TEU requires national parliaments to be notified of applications for membership of the Union. Accordingly, Art. 12 TEU refers to the national parliaments as "taking part in the revision procedures of the Treaties" and "being notified of applications for accession". As far as the revision procedure is concerned, Art. 48(7) TEU provides for the possible opposition by a national parliament to an amendment decision proposed by the European Council "within six months of the date of [the] notification [of the European Council decision]". Whereas that provision requires national parliaments to take the initiative to oppose a proposed amendment, some Member States also require the government to obtain parliamentary consent before supporting the proposed decision of the European Council. This is the case, for example, with the Austrian *Nationalrat*,[13] the German *Bundestag* and *Bundesrat*,[14] the Danish *Folketing*, the Latvian *Saeima*, the Slovakian *Národná Rada*, the UK *House of Commons* and *House of Lords*.[15] In Member States with bicameral parliaments, opposition under Art. 48(7) TEU may come from either or both chambers[16] or may require that both chambers oppose the proposed decision of the European Council.[17] In Germany, if the matter falls within the exclusive competence of the *Bund*, consent has to be obtained only from the *Bundestag*. In other cases, either the *Bundestag* or the *Bundesrat* may oppose a European Council decision based on Art. 48(7) TEU.[18] Regional parliaments may be involved in Member States with a federal

---

[12] See, apart from the approval by Member States of amending Treaties or European Council amending decisions "in accordance with their respective constitutional requirements" (Art. 48(4) and (6)), the notification to national parliaments of proposals for amendment of the Treaties (Art. 48(2)), the participation of representatives of national parliaments in the Convention (Art. 48(3)) and the possibility for a national parliament to oppose initiatives taken by the European Council pursuant to Art. 48(7) TEU.

[13] In Austria, the *Nationalrat*, after having obtained the consent of the *Bundesrat*, authorises the motion of the government. The authorisation requires a two-thirds majority in each Chamber. See Art. 23i of the bill implementing the Lisbon Treaty. See the Annex to the COSAC Thirteenth Biannual Report (n. 1, *supra*), at 30.

[14] In its judgment of June 30, 2009 (see para. 4–008, *supra*), the *Bundesverfassungsgericht* held that the law implementing the Lisbon Treaty (the "Extending Act") was unconstitutional on the ground that the powers of the *Bundestat* and *Bundesrat* had to be enhanced. It found that Art. 48(7) TEU "is not a sufficient equivalent to the requirement of ratification" and accordingly, the idea of tacit parliamentary consent to adopt a Treaty amendment was rejected. The application of Art. 48 (7) TEU requires the passing of a law within the meaning of Art. 23(1), second sentence, of the Basic Law. In addition, consent may not be given in an abstract fashion. As a result, the *Bundesverfassungsgericht* limited the flexibility sought by Art. 48(7) TEU. The same applies to the special passarelle clause laid down in Art. 88(3) TFEU. See the judgment of June 30, 2009, 2 BvE 2/08, para. 414. See also the Annex to the COSAC Thirteenth Bi-annual Report (n.1, *supra*) at 183, and Kiiver, "German Participation in EU Decision- Making after the Lisbon Case: A Comparative View on Domestic Parliamentary Clearance Procedures" (2009) G.L.J. 1287–1296.

[15] See s. 6 of the European Union (Amendment) Act 2008.

[16] For example, this is the case with the Belgian, Czech and Irish and UK Parliaments. See the COSAC Thirteenth Biannual Report (n. 1, *supra*), at 28.

[17] For example, this is the case for France and Spain: *ibid*. In Slovenia, in the event that the two chambers have conflicting views, the view of the lower chamber prevails: *ibid*.

[18] See also Annex to the COSAC Thirteenth Bi-annual Report (n. 1, *supra*), at 199–200.

structure. That raises the question, for example, in Belgium, as to whether all regional parliaments have the right to oppose a decision of the European Council based on Art. 48(7) TEU.[19]

II. THE MEMBER STATES AS ACTORS IN DECISION-MAKING

A. THE ROLE OF THE NATIONAL GOVERNMENTS

Interaction between administrations. Decision-making in the context of the Union is based on action by the Member States. The Heads of State or Government of the Member States meet and take decisions within the framework of the European Council. Ministers in national (or regional)[20] governments, in their capacity as members of the Council, take the main decisions in the context of the Union, often together with the European Parliament. National civil servants and Union officials meet in order to carry out preparatory work for decision-making in the Council (see paras 13–055—13–059). This gives rise to a relationship which facilitates the subsequent implementation of Union acts. In many cases, the same national civil servants are members of committees which supervise ex post the way in which the Commission or other Union bodies implement those acts, or they may prepare the necessary implementing measures themselves. This interaction between national civil servants and Union officials gives the lie to the widespread idea that decision-making is in the hands of "Eurocrats".[21]

14–004

In the case of some acts, the Treaties make express recourse to the "governments of the Member States".[22] Where the Treaties refer to "common accord of the governments of the Member States", the representatives of the national governments[23] adopt the act in question, yet in coming together to adopt it they do not constitute a body of the Union. Consequently, such meetings have to be distinguished from the Council, which is a Union institution. Since the Lisbon

---

[19] See Declaration (No. 51), annexed to the Lisbon Treaty, by the Kingdom of Belgium on national Parliaments ([2010] O.J. C83/355) and the literature referred to in para. 14–010, *infra*.

[20] For the involvement of devolved public authorities, see paras 14–014—14–017, *infra*.

[21] See Schockweiler, "La dimension humaine et sociale de la Communauté européenne" (1993) 4 R.M.U.E. 11, at 35–36. For an assessment from a "democratic" standpoint, see para. 16–004 *et seq.*, *infra*. See also Buitendijk and Van Schendelen, "Brussels Advisory Committees: A Channel for Influence" (1995) E.L.Rev. 37–56.

[22] See the references to the "governments of the Member States" (Art. 99 TFEU [*ex Art. 79 EC*]; Art. 127(3) TFEU; Art. 130 TFEU; Art. 253 TFEU [*ex Art. 223 EC*]; Art. 240(1) TFEU; Art. 254 TFEU; Art. 255 TFEU; Art. 282(3) TFEU; Art. 341 TFEU [*ex Art. 289 EC*]) and a "conference of representatives of the governments of the Member States" (Art. 48 TEU).

[23] The representatives of the governments do not have to be members of government. For instance, on April 27, 1994 the governments left it to the Permanent Representatives to appoint a Member of the Commission for the remainder of his predecessor's term of office (Decision 94/282 of April 27, 1994, [1994] O.J. L121/41; *corrigendum* L131/26): see *Europe*, No. 6220, April 28, 1994, 5.

Treaty, decisions formerly adopted by the Council or the governments of the Member States "at the level of Heads of State or Government"[24] are adopted by the European Council (see para. 13–044).

B. THE ROLE OF THE NATIONAL PARLIAMENTS

14–005 **Indirect involvement.** The Lisbon Treaty conferred on the national parliaments the specific role in Union decision-making of ensuring that the legislator respects the principle of subsidiarity (Art. 12(b)TEU, which refers to the Protocol on the application of the principles of subsidiarity and proportionality; see para. 14–010). The national (or regional) parliaments are not directly involved in the formulation of acts of the Union. Yet, in some respects they do play a role of their own before such acts obtain their full force. This is true in the first place of a number of acts having constitutional status (see para. 14–002). Next, there is the case of directives, where the choice of the form and methods of attaining the result to be achieved is left to the "national authorities" (Art. 288, third para., TFEU).[25] It often falls to national (or regional) parliaments to transpose a directive into national law (see para. 14–011).

Indirectly, however, members of national parliaments may influence Union decision-making through their contacts with their counterparts in the European Parliament and through influence brought to bear on national ministers sitting in the Council. Article 12 TEU refers to that influence by recalling the inter-parliamentary cooperation between national parliaments and the European Parliament (Art. 12(f) TEU)[26] and the draft legislative acts forwarded by the Union institutions to national parliaments in accordance with the Protocol on the role of National Parliaments in the European Union (Art. 12(a) TEU; see para. 14–007).

14–006 **Scrutiny of governmental action in the Council.** As already observed, national parliaments may influence decision-making at Union level by bringing pressure to bear on members of the Council, who are answerable to them. In practice, the

---

[24] See the references to the "governments of the Member States at the level of Heads of State or Government" in Arts 112(2)(b) and 117(1), second subpara., EC.

[25] ECJ, Case 102/79 *Commission v Belgium* [1980] E.C.R. 1473, para. 12. For the legal force of a directive in the event that a Member State fails to implement it, see para. 17–024 *et seq.* PJCC framework decisions, which may no longer be adopted following the entry into force of the Lisbon Treaty, also left the choice of the form and methods of achieving the intended result to the "national authorities" (Art. 34(2)(b) EU).

[26] Article 10 of Protocol (No. 1), annexed to the TEU, TFEU and EAEC Treaty, on the role of National Parliaments in the European Union ([2010] O.J. C83/203) refers to a conference of Parliamentary Committees for European Affairs (COSAC) (see para. 20–014, *infra*). On January 27, 2003, COSAC adopted guidelines for relations between governments and Parliaments on Community issues, see [2003] O.J. C154/1. See also, more recently, the Guidelines for Interparliamentary Cooperation in the European Union, adopted by the Conference of Speakers of the European Union Parliaments in Lisbon on June 21, 2008.

influence of the national parliament varies greatly depending on the Member State considered.[27] Most parliaments have a standing committee to scrutinise "European" business, such as a committee on European Affairs. In bicameral systems, each of the chambers of Parliament may have its own committee[28] or the two chambers may jointly set up a common committee.[29] In other parliaments the normal departmental committees deal with the adoption, transposition and subsequent implementation of acts of the Union.

In any event, parliamentary scrutiny of the role played by the national government in decision-making is possible only if (1) the parliament is in possession of the necessary information concerning the activities of the Union, (2) influence may actually be brought to bear on a member of the Council and (3) that member may be called to account for how he or she voted in the Council. As regards the first aspect, recent Treaty amendments have significantly enhanced the national parliaments' right to information. As far as the other two aspects are concerned, the impact of a given national parliament will depend on what powers are conferred upon it under domestic law. That having been said, the parliamentary scrutiny exercised at national level plays a part in determining the democratic character of the operation of the Union (see para. 20–004).

---

[27] Raunio, "Holding governments accountable in European affairs: Explaining cross-national variation" (2005) J. Legis. Stud. 319–342.

[28] See, for instance, the committees set up in Austria by the *Nationalrat* and the *Bundesrat*, in France by the *Assemblée nationale* and the *Sénat*, in Germany by the *Bundestat* and *Bundesrat* (set up in the wake of the discussion about the EU Treaty pursuant to amendments to the Basic Law: Arts 45 and 52(3)(a), respectively) and in the United Kingdom by the House of Commons (Select Committee on European Legislation) and the House of Lords (Select Committee on the European Union). In the United Kingdom, following the First Special Report of the House of Commons Select Committee on Modernisation of November 1, 1999 (HC 865), major changes were implemented in the process of scrutiny of European legislation. The Committee on European Legislation of the House of Commons was replaced by the European Scrutiny Committee with enlarged terms of reference. The European Scrutiny Committee is to examine European Union documents and (a) to report its opinion on the legal and political importance of each such document and, where it considers appropriate, to report also on the reasons for its opinion and on any matters of principle, policy or law which may be affected; (b) to make recommendations for the further consideration of any such document pursuant to Standing Order No. 119 (European Standing Committees); and (c) to consider any issue arising upon any such document or group of documents, or related matters. Further relatively modest changes were introduced in 2008 following the Second Report of 2004–05, HC 465. See "The European Scrutiny System in the House of Commons, A short guide for Members of Parliament by the staff of the European Scrutiny Committee (No. 6 July 2009)", which is available, in the same way as all Select Committee reports, on the Internet at *http://www.parliament.uk* [Accessed December 10, 2010].

[29] See, for instance, the committee set up by the two chambers of the Parliament jointly in Belgium, in Ireland, in Romania and in Spain. In the Netherlands, only the *Tweede Kamer* has created a European Affairs Committee; see Del Grosso, *Parlement en Europese integratie* (Deventer, Kluwer, 2000), 293 pp. Furthermore, a standing committee on European affairs has been set up, inter alia, by the Danish *Folketing*, by the Finnish, Greek and Portuguese Parliaments, and by the Swedish *Riksdag*.

14–007   **(1) Right of the National Parliament to be informed.** The Protocol to the Treaties on the role of National Parliaments provides that all Commission consultation documents (green and white papers and communications) are to be forwarded directly by the Commission to (both chambers of) the national parliaments upon publication.[30] In addition, all proposals and other draft legislative acts presented to the European Parliament and to the Council must simultaneously be sent to (both chambers of[31]) the national parliaments.[32] The national parliaments must also be informed in advance if the Commission is to submit a proposal for application of the flexibility clause[33] or if the European Council intends to make use of the possibility to introduce, in a given field, qualified majority voting or the ordinary legislative procedure.[34] They also receive an annual report from the Court of Auditors at the same time as the European Parliament and the Council.[35]

The national parliaments obtained this autonomous right to receive legislative proposals only upon the entry into force of the Lisbon Treaty. Before, it was merely provided that Commission proposals for legislation were to be made available in good time "so that the government of each Member State may ensure that its own national parliament receives them as appropriate".[36] This did not give the national parliament any autonomous right of information, although in some Member States the government was bound under domestic law to provide the national parliament or the competent parliamentary committee with

---

[30] Article 1 of Protocol (No. 1) on the role of National Parliaments in the European Union (n. 26, *supra*), which replaced Protocol (No. 9), annexed by the Amsterdam Treaty to the EU Treaties and the Community Treaties (n. 36, *infra*). Article 1 of the Protocol adds that the Commission must also forward the annual legislative programme as well as any other instrument of legislative planning or policy to national parliaments, at the same time as to the European Parliament and the Council.

[31] See Art. 8 of Protocol (No. 1) on the role of National Parliaments in the European Union (n. 26, *supra*). As far as Belgium is concerned, this refers not only to the chambers of the federal parliament, but also to the parliamentary assemblies of the Communities and of the Regions (see the Declaration by the Kingdom of Belgium on national Parliaments (n. 19, *supra*)).

[32] Article 2 of Protocol (No. 1) on the role of National Parliaments in the European Union (n. 26, *supra*). The protocol defines "draft legislative act" to cover proposals from the Commission, initiatives from a group of Member States, initiatives from the European Parliament, requests from the Court of Justice, recommendations from the European Central Bank and requests from the European Investment Bank for the adoption of a legislative act (Art. 2, second para.).

[33] See Art. 352(2) TFEU, which refers to the procedure for monitoring the subsidiarity principle laid down in Protocol (No. 2) on the application of the principles of subsidiarity and proportionality (n. 53, *infra*; see para. 7–031, *supra*).

[34] Article 6 of Protocol (No. 1) on the role of National Parliaments in the European Union (n. 26, *supra*), which refers to the powers that Art. 48(7) TEU confers on the European Council in that respect. National parliaments must be informed of the initiative of the European Council at least six months before any decision is adopted.

[35] Article 7 of Protocol (No. 1) on the role of National Parliaments in the European Union (n. 26, *supra*).

[36] See Point 2 of Protocol (No. 9) on the role of National Parliaments in the European Union, annexed by the Amsterdam Treaty, [1997] O.J. C340/113.

all Commission proposals[37] and to inform parliament of the stance which it intended to take in the Council.[38] In several of the Member States which acceded to the Union in 2004, the Constitution was amended not only to allow for accession but also to impose on the national government a duty to inform the national parliament in advance on the decisions to be taken at the level of the Union.[39] In any case, the duty to inform the national parliaments results in numerous documents being sent to these parliaments, where the information may be sifted by the general "European" committee or by the normal departmental committees (which is often more effective).

(2) Influence on the national government. In order to allow enough time for discussion of draft legislative acts, the Protocol on the role of National Parliaments

14–008

---

[37] In Belgium, the government entered into such an obligation vis-à-vis both chambers of the parliament and the parliaments of the Communities and Regions (Art. 92 *quater* of the special Law of August 8, 1980 on institutional reform, see Louis and Alen, n. 5, *supra*, at 84–85). Commission legislative proposals were also made available, inter alia, to the Danish *Folketing*, the German *Bundesrat* (Para. 2 of the *Gesetz zur EEA, BGBl.* II, 1986, 1102), the House of Commons and the House of Lords, both Chambers of the Austrian Parliament, the Netherlands *Tweede Kamer*, the French *Sénat* and *Assemblée* (Law No. 90–385 of May 10, 1990 and Art. 88–4 of the Constitution), the Italian Parliament (*Legge-Fabbri* of April 16, 1987), the Portuguese parliament (Law No. 20/94 of June 15, 1994) and the Finnish Parliament. For the practice in Belgium, see Gilliaux, *Les directives européennes et le droit belge* (Brussels, Bruylant, 1997), at 105–110; for the Netherlands, see Hessel and Mortelmans, *Het recht van de Europese Gemeenschappen en de decentrale overheden in Nederland* (Deventer, Tjeenk Willink, 1997), at 95–97; for France, see Sauron, "Le contrôle parlementaire de l'activité gouvernementale en matière communautaire en France" (1999) R.T.D.E. 171–200. In the Netherlands, the government had to publish certain draft decisions to be taken in the area of freedom, security and justice and submit them to the parliament before they were adopted: Art. 3 of the *Rijkswet* of July 10, 2008 ratifying the Lisbon Treaty, *Stb.* 2008, 301 (see previously Arts 3 and 4 of the Rijkswet of December 19, 2001 ratifying the Treaty of Nice, *Stb.*, 2001, 617; Art. 3(1) of the *Rijkswet* of December 17, 1992 ratifying the EU Treaty, *Stb.*, 1992, 692, and Art. 3 of the *Rijkswet* of December 24, 1998 ratifying the Treaty of Amsterdam, *Stb.*, 1998, 737). See already Curtin and Pouw, "Samenwerking op het gebied van justitie en binnenlandse zaken in de Europese Unie: pre-Maastricht-nostalgie?" (1995) S.E.W. 579, at 596–599.

[38] In the United Kingdom, all "European Union documents" must be laid before Parliament within two working days of their arrival at the Foreign and Commonwealth Office. "European Union document" means for this purpose: (i) any proposal under the Community Treaties for legislation by the Council or the Council acting jointly with the European Parliament; (ii) any document which is published for submission to the European Council, the Council or the European Central Bank; (iii) any proposal for a common strategy, a joint action or a common position under Title V of the Treaty on European Union which is prepared for submission to the Council or to the European Council; (iv) any proposal for a common position, framework decision, decision or a convention under Title VI of the Treaty on European Union which is prepared for submission to the Council or to the European Council; (v) any document (not falling within (ii), (iii) or (iv) above) which is published by one Union institution for or with a view to submission to another Union institution and which does not relate exclusively to consideration of any proposal for legislation; (vi) any other document relating to European Union matters deposited in the House by a Minister of the Crown.

[39] See Art. 10b of the Czech Constitution, Art. 35/A of the Hungarian Constitution, Art. 3a of the Slovak Constitution and Arts 3 and 4 of the Constitutional Act on the Membership of Lithuania in the European Union.

requires there to be an eight-week period between the time when a Commission draft is made available in all languages to the European Parliament and the Council and the date when it is placed on a Council agenda for decision (see para. 16–018). As for the influence of parliamentary scrutiny on the position taken by the government, Denmark has organised its governmental structure in such a way that a Minister must defend in the Council the point of view approved by the parliamentary committee on European affairs.[40] The Finnish, Estonian and Swedish Governments are placed under a similar obligation vis-à-vis their national parliaments.[41] In Germany,[42] in light of the judgment of the *Bundesverfassungsgericht* on the Lisbon Treaty,[43] prior parliamentary assent is required for the simplified revision procedure and other decisions by which the European Council or the Council would decide to render the ordinary legislative procedure or qualified majority voting applicable[44] as well as for other important decisions (even if the Treaty provisions themselves do not provide for the intervention of national parliaments), such as the exercise of the flexibility clause.[45] In addition, in order to defend the interests of the *Länder*, the German *Bundesrat* may commit the Federal Government to follow its opinion in certain circumstances.[46] In Austria, depending on whether the matter comes within the

---

[40] The Minister submits a draft negotiating mandate to the parliamentary committee, in which each Member has the same number of votes as the number of Members of parliament which he or she represents. That mandate constitutes only a political undertaking; see Hagel-Sørensen and Rasmussen, "The Danish Administration and its Interaction with the Community Administration" (1985) C.M.L.Rev. 273, at 279–286; Rasmussen, "Über die Durchsetzung des Gemeinschaftsrechts in Dänemark" (1985) EuR. 66–74.

[41] Basilien-Gainche, "Parlements Scandinaves et affaires européennes: Quand le contrôle de l'action gouvernementale devient modèle" (2009) R.M.C.U.E. 527–531; Bernitz, "Sweden and the European Union: On Sweden's Implementation and Application of European Law" (2001) C.M.L.Rev. 903, at 915; Aalto, "Accession of Finland to the European Union: First Remarks" (1995) E.L.Rev. 625–626.

[42] See Kiiver (n.14, *supra*), at 1289.

[43] Judgment of June 30, 2009, 2 BvE 2/08, paras 315–321 (see n. 14, *supra*).

[44] See Arts 31(3) and 48(7) TEU and Arts 81(3), 153(2), fourth subpara., 192(2), second subpara, 312(2), second subpara., and 333(1) and (2) TFEU.

[45] Article 352 TFEU. See also Arts 82(2), second subpara., and 83(1), third subpara., TFEU.

[46] Depending on whether the Federal State has exclusive competence, whether it has actually exercised a non-exclusive power in respect of matters where the *Länder*, the structure of Land authorities, or Land administrative procedures are primarily affected, or whether, in contrast, the *Länder* have exclusive competence: Art. 23(4) and (5) of the Basic Law provide respectively for a simple opinion of the *Bundesrat*, for an opinion to which the Federal Government has to pay the greatest possible respect, or for direct participation of a representative of the *Länder* in the Council proceedings. As far as the second type of opinion is concerned, the implementing Law of March 12, 1993 (*Gesetz über die Zusammenarbeit von Bund und Ländern in Angelegenheiten der Europäischen Union*)—as amended by Art. 2 of the Law of September 5, 2006—provides that, in the event that there continues to be disagreement with the Federal Government, the *Bundesrat* may resolve by a two-thirds majority to confirm the opinion, whereupon the Federal Government will be bound thereby. It may then adopt a position conflicting with that opinion in the Council only if such action is required in the overriding interests of the State. Some German commentators consider that a binding mandate is contrary to the Basic Law. Since it makes it more difficult to reach a compromise in the Council, it is also argued by some that it is contrary to the principle of cooperation in good faith: see Badura,

competence of the *Länder* or the federal authorities, the Council representative is bound by a common position adopted by the *Länder* or one of the federal legislative chambers.[47] Consent from the Netherlands parliament must be obtained in relation to certain acts of the Council to be adopted in the area of freedom, security and justice that are not subject to the ordinary legislative procedure.[48]

In other Member States, the parliament does not have the power to confer a specific mandate on the national government but has a right to be consulted on certain

---

"Willensbildung und Beschluβverfahren in der Europäischen Union" (1994) EuR. Beiheft 1, 9, at 16–17 (together with the discussion at 41–42); Everling, "Überlegungen zur Struktur der Europäischen Union und zum neuen Europa-Artikel des Grundgesetzes" (1993) D.Vbl. 936, at 946; Wiedmann, "Föderalismus als europäische Utopie. Die Rolle der Regionen aus rechtsvergleichender Sicht. Das Beispiel Deutschlands und Frankreichs" (1992) A.ö.R. 46, at 62; Ress, "Die Europäischen Gemeinschaften und der deutsche Föderalismus" (1986) Eu.GR.Z. 549, at 552–554. See also the works cited in para. 3–010, *supra*, concerning the amendment of the German Basic Law prior to the ratification of the EU Treaty. For a critical commentary on the present arrangements, see Herdegen, "After the TV Judgment of the German Constitutional Court: Decision-making within the EU Council and the German *Länder*" (1995) C.M.L.Rev. 1369–1384. Following the Lisbon-judgment of the *Bundesverfassungsgericht*, Art. 23(6) of the Basic Law was amended in 2006. It now lists explicitly "school education, culture [and] broadcasting" as matters of exclusive competence of the *Länder*. More recently, see Suszycka-Jasch and Jasch, "The participation of the German Länder in formulating German EU-policy" (2009) G.L.J. 1215–1256; Panara, "The German Länder in the process of European integration between *Föderalismusreform* and Reform Treaty" (2008) E.Pub.L. 585–614.

[47] In matters coming within the legislative competence of the *Länder*, the representative in the Council is bound in principle by a position on which the *Länder* have reached agreement among themselves. That position may be departed from only on compelling grounds relating to foreign policy and integration. A similar obligation exists with regard to positions adopted by the lower house (*Nationalrat*) in matters coming within the legislative competence of the federal authorities and by the upper house (*Bundesrat*) as regards Union measures having to be implemented by a constitutional law. In discussing measures which would result in an amendment to Austrian constitutional provisions, the Austrian Minister may diverge from the position adopted by the national parliament only if the *Nationalrat* does not intimate its opposition within a specified time. See Thun-Hohenstein and Cede, *Europarecht—Das Recht der Europäischen Union unter besonderer Berücksichtigung des EU-Beitritts Österreichs* (Vienna, Manz, 1995), 235–237; Egger, "L'Autriche—Etat membre de l'Union européenne. Les effets institutionnels" (1996) R.M.C.U.E. 380, at 383; Griller, "Verfassungsfragen der österreichischen EU-Mitgliedschaft" (1995) Z.f.RV. 89, at 102–107; Seidl-Hohenveldern, "Constitutional Problems involved in Austria's Accession to the EU" (1995) C.M.L.Rev. 727, at 735–736. For the (limited) impact of the binding opinions of the *Nationalrat* in practice, see Pollak and Slominski, "Influencing EU Politics? The Case of the Austrian Parliament" (2003) J.C.M.S. 707–729.

[48] See Art. 3(2) of the *Rijkswet* of July 10, 2008 (n. 37, *supra*). For previous systems, see Van Traa, "De rol van het Nederlandse parlement bij de procedures van Titel V en VI van het Verdrag van de Europese Unie", in *Diversiteit van de besluitvorming van de Europese Unie* (The Hague, T.M.C. Asser Instituut, 1995), at 68–75; Besselink, "An Open Constitution and European Integration: The Kingdom of the Netherlands" (1996) S.E.W. 192, at 196. For the changes introduced by the Lisbon Treaty, see Besselink and van Mourik, "The Netherlands—The Roles of the National Parliament and the European Parliament in EU Decision-Making: The Approval of the Lisbon Treaty in the Netherlands" (2009) 15 E. Pub. L. 307–318.

issues before the government defines its position.[49] For example, in the United Kingdom parliament, pursuant to a House of Commons resolution of October 24, 1990 (which also applies to the House of Lords), Ministers should not give agreement to any proposals for Union legislation which have not been cleared by the European Scrutiny Committee or on which, when they have been recommended by the Committee for debate, the House has yet to reach a resolution.[50]

14–009 **(3) Accountability of the national government.** Even if a government is not specifically obliged to take account of the views of the national parliament, the parliament may hold it politically answerable for the positions which it takes up within the Council. In this connection, Art. 10(2) TEU recalls that the governments representing the Member States in the European Council and the Council are "themselves democratically accountable either to their national parliaments, or to their citizens". To that end it is crucial for the Council to meet in public when it deliberates and votes on a draft legislative act (Art. 16(8) TEU). As a result, national parliaments may see how the members of the Council have acted.[51] Besides, the agendas and the outcome of meetings of the Council, including the minutes of meetings where the Council is deliberating on draft legislative acts, are forwarded directly to national Parliaments, at the same time as to Member States' governments.[52]

14–010 **Subsidiarity scrutiny of Union legislative acts.** The Lisbon Treaty vested new powers in national parliaments to check *ex ante* and *ex post* whether Union legislative acts comply with the principle of subsidiarity (see para. 7–031). Since the Protocol on the application of the principles of subsidiarity and proportionality[53] does not specify the internal procedures that national parliaments must follow in order to exercise these new powers, important differences exist as between the national parliaments.[54]

As to *ex ante* control, that is to say, when the national parliament considers whether to send the Union institutions a reasoned opinion on whether a given draft legislative act complies with the principle of subsidiarity (Art. 6 of the Protocol),

---

[49] For instance, this is true of the German *Bundestag* (Basic Law, Art. 23(3), and the implementing Law of March 12, 1993—as amended by Art.2 of the Law of September 5, 2006—and of the House of Commons and the House of Lords (see following ns). The former French Prime Minister Balladur entered into a similar undertaking: see *Europe*, No. 6264, July 1, 1994, 4; see now the "Circulaire du Premier ministre du 13 décembre 1999 relative à l'application de l'article 88–4 de la Constitution"; for an application, see *Europe*, No. 6334, October 10/11, 1994, 4, and No. 6335, October 12, 1994, 1.

[50] The scrutiny reserve resolution is printed with the House's Standing Orders, which are available at *http://www.parliament.uk* [Accessed December 10, 2010].

[51] For the limitations to this democratic control, see paras 20–010—20–012, *infra*.

[52] Article 5 of Protocol (No. 1) on the role of National Parliaments in the European Union (n. 26, *supra*).

[53] Protocol (No. 2), annexed to the TEU and TFEU, on the application of the principles of subsidiarity and proportionality ([2010] O.J. C83/206).

[54] See also the COSAC Thirteenth Bi-annual Report (n. 1, *supra*).

national parliaments may intervene in different ways. First, in some Member States, the plenary session of the parliament takes the final decision as to whether a reasoned opinion should be issued, regardless of any diverging views expressed by the parliamentary committee(s) in charge of monitoring compliance with the principle of subsidiarity.[55] Secondly, some national parliaments/chambers have decided that the plenary session will intervene only where the parliamentary committee(s) responsible for monitoring compliance with the principle of subsidiarity find(s) a given proposal to be contrary to that principle.[56] Finally in some national parliaments, the decision is normally adopted by committee but the plenary may recall the final vote.[57] In contrast, in some Member States, the plenary does not play any role in so far as it has delegated the task of sending reasoned opinions to the committee on European Affairs.[58] As far as the involvement of regional parliaments is concerned, the Protocol leaves it to the national parliament to consult, where appropriate, regional parliaments with legislative powers.[59] However, Belgium has gone further by putting the parliaments of its autonomous regions ("Regions" and "Communities") on an equal footing with the chambers of the federal parliament when it comes to the application of the Protocol. In a declaration attached to the Lisbon Treaty, Belgium has made clear that, in accordance with its constitutional law, the parliamentary assemblies of its autonomous regions act, in terms of the competences exercised by the Union, as components of the "national parliamentary system".[60]

As far as *ex post* control is concerned, Art. 8 of the Protocol provides that Member States may notify "in accordance with their legal order" an action for annulment—as provided for by Art. 263 TFEU—on grounds of infringement of the principle of subsidiarity on behalf of their national parliaments or a chamber thereof. In most Member States, the decision to bring such action for annulment lies in the province of the national parliament or parliamentary chamber as such.[61]

---

[55] *Ibid.*, at 21 (Dutch *Tweede Kamer* and Finnish *Eduskunta*).

[56] *Ibid.* (Polish *Senat* and Lithuanian *Seimas*).

[57] *Ibid.* (Spanish *Congreso de los Diputados* and *Senato* and Belgian *Kamer van volksvertegenwoordigers/Chambre des représentants*).

[58] *Ibid.*, (Danish *Folketin*, Italian *Camera dei Diputati*, Bulgarian *Narodno Sabranie*, and Latvian *Saeima*.

[59] Protocol (No. 2) on the application of the principles of subsidiarity and proportionality (n. 53, *supra*), Art. 6.

[60] Declaration (No. 51), annexed to the Lisbon Treaty, by the Kingdom of Belgium on national Parliaments ([2010] O.J. C83/355). See De Becker, "Belgium—The State and the Sub-State Entities Are Equal, but is the State sometimes More Equal than the Others?", in Panara and De Becker (eds), *The Role of the Regions in European Governance* (Springer, Heidelberg, 2010); Pas, "The Belgian 'National Parliament' from the Perspective of the EU Constitutional Treaty", in Kiiver (ed.), *National and Regional Parliaments in the European Constitutional Order* (Europa Law, Groningen, 2006), 57–76; Van Looy, "Het Vlaams Parlement als 'nationaal parlement' in de Europese Unie (Ceci n'est pas une fiction)" (2007) *Tijdschrift voor Wetgeving* 28–49.

[61] See the COSAC Thirteenth Bi-annual Report (n. 1, *supra*), at 29. In Luxembourg, the Conference of Presidents of the *Chambre des Deputés* may take a decision to bring an action for annulment where it is not possible to call in the plenary assembly before the expiry of the time limit laid down in Art. 263 TFEU (see also the Annex to the COSAC Thirteenth Bi-annual Report, at 338).

However, the French government must notify an action for annulment to the Court of Justice where sixty members of the *Sénat* or of the *Assemblée Nationale* support an initiative to bring such an action.[62] Likewise, in Germany, the *Bundestag* is bound to bring an action for annulment at the request of one-fourth of its members.[63] In addition, while in most cases, the committee on European Affairs drafts a report on the basis of which the plenary session votes, in some Member States, a certain number of members may call on the plenary to intervene.[64] For example, in the United Kingdom, a single member of the *House of Lords* may move a motion for the House to take a decision.[65] Where the national parliament votes in favour of bringing an action for annulment, the national government often has no choice but to start (or notify) proceedings before the Court of Justice.[66] However, in the Netherlands, Spain, and Sweden, such a request is not legally binding.

14–011   Scrutiny of implementing acts. The option available to national parliaments of securing influence by controlling their government's position in the Council continues in practice to be limited to the legislative activity of the Union. Indeed, it appears impossible for national parliaments to monitor the numerous acts by which the Commission or the Council implement Union legislation.[67] To a certain extent, however, such control is carried out by civil servants from the various national ministerial departments who monitor the Commission's executive activities under the "comitology" system or sit in the working parties of the Council (see para. 17–012 *et seq.*). It is only with respect to the area of freedom, security and justice, that the Treaties now provide for a role to be played by national authorities, in collaboration with the Commission, in the evaluation of

---

[62] See Art. 88–6 of the French Constitution.

[63] See Art. 23 (1a) of the Basic Law.

[64] See the COSAC Thirteenth Bi-annual Report (n. 1, *supra*), at 29. For example, s.109d of the Rules of Procedure of the Czech *Poslanecká sněmovna* provides that a group of at least 41 deputies may call on the plenary to adopt a resolution to bring an action for annulment. The same applies to 17 Senators of the Czech *Senát*. Likewise, in Spain, two parliamentary groups or a fifth of the members of the *Congreso de los Diputados* or the *Senado* may call in their respective plenary to take a final decision. See the Annex to the COSAC Thirteenth Bi-annual Report, at 88 and 465.

[65] *Ibid.*, at 29. See the Annex to the COSAC Thirteenth Bi-annual Report, at 512.

[66] *Ibid.*, at 29. See, for example, the Austrian *Nationalrat*, the Czech *Poslanecká sněmovna* and the *Senát*, the French *Assemblée Nationale* and *Sénat*, the German *Bundesrat* and *Bundesrat*, the Irish Houses of the *Oireachtas*, the Polish *Sejm* and the *Senat*.

[67] In a memorandum dated January 19, 1998 from the President of the Council (the United Kingdom having the Presidency at the material time), the UK government considered that the Commission's implementing legislation does not lend itself to detailed scrutiny because it is too voluminous and often technical, administrative or ephemeral, but that arrangements should be made to maintain an overview of the Commission's delegated legislative role. There could also be more involvement of individual Departmental Select Committees. In its 7th Report, the House of Commons Select Committee on Modernisation considered that scrutiny of Commission legislation was "fine in principle provided that no excessive burden is imposed" thereby. In practice such scrutiny "would operate 2 or 3 times a year" (i.e. on a limited scale).

the implementation of the Union policies by the Member States (Art. 70 TFEU) and that national parliaments, together with the European Parliament, are called upon to evaluate the activities of Eurojust and Europol (second subpara. of Arts 85(2) and 88(2) TFEU).[68]

III. The Member States' Role in Implementing EU Law

Implementing Union law. The Member States are responsible for implementing Union law except where this task has been expressly assigned to a Union institution, body, office or agency (see para. 17–002). Each Member State itself determines which bodies are to implement Union law (including the transposition of directives) and at what level of authority this is to take place (see para. 17–003). In many Member States this has resulted in changes in the domestic legal system, affecting both the organisation of the national administration and internal constitutional relationships.[69] For instance, in many cases the executive has been entrusted with the task of implementing directives.[70] When new Member States accede to the Union, the task of adjusting national law to Union law is sometimes left to the national government to carry out by means of subordinate legislation[71]

14–012

---

[68] See also Art. 12(c) TEU (refers to "national parliaments" being involved, even though Art. 70 TFEU mentions only evaluation by "Member States" and speaks of the national parliaments and the European Parliament being informed of the contents and the results of the evaluation).

[69] See Jans, de Lange, Prechal and Widdershoven, *Europeanisation of Public Law* (Groningen, Europa Law Publishing, 2007), 418 pp.; Knill, *The Europeanisation of National Administrations* (Cambridge, Cambridge University Press, 2001), 272 pp.; Snyder, "The Effectiveness of European Community Law: Institutions, Processes, Tools and Techniques" (1993) M.L.R. 19, at 38–39. See especially the position of devolved authorities; para. 11–017 *infra*.

[70] Thus in France the incorporation of numerous directives is left to the executive as a result of the narrow interpretation put on the scope of "*lois*" and the broad interpretation given to the scope of "*règlements*" (Constitution, Arts 34 and 37): Laprat, "Réforme des traités; le risque du double déficit démocratique. Les Parlements nationaux et l'élaboration de la norme communautaire" (1991) R.M.C. 710, at 713. For the practice in Belgium, see Gilliaux (n. 37, *supra*). Sometimes, too, the national parliament authorises the government to implement directives. This is the case in Italy, Portugal and Spain: Laprat, *ibid.*, at 713. Under the La Pergola Law of March 9, 1989, the Italian Parliament passes an annual "*legge comunitaria*" authorising the government to take the necessary measures in order to transpose Union obligations into national legislation; see Zampini, "L'Italie, en amont du manquement . . . Un problème de compétences entre l'exécutif, le parlement et les régions" (1994) R.T.D.E. 195–228; Tizzano, "La nouvelle loi italienne pour l'exécution des obligations communautaires" (1990) R.M.C. 532–540. *Cf.* the use of orders in council in the United Kingdom.

[71] In Spain, Law No. 47/85 of December 27, 1985 authorised the government to adopt all such "*decretos legislativos*" as were necessary in order to implement Community law; see Arpio Santacruz, "Spanish Adaptation to Community Law: 1986–1988" (1991) E.L.Rev. 149, at 150. In Ireland, after the High Court held in *Meagher v Minister for Agriculture and Food* that s. 3(2) of the European Communities Act 1972 was unconstitutional for empowering the executive to enact subordinate legislation amending or repealing primary legislation in order to implement Community law, the Supreme Court set the decision aside on the basis of Art. 29.4.5 of the Constitution, according to which no provisions of the Constitution invalidate laws enacted, acts

or national parliaments may put in place a "fast-track" legislative procedure.[72] Article 4(3) TEU [*see ex Art. 10 EC*] puts the Member States under a duty, not only to take all necessary implementing measures, but also to adjust domestic law so as to ensure the effectiveness (*"effet utile"*) of Union law (see para. 7–045). Various public bodies are also caught by that obligation in view of their close organisational or functional connection with the public authorities.[73] However, at Union level it is only the "Member State", represented by the national government, which is liable for any breaches of the obligation to implement Union law.

IV. THE MEMBER STATES' ROLE IN CONNECTION WITH THE JUDICIAL IMPLEMENTATION AND ENFORCEMENT OF EU LAW

14–013 **Judicial enforcement of Union law.** The national courts play an essential part in dealing with Union law. They determine, for instance, all disputes arising in each Member State in relation to the application of Union law.[74] As a result of the decentralised enforcement of Union law, each national court is a "Union court". Moreover, the Member States' judiciary is to provide remedies sufficient to ensure effective legal protection in the fields covered by Union law (Art. 19(1) TEU). When interpreting Union law, national courts have to take account of the characteristics of that law, such as its own terminology and the co-existence of several, equally authentic linguistic versions (see paras 21–060—21–061). If necessary, national courts may, and in some circumstances, must make a reference for a preliminary ruling to the Court of Justice.[75] If national judicial authorities apply national law in a way which is contrary to Union law, this may in certain circumstances find an action by the Commission against the Member State in

---

done or measures adopted by the State necessitated by membership of the Communities. In some cases, it held, it was proper for Community obligations to be discharged by administrative rather than legislative procedures (*Meagher v Minister for Agriculture and Food* [1994] 2 C.M.L.R. 654–657 and 663–680). See "Application of Community law by national courts", Annex VI to the Commission's eleventh annual report to the European Parliament on monitoring the application of Community law—[1994] O.J. C54/176.

[72] For example, this was the case for Cyprus, Poland and Lithuania. See the relevant sections in Kellermann, Czuczai, Blockmans, Albi and Douma (eds), *The impact of EU accession on the legal orders of new EU Member States and (pre-)candidate countries: hopes and fears* (The Hague, TMC Asser Press, 2006), 465 pp.

[73] As far as the direct effect of directives is concerned, see para. 22–083, *infra*; for a study of the instrumental approach to the concept of the "State", see Hecquard-Théron, "La notion d'Etat en droit communautaire" (1990) R.T.D.E. 693–711.

[74] This is because only specific forms of action may be brought before the Court of Justice, the General Court and the specialised courts; see paras 13–078—13–088, *supra*.

[75] See Lenaerts, Arts and Maselis, *Procedural Law of the European Union* (3rd edn, London, Sweet & Maxwell, 2012), Ch. 3. An information note on references by national courts for preliminary rulings may be found on the website of the Court of Justice under "Court of Justice" and "Procedure"; see also [2009] O.J. C297/1.

question for infringement of Union law.[76] A sufficiently serious breach of Union law by a judicial authority ruling at last instance may give rise to entitlement to compensation for the damage resulting from that breach (see para. 21–004).

As far as former non-Community acts of the Union are concerned, the role played by the national courts depends on the status of those acts in the national legal order (see para. 23–004 *et seq.*).

V. THE ROLE PLAYED BY DECENTRALISED AUTHORITIES OF THE MEMBER STATES

Decentralisation within the Member States. Most Member States have one form or another of geographical decentralisation, as a result of which real decision-making powers are vested in regional or local authorities. In those Member States described as "federal" (Austria, Belgium, Germany) or "regionalised" (Italy, Spain), the Constitution allows the regions to take certain decisions independently with regard to particular spheres. Some Member States confer less extensive powers on their regions (France) or provide for a form of decision-making autonomy for specific parts of the national territory (Finland, Portugal, United Kingdom). In other Member States still, (territorial) decentralisation is limited to giving powers of their own to local authorities and purely administrative units. Except for the case of Germany, the devolution of powers to a regional level of authority has occurred only in recent decades; in some Member States the question of devolution is completely off the agenda,[77] although the position has completely changed in the United Kingdom as a result of the creation of a Scottish Parliament, a National Assembly for Wales and a Northern Ireland Assembly (Scotland Act 1998; Government of Wales Act 1998; Northern Ireland Act 1998).[78] In view of the different forms of territorial decentralisation in the Member States, it is impossible to define the intermediate level of authority in a uniform way with a view to involving citizens more

14–014

---

[76] See ECJ, Case C-129/00 *Commission v Italy* [2003] E.C.R. I-14637, paras 29–33; ECJ, Case C-154/08 *Commission v Spain* [2009] E.C.R. I-187*, summ. pub., paras 125 and 126 (not isolated or numerically insignificant judicial decisions but a widely-held judicial construction which has not been disowned by the Supreme Court, but rather confirmed by it, would be covered).

[77] See Van Ginderachter, "Le rôle des régions dans la construction européenne" (1992) R.M.C.U.E. 777–780. For the question of territorial decentralisation in the Netherlands, see Besselink, Albers and Eijsbouts, "Subsidiarity in Non-Federal Contexts: The Netherlands and the European Union" (1994) S.E.W. 275–320; Hessel and Mortelmans (n. 37, *supra*), 504 pp.

[78] As far as the United Kingdom is concerned, see s.29 (Legislative Competence), s.34 (ECJ References) and s.57 (Community Law and Convention Rights) of the Scotland Act 1988, s.59 (implementation of Community law), s.80 (Community law), s.94 (Legislative Competence) and s.100 (ECJ References) of the Government of Wales Act 2006 (depending on the outcome of the 2011 referendum, s.94 and s.100 might be replaced by s.108 and s.113 respectively) and s.6 (Legislative Competence), s.12 (Reconsideration where reference made to ECJ) and s.24 (Community Law, Convention Rights etc.) of the Northern Ireland Act 1998. Other relevant provisions are Sch. 5 on Reserved Matters (especially para. 7(2) and Sch. 4 on Enactments Protected from

closely in action taken by the Union.[79] Since the Treaties govern only the relationship between the Member States (and their nationals) and the relationship between
the Union and the Member States (and their nationals), regional and local authorities, as "parts" of the national authority, are subject to the same duty to implement
and apply Union law (see para. 7–042).[80]

14–015 **Involvement of regional authorities.** The Union's policies are attuned in many
instances to the regions. Since the Lisbon Treaty, the Union is under a general obligation to respect the fundamental political and constitutional structures of the
Member States as regards "regional and local self-government" (Art. 4(2) TEU).[81]
In various areas, the Treaties require the Union to take account of specific regional
situations.[82] In addition, the Union grants aid to certain regions as part of its action
to strengthen economic and social cohesion (see para. 11–055). In so far as the
Member States concerned make the necessary internal arrangements to this effect,
regional authorities are involved in implementing that aid policy.[83] Furthermore,

---

Modification of the Scotland Act 1998, Sch. 3 on Transfer etc. of Functions of the Governments of
Wales Act 2006, and Sch. 2 on Exempted Matters and Sch. 3 on Reserved Matters of the Northern
Ireland Act 1998. See Heggie, "The Scottish Parliament and the EU Constitution; Moving beyond
the principle of partnership", in Ph. Kiiver (ed.), *National and Regional Parliaments in the European
Constitutional Order*, (Groningen, Europa Law Publishing, 2006), 31–45.

[79] This is one of the aims of the TEU: see Art. 1, second para., TEU. See also Scott, Peterson and
Millar, "Subsidiarity: A 'Europe of the Regions' v the British Constitution" (1994) J.C.M.S. 47–67.

[80] See, in this respect, the Declaration by the Kingdom of Belgium on national Parliaments (n. 19, *supra*,
in which Belgium makes it clear that "in accordance with its constitutional law, not only the Chamber
of Representatives and Senate of the Federal Parliament but also the parliamentary assemblies of the
Communities and the Regions act, in terms of the competences exercised by the Union, as components of the national parliamentary system or chambers of the national Parliament" (see the literature
referred to in n. 60, *supra*). See also the Statement by the Kingdom of Belgium on the signing of
treaties by the Kingdom of Belgium as a Member State of the European Union ([1998] O.J. C351/1),
in which that Member State declared that, irrespective whether a Federal, Regional or Community
Minister signs a treaty for Belgium, the Kingdom as such will in all cases be bound, in respect of its
whole territory, by the provisions of the treaty and that the Kingdom alone, as such, will bear full
responsibility for compliance with the obligations entered into in the treaties concerned.

[81] See the discussion of the principle of proportionality, para. 7–040, *supra*; for the extent to which the
principle of subsidiarity requires account to be taken of devolved authorities, see para. 7–031, *supra*.
Some commentators infer from Art. 4(3) TEU an obligation for the Union to take account of the federal structure of Member States; see *cf.* Van Nuffel, *De rechtsbescherming van nationale overheden in
het Europees recht* (Deventer, Kluwer, 2000), at 288–294; Epiney, "Gemeinschaftsrecht und
Föderalismus: 'Landes-Blindheit' und Pflicht zur Berücksichtigung innerstaatlicher
Verfassungsstrukturen" (1994) EuR. 301–324.

[82] See Art. 13 TFEU ("regional heritage"); Art. 39(2)(a) TFEU ("structural and natural disparities
between the various agricultural regions"); Art. 46(d) TFEU ("employment in the various regions");
Art. 91(2) TFEU ("standard of living and level of employment in certain regions"); Art. 96(2) TFEU
("appropriate regional economic policy"); Art. 167(1) TFEU ("regional diversity" of culture);
Art. 191(2) and (3) TFEU (diversity of situations and environmental situations in the various regions).

[83] See Hessel and Mortelmans, "Decentralised Government and Community Law: Conflicting
Institutional Developments" (1993) C.M.L.Rev. 905, at 920–925 and 932–934.

the Union is increasingly empowered to conduct policies in areas which in federal systems are predominantly dealt with at the regional level of authority (the environment and matters affecting people, such as education, culture and public health). It is then the regions which have to implement the policies. As a result, they are increasingly asking for a say in the Union formulation of the policies, in like manner to members of the national government and national civil servants.[84] However, direct participation of the regions in Union decision-making is difficult to arrange given the great disparities as between Member States in this area of the structure of the State.[85]

Participation of regions in EU decision-making. In order to involve the responsible regional ministers in decision-making, Art. 16(2) TEU allows them to represent their Member State in the Council, provided that they are authorised to commit the national government and cast its vote (see paras 13–044—13–045). Regional ministers may avail themselves of this possibility if the national legal system makes provision for such authorisation. Such an authorisation may be granted to Ministers of regional authorities for individual Council meetings or by a general authority.[86] At the same time, it has to be agreed who is to sit in the Council and

14–016

---

[84] Reich, "Zum Einfluss des europäischen Gemeinschaftsrechts auf die Kompetenzen der deutschen Bundesländer" (2001) Eu.GR.Z. 1–18.

[85] See, for instance, Scherpereel, "Sub-national authorities in the EU's post-Socialist states: joining the multi-level polity?" (2007) *European Integration* 23–46; Magnon, "Le statut constitutionnel des collectivités infra-étatiques dans l'Union européenne" (2006) R.A.E. 395–404; Nanclares, "Comunidades autonomas y Union Europea hacia una mejora de la participacion directa de las comunidades autonomas en el proceso decisorio comunitario" (2005) R.D.C.E. 759–805; Garcia, "La Corse dans l'Union européenne" (2001) R.M.C.U.E. 314–322; Speer, "Innerstaatliche Beteiligung in europäischen Angelegenheiten—Der Fall Spanien" (2000) D.ö.V. 895–905; Feral, "Les incidences de l'intégration européenne sur les collectivités territoriales françaises" (1994) R.M.C.U.E. 53–57; Neβler, "Die 'neue Ländermitwirkung' nach Maastricht" (1994) EuR. 216–229; Vaucher, "Réalité juridique de la notion de région communautaire" (1994) R.T.D.E. 525–550; Wuermeling, "Das Ende der 'Länderblindheit': Der Ausschuβ der Regionen nach dem neuen EG-Vertrag" (1993) EuR. 196–206. For the status of local authorities, see Fleurke and Willemse, "Effects of the European Union on sub-national decision-making: enhancement or constriction?" (2007) *European Integration* 69–88; Hobe, Biehl and Schroeter, "Der Einfluβ des Rechts der Europäischen Gemeinschaften/Europäischen Union auf die Struktur der kommunalen Selbstverwaltung" (2003) D.ö.V. 803–812; Schmidt, "Sind die EG und die EU an die Europäischen Charta der kommunalen Selbstverwaltung gebunden?" (2003) EuR. 936–948; Ehlers, "Kommunalaufsicht und europäisches Gemeinschaftsrecht" (2001) D.ö.V. 412–417; Le Mire, "Les répercussions de la construction européenne sur les collectivités locales" (1991) R.M.C. 785–796.

[86] A general authority is given in Belgium by Art. 81(6) of the special Law of August 8, 1980 on institutional reform, which empowers the governments of the Belgian Communities and Regions to commit the State in the Council where one of their members represents Belgium pursuant to a cooperation agreement. See Ingelaere, "De Belgische deelstaten en de Europese Unie", in Geudens and Judo (eds), *Internationale betrekkingen en federalisme: staatsrechtconferentie 2005* (Brussels, Larcier, 2006), 149–161; Ingelaere (n. 5, *supra*), at 69–72; Louis and Alen (n. 5, *supra*), at 93–96. As for representing the interests of the German and Austrian *Länder*, see n. 46 and n. 47, *supra*, respectively. For the participation of Scottish Ministers and Welsh Secretaries, see the White Papers, *Scotland's Parliament* (Cmn. 3658) and *A Voice for Wales*. For the participation of Scottish

how the Member State's votes are to be cast, especially where the regions' views differ.[87] This also applies to the representation of the "Member State" within the numerous working parties and committees which prepare the Council's work and within the committees which assist the Commission with the implementation of Union law. In this connection, too, a Member State may designate members of regional authorities, provided that it is understood that those persons represent the Member State as a whole.[88] Likewise, regional delegates may be integrated into permanent representations to the EU.[89] Given that the regions therefore depend in the first instance on whether a compromise can be reached within their Member State, the system of direct representation in the Council and other bodies cannot always be used to defend their interests.[90] Moreover, even if a federal State—with one vote—defends the interests of its regions, the views of Member States

and Welsh Ministers, see the Memorandum of Understanding between the United Kingdom Government, the Scottish Ministers, the Welsh Ministers and the Northern Ireland Executive Committee of March 2010 and the Concordat on co-ordination of European Union policy issues, according to which Ministers of the devolved administrations are able to participate in Council meetings and speak for the United Kingdom. See also Carter and McLeod, "The Scottish Parliament and the European Union: Analysing Regional Parliamentary Engagement", in Bernitz and Weatherill (eds), *The Role of Regions and Sub-National Actors in Europe* (Oxford, Hart Publishing, 2005) 67–87; Boch, "Devolution and Community Law", in Hoskins and Robinson (eds), *A True European. Essays for Judge David Edward* (Oxford, Hart, 2003), 47–66; Evans, "Regional Dimensions to European Governance" (2003) I.C.L.Q. 21–51, "UK devolution and EU law" (2003) E.L.Rev. 475–492 and Stumpf, "Mitglieder von Regionalregierungen im EU-Ministerrat. Ein Vergleich zwischen den Rahmenbedingungen nach europäischem, deutschem und britischem Recht" (2002) EuR. 275–290; Clark, "Scottish Devolution and the European Union" (1999) Pub.L. 504–524. For the (not yet realised right of participation of) Spanish *Comunidades autónomas* in comparison with Scotland, see Ross and Salvador Crespo, "The effect of devolution on the implementation of European Community law in Spain and in the United Kingdom" (2003) E.L.Rev. 210–230. In Italy, Art. 117(5) of the Constitutional Law of October 18, 2001 provides for the participation of the regions and autonomous provinces in decisions regarding the elaboration of legislative acts at Community level.

[87] In this way, the Belgian federal authority and the Belgian Communities and Regions concluded a cooperation agreement on March 8, 1994 pursuant to Art. 92 *bis*(4*bis*) of the special Law of August 8, 1980 on the representation of the Kingdom of Belgium in the Council of Ministers of the European Union, *Belgisch Staatsblad/Moniteur belge*, November 17, 1994; see Lejeune, "Le droit fédéral belge des relations internationales" (1994) 3 R.G.D.I.P. 578, at 610–615. For more details on the possibility of participation by decentralised authorities, see Van Nuffel (n. 81, *supra*), at 472–488.

[88] See the Commission's answer of April 10, 2003 to question E-0777/03 (Bautista Ojeda), [2003] O.J. C11E/116.

[89] Regions may also be represented by delegations independent from that of the central Member State. However, for the purposes of determining entitlement to an expatriation allowance in accordance with the second indent of Art. 4(1)(a) of Annex VII to the Staff Regulations, "work done for another State" only covers work done for the permanent representation of a Member State and not work done for political subdivisions of that State (ECJ, Case C-7/06 P *Salvador García* [2007] E.C.R. I-10265; ECJ, Case C-8/06 P *Herrero Romeu* [2007] E.C.R. I-10333; ECJ, Case C-9/06 P *Salazar Brier* [2007] E.C.R. I-10357; ECJ, Case C-10/06 P *de Bustamante* [2007] E.C.R. I-10381).

[90] The fact that two compromises have to be reached (domestically and within the Council) has, of course, implications for the political control which can be exercised within a given region by the representative assembly over the regional government.

of a more centralised persuasion may yet win the day in the Council or the relevant body.[91]

Regional authorities may have their say in decision-making directly through the Committee of the Regions (Arts 300 and 305–307 TFEU; see para. 13–110). The Committee's terms of reference are purely advisory, but it may nevertheless bring specific interests of the regions to the attention of the institutions which have a determinative influence on decision-making (Commission, Council and, sometimes, the European Parliament). The Committee also has the right to bring legal proceedings against acts of the institutions for infringement of the principle of subsidiarity (see para. 13–110). Despite its title, however, the Committee also has representatives of local authorities among its members and hence its positions also take account of their special interests.

Participation of regions in implementation. The Member States are at liberty   14–017
to leave implementation of some aspects of Union law to devolved bodies, provided that allocation of powers enables the Union measures to be implemented
correctly. The mere fact that different regional bodies of a Member State lay
down different rules for the implementation of Union rules encompassing minimum requirements does not constitute discrimination contrary to Union law.[92]

If a Member State is held liable for the conduct or failure to act of a decentralised body, it is not entitled, however, to hide behind the domestic division of powers or federal structure in order to avoid the Court of Justice making a finding of an infringement[93] or to escape its obligation to bring such infringement to an end.[94] Consequently, a Member State may not rely on the defence that, under national con-stitutional law, the federal executive has no authority to give instructions to a devolved legislative authority which is in breach of its Treaty obligations.[95] By con-trast, the fact that a devolved legislative authority is sufficiently autonomous under national constitutional law may be relevant for purposes of establishing a breach of Union law, in particular in the field of State Aid.[96] Each Member State must ensure

---

[91] Wiedmann (n. 46, *supra*), at 47.

[92] ECJ, Case C-428/07 *Horvath* [2009] E.C.R. I-6355, paras 47–57.

[93] For an early case, see ECJ, Case 69/81 *Commission v Belgium* [1982] E.C.R. 153, para. 5. See, more recently, ECJ, Case C-247/98 *Commission v Spain* [2000] E.C.R. I-2823, para. 20; ECJ, Case C-383/00 *Commission v Germany* [2002] E.C.R. I-4219, para. 18; ECJ, Case C-388/01 *Commission v Italy* [2003] E.C.R. I-721, paras 25–26; ECJ, Case C-357/03 *Commission v Austria*, not reported, para. 10; ECJ, Case C-358/03 *Commission v Austria* [2004] E.C.R. I-12055, para. 13;.

[94] ECJ, Case 96/81 *Commission v Netherlands* [1982] E.C.R. 1791, para. 12; ECJ, Joined Cases 227–230/85 *Commission v Belgium* [1988] E.C.R. 1, paras 9–10.

[95] ECJ, Case C-323/96 *Commission v Belgium* [1998] E.C.R. I-5063, paras 40–42 (in which judgment was given against Belgium because the Flemish Parliament had infringed Community rules on the award of public contracts).

[96] See ECJ, Case C-88/03 *Portugal v Commission* [2006] E.C.R. I-7115; ECJ, Joined Cases C-428/06, C-429/06, C-430/06, C-431/06, C-432/06, C-433/06 and C-434/06 *Unión General de Trabajadores de la Rioja* [2008] E.C.R. I-6747 (aid measures adopted by a sufficiently autonomous region could be held to be not selective, and hence would not constitute State Aid prohibited by Union law). See also para. 11–019.

that individuals obtain reparation for damage caused to them by non-compliance with Union law, whichever public authority is responsible for the breach and whichever public authority is in principle, under the law of the Member State concerned, responsible for making reparation.[97] The constitutional system of each Member State must ensure that Treaty obligations are complied with.[98] In some Member States, the national authorities may take the place of the region in breach and do what is necessary in order to bring infringements of the Treaties to an end.[99] Such mechanism will normally require a prior finding of infringement by the Court of Justice.[100] Furthermore, the national authorities may sometimes recover from the region concerned all costs incurred as a result of the infringement (including any damages which have had to be paid).[101] Just as the Commission may bring an action for failure to fulfil Treaty obligations only against the national authorities, only the national authorities may rely upon procedural possibilities which are available to a "Member State" in order to challenge a Union act.[102]

Although the Treaties do not impose any obligation to

---

[97] ECJ, Case C-302/97 *Konle* [1999] E.C.R. I-3099, para. 62 (a territorial decentralised body may be held liable); ECJ, Case C-424/97 *Haim* [2000] E.C.R. I-5123, paras 61–62 (a functionally decentralised body may be held liable); ECJ, Case C-224/01 *Köbler* [2003] E.C.R. I-10239, paras 44–47 and 50 (the Member State must designate the court competent to determine disputes concerning the reparation of damage resulting from judicial decisions). See Anagnostaras, "The allocation of responsibility in State liability actions for breach of Community law: a modern Gordian knot?" (2001) E.L.Rev. 139–158. For the question as to whether a Belgian regional authority can be held to account, see Verhoeven, "The application in Belgium of the duties of loyalty and cooperation" (2000) S.E.W. 328, at 331–332.

[98] Section 35 of the Scotland Act 1998 provides that if a Scottish Bill contains provisions which the Secretary of State has reasonable grounds to consider incompatible with international obligations or affects reserved matters, he may make an order preventing submission of the Bill for Royal Assent. For the transposition of directives in Belgium, see Gilliaux (n. 37, *supra*), at 16–31.

[99] Pursuant to Art. 169 of the consolidated Belgian Constitution, Art. 16(3) of the special law of August 8, 1980 on institutional reform provides that the State shall act instead of a Belgian Community or Region where judgment is given against the State by an international or supranational court following a failure on the part of the Community or Region concerned to comply with an international or supranational obligation. For that substitution mechanism, see Ingelaere (n. 5, *supra*), at 76–79; Lejeune (n. 87, *supra*), at 619–621; for the limits to the State's ability to act in the place of the Community or Region, see Louis and Alen (n. 5, *supra*), at 99–103.

[100] ECJ (judgment of October 28, 2004), Case C-357/03 *Commission v Austria*, not reported, para. 8.

[101] For Belgium, see Ingelaere (n. 5, *supra*), at 78, and Lejeune (n. 87, *supra*), at 611–622; for the substitution of the State and the recovery of costs in Austria, see Schäffer, "Europa und die österreichische Bundesstaatlichkeit" (1994) D.ö.V. 181, at 192; for Germany, see Härtel, "Durchsetzbarkeit von Zwangsgeld-Urteilen des EuGH gegen Mitgliedstaaten" (2001) EuR. 617, at 628–630; for the possibility of substitution (in the broad sense) in Spain and the United Kingdom, see Ross and Salvador Crespo (n. 86, *supra*), at 218–227.

[102] ECJ (order of March 21, 1997), Case C-95/97 *Région Wallonne v Commission* [1997] E.C.R. I-1787, paras 6–8. For this issue, see Van Nuffel, "What's in a Member State? Central and Decentralised Authorities before the Community Courts" (2001) C.M.L.Rev. 871–901. For more details, see Lenaerts, Arts and Maselis, *Procedural Law of the European Union* (3rd edn, London, Sweet & Maxwell, 2012), Ch.7.

"rule on the division of competences by the institutional rules proper to each Member State, or on the obligations which may be imposed on federal and [federated] authorities respectively"

they do impose requirements with regard to the effectiveness of the domestic arrangements, that is to say, as to

"whether the supervisory and inspection procedures established according to the arrangements within the national legal system are in their entirety sufficiently effective to enable the Union requirements to be correctly applied".[103]

To this end, domestic law often has to be adapted. Thus the requirement to notify the Commission of all implementing measures already adopted puts the Member State under a duty not merely to rely on a general principle of loyalty of the federated entities towards the federation (e.g. the German *Grundsatz des bundesfreundlichen Verhaltens*) but expressly to require the federated entities (e.g. the *Länder*) to notify the measures they take to the federation.[104] On the other hand, decentralised authorities should apply Union provisions having direct effect even if this means refraining from applying provisions emanating from a superior authority within their Member State.[105]

---

[103] ECJ, Case C-8/88 *Germany v Commission* [1990] E.C.R. I-2321, para. 13.
[104] ECJ, Case C-237/90 *Commission v Germany* [1992] E.C.R. I-5973, paras 23, 25 and 29.
[105] ECJ, Case 103/88 *Fratelli Costanzo* [1989] E.C.R. 1839, paras 31–33.

CHAPTER 15

THE RELATIONSHIP BETWEEN
THE ACTORS

Interaction. The European Union constitutes a level of government in its own right: institutions of the Union draw up legislation which has to be implemented and complied with within the Member States by the public authorities and their citizens. For the sound functioning of the Union, it is important to have clear rules on the normative relationship between acts adopted at Union level, on the one hand, and national law, on the other. From a political point of view, however, the way in which the various interests existing both within the Member States and across borders are reconciled through the interplay of Union decision-making is equally important. In this connection, attention should be paid to the specific interests which are structurally embodied in the institutions of the Union and to the balance between institutions required by the Treaties. The same State functions that maintain the Member States in equilibrium as State authorities are also reflected at Union level.

15–001

I. RELATIONSHIP BETWEEN THE INSTITUTIONS OF
THE UNION AND THE MEMBER STATES

Primacy of Union law. Both the provisions of the Treaties and the secondary legislation based on it have primacy over the rules of national law of each of the Member States. This primacy arises out of the case law of the Court of Justice, according to which the objectives of the Treaties could not be achieved uniformly and effectively if the effect of Union law differed from Member State to Member State on the basis of national law (see paras 21–004—21–019).[1] In order to secure compliance with Union law, the Court of Justice has recognised the right of citizens (and other legal subjects) to rely directly on provisions of Union law as against national authorities and, in some cases, as against other citizens (as other legal subjects) (see paras 21–055—21–058). These principles of "primacy" and "direct effect" have now been generally accepted within the national legal systems (see paras 21–020—21–052).

15–002

---

[1] See also Declaration (17), annexed to the Lisbon Treaty, concerning primacy ([2010] O.J. C83/344).

For former non-Community Treaty provisions and secondary legislation, the relationship with national rules generally emerges from the form and content of the relevant provisions. The Court of Justice has only limited jurisdiction with respect to former non-Community legislation (see paras 13–084—13–086).

15–003   **Sincere cooperation.** The corollary of Art. 4(3) TEU [*see ex Art. 10 EC*] is the general principle that the Member States should do everything necessary to ensure fulfilment of their obligations under Union law and to abstain from any measure which might jeopardise the attainment of the objectives of the Union. This principle of sincere cooperation also holds good for the Union institutions, which must cooperate in good faith with the Member States and amongst each other in attaining the objectives of the Union (see Art. 13(2), second sentence, TEU; see further paras 7–039—7–049). In addition, the Member States' national policy sphere is protected by the principle of conferral and the principles of subsidiarity and proportionality (Art. 5 TEU; see paras 7–009—7–041). In that connection, the Lisbon Treaty requires the Union to respect the Member States' "national identities, inherent in their fundamental structures, political and constitutional, inclusive of regional and local self-government" as well as "their essential State functions, including ensuring the territorial integrity of the State, maintaining law and order and safeguarding national security" (Art. 4(2) TEU, see para. 7–040).

II. Representation of Interests through Institutions and Member States

15–004   **Representation of interests.** The Member States are not only the object of European decision-making but, as a result of the involvement of the national (or regional) governments in the Council, also one of the actors involved in decision-making. Citizens, too, are not only the "objects" of European legislation, but, in electing the members of the European Parliament, they determine the composition of one of the actors participating in the Union's decision-making process. In contradistinction to traditional intergovernmental organisations, the interests of European citizens are defended not only by international action on the part of national authorities, but also by a directly representative institution—the European Parliament—and by other institutions, bodies, offices and agencies which carry out their tasks independently of national interests in the general interest of the Union.[2] To that effect, the Union institutions engage in regular dialogue with representative associations and civil society (Art. 11(2) TEU), whilst citizens can also take the initiative of inviting the Commission to submit proposals for legislation (Art. 11(4) TEU, see para. 16–016).

---

[2] For an outstanding analysis, see already Jacqué, "Cours général de droit communautaire", *Collected Courses of the Academy of European Law I*, 1990, 237, at 289.

Union and national interests. It emerges from the structure of the Treaties that 15–005
every time action on the part of the Union significantly affects the interests of the
Member States, the relevant decision is reserved for the governments in the
European Council or the Council. In the case of certain "constitutive" acts, such
as, of course, amendments to the Treaties, the matter is ultimately decided by
the national parliaments or even by referendum, where the Treaties refer to the
"constitutional requirements" of each Member State.

As a counterbalance to the defence of "national" interests, the Treaties provide
for the involvement of the other Union institutions with a view to identifying and
defending the "common" interest. Thus, the Commission takes views on the basis
of its independent position and the European Parliament voices the majority
views of its directly elected Members. The remaining Union institutions likewise
perform tasks intended to safeguard particular common interests.[3]

It is no surprise therefore that Union decision-making is designed to reconcile
"national" and "common" interests through interaction between the Council, the
Commission and the European Parliament. Where decisions are taken by intergovernmental procedures, the (European) Council's large degree of independence
in reaching a decision results in a compromise being struck between purely
"national" positions. Where the common interest prevails, the Treaties place the
power in the hands of an independent Union institution. Accordingly, the
Commission acts alone in monitoring compliance with Treaty obligations.

Individual interests. When it comes to the representation of interests specific to 15–006
citizens of the Union (and other individuals), the Treaties rely, on the one hand,
on the ways in which individuals may make their voices heard in their own
Member States and, on the other, on the say which individuals and interest groups
have at Union level, namely involvement in decision-making via the European
Parliament and through administrative and judicial remedies. "Democratic
scrutiny" of Union policy is therefore exercised both at national and at Union
level (see paras 20–004—20–021).

III. Balance Between the Institutions

Institutional balance. Since the institutions of the Union act as a mouthpiece for 15–007
national or common interests, the allocation of powers among the institutions is
based on a delicate balance between the interests which they represent. That
"institutional balance" is based on

> "a system for distributing powers among the different [Union] institu-
> tions, assigning to each institution its own role in the institutional structure

---

[3] See, for instance, compliance with the law (Court of Justice); due and proper management of the
Union's resources (Court of Auditors); maintenance of price stability (ECB).

of the [Union] and the accomplishment of the tasks entrusted to the [Union]".[4]

The rule set out in Art. 13(2) TEU that

"[e]ach institution shall act within the limits of the powers conferred upon it in the Treaties and in conformity with the procedures, conditions and objectives set out in them"

must be read in the light of the principle of institutional balance. This means that each institution

(1) has the necessary independence in exercising its powers;

(2) may not unconditionally assign its powers to other institutions, bodies, offices or agencies; and

(3) must pay due regard to the powers of the other institutions.

It must be possible to impose a sanction for any failure to observe that institutional balance. This is why the Court of Justice is prepared to review the institutions' compliance with their powers.[5] The principle of sincere cooperation (Art. 4(3) TEU; see para. 7–042 *et seq.*) also puts the Member States under a duty to comply with the principle of institutional balance, while, in turn, requiring the institutions to have due regard to the powers of the Member States. The "balance" which has to be guaranteed does not necessarily mean that the most "balanced" relationship between the different interests at stake has to be achieved, but reflects the balance of power laid down in the Treaties.[6]

15–008   **(1) Power of internal organisation.** Each institution is empowered to determine its own organisation and manner of operation within the limits of the rules laid down in the Treaties.[7] In order to enable it to function smoothly an institution is

---

[4] ECJ, Case C-70/88 *European Parliament v Council* [1990] E.C.R. I-2041, para. 21.

[5] *Ibid.*, paras 22–23; ECJ, Case 294/83 *Les Verts v European Parliament* [1983] E.C.R. 1339, para. 25. Examples are the Court's judgments in litigation on the correct legal basis for Union acts (see paras 7–009—7–025, *supra*) or on the extent of powers to adopt implementing acts (see para. 17–019, *infra*).

[6] See Jacqué (n. 2, *supra*), at 292. See the appraisal of those relationships from the point of view of the separation of powers in paras 15–011—15–013, *infra*, and from the democratic standpoint in para. 20–004 *et seq.*, *infra*.

[7] This is true even if the act establishing the institution does not make express provision to this effect. The Court of Auditors was a case in point before the addition of the fifth subpara. of Art. 248(4) EC [*now Art. 287(4) TFEU*] (see para. 13–105, *supra*). However, the Council has to approve the Rules of Procedure of the Court of Justice and of the General Court (Art. 253, sixth para., and Art. 254, fifth para., TFEU) and, at present, also the Rules of Procedure of the Court of Auditors (Art. 287(4), fifth subpara., TFEU). For the extent of this power, see ECJ, Case C-58/94 *Netherlands v Council* [1996] E.C.R. I-2169, paras 37–43.

entitled to introduce its own internal decision-making procedure and establish procedures for monitoring whether its internal operations are in order. In so doing, an institution must take care to comply with principles enshrined in the Treaties.[8] Even Union bodies such as the European Investment Bank must comply with the limits which Union law places on the power of internal organisation. According to the Court of Justice, the ECB[9] and the EIB exceeded those limits by introducing their own systems for combating fraud which precluded the investigatory powers conferred on the independent body OLAF by the Union legislature with regard to all Union institutions and bodies.[10] The institutions' independence is protected by privileges and immunities granted to them and their members (see paras 13–128 and 13–156). What is more, Art. 4(3) TEU requires Member States to abstain from any measure which might interfere with the internal functioning of the Union institutions.[11] That article, together with Art. 13(2) TEU, also prescribes a reciprocal duty to cooperate in good faith on the part of the institutions and the Member States. This means, for instance, that in their internal organisation the institutions have to take account of the powers of the Member States and of the other institutions. Accordingly, it has been held that in its resolutions on the question of its places of work the European Parliament has to respect the national governments' power to determine the seats of the institutions, together with the existing provisional decisions and the definitive decision on the location of the seats of the institutions.[12] The institutions are not entitled to rely on their privileges and immunities in order to neglect their duty to cooperate with the national authorities in view of the purely functional character of those rights conferred on the Union.[13]

---

[8] With regard to the decision-making procedure, see ECJ, Case 5/85 *AKZO Chemie v Commission* [1986] E.C.R. 2585, paras 37 and 40, and the other judgments with regard to the principle of collective responsibility as it affects the Commission; para. 13–075, *supra*; with regard to monitoring internal operations, see ECJ, Case C-15/00 *Commission v European Investment Bank* [2003] E.C.R. I-7281, paras 67–68.

[9] Traditionally the European Central Bank was an independent body of the European Communities. The Lisbon Treaty included the European Central Bank among the institutions of the Union (see Art. 13(1) TEU, albeit with a legal personality of its own (Art. 282(3) TFEU)).

[10] ECJ, Case C-11/00 *Commission v European Central Bank* [2003] E.C.R. I-7147, paras 172–182; ECJ, Case C-15/00 *Commission v European Investment Bank* [2003] E.C.R. I-7281, paras 67–68.

[11] See ECJ, Case 208/80 *Lord Bruce of Donington* [1981] E.C.R. 2205, paras 14 and 19 (see para. 13–157, *supra*); ECJ, Case 230/81 *Luxembourg v European Parliament* [1983] E.C.R. 255, para. 37. See also ECJ, Case C-345/95 *France v European Parliament* [1997] E.C.R. I-5215, para. 32.

[12] ECJ, Case 230/81 *Luxembourg v European Parliament* [1983] E.C.R. 255, para. 38; ECJ, Case C-345/95 *France v European Parliament* [1997] E.C.R. I-5215, para. 31. See also ECJ, Case 294/83 *Les Verts v European Parliament* [1986] E.C.R. 1339, paras 25 and 51–55 (the European Parliament had introduced a scheme for the reimbursement of election campaign expenses unlawfully since the Act on the Direct Election of the European Parliament left such matters to the Member States to determine).

[13] ECJ, Case C-2/88 Imm. *Zwartveld and Others* [1990] E.C.R. I-3365, para. 21. For the nature of the privileges and immunities, see para. 13–128, *supra*.

15–009   **(2) Limits to the delegation of powers.** An institution may not upset the institutional balance by assigning the powers conferred on it to other bodies. The Court of Justice has explained this principle by reference to Art. 3 ECSC, which entrusted the tasks of the ECSC to the "institutions of the Community . . . within the limits of their respective powers, in the common interest". The Court held that

> "there can be seen in the balance of powers which is characteristic of the institutional structure of the Community a fundamental guarantee granted by the Treaty in particular to the undertakings and associations of undertakings to which it applies. To delegate a discretionary power, by entrusting it to bodies other than those which the Treaty has established to effect and supervise the exercise of such power each within the limits of its own authority, would render that guarantee ineffective".[14]

This does not preclude an institution from delegating "implementing" powers to other bodies in circumstances not detracting from the balance between the institutions (see para. 17–021).

15–010   **(3) Respect for each other's independence.** In their relationship with each other and in exercising their powers, the institutions must take care not to jeopardise each other's independence.[15] The practice adopted by an institution may not have the effect of depriving other institutions of a prerogative granted to them by the Treaties themselves.[16] This is true in particular of the European Parliament's power to take part in the Union's legislative process, which constitutes "an essential factor in the institutional balance intended by the [Treaties]".[17] The reason is that

> "[a]lthough limited, it reflects at [Union] level the fundamental democratic principle that the peoples should take part in the exercise of power through the intermediary of a representative assembly".[18]

As has already been noted, institutional balance requires a sanction to be able to be brought to bear on any practice by which an institution exercises its powers without due regard for the other institutions' powers. Yet, before the EC Treaty

---

[14] ECJ, Case 9/56 *Meroni v High Authority* [1957 and 1958] E.C.R. 133, at 152. See Lenaerts, "Regulating the Regulatory Process: 'Delegation of Powers' in the European Community" (1993) E.L.Rev. 23, at 40–49.

[15] See ECJ, Case 25/70 *Köster* [1970] E.C.R. 1161, paras 4 and 8–9; ECJ, Opinion 1/59 *Procedure for amendment pursuant to the third and fourth paras of Article 95 of the ECSC Treaty* [1959] E.C.R. 259, point (e), at 273.

[16] ECJ, Case 149/85 *Wybot* [1986] E.C.R. 2391, para. 23.

[17] ECJ, Case 138/79 *Roquette Frères v Council* [1980] E.C.R. 3333, para. 33, and ECJ, Case 139/79 *Maïzena v Council* [1980] E.C.R. 3393, para. 34.

[18] *Ibid.* See also Art. 10(2) TEU ("[c]itizens are directly represented at Union level in the European Parliament").

was amended by the EU Treaty, the European Parliament, according to the wording of Art. 173 EEC, had no right to bring an action for annulment against acts of the Council or the Commission in order to safeguard its prerogatives. In a 1990 judgment the Court of Justice held that the absence of such a right

> "may constitute a procedural gap, but it cannot prevail over the fundamental interest in the maintenance and observance of the institutional balance laid down in the Treaties establishing the European Communities".[19]

It went on to hold that an action for annulment brought by the Parliament against an act of the Council or the Commission would be admissible provided that the action sought only to safeguard the Parliament's prerogatives and was founded only on submissions alleging their infringement.[20] Consequently, the need to preserve the institutional balance laid down in the Treaties may exceptionally move the Court to take corrective action by way of an interpretation of the relevant provisions of the Treaties.[21] As far as the judiciary is concerned, institutional balance does not impede the courts from interpreting the Treaties as giving natural and legal persons a general right to compensation from the State for damage resulting from an infringement of Union law.[22]

IV. THE ALLOCATION OF THE CLASSICAL FUNCTIONS OF A STATE

Checks and balances. Union decision-making gives rise to both legislative and implementing acts (see para. 16–003); additionally, it often requires legislative or implementing action in the Member States (see para. 17–003). The judicial resolution of disputes arising in connection with the application of Union law falls in principle to the national courts, but in certain clearly defined cases is entrusted to the Court of Justice, the General Court and the specialised courts (see paras 13–078—13–088). Within the national legal systems, the principle of separation of powers (at least in theory) requires the legislative, executive and judicial functions to be allocated to different organs of the State in order to avoid citizens having to face an administration which holds all the powers without their exercise

15–011

---

[19] ECJ, Case C-70/88 *European Parliament v Council* [1990] E.C.R. I-2041, para. 26. See also ECJ, Case C-106/96 *United Kingdom v Commission* [1998] E.C.R. I-2729, paras 21–37 (annulment of a Commission decision implementing expenditure for which the Council had not adopted a basic act on the ground that the Commission had thereby infringed Art. 7(1) EC; see also para. 13–147, *supra*).

[20] *Ibid.*, para. 27. In this connection the Court reversed its ruling in ECJ, Case 302/87 *European Parliament v Council* [1988] E.C.R. 5615, paras 8–28. See the discussion in para. 13–013, *supra*, and the amendments which have since been made to Art. 230, third para., EC [*now Art. 263, third para., TFEU*].

[21] Jacqué (n. 2, *supra*), at 294.

[22] ECJ, Joined Cases C-46/93 and C-48/93 *Brasserie du Pêcheur and Factortame* [1996] E.C.R. I-1029, paras 24–30.

being subject to any political or judicial review. That principle does not signify that each function has to be carried out completely independently by a single public authority. Instead it is effectuated through a system of checks and balances designed to ensure that public authorities are required to cooperate with each other or to supervise each other. The question arises as to how that system is constituted in the Union legal order.[23]

15–012 **Legislative and executive powers.** Union institutions have a legislative function where the Treaties provide a legal basis; sometimes the Treaties also require action on the part of national institutions (see para. 14–005). The European Parliament is generally involved in the Union legislative process, most prominently under the ordinary legislative procedure, in addition to the Council. Implementation of legislation generally falls to the Commission, which can also be authorised to supplement or amend certain non-essential elements of a legislative act (see para. 17–009). Given that the power to take legislative decisions virtually always lies with the Council, albeit mostly on an equal footing with the European Parliament, it does not square with the principle of separation of powers that it should also perform executive tasks yet not be subject to effective political supervision. In contrast, the executive function performed by the Commission is completely compatible with that institution's role in the legislative process in so far as it consists principally of its right to initiate legislation, a right which in systems characterised by separation of powers is likewise generally vested in the executive. Both at Union and Member State level, the principle of democracy requires that the administration be subject to the instructions of the government which is accountable to its parliament (see paras 20–010 and 20–011). Where some independent bodies may have regulatory functions or carry out tasks that must be free from political influence, these authorities must nonetheless be required to comply with the law and their acts must be subject to review by the competent courts.[24]

Where national authorities are involved in the adoption of Union legislation, the constitutional rules of each Member State determine whether legislative or executive bodies are responsible for the necessary decision-making. An example is the transposition of directives into national law.

15–013 **Judicial powers.** The independence of the judiciary is guaranteed in the Union legal order. The Union's political institutions have no influence on the course of pending proceedings; they are, however, under a duty to cooperate with judicial authorities.[25] In view of the principle of the primacy of Union law, both the Union and national courts have frequently to rule on the compatibility of national law with Union law.

---

[23] For an analysis of the Community legal order in the light of that principle, see Lenaerts, "Some Reflections on the Separation of Powers in the European Community" (1991) C.M.L.Rev. 11–35.

[24] ECJ (judgment of March 9, 2010), Case C-518/07 *Commission v Germany*, not yet reported, paras 41–56.

[25] For the duty to cooperate as far as Union institutions are concerned, see ECJ, Case C-2/88 Imm. *Zwartveld and Others* [1990] E.C.R. I-3365, paras 21–22 (para. 7–047, *supra*).

When national courts have to make such rulings, Art. 4(3) TEU puts them under a duty to set aside legislative measures which are incompatible with Union law even if the court hearing the case normally has no jurisdiction to review whether such measures are constitutional under domestic law. Furthermore, the Treaties give natural and legal persons the right to obtain compensation before national courts for damage caused to them by a Member State as a result of breaches of Union law, even if the national legislature was responsible for the breach in question.[26] In this way, Union law has an influence on the scope of the division of powers under the national legal systems.[27] At Union level, the requirement for adequate legal protection entails that all acts of Union institutions, regardless whether they are of a legislative or executive nature, must be able to be reviewed for conformity with the Treaties. Since the Union is intended to be a "[Union] based on the rule of law",

> "neither its Member States nor its institutions can avoid a review of the question whether the measures adopted by them are in conformity with the basic constitutional charter, the [Treaties]".[28]

Consequently, the principle of separation of powers does not preclude judicial review of measures adopted by the European Parliament.[29]

---

[26] ECJ, Joined Cases C-46/93 and C-48/93 *Brasserie du Pêcheur and Factortame* [1996] E.C.R. I-1029, paras 31–36.

[27] See the judgments cited in the discussion of the principle of sincere cooperation, ns to paras 7–045 and 7–048, *supra* and the associated text. See also Barav, "Omnipotent Courts", in Curtin and Heukels (eds), *Institutional Dynamics of European Integration. Essays in Honour of Henry G. Schermers*, Vol. II (Dordrecht, Martinus Nijhoff, 1994), 265–302.

[28] ECJ, Case 294/83 *Les Verts v European Parliament* [1986] E.C.R. 1339, para. 23. For a discussion, see Lenaerts, "Case 294/83 *Parti écologiste 'Les Verts' v European Parliament* [1986] E.C.R. 1339. The Basic Constitutional Charter of a Community Based on the Rule of Law", in Poiares Maduro and Azoulai (eds), *The Past and Future of EU Law. The classics of EU Law Revisited on the 50th Anniversary of the Rome Treaty* (Oxford, Hart Publishing, 2009), 295–342.

[29] *Ibid.*, paras 24–25. See in particular ECJ, Case 230/81 *Luxembourg v European Parliament* [1983] E.C.R. 255, paras 14, 16 and 19.

Part IV

THE DECISION-MAKING PROCESS
WITHIN THE EUROPEAN UNION

CHAPTER 16

LEGISLATION

Decision-making. Decision-making within the European Union is based on interaction between the European Parliament, the Council and the Commission. The Treaties prescribe different decision-making procedures depending on the extent to which the Member States have agreed in each given field that the national or regional governments—represented in the Council—will share their power of decision with the European Parliament and the Commission. In this connection, a distinction should be made between decision-making which leads to the adoption of legislative acts (Ch. 16) and decision-making for the purpose of implementing legislation (Ch. 17). Since the Lisbon Treaty, a uniform system of decision-making exists in all areas of Union competence. Only CFSP decision-making still exhibits particular features and will, therefore, be dealt with separately (Ch. 18). In areas of Union competence in which not all Member States participate, decision-making is restricted to the participating Member States (Ch. 19). Following the analysis of the various decision-making procedures, some factors designed to legitimate the decision-making process are analysed, in particular from the point of view of its efficiency and the extent to which it is democratic and transparent in nature (Ch. 20).

16–001

I. GENERAL PRINCIPLES

A. DEFINITION OF LEGISLATION

Traditional position. Before the Lisbon Treaty, the Treaties did not define "legislation" at Union level, nor the Union's "legislative" process. Nevertheless, it has always been clear that many legally binding acts adopted at Union level were of a legislative nature. In previous editions of this book, Union "legislative acts" were defined as (legally binding) acts based on an article of the Treaties and formulated in general, abstract terms. Even though the Treaties did not formally confer any "legislative" power on the Community institutions, it was clear that legislative acts were to be adopted by the Council in association with the Commission and, often, also with the participation of the European Parliament. Since there was no formal legislative process, there were also no specific instruments for legislative action. The Union institutions used the same instruments for the adoption of both legislative acts and implementing acts, that is to say legally

16–002

binding acts that are based on legislative acts (or on earlier implementing acts). Since legislative and implementing acts were adopted in the form of any one of the legal instruments mentioned in Art. 249 EC, it was impossible to classify the acts which those institutions adopted as legislative or implementing measures on the basis of their form.[1]

16–003   **Formal distinction.** The Lisbon Treaty introduced a clear distinction between legislative and other acts of the Union with the aim of making decision-making at Union level more democratic and transparent. The Treaties now unambiguously use the term "legislative act" for legal acts based on an article in the Treaties and adopted pursuant to a legislative procedure, i.e. under the "ordinary legislative procedure" or, in specific cases, under a "special legislative procedure" (Art. 289(1) to (3) TFEU; see paras 16–022). Other legally binding acts of a general nature that are directly based on the Treaties therefore do not qualify as "legislative acts" in the strict sense of the Treaties even if some are—from the point of view of their content—of a legislative nature.[2] The qualification of acts to be adopted as "legislative acts" has direct consequences for the operation of the institutions[3] and the scrutiny exercised by national parliaments of respect for the principle of subsidiarity.[4] Besides legislative acts, the Union institutions adopt acts for the implementation of legally binding acts of the Union. These acts are divided into two categories and designated by a specific adjective in their title (see para. 22–062). It follows that legislative acts are now formally distinguished from other acts adopted by the institutions of the Union.

The EU Constitution had proposed to go one step further and distinguish between legal instruments to be used for legislative acts and non-legislative acts respectively (see para. 22–063). The 2007 Intergovernmental Conference that agreed on the Lisbon Treaty decided not to adopt that distinction but, as is clear from the foregoing, preserved the clear distinction between legislation and implementation.

---

[1] Therefore, implementing acts of a general nature needed to be distinguished from legislative acts in the first place by reason of their legal basis: they constituted "legislative" acts if they were directly based on a Treaty article and "implementing acts" if they were based on legislative acts or on earlier implementing acts (see para. 17–006, *infra*).

[2] See para. 16–038, *infra*.

[3] See the obligation for the Council to meet in public, which applies only when it deliberates and votes on draft legislative acts (Arts 16(8) TEU and 15(2) TFEU).

[4] The fact that acts adopted pursuant to such procedure are not "legislative acts" implies that they are not subject to the requirement that draft-legislative acts must be forwarded to national parliaments (Art. 2 of Protocol (No. 1) on the role of National Parliaments in the European Union, see para. 14–007, *supra*) or to scrutiny of compliance with the principle of subsidiarity (Art. 3 of Protocol (No. 2) on the application of the principles of subsidiarity and proportionality, see para. 7–031, *supra*).

The Union may adopt legislative acts in all of the fields for which it is compe-tent,[5] except for the common foreign and security policy where the adoption of "legislative acts" is expressly ruled out (Arts 24(1), first subpara., and 31(1) TEU).

B. BASIC OUTLINE OF LEGISLATIVE PROCESS

Legislative procedures. As mentioned above, the Lisbon Treaty introduced the "ordinary legislative procedure", which consists in the joint adoption by the European Parliament and the Council of a regulation, directive or decision on a proposal from the Commission (Art. 289(1) TFEU, referring to the procedure laid down in Art. 294 TFEU). In specific cases provided for by the Treaties, the adoption of a regulation, directive or decision by the European Parliament, with the participation of the Council, or by the Council, with the participation of the European Parliament, is to constitute a "special legislative procedure" (Art. 289(2) TFEU).[6]

16–004

The co-existence of the "ordinary legislative procedure" and various forms of "special legislative procedures" shows that the Treaties do not prescribe a general procedure for the adoption of legislative acts.[7] Instead, each Treaty article which provides for action by the Union lays down how that action is to be carried out. This may be done by mere reference to the fact that the action is to be adopted "in accordance with the ordinary legislative procedure" (set out in Art. 294 TFEU) or by setting out the concrete procedural steps to be taken, "in accordance with a special legislative procedure". Some other Treaty articles set forth the pro-cedural steps to be taken for the adoption of general acts without qualifying them as a "legislative procedure" (see para. 16–038). As a result, acts adopted under those articles are not "legislative acts" in the strict sense of the Treaties. The pro-cedure that most commonly applies in all fields of action of the Union, except for the CFSP, is the ordinary legislative procedure (see para. 16–022). It should be noted that the European Council may decide—on its own initiative and by a unan-imous vote—that, in some cases where the Treaties provide for legislation to be adopted under a special legislative procedure or where the Treaties provide for the

---

[5] The reference in Arts 2(1) TFEU (exclusive competences) and 2(2) TFEU (shared competences) to the Union's competence to "legislate and adopt legally binding acts" does not seem to rule out the adoption of legislative acts in other areas, such as the areas where the Union is to support, coordi-nate or supplement Member States' action (Arts 2(5) and 6 TFEU). Given the content of the Union's competence in the areas covered by Art. 2(3) and (5) (coordination of economic and employment policies) the adoption of legislative acts in these areas seems unlikely.

[6] See Best, "Legislative procedures after Lisbon: fewer, simpler, clearer" (2008) M.J.E.C.L. 85–96. For overviews of the various legislative procedures before the Lisbon Treaty, see Raworth, *The Legislative Process in the European Community* (Deventer, Kluwer, 1993), at 129–149; Piris, "After Maastricht, are the Community Institutions More Efficacious, More Democratic and More Transparent?" (1994) E.L.Rev. 449–487.

[7] In contrast, a general procedure exists for Union participation in international agreements (Art. 218 TFEU [*ex Art. 300 EC*]; see para. 26–002 *et seq.*).

Council to act unanimously in a given area, decisions will in future be taken under the ordinary legislative procedure or by qualified majority vote, as the case may be (Art. 48(7) TEU, see paras 5–005—5–009).

Where a Treaty provision sets out the procedure to be followed for the adoption of a legislative act, the institutions concerned are to act within the limits of the powers conferred upon them by the Treaties. Therefore, the institutions may not—for the purpose of making the procedural rules concerned more or less stringent—determine another procedure for the adoption of such legislative act.[8]

16–005   **Interaction between the political institutions.** Virtually all legislative procedures involve the European Parliament, the Council and the Commission.[9] As far as "legislative acts" are concerned, the Lisbon Treaty has clearly assigned the legislative role to the European Parliament and the Council acting jointly.[10] Under the ordinary legislative procedure, the European Parliament and the Council act on the same footing; where a special legislative procedure applies, the European Parliament often does not have the same degree of involvement. Where a Treaty article provides for the adoption of legislative acts, the European Parliament and the Council are, as a general rule, entitled to legislate only if the Commission exercises its right of initiative (Art. 17(2) TEU; see para. 16–015). Where the Treaties provide for general rules to be adopted, without qualifying the procedure as "legislative", the decision-making power is mostly left to the Council, even though the European Parliament may be involved in one way or another in the decision-making process (see para. 16–040 *et seq.*). In addition, there are a number of advisory committees, consultation of which may or may not be compulsory (see para. 16–046).

As far as acts concerning relations between the institutions are concerned, the Treaties provide for the possibility to conclude interinstitutional agreements.[11] Besides, the Commission is empowered to adopt acts of a general nature itself within the limits of a power conferred on it to that end by a Treaty provision.[12] The same applies to the European Central Bank.[13]

---

[8] ECJ, Case C-133/06 *European Parliament v Council* [2008] E.C.R. I-3189, paras 54–61.

[9] See Hosli, "Who has power in the EU? The Commission, Council and Parliament in legislative decision-making" (2006) 44 J.C.M.S. 391–417.

[10] See Art. 289(1)–(2) TFEU. Accordingly, the TEU confers the "legislative function" both on the European Parliament (see Art. 14(1) TEU) and the Council (see Art. 16(1) TEU), while ruling out any legislative functions for the European Council (Art. 15(1) TEU).

[11] Article 295 TFEU (see paras 22–107—22–108, *infra*).

[12] Articles 105(3) and 106(3) TFEU (competition) and Art. 108(4) TFEU (State Aid). See ECJ, Joined Cases 188–190/80 *France, Italy and United Kingdom v Commission* [1982] E.C.R. 2545, paras 4–7 (following an application of Art. 86(3) EC [*now Art. 106(3) TFEU*]; see para. 11–017, *supra*). For the field of application of the Commission's power to take decisions, see also para. 13–065, *supra*.

[13] Article 132(1) TFEU.

No duty to legislate. The power of the Union's institutions to legislate is not 16–006 associated with a correlative duty to do so. A duty to legislate does arise, however, where the Treaties commit an institution to adopting a particular act.[14] If the substance of the obligation is sufficiently clearly defined in the Treaties, a failure to comply with it will constitute an omission against which an action for failure to act will lie.[15] If neither the Council nor the European Parliament is under a duty to act, those institutions are in principle not bound to any time at which they must take a decision on a Commission proposal.[16]

Role of Member States. The Member States as such are not involved in the 16–007 Union legislative process. It is only exceptionally that the Treaties make express mention of the "governments of the Member States" (see para. 14–004). Besides, some Union measures tantamount to an amendment of the Treaties also have to be approved by the national parliaments in order for them to obtain the force of law (see paras 5–002—5–008). However, national parliaments may also be involved in Union legislative decision-making in a somewhat indirect way (see paras 14–005—14–011).

The Union is not entitled simply to transfer its legislative power in whole or in part to the Member States.[17] However, in areas where the Union has exclusive competence, Member States are able to legislate or adopt legally binding acts "if so empowered by the Union or for the implementation of Union acts" (Art. 2(1) TFEU). This means that the Union may, in the policy areas concerned, delegate specific powers to the Member States (see para 7–022). Where the Union has already legislated in other areas, any decision as to whether to leave the matter henceforth entirely or partly to the Member States is subject to the requirements of Art. 5 TEU (legal basis, subsidiarity and proportionality) and may be revoked at any time.[18]

Participatory democracy. In the EU Constitution it was stated that the democratic 16–008 life of the Union relies, not only on the principle of "representative democracy" (in other words, the participation of the citizens through their representatives in the

---

[14] For an obligation to act, see, inter alia, Art. 215(1) TFEU; para. 25–050, *infra*. Before the Lisbon Treaty, a duty to legislate also arose where a number of Treaty articles committed an institution to adopting a particular act within a specified time (see: Arts 61, 62 and 63 EC and Arts 67 EC; Art. 104(14), third subpara., EC; Art. 255(2) EC; Art. 286(2) EC). The Lisbon Treaty repealed these provisions or deleted the time-limit formerly laid down therein (the same had already happened with Arts 6, 7 and 8 of the Amsterdam Treaty).

[15] For such an obligation on the part of the Council, see ECJ, Case 13/83 *European Parliament v Council* [1985] E.C.R. 1513, para. 64 (concerning the obligation arising under Art. 71(2) EC; see para. 11–008, *supra*).

[16] See the Commission's answer of November 20, 1998 to question P-3242/98 (Jarembowski), [1999] O.J. C297/62. For a commentary, see Schorkopf, "Die Untätigkeit des Rates der Europäischen Union im Gesetzgebungsverfahren" (2000) EuR. 365–379.

[17] Lenaerts, "Regulating the Regulatory Process: 'Delegation of Powers' in the European Community" (1993) E.L.Rev. 23, at 28–32.

[18] Paras 7–009—7–041, *supra*.

European Parliament and in the national parliaments), but also on the principle of "participatory democracy" (Arts I-46 and I-47). Ultimately, the Treaty of Lisbon did not introduce the term "participatory democracy", but it did take over most of the provisions that provided the principle of "participatory democracy" with content (see para. 20–006).

C. DECISION-MAKING POWER

1. Participation of the Council

16–009   **Council.** Under the ordinary legislative procedure, the European Parliament and the Council are put on the same level as regards their political power. In most of the special legislative procedures and the non-legislative procedures, the decision-making power is however mainly concentrated in the Council. Therefore, the Council remains the chief legislating institution. The majority of Treaty articles provide for acts of a general nature to be adopted by the Council either unanimously or by a qualified majority (for details of voting in the Council, see para. 13–050 *et seq.*). If the article in question does not specify that the Council has to vote by a particular majority, the act has to be adopted by a qualified majority (Art. 16(3) TEU).[19] In exceptional cases, the Treaties require some other majority, for instance, where not all the members of the Council participate in voting.[20] A simple majority vote is needed for procedural matters (Art. 240(3) TFEU) and for acts relating to internal organisation or relations with other institutions.[21] The requirement for the Council to act unanimously generally reflects Member States' concern to preserve the last word in sensitive matters or in areas in which the Union only recently obtained competence to act. Accordingly, when the Union was given competence to act in the various fields covered by the area of freedom, security and justice, the initial provisions of the EU Treaty required the Council to adopt decisions by unanimity. Some Treaty amendments later, the Lisbon Treaty introduced qualified majority voting in many of these fields, while again

---

[19] Before the Lisbon Treaty, Art. 205 EC required a simple majority in such a case.

[20] Special majority requirements for such cases are laid down in Art. 238(3)(a) TFEU (where the Council acts on a proposal from the Commission or the High Representative) and Art. 238(b) TFEU (other cases). See Art. 46(3), third subpara., and (4), third subpara., TEU (permanent structured cooperation in the framework of the common security and defence policy); Art. 50(4), second subpara., TEU (arrangements relating to the withdrawal of a Member State); Art. 121(4), third subpara., TFEU (recommendations to a Member State regarding its economic policy); Art. 126(13), third subpara., TFEU (excessive government deficits); Art. 136(2), second subpara., TFEU, Art. 138(3), second subpara., TFEU, Art. 139(4), second subpara., TFEU and Art. 140(2), third subpara., TFEU (certain decisions relating to the eurozone); Art. 330, third para., TFEU (enhanced cooperation); Art. 354, second and third paras, TFEU (suspension of Treaty rights).

[21] Articles 150, 160, 240(2), second subpara., 241, 242, 245, second para., 247 and 337 TFEU. See, with regard to the last competence, ECJ, Case C-426/93 *Germany v Council* [1995] E.C.R. I-3723, paras 10–22.

adding new fields for which the Council had to decide by unanimity (see para. 10–012 *et seq.*). The gradual replacement of unanimity by qualified majority voting has been a characteristic of the European integration process from the very beginning. Indeed, in order to enable all necessary measures to be adopted during the transitional period provided for by the EEC Treaty, a number of articles provided for decision-making to be carried out in stages, with decisions having to be taken unanimously in the first or in the first and second stages and by a qualified majority vote thereafter.[22]

Impact of voting requirements. Where a Treaty article requires an act of the Council to be adopted unanimously, each Member State has a decisive say in the outcome of the legislative process: either the Council adopts a piece of legislation to which each Member State can reconcile itself, or no text at all. Where, in contrast, the Council takes its decision by a qualified majority vote, the interaction with the Commission and the European Parliament ensures that there is a genuine three-way dialogue. In such a case, the Commission (by means of a proposal)— and possibly the European Parliament (by means of amendments and the possible use of its veto in the ordinary legislative procedure)—is in a position to present to the Council a legislative text which does not necessarily have to meet with the approval of every Member State.   **16–010**

Consequently, the requirement for a unanimous vote does not only make it more difficult for agreement to be reached between the Member States in the Council, it also deprives the Commission of the room for manoeuvre which its right to make proposals affords it in a procedure requiring only a qualified majority vote (see para. 16–020). The reason for this is that under such a procedure the Council has to vote unanimously on any amendment which it makes to the proposal from the Commission (Art. 293(1) TFEU [*ex Art. 250(1) EC*]), whereas only a qualified majority is required to adopt the proposal. By the same token, a requirement for a unanimous vote tends to diminish the influence which the European Parliament can bring to bear directly or indirectly (where the Commission accepts its amendments).

2. Participation of the European Parliament

Degrees of involvement. Notwithstanding its direct democratic legitimacy, the European Parliament does not invariably take part in the legislative process. The European Parliament acts as a fully-fledged legislator under the ordinary legislative procedure, which is the procedure for adopting legislative acts applicable in   **16–011**

---

[22] The relevant articles (or the clause on the transitional period) were repealed by the Treaty of Amsterdam as part of the exercise of simplifying the Treaties. The system was retained, however, in Art. 67(1) and (2) EC (whereby, after five years, the Council was to determine the field covered by the co-decision procedure, entailing voting by qualified majority) and Art. 67(4) EC (automatic application of the co-decision procedure after that period).

most fields of competence of the Union. However, in addition to the ordinary legislative procedure, there are special legislative procedures, which provide for different degrees of participation of the European Parliament: consultation and consent (see paras 16–034 *et seq.*). Furthermore, there are some other forms of participation in decision-making and some Treaty articles which provide for no input of the Parliament in decision-making or simply for it to be informed of the measures adopted (see paras 16–040 *et seq.*).

16–012   **From consultation to cooperation.** It was not until the 1980s that the European Parliament succeeded in increasing its say in Community decision-making.[23] For a long time, the Parliament's only right was to be consulted in certain cases and to deliver a non-binding opinion.[24] Grant of decision-making power in the budgetary procedure in 1970 gave the Parliament a means of blocking other institutions' decisions with financial implications. One year after the first direct elections to the European Parliament, the Court of Justice clarified for the first time the scope of the Parliament's right to be consulted. In the judgments of October 29, 1980 in the isoglucose cases, the Court of Justice held that consultation of the Parliament constituted an essential procedural requirement and annulled a regulation which the Council had adopted without consulting the Parliament.[25]

In 1987 the Single European Act then increased Parliament's say by introducing "assent" and "cooperation" procedures and extending majority voting in the Council, which enlarged the Commission's scope for taking over parliamentary amendments.[26] Assent, which gave the European Parliament a veto, was introduced for the accession of new Member States and the conclusion of association agreements (see para. 16–037). That procedure still applies in various fields, but since the Lisbon Treaty it has been renamed as "consent". The "cooperation" procedure[27] was introduced to increase the European Parliament's involvement in the Community's legislative process[28] and to make it possible for the Council to act

---

[23] For a survey of the increasing parliamentary involvement in decision-making, see Corbett, Jacobs and Shackleton, "The European Parliament at Fifty: A View from the Inside" (2003) J.C.M.S. 353–373; De Gucht (with the collaboration of Keukeleire), *Besluitvorming in de Europese Unie* (Antwerp, Maklu, 1994), at 44–59.

[24] The ECSC Treaty also required the European Parliament to give its approval in the "minor amendment" procedure provided for in Art. 95 (*cf.* para.5–009, *supra*).

[25] ECJ, Case 138/79 *Roquette Frères v Council* [1980] E.C.R. 3333, paras 33–37, and ECJ, Case 139/79 *Maïzena v Council* [1980] E.C.R. 3393, paras 34–38.

[26] In addition to the general commentaries on the Single European Act (para. 3–006, *supra*), see Bieber, "Legislative Procedure for the Establishment of the Single Market" (1988) C.M.L.Rev. 711–724; Domestici-Met, "Les procédures législatives communautaires après l'Acte unique" (1987) R.M.C. 556–571.

[27] Initially, the EEC Treaty provided that in such a case the Council was to act "by a qualified majority on a proposal from the Commission in cooperation with the European Parliament". Subsequently, the procedure was set out in Art. 252 of the EC Treaty and referred to in that Treaty as the "procedure laid down in Article 252 of the Treaty".

[28] ECJ, Case C-300/89 *Commission v Council* [1991] E.C.R. I-2867, para. 20.

by a qualified majority rather than by a unanimous vote. The move to qualified majority voting made for the flexibility which was considered necessary in order to adopt the substantial corpus of legislation for achieving the internal market (see para. 9–009). The cooperation procedure was made up of two stages. In the first stage, the European Parliament gave its opinion on the Commission proposal, after which the Council adopted a common position. In the second stage, the European Parliament could propose amendments to that common position or reject it. Compared with the procedure of mere "consultation", the possibility afforded by the cooperation procedure to propose amendments allowed the Parliament to have a real influence on decision-making. The Parliament's say in this procedure, however, was weak in two respects: it could not submit its amendments directly to the Council (with a view to their being approved by a qualified majority)[29] and could not prevent an act which it viewed with disfavour from being adopted.[30] In order to give the European Parliament a greater say in precisely those two respects, the EU Treaty introduced the co-decision procedure (now the ordinary legislative procedure). Meanwhile, the Lisbon Treaty has abolished the cooperation procedure[31] and replaced it by the ordinary legislative procedure[32] or the consultation procedure.[33]

From co-decision to the ordinary legislative procedure. In 1993, the EU Treaty   **16–013**
introduced the co-decision procedure, which afforded the European Parliament more of a say by coupling the right to propose amendments with a right of veto. This is the procedure which the Lisbon Treaty has renamed the "ordinary

---

[29] In the second stage, the Council had to act unanimously if it wished to diverge from the Commission proposal. Consequently, where the Commission was prepared to take the Parliament's amendments over in an amended version of its proposal, the chance for the Parliament of its amendments being adopted by the Council was higher than when the Commission did not amend its initial proposal. In the latter case, Parliament's amendments could be adopted by the Council only by unanimity, that is to say, only if no Member State opposed them.

[30] If the Commission did not withdraw its proposal, the Council could still adopt by a unanimous vote a common position rejected by the Parliament. In the Framework Agreement of May 26, 2005 on relations between the European Parliament and the Commission, [2006] O.J. C117E/125 (annexed to the Rules of Procedure of the European Parliament) the Commission undertook to withdraw a legislative proposal in that event unless there were important reasons for not doing so. In the first seven cases in which the Parliament rejected a Council common position, the Council adopted three common positions by a unanimous vote; on one occasion, the Commission withdrew its proposal and replaced the original one by new proposals: see the Commission's answer of August 5, 1996 to question E-1861/96 (Schleicher), [1996] O.J. C356/106. For a case study, see Earnshaw and Judge, "The European Parliament and the Sweeteners Directive: From Footnote to Inter-Institutional Conflict" (1993) J.C.M.S. 103–116.

[31] In most policy areas where the cooperation procedure was in force, the Amsterdam Treaty had already replaced it by the co-decision procedure. However, since the Member States refused to alter the provisions governing EMU, the cooperation procedure provided for in Art. 252 EC remained in force in that area.

[32] Article 121(6) TFEU [ex Art. 99(5) EC].

[33] Articles 125 TFEU [ex Arts 102(2) and 103(2) EC] and Art. 128(2) TFEU [ex Art. 106(2) EC].

legislative procedure", while using the term "special legislative procedure" for procedures in which the European Parliament is merely consulted or is to give its consent. When it introduced the co-decision procedure, the EU Treaty also reordered the field of application of the various legislative procedures so as to increase parliamentary involvement across the board. In various policy areas, a procedure involving a greater say on the part of the Parliament, sometimes even the new co-decision procedure, replaced a procedure under which the Parliament had no or only a small say. However, the fact that the Parliament's role was increased piecemeal in stages meant that its say in the legislative process differed from case to case, which made it difficult to have a clear insight into its legislative role.[34] Where, in addition, the different aspects of a given policy area were governed by different procedures, there was also a threat to the coherence of the policy concerned.[35] The Treaty of Amsterdam improved matters in this respect by confining the cooperation procedure to aspects of EMU and largely replacing it by co-decision. The Lisbon Treaty further increased the say of the European Parliament by making the ordinary legislative procedure (co-decision) applicable in most fields of action of the Union, including police and judicial cooperation in criminal matters (PJCC).

16–014   **Essential procedural requirement.** The European Parliament's participation in Union rule-making reflects at Union level the fundamental democratic principle that the peoples should take part in the exercise of power through the intermediary of a representative assembly. It was on this ground that the Court of Justice held that procedures providing for the involvement of the Parliament were essential procedural requirements for the adoption of legislative acts and that if those procedures were disregarded the acts in question could be declared void.[36] The European Parliament's prerogatives are infringed where an act is wrongly adopted on a legal basis which does not provide for the same involvement of the Parliament as the correct legal basis. This also applies where an act is wrongly adopted on a legal basis which does not provide for consultation of the Parliament, even if the institution which adopted the act has opted to consult it.[37] As more and more Treaty articles require the European Parliament to be involved in decision-making and the various legislative procedures call for different degrees of involvement, the Parliament is keeping an increasingly steady eye on the choice of legal basis made by the Commission and—in the second place—by the Council. This explains the rising number of cases brought before the Court of Justice by the Parliament.[38]

---

[34] See the criticism of Boest, "Ein langer Weg zur Demokratie in Europa. Die Beteiligungsrechte des Europäischen Parlaments bei Rechtsetzung nach dem Vertrag über die Europäische Union" (1992) EuR. 182, at 191.

[35] De Gucht and Keukeleire (n. 23, *supra*), at 58.

[36] ECJ, Case 138/79 *Roquette Frères v Council* [1980] E.C.R. 3333, para. 33, and ECJ, Case 139/79 *Maïzena v Council* [1980] E.C.R. 3393, para. 34; ECJ, Case C-300/89 *Commission v Council* [1991] E.C.R. I-2867, para. 20.

[37] ECJ, Case C-316/91 *European Parliament v Council* [1994] E.C.R. I-625, para. 16.

[38] Now under Art. 263, second para., TFEU [*ex Art. 230, third para., EC*].

D. RIGHT OF INITIATIVE

Right of initiative. Since the Lisbon Treaty, the Treaties expressly provide that Union legislative acts may be adopted only on the basis of a Commission proposal, except where the Treaties provide otherwise; other acts are to be adopted on the basis of a Commission proposal where the Treaties so provide (Art. 17(2) TEU). These provisions confirm the system laid down in the initial Community Treaties where generally the Commission was the only institution empowered to submit a proposal for legislation, with the result that the other institutions could not legislate in the absence of a prior proposal from the Commission.[39] Apart from the CFSP,[40] the Commission's right of initiative covers all the fields of competence of the Union. Generally, a formal "proposal" is needed, as is the case under the ordinary legislative procedure, which applies in most fields of Union action, but sometimes a recommendation[41] suffices.

 In specific cases provided for by the Treaties, legislative acts may be adopted on the initiative of a group of Member States or of the European Parliament,[42] on a recommendation from the European Central Bank[43] or at the request of the Court of Justice[44] or the European Investment Bank.[45] The right of initiative of a group of Member States mainly applies in the field of PJCC,[46] where the

16–015

---

[39] The ECSC system was different in so far that the Commission was empowered to adopt acts itself, except in exceptional cases where the Council took the decision on a proposal from the Commission: see, for instance, Art. 59(2) and (5) ECSC.

[40] For the right of initiative in the CFSP, see the relevant paras of Ch. 18.

[41] See for authorisation to conduct international negotiations: Art. 207(3), second subpara., TFEU and Art. 218(3) TFEU. See also Art. 121(2), first subpara., and (4), first subpara., TFEU; Art. 126(7) TFEU; Art. 219(1), (2) and (3) TFEU; Art. 143(1), second subpara., TFEU; Art. 144(2) TFEU (economic and monetary provisions); Art. 148(4) TFEU (employment).

[42] See Art. 7(1) TEU. See the decisions taken on the basis of a proposal from the European Parliament (Art. 223(1) TFEU [*ex Art. 190(4) EC*]), and the Act on the Direct Election of the European Parliament, Art. 14.

[43] See Art. 129(3) and (4) TFEU (regarding the Statute of the ESCB and of the ECB); Art. 219 (1) and (2) TFEU (agreements concerning monetary or foreign exchange regime matters). These measures may also be taken at the initiative of the Commission after consulting the ECB (*ibid.*).

[44] See Art. 252, first para., TFEU (decision to increase the number of Advocates-General); Art. 257, first para., TFEU (establishment of specialised courts); and Art. 281, second para., TFEU (amendment of the Statute of the Court of Justice of the European Union). In the last two cases, the measures concerned may also be taken at the initiative of the Commission after consulting the ECJ (*ibid.*).

[45] Article 308, third para., TFEU (amendment of the Statute of the EIB). This measure may also be taken at the initiative of the Commission after consulting the European Parliament and the EIB (*ibid.*).

[46] See, however, also Art. 7(1) TEU (on a proposal by one-third of the Member States, the European Parliament or the Commission) and (2) (on a proposal from one-third of the Member States or the Commission). See also Art. 108(2), third subpara., TFEU, which exceptionally provides for the adoption of a measure on the application of a Member State. Article 67(1) EC provided for action on a proposal from the Commission or on the initiative of a Member State, but only during a transitional period of five years following the entry into force of the Amsterdam Treaty, after which the Council was invariably to act on a proposal from the Commission; see Art. 67(2) EC.

Commission shares the right of initiative with the Member States, which may submit an initiative provided that it emanates from a group consisting of at least a quarter of the Member States.[47] As a result, in that field the Commission cannot influence decision-making to the same extent as in fields in which it has the exclusive right of initiative and the prerogatives associated with that right (see para. 16–018).

In sum, legislative acts of the Union are generally adopted on a proposal from the Commission, although in specific cases the right of initiative falls to a group of Member States, the European Parliament, the European Central Bank, the Court of Justice or the European Investment Bank.[48] Only exceptionally may Union acts be adopted by the Council in the absence of any such initiative.[49] This is undoubtedly due to the fact that the acts in question are "legislative acts" properly so called.

16–016   **Citizens' initiative.** A remarkable innovation introduced by the Lisbon Treaty is the possibility for a group of citizens to invite the Commission to initiate legislation. At the initiative of at least one million citizens coming from a significant number of Member States, the Commission may be invited to submit "any appropriate proposal" on matters where citizens consider that a legal act of the Union is required for the purpose of implementing the Treaties (Art. 11(4) TEU). The European Parliament and the Council, acting by means of regulations in accordance with the ordinary legislative procedure, are to establish the procedures and conditions required for such a citizens' initiative, including the minimum number of Member States from which it must come (Art. 24 TFEU).[50] However, these provisions do not oblige the Commission to comply with such a request.

16–017   **No right of initiative for the Council or European Parliament.** Except for the cases mentioned above, the Commission is the only institution entitled to submit proposals for legislation and neither the European Parliament nor the Council

---

[47] Article 76 TFEU. Before the Lisbon Treaty, in the field of PJCC, any Member State could submit a proposal on an individual basis (Art. 34(2) EU). In connection with JHA cooperation, initiatives often—but not invariably—appeared to stem from the Member State occupying the Presidency; see, for instance, as regards the period July 1, 1996 to June 30, 1997 the Council's answer of November 17, 1997 to question E-2405/97 (Nassauer), [1998] O.J. C102/39.

[48] See, in this connection, the definition of "draft legislative acts" in Art. 2, second subpara., of Protocol (No. 1), annexed to the EU, TFEU and EAEC Treaty, on the role of National Parliaments in the European Union ([2010] O.J. C83/203) and Art. 3 of Protocol (No. 2), annexed to the TEU and TFEU, on the application of the principles of subsidiarity and proportionality ([2010] O.J. C83/206).

[49] Articles 160, 243, 286(7), 301, third para., TFEU [*ex Arts 144; 210; 247(8); 258, fourth para., EC*]. See also Art. 354, third para., TFEU and Art. 7(3) TEU. See also Art. 4, second para., of Protocol (No. 19), annexed to the TEU and TFEU, integrating the Schengen *acquis* into the framework of the European Union, [2010] O.J. C83/290 (para. 10–010, *supra*).

[50] See the Proposal for a regulation of the European Parliament and of the Council on the citizens' initiative (COM(2010) 119).

may force it to submit a proposal (see para. 16–021). The Commission, as an independent expert institution, has the capacity to ensure that every legislative initiative is technically correct and also in the interest of the Union. No provision is made for a right of initiative on the part of the Council. As such, the Treaties seek to offer a constitutional guarantee aiming to avoid the introduction of legislative initiatives that might take a step backwards in the integration process and thereby damage the nucleus of the Union *acquis*. After all, measures adopted by the Council are the outcome of negotiations between the Member States, which in any concrete policy context defend their own interests and are not necessarily concerned in the first place with the EU's integration process. The fact that initially the European Parliament was given little or no part to play in the legislative process, meant that it obtained no right of initiative.[51] In view of the democratic legitimacy of the directly elected European Parliament, it would seem justified to confer a right of initiative also on the European Parliament, possibly combined with a duty to consult the Commission.[52]

Formulating proposals. The right to propose legislation means that the Commission can decide whether or not the Union should act and, if so, on what legal basis, in what legal form (if the legal basis permits a choice) and what content and implementing procedures the proposal should embody. Especially where the adoption of a legislative act is characterised by a wide discretion, the Commission itself decides when it is appropriate to formulate and submit legislative proposals.[53]   **16–018**

In so doing, it adheres to an annual legislative programme drawn up in consultation with the European Parliament and the Council.[54] Usually, the Commission makes contact with interest groups affected and the administrative authorities in the Member States before it adopts its proposal. Representatives of interest groups

---

[51] The European Parliament has such a right only under Art. 223(2) TFEU (laying down the regulations and general conditions governing the performance of the duties of its Members); Art. 226, third para., TFEU (determining the detailed provisions governing the exercise of the right of inquiry); Art. 228(4) TFEU (Ombudsman Regulations). See also the discussion of Art. 225 TFEU (para. 16–021, *infra*).

[52] After repeated calls (see the resolutions of July 9, 1981 ([1981] O.J. C234/64), October 8, 1986 ([1986] O.J. C283/39) and March 14, 1990 ([1990] O.J. C96/114)), the European Parliament is at present no longer pressing for such a right of initiative; see Lenaerts and De Smijter, "On the Democratic Representation through the European Parliament, the Council, the Committee of the Regions, the Economic and Social Committee and the National Parliaments", in Winter, Curtin, Kellermann and De Witte (eds), *Reforming the Treaty on European Union—The Legal Debate* (The Hague, T.M.C. Asser Institute/Kluwer, 1996), 173, at 182.

[53] CFI, Case T-571/93 *Lefebvre and Others v Commission* [1995] E.C.R. II-2379, paras 32–39.

[54] See the Interinstitutional Agreement between the European Parliament, the Council and the Commission of December 16, 2003 on better law-making, points 3 *et seq.* ([2003] O.J. C321/1). As far as the Parliament is concerned, the matter is governed by Rule 35 of the EP Rules of Procedure.

themselves also regularly contact Members of the Commission or its administration.[55] Since the Lisbon Treaty, the Commission is generally required to

> "carry out broad consultations with parties concerned in order to ensure that the Union's actions are coherent and transparent" (Art. 11(3) TEU).

According to the Protocol on the application of the principles of subsidiarity and proportionality, the Commission has to consult widely before proposing legislation.[56] It must justify the relevance of its proposals with regard to the principle of subsidiarity and its proposals should contain a detailed statement making it possible to appraise compliance with these principles.[57] In the case of major proposals for legislation, the Commission may carry out a prior impact assessment.[58] In some cases, the Commission may decide to have recourse to self-regulation by the economic operators, social partners or associations concerned.[59] In response

---

[55] For contacts with interest groups, see the Commission's communication "European Transparency Initiative—A framework for relations with interest representatives" of May 27, 2008, which sets out a code of conduct for lobbying organisations and provides for the setting up of a register for such organisations. See further the European Parliament's code of conduct regarding interest groups (Annex X to the Rules of Procedure, Provisions governing the application of Rule 9(4)—Lobbying in Parliament). See Richez, "Lobbying européen et lobbying américain: vers une plus grande convergence des pratiques" (2005) R.M.C.U.E. 601–605; McLaughlin, Jordan and Maloney, "Corporate Lobbying in the European Community" (1993) J.C.M.S. 191–212; Rideau, "Les groupes d'intérêt dans le système institutionnnel communautaire" (1993) 3 R.A.E. 49–73. For studies of lobbying in practice, see Pedler and Van Schendelen (eds), *Lobbying the European Union* (Aldershot, Dartmouth, 1994), 311 pp.

[56] Protocol (No. 2), annexed to the TEU and TFEU, on the application of the principles of subsidiarity and proportionality ([2010] O.J. C83/206), Art. 2 (which makes an exception for "cases of exceptional urgency").

[57] *Ibid.*, Art. 5. The reasons for concluding that a Union objective can be better achieved at Union level are to be substantiated by qualitative and, wherever possible, quantitative indicators. At the same time, the Protocol requires the Commission to take duly into account the need for any burden, whether financial or administrative, falling upon the Union, national governments, local authorities, economic operators and citizens to be minimised and commensurate with the objective to be achieved: *ibid.* (see also the discussion of the principles of subsidiarity and proportionality in paras 7–026—7–041, *supra*).

[58] In the case of major items of draft legislation, the Commission is to implement an integrated impact-assessment process, combining in one single evaluation the impact assessments relating inter alia to social, economic and environmental aspects: point 29 of the Interinstitutional Agreement of December 16, 2003 on better-lawmaking (see n. 54, *supra*). Where the ordinary legislative procedure applies, the European Parliament and Council may, on the basis of jointly defined criteria and procedures, also have impact assessments carried out prior to the adoption of any substantive amendment: *ibid.*, point 30. See also the Communication from the Commission to the Council and the European Parliament of March 16, 2005—Better Regulation for Growth and Jobs in the European Union, COM(2005)0057 final. For the Impact Assessment Board (IAB) established at the Commission, see *http://ec.europa.eu/governance/impact/iab/iab_en.htm* [Accessed February 4, 2011].

[59] Criteria for the application of self-regulation or co-regulation (by which a Union act leaves achievement of its aims to the parties concerned; para. 17–001, *infra*) are set out in points 16 to 25 of the Interinstitutional Agreement of December 16, 2003 (see n. 54, *supra*).

to the demand for democracy, transparency and subsidiarity, the Commission increasingly issues consultative documents, "green papers", in order to encourage political debate. Packages of related proposals for legislation are published in the form of "white papers".[60]

Publication of initiatives. The Commission formulates each proposal which it wishes to submit as a text ready to be adopted, and publishes it in the *Official Journal* (part C). Such proposals and other preparatory documents on general matters which have been approved within the Commission are referred to as "COM documents". If they are not already available on the Commission's website, they may be obtained on request.[61] Initiatives for the adoption of a PJCC legislative act submitted to the Council by a group of Member States or the Commission are also published in the *Official Journal*.[62]   **16–019**

According to the Protocol on the role of National Parliaments in the European Union, all Commission documents (green and white papers and communications) are to be forwarded to national parliaments upon publication.[63] Draft legislative acts must also be forwarded to national parliaments.[64] In order to allow enough time for discussion of the draft legislative act, the Protocol requires there to be an eight-week period between the time when a draft is made available in all languages to the European Parliament and the Council and the date when it is placed on a Council agenda for decision (adoption of an act or of a position under a legislative procedure).[65] Before making any legislative initiative, the Commission is invariably to notify the European Parliament.[66] Moreover, in all fields where the

---

[60] Thus, the Commission's White Paper on European Governance contained proposals designed to get more people and organisations involved in shaping and delivering Union policy: [2001] O.J. C287/1.

[61] Documents published by the Commission's general secretariat (SEC documents) are not always publicly available, but they are now issued as far as possible in the form of COM documents. COM documents are available from Eur-Lex: *http://eur-lex.europa.eu/en/index.htm* [Accessed December 11, 2010].

[62] Council Rules of Procedure, Art. 17(1)(c). Other initiatives for PJCC acts are published in the *Official Journal*, unless decided otherwise (Council Rules of Procedure, Art. 17(2)(a)).

[63] Protocol (No. 1), annexed to the EU, TFEU and EAEC Treaty, on the role of National Parliaments in the European Union ([2010] O.J. C83/203), Art. 1. The Commission is also to forward the annual legislative programme, as well as any other instrument of legislative planning or policy, to national parliaments, at the same time as it forwards them to the European Parliament and the Council (*ibid.*).

[64] *Ibid.*, Art. 2.

[65] *Ibid.*, Art. 4; see Art. 3(3) of the Council Rules of Procedure. The Council may derogate from the eight-week period in cases of urgency. For such an exception (in a decision not adopted on the initiative of the Commission), see recital 14 in the preamble to the Council Decision of July 16, 2003 on the granting of aid by the Belgian Government to certain coordination centres established in Belgium ([2003] O.J. L184/17).

[66] Framework Agreement of October 20, 2010 on relations between the European Parliament and the Commission, [2010] L304/47.

European Parliament acts in a legislative capacity, or as a branch of the budgetary authority, it is to be informed, on a par with the Council, at every stage of the legislative and budgetary process.[67]

16–020   **Amending or withdrawing a proposal.** When the Commission is entitled to submit a formal "proposal", it has a significant influence over the course of decision-making. So long as the Council has not acted, the Commission is entitled to amend its proposal at any time during the procedure leading to the adoption of a Union act (Art. 293(2) TFEU). It may therefore amend its proposal at any time while it is under discussion in the Council (and before that in the working parties and Coreper). In view of the flexibility demanded by the legislative procedure with a view to achieving a convergence of views between the institutions, no formalities have to be complied with in order to amend a proposal and amendments do not have to be made in writing.[68] Thus, an "amendment of a proposal" may consist in a Member of the Commission's approving a compromise proposal put forward by the Presidency of the Council, even if it involves a significant change to the original proposal.[69] Since the right not to submit a proposal is a corollary of the right of initiative, the Commission may also withdraw its proposal at any time,[70] except in the ordinary legislative procedure from the second reading onwards.

As has been noted, where the Council has to adopt an act on a proposal from the Commission, the former may amend the proposal only by a unanimous vote (Art. 293(1) TFEU), except in a few particular cases.[71] Consequently, except in those cases, as soon as one Member State is in agreement with a Commission proposal, the Council has to reach agreement on the proposal which has been submitted and which may be constantly amended by the Commission until it obtains the support of a sufficient majority. If the Council is unanimous in wishing to adopt an act which differs in some way from the Commission's proposal, the latter may deprive the Council of its power of decision by withdrawing the proposal. The Commission's room for manoeuvre is significantly greater where the Council has to act by a qualified majority than when it is required to take a unanimous decision. In the first case, the Commission will amend its proposal during the negotiations in the Council just sufficiently in order to obtain the number of votes required; in the second case, the Commission has to comply with the wishes of all the Member States, either by amending its proposal itself or by adhering to its proposal and seeing the Council possibly alter it by a unanimous vote. If the

---

[67] See already Framework Agreement of May 26, 2005 on relations between the European Parliament and the Commission, [2006] C117E/125, points 8 and12.

[68] ECJ, Case C-280/93 *Germany v Council* [1994] E.C.R. I-4973, para. 36.

[69] ECJ, Case 445/00 *Austria v Council* [2003] E.C.R. I-1461, paras 16–17 and 44–47.

[70] See the Commission's answer of January 23, 1987 to question 2422/86 (Herman), [1987] O.J. C220/6.

[71] Article 293(1) TFEU makes an exception for the cases referred to in Art. 294(10) and (13) TFEU (the conciliation phase of the ordinary legislative procedure) and in Arts 310, 312, 314 and Art. 315, second para., TFEU (certain budgetary provisions).

Council wishes to depart from the Commission's proposal, it cannot introduce just any provision. The Council will not exceed its power to make amendments if the changes it makes remain within the scope of the act as defined in the original Commission proposal.[72]

In those policy areas where the Treaties give the Commission the initiative in the form of a recommendation, it does not have the same influence on decision-making. When the Council has received the recommendation, it can still decide by the same majority even if it does not take up the recommendation and the power to take the decision cannot be removed from it.[73]

No obligation. In principle, the Commission cannot be compelled to submit a proposal, although, in some instances, the Treaties require the Commission to examine whether it should submit a proposal.[74] In addition, Art. 241 TFEU does empower the Council (acting by a simple majority vote) to   **16–021**

"request the Commission to undertake any studies the Council considers desirable for the attainment of the common objectives, and to submit to it any appropriate proposals",

whilst Art. 225 TFEU confers on the European Parliament "acting by a majority of its component Members" the right to

"request the Commission to submit any appropriate proposal on matters on which it considers that a Union act is required for the purpose of implementing the Treaties".

Because the Commission's right to make proposals is essentially in the nature of a "power", no general obligation for the Commission to submit proposals at the request of the Council or the Parliament may be inferred from those articles.[75] However, since the Lisbon Treaty, those articles explicitly require the

---

[72] ECJ, Case C-408/95 *Eurotunnel and Others* [1997] E.C.R. I-6315, paras 37–39; see also ECJ, Case 355/87 *Commission v Council* [1987] E.C.R. 1517, paras 42–44 (amendments tested against the "subject-matter" and the "objective" of the proposal).

[73] ECJ, Case C-27/04 *Commission v Council* [2004] E.C.R. I-6649, para. 80 (where Commission recommendations—and not proposals—are placed before the Council, it may modify the measure recommended by the majority required for the adoption of that measure). See also *ibid.*, para. 92 (Council decision taken on a recommendation from the Commission cannot be modified without a fresh recommendation from the Commission).

[74] Article 114(7) and (8) TFEU [*ex Art. 95(7) and (8) EC*].

[75] See to this effect Lauwaars, *Lawfulness and Legal Force of Community Decisions* (Leyden, Sijthoff, 1973), at 108–109; for a different view, see Harnier, in von der Groeben, Thiesing and Ehlermann (eds), *Kommentar zum EWG-Vertrag* (Baden-Baden, Nomos, 1991), 4307. See also CFI (Order of March 30, 2006), T-2/04 *Korkmaz* [2006] E.C.R. II-32 (no action for annulment possible against the Commission's refusal to submit to the Council a proposal for an appropriate measure).

Commission to inform the Council and the European Parliament, respectively, of its reasons if it does not submit a proposal.[76] Even before that, the Commission gave the European Parliament and the Council an undertaking to take account of any requests made and to provide a prompt and sufficiently detailed reply to the parliamentary committees concerned and to the Council's preparatory bodies.[77] Similarly, the Commission is not obliged to comply with a request addressed to it by Member States wishing to establish enhanced cooperation between themselves. If the Commission fails to submit a proposal to the Council, "it shall inform the Member States concerned of the reasons for not doing so" (Art. 329(1), first subpara., TFEU).[78] By the same token, the Commission is not obliged to comply with a request for a proposal submitted by citizens in accordance with Art. 11(4) TEU (para. 16–015, *supra*).

An obligation to submit a proposal does exist in those exceptional cases in which the Treaties impose an obligation to legislate (see para. 16–006). In such case, a refusal on the part of the Commission to submit a proposal may be challenged by an action for failure to act (Art. 265 TFEU). The Commission is also bound to "submit its conclusions to the Council without delay" in the event that the Council or a Member State requests it to make a recommendation or a proposal pursuant to Art. 135 TFEU in order to enable the Council to legislate on specific matters relating to EMU. Having regard to the cautious wording of that article, it does not require the Commission formally to submit a proposal.

Nevertheless, the Commission has to fulfil its duty to cooperate with the Council.[79] The European Parliament can call the Commission to account for any abuse of its right to submit proposals when it makes the Commission answer for its policy (see para. 13–009). Since the Treaties conferred the right of initiative on the Commission alone and the task of proposing legislation falls to it in its own right, it would seem inappropriate for the European Parliament to compel it to use that right in a particular way by threatening it with a motion of

---

[76] Unlike Arts 192 and 208 EC.

[77] Point 14 of the framework agreement of May 26, 2005 (n. 66, *supra*) and point 9 of the interinstitutional agreement of December 16, 2003 on better law-making (n. 54, *supra*); see formerly point 3.3 of the Code of Conduct agreed between the European Parliament and the Commission on March 15, 1995, [1995] O.J. C89/69. For action taken by the Commission on the European Parliament's first four legislative initiatives, see its answer of August 1, 1996 to question E-1859/96 (Schleicher), [1996] O.J. C345/110.

[78] Similarly, the Commission was not obliged to comply with a request made by a Member State for the Commission to submit a proposal for the implementation of former Title IV of the EC Treaty, as it was merely provided that the Commission "shall examine" any such request (Art. 67(2), first indent, EC).

[79] In practice, formal recourse to Art. 241 TFEU is replaced by dialogue between the two institutions. See the Council's answer of May 14, 1992 to question No. 607/92 (Dury), [1992] O.J. C159/64. See also Art. 218(1) EC which provided that "[t]he Council and the Commission shall consult each other and shall settle by common accord their methods of cooperation".

censure.[80] In this light, the European Parliament's legitimate pretension to a right of initiative to supplement its right to request a proposal under Art. 225 TFEU militates in favour of amendment of the Treaties.

II. THE ORDINARY LEGISLATIVE PROCEDURE

Ordinary legislative procedure. The ordinary legislative procedure for the adoption of legislative acts, set out in Art. 294 TFEU, provides for a direct dialogue between the European Parliament and the Council and makes adoption of acts dependent upon the approval of both institutions. If the institutions reach agreement, the final act is adopted as a regulation, directive or decision of both the European Parliament and the Council, signed by both Presidents (see Art. 297(1), first subpara., TFEU). 16–022

The ordinary legislative procedure replaces the former "co-decision procedure" set out in Art. 251 EC.[81] That procedure was introduced by the EU Treaty to give the European Parliament a greater say in the legislative process (see para. 3–014). Since the Treaty of Amsterdam, it applied to a major part of the policy areas in which Community legislation was adopted.[82] The ordinary legislative procedure now applies to virtually all fields of action of the Union where the Council has to decide by qualified majority,[83] including PJCC, where the European Parliament and the Council may adopt acts on the initiative of a group of Member States.[84] However, it does not apply in the context of the CFSP.[85]

---

[80] Compare the reasoning of the Court of Justice in conferring a right on the European Parliament to bring an action for annulment in the event of a breach of its prerogatives (now also recognised by Art. 263 TFEU) so as not to have to rely on forcing the Commission to bring an action: ECJ, Case C-70/88 *European Parliament v Council* [1990] E.C.R. I-2041, paras 19–27; see Lenaerts, "Some Reflections on the Separation of Powers in the European Community" (1991) C.M.L.Rev. 11, at 23–25.

[81] For the practical arrangements of the co-decision procedure, see the Joint Declaration of the European Parliament, the Council and the Commission on practical arrangements for the codecision procedure, [2007] O.J. C145/5.

[82] The extension of the scope of the co-decision procedure was already contemplated by the former Art. 189b(8) EC; see the report from the Commission of July 3, 1996 provided for in that provision, (1996) 7/8 EU Bull. point 2.3.1., and the resolution of the European Parliament of November 14, 1996, [1996] O.J. C362/267. For an assessment, see Silvestro and Albani Liberali, "La codécision a été un succès, il faut aller de l'avant" (1997) R.M.C.U.E. 166–169; Boyron, "Maastricht and the Codecision Procedure: A Success Story" (1996) I.C.L.Q. 293–318. See the European Parliament's resolution of July 16, 1998 on the new co-decision procedure after Amsterdam, [1998] O.J. C292/140. For the limited extension of the scope of the co-decision procedure resulting from the Treaty of Nice, see Dashwood, "The Constitution of the European Union after Nice: law-making procedures" (2001) E.L.Rev. 215–238.

[83] However, in some cases the Council acts by qualified majority under a special legislative procedure (para. 16–034, *infra*); see e.g. Art. 311 TFEU.

[84] See, for example, Arts 81 to 89 TFEU in conjunction with Art. 76 TFEU.

[85] See Art. 24(1), second subpara., TEU and 31(1), first subpara., TEU, stating that the adoption of legislative acts under the CFSP shall be excluded.

16–023 **First reading in Parliament.** The ordinary legislative procedure normally begins with a proposal from the Commission,[86] which is submitted to the European Parliament and the Council (see Art. 294(2) TFEU). The President of the Parliament refers the matter to the competent parliamentary committee (EP Rules of Procedure, Rule 43). The committee verifies whether the proposed act has the correct legal basis, whether it respects the principles of subsidiarity and proportionality and fundamental rights and whether sufficient financial resources are provided (EP Rules of Procedure, Rules 36 to 38a). Generally, the committee adopts a report comprising any draft amendments, a draft legislative resolution and an explanatory statement (EP Rules of Procedure, Rule 45), on which the Parliament holds a vote at the plenary session (EP Rules of Procedure, Rule 55).[87] The Commission is requested to state its position on draft amendments at the committee stage (EP Rules of Procedure, Rule 54) and after the vote at the plenary session (EP Rules of Procedure, Rules 56 and 57). If the Commission declares that it is not prepared to accept all the amendments or that it is not prepared to withdraw a proposal not approved by the Parliament, the Parliament may postpone the vote.[88] In order for the Parliament to give its opinion more expeditiously, its President, a parliamentary committee, a political group, at least 40 MEPs, the Commission or the Council may request that a debate on a proposal be treated as urgent. In the event that the Parliament accepts such a request, the question is placed on the agenda as a priority item and debate may take place at the plenary session without a (written) report from the responsible committee (EP Rules of Procedure, Rule 142). The European Parliament communicates the position it adopts at first reading to the Council (Article 294(3) TFEU).

16–024 **First reading in Council.** If the Council approves the European Parliament's position, it may adopt the proposed act by a qualified majority in the wording that

---

[86] For the exceptional cases in which the initiative does not emanate from the Commission, see para. 16–031, *infra*.

[87] Rule 46 of the EP Rules of Procedure sets out two simplified procedures which the chair of a committee may follow provided that no objection is made by at least one-tenth of the Members of the responsible committee. First, he or she may move that the committee approve a proposal without amendments (Rule 46(1)). Secondly, he or she may move that the chair draw up a report including amendments, which is deemed to have been adopted if no objection is made. In the latter case, the draft legislative resolution is put to a vote in the plenary session without debate (Rule 46(2)). Furthermore, under Rule 138 any legislative proposal adopted in committee with fewer than one-tenth of the members of the committee voting against is placed on the draft agenda of Parliament for a single vote without amendment, unless political groups or one-tenth of the Members of Parliament have requested in writing that the item be open to amendment. Such items are without debate unless Parliament decides otherwise on a proposal from the Conference of Presidents, or if requested by a political group or at least forty Members.

[88] See EP Rules of Procedure, Rule 54(2) (postponement of the vote in the competent committee), 57(2) and 59(4) (referral of the matter back to the competent committee by the Parliament).

Figure 2: Ordinary Legislative Procedure (Art. 294 TFEU)

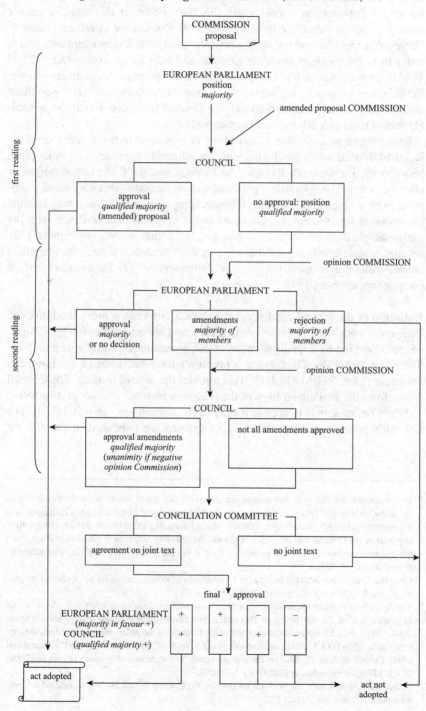

corresponds to the position of the European Parliament (Art. 294(4) TFEU).[89] As far as the Commission is concerned, this means that, at this stage, it cannot oppose an act on which the Parliament and the Council are in full agreement.[90] However, it must be noted that, in principle, the Council may adopt acts which differ from the proposal from the Commission only by unanimity (Art. 293(1) TFEU). Hence, where the European Parliament proposes amendments to the Commission proposal and where the Commission does not take over these amendments in an amended proposal, the Council (complying with the applicable voting requirement) must act unanimously.

Even though no provision to this effect is contained in the Treaties or in the Rules of Procedure of the Parliament, an informal "trilogue" may take place between the European Parliament, the Council and the Commission before or after the vote in the responsible parliamentary committee. This may allow a proposal to be adopted at first reading ("first-reading agreement),[91] as it may lead the Commission for instance to change its initial proposal in accordance with the European Parliament's wishes. Interestingly, a first-reading agreement only requires a simple majority of the votes in the European Parliament, whereas a second-reading agreement requires the Parliament to vote by a majority of its component members.

16–025 **Initiation of the second reading.** If the Council does not approve the European Parliament's position—whether or not it proposed any amendments—the Council adopts a position by a qualified majority (or, again, unanimously where its position differs from the Commission's proposal) for submission to the European Parliament (Art. 294(6) TFEU).[92] This initiates the second reading. The Council is to inform the Parliament fully of the reasons which led it to adopt its position and the Commission is to apprise it fully of its position (Art. 294(6) TFEU). The Council's position and the statement of reasons are published in the *Official*

---

[89] In that respect, the Treaty of Amsterdam simplified the procedure which, in the version provided for in the original EU Treaty, invariably required both an opinion of the European Parliament and a "common position" (former Art. 189b(2), second subpara., EC). Under that procedure, final approval of the Council was possible only in the second stage, after the Parliament had approved the common position or failed to pronounce upon it in time (former Art. 189b(2), third subpara., points (a) and (b), EC).

[90] Once the Council has adopted an act, the Commission of course can no longer withdraw its proposal; see Art. 293(2) TFEU [*ex Art. 250(2) EC*].

[91] See the code of conduct for negotiating in the context of the ordinary legislative procedures set out in Annex XX of the EP Rules of Procedure. For two examples among many, see Directive 2004/48/EC of the European Parliament and of the Council on the enforcement of intellectual property rights, [2004] O.J. L157/45 and Regulation (EC) No. 593/2008 of the European Parliament and of the Council of June 17, 2008 on the law applicable to contractual obligations (Rome I), [2008] O.J. L 177/6, *corrigendum* in [2009] O.J. L 309/87.

[92] Before the Lisbon Treaty, the position adopted by the Council in first reading was called a "common position" (see Art. 251(2) EC).

Journal.[93] When the President of the Parliament announces the Council's position at the plenary session, it is deemed to have been referred to the committee responsible at first reading, which draws up a recommendation for the second reading on behalf of the plenary session (EP Rules of Procedure, Rule 63). The recommendation may propose that the Parliament approve the Council's position, adopt amendments or reject it.[94]

Adoption or rejection by Parliament at second reading. If, within three months of the communication of its position by the Council, the European Parliament approves it or has not taken a decision, the act in question is deemed to have been adopted in the wording which corresponds to the Council's position (Art. 294(7), point (a), TFEU). Within that period, the European Parliament may, however, decide to reject the Council's position. If it does so decide by a majority of its component Members, the proposed act is deemed not to have been adopted (Art. 294(7), point (b), TFEU).[95] If the Parliament rejects the Council's position, this may be the end of the matter.[96]

16–026

Amendments by Parliament at second reading. Within the same three-month period, the European Parliament may also propose amendments to the Council's position by a majority of its component Members (Art. 294(7), point (c), TFEU). In its Rules of Procedure, the Parliament has limited its right to move amendments to those which seek to restore wholly or in part the position adopted by the Parliament in its first reading, to amendments designed to reach a compromise between the Council and the Parliament and to amendments which alter parts of the Council's position not covered by the proposal submitted at first reading and do not amount to a substantial change or which take account of a new fact or legal situation which has arisen since the first reading (EP Rules of Procedure, Rule 66(2)).[97] The Parliament forwards the amended text to the Council and the Commission, whereupon the latter delivers an opinion on the amendments (Art. 294 (7), point (c), TFEU).

16–027

---

[93] Council Rules of Procedure, Art. 17(1)(b).

[94] A proposal to amend or reject the Council's position may also be made by a political group or by at least 40 MEPs (EP Rules of Procedure, Rules 65(1) and 66(1)).

[95] The Treaty of Amsterdam abolished the possibility for the Council to convene a meeting of the Conciliation Committee in these circumstances. The proposed act was then only deemed not to have been adopted if the European Parliament rejected it again by an absolute majority of its component Members (former Art. 189b(2)(c) EC).

[96] In the case of the Proposal for a directive of the European Parliament and of the Council on the patentability of computer-implemented inventions (COM(2002) 92 final) the European Parliament rejected, by 648 votes to 14 with 18 abstentions, the Council's common position on the software patent directive. Before the vote, the rapporteur Michel Rocard said that the Parliament was split fifty-fifty on the issue and all political groups had decided to reject the text rather than risk a result they could not accept.

[97] The President of Parliament may waive these rules if new elections have taken place since first reading, EP Rules of Procedure, Rule 66(3).

16–028   **Adoption by Council at second reading.** If, within three months of the matter being referred to it, the Council, acting by a qualified majority, approves all the European Parliament's amendments, the act in question is deemed to have been adopted (Art. 294(8), point (a), TFEU). Since the Council does not decide on a proposal from the Commission in the second reading, whether a particular parliamentary amendment succeeds does not depend on whether the Commission is prepared to take it over. Nonetheless, in the second reading the Commission still has a certain influence in that if it delivers a negative opinion, the Council has to act unanimously (Art. 294(9) TFEU).[98] Given that the Commission's intervention in the second reading phase is limited to delivering an opinion and that the second reading is centred on the Council's position, the Commission can no longer amend, let alone withdraw, its proposal. As in first reading, an informal trilogue may take place so as to enable the Council to accept all the Parliament's second-reading amendments.[99]

16–029   **Conciliation.** If the Council is minded not to adopt all the amendments, the President of the Council, in agreement with the President of the Parliament, convenes within six weeks a Conciliation Committee, composed of the members of the Council or their representatives and an equal number of members representing the Parliament (Art. 294(8), point (b), and (10), TFEU).[100] The Conciliation Committee has the task of "reaching agreement on a joint text" within six weeks of its being convened on the basis of the positions of the European Parliament and the Council at second reading (Art. 294(10) TFEU). In order to find a solution, the Committee is to reconcile the points of view of the Parliament and the Council on the basis of examination of all the aspects of the disagreement.[101] Agreement

---

[98] The Commission undertakes to take the utmost account of parliamentary amendments unless there are important grounds for not doing so, in which case it has to explain its decision: point 37 of the framework agreement of October 20, 2010 (n. 66, *supra*).

[99] See the code of conduct for negotiating in the context of the ordinary legislative procedures set out in Annex XX of the EP Rules of Procedure. For an example of a second-reading agreement, see Directive 2001/29/EC of the European Parliament and of the Council of May 22, 2001 on the harmonisation of certain aspects of copyright and related rights in the information society, [2001] O.J. L167/10.

[100] The Conciliation Committee does not constitute a delegation of the Council as an institution but represents the views of the "members of the Council". See the Joint declaration of the European Parliament, the Council and the Commission on practical arrangements for the co-decision procedure, [2007] O.J. C145/5. For the composition (on the European Parliament side) and the mode of operation of the committee, see para. 13–022, *supra*.

[101] Before the Lisbon Treaty, Art. 251(4) EC provided that, in fulfilling the task of reaching agreement on a joint text, the Committee was to address the common position "on the basis of the amendments proposed by the European Parliament". For the Court, however, this provision did not limit the wide discretion of the Committee to reconcile the points of view of the Parliament and the Council on the basis of examination of all the aspects of their disagreement: ECJ, Case C-344/04 *IATA and ELFAA* [2006] E.C.R. I-403, paras 57–59. Neither is the Committee restricted in its negotiations to what is set out in the Commission's proposal; in order to safeguard the Commission's right of initiative, the joint text should, however, have the same subject-matter as the original Commission proposal.

is reached by a qualified majority of members of the Council or their representatives and a majority of the members representing the Parliament. The Commission takes part in the Conciliation Committee's deliberations and takes all necessary initiatives with a view to reconciling the positions of the Parliament and the Council (Art. 294(11) TFEU). This means that the Commission is not entitled to withdraw its proposal at this stage.[102]

If the Conciliation Committee approves a joint text, the act has to be finally adopted in a third reading by the European Parliament by a majority of the votes cast and by the Council by a qualified majority.[103] If one of the two institutions fails to approve the proposed act within six weeks of its approval by the Committee, it is deemed not to have been adopted (Art. 294(13) TFEU).[104] Likewise, if the Conciliation Committee fails to reach agreement within the time-limit, the proposed act is deemed not to have been adopted (Art. 294(12) TFEU). Consequently, neither the Council nor the European Parliament can force through an act which has not been approved by the other institution.[105]

Time-limits. As far as the time-limits are concerned, all three-month periods may be extended by a maximum of one month and all six-week periods by no more than two weeks at the initiative of the European Parliament or the Council (Art. 294(14) TFEU).   **16–030**

Commission acting as broker. The tortuous ordinary legislative procedure has the merit of enabling the European Parliament to defend its point of view directly to the Council. After it has submitted its proposal, the Commission has only a   **16–031**

---

[102] Glaesner, "Willensbildung und Beschlußverfahren in der Europäischen Union" (1994) EuR 1994, Beiheft 1, 25, at 26.

[103] The Council acts by a qualified majority even where the joint text finally adopted diverges from the Commission proposal (see Art. 293(1) TFEU, which makes an exception for Art. 294(10) and (13) TFEU).

[104] See the negative outcome on March 1, 1995 of the vote in the plenary session of the European Parliament on a joint text of a directive on legal protection of biotechnological inventions on which agreement had already been reached between the European Parliament and Council delegations in the Conciliation Committee, [1995] O.J. C68/26, and the negative vote on July 4, 2001 on a joint text of a directive on company law concerning takeover bids, [2002] O.J. C65 E/57.

[105] Under the first version of the co-decision procedure, the Council was entitled to confirm, by a qualified majority, the common position to which it had agreed before the conciliation procedure was initiated, possibly with amendments proposed by the Parliament. In that event, the act was finally adopted unless, within six weeks of the date of confirmation by the Council, the European Parliament rejected the text by an absolute majority of its component Members, in which case the proposed act was deemed not to have been adopted (see former Art. 189b(6), second sentence, EC). For an example, see the decision of the European Parliament of July 19, 1994 rejecting the text on the application of open network provision (OPN) to voice telephony which the Council had confirmed following conciliation in accordance with Art. 189b(6) EC ([1994] O.J. C261/13).

limited role to play, although it does act in practice as an honest broker in formal and informal conciliation procedures.[106] The Commission formally determines the course of the procedure only if it refuses in the first reading to take over the amendments of the European Parliament in an amended proposal or if it delivers a negative opinion in the second reading on the amendments proposed by the Parliament, hence making the Council's adoption of those amendments conditional upon its approving them by a unanimous vote. Accordingly, the Commission's position will prevail—provisionally—if at least one Member State agrees with it. There would appear to be little likelihood of the Commission's withdrawing its proposal as it would thereby openly put the Parliament out of play. If the Commission does not withdraw its proposal, it disqualifies itself from opposing the result of the decision-making process at a later stage. This is because once the Council fails to adopt all of the Parliament's amendments, the President of the Council is obliged to convene the Conciliation Committee. The Commission does take part in the proceedings of that committee, but its final judgement of the "joint text" approved by the committee if the conciliation process is successful has no influence on the necessary majorities which need to be mustered in the Council and the Parliament in order to adopt the definitive act "in accordance with the joint text" (see para. 16–029).

The Commission plays a more limited role where a legislative act emanates from the initiative of a group of Member States, a recommendation by the European Central Bank or a request of the Court of Justice. In that event, the Commission does not participate in the first and second reading and it is not obliged to take part in the proceedings of the Conciliation Committee. Accordingly, it may not compel the Council to take its decision unanimously. However, the Commission may give an opinion at the request of the European Parliament or the Council or on its own initiative (but without this having any impact on the voting requirements in the Council) and it may take part in the Conciliation Committee if it deems it necessary (Art. 294(15) TFEU).

16–032   **Two legislative chambers.** In theory, the Parliament occupies a strong negotiating position vis-à-vis the Council in that it may bring an end to the decision-making process by rejecting the Council's position. Nevertheless, the Parliament does not exercise its right to reject the Council's position lightly.[107] Rejection requires a majority vote of the Parliament's component Members. What is more, it serves no purpose for the Parliament to reject a Council's position when the Parliament would like the Union to legislate in the area concerned: in such a case, the Parliament is obliged to "co-decide" with the Council. The decisive influence

---

[106] See Borras, "The European Commission as network broker" (2007) 11 *European Integration (online papers)* 1–14.

[107] For the first two cases, see ns 104 and 105, *supra*.

exercised by the Parliament is not based solely on its "negative" veto.[108] The Council cannot in fact adopt any act which has not been expressly or impliedly approved by the Parliament. Together with the possibility of an informal "trilogue", the Conciliation Committee has developed into a successful way of striking compromises, in consultation with the Commission, between the two legislative chambers.[109]

Voting requirements and alarm bell. The ordinary legislative procedure is char- 16–033 acterised by the possibility of the Council to agree by qualified majority with a position adopted by the European Parliament. It is only at first and second reading that the Council may be required to act unanimously where the Commission does not take over, or gives a negative opinion on, amendments proposed by the European Parliament. However, before the Lisbon Treaty, the Council was to act unanimously throughout the co-decision procedure in some instances.[110] In those cases, the Lisbon Treaty provides for qualified majority in the Council.[111] However, with respect to the coordination of national social security systems (Art. 48 TFEU), it introduces an "alarm bell procedure" or "emergency brake",[112] allowing any Member State which considers that a draft legislative act would affect important aspects or the financial balance of its social security system to request that the matter be referred to the European Council. In that event, the ordinary legislative procedure will be suspended for a period of up to four months,

---

[108] This was the case with the procedure laid down in Art. 189b EC as introduced by the original EU Treaty; n. 105, *supra*.

[109] In the German federal legislative process, a *Vermittlungsauschuss* (conciliation committee), which negotiates as between the directly elected *Bundestag* and the *Bundesrat*, consisting of representatives of the *Länder* governments, operates with some success. The Union conciliation system was modelled on the German system, but is not completely comparable to it since the directly-elected *Bundestag* retains the principal legislative powers. See Foster, "The New Conciliation Committee under Article 189b EC" (1994) E.L.Rev. 185–194.

[110] See Art. 42 EC (social security); Art. 47(2), second sentence, EC (access to professions) and Art. 151(5) EC (incentive measures in the field of culture). Although this restricted to a considerable extent the leeway for reaching agreement between the institutions, it meant that the Treaty did not regard the requirement for unanimity as being incompatible with the co-decision procedure. See in this connection (where the Court held the correct legal basis to be a combination of Art. 159, third para., EC [*now Art. 175, third para., TFEU*] (co-decision procedure) and Art. 308 EC [*now Art. 352 TFEU*] (requiring unanimity; Art. 352 TFEU now refers to the ordinary legislative procedure)). By contrast, see the incompatibility found by the Court of Justice in the case of the cooperation procedure, para. 16–012, *supra*. See Dashwood, "Community Legislative Procedures in the Era of the Treaty on European Union" (1994) E.L.Rev. 343, at 362.

[111] See Art. 53 TFEU (access to professions) and Art. 167(5) TFEU (incentive measures in the field of culture).

[112] See Dougan, "The Treaty of Lisbon 2007: Winning Minds, not Hearts" (2008) C.M.L.Rev. 617–703, at 643.

during which the European Council may decide (by consensus[113]) to refer the draft back to the Council to have the decision-making procedure resumed, not to take action or to request the Commission to submit a new proposal, in which case the act originally proposed will be deemed not to have been adopted. Likewise, an "alarm bell procedure" has been introduced for certain harmonisation measures with respect to national criminal law that the European Parliament and the Council now adopt in accordance with the ordinary legislative procedure (Arts 82(3) and 83(3) TFEU). It enables any Member State which considers that a draft directive would affect fundamental aspects of its criminal justice system to request that the draft directive be referred to the European Council. In that event, the ordinary legislative procedure will likewise be suspended for a period of up to four months, during which the European Council may decide by consensus to refer the draft back to the Council to have the decision-making procedure resumed. Within the same timeframe, in case of disagreement, and if at least nine Member States wish to establish enhanced cooperation on the basis of the draft directive concerned, they are to notify the European Parliament, the Council and the Commission accordingly. In such a case, the authorisation to proceed with enhanced cooperation will be deemed to be granted.[114] In practice, this means that no separate decision of the Council, acting by a qualified majority, on a proposal from the Commission and after obtaining the consent of the European Parliament is needed for the Member States concerned to be authorised to adopt, as Union law applicable to them, the draft directive. It is to be expected that the automatic authorisation to proceed with enhanced cooperation constitutes a powerful incentive for the European Council to try hard to reach a consensus. If it nevertheless fails to do so, the further development of Union policy in this sensitive field will still not be blocked.

III. SPECIAL LEGISLATIVE PROCEDURES

A. PARTICIPATION OF THE COUNCIL

16–034   **Unanimity or qualified majority.** Article 289(2) TFEU regards the instances in which the Council does not decide jointly with the European Parliament as "special legislative procedures", that is to say those cases in which legislation is to be adopted "by the European Parliament with the participation of the Council" or "by the latter with the participation of the European Parliament". The second option is the more frequent: in this case the Council has the power of decision,

---

[113] See Declaration (No. 23), annexed to the Lisbon Treaty, on the second para. of Art. 48 of the Treaty on the Functioning of the European Union ([2010] O.J. C83/346), which recalls that in this case, in accordance with Art. 15(4) TEU, the European Council acts by consensus.

[114] Articles 82(3), second subpara., and 83(3), second subpara., TFEU, which refer to Art. 20(2) TEU and 329(1) TFEU. See para. 19–008, *infra*.

acting unanimously or by a qualified majority, whilst the European Parliament is consulted[115] (see para. 16–035) or has to give its consent[116] (see para. 16–037). It is only in a few cases that the Treaties provide that legislation is to be adopted "by the European Parliament with the participation of the Council". In that event, the European Parliament acts "with the approval of the Council"[117] or "after obtaining the consent of the Council".[118]

In the field of PJCC, the Union now acts in principle under the ordinary legislative procedure. However, in specific cases, a special legislative procedure applies. The Council is to decide by unanimity after obtaining the consent of the European Parliament on some important decisions with respect to judicial cooperation,[119] whilst some sensitive aspects of police cooperation require the Council to decide by unanimity after consulting the European Parliament.[120]

---

[115] See Arts 21(3) (measures concerning social security or social protection), 22(1) and (2) (arrangements concerning participation in municipal elections and elections to the European Parliament), 64(3) (measures constituting a step backwards as regards the liberalisation of the movement of capital to or from third countries), 77(3) (provisions concerning passports identity cards, residence permits or any other such document), 81(3) (measures concerning family law with cross-border implications), 87(3) (operational cooperation between police authorities), 89 (operations of police authorities in other Member States), 113 (harmonisation of legislation concerning indirect taxation), 115 (harmonisation of rules directly affecting the internal market), 118, second para. (creation of European intellectual property rights), 126(14), second subpara. (provisions replacing the Protocol on excessive deficit procedure), 127(6) (conferral of specific tasks on ECB), 153(2), third subpara. (certain measures on social policy), 192(2), first subpara. (certain measures on environment), 194(3) (certain measures on energy), 203 (association of OCTs), 262 (conferral of jurisdiction in relation to European intellectual property rights), 308, third para. (amendments to Statute of European Investment Bank), and 311, third para., TFEU (provisions on own resources of the Union), where the Council is to decide unanimously, and Art. 23, second para. (measures facilitating diplomatic protection), and 182(4) TFEU (specific programmes implementing multi-annual framework programmes) where the Council is to decide by a qualified majority vote.

[116] See Arts 19(1) (combating discrimination), 25 (strengthening of or adding to rights of citizens of the union), 82(2)(d) (identification of specific aspects of criminal procedure), 86(1) (establishment of European Public Prosecutor's Office), 311, fourth para. (implementing measures for the Union's own resources system), and 352 TFEU (flexibility clause), where the Council is to decide unanimously, and Art. 311, fourth para., TFEU, where the Council is to decide by a qualified majority.

[117] See Art. 223(2) TFEU (adoption of regulations and general conditions governing the performance of the duties of MEPs) and Art. 228(4) TFEU (adoption of Ombudsman regulations). In both cases the European Parliament is to act "after seeking an opinion from the Commission".

[118] See Art. 226, third para., TFEU (detailed provisions on the right of inquiry), which also requires the European Parliament to obtain the consent of the Commission.

[119] See, e.g., the establishment of a European Public Prosecutor's Office (Art. 86(1) TFEU). See also, even though not formally described as "special legislative procedure", the procedure to be followed for extension of the scope of application of judicial cooperation to aspects of criminal procedure not currently mentioned in the Treaties (Art. 82(2)(d) TFEU) and the identification of additional areas of crime in respect of which minimum rules may be established (Art. 83(1), third subpara., TFEU).

[120] See, e.g., operational cooperation between police authorities (Art. 87(3) TFEU) and operations on the territory of another Member State (Art. 89 TFEU).

B. Participation of the European Parliament

1. Consultation

16–035   **Duty to consult.** Several Treaty articles require the Council to act in accordance with a special legislative procedure, after consulting the European Parliament.[121] In such case, the Council requests an opinion, which is adopted in accordance with the procedure for the first reading under the ordinary legislative procedure described above. As long ago as 1980, the Court of Justice held that consultation of the Parliament constitutes an essential procedural requirement[122] (see para. 16–012).

The fact that it is compulsory to consult the Parliament means that the Council must exhaust all the possibilities of obtaining its opinion in time.[123] The Court of Justice adverted to the possibility for the Council to request the Parliament to declare the consultation a matter of urgency (see para. 16–024) or for a request to be made for the Parliament to meet in an extraordinary session (Art. 229, second para., TFEU). Before the Parliament has delivered its opinion, the Council may consider the Commission's proposal or attempt to arrive at a common approach or even a common position within the Council provided that it does not adopt its final position before it is apprised of the Parliament's opinion.[124]

For its part, the Parliament is under a duty to cooperate in good faith with the Council. Accordingly, the Parliament was not entitled to challenge the Council for adopting a regulation on December 21, 1992 which had to be adopted for political and technical reasons before the end of 1992, without waiting for the Parliament to give its opinion. The Parliament had decided to deal with the proposal for a regulation as a case of urgency on December 18, 1992, during its last session of the year. However, the Parliament decided to adjourn that session without having debated the proposal and it was impossible to convene an extraordinary session of the Parliament before the end of the year.[125]

The Council is bound to consult the Parliament and to allow it a reasonable time to deliver its opinion, but it is not under any duty to state in what way, if any, it took account of it. It is sufficient that the act adopted by the Council refers to the opinion requested (Art. 296, second para., TFEU; see para. 22–065).

---

[121] See n. 115, *supra.*

[122] ECJ, Case 138/79 *Roquette Frères v Council* [1980] E.C.R. 3333, paras 33–37, and ECJ, Case 139/79 *Maïzena v Council* [1980] E.C.R. 3393, paras 34–38.

[123] *Ibid.*, paras 36 and 37.

[124] ECJ, Case C-417/93 *European Parliament v Council* [1995] E.C.R. I-1185, para. 10.

[125] ECJ, Case C-65/93 *European Parliament v Council* [1995] E.C.R. I-643, paras 24–28 (in which an action for annulment of Council Regulation No. 3917/92 extending into 1993 the application of generalised tariff preferences in respect of products originating in developing countries, [1992] O.J. L396/1, was dismissed); see Van Nuffel (1995) Col.J.E.L. 504, at 511–515. See also the discussion of the duty to cooperate in good faith in para. 7–046, *supra.*

Reconsultation of the Parliament. If the European Parliament is consulted at an   **16–036**
early stage in the legislative process, it is possible that the proposal on which it
delivered its opinion will be amended in the course of further discussion in Council
working groups and Coreper. Further consultation will then be unnecessary if the
amended proposal as a whole corresponds essentially to the original proposal (e.g.
amendments made regarding only technical aspects or methods)[126] or where the
amendments made modified the proposal essentially in the manner indicated by the
Parliament.[127] It cannot be argued, however, that the amendments were essentially
in line with what the Parliament was proposing on the basis of opinions not adopted
by the Parliament as a whole but only by parliamentary committees.[128]

Since proper consultation of the European Parliament in the cases provided for
by the Treaties constitutes one of the means enabling it to play an effective role
in the legislative process of the Union, the Council cannot avoid reconsulting the
Parliament on the ground that it was sufficiently informed as to the Parliament's
opinion on the essential points at issue.[129] If it could, this would seriously undermine the maintenance of the institutional balance intended by the Treaties and
would amount to disregarding the influence that due consultation of the
Parliament can have adoption of the measure in question.[130] If the Council fails
to reconsult the Parliament on a proposal after substantial amendment, the act in
question will not have been lawfully adopted and may be annulled.[131]

---

[126] ECJ, Case 41/69 *ACF Chemiefarma v Commission* [1970] E.C.R. 661, paras 68–70; ECJ, Case
817/79 *Buyl v Commission* [1982] E.C.R. 245, paras 23–24; ECJ, Case 828/79 *Adam v
Commission* [1982] E.C.R. 269, paras 24–25; ECJ, Case 1253/79 *Battaglia v Commission* [1982]
E.C.R. 297, paras 24–25. See, e.g., ECJ, Case C-280/93 *Germany v Council* [1994] E.C.R. I-4973,
paras 38–42; ECJ, Case C-417/93 *European Parliament v Council* [1995] E.C.R. I-1185, paras
16–26; ECJ, Case C-58/01 *Océ van der Grinten* [2003] E.C.R. I-9809, paras 101–102; see Van
Nuffel (n. 125, *supra*), at 505–509. A change in the legal form of a measure (directive rather
than a regulation) does not constitute a substantial change, see CFI, Joined Cases T-125/96 and
T-152/96 *Boehringer Ingelheim Vetmedica v Council and Commission* [1999] E.C.R. II-3427,
para. 133.

[127] ECJ, Case C-331/88 *Fedesa and Others* [1990] E.C.R. I-4023, para. 39; ECJ, Joined Cases C-13
to C-16/92 *Driessen and Others* [1993] E.C.R. I-4751, paras 23–25; ECJ, Case C-408/95
Eurotunnel and Others [1997] E.C.R. I-6315, paras 46–63. The European Parliament itself has
determined that the Council may reconsult it "where, through the passage of time or changes in
circumstances, the nature of the problem with which the proposal is concerned substantially
changes" (EP Rules of Procedure, Rule 59).

[128] ECJ, Case C-388/92 *European Parliament v Council* [1994] E.C.R. I-2067, para. 17.

[129] ECJ, Case C-21/94 *European Parliament v Council* [1995] E.C.R. I-1827, paras 24–26.

[130] *Ibid.*, para. 26; see also ECJ, Case C-392/95 *European Parliament v Council* [1997] E.C.R. I-3213,
para. 22.

[131] E.g., ECJ, Case C-65/90 *European Parliament v Council* [1992] E.C.R. I-4593, paras 20–21; ECJ,
Case C-388/92 *European Parliament v Council* [1994] E.C.R. I-2067; ECJ, Case C-21/94
European Parliament v Council [1995] E.C.R. I-1827, paras 17–28; ECJ, Case C-392/95 *European
Parliament v Council* [1997] E.C.R. I-3213, paras 14–24. See also CFI, Case T-164/97 *Busaca and
Others v Court of Auditors* [1998] E.C.R.-SC II-1699, paras 79–102.

2. Consent

16–037 **Parliament's veto.** Since the Single European Act, a number of Treaty articles have required proposed acts to be given the consent of the European Parliament.[132] This means that the act comes into being only if the Parliament approves it. The Parliament takes its decision on the basis of a report from the responsible parliamentary committee recommending that the proposal as a whole be adopted or rejected (EP Rules of Procedure, Rule 81(1)). Given that no amendments may be proposed, consent constitutes de facto a right of veto. Initially, consent was required outside the legislative process proper only for the accession of new Member States and the conclusion of association agreements.[133] Exceptionally, the Parliament succeeded in having a real influence on the Union's external policy by attaching conditions to its consent.[134]

At present, the Parliament's consent is required for important international agreements (Art. 218(6) TFEU; see para. 26–012),[135] for revisions of the Treaties (Art. 48(3), second subpara., and (7), fourth subpara., TEU), for the accession of new Member States (Art. 49 TEU), for agreements relating to the withdrawal of a Member State (Art. 50(2) TEU) and for the adoption of acts under the "flexibility clause" of Art. 352 TFEU [*ex Art. 308 EC*]. In the latter case, it may happen that a legislative act finds its legal basis in a specific Treaty article, providing for the ordinary legislative procedure combined with Art. 352 TFEU, because not all the aspects of the legislative act in question are covered by the specific Treaty article. In such a situation, the Council is to act by unanimity throughout the several stages of the procedure based on Art. 294 TFEU, while making sure that the European Parliament gives its "consent" before the final adoption of the act.[136]

Parliamentary consent also forms part of the procedure for the adoption of some "organic" acts[137] and of the procedure for temporarily suspending the rights of a Member State.[138] The Council may authorise Member States to proceed with

---

[132] Before the Lisbon Treaty, the Treaties consistently required the Council to obtain the "assent" of the European Parliament.

[133] See Arts 237 and 238 EEC.

[134] See the discussion of the part played by the European Parliament in the procedure for the conclusion of international agreements in para. 26–013, *infra*.

[135] The Parliament has reserved the right to adopt recommendations at any stage of the international negotiations (EP Rules of Procedure, Rule 90(5)).

[136] For an example, see ECJ, Case C-166/07 *European Parliament v Council* [2009] E.C.R. I-7135.

[137] See Art. 14(2), second subpara., TEU; Art. 17(7), third subpara., TEU; Art. 82(2), second subpara., (d), TFEU; Art. 83(1), third subpara., TFEU; Art. 86(4) TFEU; Art. 127(6) TFEU; Art. 223(1), second subpara., TFEU; Art. 226, third subpara., TFEU

[138] Article 7(1), (2) and (5) TEU and Art. 354, fourth para., TFEU (with a majority of three-fifths of the votes cast and a majority of the members).

enhanced cooperation between themselves only after obtaining the consent of the European Parliament.[139]

Parliamentary consent is now also required in a number of cases in which acts are adopted by the Council under a special legislative procedure.[140] A particular form of special legislative procedure exists for the adoption of the budget (Art. 314 TFEU; see para. 13–141 *et seq.*).

IV. OTHER PROCEDURES

Non-legislative procedures. Since the Lisbon Treaty, only the ordinary legislative procedure and the special legislative procedures lead to the adoption of "legislative acts" (see para. 16–003). Some Treaty articles set out the procedural steps to be taken for the adoption of acts of a general nature without qualifying them as a "legislative procedure". Some of those non-legislative procedures do not differ from special legislative procedures.[141] With respect to some Treaty provisions, the acts to be adopted may also be of a similar "legislative" nature to acts adopted pursuant to legislative procedures.[142] However, given the formal definition applied by the Treaties, those acts are not "legislative acts" in the strict sense of the Treaties (see para. 16–003). Whereas most often the Council is the institution designated to adopt such acts, on a proposal of the Commission, there are some Treaty provisions that directly empower the Commission or the European Central Bank to adopt non-legislative acts of a general nature.[143]

16–038

Various institutional configurations. In those cases where the Council is to adopt acts outside the ordinary legislative procedure and the special legislative procedures, the involvement of the European Parliament is not always guaranteed (see para. 16–040). That will be the case where the Treaties require the political Union institutions to agree amongst themselves on certain arrangements (see para. 16–042). A different procedure is the possibility for the social partners to conclude collective agreements (see para. 16–044). Finally, it is worth looking at the specific

16–039

---

[139] Article 329(1), second subpara., TFEU. For the first ever instance of enhanced cooperation, see the decision on the Proposal for a Council Decision authorising enhanced cooperation in the area of the law applicable to divorce and legal separation (COM(2010)105 final), to which the Parliament gave its consent by legislative resolution of June 16, 2010.

[140] See n. 116, *supra.*

[141] E.g., Arts 74 and 103 TFEU (Council acts on a Commission proposal, by qualified majority, and after consulting the European Parliament).

[142] E.g., Article 103 TFEU, which forms the legal basis for the adoption of instruments such as Regulation No. 1/2003 (see para. 11–013) and Art. 155(2) TFEU, pursuant to which the Council may implement agreements concluded at Union level by management and labour (see para. 16–044). See Dougan (n. 112, *supra*), at 647.

[143] See para. 16–005, *supra.*

input of various other bodies in (legislative or non-legislative) procedures leading to the adoption of general Union acts (see paras 16–045—16–046).

A. OTHER INVOLVEMENT OF EUROPEAN PARLIAMENT

16–040 **Consultation.** Some non-legislative procedures require the Council to consult the European Parliament before adopting non-legislative acts of a general nature.[144] Still, other articles in the Treaties provide for no involvement of the European Parliament in the adoption of such acts.[145] In such a case, the Council (or the Commission) may validly act without consulting the Parliament. Nevertheless, the political institutions may still seek its opinion.[146] An institution may even undertake to consult the European Parliament as much as possible.[147]

16–041 **Information.** On the other hand, a number of provisions on financial and economic matters require the Council (or the Commission) merely to "inform" the European Parliament of acts adopted.[148] In such cases, the European Parliament is informed only after the measure has been adopted and therefore can have no influence on decision-making. The other political institutions have often committed themselves to keeping the European Parliament informed, in particular in the field of external relations. Accordingly, the Council has undertaken to inform the Parliament about trade agreements.[149] The Commission has undertaken to ensure, within its means, that the European Parliament is kept informed and is fully associated with the preparation, negotiation and conclusion of international agreements and accession negotiations[150] and the preparation and conduct of intergovernmental conferences.[151]

---

[144] See Arts 74, 78(3), 81(3), 95(3), 103(1), 109, 125(2), 128(2), 140(2), 150, 160, 188, first para., 322(2) and 349 TFEU.

[145] See Arts 31, 66, 107(3)(e), 112, 122(1), 126(6) to (9), 143(2), 242 and 243 TFEU. See also all the Treaty articles conferring a power of decision on the Commission (para. 13–065, *supra*).

[146] ECJ, Case 165/87 *Commission v Council* [1988] E.C.R. 5545, para. 20.

[147] See already the Commission's communication to the European Parliament of June 8, 1973 ((1973) 6 EC Bull. point 1201) and the Council's answer of May 25, 1984 to question 2277/83 (Lady Elles), [1984] O.J. C173/17.

[148] See the obligation for the Council under Art. 121(2), third subpara., TFEU and for its President under Art. 121(5) TFEU (which also puts the Commission under a duty), Art. 122(2) TFEU; Art. 126(11), second subpara., TFEU; Art. 219(1) TFEU; Art. 134(3) TFEU; see also Art. 155(2) TFEU.

[149] See the Luns-Westerterp procedures, paras 26–004 and 26–006, *infra*.

[150] Points 23–31 of Annex II ("Forwarding of confidential information to the European Parliament") and III ("Negotiation and conclusion of international agreements") to the framework agreement of October 20, 2010 (n. 66, *supra*).

[151] See already Point 12 of the Framework Agreement of May 26, 2005 (n. 66, *supra*).

B. Interinstitutional agreements

Interinstitutional agreements. In addition, the European Parliament has a claim to be involved in decision-making where other institutions have committed themselves to allowing it to play a part. For a long time, interinstitutional agreements have been concluded between the European Parliament and other institutions, on the basis of specific Treaty provisions.[152] Since the Lisbon Treaty, the Treaties expressly provide for the possibility for the European Parliament, the Council and the Commission to conclude interinstitutional agreements which may be of a binding nature (Art. 295 TFEU; see para. 22–107). Also outside those provisions, various interinstitutional agreements have been concluded in which the European Parliament, the Council and the Commission enter into obligations which are binding upon them in so far as they do not infringe provisions of the Treaties or detract from the institutional balance sought thereby.[153] Such agreements may flesh out decision-making procedures or simplify them. Accordingly, in a 1975 Joint Declaration the three institutions agreed on a "conciliation procedure" between the Council and the European Parliament with the active assistance of the Commission for

16–042

> "Community acts of general application which have appreciable financial implications and of which the adoption is not required by virtue of acts already in existence".[154]

Conciliation was to be initiated at the request of the Parliament or the Council if the Council was minded to depart from the Parliament's opinion.[155] Although this type of conciliation took place only sporadically, it was expressly declared to be applicable in some Union measures.[156]

---

[152] See Art. 287(3), third subpara., TFEU [*ex Art. 248(3), third subpara., EC*]; before the Lisbon Treaty, see also Arts 193, third para.; 218(1); 272(9), fifth subpara., EC, which authorised the institutions concerned to determine relations *inter se* by "common accord" or by agreement.

[153] See the arrangements relating to the budgetary procedure (para. 13–138, *supra*) and the various agreements fleshing out the Treaties, more specifically the agreement on procedures for implementing the principle of subsidiarity (para. 7–026, *supra*) and the joint declaration on practical arrangements for the new co-decision procedure (n. 81, *supra*). See Driessen, *Interinstitutional Conventions in EU Law* (London, Cameron May, 2007), 315 pp.; Monar, "Interinstitutional Agreements: The Phenomenon and Its New Dynamics After Maastricht" (1994) C.M.L.Rev. 693–719; Reich, "La mise en oeuvre du Traité sur l'Union européenne par les accords interinstitutionnels" (1994) R.M.C.U.E. 81–85.

[154] Joint Declaration of the European Parliament, the Council and the Commission of March 4, 1975 ([1975] O.J. C89/1), points 1 and 2.

[155] *Ibid.*, points 3 and 4.

[156] See Financial Regulation, Art. 184, for amendments to that regulation (conciliation procedure if requested by the European Parliament) and the implementing measures based on Art. 14 of the Act on the Direct Election of the European Parliament (see the declaration relating to that article). See also the resolution of the European Parliament on the consultation procedure of February 16, 1989 ([1989] O.J. C69/51).

C. INVOLVEMENT OF THE SOCIAL PARTNERS

16–043 **Dialogue between management and labour.** From the outset, workers' and employers' representatives have had an advisory role in Community decision-making as members of the European Economic and Social Committee (EC/EAEC) and of the ECSC Consultative Committee (see paras 13–107—13–108). The advisory Employment Committee and the Social Protection Committee have to consult "management and labour" in fulfilling their mandates (Arts 150, second para., and 160, second para., TFEU). The social partners meet regularly for "tripartite consultation" with representatives of the Council and the Commission.[157] The consultation of workers or their representatives is a general principle of labour law which is common to all the Member States and also applies to Union institutions and bodies.[158] At the same time, collective bargaining between employers and workers, together with the right of association, constitute matters in respect of which the Union is to encourage cooperation between the Member States (see Art. 160 TFEU), in particular through the establishment of a European works council in undertakings and groups with a Union dimension (see para. 11–044).

The Union recognises and promotes the role of the social partners at its level, taking into account the diversity of national systems and facilitates dialogue between the social partners, while respecting their autonomy (Art. 152 TFEU). This dialogue between management and labour may potentially lead to "contractual relations".[159] The last-mentioned method of decision-making was developed in the Social Agreement (see para. 11–043), the provisions of which were incorporated into the EC Treaty by the Treaty of Amsterdam. Under Art. 154 TFEU, when the Commission is minded to submit proposals in the social policy field, it has to consult management and labour twice: for the first time, on the possible direction of Union action and, for the second time, if it considers Union action advisable, on the content of the envisaged proposal (Art. 154(2) and (3) TFEU). On the occasion of such consultation, management and labour may inform the Commission of their wish to deal with the matter by agreement or by other contractual relations. They have nine months to conclude the procedure, although an extension may be decided upon jointly with the Commission (Art. 154(4) TFEU). However, the Commission is not obliged to take account of the advice given by

---

[157] This consultation is ongoing and culminates in a "Social Summit" held prior to meetings of the European Council; see Council Decision 2003/174/EC of March 6, 2003 establishing a Tripartite Social Summit for Growth and Employment ([2003] O.J. L70/31). Since the Lisbon Treaty, Art. 152, second para., explicitly provides that "[t]he Tripartite Social Summit for Growth and Employment shall contribute to social dialogue". See Branch, "The Evolution of the European Social Dialogue Towards Greater Autonomy: Challenges and Potential Benefits" (2005) Int. J. Comp. L.L.I.R. 321–346.

[158] CFI, Case T-192/99 *Dunnett and Others v European Investment Bank* [2001] E.C.R. II-813, paras 85, 89 and 90.

[159] Article 155 TFEU [*ex Art. 139 EC*].

management and labour or of their wish to deal with a particular matter amongst themselves.[160] According to the Interinstitutional Agreement between the European Parliament, the Council and the Commission on better law-making, regulation may be entrusted to the social partners where it represents added value for the general interest, but not where fundamental rights or important political options are at stake or in situations where the rules must be applied in a uniform fashion in all Member States. Furthermore, the principles of competition and the unity of the internal market must not be affected.[161]

Negotiating agreements. In the event that management and labour wish to nego-   **16–044**
tiate an agreement, the negotiation stage is left solely to them. The Treaties do not determine between which social partners negotiations are to be conducted at Union level.[162] The Commission did decide, however, to set up Sectoral Dialogue Committees (composed of equal numbers of representatives of the two sides of industry) promoting dialogue between the social partners at European level.[163] The Treaties provide that if management and labour conclude an agreement, it may be implemented by the Union or by the Member States.

The Union is empowered to implement such an agreement if the signatory parties make a joint request to that effect, provided that it relates to matters covered by Art. 153 TFEU (Art. 155(2), first subpara., TFEU). In that event, the Council is to act by a qualified majority on a proposal from the Commission; if, however, the agreement contains one or more provisions relating to one of the areas for which Art. 153(2) TFEU requires unanimity, the Council has to decide by a unanimous vote (Art. 155(2), second subpara., TFEU). The Council implemented the first agreements concluded by management and labour by means of directives.[164]

---

[160] Watson, "Social Policy After Maastricht" (1993) C.M.L.Rev. 481, at 503. See also the discussion of the principle of subsidiarity, para. 7–057, *supra*.

[161] These principles, together with those of transparency and representativeness, are stipulated for "co-regulation" and "self-regulation" in point 17 of the Interinstitutional Agreement of December 16, 2003 on better law-making (n. 54, *supra*).

[162] CFI, Case T-135/96 *UEAPME v Council* [1998] E.C.R. II-2335, paras 75–79.

[163] See Commission Decision of May 20, 1998, [1998] O.J. L225/27. As far as the "tripartite social summit" is concerned, the Council has provided a number of guidelines on the composition of delegations of workers' and employers' representatives; see Art. 3(2) of Decision 2003/174/EC (n. 157, *supra*).

[164] At cross-industry level, see Council Directive 2010/18/EU of March 8, 2010 implementing the revised Framework Agreement on parental leave concluded by BUSINESSEUROPE, UEAPME, CEEP and ETUC, [2010] O.J. 2010 L68/13 (agreement of June 18, 2009 annexed thereto), replacing Council Directive 96/34/EC of June 3, 1996 on the Framework Agreement on parental leave concluded by UNICE, CEEP and the ETUC, [1996] O.J. L145/4 (agreement of December 14, 1995 annexed thereto) and Council Directive 97/81/EC of December 15, 1997 concerning the Framework Agreement on part-time work concluded by UNICE, CEEP and the ETUC, [1998] O.J. L14/9 (agreement of June 6, 1997 annexed thereto). Whereas the first of those directives is based on Art. 155(2) TFEU, the two others were still based on Art. 4(2) of the Social Agreement. See also Council Directive 1999/70/EC of June 28, 1999 concerning the framework agreement on fixed-term work concluded

As a result, the provisions of the agreements are binding on Member States as regards the result to be achieved, but they retain the power to determine the form and methods.[165] The Commission and the Council are in no case obliged to implement agreements at the request of signatory parties. However, the Council has no power to amend an agreement concluded as between the social partners; it merely decides whether a Union-level agreement is to have legislative status. The European Parliament has only the right to be informed (Art. 155(2) TFEU). In the absence of any direct involvement of the European Parliament, the democratic legitimacy of such legislation rests on the role played by the social partners as well as on the necessary approval by the Council of the outcome of the negotiations.[166] In order to secure compliance with the principle of democracy, the Commission and the Council must check the representative nature of the social partners concerned in the light of the content of each agreement.[167]

---

by ETUC, UNICE and CEEP, [1999] O.J. L175/43 (agreement of March 18, 1999 appended as an annex), which was based on Art. 139(2) of the EC Treaty. The parties to the agreements in question are the umbrella organisations for workers (ETUC) and employers in the private (UNICE, now BUSINESSEUROPE) and public (CEEP) sectors. A number of sectoral instruments were based on Art. 139(2) of the EC Treaty, e.g., Council Directive 1999/63/EC of June 21, 1999 concerning the Agreement on the organisation of working time of seafarers concluded by the European Community Shipowners' Association (ECSA) and the Federation of Transport Workers' Unions in the European Union (FST), [1999] O.J. L167/33 (agreement of September 30, 1998 appended as an annex) and Council Directive 2000/79/EC of November 27, 2000 concerning the European Agreement on the Organisation of Working Time of Mobile Workers in Civil Aviation concluded by the Association of European Airlines (AEA), the European Transport Workers' Federation (ETF), the European Cockpit Association (ECA), the European Regions Airline Association (ERA) and the International Air Carrier Association (IACA), [2000] O.J. L302/57 (agreement of March 22, 2000 appended as an annex).

[165] The directives in question provide that the social partners themselves may introduce the necessary implementing measures by agreement (cf. para. 17–003, infra).

[166] CFI, Case T-135/96 *UEAPME v Council* [1998] E.C.R. II-2335, paras 88–89. For a critical view of the democratic legitimacy of management and labour, see Langenbucher, "Zur Zulässigkeit parlamentersetzender Normgebungsverfahren im Europarecht" (2002) Z.Eu.P. 265–286; Betten, "The Democratic Deficit of Participatory Democracy in Community Social Policy" (1998) E.L.Rev. 20–36. Indeed, democratic legitimacy requires the involvement of Union institutions, see Britz and Schmidt, "Die institutionalisierte Mitwirkung der Sozialpartner an der Rechtsetzung der Europäischen Gemeinschaft—Herausforderung des gemeinschaftsrechtlichen Demokratieprinzips" (1999) EuR. 467–498. See EP Rules of Procedure, Rule 84, by which the Parliament seeks to play some role in this procedure.

[167] CFI, Case T-135/96 *UEAPME v Council* [1998] E.C.R. II-2335, para. 89. The Commission set out criteria to that effect in its communication on the application of the Agreement on Social Policy of December 14, 1993 (COM(93)600 final), as mentioned in the judgment in *UEAPME v Council*. In that judgment, the Court of First Instance [*now the General Court*] declared inadmissible an action brought for annulment of Directive 96/34/EC (n. 164, *supra*) by the European Union of Crafts and Small and Medium-sized Enterprises (UEAPME), which was not involved in the negotiations on the framework agreement on parental leave. See Lenaerts, "Le statut de la négociation collective dans la jurisprudence européenne" (2009) *Revue de Droit Social/Tijdschrift voor Sociaal Recht* 3, at 16–18.

If the Council does not adopt an implementing decision, the agreement in question is to be implemented in accordance with the procedures and practices specific to management and labour and the Member States (see para. 17–003). This was the case with the agreements concluded by the social partners on teleworking, work-related stress and harassment and violence at work.[168] In the absence of implementation by Union legislation, the legal force of agreements concluded between management and labour at Union level remains uncertain, particularly because the question of the framework for the negotiations leading up to the conclusion of such agreements, including guarantees as to the representative nature of the negotiators for the workers and employers concerned, is not regulated.[169]

D. INVOLVEMENT OF OTHER BODIES AND GROUPS

Dialogue and consultation. Since the Lisbon Treaty, the Union institutions are required to give citizens and representative associations the opportunity to make known and exchange their views publicly in all areas of Union action (Art. 11(1) TEU). The institutions are to "maintain an open, transparent and regular dialogue with representative associations and civil society" (Art. 11(2) TEU), in particular with the social partners[170] and with churches, religious associations or communities and philosophical and non-confessional organisations.[171] This appeal for dialogue is specifically reflected in the obligation imposed on the Commission to carry out broad consultations with parties concerned and to take note of any initiative put forward by a significant number of citizens (see para. 16–016). In addition, participation of civil society has to be ensured insofar as the Union institutions, bodies, offices and agencies are to function "as openly as possible" (Art. 15(1) TFEU; see para. 13–166 *et seq.*).

16–045

---

[168] Framework Agreement of July 16, 2002 concluded by UNICE/UEAPME, the CEEP and the ETUC on telework; Framework Agreement of October 8, 2004 concluded by UNICE/UEAPME, the CEEP and the ETUC on work-related stress; Framework Agreement of April 26, 2007 concluded by BUSINESSEUROPE/UEAPME, the CEEP and the ETUC on violence at work (all available from the website of the Commission's DG for Employment, Social Affairs and Equal Opportunities).

[169] See Vigneau, "Etude sur l'autonomie collective au niveau communautaire" (2002) R.T.D.E. 653–683, and, earlier, the issues adumbrated by Vandamme, "Quel espace contractuel pour les partenaires sociaux après le traité de Maastricht" (1992) R.M.C.U.E. 788–792; Nyssen, "Le rôle des partenaires sociaux dans l'élaboration et la mise en oeuvre du droit communautaire" (1993) Ann. Dr. Louv. 319, at 328–331; Watson (n. 160, *supra*), at 506–509; see also, Gadbin, "L'association des partenaires économiques et sociaux organisés aux procédures de décision en droit communautaire" (2000) R.T.D.E. 1–46.

[170] Article 152 TFEU (referring to "the diversity of national systems" and "their autonomy").

[171] Article 17(3) TFEU ("[r]ecognising their identity and their specific contribution"). Under Art. 17(1)–(2) TFEU, the Union must respect the status under national law of churches and religious associations or communities and that of philosophical and non-confessional organisations. See Hölscheidt and Mund, "Religionen und Kirchen im europäischen Verfassungsverbund" (2003) EuR. 1083–1094.

16–046   **Compulsory consultation.** In various areas, legislative procedures as well as non-legislative procedures involve compulsory consultation of especially constituted bodies.[172] In the first place, there are the economic and social interest groups, which can make their views known through the European Economic and Social Committee. Various Treaty articles require the institutions to consult that committee before adopting an act (see para. 13–107). The EU Treaty recognised the specific interests of regional and local authorities and set up the Committee of the Regions, which has to be consulted by the Council on certain matters. These matters are ones in respect of which policy is conducted in several Member States by decentralised authorities pursuant to rules on the devolution of powers (see para. 13–110). The opinions of those committees are in no way binding. Nevertheless, they do influence decision-making, especially where the views they contain are taken up by the Commission and/or the European Parliament, which invariably has a say in decision-making on the matters in question. Where the body concerned is composed of democratically elected representatives and it is consulted in order to enable the interests to be expressed of those at whom the eventual legal provision is aimed, the obligation to obtain an opinion may make it necessary to carry out a fresh consultation if the original proposal undergoes major changes not corresponding to changes recommended by the body in question.[173]

Treaties sometimes require institutions or bodies which are considered to have relevant expertise in the field to be consulted. Accordingly, in some cases where the Council[174] or the European Parliament and the Council[175] do not have to decide on a Commission proposal, they have nonetheless to "consult" the Commission. In economic and monetary matters, some Treaty articles require the Commission or the Council to seek the opinion of the Economic and Financial

---

[172] Obradovic, "Good governance requirements concerning the participation of interest groups in EU consultations" (2006) C.M.L.Rev. 1049–1085.

[173] The Court of First Instance [*now the General Court*] applied the obligation to consult the European Parliament (see para. 16–036, *supra*) in a case where Art. 24 of the Merger Treaty required the Commission to consult the Staff Regulations Committee on any proposal to amend the Staff Regulations: CFI, Case T-164/97 *Busaca and Others v Court of Auditors* [1998] E.C.R. II-1699, paras 79–102.

[174] Article 129(4) TFEU; Art. 302(2) TFEU; Art. 49, first para., TEU; Act on the Direct Election of the European Parliament, Art. 14. As far as application of Art. 259 EC [*now Art. 302 TFEU*] is concerned (appointment of members of the European Economic and Social Committee), the Court of Justice has held that it is sufficient for the Commission to be present at the Coreper meeting at which consensus is reached on a decision submitted to the Council as a Part A item of the agenda: ECJ, Case 297/86 *CIDA v Council* [1988] E.C.R. 3531, paras 27–30. A Commission opinion is also required by Art. 242 TFEU.

[175] Article 129(3) TFEU; Art. 281, second para., TFEU. The European Parliament lays down regulations and general conditions after seeking the "opinion" of the Commission under Art. 223(2) TFEU (performance of MEPs' duties) and Art. 228(4) of the EC Treaty (Ombudsman Regulations).

Committee,[176] whilst other articles oblige the Council[177] or the European Parliament and the Council[178] to consult the ECB. In one case, the opinion of the ECB is so crucial that the consultation has to endeavour to reach a "consensus" between the Council and the ECB (Art. 219, first sentence, TFEU). In relation to these matters, however, the Commission does not have its full right to submit proposals and the European Parliament is not always involved in the decision-making process.[179]

---

[176] For the Commission, see Art. 126(4) TFEU and Art. 143(1), second subpara., TFEU; for the Council, see Art. 134(3) TFEU and Art. 144(3) TFEU.

[177] For the ECB, see the general obligation under Arts 127(4) TFEU and the specific obligations under Arts 66, 126(14), second subpara., 127(6), 128(2), 129(4), 138, 219(1) to (3); 134(3) TFEU and Art. 48(3) TEU.

[178] See Art. 129(3) TFEU.

[179] See the cases where the Commission makes a "recommendation" (para. 16–015, *supra*) and the European Parliament is merely "informed" (para. 16–041, *supra*).

CHAPTER 17

IMPLEMENTATION OF LEGISLATION

Duty to implement. The Treaties did not set up a uniform system for the imple-   **17–001**
mentation of Union legislation: where necessary, each act determines its implementation procedures itself; where the act in question does not do so, the principle
applies in any event that

> "Member States shall take any appropriate measure, general or particular,
> to ensure fulfilment of the obligations arising out of the Treaties or
> resulting from the acts of the institutions of the Union" (Art. 4(3), second
> subpara., TEU).

Since the Lisbon Treaty, the Treaties state clearly that Member States are to adopt
"all measures of national law necessary to implement legally binding Union acts"
(Art. 291(1) TFEU). Accordingly, Union law is implemented as a rule by the
Member States. In some policy areas, specific provisions entrust Union institutions,
bodies, offices and agencies with implementing tasks. In both cases, the enforcement
of legislative and implementing rules of Union law and the imposition of sanctions
for breaches thereof fall primarily to the national administrative and judicial authorities. The Commission is empowered to conduct administrative inquiries itself and
to fine individuals only very exceptionally.[1] The following sections discuss implementation by the Member States and implementation by Union institutions, bodies,
offices and agencies.

It is also possible for Union legislation to leave it to the sectors or parties
concerned to bring about the objectives sought by that legislation. According to
what to the European Parliament, the Council and the Commission agreed in the
Interinstitutional Agreement of December 2003, it is then up to the Commission
to verify whether or not the Union legislation is being implemented.[2]

---

[1] Paras 11–001—11–016, *supra* (competition cases). For the allocation of powers of implementation,
see Möllers, "Durchführung des Gemeinschaftsrechts" (2002) EuR. 483–516.
[2] See points 18 to 21 on "co-regulation" in the Interinstitutional Agreement between the
European Parliament, the Council and the Commission of December 16, 2003 on better law-
making. An example is the implementation of Union legislation by the social partners (para. 16–044,
supra).

I. IMPLEMENTATION BY THE MEMBER STATES

17–002   **Executive federalism.** Article 4(3) TEU puts Member States under a duty to implement provisions of Union law so as to ensure fulfilment of the obligations contained therein. Member States are to adopt all measures of national law necessary to implement legally binding Union acts (Art. 291(1) TFEU).[3] Where a piece of Union legislation makes no specific provision, its implementation is a matter in the first place for the Member States.[4] In this respect the Union exhibits characteristic features of a federal system in which legislative power is assigned to the federation, but executive power is vested in the federated entities (*executive federalism, Vollzugsföderalismus*). The Treaties expressly establish such a system with regard to directives, which, after adoption by the Union legislature, are binding on the Member States as to the result to be achieved, but leave the choice of the form and methods by which they are incorporated into national law to the national authorities (Art. 288, third para., TFEU [*ex Art. 249, third para., EC*]). Although in theory, therefore, directives leave certain policy choices to the Member States, in practice they are often formulated in such detail that the Member States are left only with the task of implementing them mechanically. The obligation to implement Union legislation also applies where it is cast in a different form (e.g. that of a regulation) but its substance needs specifying or it has to be applied in individual cases in order for it to be effective.[5] In many cases, Member States also have to legislate in order to be able to apply and enforce implementing rules adopted by Union institutions, bodies, offices and agencies themselves and in order to be able to impose sanctions in the event of their breach.[6]

In implementing police and judicial cooperation in criminal matters measures, Member States can invoke the responsibilities incumbent upon them with regard to the maintenance of law and order and the safeguarding of internal security (Art. 72 TFEU). Since the Lisbon Treaty, the Treaties provide for specific forms of parliamentary control over the Union's policy in the area of freedom, security and justice. The European Parliament and the national parliaments are to be associated in the objective and impartial evaluation of the implementation of the

---

[3] See also Dubey, "Administration indirecte et fédéralisme d'exécution en Europe" (2003) C.D.E. 87–133.

[4] See CFI, Cases T-492/93 and T-492/93 R *Nutral v Commission* [1993] E.C.R. II-1023, para. 26, upheld by ECJ, Case C-476/93 P *Nutral v Commission* [1995] E.C.R. I-4125, para. 14.

[5] See, e.g., ECJ, Case 30/70 *Scheer* [1970] E.C.R. 1197, para. 10; ECJ, Case 137/80 *Commission v Belgium* [1981] E.C.R. 2393, paras 3–9 (a Member State is under a duty to adopt the necessary implementing measures so as to apply the regulation establishing the Staff Regulations of Union officials); ECJ (judgment of October 28, 2010), Case C-367/09 *SGS Belgium and Others*, not yet reported, paras 32–43.

[6] See Curtin and Mortelmans, "Application and Enforcement of Community Law by the Member States: Actors in Search of a Third Generation Script", in Curtin and Heukels (eds), *Institutional Dynamics of European Integration. Essays in Honour of Henry G. Schermers*, Vol. II (Dordrecht, Martinus Nijhoff, 1994) 423–466.

Union's policies at national level which is to be conducted by the Member States in collaboration with the Commission (Art. 70 TFEU).

Domestic organisation of implementation. The Member States carry out their task of implementing Union law in accordance with their particular constitutional traditions. Accordingly, depending on the subject-matter, the implementation of a Union provision may fall within the remit of legislative or executive bodies at national or regional level (see para. 14–017).[7] Each such body is under a duty to amend domestic law so as to make it conform with Union law.[8] The division of powers within a Member State does not preclude a breach of the duty to implement Union legislation from being invariably imputed to the State itself at Union level

17–003

> "whatever the agency of the State whose action or inaction is the cause of the failure to fulfil its obligations, even in the case of a constitutionally independent institution".[9]

The Commission may bring an action under Art. 258 TFEU [*ex Art. 226 EC*] against a Member State which fails to fulfil its obligations to implement Union law. If the Court of Justice finds that the Member State has indeed failed to fulfil its obligations, the State will be required to take the necessary measures to comply with the Court's judgment, failing which the Court may impose a flat-rate fine and/or a periodic penalty payment if second proceedings are brought (Art. 260(1) and (2) TFEU).[10] As the Court held in 1963 in *Van Gend & Loos* (see para. 1–025), individuals who have a direct interest in the correct implementation of Union law may make sure that Member States fulfil their obligations in respect of the implementation of Union law.[11] This is because, under Art. 4(3) TEU, the

---

[7] ECJ, Case 96/81 *Commission v Netherlands* [1982] E.C.R. 1791, para. 12; ECJ (judgment of October 6, 2010), Case C-389/08 *Base and Others*, not yet reported, paras 22–31.

[8] See ECJ, Joined Cases 314–316/81 and 83/82 *Waterkeyn* [1982] E.C.R. 4337, para. 14 (bodies exercising legislative power and the judiciary); ECJ, Case C-8/88 *Germany v Commission* [1990] E.C.R. I-2321, para. 13 (federated States and other territorial authorities). For judicial bodies, see para. 7–045, *supra*.

[9] ECJ, Case 77/69 *Commission v Belgium* [1970] E.C.R. 237, para. 15; ECJ, Case 8/70 *Commission v Italy* [1970] E.C.R. 961, para. 9. See also ECJ, Case 30/72 *Commission v Italy* [1973] E.C.R. 161, para. 11 (a Member State must take account in its domestic legal system of the consequences of its adherence to the Union and, if need be, adapt its budgetary procedures accordingly); ECJ, Case C-423/00 *Commission v Belgium* [2002] E.C.R. I-593 (Member State held to be in breach because a cooperation agreement between the federal authority and regional authorities was required for implementation and could not be approved by those entities in time). For liability on the part of Member States for decentralised/devolved authorities, see para. 14–017, *supra*.

[10] Where the Commission brings a case before the Court on the ground that the Member State concerned has failed to fulfil its obligation to notify measures transposing a directive, the Court can impose these sanctions without there being a need for the Commission to bring a second action (see para. 13–065).

[11] See Timmermans, "Judicial Protection Against the Member States: Articles 169 and 177 Revisited", *Institutional Dynamics of European Integration. Essays in Honour of Henry G. Schermers* (n. 6, *supra*), 391, at 397–400.

national courts are under a duty to secure the effectiveness (*effet utile*) of Union law. Individuals deriving rights from that law may have them enforced in a non-discriminatory manner by the courts. Since the 1991 judgment in *Francovich*, they may claim damages from a Member State whose breach of Union law causes them to suffer loss or damage. For the sake of the uniform application of Union law, this holds good irrespective as to whether the breach committed within the national legal order is attributable to the legislature, the executive or the judiciary (see para. 21–014).

17–004   **Implementation by the social partners.** In social matters, Member States may leave the implementation of Union provisions to be agreed between management and labour.[12] Article 153(3) TFEU provides that a Member State may entrust management and labour, at their joint request, with the implementation of directives adopted pursuant to that article and with Council decisions implementing at Union level agreements between management and labour (see Art. 155 TFEU).[13] In such case, the Member State is to ensure that management and labour introduce the necessary measures by agreement within the period prescribed for transposing the directive or decision in question, and must take any necessary measure enabling it at any time to be in a position to guarantee the results imposed by the directive or the decision (Art. 153(3), second subpara., TFEU). Accordingly, the national authorities must see to it that workers who do not benefit from the protection of the directive or decision by other means, in particular where they are not members of a trade union, where they are not covered by a collective agreement or where such an agreement does not fully guarantee the protection in question, are in fact covered.[14] Also in the case of agreements concluded by management and labour at Union level, if the Council does not adopt an implementing act, such an agreement is to be implemented "in accordance with the procedures and practices specific to management and labour and the Member States" (Art. 155(2), first subpara., TFEU). The Treaties give no indication as to whether or not there is an obligation

---

[12] See Steyger, "European Community Law and the Self-Regulatory Capacity of Society" (1993) J.C.M.S. 171–190.

[13] As regards agreements concluded at Union level, the Council implementing "decision" normally takes the form of a "directive": see para. 16–044, *supra*. Such Council "implementing" decision is not adopted pursuant to a legislative procedure and, hence, does not constitute a legislative act. Nevertheless, because of the general nature of the agreements in question and the fact that such agreements, even if approved by Council decision, need further "implementation", such a Council "implementing" decision can also be considered as constituting a procedural step in the legislative process rather than a form of "implementation", see also para. 16–038, *supra*.

[14] ECJ, Case 143/83 *Commission v Denmark* [1985] E.C.R. 427, para. 8; ECJ, Case C-306/07 *Andersen* [2008] E.C.R. I-10279, paras 25–34; ECJ (judgment of February 11, 2010), Case C-405/08 *Ingeniørforeningen i Danmark*, not yet reported, paras 39–45. See Adinolfi, "The Implementation of Social Policy Directives Through Collective Agreements?" (1988) C.M.L.Rev. 291–316.

to implement on the part of the Member States. It appears from a declaration on that Treaty provision that this was not the intention of the Contracting Parties.[15]

Uniform and full application of Union law. In the absence of common rules in the matter, the Member States act, when implementing Union law, in accordance with the procedural and substantive rules of their own national law. In so doing, however, they must always pay due regard to the requirements of the uniform application of Union law.[16] The implementation of Union law may not create unequal treatment as between persons. The need to ensure that Union law is fully applied requires Member States not only to bring their legislation into conformity with Union law but also to do so by adopting rules of law capable of creating a situation which is sufficiently precise, clear and transparent to allow individuals to know the full extent of their rights and rely on them before the national authorities.[17] Where national legislation has been the subject of different relevant judicial constructions, some leading to the application of that legislation in compliance with Union law, others leading to the opposite application, it must be held that, at the very least, such legislation is not sufficiently clear to ensure its application in compliance with Union law.[18]

17–005

In order to ensure the uniform and full application of Union law, the Union legislature may indicate precisely what implementing measures the Member States must adopt and for what sanctions they must provide. In the absence of any provision in the Union rules laying down specific sanctions, the Member States are free to adopt such sanctions as appear to them to be appropriate, including criminal sanctions.[19] In any event, the Member States must ensure that infringements of Union law are penalised under conditions, both procedural and substantive, which are analogous to those applicable to infringements of national law of a similar nature and importance and make the penalty effective, proportionate and

---

[15] Declaration (No. 27), annexed to the Amsterdam Treaty, on Art. 118b [*later Art. 139*](2) of the Treaty establishing the European Community [*now Art. 155 TFEU*] envisaged the "first" of the arrangements for application of the agreements between management and labour as taking the form of collective bargaining according to the rules of each Member State and involving "no obligation on the Member States to apply the agreements directly or to work out rules for their transposition, nor any obligation to amend national legislation in force to facilitate their implementation" ([1997] O.J. C340/136). This declaration took over the wording of Declaration (No. 2) on Art. 4(2) of the Social Agreement (the wording of which was taken over by Art. 139 EC).

[16] ECJ, Joined Cases 205–215/82 *Deutsche Milchkontor* [1983] E.C.R. 2633, para. 17.

[17] ECJ, Case C-162/99 *Commission v Italy* [2001] E.C.R. I-541, para. 22; ECJ, Case C-313/99 *Mulligan* [2002] E.C.R. I-5719, paras 46–54. The obligation to implement has been clarified in the case law principally with regard to directives; para. 22–077, *infra*.

[18] ECJ, Case C-129/00 *Commission v Italy* [2003] E.C.R. I-14637, para. 33, with annotations by Peerbux-Beaugendre (2004) R.T.D.E. 201–215; Mortelmans, van der Gronden (2004) A.Ae. 192–205 and Serena Rossi (2005) C.M.L.Rev. 829–849.

[19] ECJ, Case 50/76 *Amsterdam Bulb* [1977] E.C.R. 137, paras 32–33. For a critical view on the usefulness of criminal sanctions in environmental law, see Faure, "European Environmental Criminal Law: Do we really need it?" (2004) E.Env.L.Rev. 18–29.

dissuasive.[20] Moreover, the national authorities must proceed, with respect to infringements of Union law, with the same diligence as that which they bring to bear in implementing corresponding national laws.[21] Where national law contains a general principle according to which everyone is presumed to know the law, that principle may also be applied in the case of sanctions for infringements of Union law.[22] Member States must ensure compliance with the general principles of Union law and fundamental rights when implementing Union law.[23] Accordingly, Union law requires Member States to provide for judicial review of the acts of their authorities which collaborate administratively in the production of a decision of a Union institution (see para. 22–025).

II. IMPLEMENTATION BY INSTITUTIONS, BODIES, OFFICES AND AGENCIES OF THE UNION

A. RELATIONSHIP BETWEEN IMPLEMENTATION AND LEGISLATION

17–006   **Definition of implementation.** Acts adopted at Union level include not only rules of a legislative nature but also detailed provisions which make it possible to implement legislative provisions in practice and decisions which apply legislative and other general rules to individual situations. Traditionally, it was not easy in the Union legal order to make a formal distinction between legislation and implementation of legislation.[24] The Treaties did not set up separate legislative and executive institutions[25] and it was also impossible to classify the acts which those institutions adopt as legislative or implementing measures on the basis of their

---

[20] ECJ, Case 68/88 *Commission v Greece* [1989] E.C.R. 2965, para. 24; ECJ, Case C-326/88 *Hansen* [1990] E.C.R. I-2911, para. 17. As far as the ECSC was concerned, this followed from Art. 86 ECSC: ECJ, Case C-341/94 *Allain* [1996] E.C.R. I-4631, paras 23–24. See also the requirement for sanctions for unlawful discrimination to be effective and to have a deterrent effect, ECJ, Case 14/83 *Von Colson and Kamann* [1984] E.C.R. 1891, paras 23–24. For sanctions based on violations of humanitarian international law and human rights, see ECJ, Case C-84/95 *Bosphorus* [1996] E.C.R. I-3953, para. 26.

[21] *Commission v Greece*, cited in the preceding n., para. 25.

[22] ECJ, Case C-262/99 *Louloudakis* [2001] E.C.R. I-5547, paras 76–77. Where determination of the arrangements applicable has given rise to difficulties, however, account must be taken of the good faith of the offender when determining the penalty actually imposed on him: *ibid.*

[23] ECJ, Joined Cases 201 and 202/85 *Klensch* [1986] E.C.R. 3477, para. 8; ECJ, Case C-36/99 *Idéal tourisme* [2000] E.C.R. I-6049, para. 36.

[24] The Treaty only distinguished between "legislative" and "implementing" acts in so far as Art. 207(3) EC provided that the Council was to define the cases "in which it is to be regarded as acting in its legislative capacity" with a view to allowing greater public access to documents in those cases.

[25] Indeed, the legislative function is spread over the Council, the European Parliament and the Commission (see para. 16–005), whilst the Commission and the Council also perform executive functions (see para. 17–008).

form. The distinction between legislation and implementation of legislation was therefore determined in the first place by the type of provision which served as the legal basis for the act in question. If the act was based on an article of the Treaties, it could be regarded as a "legislative act", at least in so far as its content was also formulated in general, abstract terms. In contrast, implementing (or executive) acts were involved where they were based on legislative acts (or on earlier implementing acts). The Court of Justice stated as follows in this connection:

> "The concept of implementation [. . .] comprises both the drawing up of implementing rules and the application of rules to specific cases by means of acts of individual application".[26]

Since the Lisbon Treaty, the Treaties lay down a definition of "legislative acts" (see para. 17–011) and provide for two specific forms of Union executive acts, that is to say acts adopted by the Commission pursuant to a delegation of powers by the Union legislature and acts laid down by the Commission or the Council in the exercise of implementing powers (see paras 17–009—17–010). With the insertion of the words "delegated" or "implementing" in their title, both types of executive acts are now also formally distinguishable from the instruments used for the adoption of legislative acts (see para. 22–062).

Legislation and implementation. Implementing provisions are necessary where legislative acts cannot determine every aspect of a particular policy. For example, where the Union legislator adopts a basic regulation, directive or decision pursuant to a Treaty provision, the Commission may validly adopt an act implementing that basic act in the manner prescribed in that act. The legislative procedure laid down by that Treaty provision has no role to play any more in the adoption of the implementing measure. The only condition is that the Commission's implementing act must not go beyond implementation of the principles of the basic act.[27] Where a basic act empowers an institution to adopt general implementing provisions, this means, for example, that that institution is not empowered to alter the temporal scope of the basic act by that means.[28] An implementing act cannot derogate from the provisions of a basic act,[29] unless such derogation is expressly provided for in the basic act and consistent with its general system and essential elements.[30] Once an institution has adopted a basic act that makes provision for implementing powers, it is contrary to the Union's legislative system to apply that act to individual cases with a special procedure that derogates from the rules laid

17–007

---

[26] ECJ, Case 16/88 *Commission v Council* [1989] E.C.R. 3457, para. 11.

[27] ECJ, Case 25/70 *Köster* [1970] E.C.R. 1161, paras 6 and 7.

[28] ECJ, Case C-93/00 *European Parliament v Council* [2001] E.C.R. I-10119, paras 39–43.

[29] ECJ, Case 38/70 *Tradax* [1971] E.C.R. 145, para. 10; ECJ, Joined Cases C-14/06 and C-295/06 *European Parliament and Denmark v Commission* [2008] E.C.R. I-164, paras 50–53.

[30] ECJ, Case 230/78 *Eridania* [1979] E.C.R. 2749, para. 8. See also ECJ, Case 100/74 *C.A.M. v Commission* [1975] E.C.R. 1393, paras 27–28.

down in the basic act.[31] On the same grounds, an institution may not fail to comply in an implementing act with the conditions which it itself laid down in an earlier regulation, directive or decision upon which that act is based.[32] An act is invalid where it conflicts with the act on the basis of which it was adopted. The institutions and the Member States, and, in some circumstances, individuals, too, may obtain a court ruling on the legality of an implementing act.[33]

The fact that an implementing act is subordinate to a legislative act forms part of the general hierarchy of Union rules (see para. 22–004). In the same way that a constitutional rule of Union law always ranks higher than a legislative act a legislative act takes precedence over an implementing act.

B. IMPLEMENTATION BY THE COMMISSION OR THE COUNCIL

17–008   **Conferral of executive powers on Commission.** As regards the implementation of Union acts by Union institutions, a distinction is to be made—since the Lisbon Treaty—between two types of executive acts. On the one hand, the Lisbon Treaty introduced the possibility for the Union legislator to delegate to the Commission the power to supplement or amend certain non-essential elements of legislative acts. Here, the Commission adopts non-legislative acts of general application, called "delegated acts". On the other hand, in order to be applied, legally binding Union acts may need further implementation at the Union level. To this purpose the Commission (or exceptionally the Council) adopt "implementing acts". The Council (together with the European Parliament in matters coming under the ordinary legislative procedure) may subject the Commission to certain conditions for the exercise of its implementing powers.

1. Delegation to the Commission

17–009   **Delegated acts.** Since the Lisbon Treaty, the Treaties enable the European Parliament and the Council[34] to adopt legislative acts delegating to the Commission the power to adopt "non-legislative acts of general application" to supplement or amend certain non-essential elements of the legislative act (Art. 290(1), first subpara., TFEU). These acts bear the term "delegated" in their

---

[31] ECJ, Case 113/77 *NTN Toyo Bearing Company v Council* [1979] E.C.R. 1185, para. 21. See also ECJ, Case C-313/90 *CIRFS and Others v Commission* [1993] E.C.R. I-1125, para. 44 (an individual decision may not impliedly amend a measure of general application); ECJ, Joined Cases C-246–249/94 *Cooperativa Agricola Zootecnica S. Antonio and Others* [1996] E.C.R. I-4373, paras 30–31.

[32] E.g. ECJ, Case C-393/01 *France v Commission* [2003] E.C.R. I-5403, paras 40–60.

[33] For some examples, see ECJ, Case 22/88 *Vreugdenhil and Others* [1989] E.C.R. 2049, paras 17–25; ECJ, Case C-212/91 *Angelopharm* [1994] E.C.R. I-171, paras 31–38 (n. 69, *infra*, and associated text); ECJ, Case C-244/95 *Moskof* [1997] E.C.R. I-6441, paras 27–105; ECJ, Case C-106/97 *Dutch Antillian Diary Industry* [1999] E.C.R. I-5983, paras 65–66.

[34] Article 290(1) TFEU mentions delegation by "legislative acts". It follows that the delegation can also be given by the Council (or by the European Parliament) acting alone where that institution adopts legislation in accordance with a "special legislative procedure".

title (Art. 290(3) TFEU). In such cases, the legislative act must explicitly define the objectives, content, scope and duration of the delegation of power, which may not cover the essential elements of an area (Art. 290(1) TFEU).[35] Moreover, the legislative act must explicitly determine the conditions of application to which the delegation is subject.[36] For example, it can be provided that a delegated act may enter into force only if no objection has been expressed by the European Parliament or by the Council within a given period, or that the European Parliament or the Council may revoke the delegation (Art. 290(2) TFEU).[37] In the exercise of delegated powers, the Commission is not subject to "comitology" control by the Member States as mentioned in Art. 291 TFEU (see para. 17–012 *et seq.*). However, the Commission has announced its intention systematically to consult experts from the Member States' authorities.[38] As a legally binding act, a delegated act of the Commission may in turn determine the conditions under which it needs further implementation pursuant to Art. 291 TFEU.

2. Implementing powers

Implementing acts. Where legally binding acts of the Union need uniform conditions for their implementation, implementing powers are to be conferred on the Commission or the Council.[39] In principle, in these circumstances, the power of implementation is to be conferred on the Commission. Union acts may confer implementing powers on the Council only "in duly justified specific cases"[40] and in the field of the CFSP[41] (Art. 291(2) TFEU). Where the Commission exercises implementing powers, it has traditionally been subject to control by the Member States, which consists of the Commission's proposed implementing measures being discussed in committees of representatives of the Member States. This

17–010

---

[35] The definition of delegated acts is very similar to that of acts which under the Second Comitology Decision were subject to the regulatory procedure with scrutiny (see para. 17–017, *infra*). It should be noted that, since the entry into force of the Lisbon Treaty and as long as the Second Comitology Decision (see para. 17–012, *infra*) was not replaced by a new Comitology Regulation, the institutions agreed not to have recourse anymore to the regulatory procedure with scrutiny as laid down in the Second Comitology Decision.

[36] See the Communication of December 9, 2009 from the Commission to the European Parliament and the Council—Implementation of Art. 290 of the Treaty on the Functioning of the European Union, COM(2009)673 final.

[37] The European Parliament is to decide on such an objection or revocation by majority of its component members, and the Council by a qualified majority (Art. 290(2), second subpara., TFEU).

[38] See the Commission Communication of December 9, 2009 (n. 36, *supra*), at 6.

[39] For an example of the Treaties specifying both the power to enact legislation and the power to adopt executive acts, see Art. 43(2) and (3) TFEU (agricultural policy).

[40] If the Council takes this step, however, it must state in detail the grounds for its decision: ECJ, Case 16/88 *Commission v Council* [1989] E.C.R. 3457, para. 10; ECJ, Case C-257/01 *Commission v Council* [2005] E.C.R. I-345, paras 50–61, with case notes by Drijber (2005) S.E.W. 438–441 and Randazzo (2005) C.M.L.Rev. 1737–1750; ECJ, Case 133/06 *European Parliament v Council* [2008] E.C.R. I-3189, paras 45–50.

[41] See Arts 24 and 26 TEU.

system is known as "comitology"[42] (see para. 17–012). Since the entry into force of the Lisbon Treaty, the word "implementing" is to be inserted in to the title of implementing acts of the Commission or the Council (Art. 291(4) TFEU).[43]

17–011 **Wide interpretation of "implementation".** An implementing power will be validly conferred only if it is sufficiently specific, in the sense that its bounds must be clearly specified.[44] Implementing powers encompass both regulatory powers[45] and the power to apply rules to specific cases by means of individual decisions.[46] Moreover, the term "implementation" has to be given a wide interpretation. The Commission is authorised to adopt all the measures which are necessary or appropriate for the implementation of the basic legislation, provided that they are not contrary to it.[47] In complex areas such as the organisation of the market in agricultural products, the Council may be obliged to confer wide powers of discretion and action on the Commission.[48] Even where the Commission has no express power to this effect, its implementing provisions may impose penalties, which, within the context of the policy in question, are designed to secure the proper financial management of Union funds.[49] A measure intended to harmonise national legislation may confer powers on the Commission to compel the Member States to take temporary measures if the aims of the harmonisation would otherwise be jeopardised.[50]

17–012 **Comitology.** As already mentioned, in conferring implementing powers on the Commission, the Council and the European Parliament may subject the Commission to control by committees composed of representatives of the Member States (Art. 291(3) TFEU). Before the Lisbon Treaty, the Treaty referred to the

---

[42] The Court of Justice approved this system as long ago as ECJ, Case 25/70 *Köster* [1970] E.C.R. 1161, para. 9. See Bradley, "Comitology and the Law: Through a Glass, Darkly" (1992) C.M.L.Rev. 693–721. See also Blumann, "La Commission, agent d'exécution du droit communautaire. La comitologie", in Louis and Waelbroeck (eds), *La Commission au coeur du système institutionnel des Communautés européennes* (Brussels, Editions de l'Université de Bruxelles, 1989), 49–77; Blumann, "Le pouvoir exécutif de la Commission à la lumière de l'Acte unique européen" (1988) R.T.D.E. 23–59; Ehlermann, "Compétences d'exécution conférées à la Commission—La nouvelle décision-cadre du Conseil" (1988) R.M.C. 232–239.

[43] Since December 1, 2009, the Council thus adopts "implementing regulations" and "implementing decisions". Implementing acts of the Commission were not qualified by the term "implementing" as long as the 1999 Comitology Decision had not been replaced by a Comitology Regulation pursuant to Art. 291(3) TFEU.

[44] ECJ, Case 291/86 *Central-Import Münster* [1988] E.C.R. 3679, para. 13.

[45] ECJ, Case 41/69 *ACF Chemiefarma v Commission* [1970] E.C.R. 661, paras 60–62.

[46] ECJ, Case 16/88 *Commission v Council* [1989] E.C.R. 3457, para. 11.

[47] ECJ, Case C-159/96 *Portugal v Commission* [1998] E.C.R. I-7379, paras 40–41; ECJ, Case 403/05 *European Parliament v Commission* [2007] E.C.R. I-9045; ECJ, Joined Cases C-14/06 and C-295/06 *European Parliament and Denmark v Commission* [2008] E.C.R. I-1649 (annulment of a Commission decision exceeding the implementing powers conferred by a Council regulation).

[48] ECJ, Case 23/75 *Rey Soda v Cassa Conguaglio Zucchero* [1975] E.C.R. 1279, paras 10–11; ECJ, Case C-159/96 *Portugal v Commission* [1998] E.C.R. I-7379, paras 40–41.

[49] ECJ, Case C-240/90 *Germany v Commission* [1992] E.C.R. I-5383, paras 35–42. See also the earlier case ECJ, Case 25/70 *Köster* [1970] E.C.R. 1161, para. 7.

[50] ECJ, Case C-359/92 *Germany v Council* [1994] E.C.R. I-3681, paras 30–39.

imposition on the Commission of "certain requirements" that had to be in accordance with the "principles and rules" laid down in a decision of the Council.[51] Since the Lisbon Treaty, it is up to the European Parliament and the Council, acting in accordance with the ordinary legislative procedure and by means of a regulation, to lay down the rules and general principles for mechanisms for control by Member States of the Commission's exercise of implementing powers (Art. 291(3) TFEU).

In order to improve the efficiency of the Community decision-making process, the Council adopted the First Comitology Decision on July 13, 1987, which limited and enumerated the number of implementing procedures.[52] After the introduction of the co-decision procedure, the European Parliament expressed the wish to be able to exercise control over the implementation of acts adopted by co-decision—in addition to the control exercised by representatives of the Member States. The Council responded to this wish when it adopted the Second Comitology Decision on June 28, 1999,[53] especially after the amendments made to that decision on July 17, 2006.[54]

---

[51] According to the third indent of Art. 202 EC—added by the Single European Act—, the Council was to "confer on the Commission, in the acts which the Council adopts, powers for the implementation of the rules which the Council lays down" and "may impose certain requirements in respect of the exercise of these powers". The procedures in question had to be "consonant with principles and rules to be laid down in advance by the Council, acting unanimously on a proposal from the Commission and after obtaining the opinion of the European Parliament". In this way, the third indent of Art. 202 EC confirmed the former practice whereby the Council, acting under Art. 211 EC, conferred implementing powers on the Commission to be exercised in accordance with detailed rules laid down by the Council.

[52] Council Decision 87/373/EEC of July 13, 1987 laying down the conditions for the exercise of implementing powers conferred on the Commission, [1987] O.J. L197/33. The Council could not introduce any other procedures: ECJ, Case 16/88 *Commission v Council* [1989] E.C.R. 3457, para. 14.

[53] Council Decision 1999/468/EC of June 28, 1999 laying down the procedures for the exercise of implementing powers conferred on the Commission, [1999] O.J. L184/23. See Jacqué, "Implementing powers and Comitology", in Joerges and Vos (eds), *EU Committees: Social Regulation, Law and Politics* (Oxford, Hart Publishing, 1999), 59–69; Moteira González, "Änderung des normativen Rahmens der Komitologie" (2003) Z.Eu.S. 561–588; Lenaerts and Verhoeven, "Towards a Legal Framework for Executive Rule-Making in the E.U.? The Contribution of the New Comitology Decision" (2000) C.M.L.Rev. 645–686; Mensching, "Der neue Komitologie-Beschluss des Rates" (2000) Eu.Z.W. 268–271. See also the 31st Report House of Lords: *Select Committee on the European Union, Reforming Comitology (2002–03)* HL 135. For the conflict between the European Parliament and the Commission preceding the adoption of the Second Comitology Decision, see Blumann, "Le Parlement européen et la comitologie: une complication pour la Conférence intergouvernementale de 1996" (1996) R.T.D.E. 1–24; Nuttens, "La 'comitologie' et la Conférence intergouvernementale" (1996) R.M.C.U.E. 314–327.

[54] Council Decision 2006/512/EC of July 17, 2006 amending Decision 1999/468/EC laying down the procedures for the exercise of implementing powers conferred on the Commission, [2006] O.J. L200/11 (see the consolidated version of the Second Comitology Decision, published in [2006] O.J. C255/4). See also the Statement by the European Parliament, the Council and the Commission concerning the Council Decision of July 17, 2006, [2006] O.J. C255/1. For an assessment, see Christiansen, "The 2006 Reform of Comitology: problem solved or dispute postponed?" (2006) Eipascope 9–17; Szapiro, "Comitologie: rétrospectives et prospective après la réforme de 2006" (2006) R.D.U.E. 545–586; Van der Plas, "Rol Europees Parlement fors toegenomen door nieuw Comitologiebesluit" (2006) S.E.W. 410–424; Christiansen, "The 2006 Reform of Comitology: problem solved or dispute postponed?" (2006) Eipascope 9–17.

The Second Comitology Decision set out the "principles and rules" with which the Union legislator had to comply in adopting legislative acts that confer implementing powers on the Commission.[55] It set out the different procedures between which the Council and the European Parliament may choose when conferring implementing powers on the Commission. All procedures invariably required the Commission to submit a draft of the measures to be taken to a committee made up of representatives of the Member States and chaired by a representative of the Commission, who had no vote. According to the urgency of the matter, the Commission could lay down a time-limit within which the committee must deliver its opinion. The Second Comitology Decision required each committee to allow the public to have access to its documents (Second Comitology Decision, Art. 7(2)).[56] The Commission was to inform the European Parliament of committee proceedings on a regular basis (Comitology Decision, Art. 7(3)).[57]

After the entry into force of the Lisbon Treaty, more precisely on February 16, 2011, the European Parliament and the Council adopted a regulation pursuant to Art. 291(3) TFEU laying down the rules and general principles concerning the mechanism for control by the Member States of the Commission's exercise of implementing powers.[58] The Comitology Regulation entered into force on March 1, 2011 and replaced the Second Comitology Decision. Although taking over the basic tenets of the previous comitology system, the outlook of the comitology landscape has changed drastically as a result of the post-Lisbon distinction between delegated acts and implementing acts. As delegated acts have been taken out of the comitology system and put under direct control of the European Parliament and the Council pursuant to Art. 290(2) TFEU (see para. 17-009), comitology control mechanisms henceforth solely apply when the Commission adopts implementing acts. As a result, the Comitology Regulation has not taken

---

[55] ECJ, Case C-378/00 *Commission v European Parliament and Council* [2003] E.C.R. I-937, paras 40–42.

[56] CFI, Case T-188/97 *Rothmans v Commission* [1999] E.C.R. II-2463 (as far as access to its documents are concerned, a committee comes under the Commission).

[57] See the agreement between the European Parliament and the Commission on procedures for implementing Council Decision 1999/468/EC laying down the procedures for the exercise of implementing powers conferred on the Commission, as amended by Decision 2006/512/EC, [2008] O.J. C143/1. See also the Statement by the European Parliament, the Council and the Commission concerning the Council Decision of July 17, 2006, [2006] O.J. C255/1. For an assessment, Szapiro, "Comitologie: rétrospectives et prospective après la réforme de 2006" (2006) R.D.U.E. 545–586; Van der Plas, "Rol Europees Parlement fors toegenomen door nieuw Comiitologiebesluit" (2006) S.E.W. 410–424; Christiansen, "The 2006 Reform of Comitology: problem solved or dispute postponed?" (2006) Eipascope 9–17.

[58] Regulation (EU) No. 182/2011 of the European Parliament and of the Council of February 16, 2011 laying down the rules and general principles concerning mechanisms for control by Member States of the Commission's exercise of implementing powers, [2011] O.J. L55/13 (Comitology Regulation). Article 12 of this regulation repealed Council Decision 1999/468/EC laying down the procedures for the exercise of implementing powers conferred on the Commission, as amended by Decision 2006/512/EC, [2008] O.J. C143/1.

over all procedures existing under the former comitology system. Furthermore, where control was hitherto exercised by the Council or, where appropriate, by the Council together with the European Parliament, it is now solely the Member States that exercise control over the Commission's implementing powers. The committees composed of representatives of the Member States continue to be chaired by a representative of the Commission, which has no vote. A clear understanding of the old system is nevertheless necessary in order to grasp fully the particularities of the Comitology Regulation. Therefore, both the Second Comitology Decision (as amended in 2006) and the current Comitology Regulation will be discussed.

Different types of procedure. The Second Comitology Decision classified the committee procedures into three groups, depending on whether the Committee involved had advisory, management or regulatory powers. The 2006 amendment of the Comitology Decision added a new, fourth category, the regulatory procedure with scrutiny. The Comitology Regulation redesigned the system and the number of procedures has been reduced from four to two, namely the former advisory procedure and the new examination procedure, which has taken over elements of both the management procedure and the regulatory procedure. A procedure similar to the regulatory procedure with scrutiny has not been included in the Comitology Regulation as acts formerly governed by this procedure are now adopted as delegated acts under Art. 290 TFEU. Depending on what sort of procedure the Council (where appropriate, together with the European Parliament) sets up, the Council and the European Parliament can control the Commission's implementing role to a greater or lesser extent. As will be explained below, an advisory procedure does not really have any effect on the Commission's executive role, whilst an examination procedure (previously a management procedure or a regulatory procedure), topped off with an appeal procedure, can result in intervention on the part of the Member States (previously the Council) in the implementing process.[59] As such, the Comitology Regulation is the expression of a continuum, ranging between autonomous implementation by the Commission and implementation by the Member States themselves.

17–013

Article 2 of the Second Comitology Decision sets out criteria on the basis of which the legislator may choose a committee procedure.[60] Management measures, such as those relating to the application of the common agricultural and common fisheries policies, or to the implementation of programmes with

---

[59] In judgments predating the Single European Act, the Court of Justice raised no objection to procedures involving a management committee or a regulatory committee: ECJ, Case 25/70 *Köster* [1970] E.C.R. 1161, para. 9 (management committee); ECJ, Case 5/77 *Tedeschi* [1977] E.C.R. 1555, paras 51–56 (regulatory committee). For the importance of the choice of the type of committee, see ECJ, Case C-417/93 *European Parliament v Council* [1995] E.C.R. I-1185, paras 24–26.

[60] In addition, Art. 6 of the Second Comitology Decision described the procedure which could be applied where the basic instrument confers on the Commission the power to decide on safeguard measures. Such a procedure no longer exists under the new comitology framework. Provisions dealing with safeguard measures are now scattered throughout the Comitology Regulation.

substantial budgetary implications, had to be adopted by use of the management procedure. Measures of general scope designed to apply essential provisions of basic instruments[61] had to be adopted by use of the regulatory procedure. This method of linking an implementing measure by way of its nature and/or impact to a particular procedure is also used in Art. 2 of the Comitology Regulation. Implementing acts of general scope and other implementing acts—not of general scope—relating to programmes with substantial implications, to the common agricultural or fisheries policies, to the environment, security or safety or protection of the health or safety of humans, animals or plants, and to the common commercial policy and taxation now fall under the examination procedure. Where it is considered appropriate, and for all other implementing measures, the advisory procedure applies.[62] Although these criteria are not binding, they oblige the Union legislator to state reasons in the legislative act for any departure from those criteria.[63] Futhermore, under the old system, the regulatory procedure was also used where a basic instrument stipulated that certain non-essential provisions of the instrument could be adapted or updated by way of implementing procedures. In addition to this, the regulatory procedure with scrutiny was used for the adoption of measures of general scope designed to amend non-essential elements of a basic instrument adopted in accordance with the co-decision procedure (now the ordinary legislative procedure). For reasons explained above, these measures now constitute delegated acts and fall outside the scope of comitology control.

17–014 **Advisory procedure.** Where the Union legislator has set up an advisory committee, the Commission must obtain its opinion, but is not bound by it. However, it must take the utmost account of the conclusions drawn from the discussion within the committee and of the opinion delivered (Comitology Regulation, Art. 3 [*ex. Second Comitology Regulation, Art. 3*].

17–015 **Examination procedure.** This procedure absorbs the former management committee procedure and part of the former regulatory procedure, namely in the case of measures of general scope designed to apply essential provisions of basic instruments as defined in Art. 2(1)(b) of the Second Comitology Decision. Where the Union legislator has established an examination committee, the Commission must

---

[61] This includes measures concerning the protection of the health or safety of humans, animals or plants (Art. 2 of the Second Comitology Decision).

[62] Pursuant to Art. 2(3) of the Comitology Regulation, the advisory procedure may "in duly justified cases" apply for the adoption of implementing acts to which normally the examination procedure applies.

[63] See, under the old comitology framework, ECJ, Case C-78/00 *Commission v European Parliament and Council* [2003] E.C.R. I-937, paras 43–55 (an unreasoned choice departing from those criteria was declared void); ECJ, *Commission v European Parliament and Council* [2006] E.C.R., I-2001, paras 32–45 (no departure from those criteria found).

likewise seek its opinion. The committee delivers its opinion by qualified majority as laid down in Art. 16(4) and (5) TEU and, where applicable, Art. 238(3) TFEU, for acts to be adopted on a proposal from the Commission.[64] Under the Second Comitology Decision, similar voting requirements applied to both the management committee and the regulatory committee.[65] The outcome of the vote in the examination committee will then determine the progress of the procedure. When the committee delivers a positive opinion, the Commission adopts the implementing act (Comitology Regulation, Art. 5(2)). When the committee delivers a negative opinion, the Commission shall not adopt the implementing act. In case an implementing act would nevertheless be necessary, the chair of the committee may either submit an amended version of the draft implementing act to the same committee within two months of delivery of the negative opinion or submit the draft implementing act within one month of such delivery to the appeal committee for further deliberation (Comitology Regulation, Art. 5(3)). When the committee does not reach the required majority for either a positive or a negative opinion, no opinion shall be delivered. Under those circumstances, the Commission may adopt the implementing act unless (a) the act concerns taxation, financial services, the protection of human health or the safety of humans, animals or plants, or definitive multilateral safeguard measures, (b) the basic act provides that the draft implementing act may not be adopted where no opinion is delivered, or (c) a simple majority of the component members of the committee opposes it. In those cases the Commission shall not adopt an implementing act. If an implementing act would nevertheless be necessary, the chair of the committee may submit an amended version of the draft implementing act to the same committee within two months of the vote or submit the draft implementing act within one month of the vote to the appeal committee for further deliberation (Comitology Regulation, Art. 5(4)). When no opinion is delivered in case of draft definitive anti-dumping measures or countervailing measures and the committee opposed the draft implementing act by a simple majority of its component members, the Commission shall follow the procedure set out in Art. 5(5) second subpara. of the Comitology Regulation (Comitology Regulation, Art. 5(5) first subpara.). This procedure involves consultations with the Member States and the mandatory submission of a draft implementing act to the appeal committee.[66]

---

[64] Article 3 of Protocol (No. 36), annexed to the TEU, TFEU and EAEC Treaty, on transitional provisions ([2010] O.J. C83/322) should be taken into account here.

[65] Both committees delivered their opinion by a qualified majority as laid down in Art. 205(2) EC for decisions which the Council was required to adopt on a proposal from the Commission.

[66] Article 5(5) second subpara. Comitology Regulation: "The Commission shall conduct consultations with the Member States. 14 days at the earliest and 1 month at the latest after the committee meeting, the Commission shall inform the committee members of the results of those consultations and submit a draft implementing act to the appeal committee. By way of derogation from Art. 3(7), the appeal committee shall meet 14 days at the earliest and 1 month at the latest after the submission of the draft implementing act. The appeal committee shall deliver its opinion in accordance with Art. 6. The time limits laid down in this paragraph shall be without prejudice to the need to respect the deadlines laid down in the relevant basic acts.

The Comitology Regulation further provides for the possibility of making an accelerated procedure applicable if it is foreseeable that, for imperative grounds of urgency, the time limits for the advisory or examination committee procedure cannot be complied with (Comitology Regulation, Art. 8(1))[67]. The accelerated procedure is the standard procedure when dealing with provisional anti-dumping or countervailing measures (Comitology Regulation, Art. 8(5)).

As already mentioned, the examination procedure contains elements of both the former management procedure and the former regulatory procedure. In the case of the management procedure, when the committee had issued an opinion, the Commission then adopted the implementing measures which applied immediately, but had to communicate to the Council forthwith any measures which were not in accordance with the committee's opinion. In that event, the Commission was allowed to defer application of the measures which it had decided on for a period laid down in each basic instrument but which could in no case exceed three months (Second Comitology Decision, Art. 4(3)). The Council, acting on its own initiative by a qualified majority, could then take a different decision within that period (Second Comitology Decision, Art. 4(4)). If the Council failed to reach a decision within that time-limit, the Commission's measures entered into fore definitively.

A negative opinion from a management committee thus ipso facto gave the Council an opportunity to adopt a decision differing from the measures proposed by the Commission. Yet the fact that the management committee had delivered a negative opinion did not necessarily mean that every delegation had the same difficulties in accepting the Commission's measures, as a result of which the Council could not always muster a sufficient majority in favour of different measures. In practice, the procedure did not often produce negative opinions, since the Commission ensured that its implementing function was conducted smoothly by negotiating with the delegations on the management committee beforehand.[68]

In the case of the regulatory procedure, when the committee voted in favour of the measures envisaged, they were adopted by the Commission. If, in contrast, the committee could not muster a sufficient majority for a favourable opinion, or if no opinion was delivered, the Commission had to submit the measures envisaged to the Council as a formal proposal and inform the European Parliament

---

[67] In that case, under the accelerated procedure, the Commission is to adopt the measures, which are immediately implemented and shall remain in force for a period not exceeding six months unless the basic act provides otherwise. At the latest 14 days after its adoption, the chair shall submit the act referred to the relevant committee in order to obtain its opinion. When the examination procedure applies, in case of the committee delivering a negative opinion, the Commission is under an obligation to immediately repeal the implemented act.

[68] For the role played by management committees in agricultural policy, see Trotman, "Agricultural Policy Management: A Lesson in Unaccountability" (1995) C.M.L.Rev. 1385–1406.

(Comitology Decision, Art. 5(3), (4) and (5)).[69] Next, the Council could adopt the proposal by a qualified majority (or amend it by a unanimous vote: see Art. 293(1) TFEU [ex. Art. 250 EC]), within a period to be laid down in each basic instrument which, however, could in no case exceed three months from the date of referral to the Council. If within that period the Council had indicated by a qualified majority that it opposed the proposal, the Commission was obliged to re-examine it. It could then submit an amended proposal to the Council, re-submit its proposal or present a legislative proposal on the basis of the Treaties to modify the basic instrument.[70] If on the expiry of that period the Council had neither adopted the proposed implementing act nor indicated its opposition to the proposal for implementing measures, the proposed implementing act was to be adopted by the Commission (Comitology Decision, Art. 5(6)).[71]

Appeal committee. The appeal committee is a new actor in the comitology process. It assumes the role the Council played under the management and regulatory procedure. This is a logical consequence of the fact that it is no longer the Council but the Member States that control the Commission's exercise of implementing powers.[72] As set out above, (see para. 17-015), the Commission has the opportunity or, in certain cases, the obligation to submit a draft implementing act

17–016

---

[69] Where the basic act did not specify precisely the period within which the Commission had to submit a proposal to the Council, the Commission was entitled to seek additional advice before presenting an amended proposal, in particular where it was faced with a measure which was scientifically and politically highly complex and sensitive: ECJ, Case C-151/98 P *Pharos v Commission* [1999] E.C.R. I-8157, paras 20–27.

[70] Where the Commission did not see any possibility of the Council changing its mind, it may not have resubmitted the same proposal or an amended one, nor have submitted a legislative proposal. See ECJ (order of January 22, 2010), Case C-69/09 P *Makhteshim-Agan and Others v Commission*, not yet reported, paras 37–57 (a letter in which Commission set out that position cannot be the subject of an action for annulment as it does not produce legal effects).

[71] This procedure was comparable to variant (a) (the "*filet*") under the First Comitology Decision which did not however allow the Council to reject the proposed measures by a qualified majority. Under variant (b) (the "*contrefilet*") provided for in the First Comitology Decision, the Commission was in a weaker position, since it enabled the Council to reject the proposal by a simple majority. For the differences between these variants, see ECJ, Case C-417/93 *European Parliament v Council* [1995] E.C.R. I-1185, para. 26, and the Opinion of Advocate-General P. Léger, point 92. Compare the case note by Van Nuffel (1995) Col.J.E.L. 504, at 508, with Bradley, "Institutional Aspects of Comitology: Scenes from the Cutting Room Floor", in Joerges and Others, *EU Committees: Social Regulation, Law and Politics* (Oxford, Hart Publishing, 1999), 71, at 76–79.

[72] Compare Art. 291(3) TFEU with Art. 202 EC. This does not mean that there is no role to play for the Council, or the European Parliament. Modelled on Art. 8 of the Second Comitology Decision, both the European Parliament and the Council have a right of scrutiny over draft implementing acts when they are of the opinion that a draft implementing act exceeds the implementing powers provided for in a basic act adopted following the ordinary legislative procedure. When indicating this to the Commission, the Commission shall review the draft implementing act, taking account of the positions expressed, and shall inform the European Parliament and the Council whether it intends to maintain, amend or withdraw the draft implementing act (Comitology Regulation, Art. 11).

to the appeal committee when adoption of a draft implementing act failed under the examination procedure. The appeal committee is chaired by a representative of the Commission and delivers its opinion by qualified majority.[73] Where the appeal committee delivers a positive opinion, the Commission adopts the draft implementing act. In case of a negative opinion, the Commission may adopt the draft implementing act, unless the act concerns the adoption of definitive multilateral safeguard measures (Comitology Regulation, Art. 6(3)). In that case, the Commission always needs a positive opinion before it can adopt the draft implementing act (Comitology Regulation, Art. 6(4)).

17–017   **Former regulatory procedure with scrutiny.** Under the Second Comitology Decision, the regulatory procedure was applicable to measures of general scope designed to apply essential provisions of basic instruments and when a basic instrument stipulated that certain non-essential provisions of the instrument could be adapted or updated by way of implementing procedures. Whereas this first set of measures now falls under the examination procedure (see para. 17-015), implementing measures that amend or supplement certain non-essential provisions of the basic act now constitute delegated acts under Art. 290 TFEU and hence comitology is not applicable to them any longer. The same goes for all measures on which the regulatory procedure was applicable. This procedure dealt with implementing measures of general scope designed to amend non-essential elements of a basic instrument adopted following the co-decision procedure (now the ordinary legislative procedure). Because the European Parliament acted as co-legislator in the adoption of those basic instruments, it demanded and obtained a higher degree of involvement in the comitology process.

Where the Union legislator had set up a regulatory committee with scrutiny, the implementing measures which the Commission proposed to the Committee were scrutinised by both the Council and the European Parliament. If the committee voted by a qualified majority (determined in the same way as in the case of a management committee) in favour of the measures envisaged, they must be submitted for scrutiny to the European Parliament and the Council (Second Comitology Decision, Arts 5a(2) and (3)a)). Either institution could, within three months from the date of referral to them, oppose the adoption of the draft measure proposed by the Commission, justifying its opposition by indicating that the draft measure exceeded the implementing powers provided for in the basic instrument or that it

---

[73] By way of derogation, until September 1, 2012, the appeal committee shall deliver its opinion on draft definitive anti-dumping or countervailing measures by a simple majority of its component members (Comitology Regulation, Art. 6(5)). The special treatment of draft definitive anti-dumping measures or countervailing measures in the regulation (see also n. 66), which leads to greater scrutiny of the Commission's implementing powers, is a consequence of the fact that, under the post-Lisbon framework, the Commission can now adopt anti-dumping or countervailing measures of a definitive nature. Previously, it was the Council that adopted definitive anti-dumping or countervailing measures, while the Commission could only take such measures provisionally.

was not compatible with the aim or the content of the basic instrument or did not respect the principles of subsidiarity or proportionality (Second Comitology Decision, Art. 5a(3)b)). In that event, the Commission was not allowed to adopt the proposed measure. The Commission could then submit to the Committee an amended draft of the measures or present a legislative proposal on the basis of the Treaties to modify the basic instrument (Second Comitology Decision, Art. 5a(3)c)). If, within the said period, neither the European Parliament nor the Council opposed the draft measures, they could be adopted by the Commission.

If the committee did not muster a sufficient majority in order to deliver a positive opinion, or if no opinion was delivered, the Commission had to submit its draft to the Council as a formal proposal and had to forward it to the European Parliament at the same time (Second Comitology Decision, Art. 5a(4)). Within two months from the date of referral to it, the Council could then act on the proposal by qualified majority; within four months of the date of referral to it, the European Parliament could oppose adoption of the measure on one of the grounds mentioned above. If the Council opposed the proposed measures, they could not be adopted. In that event, the Commission had the opportunity to submit to the Council an amended proposal or present a legislative proposal on the basis of the Treaties (taking into account possible objections formulated by the European Parliament). If the Council envisaged adopting the proposed measures (or if it did not act within the two-month period), the proposed measures were submitted to the European Parliament. If the European Parliament opposed the proposed measures, they could not be adopted. In that event, the Commission could submit to the Committee an amended draft of the measures or present a legislative proposal on the basis of the Treaties. If the European Parliament did not oppose the proposed measures, they were to be adopted by the Council or by the Commission, as the case may be.

In the post-Lisbon constellation, it is still the European Parliament and the Council that exercise the supervision over the type of implementing measures covered in this paragraph, albeit outside the comitology framework (see para. 17–009).

Consultation of expert committees. In implementing legislation, not only does the Commission have to have regard to the politically sensitive nature of certain measures, but scientific and technical problems also arise. For this reason, various Union measures provide for the involvement of a scientific or technical committee with a view to their implementation. Where such a committee is set up, it must be consulted even if the instrument to be implemented does not say so in so many words, because such consultation constitutes the only guarantee that a Union measure is necessary and adapted to the objective pursued.[74] An infringement of

17–018

---

[74] ECJ, Case C-212/91 *Angelopharm* [1994] E.C.R. I-171, paras 31–38.

internal procedural rules of such a committee which are intended to ensure that Member States' representatives have the time necessary to consult the different national administrative authorities, experts or professional organisations may constitute an infringement of essential procedural requirements and result in the annulment of the measure concerned.[75]

17–019 **Control on implementation by Commission or Council.** The European Parliament has often claimed that the task of implementation should be entrusted fully to the Commission. The reason is that this would enable both the Council and the European Parliament itself to supervise the Commission by virtue of their constitutional prerogatives. Both institutions should check that the Commission does not exceed the implementing power conferred on it. If it does, the European Parliament and the Council—and also any Member State—can bring an action for annulment of Commission measures in the Court of Justice.[76] In addition, the European Parliament may hold the Commission to account politically for the way in which it fulfils its executive role (see para. 13–009). Where, in contrast, the Council itself undertakes implementation or makes it subject to a comitology procedure which results in the power of implementation reverting to it, it is not possible for the European Parliament to exercise political control to the same extent. This appears justified where the Council takes decisions not based on a measure adopted by itself, such as where it appoints the members of a committee.[77] However, as far as general implementing measures are concerned, there is a danger of the Council's evading involvement of the European Parliament in the legislative process by adopting a vague piece of legislation and then giving it a completely different scope. Although the Court of Justice may find against

---

[75] ECJ, Case C-263/95 *Germany v Commission* [1998] E.C.R. I-441, paras 31–32.

[76] For cases which were successfully brought by a Member State, see ECJ, Case C-366/88 *France v Commission* [1990] E.C.R. I-3571, paras 17–25; ECJ, Case C-303/90 *France v Commission* [1991] E.C.R. I-5315, paras 27–35; ECJ, Case C-325/91 *France v Commission* [1993] E.C.R. I-3283, paras 14–17; ECJ, Case C-159/96 *Portugal v Commission* [1998] E.C.R. I-7379, paras 25–50; ECJ, Joined Cases C-289/96, C-293/96 and C-299/96 *Denmark, Germany and France v Commission* [1999] E.C.R. I-1541, paras 53–103; ECJ, Case 89/96 *Portugal v Commission* [1999] E.C.R. I-8377, paras 12–14; ECJ, Case C-393/01 *France v Commission* [2003] E.C.R. I-5405, paras 40–60; ECJ, Case C-239/01 *Germany v Commission* [2003] E.C.R. I-10333, paras 54–76. The power of implementation was not considered to have been exceeded in ECJ, Joined Cases C-296/93 and C-307/93 *France and Ireland v Commission* [1996] E.C.R. I-795, paras 11–24; ECJ, Joined Cases C-9/95, C-23/95 and C-156/95 *Belgium and Germany v Commission* [1997] E.C.R. I-645, paras 21–41; ECJ, Case C-285/94 *Italy v Commission* [1997] E.C.R. I-3519, paras 20–46. Before the broadening of its right to bring an action for annulment (see para. 13–013, *supra*), the European Parliament could do so where the Commission measure at issue infringed a legislative act adopted under a procedure providing for the involvement of the Parliament. See, e.g., ECJ, Case C-156/93 *European Parliament v Commission* [1995] E.C.R. I-2019, paras 12–13.

[77] Beutler, Bieber, Pipkorn and Streil, *Die Europäische Union. Rechtsordnung und Politik* (Baden-Baden, Nomos, 1993), at 128.

such a practice,[78] the European Parliament lacks the necessary means of political control vis-à-vis the Council. It is in practice confined to the right to ask parliamentary questions (see para. 13–010). However, this problem has become less acute since the Lisbon Treaty extended the scope of the ordinary legislative procedure to most fields of competence of the Union. Consequently, the European Parliament very often enjoys a power of co-decision on the substance of the legislative act adopted, including the way in which it is implemented. Moreover, since the Lisbon Treaty comitology regulations are also adopted under the ordinary legislative procedure, which gives the European Parliament a decisive say as to the way in which comitology control is organised. In addition, in the cases previously covered by the regulatory procedure or the regulatory procedure with scrutiny, the fear of the European Parliament that non-legislative acts of general application based on legislative acts adopted by co-decision between the Council and the European Parliament, would end up being adopted by the Council alone, has been taken into account by the Lisbon Treaty. Indeed, the introduction of the category of "delegated acts" (Art. 290 TFEU) is specifically tailored to that situation. It will be the Commission which adopts them, at an equal distance from the Council and the European Parliament, which both have the same powers of control over the Commission when it exercises its delegated powers.

C. IMPLEMENTATION BY OTHER BODIES, OFFICES AND AGENCIES

Independent executive bodies, offices and agencies. In increasing numbers   17–020
of policy areas, the Union legislature has entrusted specific bodies, offices or agencies with executive functions. In some cases, the legislature assigns tasks to specialised departments of the Commission (see para. 13–122). In others, executive tasks are conferred on bodies, offices or agencies with legal personality in their own right and powers of their own,[79] such as the European Office for Harmonisation in the Internal Market and the Community Plant Variety Office (see para. 13–123). Delegation of the management of Union programmes to executive agencies allows the Commission to outsource certain of its own management tasks.[80] In many cases, bodies with legal personality (known as

---

[78] See, e.g., ECJ, Case C-303/94 *European Parliament v Council* [1996] E.C.R. I-2943, paras 21–33; ECJ, Case C-93/00 *European Parliament v Council* [2001] E.C.R. I-10119, paras 35–44; ECJ, Case C-403/05 *European Parliament v Commission* [2007] E.C.R. I-9045, paras 40–68; ECJ, Joined Cases C-14/06 and C-295/06 *European Parliament and Denmark v Commission* [2008] E.C.R. I-1649, paras 50–78 and the inquiry carried out by the Court of Justice in ECJ, Case 46/86 *Romkes* [1987] E.C.R. 2671, paras 15–20; ECJ, Case C-417/93 *European Parliament v Council* [1995] E.C.R. I-1185, paras 28–33; ECJ, Case C-133/06 *European Parliament v Council* [2008] E.C.R. I-3189 paras 52–59.

[79] See ECJ, Case 9/56 *Meroni v High Authority* [1957 and 1958] E.C.R. 133, at 146 *et seq.*, and the parallel judgment ECJ, Case 10/56 *Meroni v High Authority* [1957 and 1958] E.C.R. 157.

[80] Council Regulation (EC) No. 58/2003 of December 19, 2002 laying down the statute for executive agencies to be entrusted with certain tasks in the management of Community programmes, [2003] O.J. L11/1.

offices, agencies, centres and foundations) perform executive functions in coordinating or supplementing action taken by the Member States. In that case, they collect and disseminate information, set up machinery for coordinating action on the part of the competent national authorities and carry out studies with a view to developing policy further.[81] Generally what is involved is a genuine amalgam of Union *administration directe* and *indirecte*[82] in which Union and national experts administer policy areas in collaboration with interest groups.[83]

17–021   **Limits on delegation.** Delegation of powers to an independent executive body may be effected in a legislative measure based on a specific provision of the Treaties, provided that the delegation is confined to the aims and means set out in that provision.[84] That constraint is less important where the body in question is set up to "attain one of the objectives set out in the Treaties" under Art. 352 TFEU [*ex Art. 308 EC*].[85] But, even then, it may be entrusted only with clearly defined

---

[81] See the tasks assigned to other Union bodies, offices and agencies with legal personality mentioned in para. 13–123, *supra*.

[82] Lenaerts, "Regulating the Regulatory Process: 'Delegation of Powers' in the European Community" (1993) E.L.Rev. 23, at 46–47.

[83] See Chiti, "The Emergence of a Community Administration: The Case of European Agencies" (2000) C.M.L.Rev. 309–343; Vos, "Reforming the European Commission: What Role to Play for EU Agencies?" (2000) C.M.L.Rev. 1113–1134.

[84] See Regulation (EC) No. 881/2004 of the European Parliament and of the Council of April 29, 2004 establishing a European Railway Agency, [2004] O.J. L164/1 (re-published with *corrigendum*: [2004] O.J. L220/3), adopted on the basis of Art. 71(1) EC [*ex Art. 91(1) TFEU*]; Regulation (EC) No. 1406/2002 of the European Parliament and of the Council of June 27, 2002 establishing a European Maritime Safety Agency, [2002] O.J. L208/1, and Regulation (EC) No. 1592/2002 of the European Parliament and of the Council of July 15, 2002 on common rules in the field of civil aviation and establishing a European Aviation Safety Agency, [2002] O.J. L240/1, both adopted on the basis of Art. 80(2) EC [*now Art. 100(2) TFEU*]; Regulation (EC) No. 851/2004 of the European Parliament and of the Council of April 21, 2004 establishing a European Centre for disease prevention and control, [2004] O.J. L142/1, adopted on the basis of Art. 152(4)(b) EC [*now Art. 168 (4)(b) TFEU*]; Council Regulation (EEC) No. 1210/90 of May 7, 1990 on the establishment of the European Environment Agency and the European Environment Information and Observation Network, [1990] O.J. L120/1, adopted on the basis of Art. 175 EC [*now Art. 192 TFEU*]. See also Regulation (EC) No. 460/2004 of the European Parliament and of the Council of March 10, 2004 establishing the European Network and Information Security Agency, [2004] O.J. L77/1 and Regulation (EC) No. 1211/2009 of the European Parliament and of the Council of November 25, 2009 establishing the Body of European Regulators for Electronic Communications [2009] O.J. L337/1, both adopted on the basis of Art. 95 EC [*now Art. 114 TFEU*], and Regulation (EC) No. 726/2004 of the European Parliament and of the Council of March 31, 2004 laying down Community procedures for the authorisation and supervision of medicinal products for human and veterinary use and establishing a European Medicines Agency, [2004] O.J. L136/1, adopted on the basis of Arts 95 and 152(4)(b) EC; Regulation (EU) No. 439/2010 of the European Parliament and the Council of May 19, 2010 establishing a European Asylum Support Office, [2010] O.J. L132/11, adopted on the basis of Arts 74 and 78 TFEU.

[85] See most of the bodies mentioned in para. 13–123, *supra*, with the exception of the agencies mentioned in the preceding n.

executive tasks. The reason for this is that if the body had discretionary powers, the policy choices would no longer lie with the institutions which have the political responsibility under the Treaties. This would detract from the institutional balance on which the Union is based.[86] Accordingly, the Commission may not delegate the execution of a Union programme to an executive agency where this would involve "discretionary powers in translating political choices into action".[87]

Judicial Review. Neither may an institution delegate more powers than it possesses itself. Accordingly, independent executive bodies are subject to the same obligations with regard to adequate legal protection as the Union institutions. Their decisions must state the reasons on which they are based (Art. 296, second para., TFEU) and be brought to the notice of the persons to whom they are addressed (Art. 297 TFEU). In addition, decisions which produce legal effects must be amenable to judicial review.[88] Accordingly, the Court of Justice has jurisdiction in actions for annulment against acts of bodies, offices or agencies of the Union intended to produce legal effects vis-à-vis third parties (Art. 263, first para., TFEU; see para. 13–079).[89] This provision, introduced by the Lisbon Treaty, confirms longstanding case law of the Court of Justice holding that it may be inferred from the fact that the Union is "based on the rule of law" that the validity of acts of all Union bodies must be amenable to judicial review where those acts produce legal effects.[90]

17–022

---

[86] ECJ, Case 9/56 *Meroni* [1957 and 1958] E.C.R. 133, at 151 *et seq.* (cited in para. 15–009, *supra*). See also ECJ, Case 98/80 *Romano* [1981] E.C.R. 1241, para. 20 (a commission set up by the Council does not have the power to adopt acts having the force of law in view of the implementing powers vested in the Commission by the Treaties).

[87] See recitals 4 and 5 in the preamble to Regulation No. 58/2003 and Art. 6(1) thereof (n. 80, *supra*). For this constraint on the delegation of executive tasks by the Commission, see Craig, "The constitutionalisation of Community administration" (2003) E.L.Rev. 840, at 848–854; Remmert, "Die Gründung von Einrichtungen der mittelbaren Gemeinschaftsverwaltung" (2003) EuR. 134–145. A plea for more autonomous executive agencies may be found in Majone, "Delegation of Regulatory Powers in a Mixed Polity" (2002) E.L.J. 319–339.

[88] ECJ, Case 9/56 *Meroni* [1957 and 1958] E.C.R. 133, at 149–151. See, e.g., CFI, Joined Cases T-369/94 and T-85/95 *DIR International Film and Others v Commission* [1998] E.C.R. II-357, paras 110–122 (review of a decision taken by the European Film Distribution Office); CFI, Case T-411/06 *Sogelma v European Agency for Reconstruction* [2008] E.C.R. II-2771, paras 33–57 (review of that agency's decision); EGC (judgment of March 2, 2010), Case T-70/05 *Evropaïki Dynamiki v European Maritime Safety Agency*, not yet reported, paras 61–75 (annulment of a contract awarded by that agency); EGC (judgment of October 21, 2010), Case T-439/08 *Joséphidès v Commission and EACEA*, not yet reported, paras 33–38.

[89] Similarly, the Court has jurisdiction in actions for a failure to act against bodies, offices and agencies of the Union (Art. 265(1) TFEU).

[90] See ECJ, Case 294/83 *Les Verts v European Parliament* [1986] E.C.R. 1339, paras 23–25; CFI, Case T-411/06 *Sogelma v European Agency for Reconstruction* [2008] E.C.R. II-2771, paras 36–17; EGC, Case T-70/05 *Evropaïki Dynamiki v European Maritime Safety Agency* (n. 88, *supra*), paras 64–66. *Cf.* CFI (order of June 8, 1998), Case T-148/97 *Keeling v Office for Harmonisation in the Internal Market* [1998] E.C.R. II-2217, paras 26–34.

Acts setting up bodies, offices and agencies of the Union may lay down specific conditions and arrangements concerning actions brought by natural or legal persons against acts of these bodies, offices or agencies intended to produce legal effects in relation to them (Art. 263, fourth para., TFEU). Some acts provide that a Member State, a member of the governing board of the body, office or agency and any other person directly and individually concerned may have the legality of an act of the body, office or agency in question reviewed by the Commission. The Commission's express or implied approval or disapproval of the act will then constitute an act amenable to judicial review.[91] In other cases, the person concerned must first apply to a board of appeal, against whose decision an appeal will lie to the Union Court.[92] In some cases, acts provide that a direct action will lie in the Union Courts against the decision of the body, office or agency concerned.[93]

17–023   **Tasks conferred on international bodies.** The same restrictions apply where the Union delegates tasks to international bodies.[94] The distribution of powers as

---

[91] See, for example, CFI, Joined Cases T-369/94 and T-85/95 *DIR International Film and Others v Commission* [1998] E.C.R. II-357, paras 52–55 (decision of the European Film Distribution Office attributed to the Commission). See also the regulations (references in para. 13–123, *supra*) establishing the European Centre for the Development of Vocational Training (Cedefop) (Art. 18), the European Foundation for the Improvement of Living and Working Conditions (Art. 22), the European Agency for Cooperation (Art. 19), the European Agency for Health and Safety at Work (Art. 22), the Community Plant Variety Office (Art. 44), the European Office for Harmonisation in the Internal Market (Art. 118, which does not allow an act to be submitted by a member of the Administrative Board to the Commission but provides for general supervision by the Commission) and the European Centre for Disease Prevention and Control (Art. 28). See further Art. 22 of Regulation No. 58/2003 with regard to executive agencies entrusted with certain tasks in the management of Community programmes (n. 80, *supra*) and Craig (n. 87, *supra*), at 849–851.

[92] *Cf.* the Board of Appeal of the Office for Harmonisation in the Internal Market (Art. 135 of the 2009 regulation establishing the Office), the Community Plant Variety Office (Arts 45, 67 and 73 of the regulation establishing the Office as amended by Council Regulation (EC) No. 2506/95 of October 25, 1995, [1995] O.J. L258/3) and the European Aviation Safety Agency (Arts 31 to 42 of the regulation establishing the Agency and Commission Regulation No. 104/2004 of January 22, 2004, [2004] O.J. L16/20) and the Complaints Board dealing with certain disputes arising under the Convention defining the status of the European Schools, established by Art. 27 of the Convention (alongside the exclusive jurisdiction of the Court of Justice over disputes between Contracting Parties relating to the interpretation and application of the Convention: Art. 26), [1994] O.J. L212/9. For legal redress under the former statute of the European Schools, see Henrichs, "Zur rechtlichen Stellung der Europäischen Schulen und ihrer Lehrer" (1994) EuR. 358–363; for the present situation, see the Commission's answer of May 22, 1997 to question E-1435/97 (Lehne), [1997] O.J. C130.

[93] For acts of the European Monitoring Centre for Drugs and Drug Addiction and of the European Monitoring Centre on Racism and Xenophobia, see Art. 17 and Art. 15(3), respectively, of the regulations establishing those bodies. For judicial review of decisions of the European Data-protection Supervisor, see Art. 32(2) of the regulation establishing the supervisor (para. 13–123, *supra*).

[94] See Lenaerts, "Regulating the Regulatory Process: 'Delegation of Powers' in the European Community" (1993) E.L.Rev. 23, at 37–40.

between the institutions and between the Union and the Member States requires the policy choices to be laid down in the act establishing the body (the international agreement), which has to have been adopted by means of the appropriate procedure, with the result that the newly established body has executive powers only.[95] Where the body adopts acts which are binding on the Union as a party to the agreement, decision-making generally takes place by mutual agreement between all the contracting parties.[96] In principle acts of such a body may not escape any form of judicial review either.[97] The international agreement may share powers as between the Union and the other contracting parties only if this does not change the nature of the powers of the Union and of its institutions as conceived in the Treaties.[98] An international agreement between the Union and third States may devolve dispute settlement to a specific dispute-resolution system. However, in order to preserve the autonomy of the Union legal order, that dispute-resolution system may not have the effect of binding the Union and its institutions, in the exercise of their internal powers, to a particular interpretation of the rules of Union law.[99]

Delegation of powers in the Treaties. The Treaties themselves have entrusted the performance of certain tasks to independent bodies with discretionary powers. Institutionally, this is a comparatively recent development, since the Member States held on for a long time to the institutional structure to which they were accustomed and which allowed them to exercise a measure of control   17–024

---

[95] See ECJ, Opinion 1/76 *Draft Agreement establishing a European laying-up fund for inland waterway vessels* [1977] E.C.R. 741, para. 5 and 15–16.

[96] See, for example, the Council of Ministers set up by the ACP-EC Partnership Agreement (para. 25–027, *infra*) and the institutions of the European Economic Area (para. 25–031, *infra*). Nevertheless, some bodies set up by multilateral agreements take their decisions by majority vote: see Gilsdorf, "Les organes institués par des accords communautaires: effets juridiques de leurs décisions. Observations à propos notamment de l'arrêt de la Cour de justice des Communautés européennes dans l'affaire C-192/89" (1992) R.M.C.U.E. 328, at 332–333.

[97] For the interpretation by the Court of Justice of such acts, see ECJ, Case C-192/89 *Sevince* [1990] E.C.R. I-3461, paras 10–11 (para. 22–048, *infra*).

[98] ECJ, Opinion 1/92 *Draft agreement between the Community, on the one hand, and the countries of the European Free Trade Association, on the other, relating to the creation of the European Economic Area* [1992] E.C.R. I-2821, para. 41; ECJ, Opinion 1/00 *Proposed agreement between the European Community and non-Member States on the establishment of a European Common Aviation Area* [2002] E.C.R. I-3493, paras 12 and 15–27. See Castillo de la Torre (2002) C.M.L.Rev. 1373–1393.

[99] ECJ, Opinion 1/00, paras 13 and 27–45 and Castillo de la Torre (n. 99, *supra*), at 1396–1387. If the international agreement sets up its own system of case law, this may raise problems for the autonomy of the Union judicial system: see ECJ, Opinion 1/76 *Draft Agreement establishing a European laying-up fund for inland waterway vessels* [1977] E.C.R. 741, paras 21–22; ECJ, Opinion 1/91 *Draft agreement between the Community, on the one hand, and the countries of the European Free Trade Association, on the other, relating to the creation of the European Economic Area* [1991] E.C.R. I-6079, paras 37–53.

over decision-making and implementation.[100] The two most important independent bodies to which tasks were entrusted by the Treaties were the European Central Bank and the European Investment Bank. Since the Lisbon Treaty, however, the European Central Bank has become a Union institution, although it continues to be a legal person in its own right (Art. 282(3) TFEU (see para. 10–096).[101]

As an independent body, the European Investment Bank has substantial latitude with regard to policy within the confines of the powers which it derives from the Treaties and the statute appended thereto.[102] Nevertheless, the acts of the EIB are also subject to judicial supervision.[103] The Court of Justice has made it clear that the functional independence enjoyed by the European Investment Bank does not have the consequence of separating it entirely from the European Union and exempting it from every rule of Union law.[104] The fact that it is independent does not preclude the Union legislature from adopting legislative measures applying to it, for instance relating to the prevention of fraud.[105]

The Treaties also confer tasks on Eurojust and Europol in the field of judicial cooperation in criminal matters and police cooperation, respectively (see para. 13–135). The concrete field of action of these legally independent bodies is however to be determined by regulations adopted pursuant to Arts 85 and 88 TFEU. The European Parliament and the Council, by means of regulations adopted in accordance with the ordinary legislative procedure, have

---

[100] Dehousse, "Integration v Regulation? On the Dynamics of Regulation in the European Community" (1992) J.C.M.S. 383, at 389–391.

[101] For the powers of the ECB before the Lisbon Treaty, see Schütz, "Die Legitimation der Europäischen Zentralbank zur Rechtsetzung" (2001) EuR. 291–305; Zilioli and Selmayr, "The European Central Bank: An Independent Specialised Organisation of Community Law" (2000) C.M.L.Rev. 591–644; the editorial, "Executive Agencies within the EC: The European Central Bank—A Model?" (1996) C.M.L.Rev. 623–631. For some critical observations, see Amtenbrink and De Haan, "The European Central Bank: An Independent Specialised Organisation of Community Law—A Comment" (2002) C.M.L. Rev. 65–76; Magnette, "Towards 'Accountable Independence'? Parliamentary Controls of the European Central Bank and the Rise of a New Democratic Model" (2000) E.L.J. 326–340; cf. Brentford, "Constitutional Aspects of the Independence of the European Central Bank" (1998) I.C.L.Q. 75–116; Gormley and De Haan, "The democratic deficit of the European Central Bank" (1996) E.L.Rev. 95–112.

[102] See Art. 308, third para., TFEU, which refers to the Statute of the European Investment Bank, laid down in Protocol (No. 5), annexed to the TEU and TFEU, [2010] O.J. C83/251.

[103] See Art. 271(b) and (c) TFEU and ECJ, Case C-15/00 Commission v European Investment Bank [2003] E.C.R. I-7281, para. 75.

[104] ECJ, Case C-15/00 Commission v European Investment Bank [2003] E.C.R. I-7281, para. 102. See, similarly, with regard to the ECB: ECJ, Case C-11/00 Commission v European Central Bank [2003] E.C.R. I-7147, para. 135.

[105] Ibid., paras 103–109. See, similarly, with regard to the ECB: ECJ, Case C-11/00 Commission v European Central Bank [2003] E.C.R. I-7147, paras 136–144.

to determine arrangements for involving the European Parliament and national parliaments in the evaluation of the activities of Eurojust and Europol (Arts 85(1), third subpara., and 88(2), second subpara., TFEU). Another example of a body to which powers are delegated by the Treaties is the Political and Security Committee (Art. 38 TEU; see para. 18–007), which is however not a separate legal person.

CHAPTER 18

CFSP DECISION-MAKING

Specific procedures. As regards the common foreign and security policy (CFSP), the Contracting Parties did not wish to make the national governments—represented in the Council—share their power of decision with the Commission and the European Parliament in the same way as in other fields of Union action. This factor—together with the reluctance to subject action in this field to judicial control by the Court of Justice—was the main reason why the EU Treaty laid down the provisions concerning the CFSP, not in the EC Treaty, but in Title V of the EU Treaty (the Union's "second pillar"), with a regime separate from Community decision-making. The same was true of the provisions on police and judicial cooperation in criminal matters (PJCC). Whereas the Lisbon Treaty abandoned the specific status of PJCC—which is now covered by the Treaty provisions concerning the adoption of legislative and implementing acts as discussed above—it left the CFSP subject to the previously existing "specific rules and procedures",[1] which are now laid down in Ch. 2 of Title V of the TEU. According to Art. 24(1), second subpara., TEU, the CFSP is to be defined and implemented by the European Council and Council acting unanimously and put into effect by the High Representative of the Union for Foreign Affairs and Security Policy and by Member States. The adoption of legislative acts is excluded (*ibid.*). Pursuant to the same provision, the "specific role of the European Parliament and of the Commission in this area is defined by the Treaties". It is clear from the following analysis that policy-making and implementation with respect to the CFSP still preserves many characteristics of intergovernmental cooperation.[2]

18–001

I. POLICY-MAKING IN THE CFSP

Decision-making. All acts that the Union wishes to adopt under the common foreign and security policy (CFSP; see Ch. 2 of Title V of the TEU) emanate from

18–002

---

[1] See Art. 24(1), second subpara., TEU.

[2] See also the fact that the Court of Justice has only limited jurisdiction with respect to the CFSP (Art. 275 TFEU, see para. 13–086, *supra*).

the European Council and the Council.[3] The European Council is responsible for identifying the strategic interests and objectives of the Union for the CFSP and defines the general guidelines for the CFSP (Art. 26(1) TEU). The Council defines and frames the CFSP on the basis of general guidelines and strategic lines defined by the European Council (Art. 26(2), first subpara., TEU). The Council and the High Representative of the Union for Foreign Affairs and Security Policy ensure the unity, consistency and effectiveness of action by the Union (Art. 26(2), second subpara., TEU).

In principle, the European Council and the Council have to act unanimously (Art. 31(1), first subpara., TEU). Like in other fields, abstention does not prevent unanimity from being attained. An abstaining member of the Council may qualify the abstention by making a formal declaration under the second subpara. of Art. 31(1) TEU. If it makes such a declaration, the Member State is not obliged to apply the decision in question, but must accept that it binds the Union. This is termed "constructive abstention". Article 31(1) TEU provides that, in a spirit of mutual solidarity, the Member State concerned is to refrain from any action likely to conflict with or impede Union action based on the decision in question, and that the other Member States are to respect its position. It is only if the members of the Council qualifying their abstention in this way represent at least one-third of the Member States comprising at least one-third of the population of the Union, that the decision will not be adopted.[4]

By way of derogation, the Council decides by a qualified majority when adopting a decision defining a Union action or position on the basis of a decision of the European Council relating to the Union's strategic interests and objectives[5] or on a proposal of the High Representative following a specific request from the European Council and when adopting decisions implementing such decisions. It also acts by a qualified majority when appointing a special representative[6] (Art. 31(2), first subpara., TEU). Consequently, the possibility to decide by qualified majority is limited to the technical implementation of measures agreed on by all

---

[3] For a description of decision-making in this area, see Pernice and Thym, "A New Institutional Balance for European Foreign Policy?" (2003) E.For.Aff.Rev. 369, at 374–380; Müller-Brandeck-Bocquet, "The New CFSP and ESDP Decision-Making System of the European Union" (2002) E.For.Aff.Rev. 257–282. For a discussion of the procedure and practice, see Keukeleire and MacNaughtan, *The foreign policy of the European Union* (Basingstoke, Palgrave Macmillan, 2008), Ch.6.

[4] Before the Lisbon Treaty, Art. 23(1), first subpara., EU required in this connection that the members of the Council qualifying their abstention represented more than one-third of the votes, weighted in accordance with Art. 205(2) of the EC Treaty.

[5] Article 23(1) EU stated in this connection that the Council was to act by qualified majority "when adopting joint actions, common positions or taking any other decision on the basis of a common strategy". See, e.g., Council Joint Action 1999/878/CFSP of December 17, 1999 establishing a European Union Cooperation Programme for Non-proliferation and Disarmament in the Russian Federation, [1999] L331/11, adopted pursuant to Common Strategy 1999/414/CFSP of the European Union of June 4, 1999 on Russia, [1999] O.J. L157/1, and on the basis of Arts 14 and 23(2) EU.

[6] See Art. 33 TEU.

Member States. The qualified majority will be calculated in the same way as in other fields (see paras 13–052 *et seq.*). However, the introduction of qualified majority voting in the CFSP (by the Amsterdam Treaty) proved impossible unless combined with a special "alarm bell procedure". If a member of the Council declares that, for vital and stated reasons of national policy, it intends to oppose the adoption of a decision to be taken by a qualified majority, no vote is taken and the Council, acting by a qualified majority, may request that the matter be referred to the European Council for decision by unanimity (Art. 31(2), second subpara., TEU). The European Council may unanimously decide that the Council is to act by a qualified majority in other cases (Art. 31(3) TEU). However, no decision having military or defence implications may be taken by a qualified majority (Art. 31(4) TEU).

The Council takes decisions relating to procedural questions by a simple majority vote (Art. 31(5) TEU).

Initiative and preparatory tasks. Any Member State and the High Representative, possibly with the Commission's support,[7] may submit an initiative or proposal to deal with a particular question (Art. 30(1) TEU). Whereas in other areas of external policy the powers of initiative, implementation and representation are vested in the Commission, acting as a College, the Commission's role in CFSP matters is confined to supporting proposals submitted by the High Representative, who is a member of the College. Accordingly, the Commission itself does not have the (exclusive) right of initiative it has in other fields of Union policy or the prerogatives associated with that right: it cannot influence the manner in which decisions are taken in the Council by amending or withdrawing its proposal.[8] In areas concerning both the CFSP and other fields of external action the Commission and the High Representative may submit joint proposals (Art. 22(2) TEU).[9]

The Political and Security Committee (PSC) advises the Council and is the privileged interlocutor of the High Representative.[10] The Political and Security Committee meets at the place where the Council has its seat, one week before the Council meets or, if the Council so requests, together with the Council. The PSC's

18–003

---

[7] Before the Lisbon Treaty, the Commission itself could submit proposals in the field of the CFSP (Art. 22(1) EU).

[8] The Commission may take the view, however, that a question falls within another field of competence of the Union and submit a proposal based on the corresponding Treaty article (e.g. for a measure under the common commercial policy or under Union development cooperation policy). In such a case Art. 4(3) TEU may well restrict a Member State's options to adopt an initiative at the same time under the CFSP: see to that effect, with respect to the situation pre-Lisbon, Heukels and De Zwaan, "The Configuration of the European Union: Community Dimensions of Institutional Interaction", in Curtin and Heukels (eds), *Institutional Dynamics of European Integration. Essays in Honour of Henry G. Schermers*, Vol. II (Dordrecht, Martinus Nijhoff, 1994), 195, at 217.

[9] See, e.g., the joint proposal for Council Regulation (EU) No. 1286/2009 of December 22, 2009 amending Regulation (EC) No. 881/2002 imposing certain specific restrictive measures directed against certain persons and entities associated with Usama bin Laden, the Al-Qaida network and the Taliban, [2009] O.J. L 346/42.

[10] Article 38, first para., TEU.

position also appears on the agenda for Coreper meetings.[11] The Council has accelerated means of decision-making at its disposal. Thus the PSC monitors the international situation on a permanent basis in areas covered by the CFSP (Art. 38, first para., TEU). In military matters the activities of the Council and the PSC are prepared by a Military Committee (EUMC) on which the Chiefs of Defence sit. The EUMC is assisted by the Military Staff (EUMS), which is part of the General Secretariat of the Council.[12] The Military Staff performs early warning, situation assessment and strategic planning tasks.[13] In addition, the High Representative is entitled to convene a meeting of the Council at very short notice of its own motion or at the request of a Member State (Art. 30(2) TEU).[14]

18–004 **Involvement of European Parliament.** The Council is entitled to act without seeking the opinion of the European Parliament, although the High Representative, as President of the Foreign Affairs Council, must regularly consult the Parliament on the main aspects and the basic choices of the CFSP and the common security and defence policy and keep the Parliament informed of how those policies evolve (see Art. 36, first para., TEU).[15] He or she must ensure that the Parliament's views are "duly taken into consideration". Agreements have been reached between the European Parliament and the Council on the way in which the Parliament is given access to sensitive information in the field of security and defence policy.[16]

---

[11] See the annex to Council Decision 2001/78/CFSP of January 22, 2001 setting up the Political and Security Committee, [2001] O.J. L27/1.
[12] See the manner of operation and organisation set out in annexes to Council Decision 2001/79/CFSP of January 22, 2001 setting up the Military Committee of the European Union, [2001] O.J. L27/4 and to Council Decision 2001/80/CFSP of January 22, 2001 on the establishment of the Military Staff of the European Union, [2001] O.J. L27/7. The Military Staff consists of seconded military personnel headed by a three-star flag officer. The Military Committee is chaired by a four-star flag officer on appointment. See also Council Decision 2001/496/CFSP of June 25, 2001 on the rules applicable to national military staff on secondment to the General Secretariat of the Council in order to form the European Union Military Staff, [2001] O.J. L181/1.
[13] See the annex to Council Decision 2001/80/CFSP of January 22, 2001 on the establishment of the Military Staff of the European Union, [2001] O.J. L27/7.
[14] The simplified written procedure (COREU) may be used in implementing the CFSP (Council Rules of Procedure, Art. 12(2)(d); para. 13–055, *supra*).
[15] Before the Lisbon Treaty, this was a task for the Member State holding the Presidency of the Council (Art. 21 EU). According to the Interinstitutional Agreement of May 17, 2006 between the European Parliament, the Council and the Commission on budgetary discipline and sound financial management, [2006] O.J. C139/1, the Presidency is to consult the European Parliament on a yearly basis on a document established by the Council on the main aspects and basic choices of the CFSP, including the financial implications for the [Union's] budget (point 43).
[16] Interinstitutional Agreement of November 20, 2002 between the European Parliament and the Council concerning access by the European Parliament to sensitive information of the Council in the field of security and defence policy, [2002] O.J. C298/1, together with the Decision of the European Parliament of October 23, 2002 on the implementation of that agreement, [2002] O.J. C298/4, appended as Annex VIII (B and C respectively) to the EP Rules of Procedure.

For its part, the Parliament may make recommendations to the Council and the High Representative (Art. 36, second para., TEU). The parliamentary committee responsible for the CFSP prepares any recommendations and may be authorised by the President of the Parliament to draw them up using an urgency procedure (EP Rules of Procedure, Rule 97(1) and (2)). The European Parliament may adopt such recommendations relatively quickly, since in urgent cases they do not have to be translated into all the official languages for the committee stage and are deemed to have been adopted at the next plenary session if no objection is made by at least 40 of the Parliament's component Members (EP Rules of Procedure, Rule 97(3) and (4)).

II. IMPLEMENTATION OF THE CFSP

Implementation by Council and Member States. The implementation of CFSP decisions lies principally in the hands of the Member States and the Council, with the High Representative being responsible for securing their implementation (see Art. 26(3) TEU). Until the creation of the European External Action Service, it was often the Commission which provided administrative, financial and legal assistance.[17] In third countries and international conferences, the diplomatic and consular missions of the Member States and the Union delegations are to cooperate in ensuring that the policy adopted by the Council is implemented (Art. 35 TEU).

18–005

Where the international situation requires operational action by the Union, the Council adopts the necessary decisions.[18] The Council determines the way in which such decisions are to be implemented (Art. 28(1) TEU).[19] In so far as the Council does not do this, implementation of the CFSP is left to the Member States, which are to support the CFSP "actively and unreservedly in a spirit of loyalty and mutual solidarity", to "comply with the Union's action in this area" and to

> "refrain from any action which is contrary to the interests of the Union or is likely to impair its effectiveness as a cohesive force in international relations" (Art. 24(3) TEU).

In order to enable prior consultations to take place within the Council, a Member State has to provide prompt information of any plan to adopt a position or to take action pursuant to a Council decision adopted under Art. 28(1) TEU, except in the

---

[17] For the practical aspects of implementation, see Keukeleire, *Het buitenlands beleid van de Europese Unie* (Deventer, Kluwer, 1998), at 302–315. For example, the policy for the restructuring of Kosovo was carried out by the Commission in collaboration with the European Agency for Reconstruction (see para. 13–123).

[18] Before the Lisbon Treaty, such decisions took the form of "joint actions" (see Art. 14(1) EU).

[19] Accordingly, whenever it deems it necessary, the Council may, on a proposal from the High representative, appoint a special representative with a mandate in relation to particular policy issues (Art. 33 TEU).

case of measures constituting merely a national transposition of Council deci-sions. Only in cases of "imperative need arising from changes in the situation" and where the Council does not itself review its previous position may a Member State take the necessary measures as a matter of urgency in the absence of a Council decision and inform the Council immediately afterwards (Art. 28(3) and (4) TEU). If a Member State has major difficulties in implementing a Council decision adopted under Art. 28(1) TEU, it must refer them to the Council. The Council is then to seek appropriate solutions consistent with the objectives of the joint action which do not impair its effectiveness (Art. 28(3) TEU).

When the Council has adopted a decision which defines the approach of the Union to a particular matter of a geographical or thematic nature,[20] implementa-tion falls to the Member States, which are to ensure that their national policies conform to the Union positions (Art. 29 TEU). They are to uphold the Union's positions in international organisations and at international conferences (Art. 34(1) TEU).[21]

18–006 **Supervision of implementation.** The European Parliament, the Commission and the Court of Justice play a more limited role in the CFSP than in other fields of Union policy.[22] The European Parliament may call the Council to account but may not impose sanctions upon it for the conduct of its policy in view of its limited supervisory powers over that institution. However, under the budget-ary procedure, the Parliament is entitled to refuse to charge certain administra-tive or operational expenditure to the general budget.[23] In an Interinstitutional Agreement of July 16, 1997, the Council and the Commission came to an understanding with the European Parliament on the financing of the CFSP, which was taken over in the Interinstitutional Agreement of May 17, 2006.[24] Each time it adopts a decision in the field of the CFSP entailing expenses, the Council will immediately communicate an estimate of the costs envisaged (*fiche financière*) to the European Parliament.[25] The Commission, for its part, does not have the power to supervise that national implementing measures comply with the obligations imposed on Member States in the field of the CFSP.[26] Since

---

[20] Before the Lisbon Treaty, such decisions took the form of "common positions" (see Art. 15 EU).

[21] For the international representation of the Union, see para. 24–009 *et seq.*, *infra*.

[22] See the statement in Art. 24(1), second subpara., TEU.

[23] See para. 13–130, *supra*.

[24] See n. 15, *supra*. See previously: the Interinstitutional Agreement of July 16, 1997 (1997) EU Bull. point 2.3.1, and the Interinstitutional Agreement of May 6, 1999, [1999] O.J. C172/1.

[25] *Ibid.*, points 42 and 43. The *fiche financière* is to relate, inter alia, to the time-frame, staff employed, use of premises and other infrastructure, transport facilities, training requirements and security arrangements (*ibid.*).

[26] Since the Court of Justice does not in principle have jurisdiction with respect to the CFSP (Art. 275 TFEU), Art. 258 TFEU [*ex Art. 226 EC*] does not apply to the provisions on the CFSP. Because the Commission has no determinative influence on the CFSP, the European Parliament cannot pass a motion of censure under Art. 234 TFEU [*ex Art. 201 EC*] in respect of its role in this policy.

the Court of Justice has only limited jurisdiction with respect to the provisions of the CFSP, it cannot review most acts of the Council or the Member States which are based thereon.[27] As a result, parliamentary or judicial supervision of national measures implementing the CFSP takes place primarily in the Member States. At Union level, supervision of the implementation of the CFSP consists chiefly of political supervision by the Council and the High Representative, which have a duty to ensure that the policy is properly implemented by the Member States (Art. 24(3), third subpara., TEU). That supervision may also be carried out within the Political and Security Committee (Art. 38, first para., *in fine*, TEU).

Military operations. As far as security and defence policy is concerned, the Union relies on the operational capacity of Member States to deploy military forces capable of the tasks referred to in Art. 43 TEU (Art. 42(3) TEU; see para. 25–043). In order to formulate and implement Union decisions and measures with implications in the defence sphere, the Union uses the Political and Security Committee (PSC), assisted by the Military Committee and the Military Staff.[28] The PSC exercises political control and strategic direction of crisis management operations (Art. 38, second para., TEU). The operations themselves are carried out by units made available by the Member States. In this connection, the European Defence Agency assists the Council in evaluating the improvement of military capabilities (Art. 42(3), second subpara., TEU). The Council may confer on a group of Member States that are willing and capable to do so the implementation of a task in connection with the common security and defence policy (Art. 42(5) TEU). It is then for those Member States, in association with the High Representative, to agree among themselves on the management of the task (Art. 44(1) TEU). Where completion of that task entails major consequences or requires amendment of the decision determining the task, the Council is to adopt the necessary decisions (Art. 44(2) TEU).

18–007

Under the third para. of Art. 38 TEU, the Council may authorise the PSC, for the purpose and duration of a crisis management operation, to take the relevant decisions concerning the political control and strategic direction of the operation.[29] In this way, the PSC has, for example, directed military operations of the European Union in the Former Yugoslav Republic of Macedonia, in Congo and

---

[27] See para. 13–086.

[28] For their operation and organisation, see the annexes to Council Decisions 2001/79/CFSP and 2001/80/CFSP of January 22, 2001 (n. 12, *supra*).

[29] Österdahl, "The EU and its Member States, Other States and International Organisations—The Common European Security and Defence Policy after Nice" (2001) Nordic J.I.L. 341, at 346–348. What is involved therefore is a delegation authorised by the Treaty of discretionary powers; see also para. 17–024.

in Chad and the Central African Republic.[30] The same applies to police missions of the Union.[31]

The Union's security and defence policy takes account of existing forms of military cooperation and of specific positions of particular Member States (Art. 42(2), second subpara., TEU[32]). By virtue of a Protocol to the Treaties, Denmark does not participate in the elaboration and implementation of decisions and actions of the Union which have defence implications.[33] In that Protocol, however, Denmark has undertaken not to prevent the other Member States from further developing their cooperation in this area.

---

[30] See Art. 4 of Council Joint Action 2003/92/CFSP of January 27, 2003 on the European Union military operation in the Former Yugoslav Republic of Macedonia, [2003] O.J. L34/26, Arts 7 and 10 of Council Joint Action 2003/423/CFSP of June 5, 2003 on the European Union military operation in the Democratic Republic of Congo, [2003] O.J. L143/50 and Art. 6 of Council Joint Action 2007/677/CFSP of October 15, 2007 on the European Union military operation in the Republic of Chad and in the Central African Republic, [2007] O.J. L279/21. Examples of decisions taken by the PSC pursuant to those joint actions are to be found in [2003] O.J. L170/15 and L170/19 and [2008] O.J. L107/60. For a detailed overview, see Naert, *International law aspects of the EU's security and defence policy, with a particular focus on the law of armed conflict and human rights* (Antwerp, Intersentia, 2010), Ch. 3.

[31] For another example, see Art. 11(2) of Council Joint Action 2005/797/CFSP of November 14, 2005 on the European Union police mission in the Palestinian Territories, [2006] O.J. L331/21, and, for a decision taken pursuant to this joint action, [2006] O.J. L331/21.

[32] Article 42(2), second subpara., TEU refers, more in particular, to the obligations of certain Member States in connection with their membership of NATO. Article 17(4) EU referred, moreover to the Western European Union (WEU).

[33] Article 5 of Protocol (No. 22), annexed by the Lisbon Treaty to the TEU and TFEU, on the position of Denmark, [2010] O.J. C83/299. Denmark had already adopted this stance upon the introduction of the CFSP in 1993 (see para. 25–046, *infra*).

CHAPTER 19

DECISION-MAKING RESTRICTED TO PARTICULAR MEMBER STATES

Survey. In two policy areas, the Treaties formulate a system of decision-making **19–001** under which not all Member States take part in the adoption of acts,

(1) the area of freedom, security and justice (Title V of Part Three of the TFEU); and

(2) Economic and Monetary Union (Title VIII of Part Three of the TFEU).

On top of this, the system of enhanced cooperation affords an opportunity for Union acts to be adopted as between a number of Member States only. Whenever decision-making is limited to certain Member States, the Council has to adapt voting requirements accordingly. In principle, the other Union institutions and bodies take part in the decision-making with the same composition and manner of operation as in the case of decision-making involving all the Member States. The *rationale* is that Members of the Commission, the European Parliament and other bodies do not represent particular Member States. The Court of Justice, too, has the same composition when it adjudicates in disputes on the interpretation and application of acts adopted under these systems of decision-making.

I. AREA OF FREEDOM, SECURITY AND JUSTICE

Adjusted decision-making in the Council. When the Council adopts measures **19–002** under Title V of Part Three of the TFEU (area of freedom, security and justice), in principle the decision-making proceeds without the participation of Denmark, Ireland and the United Kingdom. These three Member States have been granted special status by Protocol (see paras 10–028—10–029). The provisions of Title V, measures adopted pursuant to that title, together with international agreements concluded by the Union under that title, and decisions of the Court of Justice interpreting such provisions or measures are not binding upon, or applicable in, those Member States.[1]

---

[1] Article 2 of Protocol (No. 21), annexed to the TEU and TFEU, on the position of the United Kingdom and Ireland in respect of the area of freedom, security and justice ([2010] O.J. C83/295) and Art. 2 of Protocol (No. 22), annexed to the TEU and TFEU, on the position of Denmark ([2010] O.J. C83/299).

Adjusted voting requirements apply in the case of acts adopted by the Council. Unanimous decisions are taken by all members of the Council with the exception of the representatives of the governments of the Member States concerned (Denmark, the United Kingdom and Ireland); a qualified majority is defined in accordance with Art. 238(3) TFEU (see paras 13–052 *et seq.*).[2] The composition and method of work of the other institutions and bodies remain unchanged. This also applies to measures adopted pursuant to Title V of Part Three of the TFEU which build upon the Schengen *acquis*.[3] It should be noted that Iceland, Norway and Switzerland are to be associated with the further development of the Schengen *acquis*.[4]

19–003 **Specific conditions of non-participation.** Denmark, Ireland and the United Kingdom remain outside Union policy pursuant to Title V of Part Three of the TFEU in somewhat different ways (see also paras 10–028 and 10–029).

In principle, Ireland and the United Kingdom do not take part in the adoption of acts by the Council under Title V.[5] Nevertheless, these Member States have the possibility to "opt-in" with respect to certain acts.[6] First, the Schengen Protocol allows Ireland and the United Kingdom at any time to request to accept some or all provisions of the Schengen *acquis*. The Council is to decide on this request by unanimity.[7] As regards measures that build upon the Schengen *acquis*, Ireland and the United Kingdom may also notify their wish to take part. The Court of Justice clarified that this right only exists for measures building on provisions of the Schengen *acquis* that the Member State concerned has already accepted.[8] If Ireland

---

[2] Article 1 of the Protocol on the position of the United Kingdom and Ireland in respect of the area of freedom, security and justice (preceding n.) and Art. 1 of the Protocol on the position of Denmark (preceding n.). However, until October 31, 2014, special arrangements apply for the definition of a qualified majority (see Protocol (No. 36), annexed to the TEU, TFEU and EAEC Treaty, on Transitional Provisions, [2010] O.J. C83/322 and para. 13–054).

[3] See Art. 5(1), first subpara., of Protocol (No. 19), annexed to the TEU and TFEU, integrating the Schengen *acquis* into the framework of the European Union, [2010] O.J. C83/290 ("Schengen-Protocol"). For the integration of the Schengen *acquis*, see para. 10–010, *supra*. In the event that Denmark should nevertheless participate in the adoption of measures building upon the Schengen *acquis* pursuant to Title IV, the measures concerned will not constitute "Union law" as far as Denmark is concerned, but will create an obligation under international law; see Art. 3 of the Schengen-Protocol and Art. 4 of the Protocol on the position of Denmark (n. 1, *supra*).

[4] Appropriate procedures were to be agreed with these countries in an agreement concluded by the Council by a unanimous vote (not counting the United Kingdom and Ireland): see para. 10–010, *supra*.

[5] See ECJ (judgment of October 26, 2010), Case C-482/06 *United Kingdom v Council*, not yet reported, paras 45–62.

[6] See Fletcher, "Schengen, the European Court of Justice and Flexibility Under the Lisbon Treaty: Balancing the United Kingdom's 'Ins' and 'Outs' " (2009) E.Const.L.Rev. 71–98; Dougan, "The Treaty of Lisbon 2007: Winning Minds, not Hearts" (2008) C.M.L.Rev. 617, at 684–687.

[7] Schengen-Protocol, Art. 4.

[8] ECJ, Case C-77/05 *United Kingdom v Council* [2007] E.C.R. I-11459, paras 62–68; ECJ, Case C-137/05 *United Kingdom v Council* [2007] E.C.R. I-11593, para. 50, with a case note by Rijpma, (2008) C.M.L.Rev. 835–852. The classification of an act as a proposal or initiative "build upon the Schengen *acquis*" is to rest on objective factors which are amenable to judicial review, in particular the aim and the content of the act: *ibid.*, paras 77 and 56, respectively.

or the United Kingdom does not express such wish, the other Member States are automatically authorised to apply among themselves the rules on "enhanced cooperation".[9] If Ireland or the United Kingdom does not wish to take part in the acts building on provisions of the Schengen *acquis*, it is to notify the Council, following which the decision-making process is suspended to allow the Council to decide under which conditions the Member State concerned can still be considered to take part in the relevant provisions of the Schengen *acquis*.[10] The Council will take that decision by qualified majority and within four months of having received a Commission proposal.[11] If the Council is not able to adopt a decision, the European Council may take such decision at its next meeting, at the request of any Member State, acting by a qualified majority on a proposal from the Commission.[12] If neither the Council nor the European Council has adopted any decision, the Council is to resume the procedure for adopting the measure building on the Schengen *acquis*. In that case, it is for the Commission to decide on the extent to which the Member State concerned can still be considered to be taking part in the relevant area of the Schengen *acquis*.[13]

Second, as regards other measures adopted pursuant to Title V of the Part Three of the TFEU, Ireland and the United Kingdom are entitled to take part if they notify the President of the Council in writing within three months after a proposal or an initiative has been presented to the Council that they wish to take part in the adoption and application of the proposed measure.[14] If, after a "reasonable" period has elapsed, such a measure cannot be adopted with the United Kingdom or Ireland taking part, the Council may adopt it without their participation.[15] As has already been mentioned, if Denmark, Ireland and/or the United Kingdom do not take part, the Council adopts its measures by an adjusted majority and the resultant measures are not applicable in the non-participating State(s). All the same, Ireland and the United Kingdom may at any time notify their intention to the Council and the Commission that they wish to accept such a measure; in such case the procedure provided for in the Treaties for Member States wishing to take part in an existing form of enhanced cooperation applies mutatis mutandis (Art. 331(1) TFEU; see para. 19–010).[16] These provisions also apply to measures proposed or adopted pursuant to Title V which amend an existing measure by which Ireland and the United Kingdom are bound. In such case, however, where

---

[9] Schengen-Protocol, Art. 5(1), second subpara.

[10] Dougan qualifies this as a "de facto 'expulsion' mechanism": Dougan (n. 5, *supra*), 684.

[11] *Ibid.*, Art. 5(3), which sets out that such a decision should seek to "retain the widest possible measure of participation of the Member States concerned without seriously affecting the practical operability of the various parts of the Schengen *acquis*, while respecting their coherence".

[12] *Ibid.*, Art. 5(4).

[13] *Ibid.*, Art. 5(5), which leaves it open for the Member State concerned to withdraw its notification that it does not wish to take part in the measure building on the Schengen *acquis*.

[14] Protocol on the position of the United Kingdom and Ireland in respect of the area of freedom, security and justice (n. 1, *supra*), Art. 3(1).

[15] *Ibid.*, Art. 3(2).

[16] *Ibid.*, Art. 4.

725

the Council, acting on a proposal from the Commission, determines that the non-participation of those Member States in the amended version of the existing measure makes the application of that measure "inoperable" for other Member States or the Union, it may urge them to take part in the adoption of the amending measure.[17] If within two months Ireland or the United Kingdom has not notified its intention to do so, the existing measure shall no longer be binding upon or applicable to it.[18] However, the Council may determine that Ireland or the United Kingdom, as the case may be, is to bear the direct financial consequences, if any, "necessarily and unavoidably incurred" as a result of the cessation of its participation in the existing measure.[19]

In principle, no such possibilities exist for Denmark to participate in the adoption of acts pursuant to Title V; it participates solely in the adoption of measures relating to the determination of third countries whose nationals require visas and to the uniform format for visas.[20] However, Denmark may decide to implement in national law a Council decision which builds upon the Schengen *acquis*[21] and it may conclude with the Union an international agreement regarding the application of specific measures as between Denmark and the other Member States (see para. 10–028). Moreover, Denmark has been given the option to participate more fully in the adoption and application of measures adopted under Title V. If Denmark notifies the other Member States of its wish to do so, the Schengen *acquis* will become binding on it as Union law, and it will get the possibility, under arrangements similar to the ones existing at present for the United Kingdom and Ireland, to take part in the adoption and application of a measure adopted under Title V or to accept an existing measure adopted under Title V.[22]

Denmark and Ireland may abandon the special status conferred on them by Protocol by simple notification.[23] No such possibility is provided for in the case of the United Kingdom.

II. ECONOMIC AND MONETARY UNION

19–004   **Adjusted decision-making.** As far as Economic and Monetary Union is concerned, the Union has a system of decision-making which is restricted to the Member States whose currency is the euro because they satisfied the conditions

---

[17] *Ibid.*, Art. 4a(2), first subpara.
[18] This is so unless that Member State notifies its intention to accept the measure before the entry into force of the existing measure: *ibid.*, Art. 4a(2), second subpara.
[19] *Ibid.*, Art. 4a(3).
[20] Protocol on the position of Denmark (n. 1, *supra*), Art. 6.
[21] Protocol on the position of Denmark (n. 1, *supra*), Art. 4.
[22] See Art. 8 of the Protocol on the position of Denmark (n. 1, *supra*) and the Annex to that Protocol.
[23] Article 7 of the Protocol on the position of Denmark (n. 1, *supra*) (the other Member States have to be informed) and Art. 8 of the Protocol on the position of the United Kingdom and Ireland in respect of the area of freedom, security and justice (n. 1, *supra*) (the Council has to be notified in writing).

laid down to that end (see para. 11–033). Under a Protocol to the Treaties, introduced by the EU Treaty at the time of the creation of the EMU, Denmark and the United Kingdom are in a special situation in that they are not under an obligation to take part in the third stage of EMU (see para. 11–042). The opt-out granted to Denmark means that it is regarded as a Member State with a derogation in the third stage.[24] The position of the United Kingdom is different from that of a Member State with a derogation but has the same implications for decision-making in the Council and the ECB.[25] The voting rights of Member States with a derogation are to be suspended in respect of Council acts based on provisions relating to EMU which do not apply to them (Art. 139(2) and (4) TFEU). The number of votes required to attain a qualified majority has been adjusted as a result.[26] A Protocol to the Treaties confirms that the ministers of the States participating in the euro area may meet informally amongst themselves to discuss questions related to their shared specific responsibilities for the single currency.[27] The Commission takes part in these meetings; the ECB may also be invited to take part. Meetings are chaired by a president, who is elected by the ministers of the States participating in the euro area for two and a half years, by a majority of those Member States.[28] Whenever matters of common interest are concerned, they are to be discussed by ministers of all Member States; however, decisions are to be taken by the Council in accordance with the procedures determined by the Treaties. A meeting of the ECOFIN Council comprising only representatives of Member States participating in the euro is known as the "Euro Group" or "Euro Council".[29]

In principle, Member States with a derogation do not take part in decision-making in the ECB. They are not involved in the appointment of members of the ECB's Executive Board, do not have a member on the board and do not have the

---

[24] Article 1 of Protocol (No. 16), annexed to the TEU and TFEU, on certain provisions relating to Denmark ([2010] O.J. C83/287).

[25] See Arts 6, 7 and 8 of Protocol (No. 15), annexed to the TEU and TFEU, on certain provisions relating to the United Kingdom of Great Britain and Northern Ireland (para. 11–042, *supra*).

[26] See Art. 238(3)(a) TFEU. For the transitional provisions on the calculation of the qualified majority vote until October 31, 2014, see para. 13–053.

[27] See Art. 1 of Protocol (No. 14), annexed to the TEU and TFEU, on the Euro Group ([2010] O.J. C83/283), which was added by the Lisbon Treaty. See, before the Lisbon Treaty, the resolution of the European Council of December 13, 1997 on economic policy coordination in stage 3 of EMU and on Treaty Arts 111 and 113, [1998] O.J. C35/1 (also published in (1997) 12 EU Bull. points I.9 and I.19).

[28] *Ibid.*, Art. 2.

[29] The first such meeting was held on June 5, 1998 and was chaired, not by the British Chancellor of the Exchequer (representing the Member State occupying the Presidency of the Council), but by the Austrian Finance Minister (representing the Member State which was to take over the Presidency on July 1, 1998), see *Europe*, No. 7235, June 5, 1998, 6. On October 12, 2008, the financial crisis prompted the Euro Group to meet for the first time at the level of Heads of State and Government, with the UK Prime Minister also attending. See Editorial Comments in (2009) C.M.L.Rev. 1383, at 1388.

Governor of their central bank sitting on the Governing Council.[30] Since the ECB carries out some tasks regarding the central banks of Member States with a derogation and is to deliver opinions concerning them,[31] those Member States are nevertheless involved in the decision-making in those respects. It is for this reason that the ECB has a General Council, consisting of the President and Vice-President of the ECB and the Governors of all the national central banks, to take the necessary decisions in this regard.[32] The composition and operation of the other institutions and bodies, including the Economic and Financial Committee, will remain unchanged regardless as to whether the decisions to be taken affect all the Member States or only those without a derogation.

III. ENHANCED COOPERATION BETWEEN MEMBER STATES

19-005   **Differentiated integration.** Cooperation between Member States in the area of freedom, security and justice and within the framework of the EMU are forms of differentiated integration, in that not all Member States are involved and Member States accede when they deem it appropriate to do so. Such differentiated integration could also be found in intergovernmental forms of cooperation. Examples were the European Monetary System (see para. 2–007) and the Schengen Convention (see para. 2–011) which acted as precursors to the relevant Community policies between the participating Member States.[33] As far as the CFSP is concerned, there exists a similar form of enhanced cooperation between some of the Member States where a Member State formally abstains from voting and hence does not have to apply the decision concerned, even though it accepts that it commits the Union (Art. 31(1), second subpara., TEU; see para. 18–002).

The Treaty of Amsterdam created a general framework for enhanced (formerly "closer") cooperation between Member States, which is now enshrined in Title IV of the TEU (Art. 20 TEU) and Title III of Part Six of the TFEU (Arts 326 to 334 TFEU).[34] These mechanisms enable Member States to cooperate more closely,

---

[30] Article 283 TFEU in conjunction with Art. 139(2) TFEU; ESCB Statute, Arts 10.1 and 11.2 in conjunction with Art. 42.

[31] For instance, the authorities of a Member State with a derogation are obliged under Art. 127(4) TFEU to consult the ECB on any proposed act in the latter's fields of competence.

[32] ESCB Statute, Arts 44–46.

[33] See also Benelux cooperation, para. 1–018, *supra*.

[34] Chaltiel, "Le traité d'Amsterdam et la coopération renforcée" (1998) R.M.C.U.E. 289–293; Ehlermann, "Differentiation, Flexibility, Closer Co-operation: The New Provisions of the Amsterdam Treaty" (1998) E.L.J. 246–270 and "Engere Zusammenarbeit nach dem Amsterdamer Vertrag: Ein neues Verfassungsprinzip?" (1998) EuR. 362–397; Gaja, "How Flexible is Flexibility under the Amsterdam Treaty?" (1998) C.M.L.Rev. 855–870; Kortenberg, "Closer Cooperation in the Treaty of Amsterdam" (1998) C.M.L.Rev. 833–854; Constantinesco, "Le traité d'Amsterdam. Les clauses de 'coopération renforcée'. Le protocole sur l'application des principes de subsidiarité et de proportionalité" (1997) R.T.D.E. 751–767. See also Tuytschaever, "Nauwere samenwerking volgens het Verdrag

under certain conditions, within the framework of the Union's non-exclusive competences, while making use of its institutions, and exercise those competences by applying the relevant provisions of the Treaties (see para. 19–009). Enhanced cooperation is not possible in areas of exclusive Union competence. Acts adopted in the framework of enhanced cooperation are binding only on those Member States which participate in such cooperation. They do not form part of the *acquis* which has to be accepted by candidate States for accession to the Union (Art. 20(4) TEU).

Initially, enhanced cooperation among Member States was made possible for Community matters and for PJCC only. Since the Treaty of Nice, enhanced cooperation among Member States had also been available for the CFSP, albeit subject to additional conditions.[35] However, no recourse was made to the possibility of enhanced cooperation. The Lisbon Treaty made the applicable conditions the same for all policy areas of the Union, although the procedure remains slightly different for enhanced cooperation relating to CFSP matters. In addition, the Lisbon Treaty created a framework for establishing "permanent structured cooperation" among Member States in the field of the Common Security and Defence Policy (see para. 25–045).

Substantive requirements. Member States proposing to embark on enhanced cooperation may do so only if the cooperation satisfies the requirements laid down in Arts 326 and 327 TFEU. From a substantive viewpoint, the cooperation must be aimed at furthering the objectives of the Union, at protecting its interests and at reinforcing its integration process (Art. 20(1), second subpara., TEU) and must comply with the Treaties and Union law (Art. 326, first para., TFEU). In addition, it must not undermine the internal market or economic, social and territorial cohesion, must not constitute a barrier to or discrimination in trade between Member States, and must not distort competition between them (Art. 326, second para., TFEU). At the same time, it must respect the competences, rights and obligations of those Member States which do not participate in it. Those Member States, in turn, must not impede its implementation by the participating Member States (Art. 327 TFEU).[36]   **19–006**

Formal requirements. Enhanced cooperation must concern at least nine Member States[37] and must be authorised by the Council (see para. 19–008). The   **19–007**

---

van Nice" (2001) S.E.W. 375–387; Bribosia, "Différenciation et avant-gardes au sein de l'Union européenne" (2000) C.D.E 57–115.

[35] See Arts 27a to 27e EU.

[36] Before the Lisbon Treaty, specific additional substantive requirements applied for enhanced cooperation in the field of the CFSP (see Arts 27a and 27b EU). In the case of PJCC-related enhanced cooperation, Art. 40(1) EU required that the proposed cooperation respect the powers of the Community and the objectives of PJCC and that it had the aim of enabling the Union to develop more rapidly into an area of freedom, security and justice.

[37] Before the Lisbon Treaty, eight Member States were sufficient in this connection (see Art. 43(g) EU).

Council is to give its authorisation as a last resort only, when it has established that the objectives of such cooperation cannot be attained within a reasonable period by the Union as a whole (Art. 20(2) TFEU). When enhanced cooperation is being established, it shall be open to all Member States, subject to compliance with any conditions of participation laid down by the authorising decision and, where applicable, with the acts already adopted within that framework (Art. 20(1), second para., TEU and Art. 328(1), first subpara., TFEU). The Commission and the Member States participating in enhanced cooperation are to ensure that they promote participation by as many Member States as possible (Art. 328(1), second subpara., TFEU).

19–008   **Authorisation.** Member States intending to establish enhanced cooperation in all fields outside the CFSP are to address a request to the Commission, specifying the scope and objectives of the enhanced cooperation proposed. The Commission may then submit a proposal to the Council (Art. 329(1), first subpara., TFEU).[38] If the Commission submits a proposal, the Council takes its decision by a qualified majority, after obtaining the consent of the European Parliament (Art. 329(1), first subpara., TFEU).[39] In July 2010, the Council approved for the first time, after the European Parliament had given its consent,[40] a Commission proposal authorising enhanced cooperation with respect to the law applicable to divorce and legal separation.[41] It is now for the Council to reach agreement on proposed regulation amongst the participating Member States on the basis of the relevant Treaty provision, which is Art. 81(3) TFEU.[42]

---

[38] If the Commission does not submit a proposal, it is to inform the Member States concerned of the reasons for not doing so.

[39] Before the Lisbon Treaty Art. 11(2) EC merely required the European Parliament to be consulted, except in areas covered by the co-decision procedure. Article 11(2) EC further stipulated that a member of the Council could request that the matter be referred to the European Council. That possibility was abrogated by the Lisbon Treaty.

[40] The Parliament gave its consent by legislative resolution of June 16, 2010.

[41] Council Decision 2010/405/EU of July 12, 2010 authorising enhanced cooperation in the area of the law applicable to divorce and legal separation, [2010] O.J. L189/12. On March 24, 2010, the Commission submitted a proposal for a Council regulation authorising enhanced cooperation in the area of the law applicable to divorce and legal separation (COM(2010)104 final), at the request of 14 Member States and after the Council had established in June 2008 that the objectives of the regulation proposed by the Commission in July 2006 could not be attained within a reasonable period by the Union as a whole.

[42] See the Commission proposal of March 24, 2010 for a Council regulation (EU) implementing enhanced cooperation in the area of the law applicable to divorce and legal separation, COM(2010) 105 final. Article 81(3) TFEU requires the Council to act unanimously (amongst the participating Member States), after consulting the European Parliament. Pursuant to the protocol on the position of Denmark (n. 1, *supra*), that Member State does not participate in the adoption of the proposed Regulation. By virtue of the Protocol on the position of the United Kingdom and Ireland in respect of the area of freedom, security and justice (n. 1, *supra*), the same applies to the United Kingdom and Ireland, which may however express their wish to participate.

The procedure is somewhat different for enhanced cooperation relating to CFSP matters.[43] Under Art. 329(2) TFEU the Member States make their request directly to the Council. The Council takes its decision acting unanimously after obtaining the opinion of the High Representative and the Commission, in particular on whether the enhanced cooperation proposed is consistent with the CFSP and with other Union policies, respectively.[44] The European Parliament is not consulted; the request is merely forwarded to it for information (Art. 329(2) TFEU).

A few Treaty articles on PJCC provide for a system of automatic authorisation. This is the case, first of all, in Ireland or the United Kingdom notifies its wish not to take part in measures that build upon the Schengen *acquis* (see para. 19–003). Second, the Treaties provide for automatic authorisation of enhanced cooperation within the framework of the "alarm bell" procedure provided for in Arts 82(3) and 83(3) TFEU on the harmonisation of procedural or substantive aspects of national criminal law. This procedure enables any Member State which considers that a draft directive would affect fundamental aspects of its criminal justice system, to request that the draft directive be referred to the European Council. If the European Council does not reach a consensus within the time-frame specified and if at least nine Member States wish to establish enhanced cooperation on the basis of the draft directive concerned, they have to notify the European Parliament, the Council and the Commission. In such a case, the authorisation to proceed with enhanced cooperation will be deemed to be granted.[45] The 2007 Intergovernmental Conference widened the scope of application of this automatic authorisation for enhanced cooperation so as to include certain areas in which the Council is to decide by unanimous vote, namely the establishment of a European Public Prosecutor's Office and operational cooperation between national law enforcement authorities (Arts 86(1) and 87(3) TFEU). If in these areas a unanimous vote cannot be achieved in the Council, a group of at least nine Member States may request that the voting procedure be suspended and that the draft measures be referred to the European Council. In case of disagreement within the European Council, and if at least nine Member States wish to establish enhanced cooperation, the authorisation to proceed with enhanced cooperation will be deemed to be granted.

Adjusted decision-making. The provisions on enhanced cooperation allow Member States to make use of the Union's institutions and exercise its competences by applying the relevant provisions of the Treaties (Art. 20(1), first subpara., TEU).   **19–009**

---

[43] Before the Lisbon Treaty, special procedural arrangements also applied to enhanced cooperation relating to PJCC matters (see Art. 40(a) EU).

[44] In this connection too, Art. 27c EU, provided for the possibility to have the matter referred to the European Council, which would then have to decide by unanimity. That possibility was abrogated by the Lisbon Treaty.

[45] Article 82(3), second subpara., and 83(3), second subpara., TFEU, which refer to Art. 20(2) TEU and 329(1) TFEU.

This means that the procedure to be followed is that prescribed in the Treaty provision constituting the legal basis. Although all members of the Council may take part in the relevant deliberations, only those representing participating Member States may take part in the vote (Art. 20(3) TEU and Art. 330, first para., TFEU). Where unanimity is required, this refers to the votes of the representatives of the participating Member States only. In the case of acts requiring to be adopted by a qualified majority, the number of votes required to adopt a decision is calculated in accordance with Art. 238(3) TFEU (Art. 330, second and third paras, TFEU).[46]

The Council may decide that in cases where a Treaty provision which may be applied in the context of enhanced cooperation provides for the Council to act unanimously, decisions will be taken by qualified majority. To adopt that decision, the Council is to act with the unanimous vote of all participating Member States (Art. 333(1) TFEU). Using the same procedure and after consulting the European Parliament, the Council may decide that where a Treaty article requires decisions to be adopted under a special legislative procedure, decisions will be taken under the ordinary legislative procedure (Art. 333(2) TFEU; see para. 5–009). However, none of these possibilities exist for decisions having military or defence implications (Art. 333(3) TFEU). It should be noted that Art. 333 TFEU makes it possible for a smaller group of Member States to strengthen the integration process not only by developing the substantive content of Union policy in a particular area, but also by streamlining the decision-making process towards standard Union decision-making concerning legislative acts. An example could be harmonisation or coordination of national legislation in the field of direct taxation between nine or more Member States participating in the euro.

19–010 **Participation in existing enhanced cooperation.** Any Member State wishing to become a party to an existing form of enhanced cooperation outside the CFSP is to notify its intention to the Council and the Commission (Art. 331(1), first subpara., TFEU). The Commission then decides, within four months of the date of notification, on the participation of the Member State concerned. If it considers that the conditions of participation have been fulfilled, it may adopt any transitional measures necessary with regard to the application of the acts already adopted within the framework of enhanced cooperation (Art. 331(1), second subpara., TFEU). Where the Commission considers that the conditions of participation have not been fulfilled, it is to indicate the necessary arrangements to be adopted by a specified deadline. On the expiry of that deadline, it shall re-examine the request. If the Commission still issues a negative opinion, the Member State concerned may refer the matter to the Council, which is to decide on the request, taking into account the votes of the participating Member States only, and may adopt the necessary transitional measures on a proposal from the Commission (Art. 331(1), third subpara., TFEU).

---

[46] See paras 13–050 *et seq.*, *supra.*

Where a Member State wishes to become party to an existing form of enhanced CFSP cooperation, it must notify its intention to the Council, the High Representative and the Commission (Art. 331(2), first subpara., TFEU). The Council (namely the Member States taking part in the enhanced cooperation) decides on such request after consulting the High Representative. It may, on a proposal from the High Representative, also adopt any transitional measures necessary with regard to the application of the acts already adopted within the framework of enhanced cooperation. Where the Council considers that the conditions of participation have not been fulfilled, it shall indicate the necessary arrangements to be adopted and set a deadline for re-examining the request for participation (Art. 331(2), first subpara., TFEU).

Judicial review. Enhanced cooperation is fully subject to the jurisdiction of the **19–011** Court of Justice. This means that the Court of Justice may exercise supervision as regards the Council authorisation to engage in enhanced cooperation and as regards decisions to allow a Member State to participate in enhanced cooperation after it has been established. The Court of Justice further has jurisdiction over the implementation of enhanced cooperation, which means that it may review the relevant acts adopted in the framework of enhanced cooperation.

This is different only for enhanced cooperation in the field of the CFSP, given the limited jurisdiction of the Court in that field.[47] The Court has jurisdiction, however, under Art. 40 TEU, to see to it that the implementation of CFSP enhanced cooperation does not affect Union powers in other fields and vice versa (see para. 10–086).

---

[47] Before the Lisbon Treaty, the Court's jurisdiction was also limited as regards enhanced cooperation relating to PJCC matters (see Arts 40 and 46 EU). See Donner, "De derde pijler en de Amsterdamse doolhof" (1997) S.E.W. 370.

CHAPTER 20

LEGITIMACY OF DECISION-MAKING

I. EFFICIENCY OF DECISION-MAKING

Conflicting elements. Substantial numbers of national and Union civil servants   **20–001**
work to achieve the aims of the Union smoothly and efficiently. To this end,
decisions must be able to be taken quickly. In addition, they must be applied and, if
necessary, enforced, which requires the decision-making to be sufficiently
discussed beforehand with all stakeholders. These two aspects are essential for efficient decision-making. However, in the design of the decision-making procedure
they may sometimes be in conflict with each other.[1]

Impediments to swift decision-making. The establishment of a single institu-   **20–002**
tional framework for all policy areas of the Union is designed to enable the whole
range of decisions to be adopted smoothly.[2] The extension of majority voting in
the Council has the same end in mind.

On the other hand, there is concern that the Union's acts should be accepted by
the Member States and their citizens. This is the only means of ensuring effective
application and enforcement. As a result, the Commission often engages in dialogue with affected interest groups before drawing up a proposal for an act (see
para. 16–018). In matters which the Member States recognise as being politically
sensitive, in particular the CFSP, all must consent—that is, not cast their votes
against (Art. 235(1), third subpara., TFEU and Art. 238(4) TFEU)—in order to
reach a decision. Where the EU Treaty nevertheless allows a vote to be taken by
a qualified majority for the CFSP, the Council, acting by that majority, may
request that the matter be referred to the European Council—which decides by
unanimity—if a Member State opposes the adoption of the measure in question
"for vital and stated reasons of national policy".[3] Further constraints flow from

---

[1] See the discussions of efficiency in, for instance, Piris, "After Maastricht, are the Community
Institutions More Efficacious, More Democratic and More Transparent?" (1994) E.L.Rev. 449, at
454–455; Snyder, "The Effectiveness of European Community Law: Institutions, Processes, Tools
and Techniques" (1993) M.L.R. 19–54.
[2] See the preamble to the TEU, in which the Contracting Parties declare their wish "to enhance
further the democratic and efficient functioning of the institutions so as to enable them better to
carry out, within a single institutional framework, the tasks entrusted to them".
[3] See Art. 31(2) TEU.

the decentralised implementation of many acts. It is often possible to implement them in practice only if national civil servants have had an input in drawing them up so as to take account of specific situations in the Member States. In many instances, the implementation of the principle of subsidiarity has a constraining effect on legislating at Union level in so far as it may leave certain aspects of the matter concerned to regulation by the Member States or the sectors concerned, which, overall, makes the law-making picture more complex. Lastly, involvement of representatives of the people makes it easier to gain acceptance for decisions: it is partly for this reason that decision-making should be legitimised by the contribution of the European Parliament or the national parliaments, even if this does diminish the Council's leeway to muster a sufficient majority by negotiation in order to get decisions adopted (see para. 20–004 *et seq.*)

20–003 **Impediments flowing from federal principles.** The accession of new Member States has likewise posed an increasing challenge to the efficiency of decision-making. Not only where a unanimous vote is required, but also in discussions leading up to a majority vote, the number of interlocutors is likely to make it more difficult to reach compromises.[4] In enlarging and adjusting the institutions and their bureaucratic machinery, considerations of efficiency often have to give way to federal principles such as the protected minimum representation of small Member States (see para. 20–008) and the principle of equality of the various official languages (see para. 13–161 *et seq.*).

II. DEMOCRATIC CONTENT OF DECISION-MAKING

A. SUBSTANCE OF DEMOCRATIC LEGITIMACY

20–004 **Expressions of democracy.** Democracy is one of the values upon which the Union is founded (Art. 2 TEU).[5] The basic premise of democracy is that all public authority emanates from the people. The European Parliament has interpreted this premise as follows: "Every public authority must be directly elected or answerable to a directly elected parliament".[6] The principle that the people should take part in, or supervise, decision-making underpins the public authority in every Member State and, in order for a country to be a member of the European

---

[4] See Fastenrath, "Die Struktur der erweiterten Europäischen Union", and Lautenschlager, "Die Struktur der erweiterten Europäischen Union" (1994) EuR. Beiheft 1, 101–126 and 127–146, respectively (and see the discussion in 147–150, *ibid.*); Ungerer, "Institutional Consequences of Broadening and Deepening the Community: the Consequences for the Decision-Making Process" (1993) C.M.L.Rev. 71–83.

[5] See ECJ (judgment of March 9, 2010), Case C-518/07 *Commission v Germany*, not yet reported, para. 41.

[6] Article 17(2) of the Declaration of Fundamental Rights and Freedoms, adopted by the European Parliament on April 12, 1989, [1989] O.J. C120/51.

Union, it therefore must be a parliamentary democracy.[7] Under Art. 7 TEU, certain of a Member State's rights may be suspended in the event of its seriously and persistently breaching the value of democracy.[8]

The Lisbon Treaty introduced a Title II in the TEU "Provisions on democratic principles".[9] The Title contains a provision on the equality of citizens of the Union (Art. 9 TEU; see para. 8–007) and a provision on the contribution of national parliaments to the good functioning of the Union (Art. 12 TEU; see para. 20–014). Besides, it contains provisions on two main forms of democracy, namely representative democracy and participatory democracy.

Representative democracy. The functioning of the Union is founded on representative democracy (Art. 10(1) TEU). In this connection, Art. 10(2) TEU states "Citizens are directly represented at Union level in the European Parliament" and

20–005

> "Member States are represented in the European Council by their Heads of State or Government and in the Council by their governments, themselves democratically accountable either to their national Parliaments, or to their citizens".

Accordingly, representation of citizens takes place, first and foremost, through the European Parliament. In this connection, Art. 10(4) TEU underlines the importance of European political parties (see also para. 13–024). The part played by the European Parliament in decision-making reflects at Union level the "fundamental democratic principle that the peoples should take part in the exercise of power through the intermediary of a representative assembly".[10] The importance

---

[7] Article 49 TEU refers to "[a]ny European State which respects the values referred to in Article 2"; for a precursor, see the declaration of the European Council meeting at Copenhagen on April 7 and 8, 1978 (1978) 3 EC Bull. 5 (cited among the substantive requirements for accession to the Union, para. 6–009, *supra*).

[8] See Verhoeven, "How Democratic need European Union Members be? Some Thoughts after Amsterdam" (1998) E.L.Rev. 217–234.

[9] See, generally, the contributions in Wouters, Verhey and Kiiver (eds), *European Constitutionalism beyond Lisbon* (Antwerp-Oxford-Portland, Intersentia, 2009); van Gerven, "Wanted: more democratic legitimacy for the European Union. Some Suppositions, Propositions, Tests and Observations in Light of the Fate of the European Constitution", at 147–183; Lenaerts and Cambien, "The Democratic Legitimacy of the EU after the Treaty of Lisbon", at 185–207; Harlow, "Transparency in the European Union: weighing the public and private interest", at 209–238; Verhey, "Fostering executive accountability in the EU: a key issue" at 239–258. See also Piris, *The Lisbon Treaty: A Legal and Political Analysis* (Cambridge, Cambridge University Press, 2010), Ch. 3 and Sieberson, "The Treaty of Lisbon and its impact on the European Union's democratic deficit" (2008) 14 Col.J.E.L. 445–465.

[10] ECJ, Case 138/79 *Roquette Frères v Council* [1980] E.C.R. 3333, para. 33, and ECJ, Case 139/79 *Maïzena v Council* [1980] E.C.R. 3393, para. 34. It would not be compatible with the principle of democracy if the conditions under which MEPs exercised their mandate were to be affected by the fact that they do not belong to a political group to an extent exceeding what is necessary for the attainment of the legitimate objectives pursued by the Parliament through its organisation in political groups: CFI,

attached to this by the Member States is reflected in the fact that all recent amendments to the Treaties have bolstered the role played by the European Parliament. Where the European Parliament does not take part in the adoption of an act, the people's participation in the exercise of power may be secured in another manner, in particular through the national parliaments to which the government representatives in the European Council and the Council are politically accountable.

20–006 **Participatory democracy.** In the EU Constitution it was stated that the democratic life of the Union relies, not only on the principle of "representative democracy" (in other words, the participation of the citizens through their representatives in the European Parliament and in the national parliaments), but also on the principle of "participatory democracy" (Arts I-46 and I-47).[11] The provision on the principle of "participatory democracy" was taken over by the Treaty of Lisbon, even though the Treaties no longer mention the principle explicitly.

In this connection, the Lisbon Treaty requires the Union institutions to give citizens and representative associations the opportunity to make known and exchange their views publicly in all areas of Union action (Art. 11(1) TEU). The institutions are to "maintain an open, transparent and regular dialogue with representative associations and civil society" (Art. 11(2) TEU), in particular with the social partners and with churches, religious associations and communities and philosophical and non-confessional organisations (see para. 16–045). This appeal to dialogue is specifically reflected in the obligation imposed on the Commission to carry out broad consultations with parties concerned and to take note of any initiative put forward by a significant number of citizens (Art. 11(3) and (4) TEU; see para. 16–016).

20–007 **Democracy versus federalism.** Nevertheless, decision-making in the Union does not take place in the same democratic manner as it does within a State.[12] This is because the Union organises relations between States and their peoples and has to respect the equality and the national identity of each Member State (Art. 4(3) TEU). As a result, the decision-making process has to embody

---

Joined Cases T-222/99, T-327/99 and T-329/99 *Martinez and Others v European Parliament* [2001] E.C.R. II-2823, para. 202, confirmed on the merits by ECJ, Case C-488/01 P *Martinez v European Parliament* [2003] E.C.R. I-13355 and set aside, as to the admissibility of the action brought by a political party, by ECJ, Case C-486/01 P *Front national v European Parliament* [2004] E.C.R. I-6289.

[11] See also Curtin, *Postnational Democracy. The European Union in Search of a Political Philosophy* (The Hague, Kluwer Law International, 1997), 62 pp; Peters, "European Democracy after the 2003 Convention" (2004) C.M.L.Rev. 37–85; for modern forms of democratic supervision (e.g., via the Internet), see Weiler, "The European Union belongs to its Citizens: Three Immodest Proposals" (1997) E.L.Rev. 150–156.

[12] See Verhoeven, *The European Union in Search of a Democratic and Constitutional Theory* (The Hague, Kluwer Law International, 2002), 365 pp.

"federal" guarantees.[13] For instance, owing to the concern to secure an adequate representation for the small Member States, the distribution of seats in the European Parliament and of votes in the Council does not completely mirror each Member State's share of the total population of the Union. On the other hand, decisions taken at Union level often affect the control of decision-making which the people in each Member State carry out through their national representative assembly. For reasons of efficiency, it would be inconceivable for such decisions to be subjected to the scrutiny and approval of all the national parliaments. It would seem that the resultant vacuum may be filled only by securing a sufficient parliamentary role in European decision-making itself.

Rule of law and transparency. Modern democracy does not only comprise   **20–008** participation of representative assemblies in public authority, supervision by such assemblies of public authority and direct involvement of citizens and interest groups with decision-making; it is also based on the principles of the rule of law and the correlative requirements of legal protection.[14] Accordingly, the democratic content of decision-making in the Union has to do not only with the way in which power is exercised, but also with the protection afforded to legal subjects pursuant to the rule of law.[15] This is all the more important given that many decisions of the Union are formulated by Union and national officials in the interaction between the Commission and the Council. Just as in the Member States, the growing influence of the executive inevitably goes hand in hand with a burgeoning number of tasks attributed to the public authorities.[16] This makes supervision by the courts necessary in order that, in the absence of effective parliamentary control, executive action can at least be compelled to comply with superior law. The principle of democracy does not preclude the existence of independent

---

[13] For the relationship between democracy and integration, see already Weiler, "Parlement européen, intégration européenne, démocratie et légitimité", in Louis and Waelbroeck (eds), *Le Parlement européen dans l'évolution institutionnelle* (Brussels, Editions de l'Université de Bruxelles, 1988), 325–348, especially at 335–339. For the correlation between the degree of integration of international organisations and the demand for democratisation, see Stein, "International integration and democracy: no love at first sight" (2001) A.J.I.L. 489–534.

[14] See also Art. 2 TEU, which refers to "the values of respect for human dignity, freedom, democracy, equality, the rule of law and respect for human rights". The definition of the principle of democracy in the European Parliament's Declaration of Fundamental Rights and Freedoms (n. 6, *supra*) reads as follows: "All public authority emanates from the people and must be exercised in accordance with the principles of the rule of law" (Art. 17(1)).

[15] For a qualified assessment based on a teleological approach to the question of democracy, see De Smijter, "De verschijningsvormen van de democratie in de Europese Gemeenschappen: een nuancering van het democratische tekort van de Europese Gemeenschappen", *Democratie op het einde van de 20ste eeuw* (Brussels, Belgian Royal Academy of Sciences, Letters and Fine Arts, 1994), 27–53.

[16] See the contributions in Kiiver (ed.), *National and regional parliaments in the European constitutional order* (Groningen, Europa Law Publishing, 2006), 132 pp.; Flinterman, Heringa and Waddington, *The Evolving Role of Parliaments in Europe/L'évolution du rôle des parlements en Europe* (Antwerp, Maklu/Nomos, 1994), 111 pp.

administrative authorities as long as they are required to comply with the law and subject to review by the competent courts.[17]

In addition, it is equally important for the democratic content of decision-making that information should be available about policy and that policy should be open and transparent, since this is apt to increase public interest and confidence in the exercise of power.[18] Article 10(3) TFEU mentions explicitly that decisions are to be taken as openly and closely as possible to the citizens in order to ensure for every citizen the right to participate in the democratic life of the Union. To that effect, Art. 15(1) TFEU declares that

> "[i]n order to promote good governance and ensure the participation of civil society, the Union institutions, bodies, offices and agencies shall conduct their work as openly as possible" (see para. 20–017 *et seq.*).

B. PARTICIPATION IN AND SUPERVISION OF DECISION-MAKING

1. Transparency of the division of powers

20–009 **Complex picture.** In order to involve the people in the exercise of power, it is a requirement of the democratic principle that a representative assembly, if not directly participating in decision-making, at least is able to supervise it. The members of the representative assembly (and their electors) may have an effective influence over decision-making only if it is clear in whom decision-making powers are vested and which particular powers are involved. As far as decision-making within the Union is concerned, this means that it must be clearly distinguishable whether a given power is vested in the Union or in the Member States, which institution has the ultimate power of decision and which decision-making procedure has to be followed. For a long time, the coexistence of two Communities, together with non-Community forms of policy and cooperation, itself witnessed to the fact that this sort of transparency was not an attribute of Union decision-making. The Lisbon Treaty has sought to improve the situation by eliminating the distinction between Community and non-Community action, although different rules continue to exist with respect to the CFSP (see Ch. 18–001 *et seq.*). Moreover, traditionally, the diversity of legislative procedures made decision-making an extremely complex matter as this made it more difficult to precisely determine the role played by each institution and the allocation of tasks as between the European Parliament and the national

---

[17] ECJ (judgment of March 9, 2010), Case C-518/07 *Commission v Germany*, not yet reported, para. 42.

[18] De Smijter (n. 15, *supra*), at 42–43. For the "social legitimacy" of public authority, which extends beyond its democratic aspect, see Weiler (n. 13, *supra*), at 333–335. See also the European Parliament's resolution of December 10, 1996 on participation of citizens and social players in the European Union's institutional system, [1997] O.J. C20/31.

parliaments.[19] In this connection, too, the Treaty of Lisbon simplified matters by introducing an "ordinary legislative procedure" with a clear allocation of powers between the European Parliament, the Commission and the Council. Nevertheless, other procedures of decision-making continue to exist.

2. Role of parliamentary bodies

Parliamentary control at Union level. In the light of the powers of the European Parliament, commentators traditionally referred to a "democratic deficit" in the context of decision-making within the Union. What is meant is the consequences of the transfer of powers from the national to the Union level in terms of the intensity of parliamentary control of decision-making. Matters which used to come within the competence of the national parliament or in respect of which the national government was accountable to the national parliament now come within the sphere of the Union, where the European Parliament does not invariably have a decisive say in decision-making. The European Parliament may not "co-decide" with the Council on Union legislation in all cases; in others, the Council can take a decision against the wishes of the European Parliament (see paras 16–011—16–014). Furthermore, MEPs have no right to submit proposals for legislation: only the Commission has the right of initiative (see para. 16–017). As new powers are assigned to the Union, the democratic deficit would seem to grow if the gradual, piecemeal increase in the European Parliament's powers does not keep pace with the expansion of the Union's powers.[20] However, as has already been

20–010

---

[19] See Lenaerts, "Some Reflections on the Separation of Powers in the European Community" (1991) C.M.L.Rev. 11, at 20; Piris (n. 1, *supra*), at 469–470. See also European Convention, Final Report of Working Group IX on Simplification, November 29, 2002, CONV 42/02. A clear indication of the competent institution is also beneficial for all who wish to enter into contact with the Union (e.g., third countries wishing to conclude agreements with Union institutions).

[20] See the resolution of the European Parliament of June 17, 1988 on the democratic deficit in the European Community, [1988] O.J. C187/229. See also the following learned articles: Ress, "Democratic Decision-making in the European Union and the Role of the European Parliament", in Curtin and Heukels (eds), *Institutional Dynamics of European Integration. Essays in Honour of Henry G. Schermers*, Vol. II (Dordrecht, Martinus Nijhoff, 1994), 153–176; De Burca, "Developing democracy beyond the state" (2008) 46 *Columbia Journal of Transnational Law* 221–278; Bleckmann, "Das europäische Demokratieprinzip" (2001) J.Z. 53–58; Classen, "Europäische Integration und demokratische Legitimation" (1994) A.ö.R. 238–260; Raworth, "A Timid Step Forward: Maastricht and the Democratisation of the European Community" (1994) E.L.Rev. 16–33; Schockweiler, "La dimension humaine et sociale de la Communauté européenne" (1993) R.M.U.E. 11, at 35–44; Zuleeg, "Demokratie in der Europäischen Gemeinschaft" (1993) J.Z. 1069–1074; Boest, "Ein langer Weg zur Demokratie in Europa. Die Beteiligungsrechte des Europäischen Parlaments bei Rechtsetzung nach dem Vertrag über die Europäische Union" (1992) EuR. 182–200; Reich, "Le traité sur l'Union européenne et le Parlement européen" (1992) R.M.C.U.E. 287–292.

observed, the democratic content of decision-making at Union level cannot be reduced to the degree to which the European Parliament has a say.[21]

20–011 **Parliamentary control at national level.** When legislative measures are adopted by the Council on a proposal from the Commission, whether or not after consulting the European Parliament—that is to say, in the remaining instances in which legislation is not adopted under the ordinary legislative procedure—, they do not emanate from a representative assembly but from members of national (or regional) governments. This practice need not necessarily be undemocratic, provided that members of government are subject to effective parliamentary control.[22] Whether that control takes place at the Union level or at the national level has more to do with the "federal" nature of decision-making than with its democratic content.[23]

It is a fact that, as a minister, each member of the Council is accountable to his or her national parliament. Consequently, decision-making exhibits an absolute democratic deficit only in so far as the Member States themselves do not provide for parliamentary scrutiny of action taken by members of government in the Council.[24] The national legal system can ensure that the national parliament is given the necessary information about the activities of the Council and may, possibly, constrain the responsible national minister to comply with the brief given to him or her by the national parliament (see paras 14–006—14–009).

In order to have effective parliamentary control at national level, of course, the position taken by each member of the Council and the way he or she votes must be disclosed (see para. 20–018). Where, however, they act by a majority vote, this form of political control affords no guarantee that every national parliament's view will be reflected in Union acts. It is only where the Council acts unanimously, which by and large it has to do in the field of the CFSP, that ministers may be called to account to their national parliament for every act adopted. Moreover, there is another ground on which national parliamentary control is still defective in vesting democratic legitimacy in action of the Union. This is that national parliaments have neither a mandate nor the expertise to take account of the common interest in Council decision-making.

---

[21] See also Moravcsik, "In Defence of the 'Democratic Deficit': Reassessing Legitimacy in the European Union" (2002) J.C.M.S. 603–624 (and the reply by Follesdal, "Why there is a democratic deficit in the EU: a response to Majone and Moravcsik" (2006) 44 J.C.M.S. 533–562). See also the interesting proposal by Van der Schyff, "The case for a European Senate. A model for the representation of national parliaments in the European Union" (2007) Z.ö.R. 237–258.

[22] See Auel, "Democratic accountability and national parliaments: redefining the impact of parliamentary scrutiny in EU affairs" (2007) 13 E.L.J. 487–504.

[23] De Smijter (n. 15, *supra*), at 45.

[24] This also applies to regional ministers who act in the Council (by agreement) and have to answer to their representative assemblies.

Reconciling different concepts of democracy. For those reasons, commentators **20–012** have long argued that the European Parliament should be given fully-fledged powers to initiate legislation and co-decide with the Council. The European Parliament itself urges that the whole decision-making process should be based on the dual legitimacy of the directly elected European Parliament—to defend the common interest—and of the Council, whose members are accountable to their national parliaments for the way in which they defend the national position.[25] Where the European Parliament co-decides on legislative measures, those measures reflect the will of a representative assembly at least at Union level, but, in cases involving majority voting in the Council, not necessarily the will of each national parliament.

Whether the European Parliament's involvement confers sufficient democratic legitimacy on decision-making at Union level depends on whether the representation of the people in that body is considered to be representative of European public opinion.[26] Depending on the view taken of the European Parliament, commentators argue for democratising decision-making in the Union either through stricter national parliamentary control or by means of a greater say for the European Parliament. In this way in its judgments of October 12, 1993 (the "*Maastricht-Urteil*") and June 30, 2009 (the "Lisbon" judgment), the German *Bundesverfassungsgericht* (Constitutional Court) held that although, as European integration stands, the European Parliament constitutes a supplementary democratic support for the European Union, the Union still obtains its actual democratic legitimacy from the control which the national parliaments exercise over it.[27] In the view of the European Court of Human Rights, however, the European Parliament, which derives democratic legitimation from the direct elections by universal suffrage, must be seen as reflecting concerns as to "effective political democracy" within the European Union.[28]

Dual democratic legitimacy. The changes to the decision-making process **20–013** introduced by the Lisbon Treaty build on precisely this idea of the dual democratic legitimacy of the Union.[29] In those cases where the Council decides by a qualified

---

[25] See the resolution of the European Parliament of June 17, 1988 (n. 21, *supra*), point 19, and its resolution of June 12, 1997 on the relations between the European Parliament and national parliaments, [1997] O.J. C200/153.

[26] For arguments in favour, see Ress (n. 21, *supra*), at 174–175; for arguments against, see Schockweiler, "La dimension humaine et sociale de la Communauté européenne" (1993) R.M.U.E. 11, at 41–42. See also Weiler (n. 13, *supra*), at 347; von Simson, "Was heisst in einer europäischen Verfassung 'das Volk'?" (1991) EuR. 1–18; De Smijter (n. 15, *supra*), at 47–48.

[27] See paras 39–45 of the first judgment and paras. 276 *et seq.* of the second judgment (for references to the text of the judgment and commentaries, see para. 21–030, *infra*).

[28] European Court of Human Rights, judgment of February 18, 1999, *Matthews v United Kingdom*, No. 24833/94, para. 52.

[29] For the similar changes to the decision-making process introduced by the EU Constitution, see Sommermann, "Verfassungsperspektiven für die Demokratie in der erweiterten Europäischen Union: Gefahr der Entdemokratisierung oder Fortentwicklung im Rahmen europäischer Supranationalität?" (2003) D.ö.V. 1009–1017.

majority vote, the ordinary legislative procedure now normally applies and, there-fore, the European Parliament has a decisive say (see para. 16–022). In those cases where the Council decides by unanimity, the ordinary legislative procedure gener-ally does not apply, but the national parliaments are able to exercise control over the position which the national government adopts in the Council. In this connec-tion, the Lisbon Treaty reinforces the mechanisms which facilitate control by national parliaments over the activities of their respective governments (see para. 14–006). In particular, national parliaments are entitled to exercise direct control over compliance with the principle of subsidiarity (see para. 7–031).

20–014 **Contacts between European and national parliaments.** Members of national parliaments and MEPs regularly hold meetings on their own initiative to exchange information and ideas, both at national[30] and Union level.[31] The Lisbon Treaty enshrined a Treaty provision which confirms the importance of inter-parliamentary cooperation. Article 12(f) TEU states that national parliaments contribute actively to the good functioning of the Union "by taking part in inter-parliamentary cooperation between national Parliaments and with the European Parliament". Further arrangements for this cooperation are laid down in Protocol (No. 1) on the role of National Parliaments in the European Union.[32]

The European Parliament and national parliaments must together determine the organisation and promotion of effective and regular interparliamentary coopera-tion within the Union (Protocol, Art. 9). The protocol itself provides for a "con-ference of Parliamentary Committees for Union Affairs", which may submit any contribution it deems appropriate for the attention of the European Parliament, the Council and the Commission and must promote the exchange of information and best practice between national parliaments and the European Parliament, including their special committees. The Conference may also organise interpar-liamentary conferences on specific topics, in particular to debate matters of com-mon foreign and security policy, including common security and defence policy. However, the protocol specifies that contributions from the conference do not bind national parliaments and do not prejudice their positions (Protocol, Art. 10).

---

[30] Thus, Members of the European Parliament meet national colleagues within the domestic party structure and they may be invited to attend meetings of national parliamentary committees. In sev-eral Member States, MEPs may take part in the proceedings of the advisory committees on European affairs set up by the national parliament, although generally they may not vote.

[31] The European political parties are based on national parties represented in the national parliaments. See Bonnamour, "Les relations entre Parlement européen et Parlements nationaux à la veille de la Conférence intergouvernementale de 1996" (1995) R.M.C.U.E 637–646; Scoffoni, "Les relations entre le Parlement européen et les parlements nationaux et le renforcement de la légitimité démoc-ratique de la Communauté" (1992) C.D.E. 22–41.

[32] Protocol (No. 1), annexed by the Lisbon Treaty to the TEU, TFEU and EAEC Treaty, on the role of National Parliaments in the European Union, [2010] O.J. C83/203, which replaces Protocol (No. 9), annexed by the Amsterdam Treaty to the EU Treaty and the Community Treaties, on the role of National Parliaments in the European Union, [1997] O.J. C310/113.

Such conferences have since long been held under the name of the "Conference of European Affairs Committees" (COSAC), which is regularly convened.[33]

Besides, other different forms of inter-parliamentary cooperation exist in the Union.[34] Representatives from the national parliaments and the European Parliament have met to discuss changes in the Union's institutional structure as the "Conference of Parliaments" or "assizes".[35] In order to guarantee the legitimacy and independence of the participating parliaments, such contacts were not institutionalised.[36]

Other forms of representation. The Treaties also give citizens an additional say   **20–015**
in decision-making through the institutional representation of their interests as members of economic and social groups (European Economic and Social Committee) and of regional and local communities (Committee of the Regions).[37] However, those bodies do not have the same direct legitimacy as parliamentary bodies and merely have an advisory say in the Union's decision-making process (see para. 16–045). To some extent, the influence of the European Economic and Social Committee and the Committee of the Regions was bolstered by the Lisbon Treaty in that it widened the possibilities for them to bring Court actions (see paras 13–080 and 13–111). Representatives of management and labour (the "social partners") may conclude agreements with each other on which the Union institutions may confer the force of legislation (see para. 16–044). In practice, a variety of interest groups have a critical influence on decision-making as a result of the specific information and expertise with which they provide the Commission at an early stage of the decision-making process (see para. 16–018).

---

[33] The Conference of European Affairs Committees of the Parliaments of the European Union (COSAC, standing for *Conférence des organes spécialisés en affaires communautaires*), established in Paris on November 16–17, 1989. Its tasks were defined by points 4–7 of the 1997 Protocol on the role of National Parliaments in the European Union ([1997] O.J. C340/113, point 1). For COSAC's Rules of Procedure, approved on May 5 and 6, 2003, see [2008] O.J. C27/6. For the European Parliament's delegation to COSAC, see EP Rules of Procedure, Rule 131.

[34] See, in this connection, the Guidelines for Interparliamentary Cooperation in the European Union, adopted by the Conference of Speakers of the European Union Parliaments in Lisbon on June 21, 2008. These guidelines mention six frameworks for inter-parliamentary cooperation, namely (a) the Conference of Speakers of the European Union Parliaments; (b) COSAC; (c) Joint Meetings on Topics of Common Interest; (d) Meetings of Sectoral Committees; (e) Secretaries-General, and (f) Representatives of National Parliaments to the EU. See also Rule 132 of the EP Rules of Procedure.

[35] See Declaration (No. 14) to the EU Treaty on the Conference of Parliaments. Such "assizes" met at Rome on November 27–30, 1990 (1990) 11 EC Bull. point 2.3.1.

[36] See the resolution of the European Parliament of July 12, 1990 on the preparation of the meeting with the national parliaments to discuss the future of the Community (the "Assizes"), [1990] O.J. C231/165, and Scoffoni (n. 29, *supra*), at 39–40.

[37] Lenaerts and De Smijter, "On the Democratic Representation through the European Parliament, the Council, the Committee of the Regions, the Economic and Social Committee and the National Parliaments", in Winter, Curtin, Kellermann and De Witte (eds), *Reforming the Treaty on European Union—The Legal Debate* (The Hague, T.M.C. Asser Institute/Kluwer, 1996) at 173–197.

20–016 **Democratic control on implementation.** The democratic control which is exerted over the execution of acts adopted within the Union differs depending on the authority responsible for implementation. The implementation of Union acts by the Member States falls in the first place to the national governments and hence is subject to parliamentary supervision in as much as the Member States provide for it. However, except in the field of the CFSP, national parliamentary scrutiny is coupled with supervision by the Commission and—in some instances—the European Parliament's powers of inquiry.

It is impossible for the national parliaments to scrutinise the quantity of measures which are adopted by the Union institutions in order to implement acts of the Union. The only effective forum for conducting such scrutiny would seem to be the European Parliament. In view of the limited ability of the European Parliament to supervise the Council, the most democratic procedure is to confer implementing power on the Commission, since it is accountable to the Parliament (see para. 17–019). For that reason, too, independent Union bodies, offices and agencies may be given only clearly defined executive tasks which do not detract from the Commission's political accountability (see para. 17–021). The position is different only where the Treaties themselves confer a particular position on a specific body, such as the European Investment Bank, for important reasons (see para. 17–024).

3. Transparency of decision-making

20–017 **"As open as possible".** In order to enable political scrutiny of the Union institutions' action to take place, the scrutinising institutions must be able to have sufficient insight into on-going and proposed administrative activities. Moreover, the democratic character of the institutions and public confidence in the administration is reinforced by having a transparent decision-making process.[38] In 1992, in a Declaration entitled "A Community close to its citizens", the European Council undertook to open up decision-making so as to make it more transparent and to ensure better-informed public debate on the Union's activities.[39] In 1997, the Treaty of Amsterdam took this a stage further by declaring that decisions are to be "taken as openly as possible" in the Union (Art. 1, second para., TEU; see also para. 10–159). At present, Art. 15(1) TEU, introduced by the Lisbon Treaty, states:

> "In order to promote good governance and ensure the participation of civil society, the Union institutions, bodies, offices and agencies shall conduct their work as openly as possible" (see also Art. 10(3) TEU).

---

[38] See Declaration (No. 17), annexed to the EU Treaty in 1992, on the right of access to information.
[39] Birmingham Declaration (October 16, 1992)—A Community close to its citizens (1992) 10 EC Bull. point I.8.

Openness of procedure. Most of the steps which the institutions have taken in this connection have been designed to bring about greater openness both in the preparation of decisions and during the actual decision-making process.[40] Accordingly, alongside its legislative programme, the Commission now publishes an annual work programme with a view to broader discussions, also in the national parliaments, and enables interest groups affected by a particular proposal to take part more extensively in its preparation.[41] The European Parliament meets in public (Art. 15(2) TFEU see para. 13–022). Traditionally, the Council had been reluctant to publish minutes recording the negotiations in the Council, since a majority of Member States took the view that confidentiality was necessary in order to be able to reach compromises.[42] Since the Lisbon Treaty, the Council is to meet in public when it deliberates and votes on a draft legislative act (Art. 16(8) TEU and 15(2) TFEU; Council Rules of Procedure, Art. 5(1)). The Council publishes the minutes relating to legislative deliberations, the results of votes on draft legislative acts, together with explanations of votes and statements in the minutes of the Council (see para 13–048). Council meetings dealing with non-legislative activities are in certain cases also open to the public (see para 13–048). However, the Council does not disclose documents relating to the deliberations of the committees which do the preparatory work for Council meetings.[43] Neither is there an obligation to disclose the proceedings of intergovernmental conferences on amendments of the Treaties.[44] However, in contrast, the Convention set up in 2002 to consider the future of the Union met in complete openness. Since the Lisbon Treaty a "convention stage" is included in the ordinary revision procedure for amendment of the Treaties (see para. 5–004).

20–018

Access to information. The largest possible access for citizens to information strengthens the democratic character of the institutions and the public's trust in the

20–019

---

[40] For a critical discussion, see Curtin and Meijers, "The Principle of Open Government in Schengen and the European Union: Democratic Retrogression?" (1995) C.M.L.Rev. 391–442. See also Blanchet, "Le Traité d'Amsterdam. Transparence et qualité de la législation" (1997) R.T.D.E. 915–928.

[41] See the communication on increased transparency in the work of the Commission, [1993] O.J. C63/8, and the communication of June 2, 1993 to the Council, the Parliament and the Economic and Social Committee: Openness in the Community, [1993] O.J. C166/4. See the discussion of the right of initiative in para. 16–018, *supra*.

[42] See the Council's position in CFI, Case T-194/94 *Carvel and Guardian Newspapers v Council* [1995] E.C.R. II-2765, para. 52.

[43] Some have argued that openness of Council meetings may result in the real decision-making being carried out in working parties behind closed doors or at informal meetings: Dashwood, "The Role of the Council in the European Union", in *Institutional Dynamics of European Integration. Essays in Honour of Henry G. Schermers* (n. 20, *supra*), 117, at 132–133. In view of the great importance in practice of the committees which prepare Council meetings, it is at least as relevant to have their deliberations made public, see Van Schendelen, "'De Raad beslist'. Beslist de Raad?" (1995) S.E.W. 706, at 717–718.

[44] See Curtin, "The Constitutional Structure of the Union: A Europe of Bits and Pieces" (1993) C.M.L.Rev. 17, at 18.

administration.[45] The possibility for citizens to scrutinise all the information which formed the basis of a given legislative act and, hence, to find out the considerations underpinning legislative action is a precondition for the effective exercise of their democratic rights.[46] Transparency of decision-making is therefore to be coupled with easy public access to policy documents (see paras 13–161—13–168).

4. Easier access to legislation

20–020 **Access to legislation.** In order to make it easier to find Union legislation, the European Council stressed the need to undertake official codification or unofficial consolidation of legislation at an earlier stage and to improve computerised data bases.[47] Nowadays, access may be had via the Internet to a variety of documents of the Union institutions, bodies, offices and agencies and to data bases.[48] Already on December 20, 1994, the European Parliament, the Council and the Commission agreed on an accelerated working method for codifying legislative texts without altering their substantive content.[49]

20–021 **Simplifying legislation.** On the substantive side, access to Union acts will improve if they are classified in a transparent manner. Accordingly, it was long proposed that acts should be classified either as "legislative" acts or as, more detailed, subordinate "implementing measures". This proposal was partly taken up in the Treaty of Lisbon, which introduced a formal distinction between legislative and non-legislative acts (delegated and implementing acts) (see para. 16–003). Further, there will always—and rightly—be a plea for simpler, clearer legislation.[50] In December 1998, the European Parliament, the Council and the Commission adopted guidelines for improving the drafting quality of Community

---

[45] CFI, Case T-174/95 *Svenska Journalistförbundet v Council* [1998] E.C.R. II-2289, para. 66; see also ECJ, Joined Cases C-39/05 P and C-52/05 P *Sweden and Turco v Council* [2007] E.C.R. I-4723, paras 34, 46 and 59.

[46] ECJ, Joined Cases C-39/05 P and C-52/05 P *Sweden and Turco v Council* [2007] E.C.R. I-4723, para. 46.

[47] Transparency—Implementation of the Birmingham declaration (n. 39, *supra*), point I.29.

[48] See the introduction to the source material.

[49] Interinstitutional Agreement of December 20, 1994, [1996] O.J. C102/2 (see also [1995] O.J. C43/42). In an interpretative declaration, the European Parliament stated that, where there was an amendment either to the legal basis or to the procedure for adopting the text in question, it would have to reserve its view as to whether the codification was desirable (see the resolution of January 18, 1995, [1995] O.J. C43/41). See Dragone, "La codification communautaire: technique et procédures" (1998) 1 R.M.U.E. 77–94. See further the interinstitutional agreement between the European Parliament, the Council and the Commission of November 28, 2001 on a more structured use of the recasting technique for legal acts, [2002] O.J. C77/1.

[50] See, for instance, the European Council in its declaration "Transparency—Implementation of the Birmingham declaration", Annex 3 to Part A of the Conclusions of the European Council held in Edinburgh on December 11 and 12, 1992 (1992) 12 EC Bull., point I.28.

legislation.[51] In December 2003, those institutions concluded a new agreement on better law-making which contains not only agreements on the coordination of the legislative process and on the use of alternative modes of regulation, but also commitments with regard to improving the quality of legislation, simplifying it and reducing its volume.[52] Lastly, in order to improve the accessibility of the Treaties, the Treaty of Amsterdam simplified the texts and renumbered the articles of the EU Treaty and the EC Treaty (see para. 3–023). The Lisbon Treaty again renumbered the articles of the Treaties.

---

[51] Interinstitutional Agreement of December 22, 1998 on common guidelines for the quality of drafting of Community legislation, [1999] O.J. C73/1, giving effect to Declaration (No. 39), annexed to the Amsterdam Treaty, on the quality of the drafting of Community legislation, [1997] O.J. C340/139. See Xanthaki, "The Problem of Quality in EU Legislation: What on Earth is Really Wrong?" (2001) C.M.L.Rev. 651–676; De Wilde, "Deficient European Legislation is in Nobody's Interest" (2000) E.J.L.R. 293–319 and "Gebrekkige Europese regelgeving kent alleen maar verliezers—Het interinstitutioneel akkoord van 1998: geen eindstation maar eerste tussenstation op weg naar verbetering Europese regelgeving" (2000) S.E.W. 401–413. See also the Council Resolution of June 8, 1993 on the quality of drafting of Community legislation, [1993] O.J. C166/1, and Timmermans, "How Can One Improve the Quality of Community Legislation" (1997) C.M.L.Rev. 1229–1257. A possible instrument for improving quality has been suggested by Van Damme, "Naar een Europese Raad van State?" (2001) T.B.P. 519–523.

[52] Interinstitutional Agreement of December 16, 2003 on better law-making, [2003] O.J. C321/1. Pursuant to the principles of subsidiarity and proportionality, the Commission has also undertaken to simplify existing Community legislation: para. 7–030, *supra*. On the (limited) impact of the EU Constitution on the simplification of legislation, see Sandström, "Knocking EU Law into Shape" (2003) C.M.L.Rev. 1307–1313.

Part V

SOURCES OF LAW OF
THE EUROPEAN UNION

CHAPTER 21

EFFECTS OF UNION LAW IN THE NATIONAL LEGAL SYSTEMS

I. FORMS OF UNION LAW

Union law. "Union law" encompasses the rules enshrined in the Treaties and acts   **21–001**
adopted pursuant thereto, as applied and interpreted by the national courts and the
Court of Justice. Depending on the origin of the provisions, a distinction may be
made between constitutive norms which come into being as a result of action on
the part of the Member States themselves (primary Union law), rules created by
Union institutions and bodies (secondary or "derived" Union law) and other rules
which have been accepted by case law as being general principles of the Union's
legal order. Secondary Union law takes the form of specific instruments of Union
law (see, inter alia, Art. 288 TFEU) or of international agreements concluded by
the Union.

II. EFFECT IN THE NATIONAL LEGAL SYSTEMS

Principles. The status of Union law in the national legal systems is a matter of   **21–002**
Union law itself.[1] This means that Union law differs from the classical rule of
international law that a State itself determines, apart from the limitations to which
it expressly commits itself, the status of international commitments in its legal
system. The case law of the Court of Justice relating to the primacy and the possible direct effect of Union law has made it clear that Union law *as such* has effect
in the national legal system.[2] Both the Union and individuals are entitled to
enforce the proper application of Union law. On the ground of the need to secure
the full effect of Union law, the Court of Justice has developed in its case law
other requirements with which the national legal system must comply in order to
secure the primacy of Union law in practice.[3] Hereinafter, the requirements flowing from the principles of primacy and full effectiveness of Union law are set out,

---

[1] ECJ, Case 26/62 *Van Gend & Loos* [1963] E.C.R. 1, at 10–12.
[2] See paras 1–024 and 1–026, *supra*.
[3] In addition, the Member States are under a duty to take all necessary measures to implement
provisions of Union law; see para. 17–002, *supra*.

both from the angle of the Court's case law and from the perspective of the legal system of the Member States that are to accommodate those principles.

21–003 **CFSP.** As for legal effects, the Treaties make no distinction between acts adopted within the framework of the CFSP and acts adopted in other fields. The principle of the primacy of Union law therefore applies in full to any Union act, including these adopted within the framework of the CFSP. All the same, the Court of Justice does not have jurisdiction with respect to the provisions of the Treaties relating to the CFSP or with respect to acts adopted on the basis of those provisions (Art. 275 TFEU; see para.13–086). It is therefore up to the national courts to secure the effects of CFSP acts or to rule on their legality.

A. THE PRINCIPLES OF PRIMACY AND FULL EFFECTIVENESS OF UNION LAW

1. Requirements flowing from Union law

(a) *The principle of primacy of Union law*

21–004 **Precedence of primary and secondary Union law.** In its 1964 judgment in *Costa v ENEL* the Court of Justice first articulated the principle that Community law takes precedence over the domestic law of the Member States. The Court held that,

> "the law stemming from the Treaty, an independent source of law, could not, because of its special and original nature, be overridden by domestic provisions, however framed, without being deprived of its character as Community law and without the legal basis of the Community itself being called into question".[4]

The Court derived the primacy of Community law from the specific nature of the Community legal order, referring to the danger that, if the effect of Community law could vary from Member State to Member State in deference to subsequent national laws, this would be liable to jeopardise the attainment of the objectives set out in Art. 10 EC [*now Art. 4(3) TEU*] and give rise to discrimination prohibited by Art. 12 EC [*now Art. 18 TFEU*] (see para. 1–026). The case was concerned with the primacy of a number of provisions of primary Community law.

---

[4] ECJ, Case 6/64 *Costa v ENEL* [1964] E.C.R. 585, at 594; for the further development of the primacy of Community law, see Beljin, "Die Zusammenhänge zwischen dem Vorrang, den Instituten der innerstaatlichen Beachtlichkeit und der Durchführung des Gemeinschaftsrechts" (2002) EuR. 351–376; De Witte, "Le retour à *Costa*. La primauté du droit communautaire à la lumière du droit international" (1984) R.T.D.E. 425–454. See further, on the primacy of Union law, including the second and third pillar, Lenaerts and Corthaut, "Of Birds and Hedges: the Role of Primacy in Invoking Norms of EU Law" (2006) E.L.Rev. 287–315.

The Court subsequently also upheld the primacy of secondary Community law on the same grounds.[5]

The case law of the Court of Justice referred to was primarily concerned with the effects of Community law, i.e. the former first pillar of the Union. Since the entry into force of the Lisbon Treaty, the requirements established by the Court of Justice in its case law apply in principle to all forms of Union law (see para. 4–013). Yet, the Treaties contain no express reference to the primacy of Union law, although the framers of the EU Constitution intended to incorporate such a reference. Indeed, the EU Constitution provided in this regard that,

> "[t]he Constitution and law adopted by the institutions of the Union in exercising competences conferred on it shall have primacy over the law of the Member States" (Art. I-6).

The 2007 Intergovernmental Conference chose, however, not to incorporate such a reference. However, it is stated in a declaration annexed to the Lisbon Treaty that,

> "[t]he Conference recalls that, in accordance with well settled case law of the Court of Justice of the European Union, the Treaties and the law adopted by the Union on the basis of the Treaties have primacy over the law of Member States, under the conditions laid down by the said case law."[6]

The declaration further quotes an opinion of the Council's Legal Service on the primacy of EC law, which refers to the Court's case law according to which "this principle is inherent to the specific nature of the European Community" and states that,

> "[t]he fact that the principle of primacy will not be included in the future treaty shall not in any way change the existence of the principle and the existing case law of the Court of Justice".[7]

All this amounts to a general recognition of the principle of primacy of Union law.

Precedence over any rule of national law. As long ago as *Costa v ENEL*, the Court held that Community law could not be overridden by "domestic legal provisions, however framed".[8] Consequently, Union law (since the Lisbon Treaty) takes precedence over any rule of domestic law which is at variance with it, including

21–005

---

[5] ECJ, Case 14/68 *Wilhelm* [1969] E.C.R. 1, para. 6; ECJ, Case 11/70 *Internationale Handelsgesellschaft* [1970] E.C.R. 1125, para. 3; ECJ, Case 249/85 *Albako* [1987] E.C.R. 2345, para. 14.

[6] Declaration (No. 17), annexed to the Lisbon Treaty, concerning primacy, [2010] O.J. C83/344.

[7] Opinion 11197/07 (JUR 260).

[8] ECJ, Case 6/64 *Costa v ENEL* [1964] E.C.R. 585, at 594.

"principles of a national constitutional structure".[9] This is because if Union law were only binding on the Member States to the extent that it was consistent with their constitutional structure, a situation would ensue in which the application of Union law would differ from one Member State to another. Moreover, important principles which are common to the constitutional traditions of the Member States are subscribed to by the Union itself, notably respect for democracy, the rule of law (see para. 22–036 *et seq.*) and fundamental rights (see para. 22–017 *et seq.*).[10]

21–006 **Conflict.** The primacy of Union law signifies that national legal rules must give way to conflicting provisions of Union law. In order to determine whether such a conflict exists, the aim and purpose of the Union provision must be assessed in the light of what it contains and what—deliberately or not—it does not contain. The national provision continues to be effective solely for those aspects which the Union provision has left unaffected.[11] Often the question arises as to how far a Union act allows the Member States to adopt measures with regard to partial aspects not dealt with in the Union act. In such a case, it must be inferred from the aims and purpose of the Union act whether that act governs the area exhaustively or whether it still leaves some latitude for regulation by Member States. A matter not dealt with by the Union provision may be regulated by the Member States provided that they do not thereby undermine the aims and objects of the Union provision.[12] In the same way, it has to be determined whether a Union harmonisation measure entails "full" or "complete" harmonisation or whether it allows Member States to deviate from the Union measure (see para. 9–109). In some fields, action by the Union may preclude any competence on the part of the Member States (see para. 7–024).

(b) *The principle of interpretation in conformity with Union law*

21–007 **Avoiding conflict.** The primacy of Union law is a conflict rule which applies where a legal relationship is governed by conflicting national and Union rules. Where the application of a national rule is likely to result in a conflict with a Union rule, it must first be determined whether the rules cannot be interpreted and

---

[9] ECJ, Case 11/70 *Internationale Handelsgesellschaft* [1970] E.C.R. 1125, para. 3 (which referred in particular to "fundamental rights as formulated by the constitution of [the] State", but see Union protection of fundamental rights: para. 22–017 *et seq., infra*). An example may be found in ECJ, Case C-285/98 *Kreil* [2000] E.C.R. I-69. See also ECJ, Case 30/72 *Commission v Italy* [1973] E.C.R. 161, para. 11 (precedence over "budgetary legislation or practice").

[10] For further details, see De Witte, "Community Law and National Constitutional Values" (1991) 2 L.I.E.I. 1–22.

[11] For examples in the case law, see in particular ECJ, Case 40/69 *Bollmann* [1970] 69, paras 4–5; ECJ, Case 50/76 *Amsterdam Bulb* [1977] E.C.R. 137, paras 9–30; ECJ, Case 111/76 *Van den Hazel* [1977] E.C.R. 901, paras 13–27; ECJ, Case 255/86 *Commission v Belgium* [1988] E.C.R. 693, paras 8–11; ECJ, Case 60/86 *Commission v United Kingdom* [1988] E.C.R. 3921, para. 11; ECJ, Case 190/87 *Oberkreisdirektor des Kreises Borken and Others* [1988] E.C.R. 4689, paras 11–13.

[12] ECJ, Case C-355/00 *Freskot AE* [2003] E.C.R. I-5263, paras 18–33; ECJ, Case C-416/01 *ACOR* [2003] E.C.R. I-14083, paras 21–62.

applied in such a way as to avoid a conflict. Naturally, the Union rule must be interpreted in a uniform way in all Member States. As far as the interpretation of national law is concerned, the Court of Justice considers that Art. 4(3) TEU places all public authorities, and therefore also judicial authorities, under a duty to interpret the national law which they have to apply as far as possible in conformity with the requirements of Union law.[13] National courts must therefore consider whether national law (legislation and case law[14]) can be interpreted or applied in such a way that there is no conflict with Union law. This applies to all rules of Union law, including fundamental rights, general principles of Union law and rules of international law which are applicable in Union law.[15] Where national law is interpreted in conformity with the provisions of a directive, this practice is referred to as interpretation consistent with a directive (see para. 22–087). This duty to interpret national law in conformity with Union law is, however, limited by general principles of Union law, such as the principle of legal certainty, the principle of legality and the prohibition of retroactivity.[16]

Interpreting national law in conformity with Union law may enable public authorities to avoid situations in which national rules have to be set aside on account of a conflict with Union law.[17]

(c) Duty to set aside conflicting national rules

Inapplicability of conflicting national rules. In the 1978 judgment in **21–008** *Simmenthal* ("*Simmenthal II*"), the Court of Justice held that:

"in accordance with the principle of the precedence of Community law, the relationship between provisions of the Treaty and directly applicable measures of the institutions on the one hand and the national law of the Member States on the other is such that those provisions and measures not only by their entry into force render automatically inapplicable any conflicting provision of current national law but—in so far as they are an integral part of, and take precedence in, the legal order applicable in the territory of each

---

[13] See ECJ, Case C-106/98 *Marleasing* [1990] E.C.R. I-4135, para. 8; ECJ, Case C-262/97 *Engelbrecht* [2000] E.C.R. I-7321, para. 39; ECJ, Case C-60/02 *Criminal proceedings against X* [2004] E.C.R. I-651, paras 59–60.

[14] See ECJ, Case C-456/98 *Centrosteel* [1998] E.C.R. I-6007, paras 16–17.

[15] For the interpretation and application of national law in the light of fundamental rights, see paras 22–025—22–026, *infra*; for the interpretation and application of national law in the light of general principles of Union law, see paras 22–017, *infra*; for the interpretation and application of national law in the light of rules of international law, see paras 22–044 and 22–047, *infra*.

[16] ECJ, Case C-60/02 *Criminal proceedings against X* [2004] E.C.R. I-651, paras 61–63. See para. 22–074, *infra* (on regulations) and para. 22–087, *infra* (on directives).

[17] Interpretation in conformity with Union law also makes the question of the direct effect of Union law unnecessary (i.e. "can the provision of Union law be relied upon by the person seeking redress?"). See Betlem, "The Doctrine of Consistent Interpretation—Managing Legal Uncertainty" (2002) O.J.L.S. 397–418.

of the Member States—also preclude the valid adoption of new national legislative measures to the extent to which they would be incompatible with Community law".[18]

Consequently, Member States are under a duty not only to avoid adopting a measure conflicting with Community law—Union law since the Lisbon Treaty—and to change any existing conflicting measure,[19] but also—so long as the offending measure has not been amended—to refrain from applying it.[20] In the judgment in *Simmenthal II*, the Court of Justice held that,

> "every national court must, in a case within its jurisdiction, apply Community law in its entirety and protect rights which the latter confers on individuals and must accordingly set aside any provision of national law which may conflict with it, whether prior or subsequent to the Community rule".[21]

Where a national court is faced with a national provision that is incompatible with Union law, it must decline to apply that provision, without being compelled to make a reference to the Court for a preliminary ruling before doing so.[22] It is not for the national court to decide whether a provision of national law that is contrary to Union law should continue to apply for a transitional period for reasons of legal certainty.[23] Where the incompatibility of a provision of national law with Union law is alleged in proceedings in which the national court is asked to annul that provision, a finding of incompatibility will lead to its annulment. The duty to set aside conflicting rules applies not only to national courts, but also to public bodies, including administrative bodies.[24] In order to comply with that duty, inferior administrative authorities, such as local authorities, must refrain of their own motion from applying provisions adopted by a higher authority in breach of Union law.[25] Likewise, national authorities may not apply provisions of agreements concluded between Member States if they conflict with Union law.[26] The incompatibility of national legislation with Union provisions can be definitively

---

[18] ECJ, Case 106/77 *Simmenthal* [1978] E.C.R. 629, para. 17.

[19] See also ECJ, Case 159/78 *Commission v Italy* [1979] E.C.R. 3247, para. 22.

[20] See ECJ, Case 48/71 *Commission v Italy* [1972] E.C.R. 529, paras 6–8. *A fortiori*, a Member State is debarred from adopting specific measures to extend a provision found to be contrary to Union law: ECJ, Case C-101/91 *Commission v Italy* [1993] E.C.R. I-191, paras 22–23.

[21] ECJ, Case 106/77 *Simmenthal* (*"Simmenthal II"*) [1978] E.C.R. 629, para. 21. See also ECJ, Case 249/85 *Albako* [1987] E.C.R. 2345, para. 17; ECJ, Case C-262/97 *Engelbrecht* [2000] E.C.R. I-7321, para. 40. For directives, see also para. 22–072, *infra*.

[22] ECJ (judgment of January 19, 2010), Case C-555/07 *Kücükdeveci*, not yet reported, paras 53–55. In such a case, however, the national court cannot be prevented from making such reference either: *ibid*.

[23] ECJ (judgment of September 8, 2010), Case C-409/06 *Winner Wetten*, not yet reported, paras 53–69.

[24] ECJ, Case 103/88 *Fratelli Costanzo* [1989] E.C.R. 1839, para. 31. See, e.g., national competition authorities; para. 11–010, *supra*.

[25] ECJ, Case 103/88 *Fratelli Costanzo* [1989] E.C.R. 1839, para. 31.

[26] ECJ, Case C-469/00 *Ravil and Others* [2003] E.C.R. I-5053, para. 37.

remedied only by means of national provisions that are binding and have the same legal force as those that have to be modified.[27] Accordingly, the duty to disapply national rules incompatible with Union law applies even with regard to rules which have been declared unconstitutional by the national Constitutional Court, but have not yet lost their binding force.[28]

A national measure will not only be inapplicable if it is substantively incompatible with a provision of Union law, it may also be inapplicable if it was adopted contrary to a procedure laid down by Union law. This will be the case where a Member State failed to notify technical provisions to the Commission in accordance with a Union procedure for the provision of information.[29] A technical provision which has not been notified to the Commission will be inapplicable only if it constitutes a barrier to trade.[30]

Simmenthal. In *Simmenthal II* the Court of Justice was seised of a question 　**21–009** referred to it for a preliminary ruling by an Italian court, which, after obtaining a preliminary ruling on an earlier question,[31] had held that the imposition of certain inspection fees was incompatible with Community law and had therefore ordered the Italian tax authorities to repay them. The tax authorities appealed, relying on case law of the Italian Constitutional Court to the effect that a national law which conflicted with Community law was also incompatible with the Italian Constitution. On this view, the national court could not set aside the law in question until such time as it had been declared unlawful by the Constitutional Court. The Court of Justice ruled that,

> "a national court which is called upon, within the limits of its jurisdiction, to apply provisions of Community law is under a duty to give full effect to those provisions, if necessary refusing of its own motion to apply any conflicting provision of national legislation, even if adopted subsequently, and it is not necessary for the court to request or await the prior setting aside of such provisions by legislative or constitutional means".[32]

---

[27] See ECJ, Case-145/99 *Commission v Italy* [2002] E.C.R. I-2235, paras 37–39.

[28] ECJ, Case C-314/08 *Filipiak* [2009] E.C.R. I-11049, paras 81–85.

[29] ECJ, Case C-194/94 *CIA Security International* [1996] E.C.R. I-2201, paras 45–54; ECJ, Case C-443/98 *Unilever Italia* [2000] E.C.R. I-7535, paras 31–52; ECJ, Case C-159/00 *Sapod Audic* [2002] E.C.R. I-5031, paras 48–52 (concerning Council Directive 83/189/EEC of March 18, 1993; see para. 9–111, *supra*); Voinot, "Le droit communautaire et l'inopposabilité aux particuliers des règles techniques nationales" (2003) R.T.D.E. 91–112; Candela Castillo, "La confirmation par la Cour du principe de non-opposabilité aux tiers des règles techniques non notifiées dans le cadre de la directive 83/189/CEE: un pas en avant vers l'intégration structurelle des ordres juridiques nationaux et communautaire" (1997) R.M.C.U.E. 51–59.

[30] ECJ, Case C-226/97 *Lemmens* [1998] E.C.R. I-3711, para. 35.

[31] ECJ, Case 35/76 *Simmenthal* ("*Simmenthal I*") [1976] E.C.R. 1871.

[32] ECJ, Case 106/77 *Simmenthal* ("*Simmenthal II*") [1978] E.C.R. 629, para. 24.

21–010   *Factortame*. The Court of Justice went even further in the 1990 judgment in *Factortame I*, in which the House of Lords asked whether an English court had the power under Community law to grant an interim injunction against the Crown where a party claimed to be entitled to rights under Community law.[33] The problem had arisen after the Divisional Court of the Queen's Bench Division had applied to the Court of Justice for a preliminary ruling on the compatibility with Community law of nationality requirements imposed by the 1988 Merchant Shipping Act and the 1988 Merchant Shipping (Registration of Fishing Vessels) Regulations in order to put an end to the practice of "quota hopping" by which foreign vessels without any genuine link with the United Kingdom were using its fishing quotas. The House of Lords had to decide whether that court could suspend the relevant part of the 1988 Act and the 1988 Regulations by way of interim relief, the Court of Appeal having determined that under common law the courts had no power to suspend the application of Acts of Parliament in that way. Starting out from its judgment in *Simmenthal II* and the principle of cooperation enshrined in Art. 10 EC [*now Art. 4(3) TEU*], the Court of Justice ruled that,

> "the full effectiveness of Community law would be impaired if a rule of national law could prevent a court seised of a dispute governed by Community law from granting interim relief in order to ensure the full effectiveness of the judgment to be given on the existence of the rights claimed under Community law. It follows that a court which in those circumstances would grant interim relief, if it were not for a rule of national law, is obliged to set aside that rule".[34]

By so ruling, the Court safeguarded rights derived by individuals from Community law against action of a public authority, even where it had not been finally determined that the action in question was incompatible with Community law.[35]

---

[33] ECJ, Case C-213/89 *Factortame and Others* ("*Factortame I*") [1990] E.C.R. I-2433, paras 14–15.

[34] *Ibid.*, para. 21. On October 11, 1990, the House of Lords affirmed the interlocutory injunction against the Secretary of State. See Barav and Simon, "Le droit communautaire et la suspension provisoire des mesures nationales—Les enjeux de l'affaire *Factortame*" (1990) R.M.C. 591–597.

[35] That the United Kingdom legislation was indeed incompatible with Community law was only determined following the Court's judgment giving a preliminary ruling on questions which had already been referred to in ECJ, Case C-221/89 *Factortame and Others* ("*Factortame II*") [1991] E.C.R. I-3905 and the judgment given on an action brought by the Commission under Art. 226 EC [*now Art. 258 TFEU*], ECJ, Case C-246/89 *Commission v United Kingdom* [1991] E.C.R. I-4585. In the latter case, the President of the Court had already granted an application from the Commission for an interim order requiring the United Kingdom to suspend the nationality requirements of the legislation at issue: ECJ (order of the President of October 10, 1989), Case C-246/89 R *Commission v United Kingdom* [1989] E.C.R. I-3125. This was followed by the case concerning State liability for the breach of Community law: ECJ, Joined Cases C-46/93 and C-48/93 *Brasserie du Pêcheur and Factortame* ("*Factortame IV*") [1996] E.C.R. I-1029 (para. 21–014, *infra*).

Full effectiveness. In the judgments in *Simmenthal II* and *Factortame I*, the Court   21–011
of Justice linked the primacy of Community law with the duty of the national
court to secure the full effectiveness (*effet utile*) of Community law, even at the
expense of the legal tradition of its own Member State. Just as the primacy principle was associated with Art. 10 EC [*now Art. 4(3) TEU*] in *Costa v ENEL*, that
duty on the part of the national court was also derived from the principle of sincere cooperation enshrined in that article (see para. 7–048). As a general rule, the
full effectiveness of Union law requires Member States to nullify the unlawful
consequences of a breach of Union law.[36] Such an obligation is owed by every
organ of the Member State concerned within the sphere of its competence.[37]
Consequently, in principle any taxes levied in breach of Union law or benefits
unduly refused are to be refunded or paid out, respectively. Where consent has
been granted without duly complying with a procedure imposed by Union law,
the national court must therefore revoke or suspend that consent so that the correct procedure can be followed.[38] Over time, the Court of Justice has gradually
specified more precisely the requirements which Art. 4(3) TEU imposes on
Member States with a view to securing the "full effectiveness" in the national
legal system of rights derived from Union law.[39]

Remedies under national law. In the absence of Union rules governing the   21–012
matter, it is for the domestic legal system of each Member State to designate the
courts and tribunals having jurisdiction and to lay down the detailed procedural
rules governing actions for safeguarding rights which individuals derive from
Union law. But the Member States are nevertheless responsible for ensuring
that those rights are effectively protected in each case.[40] The principle of full

---

[36] ECJ, Joined Cases C-6/90 and C-9/90 *Francovich and Others* [1991] E.C.R. I-5357, para. 36; see
earlier with regard to the corresponding provision of Art. 86 ECSC: ECJ, Case 6/60 *Humblet*
[1960] E.C.R. 559, at 569.

[37] Case C-8/88 *Germany v Commission* [1990] E.C.R. I-2321, para. 13; ECJ, Case C-201/02 *Wells*
[2004] E.C.R. I-723, para. 64.

[38] ECJ, Case C-201/02 *Wells* [2004] E.C.R. I-723, paras 64–70.

[39] The relevant case law is only discussed in outline in the following sections. For a more exhaustive
discussion, see Lenaerts, Arts and Maselis, *Procedural Law of the European Union* (3rd edn,
London, Sweet & Maxwell, 2012), Ch. 4. *Cf.* Ross, "Effectiveness in the European Legal order(s):
Beyond Supremacy to Constitutional Proportionality?" (2006) 31 E.L.Rev. 476–498;
Delicostopoulos, "Towards European Procedural Primacy in National Legal Systems" (2003)
E.L.J. 599–613; Temple Lang, "The Duties of National Courts under Community Constitutional
Law" (1997) E.L.Rev. 3–18; Bebr, "Court of Justice: Judicial Protection and the Rule of Law", in
Curtin and Heukels (eds), *Institutional Dynamics of European Integration. Essays in Honour of
Henry G. Schermers* (Vol. II, Dordrecht, Martinus Nijhoff, 1994), 303–333; Fitzpatrick and
Szyszczak, "Remedies and Effective Judicial Protection in Community Law" (1994) M.L.R.
434–441; Snyder, "The Effectiveness of European Community Law: Institutions, Processes, Tools
and Techniques" (1993) M.L.R. 19, at 40–47; Steiner, "From Direct Effects to Francovich: Shifting
Means of Enforcement of Community Law" (1993) E.L.Rev. 3–22.

[40] See, e.g., ECJ, Case C-268/06 *Impact* [2008] ECR I-2483, paras 44 and 45; ECJ (judgment of March
18, 2010), Joined Cases C-317/08 to C-320/08 *Alassini and Others*, not yet reported, para. 47.

effectiveness of Union law implies that the national rules governing claims by which individuals seek to enforce the rights which they derive from Union law "must not be less favourable than those relating to similar domestic claims" (principle of equivalence) and must not embody requirements and time-limits "such as in practice to make it impossible or excessively difficult" to exercise those rights (principle of effectiveness).[41] It appears from *Factortame I* and a number of other judgments that the national court must, where necessary, refrain from applying the normal national legal rules in order to secure the full effectiveness of Union law.[42] Administrative bodies, too, must disapply conflicting procedural rules in order to give full effect to Union law.[43] As far as national procedural rules are concerned, account must be taken of their role in the procedure, its progress and its special features, viewed as a whole, before the various national instances, and of the basic principles of the domestic judicial system, such as protection of the rights of the defence, the principle of legal certainty and the proper conduct of procedure.[44]

The first of the two requirements mentioned above—the principle of equivalence—requires that all the rules applicable to actions apply without distinction to actions alleging infringement of Union law and to similar actions alleging infringement of national law.[45] This will be the case, for example, with time-limits for

---

[41] ECJ, Case 33/76 *Rewe* [1976] E.C.R. 1989, para. 5, and ECJ, Case 45/76 *Comet* [1976] E.C.R. 2043, paras 13–16; see also ECJ, Case 68/79 *Just* [1980] E.C.R. 501, paras 25–26; ECJ, Case 199/82 *San Giorgio* [1983] E.C.R. 3595, paras 12–17. See Girerd, "Les principes d'équivalence et d'effectivité: encadrement ou désencadrement de l'autonomie procédurale des Etats membres?" (2000) R.T.D.E. 75–102.

[42] See, e.g., ECJ, Case C-377/89 *Cotter and McDermott* [1991] E.C.R. I-1155, paras 20–22 and 26–27 (married women held entitled to benefits/compensatory payments paid to married men in respect of a spouse deemed to be dependent even though this was contrary to a prohibition of unlawful enrichment laid down by Irish law); ECJ, Case C-208/90 *Emmott* [1991] E.C.R. I-4269, paras 23–24 (Irish authorities held not entitled to rely on procedural rules relating to time-limits for bringing proceedings in an action brought against them by an individual in order to protect rights directly conferred upon him by a Community directive so long as Ireland had not properly transposed the directive into national law); ECJ, Case C-271/91 *Marshall ("Marshall II")* [1993] E.C.R. I-4367, paras 30 and 34–35 (Ms Marshall had succeeded in her claim for unlawful sex discrimination under the equal treatment directive following ECJ, Case 152/84 *Marshall ("Marshall I")* [1986] E.C.R. 723; the Court held that the limit imposed on any damages claim which might be awarded by an Industrial Tribunal under the 1975 Sex Discrimination Act was unlawful), see the case note by Curtin (1994) C.M.L.Rev. 631–652. See Hoskins, "Tilting the Balance: Supremacy and National Procedural Rules" (1996) E.L.Rev. 365–377; Szyszczak, "Making Europe More Relevant to its Citizens: Effective Judicial Process" (1996) E.L.Rev. 351–377. See also para. 21–019, *infra*.

[43] ECJ, Case C-118/00 *Larsy* [2001] E.C.R. I-5063, paras 50–53.

[44] ECJ, Joined Cases C-430/93 and C-431/93 *Van Schijndel and Van Veen* [1995] E.C.R. I-4705, para. 19. See Wattel, "National procedural autonomy and effectiveness of EC Law: challenge the charge; file for restitution, sue for damages?", (2008) 35 L.I.E.I. 109–132.

[45] See, e.g., ECJ, Joined Cases C-392/04 and C-422/04 *i-21 Germany and Arcor* [2006] E.C.R. I-8559, paras 62–72, with a case note by Taborowski (2007) 44 C.M.L.Rev. 1463–1482.

bringing proceedings, limitation periods and rules concerning the production of evidence.[46] Even if they satisfy the first requirement, national procedural rules may still be problematic where they make the exercise of rights derived from Union law virtually impossible or excessively difficult (principle of effectiveness). That will be so particularly in the case of presumptions or rules of evidence intended to place upon the taxpayer the burden of establishing that the charges unduly paid have not been passed on to other persons or of special limitations concerning the form of the evidence to be adduced, such as the exclusion of any kind of evidence other than documentary evidence.[47] Likewise, the exercise of Union rights is made impossible where a national government would be able to reject the recovery of charges levied contrary to a directive on account of excusable error.[48] The principle of effectiveness does not therefore preclude Member States from laying down reasonable time-limits for bringing proceedings in the interests of legal certainty.[49] Accordingly, where an individual claims a social security benefit to which he or she is entitled pursuant to a directive, a Member State may in principle rely on the fact that the time-limit for bringing such claim has expired, even where it had not properly transposed the directive into national law on time. In such a case, the principle of effectiveness does not prevent the Member State from restricting the retroactive effect of a claim; however, a time-limit may not be relied on where, as a result of it, an individual has no possibility at all of asserting the rights conferred upon him or her by the directive in question.[50]

In principle, Union law does not involve itself in the resolution of questions of jurisdiction to which the classification of legal situations based on Union law may

---

[46] See, e.g., ECJ, Case C-2/06 *Kempter* [2008] E.C.R. I-411, paras 54–60 (time-limits for bringing proceedings held lawful); ECJ (judgment of January 26, 2010), Case C-118/08 *Transportes Urbanos y Servicios Generales*, not yet reported, paras 33–48 (requirement for all domestic remedies to have been exhausted before an action for damages can be brought against the State for a breach of Union law established by the Court of Justice held unlawful where that condition does not apply to an action for damages against the State for a breach of the national Constitution determined by the competent national court); ECJ (judgment of April 15, 2010), Case C-542/08 *Barth* not yet reported (limitation period held to be lawful).

[47] ECJ, Case 199/82 *San Giorgio* [1983] E.C.R. 3595, para. 14.

[48] ECJ, Case C-188/95 *Fantask and Others* [1997] E.C.R. I-6783, paras 35–41.

[49] ECJ, Case C-343/96 *Dilexport* [1999] E.C.R. I-579, paras 23–28.

[50] See ECJ, Case C-338/91 *Steenhorst-Neerings* [1993] E.C.R. I-5475, para. 24, and ECJ, Case C-410/92 *Johnson* [1994] E.C.R. I-5483, paras 22–23, with a case note by Docksey (1995) C.M.L.Rev. 1447–1459 (where a rule of general application limiting the period for which arrears of social security benefits could be claimed was held not to be unlawful). But see ECJ, Case C-246/96 *Magorrian and Cunningham* [1997] E.C.R. I-7153, paras 36–47, and ECJ, Case C-326/96 *Levez* [1998] E.C.R. I-7835, paras 18–33 (unlawful limitation of a claim based on Art. 141 EC [*now Art. 157 TFEU*] to a period starting to run from a point in time two years prior to the commencement of proceedings); ECJ, Case C-62/00 *Marks & Spencer* [2002] E.C.R. I-6325, paras 33–47 (unlawful legislation retroactively curtailing the period within which repayment may be sought of sums collected in breach of the relevant directive); ECJ, Case C-147/01 *Weber's Wine World and Others*, [2003] E.C.R. I-11365 paras 86–92 (retroactive restriction on the right to repayment of duty levied but not due held unlawful where that restriction specifically related to a duty which the Court of Justice held to be contrary to Union law).

give rise in the national judicial system. However, where a directive imposes an obligation to establish a suitable right of appeal and only a national jurisdictional rule prevents the national court from protecting the rights ensuing from the directive, the national court must disapply that rule.[51] All the same, Union law recognises that, in order to ensure stability of the law and legal relations, as well as the sound administration of justice, it is important that judicial decisions which have become definitive after all rights of appeal have been exhausted or after expiry of the time-limits provided for in that regard should no longer be able to be called in question (principle of res judicata).[52] However, the Court has held that the principle of res judicata under national law may not be applied in a manner that prevents an interpretation by national courts that violates Union law from being called in question in the context of new judicial proceedings between the same parties on a similar issue, as that would be contrary to the principle of effectiveness.[53]

On the other hand, Union law does not preclude a national court from suspending enforcement of a national administrative measure adopted to implement a Union regulation which is alleged to be unlawful, provided that certain conditions laid down by Union law are satisfied, so as to ensure the uniform application of that law.[54]

(d) *Union law raised by courts of their own motion*

21–013 **Pleas raised *ex officio*.** The principle of full effectiveness of Union law does not normally require national courts to raise a plea alleging infringement of provisions of Union law of their own motion. However, national courts are under a *duty* to raise of their own motion pleas of law based on mandatory Union law which were not put forward by the parties, where such an *obligation* also exists where mandatory national rules are concerned.[55] The same *duty* applies where domestic law confers on courts and tribunals a *power* to apply mandatory rules of national law of their own motion.[56] Accordingly, where domestic law so allows, a national

---

[51] ECJ, Case C-462/99 *Connect Austria Gesellschaft für Telekommunikation* [2003] E.C.R. I-5197, paras 35–42.

[52] ECJ, Case C-119/05 *Lucchini* [2007] E.C.R. I-6199, paras 59–63 (stating a limit to the recognition by Union law of the res judicata principle in State Aid cases).

[53] ECJ, Case C-2/08 *Fallimento Olimpiclub* [2009] E.C.R. I-7501, paras 20–32.

[54] ECJ, Joined Cases C-143/88 and C-92/89 *Zuckerfabrik Süderdithmarschen and Zuckerfabrik Soest* [1991] E.C.R. I-415, paras 14–33. Broadly, those conditions are: (1) the national court must entertain serious doubts as to the validity of the measure; (2) if the question of its validity has not already been brought before the Court of Justice, the national court should refer a question for a preliminary ruling; (3) there must be urgency and a threat of serious and irreparable damage to the applicant; and (4) the national court must take due account of the Union's interest. See the other decided cases discussed in Lenaerts, Arts and Maselis, *Procedural Law of the European Union* (3rd edn, London, Sweet & Maxwell, 2012) Ch. 4.

[55] ECJ, Joined Cases C-430/93 and C-431/93 *Van Schijndel and Van Veen* [1995] E.C.R. I-4705, para. 13.

[56] *Ibid.*, para. 14; ECJ, Case C-2/06 *Kempter* [2008] E.C.R. I-411, para. 45.

court must examine of its own motion whether the national legislative or administrative authorities implementing a directive remained within the limits of their discretion.[57] In those instances where domestic law does not expressly confer on national courts a discretion to raise of their own motion a plea based on Union law, those courts have to assess whether such duty flows from the application of the above-mentioned principles of equivalence and effectiveness in the specific case under consideration. In this connection, the Court has ruled that the principle of full effectiveness does not preclude the application of rules of national law that prevent a national court—even at last instance—from raising a plea based on a breach of provisions of Union law where examination of such a plea would oblige it to abandon the passive role assigned to it by going beyond the ambit of the dispute defined by the parties themselves and relying on facts and circumstances other than those on which the party with an interest in the application of those provisions bases his or her claim.[58] Neither is there a breach of the principle of equivalence where the applicable rule of Union law does not occupy a similar position within the Union legal order as the rule of national law whose infringement national courts can raise of their own motion.[59]

In one exceptional case, the Court of Justice has qualified a provision of Union law (Art. 101 TFEU) as a rule of public policy which national courts should raise of their own motion.[60] Moreover, in litigation concerning the application of Council Directive 93/13/EEC of April 5, 1993 on unfair terms in consumer contracts, the Court has held that it follows from the provisions of that directive that the national court is competent to assess of its own motion whether a contractual term was unfair.[61]

---

[57] ECJ, Case C-72/95 *Kraaijeveld* [1996] E.C.R. I-5403, para. 60.

[58] ECJ, Joined Cases C-430/93 and C-431/93 *Van Schijndel and Van Veen* [1995] E.C.R. I-4705, paras 19–22; *cf.* the judgment of the same date in ECJ, Case C-312/93 *Peterbroeck* [1995] E.C.R. I-4599, paras 14–21 (where it was held that the national court's refusal to entertain pleas not already raised before the tax authorities was contrary to Union law); ECJ, Joined Cases C-222/05 to C-225/05 *van der Weerd and Others* [2007] E.C.R I-4233, paras 33–38; see case notes by Heukels (1996) C.M.L.Rev. 337–353, Pertegás Sender (1995/96) Col.J.E.L. 179–185 and Jans and Marseille (2008) C.M.L.Rev. 853–862; see also Prechal, "Community Law in National Courts: The Lessons from *Van Schijndel*" (1998) C.M.L.Rev. 681–706.

[59] ECJ, Joined Cases C-222/05 to C-225/05 *van der Weerd and Others* [2007] E.C.R I-4233, paras 29–32.

[60] ECJ, Case C-126/97 *Eco Swiss China Time* [1999] E.C.R. I-3055, paras 31–37 (where a national court is required to grant an application for annulment of an arbitration award founded on failure to observe national rules of public policy, it must also do so if it considers that the award in question is contrary to Art. 81 EC [*now Art. 101 TFEU*]). See De Muynck, "De openbare orde en het mededingingsrecht" (2001) N.T.E.R. 253–257; Weyer, "Gemeinschaftsrechtliche Vorgaben für das nationale Zivilverfahren" (2000) EuR. 145–166.

[61] See ECJ, Joined Cases C-240/98 and C-244/98 *Océano Grupo Editorial and Others* [2000] E.C.R. I-4941, paras 21–29; ECJ, Case C-473/00 *Cofidis* [2002] E.C.R. I-10875, paras 32–38; ECJ, Case C-168/05 *Mostaza Claro* [2006] E.C.R. I-10421, paras 24–39; ECJ, Case C-243/08 *Pannon* [2009] E.C.R. I-4713, paras 20–28; ECJ, Case C-40/08 *Asturcom Telecomunicaciones* [2009] E.C.R. I-9579, paras 48–59. See also ECJ (judgment of December 17, 2009),

(e) *Liability of the Member State for damage arising out of a breach of Union law*

21–014 *Francovich*. The Court of Justice held in *Francovich* that,

> "[t]he full effectiveness of Community rules would be impaired and the protection of the rights which they grant would be weakened if individuals were unable to obtain redress when their rights are infringed by a breach of Community law for which a Member State can be held responsible".[62]

The Court went on to state that,

> "the principle whereby a State must be liable for loss and damage caused to individuals as a result of breaches of Community law for which the State can be held responsible is inherent in the system of the Treaty"

and that a further basis for the obligation of Member States to make good such loss and damage is to be found in Art. 10 EC [*now Art. 4(3) TEU*].[63] That principle applies to any case in which a Member State breaches Community law—Union law since the Lisbon treaty—irrespective of the authority of the Member State whose act or omission was responsible for the breach.[64] Consequently, an individual may bring a damages claim in the national courts on account of an act

---

Case C-227/08 *Martín Martín*, not yet reported, paras 18–36 (national court may of its own motion invoke a plea based on Council Directive 85/577/EEC of December 20, 1985 to protect the consumer in respect of contracts negotiated away from business premises).

[62] ECJ, Joined Cases C-6/90 and C-9/90 *Francovich and Others* [1991] E.C.R. I-5357, para. 33. The principle is therefore intended both to protect the rights of individuals and to maintain the primacy of Community law; see Aboudrar-Ravanel, "Responsabilité et primauté, ou la question de l'efficience de l'outil" (1999) R.M.C.U.E. 544–558. Among numerous studies, see Davis, "Liability in damages for a breach of Community law: some reflections on the question of who to sue and the concept of the state" (2006) E.L.Rev. 69–80; Tridimas, "Liability for Breach of Community Law: Growing Up and Mellowing Down?" (2001) C.M.L.Rev. 301–332; Dantonel-Cor, "La violation de la norme communautaire et la responsabilité extracontractuelle de l'Etat" (1998) R.T.D.E. 75–91; Wissink, "De Nederlandse rechter en overheidsaansprakelijkheid krachtens *Francovich* en *Brasserie du Pêcheur*" (1997) S.E.W. 78–90; Van Gerven, "Bridging the Unbridgeable: Community and National Tort Laws after *Francovich* and *Brasserie*" (1996) I.C.LQ. 507–544; Schockweiler, "Die Hafting der EG-Mitgliedstaaten gegenüber dem einzelnen bei Verletzung des Gemeinschaftsrechts" (1993) EuR. 107–133. Some commentators consider that Union law also puts individuals under a duty to make good damage resulting from a breach of Union law; see Kremer, "Die Haftung Privater für Verstösse gegen Gemeinschaftsrecht" (2003) EuR. 696–705. This is true of competition law; see para. 11–013.
[63] ECJ, Joined Cases C-6/90 and C-9/90 *Francovich and Others* [1991] E.C.R. I-5357, paras 35–36.
[64] ECJ, Case C-224/01 *Köbler* [2003] E.C.R. I-10239, para. 31.

or omission of a legislative organ[65] or on account of decisions of judicial bodies adjudicating at last instance.[66]

Conditions for liability. The conditions under which that liability gives rise to a right to reparation from the State depend on the nature of the breach of Union law giving rise to the loss and damage.[67] The Court of Justice made it clear in *Factortame IV* that the conditions under which the State may incur liability for damage caused to individuals by a breach of Union law cannot, in the absence of particular justification, differ from those governing the liability of the Union in like circumstances.[68] With regard to an act or omission of the legislature or executive in breach of that Union law, Union law therefore confers a right of reparation where three conditions are met:

21–015

(1) the rule of law infringed must be intended to confer rights on individuals;

(2) the breach must be sufficiently serious; and

(3) there must be a direct causal link between the breach of the obligation resting on the State and the damage sustained by the injured parties.[69]

The same three conditions apply to State liability for damage resulting from the decision of a judicial body adjudicating at last instance.[70] According to the Court

---

[65] ECJ, Joined Cases C-46/93 and C-48/93 *Brasserie du Pêcheur and Factortame* [1996] E.C.R. I-1029, paras 34–36.

[66] ECJ, Case C-224/01 *Köbler*, [2003] E.C.R. I-10239, paras 30–59; ECJ, Case C-173/03 *Traghetti del Mediterraneo* [2006] E.C.R. I-5177, paras 30–40. See Ruffert (2007) C.M.L.Rev. 479–486; Breuer (2004) E.L.Rev. 243–254; Wegener (2004) EuR. 84–91, and for a somewhat critical view, Steyger (2004) N.T.E.R. 18–22 and Wattel (2004) C.M.L.Rev. 177–190. For earlier discussions of this question, see Anagnostaras, "The Principle of State Liability for Judicial Breaches: The Impact of European Community Law" (2001) E.Pub.L. 281–305; Blanchet, "L'usage de la théorie de l'acte clair en droit communautaire: une hypothèse de mise en jeu de la responsabilité de l'Etat français du fait de la fonction juridictionnelle?" (2001) R.T.D.E. 397–438; for a critical view, see Wegener, "Staatshaftung für die Verletzung von Gemeinschaftsrecht durch nationale Gerichte?" (2002) EuR. 785–800. For discussions of implications for the domestic legal systems, see also Convery, "State Liability in the United Kingdom after *Brasserie du Pêcheur*" (1997) C.M.L.Rev. 603–634; Hatje, "Die Haftung der Mitgliedstaaten bei Verstossen des Gesetzgebers gegen europäisches Gemeinschaftsrecht" (1997) EuR. 297–310.

[67] ECJ, Joined Cases C-6/90 and C-9/90 *Francovich and Others* [1991] E.C.R. I-5357, para. 38.

[68] ECJ, Joined Cases C-46/93 and C-48/93 *Brasserie du Pêcheur and Factortame* [1996] E.C.R. I-1029, paras 40–42.

[69] *Ibid.*, paras 50–51; ECJ, Case C-392/93 *British Telecommunications* [1996] E.C.R. I-1631, para. 39. These rules have applied to legislative acts of the Union since ECJ, Case 5/71 *Zuckerfabrik Schöppenstedt v Council* [1971] E.C.R. 975, para. 11: see Lenaerts, Arts and Maselis, *Procedural Law of the European Union* (3rd edn, London, Sweet & Maxwell, 2012), Ch. 11. For the parallel with the rules on liability applying to the Union, see ECJ, Case C-352/98P *Laboratoires pharmaceutiques Bergaderm and Goupil and Others* [2000] E.C.R. I-5291, paras 38–44; for breaches of fundamental rights, see Van Gerven, "Remedies for Infringements of Fundamental Rights" (2004) E.Pub.L. 261–284.

[70] ECJ, Case C-224/01 *Köbler*, [2003] E.C.R. I-10239, paras 51–53; ECJ, Case C-173/03 *Traghetti del Mediterraneo* [2006] E.C.R. I-5177, paras 42–45.

of Justice, this does not mean that the State cannot incur liability for acts of the legislature, executive or the judiciary under less strict conditions on the basis of national law.[71]

21–016 **(1) Provision conferring rights on individuals.** Among the provisions which confer rights on individuals are the Treaty provisions governing the four freedoms.[72] In *Factortame IV*, the Court of Justice made it clear that the right of reparation exists whether or not the relevant provision of Union law has direct effect.[73]

21–017 **(2) Sufficiently serious breach.** A breach of Union law will clearly be "sufficiently serious" if it has persisted despite a judgment of the Court of Justice from which it is clear that the conduct in question constituted an infringement.[74] However, the right of reparation does not depend on the existence of a prior judgment of the Court of Justice.[75] Still, although the national courts have jurisdiction to decide how to characterise the breaches of Union law at issue, the Court of Justice will indicate a number of circumstances which the national courts might take into account,[76] and it will even characterise the breach itself if it has all the information necessary to that end.[77] The national court must take account of the clarity and precision of the rule infringed, whether the infringement and the damage caused was intentional or involuntary, whether any error of law was excusable or inexcusable, and the fact that the position taken by a Union institution may

---

[71] ECJ, Joined Cases C-46/93 and C-48/93 *Brasserie du Pêcheur and Factortame* [1996] E.C.R. I-1029, para. 66; ECJ, Case C-224/01 *Köbler* [2003] E.C.R. I-10239, para. 57; ECJ, Case C-173/03 *Traghetti del Mediterraneo* [2006] E.C.R. I-5177, para. 45. See, e.g., in Belgium with respect to the regulatory activity of the administration: Cass. January 14, 2000, *Arr. Cass.*, 2000, No. 33, referred to in the Eighteenth Annual Report on monitoring Community law, COM(2001) 309 fin. According to this "Evobus" judgment, any ordinary breach of Community law by an administrative authority may constitute a "fault" for which the State can be held liable. See also Cass. December 8, 1994, *Arr. Cass.* 1994, No. 541 (the second "Anca" judgment, in which the State was held to be liable for a breach of Community law by a judicial body); see Vuye, "Overheidsaansprakelijkheid wegens schending van het Europees Gemeenschapsrecht" (2003) T.B.H. 743–763.

[72] ECJ, Case C-446/04 *Test Claimants in the FII Group Litigation* [2006] E.C.R. I-11753, para. 211; ECJ, Case C-445/06 *Danske Slagterier* [2009] E.C.R. I-2119, paras 21–26.

[73] ECJ, Joined Cases C-46/93 and C-48/93 *Brasserie du Pêcheur and Factortame* [1996] E.C.R. I-1029, paras 18–23, with case notes by Foubert (1996) Col.J.E.L. 359–372 and Oliver (1997) C.M.L.Rev. 635–680.

[74] ECJ, Joined Cases C-46/93 and C-48/93 *Brasserie du Pêcheur and Factortame* [1996] E.C.R. I-1029, para. 57.

[75] *Ibid.*, paras 91–96.

[76] *Ibid.*, paras 56 and 58–64, likewise paras 75–80 (the existence of fault may be taken into account only in order to determine whether the breach is sufficiently serious). For further clarification, see ECJ, Joined Cases C-94/95 and C-95/95 *Bonfaci and Others and Berto and Others* [1997] E.C.R. I-3969.

[77] See ECJ, Case C-392/93 *British Telecommunications* [1996] E.C.R. I-1631, para. 41; ECJ, Case C-118/00 *Larsy* [2001] E.C.R. I-5063, paras 40–49; ECJ, Case C-224/01 *Köbler*, [2003] E.C.R. I-10239, paras 101–126; ECJ, Case C-452/06 *Synthon* [2008] E.C.R. I-7681, paras 36–46.

have contributed towards the adoption or maintenance of national measures or practices contrary to Union law.[78] Accordingly, the incorrect transposition of provisions of a directive which are capable of bearing several interpretations and on which neither the Court nor the Commission has given any guidance does not necessarily constitute a sufficiently serious breach (see para. 22–092). As far as liability for judicial decisions is concerned, the national court must take account of non-compliance by the court adjudicating at last instance with its obligation to make a reference for a preliminary ruling under the third para. of Art. 267 TFEU.[79] An incorrect application of Union law by a judicial body adjudicating at last instance does not constitute a sufficiently serious breach where the answer to the question is not expressly covered by Union law, not provided by the case law of the Court of Justice and not obvious.[80] Where, however, at the time when it committed the infringement, a legislative or administrative organ of the Member State in question was not called upon to make any legislative choices and had only considerably reduced discretion, or even none at all, the mere infringement of Union law may be sufficient to establish the existence of a sufficiently serious breach.[81] Accordingly, the Court held already in *Francovich* that there is a sufficiently serious breach where a Member State fails to take any of the measures necessary to achieve the result prescribed by a directive within the period it lays down.[82] In any event, the existence and scope of the discretion available to the Member State must be determined by reference to Union law and not by reference to national law.[83]

(3) Direct causal link. Lastly, in order for the State to incur liability, there must be a direct causal link between the breach of the Union obligation resting on the State and the loss or damage sustained by those affected. It is for the national court to assess whether the loss or damage claimed flows sufficiently directly from the breach of Union law to render the State liable to make it good.[84]

21–018

Reparation for loss and damage. Provided that these conditions, prescribed by Union law itself, are met, it is on the basis of the rules of national law on liability that the State must make reparation for the consequences of the loss and

21–019

---

[78] ECJ, Case C-118/00 *Larsy* [2001] E.C.R. I-5063, para. 39; ECJ, Case C-224/01 *Köbler* [2003] E.C.R. I-10239, para. 55.

[79] ECJ, Case C-224/01 *Köbler* [2003] E.C.R. I-10239, para. 55; ECJ, Case C-173/03 *Traghetti del Mediterraneo* [2006] E.C.R. I-5177, paras 32 and 43.

[80] ECJ, Case C-224/01 *Köbler* [2003] E.C.R. I-10239, paras 121–122. This position is not altered by the fact that the national court should have made a reference for a preliminary ruling: *ibid.*, para. 123.

[81] ECJ, Case C-5/94 *Hedley Lomas* [1996] E.C.R. I-2553, para. 28 (infringement of Art. 29 EC [*now Art. 35 TFEU*], which prohibits quantitative restrictions on exports).

[82] ECJ, Joined Cases C-178/94, C-179/94, C-188/94, C-189/94 and C-190/94 *Dillenkofer and Others* [1996] E.C.R. I-4845, paras 22–26. For failure to transpose a directive, see para. 22–092, *infra*.

[83] ECJ, Case C-424/97 *Haim* [2000] E.C.R. I-5123, para. 40.

[84] ECJ, Case C-446/04 *Test Claimants in the FII Group Litigation* [2006] E.C.R. I-11753, para. 218.

damage caused.[85] It is the national legal order which determines against what (central or decentralised) authority the claim must be made (see para. 14–017) and designates the judicial authority competent to determine disputes relating to compensation for damage.[86] Naturally, the formal and substantive conditions laid down by national law must not be less favourable than those relating to similar domestic claims and must not be such as in practice to make it impossible or excessively difficult to obtain compensation.[87]

2. Incorporation in the Member States' legal systems

21–020 **Monist and dualist systems.** The principle of the primacy of Union law formulated by the Court of Justice was not automatically applied by each Member State in its domestic legal system. This was possible in the "monist" Member States, which give international legal norms as such precedence over domestic law. On that ground, those Member States accepted that Union law took precedence in its

---

[85] ECJ, Joined Cases C-6/90 and C-9/90 *Francovich and Others* [1991] E.C.R. I-5357, paras 42–43.

[86] ECJ, Case C-224/01 *Köbler* [2003] E.C.R. I-10239, paras 44–47 and 50 (concerning compensation for damage resulting from a judicial decision conflicting with Union law).

[87] See para. 21–012, *infra*, and, for the transposition of directives, para. 22–092, *infra*. Thus, it has been held that the following conditions for State liability should be set aside on the ground that they would impede effective judicial protection: a condition making reparation dependent upon the legislature's act or omission being referable to an individual situation, a condition requiring proof of misfeasance in public office (ECJ, Joined Cases C-46/93 and C-48/93 *Brasserie du Pêcheur and Factortame* [1996] E.C.R. I-1029, paras 67–73) and a rule totally excluding loss of profit as a head of damage (*ibid.*, para. 87). For the national courts' subsequent decisions in the *Brasserie du Pêcheur* and *Factortame* litigation, see the judgment of the *Bundesgerichtshof* of October 24, 1996, III ZR 127/91 (1996) Eu.Z.W. 761 (State held not liable in *Brasserie du Pêcheur* because of the lack of a causal link) and the judgment of the Queen's Bench Division of July 31, 1997 in *R. v Secretary of State for Transport, Ex p. Factortame and Others (No. 5)* [1997] T.L.R. 482 and (1998) R.T.D.E. 93–95 (State held liable for a serious breach). Cases in which damages have been granted in Member States for breaches of Community law are reported in the survey of the application of Community law by national courts annexed to the annual report of the Commission on monitoring the application of Community law which is available on the Commission's website (under "Legislation and Treaties", see "Application of EU law by the Member States" and "Infringements of EU law") and the website of the Court of Justice (under "Library and documentation") and the website of the Court of Justice (under "European Union law in Europe", see "National and international case law"). In determining the loss or damage for which reparation may be granted, the national court may always inquire whether the injured person showed reasonable care so as to avoid the loss or damage or to mitigate it (ECJ, Joined Cases C-178/94, C-179/94, C-188/94, C-189/94 and C-190/94 *Dillenkofer and Others* [1996] E.C.R. I-4845, para. 72; ECJ, Case C-524/04 *Test Claimants in the Thin Cap Group Litigation* [2007] E.C.R. I-02107, paras 124–126; ECJ, Case C-445/06 *Danske Slagterier* [2009] E.C.R. I-2119, paras 58–69). See further Emiliou, "State Liability under Community Law: Shedding More Light on the *Francovich* Principle?" (1996) E.L.Rev. 399–411. See also ECJ, Case C-66/95 *Sutton* [1997] E.C.R. I-2163, paras 28–35; ECJ, Case C-90/96 *Petrie and Others* [1997] E.C.R. I-6527, para. 31; ECJ, Case C-127/95 *Norbrook Laboratories* [1998] E.C.R. I-1531, paras 106–112.

own right in the domestic legal system.[88] By contrast, in "dualist" systems, international legal provisions do not form part of the domestic legal system unless and until they have been incorporated therein by a provision of national law. If the principle of primacy of Union law is given no legal force superior to the provision incorporating it, the process of incorporation does not necessarily secure the primacy for Union law.[89] In some Member States, the courts base the primacy of Union law not on the specific nature of the Union legal order, but on the provision of the national constitution which recognises the primacy of international law or which authorises the transfer of powers to a supranational authority.[90] This is often the case in the Member States which more recently acceded to the European Union and where the precedence of Union law has been embraced as part of the *acquis* to which the Member States subscribed upon accession.

As will be seen hereinafter,[91] it is particularly in Member States that provide for a system of constitutional review that the question arises as to whether Union law must be regarded as being subordinate to the national constitution and whether provisions of Union law may be tested against the national constitution. From the point of view of Union law, it is irrelevant what method a given Member State uses in order to provide a basis for the primacy of Union law within its domestic legal system, provided that that law actually is given precedence over

---

[88] E.g., the Benelux countries; see paras 21–021 and 21–032—21–033, *infra*. See, more recently, Austria, Cyprus, the Baltic States, Bulgaria and Poland, paras 21–040, 21–046, 21–043—21–045, 21–053 and 21–051.

[89] Compare the developments in Ireland, para 21–034, *infra*, with the state of the law in the United Kingdom and Denmark, paras. 21–034—21–035, *infra*. See, more recently, Hungary and Malta, paras 21–049 and 21–050; previously also the Czech Republic and Slovakia, paras 21–047 and 21–048.

[90] See paras 21–022—21–031 and 21–037—21–039, *infra*. For clauses governing the transfer of powers, see Albi, " 'Europe' Articles in the Constitutions of Central and Eastern European countries" (2005) C.M.L.Rev. 399–423; Lepka and Terrebus, "Les ratifications nationales, manifestations d'un projet politique européen—la face cachée du Traité d'Amsterdam" (2003) R.T.D.E. 365–388.

[91] For a more extensive survey of the primacy of Union law in the national legal systems, see Łazowski (ed.), *The Application of EU law in the New Member States—Brave New World* (The Hague, T.M.C. Asser Press, forthcoming); Kellermann, Czuczai, Blockmans, Albi and Douma (eds), *The impact of EU accession on the legal orders of new EU Member States and (pre-)candidate countries: hopes and fears* (The Hague, T.M.C. Asser Press, 2006), 465 pp.; Pescatore, "L'application judiciaire des traités internationaux dans la Communauté européenne et dans ses Etats membres", *Etudes de droit des Communautés européennes. Mélanges offerts à P. H. Teitgen* (Paris, Pedone, 1984), 355–406; Bonichot and others, "L'application du droit communautaire dans les différents Etats membres de la Communauté économique européenne" (1990) R.F.D.A. 955–986; Henrichs, "Gemeinschaftsrecht und nationale Verfassungen. Organisations- und verfahrensrechtliche Aspekte einer Konfliktlage" (1990) Eu.GR.Z. 413–423. For the most significant judgments of national courts relating to the application of Union law, see the survey annexed to each annual report of the Commission on monitoring the application of Union law and Oppenheimer, *The Relationship between European Community Law and National Law: The Cases* (Cambridge, Cambridge University Press, 2004). See also the website of the European Constitutional Law Network: *http://www.ecln.net* [Accessed December 12, 2010].

domestic law. This remark also applies to the reluctance which some Constitutional Courts have shown in accepting the primacy of Union law.[92]

(a) *Founding Member States*

(1) Belgium

21–021   *Franco-Suisse Le Ski.* In 1970, the Belgian Constitution of 1831 was amended to take account of the establishment of the Communities by the addition of Art. 25*bis* (Consolidated Constitution, Art. 34), which provides that "the exercise of specific powers may be conferred by treaty or by statute on international institutions".

Even before then, it had been argued that international law, including (then) Community law, took precedence over domestic law. In the judgment of May 27, 1971 in *Franco-Suisse Le Ski*, the Supreme Court (*Hof van Cassatie/Cour de Cassation*) accepted that view in confirming that a law could not prohibit the repayment of charges collected contrary to Art. 12 of the EEC Treaty on the ground that:

> "where there is a conflict between a domestic provision and a provision of international law which has direct effects in the domestic legal order, the rule laid down by the treaty must prevail; that priority follows from the very nature of international law laid down by treaty; this applies *a fortiori* where, as in this case, the conflict arises between a provision of domestic law and a provision of Community law; this is because the treaties which brought Community law into being established a new legal order by virtue of which the Member States limited the exercise of their sovereign powers in the areas defined in those treaties; . . . it follows from the foregoing that the Judge was obliged to refrain from applying the provisions of domestic law which conflict with [Article 12 of the EEC Treaty]".[93]

---

[92] In addition to the commentators cited above, see Schermers, "The Scales in Balance: National Constitutional Courts v. Court of Justice" (1990) C.M.L.Rev. 97–105; Darmon, "Juridictions constitutionnelles et droit communautaire" (1988) R.T.D.E. 217–251. Taking the view that some Constitutional Courts were reluctant to embrace the principle of primacy of Union law without reservations, some scholars have tried to explain the relationship between Union law and national law from a non-hierarchical perspective ("constitutional pluralism"). See Poiares Maduro, "Contrapunctual law: Europe's constitutional pluralism in action", in Walker (ed.), *Sovereignty in Transition* (Oxford, Oxford University Press, 2003) 501–537; Barents, "The Precedence of EU Law from the Perspective of Constitutional Pluralism" (2009) E.Const.L.Rev. 421–446; Avbelj and Komárek, "Four Visions of Constitutional Pluralism" (2008) E.Const.L.Rev. 524–527; Baquero Cruz, "The Legacy of the Maastricht-Urteil and the Pluralist Movement" (2008) E.L.J. 389–422; Kumm, "The Jurisprudence of Constitutional Conflict: Constitutional Supremacy in Europe before and after the Constitutional Treaty" (2005) E.L.J. 262–307; Walker, "The Idea of Constitutional Pluralism" (2002) Mod.L.Rev. 317–359.

[93] Cass., May 27, 1971, *Arr. Cass.*, 959; (1972) S.E.W. 42.

Consequently, Belgian law followed the Court of Justice in deriving the primacy of Community—now Union—law from the very nature of that law.[94]

As far as acceptance of the primacy of Union law over provisions of constitutional law is concerned, the state of Belgian law has become less clear since the Constitutional Court (*Grondwettelijk Hof/Cour constitutionnelle*) held that it has jurisdiction to assess the constitutionality of laws ratifying a treaty and treaties themselves.[95] However, the Constitutional Court has never held that Union law ranks lower than the Constitution. Moreover, the review of the constitutionality of laws by way of preliminary rulings has been expressly excluded for laws "ratifying a constituent treaty with respect to the European Union or the European Convention on Human Rights". It is worth noting that the Belgian Constitutional Court was the first constitutional court of a Member State to make preliminary references to the Court of Justice both on the interpretation and on the validity of Union law.[96] It may be argued that because of its particular nature, Union law must continue to have precedence even over the Constitution.[97] The Supreme Administrative Court (*Raad van State/Conseil d'Etat*) has held to this effect that Art. 34 of the Constitution does not only afford the constitutional basis for the transfer of powers to the European Union but also for the jurisdiction of the Court

---

[94] See Wytinck, "The Application of Community Law in Belgium (1986–1992)" (1993) C.M.L.Rev. 981–1020; Lenaerts, "The Application of Community Law in Belgium" (1986) C.M.L.Rev. 253–286.

[95] *Grondwettelijk Hof/Cour constitutionnelle* (before 2007 called *Arbitragehof/Cour d'Arbitrage*), October 16, 1991, No. 26/91, *B.S./M.B.*, November 23, 1991, *A.A.*, 1991, 271; see also *Grondwettelijk Hof/Cour constitutionnelle*, February 3, 1994, No. 12/94, *B.S./M.B*, March 11, 1994, *A.A.*, 1994, 211; *Grondwettelijk Hof/Cour constitutionnelle*, April 26, 1994, No. 33/94, *B.S./M.B.*, June 22, 1994, *A.A.*, 1994, 419. See the critical commentary by Louis, "La primauté, une valeur relative?" (1995) C.D.E. 23–28; Popelier, "Ongrondwettige verdragen: de rechtspraak van het Arbitragehof in een monistisch tijdsperspectief" (1994–95) R.W. 1076–1080; Velu, "Toetsing van de grondwettigheid en toetsing van de verenigbaarheid met verdragen" (1992–93) R.W. 481, at 487–516; for an approving commentary, see Melchior and Vandernoot, "Contrôle de constitutionnalité et droit communautaire dérivé" (1998) R.B.D.C. 3–45; Brouwers and Simonart, "Le conflit entre la Constitution et le droit international conventionnel dans la jurisprudence de la Cour d'arbitrage" (1995) C.D.E. 7–22.

[96] See, for the first question on interpretation, ECJ, Case C-93/97 *Fédération Belge des Chambres Syndicales de Médecins* [1998] E.C.R. I-4837; for the first questions on the validity of Community and pre-Lisbon third pillar law: ECJ, Case C-305/05 *Ordre des barreaux francophones et germanophone and Others* [2007] E.C.R. I-5305, and ECJ, Case C-303/05 *Advocaten voor de Wereld* [2007] E.C.R, I-3633, respectively. See Van Nuffel, "Prejudiciële vragen aan het Hof van Justitie van de Europese Unie: leidraad voor de rechtspraktijk na het Verdrag van Lissabon" (2009–2010) R.W. 1154, at 1166 and 1169–1172; Vandamme, "Prochain Arrêt: La Belgique! Explaining Recent Preliminary References of the Belgian Constitutional Court", (2008) E.Const.L.Rev. 127–148; Van Nuffel, "Het Europees recht in de rechtspraak van het Arbitragehof: prejudiciële vragen, te veel gevraagd?" (2005) T.B.P. 246–255.

[97] This view also inspired the amendment which took away the jurisdiction of the *Grondwettelijk Hof/Cour constitutionnelle* to give preliminary rulings on laws ratifying a constituent treaty relating to the European Union; see Vanden Heede and Goedertier, "Eindelijk een volwaardig Grondwettelijk Hof? Een commentaar op de Bijzondere Wet van 9 maart 2003" (2003) T.B.P. 458, at 468.

of Justice to ensure the uniform interpretation of Union law, even though this limits the legal effects of national constitutional provisions.[98]

(2) France

21–022   **Initial constitutional framework.** The recognition of the primacy of Union law in the French legal order is more complicated than Art. 55 of the 1958 French Constitution would suggest. According to that article, treaties which are approved and ratified in accordance with the relevant rules have legal force as from their publication superior to that of statutes, subject to the proviso that each treaty is complied with by the other party or parties. However, since Art. 54 of the Constitution provides that a treaty which the *Conseil constitutionnel* (Constitutional Council) declares unconstitutional may be approved and ratified only following an amendment of the Constitution,[99] treaties are subordinated to the Constitution. Initially, the French courts considered that the above-mentioned provisions of the Constitution did not allow them to give precedence to Union law. If they had to review the compatibility of a given statute with Union law, its compatibility with Art. 55 of the Constitution would in fact have been tested, whilst Art. 61 of the Constitution provided that (prior) review of constitutionality was reserved to the *Conseil constitutionnel*. Thus, the *Conseil d'Etat* (Supreme Administrative Court) refused to rule on the compatibility of a number of ministerial decrees with Union law, thereby following the opinion of the *Commissaire du gouvernement*, who had argued that such a ruling would be tantamount to reviewing the constitutionality of the statutes on which the decrees were based.[100]

21–023   **Reversal in case law of *Conseil d'Etat*.** In 1975, however, the *Conseil constitutionnel* cleared the way for reviewing the compatibility of statutes with Union law when it held in the course of reviewing the constitutionality of a given statute that it would not give a view on its compatibility with a treaty on the ground that this was a different type of review, since a law contrary to a treaty does not for that reason violate the Constitution.[101] This prompted the *Cour de cassation* (Supreme Court) to accept the primacy of Union law on the basis of Art. 55 of the

---

[98] *Raad van State/Conseil d'Etat*, November 5, 1996, No. 62.621 (*Goosse*) and No. 69.922 (*Orfinger*), discussed in "Annex VI—Application of Community law by national courts" to the Fourteenth Annual Report on monitoring the application of Community law (1996), [1997] O.J. C332/202.

[99] For the review of constitutionality by the *Conseil constitutionnel*, see Boulouis, "Le juge constitutionnel français et l'Union européenne" (1994) C.D.E. 505–522.

[100] Judgment of March 1, 1968 *Syndicat général des Fabricants de semoules de France* (1968) Rec.C.E. 149; for the opinion, see (1968) A.J.D.A. 235.

[101] Judgment of January 15, 1975 (1975) Rec.Con.const. 19; (1975) Rec.Dalloz Jurispr., 529. Meanwhile, the *Conseil constitutionnel* has introduced an exception to this case law, namely the constitutional obligation to implement directives. See *Conseil constitutionnel*, Decision No. 2006–540 DC, July 27, 2006, *Loi relative au droit d'auteur et aux droits voisins dans la société de l'information* (n. 120, *infra*).

Constitution and the specific nature of Union law.[102] Yet, the primacy of Union law could find no foothold in administrative case law so long as the *Conseil d'Etat* did not agree to revise its jurisprudence. The reversal eventually came in 1989 when, in the *Nicolo* case, the *Conseil d'Etat* reviewed the law on the organisation of the European elections in the light of Art. 227(1) of the EEC Treaty.[103] Subsequently, the *Conseil d'Etat* held in *Boisdet* that a statute conflicted with a Union regulation and annulled a ministerial decree based thereon.[104]

Respect for constitutional identity. Following the ratification of the EU Treaty **21–024** and the Treaty of Amsterdam, Art. 88 relating to France's participation in the European Community and the European Union was added to the French Constitution.[105] Article 88, however, does not refer to the status of Union law in the French legal order and, in particular, leaves the question open whether Union law takes precedence over the Constitution. Consequently, it was discussed whether the adoption of Art. 88 of the French Constitution had not placed Union law at least on an equal footing with the Constitution.[106]

It took until June 2004 for the *Conseil constitutionnel* to rely on Art. 88 in order to explain the relationship between the French Constitution and Union law in a series of cases in which it was asked to what extent the constitutionality of a statute implementing a directive could be examined.[107] It ruled that, by virtue of Art. 88 of the French Constitution,

---

[102] Judgment of May 24, 1975, *Administration des Douanes v Société des Cafés Jacques Vabre & Société Weigel et Cie* (1975) Rec.Dalloz Jurispr., 497, translated in [1975] 2 C.M.L.R. 336.

[103] Judgment of October 30, 1989 *Nicolo* (1989) Rec.C.E. 190, translated in [1990] 1 C.M.L.R. 173.

[104] Judgment of September 24, 1990, *Boisdet* (1990) Rec.C.E. 250, translated in [1991] 1 C.M.L.R. 3. See Oliver, "The French Constitution and the Treaty of Maastricht" (1994) I.C.L.Q. 1–25; Roseren, "The Application of Community Law by French Courts from 1982 to 1993" (1994) C.M.L.Rev. 315–376; Manin, "The *Nicolo* Case of the *Conseil d'Etat*: French Constitutional Law and the Supreme Administrative Court's Acceptance of the Primacy of Community Law over Subsequent National Statute Law" (1991) C.M.L.Rev. 499–519.

[105] For the introduction of this article, see the literature in notes concerning the ratification of the EU Treaty and the Treaty of Amsterdam; paras 3–010 and 3–020, *supra*.

[106] The *Conseil d'Etat* emphasised the supremacy of the Constitution in its judgment of December 3, 2001 in the *SNIP* case (*Syndicat national de l'industrie pharmaceutique*, (2002) R.F.D.A. 166; (2002) A.J.D.A. 1219; see Chaltiel, "La boîte de Pandore des relations entre la Constitution française et le droit communautaire" (2002) R.M.C.U.E. 595–599; Spiegels, "Das Verhältnis des Gemeinschaftsrechts zum französischen Recht—Nationale Souveränität und europäische Integration" (2003) EuR. 119–133. Yet, in the same judgment, the *Conseil d'Etat* confirmed the binding nature of general principles of Union law; see Castaing, "L'extension du contrôle de conventionnalité aux principes généraux du droit communautaire" (2003) R.T.D.E. 197–228.

[107] *Conseil constitutionnel*, Decision No. 2004–496 DC, June 10, 2004, *Loi pour la confiance dans l'économie numérique*; Decision No. 2004–497 DC, July 1, 2004, *Loi relative aux communications électroniques et aux services de communication audiovisuelle*; Decision No. 2004–498 DC, July 29, 2004, *Loi relative à la bioéthique*. See also Bell, "French Constitutional Council and European Law" (2005) I.C.L.Q. 735–744; Reestman, "*Conseil constitutionnel* on the Status of (Secondary) Community Law in the French Internal Order" (2005) E.Const.L.Rev. 302–317; Azoulai and

"the transposition in domestic law of a directive results from a constitutional requirement with which non-compliance is only possible by reason of an express contrary provision of the Constitution".

Accordingly, legislative measures implementing provisions of a directive benefit from constitutional immunity if these provisions have direct effect. By contrast, measures implementing provisions of a directive that leave some discretion to the legislator will be subject to full judicial scrutiny.[108] Moreover, even if legislative measures implement directly effective provisions of a directive, they may be subject to constitutional scrutiny if the directive runs counter to specific constitutional provisions that enshrine the "constitutional identity of France".[109] Although this suggests that primacy of Union law cannot be accepted without reservations (*"réserve de constitutionalité"*), it appears that only in exceptional circumstances would the constitutionality of laws implementing directly effective provisions of directives be tested.[110] In November 2004, the *Conseil constitutionnel* adopted the same conciliatory approach when it held the primacy clause of the Constitution for Europe (Art. I-6) to be compatible with the French Constitution and its notion of "constitutional identity".[111] It stressed that the primacy clause had to be read in light of the Union's commitment to respecting the national identity of the Member States. In this way, the *Conseil constitutionnel* accommodates the fact that the French Constitution is "at the summit of the domestic legal order" with the primacy of Union law.[112]

Ronkes Agerbeek, case note in (2005) C.M.L.Rev. 871–886; Chaltiel, "Nouvelles variations sur la constitutionnalisation de l'Europe—A propos de la décision du Conseil constitutionnel sur l'économie numérique" (2004) R.M.C.U.E 450–454.

[108] The *Conseil constitutionnel* also examines whether the French legislator exceeded the limits of the discretion set out by the directive: see para. 21–025, *infra*.

[109] In an official commentary to its June 2004 decision, the *Conseil constitutionnel* stated that "the constitutional identity of France" must not be found by reference to its case law, but is anchored in express provisions of the Constitution, such as the definition of the electoral body and rules on access to public employment. See *http://www.conseil-constitutionnel.fr/conseil-constitutionnel/root/bank/download/2004-496DC-ccc_496dc.pdf*.

[110] See Schoettl, "Primauté du droit communautaire: l'approche du Conseil constitutionnel" in *L'administration française et l'Union européenne: quelles influences? Quelles stratégies* (rapport public du Conseil d'État, 2007); Groussot, "Supr[i]macy *à la française*: another French exception?" (2009) Y.E.L. 89–120; Granger, "France is 'Already' Back in Europe: The Europeanization of French Courts and the Influence of France in the EU" (2008) E.Pub.L. 335–375.

[111] *Conseil constitutionnel*, Decision No. 2004–505 DC, November 19, 2004, *Traité établissant une Constitution pour l'Europe*. Champeil-Desplats, "Commentaire de la décision du Conseil constitutionnel No. 2004–505-DC du 19 novembre 2004 relative au Traité établissant une Constitution pour l'Europe" (2005) R.T.D.E. 557–580; Picheral, "La primauté du droit de l'Union aux termes de la décision No. 2004–505 DC du Conseil constitutionnel" (2005) R.A.E. 119–130; Walter, "Der französische Verwaltungsrat und das Recht der Europäischen Union" (2005) Eu.GR.Z. 77–85.

[112] See also Richards, "The supremacy of Community law before the French Constitutional Court" (2006) E.L.Rev. 499–517. However, in its opinion of December 2007 on the compatibility with the Constitution of the Lisbon Treaty, the *Conseil constitutionnel* said nothing about the question of the primacy of Union law: *Conseil constitutionnel*, Decision No. 2007–560-DC, December 20, 2007, *Traité de Lisbonne modifiant le traité sur l'Union européenne et le traité instituant la Communauté européenne*. See Simon, "Le Conseil constitutionnel et le traité de Lisbonne" (2008) *Europe* No. 2.

In the *Arcelor* case, the *Conseil d'État* considered that where an applicant argues that a decree implementing directly effective provisions of a directive is incompatible with a principle or provision of the French Constitution, the administrative judge must first examine whether the effectiveness of that constitutional principle or provision may already be guaranteed by a general principle of Union law.[113] Where there are serious grounds for believing that the directive is in breach of a general principle of Union law, the administrative judge must refer the matter to the Court of Justice.[114] Only where the effectiveness of a French constitutional principle or provision is not protected under Union law may the administrative judge examine the constitutionality of the challenged decree.[115] It follows that both the *Conseil d'État* and the *Conseil constitutionnel* oppose an unconditional primacy of Union law, but each imposes serious constraints on French judges to question the constitutionality of a law or a decree implementing directly effective provisions of a directive.

Status of directives. The French courts give precedence to acts of secondary Union law pursuant to Art. 55 of the Constitution by reference to the implied "ratification" of such acts. Traditionally, the *Conseil d'Etat* had some reservations about the primacy of directives. Since directives are binding only as to the result to be achieved on each Member State to which they are addressed, it held that no reliance could be placed upon provisions of a directive in challenging an individual administrative act.[116] However, it appears from later judgments that a claim that administrative[117] or statutory[118] provisions on which an individual

21–025

---

[113] *Conseil d'Etat*, judgment of February 8, 2007, *Société Arcelor Atlantique et Lorraine et autres* (2007). See Pollicino, "The Conseil d'Etat and the relationship between French internal law after Arcelor: Has something really changed?" (2008) C.M.L.Rev. 1519–1540; Chaltiel, "Le Conseil d'État reconnaît la spécificité constitutionnelle du droit communautaire" (2007) R.M.C.U.E. 335–338; Magnon, "La sanction de la primauté de la Constitution sur le droit communautaire par le Conseil d'Etat. Commentaire sous Conseil d'Etat, Assemblée, 8 février 2007, Société Arcelor Atlantique et Lorraine et autres" (2007) R.F.D.A. 578–589; Simon, "La jurisprudence récente du Conseil d'État: le grand ralliement à l'Europe des juges" (2007) *Europe* No. 3; Roblot-Troizier, "Un contrôle indirect de la constitutionnalité des directives communautaires" (2007) R.F.D.A. 601–603.

[114] This approach appears to be consistent with the ruling of the Court of Justice in *Melki* (n. 121, *infra*).

[115] In the case at hand, the *Conseil d'État* sought guidance from the Court of Justice, which confirmed that the directive that submitted installations in the steel sector to a greenhouse gas emission allowance trading scheme while excluding installations in the chemical and non-ferrous metal sectors was compatible with the general principle of equal treatment: ECJ, Case C-127/07 *Arcelor* [2008] ECR I-9895. Subsequently, the *Conseil d'État* applied the ruling of the Court of Justice: *Conseil d'Etat*, judgment of June 3, 2009, *Société Arcelor Atlantique et Lorraine et autres* (2009).

[116] Judgment of December 22, 1978, *Ministre de l'Intérieur v Cohn-Bendit* (1978) Rec.C.E. 524; (1979) Rec. Dalloz Jurispr., 155; translated in [1980] 1 C.M.L.R. 543.

[117] Judgment of July 8, 1991, *Palazzi* (1991) Rec.C.E. 276.

[118] Judgment of February 28, 1992, *Rothmans International France* and *Arizona Tobacco Products* (1992) Rec.C.E. 78 and 80; see also (1992) A.J.D.A. 224–226; [1993] 1 C.M.L.R. 253.

administrative act is based conflict with a directive may nevertheless be raised where the provisions are intended to implement the directive[119] and even when the directive has not yet been transposed into national law.[120] In its more recent *Arcelor* case, the *Conseil d'État* confirmed the trend towards giving full effect to the provisions of directives (see para. 21–024). For its part, the *Conseil constitutionnel* announced that, in accordance with the obligation to implement directives following from Art. 88 of the Constitution, it will examine whether legislation implementing a directive has exceeded the limits of the legislator's discretion set out by that directive.[121] Such a control will however be excluded where it would oppose "the constitutional identity of France". Moreover, due to the short time-limits within which the *Conseil constitutionnel* must exercise its *ex ante* review, it is prevented from requesting a preliminary ruling to the Court of Justice and would therefore intervene only where a legislative provision is "obviously incompatible with the directive which it is intended to transpose".[122]

---

[119] Dal Farra, "L'invocabilité des directives communautaires devant le juge national de légalité" (1992) R.T.D.E. 631–667; Simon, "Le Conseil d'Etat et les directives communautaires: du gallicanisme à l'orthodoxie?" (1992) R.T.D.E. 265–283. For a survey, see Tomlinson, "Reception of Community Law in France" (1995) Col.J.E.L. 183–231.

[120] Judgment of February 6, 1998, *Tête e.a.* (1998) Rec.C.E. 30. The national provision may nevertheless only be contested if it is "incompatible" with Union law; see, e.g., the judgment of July 27, 2001, *Compagnie générale des eaux* (2001) Droit administratif—Juris classeur 33 and Favret, "Le rapport de compatibilité entre le droit national et le droit communautaire" (2001) A.J.D.A. 727–730.

[121] *Conseil constitutionnel*, Decision No. 2006–540 DC, July 27, 2006, *Loi relative au droit d'auteur et aux droits voisins dans la société de l'information.*

[122] See Art. 61 of the French Constitution. The *Conseil constitutionnel* must give a decision within a month and, in case of urgency, within eight days. Since this tight time-limit does not apply to other French courts, the *Conseil constitutionnel* pointed out that "it is incumbent upon [them], if need be, to refer a matter to the [Court of Justice] for a preliminary ruling", *ibid.* Further, by virtue of new Art. 61–1 of the French Constitution, private parties are now entitled to challenge the constitutionality of a legislative provision in breach of their rights and freedoms as guaranteed by the French Constitution. The so-called "priority preliminary reference on the issue of constitutionality" operates under a "double filter" of admissibility ("*double système de renvoi*"). If a lower French court considers the question of constitutionality to be admissible, it must stay proceedings and make a reference to the *Conseil d'État* or the *Cour de cassation* which in turn must decide whether to refer this question to the *Conseil constitutionnel*. The latter has three months to issue a decision which is not subject to appeal. However, the *Conseil constitutionnel* has recently held that it will not test the compatibility of legislative provisions with Union law under the procedure laid down in Art. 61–1 of the French Constitution. This type of review falls within the jurisdiction of ordinary courts in cooperation with the Court of Justice. The *Conseil constitutionnel* reasoned that the purpose of the priority preliminary reference on the issue of constitutionality is to protect the rights and freedoms of individuals as guaranteed by the French Constitution. Thus this new procedure does not aim to secure the constitutional obligation to implement directives as provided for in Art. 88 of the French Constitution. See *Conseil constitutionnel*, Decision No. 2010–605 DC, May 12, 2010, *Loi relative à l'ouverture à la concurrence et à la régulation du secteur des jeux d'argent et de hasard en ligne.* In the same way, see *Conseil d'Etat*, Decision No. 312305 of May 14, 2010. See also ECJ (judgment of June 22, 2010), Joined Cases C-188/10 and C-189/10 *Melki*, not yet reported. There, the Court of Justice found that the "priority preliminary reference

(3) Germany

Acceptance of primacy. Article 24(1) of the German Basic Law (*Grundgesetz*)   **21–026**
of 1949 provides that the federation may by enactment transfer powers to "inter-
State institutions". Nevertheless, such a transfer of powers is subject to the structural principles of the German constitutional system as enshrined in Art. 79(3) of
the Basic Law. For the purposes of the approval of the EU Treaty, a provision was
added to the Basic Law declaring that the Federal Republic is to cooperate in
developing the European Union, which is subject to democratic, social and
federal principles, to the rule of law and the principle of subsidiarity and guarantees a protection of fundamental rights which is essentially comparable to that
afforded by the Basic Law (Art. 23(1)).[123] The *Bundesverfassungsgericht* (the
German Constitutional Court) has accepted the primacy of Union law by virtue
of domestic statutes approving the Treaties, hence only in so far as Union law
remains within the bounds set by the Basic Law.[124]

Solange **judgments.** This was not sufficient to guarantee the primacy of Union   **21–027**
law, however, when a (then) Community measure was challenged in a German
court on the ground that it violated fundamental rights enshrined in the Basic
Law. Although the Court of Justice answered a question referred for a preliminary
ruling by the court concerned by saying that the measure did not infringe any fundamental right,[125] the national court deemed it necessary also to bring the matter
before the *Bundesverfassungsgericht*. That court held that the transfer of sovereignty to the Community made under Art. 24 of the Basic Law could not result
in Community legislation detracting from the essential structure of the Basic Law.
Despite the judgment of the Court of Justice and the primacy of Community law,
the *Bundesverfassungsgericht* considered that it was necessary to conduct a
second review of the Community legislation in the light of the fundamental
rights guaranteed by the Basic Law *so long as* the Community legal order lacked

---

on the issue of constitutionality" would be incompatible with Union law, if it were interpreted as
precluding French courts from referring preliminary questions to the Court of Justice either before
the *Conseil constitutionnel* gave its decision or thereafter. By contrast, the Court of Justice did not
oppose an alternative interpretation of the "priority preliminary reference on the issue of constitutionality" according to which French courts are allowed (1) to refer preliminary questions to the
Court of Justice at any given time, (2) grant interim relief to the rights protected under Union law,
and (3) set aside national provisions conflicting with Union law. In addition, the Court of Justice
held that, prior to examining the constitutionality of a national provision limiting itself to implementing directly effective provisions of a directive on grounds that could also serve to test the
validity of the directive, Art. 267 TFEU requires national courts of last instance to refer a
preliminary question on the validity of the directive to the Court of Justice.

[123] For commentaries, see the works listed in notes concerning the ratification of the EU Treaty: para.
3–010, *supra*.

[124] Hanf, "Le jugement de la Cour constitutionnelle fédérale allemande sur la constitutionnalité du
Traité de Maastricht" (1994) R.T.D.E. 391, at 395–398.

[125] ECJ, Case 11/70 *Internationale Handelsgesellschaft* [1970] E.C.R. 1125, paras 3–20.

a democratically elected parliament with legislative powers and powers of scrutiny and a codified catalogue of fundamental rights.[126] In order to guarantee the uniform application of Community law, the Court of Justice confirmed for its part that observance of fundamental rights formed part of the requirements which Community acts had to satisfy in order to be valid and therefore had to be enforced within the context of Community law itself.[127] In 1986, after considering the case law of the Court of Justice, the *Bundesverfassungsgericht*, referring to the importance that the Community institutions attached to the protection of fundamental rights and democratic decision-making, declared that an additional review of Community legislation in the light of the fundamental rights guaranteed by the Basic Law was no longer necessary *so long as* the case law of the Court of Justice continued to afford the level of protection found.[128]

21–028   *Maastricht-Urteil*. The *Bundesverfassungsgericht* confirmed its conditional acceptance of the primacy of Union law on October 12, 1993 when it ruled on the constitutionality of the law ratifying the EU Treaty.[129] The *Bundesverfassungsgericht* declared once again that it secured the essential substance of the fundamental rights guaranteed by the Basic Law also with regard to action of the Union, while making it clear that the Court of Justice ensured respect for fundamental rights—within the Union field of competence—in each individual case and that the *Bundesverfassungsgericht* could therefore confine itself to a general guarantee that the standard of protection of fundamental rights would be undiminished.[130] In this *"Maastricht-Urteil"*, the Bundesverfassungsgericht added a second reservation to its acceptance of the primacy of Union law. It stated that German law accepted acts of the "European institutions and bodies" only in so far as they remained within the bounds of the Treaty provisions approved by the ratification law and made it plain

---

[126] The judgment in question is the so-called (first) *Solange* judgment of May 29, 1974, BVerfGE 37, at 271; for an English translation, see [1974] 2 C.M.L.R. 540; see Ipsen, "BVerfG versus EuGH *re* 'Grundrechte' " (1975) EuR. 1–19.

[127] ECJ, Case 44/79 *Hauer* [1979] E.C.R. 3727, paras 13–16 (in which reference is made to the judgments in *Internationale Handelsgesellschaft* and *Nold* and to the fact that the institutions recognised "that conception" in the Joint Declaration of April 5, 1977; para. 17–074, *infra*).

[128] Judgment of October 22, 1986 (*Solange II*) (1986) BVerfGE 73 at 339; for an English translation, see [1987] 3 C.M.L.R. 225; see the commentary by Frowein (1988) C.M.L.Rev. 201–206. The *Bundesverfassungsgericht* referred to the Joint Declaration of April 5, 1977 and the Declaration of the European Council of April 7 and 8, 1978 on democracy (1978) 3 EC Bull. 5. For the ensuing debate, see, among others, Ehlermann, "Zur Diskussion um einen 'Solange III'-Beschluss: Rechtspolitische Perspektiven aus der Sicht des Gemeinschaftsrechts" (1991) EuR. Beiheft 1 at 27–38; Everling, "Brauchen wir 'Solange III'?" (1990) EuR. 195–227; Tomuschat, "Aller guten Dinge sind III?" (1990) EuR. 340–361.

[129] The *"Maastricht-Urteil"*; for the text, see (1993) Eu.GR.Z. 429; (1993) EuR. 294; [1974] 1 C.M.L.R. 57. For the conditional nature of that acceptance, see Zuleeg, "The European Constitution under Constitutional Constraints: The German Scenario" (1997) E.L.Rev. 19–34.

[130] Point B.2, under b, [1994] 1 C.M.L.R. 80.

that it would itself review whether such acts remained within the bounds of the Union's principles of conferred powers, subsidiarity and proportionality.[131]

Safeguarding constitutional guarantees. In some subsequent cases, the   21–029
Bundesverfassungsgericht appeared to consider that, at a general level, the Court of Justice sufficiently guaranteed the protection of fundamental rights.[132] Moreover, the *Bundesverfassungsgericht* held that the highest federal administrative court (*Bundesverwaltungsgericht*) fell short of its obligations in respect of the legal protection guaranteed by the Basic Law by refusing to make a reference to the Court of Justice for a preliminary ruling on a matter in respect of which that Court had not been able to secure complete clarity. The highest administrative court had breached constitutional obligations in so far as it had failed to take account of a general principle of Union law, namely the principle of equal treatment of men and women.[133] In July 2005, however, the *Bundesverfassungsgericht* made it clear that it would continue to review whether legislation implementing Union measures respected the guarantees laid down in the Basic Law. It held the

---

[131] Points C.I.3. and C.II.2., under b, *ibid.*, 89 and 94, respectively. Among the many commentaries on that judgment, see; Hahn, "La Cour constitutionnelle fédérale d'Allemagne et le Traité de Maastricht" (1994) R.G.D.I.P. 107–126; Herdegen, "Maastricht and the German Constitutional Court: Constitutional Restraints for an 'Ever Closer Union' " (1994) C.M.L.Rev. 235–249; Ipsen, "Zehn Glossen zum Maastricht Urteil" (1994) EuR. 1–21; Kokott, "Deutschland im Rahmen der Europäischen Union—zum Vertrag von Maastricht" (1994) A.ö.R. 207–237; Meessen, "Maastricht nach Karlsruhe" (1994) N.J.W. 549–554; Schroeder, "Alles unter Karlsruher Kontrolle? Die Souveränitätsfrage im Maastricht-Urteil des BVerfG" (1994) Z.f.RV. 143–157; Schwarze, "La ratification du Traité de Maastricht en Allemagne, l'arrêt de la Cour constitutionnelle de Karlsruhe" (1994) R.M.C.U.E. 293–303; Tomuschat, "Die Europäische Union unter der Aufsicht des Bundesverfassungsgerichts" (1993) Eu.GR.Z. 489–496. For the role which the Court of Justice could play in this connection by giving preliminary rulings at the request of the German Constitutional Court, see Grimm, "The European Court of Justice and National Courts: The German Constitutional Perspective after the Maastricht Decision" (1997) Col.J.E.L. 229–242.

[132] Judgment of February 17, 2000 (*Alcan*) 2 BvR 1915/91, (2000) Eu.GR.Z. 17 and above all the order of June 7, 2000 (on the EU organisation of the market in bananas), BVerfGE 102, 147, (2000) EuR. 799–810; (2000) Eu.Z.W. 702–704; (2000) Eu.GR.Z. 328; (2000) N.J.W. 3124. See Grewe, "Le 'traité de paix' avec la Cour de Luxembourg: l'arrêt de la Cour constitutionnelle allemande du 7 juin 2000 relatif au règlement du marché de la banane" (2001) R.T.D.E. 1–17; Hoffmeister (2001) C.M.L.Rev. 791–804; Pernice, "Les bananes et les droits fondamentaux; la Cour constitutionnelle allemande fait le point" (2001) C.D.E. 427–440; Elbers and Urban, "The Order of the German Federal Constitutional Court of 7 June 2000 and the Kompetenz-Kompetenz in the European Judicial System" (2001) E.Pub.L. 21–32; Mayer, "Grundrechtsschutz gegen europäische Rechtsakte durch das BVerfG: Zur Verfassungsmässigkeit der Bananenmarktordnung" (2000) Eu.Z.W. 685–690; for a critical commentary, see Schmid, "All Bark and No Bite: Notes on the Federal Constitutional Court's 'Banana Decision' " (2001) E.L.J. 95–113.

[133] Judgment of January 9, 2001 (2001) Eu.GR.Z. 150–153; (2001) N.J.W. 1267; (2001) D.ö.V. 379; (2001) J.Z. 923; see Classen (2002) C.M.L.Rev. 641–652. Already in *Solange II*, the *Bundesverfassungsgericht* had held that the refusal of the highest revenue court to make a reference for a preliminary ruling was in breach of the principle of the "gesetzliche Rechter" enshrined in Art. 101 of the Basic Law ("No one may be removed from the jurisdiction of his lawful judge."). With respect to prospects for the future, see Nickel, "Zur Zukunft des Bundesverfassungsgerichts im Zeitalter der Europäisierung" (2001) J.Z. 625–632.

German law implementing the Framework Decision on the European arrest warrant[134] to be unconstitutional on the grounds that it was incompatible with the right of access to a court and the conditions for the extradition of German nationals as set out in the Basic Law.[135] It added that the German legislator would have to provide for means of ensuring that the surrender of a German national was conditional upon ascertaining, on a case-by-case basis, that the requesting Member State offer a "rule-of-law structure" that complied with the standards of Art. 23(1) of the Basic Law.[136] Although the *Bundesverfassungsgericht* was careful not to rule on whether the Framework Decision itself was contrary to the Basic Law, it did not attempt to interpret the Basic Law or the implementing legislation in a way consistent with the Framework Decision.[137]

21–030   **Lisbon Treaty judgment.** In a judgment of June 30, 2009, the *Bundesverfassungsgericht* held the law ratifying the Lisbon Treaty compatible with the Basic Law, while requiring certain amendments to be made to the laws governing the role of the *Bundesrat* and *Bundestag* (chambers of the federal parliament) within the framework of the EU decision-making process.[138] In its judgment, the *Bundesverfassungsgericht* made it clear that it would examine not only whether Union law complie with the principle of conferred powers (the "*ultra*

---

[134] Council Framework Decision 2002/584/JHA of June 13, 2002 on the European arrest warrant and the surrender procedures between Member States, [2002] L190/1.

[135] Judgment of July 18, 2005, 2 BvR 2236/04; available in English at: *http://www.bundesverfassungsgericht.de/entscheidungen/rs20050718_2bvr223604en.html* [Accessed December 13, 2010]. The *Bundesverfassungsgericht* held that the German legislator had not exercised the margin of discretion enjoyed under Art. 4 of the Framework Decision in a way consistent with Art. 19(4) (right of access to a court) and Art. 16(2) (prohibiting the extradition of German nationals unless the law "provide[s] otherwise for extraditions to a Member State of the European Union or to an international court, provided that the rule of law is observed") of the Basic Law.

[136] See Komárek, "European Constitutionalism and the European Arrest Warrant: In Search of the Limits of Contrapunctual Principles" (2007) C.M.L.Rev. 9, at 24–25.

[137] It should be mentioned that the Court of Justice had prescribed such consistent interpretation in Case C-105/03 *Pupino* [2005] E.C.R I-5285. See also Nohlen, "Case Comment" (2008) I.J.C.L. 153–161; Lebeck, "National Constitutional Control and the Limits of European Integration—The European Arrest Warrant in the German Federal Constitutional Court" (2007) Pub.L. 23–32; Hinarejos Parga, "Case Comment" (2006) C.M.L.Rev. 583–595; Mölders, "European Arrest Warrant Act is Void—the Decision of the German Federal Constitutional Court of July 18, 2005" (2005) G.L.J. 45–58.

[138] Judgment of June 30, 2009, 2 BvE 2/08, available in English at: *http://www.bundesverfassungsgericht.de/entscheidungen/es20090630_2bve000208en.html* [Accessed December 13, 2010]. See Ziller, "The German Constitutional Court's Friendliness towards European Law: On the Judgment of *Bundesverfassungsgericht* over the Ratification of the Treaty of Lisbon" (2010) E.Pub.L. 53–73; Thym, "In the name of sovereign statehood: a critical introduction to the Lisbon judgment of the German Constitutional Court" (2009) C.M.L.Rev. 1795–1822, at 1795. See also Editorial Comments (2009) C.M.L.Rev. 1023–1033; Doukas, "The verdict of the German Federal Constitutional Court on the Lisbon Treaty: not guilt6y, but don't do it again!" (2009) E.L.Rev. 866–888; Halberstam and Möllers, "The German Constitutional Court says "Ja zu Deutschland!" (2009) G.L.J. 1241–1258.

vires review" already contained in the *Maastricht-Urteil*) but also whether Union law ran the risk of depriving the Basic Law's constitutional identity of its core content ("identity review").[139] It indicated that further European integration—which under the Basic Law can only be based on a union of sovereign States (*Staatenverbund*)—may,

> "not be realised in such a way that the Member States do not retain sufficient space for the political formation of the economic, cultural and social circumstances of life".[140]

In its judgment, it rejected the idea that the amendments brought about by the Lisbon Treaty deprived Germany of its statehood. In this context, the *Bundesverfassungsgericht* pointed out that if further integration were to take place beyond the bounds set out in the Treaty of Lisbon so as to transform Germany into a component state of a federation, a constitutional reform would be unavoidable. In addition, it observed that in accordance with "the eternity clause" of the Basic Law, a new constitution should offer the same democratic guarantees as that of a national State.[141] The *Bundesverfassungsgericht* further interprets the principle of primacy of Union law in the light of its "identity review" in the sense that this principle of primacy "only applies by virtue of the order to apply the law issued by the Act approving the Treaties" and as "a conflict of law rule" may not prevail over the Basic Law's constitutional identity.[142] Yet, since Art. 23 of the Basic Law embodies the principle of "openness towards European law" (*Europarechtsfreundlichkeit*), the *Bundesverfassungsgericht* will only intervene under exceptional circumstances. The "ultra vires" review will only take place in the event of an obvious violation of the principle of conferred powers.[143] Likewise, the "identity review" will only occur "under special and narrow conditions".[144] Finally, as regards the review of the respect of the fundamental rights as set out in the Basic Law, the *Bundesverfassungsgericht* made it clear that the *Solange*

---

[139] *Ibid.*, paras 238–241.

[140] The *Bundesverfassungsgericht* identified five areas where a large-scale transfer of competences to the Union would be precluded by the Basic Law: "decisions on substantive and formal criminal law (1), on the disposition of the police monopoly on the use of force towards the interior and of the military monopoly on the use of force towards the exterior (2), the fundamental fiscal decisions on public revenue and public expenditure, with the latter being particularly motivated, inter alia, by social-policy considerations (3), decisions on the shaping of circumstances of life in a social state (4) and decisions which are of particular importance culturally, for instance as regards family law, the school and education system and dealing with religious communities (5)": *ibid.*, para. 252.

[141] In that connection, the *Bundesverfassungsgericht* expressed the view that the European Parliament was not "the representative body of the [European] people" since its members were not elected in accordance with a strict rule of democratic equality. *Ibid.*, paras 280–288.

[142] *Ibid.*, para. 343.

[143] *Ibid.*, paras 240 and 339.

[144] *Ibid.*, para. 340.

jurisprudence remains good law.[145] It should be noted that in a subsequent judgment, where it held the German law transposing an EU Directive on data protection[146] unconstitutional, the *Bundesverfassungsgericht* admitted the possibility that it might make references for preliminary rulings to the Court of Justice.[147]

(4) Italy

21–031   **Italy.** Union law has its place within the Italian legal order by virtue of the transfer of competence to international organisations authorised by Art. 11 of the 1947 Constitution.[148] Initially, the *Corte costituzionale* (the Italian Constitutional Court) held that a law which conflicted with Union law was also unconstitutional. In order to give precedence to Union law, Italian courts therefore had to raise the issue of constitutionality first before the *Corte costituzionale* in the event of a conflict between a national statute and Union law (see para. 21–009). It was not until the 1984 judgment in *Granital* that the *Corte costituzionale* changed its view and declared that, in the event that a court found that a national provision conflicted with a rule of Union law having direct effect, it should refrain from applying the domestic provision without raising the question of constitutionality.[149]

Nevertheless, the *Corte costituzionale* finds that there are still two situations in which it itself must give judgment. First, since the 1973 judgment in *Frontini*,[150] the *Corte costituzionale* has held that it has jurisdiction to give a ruling where a rule of Union law purportedly breaches fundamental principles of the Italian legal order or inviolable human rights.[151] Secondly, the *Corte costituzionale* reviews the constitutionality of domestic rules which qre allegedly expressly intended to prevent compliance with essential obligations under the Treaties.[152] In 1994,

---

[145] *Ibid.*, para. 191.

[146] Directive 2006/24/EC of the European Parliament and of the Council of March 15, 2006 on the retention of data generated or processed in connection with the provision of publicly available electronic communications services or of public communications networks and amending Directive 2002/58/EC, [2006] O.J. L105/54.

[147] Judgment of March 2, 2010, 1 BvR 256/08, para. 185

[148] See Adinolfi, "The Judicial Application of Community Law in Italy (1981–1997)" (1998) C.M.L.Rev 1313, at 1322; Luciani, "La Constitution italienne et les obstacles à l'intégration européenne" (1992) R.F.D.C. 663, at 664.

[149] Judgment No. 170/84 of June 8, 1984; for an English translation, see [1994] C.M.L.R. 756; see Barav, "Cour constitutionelle italienne et droit communautaire: le fantôme de *Simmenthal*" (1985) R.T.D.E. 313–341. More recently, see Daniele, "Après l'arrêt *Granital*: droit communautaire et droit national dans la jurisprudence récente de la Cour constitutionnelle italienne" (1992) C.D.E. 3–21; Gaja, "New Developments in a Continuing Story: The Relationship Between EEC Law and Italian Law" (1990) C.M.L.Rev. 83–95.

[150] Judgment No. 183/73 of December 27, 1973; for an English translation, see [1974] 2 C.M.L.R. 383.

[151] There was an initial application of this principle in judgment No. 232/89 of April 21, 1989 in *Fragd*; see Gaja (n. 148, *supra*), at 94; Daniele (n. 148, *supra*), at 16.

[152] For applications of this principle, see Daniele (n. 148, *supra*), at 18–19; Adinolfi (n. 147, *supra*), at 1318. The *Corte Constituzionale* made a reference for a preliminary ruling to the Court of Justice which illustrates the procedural context of its exercising jurisdiction in a case relating to Union law: ECJ, Case C-169/08 *Regione Sardegna* [2009] E.C.R. I-10821.

however, the *Corte costituzionale* refused to rule on the constitutionality of a national law in a case in which the lower court requested the ruling without first considering whether the law was compatible with Union law.[153] More recently, the *Corte costituzionale* has stressed the "special status" of Union law by refusing to apply its *Frontini* and *Granital* case law to other international treaties.[154] While Union law enjoys "a constitutional status" in so far as it prevails over the Italian Constitution with the exception of the two limitations laid down in *Frontini*, other international treaties are located in an intermediate position ("*norme interposte*"), that is, below the Italian Constitution but above secondary legislation.[155]

(5) Luxembourg

Luxembourg. Luxembourg law recognised the primacy of Union law uncondi- 21–032
tionally as an application of the priority of international law over domestic law which has been accepted since 1954.[156] Just as in the case law of the Belgian Supreme Court, precedence is given to international law on the ground of its very nature, with the result that the primacy of Union law is regarded as being the outcome of the specific nature of the Union legal order.[157] In this respect, the authorisation to transfer the exercise of competences to an international organisation (Constitution, Art. 49*bis*) is of no importance (here, too, the analogy with Belgium holds good).[158]

(6) The Netherlands

Netherlands. The primacy of Union law also found immediate acceptance in the 21–033
Netherlands legal system. This was because it already recognised the principle of the supremacy of international law even before it was codified in the 1953 Constitution. The 1983 Constitution reads as follows:

---

[153] Order of June 19, 1994, No 244/94; see Adinolfi (n. 147, *supra*), at 1317. In considering the constitutionality of a referendum to be held, the Constitutional Court itself even analysed the extent to which the referendum was in keeping with the Member State's obligations to give effect to its Union obligations; see the judgment of February 7, 2000, reported in the Eighteenth Annual Report on monitoring the application of Community law, COM (2001) 309 fin.

[154] *Corte costituzionale*, Judgments No. 348 and 349/2007 of October 22, 2007. Both judgments are available in English at: *http://www.cortecostituzionale.it/versioni_in_lingua/eng/attivitacorte/ pronunceemassime/recent_judgments_2007.asp* [Accessed December 13, 2010].

[155] Notably, where a conflict between Italian secondary legislation and the ECHR arises, the Italian judge must suspend proceedings and refer the matter to the *Corte costituzionale*, which will first examine whether the ECHR complies with the Italian Constitution. Only in the affirmative will the *Corte costituzionale* declare the Italian secondary legislation unconstitutional. See Rossi, "Corte costituzionale (Italian Constitutional Court): Decisions 348 and 349/2007 of 22 October 2007, and 102 and 103/2008, of February 12, 2008" (2009) C.M.L.Rev. 319–331.

[156] *Cour de cassation*, July 14, 1954, *Pas.lux.*, Vol. 16, 150.

[157] *Conseil d'Etat*, November 21, 1984, *Pas.lux.*, Vol. 26, 174. See Thill, "La primauté et l'effet direct du droit communautaire dans la jurisprudence luxembourgeoise" (1990) R.F.D.A. 978–980.

[158] With respect to this clause governing the transfer of powers, see Lepka and Terebus (n. 89, *supra*), at 368–369.

"Legal provisions valid within the Kingdom shall not be applied if to do so would not be compatible with provisions of treaties and acts of international organisations which are binding on any person" (Art. 94).

Since Art. 12 of the EEC Treaty therefore had precedence in domestic law in so far as it was "binding on any person", the court hearing *Van Gend & Loos* had only to ascertain through the preliminary reference to the Court of Justice whether the provision was capable of having legal effects on individuals (see para. 1–025).[159] In the Netherlands, too, acceptance of the primacy of Union law is based on recognition of the special nature of that law.[160] Article 92 of the Constitution allows powers to be transferred to international organisations.[161]

(b) *Member States having acceded before 2004*

(1) Ireland, the United Kingdom and Denmark

21–034   **Ireland.** In common with the two other States which acceded to the Community in 1973, Ireland belonged to the "dualist" school, according to which provisions of international law obtain the force of law only after they have been incorporated into the national legal system (Constitution, Art. 29.6). Consequently, in order to ensure the legal force of Community law, it was deemed necessary to adopt a law of accession. In addition, with a view to providing Community law with immunity from constitutional challenge, the Irish Constitution was amended (the "Third Amendment" to the Irish Constitution).[162] As a result, Art. 29.4.10 of the Constitution now provides

---

[159] Prechal, "La primauté du droit communautaire aux Pays-Bas" (1990) R.F.D.A. 981–982.

[160] See *Hoge Raad* (Dutch Supreme Court), judgment of November 2, 2004, AR1797 (Community regulation held valid and directly applicable on the basis of the EC Treaty and not pursuant to Arts 93 or 94 of the Constitution). See Kapteyn and VerLoren van Themaat, *Het recht van de Europese Unie en van de Europese Gemeenschappen* (Deventer, Kluwer, 2003), 443 pp.; Brouwer, "Nederlandse gedachten over de Grondwet en het verdrag" (1992–93) R.W. 1366–1370; Kellermann, "Supremacy of Community Law in the Netherlands" (1989) E.L.Rev. 175–185. Nevertheless, from time to time, the articles of the Constitution relating to international law are relied upon before the Netherlands courts: see Lauwaars, Lyklema and Kuiper, "De Nederlandse jurisprudentie met betrekking tot de algemene leerstukken van het recht der Europese Gemeenschappen" (1973) S.E.W. 3, at 19; see also *Raad van State*, Administrative Disputes Division, judgments of November 11, 1991 (1992) N.J./A.B. No. 50, and February 17, 1993 (1993) N.J./A.B. No. 424. The primacy of Union law holds good irrespective of whether the Union provision at issue has direct effect: *Raad van State*, Administrative Disputes Division, judgment of July 7, 1995, *Metten v Minister van Financiën*, No R01.93.0067, N.J.B.-Rechtspraak 426 (for an English translation, see (1996) M.J.E.C.L. 179–184); see Besselink, "Curing a 'Childhood Sickness'? On Direct Effect, Internal Effect, Primacy and Derogation from Civil Rights The Netherlands Council of State Judgment in the *Metten* Case)" (1996) M.J.E.C.L. 165–184; Besselink, "An Open Constitution and European Integration: The Kingdom of the Netherlands" (1996) S.E.W. 192–206.

[161] If an international treaty contains provisions at variance with the Constitution, the national parliament has to ratify it by a two-thirds majority (Constitution, Art. 91(3)).

[162] Collins and O'Reilly, "The Application of Community Law in Ireland 1973–1989" (1990) C.M.L.Rev. 315, at 323; Phelan, "Can Ireland Legislate Contrary to European Community Law?" (2008) E.L.Rev. 530–549.

that none of its provisions preclude national measures necessary for implementing Treaty obligations or prevent Union measures from having the force of law.[163] The Irish courts have inferred the primacy of Union law from this, even where a rule of Union law conflicts with a statutory or even a constitutional provision.[164] The Supreme Court has indicated, however, that it wishes to consider how Union law should be applied where it affects a right guaranteed by the Constitution.[165]

United Kingdom. In the United Kingdom, Union law obtains its legal force   **21–035** from an act of Parliament. This is because British law adheres to the principle of parliamentary sovereignty, which is tantamount to saying that the legislature is subject to no limitation, apart from its inability to restrict its own sovereignty.[166] Consequently, the legal force of primary and secondary Union law is based on s.2(1) of the 1972 European Communities Act. As far as the relationship with domestic law is concerned, although s.2(4) does not recognise the primacy of Union law as such, it does provide that any enactment passed or to be passed shall be construed and have effect subject to the "foregoing provisions" of that section, which include s.2(1), the effect of which is to incorporate the whole of Union law into the law of the United Kingdom. Consequently, Union law takes precedence by virtue of the 1972 Act and the courts presume that Parliament does not intend to legislate contrary to Union law. Thus the courts will construe a statute implementing a directive in conformity with the directive and are prepared in principle to abandon the normal canons of construction so as to enforce rights derived from Union law against the wording of the statute.[167] Yet, the courts shirk at

---

[163] See Hogan, "The Implementation of European Union Law in Ireland: The *Meagher* Case and the Democratic Deficit" (1994) Ir.J.E.L. 190–202. For the Supreme Court's reliance on Art. 29.4.5 of the Constitution in the *Meagher* case, see para. 14–012, *supra*.

[164] Walsh, "Reflections on the Effects of Membership of the European Communities in Irish Law", in Capotorti, Ehlermann, Frowein, Jacobs, Joliet, Koopmans and Kovar (eds), *Du droit international au droit de l'intégration. Liber Amicorum P. Pescatore* (Baden-Baden, Nomos, 1987), 806–820.

[165] Judgment of December 19, 1989, *Society for the Protection of Unborn Children Ireland* opinion of Finlay, J., [1990] 1 C.M.L.R. 689. The matter in question was Art. 40.3.3 of the Constitution concerning the right to life of the unborn child introduced by the Eighth Amendment; for the relationship of that provision to Union law and its subsequent application, see the discussion of free movement of services in para. 9–086, *supra*. In a concurring opinion, Walsh, J., considered that an amendment to the Constitution could affect the legal effects of an earlier amendment, as a result of which it would appear that the primacy of Union law as a principle does not rank above the Constitution.

[166] Collins, *European Community Law in the United Kingdom* (5th edn, London, Butterworths, 1998); Kinder-Gest, "Primauté du droit communautaire et droit anglais ou comment concilier l'impossible" (1991) R.A.E. 19–34.

[167] *Pickstone v Freemans Plc* [1989] A.C. 66; [1988] 3 W.L.R. 265 HL where Lord Oliver stated that "a construction which permits the section [of the 1983 Equal Pay (Amendment) Regulations adopted to implement the directive on equal pay] to operate as a proper fulfilment of the United Kingdom's obligation under the Treaty involves not so much doing violence to the language of the section as filling a gap by an implication which arises, not from the words used, but from the manifest purpose of the Act and the mischief it was intended to remedy" (at 125). See also *Litster v Forth Dry Dock* [1990] 1 A.C. 546; [1989] 2 C.M.L.R. 194. See in this regard Collins (n. 165, *supra*); de Búrca, "Giving Effect to European Community Directives" (1992) M.L.R. 215–240.

interpreting national law in conformity with Union law when it is a question of interpreting a statute which was not enacted to give effect to Union law.[168] If Parliament

> "deliberately passes an act with the intention of repudiating . . . any provision in [the Treaty] or intentionally of acting inconsistently with it and says so in express terms",

it would seem that United Kingdom courts would consider themselves under a duty to follow the statute.[169] However, it would appear from the *Factortame* litigation that British courts are increasingly prepared to disapply national law where it conflicts with directly enforceable Union law. The judgment of the Court of Justice holding that where necessary national courts must suspend the application of a domestic statute (see para. 21–010) was accepted by the House of Lords as a consequence of the obligations accepted by the United Kingdom when the European Communities Act was passed.[170] Meanwhile, the High Court has considered that the European Communities Act is a constitutional statute that cannot be impliedly repealed. It held that Union law, through its incorporation into UK law by the European Communities Acts, ranks supreme in the sense that anything in UK substantive law inconsistent with any of its rights and obligations flowing from Union law is abrogated or must be modified to avoid the inconsistency, even if contained in primary legislation. Only in the event that a Union measure would be repugnant to a fundamental or constitutional right guaranteed by the law of England, would the question arise as to whether the general words of the European Communities Act were sufficient to incorporate the measure and give it overriding effect in domestic law.[171]

---

[168] See the judgment of the House of Lords in *Duke v Reliance Systems Ltd* [1988] A.C. 618; [1988] 2 W.L.R. 359 HL where it had been sought to construe the provisions of the 1975 Sex Discrimination Act consistently with the directive on equal treatment prior to entry into force of the 1986 Sex Discrimination Act giving the directive effect in the United Kingdom.

[169] See *Macarthy's Ltd v Smith* [1979] 1 W.L.R. 1189; [1979] 3 All E.R. 325, at 329 (*per* Lord Denning MR).

[170] *R. v Secretary of State for Transport, Ex p. Factortame and Others* (No. 2) [1991] 1 A.C. 603. See Tatham, "The Sovereignty of Parliament after Factortame" (1993) EuR. 188–196; Akehurst, "Parliamentary Sovereignty and the Supremacy of Community Law" (1989) B.Y.I.L. 351–357. For the way in which British courts have subsequently given effect to Union law, see Arnull, "The Law Lords and the European Union: Swimming with the Incoming Tide" (2010) E.L.Rev. 57–87 (where the author also explores the consequences for Union law of the creation of the new UK Supreme Court); the overviews of the application of Community law in the United Kingdom published in (2008) R.T.D.E. 171–203, (2007) R.T.D.E. 47–73, (2006) R.T.D.E. 141–161, (2003) R.T.D.E. 471–488 and R.T.D.E. 439–466; Chalmers, "The Application of Community Law in the United Kingdom, 1994–1998" (2000) C.M.L.Rev. 83–128.

[171] Judgment of February 18, 2002 in *Thoburn v Sunderland City Council* [2002] EWHC 195 (Admin) [2003] Q.B. 151 DC.

Denmark. In Denmark, delegation of powers to international bodies is made pos-   **21–036**
sible by Art. 20 of the 1953 Constitution. Also under the Danish system, primary
and secondary Union law is given force by the statute on accession to the
European Communities. Although this does not result in Union law having force
superior to domestic law, the Danish courts interpret national law on the presumption that the legislature intended to act in conformity with Union law and to give
preference to interpretations consistent with Union law. However, just as in the
case of the United Kingdom, it cannot be taken for granted that Danish courts
would give precedence to Union law if they were faced with a statutory provision
which intentionally and expressly conflicted with Union law.[172] In its 1998 judgment on the ratification of the EU Treaty, the *Højesteret* (Danish Supreme Court)
found that Art. 20 of the 1953 Constitution must be interpreted "to the effect that
a positive delimitation must be made of the powers delegated [by Denmark to the
Union]".[173] The *Højesteret* thus considered that a broad interpretation of Art. 235
of the EEC Treaty (*now Art. 352 TFEU*) would constitute a violation of the
demand for specification contained in Art. 20 of the Constitution and, accordingly, instructed the Danish Government to exercise its veto powers where it considered that the Union was acting beyond its delegated powers. Moreover, it held
that Danish courts must comply with rulings of the Court of Justice unless they find
themselves in the "exceptional situation", whereby they are certain that a Union
act—held by the Court of Justice to be lawful—or an interpretation by the Court of
Justice of rules or principles of Union law exceeds the limits of the Danish law on
accession to the EU adopted under Art. 20 of the Constitution. In such a case, the
national courts must disapply the act, rules or principles in question.[174]

(2) Greece

Greece. As a rule, Greek courts give precedence to Union law, often on the ground   **21–037**
of both the specific nature of the Union legal order and Art. 28 of the 1975 Greek
Constitution, para. 1 of which confers superior force on international, as compared
to domestic law.[175] It should be noted, however, that, under the Constitution, the

---

[172] von Holstein, "Le droit communautaire dans le système juridique danois" (1990) R.F.D.A. 962–964; Rasmussen, "Denmark in face of her Community Obligations" (1982) C.M.L.Rev. 601, at 622–623; Gangsted-Rasmussen, "Primauté du droit communautaire en cas de conflit avec le droit danois" (1975) R.T.D.E. 700–707.

[173] Judgment of April 6 1998 (*Carlsen v Rasmussen*); for an English Translation, see [1999] 3 C.M.L.R. 854.

[174] For a short appraisal of this judgment, see K.L., "Redactionele signalen" (1998) S.E.W. 181. See the commentaries by Høegh (1999) E.L.Rev. 80–90; Hofmann (1999) Eu.GR.Z. 1–5. See also Biering, "The Application of EU Law in Denmark: 1986 to 2000" (2000) C.M.L.Rev. 925, at 928–932.

[175] Kerameus and Kremlis, "The Application of Community Law in Greece 1981–1987" (1988) C.M.L.Rev. 141–175; a critical view is taken of reliance on Art. 28 of the Constitution by Ioannou, "Recent Developments in the Application of Community Law in Greece" (1989) E.L.Rev. 461–469, and Konstadinidis, "Five Years of Application of Community Law in Greece" (1986) 2 L.I.E.I. 101–124.

conferral of powers on an international organisation may limit the "exercise of national sovereignty" only in so far as this does not encroach upon "human rights and the foundations of the democratic system" (Art. 28(6)).[176]

(3) Portugal and Spain

21–038   **Portugal.** In light of Art. 8 of the 1976 Portuguese Constitution, Portugal may be qualified as a monist system.[177] In 1982, that is even before Portugal acceded to the European Communities in 1986, Art. 8 of the Constitution was supplemented by a third para. giving effect to Community law in the domestic legal system.[178] In the same way as the Constitution recognises the force in the domestic legal system of international treaty law (Art. 8(2)) and thereby gives that law precedence over national legislation, the primacy of Union law is inferred from Art. 8(3).[179] In 2004, with a view to adapting the Portuguese Constitution to the primacy clause of the Constitution for Europe, a fourth paragraph was added to Art. 8 of the Portuguese Constitution according to which primary and secondary Union law shall apply in Portuguese internal law, while adding that for this to be the case, Union law must respect "the fundamental principles of a democratic State based on the rule of law". In 1992—in view of ratification of the EU Treaty—the Constitution had been amended to authorise Portugal to participate in the Common Foreign and Security Policy and the Area of Freedom, Security and Justice,

> "[s]ubject to reciprocity and to respect for the fundamental principles of a democratic State based on the rule of law and for the principle of subsidiarity" (Art. 7(6)).[180]

---

[176] See Konstadinidis (n. 174, *supra*), at 106.

[177] Moderne, "La question de la primauté du droit de l'Union en Espagne et au Portugal: Présentation de la question au Portugal" (2005) R.F.D.A. 51–55

[178] Pursuant to Art. 8(3) of the Constitution "rules issued by the competent bodies of international organisations of which Portugal [is a member] shall come directly into force in Portuguese internal law, on condition that this is laid down in the respective constituent treaties".

[179] See Moura Ramos, "The adaptation of the Portuguese Constitutional Order to Community Law", in Kellermann, De Zwaan and Czuczai (eds), *EU Enlargement. The constitutional impact at EU and national level* (The Hague, T.M.C. Asser Press, 2001) 131–140; Botelho Moniz, "The Portuguese Constitution and the Participation of the Republic of Portugal in the European Union" (1998) E.Pub.L. 465–478; Cruz Vilaça, Pais Antunes and Piçarra, "Droit constitutionnel et droit communautaire: le cas portugais" (1991) Riv.D.E. 301–310; Pinto, "L'application du droit communautaire au Portugal" (1990) R.F.D.A. 983–984.

[180] The Constitution was also supplemented by Art. 33(5), according to which the constitutional ban on the extradition of Portuguese nationals does not apply to Union measures. Hence, the implementation in Portugal of the Framework Decision on the European arrest warrant did not raise a constitutional conflict (in contrast to the cases decided in Cyprus and Poland, see paras 21–046 and 21–051, *infra*).

As regards the relationship between the Portuguese legal order and Union law, the *Tribunal Constitucional* (Portuguese Constitutional Court) has opted for a "hands-off" approach,[181] refusing, for example, to adjudicate over the "indirect unconstitutionality" of national law, that is, national legislation in breach of Union law.[182] In its view, it is for the Court of Justice, through the preliminary reference procedure, to rule on such cases. To date, the *Tribunal Constitucional* has not ruled on the constitutional implications flowing from a conflict between Union law and the Portuguese Constitution. The *Supremo Tribunal Administrativo* (the Supreme Administrative Court) refused to recognise the primacy of a Commission decision which ordered the withdrawal of a national court judgment conflicting with the Merger Regulation on the ground that such primacy would jeopardise the independence of the judiciary.[183] It has indeed been argued that Union law would not prevail over the "core nucleus" of the Portuguese Constitution.[184]

Spain. Bearing in mind the future accession of Spain to the European Communities, the authors of the 1978 Constitution drafted Art. 93 which authorises the transfer of certain powers to an international organisation or institution.[185] It is from this constitutional provision that the legal force of Union law derives. Generally, Spanish courts give priority to Union law on the ground of the special nature of the Union legal order, but sometimes they do invoke Art. 93 of the Constitution.[186] Initially, the *Tribunal Constitucional* (the Spanish Constitutional Court) seemed reluctant to pronounce on the application of Union law in the Spanish legal order, leaving the resolution of any conflict between domestic law and Union measures to the ordinary courts.[187] It stressed that from the fact that a

21–039

---

[181] Duarte and Gomes, "Capítulo VI Portugal", in Tajadura and de Miguel (eds), *Justicia Constitucional y Unión Europea* (Madrid, Centro de Estudios Políticos y Constitucionales, 2008) 259–290.

[182] *Tribunal Constitucional*, November 3, 1998, n° 621/98.

[183] *Supremo Tribunal Administrativo*, October 27, 1999, Case 45389-A.

[184] Miranda, "La Constitution portugaise et le traité de Maastricht" (1992) R.F.D.C. 679, at 681; Botelho Moniz (n. 178, *supra*), at 476–477; see also Gonçalves, "Quelques problèmes juridiques que pourra poser l'application du droit communautaire dans l'ordre interne portugais face à la Constitution de 1976" (1980) R.T.D.E. 662–693. This argument is based not only on Arts 7(3) and 8(4) of the Portuguese Constitution (compliance with "the fundamental principles of a democratic State based on the rule of law"), but also on Art. 277(2), which states that, although the unconstitutionality of international treaties does not prevent their internal application, such treaties will cease to apply where "such unconstitutionality results from the breach of a fundamental provision of this Constitution".

[185] Liñán Nogueras and Roldán Barbero, "The Judicial Application of Community Law in Spain" (1993) C.M.L.Rev. 1135–1154.

[186] *Cf.* Santaolalla Gadea and Martínez Lage, "Spanish Accession to the European Communities: Legal and Constitutional Implications" (1986) C.M.L.Rev. 11, at 22–23. For the first application of the principle of primacy by the highest ordinary court, in a judgment of June 13, 1991, see Abele, "Der Vorrang des Gemeinschaftsrechts in der Rechtsprechung des *Tribunal Supremo*" (1992) Eu.Z.W. 305–308.

[187] *Tribunal Constitucional*, February 14, 1991, *ibid.*, at 1139. See, prior to that judgment, Sobrina Heredia, "La réception et la place dans l'ordre juridique espagnol des normes conventionnelles internationales et des actes normatifs des organisations internationales" (1990) R.F.D.A. 965–968.

national provision was contrary to Union law, it did not follow that it was also unconstitutional.[188] The *Tribunal Constitucional* did not go behind the principle of primacy and invariably refused to review Union acts directly in the light of fundamental rights enshrined in the Constitution.[189] Yet, in 1992, the *Tribunal Constitucional* stated that Art. 93 of the Constitution may not be used as a means of circumventing a constitutional reform.[190]

However, when asked by the Spanish Government to pronounce on the question whether ratification of the Constitution for Europe, including its primacy clause, would need a constitutional reform, the *Tribunal Constitucional* held in December 2004[191] that the primacy of Union law had to be read in light of the Treaty provisions that guarantee "the existence of the States and their basic structures, as well as their values, principles and fundamental rights".[192] It considered that, as the supreme law of the land, the Constitution prevailed over international treaties, but that this does not preclude the primacy of Union law. For the *Tribunal Constitucional*, the concept of "supremacy" refers to the hierarchy of norms, whereas the "primacy" of Union law is a "conflict of laws" rule that determines the norm that takes precedence over another norm without questioning that other norm's validity. A norm which is supreme also enjoys primacy, unless the supreme norm itself states otherwise. For the *Tribunal Constitucional*, this is precisely what Art. 93 of the Constitution does, by enabling the transfer of national sovereignty to the Union. Yet, Art. 93 may not be construed as a means of depriving Spain of "the fundamental principles of the social and democratic State

---

[188] But see judgment No. 58/2004, April 19, 2004 (where the *Tribunal Constitucional* ruled that where a Spanish judge refuses to seek a preliminary ruling from the Court of Justice, he or she may commit a violation of the right to effective judicial protection as enshrined in Art. 24 of the Spanish Constitution).

[189] Liñán Nogueras and Roldán Barbero (n. 184, *supra*), at 1141–1144.

[190] *Tribunal Constitucional*, July 1, 1992 (*declaración* concerning the constitutionality of the EU Treaty, which stood to be ratified); see the references in para 3–010, *supra*.

[191] *Tribunal Constitucional*, Declaration 1/2004, December 13, 2004, available in English at: *http://www.tribunalconstitucional.es/en/jurisprudencia/restrad/Pages/DTC122004en.aspx* [Accessed December 13, 2010]. See López Castillo, Saiz Arnaiz and Ferreres Comella, *Constitución española y Constitución europea: análisis de la Declaración del Tribunal Constitucional (DTC 1/2004, de 13 de diciembre)* (Madrid, Centro de Estudios Políticos y Constitucionales, 2005); Plaza, "The Constitution for Europe and the Spanish Constitutional Court" (2006) E.Pub.L. 353–362; Alonso Garcia, "The Spanish Constitution and the European Constitution: The Script for a Virtual Collision and Other Observations on the Principle of Primacy" (2005) G.L.J. 1001–1024; Castillo de la Torre, "Tribunal Constitucional (Spanish Constitutional Court), Opinion 1/2004 of 13 December 2004, on the Treaty establishing a Constitution for Europe" (2005) C.M.L.Rev. 1169–1202; de Miguel, "Capítulo III España", in Tajadura and de Miguel (eds) (n. 180, *supra*), at 137–178.

[192] Giving its decision just one month after the decision on the Constitution of Europe by the French *Conseil constitutionnel*, the *Tribunal Constitucional* stressed that, in response to the relevant decisions of other European constitutional courts, the authors of the Constitution for Europe had adapted the primacy clause (Art. I-6) to "the common values of the constitutions of the States integrated into the Union and their constitutional traditions".

established by [its] Constitution". Hence, in the unlikely event of Union law breaching these fundamental principles and in so far as remedies available at Union level fail to re-establish the constitutional order, the *Tribunal Constitucional* would need to intervene.[193]

(4) Austria, Finland and Sweden

Austria. In Austria, Art. 9(2) of the Constitution enables specific competences to be transferred to international organisations. Since accession to the European Union was regarded as a total revision of the Constitution, it had, in accordance with the procedure laid down in Art. 44(3) thereof, to be approved in a referendum and cast in a law on accession.[194] In view of the "monist" approach taken by Austrian law with regard to provisions of international law, commentators accept that all provisions of Union law adopted after accession also enjoy primacy.[195] There is a possibility that a conflict may arise in Austria as a result of the role played by the *Verfassungsgerichtshof* in guaranteeing its own standard of fundamental rights.[196]

21–040

Finland. The Finnish Constitution makes no mention of delegating competence to any international organisation. Since the Finnish Parliament considered that, in some respects, accession to the European Union was incompatible with the Constitution, it adopted the 1994 law on accession under a procedure which also amended the Constitution.[197] Under the Finnish legal system, provisions of international law obtain the force of law only by formal incorporation. The 1994 law

21–041

---

[193] The *Tribunal Constitucional* added that the "real dimension" of the principle of primacy of Union law had to be assessed in light of the Treaty clause (now Art. 50 TEU) allowing Member States to withdraw voluntarily from the Union.

[194] Egger, "L'Autriche—Etat membre de l'Union européenne. Les effets institutionnels" (1996) R.M.C.U.E. 380–387; Griller, "Verfassungsfragen der österreichischen EU-Mitgliedschaft" (1995) Z.f.RV. 89–115; Herbst, "Austrian Constitutional Law and Accession to the European Union" (1995) E.Pub.L. 1–7; Seidl-Hohenveldern, "Constitutional Problems Involved in Austria's Accession to the EU" (1995) C.M.L.Rev. 727–731.

[195] Egger (n. 193, *supra*), at 382; Seidl-Hohenveldern (n. 193, *supra*), at 737–740. Initially, the *Verwaltungsgerichtshof* raised questions as to the application of the principle of primacy; see ECJ, Case C-224/97 *Ciola* [1999] E.C.R. I-2517, paras 21–34.

[196] See, in this connection, ECJ, *Österreichischer Rundfunk and Others* [2003] E.C.R. 1–4989. See Griller, "Wird Österreich das dreizehnte EG-Mitglied? Neutralität und Grundprinzipien des österreichischen Bundesverfassungsrechts als Prüfsteine des Beitrittsantrags" (1991) Eu.Z.W. 679, at 689; Egger (n. 193, *supra*), at 385. In practice, no problems have arisen; see Peyrou-Pistoulet, "Droit constitutionnel et droit communautaire: l'exemple autrichien" (2001) R.F.D.C. 237, at 254–255; Fischer and Lengauer, "The Adaptation of the Austrian Legal System Following EU Membership" (2000) C.M.L.Rev. 763, at 772–774.

[197] Aalto, "Accession of Finland to the European Union: First Remarks" (1995) E.L.Rev. 618, at 620–623. The four Basic Laws making up the Finnish Constitution have been replaced since March 1, 2000 by a single text. See Kulovesi, "International Relations in the New 'Constitution of Finland' " (2000) J.I.L. 513–522.

on accession to the Union incorporated the primacy and potential direct effect of Union law into Finnish law as parts of the *acquis* of the Union.[198]

21–042 **Sweden.** Sweden, in common with Finland, applies a "dualist" approach with regard to the position of international legal provisions. Chapter 10, Art. 5 of the Swedish Constitution affords a basis for the primacy of Union law. Along the lines of the case law of the German *Bundesverfassungsgericht*, that provision makes it possible to transfer decision-making power to the Union in so far as (*sålänge*) the latter affords protection of fundamental rights commensurate with that of the Constitution and the ECHR.[199] Pursuant to that provision, the Swedish Parliament has passed a law confirming the validity in Sweden of existing and future Union law and the legal effects attributed to that law by the Treaties, thereby incorporating the principle of the primacy of Union law.[200] More recently, in the *Unibet* case,[201] the *Högsta domstolen* (the Swedish Supreme Court) referred a question to the Court of Justice asking whether Ch. 11 of the Constitution, which does not provide for free-standing judicial review of legislative measures, was contrary to Union law. While it is true that the Court of Justice found no conflict between Ch. 11 and Union law, the reference made by the *Högsta domstolen* suggests that had such a conflict arisen, the latter would have set aside the constitutional provision in breach of Union law.[202]

(c) *The Member States having acceded in 2004 and 2007*

(1) Baltic States: Estonia, Latvia and Lithuania

21–043 **Estonia.** In Estonia, the primacy of Union law seems to be based both upon the precedence of international norms in general and upon the amendment to the 1992 Estonian Constitution. In common with the other Baltic States and Poland, Estonia has a "monist" legal system. With respect to the position of international law, it follows from Arts 3 and 123 of the Estonian Constitution that international

---

[198] For the application of these principles, see Ojanen, "The Impact of EU Membership on Finnish Constitutional Law" (2004) E.Pub.L. 531–564; Jääskinen, "The Application of Community Law in Finland: 1995–1998" (1999) C.M.L.Rev. 407–411. Compare this implicit incorporation with the express formulation of primacy and direct effect in the law ratifying the EEA Agreement, *ibid.*, at 626–627. For the precedence of EEA rules, see para. 25–030, *infra*.

[199] *Regeringsform*, Ch. 10, Art. 5, first subpara., in force since November 1, 1994.

[200] For a discussion as to whether the Swedish courts may consider whether the Union has acted within its competence, see Andersson, "Remedies for Breach of EC Law before Swedish Courts", in Lonbay and Biondi (eds), *Remedies for Breach of EC Law* (Chisterton, John Wiley & Sons, 1997) 203, at 204–206. In practice, Swedish courts recognise the primacy of Union law unconditionally; see Bernitz, "Sweden and the European Union: On Sweden's Implementation and Application of European Law" (2001) C.M.L.Rev. 903, at 925–927.

[201] Case C-432/05 *Unibet* [2007] ECR I-2271.

[202] See Nergelius, "2005-The Year when European Law and its Supremacy was Finally Acknowledged by Swedish Courts", in Cramér and Bull (eds), *Swedish Studies in European Law* (Oxford, Hart Publishing, 2008) 145–156.

agreements which have been ratified by the national parliament are part of the national legal order and, consequently, must be applied by the national courts.[203] According to Art. 123(2) of the Constitution, in the event of conflict between Estonian laws and international treaties ratified by the national parliament, the provisions of the treaties shall apply.[204] The same provision states, in its first paragraph, however, that the Republic of Estonia shall not conclude international treaties which are in conflict with the Constitution. In order to avoid such a conflict, the Constitution was amended in 2003 as a result of the same referendum by which the population gave its approval to accession to the European Union. According to the 2003 Amendment Act, "the Constitution of the Republic of Estonia applies taking account of the rights and obligations arising from the Accession Treaty".[205]

The *Riigikohus* (Estonian Supreme Court) seems to accept the unconditional primacy of Union law.[206] First, it rejected any jurisdiction under the abstract review procedure to declare a legislative provision unconstitutional for non compliance with Union law, while pointing out that this reading of the Estonian Constitution was to be understood without prejudice to the primacy of Union law, which only mandates setting aside the conflicting national measure in a concrete dispute.[207] In a second case, the *Riigikohus* held that,

> "within the spheres, which are within the exclusive competence of the European Union or where there is a shared competence with the European Union, the European Union law shall apply in the case of a conflict between Estonian legislation, including the Constitution, with the European Union law".[208]

---

[203] Pärn, "Estonia" in Ott and Inglis (eds), *Handbook on European Enlargement—A Commentary on the Enlargement Process* (The Hague, T.M.C. Asser, 2002), 251–255.

[204] *Ibid.*, at 251–252.

[205] For the referendum, see para. 6–006, *supra*. For some cases in which Estonian courts relied on the association agreement with the Union and principles of Union law, see *ibid.*, at 253–254 and Kerikmäe, "Estonian Constitutional Problems in Accession to the EU" in Kellermann, de Zwaan and Czuczai (eds), *EU Enlargement—The Constitutional Impact of the Enlargement at EU and National Level* (The Hague, T.M.C. Asser, 2001) 291 at 299–300.

[206] Albi, "Selected EU-Judgments of CEE Constitutional Courts: Lessons on How (not) to Amend Constitutions?" (2007) C.Y.E.L.P. 39–58; Albi, "Supremacy of EC Law in the new Member States" (2007) E.Const.L.Rev. 25–67.

[207] *Riigikohus*, Decision No. 3-4-1-1-05 of April 19, 2005, para. 49 (available in English at *http://www.nc.ee/?id=391* [Accessed December 13, 2010]). The *Riigikohus* thus considered inadmissible the request by the Chancellor of Justice to declare unconstitutional a law limiting membership of political parties to Estonian citizens on the ground that it was incompatible with Art. 19 of the EC Treaty (now Art. 22 TFEU).

[208] *Riigikohus*, Opinion No. 3-4-1-3-06 of May 11, 2006, para. 16 (available in English at *http://www.nc.ee/?id=663* [Accessed December 13, 2010]).

In the latter case, the *Riigikohus* considered that Art. 111 of the Constitution (reserving the right to issue currency to the Estonian Central Bank) had to be interpreted in conjunction with the 2003 Amendment Act which provides that the Constitution "applies taking into account of the rights and obligations arising from the Accession Treaty".[209]

21–044 **Latvia.** Before the accession of Latvia to the European Union, Art. 68 of the Latvian Constitution of 1922 was supplemented so as to allow for membership of the European Union, which had to be approved by a national referendum.[210] This provision forms the basis for the delegation of part of Latvia's State competences to the Union. In the Latvian legal order, once an international agreement has been approved by the Parliament, the provisions of the international agreement will prevail in case of conflict with rules of national law. Nonetheless, the Constitution is to take precedence over international agreements.[211] Even though the relationship between Union law and Latvian constitutional law has not been explicitly defined, Latvian courts are expected to give due effect to the primacy of Union law.[212] In its April 2009 ruling on the constitutionality of the law ratifying the Treaty of Lisbon,[213] the *Satversmes tiesa* (the Latvian Constitutional Court) observed that an unlimited transfer of competence to the Union would be incompatible with Art. 2 of the Constitution, which embodies the very foundations of the Latvian State in so far as it guarantees respect for fundamental rights, democracy, the sovereignty of the State and its people, the division of powers and the rule of law.[214] Any transfer of competences that would conflict with Art. 2 would need to be accepted by the Latvian people themselves, as the final depository of sovereignty, by means of a referendum. For the *Satversmes tiesa*, however, the Treaty of Lisbon did not provide for an unlimited transfer of competences since both Arts 4 and 5 TEU as well as the principles of conferral, subsidiarity and proportionality defined a clear legal framework whose respect the Court of Justice guaranteed.[215]

---

[209] The Estonian Parliament had asked the *Riigikohus* whether a law preparing the adoption of the euro was constitutional in the light of Art. 111 of the Constitution.

[210] According to Art. 68(4), substantial changes in the conditions of Latvia's membership in the European Union shall also be decided by a national referendum if such referendum is requested by at least half of the members of the Parliament (*Saeima*).

[211] See Luters-Thümmel, "Latvia" in *Handbook on European Enlargement—A Commentary on the Enlargement Process* (n. 202, *supra*) 267, at 268–272.

[212] See, to that effect, also Ušacka, "The Impact of the European integration process on the Constitution of Latvia" in *EU Enlargement—The Constitutional Impact of the Enlargement at EU and National Level* (n. 204, *supra*) 337, at 346.

[213] *Satversmes tiesa*, judgment of April 7, 2009, Case No. 2008–35–01, available in English at *http://www.satv.tiesa.gov.lv/?lang=2&mid=19* [Accessed December 13, 2010].

[214] *Ibid.*, para. 17.

[215] *Ibid.*, para. 18.3 (considering that the Court of Justice is no longer the "motor of European integration" but, as the constitutional umpire of the Union, now strives to accommodate the interests of the Union, Member States and individuals). Therefore the *Satversmes tiesa* dismissed the application brought by a group of citizens who argued that, by virtue of Art. 101 of the Constitution, a call for a referendum should have taken place.

Lithuania. The Constitution of Lithuania of 1992 contains a clause allowing the 21–045
Republic of Lithuania to participate in international organisations provided that
they do not contradict the interests and independence of the State (Art. 136). In
July 2004, the Constitution was supplemented by a Constitutional Act according
to which Lithuania is to share with and delegate competencies to the European
Union.[216] Article 2 of the Constitutional Act provides that the norms of the Union
acquis shall be an integral part of the Lithuanian legal order and will apply
directly when they are based on the founding Treaties of the Union. Furthermore,
it expressly states that in any case of conflict of norms the norms of the Union
acquis shall prevail over the laws of the Republic of Lithuania.[217] This reading
of Art. 2 has been consistently confirmed by the *Konstitucinis Teismas* (the
Lithuanian Constitutional Court) which considers that the Constitution establishes *expressis verbis* the "collision rule" which consolidates the primacy of
Union law whenever Union provisions based on the founding Treaties compete
with the provisions of Lithuanian legal acts "save for the Constitution itself".[218]
For the *Konstitucinis Teismas*, it seems that, in the hierarchy of norms, Union
law—just as public international law—is located above legislative statutes but
below the Constitution. Yet, before deciding a conflict between Union law and the
Constitution, it cannot be ruled out that the *Konstitucinis Teismas* would engage
in a dialogue with the Court of Justice.[219] Indeed, the *Konstitucinis Teismas* has
repeatedly pointed out that the case law of the Court of Justice—as well as that
of the ECtHR—operates as "a source of construction" in the interpretation and
application of Lithuanian law.[220]

(2) Cyprus

Cyprus. The establishment of the Republic of Cyprus as an independent and 21–046
sovereign State was the result of the Zurich and London Agreements which led

---

[216] Constitutional Act of July 13, 2004, on the Membership of the Republic of Lithuania in the
European Union. For the proposed Act, see Vadapalas and Jarukaitis, "Lithuania" in *Handbook on
European Enlargement—A Commentary on the Enlargement Process* (n. 202, *supra*), at 288.
[217] Commentators had argued earlier that the rule according to which international treaties have
supremacy over domestic laws and secondary legal acts (based on Art. 138 of the Constitution and
Art. 11(2) of the Law on international treaties) would also apply to Union law: Vadapalas,
"Delimitation of competences between the European Union and the Member States: a look from a
candidate country" in Melissas and Pernice (eds), *Perspectives of the Nice Treaty and the
Intergovernmental Conference in 2004* (Nomos, Baden-Baden, 2002), 25.
[218] See *Konstitucinis Teismas*, Ruling of December 4, 2008, on connecting the electricity network;
Decision of May 8, 2007, on applying to the Court of Justice of the European Communities;
Ruling of December 21, 2006, on the status, management and rights of the national broadcaster.
Available in English at: *http://www.lrkt.lt/Documents1_e.html* [Accessed December 13, 2010].
[219] The *Konstitucinis Teismas* has already made use of the preliminary reference procedure. See Case
C-239/07 *Sabatauskas and Others* [2008] ECR I-7523.
[220] See *Konstitucinis Teismas*, Ruling of December 21, 2006, on the status, management and rights of
the national broadcaster; Ruling of May 15, 2007, on State secrets and official secrets. Available
in English at: *http://www.lrkt.lt/Documents1_e.html* [Accessed December 13, 2010].

to the signing in 1960 of the Constitution and three Treaties,[221] two of which are incorporated into the Constitution.[222] The Cypriot legal system is considered to be "monist" in the sense that duly ratified and published treaties acquire superior force to any municipal law.[223] The case law of the *Ανώτατο Δικαστήριο* (Supreme Court of Cyprus) has recognised that self-executing international agreements are directly applicable as an integral part of the domestic legal order.[224] It has further adopted the rule that international agreements must be interpreted in accordance with international law and in conformity with the international obligations of the Republic.[225] According to some commentators, all this bodes well for the reception of Union law into the Cypriot legal order.[226] Yet, according to Art.179(1) of the Constitution of Cyprus, the Constitution is the supreme law of the Republic. Accordingly, in a judgment of November 2005 on the law implementing the Framework Decision on the European arrest warrant, the *Ανώτατο Δικαστήριο* ruled that legislation implementing Union measures could not go against constitutional guarantees, such as the provision according to which no Cypriot national may be extradited.[227] While formally recognising the primacy of Union law, the *Ανώτατο Δικαστήριο* found that, since that Framework Decision did not produce direct effects, Cyprus was only obliged to achieve the results mandated therein and should not achieve these results by

---

[221] These are the Treaty of Establishment, between the Republic of Cyprus, Greece, Turkey and the United Kingdom, the Treaty of Guarantee by which Greece, Turkey and the United Kingdom recognise and guarantee, inter alia, the independence, territorial integrity and security of the Republic of Cyprus and also the state of affairs established by the Basic Articles of the Constitution and, finally, the Treaty of Military Alliance between the Republic of Cyprus, Greece, Turkey and the United Kingdom.

[222] Under Art. 181 of the Constitution, the Treaty of Guarantee and the Treaty of Military Alliance are incorporated into the Constitution as Annexes I and II thereto. Continued exercise by the State of its legislative, executive, judicial and administrative functions, following the non-participation of Turkish Cypriots in the State organs of the Republic of Cyprus since 1964, has been achieved without constitutional amendment concerning the bi-communal structure of the State by taking temporary measures justified by the doctrine of necessity, enabling State functions and services to continue unimpeded while the above abnormal situation continues (for the partitioning of Cyprus, see para. 12–006).

[223] Emiliou, "The Constitutional impact of enlargement at EU and national level: the case of the Republic of Cyprus" in *EU Enlargement—The Constitutional Impact of the Enlargement at EU and National Level* (n. 204, *supra*) 243, at 245.

[224] *Malachtou v Armefti* (1987) 1 C.L.R. 207, at 235.

[225] *Ibid.*; see also *Shipowners Union v The Registrar of Trade Marks & Others* (1988) 3 C.L.R 457.

[226] Emiliou, "Cyprus" in *Handbook on European Enlargement—A Commentary on the Enlargement Process* (n. 202, *supra*), 239, at 249.

[227] *Ανώτατο Δικαστήριο*, judgment of November 7, 2005, (Civil Appeal No. 294/2005). The *Ανώτατο Δικαστήριο* held that Art. 11.2(f) of the Constitution (according to which no Cypriot could be extradited) did not leave much room for interpretation (*cf.* ECJ, Case C-105/03 *Pupino* [2005] E.C.R I-5285, where the ECJ held that, if possible, national law must be interpreted in conformity with Union Framework Decisions. See Tsadiras, "Cyprus Supreme Court, Judgment of November 7, 2005 (Civil Appeal no. 294/2005) on the Cypriot European Arrest Warrant Law" (2007) C.M.L.Rev. 1515–1528.

legislative means contrary to the Constitution. Following that judgment, the Constitution was supplemented in 2006 by an Art. 1A according to which no provision of the Constitution is deemed either to invalidate national laws necessary to implement Union legislation or to prevent Union legislation from having legal effect.[228] In the same way, Art. 179(1) of the Constitution now states that the supremacy of the Constitution is without prejudice to Art. 1A, that is, without prejudice to the primacy of Union law. Hence, the Cypriot constitutional legislator opted for a solution similar to that contained in Art. 29.4.10 of the Irish Constitution.

(3) Czech Republic and Slovakia

Czech Republic. The Czech Republic, in common with Hungary, Malta and the Slovak Republic, used to embrace a "dualist" system with respect to the incorporation of rules of international law.[229] Accordingly, treaty provisions were incorporated into the internal legal order only by express reference in a domestic rule of law.[230] Important constitutional amendments were necessary to allow for the accession of the Czech Republic to the European Union.[231] According to Art. 10 of the Czech Constitution, as amended in 2002, international agreements which have been ratified, approved and promulgated and which are binding upon the Czech Republic are to constitute part of the Czech legal order. Should an international agreement conflict with domestic law, the international agreement shall be applied. This not only turned the Czech legal order into a "monist" system, but also paves the way for the primacy of Union law. The new Art. 10a of the Czech Constitution authorises the transfer of powers to an international organisation or institution.[232] Article 95 of the Czech Constitution declares that national courts are bound by the laws stemming from such an organisation or institution and by international agreements constituting part of the Czech legal order and

21–047

---

[228] For the complexities of constitutional reform in Cyprus (e.g. the concept of "constitutional necessity"), see Patsalides, "Accommodating the Principle of Supremacy of Community Law to the Cypriot Legal Order—The Necessity for a Constitutional Amendment" (2006) E.Pub.L. 363–370.

[229] Balaš, "Legal and quasi-legal thresholds of the accession of the Czech Republic to the EC" in *EU Enlargement—The Constitutional Impact of the Enlargement at EU and National Level* (n. 204, *supra*) 267–277.

[230] However, in practice Czech courts were willing to interpret national law in the light of directly applicable provisions of the association agreement between the Czech Republic and the Union, even in the absence of any explicit reference to these provisions in domestic law. See the judgement of the High Court in *Olomouc* (nr. 2.A 6/96), interpreting national competition law in the light of EU competition rules. The Czech Constitutional Court confirmed this judgment (nr. III.US 31/97). See Týč, "Czech Republic" in *Handbook on European Enlargement—A Commentary on the Enlargement Process* (n. 202, *supra*) 229, at 231.

[231] Týč (n. 229, *supra*), at 236.

[232] According to Art. 10a(2) of the Czech Constitution, this transfer should take place by means of an international agreement which must be approved by Parliament unless a constitutional law requires approval by means of a referendum.

may assess the conformity of any domestic regulation with such laws or international agreements.[233]

In March 2006, the *Ústavní soud* (Czech Constitutional Court) pointed out that Union law itself determines the effect it has in the Czech legal order.[234] It recognised that Union acts are not subject to constitutional review, unless they threaten the values contained in Arts 9(2) and 9(3) of the Constitution, that is, unless they "threaten the very essence of State sovereignty of the Czech Republic" (formal limitation) or "the essential attributes of a democratic State governed by the rule of law" (substantive limitation). For fundamental rights, this means that the *Ústavní soud* will exercise its review powers if their level of protection at Union level is lower than that guaranteed by the Constitution. For the *Ústavní soud*, however, the protection offered by the Union is "not of a lower quality" than that provided in the Czech Republic.[235] In the same conciliatory spirit, in May 2006, the *Ústavní soud* interpreted some provisions of the Czech Charter of fundamental rights and fundamental freedoms in a way consistent with Union law and thereby concluded that the Czech legislation implementing the Framework Decision on the European arrest warrant was not contrary to the guarantees enshrined in that Charter.[236]

---

[233] Týč (n. 229, *supra*), at 237.

[234] *Ústavní soud*, judgment of March 8, 2006, Pl. ÚS 50/04 (challenge to a Government regulation implementing a Commission regulation on sugar quotas, inter alia, for being incompatible with fundamental rights as protected by the Czech Constitution). Available in English at *http://www.usoud.cz/view/726* [Accessed December 13, 2010].

[235] In the case at hand, the *Ústavní soud* annulled the Government regulation on the ground that it was "*ultra vires*". To this end, it relied on the case law of the Court of Justice according to which Member States may not paraphrase directly effective provisions contained in a regulation (see para. 22–073). For a comment on the Sugar Quotas Decision, see Sadurski, "'Solange, Chapter 3': Constitutional Courts in Central Europe—Democracy—European Union" (2008) E.L.J. 1–35; Šlosarčík, "Czech Republic and the European Union Law in 2004–2006" (2007) E.Pub.L. 367–378; Zemánek, "The Emerging Czech Constitutional Doctrine of European Law" (2007) E.Const.L.Rev. 418–435.

[236] *Ústavní soud*, judgment of May 3, 2006, Pl. ÚS 66/04. Available in English at *http://www.usoud.cz/view/726* [Accessed December 13, 2010]. The *Ústavní soud* relied on the ECJ's judgment in *Pupino* (see n. 136 supra) and held that, although a *contra legem* interpretation of constitutional provisions was prohibited, in the case at hand the Framework Decision could be interpreted consistently with both Art. 14(4) ("[n]o citizen may be forced to leave his homeland") and Art. 39 (principle of legality) of the Czech Charter. See Šlosarčík (n. 234, *supra*), at 374; Zemánek (n. 234, *supra*), at 427; Komárek (n. 135, *supra*), at 26. The *Ústavní soud* ruled that Art. 14(4) did not cover situations falling within the scope of the European Arrest Warrant, based on an historical reading of that provision (adopted in response to the unlawful deportations carried out by the communist regime against political dissidents) and on the case law of the Slovak Constitutional Court (which had not invalidated the Slovak legislation implementing the Framework Decision on the ground that it violated a similar provision of the Slovak Constitution). It held that Art. 14(4) did not mandate Czech citizens to be tried before a Czech court, but it only required Czech citizens to be subject in another Member State to a level of human rights protection equivalent to that guaranteed in the Czech Republic.

With respect to the Lisbon Treaty, the *Ústavní soud* was requested twice to exercise its power under Art. 87 of the Constitution to rule on the compatibility with the Constitution of a treaty submitted for ratification. Whilst it gave the green light to ratification in both cases, it reaffirmed the limits inherent in the Czech legal order to a transfer of powers to the Union. In its first decision,[237] the *Ústavní soud* recalled that such a transfer must comply with "the very essence of the Republic as a sovereign and democratic State governed by the rule of law".[238] In that context, however, it regarded the concept of "sovereignty" as a dynamic concept that is compatible with the European integration project on the ground that the Member States remain "the Masters of the Treaty".[239] In determining whether the Union has breached the core values of the Constitution, the *Ústavní soud* opined that the legislator enjoys a prominent role and that it would interfere only where "the scope of discretion was clearly exceeded".[240] In its second decision, delivered almost a year later, the *Ústavní soud* refused to provide a catalogue listing the competences that cannot be transferred to the Union without depriving the Czech Republic of its statehood[241] and reaffirmed that sovereignty may be "pooled" among the Member States[242]—thereby following an approach that stands in sharp contrast to the ruling delivered by the German Constitutional Court on the Treaty of Lisbon.[243]

Slovakia. On the way to EU membership, Slovakia had its Constitution of 1992   **21–048** thoroughly amended in 2001 so as to specify the rules by which powers were to be delegated to the European Union as well as the status of Community and Union law in the Slovak legal order, which was considered to be of a "dualist" nature.[244] As a result, Art. 7(2) of the Constitution states that Slovakia may, by

---

[237] *Ústavní soud*, judgement of November 26, 2008, Pl. ÚS 19/08. Available in English at *http://www.usoud.cz/view/726* [Accessed December 13, 2010].

[238] *Ibid.*, para. 97.

[239] *Ibid.*, para. 107. The *Ústavní soud* considered European integration even to contribute to strengthening sovereignty by enabling the Czech Republic to participate in a globalised world with a stronger voice: *ibid.*, para. 108.

[240] For a comment on the part of the judgment where the *Ústavní soud* examined in detail the constitutionality of Arts 2(1); 4(2); 352(1); 83; 216 TFEU as well as Arts 2; 7 and 48 (6) and (7) TEU, and the Charter, see Šlosarčík, "Czech Republic 2006–2008: On the President, Judges and the Lisbon Treaty" (2010) E.Pub.L. 1–16; Bříza, "The Czech Republic: The Constitutional Court on the Lisbon Treaty Decision of November 26, 2008" (2009) E.Const.L.Rev. 143–164.

[241] *Ústavní soud*, judgement of the November 3, 2009, Pl. ÚS 29/09, para. 111. Available in English at *http://www.usoud.cz/view/726* [Accessed December 13, 2010].

[242] *Ibid.*, para. 147.

[243] See the editorial, "The Czech Constitutional Court's Second Decision on the Lisbon Treaty of November 3, 2009" (2009) E.Const.L.Rev. 345–352.

[244] Kunová, "Constitutional aspects of the accession of the Slovak Republic to the European Union" in *EU Enlargement—The Constitutional Impact of the Enlargement at EU and National Level* (n. 204, *supra*) 327, at 329. The Constitutional amendments were introduced by Constitutional Act No. 90/2001 Coll.

means of an international treaty ratified and promulgated in accordance with the law, or on the basis of such a treaty, transfer the exercise of part of its sovereign powers to the European Communities and the European Union.[245] The same provision introduces the primacy of European law into the Slovak legal order where it provides that "legally binding acts of the European Communities and of the European Union shall have precedence over laws of the Slovak Republic".[246] The constitutional amendments turned the Slovak legal order into a "monist" system.[247]

(4) Hungary

21–049 **Hungary.** Hungary is considered to belong to the "dualist" school as far as the integration of international law into the national legal order is concerned.[248] According to Art. 7(1) of the Hungarian Constitution of 1949, the Hungarian legal order,

> "accepts the generally respected rules of international law, and guarantees the conformity of accepted international obligations with domestic law".

Prior to Hungary's accession to the European Union, the Hungarian Constitution did not allow for the transfer of competence to international organisations. Moreover, the Hungarian legal order recognised the direct applicability of international norms only through the incorporation of such norms into domestic law.[249] Therefore, the Constitution was supplemented by Art. 2/A, according to which Hungary,

---

[245] Boháčik, "The Slovak Republic" in *Handbook on European Enlargement—A Commentary on the Enlargement Process* (n. 202, *supra*) 323, at 325.

[246] *Ibid.*, at 325 and 329. Article 7(2) of the Constitution further specifies that "the transposition of legally binding acts which require implementation shall be realised through a law or a regulation of the Government [. . .]".

[247] *Ibid.*, at 325. See also Bobek and Kühn, "Europe yet to come: the application of EU in Slovakia", in Łazowski (ed.), *The Application of EU law in the New Member States—Brave New World* (The Hague, T.M.C. Asser Press, forthcoming) (working version available at: *http://www.ssrn.com* [Accessed December 13, 2010]) The authors argue that, since Slovakian courts are not yet familiar with Union law, the Slovakian legal system has so far "avoided constitutional dramas comparable to some other new Member States", in particular, the Czech Republic or Poland.

[248] Vàrhelyi, "Hungary" in *Handbook on European Enlargement—A Commentary on the Enlargement Process* (n. 202, *supra*), at 257–265.

[249] Accordingly, the *Alkotmánybíróságról* (Hungarian Constitutional Court) held in Decision No. 30/1998 (VI.25) that it was not sufficient for Art.62 of the association agreement with the Union to refer to the competition rules of the EC Treaty in order for the Hungarian authorities to be bound, or even allowed, to apply these rules. It was considered that it would be in breach of sovereignty if Hungary were to apply rules emanating from an organisation of which it was not a member. See Vàrhelyi, *ibid.*, at 262–264; Volkai, "The Application of the Europe Agreement and European Law in Hungary: The Judgement of an Activist Constitutional Court on Activist Notions" (Cambridge, Harvard Jean Monnet Working Paper 8/99, 1999), 39 pp.

"in its capacity as a Member State of the European Union, may exercise certain constitutional powers jointly with other Member States to the extent necessary in connection with the rights and obligations conferred by the Treaties on the foundation of the European Union and the European Communities",

whereby "these powers may be exercised independently and by way of the institutions of the European Union".

So far, the *Alkotmánybíróságról* (the Hungarian Constitutional Court) has mainly focused on preserving a clear division of competences between the Union judiciary and national courts.[250] First, it has been reluctant to examine cases where national law conflicts with Union law, reckoning that it is for ordinary courts in cooperation with the Court of Justice to resolve such conflicts.[251] Second, in light of Art. 7 of the Constitution, the *Alkotmánybíróságról* enjoys jurisdiction to review *ex ante* the constitutionality of international agreements. But, since it believes that Union law is not part of international law but of domestic law, the *Alkotmánybíróságról* has opted to not review the constitutionality of Union law. Yet, it has examined the constitutionality of domestic measures implementing Union law.[252] In March 2008, it also ruled on the constitutionality of an agreement concluded by the Union and its Member States with third countries (Norway and Iceland),[253] explaining that even though the Union was a contracting party, that agreement,

"does not change any of the competencies of the European Union or of the European Community regulated in the so called founding and amending treaties, but establishes obligations in the relations between the individual Member States and Iceland and Norway".[254]

Hence, this mixed agreement was not considered to be part of Union law, but of international law.[255]

---

[250] Varju, "On the Constitutional Issues of EU Membership and the Interplay between the ECHR and Domestic Constitutional Law Concerning the Right of Assembly and Freedom of Expression" (2009) E.Pub.L. 295–306.

[251] *Ibid.*, at 298.

[252] *Ibid.*, at 300.

[253] *Alkotmánybíróságról*, Decision 32/2008 of March 11, 2008, available in English at *http://www.mkab.hu/index.php?id=decisions#2008* [Accessed December 13, 2010].

[254] *Ibid.*, Part III.

[255] The *Alkotmánybíróságról* declared the statute ratifying the agreement unconstitutional on the ground that it breached the legality principle for criminal charges guaranteed by Art. 57(4) of the Constitution. It ruled that ratification could not take place until the Constitution had been amended. When the *Alkotmánybíróságról* gave its decision, that amendment of Art. 57(4) had already been adopted, but it could only enter into force simultaneously with the Treaty of Lisbon.

(5) Malta

21–050 **Malta.** The Maltese legal system distinguishes, in a "dualist" manner, between the national and international legal orders and does not accord international norms any legal force on their own in the domestic legal order.[256] Article 6 of the Maltese Constitution of 1964 provides that,

> "if any other law is inconsistent with this Constitution, this constitution shall prevail and the other law, to the extent of the inconsistency, shall be void".

Moreover, the Ratification of Treaties Act states that,

> "[n]o provision of a treaty shall become, or be enforceable as, part of the law of Malta except by or under an Act of Parliament".[257]

The Maltese Constitution was amended in 2003 to take account of accession to the European Union in the definition of the powers of the national parliament.[258] It took an Act of Parliament to ensure the legal force and primacy of Union law in the Maltese legal order. Pursuant to the European Union Act, the Treaties as well as "existing and future acts adopted by the European Union" shall be part of the domestic law of Malta (Art. 3(1)), whereas any provision of domestic law which is incompatible with Malta's obligations under the Treaties will be without effect and unenforceable (Art. 3(2)).[259]

(6) Poland

21–051 **Poland.** In 1997 Poland adopted a new Constitution, which allows for the transfer of certain sovereign powers to the European Union. According to Art. 90(1) of the Constitution,

> "the Republic of Poland may, by virtue of international agreements, delegate to an international organisation or international institution the competence of organs of State authority in relation to certain matters".[260]

---

[256] Frendo and Piscopo, "Malta" in *Handbook on European Enlargement—A Commentary on the Enlargement Process* (n. 202, *supra*) 291–297.

[257] See Xuereb, "Constitutional questions raised by the proposed accession of Malta to the European Union in the general context" in *EU Enlargement—The Constitutional Impact of the Enlargement at EU and National Level* (n. 204, *supra*) 229, at 230–236.

[258] Pursuant to Art. 65(1) of the Constitution of Malta, "Parliament may make laws for the peace, order and good government of Malta in conformity with full respect for human rights, generally accepted principles of international law and Malta's international and regional obligations in particular those assumed by the Treaty of Accession to the European Union signed in Athens on the 16th April, 2003".

[259] See the European Union Act of July 16, 2003: *http://www.legal-malta.com/law/laws-of-malta.htm* [Accessed December 13, 2010].

[260] See Jankowska-Gilberg, "Verfassungsrechtliche Grundlagen des Beitritts und der Mitgliedschaft Polens in der Europäischen Union" (2003) EuR. 417, at 418–427.

According to Art. 91(1) of the Constitution, a ratified international agreement shall constitute part of the domestic legal order and shall be applied directly, unless its application depends on the enactment of a statute. Moreover, Art. 91(3) of the Constitution provides that,

"[i]f an agreement, ratified by the Republic of Poland, establishing an international organization so provides, the laws established by it shall be applied directly and have precedence in the event of a conflict of laws".

These provisions form a legal basis for the primacy of Union law over provisions of national law.

However, it follows from the case law of the the the *Trybunał Konstytucyjny* (the Polish Constitutional Court[261]) that because the powers transferred to the Union are subject to constitutional procedures and limitations, the Union legal order is considered only to have a derivative nature and not to affect the supremacy of the Polish Constitution. In its ruling of May 2005 on the constitutionality of the Accession Treaty,[262] the *Trybunał Konstytucyjny* stressed the unconditional nature of the supremacy of the Constitution as provided for by Art. 8(1) of the Constitution. In the event of a collision between Union law and the Constitution,[263] Poland should thus either amend the Constitution, induce the modification of the conflicting Union norm or withdraw from the Union. Finally, for the *Trybunał Konstytucyjny*, the Member States keep the right to examine whether the Union complies with the principles of conferred powers, proportionality and subsidiarity. Where the Union infringes any of these principles, Union law may not prevail over national law.[264] Both in this judgment and in its judgment of April 2005 where

---

[261] Article 188 of the Constitution of Poland empowers the *Trybunał Konstytucyjny* to adjudicate on the "conformity of statutes and international agreements to the Constitution".

[262] *Trybunał Konstytucyjny*, judgment of May 11, 2005, No. K 18/04. The *Trybunał Konstytucyjny* rejected the idea that the Accession Treaty was in breach of the principle of sovereignty of the Polish People and that it violated the supremacy of the Constitution. A short version of the judgment is available in English at *http://www.trybunal.gov.pl/eng/summaries/wstep_gb.htm* [Accessed December 13, 2010].

[263] The *Trybunał Konstytucyjny* also pointed out that a conflict between Union law and the Constitution may not lead to the invalidity of a Constitutional norm, to its replacement by the Union measure, or to a limitation of its scope of application to areas not covered by Union law. Thus, the ruling of the *Trybunał Konstytucyjny* confirms the approach of some scholars who had questioned whether Union law could prevail over constitutional provisions. See, to this effect, Jankowska-Gilberg (n. 259, *supra*), at 427–439; Łazowski, "Poland" in *Handbook on European Enlargement—A Commentary on the Enlargement Process* (n. 202, *supra*) 299, at 306–307; Justynski, "The impact of the European integration process on the creation of the broad lines of the Constitution of the Republic of Poland and on the political practices of the country" in *EU Enlargement—The Constitutional Impact of the Enlargement at EU and National Level* (n. 204, *supra*) 279–290 (all mentioning that Arts 90 and 91 of the Constitution do not give Union law precedence over the Constitution).

[264] See Łazowski, "Polish Constitutional Tribunal: Conformity of the Accession Treaty with the Polish Constitution. Decision of May 11, 2005" (2007) E.Const.L.Rev. 148–162.

it held the national measures implementing the Framework Decision on the European arrest warrant to be incompatible with the Constitution,[265] the *Trybunał Konstytucyjny* made it clear that a conflict between national law implementing Union law and the Polish Constitution cannot be resolved by interpreting national law in conformity with Union law if such an interpretation would run counter to constitutional provisions or would lower the threshold of human rights protection guaranteed by the Constitution. In the same way as the Cypriot Supreme Court, the *Trybunał Konstytucyjny* found the national measures implementing the European arrest warrant incompatible with the constitutional provision that prohibits the extradition of nationals (Art. 55(1) of the Constitution).[266] However, in light of Art. 9 of the Constitution which embodies Poland's commitment to respecting international obligations, the *Trybunał Konstytucyjny* decided to delay the effects of its judgment so as to allow for an amendment of the Constitution, which took place in 2006.[267]

In a ruling of December 2006, the *Trybunał Konstytucyjny* stressed again that it had the final say regarding the implications of a conflict between the Constitution and Union law, but declared itself incompetent to examine whether a legislative statute was in breach of Union law.[268] For the *Trybunał Konstytucyjny*, this type of control is to be carried out by the Supreme Court,

---

[265] *Trybunał Konstytucyjny*, judgment of April 27, 2005, No. P 1/05. A short version of the judgment is available in English at *http://www.trybunal.gov.pl/eng/summaries/wstep_gb.htm* [Accessed December 13, 2010].

[266] As regards the duty to interpret national law in conformity with Union law, the *Trybunał Konstytucyjny* stressed that it was not applicable where such interpretation would worsen the legal position of individuals, for instance where they would lose the guarantee of the principle of double criminality, which is not a prerequisite for surrendering a person under the Framework Decision on the European arrest warrant. In addition, since surrender under the Framework Decision is more onerous for individuals than extradition, the *Trybunał Konstytucyjny* relied on an "*a minori ad maius*" argument to reject that Art. 55(1) of the Constitution could be interpreted so as to deny the extradition of Polish nationals while permitting their surrender. On this point, see Leczykiewicz, "Trybunal Konstytucyjny (Polish Constitutional Tribunal), Judgment of April 27, 2005, No. P 1/05" (2006) C.M.L.Rev. 1181–1191. Further, the *Trybunał Konstytucyjny* also found that Art. 55 could not be limited by the public policy derogations contained in Art. 31(3) of the Constitution. In contrast to the Czech Constitutional Court, it reasoned that the very essence of the right contained in Art. 55(1) would be jeopardised if a Polish national was not tried before a Polish court.

[267] In 2006, by adding a second para., Art. 55 of the Constitution has been accommodated to the Framework Decision on the European arrest warrant. See also Kowalik-Bańczyk, "Should We Polish It Up? The Polish Constitutional Tribunal and the Idea of Supremacy of EU Law" (2005) G.L.J. 1355–1366; Łazowski, "Constitutional Tribunal on the Surrender of Polish Citizens Under the European Arrest Warrant. Decision of April 27, 2005" (2005) E.Const.L.Rev. 418–435; Komárek (n. 135, *supra*), at 16–21; Albi (n. 205, *supra*), at 34–41.

[268] *Trybunał Konstytucyjny*, Procedural Decision of December 19, 2006, No. P 37/05. Hence, the *Trybunał Konstytucyjny* declared inadmissible a reference made by a lower court on the compatibility of a statute with a Treaty provision. A short version of the Procedural Decision is available in English at *http://www.trybunal.gov.pl/eng/summaries/wstep_gb.htm* [Accessed December 13, 2010].

administrative courts and common courts in cooperation with the Court of Justice through the preliminary rulings procedure.[269] Further, by virtue of Art. 91(2) of the Constitution, Polish courts are obliged to refuse to apply statutes in breach of directly effective provisions of Union law. They are also obliged to interpret national law in light of the wording and purpose of Union law.[270]

(7) Slovenia

Slovenia. Pursuant to the Slovene Constitution of 1991, international treaties which are ratified and published are part of the domestic legal order, ranking just below the Constitution.[271] Since it was considered not to allow for any transfer of sovereign rights to an international organisation,[272] the Slovene Constitution was supplemented in 2003 by a new Art. 3a, according to which,

21–052

> "Slovenia may transfer the exercise of part of its sovereign rights to international organisations which are based on respect for human rights and fundamental freedoms, democracy and the principles of the rule of law and may enter into a defensive alliance with States which are based on respect for these values".

According to the same provision,

> "[l]egal acts and decisions adopted within international organisations to which Slovenia has transferred the exercise of part of its sovereign rights shall be applied in Slovenia in accordance with the legal regulation of these organisations".

This would seem to incorporate the principle of the primacy of Union law in the Slovene legal order.

---

[269] Ruling on an action brought by the Polish President, the *Trybunał Konstytucyjny* found that vesting every national court with jurisdiction to make references to the Court of Justice as provided for by Art. 35(2) of the EU Treaty was not contrary to the right to a fair trial (Art. 45(1) of the Constitution). See *Trybunał Konstytucyjny*, judgment of February 18, 2009, No. Kp 3/08. A short version of the judgment is available in English at *http://www.trybunal.gov.pl/eng/summaries/wstep_gb.htm* [Accessed December 13, 2010].

[270] Łazowski, "Poland: Constitutional Tribunal on the Preliminary Ruling Procedure and the Division of Competences Between National Courts and the Court of Justice" (2008) E.Const.L.Rev. 187–197.

[271] Vehar and Ilešič, "Slovenia" in *EU Enlargement—The Constitutional Impact of the Enlargement at EU and National Level* (n. 204, *supra*) 331–339.

[272] *Ibid.*, at 338–339; Vehar, "Constitutional problems in the period of pre-accession in the Republic of Slovenia" in *EU Enlargement—The Constitutional Impact of the Enlargement at EU and National Level* (n. 204, *supra*) 369, at 370.

(8) Bulgaria and Romania

21–053 **Bulgaria.** With a view to preparing the accession to the Union, the 1991 Constitution of Bulgaria was amended in 2005. Article 4 of the Constitution was supplemented by a third para. according to which "the Republic of Bulgaria shall participate in the building and development of the European Union". That norm should pave the way for Bulgaria's ongoing participation in the European integration project.[273] Just as other Member States, Bulgaria has opted for a monist system.[274] According to Art. 5(4) of the Constitution, where a conflict arises between an international agreement that has been ratified and domestic legislation, the former prevails over the latter. Yet, Art. 5(1) states that the Constitution is the supreme law of the Republic. Arguably, a combined reading of both provisions would suggest that Union law is located above legislative statutes but below the Constitution.[275] Otherwise, the new Art. 85(4) of the Constitution would seem redundant, since it provides that,

> "the conclusion of an international treaty requiring an amendment to the Constitution shall be preceded by the passage of such an amendment".[276]

In order to facilitate the implementation of the Framework Decision on the European arrest warrant, the Bulgarian Constitution was thus amended in 2005 to allow for the extradition of Bulgarian nationals when provided for by an international agreement.[277]

21–054 **Romania.** In 2003, the 1991 Constitution was amended so as to enable Romania to participate in the process of "Euro-Atlantic integration".[278] Article 148(1) of the Constitution provides that the Chamber of Deputies and the Senate acting jointly may transfer competences to the Union[279] whereas Art. 148(2) of the Constitution states that Union law takes precedence over conflicting national laws "in compliance with the provisions of the accession act". Before these amendments were finally adopted, the *Curtea Constituțională* (the Romanian Constitutional Court) delivered an *ex officio* opinion[280] in which it held Arts

---

[273] Belov and Tanchev, "Bulgaria—Constitutional Gradualism: Adapting to EU Membership and Improving the Judiciary in the Bulgarian Constitution" (2008) E.Pub.L. 3–19, at 10–12.

[274] Tanchev and Belov, "The Republic of Bulgaria," in Kortmann, Fleuren, Voermans (eds), *Constitutional Law of 2 EU Member States: Bulgaria and Romania* (Deventer, Kluwer, 2008), I-16.

[275] *Ibid.*, at I-16.

[276] Tanchev and Peteva, "Bulgaria", in Kellermann, Czuczai, Blockmans, Albi and Douma (eds), *The impact of EU accession on the legal orders of new EU Member States and (pre-) candidate countries: hopes and fears* (The Hague, T.M.C. Asser Press, 2006), 37.

[277] See Art. 25(4) of the Constitution.

[278] Duculescu and Adam, "Romania", in Kellermann, Czuczai, Blockmans, Albi and Douma (eds) (n. 275, *supra*), at 115.

[279] This Article requires a majority of two thirds of the number of Deputies and Senators.

[280] See *Curtea Constituțională*, decision of April 16, 2003, No. 148/2003. Available in English at *http://www.ccr.ro/default.aspx?page=decisions/default* [Accessed December 13, 2010].

148(1) and (2) to be compatible with the limits to constitutional reform laid down in Art. 152 of the Constitution.[281] In its assessment of the effect of Art. 148(1) on Romania's sovereignty, the *Curtea Constituţională* held that the transfer of powers to the Union and Romania's active participation, along with the other Member States, in the Union's decision-making process do not amount to the loss of sovereignty ("the competence over competences") but involve a joint exercise of sovereign powers. In this regard, the *Curtea Constituţională* defined integration as "the shared exercise of sovereignty by the Member States". The *Curtea Constituţională* justified its dynamic definition of sovereignty by explaining that a traditional approach of rigid and indivisible sovereignty would run the risk of isolating Romania internationally in times of globalisation.[282] As for Art. 148(2), the *Curtea Constituţională* held that Union law enjoys an "intermediate position between the Constitution and other laws". This implies that the Constitution remains the supreme law of the Republic. Moreover, in 2009, the *Curtea Constituţională* rejected the idea that Art. 148 of the Constitution could be interpreted as granting it jurisdiction to review the compatibility of legislative statutes with Union law.[283] The *Curtea Constituţională* reasoned that such reading of Art. 148 would lead to an "inadmissible" situation as it would give rise to jurisdictional conflicts with the Court of Justice. Thus, the *Curtea Constituţională* concluded that it is for all other Romanian courts, which are entitled to seek guidance from the Court of Justice as provided for by Art. 267 TFEU, to carry out this type of review.

B. The direct effect of Union law

Van Gend & Loos. Ever since the 1963 judgment in *Van Gend & Loos*, it is clear that individuals may derive rights directly from Union (then Community) law.[284] In that judgment, the Court of Justice gave a preliminary ruling on a question raised by the Netherlands Tariefcommissie as to whether individuals might derive rights from Art. 12 EEC which the courts had to protect. The Court of Justice held that,   **21–055**

> "[t]o ascertain whether the provisions of an international treaty extend so far in their effects it is necessary to consider the spirit, the general scheme and the wording of those provisions".[285]

---

[281] These limits are: "the national, independent, unitary and indivisible character of the Romanian State, the republican form of government, territorial integrity, independence of justice, political pluralism and official language", as well as any amendment which "results in the suppression of the citizens' fundamental rights and freedoms, or of the safeguards thereof".

[282] Hence, the approach of the *Curtea Constituţională* mirrors that of its Czech counterpart: they both embrace the concept of "pooled-sovereignty".

[283] See *Curtea Constituţională*, decision of November 26, 2009, No. 1596/2009, para. 4; and decision of March 9, 2010, No. 239/2010.

[284] ECJ, Case 26/62 *Van Gend & Loos* [1963] E.C.R. 1, at 11–13.

[285] *Ibid.*, at 12.

The Court inferred from the special nature of the Community legal order that Community law is "intended to confer upon [individuals] rights which become part of their legal heritage" (see para. 1–025). The Court stated that,

> "[t]hese rights arise not only where they are expressly granted by the Treaty, but also by reason of obligations which the Treaty imposes in a clearly defined way upon individuals as well as upon the Member States and upon the institutions of the Community".

After inquiring into the substance and wording of Art. 12 EEC, the Court held that the prohibition laid down in that article on Member States increasing import duties or charges having equivalent effect which they already applied in their trade with each other had direct effect.[286]

21–056   **Conditions for direct effect.** The decisive test for determining whether or not a given provision has direct effect is its content. The Court of Justice has consistently held that a provision produces direct effects only if it is "clear and unconditional and not contingent on any discretionary implementing measure".[287] Although the Court has not invariably formulated that test in the same way, it refers to a provision which is sufficiently precise ("clear") and requires no further implementation (involving a margin of discretion) by Union or national authorities in order to achieve the effect sought in an effective manner ("unconditional").[288] A provision which is only given concrete scope through the enactment of measures by the institutions or the Member States does not confer any rights on individuals which national courts may enforce.[289] This will be the case for instance where a provision puts an authority under a duty to act, except for those aspects for which the authority has no discretion. A prohibition to act—like the standstill provision of Art. 12 EEC—is a plain example of a provision which affords the Member States no discretion, and hence has direct effect.

A provision has direct effect where the court is able, without the operation of other implementing measures, to reach an interpretation which may be applied to the case at issue, as a result of which individuals may enforce the rights derived from that provision.[290] The judgment in *Van Gend & Loos* already made clear that a provision does not lack sufficient clarity simply on the ground that the national court deems it necessary to make a reference to the Court of Justice on the interpretation of the provision in question. In *Van Gend & Loos*, the Court of Justice indicated that

---

[286] *Ibid.*, at 12–13.
[287] ECJ, Case 44/84 *Hurd* [1986] E.C.R. 29, para. 47.
[288] See the Opinion of Advocate-General W. Van Gerven in ECJ, Case C-128/92 *Banks* [1994] E.C.R. I-1209, at I-1236–1237.
[289] ECJ, Case 28/67 *Molkerei-Zentrale Westfalen* [1968] E.C.R. 143, at 153; ECJ, Case 13/68 *Salgoil* [1968] E.C.R. 453, at 461.
[290] See, e.g., ECJ, Case 12/81 *Garland* [1982] E.C.R. 359, paras 14–15.

"an illegal increase [of a customs duty] may arise from a rearrangement of the tariff resulting in the classification of the product under a more highly taxed heading and from an actual increase in the rate of customs duty".

That interpretation allowed the Netherlands court to apply the prohibition set out in Art. 12 EEC to the benefit of an undertaking.[291] Likewise, Art. 45 TFEU (free movement of workers) is not prevented from having direct effect because para. 3 of that article contains a reservation with regard to limitations justified on grounds of public policy, public security or public health. This is because "the application of those limitations is . . . subject to judicial control".[292]

Direct effect of primary law. The Court of Justice has repeatedly had to rule on whether provisions of the Treaties have direct effect.[293] Where a Treaty provision is recognised as having direct effect, an individual may rely upon it against Union and national authorities (vertically) and, in some cases, against other individuals (horizontally).[294] The application of the Treaties in the Member States does not depend on whether they have been transposed into the national legal system. When a Treaty provision having horizontal direct effect is invoked against an individual, the fact that the Member States have not enacted any provisions to implement this provision therefore does not preclude its application. Treaty provisions the horizontal effect of which has been recognised include Arts 101 and 102 TFEU [*ex Arts 81 and 82 EC*] (see paras 11–013 and 11–015), Art. 157 TFEU [ex *Art. 141 EC*] (see para. 11–044), and, vis-à-vis organisations not governed by public law where they lay down collective rules in the exercise of their legal autonomy, the provisions on the free movement of persons and the freedom to provide services (see paras 9–046 and 9–085). If a provision has direct effect, it will have such effect from the time when it entered into force or, as the case

21–057

---

[291] ECJ, Case 26/62 *Van Gend & Loos* [1963] E.C.R. 1, at 14–15.

[292] ECJ, Case 41/74 *Van Duyn* [1974] E.C.R. 1337, para. 7. See, with regard to Art. 56 EC [*now Art. 63 TFEU*] (free movement of capital), ECJ, Joined Cases C-163/94, C-165/94 and C-250/94 *Sanz de Lera and Others* [1995] E.C.R. I-4821, para. 43.

[293] The following articles of the Treaties appear to have direct effect: Art. 18 TFEU; Art. 28 TFEU; Art. 30 TFEU; Arts 34, 35 and 36 TFEU; Art. 37(1) and (2) TFEU; Arts 45 to 62 TFEU in general, and particularly Arts 45, 49, 56 and 57 TFEU; Art. 101(1) TFEU; Art. 102 TFEU; Art. 106(1) and (2) TFEU; Art. 108(3), last sentence, TFEU; Art. 110, first and second paras, TFEU; and Art. 157 TFEU, see Schermers and Waelbroeck, *Judicial Protection in the European Union* (The Hague, Kluwer, 2001), para.359, at 183–185. See *ibid.*, para.360, at 185 for a list of provisions to which the Court of Justice has denied direct effect.

[294] See, e.g., ECJ, Case 36/74 *Walrave* [1974] E.C.R. 1405, paras 17–25 (Arts 12, 39 and 49 EC [*now Arts 18, 45 and 56 TFEU*]); ECJ, Case 43/75 *Defrenne* [1976] E.C.R. 455, para. 39 (Art. 119 EC [*now Art. 157 TFEU*]); ECJ, Case C-281/98 *Angonese* [2000] E.C.R. I-4139, paras 30–36 (Art. 48 EC *[now Art. 45 TFEU]*); ECJ (judgment of January 19, 2010), Case C-555/07 *Kücükdeveci*, not yet reported, paras 50–56 (granting horizontal effect to the general principle of Union law relating to non-discrimination on grounds of age—Art. 21 of the Charter of Fundamental Rights of the European Union).

may be, from the end of the transitional period. In exceptional cases, however, the Court of Justice may place limitations on the temporal effect of a judgment recognising the direct effect of a provision (see para. 22–113).

21–058 **Direct effect of secondary law.** Alongside provisions of the Treaties, provisions contained in acts of Union institutions may be invoked by individuals. In principle, whether such provisions have direct effect depends on the same substantive criteria that apply to Treaty provisions.[295] However, depending on the type of act, additional factors may have to be taken into account. As far as international agreements concluded by the Union are concerned, it must always be ascertained whether the possible direct effect of their provisions is consistent with the spirit, the general scheme and the terms of the agreement.[296] Provisions of autonomous acts of the institutions in principle always have direct effect if the substantive criteria are fulfilled. Their vertical or horizontal effect further depends on the type of act in which they are laid down. Under Art. 288 TFEU [*ex Art. 249 EC*], regulations are "directly applicable" and are therefore binding, without any need for transposition, on all within the national legal order who are substantively affected thereby. Where a provision of a regulation has direct effect, an individual may therefore rely upon it also against other individuals.[297] There is no such horizontal direct effect in the case of provisions of directives, which, if they satisfy the requirements for direct effect, can embody only obligations for State bodies.[298]

21–059 **Direct applicability.** In indicating that a provision has "direct effect", the Court of Justice sometimes uses the expression "direct applicability".[299] Some commentators consider that these expressions are not strictly defined and use both of them in referring to the possibility for an individual to rely upon a provision.[300] For a clearer understanding of the effect of Union law, it is nevertheless more illuminating to make a distinction between "direct applicability" (whether a provision requires implementation *as a legal instrument*) and "direct effect"

---

[295] See ECJ, Case 9/70 *Grad* [1970] E.C.R. 825, paras 5–6; see also ECJ (judgment of April 22, 2010), Case C-486/08 *Zentralbetriebsrat der Landeskrankenhäuser Tirols*, not yet reported, para. 21–25 (same conditions apply to agreements concluded between the social partners which are implemented by a directive of the Council). For a survey of the direct effect of various provisions of Union law, see Prinssen and Schrauwen (eds), *Direct Effect. Rethinking a Classic of EC Legal Doctrine* (Groningen, Europa Law, 2002), 300 pp.; Pescatore, "The Doctrine of 'Direct Effect': An Infant Disease of Community Law" (1983) E.L.Rev. 155–177.

[296] Para. 22–045, *infra*.

[297] Para. 22–047, *infra*.

[298] Para. 22–080 *et seq.*, *infra*. For decisions, see para. 22–099, *infra*.

[299] ECJ, Case C-213/03 *Pêcheurs de l'Étang de Berre* [2004] E.C.R. I-7357, para. 39.

[300] See, for instance, Lauwaars and Timmermans, *Europees recht in kort bestek* (Deventer, Kluwer, 2003), at 22–24 and 107–109; Barents and Brinkhorst, *Grondlijnen van Europees recht* (Deventer, Kluwer, 2003), 52 pp.; see also Prechal, "Does Direct Effect Still Matter?" (2000) C.M.L.Rev. 1047–1069.

(whether the *substance* of a provision may be relied upon).[301] Where a provision is "directly applicable", and hence does not require implementation in the national legal order—which is the case with Treaty provisions and regulations—it follows, as explained above, that, where that provision fulfils the substantive conditions for "direct effect", it cannot only be relied upon against Union and national authorities but, in some cases, also against other individuals.

C. INTERPRETATION OF UNION LAW

Particularities of Union law. National courts which interpret provisions of Union law have to take account of the fact that Union law uses terminology which is peculiar to it and that legal concepts do not necessarily have the same meaning in Union law and in the law of the various Member States. It follows from the need for uniform application of Union law and the principle of equality that the terms of a provision of Union law which makes no express reference to the law of the Member States for the purpose of determining its meaning and scope must normally be given an autonomous and uniform interpretation throughout the Union, having regard to the context of the provision and the objective pursued.[302] Furthermore, Union provisions are drafted in several languages, which are equally authentic, and must be given uniform interpretation and application in the different Member States.[303]

21–060

Methods of interpretation. Often, national courts cannot limit themselves to giving a literal or grammatical interpretation of a Union provision. This will be the case, first of all, where different language versions of a provision diverge. In such a case, the provision in question must be interpreted by reference to the purpose and general scheme of the rules of which it forms a part (see para. 13–161).[304] In other cases too, it may be useful for the interpretation of a Union provision to consider the place of the provision in question in the broader legal context of which it forms part (systematic or contextual interpretation) and the objectives pursued by it (teleological or functional interpretation). The Court considers that every provision of Union law must be placed in its context and interpreted in the light of the provisions of Union law as a whole, regard being had to

21–061

---

[301] See already Winter, "Direct Applicability and Direct Effect: Two Distinct and Different Concepts in Community Law" (1972) C.M.L.Rev. 425–438.

[302] See, e.g., ECJ, Case 327/82 *Ekro* [1984] E.C.R. 107, para. 11; ECJ, Case C-13/05 *Chacón Navas* [2006] E.C.R. I-6467, para. 40; ECJ, Case C-116/08 *Meerts* [2009] E.C.R. I-10063, para. 41.

[303] ECJ, Case 283/81 *CILFIT* [1982] E.C.R. 3415, paras 18–19.

[304] E.g., ECJ, Case 30/77 *Bouchereau* [1977] E.C.R. 1999, para. 14; see, more recently, ECJ, Case C-72/95 *Kraaijeveld* [1996] E.C.R. I-5403, paras 28–31; ECJ, Joined Cases C-267/95 and C-268/95 *Merck and Beecham* [1996] E.C.R. I-6285, paras 21–24; ECJ, Case C-257/00 *Givane and Others* [2003] E.C.R. I-345, paras 29–50; ECJ, Case C-428/02 *Fonden Marselisborg Lystbådehavn* [2005] E.C.R. I-1527, paras 41–47.

the objectives thereof and to its state of evolution at the date on which the provision in question is to be applied.[305] In *Van Gend & Loos*, the Court had already considered that, for the interpretation of Treaty provisions, it was necessary to consider "the spirit, the general scheme and the wording of those provisions" (*cf.* para. 17–047, *supra*).[306] The Court applies the same methods of interpretation to provisions of secondary Union law. Accordingly, the scope of acts of Union institutions needs to be determined by taking into account their wording, context and objectives.[307] Lastly, as a rule, if the wording of secondary Union law is open to more than one interpretation, preference should be given to the interpretation which renders the provision consistent with higher ranking norms such as the Union Treaties, fundamental rights, other general principles of Union law and international law.[308] Moreover, where a provision of Union law is open to several interpretations, preference must be given to that interpretation which ensures that the provision retains its effectiveness (*effet utile*).[309]

21–062 **Tools of interpretation.** To situate a provision in its context and to determine its objectives, it is sometimes useful to consider the preamble to a Union act and the recitals contained therein, as they often clarify the content of the act. However, since the preamble to a Union act has no binding legal force, it cannot be relied on either as a ground for derogating from the actual provisions of the act in question or for interpreting those provisions in a manner clearly contrary to their wording.[310] For the interpretation of provisions of secondary Union law, regard can also be had to preparatory documents, such as Commission proposals[311] or opinions or amendments from other institutions or bodies, whether they were

---

[305] ECJ, Case 283/81 *CILFIT* [1982] E.C.R. 3415, para. 20.

[306] ECJ, Case 26/62 *Van Gend & Loos* [1963] E.C.R. 1, at 12.

[307] E.g., ECJ, Case C-212/91 *Angelopharm* [1994] E.C.R. I-171, paras 26–38; ECJ, Case C-280/04 *Jyske Finans* [2005] E.C.R I-10683, paras 31–44.

[308] ECJ, Case C-305/05 *Ordre des barreaux francophones et germanophone and Others* [2007] E.C.R. I-5305, para. 28; ECJ, Case C-101/01 *Lindqvist* [2003] E.C.R. I-12971, para. 87; ECJ (judgment of February 25, 2010), Case C-386/08 *Brita*, not yet reported, para. 39; ECJ (judgment of May 6, 2010), Case C-63/09 *Walz*, not yet reported, para. 22.

[309] See, e.g., ECJ, Case 187/87 *Saarland and Others* [1988] E.C.R. 5013, para. 19; ECJ, Case C-434/97 *Commission v France* [2000] E.C.R. I-1129, para. 21.

[310] ECJ, Case C-162/97 *Nilsson and Others* [1998] E.C.R. I-7477, para. 54; ECJ, Case C-308/97 *Manfredi* [1998] E.C.R. I-7685, para. 30; ECJ, Case C-136/04 *Deutsches Milch-Kontor* [2005] E.C.R. I-10095, para. 32.

[311] See, e.g., ECJ, Case C-402/03 *Skov* [2006] E.C.R. I-199, paras 27–29; ECJ, Case C-174/08 *NCC Construction Danmark* [2009] E.C.R. I-10567, para. 30; CFI, Joined Cases T-22/02 and T-23/02 *Sumitomo Chemical and Sumika Fine Chemicals v Commission* [2005] E.C.R. II-4065, para. 48 (Commission proposal); ECJ (judgments of February 23, 2010), Case C-310/08 *Ibrahim*, not yet reported, para. 47, and Case C-480/08 *Teixeira*, not yet reported, para. 58 (Commission's amended proposal).

incorporated in the final text of the act or not.[312] In contrast, for the purposes of the interpretation of Treaty provisions it is not normally possible to take preparatory documents into account because intergovernmental negotiations were traditionally not conducted on the basis of documents available to the public.[313]

---

[312] See, e.g., ECJ, Case C-266/05 P *Sison v Council* [2007] E.C.R. I-1233, paras 36–38; ECJ (judgment of December 23, 2009), Case C-45/08 *Spector Photo Group and Van Raemdonck*, not yet reported, para. 34 (amendments proposed by the European Parliament); ECJ, Case C-215/97 *Bellone* [1998] E.C.R. I-2191, paras 11 and 16 (opinion of the European Economic and Social Committee); ECJ (judgment of March 4, 2010), Case C-578/08 *Chakroun*, not yet reported, paras 55 and 62 (Council Presidency document).

[313] Compare CFI, Case T-156/94 *Aristrain v Commission* [1999] E.C.R. II-645, para. 40 (reference to a report of the French delegation made after the signature of the ECSC Treaty) with ECJ, Case C-61/03 *Commission v United Kingdom* [2005] E.C.R. I-2477, para. 29 (insufficient guidance found in the *travaux préparatoires* of the EAEC Treaty).

CHAPTER 22

FORMS OF UNION LAW AND
THEIR HIERARCHY

Primary and secondary law. Union law encompasses rules which arise as a   22–001
result of action both by the Member States and by Union institutions and bodies.
As has already been mentioned, the sources of Union law may therefore be
divided into primary and secondary (or derived) Union law, the latter consisting
of (international and autonomous) acts of institutions and bodies, as supplemented by fundamental rights and the general principles recognised in the Union
legal order. The discussion of the forms of Union law will be based upon this
distinction, starting with the ranking order of the various types of provisions.
Interinstitutional agreements and collective agreements are a particular form of
Union law. The same is true of certain acts of the governments of the Member
States and for the case law of the Court of Justice, the General Court and the
specialised courts, which plays an important part in constructing the Union
legal order, even though the tasks of the Union Courts are formally limited to the
interpretation and application of each of the other legal sources.

Since the entry into force of the Lisbon Treaty, the characteristics and legal
effects formerly attributed to the different forms of Community law now apply,
more broadly, to the various forms of Union law (see para. 4–013). Acts adopted
before the entry into force of the Lisbon Treaty outside the Community framework remain in force, with the specific legal regime surrounding them, until such
time as they are repealed or amended. Their legal force is discussed in Ch. 23.

I. HIERARCHY OF SOURCES OF LAW

Hierarchy. As for the primacy of Union law, the relationship between its various   22–002
sources is not expressly laid down in the Treaties. Nevertheless, the authors of the
Treaties always assumed the existence of a hierarchy of norms. This emerges
from Art. 263 TFEU [*ex Art. 230 EC*], under which an action may be brought—
in the Court of Justice or in the General Court—for the annulment of acts of
Union institutions inter alia on the ground of "infringement of the Treaties or
of any rule of law relating to their application" (see also Art. 146 EAEC).
Consequently, judicial review extends to examining whether the acts in question
are compatible with all superior rules of law.

22–003   **Primary law.** At the top of that hierarchy, there are the provisions of "primary" Union law (see paras 22–007—22–015), including fundamental rights and the general principles of law which the Court of Justice ensures are observed pursuant to Art. 19 TEU [*see ex Art. 220 EC*] (see paras 22–017—22–042). Since the institutions and bodies have to act within the powers conferred upon them by the Treaties, "secondary" or "derived" Union law is subordinate to those primary norms. Fundamental rights and general principles of law play a role in the interpretation and application of Treaty provisions and other rules of Union law.

22–004   **Secondary law.** In the field of secondary Union law, it is not the form of a given measure, but its nature which determines its place within the legal order. Special priority attaches to international law in the Union legal order. The legal force of treaties concluded by the Union is superior to that of other "derived" Union acts (see para. 22–044). Some principles of international law enshrined in treaties or having the force of customary law take precedence as general principles of Union law (see para. 22–055). Apart from international agreements concluded by the Union, there is no predetermined ranking order of the various forms of act which the institutions may adopt. Their place in the legal order is determined by their nature and not by their form. Thus, legislative measures take precedence over implementing provisions, even though, until recently, both could take the form of one of the instruments listed in Art. 288 TFEU [*ex Art. 249 EC*] (see para. 22–060).[1] Besides, a number of acts of the Council stand out as being organic in character (see para. 22–096). In so far as other acts are based upon such an organic act, they may not depart from it unless it is expressly amended.[2] Agreements concluded between institutions are binding upon the institutions concerned by virtue of the principle that an authority is bound by rules which it has itself adopted (*patere legem quam ipse fecisti*; see para. 22–108).

22–005   ***Lex posterior* and *lex specialis*.** In addition, as regards the relationship between equivalent provisions of Union law, the principle applies that a later provision (*lex posterior*) prevails over an earlier one and a specific provision (*lex specialis*) over a more general one (*lex generalis*). However, in order for this to be so, the more specific or later provision must be intended to limit or replace the general or earlier provision, respectively.[3]

22–006   **National law.** In each Member State, Union law is applied in conjunction with the applicable rules of national law. Consequently, the application of Union law

---

[1] However, since the Lisbon Treaty, implementing acts are formally distinguishable from legislative acts by their title (see para. 16–003, *supra*).

[2] E.g. with regard to the Second Comitology Decision: ECJ, Case C-378/00 *Commission v European Parliament and Council* [2003] E.C.R. I-937, paras 40–42.

[3] See, e.g., ECJ, Case C-481/99 *Heininger and Heininger* [2001] E.C.R. I-9945, paras 36–39; ECJ, Case C-444/00 *Mayer Parry Recycling* [2003] E.C.R. I-6163, paras 49–57; ECJ, Case C-439/01 *Cipra and Kvasnicka* [2003] E.C.R. I-745, paras 34–40. See also CFI, Case T-6/99 *ESF Elbe-Stahlwerke Feralpi v Commission* [2001] E.C.R. II-1523, para. 102 (ECSC Treaty as a *lex specialis*).

relies in practice on national legislative and implementing provisions and on the interpretation and application given to Union law by national case law. These national sources of law do not as such form a source of Union law, although they influence the recognition of general principles of law in Union law (see para. 22–036 *et seq.*). In exceptional cases, the Court of Justice and the General Court have to apply national law.[4] This occurs, for example, in disputes brought before the Union Court pursuant to an arbitration clause (Art. 272 TFEU [*ex Art. 238 EC*]) concerning a contract governed by the law of a particular Member State.[5] In the absence of an express reference to national law, the application of a provision of Union law may necessitate a reference to the laws of the Member States only where the Union Courts cannot identify in Union law, or in the general principles of Union law, criteria enabling them to define the meaning and scope of such a provision by way of independent interpretation.[6]

II. PRIMARY UNION LAW

A. STATUS OF PRIMARY UNION LAW

Constitutional law. Primary Union law consists of those provisions which were adopted directly by the Member States in their capacity as "constituent authority", meaning in the first place the Union Treaties and the Treaties amending or supplementing them, including the Accession Treaties and the annexed Acts of Accession. Together with fundamental rights and the general principles of Union law, these Treaty provisions constitute the "constitutional" provisions of Union law.[7] This is because they serve as the legal basis for action on the part of the Union and unquestionably take precedence over the law of the Member States.[8]

22–007

---

[4] See Lenaerts, "Interlocking Legal Orders in the European Union and Comparative Law" (2003) I.C.L.Q. 873–906; Kohler and Knapp, "Nationales Recht in der Praxis des EuGH" (2002) Z.Eu.P. 701–726.

[5] See Van Nuffel, "De contractuele aansprakelijkheid van de Europese Gemeenschap: een bevoegdheidskluwen ontward" (2000–2001) A.J.T. 157–162.

[6] See Lenaerts and Gutman, " 'Federal Common Law' in the European Union: A Comparative Perspective from the United States" (2006) A.J.C.L. 1–121. See further CFI, Case T-43/90 *Díaz García v European Parliament* [1992] E.C.R. II-2619, para. 36; CFI, Case T-172/01 *M. v Court of Justice* [2004] E.C.R. II-1075, para. 71.

[7] See ECJ, Case 294/83 *Les Verts v European Parliament* [1986] E.C.R. 1339, para. 23 ("the basic constitutional charter, the Treaty"); ECJ, Joined Cases C-402/05 P and C-415/05 P *Kadi and Al Barakaat International Foundation* [2008] E.C.R. I-6351, para. 285 ("the constitutional principles of the EC Treaty, which include the principle that all Community acts must respect fundamental rights").

[8] For the "constitutional" nature of primary Union law, see Heintzen, "Hierarchisierungsprozesse innerhalb des Primärrechts der Europäischen Gemeinschaft" (1984) EuR. 35, at 40, and the commentators cited in para. 1–027, *supra*. For the precedence of primary law over secondary Union law, see, e.g., CFI, Case T-144/99 *Institute of Professional Representatives before the European Patent Office v Commission* [2001] E.C.R. II-1087, paras 50–54; ECJ (order of the President of February 23, 2001), Case C-445/00 R *Austria v Council* [2001] E.C.R. I-1461, paras 82–93.

Where such provisions satisfy the test formulated by the Court of Justice for direct effect, they may as such confer rights on individuals (see para. 21–057). In some cases, the Court has also considered fundamental rights to be part of the Union's primary law.[9] However, the specific position of fundamental rights will be discussed below (see paras 22–017 *et seq.*).

22–008 **Adoption and amendment.** Primary Union law comes into being by mutual agreement as between the Member States and may be amended only in accordance with the proper procedure. In the case of the Treaties, that procedure is the amendment procedure prescribed by Art. 48 TEU and some simplified procedures, which in any event are based on approval by the Member States in accordance with their respective constitutional requirements.[10] Unless otherwise provided, such a Treaty will apply to the future effects of situations arising prior to the date on which it entered into effect (see para. 12–003). At the same time, the provisions of the Acts of Accession and the adjustments of secondary legislation annexed to those Acts themselves and ensuing therefrom constitute provisions of primary law, which, unless otherwise provided, may be amended or repealed only by recourse to the procedures prescribed for amending the original Treaties.[11] In the absence of express authority, provisions of secondary legislation cannot detract from provisions of primary law, such as a protocol annexed to an Act of Accession.[12] In exceptional cases only, a rule of primary law provides that it may be amended by the Union institutions acting on their own.[13]

22–009 **Judicial review.** The Court of Justice has no jurisdiction to rule on the validity of primary Union law. Since the Treaties and the amendments thereto do not constitute acts of the institutions within the meaning of Art. 13 TEU and Art. 263 TFEU [*see ex Arts 7 and 230 EC*], the Court of Justice has no power to consider their legality.[14] It may merely give preliminary rulings on the interpretation of primary Union law (see Art. 267(a) TFEU [*ex Art. 234(a) EC*]). This means that provisions constituting an integral part of the Acts of Accession are also not subject to judicial review by the Court of Justice.[15]

---

[9] ECJ, Joined Cases C-402/05 P and C-415/05 P *Kadi and Al Barakaat International Foundation* [2008] E.C.R. I-6351, para. 308.

[10] For these procedures, see paras 5–001—5–008, *supra.*

[11] See, e.g., Art. 7 of the 2003 and 1994 Acts of Accession, Art. 6 of the 1985 Act of Accession and ECJ, Joined Cases 31 and 35/86 *LAISA and Others v Council* [1988] E.C.R. 2285, para. 12.

[12] ECJ, Case C-445/00 *Austria v Commission* [2003] E.C.R. I-8549, paras 57–64.

[13] For the procedures in question, see para. 5–009, *supra.* For an application after the introduction in 1993 of a common organisation of the market in bananas, which was the subject of a special "protocol on bananas" annexed to the EEC Treaty, see ECJ, Case C-280/93 *Germany v Council* [1994] E.C.R. I-4973, paras 113–118.

[14] ECJ, Joined Cases 31 and 35/86 *LAISA and Others v Council* [1988] E.C.R. 2285, para. 12; CFI (order of July 14, 1994), Case T-584/93 *Roujansky v Council* [1994] E.C.R. II-585, para. 15, upheld by ECJ (order of January 13, 1995), Case C-253/94 P *Roujansky v Council* [1995] E.C.R. I-7.

[15] *LAISA and Others v Council* (see preceding n.), paras 13–18.

B. SURVEY OF PRIMARY UNION LAW

Union Treaties. Primary Union law comprises, first and foremost, the Union **22–010**
Treaties (the TEU, TFEU; before July 23, 2002 also the ECSC Treaty) and the
EAEC Treaty. In principle the broad field of competence of the TEU and TFEU
also embraces the atomic-energy sector. However, it follows from Art. 106a(3)
EAEC, as introduced by a Protocol to the Lisbon Treaty, that the provisions of the
TEU and of the TFEU "shall not derogate" from the provisions of the EAEC
Treaty.[16] Before the entry into force of the Lisbon Treaty, the same rule was formulated in Art. 305 EC (now repealed). As far as the atomic-energy sector is concerned, this means that the TEU and TFEU do not apply whenever the EAEC
Treaty contains a derogating provision.[17] Where the EAEC Treaty does not lay
down rules on a particular matter coming under the atomic-energy sector, the matter in question falls within the TEU and the TFEU.[18] Thus, the Treaty rules on the
free movement of workers apply to all employees in the atomic-energy sector who
are not in "skilled employment" within the meaning of Art. 96 of the EAEC
Treaty. In this way, Union law adopted pursuant to the TEU and TFEU operates as
the *lex generalis*, supplementing, where necessary, the *lex specialis* (EAEC law).

 For the sake of the coherence of Union law, the Court of Justice often looked
for assistance, when interpreting Treaty provisions, to a comparison of provisions
of the other Treaties which resolved the question at issue more clearly[19] or

---

[16] Protocol (No. 2), annexed to the Lisbon Treaty, amending the Treaty establishing the European
Atomic Energy Community, [2007] O.J. C306/199.

[17] See Cusack, "A Tale of Two Treaties: An Asssessment of the Euratom Treaty in Relation to the EC
Treaty" (2003) C.M.L.Rev. 117–142. This was also true of the ECSC Treaty as a result of Art. 305
EC, which provided that the EC Treaty should "not affect" the ECSC Treaty: see, e.g., ECJ, Joined
Cases 27 to 29/58 *Compagnie des Hauts Fournaux et Fonderies de Givors and Others v High
Authority* [1960] E.C.R. 241, at 255; ECJ, Joined Cases 188 to 190/80 *France, Italy and United
Kingdom v Commission* [1982] E.C.R. 2545, paras 30–31; ECJ, Case 239/84 *Gerlach* [1985] E.C.R.
3507, paras 10–11; ECJ, Case C-18/94 *Hopkins and Others* [1996] E.C.R. I-2281, paras 11–24.

[18] See, pursuant to Art. 305 EC, ECJ, Joined Cases 188 to 190/80 *France, Italy and United Kingdom
v Commission* [1982] E.C.R. 2545, para. 32 (the application of a directive based on Art. 86(3) EC
to public undertakings in the atomic energy sector does not derogate from the EAEC Treaty); ECJ,
Opinion 1/94 *Agreement establishing the World Trade Organisation* [1994] E.C.R. I-5267, para. 24
(in the absence of any EAEC provision relating to external trade, agreements concluded pursuant
to Art. 133 EC also extend to EAEC products).

[19] ECJ, Case C-61/03 *Commission v UK* [2005] E.C.R. I-2477, paras 30–36, and ECJ, Case C-65/04
Commission v UK [2006] E.C.R. I-2239, para. 19 (the fact that, unlike the EC Treaty, the EAEC
Treaty lacks derogatory clauses with respect to defence, shows that the EAEC Treaty was not
intended to apply to the military use of nuclear energy). See also ECJ, Case 13/60 *Geitling v High
Authority* [1962] E.C.R. 83, at 102 (interpretation of Art. 65 ECSC by analogy with Art. 81 EC);
ECJ, Case 294/83 *Les Verts v European Parliament* [1986] E.C.R. 1339, para. 24 (argument based
on Art. 38 ECSC in an interpretation of Art. 173 EEC recognising that an action for annulment could
be brought against the European Parliament). In *Continental Can*, the Court refused to take account,
in interpreting Art. 82 EC, of an *a contrario* argument based on the wording of Art. 66 ECSC: ECJ,
Case 6/72 *Europemballage and Continental Can v Commission* [1973] E.C.R. 215, para. 22.

explicitly.[20] Sometimes the Court held that principles formulated in the context of one of the Treaties were of general validity.[21] Where, however, a treaty provision introduced a divergent rule, that rule had to be complied with.[22]

The unity of Union law is further underpinned by the single nature of the institutions (see para. 1–016). The Court of Justice has interpreted the provisions concerning the institutions in the various Treaties in conjunction with each other, and where necessary, reconciling them.[23] Where an institution lays down rules on its internal functioning, it necessarily acts in the field of all the Treaties. Accordingly, Art. 38 ECSC afforded Luxembourg a sufficient legal basis to bring an action for annulment against a resolution of the European Parliament in which it decided to hold its meetings in Brussels and Strasbourg. The Parliament argued that the application was inadmissible on the ground that the resolution was based on all three Treaties and therefore could not be contested pursuant to the ECSC Treaty alone. The Court held, however, that the action would lie precisely because

---

[20] ECJ, Case C-115/08 *ČEZ* [2009] E.C.R. I-10265, paras 87–91 (prohibition by the EC Treaty of discrimination on grounds of nationality also held to be applicable within the ambit of the EAEC Treaty); ECJ, Case 9/56 *Meroni v High Authority* [1957 and 1958] E.C.R. 133, at 140–141 (reasoning by analogy from Art. 241 EC and Art. 156 EAEC in interpreting Art. 36 ECSC) (see also Case 10/56 *Meroni v High Authority* [1957 and 1958] E.C.R. 157, at 162–163, and Case 15/57 *Compagnie des Hauts Fourneaux de Chasse v High Authority* [1957 and 1958] E.C.R. 211, at 224–225, delivered on the same day); Case 266/82 *Turner v Commission* [1984] E.C.R. 1, para. 5 (reference to the second para. of Art. 34 ECSC in applying Art. 233 EC). See also ECJ, Case 314/85 *Foto-Frost* [1987] E.C.R. 4199, paras 13–18 (determination of the duty of courts, not being courts of last instance, to make a reference for a preliminary ruling under Art. 234 EC by analogy with Art. 41 ECSC) and the converse case in ECJ, Case C-221/88 *Busseni* [1990] E.C.R. I-495, paras 10–16 (reference made to Art. 234 EC and Art. 150 EAEC in order to determine the scope of Art. 41 ECSC).

[21] ECJ, Ruling 1/78 *Draft Convention of the International Atomic Energy Agency on the Physical Protection of Nuclear Materials, Facilities and Transport* [1978] E.C.R. 2151, para. 15 (reference to the EC Treaty in order to emphasise the general scope of the provisions of the EAEC Treaty relating to the common market), and para. 36 (application of the principle that there should be harmony between international action by the Community and the distribution of internal powers, which emerged from the case law on the EC Treaty, to situations governed by the EAEC Treaty); ECJ, Case C-115/08 *ČEZ* (n. 20, *supra*), para. 138 (interpretation of Art. 192 EAEC in alignment with Art. 10 EC with respect to the duty to interpret national law in conformity with Community law and to disapply conflicting rules of national law); ECJ, Case C-221/88 *Busseni* [1990] E.C.R. I-495, paras 21 and 39 (alignment of the effects of recommendations adopted under Art. 14 ECSC with those of directives adopted under Art. 249 EC); ECJ, Case C-341/94 *Allain* [1996] E.C.R. I-4631, paras 23–25 (interpretation of obligations arising under Arts 14 and 86 ECSC by reference to the case law on Art. 10 EC); ECJ, Case C-390/98 *Banks* [2001] E.C.R. I-6117, paras 70 and 73–75.

[22] ECJ, Joined Cases 16 and 17/62 *Confédération nationale des producteurs de fruits et légumes and Others v Council* [1962] E.C.R. 471, at 478 (second para. of Art. 173 EEC relating to the *locus standi* of legal or natural persons to bring an action for annulment interpreted restrictively despite the broader provisions of the ECSC Treaty); ECJ, Case C-327/91 *France v Commission* [1994] E.C.R. I-3641, paras 37–39 (the third para. of Art. 101 EAEC manifestly confers on the Commission different powers at the international level than Art.300 EC).

[23] ECJ, Case 101/63 *Wagner* [1964] E.C.R. 195, at 200–201.

the measure related simultaneously and indivisibly to the sphere of the three Treaties.[24]

As regards preliminary references, Arts 267 TFEU confers on the Court jurisdiction for the purpose of interpreting the TEU, TFEU and EAEC Treaty. Thus the fact that a national court refers questions to the Court pursuant to Art. 267 TFEU concerning the interpretation of provisions of the TEU or TFEU does not prevent the Court from adjudicating on the basis of the provisions of the EAEC Treaty.[25]

Amending Treaties. In so far as later Treaties (such as the Single European Act, the EU Treaty, the Treaty of Amsterdam, the Treaty of Nice and the Treaty of Lisbon) amended and supplemented the Union Treaties, their provisions likewise constitute primary Union law.   **22–011**

Protocols. Primary law also includes the "protocols annexed to the Treaties, which form 'an integral part' thereof" (Art. 51 TEU [*see ex Art. 311 EC*] and Art. 207 EAEC).[26] Consequently, the statutes of the Court of Justice of the European Union, the European Investment Bank and the European Central Bank, which are contained in protocols, have the same legal status as the Treaties. A protocol may therefore make changes in the Treaties and other provisions of primary law.[27] Where particular Member States are given a special position diverging from the rules of the Treaties, it is often formulated in a protocol. Important examples are, within the framework of the EMU, Protocol (No. 15) on certain provisions relating to the United Kingdom of Great Britain and Northern Ireland and Protocol (No. 16) on certain provisions relating to Denmark, as well as, with regard to the area of freedom, security and justice, Protocol (No. 21) on the position of the United Kingdom and Ireland in respect of the area of freedom, security and justice and Protocol (No. 22) on the position of Denmark. Such protocols may not derogate from basic provisions of the Treaty to which they are annexed.[28] This means that they must always be interpreted in a manner which accords with such basic provisions.[29]   **22–012**

---

[24] ECJ, Case 230/81 *Luxembourg v European Parliament* [1983] E.C.R. 255, paras 14–20. For the unity of the Staff Regulations of the various institutions, see CFI, Case T-164/97 *Busaca and Others v Court of Auditors* [1998] E.C.R.-SC II-1699, paras 48–61 (upheld on appeal, see ECJ, Case C-434/98 P *Council v Busaca and Court of Auditors* [2000] E.C.R. I-8577).

[25] ECJ, Case C-115/08 *ČEZ* (n. 20, *supra*), para. 84. That was the case even before the Lisbon Treaty, where Art. 150 EAEC served as a separate legal basis for preliminary references with respect to the EAEC Treaty (the Lisbon Treaty repealed that provision and inserted Art. 106a EAEC according to which Art. 267 TFEU applies to the EAEC Treaty).

[26] CFI, Joined Cases T-164/99, T-37/00 and T-38/00 *Leroy and Others v Council* [2001] E.C.R. II-1819, para. 58.

[27] *Ibid.*, para. 67.

[28] ECJ, Case C-280/93 *Germany v Council* [1994] E.C.R. I-4973, para. 117.

[29] In case of doubt, a protocol must be interpreted so as to avoid a conflict with general principles of law, such as the principle of equal treatment: CFI, Case T-333/99 *X v European Central Bank* [2001] E.C.R. II-3021, para. 38. For a case in which the protocol itself provides that its application squares with fundamental principles of the internal market and free movement, see ECJ, Case C-445/00 *Austria v Council* [2003] E.C.R. I-8549, paras 65–75.

22–013   **Accession Treaties.** As has already been mentioned, primary Union law encompasses all provisions which have been agreed between the Member States and the acceding State with regard to the conditions of accession and the resultant adjustments to the Treaties, namely the Accession Treaty, the Act of Accession and provisions forming an integral part thereof.[30] In interpreting those provisions, regard must be had to the foundations and system of the Union, as established by the original Treaties.[31] However, these provisions have the same legal status as the provisions of the original Treaties.

22–014   **Declarations.** In signing each of the Union Treaties and the Treaties amending them, the Member States, as an "intergovernmental conference", adopted declarations or took note of unilateral declarations made by Member States, which are annexed to the final act of the intergovernmental conference.[32] Unlike protocols, such declarations are not binding.[33] Declarations which are signed by all the Member States may nevertheless be taken into account by the Court of Justice in interpreting provisions of the Treaties,[34] at least in so far as they do not conflict with those provisions.[35] This also applies to unilateral declarations on the part of the Member States in which they define who is to be considered their nationals for Union purposes (see para. 8–005).

22–015   **Constitutional acts.** Some acts which the European Council or the Council adopt pursuant to the Union Treaties may be regarded as being primary Union law because their entry into force depends upon their being adopted by the Member States in accordance with their respective constitutional requirements. This

---

[30] ECJ, Case C-140/05 *Valeško* [2006] E.C.R. I-10025, para. 74. See further ECJ, Case C-36/04 *Spain v Council* [2006] E.C.R. I-2981 (action to test a regulation against an Act of Accession dismissed).

[31] ECJ, Case 231/78 *Commission v United Kingdom* [1979] E.C.R. 1447, para. 12; ECJ, Case C-233/97 *KappAhl Oy* [1998] E.C.R. I-8068, paras 18–21. See also, CFI, Case T-324/05 *Estonia v Commission* [2009] E.C.R. II-3681, para. 208 (Accession Treaty not to be interpreted in the light of secondary Union law, but rather the other way around).

[32] Such declarations are sometimes made after signature; see, e.g., the Declaration of May 1, 1992 of the High Contracting Parties interpreting Protocol (No. 17) annexed to the EU Treaty and the Community Treaties (n. 737 to para. 9–086, *supra*) and the declarations made by the European Council and the unilateral declarations made by Denmark at the European Council held on December 11 and 12, 1992 on the occasion of the Danish ratification of the EU Treaty ([1992] O.J. C348; para. 3–010, *supra*).

[33] Toth, "The Legal Status of the Declarations Annexed to the Single European Act" (1986) C.M.L.Rev. 803, at 812; see also the Commission's answer of December 1, 1997 to question No. E-3008/97 (Hager), [1998] O.J. C134/56.

[34] See Art. 31(2)(b) of the Vienna Convention of May 23, 1969 on the law of treaties (see n. 330, *infra*), which for the purpose of interpreting a treaty considers its context to be, inter alia, any instrument which was made by one or more parties in connection with the conclusion of the treaty and accepted by the other parties as an instrument related to the treaty. See Schermers, "The Effect of the Date 31 December 1992" (1991) C.M.L.Rev. 275, at 276.

[35] See also ECJ, Case C-233/97 *KappAhl Oy* [1998] E.C.R. I-8068, paras 22–23 (declaration made during the accession negotiations not to be used in interpreting the Act of Accession as it was not reflected in the wording of the Act).

category of acts consists, for the present, of the Decision of September 20, 1976 and the appended Act, adopted pursuant to Art. 190(4) EC [*now Art. 223(1) TFEU*], concerning the direct election of the European Parliament and the "own resources" decisions adopted under Art. 311 TFEU [*ex Art. 269 EC*] (see para. 5–008). Although they may possibly not be subject to judicial review by the Court of Justice,[36] the Court does not shirk from subordinating their provisions to the general principles enshrined in the Treaties.[37]

III. FUNDAMENTAL RIGHTS AND GENERAL PRINCIPLES OF UNION LAW

Beyond general principles. According to Art. 19(1) TEU [*ex Art. 220 EC*], the Court of Justice, the General Court and the specialised courts ensure that "in the interpretation and application of the Treaties the law is observed" (see also Art. 136 EAEC). Recognition of "the law" as a source of Union law has enabled the Court of Justice to have recourse to general principles in interpreting and applying Union law.[38] Ever since 1969 it has been clear that "fundamental human rights [are] enshrined in the general principles of [Union] law and protected by the Court".[39] Article 6(3) TEU refers to the fundamental rights guaranteed by the European Convention for the Protection of Human Rights and Fundamental Freedoms (ECHR) or resulting from the constitutional traditions common to the Member States as "general principles of the Union's law". However, since the entry into force of the Lisbon Treaty, the Union also "recognises" the rights, freedoms and principles set out in the Charter of Fundamental Rights of the European Union (Art. 6(1) TEU), which has the same legal value as the Treaties. Hence, fundamental rights have now been recognised as an autonomous source of Union law, with the same ranking as provisions of primary law.

22–016

---

[36] In any event, the European Court of Human Rights assumed in the judgment in *Matthews* that the 1976 Act on the direct election of the European Parliament as "a treaty within the Community legal order" could not be challenged before the Court of Justice: European Court of Human Rights, February 18, 1999, *Matthews v United Kingdom*, No. 24833/94, para. 33. On the basis of this finding, the United Kingdom was found to have violated Art. 3 of the First Protocol to the ECHR by excluding Gibraltar from the election of the European Parliament (see para. 22–030, *infra*).

[37] See with regard to the Third Decision on Own Resources, ECJ, Case C-284/90 *Council v European Parliament* [1992] E.C.R. I-2277, para. 31. See for further particulars Arnauld, "Normenhierarchien innerhalb des primären Gemeinschaftsrechts—Gedanken im Prozess der Konstitutionalisierung Europas" (2003) EuR. 191–216.

[38] Expressly mentioned in ECJ, Joined Cases C-46/93 and C-48/93 *Brasserie du Pêcheur and Factortame* ("*Factortame IV*") [1996] E.C.R. I-1029, paras 24–30.

[39] ECJ, Case 29/69 *Stauder* [1969] E.C.R. 419, para. 7; see also ECJ, Case 11/70 *Internationale Handelsgesellschaft* [1970] E.C.R. 1125, para. 4.

A. FUNDAMENTAL RIGHTS

1. Status of fundamental rights

22–017   **Respect for human rights.** The Treaties consider respect for human rights as one of the values on which the Union is founded (Art. 2 TEU)[40] and as an objective to which the Union must contribute in its relations with the wider world (Art. 3(5) TEU; see also Art. 21(1) and (2)(b) TEU, which refer to the "universality and indivisibility" of human rights). In addition, the TFEU refers to respect for fundamental rights in the context of the "area of freedom, security and justice" (Art. 67(1)) and to the "fundamental social rights" that the Union and the Member States are to "have in mind" in setting their policies (Art. 151).[41] For the Court of Justice, the principle that all Union acts must respect fundamental rights is one of the "constitutional principles of the [Treaties]".[42] Since the entry into force of the Treaty of Lisbon, the Treaties not only refer to fundamental rights as laid down in the European Convention for the Protection of Human Rights and Fundamental Freedoms and resulting from the constitutional traditions common to the Member States, but also directly recognise the value as primary law of the Charter of Fundamental Rights of the European Union (Art. 6(1) and (3) TEU). The fundamental rights recognised in Union law have to be respected by the Union institutions and bodies and by the Member States where they implement Union law (see para. 22–023). In addition, provisions of Union law have to be interpreted in the light of these fundamental rights.[43] A serious and persistent breach of fundamental rights on the part of a Member State may result, under the procedure set out in Art. 7 TEU, in the suspension of certain of the rights deriving from the application of the Treaties (see para. 6–017).

It should be mentioned that the original Treaties did not emphasise respect for human rights as an objective of the (then) Community, or fundamental rights as a source of (Community) law. It has been the Court of Justice which gradually stepped up the position of fundamental rights in the Community legal order since it recognised in 1969 that fundamental rights are enshrined in the "general principles" the observance of which it has to ensure.[44]

---

[40] See also ECJ (judgment of March 2, 2010), Joined Cases C-175/08, C-176/08, C-178/08 and C-179/08 *Salahadin Abdulla and Others*, not yet reported, para. 90 (integrity of the person and individual liberties are part of the "fundamental values" of the Union).

[41] The first para. of Art. 151 TFEU refers to the fundamental social rights set out in the European Social Charter (n. 53, *infra*).

[42] ECJ, Joined Cases C-402/05 P and C-415/05 P *Kadi and Al Barakaat International Foundation* [2008] E.C.R. I-6351, para. 285.

[43] See, e.g., ECJ, Case C-305/05 *Ordre des barreaux francophones et germanophone and Others* [2007] E.C.R. I-5305, paras 27–37; ECJ (judgment of March 4, 2010), Case C-578/08 *Chakroun*, not yet reported, para. 44.

[44] There is extensive literature on this subject; for some general articles, see Kühling, "Fundamental Rights", in von Bogdandy and Bast, *Principles of European Constitutional Law* (Oxford, Hart, 2010) 479, at 482 *et seq.*; Lenaerts, "Le respect des droits fondementaux en tant que principe

(a) *Fundamental rights as general principles of Union law*

Increased importance. The EC Treaty made no express mention of fundamental rights, although a fundamental right to equal treatment did underlie the prohibition of discrimination on grounds of nationality (Art. 12 EC [*now Art. 18 TFEU*]) and the principle of equal pay for men and women for equal work (Art. 141 EC [*now Art. 157 TFEU*]) (see para. 7–050). Initially, the Court of Justice merely held that it could not rule on the compatibility of Community measures with fundamental rights guaranteed by the Constitution of a Member State.[45] In the 1970 judgment in the *Internationale Handelsgesellschaft* case, the Court held, however, that "respect for fundamental rights formed an integral part of the general principles of law protected by [it]" and that the protection of fundamental rights

22–018

> "whilst inspired by the constitutional traditions common to the Member States, must be ensured within the framework of the structure and objectives of the Community".[46]

In *Nold* the Court then specified that

> "[i]n safeguarding these rights, the Court is bound to draw inspiration from constitutional traditions common to the Member States, and it cannot therefore uphold measures which are incompatible with fundamental rights recognised and protected by the Constitutions of those States. Similarly, international treaties for the protection of human rights on which the Member States have collaborated or of which they are signatories, can supply guidelines which should be followed within the framework of Community law".[47]

---

constitutionnel de l'Union européenne", in *Mélanges Michel Waelbroeck*, (Brussels, Bruylant, 1999) 423–457; McBride, "Protecting Fundamental Rights in Europe: A Legal Analysis", in Arnull and Wincott (eds), *Accountibility and Legitimacy in the European Union*, (Oxford, Oxford University Press, 2002) 259–274; Defeis, "Human rights and the European Court of Justice: an appraisal" (2008) Fordham I.L.J. 1104–1117; Toner, "Impact assessments and fundamental rights protection in EU Law" (2006) E.L.Rev. 316–341; Lenaerts, "Fundamental Rights in the European Union" (2000) E.L.Rev. 575–600; Von Bogdandy, "The European Union as a Human Rights Organisation? Human Rights and the Core of the European Union" (2000) C.M.L.Rev. 1307–1338; Alston and Weiler, "An 'Ever Closer Union' in Need of a Human Rights Policy" (1998) E.J.I.L. 658–723; Coppel and O'Neill, "The European Court of Justice: Taking Rights Seriously?" (1992) C.M.L.Rev. 669–692; Zuleeg, "Der Schutz der Menschenrechte im Gemeinschaftsrecht" (1992) D.ö.V. 937–944; and above all the reply from Weiler and Lockhart, "'Taking Rights Seriously' Seriously: The European Court and its Fundamental Rights Jurisprudence" (1995) C.M.L.Rev. 51–94 and 579–627; Rodriguez Iglesias, "The Protection of Fundamental Rights in the Case Law of the Court of Justice of the European Communities" (1995) Col.J.E.L. 169–181.

[45] ECJ, Case 1/58 *Stork* [1959] E.C.R. 17, at 26.
[46] ECJ, Case 11/70 *Internationale Handelsgesellschaft* [1970] E.C.R. 1125, para. 4.
[47] ECJ, Case 4/73 *Nold v Commission* [1974] E.C.R. 491, para. 13.

The European Parliament, the Council and the Commission associated themselves with that case law in a Joint Declaration of April 5, 1977 by expressing the "prime importance" which they attached to the protection of fundamental rights

> "as derived in particular from the constitutions of the Member States and the European Convention for the Protection of Human Rights and Fundamental Freedoms".[48]

The formulation of Community protection for fundamental rights was prompted by the Constitutional Courts of some Member States, especially Germany and Italy (see paras 21–023 and 21–031).

The EU Treaty introduced for the first time an express reference to the protection of fundamental rights. According to Art. 6(2) EU, the Union was to respect,

> "fundamental rights, as guaranteed by the European Convention for the Protection of Human Rights and Fundamental Freedoms signed in Rome on 4 November 1950 and as they result from the constitutional traditions common to the Member States, as general principles of Community law".

22–019 **Guiding sources.** In protecting fundamental rights, the Court of Justice has been guided by the constitutional traditions of the Member States and by treaties on human rights, most of all by the European Convention for the Protection of Human Rights and Fundamental Freedoms (ECHR) signed in Rome on November 4, 1950 (see para. 1–006).[49] In this respect, Art. 6(2) EU did nothing more than confirm the existing case law of the Court of Justice.[50] The legal position of the Member States with regard to the ECHR is identical inasmuch as they are all bound thereby and by the individual right to make an application to the European Court of Human Rights (see para. 1–006). The Court of Justice systematically reviews the interpretation and application of Union law in the light of provisions of the ECHR and, in so doing, refers to an ever greater extent to the case

---

[48] Joint Declaration of the European Parliament, the Council and the Commission, [1977] O.J. C103/1; see Forman, "The Joint Declaration on Fundamental Rights" (1977) E.L.Rev. 210–215.

[49] CFI, Case T-10/93 *A. v Commission* [1994] E.C.R. II-179, paras 48–49; ECJ, Case C-415/93 *Bosman* [1995] E.C.R. I-4921, para. 79; see also the earlier case ECJ, Case 222/84 *Johnston* [1986] E.C.R. 1651, para. 18.

[50] This confirmation has been the culmination of increasingly strong support for the case law of the Court of Justice, first in the Joint Declaration of the European Parliament, the Council and the Commission (see n. 48, *supra*) and secondly in the preamble to the Single European Act; see ECJ, Case 249/86 *Commission v Germany* [1989] E.C.R. 1263, para. 10; see Pipkorn, "La Communauté européenne et la Convention européenne des droits de l'homme" (1994) A.D. 463, at 464. For the status of the ECHR in the Member States, see Chryssogonos, "Zur Inkorporation der Europäischen Menschenrechtskonvention in den nationalen Rechtsordnungen der Mitgliedstaaten" (2001) EuR. 49–61.

law of the European Court of Human Rights.[51] Even in a situation in which Union law is not applicable, the Court of Justice has referred to the applicable case law of the Court of Human Rights.[52]

In order to determine the precise scope of a Union fundamental right, the Court of Justice also has regard to other conventions adopted under the aegis of the Council of Europe, such as the European Social Charter,[53] to the Community Charter of Fundamental Social Rights of Workers[54] and to agreements concluded within the ambit of the United Nations—such as the International Covenant on Civil and Political Rights of December 19, 1966 (ICCPR)[55] and the Convention on the Rights of the Child[56]—or within the framework of the International Labour Organisation.[57]

---

[51] E.g., ECJ, Case C-105/03 *Pupino* [2005] E.C.R. I-5285, para. 60; ECJ, Joined Cases C-189/02 P, C-202/02 P, C-205/02 P to C-208/02 P and C-213/02 P *Dansk Rørindustri and Others v Commission* [2005] E.C.R. I-5425, paras 215–219; ECJ, Case C-229/05 P *PKK and KNK v Council* [2007] E.C.R. I-439, paras 75–82; ECJ, Joined Cases C-402/05 P and C-415/05 P *Kadi and Al Barakaat International Foundation* [2008] E.C.R. I-6351, paras 311, 344, 360, 363 and 368; ECJ (December 2, 2009), Case C-89/08 P *Commission v Ireland and Others*, not yet reported, para. 54; ECJ (December 23, 2009), Case C-45/08 *Spector Photo Group*, not yet reported, paras 42 and 43; ECJ (judgment of March 9, 2010), Case C-518/07 *Commission v Germany*, not yet reported, para. 21.

[52] See, inter alia, ECJ, Case C-109/01 *Akrich* [2003] E.C.R. I-9607, paras 58–60 (concerning the right to respect for family life in a situation in which Union law does not confer on a national of a third country who is married to a national of a Member State the right of residence in that Member State); ECJ, C-71/02 *Herbert Karner Industrie-Auktionen*, [2004] E.C.R. I-03025, para. 51.

[53] See ECJ, Case 149/77 *Defrenne* [1978] E.C.R. 1365, para. 28; ECJ, Case C-438/05 *International Transport Workers' Federation and Finnish Seamen's Union* [2007] E.C.R. I-10779, para. 43 and ECJ, Case C-341/05 *Laval un Partneri* [2007] E.C.R. I-11767, para. 90; ECJ, Case C-268/06 *Impact* [2008] E.C.R. I-2483, para. 113. The European Social Charter was signed at Turin under the auspices of the Council of Europe on October 18, 1961 (which has been ratified by all the Member States; for the text, see ETS No. 35. It is also available from the Council of Europe website at *http://conventions.coe.int/* [Accessed December 14, 2010].) See also ECJ (judgment of March 2, 2010), Case C-135/08 *Rottmann*, not yet reported, paras 52–53 (European Convention on Nationality).

[54] ECJ, Case C-268/06 *Impact* [2008] E.C.R. I-2483, para. 112; ECJ, Case C-116/08 *Meerts* [2009] E.C.R. I-10063, para. 37. For the 1989 Community Charter of the Fundamental Social Rights of Workers, see para. 11–043, *supra*.

[55] See ECJ, Case 374/87 *Orkem v Commission* [1989] E.C.R. 3283, para. 31; ECJ, Joined Cases C-297/88 and C-197/89 *Dzodzi* [1990] E.C.R. I-3763, para. 68; ECJ, Case C-249/96 *Grant* [1998] E.C.R. I-621, paras 43–47; CFI, Case T-48/96 *Acme Industry v Council* [1999] E.C.R. II-3089, para. 30. The International Covenant on Civil and Political Rights of December 19, 1966 (UNTS, Vol. 99, p. 171) has been ratified by all the Member States.

[56] ECJ, Case C-540/03 *European Parliament v Council* [2006] E.C.R. I-5769, paras 37 and 57, with a case note by Bultermann (2008) C.M.L.Rev. 245–259; ECJ, Case C-244/06 *Dynamic Medien* [2008] E.C.R. I-505, paras 39–40. See also ECJ (judgment of March 2, 2010), Case C-135/08 *Rottmann*, not yet reported, para. 52 (1961 Convention on the Reduction of Statelessness) and para. 53 (Universal Declaration of Human Rights, adopted by the General Assembly of the United Nations on December 10, 1948).

[57] See ECJ, Case 149/77 *Defrenne* [1978] E.C.R. 1365, para. 28 (ILO Convention No. 3); ECJ, Case C-438/05 *International Transport Workers' Federation and Finnish Seamen's Union* [2007] E.C.R. I-10779, para. 43, and ECJ, Case C-341/05 *Laval un Partneri* [2007] E.C.R. I-11767, para. 90 (ILO Convention No. 87).

(b) *The Charter of Fundamental Rights of the European Union*

22–020 **Towards a European catalogue of rights.** It has long been considered in academic writings that the Union should have its own catalogue of fundamental rights which individuals could invoke directly in the context of Union law. Some commentators considered that such a catalogue could include rights not enshrined in the ECHR, namely economic and social fundamental rights and fundamental rights peculiar to the Union legal order.[58] The European Parliament formulated such a proposal in its Declaration of fundamental rights and freedoms of April 12, 1989,[59] although it was not followed through to any great extent.

The impetus for a genuine catalogue of fundamental rights of the European Union came from the Cologne European Council of June 1999,[60] which conferred the task of drawing up a Charter of Fundamental Rights on a "forum" (later called a "convention"). This body started work on February 1, 2000 under the presidency of the former German President Roman Herzog with representatives of national governments, the European Parliament and national parliaments and a representative of the President of the Commission. Representatives of the Court of Justice and the Council of Europe, including the European Court of Human Rights, were present as observers.[61] This unique formula inspired the Convention which was set up after the Treaty of Nice to reflect on the future of the Union (see para. 4–001). In September 2000 the Convention arrived at a consensus on a draft Charter which was subsequently approved by the European Council, the European Parliament and the Commission.[62]

22–021 **Charter of Fundamental Rights.** On December 7, 2000 the Charter of Fundamental Rights of the European Union was solemnly proclaimed at Nice by

---

[58] Lenaerts (n. 96, *infra*), at 376–390; Hilf, "Ein Grundrechtskatalog für die Europäische Gemeinschaft" (1991) EuR. 19–30; Pipkorn (n. 50, *supra*), at 480–481. For a different view of the relationship between the EC/EU and the ECHR, see Besselink, "Entrapped by the Maximum Standard: On Fundamental Rights, Pluralism and Subsidiarity in the European Union" (1998) C.M.L.Rev. 629–680; Toth, "The European Union and Human Rights: The Way Forward" (1997) C.M.L.Rev. 491–529.

[59] [1989] O.J. C120/51; discussed by Weiler, Lenaerts, Vanhamme and Bieber in Bieber, De Gucht, Lenaerts and Weiler (eds), *Au nom des peuples européens/In the name of the peoples of Europe* (Baden-Baden, Nomos, 1996), 171–364.

[60] Annex IV to the conclusions of the European Council held at Cologne on June 3 and 4, 1999 (1999) 6 EU Bull. point I-64.

[61] The composition and manner of operation of the forum was determined by the European Council held at Tampere on October 15 and 16, 1999 (1999) 10 EU Bull. point I.2. In addition to various governmental and non-governmental organisations, the Committee of the Regions, the Economic and Social Committee and the European Ombudsman were also heard. For its establishment, see De Búrca, "The drafting of the European Union Charter of fundamental rights" (2001) E.L.Rev. 126–138; Desomer, "Het Handvest van de grondrechten van de Europese Unie" (2001) T.B.P. 671, at 671–673.

[62] (2000) 10 EU Bull. point I.2.I and (2000) 11 EU Bull. point I.2.1.

the European Parliament, the Council and the Commission.[63] The Charter brings together rights which ensue out of the constitutional traditions and international obligations common to the Member States, the ECHR, the Social Charter, the Charter of Fundamental Social Rights of Workers, the case law of the Court of Justice and the European Court of Human Rights and Union legislation on data protection and worker participation. On the eve of the signature of the Lisbon Treaty, the Charter of Fundamental Rights was proclaimed again in Strasbourg on December 12, 2007 and published in the *Official Journal*.[64] This second publication of the Charter incorporates the changes proposed by the EU Constitution. In addition to the preamble,[65] the Charter is composed of six titles setting out rights which cut across the traditional division between political and civil rights and economic and social rights (see para. 22–034). Apart from some rights connected with citizenship of the Union (see para. 8–006), the fundamental rights set forth in the Charter may be invoked in the context of Union law by anyone, including persons who are not nationals of Member States.

Legal status. At the time of the first proclamation of the Charter, the discussion about its legal status was postponed to a subsequent intergovernmental conference.[66]

22–022

---

[63] (2000) 12 EU Bull. point I.2.2. Its proclamation preceded the meeting of the European Council held at Nice on December 7–9, 2000 and the conclusion on December 10, 2000 of the Intergovernmental Conference which reached agreement on the Nice Treaty. The text of the Charter was published in [2000] O.J. C364/1 and (2000) 12 EU Bull. Point 2.2.1. For an analysis of the content, see Grzeszick, "Das Grundrecht auf eine gute Verwaltung- Strukturen und Perspektiven des Charta-Grundrechts auf eine gute Verwaltung", (2006) 41 *Europarecht*, 161–181; Maus, "La charte des droits fondamentaux de l'Union Européenne et la protection des droits de l'homme en Europe" (2005) Z.ö.R. 297–312; Ashiagbor, "Economic and Social Rights in the European Charter of Fundamenal Rights" (2004) E.H.R.L.R. 62–72; Betten, "The EU Charter of Fundamental Rights: a Trojan Horse or a Mouse?" (2001) Int'l J.Comp.Lab.Ind.Rel. 151–164; Bribosia and De Schutter, "La Charte des droits fondamentaux de l'Union européenne" (2001) J.T. 281–293; Burgorgue-Larsen, "La charte des droits fondamentaux de l'Union européenne racontée au citoyen européen" (2001) R.A.E. 398–409; Goldsmith, "A Charter of Rights, Freedoms and Principles" (2001) C.M.L.Rev. 1201–1216; Hirsch Ballin, "Het Handvest van de Grondrechten van de Europese Unie: het eerste hoofdstuk van een Europese constitutie?" (2001) A.A. 88–93; Lenaerts and De Smijter, "A 'Bill of Rights' for the European Union" (2001) C.M.L.Rev. 273–300; Pache, "Die Europäische Grundrechtscharta—ein Ruckschritt für den Grundrechtsschutz in Europa?" (2001) EuR. 475–494; Rodriguez Bereijo, "La carta de los derechos fundamentales de la Unión Europea" (2001) 192 Not.U.Eur. 9–20; Tettinger, "Die Charta der Grundrechte der Europäischen Union" (2001) N.J.W. 1010–1015; Vitorino, "La Charte des droits fondamentaux de l'Union européenne" (2001) R.D.U.E. 27–64; Simon, "Les droits du citoyen de l'Union" (2000) R.U.D.H. 22–27.

[64] [2007] O.J. C303/1.

[65] See Busse, "Eine kritische Würdigung der Präambel der Europäischen Grundrechtecharta" (2002) Eu.GR.Z. 559–576.

[66] See the call for a debate on the status of the Charter in Declaration (No. 23), annexed to the Nice Treaty, on the future of the Union, [2001] O.J. C80/85 and the Laeken Declaration ((2001) 12 EU Bull. point I.27, where it is stated that "Thought would also have to be given to whether the Charter of Fundamental Rights should be included in the Basic Treaty" ("and to whether the European Community should accede to the European Convention on Human Rights").

Accordingly, the Charter was not incorporated in the Treaties and its provisions were not expressly given force of law in any other way. Nonetheless, this did not prevent the Charter from being regarded as being an authoritative catalogue of fundamental rights, having regard to the broad participation in drawing up the text and its subsequent approval by the national governments (within the European Council), the European Parliament and the Commission. According to many commentators, the institutions and bodies of the Union and likewise the Member States were bound to respect the Charter,[67] as it had to be regarded as confirming the general principles inherent in the rule of law which are common to the constitutional traditions of the Member States. In this connection, the Union Courts frequently referred to the provisions of the Charter even before the entry into force of the Lisbon Treaty.[68]

As has already been mentioned, the Lisbon Treaty conferred on the Charter the same legal force as the Treaties.[69] Unlike the EU Constitution, which contained the full text of the Charter, the Lisbon Treaty did not incorporate the Charter into the Treaties. Instead, Art. 6(1) TEU states that,

> "[t]he Union recognises the rights, freedoms and principles set out in the [Charter], as adapted at Strasbourg, on 12 December 2007, which have the same legal value as the Treaties".

That provision emphasises that the provisions of the Charter in no way extend the competences of the Union as defined in the Treaties. Moreover, the rights, freedoms and principles in the Charter,

> "shall be interpreted in accordance with the general provisions in Title VII of the Charter governing its interpretation and application and with due regard to the explanations referred to in the Charter, that set out the sources of those provisions" (Art. 6(1), third subpara., TEU, see para. 22–028).

---

[67] For the view that the Community institutions "bound themselves" to the European Charter, see Hirsch Ballin, "Eén wezenlijke maatstaf voor alle actoren in de Gemeenschap" (2001) S.E.W. 330–337; Alber, "Die Selbstbinding der europäischen Organen an die Europäischen Charta der Grundrechte" (2000) Eu.GR.Z. 349–353. See also the communication from the Commission on the legal nature of the Charter of fundamental rights of the European Union, COM(2000) 644 fin.

[68] See, e.g., ECJ, Case C-540/03 *European Parliament v Council* [2006] E.C.R. I-5769, paras 38 and 58; ECJ, Case C-432/05 *Unibet* [2007] E.C.R. I-2271, para. 37; ECJ, Case C-438/05 *International Transport Workers' Federation and Finnish Seamen's Union* [2007] E.C.R. I-10779, paras 90–91; ECJ, Case C-275/06 *Promusicae* [2008] E.C.R. I-271, paras 61–65; ECJ, Joined Cases C-402/05 P and C-415/05 P *Kadi and Al Barakaat International Foundation* [2008] E.C.R. I-6351, para. 335. See also CFI, Case T-177/01 *Jégo-Quéré v Commission* [2002] E.C.R. II-2365 (set aside on appeal: ECJ, Case C-263/02 P *Commission v Jégo-Quéré*, [2004] E.C.R. I-3425). The European Court of Human Rights referred to the Charter in its judgment of July 11, 2002 in *Goodwin v United Kingdom*, No. 28957/95, para. 100. See also Knook, "The Court, the Charter, and the Vertical Division of Powers in the European Union" (2005) C.M.L.Rev. 367–398.

[69] See ECJ (judgment of December 23, 2009), Case C-403/09 PPU *Detiček*, not yet reported, para. 53; ECJ (judgment of January 19, 2010), Case C-555/07 *Kücükdeveci*, not yet reported, para. 22, with a case note by Roes (2010) Col.J.E.L. 497–519; ECJ (judgment of March 4, 2010), Case C-578/08 *Chakroun*, not yet reported, para. 44.

Within the Intergovernmental Conference that negotiated the Lisbon Treaty, it proved impossible to reach consensus with regard to the reference to the Charter as a binding source of law without agreeing on derogatory arrangements for the United Kingdom and Poland, which were laid down in a protocol annexed to the Treaties.[70] According to that protocol, the Charter does not extend the ability of the Court of Justice or any court or tribunal of Poland or of the United Kingdom, to find that national measures or practices of these Member States are inconsistent with the fundamental rights, freedoms and principles that it reaffirms. Furthermore, it is expressly stated that Title IV of the Charter does not create justiciable rights in these Member States except in so far as national law has provided for such rights.[71]

2. Scope of fundamental rights' protection

Limited scope of application. The protection ensured by the Union Courts of fundamental rights as general principles of Union law only applies with respect to acts of the Union institutions and bodies and action taken by the Member States in the context of Union law. Likewise, it follows from Title VII of the Charter ("General provisions governing the interpretation and application of the Charter") that the provisions of the Charter are addressed to the institutions and bodies of the Union and to the Member States when they are implementing Union law (Art. 51(1)). With respect to the rights, freedoms and principles set out in the Charter, the protection of fundamental rights is subject to some additional constraints (see para. 22–028). **22–023**

(a) *Protection vis-à-vis institutions and bodies of the Union*

Union institutions and bodies. The institutions and bodies of the Union have to respect fundamental rights, including the rights, freedoms and principles set out in the Charter. Since respect for human rights is a condition of the lawfullness of Union acts, the Court of Justice has held that measures incompatible with respect for human rights are "not acceptable" in the Union.[72] An action can therefore be brought before the Union Courts against Union acts which violate fundamental rights.[73] If the wording of Union law is open to more than one interpretation, preference should be given to the interpretation which renders the provision consistent with the fundamental rights protected by the Union legal order (see para. 22–017). A provision of a Union act requiring implementation by the Member States may in itself violate fundamental **22–024**

---

[70] Protocol (No. 30), annexed to the TEU and TFEU, on the application of the Charter of Fundamental Rights of the European Union to Poland and to the United Kingdom, [2010] O.J. C83/313.

[71] *Ibid.*, Art. 1.

[72] ECJ, Joined Cases C-402/05 P and C-415/05 P *Kadi and Al Barakaat International Foundation* [2008] E.C.R. I-6351, para. 284.

[73] See, e.g., ECJ, Case C-404/92 P *X v Commission* [1994] E.C.R. I-4737, paras 17–25, with a case note by De Smijter (1995) Col.J.E.L. 332–338.

rights if it requires, or expressly or impliedly authorises, the Member States to adopt or retain national legislation not respecting those rights.[74]

The consequence of the fact that the ECHR is applied in the Union legal order is that the institutions and bodies of the Union have to comply with the rights it embodies. Consequently, the principles derived from Art. 6 of the ECHR apply to actions brought in the Court of Justice, the General Court and the specialised courts.[75] It does not mean, however, that the Commission is regarded as a tribunal within the meaning of Art. 6 ECHR in procedures imposing sanctions.[76]

The duty to respect fundamental rights also applies in the field of the CFSP. However, given the limited jurisdiction of the Court in this field (see para. 13–086), it cannot be judicially enforced.

(b) Protection vis-à-vis Member States

22–025 **Member States acting within the scope of Union law.** Fundamental rights are an integral part of the Union legal order. As a result of the primacy of Union law, any action on the part of the Member States taken within the scope of Union law has to comply with Union requirements with regard to the protection of fundamental rights.[77] In a 1989 judgment, the Court held that,

> "[s]ince those requirements are also binding on the Member States when they implement [Union] rules, the Member States must, as far as possible, apply those rules in accordance with those requirements".[78]

The Member States act "within the scope of Union law" where they apply Treaty provisions[79] or implement Union acts, in particular where applying or implementing regulations[80] or transposing directives into national law.[81] This also applies

---

[74] ECJ, Case C-540/03 *European Parliament v Council* [2006] E.C.R. I-5769, para. 23.

[75] ECJ, Case C-185/95 P *Baustahlgewebe v Commission* [1998] E.C.R. I-8417, paras 20–21; ECJ (decision of June 24, 2009), Case C-197/09 RX-II *EMEA*, not yet reported, paras 38–52; ECJ, Case C-385/07 P *Der Grüne Punkt—Duales System Deutschland v Commission* [2009] E.C.R. I-06155, para. 178.

[76] ECJ, Joined Cases 209–215/78 and 218/78 *Van Landewyck v Commission* [1980] E.C.R. 3125, para. 81. See Zampini, "Convention européenne des droits de l'homme et droit communautaire de la concurrence" (1999) R.M.C.U.E. 628–647; Wils, "La compatibilité des procédures communautaires en matière de concurrence avec la Convention européenne des droits de l'homme" (1996) C.D.E. 329–354.

[77] ECJ, Case 222/84 *Johnston* [1986] E.C.R. 1651, para. 18. See also Art. 51(1) of the Charter of Fundamental Rights of the European Union (para. 22–021, *infra*).

[78] ECJ, Case 5/88 *Wachauf* [1989] E.C.R. 2609, para. 19.

[79] ECJ, Case 222/86 *Heylens* [1987] E.C.R. 4097, paras 14–16 (Art. 39 EC [*now Art. 45 TFEU*]).

[80] ECJ, Case 5/88 *Wachauf* [1989] E.C.R. 2609, paras 16–22; ECJ, Case C-2/92 *Bostock* [1994] E.C.R. I-955, paras 16–27.

[81] ECJ, Case 222/84 *Johnston* [1986] E.C.R. 1651, paras 13–21; ECJ, Joined Cases C-465/00, C-138/01 and C-139/01 *Rechnungshof v Österreichischer Rundfunk and Others* [2003] E.C.R. I-4989, paras 68–91; Joined Cases C-20/00 and C-64/00 *Booker Aquaculture and Hydro Seafood GSP* [2003] E.C.R. I-7411, paras 88–92.

where a measure constitutes a necessary step in the procedure for adoption of a Union measure and the Union institutions have only a limited or non-existent discretion with regard to that measure.[82] Moreover, national rules fall within the scope of Union law if they obstruct the exercise of freedoms guaranteed by the Treaties. The Court of Justice has also reviewed the question of respect for fundamental rights in interpreting the Brussels Convention.[83] Article 51(1) of the Charter confirms this case law where it provides that the rights, freedoms and principles of the Charter apply to Member States "only when they are implementing Union law".[84]

The Court of Justice refuses to consider the compatibility with fundamental rights of a national measure which lies "outside the scope of Union law".[85] Thus, Union law had nothing to say about a deprivation of liberty after a sentence under provisions of national criminal law which were not designed to secure compliance with rules of Union law. Whilst any deprivation of liberty may impede the person concerned from exercising his or her right to free movement, a purely hypothetical prospect of exercising that right does not establish a sufficient connection with Union law.[86]

Interpretation by the Court of Justice. Where national rules fall within the scope of Union law and a reference is made to the Court of Justice for a preliminary ruling, the Court considers that it must provide all the criteria of interpretation needed by the national court to determine whether the rules are compatible with fundamental rights.[87] This will be the case, for instance, where national rules obstruct the exercise of freedoms guaranteed by the Treaties. Where a Member State then relies on a justificatory ground available under Union law, that ground

22–026

---

[82] ECJ, Case C-97/91 *Oleificio Borelli v Commission* [1992] E.C.R. I-6313, paras 9–14; ECJ, Case C-269/99 *Carl Kühne and Others* [2001] E.C.R. I-9517, paras 57–58.

[83] ECJ, Case C-7/98 *Krombach* [2000] E.C.R. I-1935, paras 35–45 (a national court may refuse to enforce a judgment on public policy grounds where there was a breach in another Contracting State of the right to defend oneself); see also ECJ, Case C-394/07 *Gambazzi* [2009] E.C.R. I-2563, paras 26–48.

[84] This does not, however, prevent national legal systems from giving direct effect to the provisions of the Charter. For a well-reasoned argument in favour of giving a strict interpretation to the term "implementing", see Eeckhout, "The EU Charter of Fundamental Rights and the Federal Question" (2002) C.M.L.Rev. 945–994.

[85] ECJ, Case 12/86 *Demirel* [1987] E.C.R. 3719, para. 28; ECJ, Case C-159/90 *Society for the Protection of Unborn Children Ireland* [1991] E.C.R. I-4685, para. 31; ECJ, Case C-177/94 *Perfili* [1996] E.C.R. I-161, para. 20; ECJ, Case C-144/95 *Maurin* [1996] E.C.R. I-2909, para. 12; ECJ, Case C-309/96 *Annibaldi* [1997] E.C.R. I-7493, paras 10–25; see also the earlier judgment ECJ, Joined Cases 60–61/84 *Cinéthèque v Fédération nationale des cinémas français* [1985] E.C.R. 2605, para. 26 ("an area which falls within the jurisdiction of the national legislator").

[86] ECJ, Case C-299/95 *Kremzow* [1997] E.C.R. I-2629, paras 16–18.

[87] ECJ, Case C-260/89 *ERT* [1991] E.C.R. I-2925, para. 42; ECJ, Case C-159/90 *Society for the Protection of Unborn Children Ireland* [1991] E.C.R. I-4685, para. 31; ECJ, Case C-2/92 *Bostock* [1994] E.C.R. I-955; ECJ, Case C-112/00 *Schmidberger* [2003] E.C.R. I-5659, para. 75.

must be interpreted in the light of the general principles of law and in particular of fundamental rights.[88] In this way, a provision of national law which obstructs the exercise of the freedom to provide services can,

> "fall under the exceptions provided for by the combined provisions of [Articles 52 and 62 TFEU] only if they are compatible with the fundamental rights the observance of which is ensured by the Court".[89]

More generally, this applies to any hindrance of the freedoms guaranteed by Arts 34, 45, 49, 56 and 63 TFEU [*ex Arts 28, 39, 43, 49 and 56 EC*], which may be justified on grounds of a mandatory requirement in the public interest recognised by case law or listed in Art. 36, 45(3), 52 or 65 TFEU [*Art. 30, 39(3), 46 or 58 EC*], as the case may be.[90] If such a national provision violates a fundamental right, it will not be covered by a potential justificatory ground and will constitute a prohibited obstruction of the free movement of goods, persons, services or capital. The Court of Justice has likewise made it clear that respect for fundamental rights may constitute in itself a ground for restricting the freedoms guaranteed by the Treaties.[91] In such a case, the competent authorities enjoy a wide margin of

---

[88] See *ERT* (preceding n.), para. 43; ECJ, Case C-62/90 *Commission v Germany* [1992] E.C.R. I-2575, para. 23; ECJ, Case C-368/95 *Familiapress* [1997] E.C.R. I-3689, paras 24–25; see Weiler, "The European Court at a Crossroads: Community Human Rights and Member State Action", in Capotorti, Ehlermann, Frowein, Jacobs, Joliet, Koopmans and Kovar (eds), *Du droit international au droit de l'intégration. Liber Amicorum P. Pescatore* (Baden-Baden, Nomos, 1987), 821–842; Waelbroeck, "La protection des droits fondamentaux à l'égard des Etats membres dans le cadre communautaire", in *Mélanges F. Dehousse. II. La construction européenne* (Paris/Brussels, Nathan/Labor, 1979), 333–335. For a critical analysis, see Huber, "The unitary effect of the Community's fundamental rights: the ERT-Doctrine Needs to be reviewed" (2008) 14 E.Pub.L. 323–333.

[89] See *ERT* (n. 87), para. 43.

[90] E.g., ECJ, Case C-60/00 *Carpenter* [2002] E.C.R. I-6279, paras 42–46 (hindrance of freedom to provide services tested against—and found in breach of—the right to respect for family life within the meaning of ECHR, Art. 8). See as far back as ECJ, Case 36/75 *Rutili* [1975] E.C.R. 1219, paras 26–32 (application of Art. 39(3) EC [*now Art. 45 TFEU*] in conjunction with implementation of Council Regulation No. 1612/68 of October 15, 1968, para. 9–062, *supra*, and Council Directive 64/221/EEC of February 25, 1964, para. 9–070, *supra*). See the balancing of an impediment to the provision of services (prohibition on providing information about abortion clinics abroad) against freedom of expression conducted in Advocate-General W. Van Gerven's Opinion in ECJ, Case C-159/90 *Society for the Protection of Unborn Children Ireland* [1991] E.C.R. I-4685, points 30–38. Cf. Lenaerts, "Le respect des droits fondementaux en tant que principe constitutionnel de l'Union européenne (n. 44, *supra*), at 430, and Duikersloot, "Nationale maatregelen, communautaire grondrechten en de vrij verkeersjurisprudentie" (1997) S.E.W. 218, at 221–224. It is for the national court to determine as a matter of fact whether the national legislation at issue is covered by derogations provided for in the ECHR with regard to particular fundamental rights (e.g., ECJ, Case C-368/95 *Familiapress* [1997] E.C.R. I-3689, paras 26–33), although the Court of Justice may itself apply the criterion of proportionality (e.g., ECJ, Case C-60/00 *Carpenter* [2002] E.C.R. I-6279, paras 42–43).

[91] ECJ, Case C-112/00 *Schmidberger* [2003] E.C.R. I-5659, paras 69–94.

discretion in order to determine whether the restrictions placed upon intra-Union trade are proportionate in the light of the protection of fundamental rights.[92]

The Member States have to comply with fundamental rights also when they implement CFSP acts of the Union.[93] However, as far as action undertaken by the Member States pursuant to the CFSP is concerned, Art. 275 TFEU precludes any review by the Court of Justice. Consequently, in that connection the Court of Justice cannot rule on whether the Member States have complied with fundamental rights. Protection of fundamental rights in that context therefore rests on the protection afforded by the national legal systems under the supervision of the institutions set up by the ECHR.

Limited jurisdiction. Some commentators argue that the Court of Justice should provide for uniform protection of human rights against all measures affecting nationals of a Member State where they exercise their right of free movement or freedom to provide services.[94] In the case of non-Union nationals, a sufficient connection with Union law and the fundamental rights secured thereby would be present if the person concerned had been admitted to the territory of the Union.[95] However, such an extension of Union protection of fundamental rights would make for a generalisation of the supervision exercised by the Court of Justice over action undertaken by Member States—even outside the substantive scope of Union law—which might affect the division of powers as between the Member States and the Union.[96]

22–027

In order to prevent the Charter from being construed in such a way that it would apply to Member State action outside the scope of Union law, Art. 51(1) of the Charter stresses that the Union institutions and bodies and the Member States are to respect the rights, observe the principles and promote the application of the Charter,

"in accordance with their respective powers and respecting the limits of the powers of the Union as conferred on it in the Treaties".

In addition, Art. 6(1), second subpara., TEU states that the provisions of the Charter "shall not extend in any way the competences of the Union as defined in the Treaties", whilst Art. 51(2) of the Charter emphasises that the Charter,

---

[92] *Ibid.*, para. 82.

[93] ECJ, Case C-354/04 P *Gestoras Pro Amnistía and Others v Council* [2007] E.C.R. I-1579, para. 51; ECJ, Case C-355/04 P *Segi and Others v Council* [2007] E.C.R. I-1657, para. 51.

[94] See the Opinion of Advocate-General F.G. Jacobs in ECJ, Case C-168/91 *Konstantinidis* [1993] E.C.R. I-1191, point 46.

[95] O'Leary, "A Case Study of the Community's Protection of Human Rights, with Particular Reference to the Free Movement of Persons" (1994) A.D. 431, at 488–460; see also Weiler, "Thou Shalt Not Oppress a Stranger: On the Judicial Protection of the Human Rights of Non-EC Nationals—A Critique" (1992) E.J.I.L. 65–90.

[96] For a comparison with the protection of fundamental rights in the United States, which is based on "federalisation", see Lenaerts, "Fundamental Rights to be included in a Community Catalogue" (1991) E.L.Rev. 367, at 368–376. See further Ruffert, "Die Mitgliedstaaten der Europäischen Gemeinschaft als Verpflichtete der Gemeinschaftsgrundrechte" (1995) Eu.GR.Z. 518–530.

"does not extend the field of application of Union law beyond the powers of the Union or establish any new power or task for the Union, or modify powers and tasks as defined in the Treaties".

(c) *Other limitations to the application of the Charter*

22–028 **Scope and interpretation of rights and principles.** Pursuant to Art. 6(1), third sub-para., TEU, the rights, freedoms and principles in the Charter shall be interpreted,

"in accordance with the general provisions in Title VII of the Charter governing its interpretation and application and with due regard to the explanations referred to in the Charter, that sets out the sources of those provisions".

These "explanations" refer to the explanations prepared under the authority of the Praesidium of the Convention which drafted the Charter in 2000 and updated under the responsibility of the Praesidium of the European Convention, which drafted the EU Constitution.[97]

In so far as rights recognised by the Charter are based on the Union Treaties, they have to be exercised under the conditions and within the limits defined by those Treaties (Art. 52(2)).[98] In so far as the Charter contains rights which correspond to rights guaranteed by the ECHR, the meaning and scope of those rights is the same as those laid down by that convention, but this does not prevent Union law from providing more extensive protection (Art. 52(3)).[99] Moreover, in so far as the Charter recognises fundamental rights as they result from the constitutional traditions common to the Member States, those rights must be interpreted "in harmony with those traditions" (Art. 52(4)) and "full account" must be taken of national laws and practices as specified in the Charter (Art. 52(6)). In this connection, it should be stressed that the Charter formulates fundamental rights, but does not lay down any rules concerning the relationship between the Union and the national legal orders. The reference to the Member States' constitutions does not mean, therefore, that the primacy of Union law over national law has been relinquished.[100]

---

[97] See the preamble to the Charter and Art. 52(7) thereof. For the explanations relating to the Charter, see [2007] O.J. C303/17.

[98] Eeckhout (n. 84), at 979–991.

[99] ECJ (judgment of October 5, 2010), Case C-400/10 PPU *McB.*, not yet reported, para. 53. For the relationship between the Charter and the ECHR, see Callewaert, "Die EMRK und die EU-Grundrechtecharta" (2003) EU.GR.Z. 198–206; Drzemczewski, "The Council of Europe's Position with Respect to the EU Charter of Fundamental Rights" (2001) Human Rights L.J. 14–32. Where a provision of the Charter affords a broader protection than the ECHR (e.g., the right to marry in Art. 9 of the Charter, which, unlike Art. 12 of the ECHR, does not refer to the gender of the partners), the provision in question may provide support for deriving broader protection from the ECHR; see European Court of Human Rights, July 11, 2002, *Goodwin v United Kingdom*, No. 28957/95, paras 94–104, more specifically para. 100.

[100] See Douglas-Scott, "The Charter of Fundamental Rights as a Constitutional Document" (2004) E.H.R.L.R. 37–50; Liisberg, "Does the EU Charter of Fundamental Rights Threaten the Supremacy of Community Law?" (2001) C.M.L.Rev. 1171–1199.

Furthermore, to the extent that provisions of the Charter do not embody rights or freedoms but "principles", Art. 52(5) restricts judicial enforcement of those provisions to the interpretation and the review of the legality of acts adopted by the institutions, bodies, offices and agencies of the Union and by the Member States—within the limits of their respective powers—with a view to implementing those principles. This does not mean, however, that acts other than those directly implementing the Charter may not be indirectly reviewed for compliance with the principles enshrined therein.[101]

Lastly, the Charter provides that its provisions may not be interpreted as restricting or adversely affecting human rights and fundamental freedoms as recognised, in their respective fields of application, by Union law and international law, by international agreements and by the Member States' constitutions (Art. 53).[102] Consequently, in applying the Charter, the norm affording the highest level of protection prevails.

(d) *Relationship with the protection offered by the European Court of Human Rights*

Protection against acts of the Union. Article 6(2) TEU provides that the Union "shall accede" to the ECHR (see para. 22–031). Even though the Union has committed itself to respecting fundamental rights, including the ECHR, it is not (yet) a party to that Convention.[103] Therefore, the European Commission of Human Rights (now abolished, see para. 1–006) considered that a petition would not lie against Community institutions.[104] The European Court of Human Rights confirmed that acts of the Community could not be tested against the ECHR, because the Community was not a party to the Convention.[105] The same indubitably

22–029

---

[101] See ECJ, Joined Cases C-175/08, C-176/08, C-178/08 and C-179/08 *Salahadin Abdulla and Others* (n. 40, *supra*), para. 54 (secondary Union law must be interpreted in a manner which respects the principles recognised by the Charter).

[102] See Alonso Garcia, "The General Provisions of the Charter of Fundamental Rights of the European Union" (2002) E.L.J. 492–514.

[103] Lawson, *Het EVRM en de Europese Gemeenschappen*, (Kluwer, Deventer, 1999), 569 pp.; Schermers, "The European Communities Bound by Fundamental Human Rights" (1990) C.M.L.Rev. 249–258.

[104] European Commission of Human Rights, July 10, 1978, *CFDT v EEC*, No. 8030/77, D.R., Vol. 13, 231. The European Commission of Human Rights took the view that a complaint made against a Member State which was merely implementing a judgment of the Court of Justice was inadmissible as the Community legal order itself guaranteed respect for the ECHR: European Commission of Human Rights, February 9, 1990, *M. & Co v Germany*, No. 13258/87, ECHR Y., 1990, 46 (complaint about the implementation by Germany of a judgment given by the Court of Justice under Art. 256 EC; declared inadmissible). In another case, however, the implementation by a Member State of a Community agricultural regulation was tested against the ECHR: European Commission of Human Rights, July 1, 1993, *Procola and Others v Luxembourg*, No. 14570/89, D.R. Vol 75, 5.

[105] Judgment of the European Court of Human Rights of February 18, 1999 in *Matthews v United Kingdom*, No 24833/94, para. 32; judgment of the European Court of Human Rights of January 20, 2009 in *Coöperatieve producentenorganisatie van de Nederlandse Kokkelvisserij v Netherlands*, No. 13645/05, B.2.

applies to Union acts in general. However, the European Court has never clarified whether lodging a complaint against all the Member States would make it possible to review Union acts in the light of the ECHR. So far, all complaints brought for this purpose against all the Member States have been dismissed by the European Court without its having ruled on its jurisdiction *ratione personae*.[106]

22–030 **Protection against Member States' implementation of Union law.** According to the European Court of Human Rights, an indirect review may nevertheless be carried out by testing the act by which a Member State gives effect to Union provisions against the Convention.[107] The European Court of Human Rights has held that the fact that the Member States have transferred powers to the Union does not, in principle, release them from their obligations to comply with the ECHR. That Court has declared that it is competent to review acts adopted within the framework of the Union against the ECHR in so far as the Union legal order itself does not afford equivalent protection.[108] In *Matthews v United Kingdom* such protection was clearly not secured since the complaint related to the exclusion of inhabitants of Gibraltar from the direct election of the European Parliament, as laid down in the Act on the direct election of the European Parliament, which, as an act of primary law, could not be reviewed by the Court of Justice.[109]

In *Bosphorus v Ireland*[110] the European Court of Human Rights was asked to rule on an alleged violation of property rights by a decision of a Member State

---

[106] See the decisions of the European Court of Human Rights of July 4, 2000 in *Guérin Automobiles v Belgium and Others*, No 51717/99; of May 23, 2002 in *SEGI and Gestoras Pro-Amnistía v Belgium and Others*, No. 6422/02 and 9916/02; of March 10, 2004 in *Senator Lines v Belgium and Others*, No. 56672/00. See also Tulkens, "L'Union européenne devant la Cour européenne des droits de l'homme" (2000) R.U.D.H. 50–57. Conversely, the General Court manifestly lacked jurisdiction to entertain an application to annul a decision of the Commission of Human Rights: CFI (order of November 16, 1995), Case T-201/95 *Zanone v Council of Europe and France*, not yet reported; appeal rejected by ECJ (order of May 23, 1996), Case C-9/96 *P Zanone v Council of Europe and France*, not yet reported.

[107] Judgment of the European Court of Human Rights of November 15, 1996 in Cantoni v France, No. 17862/91, para. 30 (review in the light of the ECHR not precluded by the fact that the national provision was based almost word for word on a Union directive).

[108] Judgment of the European Court of Human Rights of February 18, 1999 in Matthews v United Kingdom, No 24833/94, paras 33–34.

[109] In Matthews the United Kingdom was held to have violated the right to free elections enshrined in Art. 3 of the First Protocol to the ECHR. For further particulars, see Winkler, "Der Europäische Gerichtshof für Menschenrechte, das Europäisches Parlament and der Schutz der Konventionsgrundrechte im Europäischen Gemeinschaftsrecht" (2001) Eu.GR.Z. 18–27; De Schutter and L'Hoest, "La Cour européenne des droits de l'homme juge du droit communautaire: Gibraltar, l'Union européenne et la Convention européenne des droits de l'homme" (2000) C.D.E. 141–214. For the Act, see para. 13–015, supra; for the status of provisions of primary law, see paras 22–007—22–015, supra. The implementation of the judgment in the United Kingdom was contested by Spain before the Court of Justice, but application was dismissed, see ECJ, Case C-145/04 *Spain v United Kingdom* [2006] E.C.R. I-7917.

[110] Judgment of the European Court of Human Rights of June 30, 2005 in *Bosphorus v Ireland*, No. 45036/98; case notes by Jacqué (2005) R.T.D.E. 749–767; Douglas-Scott (2006) C.M.L.Rev. 243–254; Hinarejos Parga (2006) E.L.Rev. 251–259; Schohe (2006) Eu.Z.W. 33–64; Eckes (2007) E.Pub.L. 47–67.

implementing a Union act imposing economic sanctions. The Court held that Member State action taken in compliance with Union obligations is justified as long as the Union is considered to protect fundamental rights, as regards both the substantive guarantees offered and the mechanisms controlling their observance, in a manner which can be considered at least equivalent to that for which the ECHR provides.[111] However, any such presumption can be rebutted if, in the circumstances of a particular case, it is considered that the protection of Convention rights was manifestly deficient.[112] In the *Kokkelvisserij* case, the European Court of Human Rights ruled that the same presumption applies to the procedures followed within the European Union, and in particular the procedures of the Court of Justice of the European Union.[113] In that case, the European Court of Human Rights was asked to rule on the compatibility with Art. 6 of the ECHR of the fact that, in proceedings for a preliminary ruling before the Court of Justice, an association involved in the proceedings before the referring Dutch court, did not have the opportunity to respond to the Advocate-General's Opinion.

As regards the question whether the protection of Convention rights was "manifestly deficient", the European Court of Human Rights held in the *Bosphorus* case that the protection of fundamental rights by Union law could be considered to be—and to have been at the relevant time—"equivalent" to that of the Convention system.[114] Likewise, it considered in the *Kokkelvisserij* case that the applicant had not shown that the protection afforded to it was manifestly deficient and thus failed to rebut the presumption that the procedure before the Court of Justice provides equivalent protection of its rights.[115] As long as this presumption prevails, when Member States implement legal obligations

---

[111] See already *M. & Co* (see n. 104, *supra*), 145. By "equivalent" the Court means "comparable"; any requirement that the organisation's protection be "identical" could run counter to the interest of international cooperation pursued: *Bosphorus v Ireland*, para. 155. See; Lebeck, "The European Court of Human Rights on the relation between ECHR and EC-law: the limits of constitutionalisation of public international law" (2007) Z.ö.R. 195–236; Lindner, "Grundrechtsschutz in Europa- System einer Kollisionsdogmatik" (2007) EuR. 160–193; Haratsch, "Die Solange-Rechtsprechung des Europäischen Gerichtshofs für Menschenrechte. Das Kooperationsverhältnis zwischen EGMR und EuGH" (2006) Z.a.ö.R.V. 927–947; Lavranos, "Das So-Lange-Prinzip im Verhältnis von EGMR und EuGH—Anmerkung zu dem Urteil der EGMR v 30.06.2005, Rs.450 36/98" (2006) EuR. 79–92.

[112] *Bosphorus v Ireland*, para. 156.

[113] Judgment of the European Court of Human Rights of January 20, 2009 in *Coöperatieve producentenorganisatie van de Nederlandse Kokkelvisserij v Nederland*, No. 13645/05, B.3, with a case note by Van de Heyning (2009) C.M.L.Rev. 2117–2125.

[114] *Bosphorus v Ireland*, paras 159–165.

[115] *Coöperatieve producentenorganisatie van de Nederlandse Kokkelvisserij v Nederland*, B.3. The European Court of Human Rights referred to the possibility for the Court of Justice to order the reopening of the oral proceedings after the Advocate-General has read out his or her opinion (which the Court had refused to do as the applicant had submitted no precise information which made it appear useful or necessary to do so) and the possibility for the referring national court to submit a further request for a preliminary ruling if it had found itself unable to decide the case on the basis of the first such ruling.

flowing from their membership of the European Union, they are presumed to comply with the requirements of the Convention. At the same time, the European Court of Human Rights confirmed that Member States remain fully responsible under the Convention where they act outside their strict international legal obligations, for instance where they enjoy a margin of discretion under Union law.[116]

22–031 **Accession to the ECHR.** In so far as a complaint cannot (yet) be lodged in the Court of Human Rights against the Union institutions, the only protection of fundamental rights provided vis-à-vis the Union institutions consists of a review at last instance by the Court of Justice. If the issue raised has not yet been considered by the European Court of Human Rights, it is possible that the Union Court will put a different construction on the scope of the ECHR than that Court would have done.[117] Where there is conflicting case law of the Court of Justice and the European Court of Human Rights concerning the scope of the ECHR, national (and Union) authorities are liable to be squeezed between the primacy of Union law, on the one hand, and their obligations under the ECHR, on the other.[118]

That problem will be resolved when the Union accedes to the ECHR.[119] In that case, individuals will be able to contest alleged violations of fundamental rights by acts of the Union institutions before the European Court of Human Rights. The fact that domestic remedies must have been exhausted before a matter may be brought before the European Court of Human Rights will mean, as far as the

---

[116] *Bosphorus v Ireland*, para. 157.

[117] *Cf.* ECJ, Joined Cases 46/87 and 227/88 *Hoechst v Commission* [1989] E.C.R. 2859, paras 17–18 (inviolability of the home under Art. 8 of the ECHR held not to extend to business premises) and European Court of Human Rights (judgment of December 16, 1992), *Niemietz v Germany*, No. 13710/88 Series A, Vol. 251-B, 23; European Court of Human Rights (judgment of April 16, 2002), *Colas Est and Others v France*, No. 37971/97 (ECHR, Art. 8 also applies to business premises). Since then, the Court of Justice seems to accept that Art. 8 of the ECHR applies to business premises; see ECJ, Case C-94/00 *Roquette Frères* [2002] E.C.R. I-9011, para. 29 (see also n. 144, *infra*).

[118] See further Hirsch, "Schutz der Grundrechte im "Bermuda-Dreieck" zwischen Karlsruhe, Strasbourg und Luxemburg" (2006) EuR. 7–18; Eaton, "Reforming the human rights protection system established by the European Convention on Human Rights" (2005) 26 Human Rights L.J. 1–17; Rieder, "Protecting human rights within the European Union: who is better qualified to do the job—the European Court of Justice or the European Court of Human Rights" (2005) Tulane E. & Civ. L. F. 73–107; Callewaert, "Het EVRM en het communautair recht: een Europese globalisering?" (2001) N.T.E.R. 259–267; Krüger and Polakiewicz, "Vorschläge für ein kohärentes System des Menschenrechtsschutzes in Europa: Europäische Menschenrechtskonvention und EU-Grundrechtcharta" (2001) Eu.GR.Z. 92–105.

[119] See, already, the Commission communication of November 19, 1990, SEC(90) 2087 fin., supported by the European Parliament in its resolution of January 18, 1994, [1994] O.J. C44/32; see, previously, the Commission's memorandum of April 4, 1979 on the accession of the European Communities to the Convention for the Protection of Human Rights and Fundamental Freedoms (1979) EC Bull. Suppl. 2.

Union is concerned, that the Court of Justice will have to give judgment before a complaint can be considered.[120]

The accession of the Union to the ECHR was traditionally problematic from the point of view of both (then) Community law and the ECHR. In an opinion, the Court of Justice declared that accession of the Community to the ECHR would entail a substantial change in the Community's system for the protection of human rights and have fundamental implications for the Community and the Member States. In view of the constitutional significance of such a change, it could be brought about only by way of an amendment of the Treaties.[121] The Lisbon Treaty carried out the necessary Treaty amendments allowing for accession. Article 6(2) TEU provides that the Union "shall accede" to the ECHR, whilst making it clear that such accession "shall not affect the Union's competences as defined in the Treaties". As a result, under Union law, accession to the ECHR is not only a possibility, but also an obligation. From the point of view of the ECHR, accession by the Union was also problematic because the ECHR as it stood was open to accession only by the Member States of the Council of Europe. However, the accession of the Union has been made possible by amendments

---

[120] In staff cases, domestic remedies will be exhausted where the General Court dismisses an appeal against a decision of the Civil Service Tribunal. See also the "Discussion document of the Court of Justice of the European Union on certain aspects of the accession of the European Union to the European Convention for the Protection of Human Rights and Fundamental Freedoms" of May 5, 2010, available at *http://www.curia.eu* [Accessed December 14, 2010].

[121] ECJ, Opinion 2/94 *Accession by the Communities to the Convention for the Protection of Human Rights and Fundamental Freedoms* [1996] E.C.R. I-1759, paras 34–35, with notes by Bernaerts (1996) Col.J.E.L. 372–381; Gaja (1996) C.M.L.Rev. 973–989. For (in many respects well-directed) criticism, see De Schutter and Lejeune, "L'adhésion de la Communauté à la Convention européenne des droits de l'homme. A propos de l'avis 2/94 de la Cour de justice des Communautés" (1996) C.D.E. 555–606; Vedder, "Die 'verfassungsrechtliche Dimension'—die bisher unbekannte Grenze für Gemeinschaftshandeln? Anmerkung zum Gutachten 2/94, EMRK, des EuGH" (1996) EuR. 309–319; Wachsmann, "L'avis 2/94 de la Cour de justice relatif à l'adhésion de la Communauté européenne à la Convention de sauvegarde des droits de l'homme et des libertés fondamentales" (1996) R.T.D.E. 467–491; Waelbroeck, "La Cour de justice et la Convention européenne des droits de l'homme" (1996) C.D.E. 549–553. See also Chaltiel, "L'Union européenne doit-elle adhérer à la Convention européenne des droits de l'homme?" (1997) R.M.C.U.E. 34–50; Curtin and Klerk, "De Europese Unie en het Europees Verdrag voor de Rechten van de Mens. Een nieuwe fase in een lat-relatie?" (1997) N.J.B. 202–210; Salinas Alcega, "Desarrolos recentes en la protección de los derechos humanos en Europa. Nuevos elementos en una vieja controversia: la adhesión de las Comunidades Europeas a la Convención europea de salvaguarda de los derechos humanos y las libertades fundamentales" (2001) 199 Not.U.Eur. 9–36; Benoît-Rohmer, "L'adhésion de l'Union à la Convention européenne des droits de l'homme" (2000) R.U.D.H. 57–61. A Finnish proposal for the revision of the Treaties (see (2000) Eu.GR.Z. 572) was not accepted by the 2000 IGC. For the position of the European Parliament on accession to the ECHR, see the resolution of March 16, 2000 on the drafting of a European Union Charter of Fundamental Rights, [2000] O.J. C377/332, point 15. See also Krüger and Polakiewicz, "Proposals for a Coherent Human Rights Protection System in Europe" (2001) R.U.D.H. 1–14.

introduced by the Fourteenth Protocol to the ECHR.[122] The accession of the Union now requires the conclusion of an agreement that has to determine the Union's participation in the control bodies of the ECHR and ensure that individual applications are correctly addressed to the Union or the Member States.[123] On behalf of the Union, the agreement governing accession will have to be concluded by the Council, acting unanimously, after obtaining the consent of the European Parliament (Art. 218(6)(a)(ii) and (8) TFEU). The decision concluding this agreement enters into force only after it has been approved by the Member States in accordance with their respective constitutional requirements (Art. 218(8) TFEU).

3. Survey of rights protected

22–032 **Fundamental rights.** As has already been mentioned, fundamental rights enshrined in the Charter of Fundamental Rights of the European Union, the European Convention for the Protection of Human Rights and Fundamental Freedoms (ECHR), the International Covenant on Civil and Political Rights and other international conventions or following from the constitutional traditions of the Member States may be invoked in the context of Union law.

22–033 **Rights elaborated in the case law.** Even before the proclamation of the Charter of Fundamental Rights (see para. 22–021), the Court of Justice and the General Court ruled on the following fundamental rights:

  o   the principle of equal treatment[124];

  o   the right to a fair hearing (ECHR, Art. 6)[125] including the right to effective judicial control (i.e., existence of a judicial remedy; see also ECHR,

---

[122] Protocol No. 14 to the Convention for the Protection of Human Rights and Fundamental Freedoms, amending the control system of the Convention (CETS No. 194). Article 17 of the Protocol provides for the insertion of a new para. 2 in Art. 59 of the Convention, which reads: "The European Union may accede to this Convention". Following the ratification by the last member of the Council of Europe to do so (Russia), the Fourteenth Protocol entered into force on June 6, 2010.

[123] See Protocol (No. 8), annexed by the Lisbon Treaty to the TEU and TFEU, relating to Art. 6(2) of the TEU on the accession of the Union to the European Convention on the Protection of Human Rights and Fundamental Freedoms [2010] O.J. C83/273, which provides that the agreement relating to the accession of the Union to the ECHR is to make provision for preserving the "specific characteristics of the Union and Union law", in particular with regard to the Union's participation in the control bodies of the ECHR and the "mechanisms necessary to ensure that proceedings by non-Member States and individual applications are correctly addressed to the Member States and/or the Union as appropriate".

[124] Para. 7–050, *supra*.

[125] ECJ, Case 98/79 *Pecastaing* [1980] E.C.R. 691, paras 21–22; CFI, Case T-535/93 *F v Council* [1995] E.C.R.SC II-163, paras 32–35, English abstract at I-A-49. *Cf.* CFI, Case T-83/96 *Van der Wal v Commission* [1998] E.C.R. II-545, paras 45–47, set aside on appeal by ECJ, Joined Cases C-174/98 P and C-189/89 P *Netherlands and Van der Wal v Commission* [2000] E.C.R. I-1, paras 17–18; ECJ, Case C-349/07 *Sopropé* [2008] E.C.R. I-10369, paras 33–37.

Art. 13),[126] the right to legal process within a reasonable time,[127] the right to judicial review by an independent and impartial judicial body,[128] the right of reply in adversarial proceedings,[129] the presumption of innocence,[130] the right of access to a lawyer[131] and the right to call witnesses[132];

---

[126] ECJ, Case 222/84 *Johnston* [1986] E.C.R. 1651, para. 18; ECJ, Case 222/86 *Heylens* [1987] E.C.R. 4097, para. 14; ECJ, Case C-97/91 *Oleificio Borelli v Commission* [1992] E.C.R. I-6313, paras 13–14; ECJ, Case C-269/99 *Carl Kühne and Others* [2001] E.C.R. I-9517, paras 57–58; ECJ, Case C-185/97 *Coote* [1998] E.C.R. I-5199, paras 20–22; ECJ, Joined Cases C-402/05 P and C-415/05 P *Kadi and Al Barakaat International Foundation* [2008] E.C.R. I-6351, para. 335; CFI, Case T-177/01 *Jégo-Quéré v Commission* [2002] E.C.R. II-2365, para. 41 (set aside on appeal: ECJ, Case C-263/02 P *Commission v Jégo-Quéré* [2004] E.C.R. I-3425). This fundamental right does not require a court to grant interim measures with regard to the right of residence: ECJ, Joined Cases C-297/88 and C-197/89 *Dzodzi* [1990] E.C.R. I-3763, para. 68. See also Art. 47 of the Charter of Fundamental Rights of the EU (see para. 22–034, *infra*); *cf.* ECJ, Case C-50/00 P *Unión de Pequeños Agricultores v Council and Commission* [2002] E.C.R. I-6677, paras 32–45, ECJ, Case C-263/02 P *Commission v Jégo-Quéré* [2004] E.C.R. I-3425 (different approach to the completeness of the Community system of legal remedies and procedures by reference to Arts 6 and 13 of the ECHR).

[127] See the application (as a general principle of law, but applying Art. 6 of the ECHR by analogy) in CFI, Joined Cases T-213/95 and T-18/96 *SCK and FNK v Commission* [1997] E.C.R. II-1739, paras 53–64, and the application of the principle of law derived from Art. 6 of the ECHR to proceedings before the Court of First Instance [now General Court] in ECJ, Case C-185/95 P *Baustahlgewebe v Commission* [1998] E.C.R. I-8417, paras 20–22 and 26–48; ECJ, Case C-238/99 P, C-244/99 P, C-245/99 P, C-247/99 P, C-250–252/99 P and C-254/99 P *Limburgse Vinyl Maatschappij NV and Others v Commission* [2002] E.C.R. I-8375, paras 164–235; ECJ, Joined Cases C-341/06 P and C-342/06 P *Chronopost* [2008] E.C.R. I-4777, paras 44–60; ECJ, Case C-385/07 P *Der Grüne Punkt—Duales System Deutschland v Commission* (n. 75, *supra*), paras 177–188.

[128] ECJ, Case C-506/04 *Wilson* [2006] E.C.R. I-8613, paras 43–61; ECJ, Case C-308/07 P *Gorostiaga Atxalandabaso* [2009] E.C.R. I-1059, paras 41–46.

[129] ECJ (order of February 4, 2000), Case C-17/98 *Emesa Sugar* [2000] E.C.R. I-665, paras 10–18 (where the Court of Justice held that the fact that a party may not submit observations in response to the Advocate-General's opinion does not conflict with the right of all persons in adversarial proceedings to a fair hearing; see para. 13–090, *supra*); ECJ, Case C-450/06 *Varec* [2008] E.C.R. I-581, paras 44–54 (adversarial principle).

[130] ECJ, Case C-199/92 P *Hüls v Commission* [1999] E.C.R. I-4287, paras 149–150; ECJ, Case C-235/92 P *Montecatini v Commission* [1999] E.C.R. I-4539, paras 175–176; ECJ, Joined Cases C-189/02 P, C-202/02 P, C-205/02 P to C-208/02 P and C-213/02 P *Dansk Rørindustri and Others v Commission* [2005] E.C.R. I-5425, paras 69–76; ECJ, Case C-344/08 *Rubach* [2009] E.C.R. I-7033, paras 30–31; ECJ, Case C-45/08 *Spector Photo Group* (n. 51, *supra*), para. 43. The right not to be compelled to testify against oneself (enshrined as regards criminal matters in Art. 14(3)(g) of the ICCPR) has until now been enforced only in connection with complying with the rights of the defence; n. 218, *infra*).

[131] ECJ, Case C-7/98 *Krombach* [2000] E.C.R. I-1935, paras 35–46; ECJ, Case C-305/05 *Ordre des barreaux francophones et germanophone and Others* [2007] E.C.R. I-5305.

[132] ECJ, Joined Cases C-189/02 P, C-202/02 P, C-205/02 P to C-208/02 P and C-213/02 P *Dansk Rørindustri and Others v Commission* [2005] E.C.R. I-5425, paras 68–75.

- o the principle of legality in relation to crime and punishment (*nullum crimen, nulla poena sine lege*), which implies that a provision of criminal law may not be applied extensively to the detriment of the defendant[133] and that provisions of criminal law may not have retroactive effect[134] (ECHR, Art. 7);

- o retroactive imposition of a lighter penalty (ICCPR, Art. 15)[135];

- o the principle *ne bis in idem* (Art. 4 of the Seventh Protocol to the ECHR)[136];

- o the right to human dignity[137];

- o respect for private life,[138] family life,[139] the home and correspondence (ECHR, Art. 8),[140] in particular respect for a person's physical

---

[133] ECJ, Joined Cases C-74/95 and C-129/95 *Criminal proceedings against X* [1996] E.C.R. I-6609, para. 25; ECJ, Case C-266/06 P *Evonik Degussa v Commission* [2008] E.C.R. I-81, paras 38–40.

[134] ECJ, Case 63/83 *Kirk* [1984] E.-C.R. 2689, para. 22; ECJ, Case C-60/02 *Criminal proceedings against X* [2004] E.C.R. I-651, para. 63; ECJ, Joined Cases C-189/02 P, C-202/02 P, C-205/02 P to C-208/02 P and C-213/02 P *Dansk Rørindustri and Others v Commission* [2005] E.C.R. I-5425, paras 215–232; ECJ (judgment of June 29, 2010), Case C-550/09 *E and F*, not yet reported, para. 59.

[135] ECJ, Joined Cases C-387/02, C-391/02 and C-403/02 *Berlusconi and Others* [2005] E.C.R. I-3565, para. 68; CFI, Case T-48/96 *Acme Industry v Council* [1999] E.C.R. II-3089, para. 30.

[136] ECJ, Case C-238/99 P, C-244/99 P, C-245/99 P, C-247/99 P, C-250–252/99 P and C-254/99 P *Limburgse Vinyl Maatschappij NV and Others v Commission* [2002] E.C.R. I-8375, paras 59–63 (see para. 22–041, *infra*). See Wasmeier, "The development of ne bis in idem into a transnational fundamental right in EU law: comments on recent developments" (2006) E.L.Rev. 565–578.

[137] ECJ, Case C-337/98 *Netherlands v European Parliament and Council* [2001] E.C.R. I-7079, paras 70–77.

[138] For the protection of personal data, see ECJ, Case C-369/98 *Fisher and Fisher* [2000] E.C.R. I-6751, paras 32–38; ECJ, Joined Cases C-465/00, C-138/01 and C-139/01 *Österreichischer Rundfunk and Others* [2003] E.C.R. I- 4989, paras 73–90; ECJ (judgment of March 9, 2010), Case C-518/07 *Commission v Germany*, not yet reported, para. 21; for the protection of confidential information and business secrets, see ECJ, Case C-450/06 *Varec* [2008] E.C.R. I-581, para. 48. See also ECJ, Case 165/82 *Commission v United Kingdom* [1983] E.C.R. 3431, para. 13, although this judgment makes no reference to the ECHR.

[139] ECJ, Case 249/86 *Commission v Germany* [1989] E.C.R. 1263, para. 10. See in particular with regard to family reunification, ECJ, Case 12/86 *Demirel* [1987] E.C.R. 3719, para. 28; ECJ, Case C-60/00 *Carpenter* [2002] E.C.R. I-6279, paras 40–46; ECJ, Case C-109/01 *Akrich* [2003] E.C.R. I-9607, paras 58–60; ECJ, Case C-540/03 *European Parliament v Council* [2006] E.C.R. I-5769, paras 52 *et seq.*; ECJ (judgment of March 4, 2010), Case C-578/08 *Chakroun*, not yet reported, paras 44 and 63.

[140] With regard to the Commission's powers to carry out investigations in supervising compliance with the competition rules, see ECJ, Case 136/79 *National Panasonic v Commission* [1980] E.C.R. 2033, paras 19–20; ECJ, Case 5/85 *AKZO Chemie v Commission* [1986] E.C.R. 2585, paras 25–27.

integrity,[141] the right to keep one's state of health private,[142] medical confidentiality[143] and the right to inviolability of one's home[144];

o   freedom to manifest one's religion (ECHR, Art. 9)[145];

o   freedom of expression (ECHR, Art. 10)[146];

o   freedom of association (ECHR, Art. 11)[147] and freedom of peaceful assembly,[148] in particular the right to be a member of a trade union and to take part in trade union activities[149];

---

[141] CFI, Joined Cases T-121/89 and T-13/90 *X v Commission* [1992] E.C.R. II-2195, paras 53–59, set aside on appeal by ECJ, Case C-404/92 P *X v Commission* [1994] E.C.R. I-4737, paras 17–24, in which it was held that the Commission had violated Art. 8 of the ECHR in that, although a would-be official had refused an AIDS test, the Commission had nevertheless had a test performed on him from which the presence of the disease could be inferred; see also CFI, Case T-10/93 *A v Commission* [1994] E.C.R. II-179, paras 47–51; ECJ, Case C-377/98 *Netherlands v European Parliament and Council* [2001] E.C.R. I-7079, paras 70 and 78–80.

[142] CFI, Case T-176/94 *K v Commission* [1995] E.C.R.-SC II-621, para. 31, English abstract at I-A-203.

[143] ECJ, Case C-62/90 *Commission v Germany* [1992] E.C.R. I-2575, para. 23.

[144] ECJ, Joined Cases 46/87 and 227/88 *Hoechst v Commission* [1989] E.C.R. 2859, paras 17–18 (same form of words in *Dow Benelux v Commission* and *Dow Chemical Ibérica v Commission*, cited in n. 178, *infra*) and ECJ, Case C-94/00 *Roquette Frères* [2002] E.C.R. I-9011, paras 22–99 (see n. 117, *supra*). See Lienemeyer and Waelbroeck (2003) C.M.L.Rev. 1481–1497; Kranenborg, "Art. 8 EVRM en de verificatiebevoegdheden van de Commissie" (2003) S.E.W. 49–57.

[145] ECJ, Case 130/75 *Prais v Council* [1976] E.C.R. 1589, paras 6–19.

[146] ECJ, Joined Cases 43 and 63/82 *VBVB and VBBB v Commission* [1984] E.C.R. 19, para. 34; ECJ, Joined Cases 60–61/84 *Cinéthèque* [1985] E.C.R. 2605, paras 25–26; ECJ, Case C-159/90 *Society for the Protection of Unborn Children Ireland* [1991] E.C.R. I-4685, paras 30–31; ECJ, Case C-260/89 *ERT* [1991] E.C.R. I-2925, para. 44; ECJ, Case C-219/91 *Ter Voort* [1992] E.C.R. I-5485, paras 35–38; ECJ, Case C-23/93 *TV10* [1994] E.C.R. I-4795, paras 23–25; ECJ, Case C-368/95 *Familiapress* [1997] E.C.R. I-3689, paras 18 and 25–33; ECJ, Case C-112/00 *Schmidberger* [2003] E.C.R. I-5659, paras 79–80; ECJ, Case C-71/02 *Herbert Karner Industrie-Auktionen* [2004] E.C.R. I-3025, paras 50–51; ECJ, Case C-421/07 *Damgaard* [2009] E.C.R. I-2629, paras 25–28. For the relationship with the obligations imposed by the Staff Regulations of officials, see ECJ, Case C-150/98 P *Economic and Social Committee v E* [[1999] E.C.R. I-8877, paras 12–18; ECJ, Case C-274/99 P *Connolly v Commission* [2001] E.C.R. I-1611, paras 37–56; ECJ, Case C-340/00 P *Commission v Cwik* [2001] E.C.R. I-10269, paras 17–28. See also ECJ, Case C-100/88 *Oyowe and Traore v Commission* [1989] E.C.R. 4285, para. 16, which makes no reference to the ECHR.

[147] ECJ, Case C-415/93 *Bosman* [1995] E.C.R. I-4921, para. 79; CFI, Joined Cases T-222/99, T-327/99 and T-329/99 *Martinez and Others v European Parliament* [2001] E.C.R. II-2823, paras 230–235 (confirmed on the merits by ECJ (order of November 11, 2003), Case C-488/01 P, *Martinez v European Parliament* [2003] E.C.R. I-13355).

[148] ECJ, Case C-235/92 P *Montecatini v Commission* [1999] E.C.R. I-4539, para. 137; ECJ, Case C-112/00 *Schmidberger* [2003] E.C.R. I-5659, paras 79–80. See Mann and Ripke, "Überlegungen zur Existenz und Reichweite eines Gemeinschaftsgrundrechts der Versammlungsfreiheit" (2004) Eu.GR.Z. 125–133.

[149] ECJ, Case 36/75 *Rutili* [1975] E.C.R. 1219, paras 31–32 (where Arts 8, 9, 10 and 11 of the ECHR are mentioned in one breath; see also n. 155, *infra*). For officials' freedom of association recognised by the Staff Regulations, as interpreted in the light of "general principles of labour law" (with no reference to the ECHR), see ECJ, Case 175/73 *Union Syndicale v Council* [1974] E.C.R. 917, paras 14–15; ECJ, Joined Cases C-193 and C-194/87 *Maurissen v Court of Auditors* [1990] E.C.R. I-95, paras 13–38.

    o   rights of ownership or the right to property as protected by constitutional law in all Member States[150] and Art. 1 of Protocol No. 1 to the ECHR,[151] including intellectual property rights[152];

    o   the right to take collective action, including the right to strike[153];

    o   freedom to carry on an economic activity (trade or profession)[154];

    o   the right of everyone lawfully within the territory of a State to liberty of movement therein and to freely choose his or here place of residence therein (Art. 2 of Protocol No. 4 to the ECHR).[155]

22–034   **Rights enshrined in the Charter.** The Charter of Fundamental Rights of the European Union brings those and other fundamental rights together in a comprehensive document with six titles that recognise both political and civil rights and economic and social rights. Increasingly, the Union Courts refer to provisions of the Charter, alone or in parallel with the fundamental rights as mentioned before.

The first Title "dignity" confirms human dignity (Art. 1), the right to life (Art. 2), the right to integrity of the person (Art. 3), the prohibition of torture and inhuman or degrading treatment or punishment (Art. 4) and the prohibition of slavery and forced labour (Art. 5).

By way of "freedoms", Title II sets forth: the right to liberty and security (Art. 6), respect for private and family life (Art. 7),[156] protection of personal data

---

[150] ECJ, Case 4/73 *Nold v Commission* [1974] E.C.R. 491, para. 14.

[151] ECJ, Case 44/79 *Hauer* [1979] E.C.R. 3727, paras 17–30; ECJ, Case C-347/03 *Regione autonoma Friuli-Venezia Giulia* [2005] E.C.R. I-3785, paras 118–133; ECJ, Joined Cases C-402/05 P and C-415/05 P *Kadi and Al Barakaat International Foundation* [2008] E.C.R. I-6351, paras 356 and 358. For a discussion, see Lenaerts and Vanvoorden, "The right to property in the case law of the Court of Justice of the European Communities", in Vandenberghe (ed.), *Propriété et droits de l'homme/Property and human rights* (Bruges, die Keure/La Charte, 2006) 195–240.

[152] ECJ, Case C-479/04 *Laserdisken* [2006] E.C.R. I-8089, para. 65; ECJ, Case C-275/06 *Promusicae* [2008] E.C.R. I-271, para. 62.

[153] ECJ, Case C-438/05 *International Transport Workers' Federation and Finnish Seamen's Union* [2007] E.C.R. I-10779, paras 43–44; ECJ, Case C-341/05 *Laval un Partneri* [2007] E.C.R. I-11767, paras 90–91.

[154] ECJ, Case 230/78 *Eridania* [1979] E.C.R. 2749, paras 20–22; ECJ, Case 240/83 *ADBHU* [1985] E.C.R. 531, paras 9–13; ECJ, Case C-200/96 *Metronome Musik* [1998] E.C.R. I-1953, para. 21. This fundamental right has generally been raised before the Court of Justice together with the right to property, in which case the Court has considered them together (see *Nold*, n. 47, *supra*) or considered the right to carry on a trade or profession and the right to property one after another (see *Hauer* (n. 151, *supra*), paras 31–32, *Schräder* (n. 168, *infra*), para. 18 and *Germany v Council* (n. 13, *supra*), paras 81–87).

[155] ECJ, Case 36/75 *Rutili* [1975] E.C.R. 1219, para. 32; ECJ, Case C-370/05 *Festersen* [2007] E.C.R. I-1129, paras 35–37.

[156] ECJ, Case C-540/03 *European Parliament v Council* [2006] E.C.R. I-5769, para. 58; ECJ, Case C-275/06 *Promusicae* [2008] E.C.R. I-271, para. 64; ECJ, Case C-450/06 *Varec* [2008] E.C.R. I-581, para. 48; ECJ (judgment of March 4, 2010), Case C-578/08 *Chakroun* [2010], not yet reported, paras 44 and 63.

(Art. 8),[157] the right to marry and found a family (Art. 9), freedom of thought, conscience and religion (Art. 10), freedom of expression and information (Art. 11),[158] freedom of assembly and of association (Art. 12), freedom of the arts and sciences (Art. 13), the right to education (Art. 14), freedom to choose an occupation and the right to engage in work (Art. 15), freedom to conduct a business (Art. 16), the right to property (Art. 17),[159] the right to asylum (Art. 18) and protection in the event of removal, expulsion or extradition (Art. 19).

Under the heading "equality", Title III recognises: equality before the law (Art. 20), non-discrimination (Art. 21),[160] cultural, religious and linguistic diversity (Art. 22), equality between men and women (Art. 23), the rights of the child (Art. 24),[161] the rights of the elderly (Art. 25) and integration of persons with disabilities (Art. 26).

Under "solidarity", Title IV covers: workers' right to information and consultation within the undertaking (Art. 27), the right of collective bargaining and action (Art. 28),[162] the right of access to placement services (Art. 29), protection in the event of unjustified dismissal (Art. 30), fair and just working conditions (Art. 31), prohibition of child labour and protection of young people at work (Art. 32), family and professional life (Art. 33), social security and social assistance (Art. 34), health care (Art. 35), access to services of general economic interest (Art. 36), environmental protection (Art. 37) and consumer protection (Art. 38).

Title V "citizens' rights" enshrines: the right to vote and to stand as a candidate at elections to the European Parliament (Art. 39), the right to vote and to stand as a candidate at municipal elections (Art. 40), the right to good administration (Art. 41),[163] the right of access to documents (Art. 42), the European Ombudsman

---

[157] ECJ, Case C-275/06 *Promusicae* [2008] E.C.R. I-271, para. 64.

[158] CFI, Joined Cases T-309/04, T-317/04, T-329/04 and T-336/04 *TV2 Danmark and Others v Commission* [2008] E.C.R. II-2935, para. 118.

[159] ECJ, Case C-275/06 *Promusicae* [2008] E.C.R. I-271, para. 61.

[160] ECJ, Case C-303/05 *Advocaten voor de Wereld* [2007] E.C.R. I-3633, para. 46; ECJ (judgment of January 19, 2010), Case C-555/07 *Kücükdeveci*, not yet reported, para. 22.

[161] ECJ, Case C-540/03 *European Parliament v Council* [2006] E.C.R. I-5769, para. 58; ECJ, Case C-244/06 *Dynamic Medien* [2008] E.C.R. I-505, para. 41; ECJ (judgment of December 23, 2009), Case C-403/09 PPU *Detiček*, not yet reported, paras 53–54 and 58–60; ECJ (judgment of July 1, 2010), Case C-211/10 PPU *Povse*, not yet reported, para 64.

[162] ECJ, Case C-438/05 *International Transport Workers' Federation and Finnish Seamen's Union* [2007] E.C.R. I-10779, paras 43–44; ECJ, Case C-341/05 *Laval un Partneri* [2007] E.C.R. I-11767, paras 90–91.

[163] CFI, Case T-54/99 *max.mobil Telekommunikation Service v Commission* [2002] E.C.R. II-313, para. 48 (on the right to have a case handled fairly and impartially; judgment set aside on appeal: ECJ, Case C-141/02 P *Commission v T-Mobile Austria* [2005] E.C.R. I-1283); ECJ, Case C-385/07 P *Der Grüne Punkt—Duales System Deutschland v Commission* (n. 75, *supra*), para. 179, and CFI, Case T-276/04 *Compagnie maritime belge v Commission* [2008] E.C.R. II-1277, para. 39 (on the right to have a case handled within a reasonable time). See also CFI, T-48/05 *Franchet and Byk v Commission* [2008] E.C.R. II-1585, paras 257 and 273. Various aspects of the principle of sound administration are discussed below as "general principles of Union law"; see paras 22–036 *et seq., infra*.

(Art. 43), the right to petition (Art. 44), the freedom of movement and of residence (Art. 45) and diplomatic and consular protection (Art. 46).

Under the heading "justice", Title VI recognises: the right to an effective remedy and to a fair trial (Art. 47),[164] the presumption of innocence[165] and the right of defence (Art. 48), the principles of legality[166] and proportionality of criminal offences and penalties (Art. 49) and the right not to be tried or punished twice in criminal proceedings for the same criminal offence (Art. 50).[167]

22–035 **Balancing fundamental rights.** It appears from the case law that these fundamental rights are not unfettered prerogatives, but must be viewed in the light of their social function. The Union may subject the enjoyment of fundamental rights to restrictions, provided that the restrictions,

> "in fact correspond to objectives of general interest pursued by the Union and that they do not constitute a disproportionate and intolerable interference which infringes upon the very substance of the right guaranteed".[168]

Such restrictions must therefore be properly proportionate to the public-interest aim pursued (see paras 7–033 *et seq.*). The ECHR declares that certain fundamental rights are to be subject to no restriction,

> "except such as is in accordance with the law and is necessary in a democratic society in the interests of national security, public safety or the economic

---

[164] ECJ, Case C-432/05 *Unibet* [2007] E.C.R. I-2271, para. 37 (see the case note by Arnull (2007) C.M.L.Rev. 1763–1780); ECJ, Case C-47/07 P *Masdar v Commission* [2008] E.C.R. I-9761, para. 50; ECJ, Joined Cases C-402/05 P and C-415/05 P *Kadi and Al Barakaat International Foundation* [2008] E.C.R. I-6351, para. 335; ECJ, Case C-12/08 *Mono Car Styling* [2009] E.C.R. I-6653, para. 47; ECJ (judgment of March 18, 2010), Joined Cases C-317/08 to C-320/08 *Alassini and Others*, not yet reported, para. 61. See also CFI, Case T-54/99 *max.mobil Telekommunikation Service v Commission* [2002] E.C.R. II-313, para. 57 (set aside on appeal, see n. 163, *supra*); CFI, Case T-177/01 *Jégo-Quéré v Commission* [2002] E.C.R. II-2365, paras 41–51 (set aside on appeal: ECJ, Case C-263/02 P *Commission v Jégo-Quéré* [2004] E.C.R. I-3425). See also the discussion of "general principles of Union law" in para. 22–041, *infra*.

[165] E.g., CFI, Case T-474/04 *Pergan Hilfsstoffe für industrielle Prozesse v Commission* [2007] E.C.R. II-4225, para. 75; CFI, T-48/05 *Franchet and Byk v Commission* [2008] E.C.R. II-1585, para. 209.

[166] ECJ, Case C-303/05 *Advocaten voor de Wereld* [2007] E.C.R. I-3633, para. 46.

[167] E.g., CFI, Case T-223/00 *Kyowa Hakko Kogyo v Commission* [2003] E.C.R. II-2553, para. 104.

[168] ECJ, Case 265/87 *Schräder* [1989] E.C.R. 2237, para. 15; ECJ, Case C-200/96 *Metronome Musik* [1998] E.C.R. I-1953, para. 21; see also ECJ, Case 44/79 *Hauer* [1979] E.C.R. 3727, paras 23 and 30, and the other cases cited in n. 154, *supra*. The balancing of interests carried out in Case C-280/93 *Germany v Council* has come in for criticism; see Everling, "Will Europe Slip on Bananas? The Banana Judgment of the Court of Justice and National Courts" (1996) C.M.L.Rev. 401, at 416–419. For the limitations of fundamental rights resulting from economic sanctions imposed by the Union, see ECJ, Case C-84/95 *Bosphorus* [1996] E.C.R. I-3953, paras 21–26; ECJ, Joined Cases C-402/05 P and C-415/05 P *Kadi and Al Barakaat International Foundation* [2008] E.C.R. I-6351, paras 355–371 (see also para. 22–057, *infra*).

well-being of the country, for the prevention of disorder or crime, for the protection of health or morals, or for the protection of the rights and freedoms of others" (ECHR, Art. 8, para. 2; see to the same effect Arts 9, para. 2, 10, para. 2 and 11, para. 2).[169]

To the same effect, the Charter of Fundamental Rights of the European Union states that any limitation on the exercise of the rights and freedoms recognised therein must be provided for by law and respect the essence of those rights and freedoms and that, subject to the principle of proportionality, limitations may be made only if they are necessary and genuinely meet objectives of general interest recognised by the Union or the need to protect the rights and freedoms of others (Art. 52(1)).[170]

B. GENERAL PRINCIPLES OF UNION LAW

1. Status of general principles of Union law

General principles of law. As mentioned above, recognition of "the law" as a source of Union law (see Art. 19(1) TEU) has enabled the Court of Justice to have recourse to general principles in interpreting and applying Union law.[171] These principles form part of the Union legal order and hence infringement of them constitutes an "infringement of the Treaties or of any rule of law relating to their application" within the meaning of the second para. of Art. 263 TFEU [*ex Art. 230 EC*].[172] Some principles afford guidance for the Union's administration where it encounters ambiguities or lacunae in Union legislation which it has to apply. Other legal principles are constitutional in nature and the Union institutions

22–036

---

[169] See ECJ, Case 36/75 *Rutili* [1975] E.C.R. 1219, para. 32; ECJ, Case 136/79 *National Panasonic v Commission* [1980] E.C.R. 2033, para. 19; ECJ, Case C-219/91 *Ter Voort* [1992] E.C.R. I-5485, para. 38. Compare ECJ, Case C-112/00 *Schmidberger* [2003] E.C.R. I-5659, paras 79, and ECJ, Case C-71/01 *Herbert Karner Industrie-Auktionen* [2004] E.C.R. I-3025, paras 50–51; ECJ (judgment of March 9, 2010), Joined Cases C-379/08 and C-380/08 *Raffinerie Mediterrannee (ERG) and Others*, not yet reported, paras 80–91 (balance of interests performed by the Court of Justice having regard to the authority's margin of appreciation) with ECJ, Case C-368/95 *Familiapress* [1997] E.C.R. I-3689, paras 26–33 (balance of interests left to the national legal system). See also the balancing of interests conducted in CFI, Case T-176/94 *K v Commission* [1995] E.C.R.-SC II-621, paras 33–45, English abstract at I-A-203.

[170] For these and other restrictions on the rights recognised by the Charter, see Triantafyllou, "The European Charter of Fundamental Rights and the 'Rule of law': Restricting Fundamental Rights by Reference" (2002) C.M.L.Rev. 53–64.

[171] See Lenaerts and Gutiérrez-Fons, "The Role of General Principles of EU Law" in Arnull, Barnard, Dougan and Spaventa (eds), *A Constitutional Order of States: Essays in European Law in Honour of Alan Dashwood* (Oxford, Hart Publishing, forthcoming 2011).

[172] ECJ, Case 112/77 *Töpfer v Commission* [1978] E.C.R. 1019, para. 19.

must comply with them when issuing legislative measures.[173] In so far as they are applicable, they apply not only to acts of the institutions but also to measures adopted by Member States in implementing Union law.[174] As far as possible, Union acts have to be interpreted in conformity with such general principles.[175]

22–037 **Sources.** On some occasions, Treaty provisions explicitly refer to general principles as they result from the constitutional traditions of the Member States. Article 340 TFEU [*ex Art. 288 EC*] (see also Art. 188 EAEC) puts the Union under a duty to make good any damage caused by its institutions or by its servants in the performance of their duties "in accordance with the general principles common to the laws of the Member States" (this being the Union regime for non-contractual liability). The general principle thus expressed that an unlawful act or omission gives rise to an obligation to make good the damage caused also reflects the obligation on public authorities to make good damage caused in the performance of their duties.[176] The Court applies principles which it finds, if not expressly, at least implicitly in the legal traditions of the Member States.[177] The Court of Justice often recognises general principles of law as forming part of the

---

[173] ECJ, Case C-101/08 *Audiolux and Others* [2009] E.C.R. I-9823, paras 62–63; ECJ, Case C-174/08 *NCC Construction Danmark* [2009] E.C.R. I-10567, paras 42 and 45.

[174] See, for instance, ECJ, Case 77/81 *Zuckerfabrik Franken* [1982] E.C.R. 681, paras 22–29 (principles of legal certainty and proportionality); ECJ, Joined Cases 201–202/85 *Klensch* [1986] E.C.R. 3477, paras 8–10, and ECJ (judgment of January 19, 2010), Case C-555/07 *Kücükdeveci*, not yet reported, paras 53–55 (principle of equal treatment; for this principle see also para. 7–054, *supra*); ECJ, Case C-197/91 *FAC* [1993] E.C.R. I-2639, paras 23–25 (principle of lawfulness of administrative action); ECJ, Case C-28/05 *Dokter and Others* [2006] E.C.R. I-5431, paras 73–78 (rights of the defence to be respected by Member States). See Temple Lang, "The Sphere in which Member States are obliged to comply with the General Principles of Law and Community Fundamental Rights Principles" (1991) L.I.E.I. 23–35.

[175] See, e.g., ECJ, Joined Cases C-402/07 and C-432/07 *Sturgeon* [2009] E.C.R. I-10923 para. 48 (principle of equal treatment); ECJ (judgment of April 29, 2010), Case C-340/08 *M and Others*, not yet reported, para. 64 (legal certainty); CFI, Case T-334/07 *Denka International*, [2009] E.C.R. II-4205, para. 116 (precautionary principle).

[176] ECJ, Joined Cases C-46/93 and C-48/93 *Brasserie du Pêcheur and Factortame* ("*Factortame IV*") [1996] E.C.R. I-1029, paras 28–29. See Lenaerts, "Interlocking legal orders in the European Union and comparative law" (2003) I.C.L.Q. 876–879.

[177] Schwarze, "Tendances vers un droit administratif commun en Europe" (1993) R.T.D.E. 235–245; for an outstanding survey with numerous references to learned articles and textbooks, see Tridimas, *The General Principles of EU Law* (Oxford, Oxford University Press, 2006), 591 pp.; Schermers and Waelbroeck, *Judicial Protection in the European Union* (The Hague, Kluwer, 2001), para. 53–258, at 28–132; Bernitz and Nergelius (eds), *General Principles of European Community Law* (The Hague, Kluwer Law International, 2000), 244 pp.; Usher, *General Principles of EC Law* (London, Longman, 1998), 167 pp. See also Lenaerts, "Le droit comparé dans le travail du juge communautaire" (2001) R.T.D.E. 487–528 and "Interlocking Legal Orders in the European Union and Comparative Law" (n. 4, *supra*).

Union legal order without expressly referring to the constitutional traditions of the Member States. A legal principle is usually put forward where it is impliedly associated with the concepts applying in the field in the Member States. Where, however, the existence and substance of a legal principle and any possible derogations from such a principle are less clear, the Court of Justice makes more exhaustive inquiries into its status in the national legal systems or in treaties which the Member States have signed.[178] Several principles of law are moreover supported by the Charter of Fundamental Rights of the European Union.[179] Other principles are recognised in the international legal order as general principles of international law (see para. 22–055). This does not prevent the Court from recognising a principle of law which can be derived neither from common national constitutional traditions nor from treaties. One example is the right of a legal person not to be forced to give evidence against itself in a procedure under competition law.[180]

Treaty principles. Some constitutional principles are set out in the Treaties themselves, such as the principle of sincere cooperation (Art. 4(3) TEU; see para. 7–042 *et seq.*), the principle of conferral (Art. 5(2) TEU), the principle of subsidiarity (Art. 5(3) TEU; see para. 7–026 *et seq.*), the principle of proportionality (Art. 5(4) TEU; see para. 7–033 *et seq.*) the principle of institutional balance (Art. 13(2) TEU; see para. 15–007 *et seq.*) and the principle of non-discrimination (inter alia, Art. 18 TFEU; see para. 7–050 *et seq.*); others are recognised by other provisions of primary Union law.[181] In one case, the Court of Justice even applied a constitutional principle against the wording of the Treaties itself, namely that of observance of institutional balance.[182] Furthermore, the Treaties provide that the Union is to

22–038

---

[178] See, e.g., ECJ, Case 155/79 *AM & S v Commission* [1982] E.C.R. 1575, paras 18–22 (confidentiality of exchange of letters between lawyer and client; para. 22–041, *infra*); ECJ, Joined Cases 46/87 and 227/88 *Hoechst v Commission* [1989] E.C.R. 2859, paras 17–19, and the parallel judgments ECJ, Case 85/87 *Dow Benelux v Commission* [1989] E.C.R. 3137, paras 28–30, and ECJ, Joined Cases 97–99/87 *Dow Chemical Ibérica v Commission* [1989] E.C.R. 3165, paras 14–16 (the Court of Justice found that the legal systems of all the Member States provided protection against arbitrary or disproportionate intervention by public authorities in the sphere of a natural or legal person's private activities, but it did not extend the fundamental right of inviolability of the home to business premises; para. 22–033, *infra*).

[179] See CFI, Case T-54/99 *max.mobil.Telekommunikation Service v Commission* [2002] E.C.R. II-313, paras 48 and 57 (concerning the right to sound administration and the right to an effective remedy before a tribunal).

[180] ECJ, Case 374/87 *Orkem v Commission* [1989] E.C.R. 3283, paras 32–35, and the parallel judgment ECJ, Case 27/88 *Solvay v Commission* [1989] E.C.R. 3355 (this right is not derived from the common constitutional traditions of the Member States, from Art. 6 of the ECHR or from Art. 14 of the International Covenant on Civil and Political Rights, but arises out of the rights of the defence: para. 22–059, *infra*).

[181] See, e.g., the budgetary principles set out in the Financial Regulation and the Decisions on Own Resources (paras 13–131—13–133, *supra*).

[182] ECJ, Case C-70/88 *European Parliament v Council* [1990] E.C.R. I-2041, paras 26–27 (discussed in para. 15–010, *supra*). For the principle of democracy, see also para. 20–007, *supra*.

recognise the rights, freedoms and principles set out in the Charter of Fundamental Rights (Art. 6(1) TEU) and proclaim that fundamental rights, as guaranteed by the ECHR and as they result from the constitutional traditions common to the Member States, constitute general principles of the Union's law (Art. 6(3) TEU; see paras. 22–016 *et seq.*).

Reference should also be made to the values on which the Union is founded, namely the values of respect for human dignity, freedom, democracy, equality, the rule of law and respect for human rights, including the rights of persons belonging to minorities (Art. 2 TEU; see Ch. 7, paras 7–003 *et seq.*). If the European Council should determine the existence of a serious and persistent breach by a Member State of those values, certain of the rights deriving from the Treaties may be suspended as far as the Member State in question is concerned (Art. 7 TEU; see para. 6–017).

2. Survey of general principles of Union law

22–039 **Principles of sound administration.** According to the Charter of Fundamental Rights, every person has the right to have his or her affairs handled impartially, fairly and within a reasonable time by the institutions and bodies of the Union.[183] Among the principles of law classed as "principles of sound administration",[184] a prominent place is occupied by the principle of legal certainty, according to which legal rules must be clear and their application foreseeable for all interested parties.[185] This means in the first place that every Union act intended to have legal effects must be based on a provision of superior law which is expressly stated to be its legal basis (see paras 7–009—7–013). Legal certainty also requires certain requirements to be fulfilled, such as the requirement for acts to state the reasons on which they are based (see para. 22–065) and to be notified to interested

---

[183] Charter of Fundamental Rights, Art. 41(1). See para. 22–034, *supra*.
[184] See in the Charter of Fundamental Rights of the European Union in particular the right to good administration (Art. 41), the right of access to documents (Art. 42), the right to an effective remedy and to a fair trial (Art. 47), the presumption of innocence and right of the defence (Art. 48), the principles of legality and proportionality of criminal offences (Art. 49) and the right not to be punished twice in criminal proceedings for the same offence (Art. 50). See Lenaerts, "Beginselen van behoorlijk bestuur in de Europese Unie", in Opdebeek and Van Damme, *Beginselen van behoorlijk bestuur* (Bruges, die Keure, 2006) 67–98; Kanska, "Towards Administrative Human Rights in the EU—Impact of the Charter of Fundamental Rights" (2004) E.L.J. 296–326; Lais, "Das Recht auf eine gute Verwaltung unter besonderer Berücksichtigung der Rechtsprechung des Europäischen Gerichtshofs" (2002) Z.Eu.S. 447–482. For the United Kingdom, see Wade & Forsyth, *Administrative Law* (10th edn, Oxford, Oxford University Press, 2009), 898 pp. See also Popelier, "Legal Certainty and Principles of Proper Law Making" (2000) E.J.L.R. 321–342.
[185] ECJ, Case C-325/91 *France v Commission* [1993] E.C.R. I-3283, para. 26. For the application of legal rules interpreted by the Court of Justice, see ECJ, Case 43/75 *Defrenne* [1976] E.C.R. 455, paras 71–7; ECJ, Case C-143/93 *Van Es Douane Agenten* [1996] E.C.R. I-431, paras 27–33; ECJ, Case C-177/96 *Banque Indosuez and Others* [1997] E.C.R. I-5659, paras 26–31.

parties in a language which they understand.[186] Every measure of the institutions having legal effects must be clear and precise and must be brought to the notice of the person concerned in such a way that he or she can ascertain exactly the time at which the measure comes into being and starts to have legal effects.[187] Consequently, Union acts imposing obligations on individuals which are not notified to them—as well as national provisions that impose such obligations by implementing Union law—must be duly published (see para. 22–066). Union rules must enable those concerned to know precisely the extent of the obligations which are imposed on them, in particular where they are liable to have financial consequences.[188] Further expressions of the principle of legal certainty include respect for acquired rights,[189] the requirement for measures imposing penalties to have an unambiguous legal basis (*nullum crimen, nulla poena sine lege*),[190] the fact that measures having adverse effect on individuals may not be retroactive,[191] the existence of time-limits for challenging (Union) administrative acts,[192] the importance of not calling into question judicial decisions that have become definitive (res judicata)[193] and the limitation period imposed for the imposition of sanctions.[194] In accordance with the principle of legal certainty, Union law in principle does not require an administrative body with the *power* to reopen a decision that has become final to do so if that decision was based on an incorrect application of Union law (para. 7–045, *supra*).

Individuals may also rely on the principle of protection of legitimate expectations. That principle protects any legitimate expectations created by the Union authorities.[195] The existence of a mere Commission proposal for a

---

[186] ECJ, Case 66/74 *Farrauto* [1975] E.C.R. 157, para. 6.

[187] CFI, Case T-115/94 *Opel Austria v Council* [1997] E.C.R. II-39, para. 124; ECJ, Case C-470/00 P *European Parliament v Ripa di Meana and Others* [2004] E.C.R. I-4167, paras 65–71.

[188] ECJ, Case C-158/06 *ROM-projecten* [2007] E.C.R. I-5103, paras 23–31.

[189] ECJ, Case 12/71 *Henck* [1971] E.C.R. 743, paras 4–5 (where the law is subsequently changed, the provision in question must be interpreted in the light of the law as it was at the time when the provision was applied).

[190] ECJ, Case 117/83 *Könecke* [1984] E.C.R. 3291, para. 11; ECJ, Case C-308/06 *Intertanko* [2008] E.C.R. I-4057 (see also para. 22–033, *supra*).

[191] ECJ, Case 63/83 *Kirk* [1984] E.C.R. 2689, para. 22. A new rule may, however, be applied to future effects of situations which arose under earlier rules: ECJ, Case 84/78 *Tomadini* [1979] E.C.R. 1801, para. 21. For the retroactive entry into effect of Union measures, see para. 22–067, *infra*.

[192] ECJ, Case C-453/00 *Kühne & Heitz* [2004] E.C.R. I-837, para. 24.

[193] ECJ, Case C-2/08 *Fallimento Olimpiclub* [2009] E.C.R. I-7501 para. 22; ECJ (judgment of June 29, 2010), Case C-526/08 *Commission v Luxembourg* [2010], not yet reported, paras 26–27.

[194] ECJ, Case 48/69 *ICI v Commission* [1972] E.C.R. 619, para. 49.

[195] ECJ, Case 112/77 *Töpfer v Commission* [1978] E.C.R. 1019, paras 18–20; see examples in ECJ, Case 120/86 *Mulder* [1988] E.C.R. 2321, and Case 170/86 *von Deetzen* [1988] E.C.R. 2355; CFI, Case T-203/96 *Embassy Limousines & Services v European Parliament* [1999] E.C.R.-II 4239, paras 73–88. The principle of protection of legitimate expectations is often relied on in staff cases, see CFI, Case T-123/89 *Chomel v Commission* [1990] E.C.R. II-131, paras 25–31. The principle of good faith is the corollary in public international law of the principle of protection of legitimate

measure[196] or the fact that the Commission remained for a long time without taking any action after delivering a reasoned opinion before bringing an action in the Court under Art. 258 TFEU [*ex Art. 226 EC*][197] does not create a legitimate expectation. The principle of protection of legitimate expectations may oblige a Union authority to adopt transitional measures intended to protect the expectations which traders may legitimately have derived from the retention of Union rules.[198] On account of the same principle, a legal measure cannot unconditionally be retroactively withdrawn. The retroactive withdrawal of an unlawful measure is permissible provided that the withdrawal occurs within a reasonable time and that the institution from which it emanates has had sufficient regard to how far the beneficiaries of the measure might have been led to rely on its lawfulness.[199] However, a lawful measure which has conferred individual rights or similar benefits may not be retroactively withdrawn.[200] In any event, by virtue of the principle of protection of legitimate expectations, a Union institution cannot be forced to apply Union rules *contra legem*.[201]

In recent case law, the Court has also described the precautionary principle as a general principle of Union law requiring the competent authorities to take appropriate measures to prevent specific potential risks to public health, safety and the environment by giving precedence to the requirements related to the protection of those interests over economic interests.[202] It follows from the precautionary

---

expectations: CFI, Case T-115/94 *Opel Austria v Council* [1997] E.C.R. II-39, para. 93 (para. 26–006, *infra*). See Kolb, "Principles as sources of international law (with special reference to good faith)" (2006) 53 N.I.L.R. 1–36. For the principle of protection of legitimate expectations in the context of procedures for State Aid, see para. 11–026.

[196] ECJ, Joined Cases C-13 to C-16/92 *Driessen and Others* [1993] E.C.R. I-4751, para. 33.

[197] ECJ, Case C-317/92 *Commission v Germany* [1994] E.C.R. I-2039, para. 4.

[198] ECJ, Joined Cases C-182/03 and C-217/03 *Belgium and Forum 187 v Commission* [2006] E.C.R. I-5479, paras 147–167.

[199] ECJ, Joined Cases 7/56 and 3/57 to 7/57 *Algera and Others v Common Assembly* [1957] E.C.R. 81, 116; ECJ, Case 14/81 *Alpha Steel v Commission* [1982] E.C.R. 749, para. 10; ECJ, Case 15/85 *Consorzio cooperative d'Abruzzo v Commission* [1987] E.C.R. 1005, para. 12; CFI, T-251/00 *Lagardère and Canal+ v Commission* [2002] E.C.R. II-4825, paras 138–152; CFI, Case T-25/04 *González y Díez* [2007] E.C.R. II-3121, paras 94–103.

[200] ECJ, Joined Cases 7/56 and 3/57 to 7/57 *Algera and Others v Common Assembly of the ECSC* [1957] E.C.R. 81, 115, ECJ, Case 159/82 *Verli-Wallace v Commission* [1983] E.C.R. 2711, para. 8. See Lübbig, "Die Aufhebung (Rücknahme und Widerruf) von Verwaltungsakten der Gemeinschaftsorgane" (2003) Eu.Z.W. 233–236.

[201] CFI, Case T-2/93 *Air France v Commission* [1994] E.C.R. II-323, para. 102.

[202] CFI, Case T-13/99 *Pfizer Animal Health v Council* [2003] E.C.R. II-3305, paras 113–115 and Case T-70/99 *Alpharma v Council* [2003] E.C.R. II-3495, paras 134–136; CFI, Joined Cases T-74/00, T-76/00, T-83 to T-85/00, T-132/00, T-137/00 and T-141/00 *Artegodan and Others v Commission* [2002] E.C.R. II-4945, paras 182–184 (upheld on appeal: ECJ, Case C-39/03 P *Commission v Artegodan and Others* [2003] E.C.R. I-7885). See Szajkowska, "The Impact of the Definition of the Precautionary Principle in EU Food Law" (2010) C.M.L.Rev. 173–196; Heyvaert, "Facing the consequences of the precautionary principle in European Community law" (2006) 31 E.L.Rev. 185–206; Kühn, "Die Entwicklung des Vorsorgeprinzips im Europarecht" (2006) Z.Eu.S.

principle that where there is uncertainty as to the existence or extent of risks to human health, protective measures may be taken without having to wait until the reality and seriousness of those risks become fully apparent.[203]

Other general principles. The Court of Justice also has to rule very frequently on whether institutions and Member States have complied with the principles of equal treatment (see para. 7–050) and proportionality (see paras 7–033 *et seq.*). The principle of proportionality, too, has several aspects, such as the need for sanctions to be proportional to the seriousness of the infringement found[204] and for no greater burdens to be imposed on individuals than is reasonably necessary to attain the policy aim intended.[205] Under the Union legal order there is also a prohibition of the abuse of law.[206] Accordingly, an advantage granted by Union rules may not be obtained where the conditions laid down for obtaining it are created artificially and it appears from a combination of objective circumstances that, despite formal observance of the conditions laid down by those rules, the purpose of those rules has not been achieved. The application of Union legislation cannot be extended to cover abusive practices, that is to say, transactions carried out, not in the context of normal commercial operations, but solely for the purpose of wrongfully obtaining advantages

22–040

487–520; da Cruz Vilaça, "The Precautionary Principle in EC Law" (2004) E.Pub.L. 369–406; MacMaoláin, "Using the precautionary principle to protect human health: *Pfizer v Council*" (2003) E.L.Rev. 723–734; Icard, "Le principe de précaution: exception à l'application du droit communautaire?" (2002) R.T.D.E. 471–497; Alemanno, "Le principe de précaution en droit communautaire" (2001) R.T.D.E 917–953; De Sadeleer, "Le statut juridique du principe de précaution en droit communautaire: du slogan à la règle" (2001) C.D.E. 91–132; Fisher, "Is the precautionary principle justiciable?" (2001) J.Env.L. 315–334. See also Cheyne, "The precautionary principle in EC and WTO Law: searching for a common understanding" (2006) E.Env.L.Rev. 257–277; Daemen, "The European Community's Evolving Precautionary Principle—Comparisons with the United States and Ramifications for Doha Round Trade Negotiations" (2003) E.Env.L.Rev. 6–19; Ladeur, "The introduction of the precautionary principle into EU law: a Pyrrhic victory for environmental and public health law? Decision-making under conditions of complexity in multi-level political systems" (2003) C.M.L.Rev. 1455–1479.

[203] ECJ, Case C-236/01 *Monsanto Agricoltura Italia and Others* [2003] E.C.R. I-8105, paras 111–112, referring to CFI, Case T-13/99 *Pfizer Animal Health v Council* [2003] E.C.R. II-3305, paras 113–115 and Case T-70/99 *Alpharma v Council* [2002] E.C.R. II-3495, paras 134–136; CFI, Joined Cases T-74/00, T-76/00, T-83 to T-85/00, T-132/00, T-137/00 and T-141/00 *Artegodan and Others v Commission* [2002] E.C.R. II-4945, paras 182–184 (upheld on appeal: ECJ, Case C-39/03 P *Commission v Artegodan and Others* [2003] E.C.R. I-7887). See also EFTA Court, Case E-3/00 *EFTA Surveillance Authority v Norway* [2000–2001] EFTA Court Report 73, para. 25, and formerly, in connection with the principle of proportionality, ECJ, Case C-180/96 *United Kingdom v Commission* [1998] E.C.R. I-2265, paras 99–100; Case C-180/96 *National Farmers' Union and Others* [1998] E.C.R. I-2211, paras 63–34.

[204] ECJ, Case 240/78 *Atalanta* [1979] E.C.R. 2137, para. 15.

[205] ECJ, Case 9/73 *Schlüter* [1973] E.C.R. 1135, para. 22.

[206] ECJ, Case C-110/99 *Emsland-Stärke* [2000] E.C.R. I-11569, paras 50–54. See Lagondet, "L'abus de droit dans la jurisprudence communautaire" (2003) J.D.D.E. 8–12; Weber (2004) L.I.E.I. 43–55; Triantafyllou, "L'interdiction des abus de droit en tant que principe général du droit communautaire" (2002) C.D.E. 611–632.

provided for by Union law.[207] The Court of Justice also recognises the principle of unjust enrichment.[208] In addition, it has recognised force majeure as an exceptional ground for escaping the legal consequences of failing to fulfil an obligation.[209] In the field of the common agricultural policy, force majeure may be relied upon in the case of abnormal and unforeseen circumstances beyond the control of the person concerned, the consequences of which could not have been avoided in spite of the exercise of all due care.[210] In a number of cases, the Court has taken into account such principles as "natural justice", "fairness" and "equity".[211] In relations between Union institutions and bodies and their personnel, the Union Courts apply general principles of employment law.[212]

22–041   **Procedural rights.** In areas in which the Union has a wide discretion, the Court of Justice is strict in supervising that procedural requirements designed to ensure that individuals' interests have been duly taken into account have been complied with.[213] Many of the requirements flow from fundamental rights enshrined in Art. 6 ECHR and/or Art. 47 of the Charter of Fundamental Rights (see para. 22–034). The Court takes the view that in all proceedings in which sanctions, in particular fines or penalty payments, may be imposed, the right to be heard is a fundamental principle of Union law which must be respected even in the absence of any provision relating to the procedure in question.[214] The upshot of this is that

---

[207] ECJ, Case C-255/02 *Halifax and Others* [2006] E.C.R. I-1609, paras 68–69; ECJ, Case C-321/05 *Kofoed* [2007] E.C.R. I-5795, para. 38.

[208] ECJ, Case C-47/07 P *Masdar v Commission* [2008] E.C.R. I-9761, paras 44–47; CFI, Case T-171/99 *Corus UK v Commission* [2001] E.C.R. II-2967, paras 55–56 (in repaying amounts undue, the interest on those amounts must also be repaid). See also Jones, *Restitution and European Community Law* (London, Mansfield Press, 2000), 206 pp.

[209] ECJ, Case 4/68 *Schwarzwaldmilch* [1968] E.C.R. 377, at 385–387; ECJ, Case 68/77 *IFG v Commission* [1978] E.C.R. 353, para. 11.

[210] See ECJ, Case C-347/93 *Boterlux* [1994] E.C.R. I-3933, para. 34.

[211] For "fairness" and "equity", see ECJ, Case 31/75 *Costacurta v Commission* [1975] E.C.R. 1563, para. 4; ECJ, Case 94/75 *Süddeutsche Zucker* [1976] E.C.R. 153, para. 5; for other principles of law, see Schermers and Waelbroeck, *Judicial Protection in the European Union* (The Hague, Kluwer, 2001), paras 185–242, at 103–126.

[212] CFI, Case T-192/99 *Dunnett and Others v European Investment Bank* [2001] E.C.R. II-813, paras 85 and 89–90 (employees' right to be consulted about the withdrawal of a financial advantage).

[213] Drabek, "A Fair Hearing Before EC Institutions" (2001) E. Rev.Priv.L. 529–563; Lenaerts and Vanhamme, "Procedural Rights of Private Parties in the Community Administrative Process" (1997) C.M.L.Rev. 531–569.

[214] ECJ, Case 85/76 *Hoffmann-La Roche v Commission* [1979] E.C.R. 461, para. 9; see also ECJ, Case C-135/92 *Fiskano v Commission* [1994] E.C.R. I-2885, para. 39; ECJ, Case C-89/08 P *European Commission v Ireland and Others* (n. 51, *supra*), paras 50–59; ECJ, Case C-197/09 RX-II *M v EMEA* (n. 75, *supra*), paras 38–59. The principle of the right to a fair hearing, to which the principle of the right to be heard is closely linked, applies also to the Member States, in particular in the context of proceedings brought against them, such as those concerning the review of State Aid or the monitoring of Member State conduct as regards public enterprises; see ECJ, Case C-3/00 *Denmark v Commission* [2003] E.C.R. I-2643, paras 45–46.

when any administrative body adopts a measure which is liable to prejudice the interests of individuals, it is bound to put them in a position to express their point of view.[215] In order to enable them effectively to exercise the right to defend themselves, each of them must, where necessary, be informed clearly and in good time of the objections raised against them.[216] Where prior notification of the evidence adduced against a person and a prior hearing of that person would be liable to jeopardise the effectiveness of measures to be taken for the protection of imperative interests such as safeguarding public health or combating terrorism, the authorities may adopt those measures, even without first obtaining that person's views on the elements on which the measures are based. In such a case, however, the evidence adduced against that person is to be notified, in so far as reasonably possible, either concomitantly with or as soon as possible after the adoption of the initial measures.[217] Also as regards the rights of the defence, the Commission may not compel an undertaking to provide it with answers which might involve an admission on its part of the existence of the infringement which it is incumbent on the Commission to prove.[218] Union law does not require that principle to be respected in national proceedings which concern exclusively private relations between individuals and cannot lead directly or indirectly to the imposition of a penalty by a public authority.[219] The Court further recognises the "fundamental legal principle" that an official against whom disciplinary proceedings have been brought is entitled to be assisted by a lawyer, who must be allowed access to the file.[220] Letters exchanged between a lawyer and his or her client are confidential if the communications were made for the purposes and in the interests of the client's right of defence and emanate from an "independent" (that is to say, not an

---

[215] ECJ, Case 121/76 *Moli v Commission* [1977] E.C.R. 1971, para. 20; ECJ, Case 322/81 *Michelin v Commission* [1983] E.C.R. 3461, para. 7; CFI, Case T-346/94 *France-aviation v Commission* [1995] E.C.R. II-2841, paras 28–40; CFI, Case T-42/96 *Eyckeler and Malt v Commission* [1998] E.C.R. II-401, paras 76–88.

[216] ECJ, Case 17/74 *Transocean Marine Paint v Commission* [1974] E.C.R. 1063, para. 15; see also CFI, Joined Cases T-39/92 and T-40/92 *CB and Europay v Commission* [1994] E.C.R. II-49, paras 46–61.

[217] ECJ, Case C-28/05 *Dokter and Others* [2006] E.C.R. I-5431, paras 73–78; ECJ, Joined Cases C-402/05 P and C-415/05 P *Kadi and Al Barakaat International Foundation* [2008] E.C.R. I-6351, paras 336–348; CFI, Case T-228/02 *Organisation des Modjahedines du peuple d'Iran v Council* [2006] E.C.R. II-4665, paras 114–151.

[218] ECJ, Case 374/87 *Orkem v Commission* [1989] E.C.R. 3283, paras 32–35, and the parallel judgment ECJ, Case 27/88 *Solvay v Commission* [1989] E.C.R. 3355 (this right is not derived from the common constitutional traditions of the Member States, from Art. 6 of the ECHR or from Art. 14 of the International Covenant on Civil and Political Rights, but arises out of the rights of the defence: para. 22–059, *infra*).

[219] ECJ, Case C-60/92 *Otto* [1993] E.C.R. I-5683, paras 11–17.

[220] ECJ, Case 115/80 *Demont v Commission* [1981] E.C.R. 3147, paras 11–12. For access to the file in competition cases, see CFI, Case T-30/91 *Solvay v Commission* [1995] E.C.R. II-1775; CFI, Case T-36/91 *ICI v Commission* [1995] E.C.R. II-1847; CFI, Case T-37/91 *ICI v Commission* [1995] E.C.R. II-1901.

"in-house") lawyer.[221] Another principle recognised by Union law is that the Commission has to conclude an administrative procedure within a reasonable time.[222] In the field of competition law, the excessive duration of the investigation phase may compromise the rights of the defence where it would actually impede the establishment of evidence designed to refute the existence of conduct susceptible of rendering the undertakings concerned liable.[223]

The principle *ne bis in idem* means that a person cannot be adjudged or sentenced[224] for something for which he or she was already unappealably acquitted or sentenced and, for example, precludes the Union, in competition matters, from finding an undertaking guilty or bringing proceedings against it a second time on the grounds of anti-competitive conduct in respect of which it has been penalised or declared not liable by a previous unappealable Union decision.[225] Where proceedings at Union level are carried on concurrently with national proceedings with a different aim, two sanctions are not necessarily ruled out, although "a general requirement of natural justice" demands that any previous punitive decision must be taken into account in determining any sanction which is to be imposed.[226] The *ne bis in idem* principle does not preclude the Union from imposing sanctions on a person for the same facts for which he has already been sentenced or tried outside the Union unless this is precluded by an international agreement.[227]

---

[221] ECJ, Case 155/79 *AM & S v Commission* [1982] E.C.R. 1575, paras 18–22; ECJ (judgment of September 14, 2010), Case C-550/07 *Akzo Nobel Chemicals and Akonos Chemicals v Commission*, not yet reported; CFI (order of April 4, 1990), Case T-30/89 *Hilti v Commission* [1990] E.C.R. II-163, paras 13–18. See Gippini-Fournier, "Legal Professional Privilege in Competition Proceedings before the European Commission: Beyond the Cursory Glance" (2005) Fordham I.L.J. 967–1048.

[222] CFI, Joined Cases T-213/95 and T-18/96 *SCK and FNK v Commission* [1997] E.C.R. II-1739, para. 56.

[223] ECJ, Case C-105/04 P *Nederlandse Federatieve Vereniging voor de Groothandel op Elektrotechnisch Gebied v Commission* [2006] E.C.R. I-8725, paras 35–62; ECJ, Case C-113/04 P *Technische Unie v Commission* [2006] E.C.R. I-8831, paras 40–72.

[224] As a consequence, the *ne bis in idem* principle does not appear to have any place in the context of proceedings brought by the Commission against a Member State on the basis of Art. 258 TFEU; however, the res judicata principle applies: ECJ (judgment of June 29, 2010), Case C-526/08 *Commission v Luxembourg*, not yet reported, paras 25–37.

[225] CFI, Joined Cases T-305/94, T-306/94, T-307/94, T-313/94, T-314/94, T-315/94, T-316/94, T-318/94, T-325/94, T-328/94, T-329/94 and T-335/94 *Limburgse Vinyl Maatschappij NV and Others v Commission ("PVC II")* [1999] E.C.R. II-931, paras 86–97, as upheld on appeal (ECJ, Joined Cases C-238/99 P, C-244/99 P, C-245/99 P, C-247/99 P, C-250–252/99 P and C-254/99 P *Limburgse Vinyl Maatschappij NV and Others v Commission* [2002] E.C.R. I-8375, paras 59–63). See Wils, "The Principle of Ne Bis in Idem in EC Antitrust Enforcement: A Legal and Economic Analysis" (2003) World Comp. 131–148. See also ECJ, Joined Cases 18/65 and 35/65 *Gutmann v Commission* [1966] E.C.R. 103, at 119 (the principle prevents the Union from imposing two disciplinary measures for a single offence and from holding disciplinary proceedings more than once with regard to a single set of facts).

[226] ECJ, Case 14/68 *Wilhelm* [1969] E.C.R. 1, para. 11.

[227] ECJ, Case C-289/04 P *Showa Denko v Commission* [2006] E.C.R. I-5859, paras 50–63; ECJ, Case C-308/04 P *SGL Carbon v Commission* [2006] E.C.R. I-5977, paras 26–38.

Accordingly, under the Schengen Agreement a person whose case has been finally disposed of in a Member State may not be prosecuted again on the same facts in another Member State.[228]

Access to the law. In connection with the principle of open administration, Union law recognises an obligation to publish or notify binding acts to the parties concerned (see paras 22–066—22–067). The right of access to documents held by public authorities, which exists in most Member States in the form of a constitutional or legislative principle, now also exists vis-à-vis the Union institutions and bodies.[229]   **22–042**

IV. INTERNATIONAL LAW

A. INTERNATIONAL AGREEMENTS CONCLUDED BY THE UNION

1. Legal force and direct effect of international agreements

Binding force. Article 218 TFEU [*ex Art. 300 EC*] lays down the procedure by which the Union concludes agreements with third countries or international organisations (see para. 26–002 *et seq.*). Agreements concluded by the Union are binding on the Union institutions and on Member States (Art. 216(2) TFEU [*see ex Art. 300(7) EC*]).[230] The provisions of such agreements form an integral part of the Union legal order from the time when they enter into force.[231] This is in   **22–043**

---

[228] ECJ, Joined Cases C-187/01 and C-385/01 *Gözütok and Brügge* [2003] E.C.R. I-1345, paras 25–48; ECJ, Case C-467/04 *Gasparini and Others* [2006] E.C.R. I-9199, paras 22–37; ECJ, Case C-150/05 *Van Straaten* [2006] E.C.R. I-9327, paras 54–61; ECJ, Case C-436/04 *Van Esbroeck* [2006] E.C.R. I-2333, paras 18–24; ECJ, Case C-469/03 *Miraglia* [2005] E.C.R. I-2009, paras 28–35; ECJ, Case C-297/07 *Bourquain* [2008] E.C.R. I-9425, paras 33–52; ECJ, Case C-491/07 *Turanský* [2008] E.C.R. I-11039, paras 30–45 (on the *ne bis in idem* principle laid down in Art. 54 of the Convention implementing the Schengen Agreement). See Fletcher, "Some Developments to the *ne bis in idem* Principle in the European Union: *Criminal proceedings against Hüseyin Gözütok and Klaus Brügge*" (2003) Mod.L.Rev. 769–780; Ongena, "De '*ne bis in idem*'-regel en de Schengenlanden" (2003) N.J.Wb. 762–768.

[229] ECJ, Case C-58/94 *Netherlands v Council* [1996] E.C.R. I-2169, paras 34–40. The right of access to documents must be regarded as being a general principle of Union law, see in particular Broberg, "Access to documents: a general principle of Community law" (2002) E.L.Rev. 194–205. For access to documents, see para. 13–167, *supra*.

[230] For a survey of the status of international law in the Union legal order, see Vanhamme, *Volkenrechtelijke beginselen in het Europees recht* (Groningen, Europa Law, 2001), 435 pp.

[231] ECJ, Case 181/73 *Haegeman* [1974] E.C.R. 449, para. 5; ECJ, Case 104/81 *Kupferberg* [1982] E.C.R. 3641, paras 11–13. For obligations entered into by the Union under international law through mere signature, see para. 26–006, *infra*. As far as the temporal effect of international agreements is concerned, unless otherwise provided, an international agreement applies to the future effects of situations which arose before the agreement entered into force: ECJ, Case C-162/00 *Pokrzeptowicz-Meyer* [2002] E.C.R. I-1049, paras 48–51.

accordance with the "monist" approach: agreements concluded by the Union form part of the Union legal order without there being any necessity to transpose them into internal provisions of Union law.[232] Agreements not concluded by the Union but by the Member States also have binding force if the Union has assumed, under the Treaties, the powers previously exercised by the Member State in the field to which the agreement applies.[233] This was the case with the General Agreement on Tariffs and Trade (GATT; see para. 25–011), since the powers in connection with the application of that agreement were conferred on the Community by the EC Treaty and the Community itself subsequently took part in the tariff negotiations.[234] An agreement concluded by the Member States is also binding on the Union when the Treaties provide that the Union must exercise its powers in accordance therewith. Examples are provided by the Geneva Convention and the Protocol relating to the status of refugees and other relevant treaties, which are binding on the Union in the matter of asylum policy (Art. 78(1) TFEU [*ex Art. 63(1) EC*]).[235]

22–044 **Precedence over secondary law.** Furthermore the rules ensuing from agreements binding on the Union rank higher than acts of the Union institutions. According to the Court, "those agreements have primacy over secondary [Union] legislation".[236] As early as 1972, the Court considered itself bound to

---

[232] Although the Court of Justice derives its jurisdiction to review such agreements from their nature as "acts of institutions", see Rideau, "Les accords internationaux dans la jurisprudence de la Cour de Justice des Communautés européennes: Réflexions sur les relations entre les ordres juridiques international, communautaire et nationaux" (1990) R.G.D.I.P. 289, at 308–312. See also Bourgeois, "Effects of International Agreements on European Community Law: Are the Dice Cast?" (1984) Mich.L.Rev. 1250–1273; Pescatore, "L'application judiciaire des traités internationaux dans la Communauté européenne et dans ses Etats membres", *Etudes de droit des Communautés européennes. Mélanges offerts à P. H. Teitgen* (Paris, Pedone, 1984), at 355–406 (who also surveys the situation in the Member States; see also in this connection para. 21–020 *et seq., supra*).

[233] ECJ, Case C-379/92 *Peralta* [1994] E.C.R. I-3453, para. 16.

[234] ECJ, Joined Cases 21–24/72 *International Fruit Company* [1972] E.C.R. 1219, paras 10–17 (para. 25–011 *infra*). Likewise, the Community replaced the Member States with respect to commitments arising from the Convention of December 15, 1950 on the Nomenclature for the Classification of Goods in Customs Tariffs and from the Convention of the same date establishing a Customs Cooperation Council: ECJ, Case 38/75 *Nederlandse Spoorwegen* [1975] E.C.R. 1439, para. 21. In contrast, the Union has not assumed all the powers previously exercised by the Member States in the field of application of the Convention for the Unification of Certain Rules Relating to International Carriage by Air ("Warsaw Convention") (ECJ, Case C-301/08 *Bogiatzi*, [2009] E.C.R. I-10185, paras 25–33) or in the field of application of the International Convention for the Prevention of Pollution from Ships of 1973, as supplemented by the Protocol of February 17, 1978 ("Marpol 73/78") (ECJ, Case C-308/06 *Intertanko* [2008] E.C.R. I-4057, para. 48). Those conventions are not, therefore, part of the Union legal order.

[235] ECJ, Joined Cases C-175/08, C-176/08, C-178/08 and C-179/08 *Salahadin Abdulla and Others* (n. 40, *supra*), paras 51–53; ECJ (judgment of June 17, 2010), Case C-31/09 *Bolbol*, not yet reported, para. 38.

[236] ECJ, Case C-308/06 *Intertanko* [2008] E.C.R. I-4057, para. 42.

"examine whether [the] validity [of acts of the institutions] may be affected by reason of the fact that they are contrary to a rule of international law".[237]

In its *Kadi* judgment of 2008, however, the Court clarified that agreements binding on the Union cannot have primacy over provisions of primary Union law, including fundamental rights.[238] In view of the fact that international agreements concluded by the Union rank higher than provisions of secondary Union legislation, such provisions must, so far as is possible, be interpreted in a manner that is consistent with those agreements.[239] Since agreements concluded by the Union are binding on the Member States, their provisions also take precedence over national law. The Court of Justice takes the view that

> "[i]t follows from the [Union] nature of such provisions that their effect in the [Union] may not be allowed to vary according to whether their application is in practice the responsibility of the [Union] institutions or of the Member States and, in the latter case, according to the effects in the internal legal order of each Member State which the law of that State assigns to international agreements concluded by it".[240]

Accordingly, the supervision exercised by the Commission in ensuring that Member States comply with Union law also extends to making sure that they comply with international agreements binding on the Union. In the case of mixed agreements, concluded jointly by the Union and the Member States, the same is true for those provisions coming within the scope of Union competence.[241] In giving effect to Union law, the Member States must apply national rules as far as possible in the light of the wording and the purpose of such agreements.[242] In practice, it is exceptional for the Court of Justice to find that a national provision is incompatible with an agreement concluded by the Union.[243] Moreover, the

---

[237] ECJ, Joined Cases 21–24/72 *International Fruit Company* [1972] E.C.R. 1219, para. 6.

[238] ECJ, Joined Cases C-402/05 P and C-415/05 P *Kadi and Al Barakaat International Foundation* [2008] E.C.R. I-6351, paras 285 and 308–309.

[239] ECJ, Case C-61/94 *Commission v Germany* [1996] E.C.R. I-3989, para. 52; ECJ, Case C-284/95 *Safety High Tech* [1998] E.C.R. I-4301, para. 22; ECJ, Case C-341/95 *Bettati* [1998] E.C.R. I-4355, para. 20; CFI, Case T-256/97 *BEUC v Commission* [2000] E.C.R. II-101, paras 65–73; ECJ, Case C-286/02 *Bellio F.lli* [2004] E.C.R. I-3465, para. 33; ECJ, Case C-335/05 *Řízení* [2007] E.C.R. I-4307, paras 14–21; ECJ, Case C-228/06 *Soysal and Savatli* [2009] E.C.R. I-1031, para. 59; ECJ (judgment of May 6, 2010), Case C-63/09 *Walz*, not yet reported, para. 22.

[240] ECJ, Case 104/81 *Kupferberg* [1982] E.C.R. 3641, para. 14. See also ECJ, Case 38/75 *Nederlandse Spoorwegen* [1975] E.C.R. 1439, para. 16.

[241] ECJ, Case C-239/03 *Commission v France* [2004] E.C.R. I-9325, paras 23–31; ECJ, Case C-459/03 *Commission v Ireland* [2006] E.C.R. I-4635; paras 83–86 and 121.

[242] ECJ, Case C-53/96 *Hermès International* [1998] E.C.R. I-3603, para. 28.

[243] See, e.g., ECJ, Joined Cases 194 and 241/85 *Commission v Greece* [1988] E.C.R. 1037 (infringement of the Second EEC-ACP Convention); ECJ, Case C-469/93 *Chiquita Italia* [1995] E.C.R. I-4533, paras 54–63 (infringement of Protocol No. 5 to the Fourth ACP-EEC Convention); ECJ,

Court has only once as yet found an act of a Union institution to be incompatible with such an agreement.[244]

The precedence of international agreements concluded by the Union also applies in the field of the CFSP. However, it cannot be judicially enforced given the limited jurisdiction of the Court in this field (see para. 13–086).

22–045   **Direct effect.** In judicial proceedings, individuals may rely on a provision of an agreement concluded by the Union only if the provision in question has direct effect.[245] The test is whether,

> "regard being had to its wording and the purpose and nature of the agreement itself, the provision contains a clear and precise obligation which is not subject, in its implementation or effects, to the adoption of any subsequent measure".[246]

Accordingly, a provision of an agreement concluded by the Union will have direct effect if it fulfils the general, Union-law requirements for direct effect (see para. 21–056) and where, in addition, direct effect is compatible with the purpose and nature (sometimes expressed as "the spirit, the general scheme and the terms"[247]) of the agreement in question. It may also have been indicated in the agreement what effect its provisions are to have in the internal legal order of the Contracting Parties.[248]

Case C-61/94 *Commission v Germany* [1996] E.C.R. I-3989, paras 18–58 (infringement of the International Dairy Arrangement concluded under the GATT); ECJ, Case C-465/01 *Commission v Austria* [2004] E.C.R. I-8291 (infringement of the EEA Agreement and other association agreements with third countries); ECJ, Case C-239/03 *Commission v France* [2004] E.C.R. I-9325, paras 33–87 (infringement of the Convention for the protection of the Mediterranean Sea against pollution). For the failure to fulfil an obligation arising under the EEA Agreement to accede to an international convention, see ECJ, Case C-13/00 *Commission v Ireland* [2002] E.C.R. I-2943, paras 14–23.

[244] See CFI, Case T-115/94 *Opel Austria v Council* [1997] E.C.R. II-39, paras 122–123 (the regulation in question was annulled because it breached the EEA Agreement and that constituted an infringement of the legitimate expectations of the undertaking concerned, para. 26–006, *infra*).

[245] ECJ, Joined Cases 21–24/72 *International Fruit Company* [1972] E.C.R. 1219, para. 8. In this connection, see Tornay, "L'effet direct des traités internationaux dans l'ordre juridique de l'Union européenne" (2006) 2 R.D.U.E. 325–368; Vanhamme, "Inroepbaarheid van verdragen en volkenrechtelijke beginselen voor de Europese rechter: stand van zaken" (2001) S.E.W. 247–256; Manin, "A propos de l'accord instituant l'Organisation mondiale du commerce et de l'accord sur les marchés publics: la question de l'invocabilité des accords internationaux conclus par la Communauté européenne" (1997) R.T.D.E. 399, at 416–422; Cheyne, "International Agreements and the European Community Legal System" (1994) E.L.Rev. 581–598 (and the articles cited in para. 21–058, *supra*).

[246] ECJ, Case 12/86 *Demirel* [1987] E.C.R. 3719, para. 14.

[247] See ECJ, Joined Cases 21–24/72 *International Fruit Company* [1972] E.C.R. 1219, para. 20; ECJ, Case 87/75 *Bresciani* [1976] E.C.R. 129, para. 16.

[248] ECJ, Case 104/81 *Kupferberg* [1982] E.C.R. 3641, para. 17.

The Court has in many cases held the following to have direct effect: provisions of association agreements concluded by the Union,[249] free-trade agreements[250] and cooperation agreements.[251] A provision is not prevented from having direct effect on the ground that such effect is recognised unilaterally by the Union, but not by the other party to the agreement.[252] Neither is direct effect ruled out on the ground that the agreement provides for a special institutional framework for consultations and negotiations in relation to the implementation of the agreement or for safeguard clauses enabling the parties to derogate from certain provisions of the agreement in specific circumstances.[253]

In earlier case law, the Court considered that even if an agreement concluded by the Union contains provisions which do not have direct effect, in the sense that they do not create rights which individuals can rely on directly before courts, that fact does not preclude review by the courts of compliance of Union legislation with the obligations incumbent on the Union as a party to that agreement.[254] However, more recently the Court has ruled that it will review the validity of Union legislation in the light of an international agreement only where the nature

---

[249] See ECJ, Case 87/75 *Bresciani* [1976] E.C.R. 129, paras 16–25 (1963 Yaoundé Convention, Art. 2(1)); ECJ, Case 17/81 *Papst & Richarz* [1982] E.C.R. 1331, paras 25–27 (Association Agreement concluded with Greece, Art. 53(1)); ECJ, Case C-432/92 *Anastasiou and Others* [1994] E.C.R. I-3087, paras 23–27 (provisions of a Protocol to the Association Agreement concluded with Cyprus); ECJ, Case C-469/93 *Chiquita Italia* [1995] E.C.R. I-4533, paras 30–36 and 57 (Fourth ACP-EC Convention and Protocol No. 5 thereto); CFI, Case T-115/94 *Opel Austria v Council* [1997] E.C.R. II-39, para. 102 (EEA Agreement, Article 10); ECJ, Case C-63/99 *Gloszcuk and Gloszcuk* [2001] E.C.R. I-6369, paras 29–38, and ECJ, Case C-62/00 *Pokrzeptowicz-Meyer* [2002] E.C.R. I-1049, paras 20–30; ECJ, Case C-235/99 *Kondova* [2001] E.C.R. I-6427, paras 30–39; ECJ, Case C-257/99 *Barkoci and Malik* [2001] E.C.R. I-6557, paras 30–39; ECJ, Case C-438/00 *Kolpak* [2003] E.C.R. I-4135, paras 24–30 (articles on establishment in Europe Agreements with Poland, Bulgaria, the Czech Republic and Slovakia, respectively).

[250] See ECJ, Case 104/81 *Kupferberg* [1982] E.C.R. 3641, para. 26 (Agreement concluded with Portugal, Art. 21, first para.).

[251] See ECJ, Case C-18/90 *Kziber* [1991] E.C.R. I-199, paras 15–23 (Agreement concluded with Morocco, Art. 41(1); confirmed by ECJ, Case C-58/93 *Yousfi* [1994] E.C.R. I-1353, paras 16–19); and ECJ, Case C-126/95 *Hallouzi-Choho* [1996] E.C.R. I-4807, paras 19–20, and ECJ, Case C-416/96 *El-Yassini* [1999] E.C.R. I-1209, paras 25–32 (Agreement concluded with Morocco, Art. 40); ECJ, Case C-103/94 *Krid* [1995] E.C.R. I-719, paras 21–24 (Agreement concluded with Algeria, Art. 39(1); upheld in ECJ, Case C-113/97 *Babahenini* [1998] E.C.R. I-183, para. 17); ECJ, Case C-162/96 *Racke* [1998] E.C.R. I-3655, paras 30–36 (Agreement concluded with Yugoslavia, Art. 22(4)); ECJ, Case C-37/98 *Savas* [2000] E.C.R. I-2927, paras 46–55 (Additional Protocol of the Agreement concluded with Turkey, Art. 41(1)); ECJ, Case C-265/03 *Simutenkov* [2005] E.C.R. I-2579 (Agreement concluded with Russia, Art. 23(1); see the case note by Hillion (2008) C.M.L.Rev. 815–833.); ECJ, Case C-97/05 *Gattoussi* [2006] E.C.R. I-11917, paras 24–28 (Agreement concluded with Tunesia, Art. 64(1)).

[252] See ECJ, Case 104/81 *Hauptzollamt Mainz v Kupferberg* [1982] E.C.R. 3641, para. 18.

[253] *Ibid.*, paras 20–21; see also ECJ, Case C-192/89 *Sevince* [1990] E.C.R. I-3461, para. 25; ECJ, Case C-469/93 *Chiquita Italia* [1995] E.C.R. I-4533, para. 36; ECJ, Case C-265/03 *Simutenkov* [2005] E.C.R. I-2579, para. 24. For GATT and the WTO, see, however, para. 22–047, *infra*.

[254] ECJ, Case C-377/98 *Netherlands v European Parliament and Council* [2001] E.C.R. I-7079, para. 54.

and the broad logic of the agreement do not preclude this and, in addition, the provisions of the agreement appear, as regards their content, to be unconditional and sufficiently precise.[255] Consequently, an international agreement binding on the Union and the Member States can be invoked to review the validity of Union legislation only where its provisions have direct effect. The Court ruled out such effect with respect to the GATT/WTO Agreement (see para 22–047) and the United Nations Convention on the Law of the Sea.[256]

2. Legal force and direct effect of decisions adopted by organs set up by international agreements

22–046   **International organs.** The Court of Justice has further held that the legal force and possible direct effect of international agreements also apply to decisions adopted by institutions set up by the agreement which are responsible for implementing it. In Opinion 1/91 the Court noted that

> "international agreements concluded by means of the procedure set out in [Article 300] of the Treaty [*now Article 218 TFEU*] are binding on the institutions of the Community and its Member States and that, as the Court of Justice has consistently held, the provisions of such agreements and the measures adopted by institutions set up by such agreements become an integral part of the Community legal order when they enter into force".[257]

The Court thereby confirmed that such provisions and measures are directly applicable. The Court had in fact previously held that decisions adopted by an association council set up by an association agreement were directly applicable on the ground that they were "directly connected with the Association Agreement".[258] That consideration generally holds good for decisions of institutions set up by any agreement concluded by the Union, such as decisions of a joint committee established by a trade agreement.[259]

---

[255] ECJ, Case C-344/04 *IATA and ELFAA* [2006] E.C.R. I-403, para. 39; ECJ, Case C-308/06 *Intertanko* [2008] E.C.R. I-4057, para. 45; ECJ, Joined Cases C-120/06 P and C-121/06 P *FIAMM and Others v Council and Commission* [2008] E.C.R. I-6513, para. 110.

[256] ECJ, Case C-308/06 *Intertanko* [2008] E.C.R. I-4057, paras 54–65.

[257] ECJ, Opinion 1/91 *Draft agreement between the Community, on the one hand, and the countries of the European Free Trade Association, on the other, relating to the creation of the European Economic Area* [1991] E.C.R. I-6079, para. 37. This applies in principle for new EU Member States as from the date of accession; see the Council's answer of February 13, 1997 to question No. E-1794/96 (Balfe), [1997] O.J. C105/3.

[258] ECJ, Case 30/88 *Greece v Commission* [1989] E.C.R. 3711, para. 13, *in fine*; ECJ, Case C-192/89 *Sevince* [1990] E.C.R. I-3461, para. 9.

[259] Nevertheless, it is often the practice in the Union to transpose into Union law decisions taken by a joint committee set up by an agreement or by a cooperation or association council: see, for example, Art. 1 of Council Regulations (EEC) Nos 2229/91, 2230/91 and 2231/91 of June 17, 1991

Provisions of such decisions have direct effect if they satisfy the requirements which provisions of the agreement itself must meet in order to have direct effect.[260] In this way, the Court of Justice has held that a number of provisions of decisions of the Association Council set up by the EEC-Turkey Agreement have direct effect.[261]

An international agreement may further provide for its own system of courts, including a court with jurisdiction to settle disputes between the Contracting Parties to the agreement and, as a result, to interpret its provisions.[262] In such a case, the decisions of such a court will be binding on Union institutions, including the Court of Justice.[263]

---

on the application of Decisions Nos 1/91, 2/91 and 3/91, respectively, of the EEC-Israel Cooperation Council, [1991] O.J. L211: "Decision No 1/91 [2/91 or 3/91] of the EEC-Israel Cooperation Council shall apply in the Community". See Gilsdorf, "Les organes institués par des accords communautaires: effets juridiques de leurs décisions. Observations à propos notamment de l'arrêt de la Cour de justice des Communautés européennes dans l'affaire C-192/89" (1992) R.M.C.U.E. 328, at 331–334. For the EEA Agreement, see para. 25–029, *infra*.

[260] ECJ, Case C-192/89 *Sevince* [1990] E.C.R. I-3461, para. 14. For acts of bodies set up by multilateral agreements (under which the Union does not always have a right of veto), implementing measures are, however, generally still required: see Gilsdorf (n. 259, *supra*), at 336–337.

[261] *Ibid.*, paras 17–26; ECJ, Case C-237/91 *Kus* [1992] E.C.R. I-6781, paras 27–36; ECJ, Case C-355/93 *Eroglu* [1994] E.C.R. I-5113, paras 11 and 17; ECJ, Case C-171/01 *Wählergruppe Gemeinsam* [2003] E.C.R. I-4301, paras 54–67; ECJ, Case C-467/02 *Cetinkaya* [2004] E.C.R. I-10895, paras 30–31; ECJ, Case C-373/03 *Aydinli* [2005] E.C.R. I-6181, paras 24–25; ECJ, Case C-374/03 *Gürol* [2005] E.C.R. I-6199, paras 19–26; ECJ, Case C-325/05 *Derin* [2007] E.C.R. I-6495, paras 51–52. In the case of Decision No 3/80, direct effect was not accepted for those provisions requiring implementing measures: *cf.* ECJ, Case C-227/94 *Taflan-Met* [1996] E.C.R. I-4085, paras 23–38, and ECJ, Case C-262/96 *Sürül* [1999] E.C.R. I-2685, paras 48–74. Likewise, direct effect was not accepted for provisions of Decision No. 1/95 that require implementing measures or merely allow or encourage a Contracting Party to take action: ECJ, Case C-372/06 *Asda Stores* [2007] E.C.R. I-11223, paras 85–89.

[262] ECJ, Opinion 1/91 *Draft agreement between the Community, on the one hand, and the countries of the European Free Trade Association, on the other, relating to the creation of the European Economic Area* [1991] E.C.R. I-6079, paras 39–40.

[263] *Ibid.*, para. 39. In that Opinion, the Court held, however, that the system of court machinery provided for in the (first) draft agreement creating the European Economic Area was contrary to Art. 220 EC [*see now Art. 19 TEU*] and, more generally, to the foundations of the Community; ns to para. 25–029, *infra*. In interpreting a provision of Union law, the Court of Justice will take a lead from the construction put on it by the EFTA Court (where the provision also applies in the EFTA States by virtue of the EEA Agreement): see e.g., ECJ, Case C-13/95 *Süzen* [1997] E.C.R. I-1259, para. 10; ECJ, Joined Cases C-34–36/95 *De Agostini and TV Shop* [1997] E.C.R. I-3843, para. 37; ECJ, Case C-172/99 *Liikenne* [2001] E.C.R. I-745, para. 2; ECJ (judgment of April 1, 2004), Case C-286/02 *Bellio F.lli* [2004] E.C.R. I-3465, paras 34 and 57–60; CFI, Case T-115/94 *Opel Austria v Council* [1997] II-39, para. 108; CFI, Case T-13/99 *Pfizer Animal Health v Council* [2003] E.C.R. II-3305, paras 115 and 143, and CFI, Case T-70/99 *Alpharma v Council* [2003] E.C.R. II-3495, paras 136 and 156. For another example, see the dispute-settlement machinery of the World Trade Organisation: para. 25–014, *infra*.

3. Status of agreements concluded within the framework
of the GATT/WTO

22–047 **GATT and WTO.** The superior legal force of international agreements concluded by the Union causes them to fetter the freedom of action of the Union
institutions and the Member States. The situation is somewhat different as regards
the international rules which arise within the framework of the General
Agreement on Tariffs and Trade (GATT; see para. 25–011) and the World Trade
Organisation (WTO; see paras 25–012—25–015), which do not have the same
effect in the Union legal order.

As far as GATT rules are concerned, the Court has held that,

> "an obligation to recognise them as rules of international law which are
> directly applicable in the domestic legal systems of the Contracting Parties
> cannot be based on the spirit, general scheme or terms of GATT".[264]

The Court further stated that;

> "GATT, which according to its preamble is based on the principle of negoti-
> ations undertaken on the basis of 'reciprocal and mutually advantageous
> arrangements', is characterised by the great flexibility of its provisions, in
> particular those conferring the possibility of derogation, the measures to be
> taken when confronted with exceptional difficulties and settlement of con-
> flicts between the Contracting Parties".[265]

Because of these special features, the Court has never held any GATT rule to have
direct effect.[266] According to the Court, such direct effect is necessary, not only
in order to derive rights from the rules, but also to serve as a condition so as to
enable individuals to rely on them in order to contest the validity of Union acts
or the application of national provisions.[267] Commentators had assumed that
Member States and institutions could in fact invoke for that purpose GATT

[264] ECJ, Case C-280/93 *Germany v Commission* [1994] E.C.R. I-4973, para. 110.
[265] *Ibid.*, para. 106; for the first such *dictum*, see ECJ, Joined Cases 21–24/72 *International Fruit Company* [1972] E.C.R. 1219, para. 21.
[266] ECJ, Joined Cases 21–24/72 *International Fruit Company* [1972] E.C.R. 1219, paras 19–27; ECJ, Case 9/73 *Schlüter* [1973] E.C.R. 1135, paras 29–30; ECJ, Case 266/81 *SIOT* [1983] E.C.R. 731, para. 28; ECJ, Joined Cases 267–269/81 *SPI and SAMI* [1983] E.C.R. 801, para. 23; ECJ, Case C-469/93 *Chiquita Italia* [1995] E.C.R. I-4533, paras 26–29.
[267] See Rideau (n. 232, *supra*), at 356–362. *Cf.* regulations or directives without direct effect which may nevertheless be sufficiently clear to warrant at least a review of the compatibility of a national provision with their provisions (paras 22–074 and 22–090, *infra*, respectively). In a solitary case, the Court of Justice did dismiss a claim that a number of regulations were incompatible with pro-visions of GATT on substantive grounds without raising the question as to whether those provisions had direct effect: ECJ, Case 112/80 *Dürbeck* [1981] E.C.R. 1095, paras 45–46.

provisions without direct effect.[268] However, the Court of Justice made it clear that the special features of GATT also preclude the Court from taking account of GATT rules in assessing the legality of a regulation in annulment proceedings brought by a Member State under Art. 263 TFEU [*ex Art. 230 EC*].[269]

Likewise, the Court of Justice will not review the legality of Union acts in the light of agreements concluded under the auspices of the WTO.[270] Although the

---

[268] See Hahn and Schuster, "Zum Verstoss von gemeinschaftlichem Sekundärrecht gegen das GATT—Die gemeinsame Marktorganisation für Bananen vor dem EuGH" (1993) EuR. 261, at 280–281; Petersmann, "Application of GATT by the Court of Justice of the European Communities" (1983) C.M.L.Rev. 397, at 415–437.

[269] ECJ, Case C-280/93 *Germany v Commission* [1994] E.C.R. I-4973, para. 109, with a case note by Foubert (1995) Col.J.E.L. 312–319. For a critical view, see Petersmann, "Proposals for a New Constitution for the European Union: Building-Blocks for a Constitutional Theory and Constitutional Law of the EU" (1995) C.M.L.Rev. 1123, at 1164–1170; Everling (n. 623, *infra*), at 421–423; for a less critical view, see Dony, "L'affaire des bananes" (1995) C.D.E. 461, at 487–491. The Court of Justice does accept that the Commission may bring an action under Art. 258 TFEU [*ex Art. 226 EC*] against a Member State which infringes an agreement concluded in connection with GATT, see ECJ, Case C-61/94 *Commission v Germany* [1996] E.C.R. I-3989, para. 52, with a case note by Eeckhout (1998) C.M.L.Rev. 557–566.

[270] ECJ, Case C-149/96 *Portugal v Council* [1999] E.C.R. I-8395, paras 34–52; see also ECJ, Joined Cases C-300/98 and C-392/98 *Parfums Christian Dior and Others* [2000] E.C.R. I-11307, paras 41–44; ECJ (order of May 2, 2001), Case C-307/99 *OGT Fruchthandelsgesellschaft* [2001] E.C.R. I-3159, paras 24–28; ECJ, Case C-377/98 *Netherlands v European Parliament and Council* [2001] E.C.R. I-7079, para. 52; ECJ, Joined Cases C-27/00 and C-122/00 *Omega Air* [2002] E.C.R. I-2569, paras 89–97; CFI, Case T-2/99 *T. Port v Council* [2001] E.C.R. II-2093 and Case T-3/99 *Banana trading v Council* [2001] E.C.R. II-2123, paras 51 and 43, respectively. For a relatively approving view of the case law commencing with Case C-149/96 *Portugal v Council*: Kuijper and Bronckers, "WTO law in the European Court of Justice" (2005) C.M.L.Rev. 1313–1355; Mengozzi, "Les droits et les intérets des entreprises, le droit de l'OMC et les prérogatives de l'Union européenne: vers une doctrine communautaire des 'political questions' " (2005) R.D.U.E. 229–238; Pischel, "Trade, Treaties and Treason: Some Underlying Aspects of the Difficult Relationship Between the EU and the WTO" (2001) E.For.Aff.Rev. 103–133; von Bogdandy, "Rechtsgleichheit, Rechtssicherheit und Subsidiarität im transnationalen Wirtschaftsrecht" (2001) Eu.Z.W. 357–365; Berrod, "La Cour de justice refuse l'invocabilité des accords OMC: essai de régulation de la mondialisation" (2000) R.T.D.E. 419–450; Rosas, (2000) C.M.L.Rev. 797–816. For a critical view, see De Mey, "Recent developments on the invocability of WTO law in the EC: a wave of mutilation" (2006) E.For.Aff.Rev. 63–86; Ott, "Der EuGH and das WTO Recht: Die Entdeckung der politischen Gegenseitigkeit—altes Phänomen oder neuer Ansatz?" (2003) EuR. 504–521; Bronckers, "La jurisprudence des juridictions communautaires relatives à l'OMC demande réparation: plaidoyer pour les droits des Etats membres" (2001) C.D.E. 3–14; Royla, "WTO-Recht—EG-Recht: Kollision, Justiziabilität, Implementation" (2001) EuR. 495–521. In favour of a possibility of reviewing Union law in the light of WTO provisions, see, in particular, Beneyto, "The EU and the WTO. Direct Effect of the New Dispute Settlement System?" (1996) Eu.Z.W. 295–299; for a somewhat more cautious view, see Trachtman, "Bananas, Direct Effect and Compliance" (1999) E.J.I.L. 655–678; Eeckhout, "The Domestic Legal Status of the WTO Agreement: Interconnecting Legal Systems" (1997) C.M.L.Rev. 11–58; Kuijper, "The New WTO Dispute Settlement System: The Impact on the European Community" (1995) J.W.T. 49, at 62–64; Manin (n. 245, *supra*), at 399–428.

WTO Agreement replaced GATT with stringent dispute-settlement machinery, the Court of Justice has refused to recognise the WTO accords as rules binding on the Union institutions so as to allow the institutions every latitude to resolve disputes with trading partners within the framework of the WTO, possibly through negotiation.[271] For those reasons, it is also not possible to review Union acts in the light of rulings of the WTO Dispute Settlement Body (see para. 25–015) on the compatibility of Union acts concerned with WTO obligations.[272]

The Court of Justice considers itself under an obligation to review the legality of a contested Union act in the light of the GATT/WTO rules in two circumstances only.[273] First, it will conduct such a review where the Union intended to implement a particular obligation entered into within the framework of the GATT/WTO, which is the case, for example, with the anti-dumping regulation adopted in order to comply with the international obligations assumed by the Union as a result of Art. VI of GATT and the GATT Anti-Dumping Code adopted for the purpose of implementing that article.[274] Secondly, a Union act will be reviewed in the light of the GATT/WTO rules where it expressly refers to specific

---

[271] Case C-149/96 *Portugal v Council*, cited in the preceding n., paras 36–46.

[272] ECJ, Case C-104/97 P *Atlanta v Council and Commission* [1999] E.C.R. I-6983, para. 20; CFI, Case T-254/97 *Fruchthandelsgesellschaft Chemnitz v Commission* [1999] E.C.R. II-2743, paras 28–30; CFI, Case T-18/99 *Cordis Obst und Gemüse Großhandel v Commission* [2001] E.C.R. II-913, paras 44–60, CFI, Case T-30/99 *Bocchi Food Trade International v Commission* [2001] E.C.R. II-943, paras 49–65, and CFI, Case T-52/99 *T. Port* [2001] II-981, paras 44–60; CFI, Joined Cases T-64/01 and T-65/01 *Afrikanische Frucht-Compagnie and Internationale Fruchtimport Gesellschaft Weichert v Council and Commission* [2004] E.C.R. II-521, paras 139–142. See in this connection, Rosas, "Implementation and Enforcement of WTO Dispute Settlement Findings: An EU Perspective" (2001) J.I.E.L. 131–144; Zonnekeyn, "The Status of Adopted Panel and Appellate Body Reports in the European Court of Justice and the Court of First Instance" (2000) J.W.T. 93–108; Lavranos, "Die Rechtswirkung von WTO panel reports im Europäischen Gemeinschaftsrecht sowie im deutschen Verfassungsrecht" (1999) EuR. 289–308. Nevertheless, the Court of Justice has held that the Court of First Instance [*now the General Court*] should provide separate reasons as to why the legality of an act could not be reviewed in the light of a decision of the WTO Dispute Settlement Body; see ECJ, Case C-93/02 P *Biret International v Council* [2003] E.C.R. I-10497, paras 51–66, and ECJ, Case C-94/02 P *Etablissements Biret v Council* [2003] E.C.R. I-10565, paras 54–69 (making it clear that the legality of a Union act may not be affected in any event by such a decision before the expiry of the reasonable time which the Union has to comply with its WTO obligations). See Wiers in (2004) L.I.E.I. 143–151.

[273] ECJ, Case C-280/93 *Germany v Commission* [1994] E.C.R. I-4973, para. 111; ECJ, Case C-149/96 *Portugal v Council* [1999] E.C.R. I-8395, para. 49.

[274] ECJ, Case C-69/89 *Nakajima v Council* [1991] E.C.R. I-2069, paras 29–31; ECJ, Case C-76/00 P *Petrotub and Republica v Council* [2003] E.C.R. I-79, paras 52–63; CFI, Case T-162/94 *NMB France and Others v Commission* [1996] E.C.R. II-427, paras 99–107; CFI, Case T-19/01 *Chiquita* [2005] E.C.R. II-315, paras 156–171. See Desmedt, "L'accès des particuliers aux droits et obligations de l'OMC dans la CE" (2003) T.B.H. 357–372; Zonnekeyn, "The ECJ's *Petrotub* Judgment: Towards a Revival of the "*Nakajima* Doctrine"?" (2003) L.I.E.I. 249–266.

GATT/WTO provisions.[275] Accordingly, a measure adopted by the Union in order to comply with reports adopted under the WTO dispute settlement machinery cannot be reviewed in the light of those reports if the measure does not refer expressly to specific obligations ensuing from those reports.[276] The same applies with regard to the review of Union rules which are amended on the basis of Council Regulation (EC) No. 1515/2001,[277] which permits the Council to bring Union anti-dumping and anti-subsidy measures into line with a report drawn up by the Dispute Settlement Procedure by means of a simplified procedure (see para. 25–014). Such rules cannot be reviewed in the light of WTO rules if it is clear from the subsequent regulations that the Union did not in any way intend to give effect to a specific obligation assumed in the context of the WTO.[278]

The fact that WTO provisions lack direct effect does not preclude the Court of Justice from having jurisdiction to interpret such provisions for the purpose of responding to the needs of the judicial authorities of the Member States where they are called upon to apply their national rules which fall within the scope of those provisions.[279] It does not release national courts from their obligation to apply national rules as far as possible in the light of the wording and purpose of those provisions. In fields in which the Union has not yet legislated, Union law does not preclude the legal order of a Member State from according to individuals the right to rely directly on those provisions or from obliging the courts to apply those provisions of their own motion.[280]

4. Interpretation and reviewing the legality of international agreements

Judicial review. Where the Union acts externally by means of international agreements, that action itself is subject to judicial supervision. Before it is

22–048

---

[275] ECJ, Case 70/87 *Fediol v Commission* [1989] E.C.R. 1781, paras 18–22, at 1830 (GATT rules invoked as part of international law with a view to a finding whether conduct constituted an illicit trade practice within the meaning of Regulation No. 2641/84; for that regulation, see para. 25–008, *infra*).

[276] ECJ, Case C-377/02 *Léon Van Parys* [2005] E.C.R. I-1465, paras 41–54, see the case notes by Egli (2006) 100 A.J.I.L. 449–454 and Masson (2006) R.M.C.U.E. 189–194; ECJ, Joined Cases C-120/06 P and C-121/06 P *FIAMM and Others v Council and Commission* [2008] E.C.R. I-6513, paras 114–124. See Peers, "WTO dispute settlement and Community law" (2001) E.L.Rev. 605–610; Zonnekeyn, "The Latest on Indirect Effect of WTO Law in the EU Legal Order. The *Nakajima* case-law misjudged?" (2001) J.I.E.L. 597–608

[277] Council Regulation (EC) No. 1515/2001 of 23 July 2001 on the measures that may be taken by the Union following a report adopted by the WTO Dispute Settlement Body concerning anti-dumping and anti-subsidy matters, [2001] O.J. L201/10.

[278] ECJ, Case C-351/04 *Ikea Wholesale* [2007] E.C.R. I-7723, paras 29–35.

[279] E.g. ECJ, Case C-245/02 *Anheuser-Busch* [2004] E.C.R. I-10989, paras 40–46; ECJ, Case C-347/03 *Regione autonoma Friuli-Venezia Giulia* [2005] E.C.R. I-3785, paras 103–115.

[280] ECJ, Joined Cases C-300/98 and C-392/98 *Parfums Christian Dior and Others* [2000] E.C.R. I-11307, paras 45–49, ECJ, Case C-89/99 *Schieving-Nijstadt* [2001] E.C.R. I-5851, paras 54–73; ECJ, Case C-431/05 *Merck Genéricos* [2007] E.C.R. I-7001, paras 34–48. For the indirect force of WTO rules in the Union legal order, see Snyder, "The Gatekeepers: The European Courts and WTO law" (2003) C.M.L.Rev. 313–367.

concluded, the "agreement envisaged" may be referred to the Court of Justice for its opinion (Art. 218(11) TFEU [*ex Art. 300(6) EC*]); see paras 26–017—26–018). When the agreement enters into force, it becomes ipso facto part of the Union legal order.

As an "act of the institutions", the agreement comes within the jurisdiction of the Court to give preliminary rulings on its interpretation and validity under Art. 267 TFEU [*ex Art. 234 EC*].[281] With regard to mixed agreements concluded by the Union and its Member States on the basis of joint competence and without any allocation between them of their respective obligations towards the other contracting parties, the Court has jurisdiction to define the obligations which the Union has thereby assumed and, for that purpose, to interpret the provisions of the Agreement.[282] The Court even considers that it has jurisdiction to interpret provisions of mixed agreements, which, in accordance with the internal division of powers between the Union and the Member States, are to be implemented by the Member States in so far as the application of national provisions falling within the scope of Union law are concerned.[283] In any event, in the case of mixed agreements, the interpretative jurisdiction applies only as far as the Union is concerned.[284] As regards the interpretation of agreements concluded by the Union with third States, the Court has stressed that, where such an agreement contains provisions which are identical or comparable to provisions of the Treaties, the interpretation given to the Treaty provisions cannot be automatically applied by analogy to the interpretation of the agreement, unless there are express provisions to that effect laid down by the agreement itself.[285]

According to the Court of Justice, it is also possible to bring an action for annulment under Art. 263 TFEU against the act whereby the Union institutions

---

[281] For the first instance in the case law, see ECJ, Case 181/73 *Haegeman* [1974] E.C.R. 449, paras 4–6.

[282] ECJ, Case C-431/05 *Merck Genéricos* [2007] E.C.R. I-7001, paras 31–33.

[283] ECJ, Case 12/86 *Demirel* [1987] E.C.R. 3719, paras 8–12; ECJ, Case C-53/96 *Hermès International* [1998] E.C.R. I-3603, paras 22–29; ECJ, Joined Cases C-300/98 and C-392/98 *Parfums Christian Dior and Others* [2000] E.C.R. I-11307, paras 32–40; ECJ, Case C-245/02 *Anheuser-Busch* [2004] E.C.R. I-10989, para. 41. See Lenaerts, Arts and Maselis, *Procedural Law of the European Union* (3rd edn, London, Sweet & Maxwell, 2012), Ch. 6 (interpretation) and Ch. 10 (rulings on validity); Koutrakos, "The Interpretation of Mixed Agreements under the Preliminary Reference Procedure" (2002) E.For.Aff.Rev. 25–52; Neframi, "La compétence de la Cour de justice pour interpréter l'Accord TRIPS selon l'arrêt 'Parfums Christian Dior' " (2001) R.D.U.E. 491–519; Van Nuffel and Vanovermeire, "Over de bevoegdheid van het Hof van Justitie tot uitlegging van TRIPs en de directe werking van artikel 50 lid 6 TRIPs" (2001) T.B.H. 445–454; Heliskoski, "The Jurisdiction of the European Court of Justice to Give Preliminary Rulings on the Interpretation of Mixed Agreements" (2000) Nordic J.Int'l Law 395–412.

[284] See for the EEA Agreement, ECJ, Case C-321/97 *Andersson and Andersson* [1999] E.C.R. I-3551, paras 26–33; ECJ, Case C-140/97 *Rechberger and Greindl* [1999] E.C.R. I-3499, paras 37–38; ECJ, Case C-300/01 *Salzmann* [2003] E.C.R. I-4899, paras 65–71.

[285] See para. 1–019; for more recent applications: ECJ, Case C-351/08 *Grimme* [2009] E.C.R. I-10777, paras 27–29; ECJ (judgment of February 11, 2010), Case C-541–108 *Fokus Invest*, not yet reported, paras 28 and 34.

sought to conclude an agreement.[286] However, the annulment of such an act does not release the Union from its international obligations. In order to guarantee the rights of the contracting parties, the law of treaties confines the possibilities of annulment to cases in which the Union's consent was expressed in circumstances involving a manifest violation of a rule regarding competence which is of fundamental importance.[287] It is therefore advisable that the Union Court should invariably accompany the annulment of consent to an international agreement with a declaration that its legal effects remain unaffected.[288]

In order to secure uniform application of Union law, the Court of Justice likewise has jurisdiction to give preliminary rulings—subject to the same conditions—on the validity and interpretation of decisions of authorities established by agreements concluded by the Union.[289]

Since, in principle, the Court of Justice does not have jurisdiction with respect to action taken by the Union within the framework of the CFSP (see para. 13–086), international agreements concluded in that field are not subject to the jurisdiction of the Court.

B. INTERNATIONAL AGREEMENTS CONCLUDED BY MEMBER STATES WITH THIRD COUNTRIES

1. Agreements concluded after the Treaties entered into force

Member States' agreements. The Treaties do not preclude international competence on the part of the Member States in respect of matters which do not fall

22–049

---

[286] ECJ, Case C-327/91 *France v Commission* [1994] E.C.R. I-3641, paras 14–17; ECJ, Opinion 3/94 *Framework Agreement on Bananas* [1995] E.C.R. I-4577, para. 22; ECJ, Case C-360/93 *European Parliament v Council* [1996] E.C.R. I-1195; ECJ, Case C-122/95 *Germany v Council* [1998] E.C.R. I-973, para. 42; see also the earlier case ECJ, Opinion 1/75 *Draft Understanding on a Local Cost Standard drawn up under the auspices of the OECD* [1975] E.C.R. 1355, at 1361. For criticism, see Leray and Potteau, "Réflexions sur la cohérence du système de contrôle de la légalité des accords internationaux conclus par la Communauté européenne" (1998) R.T.D.E. 535–571; Kaddous, "L'arrêt *France* c. *Commission* de 1994 (accord concurrence) et le contrôle de la 'légalité' des accords externes en vertu de l'art. 173 CE: la difficile réconciliation de l'orthodoxie communautaire avec l'orthodoxie internationale" (1996) C.D.E. 613–633.

[287] See Art. 46(2) of the Vienna Convention of March 21, 1986 on the Law of Treaties between States and International Organisations or between International Organisations (n. 331, *infra*).

[288] Vanhamme (n. 230, *supra*), at 311–315, and Kapteyn, "Quelques réflexions sur le contrôle de la constitutionnalité des accords conclus par la Communauté avec des pays tiers" in Rodriguez Iglesias, Due, Schintgen and Elsen (eds), *Mélanges en hommage à Fernand Schockweiler* (Baden-Baden, Nomos, 1999), 275–285, who refer in this connection to the possibilities afforded by Art. 231 EC [*now Art. 264 TFEU*].

[289] ECJ, Case C-192/89 *Sevince* [1990] E.C.R. I-3461, paras 10–11 (decision of an association council; see also the judgments cited in n. 261, *supra*); ECJ, Case C-188/91 *Deutsche Shell* [1993] E.C.R. I-363, paras 17–18 (decision of a joint committee). As regards reviewing the validity of such decisions, see Lenaerts, Arts and Maselis, *Procedural Law of the European Union* (3rd edn, London, Sweet & Maxwell, 2012), Ch. 10.

within the exclusive competence of the Union. In respect of matters for which the Union has exclusive competence, a Member State can no longer conclude agreements with third States unless it has a special authorisation (see with regard to the common commercial policy, para. 25–006).

Agreements which Member States conclude with third countries or international organisations are not binding on the Union.[290] The Court of Justice has no jurisdiction to give rulings on the interpretation of provisions of international law which are binding on Member States outside the framework of Union law[291] and has no power to determine whether a national provision is compatible with such an agreement.[292] Agreements concluded by Member States are binding on the Union, however, where the Treaties refer to them or where, under the Treaties, the Union has taken over the powers formerly vested in the Member States with regard to the application of such agreements (see para. 22–043). In order to ensure that Union law is uniformly applied, the Court may interpret provisions of such agreements with effect from the time at which the Union was substituted for the Member States.[293] Where an agreement is binding upon all the Member States, but not upon the Union, the Court will still endeavour to interpret Union legislation "taking into account" the international agreement.[294]

The duty of sincere cooperation places a Member State under a duty to exercise its international powers without detracting from Union law[295] or from its effectiveness (*effet utile*) (see para. 7–048). Accordingly, a Member State must implement its international obligations with third countries—or with other Member States—in such a way as to take account of the obligation to treat its own nationals and nationals of other Member States in the same way.[296]

---

[290] For a discussion of agreements concluded as between Member States, see para. 23–014 *et seq., infra.*

[291] ECJ, Case 130/73 *Vandeweghe* [1973] E.C.R. 1329, para. 2.

[292] ECJ, Case C-379/92 *Peralta* [1994] E.C.R. I-3453, paras 16–17.

[293] ECJ, Joined Cases 267–269/81 *SPI and SAMI* [1983] E.C.R. 801, paras 14–19. See also ECJ, Case C-439/01 *Cipra and Kvasnicka* [2003] E.C.R. I-745, paras 23–24 (interpretation given of the AETR agreement as it was concluded by the Member States in the interest and on behalf of the Community).

[294] ECJ, Case C-308/06 *Intertanko* [2008] E.C.R. I-4057, para. 52 (on the basis of "the customary principle of good faith, which forms part of general international law, and of Article 10 EC [now Article 4(3) TEU]").

[295] See, e.g., ECJ, Joined Cases C-176/97 and C-177/97 *Commission v Belgium and Luxembourg* [1998] E.C.R. I-3557 (agreement held to be contrary to a Community regulation); ECJ (judgment of April 20, 2010), Case C-246/07 *Commission v Sweden*, not yet reported (proposed amendment to an agreement held contrary to the principle of cooperation in good faith).

[296] ECJ, Case C-307/97 *Saint Gobain ZN* [1999] E.C.R. I-6161, paras 57–58; ECJ, Case C-55/00 *Gottardo* [2002] E.C.R. I-413, paras 33–34; ECJ (judgment of January 21, 2010), Case C-546/07 *Commission v Germany*, not yet reported, paras 40–42. This obligation does not apply where such equal treatment would call in question the balance and reciprocity of the relevant international agreement: *Saint Gobain ZN*, para. 59, and *Gottardo*, para. 36; ECJ, Case C-376/03 *D* [2005] E.C.R. I-5821, paras 58–63. See De Pauw, "Zijn bilaterale socialezekerheidsverdragen tussen EU-lidstaten en derde landen auomatisch van toepassing op alle EU-onderdanen?" (2002) J.T.T. 257–261.

2. Agreements concluded before the Treaties entered into force

Pre-existing international obligations. In establishing the Communities, the   **22–050**
Member States sought to create reciprocal rights and obligations without detracting from their existing international obligations. For this reason, they assumed
that agreements which they had concluded with third countries before the
Community Treaties entered into force in principle were not set aside by provisions of the Treaties. Article 307 EC [*now Art. 351 TFEU*] and Arts 105–106
EAEC which were adopted to this end still apply to agreements concluded at an
earlier date by which Member States continue to be bound and to agreements
which new Member States entered into before accession.[297] Of course, this
does not mean that all the advantages which the Treaties confer on the Member
States, notably the introduction of a customs union, may be extended to third
States as a result of the application of agreements concluded prior to accession
(see Art. 351, third para., TFEU). Article 350 TFEU [*ex Art. 306 EC*] allows for
preference to be given to agreements connected with the Benelux Economic
Union.[298]

Precedence of international obligations. The first para. of Art. 351 TFEU   **22–051**
[*ex Art. 307 EC*] allows for preference to be given to,

> "[t]he rights and obligations arising from agreements concluded before 1
> January 1958[299] or, for acceding States, before the date of their accession,
> between one or more Member States on the one hand, and one or more third
> countries on the other"

by providing that they "shall not be affected by the provisions of the Treaties".
This means that national courts may ensure that third countries' rights under earlier agreements are honoured and that the correlative obligations of Member States
are fulfilled.[300] Article 351 TFEU allows for derogations from any rule of Union
law, including primary law, with the exception of principles that form part of the

---

[297] See most recently Art. 6(12) of the 2003 Act of Accession and of the 2005 Act of Accession.

[298] Article 350 TFEU is designed to prevent the application of Union law from causing the disintegration of the Benelux Union or from hindering its development. Consequently, Benelux rules may
be applied in derogation from Union rules only in so far as the Benelux Union is further advanced
than the internal market. Compare ECJ, Case 105/83 *Pakvries* [1984] E.C.R. 2101, para. 11
(priority given to Benelux customs arrangements) with ECJ, Case C-473/93 *Commission v
Luxembourg* [1996] E.C.R. I-3207, paras 42–43 (priority given to Community law as it was held
to "go further" than the relevant provision of the Benelux Treaty).

[299] This is the date of entry into force of the original EEC Treaty, which subsequently became the EC
Treaty (see para. 1–013, *supra*).

[300] ECJ, Case 10/61 *Commission v Italy* [1962] E.C.R. 1, para. 10.

very foundations of the Union legal order.[301] Article 351 TFEU does not apply to a legal relationship with a third country which was not a party to the international agreement in question before the EC Treaty entered into force[302] or the relevant date of accession. In any event, the international obligations in question must be obligations whose performance may still be required by the third country.[303]

Consequently, in the event of a conflict between any provision of Union law and an international obligation originating in a prior agreement concluded between a Member State and a third country, Art. 351 TFEU allows for the Member State to ensure that the international obligation is complied with. By the same token, a provision of national law which is necessary in order to ensure the performance by the Member State concerned of such an international obligation may be applied even though it conflicts with a provision of Union law.[304] Where a treaty permits a Member State to take a measure which appears to conflict with Union law, yet does not put it under an obligation to do so, the Member State should refrain from such action.[305] The national court has to determine the extent to which the international obligations of the Member State are compatible with Union law.[306] As far as possible, it must interpret those obligations in a manner compatible with Union law.[307]

The application of Art. 351 TFEU is subject, however, to two important limitations. First, a Member State is not entitled to rely on that article in order to derive rights vis-à-vis other Member States, contrary to Union law, from agreements concluded before the EC Treaty entered into force or before the date of accession.[308] In principle, this also holds good for multilateral agreements to which third countries—as well as Member States—are parties.[309] If, however, the multilateral agreement itself does not leave any room for the application of derogating provi-

---

[301] ECJ, Joined Cases C-402/05 P and C-415/05 P *Kadi and Al Barakaat International Foundation* [2008] E.C.R. I-6351, paras 301–304 (which mentions in this connection the protection of fundamental rights, including the review by the Union judicature of the lawfulness of Union measures in the light of such rights).

[302] ECJ, Joined Cases C-364/95 and C-365/95 *T Port* [1998] E.C.R. I-1023, paras 59–65.

[303] See, e.g., in the case of a division of a third country: ECJ, Case C-216/01 *Budějovický Budvar* [2003] E.C.R. I-13617, paras 146–167.

[304] ECJ, Case C-158/91 *Levy* [1993] E.C.R. I-4287, para. 22.

[305] ECJ, Case C-324/93 *Evans Medical* [1995] E.C.R. I-563, para. 32; ECJ, Case C-124/95 *Centro-Com* [1997] E.C.R. I-81, paras 54–60.

[306] ECJ, Case C-158/99 *Levy* [1993] E.C.R. I-4287, para. 21.

[307] De Smijter and Vanhamme, "Een analyse van het arrest *Levy* en zijn implicaties voor de interpretatie van artikel 234 EG-Verdrag" (1993-1994) R.W. 1387, at 1390.

[308] See, e.g., ECJ, Case C-475/93 *Thévenon* [1995] E.C.R. I-3813 (Regulation No. 1408/71 held to replace a convention between France and Germany); ECJ, Case C-478/07 *Budějovický Budvar*, [2009] E.C.R. I-7721, para. 99 (bilateral agreements between the Czech Republic and Austria).

[309] ECJ, Case 10/61 *Commission v Italy* [1962] E.C.R. 1, at 10 (concerning GATT); ECJ, Case 812/79 *Burgoa* [1980] E.C.R. 2787, para. 11; ECJ, Case 121/85 *Conegate v HM Customs and Excise* [1986] E.C.R. 1007, para. 25; ECJ, Case 286/86 *Deserbais* [1988] 4907, paras 17–18; ECJ, Case C-473/93 *Commission v Luxembourg* [1996] E.C.R. I-3207, paras 39-40; ECJ, Case C-301/08 *Bogiatzi* (n. 234, *supra*), para. 19 (Warsaw Convention).

sions as between any States party to it, it may be that application of Union law as between Member States will "jeopardise non-member countries' rights"[310] under the agreement.[311] In such a case, the first para. of Art. 351 TFEU may perhaps result in the multilateral agreement being given precedence.[312] Second, Art. 351 TFEU does not alter the type of rights which arise out of agreements concluded by Member States.[313] This means that an individual cannot rely on that article in order to invoke a provision of an agreement which does not have direct effect.[314] In that sense, Art. 351 TFEU does not have the effect of conferring on individuals who rely on a prior agreement rights which the national or the Union courts must protect.[315]

Obligation to eliminate incompatibilities. To the extent that agreements concluded prior to the entry into force of the EC Treaty or the date of accession are not compatible with the Treaties, the second para. of Art. 351 TFEU requires the Member State(s) concerned to take all appropriate steps to eliminate the incompatibility. Such "incompatibility" exists not only where a prior agreement conflicts with an existing provision of Union law, but also where the agreement may impede the Union institutions from effectively exercising competences such as the power to adopt restrictive measures with respect to third countries.[316] The Member States are to take "all appropriate steps to eliminate the incompatibilities established" and, where necessary, to "assist each other to this end" or to "adopt a common attitude". Accordingly, the Member State(s) in question must start negotiations with a view to adapting the prior agreement. If such negotiations are unsuccessful, the Member State(s) will have, if possible,[317] to denunciate the agreement.[318] Where several Member States are confronted with the same incom-

22–052

---

[310] The expression was used by Advocate-General J. Mischo in his Opinion in ECJ, Case C-221/89 *Factortame and Others* ("*Factortame II*") [1991] E.C.R. I-3905, point 15.

[311] In his Opinion in *Factortame II*, cited in the preceding n., the Advocate-General considered whether this was the case, but expressly dismissed this possibility: *ibid.*, point 16, last para. See also ECJ, Case C-158/91 *Levy* [1993] E.C.R. I-4287, paras 13–22.

[312] For a discussion of this eventuality, see Lenaerts and De Smijter, "Some Reflections on the Status of International Agreements in the Community Legal Order", in *Mélanges en hommage à Fernand Schockweiler* (n. 288, *supra*), 347, at 363.

[313] ECJ, Case 812/79 *Burgoa* [1980] E.C.R. 2787, para. 10.

[314] ECJ (order of May 2, 2001), Case C-307/99 *OGT Fruchthandelsgesellschaft* [2001] E.C.R. I-3159, paras 29–30.

[315] *Ibid.*; CFI, Case T-2/99 *T Port* [2001] II-2093, para. 83, and Case T-3/99 *Bananatrading* [2001] E.C.R. II-2123, para. 78.

[316] ECJ, Case C-205/06 *Commission v Austria* [2009] E.C.R. I-1301, paras 35–40; ECJ, Case C-249/06 *Commission v Sweden* [2009] E.C.R. I-1335, paras 36–41; ECJ, Case C-118/07 *Commission v Finland* [2009] E.C.R. I-10889, paras 29–32.

[317] ECJ, Case C-203/03 *Commission v Austria* [2005] E.C.R. I-935, paras 61–64.

[318] ECJ, Case C-62/98 *Commission v Portugal* [2000] E.C.R. I-5171, paras 49–50, and C-84/98 *Commission v Portugal* [2000] E.C.R. I-5215, paras 58–59. See Klabbers, "Moribund on the Fourth of July? The Court of Justice on prior agreements of the Member States" (2001) E.L.Rev. 187–197; Manzini, "The Priority of Pre-Existing Treaties of EC Member States within the Framework of International Law" (2001) E.J.I.L. 781–792.

patibility, it is for the Commission to take any steps which may facilitate mutual assistance between the Member States concerned and their adoption of a common attitude.[319] A Member State which fails to take all necessary steps to eliminate incompatibilities will be in breach of its obligations under Union law. Despite this, the application of the prior agreement will continue to be assured under the first para. of Art. 351 TFEU since that provision is primarily designed to protect the rights of third countries.[320]

22–053 **Impact on Union institutions.** After the entry into force of the Community Treaties, agreements concluded by Member States did not become binding on the Community (or, later, the Union) save where the Treaties referred thereto or, exceptionally, where the Communities (or, later, the Union) substituted themselves for the Member States (see para. 22–049). The first para. of Art. 351 TFEU refers only to obligations of Member States. Nevertheless,

> "it would not achieve its purpose if it did not imply a duty on the part of the institutions of the [Union] not to impede the performance of the obligations of Member States which stem from a prior agreement. However, that duty of the [Union] institutions is directed only to permitting the Member State concerned to perform its obligations under the prior agreement and does not bind the [Union] as regards the third country in question".[321]

Consequently, although an institution cannot compel a Member State to back out of its obligations under a prior agreement, Art. 351 TFEU does not debar the Union from taking action at variance with those obligations.[322]

C. OTHER RULES OF INTERNATIONAL LAW

22–054 **International law.** It is clear from the provisions of Art. 351 TFEU [*ex Art. 307 EC*] itself that it is the Union's intention to fit in with international law. The Court of Justice has declared that the Union must respect international law in the exercise of its powers[323] and will therefore examine whether the validity of acts of the Union institutions is affected by reason of the fact that they are contrary to "a rule of

---

[319] ECJ, Case C-205/06 *Commission v Austria* [2009] E.C.R. I-1301, para. 44; ECJ, Case C-249/06 *Commission v Sweden* [2009] E.C.R. I-1335, para. 44; ECJ, Case C-118/07 *Commission v Finland* [2009] E.C.R. I-10889, para. 35.

[320] ECJ, Case C-216/01 *Budějovický Budvar* [2003] E.C.R. I-13617, para. 172.

[321] ECJ, Case 812/79 *Burgoa* [1980] E.C.R. 2787, para. 9.

[322] Petersmann, "Artikel 234", in von der Groeben, Thiesing and Ehlermann (eds), *Kommentar zum EWG-Vertrag* (Baden-Baden, Nomos, 1991), 5738; for a case study, see Grimes, "Conflicts between EC Law and International Treaty Obligations: A Case Study of the German Telecommunications Dispute" (1994) Harv.I.L.J. 535, at 548–549.

[323] ECJ, Case C-286/90 *Poulsen and Diva Navigation* [1992] E.C.R. I-6019, para. 9; ECJ (judgment of February 25, 2010), Case C-386/08 *Brita*, not yet reported, paras 39–41.

international law".[324] The powers of the Union must also be exercised in observance of the undertakings given in the context of the United Nations and other international organisations.[325] Since the Lisbon Treaty, the Treaties expressly mention "respect for the principles of the United Nations Charter and international law" among the objectives of the Union's external action (Art. 21(1), first para., TEU).

1. Customary international law and general principles of law

Principles of international law. Not only provisions of international agreements binding on the Union act as sources of Union law. Mention has already been made of the general principles of law, among which the Court of Justice includes fundamental rights, inter alia, as enshrined in treaties on human rights concluded by the Member States (see para. 22–019). In interpreting and applying Union law, the Court of Justice also takes customary international law into account[326] and principles of international law, such as the fact that a State is precluded from refusing its own nationals the right of entry to its territory,[327] the principle that no one is arbitrarily to be deprived of his or her nationality[328] and the territoriality principle as limiting the extent of the Union's powers.[329] In considering the scope of obligations arising under international agreements, the Court of Justice complies with the rules of customary international law, a notable example being the rules of the "law of treaties" codified in the 1969 Vienna Convention on the law of Treaties[330] and the 1986 Vienna Convention on the Law of Treaties between States and

22–055

---

[324] ECJ, Joined Cases 21–24/72 *International Fruit Company* [1972] E.C.R. 1219, para. 6 (quoted in para. 22–044, *supra*). For a survey, see Meessen, "The Application of Rules of Public International Law within Community Law" (1976) C.M.L.Rev. 485–501 and, more recently, Vanhamme (n. 230, *supra*), at 255–330.

[325] ECJ, Joined Cases C-402/05 P and C-415/05 P *Kadi and Al Barakaat International Foundation* [2008] E.C.R. I-6351, paras 291–297.

[326] ECJ, Case C-286/90 *Poulsen and Diva Navigation* [1992] E.C.R. I-6019, paras 10, 13–16 and 25–29 (customary law in the context of the law of the sea). See also, by implication, ECJ, Case C-221/89 *Factortame and Others* ("*Factortame II*") [1991] E.C.R. I-3905, paras 15–16.

[327] ECJ, Case 41/74 *Van Duyn* [1974] E.C.R. 1337, para. 22.

[328] ECJ (judgment of March 2, 2010), Case C-135/08 *Rottmann*, not yet reported, para. 53 (principle confirmed in the Universal Declaration of Human Rights and the European Convention on nationality).

[329] ECJ, Joined Cases 89, 104, 114, 116–117 and 125–129/85 *Åhlström v Commission* [1988] E.C.R. 5193, para. 18; CFI, Case T-102/96 *Gencor v Commission* [1999] E.C.R. II-753, paras 89–108. For more on the territorial scope of the Treaties, see paras 12–006 *et seq., supra*.

[330] Vienna Convention of May 23, 1969 on the law of treaties (in force since January 27, 1980). Although this convention has not been ratified by all Member States (the United Kingdom has ratified it; for the text, see UNTS No. 58 (1980) Vol. III; Misc. 1971; Cmnd. 4818), it is deemed to be a codification of customary international law. See Kuijper, "The Court and the Tribunal of the EC and the Vienna Convention on the Law of Treaties 1969" (1998) L.I.E.I. 1–23. For an application, see ECJ, Opinion 1/91 *Draft agreement between the Community, on the one hand, and the countries of the European Free Trade Association, on the other, relating to the creation of the European Economic Area* [1991] E.C.R. I-6079, para. 14; ECJ, Case C-432/92 *Anastasiou and*

International Organisations or between International Organisations.[331] Thus, Union law applies the international-law principle of good faith, which debars a contracting party from taking any measure incompatible with an international agreement after it has been ratified but before it has entered into force,[332] the rules concerning the suspension and termination of an agreement on the ground of a fundamental change of circumstances (*rebus sic stantibus* clause)[333] and the principle of the relative effect of treaties, according to which treaties do not impose any obligations, or confer any rights, on third States (*pacta tertiis nec nocent nec prosunt*).[334] In connection with a question of the succession of States (following the break-up of Czechoslovakia), the Court of Justice referred to the international practice based on the continuity of treaties.[335] The Court sometimes finds it useful in interpreting provisions of Union law to refer to agreements concluded by the Member States[336] and decisions of international organisations,[337] although it does

---

Others [1994] E.C.R. I-3087, paras 43 and 50; ECJ, Case C-466/98 *Commission v United Kingdom* [2002] E.C.R. I-9427, para. 24; and ECJ, Case C-268/94 *Portugal v Council* [1996] E.C.R. I-6177, paras 19 and 27, where it was referred to as "international law"; for the application of such a rule before codification, see ECJ, Case 10/61 *Commission v Italy* [1962] E.C.R. 1, at 10.

[331] Vienna Convention of March 21, 1986 on the Law of Treaties between States and International Organisations or between International Organisations. This Convention also largely codifies customary international law. See Manin, "The European Communities and the Vienna Convention on the Law of Treaties between States and International Organisations or between International Organisations" (1987) C.M.L.Rev. 457–481.

[332] Vienna Convention 1969, Art. 18(a) as applied in CFI, Case T-115/94 *Opel Austria v Council* [1997] E.C.R. II-39, paras 90–123 (with regard to an agreement concluded by the Community, see para. 26–006, *infra*); see also ECJ, Case C-27/96 *Danisco Sugar* [1997] E.C.R. I-6653, paras 20 and 31; ECJ, Case C-308/06 *Intertanko* [2008] E.C.R. I-4057, para. 52; ECJ, Case C-203/07 P *Greece v Commission* [2008] E.C.R. I-8161, para. 64.

[333] Vienna Convention 1969, Art. 62, applied in ECJ, Case C-162/96 *Racke* [1998] E.C.R. I-3655, paras 37–60 (applied by the Council in suspending and denouncing the Cooperation Agreement with Yugoslavia). The Court of Justice conducts its review in the light only of provisions which may be regarded as a codification of existing customary law: *ibid.*, paras 24 and 59; see the case notes by Klabbers (1999) C.M.L.Rev. 179–189 and Berramdane (2000) C.D.E. 253–279.

[334] Vienna Convention 1969, Art. 34, applied in ECJ, Case C-386/08 *Brita* (n. 323, *supra*), paras 40–53 (with regard to the EC-Israel Association Agreement and its non-application to products originating in the West Bank, which are covered by the EC-PLO Association Agreement).

[335] ECJ, Case C-216/01 *Budějovický Budvar* [2003] E.C.R. I-13617, paras 150–166.

[336] See ECJ, Case 92/71 *Interfood* [1972] E.C.R. 231, para. 6 (agreements concluded at the 1960 and 1961 Tariff Conferences). In particular, this applies to the international agreements which constituted the inspiration for the common customs tariff; see, e.g., ECJ, Case 38/77 *Enka* [1977] E.C.R. 2203, paras 24–29 (Convention of December 15, 1950 on the Valuation of Goods for Customs Purposes). See also ECJ, Case 24/86 *Blaizot* [1988] E.C.R. 379, para. 17 (1961 European Social Charter).

[337] For provisions of the FAO and the World Health Organisation, see ECJ, Case 92/74 *Van den Berg* [1975] E.C.R. 599, paras 2–9; ECJ, Case 178/84 *Commission v Germany* [1987] E.C.R. 1227, paras 44 and 52; for explanatory notes and classification opinions of the International Customs Cooperation Council, see ECJ, Case 14/70 *Bakels v Oberfinanzdirektion München* [1970] E.C.R. 1001, paras 6–11; for recommendations of the International Commission on Radiological Protection, see ECJ, Case C-376/90 *Commission v Belgium* [1992] E.C.R. I-6153, paras 21–26.

not treat them as binding. This is obviously not possible where an agreement conflicts with a higher principle of Union law.[338]

2. Obligations in connection with the United Nations

United Nations. All the Member States of the Union are members of the United
Nations (UN). The United Nations Charter[339] provides that membership is open
only to "States", which precludes the Union from joining.[340] As members of the
UN, all the Member States are represented in the General Assembly. In the
Security Council, France and the United Kingdom have permanent membership
and the right of veto (UN Charter, Art. 27(1) and (3)); other Member States may
sit thereon as one of the ten non-permanent members. The Union may accede to
an agreement concluded under the auspices of the UN where that agreement so
permits.[341] Where Member States have to give effect to obligations arising for
them under the UN Charter (e.g., resolutions of the Security Council adopted
under Chapter VII of the UN Charter), they cannot avoid those obligations by
claiming that certain powers have been transferred to the Union.[342] As far as such
cases are concerned, the Treaties not only provides that in principle pre-existing
international obligations take precedence (Art. 351, first para., TFEU; see para.
22–051), but it also allows the Member States, after prior consultation, to waive
Union obligations so as to enable a Member State to carry out "obligations it has
accepted for the purpose of maintaining peace and international security" (Art.
347 TFEU [*ex Art. 297 EC*]; see para. 12–011).

22–056

---

[338] CFI, Case T-192/96 *Lebedef v Commission* [1998] E.C.R.-SC II-1047, para. 77 (English abstract
at IA-363) (ILO Convention).

[339] United Nations Charter, signed at San Francisco on June 26, 1945 (*TS* 67 (1946); Cmd 7015;
United Nations Act 1946).

[340] UN Charter, Arts 3 and 4.

[341] E.g. the Agreement of the United Nations Economic Commission for Europe concerning the adoption of uniform technical prescriptions for wheeled vehicles, equipment and parts which can be
fitted to and/or be used on wheeled vehicles and the conditions for reciprocal recognition of
approvals granted on the basis of these prescriptions, approved by Council Decision of November
27, 1997, [1997] O.J. L346/78.

[342] See Art. 103 of the UN Charter, which provides that States' obligations under the Charter are to
prevail over their obligations under any other international agreement, and Art. 48(2) of the
Charter, which provides that Members of the UN are to carry out decisions for the maintenance of
international peace and security "directly and through their action in the appropriate international
agencies of which they are members". As far as UN obligations are concerned, the Union cannot
be regarded as having been substituted for the Member States; unlike in the case of GATT (para.
22–043, *supra*), all competence in that connection has not been transferred to the Union and the
Union does not act as an equal partner within the organisation. See Stein, "European Political
Cooperation (EPC) as a Component of the European Foreign Affairs System" (1983) Z.a.ö.RV. 49,
at 66; Petersmann, "Internationale Wirtschaftssanktionen als Problem des Völkerrechts und des
Europarechts" (1981) Z.Vgl.RW. 1, at 26.

22–057 **Legal status of UN obligations.** Since all EU Member States are bound by the obligations arising under the UN Charter, the question may be asked as to whether the Union itself is so bound.[343] The Union Courts had to deal with that issue in the *Kadi* case, where an individual challenged the lawfulness in the light of fundamental rights of the EU regulations ordering the freezing of his funds so as to give effect to a resolution adopted by the UN Security Council under Ch. VII of the UN Charter. The Court of First Instance held that both international law and Union law required the Union institutions to implement the Security Council resolution, without there being any possibility of judicial review of the lawfulness of such implementing measure in the light of fundamental rights.[344] The Court of Justice set aside this judgment as it considered that the Union courts have to review the lawfulness of all Union acts in the light of fundamental rights, even acts that are designed to give effect to a Security Council resolution adopted under Ch. VII of the UN Charter.[345] Whereas the Court did not accept the primacy of the UN Charter over provisions of primary Union law and fundamental

---

[343] According to Art. 2(6) of the UN Charter, "[t]he Organisation shall ensure that States which are not Members of the United Nations act in accordance with [the principles set out in that article] so far as may be necessary for the maintenance of international peace and security".

[344] CFI, Case T-315/01 *Kadi v Council and Commission* [2005] E.C.R. II-33649, paras 181–225, see also CFI, Case T-301/01 *Yusuf and Al Barakaat International Foundation v Council and Commission* [2005] E.C.R. II-3533, with a case note by Tomuschat in (2006) C.M.L.Rev. 537–551. According to the CFI, it was empowered only to check, indirectly, the lawfulness of the resolutions of the Security Council in question with regard to *jus cogens*: *ibid.*, paras 226–291 (the CFI found that there had been no breach of principles of *jus cogens*). For a discussion, see Bianchi, "Assessing the effectiveness of the UN Security Council's Anti-terrorism Measures: the quest for legitimacy and cohesion" (2007) 17 E.J.I.L. 881–919; Klabbers, "Kadi Justice at the Security Council" (2007) I.O.L.R. 293–304; Brown, "Kadi v Council of the European Union and Commission of the European Communities: Executive Power and Judicial Supervision at European Level" (2006) E.H.R.L.R. 456–469; Bore Eveno, "Le controle juridictionnel des resolutions du conseil de sécurité: Vers un constitutionnalisme international?" (2006) 110 R.G.D.I.P. 827–860; Karayigit, "The Yusuf and Kadi Judgments: the scope of the EC Competences in respect of restrictive measures" (2006) 33 L.I.E.I. 379–404; Ohler, "Die Verhängung von "smart sanctions" durch den UN-Sicherheitsrat—eine Herausforderung für das Gemeinschaftsrecht" (2006) 41 EuR. 848–865; Van Ooik and Wessel, "De Yusuf en Kadi-uitspraken in perspectief. Nieuwe verhoudingen in de interne en externe bevoegdheden van de Europese Unie" (2006) S.E.W. 230–241; Vlcek, "Acts to Combat the Financing of Terrorism: Common Foreign and Security Policy at the European Court of Justice" (2006) E.For.Aff.Rev. 491–507.

[345] ECJ, Joined Cases C-402/05 P and C-415/05 P *Kadi and Al Barakaat International Foundation* [2008] E.C.R. I-6351, paras 280–327. For a discussion, see De Burca, "The EU, the European Court of Justice and the International Legal Order after Kadi" (2009) Harv.I.L.J. 1–49; Halberstam and Stein, "The United Nations, the European Union, and the King of Sweden: Economic Sanctions and Individual Rights in a Plural World Order" (2009) C.M.L.Rev. 13–72; Janssens, "Het Kadi-arrest van het Hof van Justitie inzake terrorismelijsten" (2009) R.W. 1410; Thouvenin, "Le juge international peut-il contrôler la légalité des sanctions adoptées par le Conseil de sécurité?" (2009) R.M.C.U.E. 373–379; Tridimas and Gutiérrez-Fons, "EU Law, International Law and Economic Sanctions against Terrorism: The Judiciary in Distress?" (2009) Fordham I.L.J. 660–730; d'Argent, "Arrêt 'Kadi': le droit communautaire comme droit interne" (2008) J.D.E. 265; Hinojosa Martinez, "The legislative role of the Security Council in its fight against terrorism:

---

rights,[346] it confirmed that the powers of the Union have to be exercised in observance of the undertakings given in the context of the United Nations[347] and that in the implementation of a resolution of the UN Security Council, due account is to be taken of the terms and objectives of the resolution and of the relevant UN obligations relating to such implementation.[348] Where the Union itself does not act, the Union institutions must in any event put the Member States in a position to comply with their pre-existing international obligations (see para. 22–053). Where only the Union has the power to give effect to UN obligations, for instance in order to impose economic sanctions, it should take the necessary steps to that effect.[349] Where the Union decides to implement a binding UN resolution, the damage resulting from the economic sanctions imposed by the resolution cannot be attributed to the Union.[350]

Review in the light of UN obligations. Another question is whether, in interpreting and applying provisions of Union law, the courts may test them against the UN Charter and resolutions adopted pursuant to that instrument. This is the case where a Union measure purports to give effect to a UN obligation (e.g., with a view to implementing sanctions imposed by the Security Council).[351] In addition, an individual may invoke obligations contained in provisions having direct effect, such as some Security Council resolutions imposing sanctions.[352] Furthermore, it

22–058

---

legal, political and practical" (2008) 57 I.C.L.Q. 333–359. For a discussion of earlier case law, see Canor, " 'Can Two Walk Together, Except They Be Agreed?' The Relationship between International Law and European Law: The Incorporation of United Nations Sanctions against Yugoslavia into European Community Law through the Perspective of the European Court of Justice" (1998) C.M.L.Rev. 137, at 161–187.

[346] According to the Court, "it is not a consequence of the principles governing the international legal order under the United Nations that any judicial review of the internal lawfulness of the contested regulation in the light of fundamental freedoms is excluded by virtue of the fact that that measure is intended to give effect to a resolution of the Security Council adopted under Chapter VII of the Charter of the United Nations": *ibid.*, para. 299. In carrying out judicial review of the contested regulation, the Court found that the inclusion of individuals on a list of persons whose assets were to be frozen, without any guarantee of the communication of the inculpatory evidence against them or as to their being heard, albeit a later date, and without any possibility for the Court itself to remedy that infringement, constituted a breach of those individuals' rights of defence, right to effective judicial review and right to property: ibid., paras 333–371.

[347] *Ibid.*, paras 291–297.

[348] *Ibid.*, paras 296–297. See already ECJ, Case C-177/95 *Ebony Martime and Loten Navigation* [1997] E.C.R. I-1111, paras 20–21 and 31; ECJ, Case C-371/03 *Aulinger* [2006] E.C.R. I-2207, para. 30.

[349] Petersmann (n. 342, *supra*), at 26–27.

[350] CFI, Case T-184/95 *Dorsch Consult v Council and Commission* [1998] E.C.R. II-667, para. 74.

[351] ECJ, Case C-84/95 *Bosphorus* [1996] E.C.R. I-3953, paras 13–15. See Canor, " 'Can Two Walk Together, Except They Be Agreed?' The Relationship between International Law and European Law: The Incorporation of United Nations Sanctions against Yugoslavia into European Community Law through the Perspective of the European Court of Justice" (1998) C.M.L.Rev. 137–187. More generally on the compatibility with international law of sanctions adopted by the Union, see Karagiannis, "Sanctions internationales et droit communautaire" (1999) R.T.D.E. 363–394.

[352] See Angelet, "La mise en oeuvre des mesures coercitives économiques des Nations-Unies dans la Communauté européenne" (1993) B.T.I.R. 500, at 502–505 and 528.

would appear that the Court of Justice is prepared to take account of rulings of the International Court of Justice in interpreting Union law.[353]

V. AUTONOMOUS MEASURES ADOPTED BY INSTITUTIONS (AND BODIES)

22–059   **Range of instruments.** The first para. of Art. 288 TFEU [*ex Art. 249 EC*] states that, to exercise the Union's competences, the institutions are to adopt regulations, directives, decisions, recommendations and opinions. Nevertheless, the institutions of the Union make use of instruments other than those listed in the second to the fifth paras of Art. 288 TFEU (see para. 22–102 *et seq.*).

The Treaties do not offer much guidance with regard to the possibility for the institutions to choose between those different instruments, although they set out a number of formal requirements to be satisfied by acts of the institutions, some of which—pursuant to general principles of Union law—also apply to acts of other bodies.[354]

A. FORMAL REQUIREMENTS

1. Choice between different instruments

22–060   **Instruments with different legal effects.** Article 288 TFEU defines the instruments available to the Council, the European Parliament and the Commission: regulations, directives, decisions, recommendations and opinions. Article 161 EAEC lists the same instruments for use by the Council and the Commission. Rules adopted under the ECSC Treaty could take the form of decisions, recommendations and opinions (Art. 14 ECSC), but the terminology of the ECSC Treaty did not correspond to that of the later Community Treaties.[355] As will be

---

[353] ECJ, Case C-432/92 *Anastasiou and Others* [1994] E.C.R. I-3087, para. 49; ECJ, Case C-162/96 *Racke* [1998] E.C.R. I-3655, paras 24 and 50. See Higgins, "The ICJ, the ECJ and the integrity of international law" (2003) I.C.L.Q. 1–20.

[354] For a general discussion of acts of the institutions and bodies, see Lauwaars, *Lawfulness and Legal Force of Community Decisions* (Leyden, Sijthoff, 1973), 5–54 (discussion of legal instruments) and 148–176 (formal requirements); Louis, "Les actes des institutions", in Louis, Vandersanden, Waelbroeck and Waelbroeck, *Commentaire Mégret—Le droit de la CEE. 10. La Cour de justice. Les actes des institutions* (Brussels, Editions de l'Université de Bruxelles, 1993), 475–540.

[355] ECSC *decisions* were binding in their entirety (Art. 14, second para., ECSC) and could be general or individual in character (see Art. 33, second para., ECSC). ECSC general decisions corresponded to EC and EAEC regulations and ECSC individual decisions to EC and EAEC decisions. ECSC *recommendations* were binding as to the aims to be pursued, but left the choice of the appropriate methods of achieving those aims to those to whom the recommendations were addressed (Art. 14, third para. ECSC). They could therefore be equated with EC and EAEC directives (except that the latter may be addressed only to Member States). ECSC *opinions* had no binding force (Art. 14, fourth para., ECSC) and hence corresponded to EC and EAEC recommendations and opinions.

shown in the survey below, it is clear from the definitions given in the relevant articles that the instruments which they list do not have the same legal effects.

Besides the instruments listed in Art. 288 TFEU, some Treaty articles also mention other instruments, such as, for instance "guidelines" or "incentive measures". In addition to the instruments explicitly mentioned by the Treaties, the institutions also commonly use other instruments, the legal effects of which have to be determined on a case-by-case basis.

In the field of the CFSP, the Treaties provide only for decisions to be used, together with general guidelines (see Art. 25 TEU).

Choice. The institutions are not always free to choose just any of those instruments when exercising their powers. First, they have to be guided by the article of the Treaty which serves as the legal basis for the action to be taken (see para. 7–011). Some Treaty articles restrict action on the part of the Union to one or more specific instruments (e.g. "directives" or "directives or regulations"), whilst others authorise any "measures" or "provisions" to be adopted. As far as legislative acts are concerned, the Treaties expressly provide that the European Parliament and the Council must refrain from adopting acts not provided for by the relevant legislative procedure in the area in question (Art. 296, third para., TFEU, introduced by the Lisbon Treaty). Furthermore, the institutions and bodies have to consider the legal effects of the instrument which they intend to adopt. In particular, they must decide whether they want to enact directly binding, exhaustive provisions (e.g. by way of a regulation) or rather leave the Member States with certain choices when implementing an act (e.g. by adopting a directive), or whether instead they wish to adopt provisions that are not legally binding (e.g. by means of a recommendation). Where the Treaties do not specify the type of act to be adopted, the institutions have to select the appropriate instrument on a case-by-case basis, in compliance with the applicable procedures and with the principle of proportionality (Art. 296, first para., TFEU, introduced by the Lisbon Treaty). The principle of proportionality precludes the Union from adopting instruments which restrict the powers of the Member States and other legitimate interests more than is necessary for the achievement of its objectives (see para. 7–038). Consequently, in some circumstances, preference should be given to instruments which are not directly applicable, such as directives, or even not binding at all, such as recommendations.

22–061

2. Distinction between legislative acts and non-legislative acts

Distinguishing between legal instruments. Regulations, directives and decisions may be used both for legislative acts and for acts implementing legislative acts or implementing other implementing acts. Formerly, the title of a Community act did not disclose whether it was a legislative act or an implementing act. Since the entry into force of the Lisbon Treaty, however, Union legislative acts are distinguished from non-legislative acts by means of their title. Indeed, as already proposed in the EU Constitution, all acts of the Council or the

22–062

Commission adopted to implement a legally binding Union act will henceforward have the word "implementing" in their title (Art. 291(4) TFEU: e.g. "implementing regulation",[356] "implementing directive" or "implementing decision"). Where a legislative act delegates powers to the Commission, the delegated acts adopted by that institution will be designated as such (Art. 290(3) TFEU: e.g. "delegated regulation", "delegated directive" or "delegated decision"). Regulations, directives and decisions not so designated will constitute legislative acts if they are based on an article in the Treaties and adopted pursuant to a legislative procedure (see para. 16–003).[357] A distinct regime applies as far as CFSP is concerned. As proposed in the EU Constitution, the normal CFSP instrument is the "decision", which in this area is not a legislative act (Arts 24(1), second subpara., and 31(1), first subpara., TEU).

22–063   **Classification proposed by the EU Constitution.** The distinction made by the Lisbon Treaty between legislative and implementing or delegated acts constitued the response to a long-standing claim for a substantive distinction to be made between legislative and implementing acts which should be reflected in distinct legal instruments with an internal hierarchy.[358] In this connection, the European Parliament generally proposed that it and the Council should be empowered to adopt legislative acts and the Commission to adopt implementing measures. The Intergovernmental Conference of 2003 responded—at least to a certain extent—to the call for a transparent system of legislative acts[359] by proposing a new system of legislative instruments in the EU Constitution.

The EU Constitution defined two instruments for legislative action by the Union: the "European law", corresponding to the present regulation,[360] and the "European

---

[356] For the first example, see Council implementing Regulation (EU) No. 1202/2009 of December 7, 2009 imposing a definitive anti-dumping duty on imports of furfuryl alcohol originating in the People's Republic of China following an expiry review pursuant to Art. 11(2) of Regulation (EC) No. 384/96, [2009] O.J. L323/48.

[357] It should be noted by way of exception, that "implementing regulations" for the European Social Fund and the European Regional Development Fund are to be adopted in accordance with the ordinary legislative procedure, see Arts 164 and 178 TFEU.

[358] For a discussion, see Lenaerts, "A Unified Set of Instruments" (2005) E.Const.L.R. 57–61; Lenaerts and Desomer, "Towards a Hierarchy of Legal Acts in the Union? Simplification of Legal Instruments and Procedures" (2005) E.L.J. 744–765. See as long ago as April 18, 1991 the resolution of the European Parliament on the nature of Community acts, [1991] O.J. C129/136, and, more recently, the resolution of the European Parliament of December 17, 2002 on the typology of acts and the hierarchy of legislation in the European Union, [2004] O.J. C31E/126.

[359] Previous Intergovernmental Conferences did not act upon the request to undertake such a discussion contained in Declaration (No. 16), annexed to the EU Treaty, on the hierarchy of Community acts. See Kovar, "La déclaration No 16 annexée au Traité sur l'Union européenne: chronique d'un échec annoncé?" (1997) C.D.E. 3–11; Monjal, "La Conférence intergouvernementale de 1996 et la hiérarchie des normes communautaires" (1996) R.T.D.E. 681–716; Tizzano, "La hiérarchie des normes communautaires" (1995) 3 R.M.U.E. 219–232.

[360] Article I-33(1), second subpara., of the EU Constitution defined it as "a legislative act of general application" that "shall be binding in its entirety and directly applicable in all Member States".

framework law", corresponding to the present directive.[361] For non-legislative action, institutions were to use a "European regulation" or a "European decision". The former would have been an act of general application for the implementation of legislative acts, other implementing acts and certain specific provisions of the EU Constitution[362] and would either have had legal effects similar to those of the existing regulation or effects similar to those of a directive.[363] The "European decision" was defined as an act "binding in its entirety", which, where specifying the persons to whom it was addressed, would be binding only on them—the same definition introduced by the Lisbon Treaty for "decisions".[364] As has already been mentioned, the EU Constitution also introduced the idea of calling European regulations and European decisions implementing other legally binding acts, "implementing regulations" and "implementing decisions" and of calling European regulations adopted pursuant to a delegation of power from the legislator "delegated European regulations". Eventually, the Intergovernmental Conference of 2007 took over only the latters changes, together with the new definition of "decisions".

3. Manner in which acts come into being

Authentication. Legislative acts adopted under the ordinary legislative procedure have to be signed by the President of the European Parliament and by the President of the Council; legislative acts adopted under a special legislative procedure have to be signed by the President of the institution which adopted them (Art. 297(1) TFEU [*ex Art. 254(1) EC*]).[365] Non-legislative acts adopted in the form of regulations, directives or decisions, when the latter do not specify to whom they are addressed, have to be signed by the President of the institution which adopted them (Art. 297(2) TFEU).

22–064

Authenticating a measure by dating it and appending the requisite signatures confirms that the terms of the authenticated instrument correspond to those of the

---

[361] Article I-33(1), third subpara., of the EU Constitution defined it as "a legislative act binding, as to the result to be achieved, upon each Member State to which it is addressed" which was to "leave to the national authorities the choice of form and methods".

[362] Article I-33(1), fourth subpara., of the EU Constitution did not expressly provide for European regulations to implement other implementing acts. That could however be inferred from Art. I-37(2) (referring in general terms to the implementation of all "legally binding Union acts").

[363] Pursuant to Art. I-33(1), fourth subpara., of the EU Constitution, such a European regulation would be "binding in its entirety and directly applicable in all Member States" or "binding, as to the result to be achieved, upon each Member State to which it is addressed" but leaving "to the national authorities the choice of form and methods".

[364] *Cf.* Art. I-33(1), fifth subpara., EU Constitution and Art. 288, fourth subpara., TFEU; see *infra*, para. 22–102. However, the TFEU also allows "decisions" to be used for legislative action (see Art. 289(1) TFEU).

[365] Article 15 of the Council Rules of Procedure provides that the text of acts adopted by the Council and that of the acts adopted by the European Parliament and the Council in accordance with the ordinary legislative procedure is to bear the signatures of the President-in-Office and the Secretary-General of the Council.

act adopted and enables the competence of the authority issuing the measure to be verified.[366] Authentication renders the instrument enforceable and ensures that it is incorporated into the Union legal order.[367] Thereafter, a measure may be amended only in accordance with the rules on competence and procedure, apart from simple corrections of spelling and grammar.[368]

The specific authentication procedures laid down in the rules of procedure of the Council and the Commission[369] may be regarded as being essential procedural requirements within the meaning of the second para. of Art. 263 TFEU, which, if infringed, may give rise to an action for annulment.[370]

4. Statement of reasons

22–065   **Obligation to state reasons.** Legal acts must state the reasons on which they are based and refer to any proposals, initiatives, recommendations, requests or opinions required by the Treaties (Art. 296, second para., TFEU [*ex Art. 253 EC*]). The duty to state reasons constitutes an essential procedural requirement within the meaning of the second para. of Art. 263 TFEU and may be raised by the Court of Justice or the General Court of its own motion.[371] If the Court finds the statement of reasons to be inadequate, it will annul the contested act.[372] The Court of Justice has held that the duty to state the reasons on which acts are based does not take,

---

[366] CFI, Joined Cases T-79/89, T-84/89, T-85/89, T-86/89, T-89/89, T-91/89, T-92/89, T-94/89, T-96/89, T-98/89, T-102/89 and T-104/89 *BASF and Others v Commission* [1992] E.C.R. II-315, para. 75.

[367] *Ibid.* In that case, the Court of First Instance [*now the General Court*] considered that the defects of the relevant Commission decision, inter alia, on account of failure to comply with the authentication procedure, were so manifest and serious as to render the decision non-existent: *ibid.*, para. 96, at II-362. On an appeal brought by the Commission, the Court of Justice held that the irregularity was not of such obvious gravity that the decision had to be treated as legally non-existent; accordingly, the Court of Justice set aside the judgment and annulled the Commission decision at issue for infringement of essential procedural requirements: ECJ, Case C-137/92 P *Commission v BASF and Others* [1994] E.C.R. I-2555, paras 48–55 and 75–78. See also CFI, Joined Cases T-80/89, T-81/89, T-83/89, T-87/89, T-88/89, T-90/89, T-93/89, T-95/89, T-97/89, T-99/89, T-100/89, T-101/89, T-103/89, T-105/89, T-107/89 and T-112/89 *BASF and Others v Commission* [1995] E.C.R. II-729, paras 108–126; CFI, Case T-32/91 *Solvay v Commission* [1995] E.C.R. II-1825, paras 49–54; CFI, Case T-37/91 *ICI v Commission* [1995] E.C.R. II-1901, paras 88–93.

[368] CFI, Joined Cases T-79/89, T-84/89, T-85/89, T-86/89, T-89/89, T-91/89, T-92/89, T-94/89, T-96/89, T-98/89, T-102/89 and T-104/89 *BASF and Others v Commission* [1992] E.C.R. II-315, para. 35; see also ECJ, Case 131/86 *United Kingdom v Council* [1988] E.C.R. 905, paras 34–39.

[369] For references to the rules of procedure, see the discussion of the operation of the Council and the Commission in paras 13–047 and 13–074, *supra*, respectively.

[370] ECJ, Case C-137/92 P *Commission v BASF and Others* [1994] E.C.R. I-2555, para. 76 (requirement for authentication laid down in the Commission's Rules of Procedure). See more recently ECJ, Case C-107/99 *Italy v Commission* [2002] E.C.R. I-1091, paras 47–48. See Lenaerts, Arts and Maselis, *Procedural Law of the European Union* (3rd edn, London, Sweet & Maxwell, 2012), Ch. 7.

[371] ECJ, Case 18/57 *Nold v High Authority* [1959] E.C.R. 41, at 51–52. See Lenaerts, Arts and Maselis, *Procedural Law of the European Union* (3rd edn, London, Sweet & Maxwell, 2012), Ch. 7.

[372] See, for example, CFI, Case T-38/92 *AWS Benelux BV v Commission* [1994] E.C.R. II-213, paras 26–36.

"merely formal considerations into account but seeks to give an opportunity to the parties of defending their rights, to the Court of exercising its supervisory functions and to Member States and to all interested nationals of ascertaining the circumstances in which the [institution] has applied the Treaty".[373]

To this end, the statement of reasons must "disclose in a clear and unequivocal fashion the reasoning followed by the [Union] authority which adopted the measure in question".[374]

Although where a given decision follows a well-established line of decisions, the reasons on which it is based may be given in a summary manner, the Union authority must give an explicit account of its reasoning if the decision goes appreciably further than previous decisions.[375] Where the Union institutions have discretion (power of appraisal), sufficient reasoning is of even more fundamental importance in order to enable the Court to verify whether the factual and legal matters upon which the exercise of the power of appraisal depended were present.[376] The extent of the requirement to state reasons is also influenced by the type of instrument employed by the institution.[377] In the case of a measure of general application, the Court of Justice has held that the statement of reasons may be confined to indicating the general situation which led to its adoption and the general objectives which it is intended to achieve.[378] However, it is a requirement of the principle of subsidiarity that an institution must state its grounds for considering that the objectives of its action cannot be sufficiently achieved by the Member States (Art. 5(3) TEU; see para. 7–030).

In order to make it clear that an act was produced in accordance with the procedure prescribed for the adoption of acts of the type in question, Art. 296, second para., TFEU [*ex Art. 253 EC*] provides that it must refer to any proposals, initiatives, recommendations, requests or opinions required by the Treaties. There is no need to mention whether and why a given proposal or opinion was or was not followed.[379] In regulations, directives and decisions, the Council cites

---

[373] ECJ, Case 24/62 *Germany v Commission* [1963] E.C.R. 63, at 69.

[374] ECJ, Case C-350/88 *Delacre and Others v Commission* [1990] E.C.R. I-395, para. 15.

[375] *Ibid.*

[376] ECJ, Case C-269/90 *Technische Universität München* [1991] E.C.R. I-5469, paras 14 and 27.

[377] For regulations, see, for instance, ECJ, Case 5/67 *Beus* [1968] E.C.R. 83, at 95; for decisions, see ECJ, Case 16/65 *Schwarze* [1965] E.C.R. 877, at 888, and ECJ, Case C-350/88 *Delacre and Others v Commission* [1990] E.C.R. I-395, para. 16. See also Lenaerts, Arts and Maselis, *Procedural Law of the European Union* (3rd edn, London, Sweet & Maxwell, 2012), Ch. 7.

[378] ECJ, Case C168/98 *Luxembourg v European Parliament and Council* [2000] E.C.R. I-9131, paras 62–68.

[379] ECJ, Case 4/54 *ISA v High Authority* [1954 to 1956] E.C.R. 91, at 100 (concerning Art. 15 ECSC); ECJ, Case C-62/88 *Greece v Council* [1990] E.C.R. I-1527, para. 29 (concerning Art. 190 [*later Art. 253*] EC [*now Art. 296 TFEU*]).

proposals submitted and "opinions obtained", which does not restrict it to opinions which it was required to obtain.[380]

5. Publication or notification—entry into effect

22–066 **Publication and notification.** Article 297 TFEU [*ex Art. 254(1) and (2) EC*] provides that legislative acts have to be published in the *Official Journal of the European Union*, together with regulations and directives which are addressed to all Member States, as well as decisions which do not specify to whom they are addressed.[381] Those acts are printed in Part L (Legislation) of the *Official Journal*.[382] Other directives, decisions which specify to whom they are addressed and recommendations have to be notified to their addressees.[383] Unless the Council or Coreper decides otherwise, they are published in the *Official Journal*.[384] The same applies to opinions.[385] The Council or Coreper decides, on a case-by-case basis, whether to publish other Council acts, such as conclusions or resolutions.[386] The European Central Bank may decide to publish its decisions, recommendations and opinions.[387] It has in fact opted to publish these and other legal instruments (guidelines and decisions) in the *Official Journal*.[388] As far as bodies set up by agreements concluded between the Union and third countries are

---

[380] See Council Rules of Procedure, Annex VI, "Provisions concerning the forms of acts". Article 296 TFEU does not require acts to refer to any subsequent amendment of the Commission proposal, unless the Commission withdrew its original proposal and replaced it by a new one: ECJ, Case C-280/93 *Germany v Council* [1994] E.C.R. I-4973, para. 37. Neither is there a requirement for a summary of the facts establishing that each of the institutions involved in the legislative procedure observed its procedural rules: ECJ, Case C-377/98 *Netherlands v European Parliament and Council* [2001] E.C.R. I-7079, paras 86–87.

[381] See, with regard to European Council Decisions, Art. 12(1) of the European Council Rules of Procedure. The obligation to publish does not cover however decisions taken by a Union institution or bodies which are only intended to have legal effects within that institution or body, such as decisions on the structure of the services, decisions to launch a study, etc.

[382] Before the amendment made by the EU Treaty to Art. 254 EC, directives did not have to be published. In practice, they were published in the *Official Journal*, Part L, under the heading "acts whose publication is not obligatory". Likewise, PJCC acts were published under Declaration (No. 9) on Art. K.6 *[later Art. 34]*(2) EU ([1997] O.J. C340/133). ECSC acts were also published in this way pursuant to Art. 15 ECSC.

[383] Article 297(2), third subpara., TFEU [*ex Art. 254(3) EC*]; Council Rules of Procedure, Art. 18(1) and (2)(a).

[384] The only exception is CFSP decisions: the Council or Coreper decides whether these should be published on a case-by-case basis (Council Rules of Procedure, Art. 17(3); see also Art. 17(4)).

[385] Council Rules of Procedure, Art. 17(2)(b).

[386] Council Rules of Procedure, Art. 17(4)(c).

[387] Article 132(2) TFEU [*ex Art. 110(2), fifth subpara., EC*].

[388] See the preamble to the Decision of the ECB of November 10, 2000 on the publication of certain legal acts and instruments of the ECB, [2001] O.J. L55/68.

concerned, the Council decides, when such an agreement is concluded, whether their decisions should be published in the *Official Journal*.[389]

The Court of Justice has held that it is a fundamental principle of the Union legal order that a measure adopted by the public authorities shall not be applicable to those concerned before they have the opportunity to make themselves acquainted with it.[390] This means that proceedings cannot be brought against individuals for breach of an obligation arising under a regulation where it was not adequately brought to their attention.[391] Union acts which have to be published in the *Official Journal* cannot be enforced against natural persons in a Member State if they have not yet been published in the *Official Journal* in the official language of that Member State. In the absence of any rules in that regard in Union law, it is not sufficient that the act in question is available in that language on the Internet or that the persons concerned could have learned of the act by other means.[392] However, where a Member State has implemented under national law provisions of a Union act which was not published in the official language of that Member State, those provisions can be enforced against individuals.[393] The principle of legal certainly precludes reliance on a decision addressed to a Member State—which does not have to be published in the *Official Journal*—against individuals, if its content was not made known to them.[394] A rule which complements a Union act without however being stated in that act may be relied on against individuals where they may be deemed to have been aware of it in the light of the circumstances, for instance because it was stated in national legislation.[395]

Entry into effect. Acts which have to be published in the *Official Journal* pursuant to Art. 297(1) and (2) TFEU enter into force on the date specified therein or, in the absence of such date, on the twentieth day following that of their publication. Other directives and decisions take effect upon notification (Art. 297(2), third subpara., TFEU). The unity and uniform application of Union law require that, save as otherwise expressly provided, a regulation should enter into force

22–067

---

[389] Council Rules of Procedure, Art. 17(5).

[390] ECJ, Case 98/78 *Racke* [1979] E.C.R. 69, para. 15; see also the parallel judgment of the same date in Case 99/78 *Decker* [1979] E.C.R. 101.

[391] ECJ, Case C-469/00 *Ravil* [2003] E.C.R. I-5053, paras 91 to 100, and ECJ, Case C-108/01 *Consorzio del Prosciutto di Parma and Others* [2003] E.C.R. I-5121, paras 88–96; ECJ, Case C-345/06 *Gottfried Heinrich* [2009] E.C.R. I-1659, paras 41–63 (annex to a regulation which had not been published held to have no binding force vis-à-vis individuals).

[392] ECJ, Case C-161/06 *Skoma-Lux* [2007] E.C.R. I-10841, paras 15–51; ECJ, Case C-140/08 *Rakvere Lihakombinaat* [2009] E.C.R. I-10533, paras 31–32.

[393] ECJ, Case C-560/07 *Balbiino* [2009] E.C.R. I-4447, paras 31–32; ECJ, Case C-140/08 *Rakvere Lihakombinaat* (preceding n.), paras 33–34.

[394] ECJ, Case C-158/06 *ROM-projecten* [2007] E.C.R. I-5103, paras 23–31.

[395] ECJ, Case C-469/00 *Ravil* [2003] E.C.R. I-5053, paras 101–103.

on the same date in all the Member States, regardless of any delays in the distribution of the *Official Journal*. In the absence of evidence to the contrary, a regulation is to be regarded as having been published throughout the Union on the date borne by the issue of the *Official Journal* containing the text of that regulation.[396] If an institution deliberately backdates an act, it infringes the principle of legal certainty.[397] In general, the principle of legal certainty precludes a Union measure from taking effect from a point in time before its publication. Exceptionally, a measure may so take effect on the dual condition that the purpose to be achieved so demands and the legitimate expectations of those concerned are duly respected.[398] In accordance with the principles of legal certainty and protection of legitimate expectations, new rules apply immediately to the future effects of a situation which arose under the old rules[399]; they can apply to situations existing before their entry into force only in so far as it clearly follows from their terms, objectives or general scheme that such effect must be given to them.[400] In contrast, procedural rules are generally held to apply to all disputes pending at the time when they enter into force.[401] The same principles hold good for the application of the Treaties (see para. 12–003) and for international agreements concluded by the Union (see para. 22–043).

6. Enforcement

22–068 **Enforcement.** The Union is not competent to enforce compliance with its acts itself. However, acts of the Council, the Commission or the European Central Bank which impose a pecuniary obligation on natural or legal persons, with the exception of States, are enforceable by virtue of the first para. of Art. 299 TFEU [*ex Art. 256 EC*]. The same is true of judgments of the Court of Justice or the General Court, which Art. 280 TFEU declares enforceable under the conditions laid down in Art. 299 TFEU.[402] The national authority designated for this purpose by each Member State must append an order for enforcement without any formality other than

---

[396] ECJ, Case 98/78 *Racke* [1979] E.C.R. 69, paras 16–17.

[397] CFI, Case T-115/94 *Opel Austria v Council* [1997] E.C.R. II-39, paras 127–132 (see also para. 22–039, *supra*).

[398] ECJ, Case 98/78 *Racke* [1979] E.C.R. 69, para. 20; ECJ, Case C-110/97 *Netherlands v Council* [2001] E.C.R. I-8763, paras 151–157.

[399] ECJ, Case 270/84 *Licata v Economic and Social Committee* [1986] E.C.R. 2305, para. 31; ECJ, Case C-160/00 *Pokrzeptowicz-Meyer* [2002] E.C.R. I-1049, para. 50.

[400] ECJ, Case 21/81 *Bout* [1982] E.C.R. 381, para. 13; ECJ, Case C-34/92 *GruSA Fleisch* [1993] E.C.R. I-4147, para. 22. For futher details, see Kaleda, "Immediate Effects of Community Law in the New Member States: Is there a Place for a Consistent Doctrine?" (2004) E.L.J. 102–122.

[401] See ECJ, Joined Cases 212/80 to 217/80 *Meridionale Industria Salumi and Others* [1981] E.C.R. 2735, para. 9; ECJ, Case C-61/98 *De Haan* [1999] E.C.R. I-5003, para. 13; ECJ, Case C-201/04 *Molenbergnatie* [2006] E.C.R. I-2049, para. 31; CFI, Case T-334/07, *Denka International v Commission* [2009] E.C.R. II-4205, para. 45.

[402] See also Arts 164 and 159, respectively, EAEC.

verification of the authenticity of the decision.[403] Enforcement then takes place in accordance with the applicable national rules of civil procedure (Art. 299, second para., TFEU). Enforcement may be suspended only by an order of the Court of Justice or the General Court. However, supervising the manner of enforcement falls to the national courts (Art. 299, fourth para., TFEU).

7. Judicial Review

Judicial review. The legality of a Union act which produces legal effects may be reviewed by the Court of Justice or the General Court when a direct action is brought against it (Art. 263 TFEU [*ex Art. 230 EC*]), where an objection of illegality is raised (Art. 277 TFEU [*ex Art. 241 EC*]) or where a national court makes a reference to the Court of Justice for a preliminary ruling on its validity (Art. 267, first para., indent (b), TFEU [*ex Art. 234, first para., indent (b) EC*]). In addition, the Court of Justice may rule on the interpretation of any "act of the institutions" (*ibid.*).[404] However, the Court has only limited jurisdiction in the field of the CFSP (see para. 13–086).

22–069

B. Regulations

Definition. A regulation has general application and is binding in its entirety and directly applicable in all the Member States (Art. 288, second para., TFEU). Sometimes the Union may only act by way of regulations,[405] whereas other Treaty articles provide for the possible use of regulations, alongside other instruments.[406]

22–070

General application. The fact that a regulation has general application means that it is "applicable to objectively determined situations and involves legal consequences for categories of persons viewed in a general and abstract manner".[407]

The field of application of a regulation is not individually tailored to specific individuals or situations. A measure does not lose its

22–071

---

[403] In the United Kingdom, application to append an order for enforcement to a judgment is made to the Secretary of State; the High Court in England or Wales or in Northern Ireland or the Court of Session in Scotland registers the judgment (Enforcement of Community Judgments) Order 1972, (SI 1972/1590), Art. 3(1); see also European Communities Act, s. 3(3).

[404] For the system of legal redress, see ECJ, Case 294/83 *Les Verts v European Parliament* [1986] E.C.R. 1339, para. 23 *et seq.*, and the detailed discussion in Lenaerts, Arts and Maselis, *Procedural Law of the European Union* (3rd edn, London, Sweet & Maxwell, 2012), of actions for annulment (Ch. 7), the objection of illegality (Ch. 9) and the preliminary ruling procedure (Ch. 6—interpretation—and Ch. 10—review of validity).

[405] For legislative action, see, e.g., Arts 14, 15, 24, 75, 85(1), 86(1), 88(2), 118, second subpara., 121(6), 127(6), 177, 197(2), 207(2), 214(5), 224, 226, 228(4), 257, 291(3), 298(2), 311, fourth subpara., 312(2), 322(1), 336, 349, 352(1) TFEU; for implementing acts, e.g., Arts 45(3)(d), 109 and 132(1), first indent, TFEU.

[406] For legislative action, see, e.g., Art. 46 TFEU; for other action, see, e.g., Art. 103(1) and 132(1) TFEU.

[407] ECJ, Case 6/68 *Zuckerfabrik Watenstedt v Council* [1968] E.C.R. 409, at 415.

"character as a regulation simply because it may be possible to ascertain with a greater or lesser degree of accuracy the number or even the identity of the persons to whom it applies at any given time as long as there is no doubt that the measure is applicable as the result of an objective situation of law or of fact which it specifies and which is in harmony with its ultimate objective".[408]

The general scope of a regulation differentiates it from a decision, which may have individual scope (see para. 22–097). Whether a given act has general or individual scope determines whether a natural or legal person may bring an action for its annulment pursuant to the fourth para. of Art. 263 TFEU. This is because, according to that provision, an action for annulment may be brought by any natural or legal person, on the one hand, against acts having individual scope or similar effects ("against an act addressed to that person or which is of direct and individual concern to them") and, on the other, against acts of general application provided that the action is brought against a "regulatory act which is of direct concern to them and does not entail implementing measures".[409]

22–072   **Binding in its entirety.** A regulation is binding in its entirety, which means that, unlike a directive, it is intended to subject a situation to rules which are all-embracing and, where necessary, precise. Where a regulation is adopted under the Treaties as a legislative act, it sometimes remains deliberately vague in conferring executive tasks (expressly) on the Union institutions or (implicitly or expressly) on the Member States. Regulations are generally adopted as implementing measures in areas in which Union legislation imposes extensive administrative tasks on the Union, such as the common agricultural policy and the application of the Common Customs Tariff.

22–073   **Direct applicability.** Regulations are directly applicable in all Member States. A regulation automatically forms part of the (highest) provisions of a Member State's legal order without it being necessary to transpose it in any way. Indeed, formal incorporation of provisions of a regulation into the national legal order is regarded as impermissible on the ground that it would bring into doubt "both the legal nature of the applicable provisions and the date of their coming into force".[410] Nevertheless, the direct applicability of regulations does not preclude a

---

[408] *Ibid.*; ECJ, Case 101/76 *Koninklijke Scholten Honig v Commission* [1977] E.C.R. 797, para. 23.

[409] See the discussion in Lenaerts, Arts and Maselis, *Procedural Law of the European Union* (3rd edn, London, Sweet & Maxwell, 2012), Ch. 7; Lenaerts, "Le traité de Lisbonne et la protection juridictionnelle des particuliers en droit de l'Union" (2009) C.D.E. 711, at 717–728.

[410] ECJ, Case 39/72 *Commission v Italy* [1973] E.C.R. 101, paras 16–17; see also ECJ, Case 34/73 *Variola* [1973] E.C.R. 981, para. 11; ECJ, Case 50/76 *Amsterdam Bulb* [1977] E.C.R. 137, paras 4–7.

power on the part of the Member States to take the necessary implementing measures.[411] Indeed, Member States are obliged to take such measures.[412]

Direct effect. Individuals are always entitled to rely on any regulation before the national courts with a view to having national law which is incompatible therewith disapplied. In addition, provisions of a regulation may have direct effect. The Court of Justice has held that,   22–074

> "by reason of their nature and their function in the system of the sources of Community law, regulations have direct effect and are, as such, capable of creating individual rights which national courts must protect".[413]

The case law does not always draw a distinction between direct applicability of a regulation and the direct effect of its provisions. Nevertheless, it may be taken that a provision of a regulation will have *direct effect* only if it satisfies the same requirements as apply to Treaty articles; in other words, it must be "clear and precise" and must not "leave any margin of discretion to the authorities".[414] The fact that a regulation is *directly applicable* means that it is applied "in favour of or against those subject to it" without having been transposed into national law.[415] This means that a regulation may not only entail rights for individuals, but also directly impose obligations upon them. Consequently, where a provision of a regulation has *direct effect*, individuals may derive rights from it against both national authorities and other individuals.[416] Even where on account of its content a regulation does not have direct effect, national provisions must nevertheless be interpreted as far as possible in the light of its wording and

---

[411] ECJ, Case 230/78 *Eridania* [1979] E.C.R. 2749, para. 35; ECJ, Case C-403/98 *Azienda Agricola Monte Arcosu* [2001] E.C.R. I-103, para. 26; ECJ, Case C-278/02 *Handlbauer* [2004] E.C.R. I-6171, paras 25–26 (para. 17–002, *supra*).

[412] As regards temporary exceptions to the application of a regulation, the Court has been cautious not to declare the *Inter-Environnement Wallonie* case law about the obligations during the period for transposition of a directive (see para. 22–079, *infra*) applicable, see ECJ (judgment of April 22, 2010), C-122/09 *Enosi Efopliston Aktoploïas and Others*, not yet reported, paras 13–17 (where it was held that, assuming that this obligation applied, it had not, in any event, been infringed).

[413] ECJ, Case 43/71 *Politi* [1971] E.C.R. 1039, para. 9; ECJ, Case 93/71 *Leonesio* [1972] E.C.R. 287, para. 5; see also paras 22–23.

[414] ECJ, Case 9/73 *Schlüter* [1973] E.C.R. 1135, para. 32, at 1158; ECJ, Case C-403/98 *Azienda Agricola Monte Arcosu* [2001] E.C.R. I-103, paras 26–28. See Bleckmann, "L'applicabilité directe du droit communautaire", in *Les recours des individus devant les instances nationales en cas de violation du droit européen: Communautés européennes et Convention des droits de l'homme*, (Brussels, Larcier, 1978), 85, at 110; Easson, "The 'Direct Effect' of EEC Directives" (1979) I.C.L.Q. 319, at 321–322; for the debate amongst academics, see Louis (n. 354, *supra*), at 493–496.

[415] ECJ, Case 34/73 *Variola* [1973] E.C.R. 981, para. 10. See also para. 22–084, *infra*.

[416] See ECJ, Case C-253/00 *Muñoz and Superior Fruiticola* [2002] E.C.R. I-7289, paras 27–32, with a case note by Biondi (2003) C.M.L.Rev. 1243–1250.

objectives.[417] This principle of consistent interpretation is limited, however, by the general principles of Union law, such as the principle of legal certainty, the principle of legality and the prohibition of retroactivity. Where a regulation empowers Member States to impose sanctions for infringements of the regulation, it cannot, of itself and independently of a national law adopted by a Member State for its implementation, have the effect of determining or aggravating the liability in criminal law of persons who act in contravention of the provisions of that regulation.[418] Moreover, a provision may be relied on against individuals only if they were capable of knowing about it.[419]

C. DIRECTIVES

22–075   **Definition.** A directive is binding, as to the result to be achieved, upon each Member State to which it is addressed, but leaves to the national authorities the choice of form and methods (Art. 288, third para., TFEU).[420] Normally, directives are addressed to all Member States. However, a directive may also be addressed to only one Member State.[421] By leaving the Member States free to determine themselves the way in which the intended result is achieved within the national legal system, directives reflect the idea of subsidiarity.[422] Consequently, directives are an appropriate means of introducing Union rules which call for existing national provisions to be amended or fleshed out before the new rules can be applied.[423]

---

[417] See the case note by Kronenberger to the judgment in ECJ, Case C-403/98 *Azienda Agricola Monte Arcosu* [2001] E.C.R. I-103 in (2001) C.M.L.Rev. 1545–1556.

[418] ECJ, Case C-60/02 *Criminal proceedings against X* [2004] E.C.R. I-651, paras 61–63.

[419] Para. 22–067, *supra*.

[420] The legal force of a directive is equivalent to that of a recommendation made pursuant to the ECSC Treaty: ECJ, Case C-221/88 *Busseni* [1990] E.C.R. I-495, para. 21; ECJ, Case C-18/94 *Hopkins and Others* [1996] E.C.R. I-2281, paras 25–29. However, such a recommendation could be addressed to persons other than Member States (see Art. 14, third para., ECSC).

[421] See, e.g., Council Directive 79/174/EEC of February 6, 1979 concerning the flood protection programme in the Hérault Valley, [1979] O.J. L38/18 (based on Art. 43 *[later Art. 37]* EC *[now Art. 43 TFEU]* and addressed only to France).

[422] For the directive as a possible instrument amenable to Member States, see Van Nuffel, *De rechtsbescherming van nationale overheden in het Europees recht* (Deventer, Kluwer, 2000), at 246–264. See further Prechal, *Directives in European Community Law. A Study on EC Directives and their Enforcement by National Courts. A Study of Directives and Their Enforcement in National Courts* (Oxford, Oxford University Press, 2005), 424 pp. (which explains all aspects of directives).

[423] The Treaties require directives to be used, inter alia, in Arts 23; 50(1); 52(2); 53(1); 59(1); 82(2); 83(1) and (2); 115; 116, second para.; 153(2), first subpara., indent (b), TFEU *[Arts 20;44(1); 46(2); 47(1) and (2); 52(1); 94; 96, second para.; 137(2), first subpara., indent (b), EC]*. Alongside other Treaty articles which do not prescribe the use of any particular legislative instrument (para. 22–103, *infra*), the following are among the articles of the Treaties which provide for the possible use of directives: Arts 46; 103(1); 106(3); 143(2) TFEU *[ex Arts 40; 83(1); 86(3); 119(2) EC]*.

1. The transposition of directives into national law

Implementation. Unlike regulations, directives are not directly applicable in Member States' domestic legal systems. They obtain their full legislative status only after they have been implemented in national law.[424] Union legislative practice shows that there may be great differences in the results which must be achieved. Some directives require legislative measures to be adopted at national level and compliance with those measures to be the subject of judicial or administrative review. Other directives provide that the Member States are to take the necessary measures to ensure that certain objectives formulated in general and unquantifiable terms are attained, whilst leaving the Member States some discretion as to the nature of the measures to be taken. Furthermore, other directives require the Member States to obtain very precise and specific results within a specified period.[425]

22–076

Requirements of legal certainty. The provisions of directives must be implemented with unquestionable binding force, and the specificity, precision and clarity necessary to satisfy the requirements of legal certainty.[426] For the purpose of considering whether a directive has been correctly implemented, the scope of national laws, rules or administrative provisions must be assessed in the light of the interpretation given to them by national courts.[427] In order to secure the full application of directives in law and not only in fact, Member States must make sure that there is a clear legal framework for the area in question, even where there is no practice in the Member State which is incompatible with the directive in question[428] or an activity referred to in a directive does not (yet) exist in a Member State.[429] Indeed, given the fact that situations may change at a given point in time, all legal persons in the Union, including those in the Member State concerned, need to know, with clarity and precision, what are, in all circumstances, their rights and obligations.[430] It is only where

22–077

---

[424] ECJ, Case 102/79 *Commission v Belgium* [1980] E.C.R. 1473, para. 12.

[425] ECJ, Case C-60/01 *Commission v France* [2002] E.C.R. I-5679; paras 25–28; ECJ, Case C-32/05 *Commission v Luxemburg* [2006] E.C.R. I-11323, paras 37–40.

[426] This is settled case law of the Court of Justice; see, e.g., ECJ, Case C-159/99 *Commission v Italy* [2001] E.C.R. I-4007, para. 32. See Sales, "La transposition des directives communautaires: une exigence de valeur constitutionnelle sous réserve de constitutionnalité" (2005) R.T.D.E. 597–621.

[427] ECJ, Case C-382/92 *Commission v United Kingdom* [1994] E.C.R. I-2435, para. 36: ECJ, Case C-300/95 *Commission v United Kingdom* [1997] E.C.R. I-2649, para. 37. The legal framework will not be considered clear enough where the case law is not sufficiently settled, see, e.g., ECJ, Case C-372/99 *Commission v Italy* [2002] E.C.R. I-819, paras 20–28. For the implementation of directives by collective agreements concluded by management and labour, see para. 17–003.

[428] ECJ, Case C-339/87 *Commission v Netherlands* [1990] E.C.R. I-851, para. 25 (which refers to a "specific legal framework").

[429] ECJ, Case C-372/00 *Commission v Ireland* [2001] E.C.R. I-10303, para. 11; ECJ, Case C-441/00 *Commission v United Kingdom* [2002] E.C.R. I-4699, para. 15.

[430] ECJ (judgment of January 14, 2010), Case C-343/08 *Commission v Czech Republic*, not yet reported, para. 41.

transposition of a directive is pointless for reasons of geography that it is not mandatory.[431]

In this respect, a Member State does not fulfil its obligations by maintaining an administrative practice which, albeit consonant with the directive, may be changed as and when the authorities please and is not sufficiently publicised.[432] Nor is it sufficient to make a general reference to the applicable Union provisions and to the primacy of Union law.[433] In order to achieve the clarity and precision needed to meet the requirement of legal certainty, it is not sufficient that the settled case law of a Member State interprets the provisions of national law in a manner deemed to satisfy the requirements of a directive.[434] The principle of legal certainty requires appropriate publicity for the national implementing measures in such a way as to enable the persons concerned by such measures to ascertain the scope of their rights and obligations in the particular area governed by Union law.[435]

Nevertheless, transposition of a directive into national law does not necessarily require that "its provisions be incorporated formally and verbatim in express, specific legislation"; sometimes,

> "a general legal context may, depending on the content of the directive, be adequate for the purpose provided that it does indeed guarantee the full application of the directive in a sufficiently clear and precise manner so that, where the directive is intended to create rights for individuals, the persons concerned can ascertain the full extent of their rights and, where appropriate, rely on them before the national courts".[436]

Accordingly, the existence of general principles of constitutional or administrative law may, exceptionally, make transposition by means of statutory or administrative

---

[431] ECJ, Case C-372/00 *Commission v Ireland* [2001] E.C.R. I-10303, para. 13; ECJ, Case C-441/00 *Commission v United Kingdom* [2002] E.C.R. I-4699, para. 17.

[432] ECJ, Case 102/79 *Commission v Belgium* [1980] E.C.R. 1473, para. 11; ECJ, Case C-102/08 *SALIX* [2009] E.C.R. I-4629, para. 43. See Curtin, "Directives: The Effectiveness of Judicial Protection of Individual Rights" (1990) C.M.L.Rev. 709–739, especially, at 716–718.

[433] ECJ, Case C-96/95 *Commission v Germany* [1997] E.C.R. I-1653, paras 32–41.

[434] ECJ, Case C-144/99 *Commission v Netherlands* [2001] E.C.R. I-3541, paras 20–21; ECJ, Case C-292/07 *Commission v Belgium* [2009] E.C.R. I-59, para. 122.

[435] ECJ, Case C-415/01 *Commission v Belgium* [2003] E.C.R. I-2081, paras 26–26 (duty to publish maps demarcating special protection areas in order to implement the directive on protection of birds).

[436] ECJ, Case 363/85 *Commission v Italy* [1987] E.C.R. 1733, para. 7; ECJ, Case C-131/88 *Commission v Germany* [1991] E.C.R. I-825, para. 6; ECJ, Case C-361/88 *Commission v Germany* [1991] E.C.R. I-2567, para. 15. Recent examples are afforded by ECJ, Case C-478/99 *Commission v Sweden* [2002] E.C.R. I-4147, paras 10–24, and ECJ, Case C-233/00 *Commission v France* [2003] E.C.R. I-6625, paras 75–87; ECJ, Case C-388/07 *Age Concern England* [2009] E.C.R. I-1569, paras 41–52.

measures unnecessary.[437] The Court has also held that a provision which concerns only the relations between the Member States and the Commission does not, in principle, have to be transposed.[438]

Time-limit for implementation. Generally, a directive will not only specify the date by which it enters into effect, but it will also lay down a time-limit within which the Member States must adopt the necessary measures and put them into effect in order to reach the result envisaged by the directive.[439] As a result, a directive imposes an "obligation to achieve a result" (*obligation de résultat*), which must be fulfilled before the end of the period laid down by the directive.[440] A Member State cannot rely upon domestic difficulties or provisions of its national legal system, even of its Constitution, for the purpose of justifying a failure to comply with obligations and time-limits resulting from directives.[441] This is because the governments of the Member States participate in the preparatory work for directives and must therefore be in a position to prepare within the period prescribed the legislative provisions necessary for their implementation.[442] The fact that a directive is belatedly transposed into national law may not cause the date to be postponed by which the obligations imposed by the directive have to be fulfilled.[443] That provisions of a given directive qualify for direct effect does not release the Member State to which it is addressed from the obligation to adopt implementing measures satisfying the purpose of the directive in good time.[444] A Member State does not fulfil its obligation to implement a directive by

22–078

---

[437] ECJ, Case 29/84 *Commission v Germany* [1985] E.C.R. 1661, para. 23; for an application, see ECJ, Case 248/83 *Commission v Germany* [1985] E.C.R. 1459, paras 18–19 and 30. See Siems, "Effektivität und Legitimität einer Richtlinienumsetzung durch Generalklauseln" (2002) Z.Eu.P. 747–753.

[438] ECJ, Case C-32/05 *Commission v Luxemburg* [2006] E.C.R. I-11323, para. 35. The Court added, however, that, given that the Member States are obliged to ensure that Union law is fully complied with, it is open to the Commission to demonstrate that compliance with a provision of a directive governing those relations requires the adoption of specific transposing measures in national law (*ibid.*).

[439] According to point 33 of the Interinstitutional Agreement between the European Parliament, the Council and the Commission of December 16, 2003 on better lawmaking, [2003] O.J. C321/1, the institutions will ensure that all directives include a binding time-limit for transposition that is as short as possible and generally does not exceed two years.

[440] ECJ, Case 8/81 *Becker v Finanzamt Münster-Innenstadt* [1982] E.C.R. 53, para. 18.

[441] ECJ, Case 100/77 *Commission v Italy* [1978] E.C.R. 879, para. 21.

[442] ECJ, Case 301/81 *Commission v Belgium* [1983] E.C.R. 467, para. 11; ECJ, Case C-319/99 *Commission v France* [2000] E.C.R. I-10439, para. 10. If the prescribed period proves too short, all that a Member State can do is take the appropriate initiatives at Union level with the responsible institutions in order to obtain the necessary extension of the period: ECJ, Case 52/75 *Commission v Italy* [1976] E.C.R. 277, para. 12/13.

[443] ECJ, Case C-396/92 *Bund Naturschutz in Bayern and Others* [1994] E.C.R. I-3717, paras 18–19; see also ECJ, Case C-208/90 *Emmott* [1991] E.C.R. I-4269, paras 23–24.

[444] ECJ, Case 102/79 *Commission v Belgium* [1980] E.C.R. 1473, para. 12.

merely relying on the duty of national courts to disapply conflicting national provisions.[445]

22–079 **Obligations during the period prescribed for implementation.** Before the period prescribed for implementing a directive has expired, there is no obligation for Member States to adopt transposition measures. However, as a result of Art. 4(3) TEU [*see ex Art. 10 EC*], they must refrain from taking any measures which might seriously compromise attainment of the objective pursued by the directive after the period for transposition has expired. It is for the national court to assess whether that is the case by considering, in particular, the effects in practice of applying the incompatible provisions and of their duration in time.[446] The same applies where a directive provides for a transitional period, during which it does not yet need to be fully transposed.[447]

If the provisions in issue are intended to constitute full and definitive transposition of the directive, their incompatibility might give rise to the presumption that the result prescribed by the directive will not be achieved within the period prescribed if it is impossible to amend them in time.[448] Incompatibility of national measures or non-transposition of certain provisions will not necessarily compromise the result required where a Member State adopts transitional implementing provisions or implements the directive in stages.[449] However, a provision of national law can compromise the result prescribed by the directive, regardless of whether it is concerned with the transposition of the directive or not.[450] This holds true even for constitutional amendments.[451]

The obligation not to take any measures which may seriously compromise the aims of a directive even before its transposition applies to national public authorities, but not to individuals.[452] If such measures are adopted nevertheless, they may be

---

[445] ECJ, Case C-197/96 *Commission v France* [1997] E.C.R. I-1489, paras 13–16; ECJ, Case C-207/96 *Commission v Italy* [1997] E.C.R. I-6869, paras 26–27.

[446] ECJ, Case C-129/96 *Inter-Environnement Wallonie* [1997] E.C.R. I-7411, paras 45–47; ECJ, Case C-14/02 *ATRAL* [2003] E.C.R. I-4431, paras 58–60. See Prechal (n. 422 *supra*), at 24–26; Gilliaux, *Les directives européennes et le droit belge* (Brussel, Bruylant, 1997), at 142–145; Klamert, "Judicial implementation of directives and anticipatory indirect effect: connecting the dots" (2006) C.M.L.Rev. 1251–1275.

[447] ECJ, Case C-316/04 *Stichting Zuid-Hollandse Milieufederatie* [2005] E.C.R. I-09759, para. 42; ECJ, Case C-138/05 *Stichting Zuid-Hollandse Milieufederatie* [2006] E.C.R. I-8339, paras 42–44.

[448] ECJ, Case C-129/96 *Inter-Environnement Wallonie* [1997] E.C.R. I-7411, para. 48; ECJ, Case C-422/05 *Commission v Belgium* [2007] E.C.R. I-4749, paras 62–68.

[449] ECJ, Case C-129/96 *Inter-Environnement Wallonie* [1997] E.C.R. I-7411, para. 49.

[450] ECJ, Case C-14/02 *ATRAL* [2003] E.C.R. I-4431, paras 58–59; ECJ, Case C-144/04 *Mangold* [2005] E.C.R. I-9981, paras 66–72; for a discussion of the latter case, see Masson (2007) 13 E.Pub.L. 587–593; Riesenhuber (2007) E.R.C.L. 63–71; Bauer (2006) N.J.W. 6–12; Foubert (2006) S.E.W. 247–251.

[451] ECJ, Joined Cases C-378/07 to C-380/07 *Angelidaki and Others* [2009] E.C.R. I-3071, paras 206–207.

[452] CFI, Joined Cases T-172/98, T-175/98 to T-176/98 *Salamander and Others v European Parliament and Council* [2000] E.C.R. II-2487, para. 57.

disapplied by the national courts. National courts are not obliged to do so however in procedures brought by individuals in reliance on the direct effect of a directive.[453] In any event, measures adopted before the period for transposition has expired in order to implement a directive must be interpreted as far as possible in a way that is not liable to compromise the result prescribed by the directive (see para. 22–087).

2. The direct effect of provisions of an unimplemented or incorrectly implemented directive

Conditions for direct effect. Since directives leave the choice of "form and methods" to the Member States, they leave in principle the competent national authorities some discretion. All the same, they often contain clear, unconditional provisions necessitating no further implementation entailing any policy choices. If a Member State fails to transpose a directive into national law or fails to transpose it properly, the Court of Justice will hold that an individual may nevertheless derive rights from those of its provisions which satisfy the substantive requirements which must be met in order for Treaty provisions to have direct effect, that is the provisions of the directive which are "unconditional and sufficiently precise" (see para. 21–056).[454] According to the Court, directives must be capable of having direct effects in relations between individuals and Member States because,

22–080

> "the effectiveness [*effet utile*] of such a measure would be weakened if nationals of that State could not invoke it in the courts and if the national courts could not take it into consideration as part of Community law".[455]

In this way, a credit negotiator was entitled to rely against the German tax authorities on a tax exemption provided for in the Sixth VAT Directive even though the directive had not yet been implemented in Germany.[456] Whereas the Court initially based this case law on the need to preserve the *effet utile* of directives, more recent case law tends to emphasise the fact that a Member State which has not (correctly) implemented a directive within the prescribed period may not rely on its own failure to perform the obligations which the directive entails (i.e. on

---

[453] ECJ, Case C-157/02 *Rieser Internationale Transporte and Asfinag* [2004] E.C.R. I-1477, para. 67.

[454] ECJ, Case 8/81 *Becker* [1982] E.C.R. 53, para. 25; ECJ, Case 152/84 *Marshall* ("*Marshall I*") [1986] E.C.R. 723, para. 46; ECJ, Case 103/88 *Fratelli Costanzo* [1989] E.C.R. 1839, para. 29. For an example of provisions of a directive held not to be sufficiently precise, see ECJ (judgment of January 14, 2010), Case C-471/07 *AGIM and Others*, not yet reported, paras 26–29.

[455] ECJ, Case 41/74 *Van Duyn* [1974] E.C.R. 1337, para. 12. For the first cases in which the Court found that directives, in common with regulations, could have direct effects for individuals: ECJ, Case 9/70 *Grad* [1970] E.C.R. 825, para. 5, and ECJ, Case 33/70 *SACE* [1970] E.C.R. 1213, para. 15.

[456] ECJ, Case 8/81 *Becker* [1982] E.C.R. 53, para. 49.

the basis of the principle *nemo auditur*) (see para. 22–082).[457] In order for a provision of a directive to have direct effect, the Court of Justice has held that, in addition to the aforementioned substantive requirements, the following two conditions must be satisfied: (i) the period prescribed for implementing the directive must have expired and (ii) the individual must rely upon the relevant provisions against a State body.

(a) *Expiry of the time-limit*

22–081 **Expiry of the time-limit.** A directive cannot have any direct effect until the period prescribed for implementing it in the national legal system has expired. Direct effect arises only at the end of the prescribed period, provided that the Member State is then in breach of its obligation to transpose the directive.[458] Sometimes a directive prescribes not only a date by which Member States must amend their national provisions, but also a date as from which the amended provisions must be applied. In such a case, the directive cannot produce any effects enforceable by the national courts before the second date has gone by.[459] As soon as a Member State has implemented the directive, its effects reach individuals through the intermediary of the implementing measures, and there is no need to rely directly on its provisions,[460] unless the implementing measures are incorrect or inadequate.[461] Individuals are also entitled to rely directly on the provisions of a directive where national measures correctly implementing the directive are not being applied in such a way as to achieve the result sought by it.[462]

(b) *Direct effect only against a Member State*

22–082 **Effects against a Member State.** An individual may invoke directly effective provisions of a directive only against a Member State which either failed to implement the directive within the prescribed period or implemented it incorrectly. The Court of Justice has held that

> "a Member State which has not adopted the implementing measures
> required by the directive in the prescribed periods may not rely, as against

---

[457] See Emmert and Pereira de Azevedo, "L'effet horizontal des directives. La jurisprudence de la CJCE: un bateau ivre?" (1993) R.T.D.E. 503, at 506–517. For examples, see ECJ, Joined Cases C-388/00 and C-429/00 *Radiosistemi* [2002] E.C.R. I-4301, paras 49–66; ECJ, Joined Cases C-465/00, C-138/01 and C-139/01 *Österreichischer Rundfunk and Others* [2003] E.C.R. I-4919, paras 99–100; ECJ, Case C-157/02 *Rieser Internationale Transporte and Asfinag* [2004] E.C.R. I-1477, para. 67.

[458] ECJ, Case 148/78 *Ratti* [1979] E.C.R. 1629, paras 43–44; see also ECJ, Joined Cases C-140/91, C-141/91, C-278/91 and C-279/91 *Suffriti and Others* [1992] E.C.R. I-6337, paras 11–13.

[459] ECJ, Case C-316/93 *Vaneetveld* [1994] E.C.R. I-763, paras 18–19.

[460] ECJ, Case 270/81 *Felicitas* [1982] E.C.R. 2771, paras 24–26.

[461] ECJ, Joined Cases C-253/96 to C-258/96 *Kampelmann and Others* [1997] E.C.R. I-6907, paras 42–45.

[462] ECJ, Case C-62/00 *Marks & Spencer* [2002] E.C.R. I-6325, para. 27.

individuals, on its own failure to perform the obligations which the directive entails".[463]

The Court's aim is to "prevent the State from taking advantage of its own failure to comply with [Union] law"[464] and therefore reflects the civil law principle *nemo auditur turpitudinem suam allegans* and the common law doctrine of estoppel.[465]

Broad interpretation of the term "Member State". In its judgment in *Marshall I*, the Court held that   **22–083**

> "where a person involved in legal proceedings is able to rely on a directive as against the State he may do so regardless of the capacity in which the latter is acting, whether employer or public authority. In either case it is necessary to prevent the State from taking advantage of its own failure to comply with [Union] law".[466]

By putting a broad construction on the term "State", the Court of Justice considerably extended the situations in which an individual may rely on a directly effective provision of a directive. An individual may so rely against

> "organisations or bodies which were subject to the authority or control of the State or had special powers beyond those which result from the normal rules applicable to relations between individuals".[467]

This has been held to include not only central authorities, such as tax authorities,[468] but also geographically decentralised authorities, such as local and regional authorities,[469] and functionally decentralised authorities.[470] Furthermore, it also includes bodies, whatever their legal form, which have been made responsible,

---

[463] ECJ, Case 148/78 *Ratti* [1979] E.C.R. 1629, para. 22.

[464] ECJ, Case 152/84 *Marshall* ("*Marshall I*") [1986] E.C.R. 723, para. 49; ECJ, Case C-91/92 *Faccini Dori* [1994] E.C.R. I-3325, para. 22.

[465] See Van Gerven, "The Horizontal Effect of Directive Provisions Revisited: The Reality of Catchwords", in Curtin and Heukels (eds), *Institutional Dynamics of European Integration. Essays in Honour of Henry G. Schermers* (Vol. II, Dordrecht, Martinus Nijhoff, 1994) 335, at 343–345.

[466] ECJ, Case 152/84 *Marshall I* [1986] E.C.R. 723, para. 49.

[467] ECJ, Case C-188/89 *Foster and Others* [1990] E.C.R. I-3313, para. 18.

[468] ECJ, Case 8/81 *Becker* [1982] E.C.R. 53, para. 49, and ECJ, Case C-221/88 *Busseni* [1990] E.C.R. I-495, para. 30

[469] ECJ, Case 103/88 *Fratelli Costanzo* [1989] E.C.R. 1839, paras 31–32; ECJ, Joined Cases C-253/96 to C-258/96 *Kampelmann and Others* [1997] E.C.R. I-6907, paras 36–47.

[470] E.g. a constitutionally independent public authority charged with the maintenance of public order and safety (ECJ, Case 222/84 *Johnston* [1986] E.C.R. 1651, paras 56–57) or a public body responsible for the provision of health care (ECJ, Case 152/84 *Marshall I* [1986] E.C.R. 723, para. 49–50).

pursuant to a measure adopted by the State, for providing a public service under the control of the State and have for that purpose special powers beyond those which result from the normal rules applicable in relations between individuals.[471] It appears, therefore, that an individual may rely on rights derived from a directive regardless of the capacity of the body concerned or whether that body was entrusted with the implementation of the directive in national law.

22–084   **No horizontal direct effect.** Also in *Marshall I*, the Court of Justice made it clear that

> "a directive may not of itself impose obligations on an individual and that a provision of a directive may not be relied upon against such a person".[472]

A directive may therefore have vertical but not horizontal direct effect. The Court based its view on the binding nature conferred by Art. 249 EC [*now Art. 288 TFEU*] on a directive only in relation to "each Member State to which it is addressed".[473] Furthermore, the Court of Justice explained in *Faccini Dori* that

> "[t]he effect of extending that case law [on the direct effect of directives] to the sphere of relations between individuals would be to recognise a power in the Community to enact obligations for individuals with immediate effect, whereas it has competence to do so only where it is empowered to adopt regulations".[474]

In *Faccini Dori*, the Court was faced with the fact that Italy had failed to transpose Directive 85/577 to protect the consumer in respect of contracts negotiated away from business premises. The Court held that a consumer could not rely upon her right to cancel a contract within seven days as against the trader with whom she had concluded it in Italy, even though the directive conferred that right unconditionally and sufficiently precisely.[475] It follows that a directly

---

[471] ECJ, Case C-188/89 *Foster and Others* [1990] E.C.R. I-3313, para. 20; ECJ, Case C-157/02 *Rieser Internationale Transporte and Asfinag* [2004] E.C.R. I-1477, para. 22–29; ECJ, Case C-356/05 *Farrell* [2007] E.C.R. I-3067, para. 40. For a discussion of the criterion "public body", see the note to the judgment in *Foster* by Szyszczak (1990) C.M.L.Rev. 868–871; Curtin, "The Province of Government: Delimiting the Direct Effect of Directives in the Common Law Context" (1990) E.L.Rev. 195–223; Prechal, "Remedies after *Marshall*" (1990) C.M.L.Rev. 451, at 457–462.

[472] ECJ, Case 152/84 *Marshall I* [1986] E.C.R. 723, para. 48.

[473] *Ibid.*

[474] ECJ, Case C-91/92 *Faccini Dori* [1994] E.C.R. I-3325, para. 24.

[475] *Ibid.*, paras 18 and 30; see also ECJ, Case C-192/94 *El Corte Inglés* [1996] E.C.R. I-1281, paras 15–21.

effective provision of a directive cannot be enforced by an individual as against another individual and, *a fortiori*, not by a public authority against an individual.[476]

In addition, an individual may not rely on a directly effective provision of a directive against a public authority where this would directly lead to the directive imposing obligations on another individual.[477] Accordingly, the Court held in its judgment in *Wells* that an individual may not rely on a directive against a Member State where it is a matter of a State obligation directly linked to the performance of an obligation falling, pursuant to that directive, on a third party.[478] Mere adverse repercussions on the rights of third parties, even if the repercussions are certain, do not justify preventing an individual from invoking the provisions of a directive against the Member State concerned.[479]

Directives versus regulations. The fact that the rights enshrined in a directive can be enforced only if the directive has been transposed or, in the absence of (correct) transposition, only against a public body hampers the uniform application through the Union of Union legislation adopted in the form of a directive. Whereas an individual can rely unconditionally as against another individual on rights conferred by a regulation, this is possible in the case of a directive only if the directive has been correctly implemented in the Member State in question. This means that individuals in Member States which have not transposed the directive correctly do not enjoy the same rights as individuals in the rest of the Union. Moreover, failure to transpose a directive may mean that it is applied to **22–085**

---

[476] ECJ, Joined Cases 372–374/85 *Traen* [1987] E.C.R. 2141, para. 24; ECJ, Case 14/86 *Pretore de Salò v Persons Unknown* [1987] E.C.R. 2545, paras 19–20; ECJ, Case 80/86 *Kolpinghuis Nijmegen* [1987] E.C.R. 3969, paras 9–10; ECJ, Case C-168/95 *Arcaro* [1996] E.C.R. I-4705, paras 33–38; ECJ (order of September 19, 2001), Case C-18/00 *Perino*, not reported, paras 22–26; ECJ (judgment of October 7, 2010), Case C-224/09 *Nussbaumer*, not yet reported, para. 30.

[477] ECJ, Case C-97/96 *Daihatsu Deutschland* [1997] E.C.R. I-6843, paras 24–25. See also (with regard to an ECSC recommendation) ECJ, Case C-221/88 *Busseni* [1990] E.C.R. I-495, paras 23–26, in which the ECSC was equated with an individual for the purposes of invoking a provision according preferential treatment in proving certain debts owed to it by an insolvent undertaking. The Court noted that the ECSC's claim for preferential treatment would affect the rights of all other creditors of the undertaking whose debts did not enjoy the same preferential status and therefore ruled that the ECSC's preferential status was not to prejudice the rights of creditors other than the State.

[478] ECJ, Case C-201/02 *Wells*, [2004] E.C.R. I-723, paras 56 and 58.

[479] *Ibid.*, para. 57. In the case at hand, an individual challenged the decision by which national authorities had given permission for mining operations at a quarry without the environmental impact assessment laid down by a Community directive having first been carried out. The Court considered that the adjoining landowner could invoke the directive even if the fact that mining operations had to be halted to await the results of that assessment was a consequence of the belated performance of the State's obligations. It held that the obligation on the Member State to ensure that the competent authorities carried out the environmental impact assessment was not directly linked to the performance of any obligation which would fall on the quarry owners. *Ibid.*, para. 58. See also ECJ, Joined Cases C-152/07 to C-154/07 *Arcor and Others* [2008] E.C.R. I-5959, paras 34–43. See further para. 22–090, *infra*.

similar fact situations differently within a Member State, for instance where certain individuals may assert their rights by making a claim against a public authority (for instance, public-sector employees) whilst others may not enforce the same rights in a private legal relationship (for instance, private-sector employees).[480] Some commentators consider that it is necessary in the interest of uniform, equal application of Union law that an individual should be able to rely as against other individuals on clear and unconditional provisions of a directive which has not been (properly) implemented.[481] However, it appears from *Faccini Dori* that a directive does not acquire the same legal force as a regulation after the period prescribed for implementing it has run out.[482]

3. Other effects of an unimplemented or incorrectly implemented directive

22–086   **Principles ensuring effectiveness.** Where a provision of a directive has not been (correctly) implemented, the absence of direct effect does not exclude this provision from having certain "effects" on the legal position of the authorities or individuals concerned. To that end, the case law has formulated a number of Union-law principles.[483] Thus, the national courts must:

---

[480] The Court of Justice accepted that consequence in ECJ, Case 152/84 *Marshall I* [1986] E.C.R. 723, para. 51. The prohibition of discrimination laid down *in the Treaties* may well apply in relations between individuals because that prohibition has direct effect and, as a Treaty provision, is applicable without further qualification in the national legal systems: ECJ, Case 36/74 *Walrave* [1974] E.C.R. 1405, para. 18 *et seq.*

[481] See the Opinion of Advocate-General W. Van Gerven in ECJ, Case C-271/91 *Marshall II* [1993] E.C.R. I-4367, point 12; the Opinion of Advocate-General F.G. Jacobs in ECJ, Case C-316/93 *Vaneetveld* [1994] E.C.R. I-763, point 18 *et seq.*, and the Opinion of Advocate-General C.O. Lenz in ECJ, Case C-91/92 *Faccini Dori* [1994] E.C.R. I-3325, points 43 *et seq.*; see also Emmert and Pereira de Azevedo (n. 457, *supra*), and Barents, "Some Remarks on the 'Horizontal' Effects of Directives", in O'Keeffe and Schermers (eds), *Essays in European Law and Integration*, (Deventer, Kluwer, 1982), 97–104; Wyatt, "The Direct Effect of Community Social Law—Not Forgetting Directives" (1983) E.L.Rev. 241–248; for the contrary view, see Timmermans, "Directives: Their Effect within the National Legal Systems" (1979) C.M.L.Rev. 533, at 541–544; for arguments for and against, see Easson, "Can Directives impose Obligations on Individuals" (1979) E.L.Rev. 67–79.

[482] For a commentary on this judgment, see Tridimas, "Horizontal Effect of Directives: A Missed Opportunity" (1994) E.L.Rev. 621–636, and the note by Robinson (1995) C.M.L.Rev. 629–639. Even though this case law was confirmed, the academic debate continued, see Betlem, "Medium Hard Law—Still No Horizontal Direct Effect of European Community Directives After *Faccini Dori*" (1995) Col.J.E.L. 469–496; Emmert and Pereira de Azevedo, "Les jeux sont faits: rien ne va plus ou une occasion perdue par la CJCE" (1995) R.T.D.E. 11–21.

[483] See von Danwitz, "Rechtswirkungen von Richtlinien in der neueren Rechtsprechung des EuGH" (2007) 62 J.Z. 697–706; Lenz, Tynes and Young, "Horizontal What? Back to Basics" (2000) E.L.Rev. 509–522; Schockweiler, "Les effets des directives dans les ordres juridiques nationaux" (1995) 2 R.M.U.E. 9–26; Plaza Martin, "Furthering the Effectiveness of EC Directives and the Judicial Protection of Individual Rights Thereunder" (1994) I.C.L.Q. 26–54.

(1) construe national law as far as possible in a way which is consistent with the directive; and

(2) in principle, give the directive in question precedence over conflicting rules of national law;

(3) where, in spite of this, the result required to be obtained by the directive cannot be attained, the Member State will be required to make good the damage caused to individuals as a result of its failure to transpose the directive, provided that certain conditions are fulfilled.

Where necessary, the national court should first refer to the Court of Justice for a preliminary ruling on the interpretation of the directive (Art. 267 TFEU [*ex Art. 234 EC*]), without being either compelled to make, or prevented from making, a reference before taking one of the steps mentioned above.[484]

(a) *Interpretation in conformity with the directive*

Interpretation in conformity with the directive. In the first place, national courts must make use of the methods of interpretation available to them under national law so as to interpret national law as far as possible in conformity with the directive. The Court of Justice has held that,

> "the Member States' obligation arising from a directive to achieve the result envisaged by the directive and their duty under Article 10 of the Treaty [*see now Article 4(3) TEU*] to take all appropriate measures, whether general or particular, to ensure fulfilment of that obligation, is binding on all the authorities of Member States including, for matters within their jurisdiction, the courts. It follows that, in applying the national law . . ., national courts are required to interpret their national law in the light of the wording and the purpose of the directive in order to achieve the result referred to in the third paragraph of Article 189 [*now Article 288 TFEU*]".[485]

The Court has made it clear that this applies not only in applying "the provisions of a national law specifically introduced in order to implement" the directive[486] but "whether the provisions in question were adopted before or after the directive".[487] National courts are required to consider national law as a whole in order

22–087

---

[484] ECJ (judgment of January 19, 2010), Case C-555/07 *Kücükdeveci*, not yet reported, paras 53–55.
[485] ECJ, Case 14/83 *Von Colson and Kamann* [1984] E.C.R. 1891, para. 26; ECJ, Case 79/83 *Harz* [1984] E.C.R. 1921, para. 26.
[486] *Ibid.*
[487] ECJ, Case C-106/89 *Marleasing* [1990] E.C.R. I-4135, para. 8; ECJ, Case C-188/07 *Commune de Mesquer* [2008] E.C.R. I-4501, paras 80–85.

to assess to what extent it may be applied so as not to produce a result contrary to that sought by the directive.[488]

The general obligation owed by national courts to interpret national law in conformity with the directive exists only once the period for its transposition has expired. However, before that date, national courts are under a duty, in accordance with *Inter-Environnement Wallonie* (see para. 22–079), to refrain as far as possible from interpreting national law in a manner which might seriously compromise the attainment of the objective pursued by the directive after the period for transposition has expired.[489]

After the expiry of the time-limit for implementation, the national court is under a duty also to interpret in the light of the directive rules of law not adopted specifically in order to transpose the directive at least with respect to facts which occurred after the expiry of that time-limit.[490] Pursuant to a principle of national law according to which more favourable provisions of criminal law have retroactive effect, national courts may set aside domestic provisions which conflict with a directive (whether transposed or not) in respect of offences which occurred before the period prescribed for transposition had expired.[491]

22–088 **Possibility of interpretation in conformity with the directive.** The national court must interpret national law "as far as possible" in conformity with the directive.[492] The relevant provision of national law must, however, be amenable to such interpretation.[493] The national court is therefore not obliged to make an interpretation *contra legem*.[494] The obligation to interpret national law in conformity with a directive is also

---

[488] ECJ, Case C-131/97 *Carbonari and Others* [1999] E.C.R. I-1103, paras 49 and 50; ECJ, Joined Cases C-397/01 to C-403/01 *Pfeiffer* [2004] E.C.R. I-8835, para. 115; ECJ, Case C-12/08 *Mono Car Styling* [2009] E.C.R. I-6653, para. 62.

[489] ECJ, Case C-212/04 *Adeneler* [2006] E.C.R. I-6057, para. 113–123; ECJ (Order of June 12, 2008), Case C-364/07 *Vassilakis and Others*, not reported, paras 53–71; ECJ, Joined Cases C-378/07 to C-380/07 *Angelidaki and Others* [2009] E.C.R. I-3071, paras 197–201; ECJ (judgment of January 14, 2010), Case C-304/08 *Plus Warenhandelsgesellschaft*, not yet reported, para. 29. Where the directive provides for the application of certain provisions from the date of its entry into force, national provisions that fall within the scope of that directive may have to be interpreted in conformity therewith: ECJ, Case C-81/05 *Cordero Alonso* [2006] E.C.R. I-7569, paras 27–34.

[490] ECJ, Case C-456/98 *Centrosteel* [1998] E.C.R. I-6007, para. 17; ECJ, Joined Cases C-397/01 to C-403/01 *Pfeiffer* [2004] E.C.R. I-8835, para. 117.

[491] ECJ, Case C-230/97 *Awoyemi* [1998] E.C.R. I-6781, paras 32–45.

[492] ECJ, Case C-106/89 *Marleasing* [1990] E.C.R. I-4135, para. 8.

[493] ECJ, Case C-334/92 *Wagner Miret* [1993] E.C.R. I-6911, para. 22.

[494] ECJ, Case C-212/04 *Adeneler* [2006] E.C.R. I-6057, para. 110.

"limited by the general principles of law which form part of [Union] law and in particular the principles of legal certainty and non-retroactivity".[495]

However, within these limits, national courts must where necessary adjust the existing case law. They must do whatever lies within their jurisdiction, to ensure a result which is consistent with the directive.[496] For the same reason, national courts may be required in certain circumstances to disapply rules of national law which conflict with the provisions of the directive in question (see para. 22–090).

Consequences for individuals. The obligation to interpret national law in conformity with directives holds good irrespective as to whether their provisions have direct effect. As a result of such an interpretation of national law, the provisions of the directive in question may also be effective vis-à-vis individuals.[497] In such a case, there is no question of a non-implemented directive imposing obligations on individuals since any obligation falling on individuals would be based on the provisions of national law.[498] The duty to interpret domestic law in conformity with Union law comes up against a limitation, however, where such an interpretation would mean that obligations imposed by a non-implemented directive could be relied upon as against an individual.[499] This is the case, for instance, where such an interpretation would have the effect of determining or aggravating, on the basis of a directive (in the absence of a law adopted for its implementation), the liability in criminal law of persons acting in contravention of the

22–089

---

[495] ECJ, Case 80/86 *Kolpinghuis Nijmegen* [1987] E.C.R. 3969, para. 13; for an application, see ECJ, Case 14/86 *Pretore de Salò v Persons Unknown* [1987] E.C.R. 2545, para. 20; ECJ, Joined Cases C-74/95 and C-129/95 *Criminal proceedings against X* [1996] E.C.R. I-6609, paras 25 and 31. For the limits which national law may place on the ability to interpret national law in conformity with a directive, see Schürnbrand, "Die Grenzen richtlinienkonformer Rechtsfortbildung im Privatrecht" (2007) 62 J.Z. 910–918; Roth, "Die richtlinienkonforme Auslegung" (2005) E.W.S. 385–396; De Búrca (n. 61, *supra*), at 215–240 (case law in the United Kingdom); Jarass, "Richtlinienkonforme bzw. EG-rechtskonforme Auslegung nationalen Rechts" (1992) EuR. 211, at 220–223. For national case law holding interpretation consistent with a directive to be possible/impossible, see Verhoeven, "The application in Belgium of the duties of loyalty and cooperation" (2000) S.E.W. 328, at 332–334.

[496] ECJ, Joined Cases C-397/01 to C-403/01 *Pfeiffer* [2004] E.C.R. I-8835, paras 116–118.

[497] Interpreting national law in the light of the directive may result in an individual being held to comply with certain obligations under national law or in that individual being precluded from effectuating claims against another individual. See ECJ, Case C-106/89 *Marleasing* [1990] E.C.R. I-4135, paras 6–9; ECJ, Case C-421/92 *Habermann-Beltermann* [1994] E.C.R. I-1657, paras 8–10; ECJ, Case C-472/93 *Spano and Others* [1995] E.C.R. I-4321, paras 17–18; ECJ, Case C-129/94 *Ruiz Bernáldez* [1996] E.C.R. I-1829, paras 1–26; ECJ, Joined Cases C-240/98 to C-244/98 *Océano Grupo Editorial and Others* [2000] E.C.R. I-4941, paras 20–32; ECJ, Case C-456/98 *Centrosteel* [2000] E.C.R. I-6007, paras 13–18. See also Ress (n. 544), at 489–496.

[498] ECJ, Case C-321/05 *Kofoed* [2007] E.C.R. I-5795, para. 45.

[499] See ECJ, Case C-355/96 *Silhouette International Schmied* [1998] E.C.R. I-4799, paras 32–37.

directive's provisions.[500] Even where criminal liability arises under legislation adopted for the specific purpose of implementing a directive, the national court must take account of the principle that criminal proceedings may not be brought in respect of conduct which is not clearly defined as culpable by law.[501] In proceedings between individuals, it is up to the national court to determine whether, in the absence of direct effect, the provisions of national law can be interpreted to achieve the result claimed by the applicant,[502] if necessary by disapplying conflicting rules of national law.[503] If the application of interpretative methods recognised by national law enables a provision of domestic law to be construed in such a way as to avoid conflict with another rule of domestic law or the scope of that provision to be restricted to that end by applying it only in so far as it is compatible with the rule concerned, the national court is bound to use those methods in order to achieve the result sought by the directive.[504]

(b) *Disapplication of conflicting national law*

22–090 **Disapplication.** Secondly, it follows from the primacy of Union law that the provisions of a directive must enjoy precedence over conflicting rules of national law. This obligation arises because of the primacy of Union law[505] and therefore holds good irrespective as to whether the provisions of the directive relied upon have direct effect. The provisions need only be sufficiently clear as to serve as a yardstick.[506] This applies in the first place to measures taken specifically with a view to implementing a directive. The national court must consider,

> "whether the competent national authorities, in exercising the choice which is left to them as to the form and the methods of implementing the directive, have kept within the limits as to their discretion set out in the directive".[507]

---

[500] ECJ, Case 14/86 *Pretore di Salò v Persons Unknown* [1987] E.C.R. 2545, para. 20; ECJ, Case 80/86 *Kolpinghuis Nijmegen* [1987] E.C.R. 3969, paras 13–14; ECJ, Case C-168/95 *Arcaro* [1996] E.C.R. I-4705, para. 42.

[501] ECJ, Joined Cases C-74/95 and C-129/95 *Criminal proceedings against X* [1996] E.C.R. I-6609, para. 25 (which refers to Art. 7 of the ECHR).

[502] See, e.g., ECJ, Case C-343/98 *Collino and Chiaperro* [2000] E.C.R. I-6659, paras 20–24.

[503] See, e.g., ECJ, Case C-456/98 *Centrosteel* [2000] E.C.R. I-6007, para. 17.

[504] ECJ, Joined Cases C-397/01 to C-403/01 *Pfeiffer* [2004] E.C.R. I-8835, para. 116; ECJ, Case C-12/08 *Mono Car Styling* [2009] E.C.R. I-6653, para. 63.

[505] See ECJ (judgment of January 19, 2010), Case C-555/07 *Kücükdeveci*, not yet reported, para. 54.

[506] See ECJ, Case C-72/95 *Kraaijeveld and Others* [1996] E.C.R. I-5403, paras 59–61; ECJ, Case C-435/97 *World Wildlife Fund* [1999] E.C.R. I-5613, paras 69–71; ECJ, Case C-287/98 *Linster and Others* [2000] E.C.R. I-6917, paras 31–39. See also Manin, "L'invocabilité des directives: Quelques interrogations" (1990) R.T.D.E. 669–693; for the application of such a test in France, see para. 21–028, *supra*.

[507] ECJ, Case 51/76 *Verbond van Nederlandse Ondernemingen* [1977] E.C.R. 113, paras 22–24; ECJ, Case 38/77 *Enka* [1977] E.C.R. 2203, paras 10 and 17–18. This is also true of individual decisions: ECJ, Case 36/75 *Rutili* [1975] E.C.R. 1219, paras 17–20.

If national law confers on courts and tribunals discretion to apply mandatory rules of law of their own motion, they must examine *ex proprio motu* whether the national authorities remained within the limits of their discretion under the directive.[508] However, the review to be conducted of national law in the light of the directive extends further than measures taken to implement it; it covers all rules governing the application of the directive in the national legal system, including rules which applied before the directive was adopted.[509] In this connection, a national court may also be obliged to disapply national procedural or jurisdictional rules which would impede the protection of rights contained in the directive (see para. 21–012). In principle, the obligation to refrain from applying conflicting rules of national law exists only after the deadline for implementing the directive has expired.[510]

Public authorities other than the courts must also refrain from applying national rules which conflict with a directive. For instance, a local authority has been held to be under a duty to refrain from applying conflicting provisions of a national law.[511] Moreover, all the authorities of a Member State must take, according to their respective powers, all the general and particular measures necessary to ensure that the result sought by the directive is achieved.[512]

Consequences for individuals. The Court of Justice has clarified the obligation to disapply conflicting rules of national law in a number of cases where provisions of an unimplemented or incorrectly implemented directive have been invoked against a public authority. In such a "vertical" context, the disapplication of conflicting rules of national law may indirectly have repercussions on the legal position of private parties who infer rights from those rules or are exempted under those rules from certain obligations. This will be the case, e.g., where an individual challenges the legality of decisions (on grounds of incompatibility with a Union directive) by which national authorities approve private projects having an effect on the environment[513] or grant a marketing authorisation to a competitor.[514] The same will be true where national rules are disapplied because they were adopted contrary to a duty of notification imposed by a Union directive.[515]

22–091

---

[508] ECJ, Case C-72/95 *Kraaijeveld and Others* [1996] E.C.R. I-5403, paras 57–58.

[509] ECJ, Case 21/78 *Delkvist* [1978] E.C.R. 2327, paras 13–16. For the inapplicability of rules adopted contrary to a duty of notification laid down by a directive, see n. 515, *infra*.

[510] ECJ, Case C-157/02 *Rieser Internationale Transporte and Asfinag* [2004] E.C.R. I-1477, paras 67–68. For the situation during the period for implementation, see para. 22–078, *supra*.

[511] ECJ, Case 103/88 *Fratelli Costanzo* [1989] E.C.R. 1839, para. 33.

[512] ECJ, Case C-72/95 *Kraaijeveld and Others* [1996] E.C.R. I-5403, para. 61; ECJ, Case C-435/97 *World Wildlife Fund* [1999] E.C.R. I-5613, para. 70.

[513] E.g. the cases cited in the preceding n.; see also ECJ, Case C-201/02 *Wells* [2004] E.C.R. I-723, cited in para. 22–083, *supra*).

[514] E.g., ECJ, Case C-201/94 *Smith & Nephew and Primecrown* [1996] E.C.R. I-5819, paras 35–39.

[515] ECJ, Case C-194/94 *CIA Security International* [1996] E.C.R. I-2201, paras 32–55; ECJ, Case C-443/98 *Unilever Italia* [2000] E.C.R. I-7535, paras 45–51. See Weatherill, "Breach of directives and breach of contract" (2001) E.L.Rev. 177–186.

Similarly, a national court may be confronted with conflicting rules of national law in litigation between individuals. Where the national court decides to ask the Court of Justice for a preliminary ruling, it may be prompted by the Court's answer to disapply the conflicting provisions of national law.[516] Furthermore, Union law may also require a national court to disapply conflicting rules of national law where an individual invokes provisions of an unimplemented or incorrectly implemented directive against an individual.[517] Likewise, the Court confirmed in *Kücükdevici*—in proceedings between an employee and her former (private) employer—that the principle of non-discrimination on grounds of age, as a general principle of Union law recognised in Art. 21 of the Charter of Fundamental Rights of the European Union and given further expression in Directive 2000/78, requires the national court to disapply any contrary provision of national law.[518] Thus, the disapplication of the conflicting national provision— the prohibition on taking into account in calculating the period of notice for dismissals any period of employment completed by the employee before reaching the age of 25—led to the imposition on the employer of the obligation not to discriminate on grounds of age, as expressed both in a general principle of Union law and in Directive 2000/78. This ruling of the Court shows that to the extent that directives give concrete content to a general principle of Union law enshrined in the Charter of Fundamental Rights of the European Union and that principle lends itself to application between private parties, the horizontal effect of that principle, as understood on the basis of the directive, may lead to the disapplication of contrary national provisions. As such, this situation is to be distinguished from that in which the disapplication of national provisions would lead to the imposition on an individual, without any basis in national law, of an obligation laid down solely by a directive which had not been (correctly) implemented.[519] In

---

[516] See, e.g., ECJ, Case C-85/94 *Piageme and Others* [1995] E.C.R. I-2955, paras 1–31; ECJ, Case C-441/93 *Pafitis and Others* [1996] E.C.R. I-1347, paras 1–70;ECJ, Case C-180/95 *Draehmpaehl* [1997] E.C.R. I-2195, paras 16–43; ECJ, Case C-215/97 *Bellone* [1998] E.C.R. I-2191, paras 9–18.

[517] See ECJ, Joined Cases C-397/01 to C-403/01 *Pfeiffer* [2004] E.C.R. I-8835, para. 116. (litigation between employees and private employer). The Court considered disapplication of conflicting provisions of national law as an "interpretative method" to be used by national courts in order to achieve the result sought by the directive where such a method is recognised by national law (*ibid.*).

[518] ECJ (judgment of January 19, 2010), Case C-555/07 *Kücükdeveci*, not yet reported, paras 51–55.

[519] See ECJ (order of 24 October 2002), Case C-233/01 *Riunione Adriatica di Securtà* [2002] E.C.R. I-9411, paras 20–21 (interpretation cannot enable the national court to give judgment against an individual for the payment of a debt which the Court held not to be based on national law). See also Lenaerts and Corthaut, "Towards an Internally Consistent Doctrine on Invoking Norms of EU Law", in Prechal and Van Roermund (eds), *The Coherence of EU Law. The Search for Unity in Divergent Concepts* (Oxford, Oxford University Press, 2008) 495–515; Straetmans, *Consument en markt*, (Deurne, Kluwer, 1998), 255–265; A[rnull], "Editorial: The Incidental Effect of Directives" (1999) E.L.Rev. 1–2; Lackhoff and Nyssens, "Direct Effect of Directives in Triangular Situations" (1998) E.L.Rev. 397.

a setting of that kind, disapplication of national provisions is not required by Union law, nor may it have the effect of determining or aggravating, on the basis of the directive and in the absence of a national law enacted for its implementation, the liability in criminal law of persons who act in contravention of that directive's provisions.[520]

(c) State liability for damages

State liability. An individual may obtain redress for loss or damage sustained as the result of the non-transposition of a directive by bringing a damages claim against the Member State. The fate of the claim no longer depends on the extent to which national law recognises that the State may be liable for legislative action or inaction. Following the judgment in *Francovich* (see para. 21–014), it has become clear that liability for loss or damage caused by a breach of Union law constitutes a general principle of Union law. The Court of Justice has indicated that it would be possible to bring a damages claim where an individual could not rely on the provisions of a non-implemented directive on the ground that such provisions required additional implementing measures and hence could not have direct effect,[521] that the national law could not be interpreted in conformity with the directive[522] or that the provisions—albeit satisfying the substantive requirements for direct effect— were invoked as against another individual.[523] This does not mean that there is no right to damages also where a provision having direct effect is infringed.

22–092

Conditions. In *Francovich* the Court set out the conditions under which Member States are bound under Union law to make good loss or damage suffered by individuals as a result of a failure to transpose a directive.[524] In later case law, the Court extended these conditions to all breaches of Union law. As a result, in the case of directives that were not or incorrectly implemented, State liability will

22–093

---

[520] ECJ, Case C-168/95 *Arcaro* [1996] E.C.R. I-4705, paras 39–43; ECJ, Joined Cases C-387/02, C-391/02 and C-403/02 *Berlusconi and Others* [2005] E.C.R. I-3565, paras 71–78. See Gelter, "Judicial federalism in the ECJ's Berlusconi case: toward more credible corporate governance and financial reporting" (2005) 46 Harv.I.L.J.487–505.

[521] ECJ, Joined Cases C-6/90 and C-9/90 *Francovich and Others* [1991] E.C.R. I-5357, paras 26–27.

[522] ECJ, Case C-334/92 *Wagner Miret* [1993] E.C.R. I-6911, para. 22; ECJ, Case C-111/97 *Evobus Austria* [1998] E.C.R. I-5411, paras 14–21.

[523] ECJ, Case C-91/92 *Faccini Dori* [1994] E.C.R. I-3325, para. 25; ECJ, Case C-192/94 *El Corte Inglés* [1996] E.C.R. I-1281, para. 22. Compare ECJ, Case C-97/96 *Daihatsu Deutschland* [1997] E.C.R. I-6843, paras 24–26 (where, with regard to a dispute between private legal persons, the Court of Justice did not consider it necessary to inquire into the direct effect of the directive and merely referred to the possibility of a damages claim) with ECJ, Joined Cases C-253/96 to C-258/96 *Kampelmann and Others* [1997] E.C.R. I-6907, para. 46 (where, with regard to disputes between individuals and public undertakings, the Court inquired into direct effect and did not discuss the damages claim).

[524] ECJ, Joined Cases C-6/90 and C-9/90 *Francovich and Others* [1991] E.C.R. I-5357, paras 39–41.

exist under the same three conditions that apply for breaches of Union law in general (see para. 21–015):

(1) the rule of law infringed must be intended to confer rights on individuals;

(2) the breach must be sufficiently serious; and

(3) there must be a direct causal link between the breach of the obligation resting on the State and the damage sustained by the injured parties.[525]

As to the second condition, the decisive criterion for a breach of Union law to be regarded as sufficiently serious is whether the Member State has manifestly and gravely disregarded the limits of its discretion.[526] Where a Member State fails to take any of the measures necessary to achieve the result prescribed by the directive within the period it lays down, this in itself will constitute a sufficiently serious breach of Union law.[527] In the case of an incorrectly implemented directive, the breach will be "sufficiently serious" where the Member State manifestly and gravely disregarded the limits on the exercise of its discretion.[528] Factors which the competent court may take into consideration include in particular the clarity and precision of the rule breached, and the scope of the discretion left to the national authorities. Where, however, at the time when it committed the infringement, a Member State was not called upon to make any legislative choices and had only considerably reduced discretion, or even none at all, the mere infringement of Union law may be sufficient to establish the existence of a sufficiently serious breach.[529] Such a breach of Union law may exist on the basis of the wrong transposition of only one sufficiently clear provision of a directive.[530] Where a directive leaves a degree of discretion to Member States, resulting in their having to make choices when legislating to transpose the directive, the national court hearing a claim for reparation must take account of all the factors which characterise the

---

[525] ECJ, Case C-392/93 *British Telecommunications* [1996] E.C.R. I-1631, para. 39. These rules have applied to legislative acts of the Union since ECJ, Case 5/71 *Zuckerfabrik Schöppenstedt v Council* [1971] E.C.R. 975, para. 11: see Lenaerts, Arts and Maselis, *Procedural Law of the European Union* (3rd edn, London, Sweet & Maxwell, 2012), Ch. 11. For the parallel with the rules on liability applying to the Union, see ECJ, Case C-352/98P *Laboratoires pharmaceutiques Bergaderm and Goupil v Commission* [2000] E.C.R. I-5291, paras 38–44; for breaches of fundamental rights, see Van Gerven, "Remedies for Infringements of Fundamental Rights" (2004) E.Pub.L. 261–284.

[526] ECJ, Case C-470/03 *A.G.M.-COS.MET* [2007] E.C.R. I-2749, para. 80, see the case note by Bouhier (2007) R.T.D.E. 693–719.

[527] ECJ, Joined Cases C-178/94, C-179/94, C-188/94, C-189/94 and C-190/94 *Dillenkofer and Others* [1996] E.C.R. I-4845, para. 26; ECJ, Case C-150/99 *Stockholm Lindöpark* [2001] E.C.R. I-493, paras 36–41.

[528] ECJ, Case C-392/93 *British Telecommunications* [1996] E.C.R. I-1631, paras 39–45.

[529] ECJ, Case C-5/94 *Hedley Lomas* [1996] E.C.R. I-2553, para. 28; ECJ, Case C-452/06 *Synthon* [2008] E.C.R. I-7681, paras 36–45.

[530] ECJ, Case C-140/97 *Rechberger and Greindl* [1999] E.C.R. I-3499, paras 51–53.

situation put before it. Those factors include, in particular, in addition to the clarity and precision of the rule infringed and the measure of discretion left by that rule to the national authorities, whether the infringement or the damage caused was intentional or involuntary, whether any error of law was excusable or inexcusable, and the fact that the position taken by a Union institution may have contributed towards the adoption or maintenance of national measures or practices contrary to Union law.[531] Accordingly, the incorrect transposition of provisions of a directive capable of bearing several interpretations on which neither the Court of Justice nor the Commission have given a ruling does not constitute a sufficiently serious breach.[532]

There is no need for the existence of intentional fault or negligence on the part of the organ of the State for the breach to entail a right to damages, provided that the aforementioned three conditions are satisfied.[533] Nor is reparation dependent on a prior finding by the Court of Justice of an infringement of Union law attributable to the State.[534]

Reparation of damage. Retroactive application in full of the measures implement-   **22–094**
ing the directive constitutes proper reparation, unless the beneficiaries establish the existence of complementary loss resulting from failure to implement the directive in time, in which case such loss must also be made good.[535] Bringing a claim for damages may be made subject to a reasonable limitation period (such as one year commencing from the entry into force of the measure transposing the directive), provided that the relevant procedural rule is not less favourable than those relating to similar domestic claims.[536] Naturally, the formal and substantive conditions laid down by national law must not be less favourable than those relating to similar domestic claims and must not be such as in practice to make it impossible or excessively difficult to obtain compensation (see para. 21–019).

D. DECISIONS

Definition. A decision is "binding in its entirety". A decision "which specifies   **22–095**
those to whom it is addressed" is "binding only on them" (Art. 288, fourth para.,

---

[531] ECJ, Case C-278/05 *Robins and Others* [2007] E.C.R. I-1053, paras 77–81.

[532] ECJ, Case C-392/93 *British Telecommunications* [1996] E.C.R. I-1631, paras 42–46; see also ECJ, Joined Cases C-283/94, C-291/94 and C-292/94 *Denkavit and Others* [1996] E.C.R. I-5063, paras 50–53; ECJ, Case C-319/96 *Brinkmann Tabakfabriken* [1998] E.C.R. I-5255, paras 30–31.

[533] For lack of a direct causal link between the infringement of Union law and the damage, see ECJ, Case C-319/96 *Brinkmann Tabakfabriken* [1998] E.C.R. I-5255, para. 29.

[534] *Dillenkofer and Others*, cited in n. 530, paras 27–28; ECJ, Case C-445/06 *Danske Slagterier* [2009] E.C.R. I-2119, paras 37–38.

[535] ECJ, Joined Cases C-94–95/95 *Bonifaci and Others and Berto and Others* [1997] E.C.R. I-3969, paras 51–54; ECJ, Case C-373/95 *Maso and Others* [1997] E.C.R. I-4051, paras 39–42.

[536] ECJ, Case C-261/95 *Palmisani* [1997] E.C.R. I-4025, paras 28–40.

TFEU). It follows that a decision is not necessarily addressed to specific persons and can be general in scope.

22–096 **"Sui generis" decisions.** This definition, introduced by the Lisbon Treaty, is wider in scope than the one contained in Art. 249, fourth para., EC, which provided that "a decision shall be binding in its entirety upon those to whom it is addressed". Accordingly, a decision in the sense of Art. 249 EC necessarily had specific addressees.

All the same, the institutions often used "decisions" for binding acts which did not satisfy this definition. These "decisions" were sometimes referred to as "*sui generis* decisions" (termed in Dutch a *besluit* and in German a *Beschluss* and hence differing from the terms *beschikking* and *Entscheidung* used in Art. 249 EC). The Council often used instruments so styled where it adopted a legislative act on the basis of a Treaty provision, such as Art. 308 EC [*now Art. 352 TFEU*], which does not prescribe any particular instrument.[537] The institutions also adopted various such decisions in connection with their internal organisation or in order to adopt the statutes of other bodies.[538] Furthermore, the Council used such instruments to amend certain provisions of the Treaties[539] and to adopt rules of an organic nature, such as the Comitology Decisions.[540] Generally, too, the Community approved an international agreement by means of such a "decision".[541]

Since the Lisbon Treaty, such "*sui generis* decisions" are adopted as decisions under the fourth para. of Art. 288 TFEU.

22–097 **Individual or general scope.** It is clear from the definition in Art. 288 TFEU that a decision will often, but not necessarily, be a measure of individual scope. As a

---

[537] See, e.g., Council Decision 87/327/EEC of June 15, 1987 adopting the European Community Action Scheme for the Mobility of University Students (Erasmus), [1987] O.J. L166/20, which was based on Arts 128 and 235 EEC. It was replaced by Decision 89/663/EEC of December 14, 1989, based on Art. 128 EEC, [1989] O.J. L395/23.

[538] See, for example, the Council's Rules of Procedure (see para. 13–047, *supra*); see also the Ombudsman Regulations adopted by the European Parliament (see para. 13–118, *supra*). See also the Council Decision of March 29, 1994 concerning the taking of [a] Decision by qualified majority by the Council, [1994] O.J. C105/1 (the "Ioannina Compromise"), which, however, did not have any binding legal effects (para. 13–051, *supra*).

[539] Para. 5–009, *supra*. Council decisions which have to be adopted by the Member States in accordance with their respective constitutional requirements constitute "primary Community law", para. 22–015, *supra*.

[540] Council Decision 87/373/EEC of July 13, 1987 laying down the conditions for the exercise of implementing powers conferred on the Commission, [1987] O.J. L197/33, and Council Decision 1999/468/EC of June 28, 1999 laying down the conditions for the exercise of implementing powers conferred on the Commission, [1999] O.J. L184/33 (para. 17–012, *supra*). See also Council Decision 88/591/ECSC, EEC, Euratom of October 24, 1988 establishing a Court of First Instance, [1988] O.J. L319/1 (para. 13–077, *supra*).

[541] See para. 26–007, *infra*.

measure of individual scope, a decision is an appropriate normative instrument for executive acts of the institutions. Accordingly, when supervising compliance with the competition rules, the Commission addresses decisions to the undertakings and Member States concerned.[542] With regard to Art. 106(3) TFEU [ex *Art. 86(3) EC*]—which entitles the Commission to adopt both directives and decisions—the Court of Justice has explained that directives enable the Commission to specify in general terms the obligations arising for Member States under the Treaties, while the possibility of adopting decisions empowers the Commission to determine that a given State measure is incompatible with the rules of the Treaties and to indicate what measures the State to which the decision is addressed must adopt in order to comply with its obligations under Union law.[543]

A decision may be addressed to individuals and Member States alike. A decision addressed to all the Member States will often constitute a legislative act.[544] An innominate act addressed by an institution to a particular person may constitute a decision only if it is intended to produce legal effects.[545]

Binding force. A decision is binding in its entirety. Decisions with specific addressees are binding only on the latter.[546] The principle of legal certainty precludes reliance on a decision addressed to a Member State against the beneficiary of that decision, if the decision was not published and its content not made known to the beneficiary.[547] Decisions addressed to the Member States are binding on all institutions of the State concerned, including the judiciary. Accordingly, they are under a duty by virtue of the primacy of Union law to refrain from applying any national provisions which would be likely to hinder the implementation of a decision.[548]   **22–098**

Direct effect. In certain circumstances the provisions of a decision may also have direct effect in the sense that an individual may rely on it in a dispute with a public authority.[549] The Court of Justice has held that,   **22–099**

---

[542] Arts 105(2) and 106(3) TFEU [*Arts 85(2) and 86(3) EC*]. See also the Treaty articles requiring the Commission to use a decision as a normative instrument: Arts 95(4) and 96(2), second subpara., TFEU [*ex Arts 75(4) and 76(2), second subpara., EC*].

[543] See ECJ, Joined Cases C-48/90 and C-66/90 *Netherlands and Others v Commission* [1992] E.C.R. I-565, paras 26–27.

[544] See, e.g., Council Decision 98/415/EC of June 29, 1998 on the consultation of the European Central Bank by the national authorities on draft legislative provisions, [1998] O.J. L189/42 (adopted pursuant to Art. 105(4) EC [*now Art. 127(4) TFEU*] and Art. 4 of the ESCB Statute). For decisions addressed to the Member States, see Mager, "Die staatengerichtete Entscheidung als supranationale Handlungsform" (2001) EuR. 661–681.

[545] See Lenaerts, Arts and Maselis, *Procedural Law of the European Union* (3rd edn, London, Sweet & Maxwell, 2012), Ch. 7.

[546] CFI (order of the President of June 8, 2009), Case T-173/09 R *Z v Commission* [2009] E.C.R. II-67*, summ. pub., paras 28–31.

[547] ECJ, Case C-158/06 *ROM-projecten* [2007] E.C.R. I-5103, paras 23–31.

[548] ECJ, Case 249/85 *Albako* [1987] E.C.R. 2345, para. 17.

[549] *Ibid.*, para. 10. See Verhoeven, "De rechtstreekse werking van de communautaire beschikking" (2008) A.Ae. 214–216.

"[p]articularly in cases where, for example, the Union authorities by means of a decision have imposed an obligation on a Member State or all the Member States to act in a certain way, the effectiveness (*effet utile*) of such a measure would be weakened if the nationals of that State could not invoke it in the courts and the national courts could not take it into consideration as part of Union law".[550]

The Court added that

"in each particular case, it must be ascertained whether the nature, background and wording of the provision in question are capable of producing direct effects in the legal relationship between the addressee of the act and third parties".[551]

In the same way as provisions of a directive, provisions of a decision may have direct effect only if they are precise and unconditional and the period, if any, within which a Member State had to comply with it has expired.[552] In common with directives, decisions addressed to one or more Member States do not have "horizontal direct effect". Decisions which have the Member States as their sole addressees, and hence are binding only upon the Member States, cannot be relied upon by an individual in the context of legal proceedings against another individual.[553]

E. RECOMMENDATIONS AND OPINIONS

22–100   **No binding force.** According to the fifth para. of Art. 288 TFEU, recommendations and opinions have no binding force.[554]

Recommendations are adopted by the Council or, in the specific cases provided for in the Treaties, by the Commission or the European Central Bank (Art. 292 TFEU).[555] Where the Council adopts recommendations, it must act on a proposal

---

[550] ECJ, Case 9/70 *Grad* [1970] E.C.R. 825, para. 5.

[551] *Ibid.*, para. 6. See also the parallel judgments ECJ, Case 20/70 *Lesage* [1970] E.C.R. 861, paras 5–6, and ECJ, Case 23/70 *Haselhorst* [1970] E.C.R. 881, paras 5–6.

[552] ECJ, Case C-156/91 *Hansa Fleisch Ernst Mundt* [1992] E.C.R. I-5567, paras 15–20.

[553] ECJ, Case C-80/06 *Carp* [2007] E.C.R. I-4473, paras 20–22.

[554] This was also true of ECSC opinions (Art. 14, fourth para., EC), but not of ECSC recommendations (see para. 22–075).

[555] As regards the Council, see, inter alia, Arts 121(2), third subpara., and (4), first subpara.; 148(4); 165(4), second indent; 167(5), second indent; 168(6); 319(1) TFEU [*ex Arts 99(2), third subpara., and (4), first subpara.; 128(4); 149(4), second indent; 151(5), second indent; 152(4), second subpara.; 276(1)EC*]; as a stage in a supervisory procedure: see Art. 126(7) TFEU [*ex Art. 104(7) EC*]; as regards the Commission: see para. 13–065, *supra* (participation in decision-making) and para. 16–015, *supra* (right of initiative); as regards the ECB, see Art. 129(3) and (4) TFEU; Art. 219(1) and (2) TFEU and Art. 289(4) TFEU.

from the Commission in all cases where the Treaties provide that it shall adopt acts on a proposal from the Commission. In those areas in which unanimity is required for the adoption of a Union act, it must act unanimously (Art. 292 TFEU). The Court of Justice has held that [EU] recommendations are "measures which, even as regards the persons to whom they are addressed, are not intended to produce binding effects", and

> "generally adopted by the institutions of the [Union] when they do not have the power under the [Treaties] to adopt binding measures or when they consider that it is not appropriate to adopt more mandatory rules".[556]

They do not create rights upon which individuals may rely before a national court.[557]

Union legislation may leave certain decisions to national authorities while allowing the Commission to express an opinion. Such an opinion has no legal effects and is not binding upon the national authorities.[558]

Some legal effect. Nevertheless, a recommendation may not be regarded as having no legal effect at all. The Court of Justice has observed that   **22–101**

> "[t]he national courts are bound to take recommendations into consideration in order to decide disputes submitted to them, in particular when they cast light on the interpretation of national measures adopted in order to implement them or where they are designed to supplement binding [Union] provisions".[559]

Where several interpretations of national or Union provisions are possible, it would appear that the principle of sincere cooperation (Art. 4(3) TEU [*see ex Art. 10 EC*]) requires the national courts to adopt the interpretation which best corresponds to the aim of the recommendation.[560]

F. OTHER ACTS

Atypical instruments. The list of instruments in Art. 288 TFEU does not prevent the Union institutions from producing legal effects by means of other   **22–102**

---

[556] ECJ, Case C-322/88 *Grimaldi* [1989] E.C.R. 4407, paras 13 and 16.
[557] *Ibid.*, para. 16.
[558] ECJ, Case 133/79 *Sucrimex and Westzucker v Commission* [1980] E.C.R. 1299, para. 16; ECJ (order of the Court of May 17, 1989), Case 151/88 *Italy v Commission* [1989] E.C.R. 1255, para. 22.
[559] ECJ, Case C-322/88 *Grimaldi* [1989] E.C.R. 4407, para. 18; ECJ (judgment of March 18, 2010), Joined Cases C-317/08 to C-320/08 *Alassini and Others*, not yet reported, para. 40.
[560] For other legal effects which may arise out of non-binding acts, see para. 22–104, *infra*.

instruments.[561] Some Treaty provisions refer to "general orientations",[562] "guidelines"[563] or "incentive measures".[564] The latter take the form in practice of decisions and action programmes (see paras 11–048 and 11–051, *supra*), whereas guidelines often take the form of recommendations and decisions (see paras 11–034 and 11–046, *supra*). The European Council is to define the "general guidelines" for the CFSP[565] and the strategic guidelines for legislative and operational planning within the area of freedom, security and justice.[566] Other Treaty provisions, more generally, authorise the adoption of "provisions",[567] "measures",[568] "rules" or "arrangements".[569] Pursuant to its Statute, the ECB has the power to issue, besides "decisions", "guidelines and "instructions" for national central banks.[570] The institutions often have recourse to "resolutions", "declarations", "conclusions" and other atypical instruments, which are not always intended to have legal effects.[571] The Commission, for its part, is increasingly using "communications", "guidelines" and "codes of conduct" in which it sets out the way in which it intends to exercise its power of decision in particular sectors.[572]

---

[561] See ECJ, Case 22/70 *Commission v Council* [1971] E.C.R. 263, paras 41–42.

[562] Article 219(2) TFEU [*ex Art. 111(2) EC*].

[563] See, inter alia, Arts 5; 26(3); 68 TFEU and Arts 121(2); 148(2); 171(1), first indent, TFEU [*ex Arts 99(2); 128(2); 155(1), first indent, EC*].

[564] Articles 19(2); 149; 165(4), first indent; 167(5), first indent; 168(5) TFEU [*ex Arts 13(2); 129; 149(4), first indent; 151(5), first indent; 152(4)(c) EC*].

[565] Arts 25(a) and 26(1) TEU [*ex Arts 12 and 13 EU*].

[566] Article 68 TFEU.

[567] See, inter alia, Art. 21(2); 25, second para.; 91(1)(d); 55(3); 133; 223(4), second subpara., TFEU [*Art. 18(2); 22, second para.; 71(1)(d); 75(3); 93; 190(4), second subpara., EC*].

[568] See, inter alia, Arts 19; 26; 48; 64(2); 114(1); 116, second para., *in fine*; 122(1); 157(3); 168(4)(a) and (b); 169(3); 171(1), second indent, TFEU [*ex Arts 13; 14; 42; 57(2); 60(1); 95(1); 96, second para., in fine; 100(1); 135; 137(2), third subpara.; 141(3); 152(4)(a) and (b); 153(3); 155(1), second indent; EC*].

[569] See, inter alia, Arts 18, second para., and 22(1) and (2) TFEU [*ex Arts 12, second para., and 19(1) and (2) EC*]; see also the reference to "rules" in Art. 91(1)(a) TFEU [*ex Art. 71(1)(a) EC*].

[570] ECB Statute, Art. 12(1).

[571] For the function of such informal acts, see Everling, "Zur rechtlichen Wirkung von Beschlüssen, Entschliessungen, Erklärungen und Vereinbarungen des Rates oder der Mitgliedstaaten der Europäischen Gemeinschaft", in Lüke, Ress and Will (eds), *Rechtsvergleichung, Europarecht und Staatenintegration. Gedächtnisschrift für L.-J. Constantinesco* (Cologne, Heymann, 1983), 133, at 144–147; Senden, "Reguleringsintensiteit en regelgevingsinstrumentarium in het Europees Gemeenschapsrecht. Over de relatie tussen wetgeving, soft law en de open methode van coördinatie" (2008) S.E.W. 43–57; Rubio, "Les instruments de soft law dans les politiques communautaires: vecteur d'une meilleure articulation entre la politique de la concurrence et la politique de cohésion economique et sociale" (2007) 43 R.T.D.E. 597–608; Klabbers, "Informal Instruments before the European Court of Justice" (1994) C.M.L.Rev. 997, at 1003–1004. For their status in the national legal systems, see, e.g., Gautier, "Le Conseil d'Etat français et les actes 'hors nomenclature' de la Communauté européenne" (1995) R.T.D.E. 23–37.

[572] E.g., with regard to competition policy, see paras 11–014, 11–016 and 11–022, *supra*; see Cosma and Whish, "Soft Law in the Field of EU Competition Policy" (2003) E.Bus.L.Rev. 25–56. See also the European Parliament's resolution of September 4, 2007 on institutional and legal implications of the use of "soft law" instruments (P6_TA(2007)0366).

Legal effects. The precise legal effects of an act must be determined in the light   **22–103**
of its content. Accordingly, the Court held in the *AETR* judgment that the
Council's "proceedings" of March 20, 1970 regarding the stance to be adopted by
the national governments in negotiations on an international transport agreement,

> "could not have been simply the expression or the recognition of a voluntary
> coordination, but were designed to lay down a course of action binding on
> both the institutions and the Member States".[573]

It will clearly appear from many atypical instruments whether the institution
which issued them intended to adopt legally binding norms.[574] It follows from
Art. 12(1) of the Statute of the ECB that the "guidelines" and "instructions"
issued by it may contain legally binding provisions.[575]

Besides, such "atypical" acts have legal effects if they create in individuals a
legitimate expectation that the institution will adhere to this policy line.[576] This
also applies in the relationship between institutions and the Member States.
Accordingly, the Commission is bound by the guidelines and notices that it issues
in the area of supervision of State Aid where they do not depart from the rules in
the Treaties and are accepted by the Member States.[577] In addition, a non-binding
act by which an institution regards itself as being bound must be viewed as a rule
of conduct from which the institution may diverge only if it gives reasons for
doing so, on account of the principle of protection of legitimate expectations[578]
and the principle of equal treatment.[579] In some cases, an institution is not

---

[573] ECJ, Case 22/70 *Commission v Council* [1971] E.C.R. 263, para. 53.

[574] See the survey produced by Borchardt and Wellens, "Soft law in het Gemeenschapsrecht" (1987) S.E.W. 663, at 700–709 (and the discussion of that survey in (1988) S.E.W. 243–248). Klabbers argues that there is a presumption that even "informal" instruments are binding (n. 571, *supra*), at 1019–1023.

[575] Gaiser, "Gerichtliche Kontrolle im Europäischen System der Zentralbanken" (2002) EuR. 517, at 521–522 and 533–534. According to Art. 14.3 of the Statute of the European System of Central Banks, the national central banks "shall act in accordance with the guidelines and instructions of the ECB".

[576] ECJ, Case C-313/90 *CIRFS v Commission* [1990] E.C.R. I-1125, paras 34 and 36; ECJ, Joined Cases C-189/02 P, C-202/02 P, C-205/02 P to C-208/02 P and C-213/02 P *Dansk Rørindustri and Others v Commission* [2005] E.C.R. I-5425, paras 62–65; CFI, Case T-380/94 *AIUFFASS and AKT v Commission* [1996] E.C.R. II-2169, para. 57; CFI, Case T-105/95 *WWF UK v Commission* [1997] E.C.R. II-313, paras 53–55; CFI, Case T-149/95 *Ducros and Others v Commission* [1997] E.C.R. II-2031, paras 61–62. See Tournepiche, "Les communications: instruments privilégiés de l'action administrative de la Commission européenne" (2002) R.M.C.UE. 55–62.

[577] ECJ, Case C-288/96 *Germany v Commission* [2000] E.C.R. I-8237, paras 62–65; ECJ, Case C-409/00 *Spain v Commission* [2003] E.C.R. I-1487, para. 95; ECJ, Case C-91/01 *Italy v Commission* [2004] E.C.R. I-4355, para. 45.

[578] ECJ, Case 81/72 *Commission v Council* [1973] E.C.R. 575, paras 10–11.

[579] ECJ, Case 148/73 *Louwage v Commission* [1974] E.C.R. 81, para. 12 (internal directive of the Commission); CFI, Case T-10/93 *A v Commission* [1994] E.C.R. II-179, para. 60 (Conclusions of the Council and the Ministers for Health); CFI, Case T-374/04 *Germany v Comission* [2007] E.C.R. II-4431, paras 109–111 (Guidance contained in a Communication of the Commission).

empowered to adopt acts embodying obligations. Where it nevertheless adopts an act with legal effects, the Court of Justice may declare it void.[580] If an atypical act which has no legal basis either in the Treaties or in any legal act adopted under them is at variance with the provisions of a regulation, the latter take precedence.[581]

As has been mentioned, the institutions may adopt resolutions, conclusions and other instruments if they wish to adopt a non-binding act. In many cases, such acts are published in the *Official Journal* (Part C). They form part of the "declarations or resolutions of, or other positions taken up by" the Council, in respect of which new Member States are placed "in the same situation as the [original] Member States" by virtue of the Act of Accession. New Member States undertake to "observe the principles and guidelines deriving from those declarations, resolutions or guidelines" and to take "such measures as may be necessary to ensure their implementation".[582] The Act of Accession itself "does not attach any additional legal effect" to those measures.[583]

22–104 **Resolutions and conclusions.** A "resolution" generally contains a statement of intention with regard to a policy programme which an institution wishes to have achieved.[584] In several cases, the Court of Justice has held that a given "Council resolution" had no binding force[585] or that "Council conclusions" did not produce any legal effect that could be relied upon before it.[586] All the same, even non-binding "resolutions" or "conclusions" can have some legal effects. For one thing, they may be useful for the purposes of interpreting Treaty provisions and binding

---

[580] See ECJ, Case C-303/90 *France v Commission* [1991] E.C.R. I-5315, paras 15–35 (annulment of a Commission code of conduct); ECJ, Case C-325/91 *France v Commission* [1993] E.C.R. I-3283, paras 14–30 (annulment of a Commission communication on the ground that it did not state the legal basis from which it derived legal force); ECJ, Case C-57/95 *France v Commission* [1997] E.C.R. I-1627 (annulment of a communication by which the Commission purported to impose obligations not already contained in the EC Treaty).

[581] ECJ, Case C-110/03 *Belgium v Commission* [2005] E.C.R. I-2801, para. 33.

[582] 2003 Act of Accession, Art. 5(3); 2005 Act of Accession, Art. 3(2); see the similarly worded Art. 3(3) of the 1972, 1979 and 1985 Acts of Accession and Art. 4(3) of the 1994 Act of Accession (for references, see paras 6–001—6–007, *supra*).

[583] ECJ, Case 44/84 *Hurd* [1986] E.C.R. 29, para. 30, at 79.

[584] See, e.g., the environment action programmes, such as the one provided for in a resolution of February 1, 1993 of the Council of the European Communities and of the representatives of the governments of the Member States, meeting in the Council, [1993] O.J. C138/1. The Court of Justice has held that this action programme "does not lay down rules of a mandatory nature": ECJ, Case C-142/95 P *Associazione Agricoltori della Provincia di Rovigo and Others* [1996] E.C.R. I-6669, paras 29–32.

[585] See ECJ, Joined Cases 90–91/63 *Commission v Luxembourg and Belgium* [1964] E.C.R. 625, at 631; ECJ, Case 9/73 *Schlüter* [1973] E.C.R. 1135, para. 40; ECJ, Case 59/75 *Manghera* [1976] E.C.R. 91, para. 21.

[586] See ECJ, Joined Cases C-182/03 and C-217/03, *Belgium and Forum 187 v Commission* [2006] E.C.R. I-5479, para. 151.

acts of Union law,[587] although they cannot alter such provisions or acts.[588] Thus, the Court of Justice has had regard to Council resolutions in determining what matters are covered by a policy area assigned to the Union by the Treaties.[589] It is for this reason that, traditionally, whenever they wish to avoid a resolution or a conclusion having effects on the way in which the allocation of powers as between the Union and the Member States is interpreted, the members of the Council adopt the relevant act in the form of a "resolution of the Council and the representatives of the Governments of the Member States, meeting within the Council".[590] Only on one occasion has the Court of Justice held a Council resolution to have binding force, when it found that it was an application of the duty of cooperation imposed by Art. 10 EC [see now Art. 4(3) TEU]. The resolution in fact determined the procedure whereby Member States wished to take the necessary conservation measures in respect of fishery resources in the North Sea.[591] In that case, the resolution contributed to the legitimacy of the temporary measures which the Member States were authorised to take in the absence of a common fisheries policy.[592]

Unilateral declarations. The non-binding acts discussed above must be distinguished from declarations made in the minutes of meetings by institutions or Member States on the occasion of the adoption of Union acts. No reliance may be placed on a unilateral declaration of a Member State for the purposes of interpreting a Union act on the ground that

> "the objective scope of rules laid down by the common institutions cannot be modified by reservations or objections which Member States may have made at the time the rules were being formulated".[593]

22–105

---

[587] Everling, "Probleme atypischer Rechts- und Handlungsformen bei der Auslegung des europäischen Gemeinschaftsrechts", in Bieber and Ress (eds), *Die Dynamik des Europäischen Gemeinschaftsrechts/The dynamics of EC-Law* (Baden-Baden, Nomos, 1987), 417–433.

[588] ECJ, Case 59/75 *Manghera* [1976] E.C.R. 91, para. 21.

[589] See ECJ, Case 293/83 *Gravier* [1985] E.C.R. 593, para. 22 (access to vocational training); ECJ, Joined Cases 281/85, 283–285/85 and 287/85 *Germany, France, Netherlands, Denmark and United Kingdom v Commission* [1987] E.C.R. 3203, para. 17 (migration policy).

[590] E.g. the Resolution of the Council and the Representatives of the Governments of the Member States, meeting within the Council of November 20, 2008 on the health and well-being of young people and the Conclusions of the Council and of the Representatives of the Governments of the Member States, meeting within the Council of November 21, 2008 on preparing young people for the 21st century: an agenda for European cooperation on schools ([2008] O.J. C319/1 and C319/20, respectively).

[591] What was at issue was the Hague Resolution of November 3, 1976, see ECJ, Case 141/78 *France v United Kingdom* [1979] E.C.R. 2923, paras 8–11; ECJ, Case 32/79 *Commission v United Kingdom* [1980] E.C.R. 2403, para. 11 ("It is not contested that this resolution is binding on the Member States"); ECJ, Case 804/79 *Commission v United Kingdom* [1981] E.C.R. 1045, paras 23–31.

[592] See also ECJ, Case 61/77 *Commission v Ireland* [1978] E.C.R. 417, para. 66.

[593] ECJ, Case 143/83 *Commission v Denmark* [1985] E.C.R. 427, para. 13; see also ECJ, Case 38/69 *Commission v Italy* [1970] E.C.R. 47, para. 12. For the significance of such declarations in practical decision-making, see Everling (n. 623, *infra*), at 134. For their use in interpreting Union acts, see Schønberg and Frick, "Finishing, refining, polishing: on the use of *travaux préparatoires* as an aid to the interpretation of Community legislation" (2003) E.L.Rev. 149–171.

A declaration made by Member States, acting together, or the institutions concerned cannot have any bearing on the objective scope of a Union act.[594] Such a declaration may be used to interpret such an act only where reference is made to its content in the wording of the act in question,[595] since legislation is addressed to those affected by it and they must be able to rely on what it contains.[596] The Court of Justice may have regard to a joint declaration in order to "confirm" the interpretation having to be given to the Union act at issue.[597] Individual declarations of one or more Member States may have factual importance, in particular where they contain details of the manner in which the adoption of an act was discussed in the Council. In that event, the Court of Justice and the General Court may take the declarations into account in order to determine the content of the discussion and then to review it.[598] In view of the uncertainty to which such explanatory statements may lead, the European Parliament has asked that statements relating to legislative acts not be made.[599]

22–106   **Institutional practice.** As far as the institutions' practice is concerned, the Court has plainly stated that,

> "[a] mere practice on the part of the Council cannot derogate from the rules laid down in the Treaty. Such a practice cannot therefore create a precedent binding on Union institutions with regard to the correct legal basis".[600]

---

[594] ECJ, Case 237/84 *Commission v Belgium* [1986] E.C.R. 1247, para. 17.

[595] See ECJ, Case C-292/89 *Antonissen* [1991] E.C.R. I-745, para. 18; ECJ, Case C-25/94 *Commission v Council* [1996] E.C.R. I-1469, para. 38; ECJ, Case C-329/95 *VAG Sverige* [1997] E.C.R. I-2675, para. 23; ECJ, Case C-245/02 *Anheuser-Busch* [2004] E.C.R. I-10989, paras 78–80. See also ECJ, Case C-368/96 *Generics* [1998] E.C.R. I-7967, paras 26–35 (general concept used in a directive interpreted in accordance with criteria set out in minutes of the Council).

[596] ECJ, Joined Cases C-283/94, C-291/94 and C-292/94 *Denkavit and Others* [1996] E.C.R. I-5063, para. 29.

[597] ECJ, Case 136/78 *Auer* [1979] E.C.R. 437, para. 25 (declaration of the Council); ECJ, Case C-310/90 *Egle* [1992] E.C.R. I-177, para. 12 (joint declaration by the Commission and the Council). See also ECJ, Case 324/82 *Commission v Belgium* [1984] E.C.R. 1861, para. 33.

[598] CFI, Case T-194/94 *Carvel and Guardian Newspapers v Council* [1995] E.C.R. II-2765, paras 74–77.

[599] See the "declaration" appended to the Interinstitutional Agreement of December 22, 1998 on common guidelines for the quality of drafting of Community legislation, [1999] O.J. C73/1 (and a declaration to a different effect by the Council). See also the earlier resolution of the European Parliament of October 12, 1995 on the transparency of Council Decisions and the Community's legislative procedures, [1995] O.J. C287/179, and the Council's answer of December 21, 1995 to question No. P-2829/95 (Kristoffersen), [1996] O.J. C56/44.

[600] ECJ, Case 68/86 *United Kingdom v Council* [1988] E.C.R. 855, para. 24; ECJ, Case 131/86 *United Kingdom v Council* [1988] E.C.R. 905, para. 29. See also the articles in Bieber and Ress (eds), n. 587, *supra*.

Under certain circumstances a constant practice—for instance based on a non-binding act by which an institution regards itself as being bound—must be viewed as a rule of conduct from which the institution may diverge only if it gives reasons for doing so, on account of the principle of protection of legitimate expectations and the principle of equal treatment (see para. 22–103).

VI. INTERINSTITUTIONAL AGREEMENTS

Agreements between institutions. The institutions have long determined relations inter se by way of interinstitutional agreements, on the basis of specific Treaty provisions.[601] The Lisbon Treaty introduced an express legal basis for the European Parliament, the Council and the Commission to conclude interinstitutional agreements which may be of a binding nature (Art. 295 TFEU). The European Parliament, the Council and the Commission are increasingly concluding agreements, initially mainly to improve the flow of information to the Parliament and to increase its participation in decision-making.[602] In the meantime, agreements have been reached on other matters, institutional and otherwise.[603] The first agreements sometimes took the form of an exchange of letters

22–107

---

[601] See *ex Arts 193, third para.; 218(1); 248(3), third subpara.; 272(9), fifth subpara., EC*, which authorised the institutions concerned to determine relations inter se by "common accord" or by agreement. See also Art. 287(3), third subpara., TFEU [*ex Art. 248(3), third subpara., EC*]. For a detailed discussion, see Driessen, *Interinstitutional conventions in EU law* (London, Cameron May, 2007), 334 pp.

[602] For the relationship between the Council and the European Parliament, see the (never officially published) Luns procedure of 1964 and the 1973 Westerterp procedure (para. 26–004, *infra*) and the Interinstitutional Agreement of November 20, 2002 concerning access by the European Parliament to sensitive information of the Council in the field of security and defence policy (see para. 18–004, *supra*). The following in particular have arisen as between the European Parliament, the Council and the Commission: the Joint Declaration of March 4, 1975, [1975] O.J. C89/1 (on the consultation procedure, para. 16–042, *supra*); the Joint Declaration of June 30, 1982 and the Interinstitutional Agreements of June 29, 1988, October 29, 1993, May 6, 1999 and November 7, 2002 on budgetary procedure (see para. 13–138, *supra*); the Joint Declaration on the implementation of the new co-decision procedure (n. 109 to para. 16–023, *supra*), the Joint Declaration on the Socrates decision of March 4, 1995 (see para. 11–048, *supra*) and the Interinstitutional Agreement of July 16, 1997 on the financing of the CFSP (see para. 18–006, *supra*). Between the European Parliament and the Commission codes of conduct were concluded in 1990 ((1990) 4 EC Bull. I.6.1) and on March 15, 1995 (see notes to para 16–021, 16–05 *et seq.*, *supra*, and 26–004, *infra*) and a framework agreement on relations between the European Parliament and the Commission on May 26, 2005 ([2006] O.J. C117E/125) and October 20, 2010 ([2010] O.J. L304/47) (replacing the framework agreement on relations between the European Parliament and the Commision of July 5, 2000 ([2001] O.J. C121/122 and (2000) 7/8 EU Bull. point 2.2.1)).

[603] See the Joint Declaration of the European Parliament, the Council and the Commission of April 5, 1977 on fundamental rights (see para. 22–018, *supra*); the Joint Declaration against racism and xenophobia of the European Parliament, the Council, the representatives of the Member States, meeting in the Council, and the Commission of June 11, 1986, [1986] O.J. C158) and (as agreed

between the institutions concerned; subsequently, they have generally been officially published. In a declaration annexed to the Treaty of Nice, the Intergovernmental Conference then in session spoke out against the practice of the European Parliament and the Commission concluding agreements between themselves, that is to say without involving the Council in the agreement.[604] Other bodies also make use of agreements.[605]

22–108   **Legal force.** The institutions can use an interinstitutional agreement to simplify the implementation of procedures laid down in the Treaties, without actually amending those procedures or altering the balance as between the institutions.[606] Where the Treaties do not expressly provide for an agreement to be reached, the legal force of an agreement will depend on whether the institutions intended it to be binding.[607] The institutions may merely have intended to coordinate their positions as a first step towards the adoption of subsequent binding

---

between the European Parliament, the Council and the Commission) the Interinstitutional Declaration of October 25, 1993 on democracy, transparency and subsidiarity ([1993] O.J. C329/135, and (1993) 10 EC Bull. point 2.2.1); the Interinstitutional Agreement of December 20, 1994 on the codification of legislation and the Interinstitutional Agreement of November 28, 2001 on a more structured use of the recasting technique for legal acts (see para. 20–020, *supra*; the Interinstitutional Agreement of December 22, 1998 on common guidelines for the quality of drafting of Community legislation (see para. 20–021, *supra*)), the Interinstitutional Agreement of May 25, 1999 concerning internal investigations by the European Anti-fraud Office (OLAF), [1999] O.J. L136/15); the Interinstitutional Agreement of February 28, 2002 on the financing of the Convention on the future of the European Union, [2002] O.J. C54/1 (extended by Interinstitutional Agreement of December 12, 2002, [2002] O.J. C320/1) and the Interinstitutional Agreement of December 16, 2003 on better law-making (see para. 20–021). As between the Commission and the Council, see the Code of Conduct of December 6, 1993 on public access to documents (see para. 13–167, *supra*).

[604] According to Declaration (No. 3), annexed to the Nice Treaty, on Art. 10 of the Treaty establishing the European Community ([2001 C80/77]), interinstitutional agreements "may be concluded only with the agreement of these three institutions". See Tournepiche, "La clarification du statut juridique des accords interinstitutionnels" (2002) R.T.D.E. 209–222.

[605] E.g., the agreement of December 13, 2001 between the ECB and Europol on combating counterfeiting, [2002] O.J. C23/9 and, for the same purpose, the cooperation agreement of March 29, 2004 between the ECB and the International Criminal Police Organisation (Interpol), [2004] O.J. C134/9 and the agreement of June 9, 2004 between Europol and Eurojust on information exchange (*Europe*, No. 8722, June 10, 2004, p. 10).

[606] Para. 15–007, *supra*; see also Declaration (No. 3), annexed to the Nice Treaty, (n. 604, *supra*). That declaration stated expressly that "[s]uch agreements may not amend or supplement the provisions of the Treaty". This reflected a lack of trust on the part of the Member States in connection with the agreement concluded between the Commission and the European Parliament on July 5, 2000 (see n. 602, *supra*). According to that declaration, such an agreement should not be possible in the future, since it stated that agreements "may be concluded only with the agreement of these three institutions". This would have given the Council a veto.

[607] Monar, "Interinstitutional Agreements: The Phenomenon and its New Dynamics after Maastricht" (1994) C.M.L.Rev. 693, at 697–703. The Interinstitutional Agreement of December 22, 1998 on common guidelines for the quality of drafting of Community legislation (n. 599, *supra*) expressly provides that the guidelines set out therein "are not legally binding".

acts.[608] An indication is afforded, in the first place, by the title chosen by the institutions: declaration, *modus vivendi*, code of conduct or agreement (which is stricter). In addition, the legal force of an agreement may be derived from its content. Accordingly, the fact that the content of an interinstitutional agreement is purely political may preclude its being binding.[609] In contrast, other agreements appear to lay down binding rules of conduct.[610] There are indications in decided cases that the Court of Justice accepts in principle that interinstitutional agreements have binding force.[611] Sometimes such an agreement is referred to in order to confirm the Court's interpretation of Union law.[612] Moreover, an interinstitutional agreement can be binding in so far as it is an expression of the principle of sincere cooperation enshrined in Art. 4(3) TEU [*ex Art. 10 EC*].[613] On that basis, the Court of Justice has recognised the binding nature of arrangements concluded between the Commission and the Council to decide on the participation of the Union and the Member States in international organisations where, in areas of shared competences, the Union and the Member States have to agree on the exercise of the voting rights.[614]

---

[608] ECJ, Case C-58/94 *Netherlands v Council* [1996] E.C.R. I-2169, paras 23–27 (on the Code of Conduct concerning public access to Council and Commission documents; see para. 13–167, *supra*). However, an institution is bound by a code of conduct vis-à-vis third parties where it adopted the code by decision and thereby voluntarily assumed a series of obligations for itself (*patere legem quam ipse fecisti*), see CFI, Case T-105/95 *WWF UK v Commission* [1997] E.C.R. II-313, paras 53–55.

[609] See the assessment of the Joint Declaration on fundamental rights in the Commission's answer of June 1, 1977 to question No. 170/77 (Maigaard), [1977] O.J. C180/18 and the Council's answer of September 23, 1977 to question No. 128/77 (Dondelinger), [1977] O.J. C259/4, to the effect that, more generally, joint declarations are "political undertakings" and "in the final instance it would be for the Court of Justice to assess their legal implications" (see also the answer of the same date to question No. 169/77 (Maigaard, *ibid.*, concerning the conciliation procedure).

[610] Point 2 of the Interinstitutional Agreement of May 17, 2006 on budgetary discipline and improvement of budgetary procedure ([2006] O.J. C139/1) states that "the budgetary discipline is binding on all the institutions for as long as the Agreement is in force". This applies *a fortiori* to the agreement between the ECB and Europol of December 13, 2001 (n. 605, *supra*), since it provides in Art. 10 for dispute resolution by arbitration.

[611] See ECJ, Case 211/80 *Advernier v Commission* [1984] E.C.R. 131, para. 22 (reference to the Joint Declaration of March 4, 1975); ECJ, Case 34/86 *Council v European Parliament* [1986] E.C.R. 2155, para. 50 (reference to the Joint Declaration of June 30, 1982).

[612] Case 44/79 *Hauer* [1979] E.C.R. 3727, para. 15 (Joint Declaration on fundamental rights); CFI, Case T-194/94 *Carvel and Guardian Newspapers v Council* [1995] II-2765, para. 66 (Code of Conduct on public access to documents).

[613] Hilf, "Die rechtliche Bedeutung des Verfassungsprinzips der parlamentarischen Demokratie für den europäischen Integrationsprozess" (1984) EuR. 9, at 24–25; Monar (n. 607, *supra*), at 700; Bieber, "The Settlement of Institutional Conflicts on the Basis of Article 4 of the EEC Treaty" (1984) C.M.L.Rev. 505, at 520–521.

[614] ECJ, Case C-25/94 *Commission v Council* [1996] E.C.R. I-1469, paras 48–49.

VII. ACTS OF MEMBER STATE GOVERNMENTS AND CONVENTIONS BETWEEN THE MEMBER STATES

22–109   **Acts with a Union basis.** In some cases, the Member States act in order to carry out a task expressly conferred on the national governments by the Treaties. Alongside amendment of the Treaties, which is the task of a "conference of representatives of the governments of the Member States" (Art. 48(4) TEU), decisions of the "governments of the Member States" are used chiefly to appoint members of the Court of Justice and the General Court[615] and to fix the seats of institutions and bodies.[616] In view of the fact that such acts have their legal basis in the Treaties and are essentially connected with the functioning of the Union, they must be regarded as being Union law. However, given the fact that these are acts of the governments of the Member States and not of the Council, they are probably not amenable to judicial review by the Court of Justice.[617]

22–110   **Conventions and agreements between Member States.** In matters coming within their competence, Member States may exercise their powers individually or collectively[618]; in so doing they may therefore conclude agreements amongst themselves.[619] If such agreements do not have a basis in the Treaties, they do not form part of Union law and cannot be interpreted by the Court of Justice. Before the entry into force of the Lisbon Treaty, the EC Treaty provided in Art. 293 for some matters to be dealt with by "negotiations" between the Member States. In the field of police and judicial cooperation in criminal matters (PJCC), Art. 35 EU allowed the Council to establish "conventions" which it then recommended to the Member States for adoption in accordance with their respective constitutional requirements (see para. 23–015). Even though the conventions concluded pursuant to Art. 293 EC did not constitute Community law, the Member States often conferred jurisdiction on the Court of Justice to interpret their provisions. Such conventions—as well as some other conventions concluded in connection with Community law—were considered "inseparable from the attainment of the objectives of the EC Treaty" (see para. 23–014). The same applied to PJCC conventions with respect to which—under Art. 35 EU—the Court of Justice has jurisdiction to interpret their provisions, as well as to conventions concluded by the Member States—before the Treaty of Amsterdam—in the field of justice and

---

[615] See Art. 19(2), third subpara., TEU and Arts 253 and 254 TFEU.

[616] Article 341 TFEU.

[617] Para. 22–009, *supra*; see also Schermers and Waelbroeck, *Judicial Protection in the European Union* (The Hague, Kluwer, 2001), para. 670, at 329–330.

[618] ECJ, Joined Cases C-181/91 and C-248/91 *European Parliament v Council* [1993] E.C.R. I-3685, para. 16 (concerning humanitarian aid).

[619] For a survey, see De Witte, "Internationale verdragen tussen lidstaten van de Europese Unie" in *Mededelingen van de Nederlandse Vereniging voor Internationaal Recht*, 2001, 79–131.

home affairs (JHA), which were held to be "inseparable from the attainment of the objectives of the EU Treaty" (see para. 23–015). New Member States undertook in the Act of Accession to accede both to the conventions concluded pursuant to Art. 293 EC and to PJCC/JHA conventions.[620] New Member States also have to accede to international agreements which the Union and the Member States conclude jointly and to "internal" agreements which the Member States have concluded with each other for the purposes of implementing such international agreements.[621]

Since the entry into force of the Lisbon Treaty, the Treaties no longer mention conventions between Member States as a policy instrument of the Union. This does not prevent existing conventions from keeping their legal force, including any interpretative jurisdiction conferred on the Court of Justice. Moreover, the possibility cannot be ruled out that Member States will continue to conclude conventions amongst themselves. Even though such conventions cannot be classified as either norms of primary Union law or provisions of secondary Union law, they undoubtedly give shape to the Union legal order in a broader sense.[622]

Decisions by Member State governments meeting within the Council. Ever since the early years of the Communities, the Member States' governments have concluded agreements among themselves which are not based on the Treaties and which they do not wish to cast as a formal convention. The Ministers take such decisions at normal meetings of the Council as "representatives of the Governments of the Member States meeting within the Council".[623] Those decisions have sometimes also been taken at the level of the Heads of State or Government within the European Council. Before the entry into force of the Lisbon Treaty, such decisions were often closely related to decisions taken by the   **22–111**

---

[620] 2005 Act of Accession, Art. 3(3); 2003 Act of Accession, Art. 5(2); 1994 Act of Accession, Art. 4(2).

[621] See Art. 6(2) to (6) and (11) of the 2005 Act of Accession; Art. 6(2) to (6) and (11) of the 2003 Act of Accession; Art. 5(2) and (3) of the 1994 Act of Accession.

[622] An example could be conventions concluded between Member States aiming to avoid double taxation, see ECJ, Case C-265/04 *Bouanich* [2006] E.C.R. I-923, para. 49; ECJ, Case C-513/04 *Kerckhaert and Morres* [2006] E.C.R. I-10967, para. 23; ECJ, Case C-414/06 *Lidl Belgium* [2008] E.C.R. I-3601, para. 22.

[623] One of the earliest instances of this was the adoption of the so-called "acceleration decisions" of May 12, 1960 and May 15, 1962, para. 9–008, *supra*. For such decisions in general, see Mortelmans, "The Extramural Meetings of the Ministers of the Member States of the Community" (1974) C.M.L.Rev. 62–91. For a study of their legal force, see Everling, "Zur rechtlichen Wirkung von Beschlüssen, Entschliessungen, Erklärungen und Vereinbarungen des Rates oder der Mitgliedstaaten der Europäischen Gemeinschaft", in Lüke, Ress and Will (eds), *Rechtsvergleichung, Europarecht und Staatenintegration. Gedächtnisschrift für L.-J. Constantinesco* (Cologne, Heymann, 1983), 133, at 147–156; Borchardt and Wellens, "Soft law in het Gemeenschapsrecht" (1987) S.E.W. 663–727; Pescatore, "Remarques sur la nature juridique des 'décisions des représentants des Etats membres réunis au sein du Conseil' " (1966) S.E.W. 579–586; Schermers, "Besluiten van de Vertegenwoordigers der Lid-Staten: Gemeenschapsrecht?" (1966) S.E.W. 545–579.

Council pursuant to the Treaties and intended to achieve uniformity in Member States' policies on non-Community aspects of European integration. The Member States had recourse to this type of cooperation where efficient action by the Community required touching upon matters not cited in the Treaties as falling within the jurisdiction of the Community.[624] Where a matter fell partly within the jurisdiction of the Member States and partly within the jurisdiction of the Community (or where no consensus could be reached as to with whom jurisdiction lay), decisions often took the hybrid form of "decisions of the Council and of the Ministers of the Member States meeting within the Council". Where subsequent Treaty amendments brought a matter within the scope of the Community's competences, earlier resolutions of the Ministers meeting within the Council could if necessary be elaborated into binding Community law. This happened, for instance, with the areas of education, culture, public health and consumer protection, where the EU Treaty gave competence to the Community, or in matters of employment and the movement of nationals of third countries, where the Amsterdam Treaty conferred new powers on the Community.[625] After the entry into force of the Lisbon Treaty, the Member States' governments still have recourse to decisions "of the Council and of the Representatives of the Governments of the Member States, meeting within the Council" whenever a matter falls partly within the jurisdiction of the Member States and partly within the jurisdiction of the Union, or where no consensus exists as to with whom jurisdiction lies.[626]

Decisions taken by the Member States' governments meeting in the Council take various forms (acts, declarations, resolutions, findings), from which it is often clear that the Member States' intention is to adopt a non-binding act.[627] The purpose and content of these acts determine whether—and if so, what—legal effects ensue from such acts. The fact that new Member States accede by means of the Act of Accession to "decisions and agreements adopted by the Representatives of

---

[624] See the influence of the common commercial policy on EPC (para. 2–003, *supra*), of the free movement of persons on internal security policy (para. 2–010, *supra*) and on education policy (para. 11–048, *supra*) and of the free movement of goods on cultural, public health and environmental policies (paras 9–034 and 9–042, *supra*). See for the dynamic development of Community powers and cooperation between Member States, the articles in Bieber and Ress (eds), *Die Dynamik des Europäischen Gemeinschaftsrechts/ The Dynamics of EC Law* (Baden-Baden, Nomos, 1987), 457 pp.

[625] For the changing nature of these forms of decision in the sphere of education, see Van Craeyenest, "La nature juridique des résolutions sur la coopération en matière d'éducation", in De Witte (ed.), *European Community Law of Education* (Baden-Baden, Nomos, 1989), 127–133.

[626] E.g. the Resolution of the Council and of the Representatives of the Governments of the Member States, meeting within the Council, on the active inclusion of young people: combating unemployment and poverty, [2010] O.J. C137/1.

[627] See, for example, the Declaration by the Council and the representatives of the Governments of the Member States, meeting within the Council, of December 16, 1997 on respecting diversity and combating racism and xenophobia, [1998] C1/14.

the Governments of the Member States meeting within the Council"[628] does not confer any additional legal effects on such acts.[629] Nevertheless, the Member States may lay down agreements in such acts which are binding under international law. In such a case, each Member State decides for itself whether the agreements in question are subject to the same ratification procedure as treaties and what legal force is to be given to them under national law.[630] This is also true of acts adopted by the national governments at the level of the Heads of State or Government, whether meeting within the European Council[631] or as the European Council.[632]

The obligations which the Member States assume in decisions taken "within the (European) Council" may not be enforced as such by the Court of Justice. In common with joint declarations made in the Council, however, such acts do have interpretative value in "confirming" obligations arising for the Member States under Union law (see para. 22–105), although the acts in question cannot detract in any way from Treaty provisions.[633] In addition, the principle of sincere cooperation requires Member States not to take any measure by such an act which "could jeopardise the attainment of the Union's objectives" (Art. 4(3) TEU; see paras 7–048 et seq.). This suggests that the Commission could bring an action under Art. 258 TFEU against acts by which the national governments detracted from their Treaty obligations.[634]

VIII. COLLECTIVE AGREEMENTS

Collective agreements. Article 155 TFEU [*ex Art. 139 EC*] refers to an instrument which does not emanate from a Union body. Under para. 1 of that article, **22–112**

---

[628] Article 3(1) of the 2005 Act of Accession; Art. 5(1) of the 2003 Act of Accession; Art. 4(1) of the 1994 Act of Accession.

[629] Para. 22–103, *supra*; for the opposite view, see Schermers and Waelbroeck, *Judicial Protection in the European Union* (The Hague, Kluwer, 2001), paras 670–671, at 330 (who took the view that since the Act of Accession refers to those decisions, it recognises them as being Community law).

[630] See Everling (n. 623, *supra*), at 136. For the Netherlands, see Besselink, "An Open Constitution and European Integration: The Kingdom of the Netherlands" (1996) S.E.W. 192, at 205.

[631] Decision of the Heads of State and Government, meeting within the European Council, concerning certain problems raised by Denmark on the Treaty on European Union, [1992] O.J. C348/2.

[632] Article 5(2) of the 2005 Act of Accession, Art. 5(3) of the 2003 Act of Accession and Art. 4(3) of the 1994 Act of Accession place "declarations or resolutions of, or other positions taken up by" the European Council on the same footing as those of the Council (para. 22–103, *supra*). For a commentary dealing specifically with the legal force of resolutions of the European Council, see Martenczuk, "Der Europäische Rat und die Wirtschafts- und Währungsunion" (1998) EuR. 151, at 155–157.

[633] ECJ, Case 43/75 *Defrenne* [1976] E.C.R. 455, para. 57, at 478 (concerning a resolution of a conference of the Member States). In this way, the Court of Justice may also interpret the actual provisions of such acts.

[634] Schermers (n. 623, *supra*), at 562 and 575.

should management and labour so desire, the dialogue between them at Union level may lead to contractual relations, including agreements. At present, collective agreements do not have the same legal force throughout the Union in relation to the parties thereto, let alone third parties. Consequently, in the absence of Union provisions relating to this matter, the legal force of any collective agreements concluded as such at Union level remains unclear (see para. 16–044). That is different where such agreements are implemented by Union acts. Accordingly, the agreements implemented by means of directives are binding on Member States as regards the result to be achieved, but they retain the power to determine the form and methods (see para. 16–044). In such a case, the provisions of such an agreement have direct effect under the same conditions as directives.[635] Likewise, national courts are bound to interpret domestic law, so far as possible, in the light of the wording and the purpose of such agreement.[636]

IX. THE CASE LAW OF THE UNION COURTS

22–113 **Source of law.** In the Union legal order, the case law of the Court of Justice, the General Court and the specialised courts constitutes an important source of law. Although they play a crucial role in developing the law, their task is formally limited to interpreting and applying each of the other sources of law discussed above.

The interpretation which the Union Courts give to a rule of Union law defines the meaning and scope of that rule as it must be or ought to have been understood and applied from the time of its coming into force.[637] It follows that a rule of Union law interpreted in this way must be applied to legal relationships which arose or were formed before the Court gave its ruling on the question on interpretation.[638] In practice, however, such an interpretation may have unexpected effects. A judicial ruling holding that a provision has direct effect may, for instance, impose considerable burdens where authorities or individuals are faced with unforeseen claims from individuals. Accordingly, in exceptional cases, the Court of Justice will impose restrictions on grounds of legal certainty on the *ex tunc* effect of its preliminary rulings on Union law.[639] The Court may thus restrict

---

[635] ECJ, Case C-268/06 *Impact* [2008] ECR I-2483, para. 58; ECJ, Joined Cases C-378/07 to C-380/07 *Angelidaki and Others* [2009] E.C.R. I-307, para. 195; ECJ, (judgment of April 22, 2010), Case C-486/08 *Zentralberiebsrat der Landeskrankenhäuser Tirols*, not yet reported, paras 21–25.

[636] ECJ (judgment of June 24, 2010), Case C-98/09 *Sorge*, not yet reported, paras 51–53.

[637] ECJ, Case C-347/00 *Barreira Pérez* [2002] E.C.R. I-8191, para. 44; ECJ, Joined Cases C-453/02 and C-462/02 *Linneweber and Akritidis* [2005] E.C.R. I-1131, para. 41; ECJ, Case C-292/04 *Meilicke and Others* [2007] E.C.R. I-1835, para. 34. See also, Lenaerts, Arts and Maselis, *Procedural Law of the European Union* (3rd edn, London, Sweet & Maxwell, 2012), Ch. 6.

[638] ECJ, Case C-453/00 *Kühne & Heitz* [2004] E.C.R. I-837, paras 21–22; case note by Caranta, (2005) 42 C.M.L.Rev. 179–188.

[639] See in this connection, Bribosia and Rorive, "Le droit transitoire jurisprudentiel des juridictions européennes" (2002) R.D.ULB. 125–152.

the direct effect of a provision to claims relating to periods starting on the date on which its judgment was given.[640] Such a restriction may be allowed only in the actual judgment ruling upon the interpretation sought.[641] It is clear from this alone that the interpretation which the Union Courts give to rules of Union law is not always merely declaratory, but contributes in real terms to the development of that law.[642]

---

[640] See, e.g., in connection with the direct effect of the interpretation given by the Court of Justice to Art. 141 EC [*now Art. 157 TFEU*], ECJ, Case 43/75 *Defrenne v Sabena* [1976] E.C.R. 455, paras 71–75. *Cf.* ECJ, Case C-262/88 *Barber v Guardian Royal Exchange Insurance Group* [1990] E.C.R. I-1889, paras 40–45, in which the Court restricted its interpretation that pensions paid by contracted-out occupational pension schemes constituted "pay" within the meaning of Art. 141 to future pensions as well as to pensions in respect of which legal proceedings had been brought, or an equivalent claim had been made, before the date of the judgment. The EC Treaty was supplemented by a Protocol (No. 17) concerning Art. 119 [*later Art. 141*] of the Treaty establishing the European Community ([1992] O.J. C224/104), which imposed a particular interpretation of the effects *ratione temporis* of the judgment in *Barber*. According to the Protocol, pensions so interpreted cover only benefits attributable to periods of employment after that date, except where claims have been made within the meaning of the judgment. For judgments delivered before the Protocol entered into force, see ECJ, Case C-109/91 *Ten Oever* [1993] E.C.R. I-4879, para. 19; and thereafter ECJ, Case C-152/91 *Neath v Steeper* [1993] E.C.R. I-6935, paras 13–18; ECJ, Case C-200/91 *Coloroll Pension Trustees* [1994] E.C.R. I-4389 (no reference to the Protocol); ECJ, Case C-57/93 *Vroege* [1994] E.C.R. I-4541, paras 35–43; ECJ, Case C-128/93 *Fisscher* [1994] E.C.R. I-4583, paras 47–50; ECJ, Case C-147/95 *Evrenopoulos* [1997] E.C.R. I-2057, paras 30–40 (clarification of the Protocol). For a critical view of the technique whereby the Member States sought to "correct" the case law of the Court of Justice by means of a protocol, see Curti Gialdino, "Some Reflections on the *Acquis Communautaire*" (1995) C.M.L.Rev. 1089, at 1117–1120. The limitation of the possibility of relying on the direct effect of Art. 141 EC did not prevent claimants from relying on national provisions laying down a principle of equal treatment; see ECJ, Case C-50/96 *Schröder* [2000] E.C.R. I-743, paras 46–50; ECJ, Joined Cases C-234/96 and C-235/96 *Vick and Conze* [2000] E.C.R. I-799, paras 46–50, and ECJ, Joined Cases C-270/97 and C-271/97 *Sievers and Schrage* [2000] E.C.R. I-929, paras 48–52.

[641] ECJ, Case C-437/97 *EKW and Wein & Co.* [2000] E.C.R. I-1157, para. 57; ECJ, Case C-292/04 *Meilicke and Others* [2007] E.C.R. I-1835, para. 36.

[642] For an account of case law as a source of law, see Schermers and Waelbroeck, *Judicial Protection in the European Union* (The Hague, Kluwer, 2001), paras 260–266, at 133–137.

CHAPTER 23

LEGAL FORCE OF PRE-LISBON NON-COMMUNITY LAW

Survey. Before the entry into force of the Lisbon Treaty, a distinction was made **23–001** between Community law, which referred to the Community Treaties and the acts adopted pursuant thereto, and non-Community law, which meant legal provisions adopted outside the Community framework. The term non-Community law referred in the first place to the "intergovernmental" provisions of the EU Treaty (in particular, Titles V and VI on the common foreign and security policy and on police and judicial cooperation in criminal matters, respectively) and measures adopted pursuant to those provisions. Those measures took the form of particular legal instruments that were not used within the Community framework. Conventions concluded between the Member States pursuant to a number of provisions of the EC Treaty, Art. 293 EC in particular, were also to be classified as acts of non-Community law, since those conventions were not subject to the provisions of the Community Treaties.

Since the entry into force of the Lisbon Treaty, the European Union no longer acts through either measures of Community law or non-Community measures. The Union's action in each of its fields of competence now gives rise to measures of "Union law" (see para. 4–012). However, pursuant to Art. 9 of the Protocol on transitional provisions, acts adopted before December 1, 2009 on the basis of the EU Treaty remain in force and their legal effects are preserved until those acts are repealed, annulled or amended in implementation of the present Treaties (see para. 4–014). The same applies to agreements concluded by the Member States on the basis of the former Arts 24 and 38 EU. Consequently, for those acts the special legal regime applicable to non-Community acts remains in place. Accordingly, with regard to those acts the former non-Community provisions of the EU Treaty remain in force, which means, inter alia, that the Commission and the Court only have limited legal powers in respect of them (see para. 4–014). In the case of PJCC acts, the limited powers of Commission and Court will cease to apply in any event on December 1, 2014 (see para. 4–014).

This chapter examines the legal force of the various non-Community acts adopted before December 1, 2009. Where appropriate, the prefix "pre-Lisbon" will be used to distinguish those acts from acts adopted after the entry into force of the Lisbon Treaty. This chapter also considers conventions which Member States have concluded amongst themselves in connection with—but not based on—Community law or in connection with—and based on—the provisions on

935

PJCC. As far as the latter conventions are concerned, the Court's jurisdiction to interpret their provisions continues to be based on the former Art. 35 EU.

I. DISTINGUISHING NON-COMMUNITY FROM COMMUNITY LAW

23–002 **Non-Community acts.** Pursuant to the provisions of Title V (common foreign and security policy, CFSP) and Title VI (police and judicial cooperation in criminal matters, PJCC) of the EU Treaty, the Union institutions adopted acts which did not constitute Community law (see paras 3–015 and 3–016). Acts which were not based on the Community Treaties did not normally have the same legal force as acts of Community law. The most important difference is that the legal status of Community acts could be clearly inferred from the case law of the Court of Justice, which had recognised the primacy and the possible direct effect of provisions of Community law. This did not happen in the case of non-Community acts, given the limited jurisdiction of the Court of Justice with regard to them. Nevertheless, where the Court of Justice is competent to pronounce on the legal consequences of non-Community acts, it is possible that similar legal effects may be attributed to those acts except when the Treaties provide otherwise.[1] The Court may give rulings, for instance, on pre-Lisbon PJCC acts vis-à-vis Member States that have accepted the Court's jurisdiction to give preliminary rulings on the interpretation of such acts (see para. 23–012). The legal effects attached to non-Community acts which fall outside the Court's jurisdiction—CFSP acts or PJCC acts vis-à-vis Member States which have not accepted the Court's jurisdiction in this regard—depend on the form, the content and the purpose of each act. The legal effects if such acts have to be appraised in the light of international law.[2]

23–003 **Legal basis.** The legal basis of a given act determines whether it is a Community or a non-Community act. Pre-Lisbon acts adopted pursuant to Title V or Title VI of the EU Treaty are clearly non-Community acts. As far as other acts are concerned, the situation is less straightforward, in particular in the case of acts of the institutions or agreements between the governments of the Member States where it is not clear whether they were based on the EC Treaty. In such a case, it must first be determined what the correct—Community or non-Community—legal basis is for the act. The Court of Justice made this clear in the *AETR* judgment in holding that the Council's "proceedings" relating to the AETR negotiations

---

[1] Article 34 EU denies direct effect to PJCC framework decisions and decisions.

[2] Accordingly, Member States may in principle refer disputes relating to such acts to the International Court of Justice where they have no connection with pre-Lisbon Community law or (present) Union law. According to Art. 292 EC, this was not possible in the case of "a dispute concerning the interpretation or application of this Treaty" (see, e.g., ECJ, Case C-459/03 *Commission v Ireland* [2006] E.C.R. I-4635); the same is true under Art. 344 TFEU of any dispute concerning the interpretation or application of "the Treaties".

(see para. 22–103) constituted an act against which an action for annulment would lie under the first para. of Art. 230 EC, which was only applicable to Community acts. It stated that,

> "[t]o decide this point, it is first necessary to determine which authority was, at the relevant date, empowered to negotiate and conclude the AETR. The legal effect of the proceedings differs according to whether they are regarded as constituting the exercise of powers conferred on the Community, or as acknowledging a coordination by the Member States of the exercise of powers which remained vested in them".[3]

It is not enough for a pre-Lisbon act to be described as a "decision of the Member States" in order for it to escape categorisation as a "Community act". It must also be determined whether, having regard to its content and all the circumstances in which it was adopted, the act in question was a measure of the Member States, collectively exercising their powers, or of the Council, adopted by the Member States in their capacity as members of the Council.[4]

II. ACTS OF THE EUROPEAN COUNCIL AND THE COUNCIL PURSUANT TO THE CFSP AND PJCC

Specific instruments. For areas coming under the common foreign and security policy (CFSP), Title V of the EU Treaty prescribed specific instruments. Besides "principles", "general guidelines" and "common strategies" decided on by the European Council (Art. 13(1) and (2) EU),[5] what was involved was mainly "joint actions" and "common positions" adopted by the Council, as well as agreements concluded by the Council at international level (see para. 23–013). What was formerly adopted in the form of common positions and joint actions now takes the form of a decision determining the actions to be undertaken or positions to be taken by the Union, and acts adopted for their implementation also take the form of decisions (Art. 25(b) TEU). Title VI of the EU Treaty set out the specific instruments to be used for action in the context of PJCC, namely "common positions", "framework decisions" and "decisions", alongside agreements concluded by the Council at international level (see para. 23–013) and the PJCC conventions

23–004

---

[3] ECJ, Case 22/70 *Commission v Council* [1971] E.C.R. 263, paras 3–4.

[4] ECJ, Joined Cases C-181/91 and C-248/91 *European Parliament v Council* [1993] E.C.R. I-3685, paras 12–14 (where reference is made to the *AETR* judgment).

[5] But a "common strategy" did have consequences as regards the procedure to be followed by the Council; see para. 18–002. For that instrument, see Spencer, "The EU and Common Strategies: The Revealing Case of the Mediterranean" (2001) E.For.Aff.Rev. 31–51. For a survey of CFSP instruments, see Dashwood, "External Relations Provisions of the Amsterdam Treaty" (1998) C.M.L.Rev. 1019, at 1030–1033.

which Member States concluded amongst themselves (see para. 23–015).[6] Since the EU Treaty did not establish any ranking order between these different instruments, the Council had a choice between several instruments for the purpose of regulating a subject-matter, subject to the limits imposed by the nature of the instrument selected. Accordingly, the fact that a matter was regulated by conventions between the Member States did not prevent the Council from adopting a framework decision to replace the relevant provisions of those conventions.[7] In addition, the European Council and the Council often adopted declarations or positions containing merely a political assessment or a declaration of intent. Some resolutions or recommendations of the Council, however, set out detailed agreements.[8]

23–005   **Formal requirements.** With the exception of conventions and agreements, which were concluded between the Member States, pre-Lisbon CFSP and PJCC instruments were not subject to any special procedure of approval and ratification by the Member States.[9] They obtained their legal force from their approval by the Council (or the European Council). They constituted instruments of international law, which, in principle, had to be applied by each Member State as from their entry into force (for framework decisions, however, see para. 23–009). Whenever the Council adopted such acts, it could decide by unanimous vote to publish them in the *Official Journal.*[10] PJCC instruments were to be published in the *Official Journal* in any event.[11]

23–006   **Effects within the national legal order.** The Member States determine the status and legal effects of pre-Lisbon non-Community acts within their domestic

---

[6] See Van den Brink, "Besluiten in de tweede en derde pijler van de Europese Unie: van eigenheid naar eenvormigheid?" (2003) Themis 243–253. Initially, both Title V (CFSP) and Title VI (JHA cooperation) of the EU Treaty referred to both common (or joint) positions (former Arts J.2 and K.2) and joint action (former Arts J.3 and K.3). The Treaty of Amsterdam replaced joint action in Title VI (henceforth PJCC) by framework decisions and decisions (see Art. 34(2) EU).

[7] ECJ, Case C-303/05 *Advocaten voor de Wereld* [2007] E.C.R. I-3633, paras 37–42.

[8] See, e.g., in the context of JHA cooperation the recommendation concerning transit for the purposes of expulsion and the addendum thereto, both of which antedated the entry into force of the EU Treaty, but were published as annexes to the Council recommendation of December 22, 1995 on concerted action and cooperation in carrying out expulsion measures, [1996] O.J. C5/3.

[9] See also Art. 2 of the 1994 and 2003 Acts of Accession: "From the date of accession, the provisions of the original Treaties and the acts adopted by the institutions and the European Central Bank before accession shall be binding on the new Member States and shall apply in those States under the conditions laid down in those Treaties and in this Act" (see, similarly, Art. 2 of the 2005 Act of Accession).

[10] See Art. 17(3) and (4). The decisions were published in Part L of the *Official Journal.*

[11] See Art. 17(1)(d) and (e) of the previous version of the Council Rules of Procedure, adopted by Council Decision of March 22, 2004 ([2004] O.J. L106/22) (publication of framework decisions, decisions and agreements).

legal systems,[12] although they have to take account of what was determined by the EU Treaty itself with respect to the legal effects of these acts and by the case law of the Court of Justice. This is true in particular of pre-Lisbon PJCC acts, given the jurisdiction of the Court of Justice to give preliminary rulings on the interpretation of a PJCC framework decision, decision or an implementing measure[13] (Art. 35(1) EU), if the Member State in question has accepted the Court's jurisdiction in this regard (Art. 35(3) EU; see para. 13–085).[14] Moreover, the Court is competent to rule on disputes between Member States concerning the interpretation or the application of pre-Lisbon PJCC acts (Art. 35(7), first sentence, EU). All this has enabled the Court to clarify the legal effects of some of these legal instruments within the legal order of the Member States. The Court has also made it clear that, since Art. 6 EU provides that the Union respects fundamental rights, Union acts adopted under Titles V and VI of the EU Treaty have to be interpreted in conformity with fundamental rights.[15]

Any further legal effects that may be attached to pre-Lisbon non-Community acts in the internal legal order of the Member States are to be determined by the Member States themselves. In "monist" Member States (such as Belgium and the Netherlands), binding pre-Lisbon CFSP and PJCC acts may take precedence over domestic law as acts governed by international law. If their provisions have direct effect (under national law), they can be relied upon by individuals before domestic courts.[16] It was precisely in order to avoid this that Art. 34(2)(b) and (c) EU declared that PJCC framework decisions and decisions did not entail direct effect. Nevertheless, the Court of Justice clarified that this does not preclude interested parties from invoking them before national courts, as otherwise the jurisdiction of the Court to give preliminary rulings under Art. 35 EU would be deprived of most of its effectiveness (see para. 23–012). A survey of the factors that Member States have to take into account in determining the legal effects of the various pre-Lisbon non-Community acts in their internal legal order is set out below.

---

[12] For the former "third pillar", see Griller, "Die Unterscheidung von Unionsrecht und Gemeinschaftsrecht nach Amsterdam" (1999) EuR. Beiheft 1, 45, at 64–68; Müller-Graff, "The Legal Bases of the Third Pillar and its Position in the Framework of the Union Treaty" (1994) C.M.L.Rev. 493, at 508–509.

[13] See, e.g., ECJ, Case C-404/07 *Katz* [2008] E.C.R. I-7607, paras 10 and 27; ECJ, Case C-66/08 *Kozałowski* [2008] E.C.R., paras 12 and 29. Article 35(1) EU did not mention PJCC common positions, which were also excluded from judicial review under Art. 35(6) EU, but could be the subject of a ruling on their interpretation or application under Art. 35(7) EU, first sentence.

[14] However, the Court had no jurisdiction to review the validity or the proportionality of operations carried out by the police or other law enforcement services of a Member State or the exercise of the responsibilities incumbent upon Member States with regard to the maintenance of law and order and the safeguarding of internal security: Art. 35(5) EU.

[15] ECJ, Case C-105/03 *Pupino* [2005] E.C.R. I-5285, paras 58–59; ECJ, Case C-354/04 P *Gestoras Pro Amnistía and Others v Council* [2007] E.C.R. I-1579, para. 51; ECJ, Case C-355/04 P *Segi and Others v Council* [2007] E.C.R. I-1657, para. 51; ECJ, Case C-404/07 *Katz* [2008] E.C.R. I-7607, paras 48–49.

[16] For similar observations concerning the German legal system, see Meyring, "Intergovernmentalism and Supranationality: Two Stereotypes for a Complex Reality" (1997) E.L.Rev. 221, at 238–242.

23–007 **Common position.** Common positions defined the approach of the Union to a particular matter (Arts 15 and 34(2)(a) EU). In the case of the CFSP, the matter was referred to as being "of a geographical or thematic nature" (Art. 15 EU).[17] According to the Court of Justice, a common position requires the compliance of the Member States by virtue of the principle of sincere cooperation, which means in particular that Member States are to take all appropriate measures, whether general or particular, to ensure fulfilment of their obligations under Union law.[18] The EU Treaty specified that Member States were to ensure that their national policies conformed to common positions (Art. 15 EU).[19] In this connection, Member States were to "uphold" and "defend" common positions in international organisations and at international conferences (Arts 19(1)[20] and 37, first para., EU, respectively). However, a common position was not supposed to produce legal effects of itself in relation to third parties.[21] That explains why, under the system established by Title VI of the EU Treaty, common positions—in contradistinction to framework decisions and decisions—cannot be the subject of an action for annulment before the Court of Justice and why the Court's jurisdiction to give preliminary rulings does not include rulings on the validity and interpretation of common positions, unlike other pre-Lisbon PJCC acts. However, national courts can ask the Court of Justice to give a preliminary ruling on a common position where the latter, because of its content, has a scope going beyond that assigned by the EU Treaty to that kind of act. It then falls to the Court to find, where appropriate, that the common position was intended to produce legal effects in relation to third parties, to give it its proper categorisation and to give a preliminary ruling.[22]

23–008 **Joint action.** Joint actions, as part of the CFSP, addressed specific situations where operational action of the Union was deemed to be required. They committed the Member States in the positions they adopted and in the conduct of their activity (Art. 14(3) EU).[23] Even if there was a change in circumstances having a substantial effect on a question subject to a joint action, the action was to stand until such time as the Council decided to review its principles and objectives (Art. 14(2)).[24] All this does not preclude joint actions from having legal effects vis-à-vis third parties.

---

[17] See the present Art. 29 TEU.
[18] ECJ, Case C-354/04 P *Gestoras Pro Amnistía and Others v Council* [2007] E.C.R. I-1579, para. 52; ECJ, Case C-355/04 P *Segi and Others v Council* [2007] E.C.R. I-1657, para. 52.
[19] See the present Art. 29 TEU.
[20] See the present Art. 34(1) TEU.
[21] ECJ, Case C-354/04 P *Gestoras Pro Amnistía and Others v Council* [2007] E.C.R. I-1579, para. 52; ECJ, Case C-355/04 P *Segi and Others v Council* [2007] E.C.R. I-1657, para. 52.
[22] *Ibid.*, paras 35–43.
[23] See the present Art. 28(2) TEU. See Dashwood, "The Law and Practice of CFSP Joint Actions" in Cremona and De Witte (eds), *EU Foreign Relations Law—Constitutional Fundamentals* (Oxford, Hart, 2008) 53–77; Münch, "Die gemeinsame Aktion im Rahmen des GASP: Inhalt, Rechtsnatur und Reformbedürftigkeit" (1996) EuR. 415–433.
[24] See the present Art. 28(1), second subpara., TEU.

Framework decision. A framework decision was a PJCC instrument for the   **23–009**
approximation of the laws and regulations of the Member States (Art. 34(2)(b)
EU). Framework decisions were binding upon Member States as to the result to
be achieved but left to the national authorities the choice of form and methods.[25]
Article 34(2)(b) EU further provided that framework decisions did not entail
direct effect. According to the Court of Justice, it followed from the fact that the
wording of Art. 34(2)(b) EU was identical to that of Art. 249 EC, third para., EC
that framework decisions were binding in nature. The binding character of framework decisions places on national authorities, and particularly national courts, an
obligation to interpret national law as far as possible in the light of the wording
and purpose of the framework decision in order to attain the result which it pursued.[26] This duty derives from the principle of sincere cooperation, which,
according to the Court of Justice, also applies within the framework of the pre-
Lisbon PJCC. Moreover, the Court has held that the jurisdiction of the Court to
give preliminary rulings under Art. 35 EU would be deprived of most of its effectiveness if individuals were not entitled to invoke framework decisions in order to
obtain a conforming interpretation of national law before the courts of the
Member States.[27] As in the case of directives, the obligation on the national court
to interpret national law in conformity with a framework decision is limited by
general principles of Union law, in particular those of legal certainty and non-
retroactivity, and cannot serve as the basis for an interpretation of national law
contra legem.[28]

Decision. As far as PJCC was concerned, the EU Treaty empowered the Council   **23–010**
to adopt "decisions" for any other purpose consistent with the objectives of
Title VI, excluding any approximation of the laws and regulations of the Member
States (Art. 34(2)(c) EU).[29] Such decisions were binding and did not entail direct
effect (*ibid.*). Again, the fact that decisions were binding on the Member States
does not preclude them from having legal effects vis-à-vis third parties. The fact
that the Court of Justice is competent, under certain circumstances, to determine

---

[25] An analogy could be drawn with the description of directives in Art. 249 EC (para. 22–075, *supra*).
For an appraisal of this instrument, see Borgers, "Implementing framework decisions" (2007)
C.M.L.Rev. 1361–1386; Monjal, "Le droit dérivé de l'Union européenne en quête d'identité"
(2001) R.T.D.E. 335–369.
[26] ECJ, Case C-105/03 *Pupino* [2005] E.C.R. I-5285, paras 33–34 and 43.
[27] *Ibid.*, paras 35–43. See Monjal, "La décision-cadre instaurant le mandat d'arrêt européen et l'ordre
juridique français: la constitutionnalité du droit dérivé de l'Union européenne sous contrôle du
Conseil d'Etat" (2003) R.D.U.E. 109, at 178–187.
[28] ECJ, Case C-105/03 *Pupino* [2005] E.C.R. I-5285, paras 44–47.
[29] The EU Treaty did not mention decisions amongst the CFSP instruments. The Member States,
however, adopted familiar forms of act such as a "decision of the representatives of the
Governments of the Member States", see Decision (96/409/CFSP) of the representatives of the
Governments of the Member States, meeting within the Council, of June 25, 1996 on the establishment of a temporary travel document [1996] O.J. L168/4.

their interpretation and validity under the preliminary ruling procedure, implies that individuals are entitled to invoke decisions before the courts of the Member States.

23–011 **Other acts.** Among the various PJCC instruments, Art. 34 EU mentioned conventions concluded between the Member States (see para. 23–015). In addition, Art. 34 EU referred to measures adopted by the Council to implement PJCC decisions and PJCC conventions.[30] The content of such measures determines whether they have legal effects not just vis-à-vis the Member States, but also vis-à-vis third parties. As far as pre-Lisbon CFSP instruments are concerned, legal effects vis-à-vis third parties seem to be excluded in the case of "principles", "general guidelines" and "common strategies" adopted by the European Council (Art. 13(1) and (2) EU). As a rule, recommendations, resolutions or declarations adopted by the Council in the pre-Lisbon framework of the CFSP or PJCC are not intended to have legal effects.[31]

23–012 **Judicial review.** According to Art. 10(1) of the Protocol on transitional provisions, annexed by the Lisbon Treaty to the TEU and TFEU, with respect to PJCC acts adopted prior to the entry into force of the Lisbon Treaty, the Court of Justice has only the powers attributed to it before December 1, 2009 (see para. 4–014). Consequently, pre-Lisbon Council action under PJCC is subject to judicial review by the Court of Justice in accordance with Art. 35 EU. Direct review takes place where a Member State or the Commission brings an action challenging the legality of framework decisions or decisions (Art. 35(6) EU). Indirect review is possible with respect to the validity of framework decisions, decisions and implementing measures where the Court of Justice gives a preliminary ruling on a question from a national court on the validity of such an act (Art. 35(1), (2) and (3) EU). National courts may refer questions to the Court only where the Member State in question has accepted the Court's jurisdiction in this regard by making a formal declaration (see para. 13–085). In this way, the Court of Justice may rule on PJCC provisions, including provisions of the Schengen *acquis* which have been transposed into "Union law".[32] It follows from Art. 6(2) EU that non-Community action on the part of Community institutions and bodies—under the

---

[30] Article 34(2)(c) and (d), second para., EU, respectively. These measures were adopted by the Council by a qualified majority of votes or by a majority of two-thirds of the contracting parties, respectively (*ibid.*).

[31] For an example, see Council Decision 2005/876/JHA of November 21, 2005 on the exchange of information extracted from the criminal record, [2005] O.J. L322/33.

[32] The first time was by ECJ, Joined Cases C-187/01 and C-385/01 *Gözütok and Brügge* [2003] E.C.R. I-1345 (interpretation of the *ne bis in idem* principle enshrined in Art. 54 of the Convention of June 19, 1990 implementing the Schengen Agreement). For the incorporation of the Schengen *acquis*, see para. 10–010, *supra*.

CFSP or police and judicial cooperation in criminal matters (PJCC)—must also respect fundamental rights.[33]

Article 46 EU did not exclude the jurisdiction of the Court of Justice to ensure, under Art. 47 EU, that no provision in Title V or Title VI of the EU Treaty detracted from the Community Treaties. As a result, the Court still had the power to pronounce on action by the institutions which was alleged to constitute an infringement of Community law even if the action was undertaken pursuant to the CFSP or PJCC. Accordingly, the Court had jurisdiction under Art. 47 EU to examine whether an act of the Council which was formally based on Title V or VI of the EU Treaty, but related to a matter coming within the Community's competence, should not instead have been adopted on the basis of a provision of the Community Treaties and in accordance with the procedure prescribed thereby.[34]

For pre-Lisbon action taken by Member States in connection with PJCC, Art. 35 EU did not expressly provide for judicial supervision. However, when the Court of Justice interprets PJCC framework decisions, decisions, conventions or measures implementing them (see Art. 35(1) EU), or rules on disputes between Member States regarding the interpretation or application of PJCC acts or on disputes between Member States and the Commission on the interpretation or application of PJCC conventions (See Art. 35(7) EU),[35] it may indicate how such interpretation and application can be kept compatible with PJCC provisions and fundamental rights.

III. INTERNATIONAL AGREEMENTS CONCLUDED BY THE UNION IN CONNECTION WITH THE CFSP AND PJCC

Agreements concluded by the Union. In accordance with Art. 24 and Art. 38 EU, the Council concluded international agreements with one or more States or international organisations in connection with the CFSP and PJCC. All agreements which the Council concluded on behalf of the EU referred to the European Union[36] as one of the participating parties, which suggests that, internationally, **23–013**

---

[33] ECJ, Case C-303/05 *Advocaten voor de Wereld* [2007] E.C.R. I-3633, para. 45. See Wölker, "Grundrechtsschutz durch den Gerichtshof der Europäischen Gemeinschaften und nationale Gerichte nach Amsterdam" (1999) EuR. Beiheft 1, 99–116; Wachsmann, "Le Traité d'Amsterdam. Les droits de l'homme" (1997) R.T.D.E. 883, at 888.

[34] ECJ, Case C-170/96 *Commission v Council* [1998] E.C.R. I-2763; ECJ, Case C-176/03 *Commission v Council* [2005] E.C.R. I-7879; ECJ, Case C-440/05 *Commission v Council* [2007] E.C.R. I-9097; ECJ, Case C-91/05 *Commission v Council* [2008] E.C.R. I-3651.

[35] In order for the Court to have this power, the Council must have failed to settle the dispute within six months of its being referred to that institution by one of its members (Art. 35(7), second sentence, EU).

[36] See, e.g., the Agreement between the European Union and the North Atlantic Treaty Organisation on the security of information, approved by Council Decision 2003/211/CFSP of February 24, 2003, [2003] O.J. L80/35, the Agreements between the European Union and the United States of America on extradition and mutual legal assistance in criminal matters, approved by Council

not only the Member States severally were bound, but also the Union as such. Agreements concluded in accordance with Art. 24 EU were binding on the institutions of the Union (Art. 24(6) EU).[37] Article 24 EU provided that no agreement,

> "shall be binding on a Member State whose representative in the Council states that it has to comply with the requirements of its own constitutional procedure".[38]

The other members of the Council could nevertheless agree that the agreement was to apply provisionally to them (Art. 24(5) EU). Agreements concluded under Art. 24 EU were published in the *Official Journal*, unless the Council decided otherwise.[39] Under Art. 46 EU, the Court of Justice had no jurisdiction to rule on the validity or interpretation of such agreements.[40]

IV. CONVENTIONS CONCLUDED BETWEEN THE MEMBER STATES

23–014 **Conventions connected with Community law.** Article 293 EC invited the Member States to "enter into negotiations with each other" with a view to laying

---

Decision 2003/516/EC of June 6, 2003, [2003] O.J. L181/25 and concluded on behalf of the Union by Council Decision 2009/820/CFSP of October 23, 2009, [2009] O.J. L291/40 and the Agreement between the European Union and the Republic of Iceland and the Kingdom of Norway on the application of certain provisions of the Convention of May 29, 2000 on Mutual Assistance in Criminal Matters between the Member States of the European Union and the 2001 Protocol thereto, approved by Council Decision 2004/79/EC of December 17, 2003, [2004] O.J. L26/1. See Mitsilegas, "The external dimension of EU Action in Criminal Matters" (2007) E.For.Aff.Rev. 457–497; Georgopoulos, "What Kind of Treaty-Making Power for the EU? Constitutional Problems Related to the Conclusion of the EU-US Agreements on Extradition and Mutual Legal Assistance" (2005) E.L.Rev. 190–208. See also the Agreement between the European Union and the United States of America on the processing and transfer of Passenger Name Record (PNR) data by air carriers to the United States Department of Homeland Security (DHS), which provisionally applies as of the date of its signature (see Council Decision 2007/551/CFSP/JHA of July 23, 2007, [2007] O.J. L204/16). That agreement replaces an earlier agreement between the EC and the USA, concluded under Art. 95 EC [*now Art. 114 TFEU*], which was denounced by the EC (see [2006] O.J. C219/1) after the Court of Justice ruled that it could not have validly been adopted under the first pillar (see ECJ, Joined Cases C-317/04 and C-318/04 *European Parliament v Council and Commission* [2006] E.C.R. I-4721, para. 9–112, *supra*).

[37] However, the Agreement between the European Union and NATO on the Security of Information restricts its application as far as the EU is concerned to the Council of the European Union, the Secretary-General/High Representative and the General Secretariat of the Council and the Commission (Agreement, Art. 3; n. 36, *supra*).

[38] Such a declaration was made, for example, by twelve Member States with regard to the agreements with the USA on extradition and mutual legal assistance in criminal matters (n. 36, *supra*). See Genson, "Les accords d'extradition et d'entraide judiciaire signés le 25 juin 2003 à Washington entre l'Union européenne et les Etats-Unis d'Amérique" (2003) R.M.C.U.E. 427–432.

[39] Article 17(1)(h) of the previous version of the Council Rules of Procedure, adopted by Council Decision of March 22, 2004 ([2004] O.J. L106/22).

[40] Since the provisions of Art. 24 EU applied to such agreements in the sphere of PJCC, the Court of Justice also had no jurisdiction in regard to them.

down arrangements in matters such as the abolition of double taxation, the mutual recognition of companies or the reciprocal recognition and enforcement of national judgments. In these areas, but also in other fields, the Member States have concluded conventions amongst themselves with a connection to fields of Community competence, but without their constituting Community law. Conventions signed between Member States could be published in the *Official Journal*.[41] For the Court of Justice, the mere fact that a provision of Community law authorised Member States to cooperate was not enough to justify the view that an agreement concluded by Member States for that purpose formed an integral part of Community law.[42] The Court of Justice held that Art. 293 EC was

> "not intended to lay down a legal rule directly applicable as such, but merely defined a number of matters on which the Member States are to enter into negotiations with each other 'so far as is necessary' ".[43]

Conventions concluded in this way were not acts of the institutions, but remained agreements governed by international law to which Art. 234 EC [*now Art. 267 TFEU*] did not apply.[44]

However, the Member States could provide in the convention itself or in a protocol thereto for the Court of Justice to have jurisdiction to interpret its provisions, as was the case with the Brussels Convention on jurisdiction and enforcement of judgments in civil and commercial matters, which was concluded pursuant to Art. 293 EC.[45] According to the Court of Justice, provisions of a convention concluded on the basis of that article and within the framework defined by it were "linked to

---

[41] Article 17(1)(e) and (f) of the previous version of the Council Rules of Procedure, adopted by Council Decision of March 22, 2004 ([2004] O.J. L106/22), required such publication for conventions between Member States which were signed on the basis of Art. 293 EC or established by the Council in accordance with Art. 34(2) EU.

[42] ECJ (order of November 12, 1998), Case C-162/98 *Hartmann* [1998] E.C.R. I-7083, paras 11–12, and ECJ (order of November 12, 1998), Case C-194/98 *Pörschke*, not yet reported, paras 11–12.

[43] ECJ, Case 137/84 *Mutsch* [1985] E.C.R. 2681, para. 11; ECJ, Case C-336/96 *Gilly* [1998] E.C.R. I-2793, para. 15.

[44] ECJ, Case 56/84 *Von Gallera* [1984] E.C.R. 01769, para. 4; ECJ (judgment of September 30, 2010), Case C-132109 *Commission v Belgium*, not yet reported, paras 43–45.

[45] Brussels Convention of September 27, 1968 on jurisdiction and the enforcement of judgments in civil and commercial matters (the Brussels Convention, often referred to as the Judgments Convention, now replaced by Regulation (EC) No. 44/2001; see para. 10–017, *supra*). Questions on the interpretation and application of the Convention could be referred to the Court of Justice for a preliminary ruling pursuant to the Luxembourg Protocol of June 3, 1971 on its interpretation ([1978] O.J. L304/36). Provision was also made for the Court of Justice to interpret the Brussels Convention of February 29, 1968 on the mutual recognition of companies and bodies corporate (see n. 276 to para. 9–068, *supra*) under a protocol of June 3, 1971 appended thereto, which, like the Convention itself, has not entered into force. The Court of Justice has no such jurisdiction in respect of the third convention adopted pursuant to Art. 293 EC: Brussels Convention of July 23, 1990 on the elimination of double taxation in connection with the adjustment of profits of associated enterprises, [1990] O.J. L225/10.

the E[E]C Treaty".[46] As a result, the Court of Justice reviewed a national provision of procedural law forming part of the provisions to which the Brussels Convention referred in the light of the prohibition of discrimination laid down in Art. 12 EC [*now Art. 18 TFEU*] and found that the provision in question was contrary thereto.[47]

Although they were not part of Community law, conventions contemplated by Art. 293 EC and those that were "inseparable from the attainment of the objectives of the EC Treaty" as well as

> "the protocols on the interpretation of those conventions by the Court of Justice, signed by the present Member States of the Community"

constituted part of the *acquis communautaire*.[48] New Member States undertook in the Act of Accession to accede to such conventions and to enter into negotiations with the other Member States in order to make the necessary adjustments thereto.[49] These conventions also included the 1980 Rome Convention on the law applicable to contractual obligations, which the Member States concluded outside the framework of Art. 293 EC. A protocol annexed to this Convention conferred jurisdiction on the Court of Justice to interpret it.[50] In the case of both the Brussels Convention and the Rome Convention, this has allowed the Court to secure consistency with Community law.[51] On this basis, the Brussels and Rome Conventions have been considered to give shape to the Community legal order in a broader sense.[52] Since the entry into force of the Lisbon Treaty, such conventions contribute to the development of the Union legal order.

---

[46] ECJ, Case C-398/92 *Mund & Fester* [1994] E.C.R. I-467, para. 12.

[47] *Ibid.*, paras 13–22.

[48] 2003 Act of Accession, Art. 5(2) and 1994 Act of Accession, Art. 4(2). The 2005 Act of Accession limited itself to listing the conventions to which the new Member States had to accede, see Art. 3(3). The 1972 and 1979 Acts of Accession mentioned only the Art. 293 [EC] conventions, whilst Art. 3(2) of the 1985 Act of Accession also referred to conventions which "are inseparable from the attainment of the objectives of that Treaty and thus linked to the Community legal order" (for the references of the Acts of Accession, see paras 6–002—6–007, *supra*).

[49] 2005 Act of Accession, Art. 3(3); 2003 Act of Accession, Art. 5(2); 1994 Act of Accession, Art. 4(2).

[50] Rome Convention of June 19, 1980 on the law applicable to contractual obligations (see para. 10–018, *supra*; now replaced by Regulation (EC) No. 592/2008), the Protocol of December 19, 1988 on interpretation of the Convention by the Court of Justice, [1989] O.J. L48/1 and the Protocol of December 19, 1988 conferring on the Court of Justice of the European Communities certain powers to interpret the Convention, [1989] L48/17. See also the powers conferred on the Court by Arts 5 and 73 of the Luxembourg Convention for the European patent for the common market (Community Patent Convention), [1976] O.J. L17/1. That convention has been signed by nine Member States including the United Kingdom. Denmark and Ireland have been unable to ratify it.

[51] The first preliminary ruling on the Rome Convention was given in ECJ, Case C-133/08 *ICF* [2009] E.C.R. I-9687.

[52] See Van Houtte, "Het Europees Overeenkomstenverdrag" in Van Houtte and Pertegás Sender (eds), *Europese IPR-verdragen* (Leuven, Acco, 1997), 190 pp.

PJCC conventions. Under Art. 34(2)(d) EU, the Council was competent to estab-   **23–015**
lish conventions in the field of police and judicial cooperation in criminal matters
(PJCC), which it recommended to the Member States for adoption in accordance
with their respective constitutional requirements.[53] Unless they provided otherwise,
such conventions, once adopted by at least half of the Member States, entered into
force for those Member States (Art. 34(2)(d) EU). Such conventions were also published in the *Official Journal*.[54] These PJCC conventions were considered "inseparable from the attainment of the objectives of the EU Treaty"[55] and new Member
States undertook in the Act of Accession to accede thereto.[56] Within the Member
States which are party to them, PJCC conventions have the same legal force as other
international conventions, except that the Court of Justice may have jurisdiction to
rule on their interpretation. If the Member State concerned has accepted the jurisdiction of the Court of Justice, that Court can give preliminary rulings on the interpretation of such conventions (Art. 35(1) EU). In any case, the Court is empowered
to rule on any dispute between Member States regarding the interpretation or the
application of such conventions whenever the dispute cannot be settled by the
Council within six months of its being referred to that institution, and on any dispute between Member States and the Commission regarding the interpretation or
the application of such conventions (Art. 35(7) EU).

    Even before the introduction (by the Treaty of Amsterdam) of Art. 35 EU, the EU
Member States concluded conventions in the sphere of justice and home affairs
(JHA), in respect of which, under the former Art. K.3 of the EU Treaty, the Council
conferred jurisdiction on the Court of Justice to interpret provisions of conventions
and to rule on any disputes regarding their application. Those conventions are still in
force and new Member States are to accede to them. Most JHA conventions which
recognise the jurisdiction of the Court of Justice provide for a first stage in which
disputes between Member States about the interpretation and application of the convention are to be discussed in the Council. After six months, a party to the dispute
may refer the case to the Court of Justice.[57] Furthermore, any dispute between one

---

[53] See also Art. 3 of the 1994 Act of Accession. See the Convention of May 29, 2000 on Mutual
Assistance in Criminal Matters between the Member States of the European Union, established in
accordance with Art. 34 of the EU Treaty by Council Act of May 29, 2000, [2000] O.J. C197/1.

[54] Article 17(1)(e) of the previous version of the Council Rules of Procedure, adopted by Council
Decision of March 22, 2004 ([2004] O.J. L106/22).

[55] See the first indent of Art. 3(4) of the 2003 Act of Accession.

[56] 2005 Act of Accession, Art. 3(3); 2003 Act of Accession, Art. 5(2); 1994 Act of Accession, Art. 4(2).

[57] See Art. 27 of the Convention on the use of information technology for customs purposes, [1995]
O.J. C316/42; Art. 8 of the Convention on the protection of the European Communities' financial
interests, [1995] O.J. C316/51; Art. 8 of the Protocol of September 27, 1996 to the Convention on
the protection of the European Communities' financial interests, [1996] O.J. C313/2); Art. 13 of
the Second Protocol to the Convention on the protection of the European Communities' financial
interests, [1997] O.J. C221/12 and Art. 12(1) of the Convention on the fight against corruption
involving officials of the European Communities or officials of Member States of the European
Union, [1997] O.J. C195/2. Article 40(2) of the Europol Convention (now replaced by the Europol
Council Decision; see para. 10–027, *supra*;) provided that if disputes were not settled within six
months, the Member States party to the dispute were to decide, by agreement amongst themselves,

or more Member States and the Commission concerning the application of the convention which cannot be settled by negotiation may be brought before the Court of Justice. Each such convention (or a protocol thereto) permits Member States to recognise the jurisdiction of the Court of Justice to give preliminary rulings on its interpretation.[58] Member States may elect to allow references for preliminary rulings to be made only by courts of last instance or by any court or tribunal.[59] Some JHA conventions conferred on the Court of Justice the same interpretative jurisdiction as the Brussels and Rome Conventions by separate protocols.[60] Where the Court of Justice has been given jurisdiction to interpret provisions of such conventions and to rule on any disputes relating to their application, it may secure consistency with other provisions of Union law.

23–016 **Legal effects post Lisbon.** Since the entry into force of the Lisbon Treaty, the Treaties no longer mention conventions between Member States as a policy instrument of the Union. This does not prevent existing conventions from preserving their legal force, including any interpretative jurisdiction conferred on the Court of Justice. Moreover, the possibility cannot be ruled out that Member States will continue to conclude conventions amongst themselves (see para. 22–110).

---

the modalities according to which they were to be settled. It appears from a declaration on Art. 40(2) ([1995] O.J. C316/32) that all the Member States, with the exception of the United Kingdom, agreed that in such cases they would systematically submit the dispute to the Court of Justice.

[58] See the arrangements laid down in the Protocols on the interpretation, by way of preliminary rulings, by the Court of Justice of the European Communities of the Convention on the establishment of a European Police Office, [1996] O.J. C299/1, of the Convention on the protection of the European Communities' financial interests, [1997] O.J. C151/2 (the latter protocol also being applicable to the Second Protocol to the Convention: [1997] O.J. C221/12) and of the Convention on the use of information technology for customs purposes ([1997] O.J. C151/16). Similar rules are set out in Art. 12(3) to (6) of the Convention of May 26, 1997 on the fight against corruption involving officials of the European Communities or officials of Member States of the European Union, [1997] O.J. C195/2 and Art. 26(3) to (7) of the Convention of December 18, 1997 on mutual assistance and cooperation between customs administrations, [1998] O.J. C24/2.

[59] As far as the Europol Convention was concerned, the first option was chosen by France and Ireland, the second by, for instance, Belgium, the Netherlands and Sweden: see the declarations in [1996] O.J. C299/2, and (for Sweden) in [1997] O.J. C100/1. As regards the financial interests and customs information technology conventions, the first option has been chosen by Ireland and Portugal (and by France in the case of the latter convention) and the second by the Netherlands ([1997] O.J. C151/14 and C151/28). In the case of the customs cooperation convention, Ireland has chosen the first option and Austria, Germany, Greece and Italy the second ([1998] O.J. C24/21).

[60] These conventions are the Convention of May 28, 1998 on Jurisdiction and the Recognition and Enforcement of Judgments in Matrimonial Matters ("Second Brussels Convention"; see para. 10–017, *supra*; replaced by Regulation (EC) No. 2201/2003), with the Protocol on the interpretation by the Court of Justice of the European Communities of that Convention, [1998] O.J. C221/20 (explanatory report at [1998] O.J. C221/65), and the Convention of May 26, 1997 on the service in the Member States of the European Union of judicial and extrajudicial documents in civil or commercial matters (see para. 10–017, *supra*; replaced by Regulation (EC) No. 1393/2007), with the Protocol on the interpretation by the Court of Justice of the European Communities of the Convention, [1997] O.J. C261/17 (explanatory report at [1997] O.J. C261/38).

Part VI

THE EXTERNAL RELATIONS OF THE EUROPEAN UNION

CHAPTER 24

THE POSITION IN INTERNATIONAL LAW OF THE UNION

International position. According to Art. 21(1), first subpara., TEU, the Union's action on the international scene,   **24–001**

> "shall be guided by the principles which have inspired its own creation, development and enlargement, and which it seeks to advance in the wider world".

In order to secure "cohesive force" for the Union in international relations,[1] the EU Treaty created a framework for a common foreign and security policy (CFSP, Title V). That framework came to supplement the powers for external action which the Communities had been exercising ever since their establishment. The Lisbon Treaty created a single legal regime for all external action of the Union. Specific rules continue to exist, however, for the CFSP. As a result, there will always be a need to ensure consistency between that field of action of the Union and the other areas of its external action.

This part starts with a discussion of the position in international law of the Union (this chapter), which is followed by a survey of the external competences of the Union (Ch. 25) and the procedure for concluding international agreements (Ch. 26). Next, the consistency of the CFSP and other Union external action is reviewed (Ch. 27).[2]

---

[1] See Art. 11(2) EU.

[2] For detailed discussions of the external relations of the EU, see De Baere, *Constitutional Principles of EU External Relations* (Oxford, Oxford University Press, 2008), 330 pp.; Koutrakos, *EU International Relations Law* (Oxford/Portland, Hart Publishing, 2006), 542 pp.; Hill and Smith, *International Relations and the European Union,* (Oxford, Oxford University Press, 2005), 469 pp.; Eeckhout, *External Relations of the European Union, Legal and Constitutional Foundations* (Oxford, Oxford University Press, 2004), 490 pp.; Cannizzaro, *The European Union as an Actor in International Relations* (The Hague, Kluwer, 2002), 364 pp. For a discussion of the changes introduced by the Lisbon Treaty, see Wouters, Coppens and De Meester, "The European Union's External Relations after the Lisbon Treaty", in Griller and Ziller (eds), *The Lisbon Treaty. EU Constitutionalism without a Constitutional Treaty* (Vienna, Springer, 2008), 143–203. For a historical overview, see Kuijper, "Fifty Years of EC-EU External Relations: Continuity and the Dialogue between Judges and Member States as Constitutional Legislators" (2008) Fordham I.L.J. 1571–1602.

I. INTERNATIONAL LEGAL PERSONALITY

24–002 **Legal personality.** Article 47 TEU expressly confers legal personality on the European Union. Just like the Member States, the Union, as a legal person, has the capacity to exercise rights in international legal transactions and enter into obligations over the whole field of its objectives.[3] This means that the Union may, in principle, conclude agreements with third countries and international organisations, be held liable under international law if it breaches its obligations and may take action itself where its rights are infringed. If a Union institution concludes an agreement, the agreement will be binding on the Union and it will be liable for its performance.[4] The Union's international capacity is governed by the rules of international law[5]; however, the division of powers as between the Union and the Member States is a matter of Union law.[6]

Before the Lisbon Treaty, the Treaties only expressly conferred legal personality on the European Community and the European Atomic Energy Community (see Art. 281 EC and Art. 184 EAEC). The European Community has now been replaced and succeeded by the European Union (see Art. 1, third subpara., TEU). The EAEC continues to exist as a separate entity with legal personality (see para. 4–009).

By contrast, before the Lisbon Treaty, the EU Treaty did not expressly endow the European Union with legal personality.[7] However, in order for an international organisation to have legal personality, it does not necessarily have to be expressly conferred on the organisation by the treaty establishing it. Legal personality may be inferred from the powers and means whereby the contracting parties endow a given organisation with independent status.[8] In view of the considerable autonomy

---

[3] See ECJ, Case 22/70 *Commission v Council* [1971] E.C.R. 263, paras 13–14; ECJ, Joined Cases 3, 4 and 6/76 *Kramer* [1976] E.C.R. 1279, para. 17/18.

[4] ECJ, Case C-327/91 *France v Commission* [1994] E.C.R. I-3641, paras 24–25.

[5] See, inter alia, the Vienna Convention of March 21, 1986 on the Law of Treaties between States and International Organisations or between International Organisations (para. 22–033, *supra*).

[6] ECJ, Ruling 1/78 *Draft Convention of the International Atomic Energy Agency on the Physical Protection of Nuclear Materials, Facilities and Transports* [1978] E.C.R. 2151, para. 35. See also Wessel, "The EU as a Party to International Agreements: Shared Competences, Mixed Responsibilities", in Dashwood and Maresceau (eds), *Law and Practice of EU External Relations* (Cambridge: Cambridge University Press, 2008) 152–187; Groux and Manin, *The European Communities in the International Legal Order* (Luxembourg, Office for Official Publications of the EC, 1985), 163 pp.; Lachmann, "International Legal Personality of the EC: Capacity and Competence" (1984) L.I.E.I. 3–21.

[7] Pliakos, "La nature juridique de l'Union européenne" (1993) R.T.D.E. 187, at 212–213; for the recognition of legal personality, see Ress, "Democratic Decision-Making in the European Union and the Role of the European Parliament", in Curtin and Heukels (eds), *Institutional Dynamics of European Integration. Essays in Honour of Henry G. Schermers* Vol. II (Dordrecht, Martinus Nijhoff, 1994), 153, at 156; for a somewhat less categorical view, see Wessel, "The Inside Looking Out: Consistency and Delimitation in EU External Relations" (2000) C.M.L.Rev. 1135–1171; von Bogdandy, "The Legal Case for Unity: The European Union as a Single Organisation with a Single Legal System" (1999) C.M.L.Rev. 887–910.

[8] Schermers and Blokker, *International Institutional Law* (The Hague, Martinus Nijhoff, 1995), paras 1562–1570, at 976–981.

conferred upon the European Union, it was increasingly argued in legal literature that the Union was to be regarded as having legal personality under international law.[9] That was the case in particular after the Treaty of Amsterdam introduced in Art. 24 EU the power of the Council to conclude agreements with third countries and international organisations. In the agreements concluded by the Council on behalf of the Union before the Lisbon Treaty, the European Union was already indicated as a participating party bound by the agreements (see para. 22–110).

Membership of international organisations. As already stated, the Union (and the EAEC) has at present the capacity to conclude agreements, including multilateral agreements establishing an international organisation.[10] In some cases, the Union may conclude agreements only together with the Member States (see para. 25–059). It may likewise accede to an international organisation, provided that the statutes of the organisation permit non-States to join.[11] In some instances, the Union has taken the place of its Member States; generally, it becomes a member alongside the Member States, as in the case of certain commodities agreements,[12] the Food and Agricultural Organisation (FAO)[13] and the World Trade Organisation (WTO).[14] In the event

24–003

---

[9] See Österdahl, "The EU and its Member States, Other States and International Organisations—The Common European Security and Defence Policy After Nice" (2001) Nordic J.I.L. 341–350; Wessel, "De Europese Unie in de internationale rechtsorde" (2001) Mededelingen van de Nederlandse Vereniging voor Internationaal Recht 11–37. For a cautious view, see Grard, "La condition internationale de l'Union européenne après Nice" (2000) R.A.E. 374, at 375–378. See also Tiilikainen, "To Be or Not to Be? An Analysis of the Legal and Political Elements of Statehood in the EU's External Identity" (2001) E.For.Aff.Rev. 223–241.

[10] ECJ, Opinion 1/76 *Draft Agreement establishing a European laying-up fund for inland waterway vessels* [1977] E.C.R. 741, para. 5. For internal limitations on powers in this connection, see para. 17–023, *supra*.

[11] Various international organisations, particularly those established before the Communities, do not allow non-States to be members, but permitted the Communities—and now the Union—to take part in their activities without voting rights as an "observer" or with some similar status. See, for instance, the Council of Europe (resolution of the Committee of Ministers of May 1951); the UN General Assembly (Resolution 3208 (XXIX) of October 11, 1974); the International Labour Organisation (ILO Constitution, Art. 12(2)). For representation at the UN, see the Council's answer of November 30, 2000 to question E-2810/00 (Titford), [2001] O.J. C113E/181. See also the website of the EU delegation to the UN: *http://www.eu-un.europa.eu/* [Accessed December 15, 2010]. See further the contributions in Wouters, Hoffmeister and Ruys (eds), *The United Nations and the European Union: an ever stronger partnership* (The Hague, T.M.C. Asser Press, 2006), 434 pp.

[12] Barents, "The European Communities and the Commodity Organisations" (1984) 1 L.I.E.I. 77–91.

[13] The Community acceded thereto in 1991. See Frid, "The European Economic Community: A Member of a Specialised Agency of the United Nations" (1993) E.J.I.L. 239–255; Schwob, "L'amendement à l'acte constitutif de la FAO visant à permettre l'admission en qualité de membre des organisations d'intégration économique régionale et la Communauté économique européenne" (1993) R.T.D.E. 1–38.

[14] See para. 25–015, *infra*. See also Gstöhl, " 'Patchwork Power' Europe: The EU's Representation in International Institutions" (2009) E.For.Aff.Rev. 385–403; Hoffmeister, "Outsider or Frontrunner? Recent Developments under International and European Law on the Status of the European Union in International Organizations and Treaty Bodies" (2007) C.M.L.Rev. 41–66; Leenen, "Participation of the EEC in International Environmental Agreements", and Koers, "The European Economic Community and International Fisheries Organisations" (1984) 1 L.I.E.I. 93–111 and 113–131, respectively.

that the Union becomes a member of an international organisation alongside the Member States, that organisation has to decide whether the Union should have voting rights of its own or whether it may exercise the Member States' rights on terms to be determined.[15] In the latter case, before any meeting of the organisation it will require a declaration to be made indicating whether competence lies with the Union or the Member States in respect of a particular item of the agenda and who is to exercise the right to vote.[16] The Union and the Member States have to coordinate their positions in advance (see para. 24–007). Where the Union is empowered under Union law to conclude an agreement in the context of the International Labour Organisation but cannot do so itself under the ILO Constitution, it may exercise its external competence through the medium of the Member States acting jointly in the Union's interest.[17]

24–004 **Liability under international law.** The Union is liable for consequences of its international action. A party which has been adversely affected thereby can sometimes obtain redress through Union judicial procedures. The Union institutions may also award it compensation pursuant to their own powers of decision. For its part, the Union is entitled to act where its rights under a treaty are infringed. For instance, it may adopt economic sanctions pursuant to its competence in the sphere of commercial policy (see para. 25–049). However, as a non-State, the Union is not entitled to bring proceedings in the International Court of Justice.[18] A dispute may only be resolved in the manner agreed by the Contracting Parties or in accordance with the procedure provided for in the treaty in question, which will generally be based on negotiations or arbitration.[19] Since agreements concluded by the Union are binding on its institutions and on the Member States (Art. 216(2) TFEU [*see ex Art. 300(7) EC*]), it is incumbent on both the institutions and the Member States to ensure that the obligations arising under such agreements are complied with.[20] In so doing, the Member States fulfil,

---

[15] Govaere, Capiau and Vermeersch, "In-Between Seats: The Participation of the European Union in International Organisations" (2004) E.For.Aff.Rev. 155–187; Neuwahl, "Shared Powers or Combined Incompetence? More on Mixity" (1996) C.M.L.Rev. 667–687; Sack, "The European Community's Membership of International Organisations" (1995) C.M.L.Rev. 1227–1256.

[16] ECJ, Case C-25/94 *Commission v Council* [1996] E.C.R. I-1469. See Lenaerts and De Smijter, "The United Nations and the European Union: Living Apart Together" in Wellens (ed.), *International Law: Theory and Practice. Essays in Honour of Eric Suy* (The Hague, Martinus Nijhoff, 1998), 439, at 443–447.

[17] ECJ, Opinion 2/91 *Convention No. 170 of the International Labour Organisation concerning safety in the use of chemicals at work* [1993] E.C.R. I-1061, para. 5. See, for instance, Council Decision 2005/367/EC of April 14, 2005 authorising Member States to ratify, in the interests of the European Community, the Seafarers' Identity Documents Convention of the International Labour Organisation (Convention 185), [2005] O.J. L136/1.

[18] Article 34(1) of the Statute of the International Court of Justice, to which all members of the United Nations are party ipso facto (UN Charter, Art. 93(1); for the UN Charter, see para. 22–056, *supra*).

[19] Groux and Manin (n. 6, *supra*), at 161–168.

[20] ECJ, Case 104/81 *Kupferberg* [1982] E.C.R. 3641, para. 11 (for the legal force of agreements concluded by the Union, see para. 22–043, *supra*).

"an obligation not only in relation to the third country concerned but also and above all in relation to the [Union] which has assumed responsibility for the due performance of the agreement".[21]

It probably cannot be inferred from this that the Member States are vicariously liable under international law for obligations entered into by the Union.[22]

II. INTERNATIONAL REPRESENTATION

A. DIPLOMATIC RELATIONS OF THE UNION

Accreditations. Third countries wishing to maintain permanent contacts with the European Union apply to the Union for accreditation of a diplomatic mission. The credentials of heads of missions from third countries accredited to the European Union are presented to the President of the Council and the President of the Commission, who meet for the occasion.[23] The Member State in whose territory the institutions of the Union are established accords such missions the "customary diplomatic immunities and privileges" (Protocol on Privileges and Immunities, Art. 16).[24] In addition to their normal diplomatic functions, those missions often represent their countries on the advisory bodies set up by trade or association agreements concluded with the Union (see paras 25–009 and 25–020).[25]   **24–005**

Union delegations. Article 221 TFEU provides for "Union delegations" which are to represent the Union in third countries and at international organisations. This right for the Union to open its own diplomatic representations was introduced by the Lisbon Treaty. Before, the Union/Communities did not set up diplomatic missions. Nevertheless, pursuant to its power of internal organisation and   **24–006**

---

[21] *Ibid.*, para. 13. Accordingly, the Commission may bring an action under Art. 258 TFEU [*ex Art. 226 EC*] against a Member State which has failed to fulfil its obligations under an agreement concluded by the Union: ECJ, Case C-13/00 *Commission v Ireland* [2002] E.C.R. I-2943, paras 14–20.

[22] Groux and Manin (n. 6, *supra*), at 153–156; Manin, "L'article 228, paragraphe 2, du traité C.E.E.", *Etudes de droit des Communautés européennes. Mélanges offerts à P.-H. Teitgen* (Paris, Pedone, 1984), 289, at 302–304.

[23] Luxembourg Compromise of January 28 and 29, 1966, Part a(3), (1966) 3 Bull.CE, 10. For the list of missions accredited to the EU and to the EAEC and the international organisations and other representations to the Commission, see the website of the Commission's Protocol Service: *http://ec.europa.eu/dgs/secretariat_general/corps* [Accessed December 15, 2010].

[24] Protocol (No. 7), annexed to the TEU, the TFEU and the EAEC Treaty, on the Privileges and Immunities of the European Union, [2010] O.J. C83/266 (see the discussion in para. 13–128, *supra*).

[25] Louis, *The Community Legal Order* (Brussels/Luxembourg, Office for Official Publications of the EC, 1993), at 75–76.

its power to conduct negotiations on agreements,[26] the Commission had established delegations in more than one hundred and fifty three countries and with international organisations based in Geneva, Nairobi, New York, Paris, Rome and Vienna.[27] Whether or not under an agreement concluded with the Communities, such delegations were generally granted the customary diplomatic privileges and immunities.[28] For its part, the General Secretariat of the Council set up liaison offices in Geneva and New York in order to maintain contacts with the international organisations based in those cities.[29]

Since the Lisbon Treaty, these delegations no longer depend on the Commission (or the Council), but are placed under the authority of the High Representative of the Union for Foreign Affairs and Security Policy and act in close cooperation with Member States' diplomatic and consular missions (Art. 221(2) TFEU). The High Representative decides to open or close a delegation in agreement with the Council and the Commission.[30] The Union delegations have been integrated into the European External Action Service (EEAS), which comprises officials of the Council and the Commission as well as staff seconded from the diplomatic services of the Member States (see para. 13–121). Staff in delegations comprise EEAS staff and, where appropriate for the implementation of the Union budget and Union policies, Commission staff.[31] Each Head of Delegation has authority over all staff in the delegation, whatever their status, and for all its activities.[32] The Head of Delegation receives instructions from the High Representative and the EEAS. In areas where the Commission exercises external powers, that institution may also issue instructions to delegations.[33]

B. REPRESENTATION OF THE UNION

24–007   **Usual forms.** Outside the framework of the CFSP (see paras 24–009 *et seq.*), the Treaties do not lay down general rules on the external representation of the Union.

---

[26] Stein, "External Relations of the European Community: Structure and Process" (1990) *Collected Courses of the Academy of European Law. I*, 1990, 115, at 134; Sauvignon, "Les Communautés européennes et le droit de légation actif" (1978) R.M.C. 176, at 180.

[27] European Commission, General Report on the Activities of the European Union 2001 (Brussels/Luxembourg, 2002), at 405 (158 accreditations). See also Brinkhorst, "Permanent Missions of the EC in Third Countries: European Diplomacy in the Making" (1984) 1 L.I.E.I. 23–33.

[28] Groux and Manin (n. 6, *supra*), at 36–38. For Commission delegations in the ACP States, see Protocol (No. 2), annexed to the ACP-EC Partnership Agreement, on Privileges and Immunities, [2001] O.J. L317/281.

[29] The European Parliament, for its part, purported to derive a "right to send diplomatic representation" from the fact that the Communities had international legal personality (see resolution of November 17, 1960, [1960] J.O. 1496; see also the resolution of April 14, 1989, [1989] O.J. C120/340).

[30] Council Decision 2010/427/EU of July 26, 2010 establishing the organisation and the functioning of the European External Action Service ([2010] O.J. L201/30), Art. 5(1).

[31] *Ibid.*, Art. 5(2).

[32] *Ibid.*, Art. 5(2).

[33] *Ibid.*, Art. 5(3).

The way in which the Union manifests itself externally coincides with the powers which each institution has to act externally. Accordingly, in most cases the Commission has the right to negotiate agreements which the Union wishes to conclude, although the Council has some leeway to nominate another negotiator (see para. 26–004).[34] Likewise, the Commission is responsible, together with the High Representative, for establishing all appropriate forms of cooperation with the organs of the United Nations and its specialised agencies, the Council of Europe, the OSCE, the OECD and other international organisations (Art. 220 TFEU).[35]

In fact, there are various ways in which the Union may be involved in international discussions. Where international discussions are concerned with subjects which fall within the competence of the Union, a delegation from the Commission will normally attend. In the event that the discussions also cover subjects within the competence of the Member States, they will generally insist on their own representatives being present. In such a case, "unity in the international representation of the Union" requires there to be close cooperation between the Member States and the Union institutions, both in the process of negotiating and concluding agreements and in the fulfilment of the obligations entered into.[36] The Member States are invariably represented alongside the Union in international organisations whose sphere of action is more broadly defined than the competences of the Union. In order to take part in the activities of such an organisation, the duty to cooperate which is incumbent on the Union and its Member States, is reflected in practice in arrangements agreed upon by the Commission and the Council. Such arrangements primarily seek to achieve a common position on the part of the Union and the Member States and to formulate agreements as to how that position is to be represented in the organisation and how voting rights are to be exercised.[37] A breach of such an arrangement may result in the

---

[34] See Art. 218(3) and Art. 101, second and third paras, EAEC. However the Commission is always the negotiator for agreements falling within the scope of the Common Commercial Policy (Art. 207(3) TFEU). By contrast, the Commission is merely "associated" with negotiations of an agreement concerning monetary or foreign exchange regime matters (Art. 219(3) TFEU) (paras 26–004—26–008, *infra*).

[35] The Commission and the Council consult each other on the desirability, the methods and the nature of such relations: Part a(5) of the Luxembourg Compromise (n. 23, *supra*).

[36] ECJ, Opinion 2/91 *Convention No. 170 of the International Labour Organisation concerning safety in the use of chemicals at work* [1993] E.C.R. I-1061, para. 36, at I-1083; ECJ, Opinion 1/94 *Agreement establishing the World Trade Organisation* [1994] E.C.R. I-5267, para. 108; ECJ, Opinion 2/00 *Cartagena Protocol* [2001] E.C.R. I-9713, para. 18; ECJ (judgment of April 20, 2010), Case C-246/07 *Commission v Sweden* [2010] E.C.R., not yet reported, para. 73. See also ECJ, Ruling 1/78 *Draft Convention of the International Atomic Energy Agency on the Physical Protection of Nuclear Materials, Facilities and Transports* [1978] E.C.R. 2151, paras 34–36.

[37] Such arrangements may be enshrined in the decision by which the Union concludes the relevant international agreement; see, e.g., Art. 3 of Council and Commission Decision (98/181/EC, ECSC, Euratom) of September 23, 1997 on the conclusion, by the European Communities, of the Energy Charter Treaty and the Energy Charter Protocol on energy efficiency and related environmental aspects, [1998] O.J. L69/1; Art. 3 of Council Decision (98/216/EC) of March 9, 1998 on the conclusion, on behalf of the European Community, of the United Nations Convention of June 17, 1994 to combat desertification in countries seriously affected by drought and/or desertification, particularly in Africa, [1998] O.J. L83/1.

annulment of the decision by which the institution concerned determined its action in the organisation in question.[38]

In practice, the Union's representation is determined in accordance with the division of powers, internal agreements and the political sensitivity of the subject-matter. Before the Lisbon Treaty, the representation of the Communities and the Union gave rise to one of the following permutations.[39] In some cases, a delegation led by the Commission and including representatives of all the Member States and Commission and Council officials acted for the Communities and the Member States (for example, in GATT/WTO negotiations). The Commission delegation sometimes included representatives of the Member State holding the Presidency of the Council for the time being or, possibly, representatives of all the Member States. In other cases, the Commission (together with officials of the Council) and representatives of the Member States acted in split delegations (for example, at the OECD). Finally, in matters coming within the CFSP and police and judicial cooperation in criminal matters (PJCC), the Union was represented by the Presidency of the Council, assisted by the Secretary-General of the Council—the High Representative for the CFSP.[40] The Lisbon Treaty confers the task of representing the Union in CFSP matters on the High Representative of the Union for Foreign Affairs and Security Policy, which means that in the above-mentioned permutations the High Representative may take over the role formerly carried out by the Member State holding the Presidency of the Council. There are different constellations still where the Union may be represented by a Commission delegation either in parallel with Member States' representations or including representatives of the Member States.

24–008 **Economic and monetary affairs.** The Treaties contain specific provisions on the Union's external representation as regards matters concerning the euro. "In order to secure the euro's place in the international monetary system", the Council, on a proposal from the Commission and after consulting the ECB, is to adopt common positions on matters of particular interest for economic and monetary union within the competent international financial institutions and conferences (Art. 138(1) TFEU.[41]) The Council is also to adopt, on the basis of the same procedure, appropriate measures to ensure unified representation within the international financial institutions and conferences (Art. 138(2) TFEU). In this way the Council can carry out this representation itself or leave it to the Commission, the European Central Bank or, where the power lies with the Member States,

---

[38] ECJ, Case C-25/94 *Commission v Council* [1996] E.C.R. I-1469, paras 48–51.

[39] The survey is taken from Groux and Manin (n. 6, *supra*), at 42. See also Sack (n. 15, *supra*), at 1252–1256.

[40] See Art. 18(1) and (3) EU.

[41] See the arrangements relating to implementation of this Treaty provision in the Resolution of the European Council of December 13, 1997 on economic policy coordination in stage three of EMU and on Arts 111 and 113 of the EC Treaty, [1998] O.J. C35/1, Part II.

the Presidency of the Council or those Member States belonging to a particular international organisation.[42]

For Council decisions in this connection, only the Member States whose currency is the euro take part in the vote (Art. 138(3), first subpara., TFEU).[43]

CFSP. In matters coming within the CFSP, the Union is represented by the High Representative of the Union for Foreign Affairs and Security Policy, who is to conduct political dialogue with third parties on the Union's behalf and express the Union's position in international organisations and at international conferences (Art. 27(2) TEU).[44] On a proposal from the High Representative, the Council may appoint a special representative with a mandate in relation to particular policy issues (Art. 33 TEU [*ex Art. 18(5) EU*]).[45] The High Representative is assisted by the European External Action Service (Art. 27(3) TEU).

24–009

Alongside the High Representative, the President of the European Council represents the Union in CFSP matters "at his or her level and in that capacity". This seems to be the case where the Union needs to be represented vis-à-vis foreign Heads of State or Government. In any event, the representation of the Union by the President of the European Council may not encroach upon the powers of the High Representative (Art. 15(6), second subpara., TEU).

Agreements of the Union with third States or international organisations in the field of the CFSP are normally negotiated by the High Representative (see para. 26–004).

The diplomatic and consular missions of the Member States and the Union delegations in third countries and at international conferences, together with their representatives in international organisations, are to cooperate in ensuring that CFSP measures are complied with (Art. 35, first para., TEU).

Cooperation. Representation of the Union is based completely on coordination of the Union delegations and the representations of the Member States. Under the

24–010

---

[42] Herrmann, "Monetary Sovereignty over the Euro and External Relations of the Euro Area: Competences, Procedures and Practice" (2002) E.For.Aff.Rev. 1–24; Weiss, "Kompetenzverteilung in der Währungspolitik und Aussenvertretung des Euro" (2002) EuR. 165–191; Lebullenger, "La projection externe de la zone euro" (1998) R.T.D.E. 459–478. For representation by the ECB, see ESCB Statute, Art. 6. For possible arrangements in the framework of the IMF, see Bini Smaghi, "A single EU seat in the International Monetary Fund?", in Jørgensen (ed.), *The European Union and International Organizations* (London-New York, Taylor & Francis, 2009), 61 *et seq.*

[43] A qualified majority is defined in accordance with Art. 238(3)(a) TFEU (Art. 138(3), second subpara., TFEU; see paras 13–053 and 13–054, *supra*).

[44] Before the Lisbon Treaty, the Union was represented by the Presidency of the Council. The Presidency was assisted by the Secretary-General of the Council—the High Representative for the CFSP—and, if need be, by the next Member State to hold the Presidency; the Commission was to be "fully associated in [those] tasks" (Art. 18(1) to (4) EU).

[45] The European Union has already appointed several "special envoys"; see the discussion of the CFSP in para. 25–042, *infra*. These special representatives carry out their mandate under the authority of the High Representative (Art. 33 TEU).

second and third paras of Art. 35 TEU, they are to step up their cooperation by exchanging information, carrying out joint assessments and contributing to the implementation of the diplomatic and consular protection of citizens of the Union in accordance with Art. 20(2)(c) TFEU and the measures adopted pursuant to Art. 23 TFEU (see para. 18–013). Already in the days of European Political Cooperation, the Foreign Ministers had agreed on arrangements for cooperation in the form of regular meetings between diplomats and officials both *in situ* and in the Political Committee (now the Political and Security Committee).[46]

24–011 **Coordination.** Member States are under a duty to coordinate their action in international organisations and at international conferences and to uphold the Union's positions in such forums, even in organisations or conferences in which not all Member States participate. The High Representative is responsible for organising that coordination (Art. 34(1) TEU). Moreover, Member States which are represented in international organisations or conferences in which not all Member States participate must keep the non-participating Member States and the High Representative informed of any matter of common interest. This also applies to the Member States which are members of the United Nations Security Council "without prejudice to their responsibilities under the provisions of the United Nations Charter".[47] This would appear to authorise those Member States to adopt a position independently in respect of matters on which the Union has not yet reached a position where the Security Council is required to reach an urgent decision.[48]

---

[46] Decision of the Ministers of Foreign Affairs, meeting within the framework of European Political Cooperation, of February 28, 1986 (1986) 1 EPC Bulletin doc. 86/090, 108, II.

[47] Article 34(2) TEU. When the Union has defined a position on a subject which is on the United Nations Security Council agenda, those Member States which sit on the Security Council are to request that the High Representative be asked to present the Union's position (Art. 34(2), third sub-para., TEU).

[48] Article 103 of the UN Charter provides that the obligations of Members of the United Nations under the Charter are to prevail over their obligations under any other international agreement. Those obligations include "prompt and effective action by the United Nations", in respect of which Art. 24 of the UN Charter provides that "primary responsibility for the maintenance of international peace and security" is conferred on the Security Council. See Eaton, "Common Foreign and Security Policy" in O'Keeffe and Twomey (eds), *Legal Issues of the Maastricht Treaty* (London, Chancery, 1994), 215, at 223. For the priority of those obligations over Union obligations, see Art. 347 TFEU [*ex Art. 297 EC*] (para. 12–011, *supra*).

CHAPTER 25

THE EXTERNAL POWERS OF THE UNION

External powers. The Lisbon Treaty has brought the external powers of the   25–001
Union together in one part of the TFEU relating to "external action by the
Union". Besides provisions on, inter alia, the common commercial policy, development cooperation and cooperation with third countries and humanitarian aid
(Arts 206 to 214 TFEU), it contains a legal basis for the adoption of restrictive
measures against third countries and non-State entities (Art. 215 TFEU) and a
solidarity clause, under which the Union and its Member States are to act jointly
in a spirit of solidarity if a Member State is the object of a terrorist attack or the
victim of a natural or man-made disaster (Art. 222 TFEU; see para. 11–064).
However, the TFEU does not contain the provisions relating to the CFSP, which
are found in Ch. 2 of Title V of the TEU (Arts 23 to 46 TEU). The CFSP does
not consist of a list of powers, but formulates aims and instruments with a view
to pursuing a "foreign policy" alongside and in connection with other external
Union action. As far as the EAEC is concerned, the Community has a general
power to conclude international agreements within the confines of the powers
conferred on it by the EAEC Treaty (see Art. 101, first para., EAEC).

The Union's foreign policy consists, on the one hand, of "autonomous"
measures of the Union having effects for third countries and their nationals and,
on the other hand, of treaties and agreements concluded with third countries or
international organisations ("contractual" acts). The Union may conclude an
agreement with one or more third countries or international organisations where
the Treaties so provide or where the conclusion of an agreement is necessary in
order to achieve, within the framework of the Union's policies, one of the objectives referred to in the Treaties, or is provided for in a legally binding Union
act or is likely to affect common rules or alter their scope (Art. 216 TFEU; see
paras 25–054 *et seq.*).

General provisions. Union external action in all fields is subject to the general   25–002
provisions of Ch. 1 of Title V of the TEU. Article 21(1), first subpara., TEU states
that the Union's action on the international scene has to be guided by the principles which have inspired its own creation, development and enlargement, and
which it seeks to advance in the wider world. The Union is to develop relations
and build partnerships with third countries, and international, regional or global
organisations which share these principles and to promote multilateral solutions to common problems, in particular in the framework of the United Nations

(Art. 21(1), second subpara., TEU). Article 21(2) lists the specific objectives which guide the Union in its external action, namely:

(a) safeguarding its values, fundamental interests, security, independence and integrity;

(b) consolidating and supporting democracy, the rule of law, human rights and the principles of international law;

(c) preserving peace, preventing conflicts and strengthening international security;

(d) fostering the sustainable economic, social and environmental development of developing countries, with the primary aim of eradicating poverty;

(e) encouraging the integration of all countries into the world economy, including through the progressive abolition of restrictions on international trade;

(f) helping develop international measures to preserve and improve the quality of the environment and the sustainable management of global natural resources, in order to ensure sustainable development;

(g) assisting populations, countries and regions confronting natural or man-made disasters; and

(h) promoting an international system based on stronger multilateral cooperation and good global governance.

I. THE COMMON COMMERCIAL POLICY

A. SCOPE

25-003   **Trade in goods.** Following the abolition of national customs duties and charges of equivalent effect in the early years of the Communities, the Council introduced a Common Customs Tariff and uniform customs rules for goods from or destined for third countries which are processed in the Union (see para. 9–026). In order to prevent Member States from putting their own undertakings at an advantage or otherwise introducing inequalities in the trade field, the EC Treaty and now the TFEU provides for the internal market to be underpinned by a common commercial policy (Title II of Part Five of the TFEU). The common commercial policy determines the conditions under which goods from third countries may be brought into free circulation in the Member States and goods from Member States may be exported to third countries. The Union conducts a common commercial policy pursuant to Art. 207 TFEU [*ex Art. 133 EC*] and a number of scattered

Treaty provisions.[1] The common commercial policy removes from the Member States the power to influence imports and exports to the benefit of national industry, thereby constituting a sphere of competence exclusive to the Union (see para. 7–021).

By way of measures required to be based on "uniform principles", Art. 207(1) TFEU mentions both autonomous measures (changes in tariff rates, achievement of uniformity in liberalisation measures, export policy and measures to protect trade) and the conclusion of tariff and trade agreements. This list, which is not exhaustive, does not rule out other methods of regulating external trade.[2] For the common commercial policy not to become nugatory in the course of time, it was considered not to be confined to trade liberalisation measures, which was the dominant idea at the time when the EEC Treaty was drafted, but also to encompass "more highly developed mechanisms".[3] Such mechanisms include commodity agreements, designed to regulate world trade and stabilise developing countries' export revenue,[4] and a system of generalised preferences for developing countries.[5] The Court of Justice takes the view that the common commercial policy may not be interpreted restrictively on the ground that to do so would risk causing disturbances in intra-Union trade by reason of the disparities which would then exist in certain sectors of economic relations with third countries.[6] The fact that a measure takes account of environmental protection objectives does not remove it from the sphere of commercial policy.[7] Measures will fall within the common commercial policy even if they may have effects on economic policy or other policy areas for which the Member States have competence.[8] Specific clauses in a given agreement which affect the competence of the Member States but are of a subsidiary or ancillary nature do not alter the agreement's nature as a commercial policy agreement.[9]

Accordingly, Art. 207 TFEU constitutes the legal basis for autonomous and contractual acts of the Community which specifically relate to international trade, unless they are expressly contemplated by other provisions of the Treaties, such as Art. 31 TFEU (customs tariff) or Arts 209 to 211 TFEU (development cooperation).

---

[1] See, inter alia, Arts 31 and 32 TFEU [ex Arts 26 and 27 EC] on the common customs tariff (paras 9–025 and 9–026, supra) and Arts 40 and 43 TFEU [ex Arts 34 and 37 EC], pursuant to which commercial policy measures have been taken in the context of the common agricultural policy.

[2] ECJ, Opinion 1/78 International Agreement on Natural Rubber [1979] E.C.R. 2871, para. 45.

[3] Ibid., para. 44.

[4] Ibid., paras 42–44.

[5] ECJ, Case 45/86 Commission v Council [1987] E.C.R. 1493, paras 17–20. For that system, see para. 25–032, infra.

[6] ECJ, Opinion 1/78 International Agreement on Natural Rubber, para. 45. For the differing scope attributed by the Commission and the Council to the common commercial policy, see ibid., paras 38–39, and ECJ, Case 45/86 Commission v Council [1987] E.C.R. 1493.

[7] ECJ, Case C-62/88 Greece v Council [1990] E.C.R. I-1527, paras 18–20.

[8] Opinion 1/78 International Agreement on Natural Rubber [1979] E.C.R. 2871, para. 49.

[9] Ibid., para. 56.

A Union act relates specifically to international trade if it is essentially intended to promote, facilitate or govern trade and has direct and immediate effects on trade in the products concerned.[10]

25–004   **Trade in services and intellectual property.** The common commercial policy is not confined to the external protection of the customs union. International trade in services is increasingly accounting for a greater share than trade in goods. In the context of the GATT Uruguay Round, the Community and the Member States conducted negotiations on agreements for liberalising trade in goods and services and on trade-related aspects of intellectual property (see para. 25–012 *et seq.*). In an opinion, the Court of Justice made it clear that Art. 133(1) to (4) EC did not cover all aspects of those agreements.[11] The Court held that those provisions of the EC Treaty covered services supplied across frontiers where neither the provider nor the recipient of the services moved to the other's country, but not services provided through the presence of natural persons or a commercial presence in the recipient's State or the case where the recipient travels to the provider's country.[12] As far as protection of intellectual property rights was concerned, only measures designed to prevent the import of counterfeit goods came within the ambit of the common commercial policy.[13]

The Treaty of Amsterdam empowered the Council, acting unanimously, to extend the application of Art. 133 EC to international negotiations and agreements on services and intellectual property in so far as they were not already covered thereby.[14] Its scope was not extended until the amendments made by the Treaty of Nice, which provided that provisions relating to the common commercial policy were also applicable to the negotiation and conclusion of agreements in the fields of trade in services—regardless of whether or not the provider or the recipient of the services move—and the commercial aspects of intellectual property

---

[10] ECJ, Case C-347/03 *Regione autonoma Friuli-Venezia Giulia* [2005] E.C.R. I-3785, para. 75; ECJ, Case C-411/06 *Commission v European Parliament and Council* [2009] E.C.R. I-7585, para. 71.

[11] ECJ, Opinion 1/94 *Agreement establishing the World Trade Organisation* [1994] E.C.R. I-5267; see Auvret-Finck (1995) R.T.D.E. 322–336; Bourgeois (1995) C.M.L.Rev. 763–787; Van Nuffel (1995) Col.J.E.L. 338–354; see also Pescatore, "Opinion 1/94 on 'conclusion' of the WTO-Agreement: Is there an escape from a programmed disaster?" (1999) C.M.L.Rev. 387–405; Dutheil de la Rochère, "L'ère des compétences partagées: A propos de l'étendue des compétences extérieures de la Communauté européenne" (1995) R.M.C.U.E. 461–470.

[12] *Ibid.*, paras 44–47.

[13] *Ibid.*, paras 54–60.

[14] Blin, "L'article 113 CE après Amsterdam" (1998) R.M.C.U.E. 447–456; Neframi, "Quelques réflexions sur la réforme de la politique commerciale par le traité d'Amsterdam: le maintien du *statu quo* et l'unité de la répresentation internationale de la Communauté" (1998) C.D.E. 137–159. For a critical view of the utility of this power, see Dashwood, "External Relations Provisions of the Amsterdam Treaty" (1998) C.M.L.Rev. 1019, at 1021–1023.

(Art. 133(5) EC).[15] The Lisbon Treaty confirmed that the common commercial policy covers the conclusion of tariff and trade agreements relating to both "trade in goods and services, and the commercial aspects of intellectual property" (Art. 207(1) TFEU). Article 207(1) further refers to the possibility to conclude such agreements relating to "foreign direct investment". At the same time, the Lisbon Treaty abrogated the possibility for the Council to extend the scope of the common commercial policy to those aspects of intellectual property protection that are not yet covered. External action of the Union in those areas will have to be based on another provision of the Treaties.[16]

According to Art. 207(5) TFEU [*see ex Art. 133(6) EC*], international agreements relating to services in the transport sector do not come under the common commercial policy, but remain subject to the provisions of the Treaties relating to transport.[17]

Decision-making. The European Parliament and the Council, acting by means of regulations in accordance with the ordinary legislative procedure, are to adopt the measures defining the framework for implementing the common commercial policy (Art. 207(2) TFEU).[18] The general rules of Art. 218 TFEU apply to the negotiation and conclusion of agreements with third countries or international organisations in this field, subject to the special provisions of Art. 207 TFEU (see para. 26–002 *et seq.*). Accordingly, Art. 207(3) TFEU provides that agreements in this field are always negotiated by the Commission, in consultation with a special committee, after the Council has authorised the Commission to open the necessary negotiations and has issued the necessary guidelines.[19] **25–005**

---

[15] See ECJ, Opinion 1/08 *General Agreement on Trade in Services* [2009] E.C.R. I-11129, para. 119. See Hermann, "Common Commercial Policy After Nice: Sisyphus Would Have Done a Better Job" (2002) C.M.L.Rev. 7–29; Krenzler and Pitschas, "Progress or Stagnation?: The Common Commercial Policy After Nice" (2001) E.For.Aff.Rev. 291–313 (for the German version, see (2001) EuR. 442–461); Neframi, "La politique commerciale commune selon le traité de Nice" (2001) C.D.E. 605–646; Vincent, "Les relations entre l'Union européenne et l'Organisation mondiale du commerce: du nouveau pour le praticien?" (2001) J.T.D.E. 105–110; Grard, "La condition internationale de l'Union européenne après Nice" (2000) R.A.E. 374–388).

[16] E.g. the "flexibility clause" set out in Art. 352 TFEU or the legal basis for intellectual property laid down in Art. 118 TFEU. See also pending request for an Opinion 1/09 ([2009] O.J. C220/15).

[17] Article 207(5) TFEU refers to Title VI of Part Three of the TFEU and Art. 218 TFEU. This exception confirms the case law of the Court of Justice in Opinion 1/94: ECJ, Opinion 1/94 *Agreement establishing the World Trade Organisation* [1994] E.C.R. I-5267, paras 48–49. Commercial policy measures may concern transport services if that aspect constitutes a necessary ancillary aspect of those measures (*ibid.*, para. 51) and hence it is not required that the agreement concerned relates exclusively or predominantly to trade in transport services (ECJ, Opinion 1/08 *General Agreement on Trade in Services* (n. 15, *supra*), para. 163).

[18] Before the Lisbon Treaty, these measures were also adopted by the Council by a qualified majority vote, but without any involvement of the European Parliament (see Art. 133(2) TFEU).

[19] The Treaty of Nice added as safeguards that the Council and the Commission are responsible for ensuring that the agreements negotiated are compatible with internal Union policies and rules and that the Commission must report regularly to the special committee on the progress of negotiations. Since the Lisbon Treaty, the Commission must also report to the European Parliament (Art. 207(3), second and third subparas, TFEU). See Krenzler and Pitschas (n. 15, *supra*), at 448–450.

Since the ordinary legislative procedure applies for the adoption of internal trade measures, this means that the Council decides on the conclusion of international agreements by qualified majority after obtaining the consent of the European Parliament (see Art. 207, first subpara., and Art. 218(6) TFEU). In some areas, however, the Treaties require the Council to decide by unanimity on the negotiation or conclusion of international agreements.[20] In the first place, this applies to agreements in the fields of trade in services, the commercial aspects of intellectual property and foreign direct investment where such agreements include provisions for which unanimity is required for the adoption of internal rules (Art. 207(4), second subpara., TFEU).[21] In addition, unanimity is required in the field of trade in cultural and audiovisual services where an agreement might prejudice the Union's cultural and linguistic diversity, and likewise in the field of trade in social, education or health services where an agreement might seriously disturb the national organisation of such services and prejudice the responsibility of Member States to deliver them (Art. 207(4), third subpara., TFEU).[22]

Article 207(6) TFEU provides that the exercise of competence in this field may not affect the delimitation of competence between the Union and the Member States. This seems to confirm the principle that any external action of the Union in the field of the common commercial policy is to respect the restrictions which apply to the action of the Union at the internal level, for example, in terms of voting requirements in the Council. Accordingly, external action of the Union in the field of the common commercial policy may not lead to any harmonisation of national law where the Treaties rule out any such harmonisation (Art. 207(6) TFEU).[23]

25–006 **Exclusive competence.** Article 3(1) TFEU regards the entire field of the common commercial policy as constituting an exclusive competence of the Union. Nevertheless, the Court of Justice has acknowledged that there are situations in which Member States are entitled to take part in the negotiation and conclusion

---

[20] Qualified majority voting remains the rule, however, for agreements on the transborder provision of services and protection against the importation of counterfeit goods, which, according to the case law, fall under "trade in goods".

[21] A comparison with Art. 133(5) EC shows that, since the Lisbon Treaty, unanimity is no longer required solely because the Union seeks to conclude an agreement in an area where it has not yet adopted internal measures or where a "horizontal" agreement is involved. For the scope of Art. 133(5) and (6) EC, see ECJ, Opinion 1/08 *General Agreement on Trade in Services* (n. 15, *supra*), paras 130–150.

[22] Compared to Art. 133(5) EC, this means that, since the Lisbon Treaty, unanimity will no longer be required for any single agreement that affects cultural, audiovisual, educational and social and human health services "horizontally".

[23] For areas in which the Treaties exclude such harmonisation (e.g. aspects of education and culture), see para. 7–014, *supra*.

of a trade agreement alongside the Union.[24] The Member States may participate in an agreement where financing constitutes an essential element of the scheme established thereby and is to be borne out of their budgets.[25] Furthermore, national commercial policy measures are permissible by virtue of a "specific authorisation" of the Union.[26] In this way, the Council authorised the Member States on a regular basis to renew or maintain certain bilateral agreements which they had concluded before the end of the transitional period.[27]

The explicit list of exclusive competences in Art. 3 TFEU was introduced by the Lisbon Treaty. However, it was long established that the common commercial policy—at least as regards goods[28]—constitutes an area of competence which is vested exclusively in the Union and therefore excludes in principle any national measures from the outset.[29] However, until the Lisbon Treaty, Union competence in respect of agreements on trade in services and the commercial aspects of intellectual property was not exclusive. Accordingly, in these areas Art. 133(5), fourth subpara., EC confirmed the competence of the Member States to maintain and conclude agreements with third countries or international organisations in so far as such agreements complied with Community law and other relevant international agreements. This meant that the external action of the Member States was limited only if the Community had already adopted internal or external measures in the relevant fields or when it adopted such measures. In addition, as far as trade in cultural and audiovisual services, educational services, and social and human health services was concerned, Art. 133(6) EC expressly declared that agreements relating thereto fall within the shared competence of the Community and its Member States.[30]

Where a field falls with the competence of both the Union and the Member States, the Union's external action is categorised as mixed (see para. 26–014).

---

[24] Member States are also entitled to continue negotiations which they started at a time when they still had competence in the relevant field where a new distribution of powers as between the Union and the Member States threatens to jeopardise the successful outcome of the negotiations (ECJ, Case 22/70 *Commission v Council* [1971] E.C.R. 263, paras 86–90) or where their participation is required in order to secure the Union's participation in the relevant agreement (ECJ, Joined Cases 3, 4 and 6/76 *Kramer* [1976] E.C.R. 1279, paras 34–44/45).

[25] ECJ, Opinion 1/78 *International Agreement on Natural Rubber* [1979] E.C.R. 2871, para. 60.

[26] ECJ, Case 41/76 *Donckerwolcke* [1976] E.C.R. 1921, para. 32. For a controversial application of this principle, see ECJ, Case 174/84 *Bulk Oil v Sun International* [1986] E.C.R. 559, paras 31–33 (see the discussion of exclusive competence in para. 7–022, *supra*).

[27] Council Decision 69/494 of December 16, 1969 on the progressive standardisation of agreements concerning commercial relations between Member States and third countries and on the negotiation of Community agreements, [1969] O.J. English Spec. Ed. (II) 603; the authorisation set out therein was renewed most recently by Council Decision 2001/855/EC of November 15, 2001, [2000] O.J. L320/13.

[28] This included agreements on crossborder trade in services and protection against the import of counterfeit goods (see n. 20).

[29] ECJ, Opinion 1/75 *Draft Understanding on a Local Cost Standard drawn up under the auspices of the OECD* [1975] E.C.R. 1355 (quoted in para. 7–021, *supra*).

[30] See ECJ, Opinion 1/08 *General Agreement on Trade in Services* (n. 15, *supra*), at paras 135–150.

This means that an agreement can come about only where it is concluded jointly by the Union and the Member States. Consequently, in addition to a Union decision (whether or not taken by a unanimous vote in the Council), the consent of all the Member States is required.[31]

B. AUTONOMOUS MEASURES

25–007 **Import and export regime.** Alongside the Common Customs Tariff, the Council has adopted common rules for imports[32] and exports.[33]

Initially, the import rules allowed Member States to maintain quantitative restrictions in respect of some products. The rules which the Council adopted in 1994 have liberalised imports and provide only for potential supervisory and safeguard measures on the part of the Union. Exceptional rules apply to some (former) state-trading countries, which are subject to a surveillance system.[34] Neither do the general import rules apply to textile products from third countries where imports are either governed by bilateral agreements concluded by the Union with countries accepting "voluntary" limitations on exports[35] or come under a specific import regime.[36] A special import regime has been introduced on the basis of what is now Art. 207 TFEU in order to allow manufacturers to bring certain key medicines onto the market only in developing countries at prices lower than those in developed countries. Under this regime, the import of such "tiered priced" products into the Union is prohibited.[37]

---

[31] Article 133(6), second subpara., EC confirmed these principles in the case of agreements relating to trade in cultural and audiovisual services, educational services, and social and human health services and, as far as the Community decision-making procedure was concerned, referred to Art. 300 EC [*now Art. 218 TFEU*] (see para. 21–002 *et seq.*). See ECJ, Opinion 1/08 *General Agreement on Trade in Services* [2009] E.C.R. I-11129, paras 135–136 and 138.

[32] See Council Regulation (EC) No. 260/2009 of February 26, 2009 on the common rules for imports, [2009] O.J. L84/1 (replacing Council Regulation (EC) No. 3285/94 of December 22, 1994, [1994] O.J. L349/53).

[33] See Council Regulation (EC) No. 1061/2009 of October 19, 2009 establishing common rules for exports, [2009] O.J. L291/1 (replacing Council Regulation (EEC) No. 2603/69 of December 20, 1969 establishing common rules for exports, [1969] O.J. English Spec. Ed. (II) 590).

[34] Council Regulation (EC) No. 625/2009 of July 7, 2009 on common rules for imports from certain third countries, [2009] O.J. L185/1, replacing Council Regulation (EC) No. 519/94 of March 7, 1994 on common rules for imports from certain third countries, [1994] O.J. L67/89. A transitional product-specific safeguard mechanism applies to imports originating in the People's Republic of China, see Council Regulation (EC) No. 427/2003 of March 3, 2003, [2003] O.J. L65/1.

[35] Galloway, "L'achèvement du marché intérieur pour le régime à l'importation des produits textiles dans la Communauté: politique de forteresse ou de la dissuasion" (1994) R.M.C.U.E. 362–371. Internally, the Commission manages the import regime in accordance with Council Regulation (EEC) No. 3030/93 of October 12, 1993, [1993] O.J. L275/1.

[36] Council Regulation (EC) No. 517/94 of March 7, 1994 on common rules for imports of textile products from certain third countries not covered by bilateral agreements, protocols or other arrangements, or by other specific Community import rules, [1994] O.J. L67/1.

[37] Council Regulation (EC) No. 953/2003 of May 26, 2003 to avoid trade diversion into the European Union of certain key medicines, [2003] O.J. L135/5 (adopted on the basis of Art. 133 EEC).

The Union export rules provide that, in principle, exportation to third countries is free. However, they do allow Member States to apply restrictions in their trade relations with third countries in order to protect the interests listed in Art. 36 TFEU [*ex Art. 30 EC*] as justifying restrictions on intra-Union trade in goods.[38] Although the Member States have a degree of discretion, for instance in estimating a risk to their national security, such restrictions on freedom of exportation may not exceed what is appropriate and necessary in order to protect the interest in question.[39] A Member State may no longer rely on this exception if the necessary protection of the interests in question is already ensured by a Union measure (for example, a measure imposing sanctions).[40] At the same time, Member States must place trust in each other as far as concerns export checks made by other Member States and, where necessary, cooperate with other Member States and the Commission.[41] As far as goods which may be used for both civil and military purposes (dual-use goods) are concerned, the Council has now adopted Union rules on such export checks.[42]

Turning to agricultural products, account must be taken of the instruments provided for under the common agricultural policy (see para. 11–001 *et seq.*).

Protective measures. In accordance with the rules agreed in the context of GATT and of the WTO, the Council has drawn up instruments under what is now Art.207 TFEU (which would today require the European Parliament and the Council to act in accordance with the ordinary legislative procedure) with a view to taking protective measures in respect of dumped or subsidised imports: products which are imported to the Union for an export price below their normal value (dumping) or whose export is subsidised in the country of origin, may have an anti-dumping or countervailing duty imposed on them where the marketing of the products

25–008

---

[38] Regulation No. 1061/2009 (n. 33, *supra*), Arts 1 and 24(2).

[39] See ECJ, Case C-70/94 *Werner* [1995] E.C.R. I-3189, paras 8–29; ECJ, Case C-83/94 *Leifer* [1995] E.C.R. I-3231, paras 7–30 (dual-use goods).

[40] ECJ, Case C-124/95 *Centro-Com* [1997] E.C.R. I-81, para. 46.

[41] *Ibid.*, paras 49 and 52.

[42] Council Regulation (EC) No. 1334/2000 of June 22, 2000 setting up a Community regime for the control of exports of dual-use items and technology, [2000] O.J. L159/1, now replaced by Council Regulation (EC) No. 428/2009 of May 5, 2009 setting up a Community regime for the control of exports, transfer, brokering and transit of dual-use items, [2009] O.J. L134/1. See Hohmann, "Neufassung der Dual-Use Verordnung: Änderung für die Exportwirtschaft und für global agierende Dienstleistungsanbieter" (2002) *Europäisches Wirtschafts und Steuerrecht* 70–76; Karpenstein, "Die neue Dual-Use Verordnung" (2000) Eu.Z.W. 677–680; Koutrakos, "The Reform of Common Rules on Exports of Dual-Use Goods under the Law of the European Union" (2000) E.J.L.Ref. 167–189. Previously, there was an "integrated regime" consisting of a CFSP decision and an EC regulation (see Council Decision 94/942/CFSP of December 19, 1994 on the joint action adopted by the Council concerning the control of exports of dual-use goods, [1994] O.J. L367/8 and Council Regulation (EC) No. 3381/94 of December 19, 1994 setting up a Community regime for the control of exports of dual-use goods, [1994] O.J. L367/1); before that, such goods came within the general derogation clause of the Union export rules.

concerned causes producers in the Union to suffer injury.[43] The Commission investigates whether dumping or subsidies are involved, together with the question of injury, and may impose a provisional duty where the Union interest so requires. Subsequently, the Council may impose a definitive duty within a specific time-limit, whereby a Commission proposal is to be deemed adopted unless the Council decides by a simple majority to reject it.[44]

In 1984, the Council introduced, also under what is now Art. 207 TFEU (today involving the ordinary legislative procedure), a "new commercial policy instrument", which enables the Union to take action against illicit commercial practices.[45] Following the conclusion of the Agreement establishing the World Trade Organisation in 1994 (see para. 25–012), the Council replaced that instrument by Regulation No. 3286/94, which enables the Union to enforce its rights under international trade rules, in particular those established under the auspices of the World Trade Organisation.[46] Under the procedures laid down in that "Trade

---

[43] Council Regulation (EC) No. 1225/2009 of November 30, 2009 on protection against dumped imports from countries not members of the European Community, [2009] O.J. L343/51 (replacing Council Regulation (EC) No. 384/96 of December 22, 1995 on protection against dumped imports from countries not members of the European Community, [1996] O.J. L56/1, as amended by Council Regulation (EC) No. 461/2004 of March 8, 2004, [2004] O.J. L77/12) and Council Regulation (EC) No. 597/2009 of June 11, 2009 on protection against subsidised imports from countries not members of the European Community, [2009] O.J. L188/93 (replacing Council Regulation (EC) No. 2026/97 of October 6, 1997 on protection against subsidised imports from countries not members of the European Community, [1997] O.J. L288/1, as also amended by Council Regulation (EC) No. 461/2004 of March 8, 2004, [2004] O.J. L77/12). See Giannakopoulos, *A concise guide to the EU anti-dumping/anti-subsidies procedures* (The Hague, Kluwer Law International, 2005), 231 pp.; Van Bael and Bellis, *Anti-dumping and other trade protection laws of the EC* (The Hague, Kluwer Law International, 2004), 1127 pp.; Stanbrook and Bentley, *Dumping and Subsidies* (The Hague, Kluwer Law International, 1996), 441 pp.; Vander Schueren, "New Anti-Dumping Rules and Practice: Wide Discretion held on a Tight Leash?" (1996) C.M.L.Rev. 271–297; Bourgeois (ed.), *Subsidies and International Trade* (Deventer, Kluwer, 1991), 214 pp.

[44] Articles 7 and 9 of Regulation 1225/2009 (see n. 43, *supra*). Where the import of particular products is unnecessarily restricted by a combination of anti-dumping measures or anti-subsidy measures with safeguard tariff measures which may be imposed under Regulations Nos 625/2009 (n. 34, *supra*) and 260/2009 (n. 32, *supra*) in order to obtain protection against sharply increased imports, the Council, acting by simple majority, may adjust the measures in question by virtue of Council Regulation (EC) No. 452/2003 of March 6, 2003 on measures that the Community may take in relation to the combined effect of anti-dumping or anti-subsidy measures with safeguard measures, [2003] O.J. L69/3.

[45] Council Regulation (EEC) No. 2641/84 of September 17, 1984 on the strengthening of the common commercial policy with regard in particular to protection against illicit trade practices, [1984] O.J. L252/1. See Denton, "The New Commercial Policy Instrument and *AZKO v Dupont*" (1988) E.L.Rev. 3–27; Steenbergen, "The New Commercial Policy Instrument" (1985) C.M.L.Rev. 421–439.

[46] Council Regulation (EC) No. 3286/94 of December 22, 1994 laying down Community procedures in the field of the common commercial policy in order to ensure the exercise of the Community's rights under international trade rules, in particular those established under the auspices of the World Trade Organisation, [1994] O.J. L349/71. For applications of these rules, see CFI, Case T-317/02 *FICF v Commission* [2004] E.C.R. II-4325. See Sunberg and Vermulst, "The EC Trade Barriers Regulation"

Barriers" Regulation, the Union may initiate, pursue and terminate international dispute settlement proceedings in the area of the common commercial policy. A further regulation affords the means for acting against goods infringing certain intellectual property rights.[47] The Union also provides protection against "extra-territorial" sanctions whereby third countries affect activities of persons coming under the jurisdiction of Member States.[48]

C. TRADE AGREEMENTS AND COOPERATION AGREEMENTS

Bilateral agreements. As a major economic power, the Union has trade relations with most countries in the world and makes use to this end of the powers conferred on it by Art. 207 TFEU [*ex Art. 133 EC*] as well as Arts 217 and 352 TFEU [*ex Arts 308 and 310 EC*]. A variety of agreements (trade agreements, free-trade agreements, cooperation agreements and association agreements[49]) often give rise to lasting cooperation, which is administered by bilateral cooperative bodies ("joint committees" or "joint commissions").

On the basis of Art. 133 EC [*now Art. 207 TFEU*], trade agreements have been concluded with the EFTA countries[50] and with a number of other (especially developing) countries.[51] Increasingly, "Cooperation agreements" and "Partnership and Cooperation agreements" have been concluded, which go beyond commercial cooperation, as they are also designed to secure economic cooperation or to afford

25–009

(2001) J.W.T. 989–1013. In addition, under Art. 207 TFEU, the Council (since the Lisbon Treaty together with the European Parliament) may also adopt direct protective measures; see Council Regulation (EC) No. 2238/2003 of December 15, 2003 protecting against the effects of the application of the United States Anti-Dumping Act of 1916, and actions based thereon or resulting therefrom, [2003] O.J. L333/1. For its part, the Union may withdraw or amend its anti-dumping and anti-subsidy measures using a simplified procedure; see para. 25–014, *infra*.

[47] Council Regulation (EC) No. 1383/2003 of July 22, 2003 concerning customs action against goods suspected of infringing certain intellectual property rights and the measures to be taken against goods found to have infringed such rights, [2003] O.J. L196/7.

[48] Council Regulation (EC) No. 2271/96 of November 22, 1996 protecting against the effects of extra-territorial application of legislation adopted by a third country, and actions based thereon or resulting therefrom, [1996] O.J. L309/1 (adopted on the basis of Arts 57, 133 and 308 EC [*now Arts 64, 207 and 352 TFEU*]); see Hüber, "La réaction de l'Union européenne face aux lois américaines Helms-Burton et D'Amato" (1997) R.M.C.U.E. 301–308.

[49] For association agreements concluded pursuant to Art. 217 TFEU [*ex Art. 310 EC*], see paras 25–021 *et seq.*)

[50] Para 1–018, *supra*. Trade relations of Iceland, Liechtenstein and Norway with the EU are now mainly governed by the Agreement on the European Economic Area (see para. 25–029, *infra*). As far as Switzerland is concerned, see para. 20–025a.

[51] See, e.g., the Agreement of July 15, 1975 with Mexico, [1975] O.J. L247/11, the Agreements on commercial cooperation of July 22, 1975 with Sri Lanka, [1975] O.J. L247/2 and of October 19, 1976 with Bangladesh, [1976] O.J. L319/2 and the commercial agreement in the form of an exchange of letters between the EEC and Andorra, [1990] O.J. L374/13. With regard to San Marino, the agreement concluded on December 16, 1991 on trade and customs union applies, [2002] O.J. L84/43.

a "framework" for both types of cooperation. The Union has concluded such agreements with Canada,[52] with Andorra,[53] with a number of developing and other countries in Asia[54] and Latin America,[55] with the Central and Eastern European countries[56] and other republics of the former Soviet Union[57] and with South

---

[52] Framework Agreement of July 6, 1976 for commercial and economic cooperation, [1976] O.J. L260/2.

[53] Cooperation Agreement with the Principality of Andorra, [2005] O.J. L135/14 (replacing the agreement mentioned in n. 51, *supra*).

[54] See the agreements on commercial and economic cooperation of May 21, 1985 with China ([1985] O.J. L250/2) (preceded by a "classical" trade agreement) and of June 16, 1992 with Mongolia ([1993] O.J. L41/46); the cooperation agreements of March 7, 1980 with the member countries of the Association of South-East Asian Nations (ASEAN: Indonesia, Malaysia, the Philippines, Singapore and Thailand), [1980] O.J. L144/2; accession of Brunei: [1985] O.J. L81/2; extension to Vietnam: [1999] O.J. L117/30), of June 15, 1988 with the countries party to the Charter of the Cooperation Council for the Arab States of the Gulf (United Arab Emirates, Bahrein, Saudi Arabia, Oman, Qatar and Kuwait), [1989] O.J. L54/3), of June 15, 1992 with Macao ([1992] O.J. L404/27), of December 20, 1993 with India ([1994] O.J. L223/24), of July 18, 1994 with Sri Lanka ([1995] O.J. L85/33), of July 17, 1995 with Vietnam ([1996] O.J. L136/29), of November 20, 1995 with Nepal ([1996] O.J. L137/15), of April 29, 1997 with Laos ([1997] O.J. L334/14) and Cambodia ([1997] O.J. C107/7), of November 25, 1997 with Yemen ([1998] O.J. L72/18, replacing the agreement of October 9, 1984, [1985] O.J. L26/2) and of November 24, 2001 with Pakistan ([2004] O.J. L378/22), replacing the agreement of July 23, 1985, [1986] O.J. L108/2); and the framework agreement concluded with South Korea on October 28, 1996 ([2001] O.J. L90/45). On November 9, 2009, a Partnership and Cooperation Agreement was signed between the European Community and Indonesia.

[55] See the framework cooperation agreement concluded on February 22, 1993 with the Republics of Costa Rica, El Salvador, Guatemala, Honduras, Nicaragua and Panama ([1999] O.J. L63/38); the framework agreement concluded on April 23, 1993 with the Cartagena Agreement *and* its member countries, namely Bolivia, Colombia, Ecuador, Peru and Venezuela ([1998] O.J. L127/10); the interregional framework cooperation agreement concluded on December 15, 1995 with the Southern Common Market ("Mercado Común del Sur" or "Mercosur") and its Party States (Argentina, Brazil, Paraguay and Uruguay) ([1999] O.J. L112/65). An economic partnership, political coordination and cooperation agreement of December 8, 1997 exists with Mexico ([2000] O.J. L276/45) and an association agreement was signed with Chile on November 18, 2002 ([2002] O.J. L352/1) following on from the framework cooperation agreement of June 21, 1996 ([1999] O.J. L42/46). For the agreement with the Mercosur states, see Filho, Lixinski and Giupponi (eds), *The law of Mercosur* (Oxford, Hart Publishing, 2010), 572 pp.; Grugel, "Democratization and ideational diffusion: Europe, Mercosur and social citizenship" (2007) 45 J.C.M.S. 43–68.

[56] Trade and cooperation agreements were concluded with Hungary (September 26, 1988, [1988] O.J. L327/2), Poland (September 19, 1989, [1989] O.J. L339/2), the Soviet Union (December 19, 1989, [1990] O.J. L68/3), Czechoslovakia (May 7, 1990, [1990] O.J. L291/29), Bulgaria (May 8, 1990, [1990] O.J. L291/8), Romania (October 22, 1990, [1991] O.J. L79/13), Albania (May 11, 1992, [1992] O.J. L343/1), Estonia (May 11, 1992, [1992] O.J. L403/2), Latvia (May 11, 1992, [1992] O.J. L403/11), Lithuania (May 11, 1992, [1992] O.J. L403/2) and the former Yugoslav Republic of Macedonia (April 29, 1997, [1997] O.J. L348/2). As from 1991, the agreements with central and south-eastern European countries were replaced by association agreements preparing for EU membership (see para. 25–022, *infra*).

[57] See the partnership and cooperation agreements concluded with Russia ([1997] O.J. L327/3), with Ukraine ([1998] O.J. L49/3), with Moldova ([1998] O.J. L181/3), Kazakhstan ([1999] O.J. L196/3), Kyrgyzstan ([1999] O.J. L196/48), Georgia ([1999] O.J. L205/3), Uzbekistan ([1999] O.J.

972

Africa.[58] Initially, such agreements were consistently concluded under Arts 133 and 308 EC [*now Arts 207 and 352 TFEU*]; more recent agreements have been concluded pursuant to Art. 181 EC [*see now Art. 209(2) TFEU*] (development cooperation) and Art. 181a EC [*now Art. 212 TFEU*] (economic, financial and technical cooperation), in combination with Art. 133 EC [*now Art. 207 TFEU*] (see para. 25–035).

Multilateral agreements. In addition, the Union is a party to the Food Aid Convention[59] and has approved various commodity agreements negotiated in the United Nations Conference on Trade and Development (UNCTAD).[60] Multilateral trade and tariff agreements are principally negotiated in the context of the WTO (formerly GATT; see para. 25–011—25–015).

25–010

D. PARTICIPATION IN GATT AND THE WORLD TRADE ORGANISATION

1. The Union and GATT

GATT. All the Member States are party to the General Agreement on Tariffs and Trade (GATT),[61] under which the signatory States undertake to grant products from the other signatory States "most favoured nation" treatment and to refrain from imposing any non-tariff barriers to trade not included amongst the safeguard measures permitted by GATT. The EU customs union constitutes an exception to

25–011

L229/3), Armenia ([1999] O.J. L239/3), Azerbaijan ([1999] O.J. L246/3) and Tadjikistan ([2009] O.J. L350/3). Agreements with Belarus and Turkmenistan have not yet been ratified by the Union. For the agreement with Russia, see Van Elsuwege, "The four Common Spaces: new impetus to the EU-Russia Strategic Partnership?" in Dashwood and Maresceau (eds), *Law and Practice of EU External Relations* (Cambridge, Cambridge University Press, 2008), 334–359; Nemirovskis, "Small but precious: the actual and potential direct effect of the partnership and cooperation agreement between the European Communities and the Russian Federation" (2007) E.For.Aff.Rev. 553–617; Muchanov, "Die Handelsbeziehungen zwischen der Europäischen Union und Rusland im Lichte des Völkerrechts" (2006) Z.a.ö.R.V. 737–768. With respect to that agreement, see also ECJ, Case C-265/03 *Simutenkov* [2005] E.C.R. I-2579. For the agreement with Ukraine, see Hillion, "Mapping-out the new contractual relations between the European Union and its Neighbours: learning from the EU-Ukraine 'enhanced agreement' " (2007) E.For.Aff.Rev. 169–182.

[58] Cooperation Agreement with the Republic of South Africa of October 10, 1994, [1994] O.J. L341. This agreement has been replaced by the association agreement "on trade, development and cooperation" signed on October 11, 1999 ([1999] O.J. L311/3), concluded by the Union by Council Decision 2004/441/EC of April 26, 2004 ([2004] O.J. L127/109).

[59] The Grains Trade Convention of 1995 has been extended until June 30, 2011; a new Food Aid Convention 1999 was approved by the Council by Decision of June 13, 2000, [2000] O.J. L163/37.

[60] See, e.g., Council Decision 2008/579/EC of June 16, 2008 on the signing and conclusion on behalf of the European Community of the International Coffee Agreement 2007, [2008] O.J. L186/12, and Council Decision 2002/970/EC of November 18, 2002 concerning the conclusion on behalf of the European Community of the International Cocoa Agreement 2001, [2002] O.J. L342/1.

[61] The General Agreement on Tariffs and Trade (GATT) was concluded in Geneva on October 30, 1947 by the Protocol of Provisional Application, UNTS, Vol. 55, 194; Cmnd. 7258.

the most-favoured nation clause and is expressly authorised by Art. XXIV of GATT (see para. 9–016).[62] The Union (previously, the Community) is not a GATT Contracting Party. Nevertheless, from the outset, the Community/Union has regarded itself as bound by GATT and has taken part since the introduction of the Common Customs Tariff in the multilateral negotiating rounds for the gradual liberalisation of world trade, in which it is represented by the Commission. In the 1972 judgment in the *International Fruit* case, the Court of Justice held that the Member States could not withdraw from their obligations under GATT by concluding an agreement between them (the EEC Treaty), but, on the contrary, their desire to observe those undertakings followed from the very provisions of the EEC Treaty.[63] The Court went on to point out that the Community had assumed functions inherent in the trade and tariff policy and to hold that,

"[b]y conferring those powers on the Community, the Member States showed their wish to bind it by the obligations entered into under the General Agreement".[64]

Accordingly, the Community succeeded de facto to the Member States in GATT, with the Commission defending the Community standpoint in the GATT organs, which operate on the basis of consensus. When agreements were drawn up in the context of GATT, such as those reached during the Tokyo Round (1973–1979), the Community therefore became a party to them, in some cases together with the Member States.[65] This practice is accepted by the other Contracting Parties, which, where necessary, address themselves to the Community—now to the Union—in dispute-settlement procedures.

2. The Union and the World Trade Organisation

25–012   **WTO Agreement.** On September 20, 1986, the eighth multilateral negotiating round began at Punta del Este (Uruguay Round). The negotiations were not concluded until December 15, 1993. The resulting Agreement establishing the World

---

[62] For a survey of GATT and the status of the Community, see Petersmann, "The EEC as a GATT Member: Legal Conflicts between GATT Law and European Community Law", in Hilf, Jacobs and Petersmann (eds), *The European Community and GATT* (Deventer, Kluwer, 1986) 23, at 24–39.

[63] ECJ, Joined Cases 21–24/72 *International Fruit Company* [1972] E.C.R. 1219, paras 11–13.

[64] *Ibid.*, paras 14–15. For the question as to whether GATT provisions may be pleaded, see para. 22–047, *supra*.

[65] See the Agreements on technical barriers to trade, government procurement, trade in civil aircraft, and interpretation and application of Arts VI, XVI and XXIII of the General Agreement on Tariffs and Trade, [1980] O.J. L71/29, L71/44, L71/58 and L71/72, respectively (the first and the third agreements are of the "mixed" type); for their approval, see the Council Decision of December 10, 1979, [1980] O.J. L71/1. The Commission disagreed with the categorisation of the agreements in question as "mixed"; see Bourgeois, "The Tokyo Round Agreements on Technical Barriers and on Government Procurement in International and EC Perspective" (1982) C.M.L.Rev. 5, at 21–22.

Trade Organisation (WTO) was signed on April 15, 1994 at Marrakesh by the GATT States and the Community and entered into force on January 1, 1995.[66] The WTO replaced the GATT as the framework for trade liberalisation negotiations, such as the Doha round of world trade negotiations, launched in Doha (Qatar) in November 2001.

WTO bodies. The World Trade Organisation replaced the GATT as a fully-fledged international organisation with legal personality, which has its secretariat in Geneva.[67] A Ministerial Conference, which meets at least once every two years, takes the most important decisions and delegates tasks to a General Council. In addition, there is a Council for Trade in Goods, a Council for Trade in Services and a Council for Trade-Related Aspects of Intellectual Property Rights. Representatives of all members of the WTO sit on those bodies.[68] In principle, they take their decisions by consensus, although it is possible to adopt some decisions by a majority vote.[69]   25–013

Dispute settlement. The WTO constitutes the institutional framework for trade relations in all areas covered by the agreements annexed to the WTO Agreement. First, there is the adjusted version of the General Agreement on Tariffs and Trade (GATT 1994), the General Agreement on Trade in Services (GATS) and the Agreement on Trade-Related Aspects of Intellectual Property Rights (TRIPs).[70] The second and third annexes relate to the Rules and Procedures Governing the Settlement of Disputes and the Trade Policy Review Mechanism. Responsibility for these matters lies with the General Council, sitting as the Dispute Settlement   25–014

---

[66] Agreement establishing the World Trade Organisation, including the Agreements set out in Annexes 1 to 4 thereto, approved by Council Decision 94/800/EC of December 22, 1994 concerning the conclusion on behalf of the European Community, as regards matters within its competence, of the agreements reached in the Uruguay Round multilateral negotiations (1986–1994), [1994] O.J. L336/1. The Commission had first sought the Court's opinion on the division of competence with regard to the conclusion of the WTO, see ECJ, Opinion 1/94 *Agreement establishing the World Trade Organisation* [1994] E.C.R. I-5267 (see the commentaries cited in n. 11, *supra*). See Brittan, "Uruguay Round" (1994) C.M.L.Rev. 229–234. Since then, the Council approved on behalf of the Community, as regards matters within its competence, the results of the WTO negotiations on financial services and the movement of natural persons (Decision 96/412/EC of June 25, 1996, [1996] O.J. L167/23), basic telecommunications services (Decision 97/838/EC of November 28, 1997, [1997] L347/45) and financial services (Decision 1999/61/EC of December 14, 1998, [1999] O.J. L20/38).

[67] For the WTO website, see *http://www.wto.org/* [Accessed December 15, 2010].

[68] WTO Agreement, Art. IV.

[69] WTO Agreement, Art. IX, para. 1 of which provides that where the Communities exercise their right to vote, they are to have a number of votes equal to the number of their Member States (which are WTO Members). According to a footnote to that provision, the Member States and the Communities together cannot cast more votes than the number of Member States.

[70] See Frid, "Multilateral Liberalisation of Trade in Services under the GATS" (1998) S.E.W. 410–416; Weiss, "The General Agreement on Trade in Services 1994" (1995) C.M.L.Rev. 1177–1225. See also n. 66, *supra*.

Body (DSB), and the Trade Policy Review Body (TPRB). The DSB may remit a dispute to a Panel. Panel reports are automatically adopted by the DSB, unless it decides by consensus not to do so or a party to the dispute appeals to the Standing Appellate Body. Reports of the Standing Appellate Body are also taken over automatically by the DSB unless it decides by consensus not to do so. The final decision is binding and entitles a party to impose trade sanctions if the other party to the dispute does not comply with it.[71]

Within the Union legal order, the Union is at liberty to settle disputes with its trading partners within the framework of the WTO, possibly by negotiation. Consequently, where a report of a Panel or of the Standing Appellate Body finds that there is a conflict between a Union measure and WTO obligations, that report cannot, in principle, be pleaded before the Union Courts in proceedings brought against the Union measure in question (see para. 22–047). In anti-dumping or anti-subsidy cases, however, there exists a simplified procedure which the Council can use in order to bring Union legislation into line with a report drawn up by the Dispute Settlement Body.[72]

25–015 **Division of powers.** The Member States and the Union are members of the WTO. Some matters within the scope of the WTO fall within the competence of the Member States (GATS and TRIPs), whilst others fall within the exclusive competence of the Union (see para. 25–004). As already mentioned, unity in the international representation of the Union requires there to be close cooperation between the Member States and the Union in applying the WTO Agreement. The duty to cooperate is all the more imperative where the Union or a Member State is authorised to take cross-retaliation measures but can do so effectively only in an area for which the other is competent.[73]

---

[71] Understanding on Rules and Procedures Governing the Settlement of Disputes, Annex 2 to the WTO Agreement, [1994] O.J. L336/234. See Mitchell, "Proportionality and remedies in WTO disputes" (2007) E.J.I.L. 985–1008; Lavranos, "The Communitarization of WTO dispute settlement reports: an exception to the rule of law" (2005) E.L.J. 313–338; Rosas, "Implementation and Enforcement of WTO Dispute Settlement Findings: An EU Perspective" (2001) J.I.E.L. 131–144; Cottier, "Dispute Settlement in the World Trade Organisation: Characteristics and Structural Implications for the European Union" (1998) C.M.L.Rev. 325–378; Lebullenger, "La Communauté européenne face au procéssus de réexamen du système de règlement des différends de l'Organisation mondiale du commerce" (1998) R.M.C.U.E. 629–637; Kuijper, "The New WTO Dispute Settlement System: The Impact on the European Community" (1995) J.W.T. 49–71; Petersmann, "The Dispute Settlement System of the World Trade Organisation and the Evolution of the GATT Dispute Settlement System since 1948" (1994) C.M.L.Rev. 1157–1244.

[72] Council Regulation (EC) No. 1515/2001 of July 23, 2001 on the measures that may be taken by the Community following a report adopted by the WTO Dispute Settlement Body concerning anti-dumping and anti-subsidy matters ([2001] O.J. L201/10). See Blanchard, "L'effet des rapports de l'Organe de règlement des différends de l'OMC à la lumière du règlement (CE) 1515/2001 du Conseil de l'Union européenne" (2003) R.M.C.U.E 37–48.

[73] ECJ, Opinion 1/94 *Agreement establishing the World Trade Organisation* [1994] E.C.R. I-5267, paras 108–109.

II. ASSOCIATION

Association. The Union is entitled to involve certain countries and territories 25–016
closely in its operation by means of an "association". Concerning the countries
and territories which come under the sovereignty of a Member State but are not
part of the Union, Art. 203 TFEU [*ex Art. 187 EC*] empowers the Council to
determine the details and procedure of such an association. Furthermore, Art. 217
TFEU [*ex Art. 310 EC*] authorises the Union to conclude agreements with third
countries or international organisations so as to establish an association.

A. ASSOCIATION OF OVERSEAS COUNTRIES AND TERRITORIES

Overseas countries and territories. The association of the overseas countries and 25–017
territories is the subject of Part Four of the TFEU (Arts 198 to 204 TFEU [*ex Arts
182 to 188 EC*]). Since most areas colonised by the Member States became independent in the 1960s, this scheme now applies only to certain overseas countries
and territories having special relations with Denmark, France, the Netherlands and
the United Kingdom.[74] The purpose of the association is to,

> "promote the economic and social development of the countries and territo-
> ries and to establish close economic relations between them and the Union
> as a whole" (Art. 198, second para., TFEU).[75]

To this end, the association establishes a free-trade area between the Union and
the overseas countries and territories, whereby the Member States endeavour to
apply to their trade with them the same treatment as they accord to each other, but
the overseas countries and territories determine their trade policy vis-à-vis the

---

[74] The countries and territories to which the provisions of Part Four of the TFEU are applicable (listed in
Annex II to the Treaties): Greenland, New Caledonia and Dependencies, a number of the French
C.O.M.s or *collectivités d'outre mer* (French Polynesia, Wallis and Futuna Islands, Mayotte and Saint
Pierre and Miquelon), the French Southern and Antarctic Territories, Aruba and the former
Netherlands Antilles (Bonaire, Curaçao, Saba, Sint Eustatius and Sint Maarten), Anguilla, Cayman
Islands, Falkland Islands, South Georgia and the South Sandwich Islands, Monserrat, Pitcairn, Saint
Helena and Dependencies, British Antarctic Territory, British Indian Ocean Territory, Turks and Caicos
Islands, British Virgin Islands and Bermuda. For the special status of Greenland, Aruba and the former
Netherlands Antilles, see also para. 12–007, *supra.* See, for the competence for monetary emission in
New Caledonia, French Polynesia and Wallis and Futuna, Protocol (No. 18), annexed to the Lisbon
Treaty, on France ([2010] O.J. C83/289).
[75] For the "advantages" which association confers on those countries and territories, see ECJ, Case
C-430/92 *Netherlands v Commission* [1994] E.C.R. I-5197, para. 22. The association arrangements
apply only to products originating in those countries and territories: ECJ, Case C-310/95 *Road Air*
[1997] E.C.R. I-2229, paras 29–36. The application of the association regime does not bring a territory within the sphere of application of the Treaties; see ECJ, Case C-181/97 *van der Kooy* [1999]
E.C.R. I-483, paras 32–42 (Netherlands Antilles held not to be part of the Union for the purposes
of the application of the VAT Directive).

Member States themselves, subject to the condition that they treat all the Member States in the same way (see Arts 199, points (1) and (2) and 200 TFEU). All the Member States contribute towards the development of the overseas countries and territories through the European Development Fund set up for that purpose (Art. 199, point 3 TFEU). A Convention annexed to the EC Treaty determined the substance of the association scheme for the first five years. Since then, the Council lays down provisions to this end unanimously,

> "on the basis of the experience acquired under the association of the countries and territories with the Union and of the principles set out" in the Treaties (Art. 203 TFEU).

Accordingly, the Council has to reconcile the aims of the association with the "principles"—likewise laid down in the Treaties—underlying the common agricultural policy. To this end, the Council has arranged matters so that agricultural products from overseas countries and territories are on an equal footing with Union products, but a safeguard clause enables the Union to react to a limited extent to difficulties to which free access of products originating in those countries and territories to the Union market may give rise.[76]

The association scheme is now substantively identical to that of the association agreements which the Union has concluded under Art. 217 TFEU [*ex Art. 310 EC*]. Unlike those agreements, however, the association scheme does not require any institutions of its own on account of its autonomous nature.

B. ASSOCIATION AGREEMENTS PURSUANT TO ARTICLE 217 TFEU

1. Scope of Article 217 TFEU

25–018   **Association agreements.** Article 217 TFEU [*ex Art. 310 EC*] and Art. 206 EAEC provide the legal basis for the Union to,

---

[76] Council Decision 2001/822/EC of November 27, 2001 on the association of the overseas countries and territories with the European Community, 2001 L314, p. 1, as amended by Council Decision 2007/249/EC of March 19, 2007, [2007] O.J. L109/33. Decision 2001/822 replaced Council Decision 91/482/EEC of July 25, 1991 on the association of the overseas countries and territories with the European Economic Community, [1991] O.J. L263/1 (subsequently amended by Council Decision 97/803/EC of November 24, 1997, [1997] O.J. L329/50, and extended by Council Decision 2000/169/EC of February 25, 2000, [2000] O.J. L55/67). The safeguard clause contained in that decision was declared lawful in CFI, Joined Cases T-480/93 and T-483/93 *Antillean Rice Mills and Others v Commission* [1995] E.C.R. II-2305, paras 81–97, as confirmed on appeal by ECJ, Case C-390/95 P *Antillean Rice Mills v Commission* [1999] E.C.R. I-769. For the validity of Decision 97/803/EEC, see ECJ, Case C-17/98 *Emesa Sugar* [2000] E.C.R. I-675, paras 27–67.

"conclude with one or more States or international organisations agreements establishing an association involving reciprocal rights and obligations, common action and special procedures".

Because association is defined in this way, there is a need for a degree of institutionalisation of the international cooperation so as to make it possible for decisions to be taken in common. As the Court of Justice has held, an association agreement creates "special, privileged links with a third country which must, at least to a certain extent, take part in the [Union] system".[77]

Scope of agreements. The Union has the power to "guarantee commitments towards non-member countries in all the fields covered by the [Treaties]".[78] As a result, it may conclude association agreements relating to any area coming under the Union Treaties.[79] Thus, an association agreement may cover free movement of workers who are nationals of the third country party to the agreement even though the power to adopt the necessary implementing measures is not vested in the Union.[80] On the Union side, the financing and other arrangements for implementing association agreements are often enshrined in an internal agreement concluded by the representatives of the governments of the Member States, meeting in the Council.[81]

25–C

Bodies set up by association agreement. With a view to its implementation and further development, each association agreement sets up a joint body composed, on the one hand, of members of the national governments or the members of the Council— generally supplemented by members of the Commission—and, on the other hand, of members of the government of each third country involved. That association council (sometimes called "council of ministers" or, to suit the title of the agreement, the "cooperation council") takes its decision by unanimous vote. Preparatory and executive powers may be delegated to the association (or cooperation) committee, which is made up of representatives of the members of the association council. Generally, each association engenders (by virtue of the agreement itself or of a decision of the association council) an advisory parliamentary body, consisting of Members of the European Parliament and of the parliament(s) of the third country or countrie concerned. Generally, the association council has jurisdiction to rule on any disput between the Contracting Parties relating to the interpretation or application of t

2

[77] ECJ, Case 12/86 *Demirel* [1987] E.C.R. 3719, para. 9. "Reciprocal rights and obligations" doe mean equality of contractual obligations: ECJ, Case 87/75 *Besciani* [1976] E.C.R. 129, para.

[78] *Demirel* (n. 77, *supra*), para. 9.

[79] For the rights third country nationals derive from association agreements, see Kellerman, "The of non-member state nationals under the EU association Agreements" (2008) E.J.L.Ref. 33 For a discussion (and a comparison) of the content of association agreements, see Humm räumliche Erweiterung des Binnenmarktrechts" (2002) EuR. Beiheft 1, 75–146; Lenaerts Smijter, "The European Community's Treaty-Making Competence" (1996) Y.E.L. 1, at 19

[80] ECJ, Case 12/86 *Demirel* [1987] E.C.R. 3719, para. 10.

[81] See, for instance, in the case of the ACP-EC Partnership Agreement, n. 116, *infra*.

association agreement. If a settlement cannot be reached, it is possible to have recourse to arbitration.[82]

2. Association agreements

(a) *Survey*

Association agreements. Association agreements play a fundamental role in the EU's external policy. All association agreements simplify access to the Union market for goods from the countries concerned and, at the same time, commit the Union to cooperate with them economically and financially. In all the agreements, save that concluded with Israel,[83] the Union unilaterally grants a zero tariff or (in the case of "sensitive" products, such as textiles) a reduced tariff. The third countries undertake for their part to grant products from the Union most-favoured nation status and not to apply any fiscal discrimination.[84]

Besides economic considerations, political considerations play a important part in determining whether such agreements are concluded and implemented.[85] Whereas some of these agreements prepare for a possible accession (see para. 25–022), others form part of the Union's neighbourhood policy (see para. 25–023). The two most important association agreements concluded by the Union are the ACP-EC Partnership Agreement (see paras 25–024 et seq.) and the Agreement on the European Economic Area (see paras 25–029 et seq.).

Preparation for accession. [86] The first time the Union made use of Art. 217 [at that time Art. 238 EEC] was when it concluded agreements with Greece and Turkey to prepare them for possible accession.[87] These were followed

---

Ntumba, "Les institutions mixtes de gestion des accords conclus entre la CEE et les Etats de développement (PVD)" (1988) R.M.C. 481–486; Lenaerts and De Smijter, at 156–57. A list of association and cooperation councils and of the representations may be found in the pre-1997 annual *Council Guide*, Brussels, Secretariat General of the European Union.

The Union has concluded an agreement based on reciprocal tariff reductions. On the preferential agreements and their compatibility with the GATT, see Kennedy, "Free Trade Agreements: Stretching the Limits of GATT Exceptions to ..." (1992) J.W.T. 59–78.

denunciation of the cooperation agreement with Yugoslavia in 1991: Council Regulation of November 25, 1991, [1991] O.J. L325/23. See Fransen, "The EEC and the Yugoslav Association and Cooperation Agreements" (1992) Leiden J.I.L. 215–243.

See Chap. 23 contributed by De Smijter to Lenaerts and Van Nuffel, *Constitutional Law of the European Union* (London, Sweet & Maxwell, 2004), at 924–935.

Agreement of 1963 establishing an Association between the EEC and Turkey (text published in [1973] O.J. C113/1), with an Additional Protocol of 1970 ([1977] O.J. L293/3), as fleshed out by, inter alia, (internal) Agreement of ... and a number of decisions of the Association Council (such as 2/80 ...) and 3/80, [1983] O.J. C110/60); Agreement of July 9, 1961 ... Second Series, I. External Relations (1), 3).

by association agreements with Cyprus and Malta which, just like the agreement with Turkey, envisaged the progressive establishment of a customs union.[88] The agreements with Greece, Cyprus and Malta have lapsed since their accession. Turkey and the Union have constituted a customs union since January 1, 1996.[89] This was followed by the initiation of a pre-accession strategy for Turkey.[90] On October 3, 2005 accession negotiations were officially opened (see para. 6–013).

Shortly after the disintegration of the communist structures in Central and Eastern Europe, the Union began to conclude association agreements with central European countries: in 1991 with Hungary, Poland and Czechoslovakia (since divided into two,[91]) in 1993 with Bulgaria and Romania, in 1995 with the Baltic States Estonia, Latvia and Lithuania and in 1996 with Slovenia.[92] These so-called "Europe Agreements" embodied various liberalisation measures intended to lead after a maximum of ten years to the creation of a free-trade area in industrial products between the Union and the central European countries concerned. Besides, they also contained provisions relating to the liberalisation of the movement of workers, establishment and the provision of services[93] and a chapter on "approximation of legislation" pursuant to which the associated partner was to endeavour to make its legislation compatible with that of the Union. Consequently, the Europe Agreements represented for both parties the means *par excellence* for effectively preparing the central European countries for later membership of the European Union. Accession negotiations began in 1998, which led to the accession of these European countries in 2004 and 2007 (see paras 6–006 and 6–007).

---

[88] See Agreement of December 5, 1970 between the EEC and Malta, [1971] J.O. L61/1; Agreement between the EEC and Cyprus, [1973] O.J. L133/1.

[89] Decision No. 1/95 of the EC-Turkey Association Council of December 22, 1995 on implementing the final phase of the Customs Union, [1996] O.J. L35/1.

[90] See Council Regulation (EC) No. 390/2001 of February 26, 2001 on assistance to Turkey in the framework of the pre-accession strategy, and in particular on the establishment of an Accession Partnership ([2001] O.J. L58/1) and Council Decision 2008/157/EC on the principles, priorities and conditions contained in the Accession Partnership with Turkey ([2008] O.J. L51/4). See Karakas, "Gradual Integration: an attractive alternative integration process for Turkey and the EU" (2006) 11 E.For.Aff.Rev. 311–331.

[91] Following the dissolution of Czechoslovakia on December 31, 1992, the Community signed association agreements on October 4, 1993 with both the Czech and the Slovak Republics. For the question under international law of State succession in the case of an agreement between Czechoslovakia and Austria, see ECJ, Case C-216/01 *Budějovický Budvar* [2003] E.C.R. I-13617 (see para. 22–055, *supra*).

[92] The Europe Agreements with Hungary ([1993] O.J. L347/2) and Poland ([1993] O.J. L348/2) entered into force on February 1, 1994. The Europe Agreements with Romania ([1994] O.J. L357/2), Bulgaria ([1994] O.J. L358/3), Slovakia ([1994] O.J. L359/2) and the Czech Republic ([1994] O.J. L360/2) entered into force on February 1, 1995. The Europe Agreements with Estonia ([1998] O.J. L68/3), Latvia ([1998] O.J. L26/3) and Lithuania ([1998] O.J. L51/3) entered into force on February 1, 1998. The Europe Agreement with Slovenia ([1999] O.J. L51/3) entered into force on February 1, 1999.

[93] See, e.g., ECJ, Case C–327/02 *Panayotova* [2004] E.C.R. I-11055 (agreements between the Communities and Bulgaria, Poland and Slovakia).

Since 1999, the European Union has engaged in a stabilisation and association process with regard to seven countries in the western Balkans, namely Albania, Bosnia and Herzegovina, Croatia, the Former Yugoslav Republic of Macedonia, Kosovo, Montenegro and Serbia.[94] The centrepiece of this process is the conclusion of a Stabilisation and Association Agreement between the Union and each of the countries concerned.[95] These agreements provide for the establishment of a bilateral free-trade area with the Union and further include a chapter on political dialogue and provisions on free competition, protection of intellectual property rights and the right of establishment. In addition, "European partnerships" are to be established to identify priorities for further action towards moving the western Balkan countries closer to the European Union, while also serving as a checklist against which to measure progress.[96] The stabilisation and association process has the aim of preparing these countries for accession to the European Union. Accession negotiations have been opened in 2005 with Croatia whereas the Former Yugoslav Republic of Macedonia has been recognised as a candidate Member State (see para. 6–013).

25–023 **Mediterranean Area.** Since the 1970s, the Union has concluded agreements, often styled "cooperation agreements", under what is now Art. 217 TFEU with virtually every country in the Mediterranean area.[97] Accordingly, the Union currently has

---

[94] See Grabar- Kitarovic, "The stabilization and association process: the EU's soft power as its best" (2007) E.For.Aff.Rev. 121–125; Pippan, "The Rocky Road to Europe: The EU's Stabilisation and Association Process for the Western Balkans and the Principle of Conditionality" (2004) E.For.Aff.Rev. 219–245. See further, Papadimitrou, Petrov and Greicevci, "To build a state: Europeanization, EU Actorness and state-building in Kosovo" (2007) E.For.Aff.Rev. 219–238.

[95] The stabilisation and association agreement with the Former Yugoslav Republic of Macedonia was signed on April 9, 2001 and approved by the Union by decision of February 23, 2004 ([2004] O.J. L84/1—it entered into force on April 1, 2004: [2004] O.J. L85/26); the agreement with Croatia was signed on October 29, 2001, approved on behalf of the Union by Decision of December 13, 2004 ([2005] O.J. L26/1—it entered into force on February 1, 2005); the agreement with Albania was signed on June 12, 2006 and approved by decision of February 26, 2009 ([2009] O.J. L107/165—it entered into force on April 1, 2009: [2009] O.J. L104/57); the agreement with Montenegro was signed on October 12, 2007 and approved by decision of March 29, 2010, [2010] O.J. L108/1; the agreement with Serbia was signed on April 29, 2008; the agreement with Bosnia and Herzegovina was signed on June 16, 2008. The last three agreements have not yet entered into force; pending their entry into force, interim agreements have been concluded. So far, no agreement has been concluded with Kosovo.

[96] Council Regulation (EC) No. 533/2004 of March 22, 2004 on the establishment of European partnerships in the framework of the stabilisation and association process ([2004] O.J. L86/1). See, most recently, Council Decision 2008/119 regarding Croatia ([2008] O.J. L42/51); Council Decision 2008/210/EC regarding Albania ([2008] O.J. L80/1); Council Decision 2008/211/EC regarding Bosnia and Herzegovina ([2008] O.J. L80/18), Council Decision 2008/212/EC regarding Macedonia ([2008] O.J. L80/32), Council Decision 2008/213/EC regarding Serbia ([2008] O.J. L80/46) and Council Decision 2007/49/EC regarding Montenegro ([2007] O.J. L20/16).

[97] For the first Association Agreements with Cyprus and Malta: see n. 88, *supra*.

associations with each of the Maghreb countries (Algeria, Morocco and Tunisia),[98] the Mashreq countries (Egypt, Jordan, Lebanon and Syria)[99] and Israel.[100] Pursuant to undertakings entered into by the Union at the Euro-Mediterranean Conference held in Barcelona on November 27 and 28, 1995,[101] the existing association agreements have gradually been replaced by agreements which are eventually to lead to the establishment of a Euro-Mediterranean Free Trade Area.[102] Henceforward, the Palestine Authority is to be involved.[103] The agreements with the Maghreb countries and some decisions of the EC-Turkey Association Council require the Member States to treat nationals of those countries who are lawfully on their territory in the same way as their own nationals as regards conditions of employment, remuneration and social security (see para. 10–015). Since 2004, the so-called Euro-Mediterranean Partnership has become part of a wider European Neighbourhood Policy (see para. 25–036).

(b) *The ACP-EC Partnership Agreement*

From Lomé to Cotonou. After most of the colonised areas in Africa obtained their independence, the Community concluded the association agreements signed

25–024

---

[98] See, first, the Cooperation Agreements of April 25, 1976 with Tunisia ([1978] O.J. L265/2), of April 26, 1976 with Algeria ([1978] O.J. L263/2) and of April 27, 1978 with Morocco ([1978] O.J. L264/2) and, subsequently, the "Euro-Mediterranean" Association Agreements concluded on July 17, 1995 with Tunisia ([1998] O.J. L97/2), on February 26, 1996 with Morocco ([2000] O.J. L70/2), on April 22, 2002 with Algeria ([2005] O.J. L265/2).

[99] See the Cooperation Agreements of January 18, 1977 with Egypt ([1978] O.J. L266/2), Jordan ([1978] O.J. L268/2) and Syria ([1978] O.J. L269/2) and of May 3, 1977 with Lebanon ([1978] O.J. L267/2). "Euro-Mediterranean" Association Agreements were signed with Jordan on November 24, 1997 ([2002] O.J. L129/1), with Egypt on June 25, 2001 ([2004] O.J. L304/39) and with Lebanon on June 17, 2002 ((2002) 6 EU Bull. point 1.6.75). Such an association agreement has also been initialled with Syria in 2004 and, in a revised version, in 2008, but has to date not yet been signed.

[100] See the "Euro-Mediterranean" Association Agreement of November 20, 1995 ([2000] O.J. L147/3). An association agreement had been concluded with Israel on May 11, 1975 pursuant to Art. 113 EC [*later Art. 133 EC; now Art. 207 TFEU*] ([1975] O.J. L136/3), but the additional protocols (such as the fourth protocol, [1988] O.J. L327/36) and protocols on financial and technical cooperation (such as the most recent protocol of June 12, 1991, [1992] O.J. L94/46) were based on Art. 238 EC [*later Art. 310 EC; now Art. 217 TFEU*]. For the way in which the European Parliament exercised its power of assent, see para. 26–013, *infra*.

[101] See the Barcelona Declaration and the programme of work (1995) 11 EU Bull. point 2.3.1.

[102] See the Euro-Mediterranean Agreements mentioned in ns. 98–100, *supra*. The structure for Union financial and technical aid was the Euro-Mediterranean partnership: Council Regulation (EC) No. 1488/96 of July 23, 1996 on financial and technical measures to accompany the reform of economic and social structures in the framework of the Euro-Mediterranean partnership (MEDA), [1996] O.J. L189/1, now replaced by Regulation (EC) No. 1638/2006 (see n. 167, *infra*). For a discussion, see the contributions in Osman and Philip (eds), *Le partenariat euro-méditerranéen. Le processus de Barcelone: nouvelles perspectives* (Brussel, Bruylant, 2003), 370 pp.

[103] See the Euro-Mediterranean Interim Association Agreement of February 24, 1997 on trade and cooperation between the European Community, of the one part, and the Palestine Liberation Organisation (PLO) for the benefit of the Palestine Authority of the West Bank and the Gaza Strip, of the other part, [1997] O.J. L187/1.

at Yaoundé (Cameroon) on July 20, 1963 and July 29, 1969 with the African States in question and Madagascar.[104] Following the accession of the United Kingdom, the Community entered into negotiations with a number of States in Africa, the Caribbean and the Pacific, which culminated in an association agreement being concluded with these "ACP States". The ACP-EC Convention was signed at Lomé (Togo) on February 28, 1975, following which it was renewed every five years.[105] A new ACP-EC Agreement was concluded at Cotonou (Benin) on June 23, 2000 by the Community, its Member States and 76 ACP States for a twenty-year period starting on March 1, 2000.[106] This ACP-EC "Partnership Agreement" provides for cooperation with 77 ACP States and has since been extended to cover 79 States.[107]

25–025 **Content of Partnership Agreement.** The ACP-EC Partnership Agreement is intended to promote and expedite the economic, cultural and social development of the ACP States, with a view to contributing to peace and security and to promoting a stable and democratic political environment (Art. 1, first para.). The key objectives are poverty eradication, sustainable development and the gradual integration of the ACP countries into the world economy. At the same time, the ACP-EC Partnership Agreement has a political dimension based on respect for

---

[104] [1964] J.O. 1430 and [1970] O.J. L282. English version in [1974] O.J. English Spec. Ed., Second Series I, External Relations.

[105] ACP-EC Convention of February 28, 1975, [1976] O.J. L25; Second ACP-EC Convention of October 31, 1979, [1980] O.J. L347; Third ACP-EC Convention of December 8, 1984, [1986] O.J. L86; Fourth ACP-EC Convention of December 15, 1989, [1991] O.J. L229/3 (concluded for ten years and since revised by the Convention of Mauritius of November 4, 1995, [1998] O.J. L156/3).

[106] [2000] O.J. L317/3, approved by Council Decision 2003/159/EC of December 19, 2002 ([2003] O.J. L65/27); [2005] O.J. L209/27 (after amendment by agreement of June 25, 2005, approved by Council Decision 2005/599/EC of June 11, 2005, [2005] O.J. L209/26, in accordance with Art. 95, which provides that amendments may be made at the end of each five-year period). A new amendment has been undertaken in March 2010 ([2010] O.J. L287/3); see for the authorisation of signature Council Decision 2010/648/EU of June 14, 2010, [2010] O.J. L287/1 (corrigendum: [2010] O.J. L299/46). See Babarinde and Faber, "From Lomé to Cotonou: Business as Usual?" (2004) E.For.Aff.Rev. 27–47; Arts, "ACP-EU Relations in a New Era: The Cotonou Agreement" (2003) C.M.L.Rev. 95–116; Vincent, "L'entrée en vigueur de la convention de Cotonou" (2003) C.D.E. 157–176; Petit, "Le nouvel accord de partenariat ACP-UE" (2000) R.M.C.U.E. 215–219. The ACP-EC Partnership Agreement entered into force on April 1, 2003.

[107] Somalia is considered one of the (least developed) ACP States, even though it has not signed the Partnership Agreement. South Africa participates in the Partnership Agreement subject to the qualifications set out in Protocol 3 on South Africa (the general and institutional provisions and the cooperation strategies will apply to that country, but in principle not the provisions on financial assistance and trade cooperation); however, South Africa is linked to the EC by the cooperation agreement of October 11, 1999 (n. 107, supra), which according to Protocol 3 takes precedence over the provisions of the Partnership Agreement. East Timor became the 78th State to accede to the Partnership Agreement, by virtue of Decision No. 1/2003 (2003/404/EC) of the ACP-EC Council of Ministers of May 16, 2003 ([2003] O.J. L141/25) adopted pursuant to Art. 94(1) of the Agreement. For a list of the other ACP States, see the tables in Arts (n. 106, supra), at 113, and in Matambalya and Wolf, "The Cotonou Agreement and the Challenges of Making the New EU-ACP Trade Regime WTO Compatible" (2001) J.W.T. 123, at 142. Cuba has not yet been admitted to accede to the Partnership Agreement, although it is accepted as a member by the group of ACP States.

human rights, democratic principles and the rule of law, and good governance. In the event that one of the parties fails to fulfil an obligation stemming from respect for human rights, democratic principles or the rule of law, a consultation procedure may be initiated which may result in "appropriate measures" being taken and, in the last resort, in the suspension of the Partnership Agreement.[108]

The ACP-EC Partnership Agreement seeks to gear the aid granted to the ACP States more to the degree of development of individual ACP countries or groups of countries. As far as the group of least-developed ACP States is concerned, the existing trade conditions remain largely unchanged. As regards the other ACP States, the ACP-EC Partnership Agreement provides for the conclusion of economic partnerships by the end of 2007.[109] Until that time, the non-reciprocal trade preferences were maintained: products originating in the ACP States could be imported into the Union free of customs duties, with the exception of those coming under a common organisation of the market or specific rules of the common agricultural policy, for which the Union has introduced a favourable import regime.[110] Since it proved impossible to have Economic Partnership Agreements (EPAs) concluded between regional groups of ACP countries and the Union, many ACP countries have individually signed interim EPAs with the EU as a first step towards comprehensive regional EPAs. The interim agreements secure and improve ACP access to the EU market so as to avoid the negative trade effects that would follow from the expiration of the Cotonou trade regime at the end of 2007. In 2008 the EU signed the first comprehensive EPA with the CARIFORUM States.[111] Negotiations are ongoing with the African and Pacific regions to move

---

[108] ACP-EC Partnership Agreement, Art. 96; see, e.g., as regards Liberia, Council Decision 2002/274/EC of March 25, 2002 ([2002] O.J. L96/23) and the partial suspension of the Partnership Agreement by Council Decision 2003/631/EC of August 25, 2003 ([2003] O.J. L220/3); as regards Haiti, Council Decision 2004/681/EC of September 24, 2004 ([2004] O.J. L311/30); as regards Guinea-Bissau, Council Decision 2004/680/EC of September 24, 2004 ([2004] O.J. L311/27). Article 97 of the ACP-EC Partnership Agreement provides for a similar consultation procedure for serious cases of corruption.

[109] Council Regulation (EC) No. 1528/2007 of December 20, 2007 applying the arrangements for products originating in certain States which are part of the African, Caribbean and Pacific (ACP) Group of States provided for in agreements establishing, or leading to the establishment of, Economic Partnership Agreements, [2007] O.J. L348/1. For the list of countries that have concluded negotiations on agreements leading to the establishment of an economic partnership agreement with the EC, see Annex I to the regulation. See further Geboya Desta, "EC-ACP economic partnership agreements and WTO comptability: an experiment in North-South interregional agreements?" (2006) C.M.L.Rev. 1343–1379.

[110] ACP-EC Partnership Agreement, Art. 36, as enlarged upon in Annex V.

[111] Economic Partnership Agreement between the CARIFORUM States, of the one part, and the European Community and its Member States, of the other part [2008] O.J. L289/3. The agreement has not yet entered into force; for its provisional application, see [2008] O.J. L352/62. The CARIFORUM States are Antigua & Barbuda, Bahamas, Barbados, Belize, Cuba, Dominica, Dominican Republic, Grenada, Guyana, Haiti, Jamaica, St. Kitts and Nevis, St. Lucia, St. Vincent & the Grenadines, Suriname and Trinidad & Tobago.

from interim agreements to comprehensive regional agreements. For ACP States which are not in a position to enter into economic partnership agreements, the Union is to work out an alternative framework for trade.[112]

The ACP-EC Partnership Agreement does not include any provisions on the free movement of workers, but it does oblige the Member States and the ACP countries to accord each other's nationals who are legally employed in their respective territories treatment free from any discrimination based on nationality as regards working conditions, remuneration and dismissal relative to their own nationals.[113] Each of the ACP States undertakes to accept the return and readmission of any of its nationals who are illegally present on the territory of a Member State of the EU.[114]

25–026 **Union assistance.** In cooperating on development financing, the Union grants administrative, technical and financial assistance to projects in the ACP States. Since the ACP-EC Partnership Agreement was concluded by the Union (then the Community) together with the Member States, the corresponding financial obligation falls on the Union and the Member States considered together.[115] Since the Union does not have exclusive competence in this area, the Member States lawfully elected to finance the aid from national contributions made available to the European Development Fund, which is administered by the Commission.[116] In this way, the Commission grants aid directly to the ACP States and to the overseas countries and territories referred to in Part Four of the TFEU. The ACP States choose the projects to be financed and are responsible for formulating, negotiating and concluding contracts with undertakings. The intervention of Commission representatives is intended solely to determine whether the conditions for Union financing are satisfied.[117] The European Investment Bank may also grant loans and other financial assistance.

---

[112] ACP-EC Partnership Agreement, Art. 37(6).
[113] ACP-EC Partnership Agreement, Art. 13(3). Article 274 of the Fourth ACP-EC Convention itself prohibited ACP States and EU Member States from discriminating as between nationals of different Member States or ACP States without putting them under an obligation to treat nationals of Member States and of ACP States identically: ECJ, Case 65/77 *Razanatsimba* [1977] E.C.R. 2229, paras 12–14. A Member State may reserve more favourable treatment to the nationals of a given ACP country in so far as such treatment results from the provisions of an international agreement comprising reciprocal rights and advantages: *ibid.*, para. 19.
[114] ACP-EC Partnership Agreement, Art. 13(5)(c).
[115] ECJ, Case C-316/91 *European Parliament v Council* [1994] E.C.R. I-625, paras 28–33.
[116] *Ibid.*, paras 34–38; see the Internal Agreement between the Representatives of the Governments of the Member States, meeting within the Council, on the Financing of Community Aid under the Multiannual financial framework for the period 2009 to 2013 in accordance with the ACP-EC Partnership Agreement and on the allocation of financial assistance for the Overseas Countries and Territories to which Part Four of the EC Treaty applies, [2006] O.J. L247/32, which establishes a Tenth Development Fund.
[117] As a result, undertakings which tender for or are awarded contracts do not have any contractual relationship with the Union: ECJ, Case 126/83 *STS v Commission* [1984] E.C.R. 2769, paras 10–18.

ACP bodies. Policy decisions with regard to the implementation of the ACP-EC   **25–027**
Partnership Agreement are taken at least once a year by the Council of Ministers,
consisting of the members of the Council and (one or more) members of the
Commission, on the one hand, and a member of the government of each ACP
State, on the other.[118] Tasks may be delegated to the Committee of Ambassadors,
which meets on a regular basis. That committee consists of the Permanent
Representatives of all the Member States and a representative of the Commission,
on the one hand, and the head of each ACP State's mission to the EU, on the
other.[119] In order to prepare for these meetings, both the members of the Council
and the ACP States within their own group endeavour to reach a common position. The ACP States do so in the Council of ACP Ministers set up for this purpose and in the Committee of ACP Ambassadors, both of which are based in
Brussels.[120] The ACP-EC bodies are chaired alternately by a Member State and
an ACP State.[121] The Joint Parliamentary Assembly acts as a consultative body.
It is made up of Members of the European Parliament and of Members of
Parliament of the ACP States or representatives designated by them. It meets
twice a year, alternatively in the Union and in an ACP State.[122]

Accession. A request to accede may be made only by States "whose structural   **25–028**
characteristics and economic and social situation are comparable to those of the
ACP States" and has to be approved by the Council of Ministers.[123] Any new
Member State of the European Union becomes a party to the ACP-EC Partnership
Agreement from the date of accession if the act of accession so provides or,
otherwise, by depositing an act of accession which is to be notified to all the ACP
countries.[124]

(c) *The EEA Agreement*

EEA Agreement.[125] Another major agreement which was concluded by the   **25–029**
Union under Art. 217 TFEU [at that time Art. 238 EEC] is the Agreement on the
European Economic Area (EEA Agreement) signed at Oporto on May 2, 1992,

---

[118] ACP-EC Partnership Agreement, Art. 15. For the Rules of Procedure of the ACP-EC Council of
Ministers, see [2005] O.J. L95/44.
[119] ACP-EC Partnership Agreement, Art. 16. For the Rules of Procedure of the ACP-EC Committee
of Ambassadors, see [2005] O.J. L95/51.
[120] The ACP States agreed to this in the Georgetown Agreement of June 6, 1975; the Internal
Agreement on measures and procedures to be followed for the implementation of the ACP-EC
Partnership Agreement, [2000] O.J. L317/376, applies as between the Member States.
[121] ACP-EC Partnership Agreement, first para. of Arts 15(1) and 16(1).
[122] *Ibid.*, Art. 17.
[123] *Ibid.*, Art. 94(1); for its application, see n. to para. 25–024, *supra*.
[124] *Ibid.*, Art. 94(3), second subpara. For examples, see Art. 6(4) of the 2003 Act of Accession and
Art. 6(5) of the 2005 Act of Accession.
[125] The paragraphs on the EEA build on Ch. 23 contributed by De Smijter to Lenaerts and Van Nuffel,
Constitutional Law of the European Union (London, Sweet & Maxwell, 2004), at 924–935.

which came into force on January 1, 1994.[126] The EEA Agreement has been concluded between the Community and its Member States, on the one hand, and the EFTA countries (see para. 1–018), except for Switzerland, on the other.[127] Following the accession of Austria, Finland and Sweden to the European Union in 1995, the participating states on the side of EFTA are Iceland, Liechtenstein and Norway. As regards Switzerland, relations with the European Union are governed by a series of bilateral agreements of 1999[128] and 2004.[129]

25–030   **Homogeneous application.** The EEA Agreement creates a free-trade area (not a customs union) between the Union and the three EFTA states. In other words, no customs charges are levied in the territory of the EEA for trade in goods as between the countries of the EEA, but each of the Contracting Parties[130] is entitled to retain its own import and export duties for goods coming from and going to third States. With the EEA Agreement, the three EFTA States accepted to take over a major part of the Union legislative *acquis*: this concerns the Treaty provisions and secondary Union law with respect to the free movement of goods, persons, services and capital, the competition rules and areas such as research and development, the environment, education and social policy.

---

[126] [1994] O.J. L1. Signature of the Agreement was possible only after amendments; after an adverse opinion from the Court of Justice on the compatibility of the system of judicial supervision envisaged in the draft EEA Agreement with provisions of the EEC Treaty, the Agreement was adjusted in that respect (ECJ, Opinion 1/91 *Draft Agreement between the Community, on the one hand, and the countries of the European Free Trade Association, on the other, relating to the creation of the European Economic Area* [1991] E.C.R. I-6079). In a second opinion, the Court held the revised agreement to be compatible with EC law (ECJ, Opinion 1/92 *Draft Agreement between the Community, on the one hand, and the countries of the European Free Trade Association, on the other, relating to the creation of the European Economic Area* [1992] E.C.R. I-2821).

[127] On December 6, 1992, 50.3 per cent of the total population and 18 of the 26 cantons voted against Swiss ratification of the EEA Agreement. The EEA Agreement did not come into effect as regards Liechtenstein until May 1, 1995 after the Principality had taken the necessary measures with regard to its regional union with Switzerland ([1995] O.J. L140/30; see Art. 7(1) of Decision No. 1/95 of the EEA Council of March 10, 1995, [1995] O.J. L86/58).

[128] See the agreements concluded with Switzerland in the sectors free movement of persons ([2002] O.J. L114/1), air transport ([2002] O.J. L114/73), the carriage of goods and passengers by rail and road (([2002] O.J. L114/791), trade in agricultural products ([2002] O.J. L114/132; amended by agreement of May 14, 2005, [2009] O.J. L136/2), mutual recognition in relation to conformity assessment ([2002] O.J. L114/369), certain aspects of government procurement ([2002] O.J. L114/430) and scientific and technological cooperation ([2002] O.J. L114/468).

[129] See the agreements concluded with Switzerland in the field of environment ([2006] L90/37), in the audiovisual field ([2006] O.J. L90/23), on cooperation in the field of statistics ([2006] O.J. L90/2), on the fight against fraud ([2009] O.J. L46/8), on the taxation of savings ([2004] O.J. L385/30), on the association of Switzerland to the Schengen *acquis* ([2008] O.J. L53/52) and on the participation of Switzerland in the Dublin Convention ([2008] O.J. L53/5). For a discussion, see Kaddous, "The Relations between the EU and Switzerland" in Dashwood and Maresceau (n. 57, *supra*) 227–269.

[130] As far as the EU and its Member States are concerned, "Contracting Parties" means the EU and/or the EU Member States, depending on their respective competences under the EU Treaty (EEA Agreement, Art. 2(c)).

.In order to ensure a homogeneous application of the relevant provisions, the EEA Agreement provides for on-going consultations to take place during the Union legislative process.[131] Besides, there is a parallel system of supervision and dispute settlement. The powers exercised, on the Union side, by the Commission and the Court of Justice with respect to the monitoring of the application of the provisions of the EEA Agreement by Union institutions, Member States and persons within their jurisdiction[132] are exercised, as far as the EFTA States are concerned, with respect to those States and persons within their jurisdiction by the EFTA Surveillance Authority (ESA, based in Brussels)[133] and the EFTA Court (based in Luxembourg).[134] Courts or tribunals of EU Member States and of EFTA States may seek a preliminary ruling from the Court of Justice or the EFTA Court, as the case may be.[135] In order to secure homogeneity, provisions of the EEA Agreement which are essentially identical to corresponding rules of primary or secondary Union law are interpreted by the EFTA Surveillance Authority and the EFTA Court in accordance with the case law of the Court of Justice.[136] For its part, the Court of Justice sometimes refers to the case law of the EFTA Court.[137]

---

[131] See, e.g., EEA Agreement, Art. 99(1) (in preparing Union legislation, the Commission is to seek advice from experts of the EFTA States) and Art.99(3) (continuous information and consultation process in the EEA Joint Committee).

[132] EEA Agreement, Art. 109(1). By this means the Commission carries out its Union supervisory duties (see Art. 17(1) TFEU; para. 13–063, *supra*).

[133] Article 109 of the EEA Agreement and Arts 5, 22 and 31 of the Agreement between the EFTA States on the establishment of a Surveillance Authority and a Court of Justice. For the Rules of Procedure of the Surveillance Authority, see [1994] O.J. L113/19.

[134] Articles 32 and 34 of the Agreement between the EFTA States on the establishment of a Surveillance Authority and a Court of Justice.

[135] See Art. 267 TFEU [*ex Art. 234 EC*] and Art. 34 of the Agreement between the EFTA States on the establishment of a Surveillance Authority and a Court of Justice, which contains a relatively open-ended variant of the preliminary ruling procedure provided for in Art. 267 TFEU, respectively. See Baudenbacher, "The implementation of decisions of the ECJ and of the EFTA Court in Member States' domestic legal orders" (2005) 40 Tex. Int'l L.J. 383–416. The Court of Justice cannot, however, give a ruling on the interpretation of the EEA Agreement with regard to events which occurred when the State concerned was a party to the EEA Agreement but not yet a Member State of the EU: ECJ, Case C-140/97 *Rechberger and Greindl* [1999] E.C.R. I-3499, paras 38–39, and ECJ, Case C-321/97 *Andersson and Andersson* [1999] E.C.R. I-3551, paras 26–33 (concerning Austria and Sweden, respectively).

[136] See, e.g., EFTA Court, Case E-1/94 *Restamark* [1994–1995] EFTA Court Report 15, paras 24, 32–33, 46–52, 56, 60, 64–66 and 79–80; EFTA Court, Joined Cases E-9/07 and E-10/07, *L'Oréal* [2008] EFTA Court Report 261, paras 27–37 (reversing earlier case law in the light of a recent ECJ judgment). See also Baudenbacher (n. 52), at 889–899. For a critical appraisal of the EFTA Court's case law, see Kronenberger, "Does the EFTA Court interpret the EEA Agreement as if it were the EC Treaty? Some Questions raised by the *Restamark* judgment" (1996) I.C.L.Q. 198–212.

[137] E.g., ECJ, Case C-13/95 *Süzen* [1997] E.C.R. I-1295, para. 10; ECJ, Joined Cases C-34–36/95 *De Agostini and TV Shop* [1997] E.C.R. I-3843, para. 37; ECJ, Case C-172/99 *Liikenne* [2001] E.C.R. I-745, para. 2; ECJ, Case C-286/02 *Bellio F.lli* [2004] E.C.R., I-3465, paras 34 and 57–60.

25–031   **EEA Institutions.** The institutions of the EEA are responsible for seeing to it that the EEA evolves in parallel with every new development of Union law in matters covered by the EEA Agreement. The EEA Council consists of the members of the Council of the European Union and members of the Commission and one member of government of each of the EFTA States.[138] It is responsible for giving the political impetus and laying down the general guidelines for the implementation of the Agreement.[139] The EEA Joint Committee consists of representatives of the Contracting Parties[140]; it ensures the effective implementation and operation of the Agreement. In the event of a conflict of interpretation as between a person coming under the Union legal order, on the one hand, and an EFTA State, on the other, the Union or an EFTA State may bring the dispute before the EEA Joint Committee, which will try to find a solution.[141] If the Joint Committee does not manage to settle the dispute, the matter may be brought before the Court of Justice.[142] Lastly, there is the EEA Joint Parliamentary Committee and the EEA Consultative Committee, which are advisory bodies representing, respectively, the peoples of Europe and the social partners.[143] Their main objective is to promote understanding between the Contracting Parties.

III. DEVELOPMENT COOPERATION

25–032   **Development policy.** Although competence in respect of development cooperation was first incorporated in the EC Treaty by the EU Treaty, the Community had already been pursuing its own development policy for some considerable time. Thus, the scheme for overseas countries and territories (Part Four of the EC Treaty; see para. 25–017) and the association policy with regard to countries in the Mediterranean area and the ACP States (see paras 25–021—25–026) aimed primarily to promote those countries' economic and social development. In association

---

[138] EEA Agreement, Art. 90(1), first subpara. The office of President of the EEA Council is to be held alternately, for a six-month period, by a member of the Council of the European Union and a member of the government of an EFTA State. The EEA Council is convened twice a year by its President (EEA Agreement, Art. 91).

[139] See EEA Agreement, Art. 89. The function, composition and operation of the EEA Council as prescribed by Arts 89, 90 and 91 of the EEA Agreement resemble the role played by the European Council in the European Union before the Lisbon Treaty.

[140] EEA Agreement, Art. 93(1).

[141] EEA Agreement, Art. 111(1). Note that only the Union and the EFTA States are entitled to bring a dispute on interpretation before the EEA Joint Committee, not the EU Member States.

[142] See Art. 111(3) of the EEA Agreement.

[143] The EEA Joint Parliamentary Committee consists of 66 members, one half of whom are Members of the European Parliament, the other half Members of the Parliaments of the EFTA States (EEA Agreement, Art. 95(1), and Art. 2 of Protocol 36 on the Statute of the EEA Joint Parliamentary Committee). The EEA Consultative Committee consists of equal numbers of the Union's European Economic and Social Committee and of the EFTA Consultative Committee (EEA Agreement, Art. 96(2)).

therewith, various common commercial policy measures had development policy aspects without detracting from their commercial policy nature (see para. 25–003). Above all, there were the multilateral commodity agreements, the Food-Aid Convention and the cooperation agreements concluded with developing countries (see paras 25–009 and 25–010). In addition, since 1971 the Council has granted, pursuant to an UNCTAD resolution of 1968, generalised tariff preferences by regulation for certain industrial, textile and agricultural products from developing countries, for which the common commercial policy affords a sufficient legal basis.[144] By granting tariff preferences, the Union seeks to increase the beneficiary countries' export revenue, hence promoting their economic development. Since January 1, 1995, new rules are in force which aim gradually to concentrate preferences on the least developed countries.[145] Lastly, the Council has adopted measures pursuant to Art. 308 EC [now Art. 352 TFEU] whose principal characteristic is development, namely financial and technical assistance granted to non-associated developing countries under cooperation agreements[146] and food aid.[147]

Specific powers. The powers provided for in Arts 208 to 211 TFEU [ex Arts 177 to 181 EC] have as their primary objective the reduction and, in the long term, the eradication of poverty. The Union is to take account of the objectives of development cooperation in the policies that it implements which are likely to affect developing countries (Art. 208(1), second subpara., TFEU). Union development cooperation is conducted within the framework of the principles and objectives of the Union's external action (Art. 208(1), first subpara., TFEU).[148] The specific power with regard to development cooperation makes it superfluous to make reference to Art. 352 TFEU both as far as concerns autonomous measures adopted by the Union pursuant

25–033

---

[144] ECJ, Case 45/86 Commission v Council [1987] E.C.R. 1493, paras 14–21.

[145] See Harrison, "Incentives for development: the EC's generalized system of preferences, India's WTO challenge and reform" (2005) C.M.L.Rev. 1663–1689; Peers, "Reform of the European Community's Generalised System of Preferences: A Missed Opportunity" (1995) J.W.T. 79–96. See also the multiannual scheme of generalised tariff preferences, as applied for the period January 1, 2009 to December 31, 2011 by Council Regulation (EC) No. 732/2008 of July 22, 2008, [2008] O.J. L211/1.

[146] Council Regulation (EEC) No. 443/92 of February 25, 1992 on financial and technical assistance to, and economic cooperation with, the developing countries in Asia and Latin America, [1992] O.J. L52/1, now replaced by Regulation No. 1905/2006 (see n. 153, infra).

[147] See Snyder, "The European Community's Food Aid Legislation: Towards a Development Policy", in his work New Directions in European Community Law (London, Weidenfeld, 1990), 146–176. For the present system, see n. 155, infra.

[148] Accordingly, it must contribute towards the development and consolidation of democracy and the rule of law and respect for human rights. Specific Union assistance is geared towards the promotion of these values in third countries; see Regulation (EC) No. 1889/2006 of the European Parliament and of the Council of December 20, 2006 on establishing a financing instrument for the promotion of democracy and human rights worldwide, [2006] O.J. L386/1. The promotion of regional integration is not stated to be an objective in the Treaties, but is mentioned in Art. 1 of the ACP-EC Partnership Agreement (para. 25–025, supra). See Ntumba, La Communauté économique européenne et les intégrations régionales des pays en développement (Brussels, Bruylant, 1990), 541 pp.

to Art. 209 TFEU [*ex Art. 179 EC*][149] and cooperation and other agreements concluded pursuant, inter alia, to Art. 209(2) TFEU [*see ex Art. 181 EC*].[150]

Within their respective spheres of competence, the Union and the Member States are to cooperate with third countries and the competent international organisations (Art. 211 TFEU) and must comply with the commitments and take account of the objectives they have approved in the context of the United Nations and other competent international organisations (Art. 208(2) TFEU).

In view of the broad objectives pursued by development cooperation policy, it must be possible for a measure to cover a variety of specific matters. Where a measure contains clauses concerning several specific matters, the Treaty provisions on development cooperation afford a sufficient legal basis, provided that development cooperation is the essential object of the measure and the obligations contained in those clauses are not so extensive as to constitute in fact objectives distinct from those of development cooperation.[151]

25–034   **Instruments for development cooperation.**[152] Under Art. 209(1) TFEU, measures for the implementation of development cooperation policy, including possibly multiannual cooperation programmes with developing countries or programmes with a thematic approach, are adopted by the European Parliament and the Council under the ordinary legislative procedure. Such measures may be financed by the Union[153] and may also receive support for their implementation from the funds of the European Investment Bank.[154] In pursuance of these

---

[149] See, e.g., Council Regulations (EC) Nos 1734/94 and 1735/94 of July 11, 1994 on financial and technical cooperation with the Occupied Territories, [1994] O.J. L182/4 and L182/6, which followed Council Decision 91/408/EEC of July 22, 1991 on financial aid for Israel and the Palestinian population of the Occupied Territories, [1991] O.J. L227/33 (based on Art. 235 EEC [*now Art. 352 TFEU*]).

[150] See, for instance, the Conventions with the United Nations Relief and Works Agency for Palestine Refugees (UNRWA) concerning aid to refugees in the countries of the Near East of 1993 ([1994] O.J. L9/17), of 1996 ([1996] O.J. L282/69) and of 1999 ([1999] O.J. L261/36), concluded under Art. 181 EC [*see now Art. 209(2) TFEU*] in conjunction with Art. 300(3), first subpara., EC [*now Art. 218 TFEU*]; a previous convention had been concluded pursuant to Art. 235 EC [*now Art. 352 TFEU*] ([1990] O.J. L118/36).

[151] ECJ, Case C-268/94 *Portugal v Council* [1996] E.C.R. I-6177, para. 39 (by analogy with Opinion 1/78 on the common commercial policy: para. 25–003, *supra*); ECJ, Case C-91/05 *Commission v Council* [2008] E.C.R. I-3651, paras 64–78 (Treaty provisions on development cooperation do not afford a sufficient legal basis for a measure mainly pursuing CFSP objectives).

[152] For a general discussion, see Mold, *EU development policy in a changing world: challenges for the 21st century* (Amsterdam, Amsterdam University Press, 2007), 272 pp.

[153] See Regulation (EC) No. 1905/2006 of the European Parliament and the Council of December 18, 2006 establishing a financing instrument for development cooperation, [2006] O.J. L374/41, and Regulation (EC) No. 1717/2006 of the European Parliament and the Council of November 15, 2006 establishing an Instrument for Stability, [2006] O.J. L327/1 (the latter based on both the Treaty provisions on development cooperation and on economic, financial and technical cooperation with third countries, see para. 25–035, *infra*).

[154] Article 209(3) TFEU. The EIB grants such support in the context of the ACP-EC Convention (para. 25–026, *supra*).

powers, the Union has introduced, for example, prevention and intervention systems for humanitarian aid, food aid, aid for uprooted people and aid for rehabilitation and reconstruction operations for developing countries.[155] Frequently, aid programmes of public authorities in beneficiary countries require them to have the projects supported by the Union carried out by means of specific calls for tenders.[156] Respect for human rights is a precondition for benefiting from tariff preferences[157] and plays an important role in agreements concluded by the Union in pursuance of its development cooperation policy.[158] Detailed rules for Union cooperation with third countries and competent international organisations may be incorporated in agreements between the Union and the countries or international organisations in question which are negotiated and concluded in accordance with Art. 218 TFEU. This is without prejudice to Member States' competence to negotiate in international bodies and to conclude international agreements on development cooperation themselves (Art. 209(2) TFEU).[159]

---

[155] See, for instance, Council Regulation (EC) No. 1257/96 of June 20, 1996 concerning humanitarian aid, [1996] O.J. L163/1; Council Regulation (EC) No. 1292/96 of June 27, 1996 on food-aid policy and food-aid management and special operations in support of food security, [1996] O.J. L166/1, now replaced by Regulation No. 1905/2006 (see n. 153, *supra*); Council Regulation (EC) No. 2258/96 of November 22, 1996 on rehabilitation and reconstruction operations in developing countries, [1996] O.J. L306/1, now replaced by Regulation No. 1717/2006 (see n. 153, *supra*); Regulation (EC) No. 2130/2001 of the European Parliament and of the Council of October 29, 2001 on operations to aid uprooted people in Asian and Latin American developing countries, [2001] O.J. L287/3, now repealed by Regulations No. 1717/2006 and 1905/2006 (all based on Art. 179 EC [*now Art. 209 TFEU*]). See Baroncini, "The Legal Framework of the European Community's Assistance towards Uprooted People" (2000) R.A.E. 139–166.

[156] See Kalbe, "The award of contracts and the enforcement of claims in the context of EC external aid and development cooperation" (2001) C.M.L.Rev. 1217–1267.

[157] E.g., Council Regulation (EC) No. 552/97 of March 24, 1997 temporarily withdrawing access to generalised tariff preferences from the Union of Myanmar, [1997] O.J. L85/8 (access withdrawn on account of the systematic use of forced labour in Myanmar (Burma)); Council Regulation (EC) No. 1933/2006 of December 21, 2006 temporarily withdrawing access to the generalised tariff preferences from the Republic of Belarus, [2006] O.J. L405/35.

[158] ECJ, Case C-268/94 *Portugal v Council* [1996] E.C.R. I-6177, paras 23–29. The Court considers that references to respect for human rights in agreements in the field of development policy may be an important factor in the exercise of the right of the Union—on the basis of international law—to have the agreement suspended or terminated where the third country has violated human rights (*ibid.*, para. 27). See also para. 25–025, *supra*, and Dimier, "Constructing conditionality: the bureaucratization of EC development aid" (2006) E.For.Aff.Rev. 263–280; Delaplace, "L'Union européenne et la conditionnalité de l'aide au développement" (2001) R.T.D.E 609–626; Fierro, "Legal Basis and Scope of Human Rights Clauses in EC Bilateral Agreements: Any Room for Positive Interpretation?" (2001) E.L.J. 41–68; Ward, "Framework for Cooperation between the European Union and Third States: A Viable Matrix for Uniform Human Rights Standards?" (1998) E.For.Aff.Rev. 505–536.

[159] Consequently, cooperation agreements include the following clause: "Without prejudice to the relevant provisions of the Treaties establishing the European Communities, neither this Agreement nor any action taken thereunder shall in any way affect the powers of the Member States of the Communities to undertake bilateral activities with [the third country] in the framework of economic cooperation or to conclude, where appropriate, new economic cooperation agreements with [the third country]" (see, for instance, Art. 25 of the cooperation agreement with India; n. 54, *supra*).

Development cooperation policy therefore does not constitute an exclusive competence of the Union; the Union's development cooperation policy and that of the Member States are to complement and reinforce each other.[160] Nevertheless, Member States' action is limited by exclusive Union competence with regard to the common commercial policy and by arrangements adopted by the Union internally or agreed upon at international level.[161] In order to promote the complementarity and efficiency of their action, the Union and the Member States are to coordinate their policies on development cooperation and consult each other on their aid programmes, including in international organisations and during international conferences. They may undertake joint action and are to contribute if necessary to the implementation of Union aid programmes (Art. 210(1) TFEU).[162] The Commission may take any useful initiative to promote the coordination of the policies of the Union and the Member States (Art. 210(2) TFEU).

IV. ECONOMIC, FINANCIAL AND TECHNICAL COOPERATION WITH THIRD COUNTRIES AND NEIGHBOURHOOD POLICY

25–035   **Cooperation with third countries.** The Treaty of Nice introduced a specific legal basis enabling the Union to adopt measures for economic, financial and technical cooperation with third countries other than developing countries. Article 212 TFEU [*ex Art. 181a EC*] serves as the legal basis for a whole series of measures which were formerly adopted under Art. 308 EC [*now Art. 352 TFEU*], possibly in combination with Art. 133 EC [*now Art. 207 TFEU*] (common commercial policy) or Art. 181 EC [*now Art. 211 TFEU*] (development cooperation) (see paras 25–009, 25–021 and 25–033). Such measures are to be consistent with the development policy of the Union and are to be carried out within the framework of the principles and objectives of its external action.[163] The Union's operations and those of the Member States must complement and reinforce each other (Art. 212(1) TFEU). The necessary measures are adopted by the European Parliament and the Council, acting in accordance with the ordinary legislative procedure (Art. 212(2) TFEU).[164] However, as far as urgent

---

[160] Article 208, first subpara., TFEU; see also ECJ, Case C-268/94 *Portugal v Council* [1996] E.C.R. I-6177, para. 36.

[161] See Declaration (No. 10), annexed to the EU Treaty, discussed in n. 282, *infra*.

[162] See also ECJ, Case C-316/91 *European Parliament v Council* [1994] E.C.R. I-625, paras 25–27.

[163] For the incorporation of human rights clauses, see the literature cited in n.158, *supra*. Sometimes trading partners are resistant to the incorporation of a human rights clause: see *Europe*, No. 6901, January 27–28, 1997, 10, and No. 6903, January 30, 1997, 9 (complaints from Australia).

[164] Under Art. 181a(2) EC, the Council acted by a qualified majority, except where the cooperation was to be based on an association agreement referred to in Art. 310 EC or on agreements to be concluded with candidate Member States for accession to the Union. The European Parliament was consulted. Development cooperation measures, by contrast, were adopted by the European Parliament and the Council under the co-decision procedure (Art. 179(1) EC). This had the remarkable result that the involvement of the European Parliament depended on the degree of development of the beneficiary countries. The Lisbon Treaty did away with this anomaly.

financial assistance to a third country is concerned, the necessary decisions are taken by the Council, acting by a qualified majority on a proposal from the Commission (Art. 213 TFEU).

The arrangements for Union cooperation with third countries and international organisations may be the subject of agreements between the Union and the third parties concerned, which are to be negotiated and concluded in accordance with Art. 218 TFEU (see para. 26–003 *et seq.*). This is without prejudice to the Member States' competence to negotiate in international bodies and to conclude international agreements (Art. 212(3), second subpara., TFEU). Accordingly, policy on economic, financial and technical cooperation does not constitute an exclusive competence of the Union.

European Neighbourhood Policy. An example of cooperation with non-developing third countries based on Art. 212 TFEU is the European Neighbourhood Policy (ENP). This policy was started with a view to the accession of most of the Central European countries to the EU and aims at avoiding new dividing lines in Europe by promoting stability and prosperity within and beyond the new borders of the European Union.[165] The Neighbourhood Policy builds, on the one hand, on the partnership and cooperation agreements concluded with former Soviet Republics (the "Eastern Partnership")[166] and, on the other hand, on the association agreements concluded within the framework of the Euro-Mediterranean Partnership (see para. 25–023). Existing programmes of Union assistance to these countries were replaced by a European Neighbourhood and Partnership Instrument, adopted under Arts 179 and 181a EC [*now Arts 209 and 212 TFEU*].[167]

25–036

---

[165] See the Presidency conclusions of the Copenhagen European Council of December 12 and 13, 2002. See Smith and Webber, "Political dialogue and security in the European Neighbourhood: the virtues and limits of 'new partnership perspectives' " (2008) E.For.Aff.Rev. 73–95; Comelli, Greco and Tocci, "From boundary to borderland: transforming the meaning of borders through the European Neighbourhood Policy" (2007) E.For.Aff.Rev. 203–218; Rhattat, "Du processus de Barcelone à la politique européenne de voisinage. Le dialogue interculturel dans l'espace euro-méditerranéen entre coexistence et affrontements" (2007) R.M.C.U.E. 100–107; Zaiotti, "Of friends and fences: Europe's Neighbourhood policy and the 'gated community syndrome' " (2007) 29 J.E.I. 143–162; Dodini and Fantini, "The EU neighbourhood policy: implications for economic growth and stability" (2006) 44 J.C.M.S. 507–32; Kelley, "New wine in old Wineskins: promoting political reforms through the new European neighbourhood policy" (2006) 44 J.C.M.S. 29–55; Magen, "The shadow of enlargement: can the European neighbourhood policy achieve compliance" (2006) 12 Col.J.E.L. 383–427; Densysyuk, "Politique de voisinage de l'Union euro péenne, quelles transformations sur le régime commercial régional en Europe" (2005) R.M.C.U.E. 101–114.

[166] See the references in n. 57, *supra* and the Communication of the Commission of December 3, 2008 on Eastern Partnership (COM(2008)final).

[167] Regulation (EC) No. 1638/2006 of the European Parliament and of the Council of October 24, 2006 laying down general provisions establishing a European Neighbourhood and Partnership Instrument, [2006] O.J. L310/1.

The Lisbon Treaty inserted into the Treaties a clause enabling the Union to conclude specific agreements with neighbouring States. Article 8(1) TEU provides that the Union "shall develop a special relationship with neighbouring countries", aiming to establish an area of prosperity and good neighbourliness, founded on the values of the Union and characterised by close and peaceful relations based on cooperation. Article 8(2) TEU adds that, for that purpose, the Union may conclude agreements with the countries concerned which may contain reciprocal rights and obligations as well as the possibility of undertaking activities jointly.

V. HUMANITARIAN AID

25–037   **Humanitarian aid.** The Treaty of Lisbon introduced a specific legal basis for Union action in the field of humanitarian aid. However, even before that, within the framework of development policy, the Council had created a regime for humanitarian aid to people who were victims of natural disasters, wars and outbreaks of fighting, or other comparable exceptional circumstances.[168] The Union's operations in the field of humanitarian aid are intended to provide ad hoc assistance and relief and protection for people in third countries who are victims of natural or man-made disasters, in order to meet the humanitarian needs resulting from these different situations (Art. 214(1) TFEU). Accordingly, Union aid in this connection is not restricted to developing countries.

Union action in the field of humanitarian aid is to be conducted within the framework of the principles and objectives of the external action of the Union in compliance with the principles of international law and with the principles of impartiality, neutrality and non-discrimination. The Union's measures and those of the Member States have to complement and reinforce each other (Art. 214(1) and (2) TFEU). Union humanitarian aid operations are to be coordinated and consistent with those of international organisations and bodies, in particular those forming part of the United Nations system (Art. 214(7) TFEU).

The European Parliament and the Council, acting in accordance with the ordinary legislative procedure, establish the measures defining the framework within which the Union's humanitarian aid operations are implemented. In this context, Art. 214(5) TFEU provides for the setting up of a European Voluntary Humanitarian Aid Corps. The Union may also conclude agreements with third countries and competent international organisations. This is without prejudice to the Member States' competence to negotiate in international bodies and to conclude international agreements (Art. 214(4) TFEU).

---

[168] See, for instance, Council Regulation (EC) No. 1257/96 (n. 155, *supra*).

VI. THE COMMON FOREIGN AND SECURITY POLICY (CFSP)

A. OBJECTIVES AND SCOPE OF THE CFSP

Framework. Title V of the TEU constitutes the legal basis for the Union's com-   25–038
mon foreign and security policy (CFSP).[169] Chapter 1 of that Title contains general
provisions on the Union's external action; Ch. 2 contains specific provisions on the
CFSP.[170] The CFSP was laid down in 1993 by the EU Treaty to replace European
Political Cooperation between the Member States (EPC; see para. 2–003). As far as
the content of the CFSP is concerned, the Treaties provide only that it should be
based on the development of mutual political solidarity among Member States, the
identification of questions of general interest and the achievement of an ever-
increasing degree of convergence of Member States' actions (Article 24(2) TEU).
Chapter 2 of Title V of the TEU does not determine in greater detail how the CFSP
is to take substantive shape, but elaborates the procedures and instruments pursuant
to which the institutions and the Member States may conduct a foreign and security policy.

Objectives. The Lisbon Treaty brought the CFSP and the other external powers of   25–039
the Union together in one Title containing both general provisions on the Union's
external action and specific provisions on the CFSP. Consequently, the CFSP is
related to the same principles, objectives and general provisions that have to guide
the Union in the other areas of its external action (see Art. 23 TEU, referring to
Ch. 1 of Title V of the TEU).[171]

Scope. Unlike European Political Cooperation (EPC; see para. 2–003), the CFSP   25–040
works not merely on the basis of intergovernmental cooperation between the

---

[169] For a general survey, see Eeckhout, *External Relations of the European Union, Legal and
Constitutional Foundations* (Oxford, Oxford University Press, 2004), Ch. 11; Hillion and Wessel,
"Restraining External Competences of EU Member States under CFSP" in Cremona and de Witte
(eds), *EU Foreign Relations Law. Constitutional Fundamentals* (Oxford, Hart Publishing, 2008)
79–122; Bono, "Some reflections on the CFSP legal order" (2006) C.M.L.Rev. 337–394; Thym,
"Reforming Europe's Common Foreign and Security Policy" (2004) E.L.J. 5–22; Baches Opi and
Floyd, "A Shaky Pillar of Global Stability: The Evolution of the European Union's Common
Foreign and Security Policy" (2003) Col.J.E.L. 299–332.
[170] The "specific provisions" flesh out some specific features of CFSP decision-making (see
para. 15–009) and CFSP instruments (see para. 18–022).
[171] Before the Lisbon Treaty, Art. 11(1) EU formulated specific objectives for the CFSP, which supplemented the general objectives of Art. 2 EU and corresponded to objectives set out in Art. 21(2)
TEU. For a discussion of CFSP objectives, see Keukeleire and MacNaughtan, *The foreign policy
of the European Union* (Basingstoke, Palgrave Macmillan, 2008), Ch. 6. Pursuant to these objectives, the Member States subscribed to the establishment of the International Criminal Court:
Council Common Position 2001/443/CFSP of June 11, 2001 on the International Criminal Court,
[2001] O.J. L155/19, as amended (after the ratification by all Member States of the Statute of the
International Criminal Court) by Council Common Positions 2002/474/CFSP of June 20, 2002,
[2002] O.J. L164/1, and 2003/444/CFSP of June 16, 2003, [2003] O.J. L150/67.

Member States but is primarily shaped by measures adopted by the institutions of the Union. The CFSP covers,

> "all areas of foreign policy and all questions relating to the Union's security, including the progressive framing of a common defence policy" (Art. 24(1), first subpara., TEU).

In this respect, too, the CFSP can no longer be compared to EPC, which initially avoided defence questions.[172] The Member States are to support the CFSP actively and unreservedly in a "spirit of loyalty and mutual solidarity"; to this end, they must work together and refrain from any action which is contrary to the interests of the Union (Art. 24(3) TEU).

B. SUBSTANCE OF THE COMMON FOREIGN AND SECURITY POLICY

25–041   **General framework.** The TEU does not lay down any substantive rules with which the Union's policy must comply. The Member States are to judge themselves, in the context of the European Council and the Council, whether a matter should be covered by the common policy.[173] The Contracting Parties did not wish to give a list of matters which should fall entirely within the common policy. The Ministers of Foreign Affairs of the Member States did in fact indicate factors which should be taken into account, namely geographical proximity of a given country or region, an important interest for the Union in the political and economic stability of a region or country, and threats to the security interests of the Union.[174] Only questions of security policy are specified in the Treaties (see Art. 43 TEU).

The Treaty provisions do, however, describe the procedures by which the CFSP is given shape. The Treaty of Amsterdam streamlined these procedures, whilst

---

[172] Initially, the exclusion of defence arose chiefly at the request of Ireland (not a member of NATO) and France (not part of the integrated military structure). In the Solemn Declaration of Stuttgart on European Union of June 19, 1983, however, the Heads of State or Government agreed to coordinate national positions as far as "political and economic aspects of security" were concerned (confirmed in Art. 30(6) of the Single European Act).

[173] See Art. 26(1) and Art. 28(1) TEU. For a survey of matters covered, see Hill, "Renationalising or Regrouping? EU Foreign Policy Since 11 September 2001" (2004) J.C.M.S. 143–163; for an analysis of the initial years, see Keukeleire and MacNaughtan (n. 171, *supra*), at 48–54, and other discussions in Burghardt and Tebbe, "Die Gemeinsame Aussen- und Sicherheitspolitik der Europäischen Union—Rechtliche Struktur und politischer Prozess" (1995) EuR. 1–20; Ryba, "La politique étrangère et de sécurité commune (PESC). Mode d'emploi et bilan d'une année d'application (fin 1993–1994)" (1995) R.M.C.U.E. 14–35; Willaert and Marqués-Ruiz, "Vers une politique étrangère et de sécurité commune: état des lieux" (1995) 3 R.M.U.E 35–95.

[174] See the Report of the Ministers of Foreign Affairs, approved by the European Council held at Lisbon on June 26 and 27, 1992, on the likely development of the CFSP (1992) 6 EC Bull. point I-31.

defining the CFSP instruments in more precise terms.[175] The Lisbon Treaty abrogated the special instruments formerly used for CFSP matters ("joint actions" and "common positions"). At the institutional level, it introduced the office of "High Representative of the Union for Foreign Affairs and Security Policy", who now plays a key role in the field of the CFSP. The policy line for the CFSP is determined by the European Council, which is to define the Union's strategic interests and the CFSP's objectives and general guidelines (Art. 26 (1) TEU).[176] The Council is to frame the CFSP and to take the decisions necessary for defining and implementing it on the basis of the general guidelines and strategic lines defined by the European Council (Art. 26(2) TEU). The High Representative, together with the Member States, is responsible for putting the CFSP into effect (Art. 26(3) TEU). Where the international situation requires operational action by the Union, the Council is to adopt the necessary decisions, laying down their objectives, scope, the means to be made available to the Union, if necessary their duration, and the conditions for their implementation (Art. 28(1), first subpara., TEU).[177] The decisions so adopted may be reviewed in the light of a change in circumstances (Art. 28(1), second subpara., TEU). The Council adopts decisions in order to define the Union's approach to particular matters of a geographical or thematic nature (Art. 29 TEU).[178] Where necessary, the Union may conclude an agreement with one or more States or international organisations (Art. 37 TEU).[179] In principle, the European Council and the Council take their decisions by a unanimous vote.[180] However, since the Treaty of Amsterdam, Council decisions can be

---

[175] For the decision-making procedure, see paras 18–002—18–007, *infra*; for a discussion of the various legal instruments which were adopted before the entry into force of the Lisbon Treaty, see paras 23–004 *et seq.*

[176] Before the Lisbon Treaty, the European Council was to decide on "common strategies" (Art. 13(2) EU). For the first, see Common Strategy 1999/414/CFSP of the European Union of June 4, 1999 on Russia, adopted by the European Council ([1999] O.J. L157/1), and subsequently Common Strategy 1999/877/CFSP of the European Council of December 11, 1999 on Ukraine ([1999] O.J. L331/1) and Common Strategy 2000/458/CFSP of the European Council of June 19, 2000 on the Mediterranean region ([2000] O.J. L183/5).

[177] Before the Lisbon Treaty, such decisions took the form of "joint actions" (see Art. 14(1) EU).

[178] Before the Lisbon Treaty, such decisions took the form of "common positions" (see Art. 15 EU).

[179] See, for instance, Council Decision 2009/820/CFSP of October 23, 2009 on the conclusion on behalf of the European Union of the Agreement on extradition between the European Union and the United States of America and the Agreement on mutual legal assistance between the European Union and the United States of America, [2009] O.J. L291/40. See Stessens, "The EU-US Agreement on Extradition and on Mutual legal Assistance", in Martenczuk and van Thiel (eds), *Justice, Liberty, Security: New Challenges for the External Relations of the European Union* (Brussels, VUBpress, 2009) 341–366; Sari, "The conclusion of international agreements by the European Union in the context of the ESDP", (2008) 57 I.C.L.Q. 53–86.

[180] Article 31(1), first subpara., TEU. For the possibility of "constructive abstention" of a Member State from implementing a CFSP decision, see para. 18–002, *infra*.

taken in certain cases by a qualified majority vote.[181] This will be so where the Council adopts a decision defining a Union action or position on the basis of a decision of the European Council relating to the Union's strategic interests and objectives[182] or on a proposal of the High Representative following a specific request from the European Council, when adopting decisions implementing such decisions and when appointing a special representative[183] (Art. 31(2), first subpara., TEU).

In addition to action taken within the European Council and the Council, the Member States are to consult one another on any matter of foreign and security policy of general interest (Art. 32 TEU [*ex Art. 16 EU*]). A special instance of cooperation is that between the diplomatic missions of the Member States and the Union delegations in third countries and at international organisations, which is to contribute to formulating and implementing the Union's common approach.[184]

25–042 **Foreign policy of the Union.** The introduction of a "common" foreign and security policy has not prompted the Member States to take joint action in every sphere of foreign and security policy. The CFSP primarily affords the Member States an institutional framework which facilitates the framing and execution of a common policy in matters on which all of them agree there should be joint action.

By means of CFSP decisions—common positions before the Lisbon Treaty—the Council has imposed economic sanctions against third States (see para. 25–050), formulated objectives and priorities for Union policy vis-à-vis third countries[185] and defined a common stance of the Member States for international

---

[181] See Kugelmann, "Die Gemeinsame Aussen- und Sicherheitspolitik" (1998) EuR. Beiheft 2 at 99–123; des Nerviens, "Le Traité d'Amsterdam. Les relations extérieures" (1997) R.T.D.E. 801–812; Bonino, "La réforme de la politique étrangère et de sécurité commune: aspects institutionnels" (1995) 3 R.M.U.E. 261–266.

[182] Before the Lisbon Treaty, Art. 23(1) EU stated in this connection that the Council was to act by qualified majority "when adopting joint actions, common positions or taking any other decision on the basis of a common strategy". See, e.g., Council Joint Action 1999/878/CFSP of December 17, 1999 establishing a European Union Cooperation Programme for Non-proliferation and Disarmament in the Russian Federation ([1999] O.J. L331/11), adopted pursuant to Common Strategy 1999/414/CFSP of the European Union of June 4, 1999 on Russia ([1999] O.J. L157/1) and on the basis of Arts 14 and 23(2) EU. Since a common strategy tended to consist of a list of specific actions, the possibility of deciding by a qualified majority was limited in practice to the technical implementation of matters on which there was agreement between all the Member States (See Pernice and Thym, "A New Institutional Balance for European Foreign Policy?" (2003) E.For.Aff.Rev. 369, at 375).

[183] See Art. 33 TEU.

[184] See also Art. 35 TEU, which refers to Art. 20(2)(c) TFEU and Art. 23 TFEU (on the right to diplomatic protection for citizens of the Union; see para. 8–013, *supra*).

[185] See, e.g., the Common Positions on Iraq (2003/495/CFSP of July 7, 2003, [2003] O.J. L169/72), Burma/Myanmar (2003/297/CFSP of April 28, 2003, [2003] O.J. L106/36), Rwanda (the most recent being 2002/831/CFSP of October 21, 2002, [2002] O.J. L285/3), Angola (e.g. 2002/495/CFSP of June 25, 2002, [2002] O.J. L167/9), Nigeria (e.g. 2002/401/CFSP of May 27, 2002, [2002] O.J. L139/1), Afghanistan (e.g. 2001/56/CFSP of January 22, 2001, [2001] O.J. L21/1), Libya (1999/261/CFSP of April 16, 1999, [1999] O.J. L103/1), Belarus (98/448/CFSP of

conferences[186] or the procedure for action on the part of the Union in international organisations.[187]

CFSP decisions—joint actions before the Lisbon Treaty—afford a basis for Union humanitarian aid actions,[188] for support for the restoration of democracy,[189] the rule of law[190] or a peace process[191] in specific States and for intervention in

---

July 9, 1998, [1998] O.J. L195/1), Sierra Leone (98/409/CFSP of June 29, 1998, [1998] O.J. L187/1), Albania (97/357/CFSP of June 2, 1997, [1997] O.J. L153/4), Cuba (96/697/CFSP of December 2, 1996, [1996] O.J. L322/1), East Timor (96/407/CFSP of June 25, 1996, [1996] O.J. L168/2), Burundi (95/91/CFSP of March 24, 1995, [1995] O.J. L72/1) and Ukraine (94/779/CFSP of November 28, 1994, [1994] O.J. L313/1). See also Common Position 2005/304/CFSP of April 12, 2005 concerning conflict prevention, management and resolution in Africa, [2005] O.J. L97/57, Common Position 1999/691/CFSP of October 22, 1999 on support to democratic forces in the Federal Republic of Yugoslavia, [1999] O.J. L273/1 and Common Position 98/350/CFSP of May 25, 1998 concerning human rights, democratic principles, the rule of law and good governance in Africa, [1998] O.J. L158/1.

[186] See, e.g., Council Decision 2010/212/CFSP of March 29, 2010, [2010] O.J. L90/8 (conference on nuclear weapons), Common Position 2007/469/CFSP of June 28, 2007, [2007] O.J. L176/39 (conference on chemical weapons), Common Position 2006/242/CFSP of March 20, 2006, [2006] O.J. L88/65 (conference of biological and toxin weapons), Common Position 2003/805/CFSP of November 17, 2003, [2003] O.J. L302/34 (instruments to combat the proliferation of weapons of mass destruction and means of delivery), Common Position 2001/567/CFSP of July 23, 2001, [2001] O.J. L202/1 (fight against ballistic missile proliferation) and Common Position 95/379/CFSP of September 18, 1995, [1995] O.J. L227/3 (conference on conventional weapons).

[187] E.g., Common Position 2007/762/CFSP of November 22, 2007 on participation by the European Union in the Korean Peninsula Energy Development Organisation (KEDO), [2007] O.J. L305/62.

[188] E.g., support for the conveying of humanitarian aid in Bosnia and Herzegovina (Decision 93/603/CFSP of November 8, 1993, [1993] O.J. L286/1).

[189] E.g., the dispatch of a team of observers for the parliamentary elections in the Russian Federation (Decision 93/604/CFSP of November 9, 1993, [1993] O.J. L286/3), support for the transition towards a democratic and multi-racial South Africa (Decision 93/678/CFSP of December 6, 1993, [1993] O.J. L316/45), support for the democratic transition process in the Democratic Republic of Congo (Joint Actions 96/656/CFSP of November 11, 1996, [1996] O.J. L300/1, and 97/875/CFSP of December 19, 1997, [1997] O.J. L357/1) and support for the democratic process in Nigeria (Joint Action 98/735/CFSP of December 22, 1998, [1998] O.J. L354/1). See Weber, "Die EU-Mission in Kongo: Perspektive einer Europäischen Friedenspolitik" (2006) 41 EuR. 879–889; Youngs, "European Union Democracy Promotion Politics: Ten Years On" (2001) E.For.Aff.Rev. 355–373.

[190] E.g. Council Joint Action 2008/124/CFSP of February 4, 2008 on the European Union Rule of Law Mission in Kosovo, EULEX KOSOVO, [2008] O.J. L42/92; Council Decision 2010/330/CFSP of June 14, 2010 on the European Union Integrated Rule of Law Mission for Iraq, EUJUST LEX-IRAQ, [2010] O.J. L149/12 (that mission was established by Council Joint Action 2005/190/CFSP of March 7, 2005, [2005] O.J. L62/37).

[191] See, for instance, the support given to the conflict settlement process in Georgia/South Ossetia (Joint Action 2008/450/CFSP of June 16, 2008, [2008] O.J. L157/110), the support for the implementation of the Lusaka Ceasefire Agreement and the peace process in the Democratic Republic of Congo (Common Position 2003/319/CFSP of May 8, 2003, [2003] O.J. L115/87), the support for the OAU peace process between Ethiopia and Eritrea (Council Common Position 2000/420/CFSP of June 29, 2000, [2000] O.J. L161/1), the support for the electoral process in Bosnia-Herzegovina (Joint Actions 96/406/CFSP of June 10, 1996, [1996] O.J. L168/1, as supplemented, and 98/302/CFSP of April 30, 1998, [1998] O.J. L138/3), the participation of the Union in the implementing structures of the peace plan for Bosnia-Herzegovina (Joint Action 95/545/CFSP of December 11, 1995, [1995] O.J. L309/2,

crisis-stricken areas (e.g., through the nomination of a Special Envoy of the European Union[192]). Accordingly, in 1994 the European Union agreed, in connection with the conflict in Bosnia and Herzegovina, to take over the administration of the city of Mostar for two years.[193] Pursuant to a joint action, the Member States met with the Baltic and central and eastern European States in Paris on May 26 and 27, 1994.[194] At the final conference held on March 20 and 21, 1995 in Paris, a Stability Pact was signed to promote good neighbourliness and regional cooperation in South Eastern Europe, which has been followed up by the OSCE.[195]

On the basis of joint actions adopted under Art. 14 EU, the Union has also established its own police and military missions, first in the Balkans, and later on also in Africa, Asia and the Middle East. A first EU Police Mission (EUPM) ensures the follow-on to the UN International Police Task Force from January 1, 2003 with the

---

as subsequently supplemented and extended), the support given to the Middle East peace process (Decision 94/276/CFSP of April 19, 1994, [1994] O.J. L119/1, as supplemented, and Joint Action 97/289/CFSP of April 29, 1997 on an assistance programme to support the Palestine Authority in its efforts to counter terrorist activities emanating from the territories under its control, [1997] O.J. L120/2).

[192] See Art. 33 TEU [ex Art. 18 EU]. In this way, Special Envoys were appointed for the African Great Lakes Region (most recently Joint Action 2009/128/CFSP of February 16, 2009, [2009] O.J. L46/36), for the Middle East peace process (most recently Joint Action 2009/136/CFSP of February 16, 2009, [2009] O.J. L46/65), for the Palestinian Authority (Joint Action 97/289/CFSP of April 29, 1997, [1997] O.J. L120/2), for Kosovo (most recently Joint Action 2009/605/CFSP of August 7, 2009, [2009] O.J. L206/20), for the Former Yugoslavian Republic of Macedonia (FYROM) (most recently Joint Action 2009/706/CFSP of September 15, 2009, [2009] O.J. L244/25), for Afghanistan and Pakistan (most recently Joint Action 2009/467/CFSP of June 15, 2009, [2009] O.J. L151/41), for Bosnia and Herzegovina (most recently Joint Action 2009/181/CFSP of March 11, 2009 [2009] O.J. L67/88), for the South Caucasus (most recently Joint Action 2009/133/CFSP of February 16, 2009, [2009] O.J. L46/53), for Moldova (Joint Action 2009/132/CFSP of February 16, 2009, [2009] O.J. L46/50), for Sudan (most recently Joint Action 2009/134/CFSP of February 16, 2009, [2009] O.J. L46/57), for Central Asia (Joint Action 2009/130/CFSP of February 16, 2009, [2009] O.J. L46/43), for the African Union ([2009] O.J. L322/50) and for the crisis in Georgia (Joint Action 2009/131/CFSP of February 16, 2009, [2009] O.J. L46/43).

[193] It did so on the basis of a memorandum of understanding concluded by the EU and the WEU with the local authorities ((1994) 7/8 EU Bull. point 1.3.2); see also Council Decision 94/308/CFSP of May 16, 1994 adapting and extending the application of Decision 93/603/CFSP (n. 188, supra), [1994] O.J. L134/1, as amended and supplemented); for the phasing out of the EU administration of Mostar, see Joint Action 96/476/CFSP of July 26, 1996 ([1996] O.J. L195/1); for the phasing out of EU operations in Mostar, see Council Decision 96/744/CFSP of December 20, 1996 ([1996] O.J. L340/1).

[194] See Council Decision 93/728/CFSP of December 20, 1993 concerning the joint action adopted by the Council on the basis of Art. J.3 of the Treaty on European Union on the inaugural conference of the Stability Pact ([1993] O.J. L339/1); continuation decided by Council Decision 94/367/CFSP of June 14, 1994 ([1994] O.J. L165/2).

[195] (1995) 3 EU Bull. point 1.4.4. See Benoît-Rohmer, "Conclusion du Pacte de stabilité en Europe" (1995) R.T.D.E. 273–277. There is further cooperation with the OSCE on the basis of Council Joint Action 2000/456/CFSP of July 20, 2000 regarding a contribution of the European Union towards reinforcing the capacity of the Georgian authorities to support and protect the OSCE Observer Mission on the border of the Republic of Georgia with the Chechen Republic of the Russian Federation ([2000] O.J. L183/3).

aim of establishing sustainable policing arrangements as part of support for the rule of law in Bosnia and Herzegovina.[196] Further police missions have been established in Afghanistan, Congo and the Palestinian territories,[197] as well as border assistance missions (Gaza),[198] missions in support of security sector reform (Guinea-Bissau and Congo)[199] and monitoring missions (Georgia and Indonesia).[200] In 2003 the European Union initiated the first military operations, first in the Former Yugoslav Republic of Macedonia (this operation has since been replaced by an EU police mission)[201] and subsequently in Congo[202] and Bosnia and Herzegovina.[203] Further military operations have been conducted in Congo,[204] in Chad and the Central

---

[196] Council Joint Action 2002/210/CFSP of March 11, 2002 on the EUPM in Bosnia and Herzegovina (BiH), [2002] O.J. L70/1, as renewed by Joint Action 2005/824/CFSP, [2005] O.J. L307/55, Joint Action 2007/749/CFSP, [2007] O.J. L303/40 and—since the Lisbon Treaty—by Council Decision 2009/906/CFSP of December 8, 2009, [2009] O.J. L322/22.

[197] Council Joint Action 2004/847/CFSP of December 9, 2004 on the EUPM in Kinshasa (Congo) regarding the Integrated Police Unit (EUPOL KINSHASA), [2004] O.J. L367/30; Council Joint Action 2005/797/CFSP of November 14, 2005 on the EUPM for the Palestinian Territories (EUPOL COPPS), [2005] L300/65; Council Joint Action 2007/369/CFSP of May 30, 2007 on establishment of the EUPM in Afghanistan (EUPOL AFGHANISTAN), [2007] O.J. L139/33.

[198] Council Joint Action 2005/889/CFSP of December 12, 2005 on establishing a European Union Border Assistance Mission for the Rafah Crossing Point (EU BAM Rafah), [2005] O.J. L327/28.

[199] Council Joint Action 2008/112/CFSP of February 12, 2008 on the European Union mission in support of security sector reform in the Republic of Guinea-Bissau (EU SSR GUINEA-BISSAU), [2008] O.J. L40/11; Council Joint Action 2005/355/CFSP of May 2, 2005 on the European Union mission to provide advice and assistance for security sector reform in the Democratic Republic of the Congo (EUSEC RD Congo), [2005] O.J. L112/20, as replaced most recently by Council Decision 2010/329/CFSP of June 14, 2010 on the EUPM undertaken in the framework of reform of the security sector (SSR) and its interface with the system of justice in the Democratic Republic of the Congo (EUPOL RD Congo), [2010] O.J. L149/11.

[200] Council Joint Action 2005/643/CFSP of September 9, 2005 on the European Union Monitoring Mission in Aceh (Indonesia) (Aceh Monitoring Mission—AMM), [2005] O.J. L234/13; Council Joint Action 2008/736/CFSP on the European Union Monitoring Mission in Georgia, EUMM Georgia, [2008] O.J. L248/26.

[201] Council Joint Action 2003/92/CFSP of January 27, 2003 on the European Union military operation in the Former Yugoslav Republic of Macedonia ("Concordia"), [2003] O.J. L34/26, succeeded by Council Joint Action 2003/681/CFSP of September 29, 2003 on the European Union Police Mission in the Former Yugoslav Republic of Macedonia (EUPOL "Proxima"), [2003] O.J. L249/66, and Council Joint Action 2005/826/CFSP of November 24, 2005 on the establishment of an EU Police Advisory Team (EUPAT) in the Former Yugoslav Republic of Macedonia (fYROM) [2005] O.J. L307/61.

[202] Council Joint Action 2003/423/CFSP of June 5, 2003 on the European Union military operation in the Democratic Republic of Congo ("ARTEMIS"), [2003] O.J. L143/50, launched by Council Decision 2003/432/CFSP of June 12, 2003, [2003] O.J. L147/42.

[203] Council Joint Action 2004/570/CFSP of July 12, 2004 on the European military operation in Bosnia and Herzegovina ("ALTHEA"), [2004] O.J. L252/11, launched by Council Decision 2004/803/CFSP of November 25, 2004, [2004] O.J. L353/21.

[204] See Council Joint Action 2006/319/CFSP of April 27, 2006 on the European Union military operation in support of the United Nations Organisation Mission in the Democratic Republic of the Congo (MONUC) during the election process (Operation EUFOR RD Congo), [2006] O.J. L116/98, launched by Council Decision 2006/412/CFSP of June 12, 2006, [2006] O.J. L163/16.

African Republic,[205] and in Somalia[206] as well as mixed civilian-military operations in Sudan.[207] Whereas the military operations were planned on the basis of a joint action adopted under Art. 14 EU, their actual launch was a matter of "security policy" decided on the basis of Art. 17(2) EU (see para. 25–043).

C. THE COMMON SECURITY AND DEFENCE POLICY (CSDP)

25–043 **Security policy of the Union.** The common security and defence policy (CSDP) forms an integral part of the CFSP.[208] It is to provide the Union with an operational capacity drawing on civilian and military assets to be used on missions outside the Union for peace-keeping, conflict prevention and strengthening international security in accordance with the principles of the United Nations Charter. The Union's tasks in this connection include,

"joint disarmament operations, humanitarian and rescue tasks, military advice and assistance tasks, conflict prevention and peace-keeping tasks, tasks of combat forces in crisis management, including peace-making and post-conflict stabilisation" (the "Petersberg tasks").[209]

---

[205] Council Joint Action 2007/677/CFSP of October 15, 2007 on the European Union military operation in the Republic of Chad and in the Central African Republic (Operation EUFOR Tchad/RCA), [2007] O.J. L279/21, launched by Council Decision 2008/101/CFSP of January 28, 2008, [2008] O.J. L34/39.

[206] Council Joint Action 2008/851/CFSP of November 10, 2008 on a European Union military operation to contribute to the deterrence, prevention and repression of acts of piracy and armed robbery off the Somali coast (ATALANTA), [2008] O.J. L301/33, launched by Council Decision 2008/918/CFSP of December 8, 2008, [2008] O.J. L330/19; see also Council Joint Action 2008/749/CFSP of September 19, 2008 on the European Union military coordination action in support of UN Security Council resolution 1816 (2008) (EU NAVCO), [2008] O.J. L252/39. See also Council Decision 2010/96/CFSP of February 15, 2010 on an EU military mission to contribute to the training of Somali security forces (EUTM Somalia), [2010] O.J. L4/16.

[207] Council Joint Action 2005/557/CFSP of July 18, 2005 on the European Union civilian-military supporting action to the African Union mission in the Darfur region of Sudan, [2005] O.J. L188/46.

[208] For a general appraisal, see Oppermann, "Public Opinion and the development of the European Security and Defence Policy" (2007) E.For.Aff.Rev. 149–167; Dietrich, "Die rechtlichen Grundlagen der Verteidigungspolitik der Europäischen Union" (2006) Z.a.ö.R.V. 663–697; Duke and Ojanen, "Bridging internal and external security: lessons from the European Security and Defence Policy" (2006) 28 J.E.I. 477–494; Graf von Kielsmansegg, "Die verteidigungspolitischen Kompetenzen der Europäischen Union" (2006) EuR. 182–200; Trybus, "With or without the EU Constitutional Treaty: towards a Common Security and Defence Policy" (2006) E.L.Rev. 145–166.

[209] The tasks listed in Art. 43(1) TEU are known as the "Petersberg tasks" following the Petersberg Declaration made by the WEU States on June 19, 1992. They were significantly extended by the Lisbon Treaty (compare Art. 17(2) EU with Art. 43(1) TEU). The European Parliament distinguishes between "security" and "defence", with the concept of security including the Petersberg operations and the concept of defence covering territorial defence and the protection of the vital interests of the Member States, see its resolution of May 14, 1998 on the gradual establishment of a common defence policy for the European Union, [1998] O.J. C167/190. See Graf von Kielmansegg, "The meaning of Petersberg: some considerations on the legal scope of ESDP

All these tasks are also to contribute to the fight against terrorism, inter alia, by supporting third countries in combating terrorism in their territories (Art. 43(1) TEU).

Decisions relating to the CSDP are always adopted by the Council acting unanimously on a proposal from the High Representative or an initiative from a Member State (Art. 42(4) TEU). In matters of CSDP, there is no possibility for the European Council to introduce qualified majority voting (Art. 31(3) and (4) TEU). The High Representative may propose the use of both national resources and Union instruments, together with Commission, where appropriate (Art. 42(4) TEU). The Lisbon Treaty empowered the Council to entrust the implementation of a task to a group of Member States which are willing and have the necessary capabilities for such a task (Art. 42(5) and 44 TEU).

Article 42(7) TEU provides that if a Member State is the victim of armed aggression on its territory, the other Member States have an obligation towards it to provide aid and assistance by all the means in their power, in accordance with the United Nations Charter.[210] It is emphasised, however, that, for those States which are members of NATO, that organisation is to remain the foundation of their collective defence and the forum for its implementation (see para. 25–047).

The CSDP includes "the progressive framing of a common defence policy",[211] which will lead to an actual "common defence" when the European Council, acting unanimously, so decides. In this case, the European Council is to recommend to the Member States the adoption of a decision in accordance with their respective constitutional requirements (Art. 42(2), first subpara., TEU).

Civilian and military capabilities. The capabilities to carry out the tasks mentioned above are provided by the Member States. The operational capacity for the CSDP was originally provided by the Western European Union (WEU; see para. 1–011). Since the Treaty of Nice, the WEU has been integrated into the European Union (even though not all the Member States belong to the WEU) and the European Union executes the security and defence policy itself.[212] In connection with its take-over of the WEU structures, the Council has set up an Institute

25–044

operations" (2007) 44 C.M.L.Rev. 629–648; Pagani, "A New Gear in the CFSP Machinery: Integration of the Petersberg Tasks in the Treaty on European Union" (1998) E.J.I.L. 737–749.

[210] Article 42(7) TEU was introduced by the Lisbon Treaty and took over the mutual defence clause of the Treaty establishing the Western European Union (see para. 2–006).

[211] The EU Treaty originally referred to "the eventual framing of a common defence policy, which might in time lead to a common defence" (former Article B, second indent, and Art. J.4(1)). See Collet, "Le Traité de Maastricht et la Défense" (1993) R.T.D.E. 225–233.

[212] Duke, "CESP: Nice's Overtrumped Success?" (2001) E.For.Aff.Rev. 155–175; Cammileri, "Le traité de Nice et la politique européenne de la défense" (2000) R.A.E 389–397. So far, the WEU continues to exist as an institution of collective defence in accordance with Art. V of the Treaty of Brussels (see para. 1–011, *supra*). Pursuant to Protocol (No. 11), annexed to the TEU and TFEU, on Art. 42 TEU ([2010] O.J. C83/278), the European Union is to draw up, together with the WEU, arrangements for "enhanced cooperation" between them. For the former relationship between the WEU and the EU, see Cahen, "L'Union de l'Europe occidentale (UEO) et la mise en oeuvre de la future défense commune de l'Union européenne" (1996) R.M.C.U.E. 21–35.

for Security Studies and a Satellite Centre.[213] For the purposes of implementing the CSDP, the EU has its own political and military structures (see para. 18–007), which have taken charge of the EU police missions and military operations.[214] A European Security and Defence College (ESDC) has been established, which is a network between national institutes, colleges, academies and institutions within the EU dealing with security and defence policy issues and the EU Institute for Security Studies.[215]

The Member States are under a duty to make civilian and military capabilities available to the Union for the implementation of the common security and defence policy, in order to contribute to the objectives defined by the Council (Art. 42(3) TEU). The Member States have undertaken to be in a position to deploy within sixty days forces of 50,000 to 60,000 persons to carry out the tasks set out in Art. 43 TEU and to sustain such a deployment for at least one year.[216] The EU can also have recourse to NATO assets and capabilities for its operations[217] and invite non-EU allies to participate in its operations (see para. 25–047).

Since the Lisbon Treaty, Member States undertake progressively to improve their military capabilities (Art. 42(3), second subpara., TEU). To that effect, a European Defence Agency had already been established in July 2004.[218] The European

---

[213] Council Joint Action 2001/554/CFSP of July 20, 2001 on the establishment of a European Union Institute for Security Studies, [2001] O.J. L200/1; Council Joint Action 2001/555/CFSP of July 20, 2001 on the establishment of a European Union Satellite Centre, [2001] O.J. L200/5. See also para. 13–005, *supra*.

[214] For a detailed overview, see Naert, *International Law Aspects of the EU's Security and Defence Policy, with a Particular Focus on the Law of Armed Conflict* (Antwerp, Intersentia, 2010), Ch. 3. For the joint actions governing the EU police and military missions, see para. 20–043; it should be noted that the actual launch of military operations always formed the subject of a Council "decision" based on the Treaty provisions on the common defence and security policy (formerly Art. 17(1) EU; now Art. 43 et seq. TEU)—the only exception being the launch of Operation EUFOR RD Congo by Council Decision 2006/412/CFSP of June 12, 2006, which was based solely on Council Joint Action 2006/319/CFSP of April 27, 2006 (n. 204, *supra*). See further Stewart, "Capabilities and coherence? The evolution of European Union Conflict Prevention" (2008) E.For.Aff.Rev. 229–253 ; Benoit, "Le lancement des premières opérations militaires de l'Union européenne" (2004) R.M.C.U.E. 235–240; Solana, "Politique européenne de sécurité et de défense: de l'opérationnalité aux opérations" (2003) R.M.C.U.E. 148–150.

[215] See Council Joint Action 2008/550/CFSP of June 23, 2008 establishing a European Security and Defence College (ESDC) and repealing Joint Action 2005/575/CFSP [2008] O.J. L176/20.

[216] Conclusions of the Presidency of the European Council held in Helsinki on December 10–11, 1999 (1999) 12 EU Bull. point I.9.28; see also Annex IV thereto. The European Council declared this capacity to be partially operational in the conclusions of the European Council held in Laeken on December 14–15, 2001 (2001) 12 EU Bull. point I.28 (Annex II).

[217] Presidency Report on strengthening of the common European policy on security and defence, Annex III to the Presidency conclusions of the European Council held in Cologne on June 3 and 4, 1999 (1999) 6 EU Bull. point I.62. For the necessary arrangements with NATO, see para. 25–047, *infra*.

[218] Council Joint Action 2004/551/CFSP of July 12, 2004, on the establishment of the European Defence Agency, [2004] O.J. L245/17. The full name of the European Defence Agency is "Agency in the field of defence capabilities development, research, acquisition and armaments" (*ibid.*, Art. 1; Art. 42(3), second subpara., TEU). It has its own legal personality and is based in Brussels.

Defence Agency is to identify operational requirements, to promote measures to satisfy those requirements, to contribute to identifying and, where appropriate, implementing any measure needed to strengthen the industrial and technological base of the defence sector, and to participate in defining a European capabilities and armaments policy. It is to assist the Council in evaluating the improvement of military capabilities (Art. 42(3), second subpara., TEU). Article 45(1) TEU sets out a detailed list of the tasks of the European Defence Agency. The European Defence Agency is open to participation by all Member States wishing to be part of it. It operates under the authority of the Council and carries out its tasks in liaison with the Commission where necessary (Art. 45(1) and (2) TEU).

Permanent structured cooperation. For those Member States whose military capabilities fulfil higher criteria and which have made more binding commitments to one another in this area with a view to carrying out the most demanding missions, the Lisbon Treaty created a framework for establishing "permanent structured cooperation".[219] Within this framework the Council adopts decision and recommendations by unanimity, but taking into account the votes of the representatives of the participating Member States only (Art. 46(6) TEU).

    25–045

Permanent structured cooperation is open to Member States which fulfil the criteria and have made the commitments on military capabilities set out in a Protocol annexed to the Treaties.[220] Member States wishing to participate in permanent structured cooperation have to notify their intention to the Council and to the High Representative. Within three months following the notification, the Council, acting by a qualified majority after consulting the High Representative, adopts a decision establishing permanent structured cooperation and determining the list of participating Member States (Art. 46(1)—(2) TEU). Any Member State who, at a later stage, wishes to participate in the permanent structured cooperation is to notify its intention to the Council and the High Representative. If that Member State fulfils all the criteria,[221] the Council adopts a decision confirming that Member State's participation, by a qualified majority (of the already participating Member States) and after consulting the High Representative (Art. 46(3) TEU). If a participating Member State no longer fulfils the criteria or is no longer able to meet the commitments set out in the Protocol, the Council, acting by a

---

See the website of the Agency: *http://eda.europa.eu/* [Accessed December 15, 2010]. Cooperation in the field of armaments has existed since 1996 in the context of the Western European Armament Group. See also the common list of military equipment covered by the European Union code of conduct on arms export of June 8, 1998 (e.g. the version adopted on March 10, 2008, [2008] O.J. C98/1), based on the list drawn up by the Council pursuant to Art. 346(2) TFEU [*ex Art. 296(2) EC*] (see para. 12–011, *supra*).

[219] Art. 42(6) and Art. 46 TEU.

[220] Protocol (No. 10), annexed to the TEU and TFEU, on permanent structured cooperation established by Art. 42 of the Treaty on European Union, [2010] O.J. C83/275.

[221] Article 46(3) TEU refers to the commitments mentioned in Arts 1 and 2 of the Protocol on permanent structured cooperation (see preceding n.).

THE EXTERNAL POWERS OF THE UNION

qualified majority in accordance with Art. 238(3)(a) TFEU, may adopt a decision suspending the participation of the Member State concerned (Art. 46(4) TEU). Any participating Member State may withdraw from permanent structured cooperation after notifying its intention to the Council, which shall take note that the Member State in question has ceased to participate (Art. 46(5) TEU).

D. SPECIAL STATUS OF CERTAIN MEMBER STATES

25–046 **Non-participation.** The policy of the Union must not prejudice the specific character of the security and defence policy of certain Member States (Art. 42(2), second subpara., TEU).[222] At the same time, the CFSP decision-making procedure allows Member States to make a formal declaration that they abstain in a given vote. They will then not be obliged to apply the relevant decision (Art. 31(1) TEU, see para. 18–002). Ever since the introduction of the CFSP in 1993, Denmark has made clear that it does not participate in the elaboration and implementation of decisions and actions of the Union which have defence implications, in particular the common security and defence policy (CSDP). That position is now laid down in a specific protocol to the Treaties.[223]

25–047 **NATO.** As mentioned above, for those States which are members of NATO, that organisation is to remain the foundation of their collective defence and the forum for its implementation. The CSDP must respect the obligations of certain Member States under NATO and be compatible with the policy established within that framework (Art. 42(2), second subpara., TEU).[224] This means that a CSDP action could

---

[222] For example, in a Declaration (No. 35), annexed to the 2003 Act of Accession, Malta emphasises its neutrality.

[223] Article 5 of Protocol (No. 22), annexed to the TEU and TFEU, on the position of Denmark ([2010] O.J. C83/299), replacing the Protocol on the position of Denmark, annexed to the EC Treaty and EU Treaty by the Amsterdam Treaty, which itself confirmed Part C of the Decision of the Heads of State and Government, meeting within the European Council, concerning certain problems raised by Denmark on the Treaty on European Union ([1992] O.J. C348/2). See Howarth, "The Compromise on Denmark and the Treaty on European Union: A Legal and Political Analysis" (1994) C.M.L.Rev. 765, at 776–779. Pursuant to those protocols, Denmark is not participating, e.g., in the European Union's military operations in Bosnia and Herzegovina (ALTHEA) and off the Somali coast (ATALANTA) or in Congo (see recital 19 in the preamble to Council Joint Action 2004/570/CFSP of July 12, 2004 and recital 6 in the preamble to Council Joint Action 2008/851/CFSP, n. 203 and 206, *supra*). For further applications, see Denmark's declarations relating to Council Decision 96/670/CFSP of November 22, 1996 on the implementation of a Joint Action by the Union in the Great Lakes Region ([1996] O.J. L312/3) and to Council Decision 98/547/CFSP of September 22, 1998 on the study of the feasibility of international police operations to assist the Albanian authorities, [1998] O.J. L263/1.

[224] For the North Atlantic Treaty (Washington Treaty), see para. 1–011, *supra*. See McLaren, "Europe's efforts to develop an autonomous defense capability, a constitution for Europe, and the implications for NATO" (2005) 11 Col.J.E.L. 523–556; Österdahl, "The EU and its Member States, Other States and International Organisations—The Common European Security and Defence Policy After Nice" (2001) Nordic J.I.L. 341–372; Kintis, "NATO-WEU: An Enduring Relationship" (1998) E.For.Aff.Rev. 537–562.

not be directed against a Member State of NATO.[225] There are to be permanent and continuing consultations with the non-EU European allies, covering the full range of security, defence and crisis management issues, in particular before decisions are taken on matters affecting their security interests.[226] Non-EU European allies may participate in an operation conducted by the EU for which NATO assets are deployed and should be invited to take part in operations conducted by the EU where no NATO assets are to be used.[227] The European Union aims to have a strategic partnership with NATO on the basis of which the two organisations may collaborate in crisis management while retaining their independence of decision-making. This collaboration is founded upon "permanent arrangements" between the EU and NATO.[228] These "Berlin plus" arrangements give the EU assured access to NATO's planning and logistics capabilities for its own military operations.[229]

Enhanced cooperation. The Treaties allow the Member States to establish enhanced cooperation between them in the field of the CFSP, under a procedure which is slightly different from that applicable in other fields (see para. 19–008).[230] Before the Lisbon Treaty, Art. 17(4) EU expressly provided for the development of closer cooperation between two or more Member States on a bilateral level, "in the framework of the WEU and the Atlantic Alliance", provided that such cooperation did not impede cooperation within the Union. In this way, France and the Federal Republic of Germany set up a Franco-German brigade, with headquarters in Strasbourg, as long ago as January 12, 1989. Subsequently, Belgium, Luxembourg and Spain joined this "Eurocorps", in which national units are placed under a common command. As already mentioned, the Lisbon Treaty went as far as to

25–048

---

[225] See the conclusions of the European Council held in Brussels on October 24 and 25, 2002 (2002) 10 EU Bull. point I.15, section 2.

[226] *Ibid.*, point I.15, ss. 3 to 5.

[227] *Ibid.*, point I.15, ss. 11 and 15. Accordingly, third countries have been invited to participate in the military operations of the European Union pursuant to agreements concluded on the basis of Art. 24 EU (now Art. 37 TFEU), see, e.g., the agreement between the European Union and Croatia on the participation of Croatia in the European Union military operation in the Republic of Chad and in the Central African Republic, concluded by Council Decision 2008/783/CFSP of September 15, 2008, [2008] O.J. L268/32, and the agreement between the European Union and the USA on the participation of the USA in the European Union Rule of Law Mission in Kosovo, concluded by Council Decision 2008/814/CFSP of October 13, 2008, [2008] O.J. L282/32.

[228] These arrangements are to be found in the joint declaration by the European Union and NATO of December 16, 2002 on the European Security and Defence policy (see NATO Press Release (2002) 142, available on the NATO website). NATO also concluded an agreement with the European Union on the security of information, based on Art. 24 EU (approved by Council Decision 2003/211/CFSP of February 24, 2003, [2003] O.J. L80/35).

[229] The terms "Berlin plus" refer to the ministerial meeting of the North Atlantic Council on June 3, 1996 in Berlin where it was agreed that a European Security and Defence Identity should be built within NATO. The European Council welcomed the "Berlin Plus" arrangements in the conclusions of its meeting held in Thessaloniki on June 19 and 20, 2003 (2003) 6 EU Bull. point I.23, s. 60.

[230] This was made possible by the Treaty of Nice. However, under Arts 27a to 27e EU such cooperation was not possible for matters having military or defence implications (see para. 9–007).

organise a form of enhanced cooperation by setting out the conditions for "permanent structured cooperation" between Member States (see para. 25–045).

VII. RESTRICTIVE MEASURES

25–049   **Initial way of action.** Where the Union wishes to act internationally by adopting sanctions or "restrictive measures", both CFSP and other Union powers come into play. The status under Union law of such sanctions has completely changed over the years. Initially, a decision to impose (what was then called) "economic sanctions" on a third country came to be discussed only at meetings of the Foreign Ministers under the auspices of EPC. The sanctions were then adopted at the national level as an exercise of the exceptional power provided for in Art. 297 EC [*now Art. 347 TFEU*].[231] It was not until 1982 that the Council accepted that the Union (then the Community) could adopt economic sanctions itself pursuant to its powers under the common commercial policy,[232] although not all the Member States supported this view.[233] Except where economic sanctions were adopted pursuant to a resolution of the UN Security Council, such Community measures were generally preceded by a decision taken in the context of EPC.[234]

---

[231] See the Council's answer of March 17, 1976 to question 526/75 (Patijn), [1976] O.J. C89/6; compare the Commission's answer of March 15, 1976 to question 527/75 (Patijn), which did not rule out a Community power (*ibid.*, C 89, p. 8). In this way, the Member States imposed sanctions against Rhodesia between 1966 and 1974, Iran in 1980 and South Africa in 1985–1986 (supplemented by two Community measures: an ECSC import ban and an EEC regulation). See Raux, "Les sanctions de la Communauté européenne et des Etats membres contre l'Afrique du Sud pour cause d'apartheid" (1989) R.M.C. 33–34; and a number of case studies in (1984) B.T.I.R. 150–245; Petersmann, "Internationale Wirtschaftssanktionen als Problem des Völkerrechts und des Europarechts" (1981) Z.Vgl.RW. 1–28; Schröder, "Wirtschaftssanktionen der Europäischen Gemeinschaften gegenüber Drittstaaten, dargestellt am Beispiel des Iran-Embargos" (1980) G.Y.I.L. 111–125.

[232] In this way, the EEC imposed sanctions against the USSR on account of the situation in Poland (1992), against Argentina on account of its occupation of the Falklands (1982), against South Africa (1986), against Iraq (1990), against Libya (1992), against Yugoslavia and, subsequently, against the Republics of Serbia and Montenegro (from 1991) and against Haiti (1993).

[233] Thus, some Member States declared, on the occasion of the extension of the sanctions against Argentina, that they would not implement the sanctions domestically (relying on Art. 297 EC [*now Art. 347 TFEU*]) or would prolong them by means of national measures. See Kuyper, "Community Sanctions against Argentina: Lawfulness under Community and International Law" in O'Keeffe and Schermers (eds), *Essays in European Law and Integration* (Deventer, Kluwer, 1982), at 142 and 149–151; Verhoeven, "Sanctions internationales et Communautés européennes. A propos des îles Falklands (Malvinas)" (1984) C.D.E. 259–290.

[234] UN Security Council resolutions required sanctions to be adopted against Rhodesia, Iraq, Libya, Yugoslavia and Haiti. For an inquiry into the relationship between those resolutions and the Community sanctions adopted in order to implement them, see Angelet, "La mise en oeuvre des mesures coercitives économiques des Nations-Unies dans la Communauté européenne" (1993) B.T.I.R. 500, at 501–517. See also Stein, "European Political Cooperation (EPC) as a Component of the European Foreign Affairs System" (1993) Z.a.ö.RV. 49–69; Vaucher, "L'évolution récente de la pratique des sanctions communautaires à l'encontre des Etats tiers" (1993) R.T.D.E. 39–59.

Current procedure. Since the entry into force of the EU Treaty (1993), sanctions   **25–050**
generally come under the CFSP (see now TEU, Title V). Typically, such sanctions
take the form of arms embargoes, economic or financial sanctions, including
"smart" sanctions such as the freezing of assets of specific persons and entities,
and restrictions on the admission into the EU of certain third-country nationals.
Sometimes, sanctions agreed under the CFSP may be carried out directly by the
Member States.[235] Frequently, however, a CFSP sanction has to be implemented by
a Union measure in another field of Union competence, such as the common commercial policy or police and judicial cooperation in criminal matters.[236] Article
215(1) TFEU [*ex Art. 301 EC*] states·that where a CFSP decision provides for "the
interruption or reduction, in part or completely, of economic and financial relations
with one or more third countries", the Council is to adopt the necessary measures.
In this connection, the Council acts on a proposal from the High Representative and
needs to inform the European Parliament of the measures adopted. Likewise, where
a CFSP decision so provides, the Council, acting under the same procedure, may
adopt restrictive measures against natural or legal persons and groups or non-State
entities (Art. 215(2) TFEU; introduced by the Lisbon Treaty).

Article 215 TFEU enables the Council to adopt restrictive measures where
it is "provided" in a CFSP act. This will be the case where the Council adopts a
decision under Title V of the TEU pursuant to a superior international obligation,
that is to say, binding resolutions of the UN Security Council. The Council first
adopts an act pursuant to Title V of the TEU, which is then further implemented
by the Union.[237] The fact that the Union is bound to act in this context does not

---

[235] See, e.g., the sanctions imposed pursuant to a UN Security Council resolution against Nigeria by
Common Positions of November 20, 1995 (95/515/CFSP), [1995] O.J. L298/1, and December 4,
1995 (95/544/CFSP), [1995] O.J. L309/1 (restrictions on visas for, e.g., members of the
Government and their families, sports boycott and arms embargo). For the implementation of sanc-
tions in the Netherlands, see Wijmenga, "Internationale sanctieregimes en de gewijzigde
Sanctiewet 1997" (2002) S.E.W. 42–51.

[236] E.g., Council Decision 2003/48/JHA of December 19, 2002 on the implementation of specific
measures for police and judicial cooperation to combat terrorism in accordance with Art. 4 of
Common Position 2001/931/CFSP, [2003] O.J. L16/68. See in this connection Hörmann, "Die
Befugnis der EG zur Umsetzung von Resolutionen des UN-Sicherheitsrates zur Bekämpfung des
internationalen Terrorismus" (2007) EuR. 121–133.

[237] Before the Lisbon Treaty, CFSP acts in this connection took the form of a common position which
used to be based on Art. 15 [*formerly Art. J.2*] EU [*see now Art. 29 TEU*]. See, e.g., with regard
to Burma/Myanmar, Council Common Position 2000/346/CFSP of April 26, 2000, based on
Art. 15 EU, and the connected Council Regulation (EC) No. 1081/2000 of May 22, 2000 based on
Arts 60 and 301 EC ([2000] O.J. L122/1 and L122/29, respectively). Similar CFSP/EC sanctions
were also adopted with regard to Libya (from 1993), Sudan (1994), Haiti (1994), the Federal
Republic of Yugoslavia (Serbia and Montenegro) (from 1995), Iraq (from 1996), UNITA in
Angola (from 1997), Sierra Leone (from 1997), Afghanistan (from 2000), Liberia (from 2001),
Zimbabwe and Somalia (from 2002), the Transnistrian region of the Moldovan Republic (from
2003), Belarus (from 2004), Bosnia and Herzegovina (since 2004), Croatia (since 2004), Congo
(since 2005), Ivory Coast (from 2005), Lebanon (since 2005), Syria (since 2005), North Korea
(since 2006), Iran (since 2007), Guinea (since 2009), Eritrea (since 2010) and foreign terrorist
organisations such as Al Qaida and the Taliban (since 2001).

mean that the CFSP act determines the action to be taken by the institutions. It is true that the Commission is bound to propose the "necessary measures" to the Council, but the latter determines what measures it deems necessary.[238]

The Council's competence to adopt restrictive measures in this connection is not confined to measures taken under the common commercial policy, but may also relate to other matters.[239] A very important provision in this regard is Art. 75 TFEU [*ex Art. 60 EC*], which provides for the adoption of,

> "administrative measures with regard to capital movements and payments, such as the freezing of funds, financial assets or economic gains belonging to, or owned or held by, natural or legal persons, groups or non-State entities"

where such is necessary "to achieve the objectives set out in Article 67,[240] as regards preventing and combating terrorism and related activities".[241] The framework for such measures is to be defined by the European Parliament and the Council, acting by means of regulations in accordance with the ordinary legislative procedure; the Council, on a proposal from the Commission, adopts the necessary measures to implement the framework. The Council is to act by a qualified majority, which means that decisions may be adopted that could not be embodied in the CFSP, for which unanimity is required.[242] With regard to measures adopted under Art. 75 TFEU and Art. 215 TFEU, the Treaties explicitly provide that they must include the "necessary provisions on legal safeguards" (see Art. 75, third para., TFEU and Art. 215(3) TFEU, respectively).

Before the Lisbon Treaty, the relevant provisions on restrictive measures by the Community (Art. 60(1) and 301 EC) only explicitly provided for measures to be adopted vis-à-vis "third countries". The ECJ held, however, that Arts 60(1) and 301 EC could serve as a legal basis for the adoption of sanctions not only vis-à-vis third countries, but also vis-à-vis the rulers of such a country and individuals and entities associated with or controlled, directly or indirectly, by them.[243] By

---

[238] Neuwahl, "Foreign and Security Policy and the Implementation of the Requirement of 'Consistency' under the Treaty on European Union" in O'Keeffe and Twomey (eds), *Legal Issues of the Maastricht Treaty* (London, Chancery, 1994, 227), 239.

[239] In this way, the Council prohibited the satisfaction of claims with regard to contracts and transactions, the performance of which was affected by sanctions imposed by the UN Security Council against Iraq (by Regulation (EEC) No. 3541/92 of December 7, 1992, [1992] O.J. L361/1) and against Libya (by Regulation (EC) No. 3275/93 of November 29, 1993, [1993] O.J. L295/4).

[240] Article 67 TFEU sets out the general objectives of the Union in connection with the "area of freedom, security and justice" (see para. 10–009).

[241] For applications of this provision, see n. 237, *supra*.

[242] For the sanctions procedure, see Auvret-Finck, "Les procédures de sanction internationale en vigueur dans l'ordre interne de l'Union et la défense des droits de l'homme dans le monde" (2003) R.T.D.E. 1–21.

[243] ECJ, Joined Cases C-402/05 P and C-415/05 P *Kadi and Al Barakaat International Foundation v Council and Commission* [2008] E.C.R. I-6351, paras 163–166.

contrast, they were not a valid legal basis for measures directed at persons or entities present in a third country or associated with them in the absence of any link to the governing regime of that country.[244] Such measures could be adopted, however, if the legal basis of Arts 60(1) and 301 EC was supplemented by Art. 308 EC [*now Art. 352 TFEU*].[245] The Lisbon Treaty for the first time introduced an explicit power to adopt restrictive measures against natural or legal persons and groups or non-State entities.

Before the Lisbon Treaty, the Union Courts reviewed the legality of restrictive measures implemented by Community measures, inter alia as to their compatibility with fundamental rights and procedural safeguards, but did not have jurisdiction to rule on CFSP acts providing for such restrictive measures to be taken in the first place.[246] Since the Lisbon Treaty, the Court of Justice of the European Union has jurisdiction to review the legality of CFSP decisions taken in this connection insofar as they provide for restrictive measures against natural or legal persons (see para. 13–086).

Scope of Union measures. Article 215 TFEU does not prevent the Union from imposing sanctions which go further than "the necessary measures" on the basis of some other power-conferring provision. For instance, Union sanctions may still be based on Art. 207 TFEU [*ex Art. 133 EC*]. The Council does not first have to adopt a decision under Title V of the TEU in order to adopt such sanctions.[247] Trade not subject to the Union sanctions remains subject to the general rules on exports (see para. 25–007).   25–051

Action by Member States. At the same time, a Member State retains the power under Art. 347 TFEU [*ex Art. 297 EC*] to take measures "in order to carry out obligations it has accepted for the purpose of maintaining peace and international security". Article 347 TFEU requires Member States to "consult each other" in this connection in order to prevent the functioning of the internal market from being affected. Since the entry into force of the EU Treaty, that obligation coincides with CFSP commitments (see para. 12–011). Only if sanctions imposed by a UN Security Council resolution were not implemented either by a CFSP act or   25–052

---

[244] *Ibid.*, paras 167–178.
[245] *Ibid.*, paras 194–236.
[246] See, for instance, the judgments in ECJ, Joined Cases C-402/05 P and C-415/05 P *Kadi and Al Barakaat International Foundation v Council and Commission* [2008] E.C.R. I-6351; CFI, Case T-341/07 *Sison v Council* [2009] E.C.R. II-3625; CFI, Case T-256/07 *People's Mojahedin Organization of Iran v Council* [2008] E.C.R. II-03019. See De Hert and Weis, "Terrorismelijsten en de paradox van de rechtsbescherming" (2009) S.E.W. 336–342; Almqvist, "A human rights critique of European judicial review: counter-terrorism sanctions" (2008) 57 I.C.L.Q. 303–331; Schmahl, "Effektiver Rechtsschutz gegen "targeted sanctions" des UN-Sicherheitsrats" (2006) EuR. 566–576. See further the (abundant) literature on the *Kadi*-case referred to in para. 22–057, *supra*.
[247] Gilsdorf, "Les réserves de sécurité du traité CEE, à la lumière du traité sur l'Union européenne" (1994) R.M.C.U.E. 17, at 25.

by other Union action within the prescribed period would a Member State be entitled to rely on Art. 347 TFEU in order to implement the resolution itself. On these lines, the Court of Justice has held that, in exercising their national competence to take measures of foreign and security policy, Member States must respect the rules of the common commercial policy.[248]

VIII. OTHER EXTERNAL POWERS OF THE UNION

A. EXTERNAL ASPECTS OF INTERNAL RULES

25–053 **External aspects.** Union rules have external aspects where they are applicable to nationals of third countries or to situations which are partly connected with such countries. Thus, free movement of goods is applicable to goods from third countries which are in free circulation in the Member States (Arts 28(2) and 29 TFEU); the Council adopts, with regard to third-country nationals, measures concerning border checks, asylum and immigration (Arts 77 to 80 TFEU); and the Union is empowered to lay down rules on international transport to or from Member States (Art. 91(1)(a) TFEU). The common organisations of the agricultural markets not only regulate Union production but also establish an import regime to stabilise the markets and ensure sales of Union production.[249] Measures liberalising free movement of workers, the right of establishment and free movement of services within the internal market also have implications for nationals of non-Union countries wishing to work, establish themselves or provide services in a Member State.[250]

B. INTERNATIONAL AGREEMENTS BASED ON INTERNAL POWERS

25–054 **Explicit treaty-making power.** In some cases, the Treaties expressly empower the Union to conclude international agreements. The agreements in question are first those already mentioned concerning the common commercial policy (Art. 207 TFEU), development cooperation (Art. 209(2), first subpara., TFEU; see para. 25–033); economic, financial and technical cooperation with third countries (Art. 212(3), first subpara., TFEU), humanitarian aid (Art. 214(4), first subpara., TFEU) and association agreements (Art. 217 TFEU). In addition, the Union is empowered to conclude agreements on the re-admission of third-country nationals to their countries of origin or provenance (Art. 79(3) TFEU),[251] on research and technological development

---

[248] ECJ, Case C-124/95 *Centro-Com* [1997] E.C.R. I-81, para. 27.

[249] See ECJ, Case C-280/93 *Germany v Council* [1994] E.C.R. I-4973, para. 55.

[250] See, for example, the measures with regard to freedom of establishment and freedom to provide services enumerated in ECJ, Opinion 1/94 *Agreement establishing the World Trade Organisation* [1994] E.C.R. I-5267, paras 90–94.

[251] This provision was added by the Lisbon Treaty. However, even before the Lisbon Treaty, the Union (then the Community) had already concluded agreements with third countries on immigration, on the basis of Art. 63 EC. See, e.g., the Agreements concluded between the Community (with the

(Art. 186, second para., TFEU),[252] on the environment (Art. 191(4), first subpara., TFEU)[253] and on an exchange-rate system for the euro in relation to non-Union currencies (Art. 219(1) TFEU).[254] Besides, the Treaties expressly empower the Union to conclude agreements with neighbouring countries (Art. 8(2) TEU) and to conclude agreements relating to the CFSP (Art. 37 TEU). The Union can exercise these external competences even in respect of matters which are not yet the subject of rules at Union level.[255] In these areas, both the Union and the Member States may cooperate with third countries or international organisations (see Arts 191(4), first subpara., 209(2), first subpara., 212(3), first subpara., and 214(4), first subpara., TFEU). The Union's competence in this regard does not detract from the Member States' own powers to negotiate in international fora and conclude international agreements (see Arts 191(4), second subpara., 209(2), second subpara., 212(3), second subpara., 214(4), second subpara., and 219(4) TFEU),[256] although Union action will reduce

---

exception of Denmark, as far as the first agreement is concerned; with the exception of both Denmark and Ireland, as far as the second is concerned) and the Government of the Hong Kong Special Administrative Region of the People's Republic of China (PRC) and the Macao Special Administrative Region of the PRC on the readmission of persons residing without authorisation, approved by Council Decision 2004/80/EC of December 17, 2003 ([2004] O.J. L17/23) and 2004/424/EC of April 21, 2004 ([2004] O.J. L143/97), respectively; and the Memorandum of Understanding between the European Community (with the exception of Denmark, Ireland and United Kingdom) and the National Tourism Administration of the PRC on visa and related issues concerning tourist groups from the PRC ([2004] O.J. L83/12).

[252] See, for example, the Agreement on scientific and technical cooperation between the European Community and the State of Israel, approved by Council Decision 2004/576/EC of April 29, 2004, [2004] O.J. L261/47.

[253] See, e.g., Council Decision 2005/370/EC of February 17, 2005 on the conclusion, on behalf of the European Community, of the Convention on access to information, public participation in decision-making and access to justice in environmental matters, [2005] O.J. L124/1 (Aarhuus Convention), further implemented by Regulation No. 1367/2006 of the European Parliament and of the Council of September 6, 2006, [2006] O.J. L264/13; Council Decision 2006/500/EC of May 29, 2006 on the conclusion by the European Community of the Energy Community Treaty, [2006] O.J. L198/15. See Thieme, "European Community External Relations in the Field of the Environment" (2001) E.Env.L.Rev. 252–264.

[254] See the literature cited in n. 42 to para. 24–008.

[255] ECJ, Case C-459/03 *Commission v Ireland* [2006] E.C.R. I-4635, paras 94–95.

[256] See also Declaration (No. 36), annexed to the Lisbon Treaty, on Art. 218 TFEU concerning the negotiation and conclusion of international agreements by Member States relating to the area of freedom, security and justice ([2010] O.J. C83/349), in which the Intergovernmental Conference of 2007 confirms that Member States may negotiate and conclude agreements with third countries or international organisations in the areas covered by Chs 3, 4 and 5 of Title V of Part Three ("in so far as such agreements comply with Union law") and Declarations (No. 13) and (No. 14), annexed to the Lisbon Treaty, concerning the common foreign and security policy ([2010] O.J. C83/343), in which the Conference underlines that the Treaty provisions on CFSP do not affect the "existing legal basis", "responsibilities" and "powers" of the Member States in relation to the formulation and conduct of their foreign policy, their relationship with third countries and participation in international organisations.

the scope for action on behalf of the Member States, in view of the principle of primacy.[257]

Even when a Treaty provision does not expressly confer on the Union the power to conclude an international agreement in a given area, such power may be provided for in a legally binding Union act (see Art. 216(1) TFEU). This is the case where a Union measure (legislative or non-legislative) confers on Union institutions the power to negotiate arrangements with third countries or international organisations.[258]

25–055 **Implied treaty-making power.** The Union may conclude international agreements not only in those cases where the Treaties or a legally binding Union act so provide, but also,

> "where the conclusion of an agreement is necessary in order to achieve, within the framework of the Union's policies, one of the objectives referred to in the Treaties [. . .] or is likely to affect common rules or alter their scope" (Art. 216(1) TFEU).

This Treaty provision, which was introduced by the Lisbon Treaty, codifies the external powers which—according to long-standing case law of the Court of Justice—flow implicitly from the Treaties and secondary Union law.

The Court of Justice has long held that

> "authority to enter into international commitments may not only arise from an express attribution by the [Treaties], but may also flow implicitly from [their] provisions. The Court [has] concluded, in particular, that whenever [Union] law created for the institutions of the [Union] powers within its internal system for the purpose of attaining a specific objective, the [Union] [has] authority to enter into the international commitments necessary for the attainment of that objective even in the absence of an express provision in that connection".[259]

It followed from this case law, on the one hand, that such external authority flows by implication from measures adopted by the institutions in so far as it is necessary to secure the effectiveness of those measures.[260] The Court of Justice held accordingly

---

[257] With regard to exchange-rate questions, see the authorisations conferred on Member States pursuant to Art. 111(3) EC [*now Art. 219(3) TFEU*] as mentioned in n. 219 to para. 11–040.

[258] ECJ, Opinion 1/94 *Agreement establishing the World Trade Organisation* [1994] E.C.R. I-5267, para. 95.

[259] ECJ, Opinion 2/91 *Convention No. 170 of the International Labour Organisation concerning safety in the use of chemicals at work* [1993] E.C.R. I-1061, para. 7; ECJ, Opinion 2/94 *Accession by the Communities to the Convention for the Protection of Human Rights and Fundamental Freedoms* [1996] I-1759, para. 26.

[260] Opinion 2/91, *ibid.*, para. 7; ECJ, Joined Cases 3, 4 and 6/76 *Kramer* [1976] E.C.R. 1279, para. 19/20.

in the *AETR* judgment that the Union was empowered to accede to an international agreement on working conditions in international road transport on the ground that the Council had adopted a regulation internally on the harmonisation of certain social legislation relating to road transport.[261] Hence, the international agreement in question could affect these rules or alter their scope. This corresponds to the last question mentioned in Art. 216(1) TFEU. On the other hand, it followed from this case law that where a power cannot be effectively exercised without involving third countries, the Union is entitled ipso facto to act externally, even if the first use made of the power is to conclude and implement an international agreement.[262] This was the case with an agreement on a European inland-waterways fund which could not be concluded without involving third countries whose vessels used the waterways in question.[263] In this situation, therefore, the Union has external competence because its internal competence may be exercised effectively only together with an external competence. This corresponds to the situation where an international agreement of the Union is "necessary to achieve, within the framework of the

---

[261] See the *AETR* judgment of March 31, 1971, Case 22/70 *Commission v Council* [1971] E.C.R. 263, paras 16–29 (quoted in para. 7–017, *supra*). For later examples of international competence implicitly arising out of existing Union legislation, see ECJ, Opinion 1/92 *Draft Agreement between the Community, on the one hand, and the countries of the European Free Trade Association, on the other, relating to the creation of the European Economic Area* [1992] E.C.R. I-2821, paras 39–40; ECJ, Opinion 1/94 *Agreement establishing the World Trade Organisation* [1994] E.C.R. I-5267, para. 77. In so far as the judgments of the Court of Justice of November 5, 2002 on the bilateral "open-skies" agreements hold that Union legislation on air transport confers exclusive external competence in respect of some aspects (fares, booking systems and slot allocation) (n. 263, *infra*), this also constitutes recognition of external powers arising for the Union out of internal legislation.

[262] ECJ, Opinion 1/94 *Agreement establishing the World Trade Organisation* [1994] E.C.R. I-5267, paras 82–85; ECJ, Opinion 2/92 *Third Revised Decision of the OECD on national treatment* [1995] E.C.R. I-521, paras 31–32.

[263] See ECJ, Opinion 1/76 *Draft Agreement establishing a European laying-up fund for inland waterway vessels* [1977] E.C.R. 741, para. 4. In Opinion 1/94, the Court of Justice held that such an external power did not exist for the provision of services, in respect of which the rules on freedom of establishment and freedom to provide services are not inextricably bound up with the status of nationals of a third country in the Union or of nationals of a Member State in a third country (Opinion 1/94, para. 85) or for intellectual property, in respect of which harmonisation at Union level does not necessarily have to be accompanied by agreements with third countries in order to be effective (*ibid.*, para. 100). However, the Treaty of Nice extended the common commercial policy to cover certain aspects of trade in services and intellectual property (see para. 20–003). In the judgments of November 5, 2002 on the bilateral "open skies" agreements, the Court of Justice considered that as regards freedom to provide services in the field of air transport, external competence was not necessary in order to effectively exercise internal competence: ECJ, Case C-467/98 *Commission v Denmark* [2002] E.C.R. I-9519, paras 54–64; ECJ, Case C-468/98 *Commission v Sweden* [2002] E.C.R. I-9575, paras 51–61; ECJ, Case C-469/98 *Commission v Finland* [2002] E.C.R. I-9627, paras 55–65; ECJ, Case C-471/98 *Commission v Belgium* [2002] E.C.R. I-9681, paras 65–75; ECJ, Case C-472/98 *Commission v Luxembourg* [2002] E.C.R. I-9741, paras 59–69; ECJ, Case C-475/98 *Commission v Austria* [2002] E.C.R. I-9797, paras 65–75; ECJ, Case C-476/98 *Commission v Germany* [2002] E.C.R. I-9855, paras 80–90 (at the same time the Court of Justice recognised, however, that there was external Union competence on the basis of the *AETR* case law; see ns 150 and 161).

Union's policies, one of the objectives referred to in the Treaties", as mentioned in Art. 216(1) TFEU.

It is implicit in these two situations that there is a limited parallelism between internal and external powers. On the basis of this reasoning, for example, Art. 43 TFEU [*ex Art. 37 EC*] and Art. 91 TFEU [*ex Art. 71 EC*], respectively, constitute the basis for a number of fisheries and transport agreements which the Union has concluded with third countries.[264] The judgment in *AETR* case also underscored that to the extent to which autonomous action on the part of the Member States at international level is likely to detract from Union legislation, the external competence of the Union that arises implicitly from internal legislation constitutes exclusive competence in the sense that it precludes any autonomous action on the part of the Member States (see para. 25–058). This will always be the case in the second situation mentioned above, namely where a power cannot be effectively exercised without external action.[265]

25–056 **Article 352 TFEU.** Furthermore, the Union has an additional power under the Treaties to conclude agreements if it takes "appropriate measures" under Art. 352 TFEU [*ex Art. 308 EC*] where action by the Union proves necessary, within the framework of the policies defined in the Treaties, to attain one of the objectives set out in the Treaties.[266] Article 352 TFEU may, however, be used as a legal basis only if the Treaties have not provided the necessary powers, and hence cannot be employed where the means of acting externally are already present by implication in an internal power.[267] Besides, agreements based on Art. 352 TFEU may

---

[264] For an example of disputes on the definition of external powers, see Close, "External Relations in the Air Transport Sector: Air Transport Policy or the Common Commercial Policy?" (1990) C.M.L.Rev. 107–127. For the external competence in the field of judicial cooperation in civil matters, see van Loon and Schulz, "The European Community and the Hague Conference on Private International Law" in Martenczuk and van Thiel (n. 179, *supra*) 257–301; Thoma, "La définition et l'exercice de compétences externes de la Communauté européenne au domaine de la coopération dans les matières civiles ayant une incidence transfrontalière" (2002) ERPL/REDP 397–416; Kotuby, "External Competence of the European Community in the Hague Conference on Private International Law: Community Harmonisation and Worldwide Unification" (2001) N.I.L.R. 1–30. For the lack of external competence as regards social policy, see Novitz, " 'A Human Face' for the Union or More Cosmetic Surgery? EU Competence in Global Social Governance and Promotion of Core Labour Standards" (2002) M.J.E.C.L. 231–261.

[265] ECJ, Opinion 1/03 *New Lugano Convention on jurisdiction and the recognition and enforcement of judgments in civil and commercial matters* [2006] E.C.R. I-1145, para. 115.

[266] ECJ, Case 22/70 *Commission v Council* [1971] E.C.R. 263, para. 95. See, e.g., already the seven bilateral agreements on cooperation in the field of education and training under the Erasmus Programme concluded between the EEC and Austria, Finland, Iceland, Norway, Sweden, Switzerland and Liechtenstein, respectively, and approved by Council Decisions 91/611/EEC to 91/617/EEC of October 28, 1991 on the basis of Art. 235 EEC [*now Art. 352 TFEU*], [1991] O.J. L332/1–L332/71.

[267] See Kovar, "Les compétences implicites: jurisprudence de la Cour et pratique communautaire", in Demaret (ed.), *Relations extérieures de la Communauté européenne et marché intérieur: aspects juridiques et fonctionnels* (Bruges, College of Europe/Story, 1988), 15, at 22–31; Raux, "Le recours à l'article 235 du traité CEE en vue de la conclusion d'accords externes", *Etudes de droit des Communautés européennes. Mélanges offerts à P.-H. Teitgen* (Paris, Pedone, 1984), 407, at 428.

not lead to the harmonisation of the laws of the Member States where the Treaties exclude such harmonisation (Art. 352(3) TFEU) and recourse to that article is not possible for agreements relating to the CFSP (Art. 352(4) TFEU).

International cooperation. In some areas, the Treaties declare that the Union and the Member States are empowered to foster cooperation with third countries and relevant international organisations without expressly conferring on the Union a power to conclude agreements. Examples are education and sport (Art. 165(3) TFEU [*ex Art. 149(3) EC*]), vocational training (Art. 166(3) TFEU [*ex Art. 150(3) EC*]), culture (Art. 167(3) TFEU [*ex Art. 151(3) EC*]) and public health (Art. 168(3) TFEU [*ex Art. 152(3) EC*]). In such cases, international cooperation may take place via the "(incentive) measures" provided for in the articles in question, which are intended to be consonant with the complementary nature of the powers in question.[268] In the field of trans-European networks, the Union may decide to cooperate with third countries (Art. 171(3) TFEU [*ex Art. 155(3) EC*]) in accordance with the procedure laid down in Art. 172 TFEU [*ex Art. 156 EC*]. In accordance with Art. 216(1) TFEU and the case law referred to above, it is likewise possible to infer a power for the Union to conclude any necessary international agreements in these policy areas.[269]

25–057

C. RELATIONSHIP TO THE MEMBER STATES' INTERNATIONAL POWERS

Pre-emption of national powers. As some Treaty provisions explicitly recognise (see para. 25–054), the Union's non-exclusive external powers do not deprive Member States of the power to act externally. It follows, however, from Art. 4(3) TEU [*see ex Art. 10 EC*] that

25–058

"to the extent to which [Union] rules are promulgated for the attainment of the objectives of the [Treaties], the Member States cannot, outside the framework of the [Union] institutions, assume obligations which might affect those rules or alter their scope" (judgment in the *AETR* case).[270]

---

[268] Flaesch-Mougin, "Le traité de Maastricht et les compétences externes de la Communauté européenne: à la recherche d'une politique externe de l'Union" (1993) C.D.E. 351, at 357–358.

[269] See, e.g., the Agreements, concluded by the Community in 1995 on the basis of Arts 149 and 150 EC [*now Arts 165 and 166 TFEU*], with the USA establishing a cooperation programme in higher education and vocational training, renewed by Council Decision 2001/196/EC of February 26, 2001, [2001] O.J. L71/7 and Council Decision 2006/910/EC of December 4, 2006, [2006] O.J. L346/33. See to this effect, Lenaerts, "Education in European Community Law after Maastricht" (1994) C.M.L.Rev. 7, at 39.

[270] ECJ, Case 22/70 *Commission v Council* [1971] E.C.R. 263, para. 22. In that judgment, the Court of Justice therefore held not only that Union (then Community) competence *existed* (see para. 25–055) but also that the Member States could no longer act in that area and that, as a result, the Union had *exclusive* competence (para. 7–023, *supra*).

This means that Member States retain their powers as long as the Union has not, or only partially, exercised its (non-exclusive) powers.[271] Where, however, the Union adopts a measure internally or internationally, the Member States should attune their international action in the light of that measure.

Since the Lisbon Treaty, the Treaties contain an explicit list of the Union's exclusive competences (see relevant para. 7–020). This list also refers to cases where previous action on the part of the Union may prevent the Member States from acting at the international level on their own. Largely inspired by the case law of the Court of Justice, Art. 3(2) TFEU provides that the Union,

> "shall also have exclusive competence for the conclusion of an international agreement when its conclusion is provided for in a legislative act of the Union or is necessary to enable the Union to exercise its internal competence, or insofar as its conclusion may affect common rules or alter their scope".

First of all, this provision makes clear that whenever a treaty making power is laid down in a Union legislative act, that power excludes the Member States' power to start negotiations on the same subject-matter.[272] Second, Art. 3(2) TFEU refers to the above-mentioned implied treaty-making powers by indicating that such powers exclude parallel Member State action when the conclusion of an international agreement is "necessary to enable the Union to exercise its internal competence" or "may affect common rules or alter their scope" (see para. 25–055). It follows from the Court's case law on Union rules liable to be "affected" or "altered" that Member States are no longer competent to conclude an international agreement where doing so would affect the uniform and consistent application of Union rules and the proper functioning of the system which they establish. By the same token, a Member State is debarred from submitting a proposal within an international organisation which is likely to affect the application of Union legislation in that field.[273] To determine whether Union rules are affected, account must be taken not only of the area covered by the Union rules and by the provisions of the envisaged agreement or action, but also of the nature and content of those rules

---

[271] See, for example, ECJ, Opinion 1/94 *Agreement establishing the World Trade Organisation* [1994] E.C.R. I-5267, paras 88–89 and 101–105; see Van Nuffel (n. 11, *supra*), at 348–351. See Maubernard, "L'intensité modulable' des compétences externes de la Communauté européenne et de ses Etats membres" (2003) R.T.D.E. 229–246. There is an exception where the internal Union power can only be exercised effectively together with the external power (see para. 25–055).

[272] Whereas the Union has treaty-making power whenever such power is conferred upon Union institutions in a legally binding Union act (see Art. 216(1) TFEU), that power thus constitutes an exclusive Union power only where it is laid down in a "legislative" act, that is an act adopted according to a legislative procedure.

[273] ECJ, Case C-45/07 *Commission v Greece* [2009] E.C.R. I-701, paras 20–23; ECJ (judgment of April 20, 2010), Case C-246/07 *Commission v Sweden*, not yet reported, paras 92–105.

and those provisions.[274] For instance, a Member State may not enter into international commitments falling within an area which is already largely covered by Union rules, even if there is no contradiction between those commitments and the Union rules.[275] Accordingly, the Court considered that a number of bilateral agreements relating to access to air transport ("open skies" agreements) between individual Member States, on the one hand, and the United States, on the other hand, were concluded in breach of Union law because they were contrary to Union legislation on fares and booking systems.[276] To determine whether Member States retain the power to enter into international commitments, account must also be taken of the nature of the Union rules concerned, in particular whether they contain clauses relating to the treatment of nationals of third countries[277] or to the complete harmonisation of a particular issue.[278] Union rules will not be affected by action on the part of the Member States where the Union has adopted only

---

[274] ECJ, Opinion 1/03 (n. 265, *supra*), paras 114–133, with a note by Kruger in (2006) Col.J.E.L, 189–199 and Lavranos in (2006) C.M.L.Rev. 1087–1100. See also Kuijper, "The Opinion on the Lugano Convention and the Implied Externnal relations Power of the European Community" in Martenczuk and van Thiel (n. 179, *supra*) 187–210.

[275] ECJ, Opinion 2/92 *Third Revised Decision of the OECD on national treatment* [1995] E.C.R. I-521, paras 33–36; ECJ, Opinion 2/00 *Cartagena Protocol* [2001] E.C.R. I-9713, paras 45–47.

[276] See the judgments of November 5, 2002: ECJ, Case C-467/98 *Commission v Denmark* [2002] E.C.R. I-9519, paras 75–112; ECJ, Case C-468/98 *Commission v Sweden* [2002] E.C.R. I-9575, paras 71–108; ECJ, Case C-469/98 *Commission v Finland* [2002] E.C.R. I-9627, paras 75–113; ECJ, Case C-471/98 *Commission v Belgium* [2002] E.C.R. I-9681, paras 88–126; ECJ, Case C-472/98 *Commission v Luxembourg* [2002] E.C.R. I-9741, paras 81–118; ECJ, Case C-475/98 *Commission v Austria* [2002] E.C.R. I-9797, paras 88–126; ECJ, Case C-476/98 *Commission v Germany* [2002] E.C.R. I-9855, paras 101–137. At the same time, the Court of Justice held that there had been an infringement of Art. 43 EC [*now Art. 49 TFEU*] concerning establishment in those judgments and in ECJ, Case 466/98 *Commission v United Kingdom* [2003] E.C.R. I-9427. See, similarly, the more recent judgment in ECJ, Case C-523/04 *Commission v Netherlands* [2007] E.C.R. I-3267, with a case note by Lykotrafiti in (2007) E.Comp.L.Rev. 28 578–583. For those judgments, see Franklin, "Flexibility vs. Legal Certainty: Article 307 EC and Other Issues in the Aftermath of the Open Skies Cases", (2005) E.For.Aff.Rev. 79–115; Heffernan and McAuliffe, "External relations in the air transport sector: the Court of Justice and the open skies agreements" (2003) E.L.Rev. 601–619; Slot and Dutheil de la Rochère (2003) C.M.L.Rev. 697–713. Open skies agreements with individual Member States were replaced by an Air Transport Agreement between the European Communities and its Member States, on the one hand, and the USA, on the other hand, [2007] O.J. L134/1. The agreement has not yet entered into force, but provisionally applies as from March 30, 2008 (see Art. 25 of the Agreement). See Grard, "'Ciel ouvert' entre l'Union européenne et les États Unis enfin! Déjà? Bientôt . . ." (2009) R.M.C.U.E. 145–153; Mendes de Leon, "De luchtvaart-overeenkomst tussen de EG en de VS van 2008: Les jeux ne sont pas encore faits" (2009) S.E.W. 236–243.

[277] ECJ, Case C-467/98 *Commission v Denmark* [2002] E.C.R. I-9519, para. 83 (and the parallel judgments in the "open skies" cases). In addition the Court referred to the situation where the Community expressly conferred on its institutions powers to negotiate with third countries (*ibid.*).

[278] ECJ, Opinion 1/94 (n. 11, *supra*), paras 95–96; ECJ, Case C-467/98 *Commission v Denmark* [2002] E.C.R. I-9519, para. 84

minimum requirements in the relevant field.[279] It is necessary to take into account not only the current state of Union law in the area in question but also its future development, insofar as that it is foreseeable at the time of that analysis.[280]

The upshot is that the extent of the Member States' international competence depends on whether or not the Union has exercised its internal and external powers exhaustively (principle of *pre-emption*).[281] The Member States have recognised this consequence of the judgment in the *AETR* case, even in those areas where the Treaties confirm in principle their international competence.[282] In this sense, the allocation of external powers as between the Union and the Member States changes with the intensity with which the Union exercises the power relating to the field in question. Member States cannot avoid the consequences of the principle of pre-emption by providing for mechanisms to avoid contradictions between Union law and the agreement envisaged; the absence of any conflict between Union rules and the agreement envisaged does not rule out that Union rules are affected by the agreement, and hence that Member States no longer have competence to conclude it.[283] That may be different only in those areas of shared competence mentioned in Arts 4(3) and 4(4) TFEU (research, technological development, space, development cooperation and humanitarian aid) for which the TFEU provides that "the exercise of that competence shall not result in Member States being prevented from exercising theirs".

However, even where the Union is exclusively competent, it may authorise a Member State to conclude international agreements diverging from Union measures.[284]

---

[279] ECJ, Opinion 2/91 *Convention No 170 of the International Labour Organisation concerning safety in the use of chemicals at work* [1993] E.C.R. I-1061, paras 18–21; case notes by Emiliou (1994) E.L.Rev. 76–86 and Timmermans (1994) S.E.W. 622–627

[280] ECJ, Opinion 2/91 (n. 279 *supra*), paras 25–26; ECJ, Opinion 1/03 (n. 265, *supra*), para. 126.

[281] By the same token, Protocol (No. 23), annexed by the Lisbon Treaty to the TEU and TFEU, on external relations of the Member States with regard to the crossing of external borders ([2010] O.J. C83/304), which replaces the corresponding Protocol (No. 11), annexed to the EC Treaty by the Amsterdam Treaty), confirms that Member States have competence to conclude agreements with third countries "as long as they respect Union law and other relevant international agreements". See also Declaration (No. 36) on Art. 218 TFEU (n. 256, supra). For the operation of "pre-emption", see already Lenaerts, "Les répercussions des compétences de la Communauté européenne sur les compétences externes des Etats membres et la question de la 'preemption'" in Demaret (ed.), *Relations extérieures de la Communauté européenne et marché intérieur: aspects juridiques et fonctionnels* (Bruges, College of Europe/Story, 1988) 39, at 54–62; for "pre-emption" generally, see para. 7–024, *supra*.

[282] See the Declaration, annexed to the Single European Act, on Art. 130r of the EEC Treaty and Declaration (No. 10), annexed to the EU Treaty, in which the Intergovernmental Conference considered that "the provisions of Article 109(5) [*now Article 219(4) TFEU*], Article 130r(4), second subpara., [*now Article 191(4), second subpara., TFEU*] and Article 130y [*now Article 209 TFEU*] do not affect the principles resulting from the judgment handed down by the Court of Justice in the AETR case".

[283] ECJ, Opinion 1/03 (n. 265, *supra*), paras 129–130.

[284] See, for instance, the authority granted by Regulation (EC) No. 662/2009 of the European Parliament and of the Council of July 13, 2009 establishing a procedure for the negotiation and conclusion of agreements between Member States and third countries on particular matters

Transparency. The allocation of powers as between the Union and the Member   **25–059**
States in the field of external relations constitutes a purely internal matter as far as
the Union is concerned (see para. 24–002). However, its changing nature makes contracting parties uncertain as to who is assuming the international obligations flowing
from a given agreement. Indeed, other parties have made the conclusion of an international agreement on the part of the Union conditional upon its being signed in
parallel by the Member States.[285] It is for this reason, too, that multilateral agreements often require signatory international organisations to deposit a declaration as
to the situation with regard to the internal division of powers.[286] In such a case, the
Union is subject to an obligation of international law requiring it to submit a complete declaration of its competences. Where the Council authorises the Commission
to accede to a convention, the principle of sincere cooperation to which the institutions are subject requires the Council to enable the Commission to comply with
international law by submitting a complete declaration of competences.[287]

---

concerning the law applicable to contractual and non-contractual obligations, [2009] O.J. L200/25,
and Council Regulation (EC) No. 664/2009 of July 7, 2009 establishing a procedure for the negotiation and conclusion of agreements between Member States and third countries concerning jurisdiction, recognition and enforcement of judgments and decisions in matrimonial matters, matters
of parental responsibility and matters relating to maintenance obligations, and the law applicable
to matters relating to maintenance obligations, [2009] O.J. L200/46.

[285] See Arts 2 and 3 of Annex IX to the United Nations Convention of December 10, 1982 on the Law
of the Sea ([1998] O.J. L179/113), which stipulated that the majority of the Member States had to
accede thereto before the Community could accede. See Stein, "External Relations of the European
Community: Structure and Process" (1990) *Collected Courses of the Academy of European Law. I*,
1990, 115, at 161–162; Simmonds, "The Community's Participation in the U.N. Law of the Sea
Convention", in O'Keeffe and Schermers (eds), *Essays in European Law and Integration* (Deventer,
Kluwer, 1982), 141, at 179–195. For the Convention, see para. 12–006, *supra*.

[286] See, e.g., Art. 44 of the United Nations Convention of December 13, 2006 on the Rights of Persons
with Disabilities, approved by the Community, together with an annexed declaration on (shared)
competence, by Council Decision 2010/48/EC of November 26, 2009, [2010] O.J. L23/35; Arts 29
and 30 of the Hague Convention on Choice of Court Agreements of June 30, 2005, approved by
the Community, together with the annexed declaration on (exclusive) competence, by Council
Decision 2009/397/EC of February 26, 2009, [2009] O.J. L133/1; Art. 5 of Annex IX to the United
Nations Convention of December 10, 1982 on the Law of the Sea and the Community's
Declaration concerning the competence of the European Community with regard to matters gov-
erned by that Convention and the Agreement of July 28, 1994 relating to the implementation of
Part XI of the Convention, [1998] O.J. L179/129.

[287] ECJ, Case C-29/99 *Commission v Council* [2002] E.C.R. I-11221, paras 67–71.

CHAPTER 26

THE PROCEDURE FOR CONCLUDING AGREEMENTS

Framework. The Treaties set out the procedure which the Union must follow   26–001
in concluding agreements with third countries or international organisations
(paras 21–002—21–012). In some cases, not only the Union but also the Member
States are party to such an agreement: this is the case with "mixed agreements" as
they are termed (paras 21–014—26–016). In order to avoid the Union concluding
international agreements which exceed the limits of the Treaties, the Treaties allow
an opinion to be sought from the Court of Justice before concluding an agreement
(paras 21–017—21–018).

I. FIELD OF APPLICATION OF THE PROCEDURE

Article 218 TFEU. Article 218 TFEU [*ex Art. 300 EC*] sets out the internal proce-   26–002
dure for negotiating and concluding "agreements between the Union and third countries or international organisations". That Treaty provision does not itself confer any
power on the Union to act internationally, but applies whenever the Union wishes to
conclude an agreement. As explained in the previous chapter, the Union is empowered to conclude an international agreement where the Treaties expressly so provide,[1] where it is necessary in order to achieve one of the objectives of the Union,
where it is provided for in a legally binding Union act or where it is likely to affect
common rules or alter their scope (Art. 216 TFEU). The decision by which the
Union approves a given agreement refers in its preamble not only to the Treaty provision constituting the substantive legal basis, but also to the provision of Art. 218
TFEU which sets out the applicable procedure. The term "agreement" is used here,

> "in a general sense to indicate any undertaking entered into by entities subject
> to international law which has binding force, whatever its formal designation".[2]

---

[1] See Art. 8(2) TEU; Art. 37 TEU; Art. 79(3) TFEU; Art. 186, second para., TFEU; Art. 191(4), first
subpara., TFEU; Art. 207(3) TFEU; Art. 209(2), first subpara., TFEU [*see ex Art. 181 EC*]; Art. 212(3),
first subpara., TFEU; Art. 214(4), first subpara., TFEU; Art. 217 TFEU; Art. 219(1) TFEU.
[2] ECJ, Opinion 1/75 *Draft Understanding on a Local Cost Standard drawn up under the auspices of
the OECD* [1975] E.C.R. 1355, at 1359–1360. Article 218 TFEU does not cover guidelines agreed

Articles 101 to 106 EAEC set out detailed rules for the conclusion of agreements by that Community; no such rules were contained in the ECSC Treaty.

This procedure applies in all fields of Union activity, including the CFSP and police and judicial cooperation in criminal matters.[3] Before the Lisbon Treaty, separate procedures applied for the adoption of agreements in those fields.[4]

The same procedural requirements apply to amendments of agreements and to additional or implementing protocols concluded together with or on the basis of the agreement itself.[5] In principle, the denunciation of an agreement also comes under Art. 218 TFEU.[6]

II. Procedure for the Negotiation and Conclusion of Agreements

26–003   **General outline.** Article 218 TFEU constitutes a general provision of "constitutional" import, since in conferring certain powers on the Union institutions it seeks to establish a balance between the institutions.[7]

The Council authorises the opening of negotiations, adopts negotiating directives, authorises the signing of agreements and concludes them (Art. 218(2) TFEU). The Commission is in most cases responsible for conducting the negotiations. The European Parliament, for its part, is consulted or (in the case of certain agreements)

---

with a third country which do not constitute a binding agreement: ECJ, Case C-233/02 *France v Commission* [2004] E.C.R. I-2759; see the case note by Lavranos and van Ooik (2004) S.E.W. 543–547. In some language versions of the Treaty (in particular Dutch) two different terms are used, whereas the other versions employ only one ("agreement", "Abkommen", "accord"). This has no significance. According to Declaration (No. 5) annexed to the EU Treaty, the expression "formal agreements" in Art. 111(1) EC [*now Art. 219(1) TFEU*] did not introduce a new category of international agreement.

[3] A declaration annexed to the Lisbon Treaty confirms that Member States continue to have the power to negotiate and conclude agreements in this field "in so far as such agreements comply with Union law" (Declaration (No. 36), annexed to the Lisbon Treaty, on Art. 218 TFEU concerning the negotiation and conclusion of international agreements by Member States relating to the area of freedom, security and justice, [2010] O.J. C83/349).

[4] See Arts 24 EU, pursuant to which the Council authorised the Presidency of the Council, assisted by the Commission as appropriate, to open negotiations. Agreements were concluded by the Council on a recommendation from the Presidency. Article 24(5) EU provided that no agreement was to be binding on a Member State whose representative in the Council stated that it had to comply with the requirements of its own constitutional procedure. The other members of the Council could then agree that the agreement would nevertheless apply provisionally.

[5] Accordingly, Rule 90 of the EP Rules of Procedure deals with the "conclusion, renewal or amendment of an international agreement".

[6] See, e.g., Council Decision 91/602/EEC of November 25, 1991 denouncing the Cooperation Agreement between the European Economic Community and the Socialist Federal Republic of Yugoslavia ([1991] O.J. L325/23), which was adopted in accordance with the procedure set out in Art. 238 EEC [*now Art.217 TFEU*].

[7] ECJ, Case C-327/91 *France v Commission* [1994] E.C.R. I-3641, para. 28.

has to give its consent. In any event, the European Parliament must be immediately and fully informed at all stages of the procedure (Art. 218(10) TFEU).

Throughout the procedure, the Council acts by a qualified majority. However, the Council has to take its decision by a unanimous vote where the agreement in question covers a field for which, at the internal level, unanimity is required for the adoption of a Union act, and in the case of association agreements and of cooperation agreements with States which are candidates for accession[8] (Art. 218(8) TFEU). Unanimity will also be required for the agreement by which the Union is to accede to the European Convention of Human Rights (*ibid*; see para. 22–031). In the case of agreements based on Art. 207 TFEU [*ex Art. 133 EC*] (common commercial policy), the Council decides in principle by a qualified majority vote; however, unanimity is required in some cases (see para. 25–005).

A. NEGOTIATIONS

Union Negotiatior. Negotiations for the conclusion of an international agreement start after the Council has adopted a decision authorising the negotiations. In that decision, the Council is to nominate the Union negotiator (or head of the Union's negotiating team), depending on the subject of the agreement envisaged. The Council acts on recommendations by the Commission, except where the envisaged agreement relates exclusively or principally to the CFSP, in which case recommendations emanate from the High Representative (Art. 218(2) and (3) TFEU). Before the Lisbon Treaty, agreements with third countries or international organisations were invariably negotiated by the Commission.[9] Article 218(2) and (3) TFEU leave more latitude to the Council as far as the nomination of the negotiator is concerned. Negotiations are expressly reserved to the Commission only as regards agreements in the field of the common commercial policy (Art. 207(3) TFEU). Nevertheless, it follows from Art. 17(1) TEU that, with the exception of the CFSP and other cases provided for in the Treaties,[10] it is for the Commission to ensure the Union's external representation. Accordingly, the intention behind Art. 218(2) and (3) TFEU appears to be that negotiations should be conducted, as far as the CFSP is concerned, by the High Representative, whereas, in all other areas, negotiations should normally be conducted by the Commission or, in specific cases (e.g. mixed agreements), by a "negotiating team" involving the Commission and representatives of the Council or of the Member States.

In order to enable it to make effective recommendations, the Union negotiator is empowered to conduct exploratory discussions with potential Contracting Parties.[11]

26–004

---

[8] For such agreements, see Art. 212 TFEU.

[9] See Art. 300(1), first subpara., EC. For the Commission's capacity to negotiate, see Keukeleire and MacNaughtan, *The foreign policy of the European Union* (Basingstoke, Palgrave Macmillan, 2008), Ch.6, at 86–93.

[10] E.g., Art. 219(3) TFEU (see para. 26–005).

[11] Flaesch-Mougin, "Le traité de Maastricht et les compétences externes de la Communauté européenne: à la recherche d'une politique externe de l'Union" (1993) C.D.E. 351, at 378.

The Union negotiator conducts the negotiations in consultation with a special committee which may be appointed by the Council and within the framework of such directives as the Council may issue to it (Art. 218(4) TFEU).[12] Since the Council has to approve the agreement ensuing from the negotiations, it is reasonable that the Council should be able to put across its views in this way at the outset and during the course of the negotiations. The European Parliament, for its part, must be fully informed by the Commission (or the High Representative) of its recommendations and of the progress of international negotiations.[13] The Commission has undertaken to keep the Parliament informed both during the phase of preparation of the agreements and during the conduct and conclusion of international negotiations.[14] For its part, the Council has agreed under the Luns-Westerterp procedures that the European Parliament should hold a debate before negotiations are opened and that during the negotiations for association agreements the Commission should keep in close contact with the responsible parliamentary committee.[15] In its Rules of Procedure, the European Parliament has provided that in the case of any international agreement it may request the Council not to authorise the opening of negotiations until the Parliament has stated its position on the proposed negotiating mandate and that it may adopt recommendations to be taken into account before the relevant international agreement is concluded.[16] Such acts adopted by the European Parliament are not in any way binding on the Commission or the Council, but are important where the conclusion of the agreement in question is contingent on the Parliament's consent.

---

[12] See, as regards agreements relating to the common commercial policy, Art. 207(3), third subpara., TFEU, which provides that the Commission is to regularly report to the special committee and to the European Parliament on the progress of negotiations.

[13] According to Rule 90(1) and (4) of the EP Rules of Procedure, the responsible parliamentary committee is to be informed, if necessary on a confidential basis.

[14] See points 23–29 the Framework Agreement on relations between the European Parliament and the Commission of October 20, 2010 ([2010] O.J. L304/47); see formerly point 29 of the Framework Agreement of May 26, 2005, and point 3.10 of the Code of Conduct agreed between the European Parliament and the Commission on March 15, 1995, [1995] O.J. C89/69.

[15] On March 24–25, 1964, the Council took the decision to provide information on association agreements following an exchange of letters between the President of the Council (Luns, the Dutch Foreign Minister) and the President of the European Parliament (Martino). After the then President of the Council (Westerterp) stated in November 1972 that he was prepared to make confidential information about trade agreements available to parliamentary committees, the Council laid down a number of procedural rules concerning trade agreements in a communication of October 16, 1973, which was notified to the European Parliament. These interinstitutional decisions were never published officially; for their wording, see Tomuschat, "Artikel 228", in von der Groeben, Thiesing, Ehlermann (eds), *Kommentar zum EWG-Vertrag* (Baden-Baden, Nomos, 1991), at 5666–5669; see also Rengeling, "Zu den Befugnissen des Europäischen Parlaments beim Abschluss völkerrechtlicher Verträge im Rahmen der Gemeinschaftsfassung", *Staatsrecht—Völkerrecht—Europarecht. Festschrift für H.-J. Schlochauer* (Berlin, de Gruyter, 1981), at 877–898.

[16] EP Rules of Procedure, Rule 90(2) and (5).

Monetary affairs. By way of derogation from Art. 218 TFEU, there are special   **26–005**
rules on negotiations,

> "where agreements concerning monetary or foreign exchange regime matters
> need to be negotiated by the Union with one or more States or international
> organisations" (Art. 219(3) TFEU [*ex Art. 111(3) EC*]).

In such a case, the Council is to decide on the arrangements for the negotiation
and conclusion of the agreement in question by a qualified majority on a recommendation from the Commission and after consulting the European Central Bank.
These arrangements are to ensure that the Union expresses a single position
(Art. 219(3) TFEU). Depending on the formula chosen by the Council, negotiations on these matters need not necessarily be entrusted to the Commission. The
Commission is entitled, however, to be fully associated with the negotiations.[17]

B. CONCLUSION OF AGREEMENTS

1. Initialling and signature

Division of powers. After the negotiations have closed, the text of the draft agree-   **26–006**
ment is initialled by the negotiators. The power to sign the agreement is vested in
the Council, which acts on a proposal from the Union negotiator (Art. 218(5)
TFEU). At the same time, a decision may be adopted on the provisional application of the agreement before it enters into force (*ibid.*). Where the agreement is
concerned with a matter in respect of which both the Union and the Member
States have competence, the Union and the Member States must determine
together who has the right of signature. Since that right entails the power to take
the final decision as to the content of the agreement and creates an impression in
other subjects of international law as to the division of competence as between
the Union and the Member States, the decision as to who has the right of signature is amenable to judicial review.[18]

Unlike in the case of initialling, which is intended only to fix the definitive text
of the agreement, obligations ensue from signature for a contracting party,
whether or not it signs subject to ratification. Until such time as it makes its intention clear not to become a party, a signatory State or international organisation is
obliged to refrain from acts which would defeat the object and purpose of the
agreement.[19] This international-law principle of good faith applies equally after
the agreement has been ratified and during the period prior to its entry into

---

[17] Article 219(3) TFEU. For cases in which negotiating mandates were conferred on the Member
States, see the decisions cited in n. 218 to para. 11–040, *supra*.

[18] ECJ, Case C-25/94 *Commission v Council* [1996] E.C.R. I-1469, paras 29–37.

[19] Article 18, point (a), of the Vienna Convention of March 21, 1986 on the Law of Treaties between
States and International Organisations or between International Organisations (para. 22–055, *supra*).

force.[20] It applies to the Union institutions when an agreement has been approved by the Union, the date of its entry into force is known and the Union adopts acts conflicting with provisions of the agreement.[21] Individuals may challenge such acts in reliance on the principle of protection of legitimate expectations in so far as the acts in question conflict with provisions of the agreement which have direct effect for them following the agreement's entry into force.[22]

At this stage, too, the European Parliament must be immediately and fully informed (Art. 218(10) TFEU. Under the Luns procedure, the Council agreed as long ago as 1964 to inform the responsible committee of the European Parliament confidentially and informally about each initialled association agreement before signing it. At that time, the Treaty required the European Parliament only to be consulted before the conclusion of such an agreement. Since the Single European Act, the Parliament had to consent. Moreover, from 1973 on, information has been provided about initialled trade agreements to the responsible parliamentary committee under the Westerterp procedure. Since the Lisbon Treaty, the European Parliament has to give its consent to the conclusion of such agreements (Art. 218(6), second subpara., sub (a),(v) in combination with Art.207(2) TFEU). According to the Parliament, every draft agreement should be submitted to it before signature, in order to obtain its opinion or consent.[23]

2. Power to conclude agreements

26–007 **Council.** The Council concludes agreements on a proposal of the Union negotiator. There are different rules in this respect for agreements relating to monetary and exchange-rate matters. In such cases, the Council does not decide on a proposal from the Commission but on a recommendation from the ECB or from the Commission after consulting the ECB (Art. 219(1) TFEU). Moreover, the conclusion of such agreements is subject to such arrangements as the Council decides upon pursuant to Art. 219(3) TFEU (see para. 26–005).

The Council generally "concludes" an agreement by means of a decision concluding the agreement "on behalf of the Union". The fact that the Council adopts a decision (or a regulation) to this end, does not deprive the agreement of its legal force as an international agreement concluded by the Union.[24] An agreement obtains the force of Union law after it has entered into effect

---

[20] *Ibid.*, Art. 18, point (b).

[21] CFI, Case T-115/94 *Opel Austria v Council* [1997] E.C.R. II-39, paras 90–94.

[22] *Ibid.*, para. 94 (the judgment in the *Opel Austria* case accordingly annulled a regulation imposing duties only a few days before the EEA Agreement prohibiting such duties entered into effect).

[23] EP Rules of Procedure, Rule 90(6).

[24] See Everling, "The Law of the External Economic Relations of the European Community" in Hilf, Jacobs and Petersmann (eds), *The European Community and GATT* (Deventer, Kluwer, 1986), 85, at 96; Tomuschat (n. 15, *supra*), at 5671.

internationally. Agreements concluded by the Union are published in the *Official Journal*.[25]

The Council also takes decisions to suspend an agreement, on a proposal from the Commission or the High Representative.[26] The same procedure applies where the Council establishes the positions to be adopted on the Union's behalf in a body set up by an agreement, when that body is called upon to adopt acts having legal effects, with the exception of acts supplementing or amending the institutional framework of the agreement (Art. 218(9) TFEU).[27]

Commission. The Commission (or the High Representative) is sometimes vested with the power to conclude agreements. What is involved is a small number of administrative agreements.[28]   **26–008**

Internal Union powers vested in the Commission cannot alter the allocation of powers between the Council and the Commission with regard to the conclusion of international agreements. Consequently, the Commission has no power to conclude an agreement with a third country on the application of the competition rules, even though, internally, it does have the power to adopt individual decisions in that field.[29] Even when concluding non-binding guidelines with a third

---

[25] Council Rules of Procedure, Art. 17(1)(d). This applies to agreements concluded by the Union in the field of the CFSP, unless the Council decides otherwise on the grounds of Arts 4 and 9 of Regulation (EC) No. 1049/2001 of the European Parliament and of the Council of May 30, 2001 regarding public access to European Parliament, Council and Commission documents (Council Rules of Procedure, Art. 17(1)(e)).

[26] The application of an agreement may also be suspended by and in accordance with the procedure for imposing economic sanctions. See the discussion of Art. 215 TFEU [*ex Art. 301 EC*] in paras 25–050—25–052, *supra*. Accordingly, the trade concessions under the Cooperation Agreement with Yugoslavia were suspended (Council Regulation (EEC) No. 3300/91 of November 11, 1991, [1991] O.J. L315/1) and an embargo was brought in against Haiti by way of derogation from the Fourth ACP-EC Convention (Council Regulation (EEC) No. 1608/93 of June 24, 1993, [1993] O.J. L155/2) under Art. 133 EC [*now Art. 207 TFEU*]. For the validity under international law of the suspension of the Cooperation Agreement with Yugoslavia, see ECJ, Case C-162/96 *Racke* [1998] E.C.R. I-3655 (see para. 22–055, *supra*).

[27] The European Parliament must be "immediately and fully informed" about any decision taken by the Council in this connection (see Art. 218(10) TFEU). For the Commission's undertaking to this effect, see point 20 of the Framework agreement of 26 May 2005.

[28] See Art. 220 TFEU (relations with international organisations) and Art. 6 of the Protocol on Privileges and Immunities (para. 13–128, *supra*) (agreements for the recognition by third countries of Union *laissez-passer* as valid travel documents).

[29] ECJ, Case C-327/91 *France v Commission* [1994] E.C.R. I-3641, paras 40–43 (annulling the decision whereby the Commission sought to conclude the Agreement with the United States of America regarding the application of the competition laws of the European Communities and the United States, which was signed and entered into force on September 23, 1991). Agreements on cooperation in the field of competition have since been concluded by the Council pursuant to Art. 83 EC [*now Art. 103 TFEU*] and—as far as mergers are concerned—Art. 308 EC [*now Art. 352 TFEU*]; the Commission had to conclude such agreements only as far as the ECSC was concerned: see Council and Commission Decision 95/145/EC, ECSC of April 10, 1995, [1995] O.J. L95/45 (concluding again the 1991 agreement) and Council and Commission Decision 98/386/EC, ECSC of May 29,

country, the Commission must take account of the division of powers and the institutional balance established by the Treaties.[30]

Article 218(7) TFEU allows the Council, when concluding an agreement, to authorise the Union negotiator to approve modifications on behalf of the Union where the agreement provides for them to be adopted by a simplified procedure or by a body set up by the agreement. The Council may attach specific conditions to such authorisation.

3. Involvement of the European Parliament

(a) *Consultation*

26–009 **Duty to consult.** Except for agreements which relate exclusively to the CFSP, the Council has at least to consult the European Parliament before concluding the agreement (Art. 218(6), second subpara., TFEU). For five important categories of agreements, the European Parliament must give its consent (see para. 26–012). The European Parliament also has to be consulted where no involvement whatso-ever of the European Parliament is prescribed for the adoption of internal rules. The European Parliament is not consulted, but must be "immediately and fully informed" in the event of the suspension of an agreement or the establishment of the Union position in a body set up by an agreement when that body is called upon to adopt decisions having legal effects, with the exception of decisions supplementing or amending the institutional framework of the agreement (Art. 218(9) and (10) TFEU).[31]

26–010 **Opinion of the Parliament.** The Council has to consult the European Parliament before it concludes the agreement in question. The Treaties do not provide that the Parliament's opinion must be sought before the agreement is signed, which is the view taken by the Parliament.[32] If the matter is urgent, the Council may lay down a commensurate time-limit within which the Parliament should deliver its opinion. If the Parliament fails to deliver an opinion within that time-limit, the Council may act (Art. 218(6), second subpara., sub (b), TFEU).[33] The European

---

1998, [1998] O.J. L173/26 (additional agreement with the United States); Council and Commission Decision 1999/445/EC, ECSC of April 29, 1999, [1999] O.J. L175/49 (agreement with Canada); Council Decision 2003/520/EC of June 16, 2003, [2003] O.J. L183/11 (agreement with Japan); Council Decision 2009/586/EC of February 16, 2009, [2009] O.J. L202/35 (agreement with Korea).

[30] ECJ, Case C-233/02 *France v Commission* [2004] E.C.R. I-2759, para. 40.

[31] See Dashwood, "External Relations Provisions of the Amsterdam Treaty" (1998) C.M.L.Rev. 1019, at 1024–1028.

[32] See EP Rules of Procedure, Rule 90(6).

[33] Accordingly, the agreement between the EC and the USA on the processing and transfer of PNR data by Air Carriers to the United States Department of Homeland Security, Bureau of Customs and Border Protection, was concluded by Council Decision 2004/496/EC of March 17, 2004 ([2004] O.J. L183/83), the European Parliament not being able to deliver an opinion within the time-limit laid down "in view of the urgent need to remedy the situation of uncertainty in which

Parliament adopts its opinion by a majority of votes cast. The Council is not bound in any way by that opinion. Nevertheless, if the opinion adopted by the Parliament is negative, the President of the Parliament will request the Council not to conclude the agreement in question.[34]

(b) *Consent*

Duty to obtain consent. For five categories of agreements, the Treaties make their conclusion dependent upon the prior consent of the European Parliament (Art. 218(6), second subpara., sub (a), TFEU). Before the Lisbon Treaty, the Treaties referred to the "assent" of the European Parliament (Art. 300(3) EC). Here, too, the Parliament contends that, in the absence of any provision in the Treaties, it should have to give its consent before the agreement is signed.[35] The Council and the European Parliament may, in an urgent situation, agree upon a time-limit for the consent (Art. 218(6), second subpara., sub (a), last sentence, TFEU). The European Parliament gives its consent by a majority of the votes cast on the basis of a report from the responsible committee which may merely recommend either that the whole of the proposal be either accepted or rejected; no amendments may be tabled.[36] If the European Parliament decides to withhold its consent, its President informs the Council that the agreement in question cannot be concluded.[37]

26–011

Five categories of agreements. The consent procedure applies, in the first place, to association agreements. The requirement for parliamentary consent for such agreements was introduced as long ago as the Single European Act.[38] Secondly, consent will also be required for the agreement by which the Union is to accede to the European Convention of Human Rights. This was introduced by the Lisbon Treaty. Thirdly, consent has to be obtained for other agreements establishing a specific institutional framework by organising cooperation procedures. Since most "cooperation agreements" establish bilateral bodies, this provision refers, in all likelihood, to agreements which establish a more complex institutional structure, yet are not concluded as an association agreement.[39] The fourth category of agreements requiring parliamentary consent are those having "important

26–012

---

airlines and passengers found themselves, as well as to protect the financial interests of those concerned" (see point 3 of the preamble). However, the decision was annulled by the Court because it was adopted on the wrong legal basis (see ECJ, Joined Cases C-317/04 and C-318/04, *European Parliament v Council and Commission* [2006] E.C.R. I-4721).

[34] EP Rules of Procedure, Rules 90(8) and (9).

[35] EP Rules of Procedure, Rule 90(6) which refers to the consent procedure under Rule 81 of the EP Rules of Procedure (para. 16–037, *supra*).

[36] *Ibid.*, para. 8.

[37] *Ibid.*, para. 10.

[38] However, since the EU Treaty, consent has to be given by an absolute majority of the votes cast and no longer by a majority of the component Members of the European Parliament.

[39] Flaesch-Mougin (n. 11, *supra*), at 385–386. A first instance is the WTO Agreement, para. 25–012, *supra*.

budgetary implications" for the Union.[40] The final category consists of agreements covering fields to which either the ordinary legislative procedure applies or a special legislative procedure under which the Parliament's consent is required. This last category was significantly enlarged by the Lisbon Treaty. Before the Lisbon Treaty, consent was required merely for agreements entailing amendment of an act adopted under the co-decision procedure [*now the ordinary legislative procedure*] (see Art. 300(3), second subpara., EC). Accordingly, the Council could not, by means of an international agreement, detract from internal legislation which the European Parliament and the Council had adopted under the co-decision procedure. However, so long as no internal act had been adopted, the Council was entitled to conclude international agreements in the field in question after merely consulting the European Parliament.

The enlargement of the last category also means that the consent of the European Parliament is now required for trade agreements, since the Lisbon Treaty brought the common commercial policy under the ordinary legislative procedure (Art. 207 TFEU). Article 133 EC, by contrast, made no provision for any involvement of the European Parliament. Under the Westerterp procedure (see para. 26–004) it was entitled only to have cognisance of a signed agreement, after which it could, if it deemed it appropriate, adopt an opinion on its own initiative. Nevertheless, the European Council proposed as long ago as 1983 that the European Parliament should be consulted on the conclusion of all "significant international agreements".[41]

Unlike the requirement as to majority voting in the Council (see para. 26–007), the requirement for parliamentary consent is not tied exclusively to the legal basis of the agreement in question. Criteria relating more to the importance of a given agreement (see, particularly, the fourth category) are also significant.[42] The

---

[40] In order to ascertain whether an agreement has important budgetary implications, account must be taken of whether expenditure under the agreement is spread over several years, of a comparison of the expenditure under the agreement with the amount of the appropriations designed to finance the Union's external operations and, where the agreement relates to a particular sector, of a comparison between the expenditure entailed by the agreement and the whole of the budgetary appropriations for the sector in question, taking the internal and external aspects together. See ECJ, Case C-189/97 *European Parliament v Council* [1999] E.C.R. I-4741, paras 29–33.

[41] Solemn Declaration of Stuttgart on European Union, June 19, 1983 (1983) 6 EC Bull. point 1.6.1. In practice, the Council generally requested an opinion; see, however, the European Parliament's resolution of February 1, 1996 on the failure to consult Parliament on the EU-Russia Interim Agreement, [1996] O.J. C47/26 (in which the Parliament refers to the failure to comply with a Council "undertaking"). For the European Parliament's limited influence in the case of trade agreements, see Bosse-Platière, "Le Parlement européen et les relations extérieures de la Communauté européenne après le Traité de Nice" (2002) R.T.D.E. 527–553.

[42] The possible procedures are:
(1) unanimous vote in the Council following the consent of the European Parliament, in the case of association agreements, the agreement by which the Union is to accede to the European Convention of Human Rights, cooperation agreements with candidate-Member States and all agreements relating to an area for which a unanimous vote (in the Council) is required for internal provisions, which also;

upshot of all this will probably be differences of opinion as between the Council and the Parliament.[43]

Political impact. The power of consent enables the European Parliament to have a real say in the Union's foreign policy.[44] The European Parliament has sometimes withheld its consent to additional protocols to association agreements until the negotiators agreed to provisions complying with the Parliament's wishes regarding, in particular, respect for human rights in the third country concerned.[45] Thus, in March 1988, the European Parliament withheld its consent to additional protocols to the EEC-Israel Agreement until such time as Israel complied with the requirement under a Community regulation to afford agricultural products from the occupied territories direct access to the Community.[46] Consent gives the European Parliament a means

26–013

(a) give rise to a specific institutional framework,
(b) have substantial budgetary implications or
(c) relate to an area for which the consent of the Parliament is required for internal provisions;
(2) unanimous vote in the Council after consultation of the European Parliament, in the case of agreements relating to an area for which a unanimous vote is required for internal acts which do not fall under (a), (b) or (c);
(3) qualified majority vote or unanimity in the Council with No. involvement of the European Parliament, in the case of certain CFSP agreements;
(4) qualified majority vote in the Council and consent of the European Parliament, in the case of an agreement relating to an area other than (1), (2) or (3), which also falls within either (a), (b) or (c) or (d) in which the ordinary legislative procedure applies;
(5) qualified majority vote in the Council after consultation of the European Parliament, in the case of agreements falling within an area other than (1), (2) or (3) and not coming within (a), (b), (c) or (d).

[43] Flaesch-Mougin (n. 11, *supra*), at 387.
[44] See Soriano, "Analyse de l'évolution de l'action extérieure de l'UE dans le domaine des droits de l'homme, de la démocratie et de l'Etat de droit" (2005) *Annales de droit de Liège* 5–42; Bieber, "Democratic Control of European Foreign Policy" (1990) E.J.I.L. 148–173; for a survey of this competence in the overall context of the European Parliament's scrutiny of external policy: Thym, "Parliamentary Involvement in European International Relations", in Cremona and de Witte (eds), *EU Foreign Relations Law. Constitutional Fundamentals* (Oxford, Hart, 2008) 201–232; Robles Carrillo, *El control de la Política Exterior por el Parlamento Europeo* (Madrid, Civitas, 1994), 563 pp; Bosse-Platière, "Le Parlement européen et les relations extérieures de la Communauté européenne après le Traité de Nice" (2002) 38 R.T.D.E. 527–553; Hilf and Schorkopf, "Das Europäische Parlament in den Aussenbeziehungen der Europäischen Union" (1999) EuR. 185–202.
[45] See the European Parliament's refusal to give its consent to Protocols with Syria ([1992] O.J. C39/52 and C39/55) and Morocco ([1992] O.J. C39/54). Consent was ultimately given on October 28, 1992 (but not for one of the Protocols with Syria, [1992] O.J. C305/64); for the Protocols in question, see [1992] O.J. L352/14 (Morocco) and [1992] O.J. L352/22 (Syria). On December 15, 1987, the European Parliament deferred giving its consent to two financial protocols annexed to the EEC-Turkey Agreement on similar grounds ([1988] O.J. C13/28; it gave its consent thereto on January 20, 1988, [1988] O.J. C49/52).
[46] [1988] O.J. C94/55 (consent withheld on March 9, 1988; for the political reasons, see (1988) 3 EU Bull. points 2.4.13–15); [1988] O.J. C290/60 (consent given on October 12, 1988); Silvestro, "Les Protocoles financiers CEE-Israël à l'examen du Parlement européen" (1991) R.M.C.U.E. 462–464.

of applying pressure with a view to its being more closely involved in the drawing up of agreements or of particular clauses therein. By this means, the European Parliament may obtain concessions from the Council with regard to the involvement of the Parliament going beyond the specific confines of a particular agreement.[47] More recently, on February 11, 2010, the European Parliament withheld its consent to an Agreement between the EU and the USA on the processing and transfer of Financial Messaging Data from the European Union to the United States for purposes of the Terrorist Finance Tracking Program.

III. MIXED AGREEMENTS

26–014 **Legal reasons.** External action on the part of the Union often takes the form of a mixed agreement, where both the Union and the Member States are parties.[48] Most multilateral agreements to which the Union is a party and all the present association agreements fall into this category. Close cooperation is required between the Member States and the Union institutions where the subject-matter of an agreement appears to fall partly within the competence of the Union and partly within that of the Member States (see paras 24–007, 25–006 and 25–015). In such a case, the agreement will be concluded both by the Union and by the Member States, unless the agreement does not allow international organisations such as the Union to sign and the Union exercises its external competence through the medium of the Member States.[49] The Court of Justice has also held that the Member States may participate in an agreement where the financing falls to them and constitutes an essential element of the agreement (see para. 25–006). Lastly, a Member State may participate in an international agreement alongside the Union as the international representative of certain dependent territories which are not part of the sphere of application of Union law.[50] Where the Union—possibly with its Member States—accedes to an organisation established by a multilateral treaty, complications arise not only from the allocation of competences, but also from the allocation and exercise of voting rights in organs of the organisation (see para. 24–003).

---

[47] Flaesch-Mougin (n. 11, *supra*), at 385.

[48] See, expressly, Art. 102 EAEC. For an extensive discussion, see the articles in Hillion and Koutrakos, *Mixed Agreements Revisited: The EU and its Member States in the World* (Oxford, Hart, 2010), 442 pp.; Eeckhout, *External Relations of the European Union, Legal and Constitutional Foundations* (Oxford, Oxford University Press, 2004), at 190–225; O'Keeffe and Schermers (eds), *Mixed Agreements* (Deventer, Kluwer, 1983), 248 pp.; Leal-Arcas, "The European Community and Mixed Agreements" (2001) E.For.Aff.Rev. 483–513.

[49] ECJ, Opinion 2/91 *Convention No. 170 of the International Labour Organisation concerning safety in the use of chemicals at work* [1993] E.C.R. I-1061, para. 5.

[50] ECJ, Opinion 1/78 *International Agreement on Natural Rubber* [1979] E.C.R. 2871, para. 62. The special position of the Member State concerned has no effect on the demarcation of spheres of competence within the Union: ECJ, Opinion 1/94 *Agreement establishing the World Trade Organisation* [1994] E.C.R. I-5267, paras 17–18.

Political reasons. In practice, mixed agreements also come to the fore in other 26–015
circumstances for a variety of political reasons. The contracting parties may ask
for the agreement to be concluded as a mixed agreement. In addition, Member
States often choose to be party to the agreement. In this way, the conclusion of
the agreement is not hampered by any disputes as to the extent of Union powers
and the Member States remain in a position to take implementing measures themselves. In the case of an agreement which establishes institutions with powers of
decision, the mixed form guarantees that the Member States keep their voting
rights in those institutions or that the Union—in the event that the Member States
do not exercise their voting rights themselves—has a number of votes equal to the
number of Member States.[51] Since the Member States also commit themselves
internationally by a mixed agreement, the Union, for its part, is secured as regards
the funding or other implementing measures which the agreement requires the
Member States to take.[52] Nevertheless, the fact that an agreement entails obligations and financial burdens for the Member States does not detract from the
exclusive character of a Union competence.[53] Thus, participation of the Member
States in an agreement does not as such result from their obligations to bear some
of the expenses of an international organisation like the WTO, which has only
an operating budget and not financial instruments.[54] Accession of the Member
States to such an agreement could be regarded, however, as an action pursuant to
special authorisation on the part of the Union.[55]

Consequences. In any event, a mixed agreement does not result in any shift in the 26–016
respective powers of the Union and the Member States to give effect to the obligations arising for each of them out of the agreement. At most, the conclusion of
a mixed agreement may prevent the agreement from being regarded as an exercise of power by the Union which results in a policy area being taken outside the
sphere of competence of the Member States.[56]

---

[51] For voting rights and, more generally, participation in such bodies, see Hoffmeister, "Outsider or
Frontrunner? Recent Developments under international and European law on the status of the
European Union in International Organisations and Treaty Bodies" (2007) C.M.L.Rev. 41–68;
Neuwahl, "Shared Powers or Combined Incompetence? More on Mixity" (1996) C.M.L.Rev. 667,
at 678–687; Sack, "The European Community's Membership of International Organisations"
(1995) C.M.L.Rev. 1227, at 1232–1256.

[52] Nevertheless, the Commission does not favour this form of action: see, e.g., n. 65 to para. 25–011,
supra (on the Tokyo Round Agreements).

[53] ECJ, Opinion 1/75 *Draft Understanding on a Local Cost Standard drawn up under the auspices of
the OECD* [1975] E.C.R. 1355, at 1364.

[54] ECJ, Opinion 1/94 *Agreement establishing the World Trade Organisation* [1994] E.C.R. I-5267,
para. 21.

[55] See Neuwahl, "Joint Participation in International Treaties and the Exercise of Power by the EEC
and its Member States: Mixed Agreements" (1991) C.M.L.Rev. 717, at 733.

[56] *Ibid.*, at 729–731. For liability in the case of "mixed" international obligations of the Union and
its Member States, see Björklund, "Responsibility in the EC of Mixed Agreements—Should
Non-Member Parties Care?" (2001) Nordic J.I.L. 373–402.

IV. OPINION OF THE COURT OF JUSTICE

26–017 **Objective.** Any Member State, the European Parliament,[57] the Council and the Commission may obtain the opinion of the Court of Justice as to whether an envisaged agreement is compatible with the Treaties.[58] Where the Court's opinion is adverse, the agreement may enter into force only after it has been amended or after the Treaties have been revised in accordance with one of the procedures provided for by the Treaties (Art. 218(11) TFEU [*ex Art. 300(6) EC*]).[59] The procedure for obtaining the prior opinion of the Court is intended to avoid complications which would result from a finding made in judicial proceedings that an international agreement which is binding on the Union is incompatible with provisions of the Treaties on account of its content or the procedure by which it was concluded. Such a judicial decision

> "could not fail to provoke, not only in a [Union] context but also in that of international relations, serious difficulties and might give rise to adverse consequences for all interested parties, including third countries".[60]

Article 103 EAEC provides for a similar review procedure with regard to agreements which Member States propose concluding with third States.[61] However, the EAEC Treaty does not allow the opinion of the Court of Justice to be sought on agreements concluded with third parties by the Commission on the basis of that Treaty.[62]

26–018 **Conditions.** The Court of Justice will accept as an "envisaged agreement" an agreement whose subject-matter is known, even if there is not yet agreement on the full text. Especially as regards a question of competence,

> "it is clearly in the interests of all the States concerned, including third countries, for such a question to be clarified as soon as any particular negotiations are commenced".[63]

---

[57] The European Parliament was given the right to obtain an opinion by the Treaty of Nice.

[58] Before the Lisbon Treaty, the Court of Justice only had jurisdiction to give an opinion on the compatibility of an agreement with the provisions of the EC Treaty. The EU Treaty did not confer jurisdiction on the Court to rule on the compatibility of CFSP or PJCC agreements with that Treaty. For the CFSP, see however Art. 275 TFEU.

[59] For the different revision procedures, see Ch. 5.

[60] ECJ, Opinion 1/75 *Draft Understanding on a Local Cost Standard drawn up under the auspices of the OECD* [1975] E.C.R. 1355, at 1361.

[61] See ECJ, Ruling 1/78 *Draft Convention of the International Atomic Energy Agency on the Physical Protection of Nuclear Materials, Facilities and Transports* [1978] E.C.R. 2151, paras 2–3.

[62] This does not prevent the Court of Justice from ruling, both under the Union Treaties and the EAEC Treaty, on an application for annulment of the decision by which such an agreement is approved (para. 22–048, *supra*): ECJ, Case C-29/99 *Commission v Council* [2002] E.C.R. I-11221, para. 54.

[63] ECJ, Opinion 1/78 *International Agreement on Natural Rubber* [1979] E.C.R. 2871, para. 35.

In so far as the subject-matter of the envisaged agreement is known, questions of competence may be submitted to the Court of Justice before negotiations have formally begun.[64] On the other hand, no time-limit is prescribed for making a request for an opinion and, hence, such a request may be made after the negotiations have come to an end[65] and even after the agreement has been signed but before the Union's consent to be bound by the agreement is finally expressed.[66] Once the Union has concluded an international agreement, the Court of Justice no longer has jurisdiction to give an opinion on it.[67] In such proceedings, any issues may be raised which potentially cast doubt on the substantive or formal validity of the agreement having regard to the Treaties. Questions relating to the division of competence to conclude such an agreement as between the Union and the Member States are particularly liable to be raised.[68] Since the answer to such a question depends on the scope of Union powers, the Court will also rule on the correct legal basis for the Union to use in order to approve the agreement in question.[69] However, the procedure for obtaining an opinion is not intended to solve difficulties associated with implementation of an envisaged agreement which falls within shared Union and Member State competence.[70]

---

[64] ECJ, Opinion 2/94 *Accession by the Communities to the Convention for the Protection of Human Rights and Fundamental Freedoms* [1996] E.C.R. I-1759, paras 16–18.

[65] ECJ, Opinion 1/75 *Draft Understanding on a Local Cost Standard drawn up under the auspices of the OECD* [1975] E.C.R. 1355, at 1361.

[66] ECJ, Opinion 1/94 *Agreement establishing the World Trade Organisation* [1994] E.C.R. I-5267, para. 12, at I-5392.

[67] ECJ, Opinion 3/94 *Framework Agreement on Bananas* [1995] E.C.R. I-4577, paras 8–23. This does not mean that an action for annulment cannot be brought against the decision by which the Union concluded the agreement: *ibid.*, para. 22; ECJ, Case C-122/95 *Germany v Council* [1998] E.C.R. I-973, para. 42 (see para. 22–048). See also Karagiannis, "L'expression 'accord envisagé' dans l'article 228 §6 du traité CE" (1998) C.D.E. 105–136.

[68] ECJ, Opinion 1/75 (n. 65, *supra*), at 1360; Ruling 1/78 (n. 61, *supra*), para. 5; Opinion 1/78 (n. 50, *supra*), para. 30; Opinion 2/91 (n. 49, *supra*), para. 3; ECJ, Opinion 2/92 *Third Revised Decision of the OECD on national treatment* [1995] E.C.R. I-521, paras 13–14; Opinion 1/94 (n. 50, *supra*) para. 9, at I-5391–5392; ECJ, Opinion 1/03 *New Lugano Convention on jurisdiction and the recognition and enforcement of judgments in civil and commercial matters* [2006] E.C.R. I-1145. See also Art. 107(2) of the ECJ Rules of Procedure ("The Opinion may deal not only with the question whether the envisaged agreement is compatible with the provisions of the Treaties but also with the question whether the Union or any Union institution has the power to enter into that agreement"). For further details, see Lenaerts, Arts and Maselis, *Procedural Law of the European Union* (3rd edn, London, Sweet & Maxwell, 2012), Ch. 12.

[69] ECJ, Opinion 2/92 (n. 68, *supra*), paras 9–14; ECJ, Opinion 2/00 *Cartagena Protocol* [2001] E.C.R. I-9713, paras 5–12; ECJ, Opinion 1/08 *General Agreement on Trade in Services* [2009] E.C.R. I-11129, paras 109–110; for a critical view, see Maubernard, "L''intensité modulable' des compétences externes de la Communauté européenne et de ses Etats membres" (2003) R.T.D.E. 229–264. See also Gattinara, "La compétence consultative de la Cour de justice après les avis 1/00 et 2/00" (2003) R.D.U.E. 687–741.

[70] ECJ, Opinion 2/00 *Cartagena Protocol* [2001] E.C.R. I-9713, para. 17.

CHAPTER 27

CONSISTENCY BETWEEN THE COMMON FOREIGN AND SECURITY POLICY AND OTHER EXTERNAL ACTION

I. CONSISTENCY BETWEEN THE CFSP AND OTHER POLICIES OF THE UNION

A. PRINCIPLE

Consistency. The Treaties require the Union to "ensure consistency between the different areas of its external action and between these and its other policies" (Art. 21(3), second subpara., TEU).[1] The Treaties make a clear distinction between Union action within the context of the CFSP (Ch. 2 of Title V of the TEU) and other external action on the part of the Union (in particular under Part Five of the TFEU). The field of application of Union external action under Part Five of the TFEU or based on internal competences of the Union is determined by the substantive scope of the Treaty provisions as described above (see paras 25–003—25–037 and 25–053 et seq.). In contrast, the scope of the CFSP extends to "all areas of foreign policy and all questions relating to the Union's security" (see para. 25–040). CFSP action is subject to specific rules and procedures (see Art. 24(1), second subpara., first sentence, TEU).

The legal split between CFSP action and other external action on the part of the Union does not square with what really happens at international level. Union external relations in all fields have invariably pursued "political" objectives.[2] Consequently, when the Union wishes to express a policy with regard to the

27–001

---

[1] For a general discussion of the need for consistency, see Gauttier, "Horizontal Coherence and the External Competences of the European Union" (2004) E.L.J. 23–41.

[2] See paras 25–003 (common commercial policy), 25–016 et seq. (association agreements) and 25–032—25–033 (development cooperation), *supra*. See Griller, "Die Unterscheidung von Unionsrecht und Gemeinschaftsrecht nach Amsterdam" (1999) EuR. Beiheft 1, at 45–72; Pechstein, "Das Kohärenzgebot als entscheidende Integrationsdimension der Europäischen Union" (1995) EuR. at 255–256; Krenzler and Schneider, "Die Gemeinsame Aussen- und Sicherheitspolitik der Europäischen Union—Zur Frage der Kohärenz" (1994) EuR. 144, at 152; see also Flaesch-Mougin, "Le traité de Maastricht et les compétences externes de la Communauté européenne: à la recherche d'une politique externe de l'Union" (1993) C.D.E. 351, at 375–376.

outside world, it is essential for its CFSP and other external action to be consistent. Besides, it was the need to defend Union interests more effectively through concerted action which laid to the coordination of Member States' foreign policies that developed into European Political Cooperation (EPC).[3] The Single European Act gave the Presidency of the Council and the Commission special responsibility for ensuring consistency between the external policy of the Community and the policies agreed upon in EPC.[4] When the CFSP was introduced, the EU Treaty entrusted that task to the same institutions: the Council and the Commission were responsible for ensuring consistency of the Union's external activities as a whole in the context of its external relations, security, economic and development policies (Art. 3 EU).[5] Since the Lisbon Treaty, the Council and the Commission, assisted by the High Representative, have the task of ensuring consistency between the different areas of the Union's external action (Art. 21(3), second subpara., TEU). Even when Member States enter into enhanced cooperation, the Council and the Commission have to ensure the consistency of activities undertaken in that context and the consistency of such activities with the policies of the Union (Art. 334 TFEU). Where the proposed enhanced cooperation relates to the CFSP, the High Representative has to give an opinion on whether it is consistent with the CFSP and the Commission has to give its opinion in particular on whether it is consistent with other Union policies (Art. 329(2), second subpara., TFEU).

B. GUARANTEES OF CONSISTENCY

1. Principles and objectives of the Union

27–002   **Uniform principles and objectives.** Chapter 1 of Title V of the TEU sets out uniform principles and objectives which guide the Union's external action, such as, inter alia, the objective of consolidating and supporting "democracy, the rule of law, human rights and the principles of international law"[6] (Art. 21 TEU; see also Art. 3(5) TEU). On the basis of these principles and objectives, the European Council is to identify the strategic interests and objectives of the Union (Art. 22(1) TEU). The Treaties explicitly state with regard to both CFSP and other Union

---

[3] For the interaction between the EC and EPC as the *raison d'être* for EPC, see Lak, "Interaction between European Political Cooperation and the European Community (External)—Existing Rules and Challenges" (1989) C.M.L.Rev. 281, at 285–293; Nuttall, "Interaction between European Political Cooperation and the European Community" (1987) Y.E.L. 211–249.

[4] Single European Act, Art. 30(5).

[5] See Kugelmann, "Die Gemeinsame Aussen- und Sicherheitspolitik" (1998) EuR. Beiheft 2, at 99–123.

[6] See the Commission's communication, published as "The European Union and human rights in the world" (1995) EU Bull. Suppl. 3; for a substantive appraisal of the policy of the European Union, see King, "Human Rights in European Foreign Policy: Success or Failure for Post-Modern Diplomacy" (1999) E.J.I.L. 313–337. See also the position with regard to human rights in connection with development cooperation, para. 25–033, *supra*.

external action that it "shall be guided by the principles, pursue the objectives, and be conducted in accordance with the general provisions" laid down in Ch. 1 of Title V of the TEU (Art. 23 TEU and Art. 205 TFEU, respectively).[7] These principles and objectives must equally be observed in the development and implementation of the external aspects of other Union policies (Art. 21(3), first subpara., TEU). These principles and objectives are intended to secure consistency in the Union's external action.[8]

2. A single institutional framework

Institutions. The Union has a single institutional framework which, according to Art. 13(1) TEU is to ensure the "consistency, effectiveness and continuity of its policies and actions".[9] Most acts exercising the external powers of the Union are adopted by the Council; for CFSP acts this is always the case. In so doing, it follows the general political guidelines provided by the European Council (Art. 13(2) TEU). The fact that those taking part in the decision-making are the same ensures some degree of coherence between the CFSP and other external action of the Union.

27–003

The Treaties explicitly state that the Union has to ensure consistency between the different areas of its external action and between these and its other policies.[10] The Council and the Commission, assisted by the High Representative of the Union for Foreign Affairs and Security Policy, are responsible for ensuring that consistency and have to cooperate to that effect (Art. 21(3), second subpara., TEU). As far as the CFSP is concerned, the Council and the High Representative are responsible for ensuring the "unity, consistency and effectiveness of action by the Union".[11] Within the Council, the Foreign Affairs Council configuration is responsible for ensuring the consistency of the Union's external

---

[7] See also Art. 24(2) TEU and Arts 207(1), 208(1), 212(1) and 214(1) TFEU referring to the framework of the principles and objectives of the Union's external action.

[8] See already Müller-Graff, "Einheit und Kohärenz der Vertragsziele von EG and EU" (1998) EuR. Beiheft 2, 67–80; see also Flaesch-Mougin (n. 2 *supra*), at 373–374, and Pechstein, "Das Kohärenzgebot als entscheidende Integrationsdimension der Europäischen Union" (1995) EuR. 247–258.

[9] See Wessel, "De 'tweede pijler' van de Europese Unie: een vreemde eend in de bijt?" (1995) S.E.W. 554, at 544–559; Krenzler and Schneider, "Die Gemeinsame Aussen- und Sicherheitspolitik der Europäischen Union—Zur Frage der Kohärenz" (1994) EuR. 144, at 148–155.

[10] Article 21(3), second subpara., TEU. See also the general obligation for the Union to "ensure consistency between its policies and activities, taking all of its objectives into account and in accordance with the principle of conferral of powers" (Art. 7 TFEU).

[11] Before the Lisbon Treaty Art. 18(4) EU stated that the Commission was to be fully associated with the work carried out in the CFSP field generally. For a case in which the Council emphasised the duty to ensure consistency and the fact that the Commission had been fully associated with the work on the common position to be adopted, see Common Position 94/779/CFSP of November 28, 1994 defined by the Council on the basis of the former Art. J.2 of the Treaty on European Union on the objectives and priorities of the European Union towards Ukraine, [1994] O.J. L313/1.

action (Art. 16(6), third subpara., TEU). Coordination is also provided for between Coreper, which carries out the preparatory work for Council decision-making generally, and the Political and Security Committee, which advises the Council in particular on CFSP matters (see para. 18–003). Within the Commission, the High Representative—who is one of the Commission's Vice-Presidents—ensures the consistency of the Union's external action and the coordination of the different aspects of the Union's external action (Art. 18(4) TEU). Coordination is provided for even at the stage of the preparation of policy decisions. It is important in this regard that in areas concerning both the CFSP and other fields of external action the Commission and the High Representative may submit joint proposals (Art. 22(2) TEU) and that in the field of the CFSP the Treaties provide for the possibility of a proposal submitted to the Council by the "High Representative with the Commission's support" (Art. 30(1) TEU). The European Council, for its part, identifies the strategic interests and objectives of the Union's external action.

As far as the international representation of the Union is concerned, the President of the European Council and the High Representative ensure the Union's representation in matters relating to the CFSP (see Art. 15(6), second subpara., TEU and Art. 27(2) TEU, respectively). In contrast, the Commission is generally empowered to represent the Union in other fields (Art. 17(1) TEU; see paras 24–007—24–011). In Union practice, various forms of international representation have emerged and are designed to secure unity in the external action of the Union and the Member States (see para. 24–007).

3. Political and judicial supervision

27–004 **Parliamentary control.** Only limited parliamentary scrutiny is possible with a view to ensuring that the CFSP and other external action of the Union are mutually consistent. The European Parliament may put questions to the Commission and the Council, but may not hold the Commission politically accountable for a CFSP action of the Union where that institution has no powers to influence decision-making and to supervise that the institutions and the Member States comply with obligations (see paras 18–004 and 18–006).

27–005 **Judicial review.** The Court of Justice has no direct jurisdiction to rule on the compatibility of a given Union action with the CFSP. As far as the CFSP is concerned, the Court of Justice has jurisdiction to rule only on actions for annulment brought by natural or legal persons against decisions of the Council providing for restrictive measures against natural and legal persons.[12] However, the Court of Justice has jurisdiction to ensure that implementation of the CFSP does not affect

---

[12] Article 24(1), second subpara., TEU and Art. 275, second para., TFEU. For the restrictive measures in question, see para. 25–052, *infra*.

Union powers in other areas and, conversely, that the implementation of those Union powers does not affect the CFSP.[13]

This supervisory competence corresponds to the review which the Court of Justice carried out before the entry into force of the Lisbon Treaty pursuant to Art. 47 EU with respect to the division of powers between Community and non-Community action of the Union. For the Court, a CFSP measure affected the provisions of the EC Treaty within the meaning of Art. 47 EU whenever it could have been adopted on the basis of the EC Treaty, it being unnecessary to examine whether the measure actually prevented or limited the exercise by the Community of its competences. To that effect, the Court examined whether the CFSP provisions, on account of both their aim and their content, had as their main purpose the implementation of a policy conferred by the EC Treaty on the Community and could therefore properly have been adopted on the basis of the EC Treaty.[14] Accordingly, the Court annulled a CFSP decision on the proliferation of small arms because it pursued a number of objectives falling within the Community's competence on development cooperation which were not merely incidental to the CFSP objectives also pursued by that decision.[15]

II. Consistency between the External Action of the Union and that of the Member States

Sincere cooperation. The "consistency" in foreign policy required by the Treaties is predicated on the unity which has to exist as between the action of the Union and that of its Member States. That requirement appears to be embodied in the principle of sincere cooperation which applies to the Member States and the institutions (Art. 4(3) TEU [ex Art. 10 EC]): in principle, Member States may not act in an area which falls within the exclusive competence of the Union and they may not take or maintain any action in any other field which conflicts with Union law (see para. 25–058).

27–006

This principle of sincere cooperation equally applies in the field of the CFSP, as is further emphasised by Art. 24(3) TEU [ex Art. 11(2) EU].[16] However, the Union Courts lack jurisdiction in the field of CFSP to secure compliance by the

---

[13] Articles 24(1), second subpara., and 40 TEU.

[14] ECJ, Case C-91/05 *Commission v Council* [2008] E.C.R. I-3651, para. 60. Since the question was only whether the Community was competent or not, it was not relevant whether in an area of shared competence, such as development cooperation, the measure in question could actually have been adopted by the Member States in the exercise of their competences: *ibid.*, para. 61.

[15] *Ibid.*, paras 79–110. See Hillion and Wessel, "Competence Distribution in EU External Relations after Ecowas: Clarification or Continued Fuzziness?" (2009) C.M.L.Rev. 551–586.

[16] See also Art. 32 TEU [ex Art. 16 EU], according to which the Member States are to consult one another within the European Council and the Council on any matter of foreign and security policy of general interest in order to determine a common approach, and are to ensure, through the convergence of their actions, that the Union is able to assert its interests and values on the international scene.

Member States with their CFSP obligations (see para. 13–086). It is improbable that a Member State would bring a breach of a CFSP commitment before the International Court of Justice. Whether individuals may challenge a breach by a Member State of commitments entered into under the CFSP depends on the legal force of such commitments in the national legal system. It follows that the consistency of the Member States' foreign and security policies with that of the Union has to be secured primarily within the Council and by the High Representative (see Art. 24(2), third subpara., TEU; Art. 26(2), second subpara., TEU). The fact that national diplomats and civil servants are involved in preparing decisions, together with the unanimity required in order to adopt decisions, affords a certain guarantee that action by the Member States will not be at odds with the CFSP action decided upon by the Union.

THE AUTHORS

Koen Lenaerts

Born 1954; lic.iuris, Ph.D. in law (Katholieke Universiteit Leuven); Master of Laws, Master in Public Administration (Harvard University); Lecturer (1979 to 1983) subsequently Professor of European Law, Katholieke Universiteit Leuven (since 1983); Legal secretary (*référendaire*) at the Court of Justice of the European Communities (1984 to 1985); Professor at the College of Europe, Bruges (1984 to 1989); Member of the Brussels Bar (1986 to 1989); Visiting Professor at the Harvard Law School (1989); Judge of the Court of First Instance of the European Communities (1989 to 2003); Judge of the Court of Justice of the European Union (since 2003).

Piet Van Nuffel

Born 1968; lic.iuris, Ph.D. in law (Katholieke Universiteit Leuven); Master of Laws (Harvard University); Teaching assistant and Research Fellow (1993 to 1999) and since 2008 Professor of European Law, Katholieke Universiteit Leuven; Visiting Professor at the College of Europe, Natolin (since 2004); Legal secretary (*référendaire*) at the Court of First Instance of the European Communities (1999 to 2001); Administrator at the European Commission, Directorate-General for Competition, Unit for general competition policy, economic and legal aspects (2001 to 2003); Legal secretary at the Court of Justice of the European Communities (2003 to 2009); Member of the Legal Service of the European Commission.

THE EDITORS

Robert Bray
Principal Administrator in the Secretariat of the Committee on Legal Affairs in the European Parliament.

Nathan Cambien

Born 1983; lic.iuris (Katholieke Universiteit Leuven); Magister Juris (University of Oxford); Ph.D. Fellow of the Research Foundation-Flanders and doctoral assistant, Katholieke Universiteit Leuven (since 2007).

INDEX

separate budgets, 13–131
structure, 13–132
Bulgaria
accession to EU, 21–053
application of Union law, 21–053
association agreements, 25–022
Bundesverfassungsgericht
Germany, 21–026, 21–027, 21–028,
21–029, 21–030
Cabotage
transport, 11–008
Canada
cooperation agreements, 25–009
Canary Islands
territorial scope of the Treaties, 12–007
Candidate countries
see also **Accession**
acceptance of Union *acquis*, 6–010
respect for values of the Union, 6–009
Capital movements and payments
see **Free movement of capital and
payments**
Cartels
see **Competition policy**
Case law
source of law, 22–113
Cassis de Dijon
freedom of movement, 9–012, 9–033,
9–039, 9–043, 9–044, 9–094, 9–111
CCT
see **Common Customs Tariff**
Cedefop
see **European Centre for the
Development of Vocational
Training**
Central African Republic
military operations, 25–042
Central and eastern European countries
see also individual countries
partnership and cooperation agreements,
25–009
Central banks
see also **European Central Bank;
European System of Central
Banks**
credit facilities, 11–037
economic and monetary policy, 11–039,
11–040
Ceuta and Melilla
territorial scope, 12–007
Chad
military operations, 25–042
Channel Islands
special arrangements, 12–007

Charges having equivalent effect
free movement of goods, 9–017—9–018
Charter of Fundamental Rights
see also **Fundamental rights**
adoption of, 3–026
Constitution for Europe, 4–005
establishment of, 22–020—22–021
legal status, 22–022
scope of, 22–028, 22–034
**Charter of Fundamental Social
Rights of Workers**
social policy, 11–043
Charter of Paris
CSCE, 1–011
Checks and balances
system of, 15–011
Churchill, Winston
United States of Europe, 1–003
Citizens
right of initiative, 16–016
Citizenship of the Union
contacts with Union institutions, 8–014
creation of, 8–002—8–004
diplomatic protection, 8–013
equal treatment, 7–055, 8–001,
8–007, 8–011
family members, 8–009, 8–010, 8–011
freedom of movement, 8–008,
8–009, 8–010
meaning, 8–005
participation in elections, 8–012
rights associated with, 8–006
rights of entry and residence, 8–008,
8–009, 8–010, 8–011
Civil protection
policy, 11–062
Civil Service Tribunal
see **European Union Civil Service
Tribunal**
Civil society
dialogue with, 15–004
Classical functions of a State
checks and balances, 15–011
independence of the judiciary,
15–013
legislative and executive powers,
15–012
Closer cooperation
see **Enhanced cooperation**
Coal and steel
see **European Coal and Steel
Community**
Co-decision procedure
see **Ordinary legislative procedure**

Mashreq countries
association agreements, 25–023
Measures having equivalent effect
quantitative restrictions, 9–028,
9–030—9–032
Medical and paramedical diplomas
mutual recognition of, 9–080
Mediterranean countries
association agreements, 25–023
Member States
see also **National parliaments**
actors in decision-making, as, 14–004
acts of Member State governments,
22–109
agreements between, 22–110
breach of Union law, liability for
conditions for liability,
21–015—21–018
principle of liability, 21–014
reparation for loss or damage,
21–019
constituent authority, as,
14–002— 14–003
conventions, 22–110
international powers, 25–058
list of, 6–001
national authorities, 14–001
role in implementing Union law,
14–012
Members of institutions and bodies
duties, 13–156
financial status, 13–157
independent status, 13–155
privileges and immunities, 13–156
Members of the Commission
appointment, 13–069
compulsory retirement, 13–073
independence, 13–072
retirement, 13–073
term of office, 13–071
Members of the European Parliament
(MEPs)
see **European Parliament**
Merger control
competition policy, 11–016
Merger Treaty
Single Council and Single Commission,
1–016
Migrant workers
see also **Freedom of movement for
workers**
prohibition of discrimination, 9–061—
9–062
social and tax advantages, 9–062

Military Committee
decisions, 18–007
Military cooperation,
Brussels Treaty, 1–003
common foreign and security policy,
18–007
NATO, 1–003
Military occupations
sex/gender discrimination, 7–057
Military operations
decisions, 18–007
security policy, 25–042
Military Staff
decisions, 18–007
Mixed agreements
consequences of, 26–016
reasons for, 26–014—26–015
Moldova
partnership and cooperation agreements,
25–009
Monaco
euro, 11–040
territorial scope, 12–009
Monetary cooperation
economic and monetary union, 2–006,
2–008
European Monetary System, 2–007
Monetary Cooperation Fund
management of EMS, 2–007
Monetary policy
see **Economic and monetary
policy**
Monist systems
supremacy of EU law, 21–020
Monnet, Jean
ECSC, 1–007
Montenegro
stabilisation and association process,
25–022
Morocco
association agreements, 25–023
Mostar
administration of the city, 25–042
Motion of censure
European Parliament, 13–009
Motto of the Union
symbol of the Union, 8–003
Mutual recognition
diplomas, certificates and other
evidence of formal qualifications,
9–079—9–081
National courts and tribunals
enforcement of Union law, 13–078,
14–013

Sustainable development
environmental policy, 11–059
Sweden
application of Union law, 21–042
European Free Trade Association,
1–018
Switzerland
bilateral agreements, 25–029
European Free Trade Association,
1–018
Schengen area, 2–011
Symbols of the Union
adoption of, 8–003
Syria
association agreements, 25–023
Tajikistan
partnership and cooperation agreements,
25–009
Target price
common agricultural policy, 11–004
Tariffs
see **Common commercial
policy**
Taxation
discrimination, 9–061
Technological development
policy, 11–058
Television signals
freedom of movement, 9–087
Temporal scope
Treaties, 12–003—12–005
Territorial scope
Treaties, 12–006—12–010
Terrorism
solidarity clause, 11–064
Terrorist Finance Tracking Program,
26–013
Third-country nationals
see also **Area of freedom security and
justice**
conditions of employment, 11–044
rights, 12–002
visas, 10–012
Third pillar
see **Police and judicial cooperation in
criminal matters**
Three Wise Men
report of, 3–002
Threshold price
common agricultural policy, 11–004
Tindemans Report
European Union, 3–002
Tourism
policy, 11–062

Trade
see also **European Free Trade
Association**
freedom to carry on a trade or
profession, 22–033
Trade agreements
common commercial policy,
25–009
Trade Policy Review Body (TPRB)
WTO, 25–014
Trade unions
rights in relation to, 22–033
Trademarks
see **Intellectual property**
Training
see **Vocational training**
Traité cadre
European Economic Community, 1–015
Traité–constitution
European Economic Community, 1–015
Traité–foundation
European Economic Community, 1–015
Traité-loi
European Coal and Steel Community,
1–009
Trans-European networks
policy, 11–056
Trans-frontier situation
freedom of movement, 9–057
Transitional period
common market, 9–008
protective measures, 12–012
**Translation Centre for Bodies of the
European Union**
establishment of, 13–123
Transparency
democracy, 20–008, 20–017—20–018
division of powers, 20–009
requirements, 13–166, 13–167
Transport
common transport policy
discrimination, 11–009
instruments, 11–008
scope, 11–007
Treaties
Accession Treaties, 22–013
Amending Treaties, 22–011
personal scope of, 12–001
safeguard clauses, 12–011, 12–012
structure of the basic Treaties, 4–009
temporal scope of, 12–003—12–005
territorial scope, 12–006—12–010
Treaty languages, 13–160
Union Treaties, 22–010

Treaty establishing a Single Council and a Single Commission
see **Merger Treaty**
Treaty of Amsterdam
amendments to other Treaties, 3–021
border checks, 10–004
closer cooperation, 3–022
generally, 1–016, 3–020
police and judicial cooperation, 2–010
renumbering, 3–023
Treaty of Lisbon
amendments to the institutional
framework, 4–011
constitutional innovations, 4–010
introduction of, 4–007, 4–008
negotiation and ratification, 4–008
previous Community law, 4–013
previous non–Community law, 4–014
provisions of, 4–009
structure of the basic Treaties, 4–009
transitional provisions, 4–015
Union Law, 4–012
Treaty of Maastricht
see **Treaty on European Union**
Treaty of Nice
introduction of, 3–024
provisions of, 3–025
Treaty of Rome
provisions of, 1–013
Treaty on European Union
acquis communautaire, 3–013
amendments to other Treaties, 3–014
CFSP, 3–015
consequential amendments to national
constitutions, 3–010
creation of, 3–009—3–010
decision–making, 3–018, 3–019
establishment of EU, 3–011
police and judicial cooperation in
criminal matters, 3–016
provisions of, 3–012
single institutional framework,
3–017
three pillars, 3–013
**Treaty on the Functioning of the
European Union**
establishment of, 4–009
TRIPs
generally, 25–014
Tunisia
association agreements, 25–023
Turkey
EU–Turkey Association Council,
10–015, 25–023

preparation for accession, 6–013,
25–022
**Turkish Republic of Northern
Cyprus**
see **Cyprus**
Turkmenistan
cooperation agreements, 25–009
Ukraine
partnership and cooperation agreements,
25–009
Unanimity
requirement for, 13–050
UNCTAD
commodities agreements, 25–010
Undertakings
competition rules
see **Competition policy**
Unemployment benefit
see **Social security**
Uniform visa
rules on, 10–012
Unilateral declarations
generally, 22–105
Union acquis
see also Acquis communautaire
candidate countries, 6–010
Union competences
applicable legal basis, 7–015
choice of legal basis, 7–012
common commercial policy, 25–006
distinction dependent on legal basis,
7–013
exclusive/non-exclusive, 7–020—7–022,
25–006, 25–058
express / implied competences, 7–014—
7–017
functional approach, 7–002
fundamental principles, 7–008
generally, 7–001
international agreements, 25–058
multiple legal bases, 7–016
principle of conferral, 7–009
ratione materiae, 7–010—7–011
shared competence, 7–020, 7–023,
7–024
supplementary competences,
7–018—7–019
supporting competences, 7–025
Union d'Etats
political cooperation, 2–002
Union law
see also **General principles of Union
law; Primary Union law**
breach of